THE JEWS: THEIR HISTORY, CULTURE, AND RELIGION

The original preparation of this book was made possible by funds generously made available by the American Jewish Committee.

THE JEWS

THEIR HISTORY, CULTURE AND RELIGION

Edited by

LOUIS FINKELSTEIN

Chancellor

The Jewish Theological Seminary of America

VOLUME 1

LONDON: PETER OWEN LIMITED

To

IRVING LEHMAN

1876-1945

Who in life and precept
integrated the ancient tradition
of the Hebrew prophets with the spirit
of American democracy

PETER OWEN LIMITED
50 Old Brompton Road London SW7

First published in the British Commonwealth 1961

Bound in Great Britain
Printed in the U.S.A.

CONTRIBUTORS AND MEMBERS OF THE PLANNING COMMITTEE[1]

William Foxwell Albright, *The Johns Hopkins University,* Emeritus Professor of Semitic Languages; *The Jewish Theological Seminary of America,* Louis M. Rabinowitz Visiting Research Professor of Biblical Literature, 1957-1959

Alexander Altmann, Communal Rabbi, Manchester and District; *Institute of Jewish Studies,* Honorary Director, Manchester, England

Hillel Bavli, *The Jewish Theological Seminary of America,* Seminary Professor of Hebrew Literature

Itzhak Ben-Zvi, *The State of Israel,* President

Elias J. Bickerman, *Columbia University,* Professor of Ancient History

Arturo Castiglioni, *Yale University,* Professor of the History of Medicine[2]

Israel S. Chipkin, *American Association for Jewish Education,* Executive Director[2]

David Daiches, *Cambridge University,* University Lecturer in English

Moshe Davis, *The Jewish Theological Seminary of America,* Provost, Associate Professor of American Jewish History

Ben Zion Dinur, *The Hebrew University,* Professor Emeritus of Modern Jewish History

Uriah Zevi Engelman, *American Association for Jewish Education,* Head, Department of Research and Information

Louis Finkelstein, *The Jewish Theological Seminary of America,* Chancellor, Solomon Schechter Professor of Theology

Walter J. Fischel, *University of California, Berkeley,* Department of Near Eastern Languages, Professor of Semitic Languages and Literature

Eli Ginzberg, *Columbia University,* Professor of Economics

Nathan Glazer, New York City

Judah Goldin, *The Jewish Theological Seminary of America,* Associate Professor of Aggadah

Robert Gordis, *The Jewish Theological Seminary of America,* Associate Professor of Biblical Exegesis; *Fund for the Republic,* Consultant on Religion

Simon Greenberg, *The Jewish Theological Seminary of America,* Vice-Chancellor, Vice-President of the Faculties, Professor of Homiletics and Education

Abraham S. Halkin, *The Jewish Theological Seminary of America,* Associate Professor of Jewish Literature and Institutions

Israel Halpern, *The Hebrew University,* Head, Department of Jewish History, Associate Professor of Jewish History; *Hebrew University and Yad Washem Institute for Research on the Disaster of European Jewry,* Head

[1] As of April, 1958
[2] Deceased

Melville J. Herskovits, *Northwestern University,* Professor of Anthropology, Director, Program of African Studies

Abraham J. Heschel, *The Jewish Theological Seminary of America,* Seminary Professor of Jewish Ethics and Mysticism

Milton Himmelfarb, *The American Jewish Committee,* Director, Library of Jewish Information

Oscar I. Janowsky, *City College of the City of New York,* Professor of History, Director, New York Area Studies

Mordecai M. Kaplan, *The Jewish Theological Seminary of America,* Professor of Philosophies of Religion

Milton R. Konvitz, *Cornell University,* Professor of Industrial and Labor Relations and Professor of Law

Simon Kuznets, *The Johns Hopkins University,* Professor of Political Economy

Anita Libman Lebeson, formerly Instructor in History, *University of Illinois;* College of Jewish Studies

Frederick Lehner, *West Virginia State College,* Professor of German and French

Jacob Lestschinsky, "*Jewish Daily Forward,*" *World Jewish Congress*

Saul Lieberman, *The Jewish Theological Seminary of America,* Dean, Rabbinical School, Professor of Talmud

R. M. MacIver, *Columbia University,* Lieber Professor Emeritus of Political Philosophy and Sociology

Julius B. Maller, *The State of New York Department of Audit and Control,* Chief of Research; *Yeshiva University,* School of Education, Professor of Psychology

Ralph Marcus, *The University of Chicago,* Professor of Hellenistic Culture[2]

Yudel Mark, *Jewish Education Committee of New York,* Consultant for Yiddish Schools; *Yivo Institute for Jewish Research,* Chief Editor, "*Yiddische Sprakh*"

Alexander Marx, *The Jewish Theological Seminary of America,* Jacob H. Schiff Professor of History[2]

Abraham Menes, "*Zukunft,*" Coeditor; "*Jewish Daily Forward,*" Columnist

Jacob J. Rabinowitz, *The Hebrew University,* Associate Professor of Jewish Law

Cecil Roth, *Oxford University,* Reader in Jewish Studies

Charles Singer, *University of London,* Professor Emeritus; *University College,* London, Fellow; *Oxford University,* Magdalen College, Honorary Fellow; "*History of Technology,*" Joint Editor; *American Philosophical Society,* member

Shalom Spiegel, *The Jewish Theological Seminary of America,* William Prager Professor of Medieval Hebrew Literature

Arieh Tartakower, *The Hebrew University,* Lecturer, Head, Department of Sociology of the Jews

Bernard D. Weinryb, *Dropsie College,* Professor of History and Economics; *Yeshiva University,* Professor of Jewish History and Institutions

Eric Werner, *Hebrew Union College,* Professor of Liturgical Music

Rachel Wischnitzer, *Yeshiva University,* Stern College, Assistant Professor of Fine Arts

CONTENTS

I. THE HISTORY OF JUDAISM AND THE JEWS

II. THE ROLE OF JUDAISM IN CIVILIZATION

ILLUSTRATIONS

LIST OF MAPS

PREFATORY LETTER

July 4, 1949

Dear Judge Proskauer:

Six years have passed since that memorable evening when the plan for the present book—first projected in conversations with Lewis L. Strauss, Irving Lehman and Sol M. Stroock—took final form in a discussion with you. Your understanding encouraged me to proceed with this task, which could never have been finished without your unflagging interest and support. It is now my pleasant duty to present the completed work to you.

This book is the first comprehensive description of Judaism and the Jews. While avoiding the anatomical structure and purely alphabetical organization of an encyclopedia, it is designed as a readable and unified sketch of a singular human phenomenon. The principal relevant facts concerning the people of Israel and its faith are summarized in a succession of essays, which form an ordered whole and afford penetrating glimpses into particular aspects of the subject. This book includes the first compact history of the Jews written by scholars specializing in the several fields; an apprecia- of the role of Judaism in world culture, seen from a wide variety of disciplines and skills; an initial effort toward a demography of the Jews in America; and a brief outline of the Jewish religion.

The complexity of the work, despite all efforts to achieve simplicity and uniformity, indicates the difficulty and intricacy of the subject. The history of Israel opens with the birth of Abraham, some 120 generations ago in the Mesopotamian bronze age, the period of Hammurabi, and since that time there has been scarcely a civilized dialect which does not contain some record bearing on the chronicle of this ancient people and its faith. One might almost say that no inhabited land but has witnessed Jewish heroism and martyrdom.

To compose a history of the Jews requires erudition and command of method, rarely, if ever, combined in one individual. It is one thing to reconstruct a living record of prebiblical and biblical Judaism from archaeological and literary records, and quite another to discern in an inexhaustible mass of documents, record books, living monuments or institutions, the pattern of modern Jewish life. Few scholars could master both techniques. And the sort of research that enables a man to interpret a prolix medieval work (its confusion of fact and legend, its reliance on hearsay evidence, its extravagance and vagueness) is completely different from that required for the exegesis of an obscure, but pregnant, biblical or talmudic or philosophical text.

In the course of its long, tortuous history, Judaism has profoundly affected, and been deeply affected by, cultural phenomena covering the whole range of human experience. To understand fully the place of Judaism in civilization it would be necessary to master philosophies and mental outlooks of cultures as varied as those of the ancient Canaanites, the Egypt of the Pharaohs, the Mesopotamia of the Assyrians, the Babylonians, and the Persians, the Seleucid and the Ptolemaic empires of the Greeks, the world empire of the Romans, the deserts of the Arabs, pre-Christian and Christian Europe, as well as the chaotic and complex world of our own day.

In turn, the faith and tradition of the Jews have left an indelible stamp on Western music, art, science, mathematics, medicine, philosophy, letters, education, philanthropy, law, public administration, manners, morals, and religion. The extent of this influence is not yet fully understood, for there are few scholars who know Jewish lore and, at the same time, enough of any field in Western culture to discover mutual relationships. Histories and anthologies of Western philosophy are still necessarily written with scant reference to such towering figures as Maimonides and Crescas, and none at all to the penetrating insights of the Talmud. The reconstruction of talmudic mathematics, and the analysis of its influence on that of the medieval period, are still in their initial stages; only the merest beginning has been made in the study of the relation of talmudic legal principles to the Canon Law and through it to later norms. The educational technique of the ancient Rabbinic schools, which might be of great practical value today, remains unknown except to the preoccupied, completely dedicated talmudic scholar. Students have still to describe the literary forms of Rabbinic Judaism that directly—and indirectly, through the Gospels—exerted so profound an influence on later composition. The Jewish conception of the whole of life as a work of art, a pageant of worship, in which every action must follow the score set down in the codes, yet may reflect individual ingenuity and piety, is only now beginning to be expounded. The essays in the present volume can but suggest vast areas of research in these and other fields.

While the Jews today number perhaps fewer than twelve millions, they are so scattered and differentiated that any comprehensive demography of them must be almost as complicated as that of mankind as a whole. A survey of the Jews of America alone would require great variety of sociological data and techniques. The lack of any inclusive Jewish organization makes for the formation of many different types of social relationship, mere enumeration of which would occupy many pages. There are Jews whose ancestors have lived in the United States for almost three centuries;

others who arrived but yesterday. There are many Jews who have become integrated in the life of little villages and towns; while large numbers are concentrated in populous cities. In New York City there are not only Jews who are native Americans, but also Jews whose mother tongue is French, German, Dutch, Spanish, Italian, Greek, Russian, Polish, Magyar, Hebrew or Yiddish. Even this list is incomplete! A prominent Jewish scholar once remarked that more is known about the Jews of ancient Sura and Pumbedita than about those of modern New York. He did not exaggerate. Even among authorities on Jewish communal life few are acquainted with all the groups that make up New York Jewry. No study has yet clarified the mutual relations between Jews who came to America from various parts of Europe during the Hitler persecutions, and earlier Jewish immigrants from Eastern Europe and Germany itself.

The chapters of this book dealing with the demography of the Jews should be considered only as "prolegomena," not as complete studies. It is hoped that they will stimulate and be supplemented by further inquiries, and ultimately lead schools of higher Jewish learning to introduce into their curricula such Jewish social studies.

The difficulties faced by sociologists attempting to study Jewish demography are indicated in part by the authors of those chapters. Jews who are sociologists naturally devote themselves primarily to general sociology, and indeed the demography of the Jews can be considered only as part of the whole social picture. Actually, the study of the social sciences is itself in its infancy and the number of sociologists who happen to be of the Jewish faith is small. Altogether, the study of Jewish sociology is practically non-existent today. While grateful for the material on the subject provided in the current volume, and realizing that the authors are pre-eminent in the field as it now stands, the editor can take no responsibility for their views. Each chapter is presented as reflecting the opinion of the individual author, rather than that of a composite of the contributors to the volume or of the editor himself.

The same is true with regard to the other chapters. The editor can take no responsibility for the views expressed, and is indeed in actual disagreement with a number of them. Some authors disagree with others. Each was invited to write his own chapter because of the special contribution he had to make, regardless of whether it would contradict the views of others or of the editor.

Despite its varied authorship, the inevitable lacunae, and the preliminary character of some research, the emergence of this book may be a milestone in the development of American Jewish scholarship and literature. Its Table of Contents suggests areas of research with which future Jewish scholarship may concern itself. Within certain limitations, the work is an effective summary of virtually all that is known about Judaism and the Jews. The material was prepared by the co-operating authors with scholarly objectivity and responsibility, and generally with clarity and readability. The editor found to his delight that certain chapters include original research of enduring value, some destined to change the whole course of study in their fields. He feels reasonably certain that such chapters will be studied with particular care by the scholars in those areas, as well as by the general reader. He regrets that the following chapters which he had hoped to include in this first edition were not prepared, for various reasons, in time: a history of the Jews in Moslem lands by Professor Ben Zion Dinaburg; a discussion of the cultural life of the Jews of eastern Europe in recent centuries by Dr. Abraham Menes; a chapter on the Jewish influence on mathematics and astronomy; and his own summary of the cultural life of the Jews in the Middle Ages. Each of these subjects is partly covered, however, in other chapters.

One chapter, whose omission in this edition will be especially regretted, is that describing the development of the Palestinian Jewish community, now burgeoned into the State of Israel. Both during the war and afterward the editor was in communication with several Palestinian scholars, urging them to undertake the writing of this story. Because of unsettled conditions, none of those originally approached saw his way clear to take on the assignment. When finally a chapter was written by a well known scholar, distance made it impossible to keep in sufficiently close contact with him to bring the paper in line with the over all scheme of the work. There was also a considerable number of inaccuracies, which the writer had not been able to check because of war conditions. Under these circumstances, the editor was advised to omit the chapter, and can but express the hope that this record of magnificent achievement will find its place in future editions.

The thoughtful reader will notice other important omissions. It may seem strange that there is a chapter on "Israel in Iran," but none dealing with the Ladino literature. This occurred because the editor was fortunate in having a chapter prepared by Professor Walter J. Fischel, the authority on Jewish culture in Persia, while no comparable study regarding Ladino literature could be obtained. The same applies to other areas.

Despite all efforts to bring about common approaches and common standards, a collection of essays inevitably remains an assembly of differing styles, as well as points of view. The editor has made no effort to overcome inconsistencies among the authors; on the contrary, he has drawn attention to them. He has also made no effort to persuade writers to address themselves, necessarily, to the same audience. Some essays are technical; others, without diminution of scholarly integrity and insight, are popular in presentation. Some writers have considered it their task to present merely the consensus of present scholarship, and have avoided reference to their own theories and hypotheses. In other essays, the student will find bold insights and theories, together with references to the commonly accepted views.

In addition to the chapter on Judaism and art by Mrs. Rachel Wischnitzer, there was to have been another by Professor Franz Landsberger of Hebrew Union College. However, as Professor Landsberger has in the meantime published his comprehensive work, *A History of Jewish Art*, which covers the ground in great detail, the editor agreed to release him from the task of preparing a special chapter.

The problem of anti-Semitism is dealt with only tangentially in this volume. The editor was persuaded to omit the chapters intended to cover that subject in detail. A number of studies, specifically dedicated to this problem, are now being conducted by various institutions; and the comprehensive works to emanate from them would doubtless make superfluous any summary statement in this book.

At the suggestion of Professor Harry A. Wolfson, the editor wrote a number of colleagues and friends, asking them to suggest the questions about Judaism and the Jews which they believed their acquaintances would most like to see answered. A list of the questions which were submitted by 209 educators and scholars as a result of this inquiry is published in the Appendix, together with page references indicating where in the book replies may be found.

Most of the chapters were written before 1946. Except in a few instances, there was no effort to bring them up to date, both because that would be a never ending process and because additional changes would have unduly delayed publication.

In the preparation of the book, I have, as you know, drawn freely on your own advice and on that of Dr. John Slawson and other members of the staff, of Professor Salo W. Baron, Chairman of the Committee on Library Research and Publications, and upon other members of the American Jewish Committee, which generously covered the costs of preparation. Dr. Ordway Tead of Harper & Brothers, the scholars who constituted the advisory committee on this publication, and many others were most helpful. When, as happened once or twice, my courage failed and I began to doubt that the book would ever appear, I had your urging, as well as that of my good friend, Alan M. Stroock, Vice President of the American Jewish Committee and Chairman of the Board of Directors of The Jewish Theological Seminary of America, to spur me on. All through the work, I was mindful of the joy its development would have given my teacher, the late Cyrus Adler, President of the American Jewish Committee and of the Seminary.

To Professor Alexander Marx of the Seminary we are indebted not only for suggestions basic to planning the whole sweep of the work, but for detailed advice. He spent considerable time going over with me the chapters on Jewish history, and the book has benefited enormously from his learning and insight.

Professor Judah Goldin of the State University of Iowa devoted many months to reading various manuscripts, and made suggestions for changes in style, almost all adopted by the authors. His own chapter is a delight, as well as the product of genuine and authoritative learning.

Despite all these advantages, I gravely doubt whether the book could have appeared at this time had not the Board of Directors of the Seminary granted me a leave for the current academic year; and had I not had in this as in other work the invaluable and indefatigable aid of my assistant, Miss Jessica Feingold. Her experience as assistant to the editors of various symposia of the Conference on Science, Philosophy and Religion, as well as with the publications of The Institute for Religious and Social Studies, was brought to bear on the even more difficult work of preparing the present manuscript; and she generously relieved me of every detail that could be delegated to her.

I am under further indebtedness to Mr. Devin Garrity and the Devin-Adair Company for permission to republish (with considerable changes and additions) my essay on "The Beliefs and Practices of Judaism."[1] Dr. Solomon Grayzel of the Jewish Publication Society of America made a number of valuable suggestions; and he and Dr. Maurice Jacobs were most co-operative in permitting me to draw on maps and illustrations in the possession of the Society. My friend, Dr. Franz Pick, was helpful with suggestions regarding the illustrations. In the early stages of the work Mrs. Joan Leff Lipnick and Miss Judith Rudansky served as research assistants, and considerably lessened my burden. Real apprecation is due Rabbi Gershon Cohen who checked a number of details and assisted in the final editing. Also to Miss Julie Eidesheim and Mr. Otto Albertson who read the manuscript and proofs.

And now, having ended this task, I follow the example of R. Nehuniah ben Hakkanah, great Sage of the first century, who when he entered the House of Study prayed that no error should occur through him, and when he left gave thanks for his portion.

LOUIS FINKLESTEIN

The Jewish Theological Seminary of America
New York City

[1] Louis Finkelstein, J. Elliot Ross, William Adams Brown, *The Religions of Democracy: Judaism, Catholicism, Protestantism in Creed and Life,* The Devin-Adair Company, New York, 1941, pp. 1-89.

INTRODUCTORY NOTE

The English translation of the Hebrew Scriptures issued by the Jewish Publication Society of America (1943) has been used, in general, for quotations from the Bible. However, several authors, for example, Dr. Robert Gordis, were permitted to substitute their own renderings, because these seemed basic to their argument. Similarly, in specialized articles, such as that by Professor Shalom Spiegel, diacritical marks and technical forms of transliteration have been used, whereas in the book generally transliteration has followed the system set up for popular works by the Jewish Publication Society of America. The names of modern settlements in Palestine have been cited in the spelling commonly used in Zionist English publications, though that may be out of accord with the transliteration system employed in the rest of the book. Hebrew words which have become part of the English language are spelled according to the standard English dictionaries and encyclopedias, as *Cabbala* instead of *Kabbalah.* Because of the fact that the papers were prepared at different times and in different countries, it has been impossible to achieve real consistency in spelling or transliteration. Because of the difference in pronunciation, no effort has been made to reconcile the transliteration of Hebrew with that of Yiddish. In some cases popular pronunciation has determined the transliteration, as in *Agudas* (for *Agudat*) and *kosher* (for *kasher*).

Foreign words and transliterations of foreign phrases are italicized. However, the titles of talmudic treatises are printed in Roman letters in the text, notes, and bibliographies. The abbreviation "R." is used for Rabbinic Sages, who bore the title Rabbi or Rab, and lived in talmudic times. Those who lived after the close of the Talmud are described as "Rabbi."

The notes in brackets, further distinguished by the use of letters of the alphabet, were added by the editor and his associates to guide the reader, particularly where a subject mentioned in one passage is more fully discussed in another essay. The reader will find a number of individuals and organizations mentioned in more than one place. This duplication has been allowed because each of the various authors treats a given subject differently, and the repetition seemed valuable. Sometimes chapters overlap considerably, such as those of Dr. Arturo Castiglioni and Professor Charles Singer, those of Dr. Israel S. Chipkin and Dr. Moshe Davis, or those of Dr. Davis and Mrs. Anita Libman Lebeson. However, the reader should find the overlapping helpful to a complete study of the subject.

The bibliographies are not uniform either in their comprehensiveness or in their selectivity. Similarly, the various writers are by no means uniform in their use of footnotes for detailed discussion. In some chapters the notes are numbered by sections of the chapter, notably in the articles by Professor Judah Goldin and Professor Alexander Altmann. In others the numbering is continuous for the whole chapter.

FOREWORD

July 4, 1949

The purpose of this book is to bring into focus the vast number and wide variety of data concerning Judaism and the Jews, so that they can be seen in relation to one another and to the general phenomena of human culture. Because of their circumstances, the events in which Jews have participated, and to which they have contributed, are almost as diversified as the history of the human race itself. This book is therefore necessarily a joint work. Each of the thirty-four contributors has undertaken to discuss the aspect of Judaism and the Jews with which he is best acquainted. These authors include Christian and Jew; Europeans, Israelis, and Americans; philosophers, historians, social scientists, scientists, men of art and letters, and men of affairs; rationalists and mystics; skeptics and believers. They have not met to dicuss their special contributions; no effort has been made to enforce any uniformity of concept or presentation. Any unity nonetheless emerging is due entirely to the nature of the phenomenon under discussion. If the book contains a message (and I believe it does), it is a message inherent in the extraordinary events and insights described.

In the perspective of geology or biology, it is but yesterday that Moses appeared before Pharoah to demand the release of the Israelite slaves; and but a few hours more since Abraham left Ur of Chaldees. In this short span of time, the undertaking initiated by Patriarchs and early prophets has developed trends in civilization which, it is generally agreed, contain whatever is hopeful for the destiny of man. Beginning with the promise of a Messianic age, these trends are perhaps the chief visible instruments for its attainment. What fate and achievements still await the Jewish and its derivative traditions during the long millennia to come, none dares predict. Despite the widely current fears for man's future, it seems probable that the development of his civilization will proceed with increasing speed. Indeed, if man in future directs to the advancement of his knowledge of human relations, the humanities, ethics, and religion, energies like those spent in recent centuries on study and conquest of the material world, he may in a comparatively brief period as far surpass twentieth century man as twentieth century man surpasses the Neanderthal. And if it seems unlikely that our sons and daughters will prophesy, we have Scriptural assurance that that exalted state awaits some of our more distant descendants.

The chronicle and description of the Western world's most ancient tradition, as it emerged from darkness into light, and turned each crisis into an instrument of growth, offers hope for the human race as a whole. The presentation of the facts bearing on this development would itself completely justify this book, but other, more limited, considerations have entered into its planning. The work seemed necessary to dispel widespread misinformation, and to provide authentic information about its central theme. That this should be needed may appear paradoxical. Of all the curiosities of our world, one of the strangest is that a civilization, many of whose basic ideas derive from Judaism, should have so little appreciation of its real character.

Clearly, inadequate comprehension of Judaism cannot be due to lack of knowledge of its basic literature. With the possible exception of the New Testament, no literature approaches in popularity the Scriptures, which are the cornerstone of Judaism. Everywhere men find comfort in the Psalms of David, and guide their lives by the wisdom of Solomon. Jewish rituals are retained in the religious symbolisms of half the world; Jewish theology is a potent force in the development of civilization. The prophetic conception of man and his future pervades much of the science and policy of our day.

Misunderstanding of Judaism cannot be caused by the difficulty or abstruseness of the subject. Its literature is available and may be mastered; its traditions have all been reduced to writing and printing, and handy translations in many languages are widely distributed. There is a vast literature dealing with Judaism as a faith and the Jews as a people.

The ease with which anyone may enter the most sacred portals of Judaism is, in fact, astonishing. The child of a traditional Jewish household often discovers at the age of eight or nine that the book he has been studying is none other than the Talmud on which the erudite in the faith base their opinions. With a curious delight that boy encounters in its folios the very passages his learned rabbi cites in sermon or decision, and recognizes that a child is divided from the foremost scholar in Israel not by kind but by degree of knowledge.

Even the Cabbala which seems to the uninitiate a difficult and perplexing riddle, and is usually described as such, has been superbly expounded by Professor Gershom Scholem.[1]

Despite the general knowledge of so much of Jewish literature, the fact remains that Judaism is today probably the least understood of all major religions. This truth was illustrated for me by an incident connected with the publication of this book. While the proofs were being read, the publisher kindly invited me to meet a group which was to interpret *Judaism and the Jews* (as we then proposed to call this work) to booksellers. Re-

[1] *Major Trends in Jewish Mysticism*, Schocken Books, Inc., New York, 1941.

gardless of the value of the material, some were troubled by the title. For the reading public, they argued, Judaism has merely archaeological interest, having ceased to exist more than eighteen centuries ago, with the fall of Jerusalem at the hands of Titus. In contrast, they said, the Jews are a contemporary phenomenon, of perennial interest. As frequently happens, practical considerations led to a review of the theoretical, and the present title was adopted because of its precision, as well as for its intelligibility.

Never before had I realized so clearly that the religion which I try to practice is not considered "living" by many of my countrymen. But thinking over the discussion, I recalled various incidents which confirmed that view. There was the young author of a book on "modern religion and the doctrine of human brotherhood," who had consulted me about the chapter on Islam, seeking introduction to authorities in that field, and surprised me by his omission of any chapter on Judaism. He apparently had thought Judaism a "tribal" religion, obsolete in the modern world, preserved by a few queer devotees, with no real value for modern man and no bearing on the problems of human brotherhood.

I remembered the occasion when I pleaded with the dean of a well known college on behalf of a young friend, called to take an examination on the Sabbath. Explaining my position, I reminded the dean that the American people as a whole seek to encourage religion in the young, and that to compel the young man to take his examination as scheduled might be the first step in tearing him away from his faith, and possibly from all faith. After listening to me patiently, the dean, doubtless harassed with many requests for special consideration, and (like many heads of bureaus) intolerant of the need for individual arrangements, said, "My dear friend, you really cannot expect us to run this college in accordance with your ancient wilderness customs."

The experience with both men, each religious in his own tradition, may have been similar to that of the late Henry W. Nevinson, for many years editor of the London *Nation*. In a witty and instructive passage of his last autobiographical volume, Nevinson records his feelings as he approached the shores of Palestine, where he was to tour some of the Zionist colonies:

> To an Englishman brought up last century, as I was, in a strictly Evangelical family, that land is not merely holy. It is far more intimately known than his own country. It is almost his own possession, and bewildering enthusiasts used even to hint to him that, as a descendant from "the Lost Ten Tribes," he even had some claim to that heritage.
>
> This strictly Biblical education produced among those who, like myself, belong to the last century, the peculiar illusion that both the promises and the threatenings of the Jewish lawgivers and prophets were specially designed for ourselves by a foreseeing power. We never doubted that we English Evangelicals were the Chosen People and when, every Sunday evening, we sang in

the Magnificat, "As He promised to our forefathers Abraham and his seed for ever," we gave no thought to the Jews; and when soon afterwards we sang in the Nunc Dimittis, "to be a light to lighten the Gentiles, and to be the glory of Thy people Israel," we meant that Missionary Societies would spread the light of the Gospel to negroes, Chinese, and Indians, while God's English people retained the glory. Though we heard passages from Jewish history every Sunday, and read or even sang several Jewish lyrics, I can remember only one mention of the Jews in our Prayer Book services, and that occurs in one of the Good Friday Collects. For, after admitting that God made all men and hates nothing that He has made, nor desires the death of a sinner, but rather that he should be converted and live, that Collect calls on him to have mercy upon all Jews, Turks, Infidels, and Heretics, in the hope that they may be saved among the remnant of the true Israelites. And by the true Israelites we unquestionably understood the Protestants of congregations like ours.[2]

So distinguished a Bible scholar as Rudolph Kittel revealed startling misconceptions about current Judaism. My colleague, Professor Alexander Sperber, relates how, once before leaving Leipzig for his native Rumania to celebrate the Passover, he went to say good-by to Kittel, who wondered about the reason for the journey. Sperber explained that Passover is a Jewish family festival, much as Christmas is for Christians. At this point, Kittel, whose works are still invaluable for every Bible student, remarked, "By the way, Sperber, there is a question about Passover I had always meant to ask you. Now that the Temple is destroyed, where do the Jews sacrifice the paschal lamb?" Kittel must have known that Jews have no sacrificial system today and that their worship is solely that of prayer, study, and the observance of moral and ritual commandments. But the information had been pigeonholed in his mind; in his effective consciousness, Passover had no meaning without a paschal lamb!

Such false notions about contemporary Judaism and the Jews are by no means limited to those outside the faith. The confusion seems part of modern culture, affecting Jews themselves. A famous Jewish philanthropist spent many hours arguing that my observance of the Jewish food laws was worse than nonsense; he regarded it as wicked and opposed to the very spirit of Judaism. He also supposed that because I observed these laws I was necessarily in favor of the terrorists who were then wreaking havoc in Palestine, and could not be convinced that *kashrut* is reconcilable with pacific love for all humanity, or that, from my point of view, as a ritual of communion with God, *kashrut* is irreconcilable with violence.

A distinguished scholar, himself a Jew, remarked some years ago in a discussion of the Jewish contribution to world culture, "You know that Jewish literature since the Bible contains virtually nothing original and

[2] *Last Changes, Last Chances*, Harcourt Brace and Company, New York, 1929, pp. 325-326.

significant to human thought." No better comment on his view is needed than the many chapters of this book dealing with the post-biblical literature and thought of the Jews.

The rejection of Judaism as a living monotheistic faith sometimes affects, quite unconsciously, memory of the Scriptures. Perhaps some readers of this book, asked to give the source of the rule, "And thou shalt love thy neighbor as thyself," will like Bertrand Russell in *A History of Western Philosophy*[3] think of Mark 12.31, rather than of Leviticus 19.18, the source used by Jesus.

Likewise, those in close contact with Judaism and the Jewish community frequently overlook basic traits of the faith. Ten years ago at a Philadelphia synagogue center, I spoke of the meaning of persecutions of the Jews, quoting extensively from the chapters in Isaiah on the Suffering Servant, particularly the beautiful verses,

> He was oppressed, though he humbled himself
> And opened not his mouth;
> As a lamb that is led to the slaughter,
> And as a sheep that before her shearers is dumb;
> Yea, he openeth not his mouth . . .
>
> Yet it pleased the Lord to crush
> Him by disease;
> To see if his soul would offer itself
> In restitution, that he might see his seed, prolong
> His days and that the purpose of the Lord
> Might prosper by his hand (53.7,10).

During the prolonged discussion on the nature and purpose of Judaism, one of the questioners who seemed to represent also the views of others asked with a little embarrassment why, as one of my main texts to interpret Judaism, I had taken selections from the New Testament rather than the Old.

When The Jewish Theological Seminary of America was reorganized in 1902 under the presidency of Solomon Schechter, an eminent member of the Board of Directors noticed that the pretheological students were taught, among other subjects, the treatise of the Talmud called Baba Kamma. Having read an English translation of the treatise, and remembering its contents, he told Dr. Schechter that he could not understand how the laws about one man's ox goring his neighbor's cow (the subject of one of the chapters in the treatise) could bear on Jewish theology. Dr. Schechter did not find it easy to explain even to one so interested and devoted, that in ancient Jewish society the principles of the faith were expressed with equal urgency in civil, ceremonial, and moral law.

[3] *A History of Western Philosophy*, Simon and Schuster, New York, 1945, p. 326.

In the light of such incidents it is no extravagance to call Judaism the unknown religion of our time. Its adherents live in the same cities and houses as members of other creeds; they travel in the same subways and buses; they correspond, visit, converse, and do business with their fellow Americans of all groups. Jews may be loved as individuals and respected for their gifts. Their prophets are also the prophets of Christendom and Islam. The Holy Land is equally sacred to the members of the Jewish, Christian, and Islamic faiths. Neither Christian nor Moslem theology is intelligible without a study of its Jewish antecedents. But only the rare American or European of any faith appreciates the character of the ancient Jewish tradition, is aware of its distinctive teachings and nature, and seeks to understand the relation of the modern Jew to his predecessor of biblical and talmudic times.

The general confusion about Judaism and the Jews is not dispelled by the popularity of the Bible; on the contrary, the wide knowledge of the Hebrew Scriptures may help increase misconceptions. The reader of the Bible tends, like Nevinson, to identify the Israelites with his own circle, and the Philistines with his own opponents. In mature years it is difficult to substitute for infant imagery the people who follow the faith of the prophets, study their language, and adhere rigidly to their ways.

To paraphrase Stevenson, a Jewish writer sometimes thinks that his own faith has the love of a parent for other faiths derived from it; while these faiths have for Judaism the indifference of a child. Judaism is intensely interested in the history and development of Christianity and Islam, which—to quote Maimonides—it regards as means of carrying to the ends of the earth an understanding of God's unity and the teaching of Scripture. The oldest Western religion sees the younger ones as fruits of its own planting; as part of man's endless future; as steps toward the realization of the prophetic vision of a world of peace. Christendom and Islam seem to think of Judaism as a relic of the past—quaint, valuable for the insight it offers into their origins, astounding in its defiance of the years, but still not an integral part of man's future.

Because the culture of the Western world tends to be predominantly Christian, this lack of faith in Judaism as a contemporary and permanent factor in civilization carries over into Judaism itself. Its own children sometimes doubt its meaning and its future.

Misunderstanding of Judaism as a religion easily leads to the doctrine of the "Jewish race." This curious tenet rests on the twofold foundation of scientific ignorance and linguistic ambiguity. When eminent writers, such as Disraeli and Winston Churchill, refer to the Jews as a "race," they probably have in mind the wide variety of meanings in English lexicography of the term, "race," and do not intend to imply any exclusive kinship between the Jews of today and the Israelites who came forth from

Egypt. At any rate, it is improbable that in the admixture of peoples across the centuries there are any "pure" races in the Western world. A faith which at one time won as many proselytes as Judaism, and which has lost as many of its people through assimilation, which has representatives differing as widely as the Yemenite Jews of South Arabia and the North European Jews of Germany, is hardly a "race." As Professor Melville J. Herskovits shows in Chapter 36, the efforts of anthropologists to find a common racial factor among all Jews have thus far failed, and will probably fail in the future. The Talmud maintains that the descendants of Sisera, Haman, and Titus included the foremost Jewish scholars of their time; Queen Victoria proudly regarded herself as a descendant of King David.

The usual genealogical table, which mentions only two remote ancestors and many descendants, conceals the interesting fact that an inverted table might be arranged, indicating from how many different individuals we are each descended. Theoretically the number of our ancestors in any generation is 2^n, where n represents the number of generations back. Thus the number of the ancestors of any one of us for fifty generations would be 2^{50}, or 1,125,899,906,842,624. This is a larger number of people than have lived on the face of the globe since its creation: it is obvious that there was considerable interbreeding among the ancestors of modern man, and that probably the whole world is kin.

But the racist doctrine continues to have its adherents both within Judaism and outside the fold. Wherever it spreads among Jews, it tends to destroy the Jewish faith; where it spreads outside the Jewish group, like all obscurantist divisions, it tends to weaken civilization itself.

Those who wish to understand Judaism find most difficulty in its special form of expressing ideas, its symbolism. Conventional Western words and propositions cannot convey the full meaning of Jewish ritual, moral action, and historical narrative. Because the science of religious anthropology is imperfectly developed, many are unaware that Judaism has a distinctive system of semantics. The ancient teachers of Judaism thought in pictures more often than in words, and expressed the doctrines of their faith in forms of ritual and moral behavior, or in tales of history, rather than as logical propositions. To what extent, for example, the narratives preserved in the Pentateuch and the Former Prophets were originally intended only as allegories, has been a subject of discussion for many centuries; but there never was any doubt that they were didactic in their purpose. Similarly, each form and ceremonial has its lesson; ethical behavior itself derives value not merely from the good it performs, but also from the ideas it conveys as a symbol.

In Chapter 42, dealing with Judaism as a religion, I have endeavored to clarify some of these symbolic meanings, and to suggest also what appears to be the symbolism of the system as a whole. But, in the last analysis, it is as imposisble to describe in words the ideas, say, which the Day of Atonement evokes for an observant Jew, as those which are indicated in daily life by a handshake, a kiss, a frown. The study of primitive life and early Mesopotamian and Egyptian history shows that many of the forms used by the Jews originated among peoples of earlier times. Freudians have tried to discover universal symbolism in such rituals as the blowing of the trumpet on the festival of Rosh Ha-Shanah, and the carrying of the palm branch on Sukkot. There was, of course, little difficulty in finding such meaning and origin for the ritual of circumcision. All these studies, while interesting, shed no more light on Judaism than the study of the origin of the alphabet on the ideas of Shakespeare. Whatever the genesis of the rituals of Judaism, they have developed a unique significance that is usually unrelated to their accidental, extra-religious origins.

Jewish theology needs to be *felt*, as well as understood. Its propositions are more than assertions, they are affirmations and dedications. To repeat the *Shema* each day is to develop such a sense of the Existence and the Unity of God, of His love for man, and of man's duty to love Him, as may easily move one to tears, especially on occasions such as Rosh Ha-Shanah and Yom Kippur, when one rejects mundane surroundings and surrenders entirely to the ideas of the ritual.

The practice of the 613 commandments therefore constitutes the Jewish system of theology; and no system of doctrines can be anything more than a pale reflection of this reality. As the history of the Universe and Man is to Judaism a Divine epic, so the life of each individual is his supreme work of art and his main contribution to the sum-total of the Divine creation. It follows that he who lives a righteous life is God's partner in the creation of the world.

Because the symbols in which Judaism expresses its ideas include moral as well as ceremonial actions, many who are not outwardly or even consciously religious may have a distinguished share in the faith, and may be numbered among its saints. "He who wishes to attain saintliness," says an ancient text, "should be meticulous with regard to the blessings uttered in thanks to God for the goods He has given man; but others say, with regard to the prescriptions of the treatise of Abot (which urges concentration on study of the Torah); and still others say, with regard to the civil rights of others."

The symbolism through which Judaism expresses itself may be handed down for generations without awareness of the deeper meaning; and sometimes nothing remains except an accent on certain phases of morals which may receive special emphasis in Judaism. Walter Rathenau, who was probably not an observant Jew and may not have considered himself a religious Jew in any sense, ascribed to Jewish tradition his aversion to hunting. The ancient biblical and Rabbinic concept that giving unnecessary pain to an animal is a sin, had survived in his cultural make-up. In a conversation Louis D. Brandeis remarked, "You may study the Talmud; I practice it." I understood him to mean that although he had never (so far as I know) studied the Talmud, he felt that at least part of his defense of the oppressed and his fierce devotion to human freedom derived from its religious inspiration.

While some individuals and groups thus preserve certain Jewish symbols, without appreciation of their meaning, others have sought to transmit the meaning, without the symbolism. This effort began as early as Philo, and was clearly intended to make Judaism intelligible to men who were not trained in its forms, namely, assimilated Jews, or those outside the fold. Hence, while every other field of Jewish literature is almost wholly in Hebrew, the philosophical is almost wholly in other languages. The Greek of Philo, the Arabic of Rab Saadia Gaon and Maimonides, the German of Mendelssohn, Hermann Cohen and Franz Rosenzweig, the English of Solomon Schechter and of Kaufmann Kohler, testify to the nature of their common task: the translation of Judaism from its native symbolism to that imposed by the necessities of a Hellentistic-minded, Western world.

Neither symbolism without the basic ideas of Judaism, nor propositional theology separated from its symbolism—valuable as both may be—can be adequate for the preservation and transmission of the faith or the fulfillment of its task. The totality of Judaism is based on the proposition that man is the child and servant of God, and that his mission on earth is to fulfill himself by fulfilling the Will of God. It may be said quite without blasphemy, that his mission on earth is to fulfill God; for as the human process is perfected, and better men appear on the earth, the Divine goal in creation becomes continually more manifest and is more nearly approached. It is the glory of God that His most magnificent creature, free to choose between justice and injustice, love and hate, mercy and cruelty, knowledge and ignorance, turns to the good, rather than away from it.

The prophets hoped that the Jewish people, as a kingdom of priests, would consist of individual servants of God, and also, like other groups, be in totality a composite servant. Its composite service especially requires the forms of worship, established for the individual, for the home, and the synagogue. Through these forms, above all, the group-servant retains its unity, its continuity, and its distinctiveness.

Conscious and deliberate apostasy from Judaism is, therefore, in the light of Jewish theology a heinous sin; and the ignorance of the meaning of Judaism which leads to it is one of the grave evils of the world. Whatever can give the individual Jew a better understanding of his faith, so that he will cleave to it firmly and consciously, helps mankind by helping to maintain one of its principal servants.

More complete information about Judaism may perhaps avert, in some degree, the growth of anti-Semitism. Recent research seems to indicate that its main source is not ignorance, but individual and social pathology. Dislike of groups seems to be an expression of inner unhappiness and unsettlement; and the Jews have proved a convenient target for hatred in many generations. Men who are ignorant are easily misled by those who are vicious; and it becomes the duty of any group which seeks to increase love in the world, to prevent misunderstanding of itself by offering correct information. "He who is the victim of such injustice that his neighbor will suffer punishment for injuring him," according to the Talmud, "will not be admitted to the presence of God." The reason is obvious: unless the neighbor is mentally ill, it is the duty of the person whom he misunderstands to set him right; and one has not achieved full perfection of the soul, justifying admission to the Divine Presence, if one permitted oneself to be misunderstood.

The long persistence of anti-Semitism may be due in part to the unwillingness of Jewish scholars and thinkers to deal with it. Apologetics for Judaism have been written from the days of Artapanus, 300 years before Josephus until the present; but clearly the problem cannot be solved by apologetics. Judaism needs not a defense against calumny but an effective presentation and fulfillment.

From the point of view of Judaism as a religion, anti-Semitism is of major interest because it appears as an impediment to the better understanding among men that must occur before a better world can issue from our own anarchic one. As Professor R. M. MacIver has shown in his magnificent study, *The More Perfect Union*,[4] hostility toward any group is part of a cultural trend that must be regarded as a whole. His view must be accepted as authoritative sociology; it is also excellent theology. As the ancient Sages of Israel recognized, hostility suffered by any group will be erased only when hostility, as such, ceases to dominate the minds of men.

The achievement of this goal is one of the major aims of all Western religion, and of Judaism in particular. The tensions among religious groups will not be solved by a retreat from religion, but by advancement toward it. Divisions between men, expressed in mutual hostility, have their origin in paganism and not in monotheism, though monotheism may not have succeeded in eradicating them. For the disappearance of anti-Semitism, Judaism looks to a world in which religion will have been vindicated.

So it comes about that the future of the Jews as a group and as individuals is intimately bound up with the goals of their faith. The Jews are hostages to the doctrine entrusted to them by their prophets and Sages. In a world moving toward religion, Jews may suffer hostilities surviving the pagan era; but in a world which reverts to paganism, Jews have no

[4] *The More Perfect Union*, The Macmillan Company, New York, 1948.

possibility of life. Said the fishes to the fox, in Rabbi Akiba's fable, "If we are in danger in the water, our natural element, what would happen to us on the dry land!"

Both from the viewpoint of man's spiritual advancement and the more limited one of improved understanding among men, one of the most promising trends of our day is the growth of profound religious insight throughout America. New winds have blown during the past decade, in Judaism as well as in Christianity. The materialistic emphasis widely accepted in my college days is being replaced by new spiritual insights. The wistfulness for religion, first evident in the late 1930's, is taking effective form. The theological seminaries may serve as barometers for the general community in this regard. From a number comes word that there is increasing interest in theology, and that, with philosophy, it is replacing exclusive preoccupation with politics and with social reforms. This appears equally to be true of Jewish and Christian theological seminaries in America. This new religious spirit, unreservedly loyal to the traditions from which it springs, seeks to increase better understanding and love among men rather than to set them apart. It seeks no reduction of the various faiths to a common, meaningless syncretism, but their fulfillment as separate efforts to achieve mutual appreciation among men and common service to God.

A survey of the trend would be beyond the proper limits of this work; yet so far as Judaism is concerned, the development, should it prove continuous and fulfill itself, would be of the utmost significance. Few, regarding the American Jewish scene only a decade ago, could have foreseen it. When the late Rabbi Meir Berlin, leader of the Orthodox faction of the World Zionist Organization and scion of one of the most distinguished rabbinic families of our time, visited America in 1943, he observed that there seemed little promise of a renaissance of Judaism here. But when he returned for a last visit, in 1948, he found that the renaissance he had thought impossible seemed to have begun.

In the light of Jewish history the student will not be surprised at the development. A Babylonian Jew in the first century of the Christian Era would have been astonished had he been told that within a few generations the land where Judaism seemed to be vanishing was to become the center of its learning and culture, the home of the Babylonian Talmud, and the Geonim. In the ninth century, it appeared unlikely that the Jews of Spain would produce Ibn Gabirol, Judah Ha-Levi, and Maimonides; nor was there much in the Germany and France of the days of Rabbenu Gershom to promise the development of Jewish learning, culture, and life that marked the period of Tosafists. We may be at the beginning of a new era in the Western world, when men will turn toward the eternal truths and the appreciation of religious insights, and when Judaism will again thrive as a creative force.

A resurgence of Jewish observance in our highly standardized and industrialized world may be considered in the light of a remark made by Van Wyck Brooks. Some years ago, I told him that many of my colleagues in the American rabbinate and a still larger proportion of the laity believed that the time had come to abandon or change many or most of the distinctive Jewish ceremonials as incompatible with industrial civilization. "Perhaps," he said simply, "it would be better to change industrial civilization." The aesthetic insight thus revealed by this brilliant writer may become part of the culture of our time; and the future of American Judaism may yet be as luminous a spiritual phenomenon as those of ancient Palestine and Babylonia or medieval Spain. Such a renaissance of Judaism would be another example of what Christian writers frequently call the "mystery of Israel," and what to a Jewish writer seems nothing less than the miracle of Israel.

The basic element in this mystery or miracle is the survival of Judaism. In the first century, no one would have predicted the continued life of the faith and the people for two centuries, much less two millennia.

All the forces of sociology and politics, as well as individual psychology, seemed for many centuries to converge on the extinction of Judaism. Its demands for rigid formalism of observance, its insistence on remaining a religion which must be studied in order to be followed, the suspicion and distrust of its adherents by their neighbors, the lack of any central organization, would all have seemed to spell its certain doom. No wonder that more than one talmudic authority came to the dismal conclusion that "the Torah is destined to be forgotten by Israel." But somehow the expected evils were averted. Judaism has continued to live and flourish; and it now shows, in some respects, more vitality than for many generations.

The objective student of society can easily dismiss this phenomenon as mere chance, or as the result of various forces, not completely definable. He can "explain" the miracle of the prophets, who few in number were able to preserve and advance the pure tradition of Moses, despite the apostasy of the majority and the persecutions of idolatrous kings. He can show how various human factors made the Babylonian exile an instrument of invigoration, rather than of death. After the event, he can demonstrate that, given ordinary common sense, the Maccabees were bound to defeat the Seleucids, to obtain autonomy and further life for their community; and that Rabban Johanan ben Zakkai and his colleagues were bound to establish a non-political entity for Judaism to replace the state that had perished. He can identify the forces that made for the emergence of European Judaism, precisely when that of Palestine and Babylonia began to decline; and can regard as mere accident the rise of American Judaism when that of Europe approached the frightful catastrophes of the 1930's. Similarly, the emergence of the State of Israel may be attributed to nothing more than manipulation of human forces by a determined minority, to the wisdom and generosity of statesmen, and to the heroism of soldiers in battle.

Such assumptions have their place in scientific inquiry which seeks to explain events always by what preceded them, and regards as beyond its scope the concept that they may be determined by goals toward which man and the Universe strive. There remains this puzzle: that in the astonishing record of man the chronological sequence is not necessarily the logical one, and does not necessarily explain all that calls for explanation. The reader of Jewish history in our generation may be particularly moved by this thought, as were so many previous generations. Turning the pages of the historical essays in this volume—written with scientific objectivity—it is hard to escape the conviction that all this has a Meaning, and a Purpose; and that in this remarkable tale there is, as everywhere in the Universe and Life, a manifestation of God. That manifestation is not described by the historians; and to the extent that it is a mystery, the story of the Jews remains a mystery.

The mystery is if anything intensified in the reading of this book. While errors are exposed, and much information is offered, the truth always is revealed as more miraculous than the fable, and the increase of data increases the marvel.

Having read and re-read the various chapters I feel more than ever convinced that the writers, who so generously and painstakingly gave of themselves by sharing with us their knowledge and by helping us see through the detailed facts the greatness expressed in them, have performed an act of *kiddush ha-shem*, the sanctification of the Name of God.

FOREWORD TO THE THIRD EDITION

Generous public response and great scholarly generosity made possible the present edition, which in many ways fills unfortunate gaps in the first and second. Material on the Jews in Eastern Europe has been supplied by Israel Halpern, Abraham Menes, and Bernard D. Weinryb; while Arieh Tartakower has written a whole new chapter on "The Decline of European Jewry." Besides the discussion of the rebirth of Israel prepared by Ben Zion Dinur for the second edition, this volume includes authoritative papers on the Near East and the State of Israel by its President Itzhak Ben-Zvi and by Oscar I. Janowsky. Members of the Planning Committee, notably R. M. MacIver and Eli Ginzberg, arranged expansion of Section III so that, without omission of a large proportion of material from earlier editions, the sociology and demography are strengthened by analyses from Simon Kuznets, Milton Himmelfarb, and Nathan Glazer, as well as a supplement by Jacob Lestschinsky. Other contributors to the first edition have thoughtfully corrected their chapters and have brought them up to date. Among these was Israel S. Chipkin, who lamentably died in 1955. Also recorded with sorrow is the decease of Arturo Castiglioni, Julius B. Maller, Ralph Marcus, and Alexander Marx, as well as Louis M. Rabinowitz, who provided special funds for preparation of the third edition.

Even more than its predecessors, the present edition received the earnest, devoted attention of Miss Jessica Feingold, who became, in effect, associate editor. The work could not possibly have appeared without her indefatigable co-operation.

Both the authors and the editor are most appreciative of the fine translations by Moshe Kohn (Chapters 6 and 13) and Beatrice Weinreich (Chapter 8 and the supplement to Chapter 38). In reverse, chapters from the first edition are now being published in Hebrew, the first being *Darkei Ha-Yahadut be-Amerika*, by Moshe Davis, issued in Tel-Aviv in 1953. Other chapters may soon appear in paperback form in English.

A cross section of 209 Americans indicated "What questions should be answered in the book on Judaism and the Jews?" in preparation for the 1946 edition. The same group, and a list of some 2,500, were sent the same questionnaire in 1956-1957. As a result the history of ten momentous years is covered from a unique angle in the Appendix, which also indicates the location in these volumes of the answers sought by the 745 who helpfully responded.

Despite the advances made in the third edition, it cannot possibly be complete or contemporary. Plans are already under way for an improved fourth edition. It is hoped that will consider recent archaeological finds perforce omitted from the chapters on the early history. Perhaps time will bring clarity, too, regarding recent studies in blood groupings, fingerprints, and the incidence of certain diseases—all suggesting new light on the whole problem of common ethnic type. A way may also be found to implement the 1950 suggestion of Louis Ginzberg for an investigation of the influence of Jewish law on canon law and the Code of Justinian. Another needed comprehensive study is that of Judaism as philosophy or the philosophy of Judaism. A chapter on Jewish bibliography would be invaluable. The Appendix could be enriched by study of a comparable questionnaire sent other groups, including one exclusively Jewish; analysis of the whole series could profitably be elaborated.

The present edition benefited greatly from constructive reviews, as well as oral and written suggestions. A fourth edition would also gain much from such comment.

All royalties will continue to be earmarked for subsequent improved editions, in hopes that the work may become a classic worthy of its subject and useful to generations yet unborn.

July 4, 1959

I

THE HISTORY OF JUDAISM AND THE JEWS

I

THE HISTORY OF JUDAISM AND THE JEWS

CHAPTER I

THE BIBLICAL PERIOD

By William Foxwell Albright

1. Hebrew Beginnings

Hebrew national tradition excels all others in its clear picture of tribal and family origins. In Egypt and Babylonia, in Assyria and Phoenicia, in Greece and Rome, we look in vain for anything comparable. There is nothing like it in the tradition of the Germanic peoples. Neither India nor China can produce anything similar, since their earliest historical memories are literary deposits of distorted dynastic tradition, with no trace of the herdsman or peasant behind the demigod or king with whom their records begin. Neither in the oldest Indic historical writings (the Puranas) nor in the earliest Greek historians is there a hint of the fact that both Indo-Aryans and Hellenes were once nomads who immigrated into their later abodes from the north. The Assyrians, to be sure, remembered vaguely that their earliest rulers, whose names they recalled without any details about their deeds, were tent dwellers, but whence they came had long been forgotten.

In contrast with these other peoples the Israelites preserved an unusually clear picture of simple beginnings, of complex migrations, and of extreme vicissitudes, which plunged them from their favored status under Joseph to bitter oppression after his death. Until recently it was the fashion among biblical historians to treat the patriarchal sagas of Genesis as though they were artificial creations of Israelite scribes of the Divided Monarchy or tales told by imaginative rhapsodists around Israelite campfires during the centuries following their occupation of the country. Eminent names among scholars can be cited for regarding every item of Gen. 11-50 as reflecting late invention, or at least retrojection of events and conditions under the Monarchy into the remote past, about which nothing was thought to have been really known to the writers of later days.

The archaeological discoveries of the past generation have changed all this. Aside from a few die-hards among older scholars, there is scarcely a single biblical historian who has not been impressed by the rapid accumulation of data supporting the substantial historicity of patriarchal tradition. According to the traditions of Genesis the ancestors of Israel were closely related to the nomadic and seminomadic peoples who roamed over North Arabia and contiguous lands in the last centuries of the second millennium B.C.E. and the first centuries of the first millennium. This has been strikingly confirmed by the linguistic data found in recently excavated inscriptions. Genesis derives the ancestors of Israel from Mesopotamia—archaeological evidence agrees. According to Gen. 11:31, Terah, father of Abraham, migrated from Ur-kasdim, that is, from the territory of the great Early-Babylonian city of Ur, to the region of Harran in northwestern Mesopotamia.[1] The British excavations at Ur from 1922 to 1934, illustrated by cuneiform documents from other sites, have proved that Ur was at the height of its prosperity from about 2070 to about 1960 B.C.E. (new low chronology), when it was destroyed by invading Elamites. In the eighteenth century Ur was partially restored, but during the wars between Samsu-iluna, the Amorite son of the great Hammurabi, and Ilima-Anum in the early seventeenth century it was utterly destroyed and disappears from history for centuries. We shall probably never be able to fix the date of Terah's migration from Ur to Harran, but there can be no doubt that a date about the third quarter of the twentieth century B.C.E. would suit historical indications remarkably well.

We lack space to outline the evidence which demonstrates beyond reasonable doubt that Hebrew tradition was correct in tracing the Patriarchs directly back to the Balikh Valley in northwestern Mesopotamia. This evidence consists of explicit references to cities like Harran and Nahor (Gen. 24:10), both of which were flourishing in the nineteenth and eighteenth centuries;[2] it consists also of personal, tribal and divine names,[3] and especially of the cosmogonic narratives of Gen. 1-11.[4] The latter are peculiarly significant, because they are closely related to similar material preserved in Assyro-Babylonian tablets, whereas they bear virtually no relation whatever to Canaanite cosmogony as now known from various sources. In this connection it may be noted that the writer no longer connects the story of Babel with the time of Hammurabi and his successors (seventeenth-sixteenth centuries B.C.E.) but rather with the Babylonian stories relating to the foundation of Babylon by Sargon of Accad, several centuries earlier.[5]

We now know that the age of the Patriarchs, between the twentieth and sixteenth centuries B.C.E., was unusually well adapted for just such movements as those described in the Book of Genesis. In the twentieth and nineteenth centuries Amorite chieftains displaced native Accadian (Assyro-Babylonian) princes in most Mesopotamian districts, and the process was continued until by the time of the Mari archives in the late eighteenth century we find Amorites in nearly every important political post from the Zagros Mountains in western Iran to the Mediterranean. The term "Amorite," it must be remembered, was originally an Accadian word

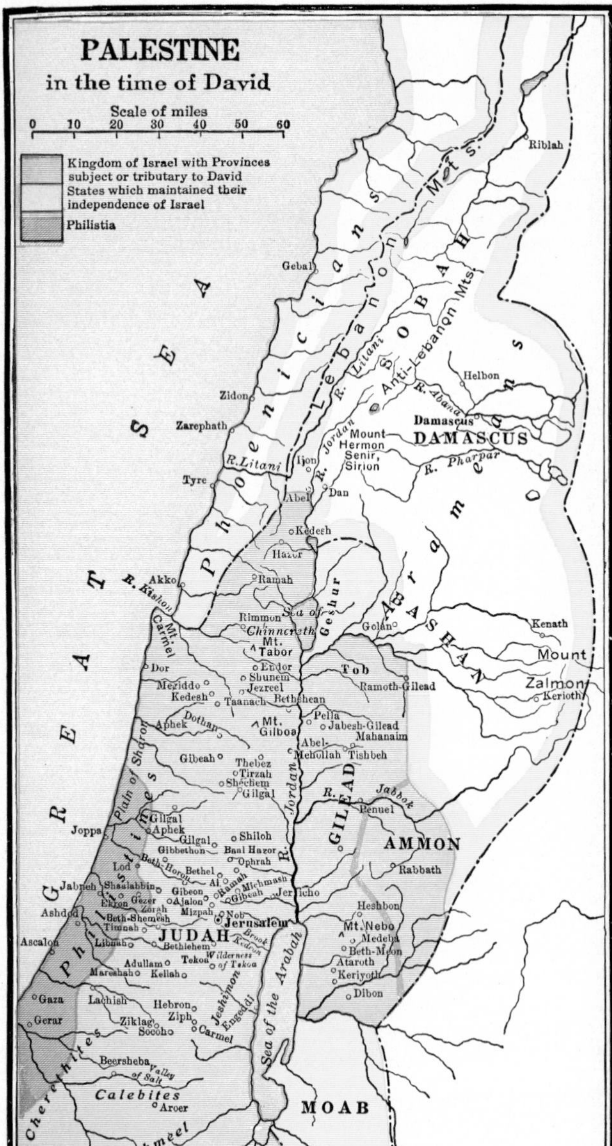
PALESTINE
in the time of David
Scale of miles
0 10 20 30 40 50 60
Kingdom of Israel with Provinces subject or tributary to David
States which maintained their independence of Israel
Philistia
GREAT SEA
Phoenicians
Lebanon Mts.
Anti-Lebanon Mts.
SOBAH
Aramaeans
Riblah
Gebal
Zidon
Zarephath
Tyre
R. Litani
Ijon
Abel
Dan
Kedesh
Hazor
Ramah
Akko
R. Kishon
Mt. Carmel
Rimmon
Sea of Chinnereth
Mt. Tabor
Geshur
Golan
BASHAN
Helbon
R. Abana
Damascus
DAMASCUS
Mount Hermon Senir, Sirion
R. Jordan
R. Pharpar
Kenath
Mount Zalmon
Kerioth
Dor
Endor
Shunem
Jezreel
Megiddo
Kedesh
Taanach
Bethshean
Tob
Ramoth-Gilead
Dothan
Aphek
Mt. Gilboa
Pella
Jabesh-Gilead
Mahanaim
Abel-Meholah
Tishbeh
Plain of Sharon
Gibeah
Thebez
Tirzah
Shechem
Gilgal
R. Jabbok
Penuel
GILEAD
Joppa
Gilgal
Aphek
Gilgal
Shiloh
Gibbethon
Baal Hazor
Ophrah
Lod
Beth-Horon
Bethel
Ai
Jabneh
Shaalabbin
Gibeon
Ramah
Michmash
Gibeah
Jericho
Ekron
Gezer
Ajalon
Zorah
Mizpah
Nob
Ashdod
Beth-Shemesh
Timnah
Jerusalem
Brook Kedron
JUDAH
Ascalon
Libnah
Bethlehem
Wilderness of Tekoa
Adullam
Tekoa
Mareshah
Keilah
Philistines
Jeshimon
Engeddi
Sea of the Arabah
AMMON
Rabbath
Heshbon
Mt. Nebo
Medeba
Beth-Meon
Ataroth
Keriyoth
Dibon
Gaza
Lachish
Hebron
Gerar
Ziklag
Ziph
Socoho
Carmel
Cherethites
Beersheba
Valley of Salt
Calebites
Aroer
MOAB
Jerahmeel
Amalekites
Idumeans
NEGEB
EDOM
SEIR

PALESTINE
Physical Map
Scale of miles
0 5 10 15 20 25
Over 3000
2000 to 3000
1000 to 2000
500 to 1000
Sea level to 500
Below sea level
Ras el Kerum
Haifa
GREAT SEA
R. ed Dufleh
Caesarea
R. el Mefjir
R. Iskanderuneh
Birket Ramadan
Plain of Sharon
Joppa
Lydda
R. Rubin
Valley of Sorek
R. Sukereir
W. el Burshein
Azotus
Plain of Philistia
Lowland
Ascalon
Val. of Zephathah
Shephela
W. esh Sheridah
W. Ghuzzeh
Beersheba
W. es Seba

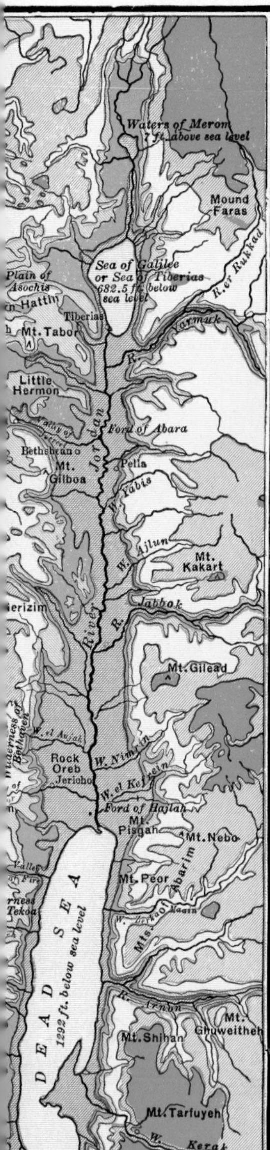

Waters of Merom
7 ft. above sea level
Mound Faras
Sea of Galilee or Sea of Tiberias 682.5 ft. below sea level
Plain of Asochis
Tiberias
Mt. Tabor
Yarmuk
Little Hermon
Ford of Abara
Bethshean
Mt. Gilboa
Jordan
Pella
W. Yabis
W. Ajlun
Mt. Kakart
Jabbok
River
Mt. Gilead
Rock Oreb
Jericho
W. Nimrin
Ford of Hajlah
Mt. Pisgah
Mt. Nebo
Mt. Peor
Abarim
DEAD SEA
1292 ft. below sea level
R. Arnon
Mt. Shihan
Mt. Ghuweitheh
Mt. Tarfuyeh
W. Kerak
Val. of Salt

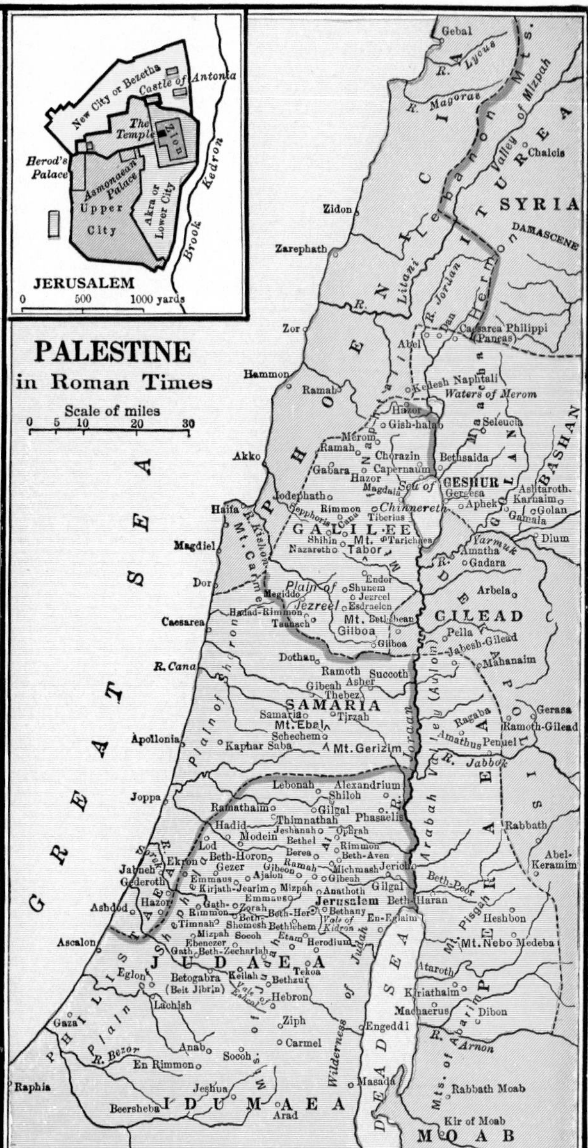

PALESTINE
in Roman Times
Scale of miles
0 5 10 20 30
JERUSALEM
0 500 1000 yards
New City or Bezetha
Castle of Antonia
The Temple
Zion
Herod's Palace
Asmonaean Palace
Upper City
Akra or Lower City
Brook Kedron
GREAT SEA
PHOENICIA
ITUREA
SYRIA
DAMASCENE
Lebanon Mts.
Valley of Mizpah
Hermon
GALILEE
SAMARIA
JUDAEA
IDUMAEA
GILEAD
PERAEA
BASHAN
GESHUR
MOAB
EDOM
GEBAL
Gebal
Zidon
Zarephath
Zor
Hammon
Akko
Haifa
Magdiel
Dor
Caesarea
R. Cana
Apollonia
Joppa
Jabneh
Ashdod
Ascalon
Gaza
Raphia
Beersheba
Akrabbim
Chalcis
Caesarea Philippi
Abel
Dan
Kedesh Naphtali
Waters of Merom
Hazor
Gish-halab
Seleucia
Chorazin
Capernaum
Bethsaida
Sea of Chinnereth
Tiberias
Magdala
Gergesa
Aphek
Ashtaroth
Karnaim
Golan
Gamala
Dium
Nazareth
Mt. Tabor
Tarichaea
Gadara
Amatha
Arbela
Endor
Shunem
Jezreel
Megiddo
Plain of Jezreel
Mt. Gilboa
Bethshean
Pella
Jabesh-Gilead
Mahanaim
Dothan
Succoth
Samaria
Mt. Ebal
Schechem
Mt. Gerizim
Tirzah
Ramoth-Gilead
Gerasa
Penuel
Shiloh
Alexandrium
Phasaelis
Jericho
Bethel
Ai
Gibeon
Gibeah
Anathoth
Jerusalem
Bethany
Bethlehem
Herodium
Emmaus
Lod
Gezer
Hebron
Tekoa
Lachish
Engeddi
Masada
Heshbon
Mt. Nebo
Medeba
Rabbath
Dibon
Machaerus
R. Arnon
Rabbath Moab
Kir of Moab
Zoar
R. Sared
DEAD SEA
Plain of Sharon
Mt. Carmel
Wilderness of Judah
Arad
Carmel
Ziph
Socoh

meaning "westerner"; in the patriarchal age it was applied to all people speaking Northwest Semitic dialects, including the ancestors of the later Arameans and Israelites. Among "Amorite" personal names in these centuries we have a number characteristic also of Hebrew tradition, such as Abram, Jacob, Laban, Zebulun, Benjamin.[6] Later the name shifted considerably in meaning, being applied to themselves by Syro-Palestinian groups with which the Israelites came into direct conflict. The Mari archives, excavated by a French expedition in 1936, illustrate the freedom of movement between various parts of the Amorite world in the late eighteenth century extraordinarily well. Trade was widespread and caravans of merchants were among the commonest sights. The king of Assyria, with his capital at Assur on the Tigris, negotiated with the prince of Qatna in central Syria with a view to marrying his son to the latter's daughter, just as the humbler Abram sent his son to Nahor near Harran for a similar purpose. To protect traders and farmers against the still seminomadic kinsmen of the settled Amorites great vigilance was necessary and an elaborate system of signal fires was devised for rapid communication over distances.[7]

Numerous recent excavations in sites of this period in Palestine, supplemented by finds made in Egypt and Syria, give us a remarkably precise idea of patriarchal Palestine, fitting well into the picture handed down in Genesis. After about 2100 B.C.E. there was a progressive deterioration of material culture in the land, accompanied by rapid thinning out of occupation, certainly because of increasing pressure from nomadic and seminomadic groups in and around the country. After the twentieth century nomadic attacks blotted out sedentary occupation all but completely from southern and central Trans-Jordan; it was not until the thirteenth that it became resettled, after some seven centuries without appreciable sedentary occupation.[8] Egyptian records of the late twentieth century show that nearly all Palestine and southern Syria were organized along tribal lines, very few towns being mentioned, in strict agreement with the results of excavations. Under Egyptian protection, however, sedentary occupation developed rapidly, until by the late nineteenth century Egyptian records just published by Georges Posener prove that nearly all western Palestine and southern Syria were organized as city-states, while Trans-Jordan was still in the tribal stage of development.[9] Again archaeology confirms the data provided by written records. In this period, moreover, towns were scattered thinly through the hill country and sedentary occupation was largely restricted to the coastal plains and the broad alluvial valleys of Jezreel and the Jordan. The wanderings of the Patriarchs are thus correctly limited by tradition to the hill country and the desert Negeb; not a single city of the coastal plains or the broad valleys of the interior is mentioned (except in the extreme south). Moreover, Egyptian records and excavations at such sites as Gezer and Megiddo in Palestine, Gebal (Byblus), Qatna and Ugarit in Syria prove conclusively that Egypt then controlled Palestine and southern Syria, and that trade between Egypt and Palestine was very active.[10] The famous mural painting of Beni-Hasan, dated about the year 1892 B.C.E., portrays a visit to Middle Egypt by a little caravan of traveling Semitic smiths and musicians, who provide an excellent background from which to understand Gen. 4:20-22.[11] The picture of limited movements in the hill country of Palestine, of seasonal migration between the Negeb and central Palestine,[12] and of easy travel to Mesopotamia and Egypt is, accordingly, so perfectly in accord with conditions in the Middle Bronze Age that historical skepticism is quite unwarranted. When we add the fact that our present knowledge of social institutions and customs in another part of northern Mesopotamia in the fifteenth century (Nuzu) has brilliantly illuminated many details in the patriarchal stories which do not fit into the post-Mosaic tradition at all,[13] our case for the substantial historicity of the tradition of the Patriarchs is clinched. This does not, of course, mean that oral tradition, even though based on poetic epics as Cassuto has most recently seen, can be treated by the historian as though it were based directly on written records. In many ways the orally transmitted record is superior, but it is peculiarly exposed to the phenomena of refraction and selection of elements suited for epic narrative, regardless of their chronological order.[14] It is, accordingly, uncertain to what extent we can adopt the traditional order of events or the precise motivation attributed to them. Nor can we accept every picturesque detail as it stands in our present narrative. But as a whole the picture in Genesis is historical, and there is no reason to doubt the general accuracy of the biographical details and the sketches of personality which make the Patriarchs come alive with a vividness unknown to a single extrabiblical character in the whole vast literature of the ancient Near East.

2. The Age of Moses

There has been a persistent effort by many scholars to discredit the Israelite tradition of a prolonged sojourn in Egypt before the time of Moses. It is true that these narratives, as we have them, were modernized about the tenth century B.C.E., the personal and geographical names of older tradition being in part revised to suit contemporary Egyptian nomenclature. Since almost exactly the same thing was done some seven centuries later by the Greek translators of Genesis, the mere fact of such revision does not disprove the authenticity of the underlying tradition.[15] We now know from a mass of corroborative evidence to what a profound extent the northern part of Egypt, especially the northeastern Delta, became semitized during the period in question.[16] Semitic influences poured into Egypt during the Twelfth Dynasty, when (as noted above) Palestine, Phoenicia and part of Syria belonged to the sphere of Egyptian suzerainty. In the eighteenth century these influences increased rapidly in significance, and before the end of this century Semites had made themselves masters of much of Egypt.[17] The Hyksos conquerors are now known to have been mainly—perhaps entirely—of Northwest Semitic stock, closely akin to the Hebrews, who probably formed one of their component elements.[18] Biblical Hebrew names like Jacob and Hur figure among the lists of their chieftains and nobles. There are numerous details in Hebrew tradition which square so completely with Egyptian records that an intimate connection between the Hebrew settlement in Egypt and the Hyksos conquest may be considered certain. We cannot say more with confidence, because of the almost complete lack of Egyptian historical inscriptions during the whole Hyksos age. If this gap in our knowledge is ever filled, we shall probably owe it to some unexpected find of cuneiform tablets in Syria or Palestine.

The Hyksos were finally crushed by the founder of the Eighteenth Dynasty, Amosis I, who stormed Tanis (Zoan) and destroyed the last Semitic garrisons in Egypt about 1550 B.C.E. There is no reason to think that the Semites were driven out of the country, though some of the leaders and the more nomadic elements may have retreated to Palestine. Judging from contemporary documents, those who escaped slaughter were enslaved or were permitted to remain in the region around Tanis as serfs. There is, accordingly, every reason to regard Amosis as the "Pharaoh who knew not Joseph" of Ex. 1:8. In tradition, however, there is always a strong tendency to pass silently over periods when there is nothing exciting to report. Hence Hebrew tradition slipped without realizing the shift from Amosis to Sethos I, who began to rebuild the long-neglected city of Tanis, after his accession to the throne of the Nineteenth Dynasty in 1319 B.C.E. In the interim Semitic influence became increasingly powerful in Egypt. The worship of Canaanite gods introduced by the Hyksos, such as Baal, Horon, Resheph, and of goddesses like Ashtaroth (Astarte), Anath and Asherah (called "Holiness," Heb. *Qodesh*) increased more or less steadily until it reached a climax in the time of Moses (thirteenth century B.C.E.).[19] Specifically Hebrew deities also were worshiped, to judge from a personal name borne by a petty official of the late fourteenth century, "Sadde-'ammi," that is, "Shadde-'ammi" in later Hebrew pronunciation.[20] The god Shaddai, properly "The One of the Mountains, Mountain-god,"[21] attributed in Israelite tradition to the Patriarchs, was certainly a principal deity of Israel in the days of Moses, as we know from the fact that the name is a component of three personal names borne by Israelites living in the time of Moses. Since one of these names is identical (in reverse order of elements) with this Sadde-'ammi, it is quite likely that it belongs to a

Hebrew who was an older contemporary of Moses. Some two generations earlier there had flourished another high Egyptian official with a Semitic name who may have been Hebrew by race, Yanhamu, Egyptian commissioner in Palestine.

By 1300 B.C.E. the stage was set, culturally and religiously, for the emergence of a heroic figure like Moses. He himself bore an Egyptian name only slightly altered in the speech of later Israel, and Egyptian names such as Phinehas, Hophni and Merari were common among his relatives.[22] At that time, after intimate political and cultural contact between Egypt and Palestine for some seven centuries, there were thousands—perhaps scores of thousands—of Semites living as slaves, serfs, merchants and nobles in Egypt, with thousands of Egyptians in Palestine and Phoenicia. We have already referred to the Canaanite gods adopted into the Egyptian pantheon; hundreds of Semitic words (Canaanite and Hebrew) occur in the native Egyptian literature of the period, especially in the thirteenth century, in which no literary composition failed to be sprinkled with them. Bilingualism must have been characteristic of the Ramesside capital at Tanis, around which lay the land of Goshen. In contemporary Palestine we find no fewer than four scripts used side by side to write Canaanite, and learned scribes wrote Accadian, the medium of international communication employed at that time in the entire ancient Near East. It would, accordingly, be passing strange if Moses were not at home in both Egyptian and Canaanite, as well as in his native Hebrew (which was only a dialectal variant of Canaanite). Moreover, the entire cosmopolitan world of the day must have been familiar to his eyes and ears in and around the Egyptian capital at Tanis. The reconstruction of Tanis begun by Sethos I was continued by his son, the pharaoh of the Exodus, Rameses II, who called it "House of Rameses" (Raamses, Ex. 1:11; cf. Gen. 47:11, where "the land of Rameses" is the same district as the "plain of Tanis" in Psalm 78:12, 43).[23] Since it was the capital of Egypt and was also situated on the Egyptian frontier toward Syria, an Egyptian scribe was justified in speaking of it as the "front of every foreign country, the end of Egypt." He goes on to describe the beauty of its gorgeous buildings and the importance of its military role as the base of operations in foreign lands, where chariot horses were inspected, foot soldiers were marshaled, and warships were moored. Another scribe waxes dithyrambic in picturing the wealth and resources of the city and its environs, emphasizing also the fact that it was an important seaport. In a stele found at Beth-shan in Palestine, dated in 1292 B.C.E., it is said that "He [Rameses II] puts the Asiatics to flight, pacifying the war that had flared up everywhere; those who wish come to him together in humility at his fortress of life and prosperity, House of Rameses, Great of Victories."[24]

The religion of Egypt in the fourteenth and thirteenth centuries B.C.E.

is better known than at any other period, thanks to the great wealth of inscriptions and monumental representations which have come down to us. At the beginning of the fourteenth century Egypt was dominated by the priesthood of the god Amun at Thebes, whose synthetic figure had gradually absorbed the most important deities, such as Re of Heliopolis (Heb. On, home of Joseph's wife), and had become far more important than that of any other Egyptian deity. In fact, just at this time we find Amun-Re exalted in hymns as the father of all other gods, the maker of heaven and earth, creator of mankind. About 1375 B.C.E. the young Amenophis IV (*c.* 1377-1360), apparently influenced by his extraordinary mother, Teye, followed an unidentified adviser in breaking completely with the cult of Amun, which was replaced by a solar monotheism centering about the solar disk, Aten. For over fifteen years this monotheistic heresy held sway over Egypt, the old polytheism being repressed with such violence that later Egypt remembered the young king only as "the criminal of Akhetaten" (name of his capital at Tell el-Amarna). Though some writers have gone much too far in connecting the monotheism of Moses with the cult of the Aten, it is probable that there is some indirect connection.[25] In the first place, the people of northern Egypt were restive under the ecclesiastical tyranny of the priests of Amun and did not take kindly to its restoration after Akhenaten's death. In the second place, we have now some long hymns from the thirteenth century which show that the religion of Amun itself had been considerably modified in the preceding two centuries in the direction of syncretism and universalism, with frequent reminiscence of the style and wording of the hymns to the Aten found in numbers of the tombs of Amarna.[26]

Among the clearest illustrations of ideas common to Atenism and Mosaism are the exclusive monotheism of both (like the God of Israel in Ex. 20:3, Aten is the god "beside whom there is none other"), the emphasis on the "Teaching" ("Torah" in Israel), and the constant stress on the one God as creator of everything (Aten, like YHWH, is the god "who creates what comes into existence"). On the other hand, there were many fundamental differences, especially in ethics, between the Aten heresy of Egypt and Mosaic monotheism. Thanks to these far-reaching differences the religion of Moses was incomparably more qualified to move mankind than was the selfish sentimentalism of Amarna.

The Ramesside society in which Moses grew to manhood two generations after the collapse of the Aten heresy was probably the most cosmopolitan hitherto known to the ancient world, as we have shown above. Its religion was equally composite. In the capital itself the great Canaanite gods Baal and Horon, with the goddesses Anath and Astarte, were worshiped on a par with the native Egyptian deities Seth and Horus, Nephthys and Isis, with which they were identified. Egyptian adaptations of several

Canaanite myths have been discovered. The picture in contemporary Canaan was similar, with Egyptian temples and cults springing up all over the country, the divine craftsman Ptah of Memphis being identified with Koshar, Hathor with Baalath of Byblus, and so on.

Yet the religious picture of Moses's youth was, by and large, singularly repulsive. Among the Canaanites extremely depraved practices were inextricably bound up with religion. Ritual prostitution of both sexes was rampant, and the variety of evil practices is attested by the multiplicity of names employed to designate these "professions." The *cinaedus* (homosexual) formed a recognized guild in Canaanite temples, and there were other groups which combined dancing and singing with divination in a peculiarly unholy union. Snake worship and human sacrifice were rife. The "Creatress of the Gods" (Asherah) was represented as a beautiful naked prostitute, called "Holiness" in both Canaan and Egypt. The two other principal Canaanite goddesses, Anath and Astarte (Heb. Ashtaroth), are called "the great goddesses which conceive but do not bear," and the rape of Anath by Baal formed a standing theme in Canaanite mythology, in spite of the fact that she was at the same time regularly called "the Virgin." Anath is represented as a naked woman astride a stallion, brandishing her lance; in Canaanite literature she figures in scenes of incredible ferocity.[27]

Among the Egyptians religion stood on a considerably higher plane, but was still anything but an edifying spectacle much of the time. The worship of animals, relatively unimportant in contemporary Canaan, was characteristic of almost every part of Egypt. Egyptian myths swarmed with crudities; for instance, creation was generally described as an act of sexual self-abuse on the part of the divine creator. Moreover, the relation between religion and ethics in Egypt had deteriorated considerably since the early second millennium, as a result of the rapid spread and concomitant degradation of funerary beliefs and practices. Not long before the fifteenth century B.C.E. an elaborate mortuary ritual, restricted to kings in the Old Empire and extended to include nobles in the Middle Empire, had been further extended to cover anyone who possessed the necessary pecuniary means. In the Book of the Dead and related works we possess the funerary ritual of the Mosaic Age. In spite of the comparatively high ethical standards of the Negative Confession and the judgment before Osiris, it became possible for anyone to assure himself a happy existence in the hereafter by suitable expenditure of his substance for proper burial and for preparation of all necessary magical spells and instructions to accompany him in the journey after death. Since an astonishingly high proportion of the per capita wealth of the country was devoted to the construction of tombs and their subsequent endowment, as well as to the funerals themselves, with the costly embalming of corpses and expensive processions and entertainments that characterized them, it is easy to understand what an abuse this entire phase of Egyptian religion had become by the time of Moses. Small wonder that the new faith reacted violently against all kinds of sacred prostitution and human sacrifice, against magic and divination, and against funerary rites and cult of the dead!

As against the decadence of contemporary Egyptian and Canaanite religion, Moses drew inspiration from the simple traditions of his own Hebrew people and the stern moral code of the nomads of Midian, among whom he spent much of his early manhood before the Exodus. Rejecting all mythology (in accordance with the example of Amarna and doubtless of other abortive efforts to reform religion of which we have no direct information), Moses kept a few traditional appellations of deity, which he applied to the new figure of YHWH, which may possibly be older than he but cannot have had any prior significance. Among these names, which we know from the earliest religious poetry of Israel, such as the Oracles of Balaam,[28] were *El* ("The Powerful One"), *Elyon* or *Eli* ("The Exalted One," used by the Canaanites as an appellation of Baal, the great storm-god, king of the gods),[29] and *Shaddai* (see above). Just as the Canaanites had sometimes used the plural of *el*, "god," to indicate "totality of the gods" (as, for instance, in the Canaanite Amarna letters) so the Israelites used *Elohim* to stress the unity and universality of God.

In the Torah we have, carefully collected and arranged, a considerable body of civil and cultic legislation. These laws and regulations are couched in different wording, showing complex sources. They have been preserved for us in documents of different ages—all relatively early. Yet there is a basic similarity about their cultural and religious background which makes it impossible not to attribute their origin to the beginnings of organized Israelite monotheism—in other words, to Moses. The cultic laws never mention the Temple, while the civil laws reflect a period before the institution of the Monarchy and the appointment of magistrates by the king. Moreover, in recent decades it has become certain that the Book of the Covenant in Ex. 21-23 is part of a once much longer Hebrew analogue to the Code of Hammurabi, the Assyrian and Hittite legal codes, and similar legislation, all belonging to the period between 2000 and 1100 B.C.E.[30] The Book of the Covenant reflects an agricultural society of patriarchal type and simple mores; it is very different in these respects from both Babylonian and Hittite aristocratic feudalism, in which payments of money replace corporal punishment, especially where superiors are convicted of crimes against inferiors. It is at the same time, however, much more humane than the Draconic Middle Assyrian laws, which reflect a singularly harsh attempt to maintain traditional mores in a highly organized urban civilization. It is, in any case, incredible that the Book of the Covenant should reflect Canaanite jurisprudence in either spirit or details, though we may freely concede strong Canaanite influence on formulation and legal terminology.

If we turn to the Priestly Code, a similar situation develops; in it we have substantially the sacrificial and ritual practice of the Tabernacle as transmitted by tradition from the period before Solomon's Temple, just as in corresponding sections of the Mishna we possess a traditional account of the practice of Herod's Temple. Just how much of this ritual goes back to Moses himself would be idle to conjecture in the present state of our knowledge; the spirit and much of the detail may be considered as antedating the Conquest of Canaan—in other words, as going back to Mosaic origins.

To Albrecht Alt we owe recognition of an extremely important fact: that there is an element in both civil and cultic legislation of the Torah which was specifically Israelite and which went back to the beginnings of Israel—in other words, it was specifically Mosaic.[31] This element is the apodictic legislation which we know best from the Ten Commandments, consisting of short injunctions, mostly couched in imperative form: "Thou shalt (not)!" The apodictic laws of the Torah reflect a monotheistic system with very lofty ethical standards. It is not necessary to insist that all this legislation goes back to the Mosaic period in its present form; it was long transmitted orally, and wording must have been modified in the course of the centuries, while relatively primitive injunctions were replaced by others which were better suited to a more advanced society.

The figure of Moses completely dominates the tradition of the Exodus and the Wanderings. It is, accordingly, impossible to picture the movements in question as though they were normal displacements of nomadic tribes. On the contrary, it took both Moses's unusual qualities of leadership and a sequence of extraordinary events, vividly portrayed for us by tradition, to induce his followers to flee from their Egyptian oppressors into the desert. After many generations in the northeastern Delta the Hebrew peasants and shepherds were resigned to submit to the odious corvée and to endure the treatment by which Sethos I and his son evidently hoped to reduce the preponderance of Semites in the region around their new capital without losing the advantage of a rich source of slave labor for the state; the alternative of risking all in a desperate break for freedom and even more perilous trek through the wild desert of the Sinai Peninsula did not appeal to them. Fortunately Moses prevailed, and his mob of serfs and slaves of every possible origin (Heb. *asafsuf* and *erebrab*) became crystallized around the tribal nucleus of Israel into a new people, with a new faith and an unparalleled mission in world history.

Having successfully negotiated the difficult barriers imposed by the great Papyrus Marsh (*yam suf*) and the Egyptian frontier posts and punitive measures, the mob of Moses's followers escaped into the desert.

Though we have a number of very old traditions regarding details of their generation ("forty years") in the desert and in Trans-Jordan, it is quite impossible to reconstruct the exact sequence of events. Some things are, however, clear. Moses had great difficulty in organizing and disciplining his followers, and there were many serious setbacks, among which we hear of an abortive invasion of the extreme southern fringe of Canaan from the Israelite base at Kadesh-barnea. Since the territory south of Canaan was occupied by nomadic Amalekites, while the fertile regions of Seir and Moab were held by Hebrew tribes, akin to Israel, which were then in the process of settling down,[32] the Israelites were seriously handicapped for want of room. Moreover, they were compelled by their flocks of sheep and their accompanying asses (at a time before camels had been generally domesticated)[33] to remain close to sources of water, like the oasis of Kadesh. Hence, after it had become evident that Israel was too weak to break through the belt of strongly fortified mounds at the extreme south of Canaan, it was decided to move past Edom and Moab into Trans-Jordan, where the situation was far more favorable. And so it was: the land of the Amorites, which included later Gilead and Ammon, had not been settled long at that time, and towns were sprinkled but thinly over an extensive territory. Moreover, west of this thin zone of fortresses were the forested hills of Gilead, designed by nature for agricultural settlement, but still almost entirely virgin. It was here that the Israelites were able to win their first victories and to establish themselves solidly before invading Canaan.[34] It was here that Moses died at the height of his powers (Deut. 34:7):[35]

"His eye was not dim nor his natural force abated!"

3. THE CONQUEST OF PALESTINE

Thanks to an enormous increase in the materials at our disposal since 1930, our picture of Canaanite history and civilization at the time of the Hebrew Conquest has become far clearer than it was. To the domain of Canaanite culture then belonged the entire coastland of Palestine and Syria from the Egyptian frontier south of Gaza to the northern boundary of Ugarit, southwest of Antioch. Eastward the borders were fluctuating, and there is much confusion in tradition between Canaanites and Amorites, whose language and culture differed so little that it is hard to find a satisfactory criterion for use of these names. Originally the term "Canaan" was applied almost certainly to Phoenicia proper as the land of purple dye, whereas "Amorite" was a general term used in Mesopotamia to designate all Northwestern Semites as "Westerners." Later "Canaan" was extended southward and eastward, while "Amor" (Amurru) was adopted in the West as a designation for a large parent state in eastern Syria, to which smaller states later traced their origin. "Canaanite" higher culture, both religious and literary, went back to age-old tradition along the eastern shore of the Mediterranean, whereas "Amorite" higher culture was strongly influenced by Sumero-Accadian civilization.

At the time of the Israelite Conquest, western Palestine had been for many centuries subject to Egyptian rule. Ever since about 2000 B.C.E. it had been nominally dependent on Egypt, but in the eighteenth century the Egyptian crown became too weak to exercise any real authority in the country. Toward the end of the century Northwest Semitic tribes occupied northern Egypt, and early in the following century a Semitic empire was established with its center at Avaris, later called Tanis (Heb. Zoan).[36] After Amosis's expulsion of the Hyksos (*c.* 1550 B.C.E.) the native Egyptian pharaohs fell heir to the Hyksos heritage in Palestine and Syria. Rebellions were frequent but invariably abortive. Under the heavy hand of Egyptian bureaucrats and garrisons of slave troops, the country suffered, as may be seen from the relatively continuous decline in the arts which has been demonstrated by archaeological explorations in the past twenty-five years.[37] The exorbitant demands of the crown were greatly swelled by the attempts of Egyptian officials of all grades to enrich themselves during their periods in office. Moreover, owing both to inefficient administration and to dishonesty, supplies for the Nubian and other slave troops which maintained order in the provinces were often held up, and the unfortunate troops had to resort to pillage and banditry in order to live. Both Egyptian and cuneiform documents of the age swarm with vivid illustrations of the situation.

At the same time that the wealth of the country and the morale of its inhabitants were slowly drained away by a rapacious foreign government, the native Canaanite princes, who were allowed to continue in their places under the watchful eyes of Egyptian commissioners, were progressively weakened in power and increased in number. Between the time of the Amarna Tablets (*c.* 1400-1360 B.C.E.) and the principal phase of the Israelite conquest under Joshua, the number of autonomous princes (sometimes called "kings" in the Amarna Tablets, just as in the Book of Joshua) in southern Palestine appears to have doubled. Excavations have shown (*e.g.*, at Debir, Eglon) that some of the Canaanite "royal cities" of Joshua's time played an entirely different role in the Amarna age. At the same time there seems to have been a tendency to scatter out from the larger centers and to settle in smaller places, owing partly perhaps to the desire to escape direct Egyptian control and partly to the fact that cisterns were beginning to come into use, making it possible to establish settlements in places far from a direct source of water (stream or fountain).

The Canaanite population had a sharp class division between the hereditary nobility, largely non-Semitic, and the dependent *khupshu* class, which was only half free, being bound to the soil but possessing certain personal and property rights.[38] There was also a considerable number of trained craftsmen, whose skill and industry made their towns known abroad; but we do not know what their social status was. In addition there was a large slave population. Characteristic of the Amarna Age in all parts of Canaan was a seminomadic class which spent much of its time robbing its sedentary neighbors or in equally troublesome employment as mercenary auxiliary troops, both in Egyptian and in native service. This class or group had been known all over Western Asia since the eighteenth century as *'Apiru* (formerly known, following the cuneiform spelling, as *Khabiru*), but generally referred to in documentary sources as "bandits." To judge from contemporary allusions and personal names borne by different 'Apiru, they were extremely heterogeneous in origin; the boundary that separated them from Northwest Semitic sheepherding seminomads was at best fluid. It may be that the term "Hebrew" (Heb. *'ibri*) is derived from this *'Apiru*, though this view has certain difficulties and is often disputed.[39]

After our earlier sketch it is not necessary to go into detail here about the religion of the Canaanites; suffice it to repeat that their religious beliefs and practices were both crude and depraved. It is not, however, true that their religion was primitive in the sense of lacking organized priesthood, temple service and pantheon. Quite the contrary! Thanks to the results of the excavations of M. Schaeffer at Ugarit since 1929, supplemented and confirmed by other work elsewhere, we now know that the Canaanites had a great many temples and shrines, adorned with idols, that they had elaborate priestly institutions, and that their pantheon was no whit less highly organized than the pantheons of Egypt, Babylonia, the Hittites, or the nearly contemporary Homeric Greeks. At the head of their pantheon were the figures of El, slightly remote from the human scene, and Baal, the great storm-god, lord of the gods and creator of mankind. Since "Baal" meant properly "lord," the name also appears as a component element of other divine names, but used alone it referred only to the great cosmic figure of the storm-god.

It is no easy task to reconstruct the details of the Conquest, since the extant Israelite tradition is not uniform and our biblical sources vary considerably. Moreover, there are scarcely any inscriptions which throw direct light on the time and circumstances of the Israelite invasion; and the results of excavations are ambiguous and sometimes in apparent conflict with the tradition. However, we are much better off than we were a quarter century ago. The progress of excavation and of philological interpretation of inscriptions has made it absolutely certain, in the writer's judgment, that the principal phase of the Conquest must be dated in the thirteenth century, probably in the second half of that century. The destruction of the last Canaanite towns of Tell Beit Mirsim (probably Debir) and Beth-el (both excavated by the writer) must be dated in the thirteenth century, the latter probably preceding the former by a respectable interval. The destruction of the last Canaanite Lachish is probably to be dated in or about 1230 B.C.E., immediately before the reference to Israel as a nomadic folk conquered by Egyptian arms on a triumphal stele of Marniptah, set up in 1229 B.C.E. At all events, an Egyptian document recording the payment of local tribute in the fourth year of Marniptah or one of his two ephemeral successors, which was discovered by Starkey in 1937, requires a date for the burning of Lachish in 1230 or somewhat later. The problem of Jericho is immensely complicated by the fact that there has been no adequate systematic excavation there to clear up the somewhat obscure stratigraphic picture; we know that the last Canaanite Jericho was not destroyed before the fourteenth century, but whether it was occupied or not in the thirteenth century has not been determined with certainty.[40] If there was a Canaanite settlement there at that time it was not very important. However, it may be that Israelite oral tradition combined a story about how such a Jericho passed into Israelite hands with an older story about the destruction of a larger precursor, in much the same way as it conflated the destruction of the great Canaanite town of the third millennium at Ai (Beth-aven) with the fall of the near-by Canaanite town of the thirteenth century at Luz (Beth-el).[41]

Recent efforts to reduce the historical importance of Joshua to a minimum have been unsuccessful.[42] On the other hand, it seems probable that his military feats were somewhat exaggerated by the standard tradition in Joshua, since the capture of Hebron is elsewhere attributed to Caleb and the seizure of Debir (Kirjath-sepher) is credited to Caleb's son-in-law Othniel, the first "judge." However this may be, excavations show that there was only a short interval between the destruction of such Canaanite towns as Debir and Beth-el, and their reoccupation by Israel. This means that the Israelite invasion was not a characteristic irruption of nomads, who continued to live in tents for generations after their first invasion. Neither was the Israelite conquest of Canaan a gradual infiltration, as often insisted by modern scholars. The tradition that virtually all Canaanite towns were burned to the ground while their inhabitants and even the cattle were slaughtered is evidently exaggerated, since such towns as Gibeon, Shechem, Hepher, Tirzah and Zaphon were incorporated into the Israelite tribal system. On the other hand, we know from numerous nearly contemporary references that the practice of *herem*, "devoting to destruction," was very common in that region and period, so it would have been very strange if the wild and warlike Israelites did not follow the custom of the day. Later tradition recognized that the destruction of a large part of the Canaanite population had saved Israel from a process of acculturation which might have had disastrous consequences for the new faith.

There can be no doubt that the number of Israelites had swollen enormously since the days of the desert wanderings in the Negeb, south of Canaan, when Israel was too weak even to occupy the little fortresses on the southern fringe of the country. The religion of Moses was a missionary faith with dynamic appeal to the nomadic and seminomadic tribes of that time. After the first great victories over Sihon, converts may well have flocked to join the triumphant standards of the new faith. Among them was the Syrian diviner, Balaam, to whose brief conversion we owe the oracles which have been transmitted to us in fragmentary form in Num. 23-24.[43] There can be little doubt that the same thing happened in western Palestine. The case of the Gibeonites has been recorded by tradition. Far more significant is the fact that the Book of Joshua does not preserve any detailed tradition regarding the conquest of the land of Ephraim and Manasseh, separating Judah from Issachar and Zebulun. Since Shiloh, seat of the Tabernacle, Shechem, traditional meeting place of the first Israelite assembly after the Conquest, and Timnah, to which Joshua himself retired, were all located in this region, the lack of any canonical tradition about the mode of its occupation is very striking indeed. In other and later sources we do find a tradition about the conquest of central Palestine, but all these sources attribute the conquest to the time of Jacob, several centuries earlier.[44] We can hardly be far wrong in assuming that central Palestine was already largely peopled by seminomadic and partly settled Hebrew clans which attached themselves immediately to their relatives from beyond the Jordan and made a bloody conquest unnecessary. This would explain why such old Canaanite towns as Shechem, Hepher and Tirzah were absorbed into the Israelite clan system without particular difficulty—they were already in contractual and marriage relationship with the surrounding seminomads.[45] Archaeological explorations confirm this natural deduction, since outside of Shechem there are singularly few sites of Canaanite fortified towns in Ephraim and southern Manasseh, between Beth-el and Dothan.

4. TRIBAL RULE AND CHARISMATIC LEADERS

An impartial observer of the early twelfth century B.C.E. would probably have said that everything was against the success of the Israelite experiment. At that time Israel was still a heterogeneous amalgam of elements of very different origins, and the memory of their mixed background as state slaves in Egypt and *'Apiru* freebooters in Palestine was still vivid. The peoples of Canaan were very conscious of aristocracy and old lineage, but the Israelites had neither a class system (except in so far as the Aaronids and the children of clan leaders represented class) nor aristocratic ancestry. Among the Israelites there were few craftsmen and scant respect for the amenities of civilization: the archaeologist can scarcely be faced with a greater contrast than that between the well-built and well-drained patrician houses of the last Canaanite Beth-el and the rustic constructions and lack of drainage characteristic of all three of the earliest Israelite periods of building. The early religion of Israel had little art and probably little or no music. Against the ancient liturgy of Canaanite temples and their elaborately organized personnel appeared in sharp contrast the aesthetic barrenness of the early cult of YHWH. Against the rich mythology and the dramatic ritual of Canaanite religion stood out the lonely figure of the desert God, without mythology and virtually without ritual. Against the emotional ecstasy of orgiastic Canaanite rites there came no answering echo from the stern code of Israelite morality. Where the Canaanites were sophisticated the Israelites were harsh with the cruel severity of unspoiled nomads; where the Canaanites gloated in sadistic glee the Israelites turned away in shocked reaction against the brutalities of an oversophisticated culture.[46]

In spite of the initial successes of the Israelites between *c.* 1250 and 1225 B.C.E., they could scarcely have continued to expand if it had not been for the period of Egyptian decline which followed the death of Marniptah about 1225. For a decade three weak rulers held the façade of empire together, but the Egyptian dependencies, extremely restive under Marniptah, must have broken away almost entirely from their allegiance to Pharaoh. After this decade Egypt fell into complete anarchy for nearly a generation, as vividly portrayed in the preamble to the famous Papyrus Harris; an unnamed Syrian finally made himself chief, but no contemporary monuments elucidate the episode. It was not until 1195 B.C.E. that an energetic young king, Rameses III, was able to undertake the recovery of the Asiatic empire of Egypt. Thanks to this breathing spell the Israelites were able to establish themselves firmly in the hill country of western Palestine, from Kedesh in northern Naphtali to Debir in southwestern Judah, and from central Hauran to the Arnon in eastern Palestine (Trans-Jordan). Among territory then held and subsequently lost must be counted in particular the region north of the Arnon, which was taken by the Moabites, the land of Bashan, which was occupied by the Arameans, and at least part of the Plain of Sharon. As a result of these and other losses, the tribes of Reuben, Manasseh, Dan, Asher, and Simeon were greatly reduced in power and influence. It was not until the time of David that the lost territory was regained, and much of it was lost again within a century.

The Israelite confederation of the period of the Judges was in some ways a true amphictyony, as recognized especially by Albrecht Alt and Martin Noth.[47] Like Greek amphictyonies of a slightly later period, it consisted of a federation of distinct tribes, grouped around a central sanctuary, which exercised a strong cohesive force, unifying the tribes in religion and politics, as well as to some extent also in language and customs. Israel possessed an unusually powerful centripetal force in the Mosaic tradition. On the other hand, strong centrifugal forces were operating to break up the federation. In the first place, Israelite territory was not well suited geographically to form a political unit. Galilee was separated from Manasseh and Ephraim by the broad Plain of Jezreel, controlled by Canaanite chariotry, against which the footmen of Israel were as helpless as modern infantry against tanks. Nor were relations between Judah and Ephraim any too well knit, though the usual view that they were separated by a chain of Canaanite fortresses was probably not true during most of our period. The barrier of the Jordan Valley was not serious; it was more important that the problems and dangers which faced the tribes of Trans-Jordan were very different from those which confronted their kinsmen in western Palestine.[48] Even more of a barrier than these obvious geographical interruptions was the fact that travel from north to south was generally restricted to the narrow ridge separating the watershed of the Mediterranean from that of the Jordan: each two or three miles to the east and west of this ridge meant, as a rule, that the transverse valleys and gorges became twice as difficult to cross as they were before. Moreover, these geographical barriers favored cantonization, which perpetuated or created boundaries between dialects, customs and political orientation.

In the second place must be listed among centrifugal forces the fact that the early missionary drive which dominated Israel under Moses and Joshua soon began to weaken, though several traditions recorded in Judges and Samuel show that it did not die out entirely. Pre-Mosaic beliefs and practices emerged, and the native paganism of Canaanite and Hebrew groups which had been absorbed only partially into the Israelite confederation returned to favor. The conflict between YHWH and Baal gradually grew in popular consciousness; it is first concretely stated in the surviving tradition of Gideon, about a century and a half after the Conquest. It is still unclear to what extent Baal was identified with YHWH in the period of the Judges, but the frequency of Baal names among the families of both Saul and David (see below) makes it appear likely that syncretism between YHWH and Baal was already advocated in certain circles.

The centrifugal process was checked by foreign aggression rather than by internal evolution toward more stable political forms. Of all threats from the outside the most formidable was that of the Philistines, who invaded Palestine by sea and land about 1187 B.C.E., half a century after the climax of the Israelite invasion. In league with other seafaring peoples from the northern shores of the Mediterranean they overwhelmed the resistance of the Hittites and Canaanites, and came very close to invading Egypt itself before they were defeated. The Egyptian king made a virtue of necessity, however, allowing the Sea Peoples to establish themselves along the shores of Palestine from Gaza to Dor and probably still farther north.[49] Further strengthened by immigration across the Mediterranean, the Sea Peoples maintained close ties with Aegean lands for centuries. By the middle of the twelfth century their influence began to penetrate inland, as we know from pottery finds in the towns of the Judahite Shephelah (low hill country).[50] The report of the Egyptian envoy Wen-amun, *c.* 1080 B.C.E., shows that they were then competing actively with the Canaanite cities of Phoenicia for control of the lucrative sea trade. About the middle of the eleventh century the Philistines defeated Israel at the battle of Ebenezer and captured the Ark. Excavations indicate that the Philistines then overran and destroyed many towns in Judah and Ephraim, including Debir, Beth-zur, Shiloh.[51] The hegemony over Palestine set up at that time did not end until the victories of Saul and especially of David.

In northern Palestine the greatest danger to Israel came from the wealthy Canaanite towns that had escaped destruction. Owing to the obscurity of tradition and the fact that sites like Hazor have not yet been adequately excavated, it is impossible to reconstruct the sequence of events clearly. Archaeological work at Megiddo makes it possible to fix the date of the Song of Deborah about 1125 B.C.E. (extreme limits 1150-1075).[52] Thanks to the victory at the Kishon, the Israelites were able to ward off the threat which appears to have been created by a league between the remaining Canaanite city-states of Galilee and incoming Sea Peoples.

In Trans-Jordan there was aggression from several directions, and the waves of invasion which broke against it often flowed over into western Palestine, leaving no part of Israel secure from attack. First, somewhere in the twelfth century, came a successful Moabite invasion and occupation, brought to an end by a bold stroke carried out by a Benjamite named Ehud. Ehud is the first of the judges whose figure stands out with some clarity against the background of Israelite heroic saga. Like most of the subsequent "judges" (*shophetim*) of this period whose names are recorded in the Bible, Ehud obtained the title, not by magisterial functioning in a court, but by deeds of extraordinary martial prowess. Most of these judges were not magistrates, but military heroes and successful commanders of armies; they were respected and obeyed by their fellow countrymen, regardless of their tribal affiliation and their social origin, because they were believed to possess some special outpouring of the spirit of God which made them superior in valor and wisdom to the common man. Leaders of this type have been happily called "charismatic leaders" by Max Weber and Albrecht Alt.[53] It is probable that the Israelites adopted the use of the word *shophet* in this sense from their Canaanite precursors, since the same term appears in the sense of "prince" in earlier Canaanite mythology and it was still used in Carthage, centuries later, to designate the heads of the state. There can be no doubt, however, that there was an inner-Israelite development of the charismatic associations of judgeship. Several of the minor judges, of whom nothing is recorded but their names and the number of years during which they functioned, evidently owed their distinction to their success as intertribal arbitrators.[54] As among the nomadic and seminomadic Arabs of our own day, wisdom and impartiality in making decisions according to tribal customary law were quite enough to spread the fame of a popular arbitrator, to whom men might come scores of miles for arbitration of knotty cases. In the raw semisedentary culture of Israel in the days of the Judges, respected arbitrators and interpreters of tribal law played a highly important role in restricting lawlessness and blood feuds. It was thus no light honor when a successful military leader or a popular hero was consulted by his followers, to whom physical prowess and shrewdness in strategy carried with them social prestige and reputation for wisdom.

Early in the eleventh century the newly settled tribes of Israel were struck by an avalanche from the Syrian Desert which all but overwhelmed them. This was the first irruption of camel-riding nomads into the Fertile Crescent of which we have any historical record. Domesticated camels were so rare in early times that they never appear in our contemporary records and monuments in the earlier centuries of the second millennium.[55] Not long before our time, however, the wild tribes of inner Arabia had learned how to ride the camel over long distances and to surprise wholly unsuspecting victims asleep in remote encampments. Thus the Bedouin razzia came into existence. Year after year the wild Arab hordes poured over Palestine, forcing the Israelites into the mountains and forests, and plundering their crops and their livestock. Tradition described the hordes as "Midian and Amalek and the Bne Qedem" (Judg. 6:3). Had their depredations been allowed to continue unchecked, Israel would have been displaced from Canaan before it had completed a century and a half of occupation. Thanks to the valor and shrewdness of a man of western Manasseh named Jerubbaal (Gideon) this great danger was averted, and Palestine was saved from further Arab inundation for over four centuries. Moreover, Gideon was not only a successful charismatic leader; he was also a militant propagandist for the God of Israel, carrying the war against Baalism into the camp of the followers of Baal. The fact that his own personal name was formed with "Baal" while that of his father Joash was formed with "YHWH" vividly illustrates the confused religious situation prevailing at that time in north-central Israel.

It can scarcely have been more than a generation later when the Philistines, after a century of desultory conflict and increasing pressure on southern Israel, invaded the highlands of Ephraim in force and destroyed Shiloh, as demonstrated by the Danish excavations there. As we have noted above, this victory was followed by the destruction of other Israelite towns, and probably cost Israel much of the material wealth which it had accumulated during the preceding generation. The burning of Shiloh and loss of the Ark left the Israelite amphictyony without a central sanctuary, thus gravely endangering its stability. By their master stroke the Philistines might have made themselves permanent lords of Palestine, if it had not been for the emergence of Samuel not long afterwards. His great popular reputation as judge and diviner bridged the gap between the old charismatic and the new prophetic age; his early association with the high priest, Eli, bridged another gap between the amphictyony and the Monarchy. Just what Samuel's role in the history of Yahwism was, we do not know; but there is no reason to doubt the correctness of Israelite tradition, according to which he was a champion of monotheism in his day.

In the course of two centuries there had been great development in the material civilization and social organization of Israel, in spite of repeated blows from outside, some of them crushing in their impact. Most of the destroyed Canaanite towns had been reoccupied, and these towns became foci of agricultural clans grouped in patriarchally organized families. The average population of the major towns was much smaller than in Canaanite times, and open spaces were used for sheepfolds and grain pits. Characteristic of the age, at least in places like Debir, Beth-shemesh and Beth-el, were large rustic houses, with numerous rooms on the ground floor around an open courtyard, and other rooms upstairs. Construction and character of furnishings prove conclusively that these large houses were not aristocratic mansions, like the Canaanite buildings whose place they sometimes take, but were occupied by several smaller families, grouped around a patriarchal head. Moreover, thanks to the extremely rapid diffusion of the art of building cisterns, introduced not long before the end of the Canaanite occupation (see above), it had become possible to build new towns and villages on sites far from any spring or running stream. And so hundreds of new settlements had arisen where no Canaanite settlement had ever been; illustrations from the neighborhood of Jerusalem are Gibeah, Ramah, Geba, Michmas—to mention only a few names of towns known to go back to the period before Samuel. Considerable areas of woodland, both east and west of the Jordan, had been cleared; vast numbers of olive trees and vineyards had been planted.

Moreover, commerce was fast returning to the place it held under the Canaanites; in some respects it probably surpassed any previous record in Palestine. Camel caravans were already providing new means of transporting the wares of the desert into Palestine, not to mention the tremendous new possibilities which they provided for cheap transport over greater distances. The rapid growth of the little country of Ammon, on the very edge of the desert east of Gilead, after the time of the Conquest, in which it played no role, until it was able to threaten Israel repeatedly in the course of the eleventh century, illustrates what the camel trade already

THE RETURN OF THE ARK FROM THE HANDS OF THE PHILISTINES

The Holy Ark of the covenant, once captured by the Philistines, returned to the Israelites by Divine Power. The idol of the Philistines "was fallen upon his face to the ground before the Ark of the Lord. And the head of Dagon . . . lay cut off upon the threshold . . ." (I Samuel, 5.3,4).

From the Synagogue of Dura Europos, 245 C.E.

Wall painting, fresco, size copy by Herbert J. Gute of the Yale University Art Gallery.

meant at this time. In the Mediterranean sea trade was rapidly expanding after the interruption created by the movements of the Sea Peoples in the late thirteenth and twelfth centuries. The Report of Wen-amun, already mentioned above, vividly illustrates the rapid expansion of merchant shipping, organized in large corporations for better protection against pirates and raiders.[56] The Song of Deborah mentions the active maritime part played by members of the tribes of Dan and Asher. By the middle of the eleventh century, pottery imported from Cyprus appears again in Israelite sites, after a long interruption during which exceedingly little imported ware (except Philistine) is found.

The increase in wealth, combined with the menace of the Philistines, made a more stable political organization particularly imperative. Gideon's son Abimelech headed a Canaanite reaction at Shechem, and made himself briefly "king." Samuel attempted to establish the succession of "judges" on a stable basis by appointing his own sons to that office. Both efforts, like others which were soon forgotten, were failures: Abimelech proved to be a bloody tyrant and was ignominiously killed by a woman; Samuel's sons were corrupt in the administration of justice and became targets for the clamor of the people. The way was thus opened for a new step in the political evolution of Israel.

5. THE UNITED MONARCHY

A popular hero, Saul, was proclaimed king in spite of the initial opposition of Samuel. At the very beginning of his reign he won decisive victories over the Ammonites, Philistines and Amalekites, thus freeing Israel from immediate danger on all sides of the country. His jealous, tyrannical nature, amply illustrated by tradition, could not brook opposition, and so he was gradually forced into hostility toward every actual or potential rival for power. Early in his reign came the break with Samuel, followed shortly afterward by the quarrel with David, his son-in-law and already a popular hero on his own account. Tradition recalled these dramatic personal relationships and illustrated them vividly by anecdotes which throw a bright light on the personalities involved; tradition failed to consider underlying tendencies and policies. The conflict between Saul and David was apparently at bottom little more than a contest for popular favor and power between two charismatic leaders, but the bitterness between Samuel and Saul had a much broader base. There is no hint in our sources that Samuel took any action with regard to restoration of the tabernacle of Shiloh, and the Ark remained at Kirjath-jearim until well along in the reign of David. Saul, however, collected the surviving Elides and installed them at Nob, less than an hour's walk to the southeast of Gibeah, Saul's own residence. Here was erected some kind of structure to house the sacred objects and rites; the Ark might also have been brought here, in spite of the superstitious awe in which it was held by the people, if there had been time to plan for the transfer. As it was, we may safely infer that Saul's action had two purposes, first to strengthen his hand against Samuel, second to give him direct personal control of the high-priestly family, with its strong traditional and symbolic meaning to Israel. When Saul ordered the slaughter of all the Elides, in a fit of jealous rage because they had assisted David, he broke with orthodox Yahwism completely. His earlier piety, illustrated by the tradition that he suppressed witchcraft and necromancy in Israel (I Sam. 28:3), may even have been replaced by outright syncretism. It is in any case a curious fact that, while his eldest son was called Jonathan, a name formed with "YHWH," names formed with "Baal" occur at least three times among the younger Saulides. Saul may have been moved by considerations of political expediency in thus favoring Baalism, which was much more strongly entrenched in the north than in the south. At all events, he was sufficiently interested in maintaining control over the northern territories of Israel to meet his death in a hopeless battle to defend the Esdraelon pass against a powerful Philistine army (*c.* 1000 B.C.E.).

The writer's excavation of the remains of Saul's fortress at Gibeah illustrates the rustic simplicity of his court better than anything else can do.[57] Though strongly constructed, the fortress walls were built of hammer-dressed masonry, and its contents were extremely simple. Tradition makes clear that Saul never had a standing army of more than nominal strength, so he remained at the mercy of tribal institutions and customs throughout his reign. Under such circumstances he could win great victories over the seminomadic Ammonites and Amalekites, but he was quite unable to make any real headway against so solidly organized a confederation as the Philistine pentapolis.

The death of Saul and his sons at the disastrous battle of Gilboa opened the way for David's brilliant career. Thanks to his deeds of heroism and to his singular personal charm, attested by all relevant traditions, David enjoyed the widest popular favor, scarcely dimmed by his long service under the Philistine Achish, tyrant of Gath. He was thus as striking a charismatic figure as any in earlier Israelite history. Moreover, David had unusual gifts of mind. He was celebrated by Israelite tradition as a musician, and there can be no reasonable doubt as to the importance of his own direct and indirect contributions to Hebrew music and poetry, on which archaeological finds have recently cast very interesting light.[58] As general and statesman he was also a distinguished figure.

During David's seven-year reign in Hebron he consolidated his power and apparently waged successful war against the Philistines. Recent archaeological research strongly indicates that the casemated walls of Debir and

Beth-shemesh were built by David as part of a line of defense against the Philistines.[59] After the assassination of Saul's youngest son, Esh-baal (Ish-bosheth),[60] the heads of the northern tribes invited him to become king of reunited Israel. His own and his predecessor's experience with the fickleness of tribal support seems directly responsible for his decision to establish his new capital at a non-Israelite site on the borders of the two reunited halves of his kingdom; a brief and obscure siege was sufficient to reduce Jerusalem, thenceforward called officially "City of David." Jerusalem was quite outside of the Israelite tribal system; it owed allegiance only to the king, and it became peopled largely by his personal retainers, who had abandoned their original allegiances and were legally "slaves of the king," a term used regularly by the Israelites and their neighbors in the sense of "royal officials." This act of David was sheer political genius.[61]

Having established his court at Jerusalem, David next took measures to attach the amphictyonic tradition to himself by moving the few survivors of the Nob massacre to the city, where he erected a tabernacle in which the Ark, venerated ancient symbol of Israel's faith, was presently installed. According to tradition, David set in motion elaborate plans for building a temple on the summit of the hill overlooking Jerusalem from the north, which he had acquired from its Jebusite owner. However this may be, there can be no reasonable doubt that tradition was in part correct in attributing to David far-reaching modifications and improvements in the organization of divine worship, especially in the orchestral system.[62] Moreover, examination of the list of Levitic cities, according to which four places in each tribe were designated for the residence of priests and Levites, makes it certain that—unless the original list was a late fiction, for which it is extremely hard to find plausible grounds—it must go back to the latter part of David's reign (or the very beginning of the reign of Solomon), since it was only then that the towns in question were all part of Israel, according to historical and archaeological indications, and only then that the political background was suitable.[63] By distributing the priests and Levites over the country, David weakened them politically at the same time that he contributed to the spread of normative Yahwism.[64]

Similar considerations make it highly probable that the six cities of refuge, all of which were included among the Levitic cities, were instituted in or immediately after the reign of David.[65] This institution can have been intended only as part of a campaign to suppress the time-honored practice of blood revenge, with the resulting vendettas which have repeatedly brought total destruction to groups and communities in the tribal history of Palestine, whether under Canaanites, Israelites or Arabs. No stable government can coexist with blood feuds. David's famous census was another phase of his struggle to restrict the autonomy of the tribes by placing them under a bureaucratic administration answerable only to the crown. The redivision of Israel into new districts distinct in large part from the old tribal territories was carried into effect by Solomon, presumably in accordance with a plan initiated by his father.

As a result of David's brilliant victories over the Edomites, Moabites, Ammonites, Arameans and Philistines, he extended the nominal boundaries of Israel as far as central Syria in the northwest and the Euphrates Valley in the northeast.[66] The entire coast from Carmel to south of Joppa became Israelite, and the Philistines were reduced to paying tribute. Since much of the booty and probably all the tribute were turned in to the royal coffers, the crown became immensely wealthy. These extensive resources were used partly to support a steadily increasing army of mercenary troops and royal officials, all of whom (see above) owed personal allegiance only to the king. The functionaries of the king were organized according to the models set by the Egyptian bureaucratic system, whether borrowed directly or through Canaanite (Phoenician) intermediation.[67]

David failed signally in regulating the succession to the throne, and thus in stabilizing royal institutions in Israel. The revolt of Absalom was possible only in a society where the charismatic principle of leadership was still dominant and where the idea of constitutional legality had not yet taken root. Around Absalom gathered all the dissatisfied elements of Israel: early friends and relatives of David who were bitter because of lack of success at court; members or adherents of the house of Saul; non-Judahite Israelites who disliked the most-favored place of Judah in David's organization of the state. Even on David's deathbed an insurrection broke out, attempting to displace the palace favorite, Solomon, by the fourth son of the king, Adonijah. The attempt to crown Adonijah proved abortive, but it was a bad portent for the future unity of Israel.

Solomon's long reign (*c.* 961-922 B.C.E.)[68] has always been justly celebrated as the culmination of Israelite material history. Thanks to his inherited wealth and power, as well as to his own shrewdness in taking advantage of favorable economic circumstances, he created an impression on his contemporaries which made him a central figure of saga and legend. Among hundreds of millions of Moslems the riches and wisdom of Suleiman, who reigned over all men and jinn, still dominate story and proverb. The political setting of the age was singularly favorable: Egypt, under the last feeble rulers of the Tanite Dynasty, was in no position to interfere in Asia; Assyria, under the fainéant Tiglath-pileser II (966-935 B.C.E.),[69] was at one of the lowest points reached in a long history; the new Sidonian state with its capital at Tyre was absorbed in sea trade and commercial expansion;[70] the Arameans had been soundly defeated by David, though they began to recover during Solomon's reign. It was, therefore, quite unnecessary for Solomon to undertake any serious military operations.

As a warning against would-be aggressors he established a powerful standing army, consisting mainly of chariotry, which his father had still refused to employ. The figures in Kings and Chronicles are conflicting, but the most probable ones attribute to him 1,400 chariots, 4,000 stalls for the chariot horses, and some 12,000 horses. Even allowing for a certain amount of exaggeration, this represented a potent force, roughly equivalent to the amount of chariotry thrown by Hadad-ezer of Damascus against Shalmaneser III at the battle of Qarqar a century later. One of the chariot cities which Solomon rebuilt has been excavated; the excavators of Megiddo have estimated that there were some 450 well-built stalls for horses in that site alone.

With this assurance against foreign interference, Solomon could turn his attention to the marvelous opportunities for trade and development of the arts of civilization that were then opening up. Our sources describe commerce with Phoenicia, Egypt, South Arabia and adjacent regions, as well as with Hittite North Syria and Cilicia. By intermarriage with Egypt he became an ally of that country. He entered into close partnership with Hiram of Tyre (969-936 B.C.E.) in organizing elaborate trading expeditions on the Red Sea and the Indian Ocean, possibly also in the Mediterranean. At that time Phoenician commercial expansion was at its height, and trading colonies were established at least as far west as Sardinia (Tarshish).[71] An essential part of Phoenician colonial activity was then devoted to mining, especially in the rich copper workings of Cyprus and Sardinia. We do not yet know definitely whether Phoenician expansion had reached southern Spain as early as Hiram's time, though it does not seem impossible. We do know, however, that the name Tarshish ("Refinery"?) was applied in the following century to Nora in southern Sardinia. Thanks to Phoenician collaboration, Solomon constructed great copper refineries at Ezion-geber at the northern end of the Red Sea (Gulf of 'Aqabah), where they have been recently excavated by Nelson Glueck.[72] The copper for these refineries (as well as for the copper works mentioned in I Kings 7:45) came from recently discovered copper mines in the Ghor, both south and north of the Dead Sea. No less significant than Solomon's partnership with the Phoenicians was his commercial relationship to "all the kings of the Arabs," including the famous queen of Sheba, which here makes its first appearance in recorded history. At this time caravan trade in the desert was being revolutionized by the rapid development of the use of domesticated camels for long hauls. Solomon may well have been the first important ruler to exploit this new source of wealth.

With these new means at his disposal Solomon launched out into an elaborate series of building operations. We are well acquainted with the construction of the Temple and royal palace, thanks to the detailed—though often obscure—description in I Kings; the fortification of Gezer and Megiddo has been confirmed by excavation, and we have already alluded to the Megiddo stables and the refineries of Ezion-geber (which are not mentioned in our literary sources). Throughout Phoenician influence is dominant—in the plan of palace and Temple; in the details of hewing, laying and quoin construction which characterize Solomonic masonry in sharpest contrast to the masonry of Saul and David; in proto-Ionic pilaster capitals and other details of architectural ornamentation.[73] All of this cost a great deal, both in treasure and in labor. Solomon reduced the recently conquered Canaanites of Esdraelon, the coastal plain and the outlying districts of Galilee to state slavery (*mas ʿobed*).[74] He also presumably forced the conquered Hebrew states of Trans-Jordan (Edom, Moab and Ammon) to furnish state slaves. Since, however, these sources of cheap labor proved inadequate, he went so far as to resort to the corvée (*mas*) to enlist free Israelites in work battalions, alternating between a month in Lebanon and two months at home. If the recorded number of 30,000 Israelite conscripts is correct, it would constitute a drain on the population roughly equivalent to a draft of 5,000,000 Americans in 1945.[75] It is scarcely probable, however, that even Solomon dared employ this corvée for anything but the construction of the Temple and other buildings of common interest to all.

Solomon continued policies inaugurated apparently by David, with a view to centralization of authority in the crown, further weakening of tribal ties, and attachment of the priesthood to his person. In pursuance of the policy of centralization, the tribal divisions were replaced for administrative purposes by twelve roughly similar prefectures, sometimes more or less coterminous with the old tribes, but more often diverging sharply from them. The new prefects, whose names are listed in I Kings 4, seem to have been officials from the royal entourage; two of them are stated to have married daughters of Solomon—a clear illustration of the methods employed to secure their loyalty to the crown. It has been urged that Judah was excluded from the number of prefectures and that it enjoyed preferential treatment, but I Kings 4:19-20 seems to contradict this interpretation, which disagrees strikingly with the efforts of David to place the crown above tribal divisions.[76] A principal duty of these prefects was to furnish provisions for the royal court, each for a month. If the daily amount recorded in I Kings 5:2 ff. is correct, the average amount of provision supplied by each prefecture in a year was something like 900 *kor* of semolina, 1,800 of wheat flour, 900 oxen, 3,000 sheep, etc.[77] Since the *kor* was roughly equivalent to six bushels, this was a very heavy drain on a population which probably averaged less than 100,000 for each prefecture, including Canaanites. Small wonder that Israel rebelled after Solomon's death!

The seventy years during which David and Solomon ruled a united

Israel were a time of extraordinary material and cultural progress. A great many new towns and villages were built all over the country, and the population may easily have doubled, from a possible 400,000 to a possible 800,000 (counting only Israelites). Public security was so improved that the large subterranean grain pits which were so characteristic of the preceding age vanish from the excavated sites of the time. Architecture, art and music developed amazingly. The increased popularity of literature may be gauged by David's own reputation as psalmist, and especially by Solomon's even greater fame as poet and author of proverbs and fables. It may be doubted whether Solomon's literary craftsmanship was sufficiently appealing to subsequent generations to have survived intact, as some of David's compositions unquestionably did; but who can say how much of it may not be embedded in the postexilic anthologies of Proverbs and Canticles? In any event, it is certain that classical Hebrew prose attained definite form and canons during Solomon's reign, as vividly illustrated by the beautifully written narrative of the events preceding and accompanying the death of David and Solomon's own accession to the throne. From the forms of Egyptian names and other hints, it has frequently been surmised that such sections of the JE[77a] narratives of Genesis as the story of Joseph took their present literary form at that time. However this may be, the age was certainly characterized by a flowering of literature. Some day we may have archaeological documentation of the increasing use of the art of writing at that time; at present we have only one Hebrew inscription which can be attributed with confidence to the reign of Solomon or immediately afterwards—the Gezer Calendar, a school exercise containing a mnemonic ditty listing the periods of the agricultural year.[78] To the schoolboy in question and to his teacher we owe a debt of gratitude, since this priceless little document furnishes us invaluable data for the history of Hebrew script and spelling. Such objective contemporary data are worth far more for the critical student of the Hebrew biblical text than any amount of deduction from subjectively constructed premises.

6. From the Disruption of the Monarchy to the Revolt of Jehu

Solomon's cavalier disregard of time-honored tribal and individual rights was bound to alienate an increasing number of his subjects, especially in the northern part of the country, where blood ties and rewards of empire were much less effective than in the south. Hardly had Solomon died, *c.* 922 B.C.E.,[79] when rebellion flared up against his son, Rehoboam. The revolt was headed by Jeroboam, an Ephraimite from Zeredah, southwest of Shechem.[80] Jeroboam had been an official in charge of the Josephite corvée employed by Solomon in fortifying Jerusalem, but was forced to flee to the protection of Shishak, king of Egypt. The latter, a powerful

Libyan noble, had dethroned Psusennes II, last of the Tanite house (*c.* 935 B.C.E.), and had made himself king in his place, founding the Bubastite (Twenty-second) Dynasty. Shishak replaced the weak, quasi-priestly, rule of the Tanites by a dynamic policy of aggression, illustrated by his protection of the Edomite, Hadad, and the North Israelite, Jeroboam, against their suzerain in Jerusalem. If Rehoboam had been able to strike at once against the still unorganized North Israelites, he might have won; that the attack was not launched must probably be credited in large part to a warning from Shishak, who was doubtless already plotting to disrupt the Solomonic empire. At all events, Rehoboam was sufficiently alarmed by the threat of Egyptian invasion to abandon any projected punitive expedition and to fortify a large number of strategically located points commanding roads and valleys leading into Judah from the south and west. Fifteen of these fortified towns are listed by the Chronicler; they were admirably selected to create the strongest practicable defense line against attack by an Egyptian army.[81] When the invasion finally came, in the fifth year of Rehoboam (*c.* 918 B.C.E.), it broke with tremendous force over Judah and its Philistine and Edomite dependencies. In the great Karnak List Shishak listed over 150 places which he claimed to have taken; the presence of many Edomite names in this list has only recently been recognized.[82] Archaeological evidence confirms the accounts in Kings and Chronicles: the huge Egyptian host, consisting largely of barbarian contingents from Libya and Ethiopia, carried fire and sword over the country, utterly devastating such towns as Debir and probably Beth-shemesh. Once in Asia, Shishak proceeded to lay Israel as well as Judah waste; the correctness of the inclusion of North Israelite towns in the list has been demonstrated by the discovery of a fragment of a large triumphal stele of Shishak at Megiddo, one of the towns listed at Karnak as conquered. Having unleashed the Egyptian terror on Judah, Jeroboam was to have much the same experience as Stalin nearly three thousand years later, when the Nazis turned against Russia after conquering Poland.

Meanwhile Jeroboam proceeded with no little shrewdness to break the links connecting the northern tribes to Jerusalem. There is reason to think that he kept the administrative structure as intact as was practicable; it can scarcely be accidental that the provincial organization of North Israel in the eighth century was still modeled after the administrative reorganization of Solomon, with western Manasseh, Gilead, Dor and Megiddo forming independent prefectures.[83] Even his strangely archaic name, which probably means "May the People Multiply," is obviously modeled after the equally archaic name of his rival, Rehoboam (for Yirhab ʿam, "May the People Expand"). It must be remembered that throne names were by no means restricted to Egypt; we know six or seven dual names of kings of Judah, beginning with Solomon (Jedidiah), and at least two of kings of

Aram. It is quite possible that he selected Shechem as his first capital at least partly because it lay outside the strictly Israelite tribal system, being a Canaanite enclave in Manasseh.[84] In moving from Shechem to Tirzah, he may also have selected an old Canaanite town which was not even yet considered as strictly within the tribal system. In his religious reorganization Jeroboam had to go back to earlier precedents than those of the Davidides, since they had done their work of attaching the Elide family and the traditional system of worship to Jerusalem surpassingly well. Probably to old North Israelite practice went back the tradition portraying the invisible presence of YHWH as standing on the back of a young bull—certainly the same young bull on which the ancient storm-god of Southwestern Asia was represented as standing (usually visible, sometimes invisible) from the early third millennium B.C.E. to the fourth century C.E.[85] According to the JE tradition of Ex. 32, the golden bull-calf had already been introduced into Israelite cult by Aaron himself, during the lifetime of Moses. Conceptually this practice was no more idolatrous than the equally symbolic representation of YHWH in the Temple of Solomon as an invisible Presence enthroned on the cherubim.[86] In practice, however, the pagan associations of the young bull were likely to lead to paganizing theology and to encouragement of syncretism. The latter undoubtedly took place; we have no direct evidence for the former, and the name *'Egel-yau*, borne by an Israelite of the early eighth century whose name occurs in the Ostraca of Samaria, meant merely "Young Bull of YHWH," expressing full recognition of the fact that the bulls were not themselves gods, but were merely ministers of Deity. As sites for the chief centers of the reorganized YHWH cult Jeroboam selected Beth-el and Dan, both because of their strategic locations and because of their significance as ancient pilgrimage shrines. The priesthood of Dan claimed descent from Moses, that of Beth-el probably from Aaron—a claim rejected by the priests of Jerusalem.

Meanwhile the paganizing tendencies initiated in Jerusalem by Solomon himself, both through the complex ritual and elaborate decoration of the Temple (which now included a much greater measure of Canaanite elements than ever before) and through his uxorious toleration of foreign cults across the Kedron Valley from the Temple, were bearing fruit. Rehoboam's second successor, Asa, was only a child at the death of his brother, Abijah, and he remained for fourteen years under the regency of the queen mother, Maachah. Rehoboam's mother had been an Ammonite princess, and Maachah belonged to the family of the half-pagan Absalom, so paganism was ascendant on the distaff side. Small wonder that Maachah was an open worshiper of Asherah, the great Canaanite goddess of fertility! Fortunately the young king sided with the Yahwists, and when he became old enough to take power into his own hands, he inaugurated a drastic reformation, restoring monotheism to its old place of honor in Judah.[87] In judging the frequent triumphs of Canaanite polytheism in Israel, we must always bear in mind that polytheism had a popular appeal in many ways like that of the dominant secularism of our own day. The wealth, science and aesthetic culture of that age were lined up on the side of Canaanite religion, thanks to the unprecedented progress made by the great Phoenician cities and their smaller counterparts on the coastal plain of Palestine. Compared with Phoenicia, the lands of Judah and Israel were very poor, very rustic and far behind the spirit of the day in fashions, arts of civilization and material pleasures of life. All the sinister fascination of the elaborate proto-sciences of magic and divination was marshaled in defense of polytheism against the stern, almost savage, simplicity of Mosaic theology. When Israelite women employed the same amulets as their Canaanite friends in order to ward off evil spirits, they unconsciously made it more difficult to save their children from the perils of the Canaanite way of life. The extraordinary thing is that the way of Moses succeeded in Israel in spite of the forces drawn up against it!

Meanwhile the intermittent struggle between Judah and Israel continued. Abijah is credited with having won an important victory over Jeroboam. However, Israel's potential power was so much greater than Judah's, especially after the devastation of the latter by Shishak, that no such victories had more than ephemeral significance. Moreover, Asa had to repel at least one invasion from the direction of Egypt, probably carried out by an Ethiopian garrison commander from the Egyptian frontier fortress of Gerar. Whether Zerah "the Ethiopian" was acting on orders from Shishak's successor, Osorkon I, we are not told, but it seems likely enough. But when Baasha of Israel undertook hostile acts on the northern frontier, Asa sent envoys to Ben-Hadad of Aram, whom he readily persuaded to invade Israel from the north. The resulting invasion (*c.* 878 B.C.E.) devastated northern Galilee, and probably led—directly or indirectly—to the loss of all Israelite territory east of the Jordan and north of the Yarmuk. Thus Asa copied Jeroboam I, and brought the downfall of Israel a step nearer. Stern as the lesson was, it seems to have been learned, and relations between the two Israelite states remained, in general, friendly for the following century and a half.

Under the long reigns of Asa (*c.* 913-873 B.C.E.) and Jehoshaphat (*c.* 873-849 B.C.E.) the house of David was solidly established on the throne of Judah. Since they controlled Edom, as far as the Gulf of ʿAqabah, these kings were able to hold exclusive control over the caravan trade from Arabia, except in so far as the caravans stopped at Midianite ports farther south. The traditions concerning their wealth are probably true in substance. Monotheistic circles remembered them, particularly Jehoshaphat, for their support of YHWH against pagan deities and practices. In

Jehoshaphat's reign, according to the Chronicler, there was an exceedingly important administrative change—the replacement of the older customary law, administered by local elders, by royally appointed judges, and the establishment of a court of appeals in Jerusalem, formed of religious and tribal heads.[88] From this time on it became necessary to codify civil legislation, in order to furnish the directives without which no royal judiciary could long maintain the respect of the people.

In North Israel, on the other hand, the stability of the crown became steadily less, if possible. Jeroboam's son Nadab was assassinated in the second year of his reign and was replaced by Baasha, to whom his murder was attributed. Baasha's son, Elah, was in his turn, according to our tradition, assassinated by Zimri in the second year of his reign—a remarkable example of poetic justice. Zimri massacred all male members of the house of Baasha, but was himself burned to death in his palace by Omri; the latter was forced to fight for some time with a certain Tibni before he could become sole ruler of northern Israel (*c.* 876 B.C.E.). By this time Israel had lost eastern Palestine north of the Yarmuk to Aram (see above), and the region just north of the Arnon had been occupied by the resurgent Moabites. It is sometimes inferred from the rapid change of rulers in North Israel during the first half century after the Disruption, that its monarchy was elective. This idea is extremely improbable: it is quite enough to recognize that the idea of charismatic leadership was still very much alive, and that there was no combination of extraordinary qualities of leadership and religious sanction in North Israel to assure the permanence of a dynasty there.

Omri's prestige and qualities of leadership were such that he was able to hand the throne down to his grandsons. During the decades of the Omride Dynasty (*c.* 876-842 B.C.E.) Israel was consolidated and saved from further disintegration. Thanks to the Mesha Stele, we know that Omri reconquered Moab and resettled Israelites in the territory north of the Arnon; he also seems to have been victorious against Aram. At the same time, Omri oriented his policy westward, toward the Mediterranean and Phoenicia. In about 870 B.C.E. he transferred his capital from Tirzah, which faced eastward, to the splendid new site of Samaria, facing westward toward the Mediterranean and northwestward toward Phoenicia. Crowfoot's excavations have proved that Reisner was wrong in differentiating between a building period of Omri and a second of Ahab; actually Omri can only have begun construction of the city, which was continued by his son Ahab without interruption.[89] Omri's friendly relationship to Phoenicia was sealed by marriage of his crown prince to Jezebel, daughter of Ittobaal, the Sidonian king of Tyre (887-856 B.C.E.). One important reason for this alliance was undoubtedly the common danger to both constituted by the steady expansion of the power of Ben-Hadad, king of Aram (*c.* 880-842

B.C.E.). The alliance proved fatal to the permanence of the dynasty, but it probably brought considerable wealth to both Omri and Ahab, through the accompanying expansion of trade relations between Israel and Phoenicia. By this time North Africa and Spain, as well as Sardinia, had certainly been colonized, and Sidonian power was at its height.

Ahab, however, had to fight several wars against Aram, mainly defensive. Owing to lack of contemporary records it is quite impossible to reconstruct the complex interplay of political forces.[90] It is very important, however, to note that the threat of Assyrian expansion had again become real after the North Syrian campaign of Asshur-nasir-apli about 870 B.C.E., which followed more than a century during which there is no trace of Assyrian activity west of the Euphrates. It was not, however, until 853 that the next Assyrian king, Shalmaneser III, felt himself strong enough to make a direct attack on the powerful Syrian states of Hamath and Aram. Ben-Hadad (called Hadad-ezer, evidently his personal name, by the Assyrians) had learned of the projected invasion a long time in advance, thanks probably to the use of such telegraphic devices as fire signaling, with which the inscriptions of Mari and Lachish have made us familiar. Marshaling his forces, which included well-organized armies provided by the three main allies, the kings of Hamath, Aram and Israel, as well as small contingents from many other more insignificant sources, the Aramean met the Assyrian at Qarqar in the territory of Hamath. The battle appears to have been indecisive; at all events the Assyrians were forced to withdraw and it was not until 848 that they resumed the war against the Syrian confederates. In the interim war between Aram and Israel broke out again, resulting in the death of Ahab before Ramoth-gilead on the northeastern frontier of Israel, the site of which has been recently discovered by Nelson Glueck. The most interesting point about this battle is that Jehoshaphat of Judah was Ahab's ally against Aram, thus beginning a defensive alliance which seems to have lasted until the downfall of the Omride house.

Ahab and Jezebel will be remembered to the end of recorded history, not because of their own little personalities, but because of the towering figure of the dour Gileadite, whom they despised but also feared, and whose influence was to bring their house to ruin. We know little about the man, Elijah, but more about his great deeds, and much more about the tremendous influence which he exerted on his own and all subsequent ages. Elijah came after the prophets of YHWH had been recognized as a special class or body of inspired preachers and reformers for over a century and a half. The example of the great Samuel, who rebuked Saul, had been followed by Nathan, David's mentor, and Gad; by Ahijah the Shilonite, critic of Jeroboam, and Jehu ben Hanani, who attacked Baasha; and in Judah by Shemaiah and Azariah, little though we may know about them.

Elijah stood in the direct line of this tradition. The prophet of YHWH was still an inspired seer, whose oracles followed the ecstatic model and were seldom remembered long; the time had not come for marvelous poetic sermons, composed in advance, delivered orally and written down later by enthralled listeners or recited from generation to generation until collected into anthologies by later scholars. Pious Israelites were not far wrong in distinguishing between true prophets and false prophets of YHWH by the reaction of their words on the privileged classes; if the latter were pleased the prophet was false; if they were displeased the prophet was true.

The traditions regarding Elijah are few in number but rich in content; they paint their subject in unforgettable strokes. A man of wild places and deserts, he went for refreshment to the Mountain of God, where Moses had once brought Israel to the feet of YHWH. To him Jerusalem and Beth-el were perhaps equally objectionable from the standpoint of authentic Mosaic tradition, but tradition recalled only his vastly greater wrath at the abominations of Baalism, honored in Israel as never before. The princess of Tyre had brought with her the cult of the great Tyrian divinities, Baal-Melcarth and Asherah. It was not only to Israel that Melcarth gained access with Jezebel; a recently published stele of Ben-Hadad of Aram, dating about 850 B.C.E., contains a votive dedication to Melcarth, whose cult may possibly have been popularized in Aram by another Tyrian princess.[91] Asherah's special connection with Tyre is already attested by the Keret Epic, which was nearly six centuries older than Jezebel.[92] Against the profligate abandon of the cult of Melcarth and Asherah Elijah reacted with merciless severity. Not for him were the civilized reactions of a weak Ahab; he was a man of the desert, to whom wholesale *herem* (sacrificial destruction) was the only way to suppress the abominations of an effete agricultural civilization. To Elijah, the man of the people, justice to the poor and the widow was paramount; in those years of increasing wealth and luxury too many Israelites were forgetting the apodictic law of Moses: "Thou shalt not . . ." Not long after the prophet's death the dynasty of Omri collapsed amid torrents of blood, the inevitable end of an evil period. But for Elijah we should probably know virtually nothing of it but the names and regnal years of its kings.

7. From Jehu to the Fall of Samaria

No revolution is described in the Bible with such wealth of detail as Jehu's rebellion against the house of Omri. Several aspects of the revolution appear clearly. In the first place, it was a religious upheaval, in which the fiery propaganda of Elijah and his successor, Elisha, reached its goal, that of extirpating the cult of Baal-Melcarth from Israelite soil. In the course of the ensuing blood purge, not only all the Omrides and their more prominent supporters were liquidated; there was also a wholesale slaughter of all captured priests, prophets and votaries of Baal. Closely linked with the religious upheaval was a socioeconomic revolution, in which the poor and the landless revolted against the increasing contrast between the wealth of the new nobility and the equally new merchant class, on the one hand, and the poverty of the masses, on the other. The years of famine which dogged the Omride period had compelled the peasants to mortgage their lands and sell their children in order to eke out a bare subsistence. As a result of the symbiotic trading relationship set up by Solomon and later by Omri with Phoenicia, wealth had undoubtedly poured into Israel, as vividly illustrated by the excavations at Samaria. When hard times came to the peasants, the wealthy merchants lent them the necessary funds to tide them over—at usurious rates of interest, just as has been the practice in Palestine and Syria since time immemorial. In this unpredictable Mediterranean climate periods of rainy years alternate irregularly with periods of dry years, carrying with them constant movement of men and money, and dooming the peasantry to periodic ruin unless protected by enlightened government policy. But no famine was as long remembered as the great drought of Ahab's time, recorded also in Tyrian annals. The episode of Naboth, a particularly bad perversion of justice, became the dominant theme in the upsurge of popular discontent. Extremists like the Rechabites, who rejected agriculture and all the amenities and vices of sedentary society, joined Jehu; tradition credits the Rechabite leader, Jonadab, with an active part in the bloodiest phase of the revolution. A third aspect of the revolution was military: the army officers, led by Jehu, were dissatisfied with the weak policy of the crown, which they presumably associated with the luxurious indolence of the privileged classes and the dominance of Phoenician religion and culture.

Had Jehu been himself a great man, he might have reunited Israel and deferred the day of reckoning. Unfortunately, there is nothing in his record to suggest ability, and the situation of the Northern Kingdom declined rapidly under Jehu and his son, Joahaz. By the sanguinary thoroughness of his blood purge he had irremediably antagonized Israel's previous friends, Judah and Phoenicia. Judah's king and king's brothers had been butchered, while the deaths among Phoenicians, from Jezebel down, were extremely numerous, and the insult to Melcarth, lord of Tyre, was irrevocable in character. Deprived of help from these former allies, Israel's situation became rapidly desperate. Hazael of Aram overran and apparently annexed the whole of Israelite Trans-Jordan. In 841 Jehu docilely paid tribute to the king of Assyria, in connection with Shalmaneser's attack on Hazael, in which the Arameans suffered severely but did not capitulate. But no more help came from Assyria. After 837 B.C.E., when the Assyrians raided the northeastern end of Hazael's territory, the kingdom of Aram was not molested again until 805, shortly after the death of Hazael. Assyria had its own problems: for six years there was civil war, followed by a painful process of consolidation for eleven years, and then by the regency of Semiramis for four additional years.[93] Under Jehu's son Joahaz (*c.* 815-801 B.C.E.) Israel was devastated by the Arameans and reduced to a dependency of Aram. The king was allowed a bodyguard of only ten chariots and fifty horsemen—in contrast to Ahab's reported two thousand chariots at Qarqar. The chariot cities founded by Solomon were left empty, in particular Megiddo, which was destroyed and does not seem to have been rebuilt immediately. Hazael carried his arms southward on both sides of the Jordan, overrunning Philistia and levying a calamitous tribute on Judah.

Meanwhile Judah had also had a revolution, though a much milder affair. Ahab's sister, Athaliah, had been married to Jehoshaphat's son, Ahaziah. After the latter was killed by Jehu in 842, the queen mother seized power, killing all the Davidides who appeared to threaten her status. She was also a votary of Baal, whose high priest, Mattan, bore a typically Phoenician name, suggesting that the god in question was the same Tyrian Melcarth whose cult had already been diffused in Israel and Aram. Fortunately Jehoash, one of Ahaziah's sons, had been saved by his aunt, who was wife of Jehoiada, high priest of YHWH. When revolt finally broke out about 837 B.C.E. the young prince was set on the throne. Athaliah and Mattan were killed, but nothing is said of any further blood purge, suggesting that there was little of the intense socioeconomic feeling in Judah that had led to such excesses a few years earlier in Israel. The reign of Jehoash (*c.* 837-800 B.C.E.) was in no sense brilliant; his crushing humiliation at the hands of Hazael of Aram has been mentioned. Nor was the reign of his son, Amaziah, much more remarkable; he reconquered Edom, which had rebelled successfully against Judah half a century before, but was disastrously defeated by Joash, king of Israel. It is characteristic that both Jehoash and Amaziah were assassinated in palace revolts, and that tradition remembered both of them in terms which mix praise with blame almost equally.

The turn of Israel's fortunes was not long in coming. In 805 the young Assyrian king, Adad-nirari III, resumed aggressive policy in Syria, and by 802 Aram was prostrate, its king forced to pay no less than a hundred talents of gold and a thousand of silver to the triumphant Assyrians. About 801 Joash became king of Israel, and in the ensuing war with Ben-Hadad, Hazael's son, he recovered the territory previously lost to Aram. By the time of his death he had also reduced Judah to a vassal state, setting the stage for the brilliant reign of his son, Jeroboam II (*c.* 786-746 B.C.E.). Under the latter the Northern Kingdom reached the summit of its material power and wealth, expanding northward at the expense of Damascus and Hamath, and southward—as would appear from our obscure text, II Kings 14:28—at the expense of Judah. Archaeology contributes further details, illustrating the development of architecture at Samaria and Megiddo, as well as the flowering of the arts. During this entire period Assyria was weak, scarcely able to maintain her foothold in Syria by repeated campaigns against Hamath and Damascus. Moreover, Hamath and Damascus were themselves engaged in a bitter conflict for supremacy in Syria, vividly described in the contemporary stele of Zakir, king of Hamath. At that time Phoenician colonial expansion was at its height, and wealth poured into the treasuries of its great cities. Greek competition was actively beginning, and in less than a century the Greeks and the Assyrians were to deal terrific blows against the merchant princes of Tyre and Sidon. But Phoenicia was still a neighbor from which Israel could gain immense riches, both through the sale of Israelite products to the overcrowded Phoenician seacoast and through direct investment of capital and manpower in Phoenician enterprises. Tolls on caravans passing through Israel from Arabia were presumably also an important source of revenue.

The wealth and power of Israel under Jeroboam II meant great material progress and a notable rise in the standard of living; they also brought with them again increasing disparity between the lot of the rich and that of the poor, and increasing moral corruption, further augmented by the infiltration of inherited Canaanite customs and new Mediterranean practices into Israel over the long common border with Phoenicia. Moreover, the disastrous rout of Melcarth and his followers had by no means eradicated the older cult of Baal, especially in the old Canaanite towns which lined the plains. According to II Kings 13:6 Jehu and his son did not remove the Asherah from Samaria; we may perhaps surmise that this Asherah had existed before the importation of the cult of the Tyrian Melcarth and Asherah, and was considered as less obnoxious. However this may be, the personal names on the Ostraca from Samaria, dating from the years 778-770 B.C.E., indicate that names formed with "Baal" were still roughly in the ratio of 7:11 to names formed with "YHWH." Allowing for a certain preponderance in favor of the latter among abbreviated names, we should still have fully half as many Baal names as YHWH names. Since we can no longer reckon with the possibility that Baal was a recognized appellation of the God of Israel, it follows that Baalism was still the basic religion of a large proportion of the people of the land. The contemporary situation in Judah was very different; Baal names—which had been fairly common in the tenth century—never appear in our literary or epigraphic sources of the eighth and seventh centuries B.C.E.

This is the background against which we must set the poetic sermons of Amos and Hosea. If Morgenstern's plausible combination is correct,[94] we may date the beginning of Amos's prophetic career about 752; his last datable prophecy was delivered not long after 738 B.C.E. Hosea's poetic sermons seem to extend from before 746 to after 735. Both are fine examples of the true prophet of YHWH, who felt it as his primary function to rebuke his people and rulers for breaking the law of YHWH. In their public appearances we see scarcely a trace of the old ecstatic; in their poetic addresses there is careful preparation, but along original lines, drawing little from older poetic literature, perhaps because of the strong Canaanite element embedded in the latter. In both these prophets we find constant awareness of the JE tradition of Israel's beginnings and the Mosaic period; both show their point of view by stressing the divine *Torah*. In these prophets we do not have innovators, but reformers like Samuel and Elijah, reformers who reflect a gentler, more refined age, in which love had become more potent than hate and a cosmopolitan spirit looked at Israel and Judah almost as impartially as it considered their neighbors. It is not their zeal for monotheism, but rather their more advanced culture and their sensitivity to more refined spiritual nuances that set Amos and Hosea apart from their precursors in Israel. Hosea inveighs against all forms of religious practice which diverge from the narrow tradition of Mosaic monotheism, whether the cult of Baal, the cults of the high places, or the cults of YHWH at Beth-el and Dan. Both prophets are horrified by the selfish luxury, the immorality and the oppression of the poor that they see around them, but neither of them ever makes the modern mistake of distinguishing sharply between individual morality and social welfare. In that relatively simple age it was clear enough that each entailed the other; neither was possible alone.

Under the long reign of Uzziah (Azariah), *c.* 783-742 B.C.E., Judah reached the summit of its power. The fame of Uzziah's reign was second only to that of Solomon in succeeding generations, as we know from the Chronicler and from such testimonies as the Herodian plaque honoring the last resting place of the king's reputed bones, discovered some years ago by Eleazar Lipa Sukenik.[95] Ascending the throne as a lad of sixteen, several years after the accession of Jeroboam II, it does not seem likely that Uzziah reached the summit of his power until after the sun of Jeroboam had begun to set. Meanwhile Uzziah was busily engaged in building up economic and military strength. The Chronicler's description of his efforts to develop the economic resources of the country is most instructive, and is confirmed by archaeological indications, which prove that the most active period of construction in the Negeb was precisely in the eighth century B.C.E. The penetration of Jewish enterprise into Arabia at the time is attested by the discovery of a seal of Jotham, Uzziah's son and regent, in Glueck's recent excavations at Ezion-geber; that the king built Eloth near Ezion-geber is stated in II Chron. 26:2.[96] Uzziah's military program is also described in some detail by the Chronicler, who credits him with the introduction of siege engines into Judah. Uzziah appears to have conquered the northern and eastern part of the Philistine plain, thus controlling the important caravan routes in the Coastal Plain. The Chronicler lays great stress on his military activities in Arabia (still clearer in the Greek version), which were evidently designed to consolidate his position on the caravan routes from Arabia. About 750 Uzziah was stricken with leprosy and his place in public was taken by his son, Jotham, officially designated as regent. However, Uzziah seems still to have been the real ruler, and when Tiglath-pileser III of Assyria invaded Syria in 743 and the immediately following years, he credits him (under the alternative name Azariah) with being the head of the anti-Assyrian party in the west. This assertion is in every way reasonable. Jeroboam II, who had been the strongest ruler in the west, died about 746 and was replaced for six months by his son, Zechariah. The latter was killed in a revolt, which placed a certain Shallum on the throne for a month, after which Menahem seized the throne, following a civil war remembered for Menahem's atrocities. During this period Judah was the most stable state in Palestine and probably in all Syria, where inscriptions reveal a more or less continuous state of internecine war. Judah's wealth and military establishment were thus calculated to place her in the forefront of any plan for a coalition against the resurgent power of Assyria.

However, it was too late. Jotham was replaced by his son, Ahaz, about 735, and Ahaz found himself at once the target for an attack by Menahem's second successor, Pekah, and the latter's ally, Rezin, king of Aram. Ahaz appealed to Assyria for help, which was promptly forthcoming; Damascus was stormed by the Assyrians in 732, after a bloody war, and Aram was converted into four Assyrian provinces. Even before the fall of Damascus the Assyrian armies swept over Israel, devastating Galilee, and annexing all of Israel except Ephraim and western Manasseh (733 B.C.E.). In 732 the Assyrians appointed Hoshea as the last king of Samaria, but the Assyrian exactions were too much for him, and he rebelled about 724, relying on the very dubious promise of Egyptian assistance. Egypt was then broken up into many small city-states, and the "king" in question, Siwe or Sibe ("Star" in Egyptian), appears outside of the Bible and the Assyrian inscriptions only doubtfully on a single scarab! Hoshea was immediately taken prisoner, but the capital held out against a besieging army for over two years, falling at last in the first three months of 721. In his inscriptions Sargon II of Assyria repeatedly boasts of his conquest of Samaria and the "wide land of Beth-Omri" (official Israelite name of

Samaria).[97] He claims to have taken 27,290 Israelites into captivity. North Israel had ceased to be a political entity.

8. Judah from the Fall of Samaria to the Captivity

It was now a century and a half since the Assyrians had resumed their remorseless march of empire. It was only a quarter of a century since a revitalized Assyria had begun to crush the kingdoms of Arpad and Hamath. Every few years since then brought with it the end of some once strong native state. In 732 Damascus had fallen and the glory of Aram was but a memory; in 721 Samaria followed her long-time rival. . . . Such considerations must have made every man of Judah tremble for the future of his little state, the last barrier between Assyria and the caravan routes of the Negeb. In the new age no man was secure, and no city could hope for prolonged existence. Ahaz had indeed surrendered to his powerful allies in the war against Aram and Israel, but there is no reason to suppose that Judah's burden of taxation was at all reduced because of her favored status. However, Ahaz had saved his country from devastation, and archaeological indications point to increasing prosperity toward the end of the eighth century B.C.E. Uzziah had laid sound foundations for economic development. Moreover, it appears that the increasing prosperity of Judah was not canalized for the exclusive benefit of the aristocracy and the wealthy merchants, as was apparently true of the Northern Kingdom in the eighth century (see above). The excavations at Debir show that there was an extraordinary homogeneity of population there between 750 and 589 B.C.E., at least if we may judge from the fact that all private houses so far excavated reflect a surprisingly narrow range of variation in the social scale. The citizens of the town seem to have been almost exclusively engaged in one type of industry, to the exclusion of all others, aside from normal rural pursuits: the weaving and dyeing of woolen goods.[98] Explicit biblical statements, referring to the late pre-exilic age, show that there were other such concentrations of craftsmen in Judah, notably of potters, linenworkers, metalworkers, while in Jerusalem there were quarters devoted to bakers and goldsmiths.[99] Significantly enough, these references appear mostly in connection with genealogical lists, indicating clearly that there was a relatively direct passage from the old clan system to a new guild system. In other words, there was no period in Judah during which there was such concentration of wealth in the hands of individuals (aside from the crown) as to destroy the old social order, a fact which explains in part why there is no such bitter denunciation of the dominant social order in Isaiah or Micah as we find in Hosea. It is more than likely that some enlightened person or movement was at least partly responsible for the development of the guild system in Judah, perhaps on Phoenician models;

but its growth in a semipatriarchal society would have been unthinkable if Judah had not lagged considerably behind Israel in the evolution of ancestral Hebrew institutions, at the same time that it enjoyed nearly the same opportunities for commercial and industrial expansion.

The stage was thus set for both religious reform and political activism. On the one hand, the people found themselves faced by swiftly approaching doom, borne by swift horsemen from the north. Against the overwhelming might of Asshur only YHWH could stand; without Him His followers were helpless. On the other hand, new prosperity and new economic opportunities made men increasingly restive under the grinding taxation necessary to meet rapacious Assyrian demands for tribute and irregular levies of every kind. So when Ahaz died, some six years after the Fall of Samaria,[100] and was replaced by an energetic young prince, Hezekiah, there was a rapid change in both religious and political policy.

Owing to unwarranted depreciation of the data preserved for us by the Chronicler, most recent historians have failed fully to understand the religious situation under Hezekiah. By the latter's accession devout Yahwistic circles in Judah had progressed in their iconoclasm far beyond the policy of toleration toward popular Israelite religious practices and paganizing cultic institutions which had characterized the official attitude of the earlier Divided Monarchy. Moreover, the catastrophic collapse of Samaria, effectively utilized by the Prophets, strongly reinforced the reform party. Hezekiah proceeded, accordingly, to eliminate the high places and to destroy the altars, standing stones (*mazzebot*) and related objects, associated by the masses with local cults of YHWH; he even went so far as to destroy no less sacred an object than the copper representation of a snake which had been preserved in the Temple, and which was reputed to have been made by Moses. That this reform was only partly successful need not surprise us; such iconoclastic efforts on the part of a minority to change time-honored customs require wholehearted acceptance by the masses before they are likely to succeed.

At the same time Hezekiah and his supporters began active missionary propaganda in Northern Israel; the Chronicler tells us that it met with some success in Galilee but was unfavorably received in Ephraim. This is not surprising, since the rival sanctuary of Beth-el had been reorganized under Assyrian provincial auspices in order to compete with Jerusalem for the religious support of the people of Ephraim (II Kings 17:27-28). We may safely assume that the political aspects of this missionary propaganda were not lost on the Assyrian governors of Samaria, who were having difficulty keeping the Israelite population subjugated, as we learn from Assyrian sources.

While Sargon II of Assyria was alive, Judah apparently did not go beyond planning for future revolt. The Assyrian inscriptions inform us that the king of Ashdod, then the most important Philistine city, tried to obtain the aid of Judah in his projected rebellion. However this may be, the Assyrian general attacked Ashdod, reduced it and made it an Assyrian province in 711 B.C.E. Egyptian support, which had also been sought by the rebels of Ashdod, failed notably, eliciting bitter taunts from both Isaiah and the contemporary Assyrian historian. Even if Hezekiah had become involved in the rebellion, he withdrew in time, saving Judah from a futile stand against vastly superior power. So matters remained for about a decade, during which there were far-reaching changes in the international situation. Sargon had died and had been replaced by a greatly inferior son, Sennacherib (705). The Ethiopians, who had previously conquered Upper Egypt, had extended their power over the whole of the Nile Valley, and an energetic Ethiopian king, Shabako, had now unified Egypt again after a long period of anarchy and external weakness.[101] The Chaldean chieftain, Merodach-baladan, had re-established himself as king of Babylon and was defying Assyrian efforts to dislodge him. Under the circumstances, it was to be expected that Judah would try to throw off the onerous Assyrian yoke. In preparation for the day of decision, Hezekiah accepted the overtures made by Babylon and Egypt, intervened in Philistine affairs in order to strengthen the hands of the local rebels, and fortified Jerusalem, where he excavated the Siloam tunnel through the solid rock in order to provide the city with water in time of siege.

In 701 B.C.E. the Assyrian army invaded Palestine and crushed the rebellion, after defeating a large Egyptian and Ethiopian host which had advanced northward to relieve the beleaguered town of Ekron. The strong frontier fortress of Lachish was stormed, as vividly pictured in the Assyrian reliefs, and the fortified towns—forty-six in number, according to the Assyrians—fell in rapid succession. Hezekiah thereupon capitulated, paying an extremely heavy tribute, listed in detail by the Assyrian records, which agree substantially with the much briefer summary in Kings. According to the Assyrian annals, Sennacherib also turned over a strip of Jewish territory in the Shephelah to the three neighboring Philistine principalities. What happened subsequently we do not know, though it appears that the Jewish towns were recovered not long afterwards. Deuteronomic tradition connects a disastrous pestilence with an Assyrian invasion which took place after the accession of the Ethiopian prince Taharqo (Tirhakah) to the Egyptian throne in 689. Since Hezekiah died in 686, the invasion would have occurred between 689 and 686. Our Assyrian records close in 689 and we have no record of military doings in Sennacherib's reign thereafter. In 691, however, the Assyrians were defeated at Khalule by the Babylonians and Elamites, so it is entirely reasonable to suppose that Hezekiah then began planning a new revolt with Ethiopian aid, and that he revolted after Tirhakah's accession. This time the aged Isaiah supported the king, who was saved by the pestilence and apparently died before the Assyrians were able to put a new army into the field.[102]

The period of the two following Assyrian kings, Esarhaddon (681-669) and Asshurbanapal (669-*c.* 630 B.C.E.), represented the climax of Assyrian prestige and wealth, though signs of weakness may be discerned by the historian. Esarhaddon conquered Egypt and his son consolidated his father's conquest; his destruction of Thebes in 663 was long remembered (cf. Nah. 3:8). In 652, however, the Assyrian Empire was shaken to its foundation by a bloody civil war which broke out between Asshurbanapal and his brother and vassal, Shamash-shum-ukin, king of Babylon, and lasted until the capture of Babylon in 648. Among the states of Syria and Palestine which joined the rebellion may have been Judah (cf. II Chron. 33:11). The Arab tribes of the Syrian Desert, which had been increasing in numbers and pressing northward for several centuries, took advantage of the situation to inundate the regions east of Antilibanus and Jordan. Edom and Moab are named in the Assyrian inscriptions among the regions devastated, and though a Moabite king captured an Arab chief, whom he sent in chains to Nineveh, there can be no doubt that this catastrophe spelled the end of Moab as a strong autonomous state.[103] A vivid contemporary dirge from about 650 B.C.E., describing the fate of Moab, has been preserved in both Isaiah (15-16) and Jeremiah (48), with variations showing its popularity.

During this period Judah became infected by the prevailing syncretism, and its king, Manasseh, is said to have restored the local shrines of YHWH, which Hezekiah had destroyed, and to have returned to official recognition of Baalism as well as to the practice of divination and magic. It may be noted that no other period of cuneiform records has yielded any remotely comparable mass of tablets relating to magic and divination, and that the royal Assyrian letters of the time contain innumerable references to astrology and magic. It was practically impossible for a small vassal state to keep from being flooded with such idolatrous and superstitious practices, which were under royal Assyrian protection.

After the accession of Manasseh's young grandson, Josiah, in 640 B.C.E. the situation changed abruptly. Josiah is said to have been only eight years old at this accession, and his coming of age coincided roughly with the death of Asshurbanapal, *c.* 630.[104] In 629 he began a purge which seems to have been considerably more thoroughgoing than that of Hezekiah, including objects of local Yahwist cult as well as pagan idols and installations. It appears that this purge coincided with the removal of effective Assyrian domination, since Josiah was able to extend it into Northern Israel (though perhaps not until after some time), including Galilee as well as Ephraim and Manasseh. In particular he destroyed the cultic installations at Beth-el, which had long been in active competition, under Assyrian protection, with the Temple in Jerusalem. This purge is unthinkable unless Josiah also exercised political control of the country, either in defiance of Assyria or, more probably, as nominal vassal of the Assyrians, in somewhat the same way as the contemporary Psammetichus of Egypt. As nominal vassal, controlling the Assyrian provinces of Samaria and Megiddo as well as the tributary state of Judah, Josiah would be free to carry out his reforms; this would also explain why biblical tradition has preserved no hint of military action for the reconquest of Northern Israel. Albrecht Alt and his pupils have effectively demonstrated the importance of this phase of Israelite history.[105] Ever since Hezekiah's missionary activity in the north, the kings of Judah had kept up close relations with their northern relatives. Amon, Manasseh's short-lived son and successor, was the grandson of a notable from the Galilean town of Jotbah (Assyr. Yatbatu, Greek Jotapata). Josiah's own son, Eliakim, was grandson of another notable from the Galilean town of Rumah, near Jotbah.[106] But Necho's invasion of 609 and Josiah's death in battle with him, defending the Megiddo pass on behalf of the Babylonians (to whom he had by this time shifted his loyalty),[107] put an end to these grandiose dreams of a reunited Israel under a prince of the house of David.

9. CAPTIVITY AND RESTORATION

Judah declined rapidly after Josiah's death. Egyptian rule was superseded within seven years by Chaldean, when Eliakim (Jehoiakim) was forced to surrender to Nebuchadnezzar's army. His rebellion not long afterwards brought swift retribution, but before the Chaldean army laid siege to Jerusalem the Jewish king died or was assassinated and his young son, Jehoiachin, went into exile in his place (598 B.C.E.).

Among the most significant of the undertakings that had been sponsored by Josiah must be reckoned the authoritative collection of the historical traditions of Israel into a new corpus, based on the ancient code found in the Temple (II Kings 22:3 ff.). This code was expanded and edited (it is now known as the Book of Deuteronomy), and was supplemented by a collection of the historical traditions of the Conquest (Joshua) and subsequent periods (Judges, Samuel and Kings), with a running theological commentary which pointed out the close relationship between evildoing and Divine Retribution.[108] Begun after the finding of the ancient code (which had originally been compiled in Northern Israel and was carried to Jerusalem after the Fall of Samaria) in 622 B.C.E., this great work may not have been completed until years after Josiah's death in 609; it was then brought up to date and re-edited about 560 B.C.E. The enthusiasm shown by the Deuteronomist for the work of the prophets and the closeness of his style to that of the prose sections of Jeremiah shows that the two were written in the same period and under similar auspices; the striking similarity between the rhetorical style of the Deuteronomist and Jeremiah and that of the Lachish Letters forms a strong additional argument in favor of dating the work of the former in the last generation before the Fall of Jerusalem.

Informing the work of the Deuteronomist is a pronounced archaistic flavor, arising partly from a desire to seek salvation for the tottering land of Judah by going back to Israel's early history.[109] As a conscious effort to recapture the letter and the spirit of Moses, founder of Israel's institutions, it represents a nostalgic return to the past as the source of all good things. No longer was there facile optimism about Israel's future. As the Northern Kingdom and most of its neighbors had fallen, so would Judah unless it abandoned its evil modern ways and its sophisticated adaptations of foreign culture. Some men of Judah went to extremes; among them were the Rechabites, who went so far as to eschew all agriculture along with other innovations of civilization, attracting favorable comment from Jeremiah himself.

Jeremiah's poetic addresses to the people of Judah are couched in singularly beautiful verses, which plastically reproduce his intense hatred of paganism, paganizing ritual and all kinds of cant. In particular he attacks conventional exaltation of the Temple and its sacrificial ritual at the expense of elementary justice and kindness. Under such conditions, in which each new reign and each new deportation meant progressive deterioration of morals, only one conclusion was possible for so direct and forthright a thinker as Jeremiah: just as in the past history of Israel wickedness had invariably been followed by political catastrophe, so would it, under the prevailing circumstances, happen again. For Jeremiah the only way in which Judah could postpone a similar catastrophe was by patient submission to the will of God as manifested in Chaldean domination. Hence Jeremiah set himself against the self-styled patriots of his people, preferring to be despised as a coward and condemned as a collaborationist. It is instructive to note the extent to which Judahite chauvinism, whipped to a frenzy by the oracles of the prophets whom Jeremiah so roundly denounced (Jer. 23:9-32), went, as illustrated by the Lachish Letters. Toward the end of Zedekiah's reign we find the *sarim* (royal officials and notables) denouncing Jeremiah to the king and demanding that he be executed because of his bad influence on the morale of the people (Jer. 38:4). In Lachish Letter No. 6, a patriotic official writing to the commander of the garrison of Lachish complains bitterly about circular letters sent out by the *sarim*, alleging in identical words that "they weaken the hands" of the people.[110] Yet these were the *sarim* who wished to put Jeremiah to death!

The period 598-587 B.C.E. was charged with unmixed gloom. Jehoiachin had been accompanied into exile by the leading men of Judah and its best craftsmen. Jeremiah spoke scathingly of the qualities of the regent, Zedekiah, and his followers, whom he called "bad figs" as against the "good figs" which had been taken by the Chaldeans. But Zedekiah and his adherents stubbornly followed the path to ruin by conspiring with Psammetichus II and his son Apries against the Chaldean suzerain. From passages in Jeremiah, vividly illustrated by the Lachish Letters, we learn of the successive fall of the towns of the Negeb and the Shephelah, followed by the last siege of Jerusalem. Excavations at Debir and Lachish show the increasing poverty of the country between the two destructions of these towns in 598 and 587.[111] The population of Judah, which had probably passed 250,000 by the end of the eighth century,[112] can scarcely have been over half that number during this interval. Finally, in August, 587,[113] Jerusalem was stormed and most of the remaining notables and craftsmen were sent into Babylonian captivity.

The former mayor of the palace,[114] Gedaliah, was appointed governor of Judah by the Chaldeans, and many Jews who had fled to security before the Chaldean advance returned to the country and accepted his authority. The chiefs of the army in the field, who had hidden in the wilds during the siege, entered into negotiations with Gedaliah, but before any arrangement could be reached a certain ultrapatriotic member of the Davidic family, named Ishmael, treacherously assassinated Gedaliah, killing many of his followers, as well as the Chaldeans stationed at Mizpah. The army chiefs then collected a considerable number of the remaining Jews and fled to Egypt, where they entered into military service and were installed as garrison troops at the northern and southern boundaries. A hundred years after their flight to Egypt we begin to learn something of the fortunes of some of their descendants who were settled by the Saite kings at Elephantine (Yeb) before the Persian invasion in 525 B.C.E. Even after Gedaliah's assassination, however, there were still enough Jews of rank or skill left in the land to provoke the Chaldeans to a third deportation (582 B.C.E.).

In Jer. 52:28 ff. we have an extract from an official document of the Babylonian *golah* giving exact figures for the three deportations, whose total is there computed at only 4,600 souls. The number of those exiled in 598 is set at 3,023 instead of 8,000 (or 10,000) in Kings; the difference may be partly due to the fact that the latter was only a conjectural estimate, but may also be partly due to the heavy mortality of the starving and diseased captives during the long desert trek to Babylonia. There, however, the native energy and capacity of the captives was not slow in asserting itself. In recently published tablets from a royal archive of Nebuchadnezzar, dating in and about the year 592 B.C.E., Jehoiachin and five of his sons, as well as at least five other Jews, are mentioned among recipients of rations from the royal court. It is significant that Jehoiachin was still called "king of Judah" in official Babylonian documents.[115]

Just as Jeremiah had denounced the wickedness of Judah, urging his people to bow to the Chaldean yoke, so did his younger contemporary, Ezekiel, in the Babylonian *golah,* whose focus (outside of Babylon) was at a colony established on the Chebar Canal near Nippur in central Babylonia.[116] In spite of the corrupt text of his poems and prose sermons, their purport is clear almost throughout. The Prophet depicted the religious perversity of the men of Judah in scathing terms, employing figures of unexcelled vividness. He predicted the downfall of the state and the captivity of its population, just as Jeremiah was doing in Jerusalem. From the Jews in exile he demanded puritanical standards of morality, strict accountability of the individual for his actions, and rigid monotheism. It is significant that we hear no more of pagan practices among the Babylonian Jews, whereas the Egyptian Jews who had flouted Jeremiah, as well as many Yahwists in North Israel and Trans-Jordan during the next century, practiced syncretistic rites which at best compromised seriously with the surrounding paganism.

It is now possible, thanks to archaeological discoveries, to reconstruct the situation of the Jews in Palestine during the Exile with general clarity. All, or virtually all, of the fortified towns in Judah had been razed to the ground as thoroughly as we know to have been the case at Debir, Lachish and Beth-shemesh (to mention only those sites which have been both adequately and recently excavated; the evidence is clear for many other sites from soundings and surface explorations). We are expressly told that the Chaldean general, Nabu-zer-iddin, left many of the poor in order to harvest grapes and make wine (Jerusalem was captured early in the grape harvest). On the other hand, a number of the Jewish settlements in the Negeb (which seems to have been detached from the Judahite state in 598 B.C.E.) appear to have escaped destruction, and the Israelite towns north of the old border remained under Babylonian control, being thus saved from the fate of the towns to the south: Beth-el, for example, was occupied through this period and down probably into the late sixth century. The territory belonging to Judah in 589 was divided between the Edomites (Idumeans), who settled in the southern hill country about Adoraim (Dura) and Hebron, and the Babylonian province of Samaria (as shown recently by Albrecht Alt).[117] There was also a considerable Israelite population in Ephraim, Galilee and Trans-Jordan; and at some time before the middle of the fifth century Yahwists became hereditary governors of Samaria and Ammon.

As long as the exiled king lived there was hope for a restoration of the Jewish monarchy, and this hope appears to have flamed up brightly when the news of Jehoiachin's release from prison after the death of Nebuchadnezzar was circulated through the *golah* (captivity) (561 B.C.E.).

It is not likely that there was a long interval between his death and the fall of the Chaldean Empire before the onslaught of Cyrus in 539. Jehoiachin's three older sons, all born before 592 (as shown by recently published cuneiform documents),[118] were probably already dead by this time, leaving his fourth son, who bore the well-attested Babylonian name Sin-ab-usur,[119] to head the Davidic family and to enter into negotiations with the Persians for a restoration of the Jewish state. The enthusiastic resurgence of Jewish nationalism on a deeper religious basis, which we find at this time, is eloquently portrayed by Deutero-Isaiah, who combined Jewish nationalism with religious universalism; nowhere in earlier prophetic literature do we find such explicit recognition of the gulf existing between the One God, whose special favor had been extended to Israel, and the nonexistent deities who were mistakenly worshiped by the Gentile peoples. In this stage of the Zionism of the Restoration, there was a pure religious idealism which reminds one in certain respects of the cultural idealism of Ahad Ha-Am and Eliezer ben Yehuda in the generation before the First World War.

The substantial historicity of the Edict of Cyrus in 538 has been confirmed by modern archaeological discoveries,[120] but it is wholly unnecessary to suppose that it was followed by any wide response on the part of the Jews of the *golah*. In the first place, the latter were in general becoming well established in their new homes, as vividly illustrated by Egyptian papyri beginning in the year 495 and by Babylonian contract tablets dating from various periods (but sporadic and often uncertain until 437 B.C.E., when Jewish names become abundant in the Nippur documents).[121] In the second place, the journey was dangerous and expensive, while conditions in Judah were certainly very unsatisfactory. However, between 538 and the death of the Persian king Cambyses in 522 many Jews had undoubtedly returned to Palestine, among them Zerubbabel, son of Jehoiachin's eldest son, Shealtiel, who had replaced his uncle Sin-ab-usur as head of the Davidic house, and the hight priest, Joshua (Jeshua). They found a very small territory to call their own, stretching less than twenty-five miles in a straight line along the watershed ridge from north of Jerusalem to south of Beth-zur, with a total population which can scarcely have exceeded 20,000 in 522 B.C.E.[122] The governors and nobles of Samaria, who had regarded this district as part of their province, were openly hostile. On the other hand, there were extensive districts in Greater Palestine which were peopled wholly or partly by Jews and Israelites, and a modest flow of capital was assured by immigrants and gifts to the Holy Place.

Zerubbabel (Zer-Babil, "Offspring of Babylon," a very common Babylonian name), whose father had been born about 597 (as we know from recent finds), was not an impetuous youth, as generally assumed, but a cautious man of middle age (almost certainly born before 570). His caution irritated the fiery prophets, Haggai and Zechariah, who seized the opportunity offered by the continuous rebellions in every part of the Persian Empire which followed the accession of Darius Hystaspes in 522. Haggai's first oracle, in late August, 520, in which he spurred the men of Judah to take up the long overdue rebuilding of the Temple in earnest, was delivered about two months after the rebellion of Babylonia under a man who called himself Nebuchadnezzar.[123] Less than a month later work actually began. Haggai's second oracle (Hag. 2:1 ff.), nearly two months later, exults in the approaching downfall of Persia and the coming of a new Jewish state; in his fourth oracle (Hag. 2:20 ff.), dated in December, while the Babylonian rebellion still appeared to be successful, he explicitly declared that the imperial throne would be overturned and implied that Zerubbabel was the Lord's anointed. Most of Zechariah's prophecies are later, reflecting the situation that followed the complete triumph of Darius over his foes, when the ambiguous stand of the Jews during the previous year naturally became the target of official Persian investigation. Whether Zerubbabel died a natural death or was removed, we cannot say; there is not the slightest reason to suppose that he committed any overt act of disloyalty to the crown. In spite of the hostility of the satrap of Syria and the men of Samaria, the Temple was finished in March, 515; evidently the Persian authorities contented themselves with depriving the Davidic family of its political prerogatives, which were turned over to Joshua and his successors. We may safely credit Joshua with political astuteness in the difficult situation in which he found himself.

The disappointment felt by Jews in all parts of the Persian Empire at the failure of the restored Davidic state to materialize must have been followed, just as in similar recent situations, by decline in their interest in Judah. This shift of interest left the little priestly state of Judah unable for three generations greatly to influence currents of Jewish life in other parts of the world. Meanwhile Jewish communities were being founded in cities as remote from Jerusalem as Sardis, capital of Lydia.[124] It is true that the Temple had been rebuilt, but efforts to reconstruct the ancient city walls had been thwarted by the officials of Samaria, and Jerusalem was surrounded with ruins. In this period of some sixty years, however, the population may have doubled, and more or less normal relations between the returned exiles and the older Jewish population were certainly established. The time was ripe for a new forward step in the resurrection of Zion.

10. From Nehemiah to the Fall of the Persian Empire

It may appear strange but it is nevertheless true that the history of the Jews in the fifth century B.C.E. is in some respects more obscure than any corresponding section of Israel's history after the twelfth century B.C.E. This is due to the fact that the books of Ezra and Nehemiah have undergone unusual vicissitudes, leaving their text and the order of their contents in quite extraordinary confusion, with sharply divergent recensions to warn us against docilely following any one. It is scarcely surprising that distinguished biblical scholars have dated Ezra and Nehemiah in almost every part of the period covered by this section, or that opinions differ widely as to the order of their careers. Nor is it altogether surprising that the Ezra Memoirs have been declared by Charles C. Torrey and others to be quite apocryphal. Thanks to archaeological discoveries, particularly the Elephantine Papyri (since 1906) and the Jehoiachin tablets (1939; see above), we can now date Nehemiah in the third quarter of the fifth century with certainty and can locate Ezra with a high degree of confidence shortly after him. Our arguments and those of our precursors will be found elsewhere; here we can sketch only the results, with emphasis on the degree of probability in each case.

Among the personalities of ancient history there are few which present themselves to us as vividly as that of Nehemiah, thanks to his *apologia pro vita sua*, whose authenticity has never been doubted by any scholar of competence. Endowed with unusual energy and presumably with exceptional charm, he rose to a high rank among the court officials of Artaxerxes Longimanus (465-424), whose cupbearer he became. As long since recognized, this position required a eunuch to fill it, and there is strong collateral evidence in favor of this view.[125] Nehemiah's love for his people was so great, however, that his physical handicap became an asset and he was able to serve Israel with rare single-mindedness. On the other hand, the petulance and obstinacy that formed the reverse side of his character made it difficult for him to collaborate, and he made bitter enemies.

It appears to have been in December, 445, that Nehemiah learned from his brother Hanani and other Jews who had recently come from Jerusalem how bad the situation there really was. He seems to have been particularly moved by the news that the walls were still in ruins (see above), a fact which made it possible for Arab, Edomite or Ammonite raiders to attack the unprotected Holy City almost at will. It was apparently not until considerably later that he succeeded in arousing the interest of the king in the plight of the Jews in Palestine. To judge from the additional details preserved by Josephus, Nehemiah did not actually arrive in Palestine, armed with a bodyguard and royal rescripts, until the year 440.[126] Early in August, 439, he began the work of rebuilding the great city wall, almost exactly 148 years after its destruction by the Chaldeans (if our chronology is correct). Fifty-two days later, thanks to energetic efforts on his part and to a mass levy from all parts of the little province of Judea, the wall had been raised. However, work on the wall cannot actually have been completed in such a short time by volunteer workmen; and we may safely follow the explicit statement of Josephus that the entire work took two years and four months, especially since the latter fixes the end of the work in a month which harmonizes exactly with the month given by the Hebrew text for its beginning. The task of finishing the battlements, of building great revetments, towers, gates, etc., was not completed, then, until December, 437.[127]

Nehemiah's personal relationships were not so happy as one might expect from this brilliant initial success. That he was bitterly opposed by Sin-uballit (Sanballat), governor of Samaria, was only natural, since the latter had fallen heir to the old claims of Samaria on the territory of Judah, which had belonged to it during Chaldean times, as shown recently by Albrecht Alt.[128] Sin-uballit, in spite of his inherited Babylonian name, was a Yahwist by religion, as proved by the fact that two of his sons were named Delaiah and Shelemiah; some of his hostility may be traced to the machinations of hostile groups among the priests, prophets and nobles of Judea, about which Nehemiah complains so bitterly in his memoirs. Tobiah, governor of Ammon, who controlled central Trans-Jordan, also was hostile to Nehemiah; his Yahwism is proved by his own name, that of his son, Johanan, and the fact that his descendants in the early second century B.C.E. were still Jews.[129] That the Yahwism of Sin-uballit and Tobiah was not that of the returned exiles in Jerusalem, much less that of the Babylonian *golah*, may be considered as certain, especially after the Elephantine discoveries; it was a syncretistic structure with archaic features, presumably something like the religion of the Jewish colonists at Elephantine.[130, 130a]

An excellent idea of the population and social organization of Judea in the time of Nehemiah is provided by the census list in Neh. 7 (and Ezra 2), which may represent the original list of returned exiles, with corrected numbers and additional entries to bring it up to date. It is composed of two main groups: the returned exiles and their descendants; the inhabitants of towns in northern Judea whose forebears had presumably returned to their homes not long after the Chaldean invasion or who had never left them. Among the former are a number of families whose names prove their late origin, as is particularly clear in the case of the family of Bagoi (Bigvai), bearing a characteristic Iranian name, but also in the case of the family of Elam (evidently descended from settlers in the region around Susa) and of the family of the "Governor of Moab" (Pahath-moab).[131] Among the latter are such Judahite towns as Bethlehem and Netophah, Benjamite towns such as Ramah and Geba, and also Ephraimite towns (north of the pre-exilic border) like Beth-el and Ai; farther away were Jericho and a little group of three towns of Ephraim on the edge of the

Plain of Sharon around Lod (Lydda). Since Beth-zur, Keilah, Tekoa and other towns of Judah farther south, mentioned in the account of Nehemiah's building operations, do not appear in this census, it seems clear that this part of the province was virtually uninhabited when the exiles began to return after 538 B.C.E. On the other hand, the region around Jerusalem was already settled and offered less room for the returning Jews. Archaeological work at Beth-el has proved that it was occupied down to the latter part of the sixth century, and was then destroyed by a great conflagration; it was later reoccupied but remained thinly settled down into the fourth century.[132] Lydda and the adjoining towns may have been added to the province by Nehemiah himself. Jerusalem was peopled mainly by priests, Levites and Nethinim, etc., as well as by a certain number of wealthy persons, officials and tradesmen. The total population was over 42,000 freeborn Jews, besides over 7,000 slaves and menials, approximately 50,000 in all, of whom between 10,000 and 15,000 may have lived in and around the capital. While this was only a tiny nucleus for a Jewish state, it was already a respectable development for about a century of growth from extremely small beginnings.

Unfortunately, as indicated above, we are very unsatisfactorily informed about the date of Ezra. The most recent evidence favors a date for Ezra's mission in or about the thirty-seventh year of Artaxerxes, *i.e.*, about 428 B.C.E.[133] It is not clear whether Nehemiah was in Jerusalem at the time; he is not specifically mentioned in the Ezra Memoirs proper, and the evidence is conflicting.[134] There can, however, be little doubt that his influence was directly responsible for the royal rescript giving Ezra extensive powers in connection with his plan to reform the religious organization at Jerusalem. The view, brilliantly defended by Eduard Meyer and Hans Heinrich Schaeder,[135] that "Judaism was created by the Persian Empire," is grossly exaggerated, and has, in fact, no more real validity than the corresponding statement, sometimes heard, that "Zionism has been created by the British." We need not depreciate the role played by Cyrus and Nehemiah, by Lord Balfour and Lord Samuel, to recognize that in general there was more opposition than support among Persian and British officials. Judaism and Zionism were both developed by the Jewish people, working against great odds—so great, in fact, that without benevolent assistance at critical moments from the Persian and British imperial authorities success might have been impossible, in spite of the faith of the leaders of both movements.

Nowhere in the Ezra Memoirs proper is there a clear statement about who was then *tirshatha* (royal commissioner) of Judea,[136] but we may safely infer that it was Nehemiah himself, whose brother Hanani (Hananiah) may have taken charge during his absence (cf. Neh. 7:2), especially since the latter was still apparently at the head of Jewish affairs in Jerusalem a few years later in 419, when an edict of Arsames, Persian viceroy of Babylonia, Syria and Egypt, with regard to the orthodox observance of Passover, was forwarded through him to the Jewish colonists at Elephantine.[137] Nor have we any information about what happened between Nehemiah's governorship and the year 411 B.C.E., when we find a Persian, one Bagoas (Bagohi), named in official documents as governor of Judea, while the chief political role under him reverts to the high priest. In Nehemiah's time Eliashib, grandson of Joshua, who must have been well along in years, was high priest (until after 433 B.C.E.). When Ezra came to Jerusalem a few years later Eliashib's grandson Johanan seems already to have been high priest (cf. Ezra 10:6 with Neh. 11:23). The latter was still high priest in 408, but by that time he had probably lost the respect of all by murdering his brother Joshua in the Temple, an act which shocked the world of that day and brought severe reprisals from Bagoas. Not long afterwards he was succeeded by his son Jedaiah (Jaddua), with whom our knowledge of the succession of high priests stops until the Hellenistic period.

Ezra's greatest significance in the history of Judaism probably lay in the field of cultic reform rather than in that of political action. He seems to have played an important role in establishing the canonical Torah as the normative rule of Israel's faith. The Pentateuch was probably edited in approximately its present form by an orthodox Jewish circle in Babylonia, employing the so-called JE document from the early Monarchy, the Deuteronomic Code from the end of the Monarchy, and the Priestly Code. The last-named component of the Pentateuch represents the official tradition of the patriarchal age, the Mosaic period and the ritual law of the Tabernacle as handed down by the priests of the Temple in Jerusalem. It contains some very early material, most of it probably written down before the Exile. As it stands, however, there is little doubt that it was edited in approximately its present form during the Exile. There seems no adequate reason to deny that it was known in Jerusalem generations before Ezra, but it seems highly probable that it was Ezra who introduced the complete Pentateuch into normative Jewish use and who is largely responsible for the way in which its archaic practices were adjusted to actual ritual usage in the Temple. The latter was alone a major contribution to the future of normative Judaism.

In another direction we may credit Ezra with original literary compilation. We owe to Charles C. Torrey recognition of the fact that the style and point of view of the Ezra Memoirs (in which Ezra speaks primarily in the first person) are identical with those of the Chronicler.[138] It is, therefore, highly probable that Jewish tradition is in principle correct in identifying Ezra with the Chronicler. Since the first edition of the latter's work brings us down to the time of Johanan, and since (as we may now affirm with confidence) his genealogy of the Davidic house closes before the end of the fifth century,[139] there is no historical improbability in this tradition. All internal and linguistic objections to dating the final redaction of the Chronicler's work after the early fourth century have been disproved by recent archaeological research.[140]

The fourth century is almost wholly without dated Jewish documents. Egypt and Babylonia cease to yield any information about the further fortunes of their Jewish colonies, about which we were so well informed in the latter part of the fifth century. In Judah we lack even the names of the high priests after Jaddua, though we may suspect that the names of a Johanan and a second Jaddua have dropped out of later lists. On the other hand, archaeology has demonstrated that the Jewish state of the fourth century was recognized by the Persian authorities as a hierocratic commonwealth like that of Hierapolis in northern Syria, which enjoyed the right to levy its own taxes and to strike its own silver coins—employing the *darkemon* standard (imitating, as E. L. Sukenik has shown, contemporary Attic drachmas) which is attested in the work of the Chronicler.[141] The material culture of Jewish Palestine was already saturated with Greek influence,[142] which was soon to engulf the world and to usher in a new era, fraught with both evil and good.

NOTES

[1] It is true that the Greek translation of the third century B.C.E. renders simply "in the land of the Chaldeans," omitting any reference to Ur (cf. my remarks in *The Archaeology of Palestine and the Bible*, p. 209, n. 27). Yet the Book of Jubilees, which probably dates from the same century (cf. most recently *From the Stone Age to Christianity*, pp. 266 f.), mentions both an eponymous hero named "Ur son of Kesed," who "built Ara (misunderstood Aramaic *ar'a*, "land"?) of the Chaldeans," and Ur of the Chaldees itself (the latter repeatedly). It therefore seems to me that the most probable solution is to be sought in a different direction: the original Hebrew text may have been "Ur (in the) land of the Chaldees," which was differently abbreviated by haplography in the recensions underlying the Septuagint and the masoretic text.

[2] See my remarks and references in *From the Stone Age to Christianity*, pp. 179 ff.

[3] Cf. n. 2, as well as J. Lewy in the *Revue de l'Histoire des Religions*, 1934, pp. 44 ff.

[4] See *Jour. Bib. Lit.*, 1939, pp. 91-103.

[5] According to this cycle of legends (which I hope to discuss at a convenient opportunity) Babylon was built just "opposite" Accad, capital of Sargon I, who established a mighty empire in the twenty-fourth century B.C.E. (for this and other early Babylonian dates see especially *Bull. Am. Sch. Or. Res.*, No.

88, pp. 28-33). Its name *Babili(m)*, "Gate of God" (of which *Kadingirra* is merely the Sumerian translation), and other points in the story indicate that it was an important shrine, whose temple tower was perhaps the highest (and earliest?) structure of the kind to be erected in that age.

[6] Cf. the preceding references, to which add *Bull. Am. Sch. Or. Res.*, No. 83, p. 34.

[7] For the Mari archives in general cf. *Bull. Am. Sch. Or. Res.*, Nos. 77, pp. 20 ff., and 78, pp. 23 ff. On the two last items in the paragraph see G. Dossin, *Revue d'Assyriologie,* XXXVI, 174 ff., XXXV, 50 ff.

[8] Cf. my discussion of the situation in *The Jewish People Past and Present,* I (1946), 28, 34. On the demographic history of Trans-Jordan see Nelson Glueck, *The Other Side of the Jordan*, pp. 20 ff.

[9] See *Bull. Am. Sch. Or. Res.*, Nos. 81, pp. 16 ff., and 83 pp. 30 ff.

[10] See especially J. A. Wilson, *Am. Jour. Sem. Lang.*, LVIII (1941), 225-236, as well as my remarks in the Leland Volume (*Studies in the History of Culture,* Menasha, 1942), pp. 17-21.

[11] See my observations in *Archaeology and the Religion of Israel,* pp. 98, 200.

[12] Cf. Alt, *Palaestinajahrbuch,* XXXV (1939), 26 ff.

[13] For a comprehensive account, with bibliography, see Gordon, *Biblical Archaeologist,* III (1940), 1-12.

[14] On this subject cf. my observations, *From the Stone Age to Christianity,* pp. 33 ff.

[15] Cf. provisionally *Archaeology of Palestine and the Bible*, p. 143, and for examples (which can easily be increased in number) cf. *Jour. Bib. Lit.*, XXXVII, 132 ff. (where much is antiquated). Alan Rowe has recently discovered the Egyptian name of Joseph, which had previously been reconstructed by Spiegelberg, in an inscription of the Bubastite period.

[16] Cf. *From the Stone Age to Christianity*, p. 184.

[17] See now *Bull. Am. Sch. Or. Res.*, No. 99, pp. 13-17.

[18] Cf. my remarks in the Leland Volume (see n. 10), pp. 21 ff.

[19] Cf. *From the Stone Age to Christianity,* pp. 160, 169; *Bull. Am. Sch. Or. Res.*, No. 84, pp. 7-11.

[20] I expect to discuss this name soon; it occurs on a figurine from a tomb of the late fourteenth century B.C.E. excavated by Petrie (see his *Kahun, Gurob, Hawara,* Pl. 24), and was identified in 1910 by Burchardt (this identification is strikingly confirmed by my phonetic study of New Empire transcriptions).

[21] See my discussion, *Jour. Bib. Lit.*, LIV, 180-193.

[22] Cf. Meek, *Am. Jour. Sem. Lang.*, LVI (1939), 113-120.

[23] On the identification of Tanis with Rameses (Raamses) see now Montet, *Le drame d'Avaris* (Paris, 1941).

[24] Cf. Alan Rowe, *The Topography and History of Beth-shan,* p. 34.

[25] Cf. *From the Stone Age to Christianity*, pp. 165 ff., 205 f.

[26] *Ibid.*, p. 169; see further A. H. Gardiner, *Hieratic Papyri in the British Museum,* Third Series, I, pp. 28-37, and Adolf Erman, "Der Leidener Amonshymnus," *Sitz. Preuss. Akad. Wiss.*, 1923.

[27] Cf. *Archaeology and the Religion of Israel*, pp. 77, 86.

[28] See my paper, *Jour. Bib. Lit.*, 1944, pp. 207-233.

[29] For Elyon see Levi della Vida, *Jour. Bib. Lit.*, 1944, pp. 1-9; for Eli see the *Keret Epic*, II, iii: 5 ff. (H. L. Ginsberg, *The Legend of King Keret*, *Supplementary Studies* of the *Bull. Am. Sch. Or. Res.*, 2-3 [1946], pp. 29, 47).

[30] A striking Greek case may serve to illustrate how a block of laws from the original code (now known only from Ex. 21-23 and a few fragments elsewhere) may have survived after the rest was lost. Professor John H. Kent of Southwestern (Memphis) has called my attention to the fact that the only block of legislation from the Attic code of Draco (*c.* 621 B.C.E.) which has survived to our time was a group of laws about homicide, re-enacted in 409-408 and inscribed at that time on stone; see Bonner and Smith, *The Administration of Justice from Homer to Aristotle*, I, pp. 110 and *passim*.—For the date of the ancient Near Eastern codes see *From the Stone Age to Christianity*, p. 204; the Code of Hammurabi must now be lowered an additional sixty-four years or so (cf. n. 5, above).

[31] See Alt, "Urspruenge des israelitischen Rechts" (*Ber. Saechs. Akad. Wiss.*, 1934); cf. my review, *Jour. Bib. Lit.*, 1936, pp. 164 ff.

[32] Cf. *Jour. Bib. Lit.*, 1944, pp. 227 ff.

[33] Cf. provisionally my remarks in *From the Stone Age to Christianity*, pp. 120 f., *Archaeology and the Religion of Israel*, pp. 96 f., *Jour. Bib. Lit.*, 1945, pp. 287 f.

[34] Cf. A. Bergman, *Jour. Pal. Or. Soc.*, 1936, pp. 224-254.

[35] Cf. *Bull. Am. Sch. Or. Res.*, No. 94, pp. 32 ff.

[36] See Montet, *Le drame d'Avaris* (Paris, 1941), and my remarks on chronology, *Bull. Am. Sch. Or. Res.*, No. 99, pp. 13 ff.

[37] Cf. *Annual Am. Sch. Or. Res.*, XVII, 68.

[38] See I. Mendelsohn, *Bull. Am. Sch. Or. Res.*, No. 83, pp. 36-39; E. R. Lacheman, *ibid.*, No. 86, pp. 36 f.

[39] On the problem of the ʿApiru and the Hebrews cf. the literature cited in my *Archaeology and the Religion of Israel*, p. 200, n. 8, and by H. H. Rowley, *Pal. Explor. Quar.*, 1942-1943, pp. 41 ff. I am inclined to think that the term *ʿApiru* is derived from the Egyptian *ʿ-p-r*, "ship's complement, crew, gang of laborers," employed particularly in the Old Empire (Second to Sixth Dynasties, when sea trade between Egypt and Syria was most active).

[40] See the most recent discussion by G. E. Wright, *Bull. Am. Sch. Or. Res.*, No. 86, pp. 32-35.

[41] Cf. my remarks, *Bull. Am. Sch. Or. Res.*, No. 74, pp. 15-17.

[42] For a relatively minimal estimate of the historical role of Joshua see Alt, "Josua," in *Beih. Zeits. Alttest. Wiss.*, No. 66, pp. 13-29, followed by Noth in various papers. For a relatively maximal view see my observations, *op. cit.*, pp. 12 ff., and G. E. Wright, *Jour. Near East. Stud.*, 1946, pp. 105-114.

[43] See *Jour. Bib. Lit.*, 1944, pp. 207-233.

[44] Cf. *From the Stone Age to Christianity*, p. 211, with references.

[45] Cf. *Archaeology and the Religion of Israel*, p. 102; *Bull. Am. Sch. Or. Res.*, No. 89, pp. 16 f.

[46] For some details with regard to Canaanite religion and mythology see

Archaeology and the Religion of Israel, pp. 68-94; *From the Stone Age to Christianity,* pp. 175-179.

[47] See especially Noth, *Das System der Zwoelf Staemme Israels* (1930); cf. *Archaeology and the Religion of Israel,* pp. 102 ff.

[48] On the geographical and historical role of the Jordan see Nelson Glueck, *The River Jordan* (1946).

[49] Cf. the statement of the official record in the Papyrus Harris (Breasted, *Ancient Records,* IV, p. 201, § 403). They were probably employed as slave troops (cf. H. H. Nelson, *Early Historical Records of Ramses III,* p. 4, n. 24).

[50] See my discussion in *Tell Beit Mirsim,* I, pp. 53 ff., *Tell Beit Mirsim,* III, pp. 1 ff., 36 ff.; Elihu Grant and G. E. Wright, *Ain Shems Excavations,* V, pp. 126 ff.

[51] See *Tell Beit Mirsim,* III, pp. 36 f.

[52] In 1937 (*Bull. Am. Sch. Or. Res.,* No. 68), following study of the Megiddo excavations on the spot, I concluded that the Song of Deborah should be dated in the period when the town was in ruins, between Megiddo VII and VI, since Jud. 5:19 locates the battle "at Taanach, by the Waters of Megiddo," thus implying that Megiddo itself was not occupied at the time. In 1940 I withdrew from my position, accepting Engberg's date between VI and V, in the early eleventh century (*ibid.,* No. 78, pp. 4-9). Since then, J. Simons (*Oudtestamentische Studien,* I [1942], pp. 38-54) has also argued that the break between VI and V was more significant than that between VII and VI. In the early months of 1946 I was enabled by the courtesy of Mr. Delougaz and Mrs. Hauser to study the proofs of *Megiddo II,* as well as the pottery from the Megiddo excavations. As a result I must emphatically withdraw my acceptance of Engberg's view and return to my original position. The break between VII and VI was much more complete and more protracted than that between VI and V, while the change in character of masonry and pottery also is much greater.

[53] Cf. *From the Stone Age to Christianity,* pp. 215 ff.

[54] Cf. *loc. cit.*

[55] See above, n. 33.

[56] See B. Maisler, *Bull. Am. Sch. Or. Res.,* No. 102, p. 10.

[57] *Annual Am. Sch. Or. Res.,* IV (1924); *Bull. Am. Sch. Or. Res.,* No. 52, pp. 6-12.

[58] See provisionally *Archaeology and the Religion of Israel,* pp. 125-129.

[59] Cf. *Tell Beit Mirsim,* III, pp. 12 ff., 37.

[60] For this name see *Archaeology and the Religion of Israel,* p. 207, n. 62.

[61] See Albrecht Alt, *Zeits. Deutsch. Morg. Ges.,* 1925, pp. 13 ff.; Alt, *Die Staatenbildung der Israeliten in Palaestina,* pp. 31 ff., 53 ff.

[62] *Archaeology and the Religion of Israel,* pp. 125 ff.; John Bright, *Union Seminary Review,* LIII, 20 ff.

[63] See Samuel Klein, *Are Hakohanim Vehalviyim, Mekhqarim III, IV* (Jerusalem-Tel-Aviv, 1934); Albright, *Louis Ginzberg Jubilee Volume, English Section,* pp. 49 ff.

[64] Cf. *ibid.,* p. 59, n. 24.

[65] See *ibid.,* p. 54, with references. The fullest recent study is Max Loehr's

Das Asylwesen im Alten Testament (1930). There can, of course, be no reasonable doubt that the individual cities of refuge were employed as asylums long before the time of David; I am here speaking of the institution of six cities, not of the origin of the practice, which is doubtless very ancient.

[66] See *Archaeology and the Religion of Israel*, pp. 130 f. In Syria proper David's empire extended only to the border of Hamath in the region of Hums, but since he controlled Zobah there was no power to block him politically until he reached the Euphrates Valley. The Arameans were still partly nomadic at that time.

[67] See *Archaeology and the Religion of Israel*, pp. 108, 120, with references.

[68] For the chronology of this period see now my treatment in *Bull. Am. Sch. Or. Res.*, No. 100, pp. 16-23. My dates are approximate, but they seem more satisfactory than any other system, precisely in part because of their flexibility, which stands in sharp contrast to the involved and rigid system of Max Vogelstein (*Biblical Chronology*, Part I, 1944).

[69] For Assyrian dates see Arno Poebel, *Jour. Near East. Stud.*, 1943, p. 88.

[70] On the character of the Sidonian state see my discussion, *Studies in the History of Culture* (Leland Volume), 1942, pp. 33 f.

[71] See *Bull. Am. Sch. Or. Res.*, No. 83, pp. 14-22, and No. 95, p. 38.

[72] See Nelson Glueck, *The Other Side of the Jordan*, pp. 89-113, and for the copper mines and smelting in general see *ibid.*, pp. 50-88, and *Bull. Am. Sch. Or. Res.*, No. 90, pp. 13 f.

[73] See *Archaeology and the Religion of Israel*, pp. 142 ff.; G. E. Wright, *Biblical Archaeologist*, IV, pp. 17 ff., VII, pp. 73 ff.

[74] See I. Mendelsohn, *Bull. Am. Sch. Or. Res.*, No. 85, pp. 14 ff.

[75] This estimate is based on the following considerations. Archaeological and documentary evidences coincide in fixing the population of Judah (as a state, not merely a tribe) in 701 B.C.E. at about 250,000. The Assyrian records (whose errors probably cancel out pretty well) count a little over 200,000 people in forty-six captured fortified towns of Judah (a number of towns which agrees very well both with archaeological surveys and with the total of sixty towns of significance listed in Joshua 15, which applies to some phase of the Divided Monarchy, either the ninth century, as I believe, or the seventh, with Alt). Tell Beit Mirsim, which represents a fair cross section of the towns of Judah, had a maximum population in the eighth century of about 3,000 (*Tell Beit Mirsim*, III, p. 39). Allowing for a seminomadic population of about 50,000 in the Negeb and the hill country, as well as for about the same number in Jerusalem and its surrounding villages, we should have a total of about 250,000. This agrees very well with the Assyrian total of 200,000, which did not include the people of Jerusalem or the seminomads of the Negeb, or, for that matter, the dead and the fugitives who fled into the hills. Now archaeological evidence makes it certain that there was a very considerable expansion of the population of Judah during and after the tenth century B.C.E., when the *pax Davidica* made it possible to found many new towns and villages. Moreover, the tremendous commercial and industrial expansion under Solomon also brought about an increase of population. Furthermore, as J. L. Kelso points out to me, the introduction of the iron plow tip, replacing

tips of holm oak and copper, made it possible to increase the production of the soil very materially at that time (much as happened in Western Europe after the Dark Ages, when the introduction of the large plowshare and colter revolutionized agriculture). Now, as I have shown in detail elsewhere (*Jour. Pal. Or. Soc.*, 1925, pp. 20-25), the two census reports of Numbers probably reflect divergent recensions of the Davidic census, which in that case totaled about 600,000 Israelites, distributed among the twelve tribes. Some 125,000 of these are credited to the territory included by Joshua 15 in Judah (that is, the state, not the tribe in the narrow sense). We should, accordingly, be quite warranted in deducing that the population of the southern tribes had roughly doubled between about 975 and 701 B.C.E., especially since this deduction agrees strikingly with archaeological indications. An increase of a fourth to a third seems conservative for the generation following the Davidic census, so we may estimate that the entire native Israelite population in the middle of Solomon's reign was at least three-quarters of a million.

[76] On this subject see Alt, *Staatenbildung* (cf. above, n. 60), p. 54, n. 30, with the references, and my discussion, *Archaeology of Palestine and the Bible*, pp. 140 ff.

[77] For Babylonian parallels to Solomon's provisioning system see R. P. Dougherty, *Annual Am. Sch. Or. Res.*, V, 23 ff.

[[77a] J, E, JE, D, P are arbitrary symbols used by Bible scholars in referring to what they believe are different documents which have been incorporated into the Pentateuch.]

[78] See my treatment of this text, *Bull. Am. Sch. Or. Res.*, No. 92, pp. 16-26.

[79] For the chronology see above, n. 68.

[80] See *Bull. Am. Sch. Or. Res.*, No. 49, pp. 26 ff.

[81] See Beyer, *Zeits. Deutsch. Pal. Ver.*, 1931, pp. 113-134.

[82] Cf. *Tell Beit Mirsim*, III, p. 38, n. 14, and the literature there cited.

[83] Cf. *Jour. Pal. Or. Soc.*, 1925, pp. 37-44.

[84] On the same principle that David chose Jerusalem, which lay outside the native Israelite tribal system, as his capital, in order to free himself from tribal jealousy and intrigue as much as possible; see above, n. 61.

[85] See *From the Stone Age to Christianity*, pp. 228 ff.

[86] On the cherubim see the literature cited in *Archaeology and the Religion of Israel*, p. 216, n. 65.

[87] Cf. *Archaeology and the Religion of Israel*, pp. 157 ff. On the relationship between the queen mother, Maachah, and Kings Abijah and Asa see S. Yeivin, *Bull. Jew. Pal. Explor. Soc.*, 1943, pp. 116 ff.

[88] In the light of the steadily increasing evidence for the historicity of most of the documentary material not found in Kings which is preserved by the Chronicler, it is hypercritical to reject the clear statements of II Chron. 19:8-11. See my paper, "The Judicial Reform of Jehoshaphat," *Alexander Marx Jubilee Volume*, New York, 1950, pp. 61-82.

[89] See J. W. Crowfoot, Kathleen Kenyon and E. L. Sukenik, *The Buildings at Samaria* (1942), pp. 5 ff.

[90] For recent efforts to reconstruct the historical sequence of events and their causes cf. especially Julian Morgenstern, *Amos Studies*, I, pp. 258-348, and Alfred Jepsen, *Archiv f. Orientf.*, XIV, 153-172 (1942).

[91] See Levi della Vida and the writer, *Bull. Am. Sch. Or. Res.*, No. 90, pp. 30 ff. On the cult of Baal-Melcarth see the illuminating observations of R. de Vaux, *Bulletin du Musée de Beyrouth*, V, 7-20.

[92] Cf. most recently *Bull. Am. Sch. Or. Res.*, No. 94, p. 30 and n. 4. There are many additional passages in Keret II and Danel (Aqhat) where the appellation *Qudshu* (*Qodesh*), "Holiness," appears as name of Asherah.

[93] A different view is taken by Poebel, *Jour. Near East. Stud.*, 1943, pp. 80-84, but I cannot agree with his argument.

[94] *Amos Studies*, pp. 161 ff.

[95] See *Bull. Am. Sch. Or. Res.*, No. 44, pp. 8-10, with the references there.

[96] See Nelson Glueck, *Bull. Am. Sch. Or. Res.*, No. 72, pp. 7 ff.; No. 79, pp. 13 ff., with my remarks in n. 9.

[97] It cannot be emphasized too strongly that the expression "Jehu son of Omri" in Assyrian means simply "Jehu of Beth-Omri," as first pointed out by Ungnad, and has nothing to do with the man Omri as such: cf. *Bull. Am. Sch. Or. Res.*, No. 4 (1921), p. 8, where I first pointed out this obvious fact; *Jour. Pal. Or. Soc.*, 1925, p. 37; and for the parallel data from Aramaic and Assyrian cf. *Jour. Pal. Or. Soc.*, I, 55, n. 1.

[98] See *Tell Beit Mirsim*, III, pp. 55-62.

[99] Cf. I. Mendelsohn, *Bull. Am. Sch. Or. Res.*, No. 80, pp. 17-21.

[100] Cf. *Bull. Am. Sch. Or. Res.*, No. 100, p. 21. This date, which seems to me the only one that can be squared with our direct biblical documentation, is also held by Mowinckel and others.

[101] The chronology of the Ethiopian Dynasty is obscure until the accession of Taharqo (Tirhakah) in 689 (a date established most recently by Borchardt). The fifteenth (so in a British Museum statuette, recorded most recently by Hall, *Cambridge Ancient History*, III, 289, n. 2) year of Shabako and the third of Shebtiko are monumentally recorded, yielding minimal (but probably nearly correct) dates for their accessions in 705 and 691 B.C.E. The conquest of Lower Egypt by the Ethiopian Piankhi probably took place immediately before the accession of Shabako.

[102] The problem of Sennacherib's campaigns against Hezekiah remains very obscure; for convenient orientation see Leo Honor, *Sennacherib's Invasion of Palestine* (1926). In spite of the fact that recent German scholarship supports the one-campaign hypothesis (cf. Rudolph and Alt, *Palaestinajahrbuch*, 1929, pp. 59 ff.), I adhere to Winckler's two-campaign alternative for the reasons cited *Jew. Quar. Rev.*, XXIV, pp. 370 f. (and other reasons which cannot be listed here).

[103] Cf. my preliminary remarks, *Jour. Bib. Lit.*, 1942, p. 119.

[104] For the date see Poebel, *Jour. Near East. Stud.*, 1943, pp. 88 ff. The death of Asshurbanapal took place between 633 and 628 B.C.E.

[105] In my opinion Alt has gone too far in referring the lists of towns in Galilee (Josh. 19) to the reign of Josiah; a number of them were destroyed in the eighth century and not reoccupied.

[106] Cf. *Jour. Bib. Lit.*, 1939, pp. 184 f.

[107] On the historical situation (with references to recent literature) see *Jour. Bib. Lit.*, 1932, pp. 84 ff.

[108] See now the epochal treatment of the work of the Deuteronomist by Martin Noth, *Ueberlieferungsgeschichtliche Studien* (1943), pp. 3-110. The superfluous assumption that there was a whole Deuteronomic school which collaborated over a long period may now be discarded. However, I cannot accept Noth's date for the composition of this work about the middle of the sixth century (p. 91), since it is highly improbable that so much older historical material had survived the catastrophe of the Exile (note how little was available a century and a half later to the Chronicler!).

[109] Cf. *From the Stone Age to Christianity*, pp. 241 ff.

[110] See *Bull. Am. Sch. Or. Res.*, No. 82, p. 22.

[111] *Jour. Bib. Lit.*, 1932, pp. 78 f.; *Tell Beit Mirsim*, III, 65 f.; *Pal. Explor. Fund Quar. State.* (*Pal. Explor. Quar.*), 1937, pp. 175 ff., 235 ff.; *ibid.*, 1938, pp. 252 ff.

[112] See above, n. 75.

[113] For this date see most recently *Bull. Am. Sch. Or. Res.*, No. 100, p. 22, with references.

[114] See Hooke, *Pal. Explor. Fund Quar. State.*, 1935, pp. 195 f.

[115] Cf. *Biblical Archaeologist*, V, 49 ff.

[116] See *Jour. Bib. Lit.*, 1932, pp. 100 f.

[117] See Alt in *Festschrift Otto Procksch* (1934), pp. 5-28.

[118] See above, n. 115, for references.

[119] For this interpretation, following the Greek text, of the unintelligible "Sheshbazzar" see my observations, *Jour. Bib. Lit.*, 1921, pp. 108 ff., and for the initial *shin*, due to dissimilation (for which there are two other illustrations in this very name), see most recently *Bull. Am. Sch. Or. Res.*, No. 82, p. 17.

[120] Cf. particularly R. de Vaux, *Revue Biblique*, 1937, pp. 29-57, following in the wake of Eduard Meyer and H. H. Schaeder.

[121] See Ebeling, *Aus dem Leben der juedischen Exulanten* (1914), and Eissfeldt, *Zeits. Alttest. Wiss.*, 1935, pp. 60 f., for the material from the Murashu archives. There is a little scattered material from earlier periods, but some of it is doubtful.

[122] This rough estimate is based on the following facts: Archaeological explorations have demonstrated that there was a virtually complete break in the urban life of Judah after the Chaldean invasions and deportations which ended in 582 B.C.E. (*e.g.*, at Debir, Lachish, Beth-shemesh, Beth-zur, as well as at many other sites which have been explored more superficially). Even Beth-el, which was outside of the pre-exilic state (except under Josiah) but inside the later Persian province, was destroyed before 522 B.C.E., though it was a flourishing town during the middle of the sixth century (see provisionally *Bull. Am. Sch. Or. Res.*, No. 56, p. 14; subsequent work on the pottery has shown that we are dealing with a phase which followed the Exile but preceded the developed Persian types of the fifth century). It has long been certain from careful study of the names, etc., that the list in Ezra 2 and Neh. 7 belongs to a relatively late date in the fifth century, in strict accord with Neh. 7:5 ff., which attributes the publication of the document to Nehemiah, *c.* 440 B.C.E. It is, accordingly, clear that this document represents the revised form of the census of Judah, begun at the Restoration; it includes both the

returned exiles (and their descendants) and the Jews already established in the district. Since the entire population, including slaves, was reckoned at just under 50,000 in *c.* 440, it was probably not over two-fifths this number three generations earlier, before natural increase and continuing influx of immigrants from the *golah* had brought it up to the higher level.

[123] On the political situation at this time see especially Olmstead, *Am. Jour. Sem. Lang.*, 1938, pp. 409 ff. (note, however, that there is an error of a year in reckoning the date of the dedication of the Temple, which was March, 515, not March, 514).

[124] The native name of Sardis was *Sfarda*, written in the Lydian-Aramaic bilingual of Sardis exactly as in Obad. 20. The Aramaic inscription in question dates probably from the year 455 (Torrey, *Am. Jour. Sem. Lang.*, XXXIV, 191 ff.) and may reflect a Jewish-Aramaic community settled there (Kahle and Sommer, *Kleinasiatische Forschungen*, I, 29 f.). There can be little doubt, in my opinion, that the prophecy of Obadiah reflects the end of the sixth or the beginning of the fifth century B.C.E.

[125] Cf. R. Kittel, *Geschichte des Volkes Israel*, III, pt. 2, pp. 614 f.

[126] Thanks to the work of Howorth, Torrey and especially of Sigmund Mowinckel, *Stattholderen Nehemia* (Kristiania, 1916), it has become certain that the biblical text followed by Josephus in his account of the Restoration was the original Alexandrian translation of the second century B.C.E., the first part of which is preserved in First Esdras (Third Esdras in the Latin Bible). The extant Greek text of Nehemiah goes back only to Theodotion in the second century C.E. Torrey and others have already seen that First Esdras preserves many details which have been lost or corrupted in the Hebrew recension of Ezra (which is better in other ways). Mowinckel is, therefore, quite justified (pp. 58 ff.) in preferring Josephus's chronological data to those of the Hebrew Bible; see below, n. 127.

[127] According to the Hebrew the wall was begun fifty-two days before the twenty-fifth of Elul, *i.e.,* about the third of Ab, the fifth month. According to Josephus it was finished after two years and four months, in the ninth month, which would mean that it was begun in the fifth month.

[128] See above, n. 117.

[129] On the history of the house of Tobiah, illuminated in recent decades by the systematic study of the remains at ʿAraq el-Emir and by the Zeno Papyri, see especially the work of Vincent, Gressmann and Koenig referred to in my *Archaeology of Palestine and the Bible*, pp. 221 f., nn. 108-111.

[130] On the religion of the Jewish colony at Elephantine see most recently Albert Vincent, *La religion des Judéo-Araméens d'Éléphantine* (1937), and my observations in *Archaeology and the Religion of Israel*, pp. 168-174, as well as *Bull. Am. Sch. Or. Res.*, No. 90, p. 40 (where I take account of the new data provided by the article of U. Cassuto in *Kedem*, I, 47-52). The close cultic sympathy existing between the Jews of Elephantine and the people of Samaria is illustrated not only by the way in which the former appeal to the latter after the destruction of their temple, but also by numerous more general considerations, on which cf. also Van Hoonacker, *Une communauté judéo-araméenne à Éléphantine* (1915), pp. 73-84.

[130a Cf. below Bickerman, Elias J., "The Historical Foundations of Post-biblical Judaism," p. 83.]

131 The "governor of Moab" after whom the family in question had received its name must have flourished under the Babylonian or the Persian Empire, since the word *pehah* was borrowed by the Arameans in Late Assyrian times, whereas Moab was still ruled by its own tributary kings down at least to *c.* 645 B.C.E.

132 The official publication of this excavation will be issued soon.

133 Assuming that "seventh year" (Ezra 7:7) is haplography of "thirty-seventh year" (note that the latter would have three initial occurrences of *shin* following one another, as in Neh. 5:14). My earlier view that Ezra's mission took place in the seventh year of Artaxerxes II, in which I followed Van Hoonacker (*Jour. Bib. Lit.*, 1921, pp. 104-124), has since been replaced by a position approximating that of Bertholet (*The Archaeology of Palestine and the Bible* [1932], pp. 169 ff., 218 f., n. 98), though I have not always adhered consistently to this position. There is no adequate reason to follow Torrey and delete the reference to Nehemiah as *tirshatha* in Neh. 8:9, which deals with Ezra's reform, or to separate Neh. 10:1 from it. It follows that Nehemiah was then in Jerusalem, whether before the expiration of his twelve-year period or not. Mowinckel thought (on the basis of the chronology preserved by Josephus; see above, n. 125) that Nehemiah's twelve years as governor may have expired in the thirty-seventh year, assuming that he took office in the twenty-fifth year, but this alternative is uncertain. In any event, it seems highly probable that Ezra arrived in Jerusalem toward the end of Nehemiah's governorship. With this date would, incidentally, harmonize very well the fact that he was accompanied by the Davidide Hattush, son of Shechaniah, who was probably born between 490 and 480 B.C.E. and would thus be between fifty and sixty at this time. With it would also agree very well the reference (Ezra 10:6) to the "chamber of Johanan son of Eliashib," who was High Priest when the first edition of the work of the Chronicler was finished (Neh. 12:23), since Eliashib was still High Priest at the return of Nehemiah to the court in 432 (Neh. 13:4 ff.), whereas Johanan had apparently been High Priest for some time in 411 B.C.E., to judge from the Elephantine correspondence.

134 See the preceding note. The Ezra Memoirs proper are couched in the first person, whereas the references to Ezra in connection with Nehemiah are in the third person.

135 Cf. Eduard Meyer, *Die Entstehung des Judentums*, p. 65; Schaeder, *Esra der Schreiber*, p. 55.

136 See above, n. 134.

137 Cf. Albert Vincent, *La Religion des Judéo-Araméens d'Éléphantine,* pp. 235 ff.

138 See Torrey, *Composition and Historical Value of Ezra-Nehemiah*, pp. 16-28, etc., *Ezra Studies*, pp. 238-248; Albright, *Jour. Bib. Lit.*, 1921, pp. 119 f.; Arvid Kapelrud, *The Question of Authorship in the Ezra Narrative* (Oslo, 1944), pp. 95 ff. The last-mentioned scholar tries to avoid the conclusion which Torrey reached by severe logic, that the Ezra Memoirs are apocryphal (whereas I believe that Ezra was the Chronicler), by speaking vaguely

of "Chronicler circles." Just what "circles" of scholars we can expect in a largely agricultural community of considerably less than a hundred thousand souls is not clear. Martin Noth emphasizes this individuality of the Chronicler very strongly in his *Ueberlieferungsgeschichtliche Studien* (1943), pp. 155 ff.

[139] Cf. already *Jour. Bib. Lit.*, 1921, p. 111. Pushing back the birth of Pedaiah to before 592 B.C.E., as required by the new cuneiform evidence, and allowing (in view of the fact that not all members of the genealogical chain in I Chron. 3:17 ff. were first-born sons) between twenty-five and thirty (*i.e.*, twenty-seven and a half) years to a generation (plus a decade for the younger sons of Elioenai), we come to about 420 for the birth of the youngest son of Elioenai in our list.

[140] Cf. *The Archaeology of Palestine and the Bible*, pp. 173 ff.; *Bull. Am. Sch. Or. Res.*, No. 53, pp. 20 ff.; *Jour. Bib. Lit.*, 1942, pp. 125 f.; J. Kutsher, *Kedem*, II, 74. In the last-mentioned paper, Kutsher publishes the first of the leather rolls of Arsames, from about 410 B.C.E., and mentions different occurrences of the Persian word *pitgama* or *patgama*, which Torrey and Cowley, followed by many others, regarded as decisive evidence for the Greek date of the Chronicler, since they erroneously identified it with different Greek words!

[141] On these coins see M. Narkiss, *Matbeat Hayehudim* (Jerusalem, 1936), Book I, pp. 17-23.

[142] Cf. *From the Stone Age to Christianity*, p. 259. The material is too scattered to warrant a bibliography, but it is now very abundant.

BIBLIOGRAPHY OF BOOKS AND PAPERS CITED IN THE NOTES

ALBRIGHT, WILLIAM FOXWELL, *The Archaeology of Palestine and the Bible.* New York and Chicago, 1932.

———, *From the Stone Age to Christianity.* Baltimore, 1940.

———, *Archaeology and the Religion of Israel.* Baltimore, 1942.

———, *The Excavation of Tell Beit Mirsim in Palestine.* Annual of the American Schools of Oriental Research, Vol. XII. New Haven, 1932.

———, "Excavations and Results at Tell El-Ful (Gibeah of Saul)" in *Annual, American Schools of Oriental Research.* Vol. IV, New Haven, 1924.

———, "The Excavations of Tell Beit Mirsim, Vol. II The Bronze Age," in *ibid,* Vol. XVII, 1936-1937.

ALT, ALBRECHT, *Die Urspruenge des israelitischen Rechts.* Leipzig, 1934.

———, *Die Staatenbildung der Israeliten in Palaestina.* Leipzig, 1930.

BONNER, R. J., and SMITH, G., *The Administration of Justice from Homer to Aristotle.* Chicago, 1930-1938. 2 vols.

Chicago University, Oriental Institute, *Medinet Habu,* Vol. I, "Early Historical Records of Rameses III." Chicago, 1921-1931.

CROWFOOT, J. W., KENYON, K. M., and SUKENIK, E. L., *The Buildings at Samaria.* London, 1942.

EBELING, ERICH, *Aus dem Leben der juedischen Exulanten in Babylonien.* Berlin, 1914.

EHELOLF, HANS, and SOMMER, FERDINAND (eds.), *Kleinasiatische Forschungen.* Weimar, 1930. Vol. I.

GARDINER, ALAN H. (ed.), *Hieratic Papyri in the British Museum, Third Series.* London, 1935. Vol. I.

GINSBERG, HAROLD L., *The Legend of King Keret.* Supplementary Studies of the Bulletin American Schools of Oriental Research, Nos. 2-3. New Haven, 1946.

GLUECK, NELSON, *The Other Side of the Jordan.* New Haven, 1940.

———, *The River Jordan.* Philadelphia, 1946.

GRANT, ELIHU, and WRIGHT, G. E., *Ain Shems Excavations.* Haverford, 1931-1939. 5 vols.

HONOR, LEO L., *Sennacherib's Invasion of Palestine.* New York, 1926.

KAPELRUD, ARVID, *The Question of Authorship in the Ezra Narrative.* Oslo, 1944.

KITTEL, RUDOLF, *Geschichte des Volkes Israel.* Stuttgart, 1927-1929. 3 vols.

KLEIN, SAMUEL, *Are Hakohanim Vehalviyim in Mekhqarim,* III, IV. Jerusalem and Tel-Aviv, 1944.

LOEHR, MAX, *Das Asylwesen im Alten Testament.* Halle, 1930.

MEYER, EDUARD, *Die Entstehung des Judentums.* Halle, 1897.

MONTET, PIERRE, *Le drame d'Avaris.* Paris, 1941.

MORGENSTERN, JULIAN, *Amos Studies.* Cincinnati, 1941. Vol. I.

MOWINCKEL, SIGMUND, *Statholderen Nehemia.* Kristiania, 1916.

NOTH, MARTIN, *Das System der Zwoelf Staemme Israels.* Stuttgart, 1930.

———, *Ueberlieferungsgeschichtliche Studien.* Halle, 1943.

PETRIE, SIR WILLIAM M. F., *Kahun, Gurob and Hawara.* London, 1890.

ROWE, ALAN, *The Topography and History of Beth-shan.* Philadelphia, 1930.

SCHAEDER, HANS HEINRICH, *Esra der Schreiber.* Tuebingen, 1930.

TORREY, CHARLES C., *The Composition and Historical Value of Ezra-Nehemiah.* Giessen, 1896.

———, *Ezra Studies.* Chicago, 1910.

VINCENT, ALBERT, *La religion des Judéo-Araméens d'Éléphantine.* Paris, 1937.

ALBRIGHT, W. F., "King Joiachin in Exile," in *The Biblical Archaeologist* V, No. 4, New Haven, 1942.

———, "The Discovery of an Aramaic Inscription relating to King Uzziah," in *Bulletin of the American Schools of Oriental Research,* No. 44, Baltimore.

———, "Archaeological and Topographical Explorations in Palestine and Syria," in *ibid.,* No. 49.

———, "A New Campaign of Excavation at Gibeah of Saul," in *ibid.,* No. 52.

———, "Light on the Jewish State in Persian Times," in *ibid.,* No. 53.

———, "The Kyle Memorial Excavation at Beth-el," in *ibid.,* No. 56.

———, "Further Light on the History of Israel from Lachish and Megiddo," in *ibid.,* No. 68.

———, "The Israelite Conquest of Canaan in the Light of Archaeology," in *ibid.,* No. 74.

———, "New Light on the History of Western Asia in the Second Millennium, B.C.," in *ibid.*, Nos. 77 and 78.
———, "New Egyptian Data on Palestine in the Patriarchal Age," in *ibid.*, No. 81.
———, "The Lachish Letters after Five Years," in *ibid.*, No. 82.
———, "The Land of Damascus between 1850 and 1750 B.C.," in *ibid.*, No. 83.
———, "New Light on the Early History of Phoenician Colonization," in *ibid.*, No. 83.
———, "The Egypto-Canaanite Deity Haurôn," in *ibid.*, No. 84.
———, "A Third Revision of the Chronology of Western Asia," in *ibid.*, No. 88.
———, "Two Little Understood Amarna Letters from the Middle Jordan Valley," in *ibid.*, No. 89.
———, "The Gezer Calendar," in *ibid.*, No. 92.
———, "The 'Natural Force' of Moses in the Light of Ugaritic," in *ibid.*, No. 94
———, "Egypt and Mesopotamia, *c.* 1730 B.C.," in *ibid.*, No. 99.
———, "The Chronology of the Divided Monarchy of Israel," in *ibid.*, No. 100.
———, "Israel in the Framework of the Ancient Near East," in *The Jewish People—Past and Present*. Jewish Encyclopedia Handbooks. New York, 1946.
———, "Historical and Mythical Elements in the Story of Joseph," in *Journal of Biblical Literature*, XXXVII.
———, "The Date and Personality of the Chronicler," in *ibid.*, XL.
———,"The Seal of Eliakim and the Latest Pre-exilic History of Judah with some Observations on Ezekiel," in *ibid.*, LI.
———, "The Names of Shaddai and Abram," in *ibid.*, LIV.
———, "Review of 'Die Urspruenge des israelitischen Rechts' by Albrecht Alt," in *ibid.*, LV.
———, "Review of 'Introduction to the Old Testament,' by Robert Pfeiffer," in *ibid.*, LXI.
———, "The Oracles of Balaam," in *ibid.*, LXIII, Pt. III.
———, "Review of 'Hebrew Union College Annual, 1941-1944,'" in *ibid.*, LXIV.
———, "A Revision of Early Hebrew Chronology," in *ibid.*, I.
———, "The Administrative Divisions of Israel and Judah," in *Journal of the Palestine Oriental Society*, V, Jerusalem.
———, "The List of Levitic Cities," in *Louis Ginzberg Jubilee Volume* (English Section). New York, 1945.
———, "The Role of the Canaanites in the History of Civilization," in *Studies in the History of Culture*. Menasha, Wisc. 1942.
ALT, ALBRECHT, "Die Rolle Samarias bei der Entstehung des Judentums," in *Festschrift Otto Procksch*. Leipzig, 1934.
———, "Erwaegungen ueber die Landnahme der Israeliten in Palaestina," in *Palaestinajahrbuch*, XXXV, Berlin, 1939.

———, "Nachwort ueber die territorialgeschichtliche Bedeutung von Sanheribs Eingriff in Palaestina," in *ibid.*, 1929.
———, "Jerusalems Aufsteig," in *Zeits. der Deutsch. Morgenlaendischen Gesellschaft,* LXXIX. Leipzig, 1925.
BERGMAN, ABRAHAM, "The Israelite Tribe of Half-Manasseh," in *Jour. Palestine Oriental Society,* XVI.
BEYER, PFARRER G., "Beitraege zur Territorialgeschichte von Suedwestpalaestina im Altertum," in *Zeitschrift des Deutschen Palaestina-Vereins.* Leipzig, 1931.
BRIGHT, JOHN, "The Age of King David: A Study in the Institutional History of Israel," in *Union Seminary Review,* LIII, No. 2.
DE VAUX, R., "Les Prophètes de Baal sur le Mont Carmel," in *Bulletin du Musée de Beyrouth,* V (no date, 1943 or later). Beyrouth.
———, "Les Décrets de Cyrus et de Darius sur la reconstruction du temple," in *Revue Biblique,* XLVI. Paris, 1937.
DOSSIN, GEORGES, "Signaux Lumineux au Pays de Mari," in *Revue d'Assyriologie,* XXXV. Paris, 1938.
DOUGHERTY, R. P., "Cuneiform Parallels to Solomon's Provisioning System," in *Annual, Amer. Sch. Or. Res.*, V.
EISSFELDT, OTTO, "Neue Zeugnisse fuer die Aussprache des Tetragramms als Jahwe," in *Zeits. fuer die Alttestamentliche Wissenschaft,* LIII, Berlin, 1935.
ENGBERG, R. M., "Historical Analysis of Archaeological Evidence: Megiddo and The Song of Deborah," in *Bull. Am. Sch. Or. Res.,* No. 78.
ERMAN, ADOLF, "Der Leidener Amonshymnus," in *Sitz. Preuss. Akad. Wiss.* Berlin, 1923.
GLUECK, NELSON, "Three Israelite Towns in the Jordan Valley: Zarethan, Succoth, Zaphon," in *Bull. Am. Sch. Or. Res.,* No. 90.
———, "The Topography and History of Ezion-Geber and Elath," in *ibid.*, No. 72.
GORDON, CYRUS H., "Biblical Customs and the Nuzu Tablets," in *Biblical Archaeologist,* III.
HOOKE, S. H., "A Scarab and Sealing from Tell Duweir," in *Palestine Exploration Fund Quarterly.* London, 1935.
JEPSEN, ALFRED, "Israel und Damaskus," in *Archiv fuer Orientforschung,* XIV. Berlin, 1942.
KRAMER, SAMUEL N., "Ishtar in the Nether World According to a New Sumerian Text," in *Bull. Am. Sch. Or. Res.,* No. 79.
KUTSHER, J., "An Aramaic Leather Scroll of the Fifth Century B.C.," in *Kedem, Studies in Jewish Archaeology* (Hebrew). Jerusalem, 1942.
LEVI DELLA VIDA, G., "El 'Elyon in Genesis 14:18-20," in *Jour. of Bibl. Lit.*, LXIII, Pt. I.
———, and ALBRIGHT, W. F., "Some Notes on the Stele of Ben-hadad," in *Bull. Am. Sch. Or. Res.,* No. 90.
LEWY, JULIUS, "Les Textes paléo-assyriens et l'Ancien Testament," in *Revue de l'Histoire des Religions,* CIX. Paris, 1934.

MAISLER, B., "Canaan and the Canaanites," in *Bull. Am. Sch. Or. Res.,* No. 102.

MEEK, T. J., "Moses and the Levites," in *American Journal of Semitic Languages and Literature*, LVI. Chicago, 1939.

MENDELSOHN, I., "Guilds in Ancient Palestine," in *Bull. Am. Sch. Or. Res.*, No. 80.

———, "State Slavery in Ancient Palestine," in *ibid.*, No. 85.

MOWINCKEL, S., and ALBRIGHT, W. F., "The Babylonian Matter in the Predeuteronomic Primeval History," in *Jour. Bibl. Lit.*, LVIII, 1939.

OLMSTEAD, A. T., "Darius and his Behistun Inscription," in *Amer. Jour. Sem. Lang.*, LV, 1938.

POEBEL, A., "The Assyrian King List from Khorsabad (concluded)," in *Journal of Near Eastern Studies*, II. Chicago, 1943.

ROWLEY, H. H., "Habiru and Hebrews," in *Pal. Explor. Quar.,* Jan.-April, 1942.

RUDOLPH, W., "Sanherib in Palaestina," in *Palaestinajahrbuch*. Berlin, 1929.

SIMONS, JAN J., "Caesurae in the History of Megiddo," in *Oudtestamentische Studien,* P.A.H. de Boer (ed.). Leyden, 1942.

TORREY, CHARLES C., "The Bilingual Inscription from Sardis," in *Amer. Jour. Sem. Lang.*, XXXIV.

WILSON, JOHN A., "The Egyptian Middle Kingdom at Megiddo," in *ibid.,* LVIII.

WRIGHT, G. E., "Solomon's Temple Resurrected," in *Biblical Archaelogist,* IV.

———, "The Significance of the Temple in the Ancient Near East," in *ibid.*, VII

———, "Two Misunderstood Items in the Exodus-Conquest Cycle," in *Bull. Am. Sch. Or. Res.*, No. 86.

CHAPTER 2

THE HISTORICAL FOUNDATIONS OF POSTBIBLICAL JUDAISM

By Elias J. Bickerman

I

The sacred history of the Chosen People ends chronologically with Nehemiah's prayer: "Remember us, O God, for good." With Nehemiah's name, "glorious in his memory," concludes the praise of the worthies in the Wisdom of Ben Sira, composed in Jerusalem about 190 B.C.E. Thus, even before the Maccabean revolt, the Jews recognized that after Nehemiah and his contemporary prophets, that is, toward the end of the fifth century, in the age of Socrates, the postbiblical period of Jewish history begins. That period is marked by a unique and rewarding polarity: on the one hand, the Jerusalem center and, on the other, the plurality of centers in the Diaspora. The Dispersion saved Judaism from physical extirpation and spiritual inbreeding. Palestine united the dispersed members of the nation and gave them a sense of oneness. This counterpoise of historical forces is without analogy in antiquity. There were, of course, numberless migrations and transportations of peoples and fragments of peoples; but in due time these offshoots lost connection with the main stock. The colonists brought to cities of Syria by Assyrian kings, the men of Cutha or of Erech, were very soon detached psychologically from their respective cities. Likewise, Phoenician or Greek settlements soon separated from the metropolis. At the most, the Phoenicians had refused to follow a Persian king in his campaign against Carthage, their colony.[1] But the Jewish Dispersion continued to consider Jerusalem as the "metropolis" (Philo), turned to the Holy Land for guidance, and in turn, determined the destinies of its inhabitants. Men who established the normative Judaism in Palestine—Zerubbabel, Ezra, Nehemiah—came from the Diaspora, from Babylon and Susa.

The forces which unwittingly enabled Israel to develop into a people alike at home in the ancestral land as well as in the lands of the Dispersion were largely external. When Jerusalem was conquered (597 B.C.E.) and, later (586), destroyed by the Babylonians, the court, the warriors, the craftsmen were transferred to Mesopotamia. This device of deportation, invented perhaps by the Hittites, and applied subsequently by all their successors (Babylonians, Persians, Greeks, Romans, Turks and even Anglo-Americans—as readers of Longfellow's *Evangeline* know) was by no means an attempt at extermination. The distortion of the ancient expedient is an invention of a modern, European nation in the twentieth century. Being Semites and idolators, the Babylonians simply transported a rebellious group elsewhere in order to break its natural cohesion. In new surroundings, mixed with other ethnic elements, the former enemy learned obedience and, once subdued, furnished labor, taxes and military services. Accordingly, the exiles received land to till, abandoned sites to rebuild and to settle.[2] They remained free and mostly under leadership of native chiefs. Such a *segan* (as he is called in Aramaic documents) of Phrygians, of Carians, etc., is often mentioned in cuneiform records from Babylonia. On the other hand, since the structure of Oriental monarchies was essentially feudal, there was neither the wish nor the need to assimilate. Thus, in 331 B.C.E., there was still near Nippur (in Mesopotamia) a Carian settlement of colonists transported there from Asia Minor at least two hundred years before. Likewise, the Captivity had created numerous Jewish settlements in Mesopotamia. As a later Babylonian historian tells us (according to some lost original records), King Nebuchadnezzar assigned to the captives dwelling places "in the most convenient districts of Babylonia."[3] Later, in 539, when the Persian king Cyrus conquered Babylon, he reversed, quite naturally, the policy of his adversary and allowed gods and men in Babylonian captivity to return home.

At this moment, the restoration of the Holy City, burned fifty years previously, depended on an accidental conjunction. When the Assyrians conquered Samaria in 722 they established a military colony there. As a result, the Ten Tribes, deported to Assyria, could never again come back. Since, however, there were already military colonies of the Assyrians in Palestine (Samaria, Gezer, etc.), Nebuchadnezzar did not need to send new settlers to Jerusalem. Further, although the Babylonians were savage in battle, they took no delight in useless destruction and wholesale slaughter. The remnant of Judah was not exterminated or scientifically tortured to death. Nobody desecrated the graves in Jerusalem; nobody prevented the believers from bringing meal offerings and frankincense to the burned-down House of the Lord and from weeping on its ruins. The walls of Jerusalem being broken down by the Babylonians, the ancient capital was now an open Jewish village. So, unlike the case of Samaria, there was a political vacuum which the Restoration could fill. In the same manner, for example, the Thebans, dispersed by Alexander the Great (in 334), returned eighteen years later and rebuilt their commonwealth.[4] The exceptional feature of Jewish history is the reluctance of so many of the exiled to go back. They remained in Mesopotamia but, paradoxically, continued to care for the Holy City generation after generation, for centuries and millennia. Cupbearer before Artaxerxes I, born and reared in the fifth generation in the Diaspora, Nehemiah weeps when he hears of the affliction of the children of Israel in Jerusalem. He risks disgrace to obtain royal favor for the Holy City. How are we to explain this unity between the Dispersion and Jerusalem?

Every transferred group continued, as a matter of course, to worship the ancestral gods on foreign soil. The men of Cutha, transplanted to Samaria, worshiped Nergal, and the men of Sepharvaim in Samaria continued to sacrifice their children to Adrammelech and Anamelech (II Kings 17:30).[5] "The Jewish force" in Elephantine, mercenaries established there by the Pharaohs about 600 B.C.E.,[6] continued to worship the national God on the southern frontier of Egypt. On the other hand, as a matter of course, the colonists feared and worshiped gods of the land in which they dwelt. A priest of Beth-el was sent back from the Captivity to teach the Assyrian colonists in the land of Samaria how to serve the God of Israel. But the latter was a "jealous God." Some Jews at Elephantine, the seat of the Egyptian god Khnum, seem to have accepted this sheep-headed divinity, or other pagan deities. But even to them the God of Zion, "Yahu" or "Yahu Sabaot," as they styled Him, remained the supreme divinity.[7]

The Diaspora clung to its unique God and to Jerusalem, the unique center of lawful worship. But at the same time, the God of Zion, the "great and terrible God," was not only the God of the Jews; He was the sole God in heaven and earth, the so-called deities of the pagans were nothing but vain idols. Hence, the polarity of Jerusalem and the Dispersion had its ideological counterpart in the paradoxical combination of universal monotheism and particularism, in the conception that the sole Lord of the Universe dwells on the hillock of Zion. This theological paradox held the Jews in the Dispersion together, and from all points of the compass they directed their eyes to the Lord's Temple in Jerusalem.

But here, in turn, we have to consider the political aspect of the situation. The spiritual unity of the Jews could hardly be established around Jerusalem if the whole Orient, from the Indus to Ethiopia, had not been one world obeying the orders issued by the Persian king. By its influence at the royal court, the Diaspora in Babylonia and Persia could act in behalf of Jewry everywhere and impose a uniform standard of faith and behavior. In a papyrus unearthed in Elephantine we can still read a communication, sent in 419, to the Jewish settlement at this other end of the world, giving rules as to the observance of the Feast of Unleavened Bread. These instructions were forwarded to the satrap of Egypt by King Darius of Persia. On the other hand, in their troubles with the Egyptians, the Jews in Elephantine wrote to the Jewish authorities in Jerusalem.

Or again, the re-establishment of normative Judaism after the Exile is connected by both Jewish tradition and modern scholarship with the name of Ezra, who restored the Law of Moses. But unlike Moses, Ezra's authority to promulgate and administer the Torah in Jerusalem was not derived from a Divine Revelation. Ezra arrived at Jerusalem as a Persian commissioner with a royal letter placing "the Law of thy God" on the same compulsory level as the law of the king, and threatening the offender of Mosaic precepts with death, banishment, confiscation of goods and imprisonment. In this way the perpetual character of the Torah was established and the Divine Law made known and imposed on all Jewry under the Persian scepter. When, after the dissolution of the empire of Alexander the Great, about 300 B.C.E., the unity of the political world of which the Jews were part had been broken, their religious and spiritual cohesion remained firmly established on the foundations laid down during the Persian age by Ezra and Nehemiah, King Darius and King Artaxerxes.

The imperial protection shielded the Palestinian Jewry from the Arabs and the Philistines, Edom and Moab. In the background of Jewish history in Palestine, from the time of the Judges, there was a constant drive of Aramaic and Arab nomads against the settled country whose comforts they envied. Persian, and later, Macedonian, frontier guards secured from now on the peace of the Jewish peasant. If Jerusalem had not been a part of a Gentile empire, the nomads would have driven the Jews into the sea or swallowed up Palestine, and the rock of Zion would have been the foundation of an Arabian sanctuary a thousand years before Omar's mosque.

2

Let us now take a look at Judaism in the last century of Persian rule, after Nehemiah (432) and before Alexander's conquest of Asia (332). During this period, Jerusalem and a strip of land around it formed a small district of Judea (*Yehûd*) lost in the enormous satrapy "Across the River," that is, west of the Euphrates. The district of Judea was approximately a quadrilateral, about thirty-five miles long, from Beth-el to Beth-zur, and from twenty-five to thirty miles broad, the plateau between the Dead Sea and the lowland in the west. Its area was about a thousand square miles, of which a good part was desert. Of the political history of Judea during our period there is virtually no record. An accidental notice informs us that Artaxerxes III of Persia had deported many Jews to the Caspian Sea during his campaign against Egypt. In all probability, Jerusalem, like Sidon, sided with Egypt in this conflict. A cuneiform tablet records the transport of prisoners from Sidon to Babylonia in the autumn of 345.[8] Thirteen years later Jerusalem as well as Sidon opened the gates to Alexander the Macedonian.

There was a Persian governor in Jerusalem; there was a provincial fiscus; jar handles bearing stamps of "Judea" and "Jerusalem" in Hebrew (and later Aramaic) characters show that tribute was paid in kind.[9] The governors received "bread and wine" from the people (Neh. 5:15) and since the governor had to provide a free table for his officers and the nobles of the land, each day he had to slay one ox and six choice sheep, exclusive of fowl. No wonder, then, that the governor expected a sheep as a present in behalf of suppliants (Mal. 1:8). Monetary economy, nevertheless, began to grow in Palestine. In the time of Nehemiah there are people borrowing money to pay the royal taxes. It is worth noting that Persian royal coins have not been found until now in the numerous and rich coin hoards of the fourth century in this region.[10] Likewise, the Book Ezra-Nehemiah does not mention any coin; when it mentions precious metals and objects made of the metals, it reports their weight. There is no certain record of troops from Judea in Persian service. The contingent from "the Solymian hills" in Xerxes' expedition against Greece, mentioned in the epic poem of Choerilus, a friend of Herodotus, refers probably to the "eastern Ethiopians." But the Jews had arms and had to appear with their swords, their spears and their bows by order of the governor. The latter had his personal guard, and the castle in which he lived commanded the Temple Hill.

Like every city and nation in the Persian Empire the Jews enjoyed a more or less large autonomy, amplified by bribes and diminished from time to time by arbitrary interference of the Persian authorities. For instance, when once a murder had been committed in the Temple, the governor inflicted on the Jewish nation the fine of fifty shekels for every lamb used in the daily offering; this payment was enforced for seven years, that is, probably, until a new governor came to Jerusalem. The Jews were represented by "the nobles of the Jews," the heads of the clans. On the other hand, there was the High Priest, "and his colleagues the priests who are in Jerusalem," as a document of 409 says. All the sacred personnel, the priests, Levites, singers, doorkeepers, slaves and servants of the Temple were free of tolls, tributes and customs. Here as elsewhere the Persian government favored the priesthood among its subjects as against the military aristocracy. The introduction of the Torah as "the law of the Jews" by a royal decree in 445 served the same purpose. Nevertheless, it would be erroneous to regard the district of *Yehûd* in the fourth century as an ecclesiastical state. While in Egypt, at the same date, a very large part of the soil belonged to the temples, and even a tithe of custom duties was assigned to them,[11] the sanctuary of Jerusalem does not appear to have possessed any real estate outside its own site, and the emoluments of the priests were offerings of the believers. Even the voluntary contribution of a third of a shekel by every male Israelite, established under Nehemiah to defray the expenses of public worship, fell into disuse.[12] But the influence of the priests continued to rise. In Nehemiah's time lay rulers of Judah led in public affairs, *e.g.*, in the dedication of the walls of Jerusalem, while the priests and the Levites purified the people; likewise plots against Nehemiah were devised among "the nobles of Judah." A century after him, a Greek traveler learned from his Jewish informant that public affairs of the Jews were administered by priests.[13]

It is a widely spread error that Judaism after Ezra was under the yoke of the Law, that the Jews were a community governed by an extreme strictness, that they were immune to foreign contagion and, until the Macedonian conquest, separated from the Greek world. As a matter of fact, excavations have shown that in the fifth and fourth centuries B.C.E., Palestine belonged to the belt of an eclectic, Greco-Egyptian-Asiatic culture, which extended from the Nile Delta to Cilicia.[14] The kitchen pots, as well as heavy bronze anklets worn by girls, or weapons of men, were now the same in the whole Levant, united under Persian sway. Greek painted pottery, Phoenician amulets and Egyptian idols are equally typical of Palestine in the fourth century. A Jerusalemite who went down to the coastal cities, let us say to Ascalon, could not help seeing a Greek cup showing Oedipus in conversation with the Sphinx or small bronzes of Egyptian deities. And when he returned with earthenware for his household, it might happen that he introduced into the Holy City reminiscence of a Greek mythos. An Attic black-figured cup with a sphinx has been found at Tell-En-Nashbeh, some six miles north of Jerusalem. The story, related by a pupil of Aristotle, that the master had met in Asia Minor (*c.* 345 B.C.E.) a Hellenized Greek-speaking Jew is probably a fiction, but not one which is improbable.[15] The commercial influence of Greece in Palestine was so great that the Athenian coins became the principal currency for trade transactions in the fifth century. This currency was gradually replaced in the fourth century by local imitations of the Athenian "owls." The authorities in Palestine also struck such imitations.[16] As their small denominations show, these coins were destined for local use and for business transactions on market days. Nevertheless, used by pious Jews and even bearing the stamp of a Jewish agent of the Persian government (Hezekiah), these first Jewish coins show not only the owl of the Athenian model but also human figures,[17] and even the image of a divinity seated on a winged wheel.[18] Whether the die cutter simply imitated here the Baal of the Tarsian coins or intended to represent in this way the "Lord of Hosts," these coins are hardly in accord with the biblical interdiction of "graven images." In fact, being real men and not puppets like the characters portrayed in conventional textbooks, the Jews of the

Restoration, like those of every generation, were entangled in contradictions and in conflicting patterns of real life.

They were convinced that God set them apart from the nations (Lev. 20:24), but they called Him the God of Heaven, which was the title of Ahuramazda, the deity of their Persian rulers. They regarded as Israel's heritage the whole land from Dan to Beer-sheba, even from Egypt to the Orontes (I Chron. 13:5), but did not establish friendly relations with the remnants of Ephraim who worshiped the same God and consecrated His priests according to the prescriptions of the Torah (II Chron. 13:9). In Jerusalem in the fourth century the priesthood was considered firmly organized by David himself, but among these ancient priestly families were some like the clan Hakoz, which had been regarded as of doubtful lineage only a hundred years before. The Jews imagined that they were living according to the Law of Moses, while the synagogue, unknown to the Torah, became a fundamental part of their devotional life. So "the congregation of the Lord" became the basic element of the nation[19] and a Jerusalemite could not imagine the national kings of the past acting otherwise than in agreement with the Holy Community (I Chron. 13:1; 16:1; 28:8; 29:1; II Chron. 30:4). Of still greater significance was another innovation: how the Torah came to be taught "throughout all the cities of Judah" (II Chron. 17:9). Before this the priests had kept to themselves the decision on matters of ritual and of morals. The knowledge comes from the priest's lips, says an author of the age of Ezra and Nehemiah, and law from the priest's mouth, because he is the messenger of the Lord (Mal. 2:7). But the democratization of the instruction in the Law in the fourth century opened the way to the coming of the scribe, and imperceptibly compromised the supremacy of the priest. From now on, the superiority of learned argument over authoritative decree prevailed. The First Psalm presents as the model of happiness not the officiating priest in the Temple, but rather the Sage who meditates on the Torah day and night. Scribes and Sages, clergy and laymen, the Jews were expected to be "saints," holy unto the Lord (Lev. 20:26). But the Law of God which gave the standard of holiness was imposed upon the saints by the decree of their pagan sovereign.

Another widespread and mistaken conception is that of postexilic exclusiveness.[20] As a matter of fact, in the Persian period, the Jews were first of all peoples we know to open wide the gates to proselytes. Every ancient cult was exclusive; none but the members of a family participated in the worship of its tutelary gods; no foreigner was able to sacrifice to the deities of a city.[21] When Orestes, masked as a stranger, returns to his ancestral home, he asks permission to take part in religious ceremonies, "if strangers may sacrifice with citizens."[22] In the fifth century B.C.E. the Athenians equally assume that it is a "calamity" to have an alien father.[23]

They were proud of being autochthonous, and not immigrants of mixed blood. In 333 B.C.E., when Alexander the Great was already making war in Asia, a special law was necessary in Athens to authorize the shrine of a foreign deity on the sacred soil of Pallas.[24] But the Jewish law allowed a stranger sojourning among the Jews to keep the Passover with the congregation of Israel (Ezra 6:21). "One law shall be to him that is homeborn, and unto the stranger who sojourns among you" (Ex. 12:49). And again: "The stranger who sojourns with you shall be to you as the homeborn among you, and thou shalt love him as thyself" (Lev. 19:34). An Athenian contemporary of Ezra would be astonished to hear that he has to love the *Metoeci*. Equally startling for the ancient world was the idea of proselytism, the appeal to the nations to join themselves to the Lord, which began with Second Isaiah and was repeated by later prophets again and again. "Thus says the Lord of hosts: In those days it shall come to pass, that ten men shall take hold, out of all the languages of the nations, shall even take hold of the skirt of him that is a Jew, saying: We will go with you, for we have heard that God is with you" (Zech. 8:23). So, the postexilic community establishes the new and really revolutionary principle: "Thus says the Lord: My house shall be called a house of prayer for all peoples" (Is. 56:7).

Again we meet with the fact that every historical situation is many-sided and full of contradictions. The heathens were tolerant and their gods lived amicably side by side because each nation had its own gods who did not care for other people. An Argive refugee in Athens is told not to be afraid of the Argive gods: "We have gods who fight on our side and who are not weaker than these on the side of the Argives."[25] Thus, the pagans made no efforts to convert a stranger but, for the same reason, excluded him from their own religion. Everybody was a true believer, in the opinion of the heathen, if he worshiped his ancestral gods. Thus, each city was exclusive and intolerant within its walls, but recognized the other gods outside. On the other hand, knowing that the Lord is the One True God, the Jews naturally proselytized among the heathen and admitted the converted to the universal religion. And for that same reason they were intolerant of those outside the congregation and rejected the folly of idolatry. Only a Jew was a true believer, but everybody could enter the congregation of the Chosen People.

The thought of this period is illustrated in an anonymous historical composition which now appears in the Bible as Ezra-Nehemiah and Chronicles.[25a] The arrangement reveals that the latter part of the original work (Ezra-Nehemiah) found its way into the scriptural canon before the portion (Chronicles) which related the pre-exilic history already covered by the Books of Samuel and Kings. But the work originally formed a single, continuous narrative from Adam to Nehemiah; it was still read in this edition by the compiler of a Greek version (the so-called First Esdras) in the second century B.C.E.

For the pre-exilic period the Chronicler draws for the most part on the Books of Samuel and Kings, but adds a great deal of information from other sources. Historians usually discount this additional material and blame the Chronicler for his little regard for facts. He can, for instance, state coolly that David had 1,570,000 warriors, exclusive of the troops of Levi and Benjamin (I Chron. 21:5). But the same exuberance in numbers is displayed by Assyrian records, and the source of the Chronicler (II Sam. 24) gives a number no less fantastic for David's army: 1,300,000. Fact-hunting critics overlook a very important feature of the work: its emancipation from the authority of tradition.

Oriental historiography is strictly traditional. An Assyrian reviser of royal annals may transform a booty of 1,235 sheep into one of 100,225,[26] or attribute to the king a successful campaign of his predecessor; but in the main he simply summarizes his source. The compiler of Kings closely follows his authorities, although he adds personal comments to the events. The Chronicler, like Hecataeus of Miletus or Herodotus, gives such information concerning the past as appears to him most probable, and corrects the sources in conformity with his own historical standards. For instance, when he asserts that the Levites carried the Ark in accordance with David's order (I Chron. 15:1), he interpolates something into his source (II Sam. 6:12) because he assumes as self-evident that the pious king could not but act according to the Law of Moses (Ex. 25:13). For the same reason he says "Levites" (II Chron. 5:4) when his source (I Kings 8:3) speaks of "priests" taking up the Ark under Solomon. Following his rule of historical probability, he cannot believe that Solomon turned over some cities to Hiram of Tyre (I Kings 9:12); so he changes the text: the cities were given by Hiram to Solomon (II Chron. 8:2). In the same manner, he attributes to ancient kings, David and Josiah, the organization of the priesthood and of the sacred services as they existed in his own time. Since Israel had ceased to be an independent state, the author treats with predilection all matters concerning the Temple, which now became the center of national life, and devotes a long description to religious measures of King Hezekiah which are hardly mentioned in Kings. Owing to the shift of historical interest, he passes over in silence the Northern Kingdom, which had rebelled against the house of David. He does not hesitate to use the term "Israel" when he speaks of Judah, which alone remained faithful to the covenant of the fathers.

The critics have often stressed the Chronicler's practice of viewing the past as the realization in Israel of the rules and principles of the Torah, his tendency to find the origins of the Judaism of his own day in remote antiquity. In fact, his purpose is not to give a mere chronicle but to provide a clue to the meaning and direction of Israel's history. The same attempt, with regard to Greek (and even world) history, was made by Herodotus, who wrote about a hundred years before the Chronicler. Herodotus seems to feel that the gods, envious of human greatness and happiness, use man's wrongdoings to punish him or his posterity. It is the doctrine of Nemesis, exemplified, for instance, in Polycrates's fate. The moral of history is, therefore, to remain an average man; its lesson is that of moderation and submission to destiny, the "nothing in excess" of the Seven Sages.

The Jewish author finds in divine pragmatism the principle for understanding the past; his clue is the idea of retribution. That is, of course, nothing new. Herodotus explains Croesus' fall by the sin of his ancestor in the fifth generation. In a cuneiform text Nabonidus's evildoing explains his fall and the catastrophe of Babylon.[27] But the Chronicler describes the whole of human history from this standpoint. According to his conception, the pious kings always enjoyed prosperity, while punishment necessarily befell the wicked and unfaithful ones. The idea is applied to the reinterpretation of the past with the same constancy and disregard of facts as when some modern books describe history in terms of class struggle or racial changes. From Saul to the last king, Zedekiah, the evildoers die for their transgressions. But, since the Chronicler conceives of Divine Necessity in human history as the work of the personal God and not of a machinelike Fate of the Greeks, he seeks to justify the visitations sent upon Israel. In the first place, he stresses the idea of personal responsibility. He follows and repeats (II Chron. 25:4) the principle established in Deuteronomy (24:16) that "the fathers shall not be put to death for the children, neither shall the children be put to death for the fathers; every man shall be put to death for his own sin," a conception which appears about the same time in Greece too. But the principle of collective responsibility remained active in Greece, except for Athens, with regard to political crimes.[28] In Judaism, the Book of Kings still presents the hand of God visiting the sins of the fathers upon their children and striking peoples for the transgressions of their kings. Jehoiachin is carried away and Judah is destroyed in 597 "for the sins of Manasseh" who had reigned almost fifty years before (II Kings 24:3; Jer. 15:4). The Chronicler assumes that Manasseh had received a due punishment from the Assyrians, who led him about in fetters and held on to him by a hook thrust into his nostrils (II Chron. 33:11). On the other hand, the destruction of Jerusalem in 587 is explained in Kings (II Kings 24:20) as an expression of God's anger against the last king, Zedekiah. The Chronicler adds that "all the chiefs of the priests, and the people, transgressed very greatly after all the abominations of the nations; and they polluted the house of the Lord which He had hallowed in Jerusalem" (II Chron. 36:14).

The Syrian invasion in the reign of Joash is a judgment on the people, "because they had forsaken the Lord, the God of their fathers" (II Chron. 24:24). The invasion of Shishak happened because all Israel had transgressed along with King Rehoboam (II Chron. 12:1). Consequently, the deliverance from Sennacherib is caused by the reconciliation of the people with God, and the author is fond of associating the people with the king in religious reformations (I Chron. 13:4; II Chron. 30:4f.).

This conception of personal responsibility for transgression explains the role of the prophets in Chronicles. Herodotus uses the Oriental theme of the wise counselor to show how man in his blindness neglects prudent advice and runs to his doom. The Chronicler knows that God sent His prophets "because He had compassion on His people" (II Chron. 36:15); but they mocked His messengers and despised His words. So the culprit was fully conscious of the culpability of his deed and duly warned, a proviso which later talmudic jurisprudence requires for legal conviction and punishment of a capital offender. Thus, warned by God, the wicked kings sinned with malice and God's wrath was fully justified. Accordingly, the Chronicler's standard in judging the ancient kings is their obedience to the Divine Message sent through the prophets. Jerusalem was destroyed because Israel scoffed at the warnings of the prophets. The Temple was rebuilt by Cyrus, in order that the Word of the Lord by the mouth of Jeremiah might be accomplished (II Chron. 36:22). This, "the Chronicle of the whole of sacred history," as Jerome calls it, leads to the Restoration under Persian rule. When the adversaries of Jerusalem frustrate the building of the Temple, King Darius intervenes, and the Jews dedicate the sanctuary and prosper "through the prophesying of Haggai . . . and Zechariah" (Ezra 6:14).

In keeping with ancient historiography, the recital becomes fuller when the compiler approaches his own time. But some features of the latter part of his work are peculiar. In the first place, we note that while the author considers Nehemiah's days as being in the past (Neh. 12:47), he does not continue the narrative until his own time but ends with the account of Nehemiah's measures which concluded the Restoration in 432 B.C.E. In the same way, Herodotus (and other Greek historians in the fifth century) did not deal with the events after the Persian wars.[29] Again, while for the pre-exilic period the Chronicler refers to many sources, for the Persian epoch he gives hardly anything other than a reproduction of official records: lists, letters and memoranda of royal administration, memorials of Ezra and of Nehemiah. He scarcely provides notes of his own for a chronological and logical framework. And, while he freely passes judgment on ancient persons and times, he refrains from expressing his personal views in the account of the Persian period. One is reminded of Greek *logographi* of the fifth century who, as an ancient critic says, repeated "the written records that they found preserved in temples or secular buildings in the form in which they found them, neither adding nor taking away anything."[30]

This dependence on source material leads, quite naturally, to some confusion. As the Chronicler confuses, for instance, Darius I with Darius II, he places a dossier referring to Xerxes and Artaxerxes I before their predecessor Darius I. The Chronicler quotes Ezra's and Nehemiah's accounts in their own words, a feature which involved the change from the third person to the first person and *vice versa*. This device served to authenticate the narrative and came into historical writing from the diplomatic style, where exactness of quotation was absolutely necessary. In Egypt the story of the war of King Kamose in the sixteenth century B.C.E., or the epic of the victory of Rameses II at Kadesh, *c.* 1300 B.C.E., presents the same change from a subjective account to objective praise by the hero of his own deeds.[31] The so-called "Letters to God Assur" in Assyrian historiography likewise show the use of the third person when the king is spoken of in the introduction composed by a scribe, while in the body of the text the king speaks in the first person.[32] In a Persian tract composed after the conquest of Babylon in 538 B.C.E., the so-called Cyrus cylinder, the author relates the evildoings of Nabonidus, the last king of Babylon, and the conquest of the city by Cyrus. Then, without any transition, exactly as in Ezra-Nehemiah, the author introduces Cyrus's proclamation, beginning "I am Cyrus," which gives Cyrus's own account of the events.[33] When the Chronicler quotes documents verbatim, he again follows the style of chancelleries. He introduces even in his narratives of pre-exilic history such compositions couched in official form, *e.g.*, a circular communication of King Hezekiah (II Chron. 30) and even a letter of the prophet Elijah (II Chron. 21:12).[34]

Ezra's and Nehemiah's prayers, the national confession of sins, the covenants made with God under the leadership of Ezra and Nehemiah are presented as proof that there is a difference between the wicked Jerusalem of the kings and the new Israel which decided to follow the way of righteousness. That accounts for the blessing of the present state under the protection of the Persian kings. The Temple is restored "according to the commandment of the God of Israel, and according to the decree of Cyrus, and Darius, and Artaxerxes king of Persia" (Ezra 6:14).

The whole conception of the Chronicler shows that he wrote when Persian rule seemed destined for eternity and the union between the altar in Jerusalem and the throne of Susa seemed to be natural and indestructible. The Chronicler wrote before Alexander the Great, that is, in the first half of the fourth century. Accordingly, the tendency of his work is to recommend a kind of political quietism which should please the court of Susa as well as the High Priest's mansion in Jerusalem. The idea of the

Messianic age which was destined to come after the overthrow of the Persian world power, finds no place in the work of the Chronicler. Armies are superfluous for Israel, the Jews need not fight when the Lord is with them; the Chronicler does not tire of stressing this conception. But "the Lord is with you while you are with Him" (II Chron. 15:2). Zedekiah was punished and Jerusalem destroyed not only because the king did evil and did not give heed to Jeremiah's words, but also because "he rebelled against King Nebuchadnezzar, who had made him swear by God." That is taken from Ezekiel (17:13) but the lesson could hardly escape the attention of the Chronicler's readers, subjects of the Persian king.

The Chronicler's historical work, Attic pottery unearthed in Palestine, Jewish coins bearing a Divine Image, universalism and exclusiveness, all these together create a picture of Jewish life after the Restoration rather different from what is conveyed by the conventional clichés. They indicate that life was more vivid, more diversified than the rules of conduct as formulated in Scripture might suggest.

3

A postexilic oracle, included in the Book of Isaiah (11:11) promises the return of the Diaspora from Elam, Assyria, Babylonia, Lower and Upper Egypt, from North Syria and "from the islands of the sea." This Jewish Diaspora encountered everywhere the Hellenic Diaspora. Greek trading stations existed in the fifth and fourth centuries, for example, at Ugarit (near modern Lattakie) and at the mouth of the Orontes in Syria.[35] When in 586 Jewish refugees from Palestine, Jeremiah among them, went to "Tahpanhes" in the Egyptian Delta, they entered a settlement of Greek mercenaries, established here (Daphne) by Psammetichus.[36] Payments of rations listed in a Babylonian account between 595 and 570 B.C.E. were provided not only to King Joiachin [Jehoiachin] and numerous other men of Judah in exile, but also to Ionian carpenters and shipbuilders.[37] As cuneiform business documents of the Persian period show, the Jews in the Babylonian Diaspora rubbed shoulders with men from India and Armenia and Turkestan and, of course, Lydians and Ionians.[38] When later Greek authors supposed that Pythagoras, that ancient sage of Samos, was indebted not only to Egypt and Chaldea, but to Jewish wisdom, too, when a later Jewish author thought that the Greek sages had learned loftier conceptions of God from Moses, they were probably wrong, but the surmise does not any longer appear absurd in the light of recent discoveries. One may fancy Ezekiel talking with Pythagoras in Babylon; they speak of Homer and of Moses. What a topic for an *Imaginary Conversation* in Landor's fashion!

But our information concerning the Diaspora in the Persian period is scanty and accidental. To be sure, we still have numerous records from Babylonia, written between 464 and 404 B.C.E., with many Jewish names.[39] But since these tablets are business documents of one pagan firm in Nippur, in southern Babylonia, we do not really learn anything substantial of the life of the Jews from these contracts and receipts. Nevertheless, these archives show that the *golah* of 597 and 587 still remained on the same place where the exiled had been settled by Nebuchadnezzar, namely, "by the river Chebar" (Ez. 1:1), which is the "large canal" of the cuneiform tablets, a watercourse on which Nippur was situated. The Jews in the documents often bear Babylonian and Persian names, some of them combined with the names of pagan deities. For instance, the father of a Hanana is called Ardi-Gula, that is, "servant of [the Goddess] Gula." But about seventy per cent of the Jews had genuine Hebrew names. The Jews in the district of Nippur were for the most part farmers; but they were also tax collectors and royal officials; they held military tenures and transacted business with the Babylonians and the Persians. A Jewish claimant opposes a Babylonian merchant house "in the judicial assembly of Nippur."

There were many Jewish settlements in Egypt, too; for instance, in the Delta, near Pelusium, at Memphis, and in upper Egypt. The Egyptian Diaspora was pre-exilic. Even before the Exile an oracle signifies five cities in the land of Egypt that speak the language of Canaan and swear to the Lord of Hosts (Is. 19:18), and the Second Isaiah (49:12) mentions the Jews in the land of Sinim, that is, Syene, at the first cataract of the Nile, at the southern border of Egypt. To this place Jewish mercenaries were sent by one of their kings in the beginning of the sixth century to help the Pharaoh. Guardian of the Ethiopian boundary, "the Jewish force" came into Persian service after Cambyses' conquest of Egypt (525 B.C.E.), and obeyed the Pharaohs again after the defection of Egypt in 404. Numerous documents in Aramaic of the fifth century, belonging to this military settlement, have been unearthed at Elephantine.[40]

The "Jewish force" (as the regiment is officially styled) was divided into companies, the captains of which bear Babylonian or Persian names; a Persian was "the chief of the force." The settlers received pay and rations (barley, lentils, etc.) from the royal treasury. But the colony was civilian in its way of life. The Jews at Elephantine bought and sold their tenures, transacted business, defended their claims in civil courts, although everyone, even women, was styled as belonging to the regiment. The Jews dealt with military colonists of other nations settled in the neighborhood, as well as with Egyptians. There were mixed marriages. Independently of the military organization the Jews formed a religious community of the kind later, in the Hellenistic period, called *politeuma*. A president "with his colleagues" represented the community which was gathered in "assembly" whenever wanted. The president was also the treasurer of the local Temple of the national God, whom these Jews called "Yahu" and regarded as "the God of Heaven." Likewise, their system of sacrifices and the terms referring to them were the same as in the Bible: holocaust, meal offering, incense; they offered libations and immolated sheep, oxen and goats. They observed the Passover. Their faith was rather homely and plain. They suggested in a letter that their enemy was killed, "and the dogs tore off the anklets from his legs," because they had prayed for it to the God of Heaven and fasted "with our wives and our children" in sackcloth. They did not doubt that merit before God may be obtained with expensive sacrifices, and would hardly appreciate the prophetic word that God desires mercy and not sacrifices (Hos. 6:6). But equally, they did not suspect that their place of worship was a violation of Divine Law proclaimed in Deuteronomy, which forbids altars and immolations outside of the one chosen place at Jerusalem. With the same "provincial" naïveté, they uttered blessings in the name of "Yahu and Khnum."

While the religion of the Jews of Elephantine was primitive their business activity was highly modern. They wrote, and probably talked, not Hebrew but Aramaic, which had become the common and official language of the Persian Empire. Accordingly, while contemporary demotic documents reflect Egyptian law, and while Mesopotamian settlers near Aleppo (Syria) and at Gezer (Palestine) continued to draw cuneiform deeds in harmony with the Babylonian system,[41] the Aramaic records from Elephantine manifest the formation and development of a new common law of the Levant. The form of these instruments is that of a declaration made before witnesses and reproduced in direct speech; this is modeled on Egyptian formularies. The same form is used in an Aramaic lease agreement of 515 B.C.E. entered into in Egypt by two parties not of Jewish origin. Some stipulations in business documents from Elephantine reproduce Egyptian formulae also, *e.g.*, the abandonment of the claims to a ceded property. But the term "hate" for separation of spouses is Babylonian and biblical (Deut. 21:15), although it was also borrowed by the Egyptians. Babylonian too are the contracts of renunciation arising from a previous decision of the court, the legal term for "instituting a suit" and the standard of weight. This syncretistic common law was built up partly by precedents set by the Persian king's judges, partly by way of customary agreements. The Persian court adopted, for instance, the Egyptian practice of imposing an oath (formulated by the judge) upon the party in support of the claim when there was no other evidence, even when the litigants were of different nationalities, *e.g.*, a Jew and a Persian. Everybody was required, of course, to swear by his own deity; when a Jewess became the wife of an Egyptian, she was supposed to follow the status of her husband

and she took oath by an Egyptian goddess. On the other hand, polygamy, allowed in Jewish law, was prohibited in marriage contracts of Elephantine by a stipulation agreed upon by the parties and guaranteed by a fine. While Egyptian marriage was based on mere consensus, the Jews at Elephantine still regarded a union as valid only when the bride's father received from the groom a "marriage price" (*mohar*). But this conveyance of rights to the husband became here an antiquated formality. The new common law established an almost complete equality between spouses. Both had the right to divorce at his or her pleasure, provided the declaration of "hating" was made "in the congregation." The power to divorce was given to the bride in Egyptian marriage contracts, but it was limited to the husband alone in Jewish (and Babylonian) law. Egyptian too was the status of woman with regard to her legal capacity; married or not, she was able at Elephantine to conduct business, hold property in her own right and resort to law about it. No less surprising was the stipulation that either spouse would inherit from the other when there were no children. Thus, the Aramaic papyri from Elephantine of the fifth century B.C.E. are the earliest evidence we have for the transformation of the Jewish behavior in the Dispersion. Living on equal terms with the natives, transacting business with peoples of various races, intermarrying, the Diaspora began to diverge from the course followed at Jerusalem.

But living together with other people rarely continues untroubled. Although the priest of the Egyptian god Khnum was a neighbor of the Jewish sanctuary at Elephantine for many decades, in 411 the Egyptian clergy bribed the Persian governor to order the Jewish temple destroyed. One may doubt whether that was really "the first anti-Semitic outbreak," as the action is now considered by historians. When we read the endless complaints of a certain Peteesi, an Egyptian (513 B.C.E.), about vexations he was forced to suffer from Egyptian priests on account of some litigation,[42] we are rather prepared to believe that the conflict of 411 at Elephantine was a local incident, and not a symptom of general anti-Semitism. When the Persian governor refused to allow the reconstruction of the temple, the Jews of Elephantine sent an appeal to Jerusalem. But the existence of a temple outside Zion could hardly please the authorities at Jerusalem. Consequently, in 408, the Jews of Elephantine wrote to Bagoas, the Persian governor of Judea, and to the sons of Sanballat, governor of Samaria, hinting also at a forthcoming bribe. The addressees prepared a memorandum recommending to the satrap of Egypt the reestablishment of the temple, without animal offerings, however: a compromise which would please both the Egyptians, who at this time worshiped almost every animal, and the Jerusalemites, who in this manner reduced the altar of Elephantine to a lower rank.

But there were again intrigues and counterintrigues, bribes and favors at the court of the Persian satrap of Egypt; and since, toward the end of the fifth century, Egypt rebelled against Persia, the temple at Elephantine was never rebuilt, although the Jewish military settlement continued and was ultimately taken over by Alexander the Great.

4

The Persian Empire fell in 333. When Alexander the Great proceeded down the coast of Syria toward Egypt, most peoples and cities on his route, Jerusalem among them, readily submitted to the Macedonian. The meeting of Jewish deputies, sent to offer the surrender of the Holy City, with the world conqueror later became a choice topic of Jewish legend. In fact, the Macedonian, who considered himself the legitimate heir of the Persian kings, here as elsewhere simply accepted and confirmed the statutes and privileges granted by his Iranian predecessors. But an accidental order of Alexander's deeply influenced the history of Palestine.

The city of Samaria revolted in 332, and the king, having taken it, settled Macedonians there. This punishment, inflicted on Samaria, brought about the break between Judah and Ephraim. Captured by the Assyrians in 722, the city of Samaria had become a military colony. The men from Babylonia and northern Syria transplanted here, brought along their own gods, such as the god of pestilence, Nergal of Cutha, who at the same time appeared in Sidon, a city also resettled by the Assyrians after the rebellion of 677. Being polytheists, the settlers in due course adopted the deity of the land in which they dwelt and learned to worship the God of Israel with great zeal. Since Sargon in 722 deported only the higher classes of the district of Samaria, the countryside was not denuded of the original population. Sargon himself refers to the tribute imposed on this remnant of Israel.

The newcomers intermingled and intermarried with the former inhabitants of the land of Samaria and accepted their religion. In 586, men of Shiloh and Samaria came and worshiped at the ruined site of the Temple of Jerusalem. In 520 the Samaritans claimed a share in the rebuilding of this Temple. As already noted, in 408 the Jews at Elephantine wrote to the leaders in both Jerusalem and Samaria as to coreligionists. Still later there were people of Ephraim who celebrated the Passover at Jerusalem (II Chron. 34:6). It seems that the conversion of the heathen immigrants to the service of the God of Israel was complete and that both Samaria and Jerusalem worshiped the same God with the same rites in the fourth century B.C.E. There is no mention of any pagan cult among the Samaritans. Accordingly, prophets in Jerusalem expected the redemption of both "prisoners of hope" (Zech. 9:13), Judah and Ephraim. The conflict between the two cities under Persian rule was primarily a political one.

Samaria opposed the rebuilding of the walls of Jerusalem because the resurrected capital in the south would be a natural rival of the northern fortress. In the same way, the Assyrian settlers in Sidon, who became completely assimilated with the natives, inherited their quarrel with Tyre, another Phoenician capital.

But when Alexander planted Macedonian colonists in the city of Samaria, he destroyed the fusion between "the force at Samaria" and the countryside. The new masters of the stronghold did not know anything about the God of Israel. They did not care for Nergal either. They were at home rather in Athens, where in the third century B.C.E. a pagan association crowned a certain "Samaritan" as its benefactor. If the new inhabitants were inclined to adopt some elements of the religion of the former settlers, they could hardly succeed because the God of Israel did not tolerate any rival.

It often happened that when a Greek colony was established, native villages under its control formed a union around an ancestral sanctuary. Following the same pattern, the countryside of (now Macedonian) Samaria constituted an organization, in Greek style, "Sidonians of Shechem," for the purpose of serving the God of Israel.[43] Shechem, the most ancient capital and the most sacred site of Israel, became the natural center of the confederation. The name "Sidonians," that is, "Canaanites," was probably chosen in opposition to the newcomers; it emphasized the fact that the members of the League were aboriginal inhabitants of Canaan. The geographical term "Samaritans" was appropriated by the Macedonian intruders, and the religious term "Israel" now belonged to Jerusalem. The descendants of the Assyrian settlers, men like Sanballat, Nehemiah's adversary, who had been the leaders in Palestine for four centuries and who were now dispossessed, could neither accept the predominance of the Macedonian colony nor become a dependency of Jerusalem. They repeated to the Jews, "we seek your God as you do" (Ezra 4:2), but were not prepared to recognize the demands of Jerusalem that the common Deity may not be rightfully worshiped away from the summit of Zion. As the Chronicler emphasized (II Chron. 30:10), such claims were received with derision in the north.

The new union around Shechem, therefore, founded its own sanctuary. It was consecrated to the God of both Jerusalem and Shechem, and stood on the summit of Gerizim, overlooking Shechem, on the site where the Chosen People were commanded to "set the blessing," according to the precept of Deuteronomy (11:29). Deuteronomy was originally a Jerusalemite book, published in 621 B.C.E., but since 722 B.C.E. there had been no center of the religion of the fathers outside Jerusalem, and the worshipers of God, in Samaria or elsewhere, had to seek guidance at Jerusalem. The choice of Gerizim shows the dependence of the Shechemites on Jerusalem in spiritual matters and, at the same time, it proves that only the pride of the former Assyrian aristocrats, loath to acknowledge the supremacy of the southern rival, was responsible for the foundation of the Samaritan temple, and, consequently, for the break between Judah and Ephraim. The whole controversy between Jews and Samaritans was now subordinated to the question: Which place was chosen by God for His inhabitation, Zion or Gerizim? Later propagandist inventions obscured the origin of the schism and confused its dating which, for this reason, remains controversial. The Samaritans glorified their temple by attributing its founding to Alexander the Great. The Jews associated the separation with Nehemiah's expulsion of a scion of the high-priestly family for his marriage to a Samaritan girl (Neh. 13:28). This combination provided a "rational" account for the schism, and conveniently branded the priesthood at Gerizim as illegitimate. But the Jewish tradition itself, repeated by Josephus, states that the Samaritan temple was founded at the time of Alexander the Great. The fact that it did not receive any subvention from the Macedonian rulers, as well as the fact that it belonged not to Samaria but to "that foolish nation which dwells in Shechem" (as Ben Sira says), offers the definitive proof of its foundation after the Macedonian conquest.

Jerusalem was situated far away from the main trade routes which crossed Palestine and ran along the coast. Thus, while the Greeks knew the Palestinian shore very well, no Greek writer before the time of Alexander the Great mentions the Jews, with the exception of Herodotus, who alludes to the circumcision practiced by "the Phoenicians and the Syrians of Palestine." But even after Alexander the Great, the first Greek authors who took cognizance of the Jews got their information from the Diaspora, from Jewish immigrants or Jewish soldiers in the service of Alexander and his successors. That is by no means surprising. Why should a Greek author, at a time when the whole fabulous Orient was open to his inquiry, concentrate on a Lilliputian place in the arid mountains? Let us note, by the way, that the first Greek book (by Aristotle's pupil Theophrastus) giving some exact information about Rome, appeared in 314-313 B.C.E. Some years later another student of philosophy, Hecataeus of Abdera, who had accompanied Ptolemy I of Egypt in his Syrian campaign of 312 B.C.E., published in a report of his journey the first Greek account of the Jews, based particularly on data given to the author by a Jewish priest who, in 312, accompanied the Ptolemaic army to Egypt.[44] Hecataeus's narrative was used by Theophrastus,[45] while another pupil of Aristotle, Clearchus, described what is probably a fictitious meeting between his master and a Jewish magician in Asia Minor.[46]

Let us consider the picture of the Jews as seen with Greek eyes at the end of the fourth century. For the reason just stated, a Greek writer must have had a particular motive to take an interest in the Jews. Now, the philosophers, and the school of Aristotle in particular, looked for empirical confirmation of their social theories in the newly opened Orient. Similarly, the discovery of America was utilized by European scholars of the sixteenth century to identify the Red Indians with the lost Ten Tribes. Greek scholars of Alexander's time thought that the peoples untouched by the dissolving influence of modern (that is, Greek) civilization must have conserved the purity of religion and the perfection of social organization which the philosophers attributed to man in a state of nature. On the other hand, the Greeks knew that in the Orient knowledge was the monopoly of the priestly caste. Having discovered a people led by priests and obeying the Law coming directly from the Divinity, the Greeks ranged the Jews beside the Indian Brahmans and Persian Magi. The Jews are a "philosophical race," says Theophrastus; they descend from the Indian philosophers, says Clearchus. Just as a Greek author (Megasthenes) claimed that the doctrines of the ancient Greek philosophers concerning nature had been formulated by the Indians, other writers ascribed the origins of philosophy to the Jews. Clearchus presents a Jewish sage who furnishes Aristotle with the experimental proof of the Platonic doctrine of immortality. Some decades later, Hermippus, another follower of Aristotle, mentions the (supposed) Jewish belief in the soul's immortality as a well-known fact, and adds that Pythagoras borrowed from the Jews and the Thracians his opinions about it. Since the Jews named their Deity "God of Heaven," they provided the philosophers with the desired proof that natural theology of mankind had identified God with the heavens. Likewise, monotheism, as well as the absence of divine images, agreed with the philosophical conceptions. Other data were interpreted accordingly. For instance, Theophrastus states that the Jews celebrate their festivals at night in contemplation of the stars (the order of heavenly bodies was for the philosophers the most important proof against atheism) and discourse about the Divine. In the same way, Hecataeus ascribes to the Egyptian priests philosophical conversations during the banquets where wine was not served.

The political organization of the Jews was viewed from the same standpoint, as the realization of an ideal state, governed by the Sages, the philosophers according to Plato and the priests according to the Palestinians. The Torah is presented as a narrative of the settlement of the Jews in Palestine and as their constitution. Moses, as lawgiver, could establish his system only after the conquest; so, according to Hecataeus, he had conquered the Promised Land and founded Jerusalem. As in Sparta, his system is based on military virtues of bravery, endurance and discipline. As is fit for the perfect state, the legislator forbade the sale of the land distributed among the Jews of Palestine in order to prevent the concentration of wealth and its sinister consequence, the decrease of population. This Greek interpretation of Lev. 25:23 clearly shows that Hecataeus's inquiry was oriented by his philosophic aims; he elicited from his Jewish informants answers which could serve his theory. For this reason it is a very delicate task to appreciate the earliest Greek records as testimony regarding the state of Judaism in Alexander's time. When Hecataeus affirms that the priests receive a tithe of the income of the people, he idealizes the realities. When he adds that the priests administer public affairs, he surely gives a one-sided view of the subject. But when he emphatically states that the High Priest was regarded as the mouthpiece of God and messenger of divine oracles, we suspect that the Greek writer attributes to the Jews the behavior they should have in his opinion, in order to represent the ideal scheme of the philosophical commonwealth. Hecataeus's High Priest, by the way, is chosen as the most able leader among the priests.

Some features stressed in the Greek records are worth noting. The importance of the priesthood and the role of the High Priest in Jerusalem, the obstinacy of the Jews in defense of the Law and the slander of their neighbors and foreign visitors with regard to antialien sentiments of the Jews, already point in Hecataeus's narrative to characteristic features of Hellenistic Jewry. We learn that already before 300 B.C.E. the Jews in Palestine did not tolerate pagan shrines and altars on the holy soil and that, at the same time, the Jews in the Diaspora freely scoffed at the superstitions of the Gentiles. This attitude was inevitable because the Jews were in possession of the Truth. They might have said to the pagans: We claim liberty for ourselves in accordance with your principles and refuse it to you in accordance with our principles. In the polytheist world of Hellenism, where all beliefs were admitted as different refractions of the same eternal light, the Jewish claim to the oneness of the Divine Revelation must have appeared as a provocation.

Nevertheless, Alexander and his successors accepted the Jews among the citizens of the new settlements founded in the East. When the experiment of founding commonwealths of Greek type in the Orient succeeded, later descendants of the settlers became "Aristocrats" but the first settlers were no more respected by their contemporaries than the passengers of the *Mayflower* were by the Englishmen of 1620. The conquest of Alexander, welding East and West into a single economic whole, brought wealth to Greece and to many Oriental towns. Why should a craftsman from Athens or a moneylender from Babylon enroll in the list of settlers of a new city far away, let us say Europos on the Euphrates? As the kings needed cities to safeguard the military communications and as strongholds against the indigenous population, settlers were at a premium. For instance, Alexander transferred some contingents from (still Assyrian) Samaria to Egypt, where they received allotments of land.

There is no reason to suspect Josephus's statement that the early Hellenistic rulers gave the Jews equal status with the Macedonians and Greeks who settled in the new colonies. He fails to make it clear that these privileges were individual and did not bear on the position of Jewry as a community in the new colony. This was a point on which hinged the later struggle between the Greeks and the Jews in Hellenistic cities. We do not know how Alexander and his successors reconciled Jewish exclusiveness with the obligations of the Greek citizen. Probably, the antinomy was solved in each case empirically. There were Jews, like the magician spoken of by Clearchus, who "not only spoke Greek, but had the soul of a Greek," and thus were inclined to mutual tolerance. Sometimes the king exempted the Jews; thus Alexander pardoned the Jewish soldiers who had refused to build a heathen temple in Babylon, and Seleucus I ordered money to be given for oil to those Jews, citizens of Antiochia, who were unwilling to use pagan oil. As oil was given by the "gymnasiarchs" for anointing during athletic games, the notice seems to imply that in Greek cities of the Diaspora, Jewish youth about 300 B.C.E. already took part in exercises of the "gymnasia," naked like their Hellenic comrades.[47] Physical training was the foundation of Greek life and mentality in all Greek cities, and the gymnasia became the centers of Greek intellectual activity and the principal instrument of Hellenization. Through the palaestra, by way of sports, the Jewish settlers became recognized members of the community. They learned to take pride in the city long before Paul proclaimed at Jerusalem his double title of honor, "I am a Jew, a Tarsian of Cilicia, citizen of no mean city." And conversely, the Jews of Alexandria could not but imagine that Alexander had become a worshiper of the true God at the time of his founding of their city and had brought the bones of the prophet Jeremiah to Alexandria as her palladium.[48]

5

After Alexander's death (324 B.C.E.) wars between his generals ended in the dismemberment of his empire. After 301 there were three great powers governed by Macedonian dynasties: Asia (that is substantially Syria, Mesopotamia, Persia and a large portion of Asia Minor) under the sway of the Seleucids, Egypt of the Ptolemies, and the realm of Macedonia in Europe. Thus, the political unity of the world where the Jews lived was broken. Even the Roman Empire did not re-establish the lost oneness, since an important Jewry remained in the Parthian kingdom, outside the laws of the Caesars.

Palestine became a dominion of Egypt but was reconquered by Antiochus III of Asia in 200 B.C.E. Since the government of both the Ptolemies and the Seleucids rested on the same political principles, we may view as an entity the period of Ptolemaic and Seleucid domination over Jerusalem until the Maccabean struggle, that is, some 125 years between 301 and 175 B.C.E. The district of Judea, called "the nation of Jews," under the Seleucids, was still a very small part of the province of Syria.[49] When a traveler passed the Jordan or the town of Modein in the north, or went south beyond Beth-zur, or toward the west descended into the coastal plain, he left the Jewish territory. Frontier guards, for instance, at Antipatris, customhouses, custom duties for export and import reminded the Jerusalemite of this fact. Thus, even in Palestine, the political term "Jew" did not include all the religious adherents of the Temple on Zion. With respect to religion there were many Jews and Jewries elsewhere, in Galilee or in Trans-Jordan or, for instance, where the powerful clan of the Tobiads was located. But politically these were not considered "Jews." The term "Jew" applied only to those "who lived around the Temple of Jerusalem," and so a Greek historian calls them.[50] Jerusalem was the only "city" of the Jews; other settlements in Judea were politically "villages." Judea continued to be a self-governing unit; there was no royal governor in Jerusalem, although the citadel of the Holy City was garrisoned by royal troops. The Jews, too, had to furnish contingents to the royal forces; Jewish soldiers are mentioned in Alexander's army, a Jewish regiment of cavalry under Ptolemy. It may be that fortresses on the frontier, such as that at Beth-zur, excavated recently, were occupied by native forces; about 200 B.C.E. the walls of Jerusalem were rebuilt by the Jewish authorities.

In 200 the Jewish militia helped Antiochus III to dislodge the Egyptian garrison from the citadel of Jerusalem. But more important for the central government was the collection of taxes, such as the poll tax, or taxes on houses or gate tolls, etc., to which was added the tribute, that is, the annual payment of a lump sum by the Jewish commonwealth as such. In the third century Judea, as a province of the Egyptian Empire, was part of the highly complicated system of planned economy that was built up by the Ptolemies. Like all natives of the province, "Syria and Phoenicia," the Jews had to declare their movable property and cattle for the purpose of taxation. Likewise, the Ptolemies introduced their subtle system of collecting the revenue by tax farmers. The Ptolemies favored the local notables as farmers of revenue, since in this way the native aristocracy had a stake in the Ptolemaic domination.

As regards self-government, Jerusalem was an "aristocratic" commonwealth. The "council of Elders" was the ruling body, composed of laymen and priests. But the aristocracy as a social class was priestly, just as in Hellenistic Egypt. When Antiochus III granted exemption from personal taxes to the upper class in Jerusalem, he named the council of Elders, the officers of the Temple with respect to their functions, and the sacerdotal caste as such. The intermediary between the royal government and the Jews was the High Priest, appointed by the king. Practically, the office was hereditary and was held for life. The High Priests, responsible primarily for the tribute, also became accustomed under Egyptian domination to farm the other taxes. In this way, the High Priest became the political head of the nation as well. About 190, Ben Sira spoke of the High Priest Simeon in terms appropriate to a prince: he was the glory of his people, in his time the Temple was fortified, he protected his people. As to the common people, they were sometimes summoned to the Temple court to hear official reports on the situation and to acclaim the official speaker. Nevertheless, as Ben Sira shows, the "assembly of Elders" and even the popular "assembly in the gate" continued to regulate social life and still had judicial and administrative functions.

While politically the situation of the "nation of the Jews" was essentially the same in 175 B.C.E. as had been that of the district *Yehûd* two centuries earlier, there was a decisive change as to the state of civilization.[51] There was a mixture of population and language and a diffusion of the foreign (Hellenic) culture unparalleled in the Persian period. To begin with, there were now many Hellenic cities in Palestine. The Jewish territory was practically in the midst of Hellenic cities: Ascalon, Akko (Ptolemais), Joppa (Jaffa), Apollonia and others on the coast; Samaria, Scythopolis and Gadara in the north; Pella, Gerasa, Philadelphia (Rabbath-Amana) beyond the river Jordan; and Marisa in the south. Here the Jews came into contact with Greek men, institutions, arts, soldiers from Aetolia or Macedonia, Greek poetasters and sculptors like the creator of the fine statue of the nude Aphrodite found at Carmel recently. They could see in Marisa, for instance, the Greek system of paved streets forming quadrangular blocks with a large open place at the main street, enlarged by colonnades, a view quite different from the maze that constituted an Oriental town. In Trans-Jordan there was a mixed settlement of Jewish and Greek soldiers under the command of a Jewish sheikh. There, in 259 B.C.E., a Greek from Cnidus in the service of this sheikh sold a Babylonian girl to a Greek traveler from Egypt. Among the guarantors and witnesses were a son of one Ananias and a Macedonian "of the cavalrymen of Tobias."

The Jewish territory itself was crowded with Greek officers, civil agents and traders, as the papyri show. Greek residents loaned money, bought and sold slaves, oil, wine, honey, figs, dates, while wheat was exported from Galilee. Greek caravans came up to Jerusalem too. On the other hand, the kings had inherited from the Persian monarchs crown lands, and there were in Judea estates belonging to royal courtiers. It happened, of course, as a papyrus tells, that a Greek usurer was driven out of a Jewish village when he tried to collect money for a debt; but, as this instance shows, even the village could not avoid the Greek commercial penetration. Another important factor was that now a foreign language, Greek, became that of business and administration. Even in the villages there must have been persons able to draft a contract in Greek, or to write a request in the style required for a Greek petition.

The influence of a new, foreign and technologically superior civilization acted, as usual, as a powerful dissolvent which destroyed the traditional discipline of life. The author of the Book of Jubilees[52] gives us insight into the moral situation of Palestinian Jewry after one and a half centuries of intensive contact with the Greeks. He fulminates against the evil generation who forgot the commandments and sabbaths. He repeatedly warns against associating with the pagans or eating with them. He lets Abraham implore his sons "not to take to themselves wives from the daughters of Canaan," nor to make idols and worship them. He even speaks of children of Israel "who will not circumcise their sons," and stresses the prohibition against appearing naked, that is, participating in Greek athletic games. It is particularly notable that he claims that the commandments were already observed by the Patriarchs and stresses again and again that ritual prescriptions are eternal ordinances. In fact, "every mouth speaking iniquity" already began to deny the perpetual force of the biblical regulations. As Esau says in the Book of Jubilees, "neither the children of men nor the beasts of the earth" have any oath valid forever: an echo of Greek philosophical criticism. Another contemporary writer, Ben Sira, speaks of the Jews who are ashamed of the Torah and its regulations, of ungodly men who have forsaken the Law of the Most High God. At the same time, probably unknown to Ben Sira, in Rome another adversary of Hellenism, Cato the Censor, applied himself to the reformation of the lax morals of Hellenized Rome where the newly coined word *pergraecari*, "act as a Greek," was used to signify the licentious way of life. But Cato surpassed the Jewish moralists in his antialien feelings. Ben Sira knows that wisdom has gained possession of every people and every nation, and he considers the physician ordained by God. Cato insists that Greek physicians came to Rome with the purpose of killing Romans by treatment, and under his influence Greek philosophers were expelled from Rome.

Nevertheless, it is rather difficult to gauge the impact of Greek civilization on Jewish thought in the third century B.C.E. Even if the Book of Kohelet (Ecclesiastes) was composed in this period, as the critics generally agree, it hardly shows any trace of Greek speculation. The outlook of the author is rather anti-intellectual: "he that increaseth knowledge, increaseth sorrow" (Eccl. 1:18). The whole philosophy of expediency which the author preaches, and even his lesson—make the best of the present day—belongs to the traditional teaching of wise men in the Orient. Significant only is his omission of traditional values. He does not attack these, but he emphatically denies their value: it is the same whether one sacrifices or not, "all things come alike to all" (Eccl. 9:2), "moment and chance" rule life (Eccl. 3:19). Ecclesiastes is prepared to accept anything because he doubts the value of everything. He mentions God thirty-eight times, but he also repeats thirty times that "all is vanity." It is in opposition to such a philosophy of relativity, dear to the "sons of Beliar," that the author of Jubilees stresses the heavenly origin of the traditional precepts of belief and ritual.

As it often happens, in order to uphold traditional values, their apologists themselves propose the most radical innovations. The author of the Book of Jubilees outdoes the later talmudic teaching in his severity as to the observance of ritual prescriptions. But to assert the everlasting validity of the Torah, this traditionalist places his own composition beside and even above Scripture, claims for his book a divine origin, and gives precepts which differ widely from those set forth in the Torah. The Bible says that the sun and the moon shall regulate seasons and days. In his paraphrase the author of Jubilees attacks the lunisolar calendar and strongly urges the adoption of his own system of a year of 364 days in which each holiday always falls on the same day of the week as ordained by God. Since the Jewish ecclesiastic calendar was built on the observation of the physical reappearance of the new moon, the apologist of orthodoxy simply proposes to turn upside down the whole structure of the ritual. The reason for his revolutionary idea is significant: the irregularity of the moon confuses the times. Thus, without realizing it, this traditionalist succumbs to the seduction of the Greek penchant for rationalization.

In the face of innovators, Hellenistic or pseudo-orthodox, the conservative forces, grouped around the Temple, stood fast and tried to uphold the established way of life.[53]

The literary representative of this conservative class was Jesus Ben Sira, a warm admirer of the High Priest Simeon. He realized that with him a venerable line of pious maxim writers came to an end: "I, indeed, came last of all," he says, "as one that gleaneth after the grape-gatherers." His social and religious ideas are conventional and the advice he addresses to his "son" (that is, pupil) aims at making him accept the present order. "The works of God are all good and He provides for every need in its time." Although he sharply denounces the oppressors who, by the multitude of their sacrifices, try to pacify God for sins—he that deprives the hireling of his hire sheds blood—he is convinced that poverty and wealth alike come from God. In these views, Ben Sira reproduces the traditional wisdom of the Orient. This traditional Oriental wisdom is further reflected in such general dicta as "he that runs after gold will not be guiltless." He also keeps the traditional tenets of religion, and implicitly rejects the new doctrine of the future life. He maintains that man can dominate his evil nature by strictly following the Law, he clings to the principle that the moral govern the world, that the wicked are punished, and that virtue leads to well-being while laziness and dissolution bring disaster. He strongly stresses man's own responsibility for his sins and his advice to his pupils is biblical: "with all thy strength love Him that made thee."

Historians classify, but life's strands are inextricably interwoven. The traditionalist Ben Sira is at the same time the first Jewish author to put his own name to his work and to emphasize his literary personality and individuality. He claims no prophetic inspiration, nor any apocalyptic revelation. He is bringing doctrine "for all those who seek instruction" and, like a Greek wandering philosopher of his time, proclaims: "Hear me, you great ones of the people and give ear to me, you, rulers of the congregation." He not only accepts the figure of personified wisdom (an originally Canaanite goddess), which appears in Proverbs, but puts this profane knowledge on a level with "the book of the Covenant of the Most High, the law which Moses commanded"—a rather bold effort to reconcile the synagogue with the Greek Academy, Jerusalem with Athens. Even the literary form of his book reflects the modernism which he combats. Ben Sira is fond of utilizing passages of Scripture as texts to comment upon in putting forth his own views on the subject. This practice was probably influenced by synagogue preaching.

The process of action and reaction produced in the third century B.C.E. by the suddenly intensified contact between Judaism and Hellenism led to curious changes in the usage of the Divine Name. The proper name of the national God (YHWH) ceased to be pronounced by the Jews in the course of the fifth century except in the Temple service and in taking an oath. The latter usage is attested to by a source used by Philo,[54] and it was preserved by the Samaritans as late as the fifth century of the Common Era. As the exceptions show, the motive for the disuse of the proper name was the idea that its utterance had magical power. The general belief in the magical efficacy of the proper name is well known, but in Canaan it became dominant about the beginning of the first millennium B.C.E. Thus, the Phoenician gods are anonymous[55] while the deities of the "Proto-Phoenicians" in the fourteenth century B.C.E. had proper names, as the texts of Ugarit show. The Jews accepted the idea of the unpronounceable Divine Name, only after the Exile. Their national God was now "the God in Jerusalem" or the "God of Heaven," a name which identified Him with the supreme deity of the Persians and the Syrian peoples. Accordingly, the pronunciation *Elohim* (God), and afterward *Adonai* (my Lord), was substituted for the tetragrammaton YHWH. When the Greeks came, the abstract term, "God," perfectly corresponded to their philosophical conception of the Supreme Being, *ho Theos*, the God, or *to Theion*, the Divine. So they accepted this indefinite designation for the God of the Jews. By a kind of reversed attraction, the Greek speculative term then influenced Hebrew writers. The Book of Kohelet speaks of God only as *Elohim*. One would expect, therefore, that when speaking Greek the Jews would designate their God as *ho Theos* or *to Theion*. As a matter of fact, they said *Kyrios*, a legal term meaning the legitimate master of someone or something, a word which as a substantive was not used in Greek religious language. It is simply a literal translation of the Hebrew appellative *Adonai* (the Lord), which became in the meantime the standard pronunciation of the awe-inspiring tetragrammaton. Since *Kyrios* was not intelligible to the Greeks and the term *Theos* had a rather general meaning, the Jews speaking or writing Greek in Palestine began in the third century B.C.E. to speak of their God as *Hypsistos*, "the Most High." In the same way, in the fifth century B.C.E. the Hellenized Thracians identified their supreme deity, *Sabazios*, with Zeus. And again, the Greek term reacted upon the Hebrew style. Already in Ben Sira the designation, "Most High God," is found forty-eight times, although the corresponding Hebrew term *Elyon* is very rare in the Bible. The same circumlocution is frequently used by the very anti-Greek author of the Book of Jubilees, and the same title was chosen by the Maccabean priest-kings to designate the God of Zion in their official Hebrew utterances. The Talmud quotes the formula: "In such a year of Johanan, priest of the Most High God."

But the most important result of the Greek impact on Palestinian Judaism was the formation of a Jewish intelligentsia, different from the clergy and not dependent on the sanctuary. The new class was known as "scribes." "Scribe," if not simply penman, was the technical term for a public official who entered the civil service as a profession. Accordingly, there were in the ancient Orient preparatory schools for future office-holders. From these institutions came the works of the mundane "wisdom" literature (like the biblical Proverbs), advising, as a Babylonian text says, "to fear God and the Law." But in the Hellenistic age Greek became the universal language of administration and business, and native writing and learning were rapidly becoming confined to the temples. The cuneiform documents of the Hellenistic age use the ideogram "priest" to denote the native notaries, and the latter act in Ptolemaic Egypt "in behalf" of a priest. Likewise, the native law in Ptolemaic Egypt was administered by a court of three priests. In both Egypt and Babylonia, so far as the native writing was still used, the priest was now the scribe, the judge and the sole teacher of the people, and the temples were only centers of native learning. The "Chaldeans," astrologers and astronomers who preserved the ancient science in Babylonia, were part of the clergy. At the same time as in Egypt and Mesopotamia the polytheistic Orient shrinks into a priestly dependence, there begins a cleavage between the sacerdotal and the secular interpreters of the Divine Law in Judaism. About 190 B.C.E. Ben Sira urges his hearers to honor the priest and to give him his portion according to the Law. He acknowledges the authority of the High Priest "over statutes and judgment," but it is the scribe who advises the rulers, and the assembly in the gate sits in the seat of the judge and expounds righteousness and judgment. The scribe is not a lawyer acting in behalf of a client; but like the Roman *juris periti* of the same period, a person who has such knowledge of the laws and customs as to act as authority for the judge to follow in his decisions. In both Jerusalem and Rome, the administration of justice was no longer in the hands of the priests in the third century B.C.E. Ecclesiastes mentions the "ten rulers" of the city who are not worth one Sage (Eccl. 7:19). Ben Sira mentions the jurisdiction of the popular assembly in the punishment of adultery. But for the most part he speaks of the "rulers." He advises his reader: Gain instruction so that you may "serve the potentate." Ben Sira has in mind the agents of the Macedonian kings, such as Zenon, well known on account of recently discovered papyri. As servant of his Greek master, the Jewish scribe becomes a legitimate interpreter of the Divine Law. In fact, still at the time of Malachi, that is, toward the end of the fifth century B.C.E., knowledge comes from the priest's lips and the people "seek the law at his mouth; for he is the messenger of the Lord of hosts" (Mal. 2:7). It is the priest who answers the questions concerning ritual cleanliness (Hag. 2:12). The Chronicler still regards instruction in the Law as the privilege and duty of the Levites and considers the "scribes" as a class of the Levites (II Chron. 34:13). But in the royal charter given to Jerusalem in 200 B.C.E. the "scribes of the sanctuary" form a special and privileged body. The foreign rulers of the Orient needed, of course, expert advice as to the laws and customs of their subjects. Antiochus III's proclamation concerning the ritual arrangements at Jerusalem could not be drafted without the collaboration of Jewish jurists. At the same time, the lay scribe, powerful in the council of the Greek potentates, became, owing to his influence with the foreign master, an authority in the Jewish assembly. "The utterance of a prudent man," says Ben Sira, "is sought for in the congregation," and he mentions in opposition to the scribe, the craftsman, whose opinion is not asked in the council of the people. Since all Jewish law and legal customs were derived from the Torah, the scribe became the authority as to the Law of Moses. He meditated on the Law of the Most High. But still, in the time of Ben Sira the knowledge of the Torah was considered only part of the intellectual qualifications required of the scribe. He had also to find out the hidden sense of parables and to search out the wisdom of all the ancients. Daniel, who explains the secret and meaning of royal dreams at the Babylonian court, is the ideal scribe as visualized by Ben Sira. On the other hand, the scribe is not only counselor of kings and assemblies, but also wise man and teacher. "Turn to me, you ignorant," says Ben Sira, "and tarry in my school." He promises as the fruit of his teaching the acquisition by the pupil of "much silver and gold." But he gives to his pupils "wisdom," "and all wisdom is from the Lord, and is with Him forever." So his scribe and his school of wisdom prepare for the coming of the Pharisaic scholar in the next generation. This Pharisaic scholar regards learning as the highest of human values and teaches that the fear of the Lord is the beginning of wisdom, but is prepared to serve his Master not for the sake of reward. However, between Ben Sira and the first Pharisees, there is the persecution of Antiochus and the revolution of the Maccabees.

6

The process of dispersion continued and created new ramifications of third-century Jewry. We learn, for instance, that toward the end of this century two thousand Jewish families from Babylonia were settled by the Seleucid government as military colonists in Lydia and Phrygia, and that at the beginning of the same century Ptolemy I transferred Jews and Samaritans from Palestine to Egypt. The wars between Alexander's successors brought many Jewish slaves, captured in Palestine, to the Alexandrian or Syrian markets. There was also a voluntary emigration; many went to Egypt, we are told, attracted by the humanity of the Ptolemies.

The bulk of Jewry was still established between the Euphrates and the Nile. But the fate of Alexander's empire divided the Levant into two parts. While the Jews in Egypt and, until 200 B.C.E., of Palestine owed allegiance to the Ptolemies, the Jews in the East and, after 200 B.C.E., in Palestine, were subjects of the Seleucids. The Hellenistic kingdoms were based on personal loyalty to the monarch rather than on national or territorial feeling. Since the Seleucids and the Ptolemies were perpetual rivals and antagonists who fought five wars in the third century, both dynasties tried to gain the favor of the Jews. It is significant that the biblical passage (Deut. 26:5), "A wandering Aramean was my father and he went down into Egypt," is changed to "My father forsook Syria and went down into Egypt" in the Alexandrian Greek version. Likewise, the Midrash for Passover evening, established by the authorities of the Temple under the Egyptian rule, changes the same scriptural sentence, giving to it the meaning that the "Aramean," that is, Laban, the personification of Syria, sought to destroy "my father," Jacob, so that the latter came to Egypt according to the Word of God. On the other hand, after 200 B.C.E., under the Seleucid domination, another composition in the Passover service put emphasis upon the anti-Egyptian implications of the

Exodus and upon Israel's Mesopotamian origins.[56] The fact that Jerusalem, the spiritual center of the Diaspora, belonged to one of the rival powers cast suspicion on the loyalty of the Jews under the domination of the other. In a paraphrase of the biblical history, the Book of Jubilees explains the enslavement of the Jews by Pharaoh as follows: "because their hearts and faces are toward the land of Canaan," ruled by the king of Syria.

In the light of these texts we may understand the origins of the Alexandrine version of the Bible.[56a] According to Jewish tradition, already known and standardized about 180 B.C.E., the Greek translation of the Torah was made about 280-250 B.C.E. in Alexandria upon the suggestion of King Ptolemy II. Modern critics reject the tradition without the slightest reason, and regard the undertaking as one of the Alexandrine community, intended to convert the heathen and to enable the Greek-speaking Jews to read the Scriptures.

Regardless of the auspices under which this translation was undertaken, the mere fact that the translation was made is of primary importance. Let us add that the Greek version of the Torah was soon followed by translations of other Jewish books. Throughout three centuries and more, the Jews did not cease from rendering their books into the world's common language. Psalms of the Temple and the Psalms ascribed to Solomon, the prophets of Old and the new fabricated revelations of Enoch and Moses, Job and Esther and the chronicles of the Maccabean dynasty were published in Greek. Looking back at this activity of translators, a later Rabbi explained the verse Gen. 9:27 as meaning: "Let them speak the language of Japhet in the tent of Shem."[57]

This venture of translating was unique in antiquity. There were in Greek some popular tales or missionary tracts adapted from Egyptian; some authentic traditions were preserved in Greek books which circulated under the name of Zoroaster or Ostanes. Contemporary with the Greek version of the Torah, an Egyptian priest (Manetho) and the Chaldean Berossus, and later some Phoenician authors, issued in Greek summaries "from the sacred books" of the history of their respective peoples. These compilations were, like similar works of Jewish or Roman writers, Demetrius, Fabius Pictor and later Flavius Josephus, adaptations made to Greek taste.

However, the esoteric character of priestly lore prevented a wholesale translation of the sacred books of the East. We know exactly hymns and rites of the Babylonian temples at Uruk (the biblical Erech) as used in the Hellenistic age, since we are able to decode the cuneiform signs. But the priests who copied these texts under the rule of the Seleucids abstained from translating their psalms and instructions into Greek. No wonder: in describing some rites, the author of the ancient text added: "The

Foreigner may not see it." Likewise, there is an abundant literature in Greek attributed to the Egyptian god of wisdom, Thoth, called in Greek Hermes. But these books hardly exhibit any Egyptian element, and the ignorance of their writers is such that they make "That," which is another spelling of "Thoth," refer to an independent divinity. Although the daily liturgy of Hellenized gods, such as Isis, was celebrated in Greek, the authentic sacred books of Egypt, carried by the priests in sacral processions, remained inaccessible to the Hellenes. An immense body of literature in Greek was ascribed to Zoroaster, but none of his votaries took the trouble to translate his authentic Hymns, and the Persian god Mithra always remained "unable to speak Greek."

In this way, while the Oriental religions remained unknown to a Western devotee, they lost ground in their native countries as well when the hieroglyphs and the cuneiforms began to be forgotten. In the second century B.C.E. the knowledge of sacred letters was already limited at Uruk in Babylonia to a small group of clerics. By translating liberally its literature, sacred and profane, new and old, into the world language, Judaism preserved its vitality. Moses and his law, or the revelations of Jewish seers, entered and filled in the mental world of the proselytes as if the latter had been born in Abraham's posterity. The Jews became "people of the Book" when this Book was rendered into Greek.

To return to the Greek version of the Torah, it was done with due regard for the Greek reader. The Rabbinic tradition recalls the fact that the translators at times changed their text out of deference to pagan sensitivity.

A classic instance is Lev. 11:6, where the Greek version renders the word "hare" among the unclean animals by "rough foot," because the Greek word for hare (*Lagos*) was the epithet for the ancestor of the Ptolemaic Dynasty. Even more important is the religious terminology of the translation. Although the ineffable Name was transliterated in the Greek Bible it was pronounced as *Kyrios*, the Lord. Likewise, the version omits other appellations of the God of Israel, such as *Adonai*, *Shaddai*, *Sabaot*, which continued to be used in Palestine. In their place, the version employs expressions such as "the God," "the Almighty," etc. In this way the particular God of Abraham, Isaac and Jacob becomes in Greek the Supreme Being of mankind. This representation of the original meaning corresponds to the religious trend of the Greek world. In the Greek Diaspora the local deities, let us say of Thebes or Crete, gave place to the universal Olympians, and the latter, losing their individuality, became simply different forms of the same universal deity of salvation and benefaction.

Consider another example. The term, "Torah," should be rendered in Greek by words expressing some kind of authority. But its regular rendering in the version is *Nomos*, "the Law," or better, "the constitution." Thus, the Pentateuch in Greek appeared as the legal corpus of Jewry. But while the translators tried to present Judaism as universalistic, they were no less intent on emphasizing the difference between the true religion and heathenism. For instance, they purposely used different Greek terms when speaking of the Temple or the Altar or the service of the true God and, on the other hand, when mentioning idolatry. In a hymn of praise, written in 261 B.C.E., a Greek contemporary of the translators glorified the Egyptian deity who had cured him.[58] The technical terms of praise he uses, such as *arete*, *dynamis*, *kratos* do not occur, with regard to the Lord, in the Greek Pentateuch. With the same purpose of separating the Supreme Being from the anthropomorphic idols of the Greeks, the version avoids expressions attributing human forms and passions to the Lord. For instance, Ex. 24:10 tells that the Elders coming up toward Sinai with Moses "saw the God of Israel." The Greek version reads: they saw the place "where the God of Israel had stood." But neither the Greek version of the Bible nor the works of Berossus and Manetho, written for the Greek public, attained their object. The Greeks preferred their own quite fantastic versions of Oriental history. They repeated, for instance, despite Berossus' protest, that Babylon was founded by the dissolute Queen Semiramis, and said that Judah, the ancestor of the Jews, was a son of the same legendary queen. Neither Berossus nor Manetho is quoted by Greek historians, but both were read and used as sources of astrological and magical knowledge. Likewise, the Septuagint is quoted a few times by philosophers. Later pagan speculation might, like the author of *Poimandres,* employ the biblical history of creation to express a new religious feeling. But Greek scholarship intentionally ignored the Bible as well as Berossus or Manetho because the Greeks regarded, quite naturally, their own tradition of the mythical past as trustworthy and consequently rejected as unreliable myths the contradictory Oriental accounts.

Relations between the Jews and the pagans in the Dispersion continued to be friendly or indifferent. Philosophers considered the strict observance of the Sabbath as superstition. A writer could reproduce the malicious anecdote, invented by the Idumeans, about the foolishness of the people of Jerusalem. But there is no anti-Jewish passage in Greek literature before the Maccabean struggle nor any recorded anti-Jewish action. The details of daily life of the Jews in the Diaspora before the Maccabean age are almost unknown, except for Egypt. Here we find Jews transacting business with other colonists. They were legally regarded as "Hellenes," in opposition to the native "Egyptians." There is, for instance, a judgment of a Ptolemaic court of 226 B.C.E. concerning an alleged assault. Both parties were Jews, but the legal guardian of the defendant, a Jewess, was an Athenian, the witnesses of the summons were a Thracian and a Persian, and the case was decided according to Greek law. The juridical situation of the Jews in Ptolemaic Egypt, and in the Diaspora generally, is sufficiently clear. The difficulty begins when we try to appreciate the cultural relations between Jews and pagans. The number "6" was called "Eve of Sabbath" in the slang of gamblers in Alexandria.[59] What did the Greeks know of the Jewish religion? Around 200 B.C.E. a Jewish poetaster wrote a tragedy describing the Exodus. The author (Ezekiel) follows Hellenistic dramatic techniques and imitates Euripides. But was his composition written for heathen readers or was it intended to take the place in Jewish education of Greek plays based on mythology? The most impressive witness and the most important feature of Judaism coming into contact with Hellenism was the conversion of Greeks. There were, of course, always "strangers who joined themselves unto the Lord" (Jub. 55:10), but it was only in the Hellenistic age that proselytism became widespread. To understand the phenomenon, let us note at the outset that new adherents unto the Lord were all, or almost all, Greeks or Hellenized natives of Greek cities. The people of the countryside continued to speak their native languages and stubbornly worshiped their traditional gods. An Anatolian or Egyptian peasant did not care much for any deity in Greek garb, whether from Olympus or from Zion. The Greek translation of the Pentateuch represented the Most High God of the Dispersion as speaking Greek. The Alexandrine version of the Torah was made before 250 B.C.E. No part of the Bible, however, was translated by the Jews into any tongue other than Greek—not even Latin, although some Latin formulae were used by Latin-speaking Jews in Africa and Italy in the second and third centuries C.E.

All translations of the Bible, except those into Greek, were the results of Christian missionary activity. The Ethiopian eunuch, returning from a pilgrimage to Jerusalem, was reading Isaiah (Acts 8:28) in Greek when met by the Apostle Philip on the road. Probably no Jew in Egypt ever tried to reach the natives who spoke only dialects of the Egyptian tongue. He was "Hellene" and as such he discriminated against the people who did not know Greek. Nothing seemed to him more unfair than the idea of degrading himself to the condition of the natives. On the other hand, the people of the cities were in a propitious mood to receive foreign missionaries. The new cities of the Near East were new homes for settlers whether they came from Athens or from Caria. Of course, everybody took with him to his new home his ancestral idols and did not neglect the age-old shrines of the new country's deities. But gods and men alike were upset on a new soil. There was room for unknown deities who might stir new hopes and quiet fears; and there was the fascinating appeal of the divine forces of the mysterious East, of gods who were old before the birth of Zeus.[60] Accordingly, many Oriental cults started missionary efforts among the "Hellenes." An Egyptian priest brought the worship of Serapis to Delos, the sacred island of the Greeks, at about the beginning of the third century B.C.E. A shrine was erected to the Syrian Atargatis in an Egyptian village by a Macedonian soldier in 222 B.C.E. Before the end of the third century B.C.E. the mysteries of the Persian Mithra spread among the Greeks in Egypt. Jewish propaganda followed the same road and the same pattern. The same term *proselytos* (*advena*),[61] that is "one who has arrived at or to," was used for both the converts to the Lord and the converts to the Egyptian Isis. Unfortunately, we do not have dated evidence of Jewish proselytism before the Maccabean period. But when we are told that in 139 B.C.E. Jews were expelled from Rome for attempting "to infect" Roman morals with their cult, we may postulate that proselytism in the Near East must have started before the beginning of the second century B.C.E. It seems that in early Hellenism the people who completely accepted Judaism by circumcision and baptism, and refused to take part any longer in pagan ceremonies, were rather rare. But there were numerous Hellenes who revered the Most High without observing all the prescriptions of the Torah. Some early Hellenistic texts throw light on the state of mind of such "God-fearers."[62] About 180 B.C.E. a minister of Seleucus IV of Syria attempted to extort money from the Temple treasury, but failed ignominiously. His defeat, immortalized by Raphael's *Storia di Eliodoro,* was, of course, explained in Jerusalem as a miracle. The story was told of Heliodorus who, scourged by angels, had been ordered to "declare unto all men the mighty power of God." He then testified to all men the works of the Great God, whom he had seen with his eyes. Heliodorus did not become a Jew but the stripes received at the hands of the angels convinced him that the Lord of Zion is above all gods (II Macc. 2:4). In the same way, according to Jewish legend, Alexander the Great prostrated himself before the High Priest, and Nebuchadnezzar had to recognize that the Most High God does according to His will, "in the host of heaven and among the inhabitants of the earth" (Dan. 4:32).

Since pagan cults were polytheistic, their propaganda tried to persuade men only of the relative superiority of a particular deity. The Jewish mission adopted the same pattern. For example, there is a Jewish tale of Bel and Daniel. Deceived by a trick of Bel's priests, the Persian king exclaims, "Great art thou, Bel, and there is not with him deceit." But Daniel explodes the pretended miracle, and the king recognizes that great is the Lord, God of Daniel, and there is none other beside Him. The Book of Jonah describes a Jewish missionary who calls for repentance and is sent to foreign lands, where the name of the Lord is already known and revered. The sailors on Jonah's ship are heathen, praying, every man, to his own idol, but they all fear the Lord exceedingly. These sailors, or Heliodorus of the Jewish tale, resemble the adherents of syncretistic cults who worshiped the Lord as the Supreme Master of the Universe, but placed under Him, or beside Him, other divine forces. Such were, for example, some religious societies in Asia Minor which fused the Phrygian *Sabazios* with *Sabaot*, observed the Sabbath, but refused to accept the exclusive attitude of Judaism toward pagan worship. The existence of such "God-fearers" extended the influence of Judaism, of course, and the sons of semiproselytes often became full converts. But the recognition of such followers of Judaism sapped the foundations of the latter. A Jewish latitudinarian, such as a certain Artapanus, could endeavor to identify Moses with Thot-Hermes, a central figure in Hellenistic syncretism, and ascribe to the apostle of monotheism the establishment of the Egyptian cult of animals.

On the other hand, let us again open the Book of Jonah. The people of Nineveh who were and who remained pagans did not perish because they fasted and, covered with sackcloth, cried mightily unto God. Such is the lesson of this book: God is abundant in mercy and will have pity on the great city "wherein are more than sixscore thousand persons that cannot discern between their right hand and their left hand, and also much cattle." The design of the book is not to teach the universality of Divine grace, as the critics say today. This point is already presumed by the author. But as the Rabbis explained and the Church Father, Chrysostom, saw, the question of Jonah is whether contrition per se, even that of unbelievers, is sufficient to turn away God's anger. The Jewish author of the biblical book affirms it. The universal church, as well as the mosque, answers in the negative—*extra ecclesiam nulla salus*. This answer as well as Jonah's misgivings about God's compassion are easy to understand. If the repentance of the unbeliever avails him, if he may share the favor of Heaven without assuming the yoke of the Law, why the necessity to enter the fold? Why should a Jew by birth observe the numberless minute ritual precepts which involve social disapproval and, for instance, bar him from the royal table? The generous universalism of the Book of Jonah was more dangerous to institutional Judaism than the indifference of Ecclesiastes. The confusion of the syncretists helped to inspire the reform of the Jewish religion about 175 B.C.E. under the auspices of Antiochus Epiphanes.

7

Palestine is the bulwark of Egypt. As Napoleon observed, domination over Palestine is indispensable if one wishes to protect the valley of the Nile. Accordingly, the rivalry between the court of Alexandria and that of Syria was concentrated in Palestine. Although in 200 B.C.E. the land came under the control of Syria, there was a pro-Egyptian party in every important city, including Jerusalem. Now, in 168 B.C.E., Antiochus IV, Epiphanes of Syria, who the year before had conquered Egypt and had made himself Pharaoh at Memphis with the traditional Egyptian ceremony, was compelled by Rome's order to withdraw completely from Egypt. He went back along the Phoenician coast, "groaning and in bitterness of heart," as an ancient historian says. The pro-Egyptian party made use of this opportunity to attempt to seize power. The Phoenician city of Aradus refused to admit the king and had to be taken by storm. Likewise, at Jerusalem the pro-Egyptian party struck, seized the city, drove out the Seleucid High Priest Menelaus, and again installed the High Priest Jason who had been deposed by Antiochus three years before. The king suppressed the revolt and made Jerusalem pay for the rebellion. According to the ancient code of political morals, a city was regarded as a person and had to bear collective responsibility for the deeds of its inhabitants. Usually, a rebellious city lost its rank; its walls were destroyed and it became a village, dependent on another, faithful community. The same punishment was inflicted on Jerusalem. But this measure assumed in the case of Jerusalem a revolutionary character. A Greek city or an Oriental people was a social group. Looked at from one point of view, Jerusalem appeared as a state, but from another as a church.

When Antiochus III seized the Holy City in 200 B.C.E., he, as usual, confirmed the rights and privileges of Jerusalem and, above all, the re-establishment of the traditional institutions. "All the members of the nations shall live in accordance with their traditional laws."[63] Such a formula would mean in a Greek city a guarantee of its political constitution. But in Jerusalem it signified the validity of the Mosaic law, the obligatory observance of the Sabbath, and the prohibition of pagan shrines on Jewish territory. To make Jerusalem a mere dependency of a Greek city, now established on a hill opposite the Temple, meant the abolition of the force of the Mosaic law in Judea. But this negative measure must not be confused with persecution. Nobody was any longer compelled to observe the Sabbath or other ritual precepts, but nobody was prevented from doing so. The tradition does not mention any conflict between the government and the faithful during this stage of reformation. But about a year and a half later, toward the end of 167, new royal decrees initiated the persecution. The Temple was desecrated and there was erected "the abomination of desolation." Swine's flesh was offered, and idols set up. Circumcision and the observance of Jewish feasts were forbidden, and death was declared the penalty for disobedience. Local commissioners carried out the king's orders, compelling Judea, city by city, to sacrifice to idols and to eat unclean food. The copies of the Torah were burned "and there was very great wrath upon Israel." Such a persecution is a unique phenomenon in Greek history, almost without precedent in the whole history of the ancient world. We must go back to the fourteenth century B.C.E. when the Pharaoh Ikhnaton worshiped the sun "as the only god, beside whom there is no other," or look to the persecution of the Christians under the Roman Emperor Decius (249 C.E.) to find a parallel to Epiphanes's folly. How are we to explain his action?

The First Book of Maccabees says that Antiochus "wrote to his whole kingdom, that all should be one people, and every one should leave his laws, and all the heathen consented to the commandment of the king." But there was no uniformity in religion throughout Epiphanes's kingdom; for example, Babylonian priests, as the dates on cuneiform tablets show, continued to copy ancient Chaldean religious texts at the same time as the books of the Torah were destroyed in Jerusalem. So far as we know, the persecution of Antiochus dealt with Judea only; the Dispersion was touched sporadically, on local initiative, for instance at Ptolemais (Acco). The Samaritans were harassed by an overly zealous Seleucid governor, but the molestation ceased when they stated that they were not Jews and had chosen to live in accordance with Greek customs, although they continued to observe the Sabbath and to follow the Law of Moses. Contrary to the plan ascribed to him by most modern historians, Antiochus Epiphanes did not attempt to destroy Judaism root and branch, but continued to respect the fiscal privileges of the Temple and to recognize "the nation of the Jews" presided over by the "Senate." Thus, as a matter of fact, there was no intention of forcing changes in any religion except that of the Jews living in the province of Judea, the center of which was now the Greek city of the "Acra," literally the "Citadel," established on the site of Jerusalem. On the other hand, as the accounts show, the new cult introduced into the Temple was not that of the Greek gods of Antiochus Epiphanes. Now called by the Greek name "Zeus Olympios," the God of the Temple was still the Most High God of Abraham, Isaac and Jacob. But He was now worshiped in a new manner which strangely combined lofty ideas of Greek enlightenment with the antique rites of Baal. He was no longer alone in the sanctuary. There were other deities; there were idols. But He was regarded as invisibly present on the altar and He was worshiped under the open sky. The meaning of all this is illumined by another passage of I Macc.: "In those days went there out of Israel wicked men, who persuaded many saying: let us go and make a covenant with the heathen that are round about us. For since we departed from them, many evils have found us." The Hellenizing party, heir to the latitudinarian spirit of the Book of Jonah and of the work of Artapanus, came to power in Judea with the accession of the High Priest Menelaus. Convinced that the maintenance of their peculiar customs cut the Jews off from the rest of the world, the reformers attempted to effect a fusion of Judaism and Hellenism. As Ezra and Nehemiah had imposed their views through the authority of the Persian kings in the past, similarly Menelaus had recourse to royal edicts in order to compel the Jews of Judea and Jerusalem to obedience. The legal fact that, since Ezra and Nehemiah, the Torah was enforced at Jerusalem by secular authority necessarily forced every reformer of Judaism to appeal to the heathen overlord of Jerusalem. Of course, the king and the court regarded the reform with favor. It appeared in Greek eyes as a very reasonable overthrow of meaningless and particularistic customs. The opposition to the royal decrees by the Jews, faithful to their ancestral religion, was regarded by the administration as wickedness and rebellion, and persecution resulted.

We need not dwell here on the events that followed. Everyone knows how the godly Jews, led by the Maccabees, delivered the nation and the Temple from oppression and opprobrium. The Syrians ended the persecution in the winter of 164-163 and re-established freedom of religion. In December, 164, Judah Maccabeus recovered Jerusalem and the Temple. In February, 162, after the death of Antiochus IV, the court conceded the restoration of the Temple and of the Jewish way of life "according to the customs of their forefathers." The execution of Menelaus and the appointment of a new High Priest, Alcimus, who was recognized by the most pious among the children of Israel, marks the end of the conflict.

The conflict showed that Judaism could not continue to follow the ancestral way. The reformation of Menelaus, although a folly, was a response to a living problem. In Egypt, in Babylonia, in Syria, the sacerdotal caste was the most narrow-minded element of the population, the citadel of anti-Hellenic sentiments. In Jerusalem, the priests took the lead in introducing Greek fashions, and neglecting the sacrifices they hastened to athletic games. But Judaism was not a religion of idols but of the Living God. Since the solution of Menelaus was incompatible with Judaism, what was the way to follow?

The Hellenistic civilization was supranational and universal, the same at Antioch as at Athens or Alexandria. It was not bound to a faith or a creed, but had its source in the common education. Without forsaking one's particular gods and customs, one could become a "Hellene" through a Greek school, through the assimilation of the Hellenic civilization. And this civilization, open to everyone, was that of the rulers of the world. The classic Orient was in the same position with regard to Hellenism as the East today is *vis-à-vis* Western civilization. Whether the latter brings penicillin or atomic bombs, the theory of relativity or relativity in morals, it always stands for power and is indispensable to survival; so in the ancient world was the Hellenic civilization the force of progress for good and evil. Only two peoples in antiquity accepted Hellenic civilization—the

Romans and the Jews. The others remained averse to it. The Egyptian clergy in the Hellenistic age copied in hieroglyphic writings formulae and texts of the period of Egyptian greatness, the New Empire, more than a thousand years older. As a result, the native intelligentsia in the Orient became completely Hellenized and lost every relation to the indigenous culture. No new literary work was created in cuneiform during the Greek period, but there were numerous Greek writers of Mesopotamian origin. The Oriental sanctuaries in the Greek age rigidly reproduced the traditional plan, but nobody scoffed at Oriental gods more vigorously than Lucian of Samosata, whose native tongue was Aramean. Full of pride in the glorious past, boasting that no change had ever taken place in their traditions, the Orientals set their face against all innovations—and lost the future. The difficulty was that Hellenism, although universal, was by no means cosmopolitan. The ranks of "Hellenes" were open on condition that the neophyte become a Greek and prove himself to be a Greek.[64] But the Oriental traditional attitude was diametrically opposed to Greek enlightened rationalism. Dietary laws made it impossible for a Jew to eat meat at the table of a pagan. A Syrian, an Egyptian, a Phoenician, had his own food peculiarities preventing him from accepting Greek hospitality. For instance, fish was sacred to Atargatis, and thus, forbidden food to the Syrians, a peculiarity which provoked numberless Greek "digs" at that "superstition." The sanctity of the cock was a feature of the Iranian religion,[65] while the Egyptian priests had often to follow a vegetable diet. Likewise, the refinement of the rules of uncleanness was common to all ancient religions. A mere touch of a dove made a Syrian unclean for a day. Hellenization was to be had only at the price of dropping these peculiarities and following the Greek patterns of behavior. How was one to unite in sentiment and conduct one's peculiar tradition with Greek universalism? The Jews alone among all the Orientals facing this problem were able to accept Hellenic civilization and also preserve their individuality.

It was the task of the Maccabean age and of the following generations to find solutions for this ever-recurring problem. It is beyond the scope of this essay to detail the history of this adaptation, but some general remarks about it may be allowed.[66] The solution, invented by the Maccabees and applied by the Pharisees[66a] and Rabbis, was the assimilation of Greek features which could enrich and renew Judaism. For instance, post-Maccabean Judaism adopted the most important idea of Hellenism, that of *paideia*, of perfection through liberal education. Even Ben Sira, in agreement with the general view of the ancient Orient, stated that the craftsman or the peasant "whose discourse is with bullocks," cannot gain wisdom. The Pharisees regarded universal instruction as basic to Judaism. They established a school in every village in the land of Israel; in the same way a *gymnasion* was a necessary feature of every Greek settlement. The Jewish school gave instruction in the Scripture and the Unwritten Law, cultivated the sacred language; its ideal was the scholar, versed in the Holy Writ, not the athletic gentleman of the *gymnasion*. The transformation of Judaism into a more complex civilization through the introduction of Greek concepts and methods came through the adaptation of Hellenic ideas to the problems raised for Judaism by the very contact with the universal culture. While the Egyptians ascribed to their glorious sage Imhotep sayings of Greek wisdom,[67] the Jews circulated publications in which leaders of Greek civilization, Sophocles or Orpheus, proclaimed the monotheistic faith, quoted Scripture, glorified the Sabbath and repeated injunctions not to eat any flesh with blood. Thus the Jews remained the only one people in antiquity which dealt effectively with Greek culture. It is no accident that the spiritual revolution which ended the ancient world came from Jerusalem. Jerusalem was the only living center beyond the authority of Hellenism, the one refuge of independent thought. There was a place where it was possible to stand outside the Hellenic earth, and from there, and only from there, could this earth be moved.

Notes

[1] *Herod*, III, 19.

[2] See the present writer's paper "An Edict of Cyrus," in *Journ. of Bibl. Lit.*, LXV, 1944.

[3] Berosus ap. Josephus, *Contra Apionem*, I, 150.

[4] Maurice Holleaux, *Etudes d'épigraphie et d'histoire grecques*, (Paris, 1938), I, 1.

[5] On Sephararvain cf. William Foxwell Albright, *Archaeology and the Religion of Israel* (Baltimore, 1942), p. 163.

[6] On chronology cf. Albright, *op. cit.*, p. 168.

[7] See A. Dupont-Sommer, *Revue de l'histoire des religions*, CXXX (Paris, 1945, 17-28) and *Comptes-Rendus de l'Académie des Inscriptions* (1947), pp. 175-191.

[8] Sidney Smith, *Babylonian Historical Texts* (London, 1924), p. 145.

[9] Albright, "Light on the Jewish State in Persian Times," in *Bull. Amer. Sch. Or. Res.*, No. 53, p. 20.

[10] M. Rostovtzeff, *Social and Economic History of the Hellenistic World.* (Oxford, 1941) III, 1324.

[11] On the so-called "Naucratis" inscription see the literature quoted by G. Posener in *Annales du Service des Antiquités de l'Égypte* (Paris, 1934), p. 141.

[12] See E. Bikerman, "Héliodore au Temple de Jérusalem," in *Annuaire de l'Institut de Philologie et d'Histoire Orientales* (Université de Bruxelles), 1939-1942, VII, 14.

[13] Hecataeus ap. Jos. *C. Ap.* I. 188.

[14] For archaeological evidence cf. Rostovtzeff, *op. cit.*, p. 1325, see also McCown, *Tell En-Nashbeh,* I (Berkeley, 1947).

[15] Clearchus ap. Jos. *C. Ap.* I, 176, Cf. Hans Lewy, "Aristotle and the Jewish Sage According to Clearchus of Soli," in *Harv. Theo. Rev.*, XXXI, No. 3, p. 205.

[16] A. Reifenberg, *Ancient Jewish Coins* (Jerusalem, 1947).

[17] Reifenberg, *op. cit.*, #1a. A Hebrew shekel (3.88 gr.) in silver, obv.: male head bearded; Rv.: Female head; Inscr. (in Hebrew): "one half."

[18] Reifenberg, *op. cit.*, Plate I, #3.

[19] Louis Finkelstein, *The Pharisees* (Philadelphia, 1938), II, p. 566.

[20] C. C. Torrey, *The Second Isaiah* (New York, 1928), p. 126, has already vigorously protested against this misconception. cf. Finkelstein, *op. cit.*, p. 461.

[21] It is a pity that N. D. Fustel de Coulanges's *La Cité Antique,* published in 1864, is almost unknown outside of France.

[22] Eur., *Electra,* 795.

[23] Eur., *Ion,* 588.

[24] Cf. A. D. Nock, *Conversion* (London, 1933), p. 20.

[25] Eur., *Heracl.,* 348.

[[25a] Cf. above William Foxwell Albright, "The Biblical Period," pp. 50 ff.]

[26] A. T. Olmstead, *History of Assyria* (New York, 1923), p. 580.

[27] Cf. Albright, *From the Stone Age to Christianity* (Baltimore, 1929), pp. 242 and 245.

[28] G. Glotz, *The Greek City and its Institutions* (New York, 1929), p. 258.

[29] C. N. Cochrane, *Christianity and Classical Culture* (Oxford, 1944), p. 462.

[30] Dion. Halic., *De. Thuc.* 5. I quote the translation of the passage in Lionel Pearson, *Early Ionian Historians* (Oxford, 1939), p. 3.

[31] Adolf Erman, *The Literature of the Ancient Egyptians* (London, 1927), pp. 58 and 95.

[32] Cf., too, an inscription of Shalmaneser III in D. D. Luckenbill, *Ancient Records of Assyria and Babylonia* (Chicago, 1926-1927), II. The narrative begins in the first person (#623) and continues in the third person (#624).

[33] R. W. Rogers, *Cuneiform Parallels to the Old Testament* (New York, 1912), p. 380.

[34] Such fictitious documents are already included in the Egyptian cycle of stories of Petubastis, a kind of historical novel which is presented as a work of historiography. See G. Maspero, *Popular Stories of Ancient Egypt,* (New York, 1915), pp. 242 and 256.

[35] See Rostovtzeff, *op. cit.*, III, 1326.

[36] *Herod,* II, 30 and 154.

[37] Albright, "King Joachim in Exile," in *Biblical Archaeologist,* V, No. 4, p. 51.

[38] W. Eilers, in *Zeitschr. Deutsch. Morgenlaend. Ges.,* 1940, p. 225.

[39] See S. Daiches, *The Jews of Babylonia,* (London, 1910).

[40] A. E. Cowley *Aramaic Papyri of the Fifth Century* (Oxford, 1923). Some 125 ostraca will be published by A. Dupont-Sommer in the *Corpus Inscriptionum Semiticarum.* See his papers quoted above in n. 7.

[41] E. Dhorme in *Revue d'Assyriologie,* 1928.

[42] F. L. Griffith, *Catalogue of the Demotic Papyri in the John Rylander Library* (Manchester, 1909), p. 60.

[43] See Bickerman, "Un Document relatif à la persécution d'Antiochus IV Epiphane," in *Revue de l'Histoire des Religions*, CXV, p. 188.

[44] Lewy, "Hekataios von Abdera," in *Zeitschr. Neutest. Wissen.*, XXXI, p. 117.

[45] W. Jaeger, "Greeks and Jews: The First Greek Records of Jewish Religion and Civilization," in *Journal of Religion*, XVIII, p. 38.

[46] Lewy, *op. cit.*, n. 15.

[47] We do not know whether oil was also distributed to the people who did not frequent the "gymnasia." Cf. Jeanne et Louis Robert, *Inscriptions grecques de Lydie*, p. 129.

[48] F. Pfister, "Eine juedische Gruendungsgeschichte Alexandrias," in *Sitz. Heidelberger Akad. Wissen.*, XI, July, 1914.

[49] See Bikerman, *Institutions des Séleucides* (Paris, 1938), p. 165.

[50] Polybius, XVI, 39, 5.

[51] Rostovtzeff, *op. cit.*, Index s.v. Palestine.

[52] On the Book of Jubilees: Finkelstein, "Pre-Maccabean Documents in the Passover Haggadah," in *Harv. Theo. Rev.*, XXXVI, p. 19.

[53] On the phantom of the so-called "Great Synagogue," which is often evoked by modern writers on this period, see my note in *Revue Biblique*, XXXI, 1948.

[54] W. L. Knox, *Some Hellenistic Elements in Primitive Christianity* (London, 1944), p. 48.

[55] See Bickerman, "Anonymous Gods," in *Journ. of the Warburg Inst.*, I, p. 58.

[56] Finkelstein, "The Oldest Midrash: Pre-Rabbinic Ideals and Teachings in the Passover Haggadah," in *Harv. Theo. Rev.*, XXXI, p. 291 and XXXVI, p. 19.

[[56a] Cf. below Ralph Marcus, "Hellenistic Jewish Literature," pp. 1077-1081.]

[57] S. Lieberman, *Greek in Jewish Palestine*, (Philadelphia, 1942).

[58] See Bataille's paper quoted in n. 67.

[59] P. Perdrizet, in *Bull. de l'Inst. Français d'Archéol. Orient.*, XXX, 5.

[60] See the classic book of Franz Cumont, *Les religions orientales dans le paganisme romain* (4th ed., Paris, 1929).

[61] R. Reitzenstein, *Die hellenistischen Mysterienreligionen* (3rd ed., Leipzig, 1927), p. 193.

[62] See paper quoted in n. 12.

[63] Josephus *Antt.* XII, 29. Cf. Bickerman, "La Charte Séleucide de Jérusalem," in *Rev. études juiv.*, C, 4.

[64] Bickerman, "Sur une Inscription Grecque de Sidon," in *Mélanges Syriens offerts à M. R. Dussaud,* (Paris, 1938), I, 96.

[65] Cumont in *Comptes-Rendus Acad. des Inscr.* (1942), p. 85.

[66] Cf. Bickerman, *The Maccabees* (New York, 1947), pp. 85-97.

[[66a] On the Pharisees cf., below, Judah Goldin, "The Period of the Talmud," pp. 117-158.]

[67] U. Wilcken, "Zur aegyptisch-hellenistischen Litteratur," in *Aegyptiaca*,

Festschrift fuer Georg Ebers (Leipzig, 1897), p. 142; cf. A. Bataille in *Etudes de Papyrologie,* IV (1935), 125.

BIBLIOGRAPHY

ALBRIGHT, WILLIAM FOXWELL, *Archaeology and the Religion of Israel.* Baltimore, 1942.

———, *From the Stone Age to Christianity.* Baltimore, 1940.

BICKERMAN, ELIAS, *Institutions des Séleucides.* Paris, 1938.

———, *The Maccabees.* New York, 1947.

COCHRANE, CHARLES NORRIS, *Christianity and Classical Culture.* Oxford, 1944.

COULANGES, FUSTEL N. D. de, *La Cité Antique.* 28th ed., Paris, 1924.

COWLEY, A. E., *Aramaic Papyri of the Fifth Century.* Oxford, 1923.

CUMONT, FRANZ, *Les religions orientales; dans le paganisme romain.* 4th ed., Paris, 1929.

DAICHES, SAMUEL, *The Jews of Babylonia.* London, 1910.

ERMAN, ADOLF, *The Literature of the Ancient Egyptians.* London, 1927.

FINKELSTEIN, LOUIS, *The Pharisees.* Philadelphia, 1938, 2 vols.

GLOTZ, G., *The Greek City and its Institutions.* New York, 1929.

GRIFFITH, F. L., *Catalogue of the Demotic Papyri in the John Rylander Library*, Manchester, 1909.

HOLLEAUX, MAURICE, *Etudes d'épigraphie et d'histoire grecques.* Paris, 1938.

KNOX, WILFRED L., *Some Hellenistic Elements in Primitive Christianity.* London, 1944.

LIEBERMAN, S., *Greek in Jewish Palestine.* Philadelphia, 1942.

LUCKENBILL, D. D., *Ancient Records of Assyria and Babylonia.* Chicago, 1926-1927. 2 vols.

MASPERO, G., *Popular Stories of Ancient Egypt.* New York, 1915.

MCCOWN, C. C., *Tell-En-Nasbeh.* Berkeley, 1947. Vol. I.

NOCK, A. D., *Conversion.* London, 1933.

OLMSTEAD, A. T., *History of Assyria.* New York, 1923.

PEARSON, LIONEL, *Early Ionian Historians.* New York, 1929.

REIFENBERG, A., *Ancient Jewish Coins.* 2nd ed., Jerusalem, 1947.

REITZENSTEIN, R., *Die hellenistischen Mysterienreligionen.* 3rd ed., Leipzig, 1927.

ROBERT, JEANNE ET LOUIS, *Inscriptions grecques de Lydie* (Hellenica VI). Paris, 1948.

ROGERS, R. W., *Cuneiform Parallels to the Old Testament.* New York, 1912.

ROSTOVTZEFF. M., *Social and Economic History of the Hellenistic World.* Oxford, 1941.

SMITH, SIDNEY (translator), *Babylonian Historical Texts.* London, 1924.

TORREY, CHARLES C., *The Second Isaiah.* New York, 1928.

ALBRIGHT, WILLIAM FOXWELL, "King Joachin in Exile," in *Biblical Archaeologist*, V, No. 4. New Haven, 1942.

———, "Light on the Jewish State in Persian Times," in *Bulletin of the American Schools of Oriental Research,* No. 53, Baltimore, 1934.

BATAILLE, A., "Nouveau Fragment . . . ," in *Etudes de Papyrologie,* IV. Paris, 1938.

BICKERMAN, E., "Héliodore au Temple de Jérusalem" in *Annuaire de l'Institut de Philologie et d'Histoire Orientales*, VII. Université de Bruxelles, 1939-1942.

———, "An Edict of Cyrus," in *Journal of Biblical Literature*. LXV, 1944. New Haven.

———, "Anonymous Gods," in *Journal of the Warburg Institute,* I. New York.

———, "Sur une Inscription Grecque de Sidon," in *Mélanges syriens offerts à M. R. Dussaud,* I. Paris, 1938.

———, "Un Document relatif à la persécution d'Antiochus IV Epiphane," in *Revue de l'Histoire des Religions,* CXV. Paris.

———, "La Charte Séleucide de Jérusalem," in *Revue des Etudes Juives,* C. Paris.

———, "Viri magnae Congregationis," *Revue Biblique,* Paris, 1948.

CASSUTO, U., "The Gods of the Jews of Elephantine," in *Kedem,* Studies in Jewish Archaeology (Hebrew), I, edited by E. L. Sukenik, Jerusalem, 1942.

CUMONT, F., "Le coq blanc des Mazdéens," in *Comptes-Rendus de l'Académie des Inscriptions*. Paris, 1942.

DUPONT-SOMMER, A., "Le Syncrétisme religieux des Juifs d'Eléphantine d'après un ostracon araméen inédit," in *Revue de l'Histoire des religions,* CXXX. Paris, 1945.

———, "Yahô et Yahô-Seba'ôt," in Comp. Rend. Acad. des Inscr., 1947.

EILERS, W., "Kleinasiatisches," in *Zeitschrift der Deutschen Morgenlaendischen Gesellschaft,* CXIV, 1940.

FINKELSTEIN, L., "Pre-Maccabean Documents in the Passover Haggadah," in *Harvard Theological Review*, XXVI. Cambridge, 1943.

———, "The Oldest Midrash: Pre-Rabbinic Ideals and Teachings in the Passover Haggadah," in *Harv. Theo. Rev.,* XXXI.

JAEGER, W., "Greeks and Jews: The First Greek Records of Jewish Religion and Civilization," in *Journal of Religion,* XVIII, Chicago.

LEWY, H., "Aristotle and the Jewish Sage According to Clearchus of Soli," in *Harv. Theo. Rev.,* XXXI, No. 3.

———, "Hekataios von Abdera," in *Zeitschrift fuer die Neutestamentliche Wissenschaft*, XXXI.

PERDRIZET P., "Un jeu alexandrin de l'icosaèdre," in *Bulletin de l'Institut Français d'Archéologie Orientale*. XXX, Paris.

PFISTER, F., "Eine juedische Gruendungsgeschichte Alexandrias," in *Sitzungsberichte der Heidelberger Akademie der Wissenschaften,* No. XI, July, 1914.

POSENER, G., "Notes sur le Stèle de Naucratis," in *Annales du Service des Antiquités de l'Egypte,* XXXIV, Le Caire, 1934.

WILCKEN, U., "Zur Aegyptisch-hellenistischen Literatur," in *Aegyptiaca, Festschrift fuer Georg Ebers*. Leipzig, 1897.

CHAPTER 3

THE PERIOD OF THE TALMUD
(135 B.C.E.–1035 C.E.)

By Judah Goldin

I

Legend has it that when the victorious Maccabees regained the Temple they could find nothing undefiled within the sacred precincts except a small cruse of oil, enough only for one day's lights. Miraculously, however, the lamps filled with this oil continued to burn for eight days. If there are fragments of fact under this folk tale, they are splintered beyond recognition. As a symbol, on the other hand, the story is a summary of the period that is our present concern. For the Jews of the early years of the second century B.C.E. could at first hardly suspect that what had begun as resistance to the fanatic policy of Antiochus IV would culminate within the lifetime of one of the Maccabean brothers in complete independence, to be sustained for eighty years. Even more impressive than the political phenomenon, the spiritual talents kindled within Israel at this time were to illuminate centuries of Jewish life. From the Maccabean era to the middle of the eleventh century, when the Babylonian academies fell into oblivion, the development of the Talmud and its elevation to a position of classical authority constitute the most significant achievement of the Jewish people. And this, too, may be added: the intellectual *qui vive* so characteristic of Jews throughout the Middle Ages despite contumely and persecution was the result of the Talmud.

Since the people in convocation had proclaimed the Hasmonean family as High Priests and rulers (143-142 B.C.E.),[1] it was quite natural for John Hyrcanus to take over these offices upon the unfortunate death of his father, Simon, in 135. Not one of the Maccabean brothers had died a natural death; each had met his end in the service of his people; and now the murder of Simon by his son-in-law once more threatened the security of Judea. Thus the first seven years of John Hyrcanus's rule were precarious, for himself and for the country. Only as a result of turmoil and intrigue within the Syrian court could he recover territory his father and uncles had previously held. In the course of a long administration (until

104), Syrian chaos made it possible for him even to add to the extent and power of his land.

In John Hyrcanus, however, we begin to observe a shift from the emphasis of the initial Maccabean adventure.[2] Religious freedom had been Mattathias's objective when he called upon his countrymen to revolt.[3] Self-defense, reprisals for vicious attack, a desire to be politically independent, the need for some outlets to the sea, compelled his children to continue to fight even after the Temple was once again in Jewish hands. The policies of the famous Hasmonean's grandson little by little revealed several other ambitions. Not only did John carry on wars to enlarge his territory, not only was he the first to employ heathen mercenaries in his army, but he also compelled the Idumeans whom he conquered to accept Judaism.

John Hyrcanus ruled together with an assembly of lay and priestly members, and it was this body that legislated for the whole country. There were in Palestine at the time a number of heathen settlements, and a series of laws, preserved in later sources, probably reflect minimal provisions which such inhabitants were expected to adopt.[4] These laws are the famous Noachian commandments,[5] echoes of which are later heard in New Testament teaching.[6] They required the heathen to obey the courts of the land, not to blaspheme the state religion, not to worship idols on Jewish territory, not to commit murder or robbery or unchastity, or eat flesh torn from an animal yet alive.

Men with social and spiritual interests could always find some party with which to identify themselves, since there were dozens of sects welcoming associates. Of such groups, three are better known to us than others; but even about these our information is not always sufficient or dependable.[7]

The group known as Essenes (the meaning of the name is still a puzzle)[8] were of an unworldly, ascetic character. They lived in isolated communities by themselves, far from the tumult of cities, sharing all their possessions. Private property was forbidden. Since they feared to contract ceremonial impurity they were given to frequent bathing. As symbolic of their emphasis on purity they dressed in white. In observing the Sabbath, they were much more strict than their fellow Jews. They rose very early for their prayers and encouraged long periods of silence. Apparently they had some reputation as diviners, and certain formulae, which they looked upon as sacred secrets of their colonies, they never revealed to others. Many did not marry; as a result, their membership was usually not very large, and depended on the attraction strangers might feel toward their mystic way of life. To become a member, however, was no simple affair. The candidate had to go through a rigorous probation period; only after satisfying his superiors who patiently, for years, observed him, could he qualify for full admission. Among their teachings the Essenes included a belief in immortality; and although they subscribed to a doctrine of complete determinism, they maintained that man would be judged, punished or rewarded, for his conduct.

The Sadducees (most probably derived from the priestly family known as the Zadokites) were drawn chiefly from priestly and aristocratic circles. Their following among the mass of people was limited because their wealth, haughty bearing and reputation for severity alienated many. They had close associations with a number of Hasmonean princes; through their influence at court and the economic advantages they enjoyed, there were times when their power was very great. They rejected the doctrine of determinism completely; in their opinion man was entirely free to do as he pleased. It was quite in keeping with this view therefore that they should remove God "beyond, not merely the commission, but the very sight of evil."[9] To the doctrine of resurrection, to the belief in angels, they would give no ear. Finally, they denied authority to new laws and institutions; that is, they recognized as binding scriptural law or law which was the product of simple scriptural exegesis. But they refused to acknowledge the validity of any *ad hoc* legislation, enactments in response, let us say, to historical necessity.[10] Beyond biblical support they would not venture.

The third and most famous of the parties was that of the Pharisees[10a] (generally accepted to mean, Those who withdraw—Heb. *Perushim*—from all impurity and unclean foods). They had greatest support from the mass of people.[11] The members were known for their simple, unostentatious lives; and on this score indeed they used to be taunted by the Sadducees: "It is a tradition among the Pharisees to afflict themselves in this world; yet in the world to come they shall have nothing."[12] The mockery had a *double entendre*, for it was intended to ridicule at the same time a doctrine of the Pharisees, namely, that Divine Providence was a reality and that "in the world to come" each immortal soul would be judged. Without denying that man's actions were dependent on God's will, they insisted that man is a free moral agent; as Rabbi Akiba later expressed it, "Everything is foreseen, yet freedom of the will is given."[13] They further taught that there would be a resurrection of the dead, and they subscribed to the belief in angels.

Occasionally sanctimonious prigs and deceivers attached themselves to the Pharisaic movement, "Pharisaic plagues," they were called by the Pharisees.[14] To no group were such hypocrites more repugnant than to the Pharisees themselves. "Hypocrites," exclaimed a second-century Rabbi, "shall not be admitted to the presence of God, even as the verse [Job 13:16] says, 'That a hypocrite cannot come before Him.' "[15] Such charlatans in short are as little an index of Pharisaic teaching or conduct as are counterfeits anywhere else.

What contributed so greatly to the popularity of the Pharisees was not only their proverbial urbanity but their intelligent social sense. They feared excesses in any direction and therefore strongly disapproved of severity in punishment. Furthermore, they did not look cynically upon traditions which had developed among the populace in the course of centuries. When circumstances demanded the institution of new law, they did not fear to recognize it as authoritative. Since they understood that unless the content of Scripture was continuously interpreted even the Bible would soon become a dead letter, they refused to restrict the role of interpretation. This dynamic conception made it possible to declare, for example, that the *lex talionis*, the eye for an eye of Scripture, was not intended literally, but was a brief way of stating that the victim should be compensated for the physical damages he had suffered.[16] The same conception subsequently led the Rabbis, continuing Pharisaic tradition, to read out of existence the primitive law of the rebellious son (Deut. 21:18 ff.) which gave parents so highhanded and total a power over their children.[17]

Perhaps the most significant commentary on the relative vitality of the three groups is offered by history itself—only Pharisaism fully recovered from the profound shock of events of the years 66-70.

During the early years of his administration John Hyrcanus identified himself with the Pharisaic group. But he later turned against them;[18] for there seems to have been current in their midst a sentiment against the concentration of both the priestly and the politico-military functions in one man. The sentiment was not exactly without precedent. Centuries earlier King David had been prevented from erecting a temple because his hands had shed blood.[19] At a later date one hears a prominent Rabbi say that uncut stones were ordered for the altar because iron which cut them was also used for swords, and furnishings dedicated to God must not be defiled by such metal.[20] The homily has none of the earmarks of novelty.[21] Such reminiscences were part of the popular lore. And John becoming a typical Oriental potentate discovered that his countrymen were prepared to enjoy the economic advantages of his policy, but not to forgive his trespassing upon their ideals. His own circle was not so sensitive; why should the Pharisees be less amenable? He began therefore to hound their leaders and to revoke their laws. Many of them had to flee for safety; in their midst was the principal of the leading school in the country, Joshua ben Perahiah. A colleague of Joshua's, Nittai the Arbelite, likewise the head of a school, apparently did not join the refugees; but this may have been the incident in his mind when he said, "Keep far from an evil neighbor and do not associate with the wicked."[22]

The breach between the Pharisees and the ruling house was to last for several decades and thus contribute to the weakening of the country. But before the effects on the body politic could become apparent the cleavage had to penetrate more deeply. External forces could then complete a disruption begun by internal strife and shortsightedness.

Upon John's death, his son Aristobulus assumed power. His rule lasted no longer than one year, until 103; nevertheless, in that brief interval (if Josephus may be trusted)[23] he behaved like a despot; what his father had done with the Idumeans, he did with the Itureans; and not content with the nature of his position, he declared himself king.[24] When his brother Alexander Janneus (103-76) succeeded him, the cue, in other words, was already at hand. It is not only High Priest, but King Alexander who now governs Palestine.

Like his father John in his later years, Alexander looked to the Sadducees for advisers and support. Throughout the twenty-seven years of his reign he waged one war after another; and though these campaigns enlarged his territorial holdings, they gave the country no rest. After so many years on the battlefield, invasion, and threat of invasion, the people yearned for peace. Some degree of material prosperity must have been introduced as a result of Alexander's encouragement of maritime trade, perhaps, too, by building ventures under his sponsorship.[25] But he never learned to cultivate the affection of the people at large. At one of the colorful religious ceremonies in the Temple, while officiating as High Priest, he scornfully poured a water libation at his feet, not on the altar. The mass of pilgrims who had assembled in the Temple for the festival were outraged. It was public contempt toward a practice which to them was sacred; and they pelted him, their monarch, with the citrons they had brought for the holiday procession. Pandemonium broke loose at once; whereupon the king's soldiers charged into the mob. Execution, death sentences, became so common that once more a mass flight from the country occurred. Had it not been checked, the Jews might have discovered themselves a helpless and vanishing minority in their own land. In the national emergency, therefore, a leading Sage had to re-enact an earlier law which declared Jews who abandon the Holy Land for other countries ritually unclean.[26]

It was especially the Pharisees on whom Alexander let loose his wrath. They most articulately represented the people's attitude toward him. He may very well have imagined that by crushing the Pharisees the source of his difficulties would disappear. Force, however, did not restore order, and by the time he was ready to contemplate other solutions for his domestic problem the gulf between himself and his subjects was too wide. For six years the king proved unable to subdue an uprising against him. The rebels went so far as to solicit Syrian aid against their own monarch. When on one occasion he turned pathetically to some of their representatives with the question: What ought he to do to win their sympathy? they replied that he ought to die. Until the very end he knew no peace; and it was finally the recognition of his own failure that made him say on his deathbed to his wife, "Fear neither the Sadducees nor the Pharisees; but beware of those who, living the life of Zimri, demand the rewards of Phineas."[27]

Not Alexander's sons, but his widow Alexandra Salome succeeded him on the throne. A prominent Pharisee of the period, Simeon ben Shatah, appears to have been related to her;[28] and through his influence the Pharisees returned to the Sanhedrin from which they had been excluded for more than a quarter of a century. Unfortunately, the memory of what they had suffered at the hand of the Sadducees was still fresh, and now that they were in power, the Pharisees began running down their opponents. Such retaliation ultimately could have but one result: accentuation of party differences to the point of civil war. Immediately, on the other hand, Pharisaic ascendancy contributed to several significant developments.

In the first place, the nine years of Alexandra's reign were years of peace; hostilities with neighboring countries, conquests, ceased, and the people could devote themselves thoroughly to the cultivation of their lands. The quiet and comfort that now prevailed were so impressive by contrast with the years that preceded and followed, that later only legendary terms were found adequate to describe the crops, the blessings of that interlude.[29]

In the second place, the control of the Sanhedrin by the Pharisees enabled them to put through various reforms and laws which the country needed and which their principles demanded.[30, 30a] This was most likely the interval when many details of judicial procedure, recorded in later Rabbinic compilations, were enacted. Even the popular sayings of Simeon ben Shatah and his colleague Judah ben Tabbai reflect the interest in judicial affairs. Judah, for example, always urged judges not to behave like autocratic chief justices, to treat litigants with absolute impartiality. A cross-examination of witnesses, warned Simeon, unless carefully conducted, would lead not to the fulfillment but to the perversion of justice.[31]

We get outlines of a portrait of both Simeon and the period, not alone from some stories handed down about the man—that reflect his shrewdness, his acute sense of honesty in his traffic with heathen, his adherence to principle even at the expense of his own family happiness, his vigorous impatience with superstition even when modified by piety.[32] In these, after all, fact has been so amalgamated with legend that we cannot on occasion determine where history is yielding to affection.

More telling are certain laws for whose establishment he was greatly responsible. Thus, he introduced a reform in connection with marriage laws which made it more difficult for husbands to divorce their wives.[33]

Together with his colleague he had a decree passed which put certain imported metal vessels in the same category with vessels made by local manufacturers; thereby preventing a serious crisis in the economy of the country.[34] Above all, he took effective measures to democratize education;[35] and so profound were the results of the expanded public education program which he stimulated that early in the second century a writer could exclaim, "Above all we pride ourselves on the education of our children"[36]—as though this opportunity had existed from remote antiquity.

What Alexandra herself was like it is not easy to say.[37] It is as possible to credit her with an understanding of her subjects' desires as see in her a lack of initiative. She was an old woman, sixty-two years of age, when she began to rule. And the crisis that followed is as much the product of deep-rooted forces as of personal ambitions. The dismal fraternal clash to which we must now turn was an outlet for conflicting interests. The nine years temporarily subdued that conflict, they did not resolve it.

For when Alexandra died in 67, an era of turmoil began which was the prelude to loss of political independence, subjection to rulers and governors unsympathetic to the ideals of the country, and finally the tragedy of the destruction of Temple and state. And once the momentum of decline set in, nothing, it seemed, could interrupt it.

By virtue of seniority, Hyrcanus, who had served as High Priest during his mother's reign, now expected the throne. But his younger brother Aristobulus, supported by many young people of the Sadducean group, accurately observed that Hyrcanus lacked the capacities of a king: he was timid, weak in character, without the statesman's vision. Aristobulus may have been deficient in statesmanship, but not in daring or energy. Civil war broke out; and though Hyrcanus was not without support at first, he was defeated by the hosts of his younger brother. Vanquished, the erstwhile High Priest yielded to the victor; and some sort of domestic peace might have been maintained if it had not been for the appearance of a sinister character upon the scene. The man's name was Antipater; his shadow was to hover over many years and misfortunes.

When, years before, John Hyrcanus had forced Judaism on the Idumeans he evidently conjectured that the new, though unwilling, converts could learn to identify their own destiny with that of his people. The gruesome accuracy of his *Realpolitik* was now vindicated, albeit not as John would have wished.

Antipater was of Idumean descent. During the reign of Alexander Janneus his father had served as governor of Idumea. The son, however, had larger ambitions. He perceived that the tumult within Judea could serve his own purposes if he but acted adroitly. The first step was to win the good faith of the defeated, equivocating Hyrcanus; from then on Antipater ceaselessly urged him to contest the throne that Aristobulus had usurped. Was not Hyrcanus the elder brother? Was not the crown in all justice his? Was it manly to resign so placidly? And the prodding was effective, especially since Antipater guaranteed the assistance of a neighboring Arab king.

Once more all the violence of civil war broke loose; but this time when the smoke of battle lifted Judea no longer belonged to herself. For news of what was taking place within the land was brought to Pompey, then in Asia. Here was an opportunity to gather still another country under the wings of the Roman eagle. On this occasion, however, the great warrior hardly had to make the initial move, since the country was delivered to him, as it were. In Syria envoys from Judea appeared before one of his generals, and each pressed claims. The ambassadors representing Aristobulus brought gifts, those representing Hyrcanus also came well laden. When later Pompey arrived the contestants approached him. Pompey listened to accusations and counteraccusations, but for the time being would not commit himself. Suddenly a third delegation arrived, a group representing the people at large, and these pleaded with him to rid the country of both brothers. So worn out by the feuds of the royal family were the masses that they had had their fill of their own sovereigns. If given their choice, they would have neither Hyrcanus nor Aristobulus. Weariness was all they felt, for in neither aspirant could they discern the likelihood of the peace they so earnestly wished for. Hyrcanus was without backbone, Aristobulus was surrounded by those factions intent upon destroying the queen's program. "O God, King of the universe," a certain saint, seized by one of the armies during the civil war, had cried, "since these men standing beside me are Thy people, and those who are besieged are Thy priests, I beseech Thee not to hearken to them against these men nor to bring to pass what these men ask Thee to do to those others."[38]

Eventually the great conqueror gave his decision. It had become perfectly clear to him that of the two Hyrcanus would prove more tractable to Rome. And Pompey was ready to smash opposition; what equipment he lacked, he could send for. When Aristobulus retreated with his soldiers into the Temple, Pompey drew up his forces for a siege. On a Sabbath—it may have been the Day of Atonement[39]—when the Jews refused to conduct military activities unless personally attacked, the Romans finally made a breach in the fortifications, and their general marched into the Sanctuary. Officiating priests were cut down at their posts, but the Temple itself was spared. The fashion of plundering had to wait for Crassus.[40] Then Pompey announced his terms: Aristobulus was a prisoner; Hyrcanus was to be recognized as High Priest—but no more; certain territories and seaports held by Judea (practically all the cities conquered by the Maccabees) had to be relinquished; and the country reduced to its "rural core,"[41] a conquered province, was to pay tribute to the victors. Six years later (57) even the administrative structure was radically reorganized; the province was divided into five districts by Gabinius, the Roman proconsul at Syria.

Thus independence was lost in 63. The contrast was glaring indeed between early feelings toward the Hasmoneans and the present ones. During the leadership of Judas Maccabeus the family had been regarded as alone appointed "to save Israel with their hands."[42] Now Israel was prepared to sacrifice even independence if only that might spell the end of the Hasmonean house. "Thou, O Lord, didst choose David to be king over Israel," sang an anonymous Pharisaic poet of the period as he reflected over what had occurred:[43]

And swaredst to him touching his seed that never should his kingdom fail before Thee.
But, for our sins, sinners rose up against us;
They assailed us and thrust us out;
What Thou hadst not promised to them, they took away from us with violence.
They in no wise glorified Thy honorable name;
They set a worldly monarchy in place of that which was their excellency;
They laid waste the throne of David in tumultuous arrogance.
But Thou, O God, didst cast them down, and remove their seed from the earth,
In that there rose up against them a man that was alien to our race.
According to their sins didst Thou recompense them, O God;
So that it befell them according to their deeds.
God showed them no pity;
He sought out their seed and let not one of them go free.
Faithful is the Lord in all His judgments
Which He doeth upon the earth.

Politically speaking, the step taken by the people was a major blunder:[44] was it to be expected that alien Rome, regardless of several earlier treaties of friendship,[45] would reveal deeper sensitivity to the religious ideals of the country than its native princes? To treat this incident simply as a sudden, temporary exasperation with the Hasmoneans, however, will not do; for not only this time, but on several subsequent occasions one witnesses Pharisaic leaders, whose loyalty to the nation is beyond reproach, counsel submission to Rome. "What does the emperor demand of you," Johanan ben Zakkai was to plead with the party conducting the war for independence in 66-70, "but that you send him a bow and arrow" in token of submission?[46] No less did Joshua ben Hananiah attempt to pacify the incensed populace in the second century when clamor for revolt against Hadrian rose. Should not a crane rejoice if the lion spared its neck?[47]

What led the Pharisees even in the first pre-Christian century to political miscalculation was fatigue, to be sure. Perhaps, too, they did not really know Rome. But there was another cause as well. It was a feeling that the religious tradition had to be superior to all else in the country. This need not suggest that economic or sociological factors did not apply in Israel. They undoubtedly did in the history of this people as everywhere else. Many laws and controversies over the law are unintelligible unless seen against such a background. When an early pair of Sages during the Maccabean period, José ben Joezer and José ben Johanan, decreed that Jews who migrate to foreign countries render themselves ritually unclean, the idiom is the idiom of piety; but the motive and objective are plainly to prevent an exodus from the country which threatened the survival of the Palestinian Jewish community. Again, when we hear the same men declare that glass vessels, like other vessels, are susceptible to impurity, the religious vocabulary is but their method of expressing an economic necessity—imported glass vessels, which by now had become fairly common, were either to be put on the same level with such objects as Palestine itself produced or the economy of the country would be dislocated. Or when a little later Joshua ben Perahiah, attempted to establish a boycott of Alexandrian wheat in the interests of the Palestinian "farm bloc," he too talked in ritualistic language; the Sages who outvoted him in the interest of consumers employed similar expressions.[48]

Social forces, in short, are not to be gainsaid. But they cannot cancel the purely religious determination that had by this time become widespread under Pharisaic tutelage. The Pharisees would not concede that the land was anybody's but Israel's; they were never to cease calling it the Land of Israel, *Eretz Yisrael*. Nevertheless, if the religion was in any way jeopardized they preferred to negotiate with rulers who perchance might leave the internal life of the people undisturbed. Domination by a foreign power was certainly no new phenomenon in Jewish history. In the folk experience some mode of adjustment to such a circumstance had evolved as a result of previous captivity and conquest. Even at the present juncture the majority of the four and a half million Jews in the world (Baron accepts the possibility of an eight million figure!)[49] lived outside their mother country, subject to non-Jewish government. Some privileges these Diaspora Jews possessed, but their communities cannot be called independent. This is no less true of the flourishing center in Alexandria.

The Jewish masses in Palestine, exhausted by an era of almost uninterrupted warfare of which the present intestine struggle was but the climax, concurred with Pharisaic policy. If anything, the bond between people and Pharisees now grew stronger. When about twenty years later, for example, a Hasmonean regained the throne for a brief period, he still could not compete with the Pharisaic leaders for the affection of the people. On the Day of Atonement as he emerged from the Temple, where he had been officiating as High Priest, crowds formed a procession behind him.

Suddenly they beheld the two outstanding Pharisees of the generation and immediately abandoned their prelate to pay their respects to the two Sages. And if there is more than fancy to the tradition that these Sages were of proselytic descent,[50] then not only the High Priest's rage (and the cutting retort of the two men), but also the measure of the people's devotion to the Pharisees becomes obvious. The High Priest said to them, "Welcome, O descendants of heathen!" To which they replied, "Welcome indeed to descendants of heathen who do the work of Aaron, but let there be no welcome for the descendant of Aaron who does not do Aaron's work."[51]

Repeated attempts on the part of Aristobulus and his sons to recover what they had lost met with no success. A taste of Roman domination, of Gabinius's extortions, of exploiting *negotiatores* in their midst[52] led the Jews to regret their invitation to the conquerors; and the defeated Hasmoneans were able to rally support for several revolts. But these brought only panic to the country, especially since on every occasion Rome stepped in and asserted her authority. In the meantime, as Caesar's star rose on the Roman horizon, Antipater hastened to ingratiate himself with the new dictator. From Caesar he finally (47 B.C.E.) won the appointment as procurator of Judea; the confirmation of Hyrcanus as High Priest and Ethnarch interfered little with the Idumean's schemes. To his sons as governors Antipater turned over different parts of the country. Particularly significant for this history was the appointment of his son Herod to the governorship of Galilee. Here the young man served his apprenticeship and gave notice of his character by his doings. Without recourse to law he suppressed an uprising, and when summoned before the Sanhedrin to give an account of his conduct, he appeared with lieutenants in so menacing a fashion that the judges were terror stricken. It was on this occasion that the sage Samaias (Shemayah) turned to his colleagues and predicted that their cowardice, their fear to condemn the guilty man, would only encourage him; and in the end they, too, would not be spared.

At the order of the Roman governor of Syria Herod succeeded in escaping punishment, but he nursed his grudge against the men who had dared try him. His day had not yet arrived; several reverses were still in store for him. Thanks to Parthian help Aristobulus's son Antigonus had returned to rule the country. Hyrcanus he mutilated and displaced as High Priest. But the Parthian pillage of Judea, which had accompanied Antigonus's restoration, did little to endear him to his subjects after the first enthusiasm. And during this time Herod neither retired into obscurity nor permitted his career to be eclipsed. On the contrary, those years he put to good advantage, making himself useful to the Romans, cultivating Antony, winning Galilean friends, attracting malcontents, seizing provisions for his soldiers. Finally, in the year 37, after defeating Antigonus, the Idumean entered the city of Jerusalem and put the Jewish crown on his head. The Hasmonean Dynasty, to all intents and purposes, was ended.

What caused the failure of the Hasmoneans? Some observations have in part suggested an answer, but a recapitulation may be helpful.

Under the Hasmoneans the country had certainly become richer economically than it had been before their time. Alongside agriculture, which always remained the major feature of livelihood (men raised especially wheat, dates, figs; they produced oil, wines, spices), urban centers had developed. Many engaged in handicrafts. There was trade, domestic and foreign; there were luxuries; there was an almost steady building program. Additional coastal cities had been acquired. For a while the country once again extended as far as its early Davidic boundaries. Politically Judea occupied a more significant position among nations than she had as a Syrian possession; from this prominence even Jews settled in other countries benefited; and on occasion pressure could be brought on a queen like Cleopatra to give up intentions of invading the Hasmonean realm.[53] Culturally, the country could point to sundry schools where intellectual activity was conducted. At least two advanced Pharisaic academies attracted students; there is no reason to doubt that the Sadducees maintained schools where their principles were taught and their methods adopted. We owe to this period a number of literary works. National independence stimulated a revival and development of the Hebrew language. In the light of such facts one cannot say that the Hasmoneans did nothing for their country.[54] Yet they failed to retain the loyalty of their subjects.

Fundamentally there were two reasons for this. First, they mistook party interest for national interest. Parties were not the invention of the second- and third-generation Hasmoneans. But by identifying themselves with one party or another—and usually the party that represented a minority disliked by the masses—they could not do justice to desires and interests which did not coincide with their personal tastes. That is why they could not put an end to war, though the nation was worn out by battles and troops and campaigns. The second cause inevitably emerged from the first. The Hasmoneans drifted further and further from the values and concepts of their people. Ideals cherished by the people became at best tangential to the royal house, and thus it ceased to personify the character of the nation. This did not happen suddenly; nowhere is such a phenomenon abrupt. This did not occur in any one specific incident or area of conduct. It expressed itself in various and subtle ways and steps. And when the folk discovered that the rulers had departed from the native idiom, it tired of them.[55]

It is therefore futile to say, as some recent historians have said,[56] that Herod was no worse than his predecessors—a debatable contention. But this is of secondary importance. What is important is that there was nothing in his reign to correct the two major shortcomings of the Hasmoneans. While he may have equally despised Pharisees and Sadducees, he did not rule the country with its interest uppermost in his mind. For party interest he substituted Roman interest. A king of the Jews he was, but not a Jewish king.

2

In the words of Shemayah, "Do not court the ruling powers,"[1] there is as serviceable a key to Herod's palace and reign (37-4) as the period can furnish. From the day Herod mounted the throne to his last breath fear was in the land. Fatigue had simply resigned to terror. The man was, to quote Josephus, "brutish and a stranger to all humanity."[2]

His subjects could not forget that their monarch was not one of their own,[3] that in effect he ruled over what was not his. To the Hasmoneans he was merely a usurper, and even the high priesthood he took from them. To the aristocracy he was not only a parvenu but a brigand who constantly seized their wealth, for lack of any of his own, to bribe Antony. The members of the Sanhedrin he killed almost to a man.[4] No one forgot the blood he had shed in Galilee. And his pathological character only aggravated a disposition totally incapable of inspiring confidence.

In order to reinforce his claim to the throne, Herod had married the Hasmonean princess Mariamne, granddaughter of the ill-fated Hyrcanus. With time perhaps he might have won her affection, for he loved her sincerely. But Mariamne's mother would not be placated, since Herod had passed over her son to appoint some insignificant stranger as High Priest. With the help of Cleopatra, who also distrusted Herod's every move, the mother prevailed upon Antony to have Herod appoint her Hasmonean son to the high priesthood. The young man, however, proved fatally popular with crowds. In such acclaim of the High Priest Herod heard undertones of revolt against himself. He therefore arranged to have the boy "accidentally" drowned at a party in Jericho. And at the boy's funeral the king so outdid himself in mourning that no one, least of all the mother, was deceived.[5]

Violence did not stop with the murder of Mariamne's brother. Ordered to appear before Antony to answer charges on his responsibility for this crime, Herod left instructions that if he were not acquitted his brother-in-law Joseph should murder Mariamne. During his absence Joseph informed the queen of her husband's orders. Upon his return, Herod discovered that Joseph had revealed the secret, and ordered him executed. For the present Mariamne escaped.

Again, after Augustus's victory over Antony, Herod prepared to visit the new world ruler in order to win his favor. Before departing for the conference he ordered the old Hyrcanus, Mariamne's grandfather, put to death, lest any scion of the Hasmonean house prove a rallying figure for revolt during the king's absence.

In 30-29 he had to go to Rhodes. Once more his orders were that if he failed to return Mariamne was to be slain, for he could not bear the thought of his wife possibly belonging to another. All the machinery of intrigue within the court was on this occasion, too, set off, and when Herod returned, the calumnies, the furtiveness, the whisperings so persisted that in a rage he ordered her sent to the executioner. He rued this action. But the man himself was a pitiful captive of fear, and death alone gave him release.

These were but the more sensational murders during the early period of his reign; they hardly describe the elaborate espionage system throughout the land and the staggering number brought to the sword among the masses. Even the king was not beyond disguising himself in order to mix with crowds and overhear what might be plotted against him. What his subjects thought of him was made quite clear, after his death, to Augustus. "It was not a king," said the Jewish deputies to the emperor, "whom they had to tolerate, but the most cruel tyrant that ever existed. Numerous had been his victims, but the survivors had suffered so much that they envied the fate of the dead. For he had tortured not only the persons of his subjects, but also their cities; and while he crippled the towns in his own dominion, he embellished those of other nations, lavishing the lifeblood of Judea on foreign communities. In place of their ancient prosperity and ancestral laws, he had sunk the nation to poverty and the last degree of iniquity. In short, the miseries that Herod in the course of a few years had inflicted on the Jews surpassed all that their forefathers had suffered during all the time since they left Babylon to return to their country in the reign of Xerxes."[6]

Thirty-three years on the throne are of course not a short reign and Herod was not an idle man. Especially during the years 25-13 he busied himself with an extensive construction program. He built gymnasia, theaters, and amphitheaters, temples to pagan gods (in pagan cities), fortresses and ports, dwellings for seamen, and cities. These undertakings contributed to the expansion of the country's economic facilities. They provided employment for many; they improved the appearance of various locations. The trouble was that at the same time they involved an exorbitant system of taxation, and monuments are not victuals. Funds, however, were needed not only for works projects but also for bribing Rome, for maintaining the lavish royal households and armies; and these were totally nonproductive expenditures consuming the country's wealth. Moreover, since so large a part of these projects was devoted to pagan objectives, they antagonized numerous elements in the population. Caesarea was anything but a Jewish city; the theaters—there was one even in Jerusalem!—were objects of abomination no less than pagan temples. Men by and large were happy to work; "Love work and hate lordship"[7] had been a slogan of Shemayah's which many remembered. But it was, to say the least, utter tactlessness for a king of the Jews to devote himself so zealously to pagan installations. "In the East," says Rostovtzeff,[8] ". . . Greek forms and Greek ideas remained a thin veneer over a local, purely Oriental substratum. Moreover, Greek influence in the East was confined to the cities and to the upper classes of the population, and never affected the masses. . . . Even in the Hellenistic monarchies . . . the masses of the country were never affected by Greek culture and retained persistently their old customs and habits and their traditional religious beliefs."

Hence the failure of a number of sincere measures in behalf of the people—for example, importing food for the country during the famine of 25, or remission of a percentage of the taxes in 20 and again in 14[9]—to turn the tide in Herod's favor. Hence, too, his continued unpopularity despite his undertaking to rebuild the Temple at Jerusalem on a magnificent scale. The Jews were prepared to admit that "he who has not seen Herod's Temple has never in his life beheld a stately structure."[10] But they could perceive, too, that this was no more than a baroque device on the part of their monarch to purchase their good will;[11] for even this gift he made almost meaningless by setting up an eagle on the Temple gates. In the last year of his life, two Rabbis set the spark of an unsuccessful revolt by tearing down the hated object.

In brief, regardless of what distinction his foreign policy may have achieved,[12] to his subjects his title *rex socius et amicus populi Romani* was insufferably appropriate. He was surrounded by heathen advisers and only pagan culture interested him. No wonder, therefore, that despite his extension of the country's boundaries—with Rome's permission only—the people could not but feel their lives restricted. And therefore, too, they felt that their true representatives were not in the royal palace, but in the Pharisaic academies.

An extraordinary pair of Sages were now at the head of the schools. Of the two, Shammai represented the more conservative element and temperament in the country. Himself a man of means, he was perhaps inclined to voice the interests of the well-to-do, to regard problems from their perspective. What discouraged strangers in meeting him was his short temper—one is tempted to say, his lack of a sense of humor. He found nothing strange in recommending the kind of purchasing that is possible only to the affluent. He might be at the market place on a weekday and see an attractive morsel; immediately he would acquire it for impressive Sabbath fare. If on the morrow he discovered a still more expensive delicacy, he would buy it for the Sabbath.[13] Such pious concentration on the Sabbath is admirable, but requires an income. His colleague Hillel thanked God if he had food sufficient unto the day.[14] It would be unfair to Shammai to make of him a harsh, uncivil rigorist. In fact, he was famous for the saying, "Greet all men with a cheerful countenance";[15] and significantly, from his school were derived some of the more "courtly" rules in regard to women.[16] Obviously, the man seldom rose above the limitations of respectability.

The famous Hillel, whose teachings and spirit colored Judaism so profoundly, was an admirable counterpart of his associate. The story of his life is hard to reconstruct in full despite traditions about him, for legend clings to him. The legends, however, are a touchstone of the abundant love his people bore him with good reason.

He had been born in Babylonia, but in his search for learning migrated to Palestine, where the most noteworthy Jewish schools were established. His means were very limited; only by hard labor could he save enough to support himself and meet admission fees to the academy. The story goes so far as to say that once he almost froze to death when, for lack of funds, he climbed to the skylight of the schoolhouse in order to overhear the discussions within, and was snowed under by one of those rare snowfalls in the Holy Land.[17]

In the academies of Shemayah and Abtalyon he found that store of traditions without which none could aspire to distinguished scholarship. This was not all, however. From these two "great expositors"[18] he acquired a discipline, principles of research and interpretation, whose application and perfection made possible the whole development of the Talmud. Hillel recognized the potentialities of his teachers' method; it was so constant an instrument in his personal studies and his teaching that to later generations the principles came to be known as Hillel's formulae.

What was so extraordinary about an academic discipline? The answer is that more than scholarship is involved, for the academies were not merely retreats for intellectual exercises. Law was being developed here. And law affects the society's every citizen, learned and otherwise. The kind of law, the kind of culture that would become a national possession depended often on the agenda inside the schools. To these teachers and students the hiatus between market place and lecture hall was unnatural. Consequently, the reform of a school curriculum directly impinged upon the Jewish way of life.

As we have already had occasion to observe,[19] one of the distinguishing features of the Pharisaic groups was the recognition that Scripture alone was not the whole of Judaism; that law and custom supplementary to the text of Scripture were as genuine an expression of Jewish history as were the norms and practices recorded in the holy classic. Nevertheless, even among the Pharisees some, through inclination and upbringing, were embarrassed by constant innovation, by the daring to deduce independently what earlier generations had not specifically sanctioned. On the other hand, there were Sages—and Hillel was their leader—whose vision went beyond past and present. They did not reject what had come from earlier ages; but they insisted that in each generation scholars were entitled to search the Torah thoroughly[20] and, with the assistance of reason and logic, derive new meanings and new legal prescriptions.

Thus as Hillel pursued his studies he observed that it was perfectly valid to determine from "the general" what should apply to "the particular," and *vice versa*; that analogy, inference, deduction from context were indispensable for the jurist and student.[21] In short, what he urged on his disciples was the cultivation of memory *and* reason, precedent *plus* independent reflection and judgment.

Just such an emphasis brought Hillel to prominence. A problem had been set before certain distinguished scholars and they declared that they were unable to solve it. In the audience, however, sat someone who had already met Hillel on an earlier occasion; he recommended that the accomplished Babylonian be consulted. Hillel was thereupon summoned, heard the question, and attempted to give the answer by applying his rules of interpretation: could not the immediate case be compared to other cases about which there were explicit decisions? No, insisted the Sages in charge; either there was a clear tradition or the matter had best be left in doubt. Hillel failed to move them by his argumentation; only after he declared that his decision was a tradition from his teachers Shemayah and Abtalyon did the judges yield.[22]

There was more than acute scholarship to Hillel, and this explains how one who was not a native Palestinian could rise to the leadership of his generation. His patience was proverbial and his tact unfailing. Men might wager that they could make him lose his temper, to their own loss only.[23] Proselytes rebuffed by Shammai never annoyed Hillel. He understood that the heathen with an interest in Judaism was first concerned with the ultimate, the essential message of the religion, not its minutiae. When a heathen, discouraged by Shammai, once appeared before Hillel and asked: What in a nutshell does Judaism teach? Hillel did not interpret the question as impertinence. He grasped what had escaped his less patient colleague, and replied, "What is hateful to thee never do to thy fellow man. This is the entire Torah; all else is commentary." Then he added, "Go master it."[24]

The liberal spirit so manifest in this incident is no less a characterization of the man as teacher and jurist. He welcomed everybody to his school, rich and poor, prominent and humble, pious and negligent. His followers never approved of the exclusive character of Shammai's academy.[25] Furthermore, unlike Shammai, Hillel attempted to express the larger intent of Scripture rather than its limited implications. And as a jurist he had none to equal him in his generation. We see this especially in one of his reforms; here he could translate social-mindedness into action.

Public welfare was at stake. Hillel discovered that in his day an ancient biblical law was creating excessive hardship. According to Scripture (Deut. 15:2), all loans were remitted in the seventh, sabbatical year. Now, originally—as the Bible itself reveals—cancellation of debts was demanded in order to prevent the impoverishment of the small landholder. In a rudimentary agricultural economy, loans almost always reflect the distress of the borrower. If no steps had been taken to relieve debtors, all property would gradually have fallen into the hands of a few wealthy squires, who could then reduce the masses to serfdom. By Hillel's time, however, this particular law was producing results contrary to its own intention, contrary to the interests of society. The economy of the country had become more complex. Palestine was still primarily agricultural; but a credit system had evolved in the more advanced state. Yet as the calendar approached the seventh year, men with capital refused to lend their money; they knew they could never again collect it. The letter of the law was undoing the very ideal for which it had been instituted! When Hillel "saw that the people refrained from extending loans to each other and were thus transgressing the biblical injunction, 'Beware lest a base thought enter your head—The seventh year, the year of remittance is approaching—and you grudge help to your needy brother and give him nothing,' "[26] he enacted the *prozbul*—that is, he created an instrument which enabled creditors to recover whatever sums had been borrowed from them. And the flow of credit was restored.

Like some earlier ordinances already observed in our survey, this *takkanah*, enactment, by Hillel served subsequent generations of scholars as a model for legislation. When at a later date the price of doves in Jerusalem became prohibitive, Hillel's great-grandson would not rest until a law was passed which automatically forced merchants to sell their birds at a fraction of what they had been demanding.[27] The spirit of Hillel, then, is to greet us in each age. And ultimately this was his distinction—that to the reflective-liberal point of view which he had inherited from his predecessor Shemayah and from sages like Simeon ben Shatah, Nittai the Arbelite, José of Jerusalem, he gave brilliant expression and *élan*. Conservatives would not disappear and conservativism would not lack distinguished spokesmen. But the Hillelite current could not be resisted.

So deep was the impact of both Shammai and Hillel on their age that the academies over which they presided came to be known henceforth as Bet Shammai and Bet Hillel, the Shammaite school and the Hillelite school.[28] Like scholars everywhere, the members of these respective schools engaged in all kinds of intellectual controversies. The range, no less than the number, of their interests is amazing.[29] Eventually such debates added to the content of Jewish tradition. What is more, the Shammaites and Hillelites exemplified the meaning of scholarship for future students. Lively debate, exciting sessions were to mark the school system ever after. Much in these discussions was theoretical and scholastic, particularly after Rome appropriated more and more jurisdiction to herself. But much, too, was the expression of issues stirring society, the Hillelite school (and later their followers) reflecting the needs of the mass, the Shammaite school (and later their spiritual kin) reflecting the interests of the propertied groups. Both, however, were dedicated to the folk civilization; hence, while the ruling power removed itself from the experience of the population, the Sages came to be regarded as the people's guides, "the fathers of the universe."[30]

To the Herodian family during the closing period of Herod's life we may apply an Aramaic *bon mot* by Hillel. Noticing a skull afloat on some river, Hillel had exclaimed, "Because thou didst drown others wast thou drowned; and the end of them that drowned thee will also be drowning!"[31] Plot and counterplot dogged the footsteps of the sick monarch. He had at first contemplated assigning the succession to the two sons whom his beloved Mariamne had borne him. But his sister and Antipater, another of his sons by a different wife, did not rest until they had so poisoned Herod's mind against the two boys that he demanded their execution. The death of these brothers still left Antipater's ambition unfulfilled, for he was impatient for the throne; his father, the prince felt, took long in dying. The conspiracy he now organized, however, was to be his own undoing; he was executed five days before Herod's death. Once more the monarch changed his will; he knew his days were numbered. What distressed him was that his death would be greeted by rejoicing throughout the country. So he ordered that the most distinguished popular leaders be seized for slaughter when he died. Mourning for them would not only conceal the joy at his own passing, but would lead Rome to believe that he was being lamented by devoted subjects. Fortunately the order was never obeyed; but neither did the people forget that their king had been an enemy to the end. The structure of his achievements collapsed with his death. For the country his reign left a heritage of disaster.

Herod's death merely accelerated the total subjection of Judea to Rome. Although in his last will he had named his son Archelaus as his chief successor to rule Judea, the royal candidate had to get Rome's confirmation. Before he could leave for the imperial city, however, riots broke out in Jerusalem. A delegation had called upon him to demand punishment for Herod's counselors who had urged the execution of the Rabbis inspiring revolt during Herod's last year. This Archelaus would not grant. He was prepared to consider measures for the reduction of taxes, for freeing political prisoners condemned by his father. But he was adamant in his position that Herod's favorites were to retain their offices. The mobs assembled in the city for the Passover celebrations were in no mood for discussion, and only by means of force could the uprising be crushed.

Archelaus hastened to Rome. During his absence fresh revolts broke out which required the intervention of the Syrian legate. The legion brought to establish order only exasperated the restless population, for they would not calmly look on as their treasuries and Temple were being plundered.

Meanwhile in Rome, everything was far from developing as Archelaus had hoped. Not only did he appear to press claims; but his brother Antipas was also there, he, too, accompanied by an eloquent advocate, to prove that he was the legitimate successor. To complicate matters all the more, an embassy from the people appealed to Augustus to free the country from Herodians one and all.[32] Augustus did not know how to decide the issue. At last he determined to divide the kingdom among several sons. To one, Philip, he assigned a large region of Herod's holdings where the settlements were essentially heathen. To Antipas, who had opposed Archelaus, he turned over Galilee and Perea. Archelaus received Judea, Samaria and Idumea, but not as king, only as ethnarch.

For ten years, that is, until the year 6 of the Common Era, Archelaus governed his discontented subjects. To them their ruler was another Herod, building lavishly, behaving tyrannically, appointing high priests recklessly. Finally even Augustus could no longer wink at the protests of the people and ordered the tyrant banished to Gaul. Judea was now openly annexed by the empire, to be governed by Roman procurators.

3

It was part of Roman policy to avoid as far as possible interference with the internal administration of her provinces. Laws for the country, for example, were passed by the Sanhedrin. Though the procurator was charged with the responsibility for taxation, the actual collection of taxes was left to native publicans who purchased their offices for various sums. The Temple personnel and government belonged to the priestly class. The religious sentiments of the country were, by and large, not ignored; hence legionnaires were frequently cautioned not to carry images through the Holy City. Nevertheless, the close, enforced relationship between Judea and Rome was doomed to failure, and this for several reasons.

In the first place, the distance of the province from Rome often encouraged procurators to feel that they had carte blanche to do whatever pleased them. It is true that the provincials were not denied appeal to higher authority; but it was not always easy,[1] let alone pleasant, to bring charges against the imperial governor. As a result, from his seat in Caesarea, he ruled almost like an absolute monarch. He had his troops to enforce his will; and soldiers, in the employ of an official, are not inclined to be critical of his policies toward people whom they are hired to police.

In the second place, the character of certain governors was appallingly irresponsible, and the relationship, at best packed with tension, suffered as a consequence. The Emperor Tiberius was fond of describing governors of provinces as flies on an infested sore: they served only to add to the agony of the victim.[2] And it was Judea's misfortune to be governed by a series of such men. They plundered the provincials mercilessly and to their grievances replied with further profligacy. To men like Pontius Pilate (26-36), Felix (52-60), Albinus (62-64), Florus (64-66), the country was no more than a gold mine to be exploited for private benefit.

In the third place (perhaps most important), the *Weltanschauung*, the universe of discourse of the region with which the procurators and the Roman garrisons in this instance were charged, was entirely beyond their comprehension. What was one to make of a people who resolutely stationed themselves before the governor's palace and declared that they would sooner die than permit standards with the imperial image to be carried through their sacred city?[3] How was one to be patient with an agitator who promised his followers divine tokens of deliverance if they would accompany him to the Jordan?[4] Was one seriously to believe the popular preacher who attracted crowds of simple folk by his parables and his cures, that the kingdom of which he spoke was not of this world, that he had no designs on the things which were Caesar's?

Moreover, let us not forget what were some of the impressions circulating in the empire about Jews. Some whispered that Jews made all this holy fuss over the head of an ass, that they were unwilling to accept regular forms of hospitality,[5] that it was a principle with them not to help strangers lost on the way.[6] It is not unlikely that many procurators and troops had somewhere run into such rumors which would not predispose them favorably toward the Judeans. Add to this the sensitivity of a subject people and the constant reminders of their status; the condescension of the imperial personnel and their constant annoyance with unintelligible fanaticism—and the conclusion is inescapable that a bitter clash between the two could only be postponed, not avoided.

Finally, it is not superfluous to remark that, at all times, an imperial arrangement for governing provinces is a cheerless prospect. To a contemporary, the story of England in India will immediately occur. The history of the American colonies is similarly quite suggestive. "The two great objects of Great Britain in regard to the American trade," wrote Sir Francis Bernard, a typical "proconsul" of the eighteenth century, "must be 1. To oblige her American subjects to take from Great Britain only, all the manufacture and European goods which she can supply them with: 2. To regulate the foreign trade of the Americans so that the profits thereof may finally center in Great Britain, or be applied to the improvement of her empire. Whenever these two purposes militate against each other, that which is most advantageous to Great Britain ought to be preferred."[7] Substantially the same was observed by the Rabbis— "The coffers of Caesarea were filled only by the spoils of Jerusalem."[8]

Upon the arrival of the first procurator, Coponius (6-9), tumult broke out, for he called for a census of the population. To this measure there were objections on both religious and practical grounds. The results of David's census (II Sam. 24) were a source of terror to the pious mentality; and, realistically, it was feared that the census was no more than a beginning for more intensive and exorbitant taxation. Only through the intercession of the High Priest, and no doubt his influential associates, was revolt averted for the time. But the excitement contributed to the crystallization of another party, the Zealots, whose program called for rejection of all compromise with Rome and for acknowledging only God as lord of the country. The party was a formidable one.

Six other governors came to Judea in the course of the next thirty-two years, until a grandson of Herod, Agrippa I, was permitted to return to his ancestral throne and restore a semi-independence to the country. Of these governors Pontius Pilate was the most notorious. In a letter quoted by Philo, the procurator is charged with "corruptibility, violence, robberies, ill treatment of the people, grievances, continuous executions without even the form of a trial, endless and intolerable cruelties,"[9] and a careful reading of the New Testament supports this charge. Contrary to precedent, he ordered his soldiers to enter Jerusalem with standards bearing imperial images. He appropriated Temple funds in order to construct an aqueduct. In the Herodian palace, which he maintained as his Jerusalem residence, he brazenly set up imperial shields. He put to death numerous Samaritans who had assembled to witness the miracles of a self-proclaimed prophet in their midst—for this brutality, in fact, he was removed from office. Some time before this incident, however, he had ordered the crucifixion of a carpenter of Nazareth, a certain Jesus.

Of the childhood, youth and young manhood of Jesus we know almost nothing. The events of the last three years of his life, however, were destined to raise him out of obscurity to major significance. To his followers, and most likely to himself as well, he represented the long-awaited Messiah, the Christ, at whose coming the dominion of God would be ushered in. The age devoutly wished for a consummation of the Messianic ideal. Roman tyranny, disillusionment with the worldliness of successive high priests, apocalyptic vision, prophetic tradition regularly expounded in the synagogues and schools, contributed to an atmosphere of spiritual expectancy. Shortly before the appearance of Jesus, another Jew, John, had attracted crowds by his conduct and preaching, and announced that God's reign was at hand. "The people," Josephus informs us,[10] "flocked in crowds to him, being stirred by his addresses." They were especially impressed by his appearance, for in a garment of camel's hair and leather girdle he seemed like one of the ancient prophets come back to his people. John called upon his audience to undergo baptism, to repent in readiness for the coming of the Messiah. Apparently great numbers were moved by his appeal; one of those who underwent baptism at John's call was Jesus himself; but the stir created by the Baptizer made the ruler of Galilee, Herod Antipas, suspicious, and John was executed.

Nothing indeed—short of open revolt—so terrified the ruling powers as Messianic forecasts or claims. The authorities constantly feared that the Messianic herald or pretender was but disguising his real objective, political revolution, with mystic vocabulary. This was especially the case with the Roman officials to whom the Jewish concept of a Messiah was altogether unintelligible.[11] And it was this Roman limitation in all likelihood which led Jesus to anticipate that he would have to pay for his role with his life.

On the men and women whom he attracted the Nazarene made a lasting impression. His teachings were substantially what they might have heard from any sensitively pious Sages in the synagogue or academy. Like them, too, he illustrated his messages with parables, quoted Scripture, recommended hedges around the commandments,[12] scorned hypocrisy. What distinguished him from other moralists and teachers, however, was a feeling of authority, a spirited independence of accepted sanctions. He had no intention, he protested, "to destroy the Law and the prophets." The fact is, he declared to his disciples, "till heaven and earth pass away, not an iota, not a comma, will pass from the Law until it is all in force. Therefore, whoever relaxes a single one of these commands, were it even one of the least, and teaches men so, he will be ranked least in the Realm of heaven; but whoever obeys them and teaches them, he will be ranked great in the Realm of heaven."[13] Nevertheless, in practice he frequently justified his disciples' infractions, and as a result alienated many who wholeheartedly endorsed his ultimate ideal, namely, qualifying mankind for citizenship in the Kingdom of God.

When, therefore, Jesus was apprehended on the eve of the Passover, for which festival crowds had flocked to Jerusalem and the procurator had come down with his troops from Caesarea to "keep the peace," only a few of his most faithful companions stood by him. His tragic conviction was speedy; and he was nailed to the cross.

The five years following the dismissal of Pilate in 36 were full of anxiety for the Jews, particularly after the middle of 38 when the Emperor Caligula demanded that worship be offered to him, as to a god, everywhere in the empire. This order led to a violent persecution of the Jews in Alexandria, who naturally could not obey such a law. In the Holy Land the edict raised universal consternation, and it was only the courageous prudence of the governor of Syria that spared Palestine from bloodshed. Petronius urged the emperor, subtly and tactfully, to delay having his statue set up in Jerusalem. Fortunately, both for the country and for the governor, Caligula was murdered in 41, and the order was abandoned. The incident, however, underscored in Jewish minds the realization that the relationship with Rome was utterly precarious: a Flaccus in the seat of Petronius would have brought on an explosion.

Nevertheless, three years of quiet and comparative prosperity followed. Agrippa I, thanks to his imperial cronies, was permitted to return to the throne and act as king over his grandfather's territories. Independence was far from restored to the Jews; on two separate occasions when he undertook projects without consulting Rome, the king was summarily ordered to cease his activities.[14] But the absence of a procurator was in itself a great relief; and perhaps this more than anything else led the populace, at one of the Temple celebrations, to hail their monarch as a brother, part Idumean though he was.[15]

The relative order within the country must have proved a boon to the Sages and to the academies. Intellectual activity flourished; individuals occasionally undertook the translation of biblical books;[16] and within the schools discussion was conducted vigorously. Hillelites and Shammaites found much over which to debate, but academic divergence was never permitted to disrupt the peace and unity that both schools pursued. "Notwithstanding that the ones forbade what the others permitted, that the ones declared unfit what the others declared fit, Shammaites did not refrain from wedding women of the Hillelite group, nor Hillelites from wedding women of the Shammaite group. Despite all the controversies over what is clean and what is unclean—wherein the ones declared clean what the others declared unclean—neither refrained from using what belonged to the other."[17]

The most distinguished personality of the period was Gamaliel I, Hillel's grandson. In his father's household Gamaliel had frequently heard it said that deeds were the important thing in life, that much talk would lead to sin,[18] and he himself always urged his contemporaries to keep clear of doubt and mere conjecture.[19] His title "Rabban" probably reflects the influential position he attained within the Sanhedrin, dominated for the most part by priests and their Sadducean allies. Through his influence several significant reforms were introduced in Jewish law;[20] and by the same influence he was able to save from severe sentence a number of Christian apostles whom the Sanhedrin were about to condemn.[21]

It may be that among the disciples of Rabban Gamaliel[22] was a certain Hellenistic Jew come up from Tarsus. Unlike Jesus, whose most effective apostle he was to become, Saul, or Paul, was a man of means and could undertake frequent journeys. As a result, whatever the nature of his attachment to Pharisaic teachings, considerable non-Jewish elements impressed themselves on his receptive mind. In the course of his various travels he frequently encountered groups of heathens who, in the twilight of paganism, had begun to adopt sundry Jewish beliefs and ceremonies. What hindered these people, the men especially, from adopting Judaism entirely? This question agitated Paul for a number of years until he could find an answer to his own satisfaction.

At first he hated the early Christians with a passion characteristic of all his moods. It was almost a mission with him, he confesses, to hound the believers in Jesus. Suddenly and quite mysteriously, the Tarsian continues, he experienced a conversion. The cry, "Saul, Saul, why do you persecute me?"[23] transformed the foe into a champion.

From that day to his death (sometime after 63) Paul's life was filled with turbulence, but no less with a fixed purpose. He was to be the Christ's apostle to the nations of the world; and, since the accumulated traditions of Jewish history were beyond the comprehension of these peoples, there was only one thing to do—forfeit the tradition. A few basic principles of Judaism alone were to be the requirements for admission to the fellowship of believers. These principles were to be supplemented, however, by a faith in the Messianic character of Jesus; that is, that not only was Jesus the Messiah, but that his coming had automatically terminated the efficacy or authority of Jewish law.

To the Jews such a theology was impossible: Was one to reduce a heritage of centuries and millennia to allegory? Significantly enough, two facts now came to the fore. The original followers of Jesus, on the one hand, opposed Paul with utmost bitterness, for they, too, resented his demands. On the other hand, the new schism soon had to adopt much non-Jewish idiom, because the nations had their distinctive histories as well, and converts from their midst could not, at the profession of faith, forget their upbringing. Inevitably Pauline doctrine had to come to terms with these phenomena, and when it did a new religious movement was born. It was no longer Judaism.

After the death of Agrippa the country was once again reduced to the status of a province to be governed by procurators; for the next twenty-two years they did everything to make confusion worse confounded. Fadus demanding that the High Priest's vestments be deposited, as once before, with the Romans; Tiberius Alexander symbolizing apostasy triumphant; Cumanus unable to maintain discipline among his own soldiers and aggravating Samaritan-Jewish relations; Felix outraging everyone and encouraging local banditti, and on trifling charges ordering the imprisonment of excellent persons—these men destroyed every possibility for peace and established a precedent for pillage and anarchy.

Such a state of affairs strengthened the Zealot group, and a number of extremists in their midst now abandoned restraint altogether. At every public gathering, wherever huge crowds assembled and order was at a minimum, these extremists created panic by stabbing their enemies with hidden daggers. They formed an underground movement and spread terror throughout the country. Everyone trembled at the mention of the Sicarii (they were so called because of their murders with the *sica*, dagger), for their weapons were raised not only against Romans but against any Jews suspected of counseling "collaboration." Often enough innocent people were among the victims. "When once the angel of destruction is summoned, he does not scruple to distinguish between righteous and wicked."[24]

In turn, terrorism both induced and thrived on Messianic spasms. An Egyptian Jew appeared suddenly and attracted thousands (if Josephus is right, about 30,000)[25] to himself. He promised nothing less than penetration into Jerusalem, a routing of the Roman garrison, and independence. Hopes ran high, but the procurator dashed them before the miracle began. "No sooner were these disorders reduced than the inflammation, as in a sick man's body, broke out again in another quarter."[26] Houses were looted, people slain, villages set afire. And the line between Messianic frenzy and brigandage was all the more blurred.

It is against such a background that we can understand why a number of leading Pharisees counseled against a war policy. Their hatred of Rome was as intense as that of the Zealots and of the Sicarii; but they had more than a rough estimate of Rome's power, and they beheld only too well Palestine's increasing impotence. "Pray for the peace of the [Roman] government," urged one of the Sages among the priests, "for, if it were not for the fear which it inspires, we would swallow each other alive."[27]

The Arch of Titus, An Inner Panel

The Arch still standing in Rome was erected by Titus (40 or 41-81 C.E.) to commemorate his triumph in Palestine. The inner panel represents the procession and shows Roman soldiers carrying the golden table, the musical instruments, and the seven-branched candlesticks taken from the Temple in Jerusalem.

They tried once and again to calm an upset population—"If you are engaged in planting," appealed Rabban Johanan ben Zakkai, "and suddenly have been informed that the Messiah has arrived, finish with your planting first and then go greet him"[28]—but in the tumult which now rose their pleas made no headway.

The governor who followed Felix was unable to undo the mischief of his predecessor. Although officially relations between Judea and Rome had not been broken off, pitched battles were taking place in the streets during the administration of the next procurator. He had to be recalled after two years; as a parting gift to his successor he emptied the prisons of their inmates, so that when Florus arrived in 64 he had less a province than a battlefield. His own baseness and bestiality led to rebellion on so large a scale that it was no longer possible to regard what was occurring as sporadic incidents. He plundered the people; from that he turned to plundering the Temple. The people were beyond themselves with fury. Some young wits thereupon staged a public satire by marching through the streets with baskets begging coppers for the destitute Florus. This burlesque of his dignity Florus could not forgive. He ordered a detachment of soldiers to march on Jerusalem and these proceeded to pillage, imprison and crucify indiscriminately. But he was still not pacified. He demanded that the citizens march out to greet troops summoned from Caesarea, and thus acknowledge submission to Roman authority. Only after much effort did the elders convince the mob to swallow this insult for the sake of peace. Then the troops arrived and the people cheered as ordered—but the soldiers would not respond to the salutation. It became too clear to the crowds that the whole procession had been planned as a blow to their self-respect, and a riot broke out with all the concomitants of slaughter. Nevertheless, Florus had to withdraw with his soldiers from Jerusalem because the mobs outnumbered his forces. Restoration of order was perhaps still possible; and in Agrippa II, the son of Agrippa I, there might have been found the advocate to persuade the Jews that war would be fatal for them. Agrippa II did hasten to make the appeal, for he was then returning from Alexandria; moreover, he almost succeeded in quieting the population, in proving the hopelessness of war with Rome, in drawing a promise that they would pay outstanding taxes and repair various ruins. When, however, he proceeded to urge them to submit to Florus until a successor was appointed, he was answered with cries of mockery. The country was at war.

4

The war raged for four years; indeed, it was seven years before the last resisting strongholds were taken. But the Jews were fighting a losing battle from the day they ceased to offer a sacrifice in behalf of the emperor.

Consider first the nature of the antagonist. Once Rome recognized a state of war she did not make the mistake of which Syria had been guilty in the second century B.C.E.: the mistake of underestimating the capacity and determination of the revolutionaries. Particularly after the defeat of Cestius Gallus,[1] the emperor appointed no less a general than Vespasian against the province. And when Vespasian retired from the battlefield to become emperor, he left his son, Titus, in command. Both these men used not only all possible instruments of warfare but keen strategy. When it was evident that direct attack would not subdue Jerusalem, walls were erected around the city to prevent egress and thus starve its inhabitants to submission.

In the second place, the poverty within the country was acute. Unemployment swelled the ranks of the destitute; and in 64, when the Temple was at last completed, more than eighteen thousand laborers were left idle.[2] It is significant that one of the earliest acts of the rebels was the destruction of archives where a record of debts was kept.[3] A few aristocrats, landowners and capitalists had almost all of the country's wealth[4] which the procurators had not pocketed in advance; and the rich were opposed to the war. What hastened the disaster was that the Sicarii, in vengeance, destroyed the stores and provisions that the well-to-do had laid up,[5] either in their attempt to escape the cupidity of the procurators or perhaps for just such an emergency as the revolt. Before the war was over, men and women in Jerusalem were happy if they could find scraps among the refuse, straw to boil, and worse.[6]

The wealthy and socially prominent were not the only ones who opposed war. There were others whose motives for peace were not the preservation of their private property, but whose policy willy-nilly contributed to weakening united effort. The Jewish Christians would not fight because the political aspects of this uprising were irrelevant to their Messianic scheme. The Hillelite element among the Pharisees, at least those devoted to Johanan ben Zakkai, saw no hope in the struggle.

And corresponding to this absence of unity in the population was an inability of the war advocates themselves to organize effectively. The latter were, it is true, agreed that peace with Rome was at an end. The Shammaites, for example, now forced through a number of measures calculated to deepen the gulf separating Jew from non-Jew.[7] The question, however, was this—how should the war be conducted and what personalities were to be in charge of the campaigns? There was a moderate group with its leadership; there were several Zealot groups, each with leadership of its own. And no one trusted his fellow. "Why was the first Temple destroyed?" runs the melancholy reflection in the Talmud. "Because three things . . . idolatry, unchastity, and murder [were rampant]. But why the second Temple? Were they not diligently studying Torah and fulfilling religious commandments and practicing lovingkindness? Why then was it destroyed? Because of mutual hatreds, all without cause."[8] Josephus, John of Gischala, Simeon bar Giora, Anan, Eleazar son of Simeon turned against one another the swords that should have been directed against the common enemy. The country thus bled itself to death before the blood-letting came to be applied from outside. When unity was at last achieved, it was too late.

Finally, Judea suffered from a woeful lack of professional military experience. Some of the rebel chiefs were adept at guerrilla fighting; they had the advantage of knowing their own terrain; but at planned military operations, such as a contest with Rome would require, there was little skill. The case of Josephus[8a] is instructive, even if the account of his clever stratagems is more than braggadocio. Regardless of virtues and shortcomings in his character, in a trained army he would never have risen to high command. What did he know of warfare except what some manuals taught him and desperation led him to? Yet to him, at the age of twenty-nine, was entrusted the important region of Galilee where the first thrust of the Romans was anticipated. His equivocal character and ultimate disloyalty naturally hastened defeat. The loss of that fertile portion of the Holy Land by 67 convinced many moderate supporters that victory was out of the question. All in all, the war could have only one result, tragedy.

However obvious such facts may be to moderns, or may have been to Agrippa, or to the Hillelites, to the war parties they were not altogether clear—unless we are to assume that they were totally insane. Perhaps the statement ought to be formulated thus: However vaguely or otherwise these facts were apprehended by the war parties, they did not lack other assumptions which—to them—counterbalanced unfavorable odds. The war, one must remember, proved a long one despite all handicaps. Without sources of courage the resistance could not have been so long maintained.

"What is it which inspires you with confidence to defy the Romans?" Agrippa asked the rebels;[9] and the answer emerges from the Thucydidean speech that Josephus has put into his mouth. Apparently they hoped that they would not be alone in harassing Rome. The latter years of the sixties were filled with difficulty for the empire,[10] and in the general turmoil the Jews believed that Rome would be unable to take an effective stand. Again, they felt that direct assistance would come to them from Jews in neighboring countries or the far-flung Diaspora. Especially deep was the feeling that God would not permit the heathen to devastate His Holy City and Temple. And alongside such expectations were memories of the remarkable success of the Maccabees, a mood of desperation with the *status quo* of intolerable servitude, the Messianic temper, some minor victories. Even as they had routed Florus and Cestius Gallus, cried the rebels at Johanan ben Zakkai, so would they put Vespasian's and Titus's forces to flight.[11]

And so the war was fought and thousands upon thousands lost their lives, and thousands more were seized as captives and sold as slaves,[12] and the country was ravaged, and the Temple was sent up in flames—whether with or against the will of Titus was immaterial.[13] Tradition has it that this last occurred on the ninth day in the month of Ab; and, the legend adds, when fire surrounded the magnificent structure, the priests hastened to the roofs, flung the keys up to the heavens, and cried out, "Master of the universe, here are the keys which Thou didst entrust us with; we have not proven trustworthy custodians!"[14]

Judea capta—this was the inscription on the coins minted to celebrate Titus's great victory. And if he had in mind the territory and those aspects of Jewish life closely connected with the territory, he was no doubt right. For the war produced a number of profound changes and only prophetic insight could have discerned that the present catastrophe did not spell an end to Jews and Judaism. For the destruction of the Temple meant not only that the chief institution of worship had perished, but that the capital of Jews everywhere had fallen. Even the Jews in Alexandria, with their temple of Onias, never doubted that it was but a local institution while the Jerusalem Temple was the center for world Jewry. Indeed, Onias's temple survived the great sanctuary only a little less than three years.[15] The Temple tax which had formerly been collected from all Jews was henceforth appropriated for the temple of Jupiter Capitolinus in Rome.[16] Many therefore despaired of a future. Multitudes in their grief resolved to abstain from meats and wine because these had been Temple staples; and, they felt, it was wrong for man to enjoy what could no longer be offered to God. Rabbi Joshua ben Hananiah strongly opposed such excessive mourning, true;[17] but at the sight of the ruins even he could not suppress despondency. "Woe unto us," the sob broke from him, "that this, the place where the iniquities of Israel were pardoned, is now laid waste."[18]

One immediate consequence of the end of Temple worship was the loss of considerable revenue previously enjoyed by the priests. Inevitably this loss of wealth, plus the fact that their function disappeared, meant also a loss of influence. And that wealth and influence had been no slight thing.[19] "Woe unto me because of the house of Boethus," a popular song used to run:

Woe unto me because of their clubs;
Woe unto me because of the house of Hanin,
Woe unto me because of their whisperings;
Woe unto me because of the house of Kathros,
Woe unto me because of their quills;
Woe unto me because of the house of Ishmael ben Phiabi,
Woe unto me because of their fists.
For they are High Priests,
And their sons are treasurers,
And their sons-in-law are officers,
And their slaves beat the folk with sticks![20]

Priestly gifts like the heave offerings and tithes were still given them, as Scripture had commanded; but their former income and authority were never to return.

In the course of the succeeding years a number of survivors were permitted to return to their estates. Some evidently recovered their fortunes.[21] But the majority were almost pauperized; and among these were many former magnates.[22] Since the country was now Vespasian's private property,[23] the tribute he collected from the inhabitants went into his own belt, not into improvements. For many emigration was the only escape from starvation. Thus began the pilgrimage and flight that brought the Jew to many lands where rarely before had he taken root. This was exclusive of those seized for slavery. Most of the captives were brought to Rome; whenever possible they were redeemed by their coreligionists already settled there. And so great was the influx that by the third decade of the following century Rabbi Mattiah ben Heresh could establish an advanced academy of learning here.[24]

To two groups, as distinct and active bodies, the war proved fatal. No longer do we hear of Sadducees and Essenes. Their tendencies did not disappear: attitudes, inclinations are not the product of party membership only. The point is that the cohesiveness of these groups was shattered. Transformations within the country were so radical that an exceptional adaptability was required, and this these groups lacked. The Sadducees, moreover, must have lost great numbers during the war, when the wealthy were special objects of mob hostility.

And yet the extraordinary fact remains that neither Israel nor its way of life was destroyed. The figure of the phoenix rising from ashes, overworked as it may be, is nonetheless the only one that can suggest what we are now to observe. Spiritual life and cultural values—the elements, in brief, to which a people refers when it contemplates its *raison d'être* or describes its objective in history—if anything, rose to an excellence in many ways superior to the accomplishments of the past. We may, if we wish, call such a phenomenon the mechanics of survival, and demonstrate, for example, that the emigrations that took on such proportions at that time made it possible for Jews later to find communities of their brethren in various countries, and thus blunt the sharp edge of exile. Or we may observe that an impoverished folk was truly relieved of a great economic burden when it no longer could purchase beasts for sacrificial purposes. Or, again, the disappearance of sects removed certain conflicting interests and thereby facilitated a conservation of energy and a unity of purpose. Or, finally, from the agony may have been forced a conception of destiny independent of territory. Such and other observations are undoubtedly correct. But the mechanics were not the products of accident. To an eminent degree they were the results of the foresight and determination of a group of men, especially of Rabban Johanan ben Zakkai—who never stirred without the accompaniment of the spirit of Torah.[25]

5

"It was said of Rabban Johanan ben Zakkai that he neglected neither Scripture nor Mishna nor Gemara nor *halakot* nor *agadot* nor the subtleties of the Torah nor the subtleties of the early Sages nor any of the rules of the scholars—not a word in the Torah did he neglect; confirming what Scripture says, 'That I may cause those that love me to inherit substance, and that I may fill their treasuries'" (Prov. 8:21).[1] This was not the only thing said of him; he was known always to be the first to greet his fellow man; he himself held the door open for his students; and so on and so on.[2] It was also later said of him that, like Moses, he lived to be a hundred and twenty years old.[3] The figure is more charitable than accurate; nevertheless, there are points of contact between the singular prophet and the Sage.

While the war was still in progress, Johanan ben Zakkai perceived that arms could not save Judaism. Neither would pessimism nor spiritual timidity. On the other hand, he was convinced that a vitalized tradition could; if necessary, it would be a portable homeland. During the tumult of war, when human decencies and moral scruples were cast to the winds, he ordered the immediate suspension of certain biblically enjoined ceremonies;[4] they would then have been a mockery, and the crisis called for someone with sufficient courage to declare that even so sacred an order as Scripture's was now impractical. He pleaded with the war parties to submit; when he saw that his entreaties were futile, he had himself smuggled out of the beleaguered city (in a coffin), made his way to the Roman camp, and submitted a petition—Would Rome grant him and his disciples refuge in the coastal city of Jabneh where he might establish an academy?[5] A number of refugees had already been readmitted there,[6] and Johanan's request seemed innocent enough. It was granted. "There had been books on the slope of Beacon Hill," writes Van Wyck Brooks, "when the wolves still howled on the summit."[7] The battle cries on Mt. Zion had not yet subsided when from Jabneh the voices of the scholars could be heard.

The disciples who retreated with their master to Jabneh did not remain indifferent, any more than did Johanan, to events in the Holy City.[8] But they were taught by him what new emphases to make, how to convert inherited values into new ones, where to set the foundations for the structure of Judaism that was to be rebuilt. To his grief-stricken disciple who feared that with the destruction of the Temple the future iniquities of Israel would have to go unpardoned, he declared, "My son, do not weep; we have a means of atonement as effective as this. And what is it? It is deeds of lovingkindness; as the prophet has put it, 'For I desire mercy and not sacrifice' " (Hos. 6:6).[9] When in later generations we meet scholars interpreting a term, which in earlier periods had been employed for Temple worship, as prayer,[10] it is clear that Johanan's program has succeeded.

Now the program called for more than eloquent homiletic. From his students and collaborators Johanan required craftsmanship and tools of the craft, learning accompanied by works.[11] Without scholarship action would be unguided and as unsafe as a sea voyage without a compass. Precisely this had been his criticism of the Galileans.[12] Yet scholarship could not now be permitted to relax into scholasticism. Two things above all were therefore indispensable: one, the formation of a new center and institution to be endowed with all the authority formerly exercised by the Sanhedrin in the Temple; two, the enactment of new, but necessary, laws which would confirm the authoritative character of the new center. Both were accomplished. Jabneh was declared the seat of the High Court, whence all major decisions were to be issued—here, for example, the fixing of the calendar (a most important problem in these centuries)[13] was to be determined. And a series of important *takkanot*, enactments, were at once proclaimed, to underscore that Jabneh, in everything but sacrificial offerings, was to enjoy the prerogatives of Jerusalem.

These measures evidently could not be put through without some protest. To give but one illustration: Tradition in the past had established that if the New Year occurred on a Sabbath the blowing of the ram's horn[14] could take place only in the Temple at Jerusalem, but was to be forbidden elsewhere.[15] Johanan ben Zakkai now decreed that the ceremony, in such a contingency, should be performed wherever the High Court was stationed, regardless of the city it was in.[16] Some distinguished scholars, however, opposed the unprecedented action. On what grounds, they wondered, did Johanan justify his view? "Let us put it up for discussion," they said. "First sound the ram's horn," replied Johanan ben Zakkai, "and we will discuss it afterwards." After the ceremony the scholars turned to him with "Well, let us discuss the matter." Whereupon he said, "The ram's horn has already been sounded; what point is there to a debate over a *fait accompli?*"[17]

The incident is quite representative, but must not be misunderstood as scorn of academic discussion or of the dialectic that characterizes so much of the talmudic content. Johanan ben Zakkai did not wish to discourage the Rabbinic method of study and teaching. "If thou hast studied much Torah," he used to say, "take no credit to thyself, for to this end wast thou created."[18] What he expected was a quality of realism, and learning out of season in pedantry. The issue and the occasion called for immediate action and not exegesis; and he was not afraid of opposition. In earlier days he had effectively confuted Sadducean scholars;[19] he was no less able at present against other contestants, among the Sages and elsewhere.[20]

Thus Jabneh, the city of Philistine origins, became the vineyard for scholars who loved the Torah. Here, as occasion arose, *takkanot* were issued. Here valuable traditions were collected and redacted, particularly those related to the Temple; for the purely intellectual interest in this field was accompanied by a hope that soon again the Temple might be rebuilt, and the restoration of its worship depended upon authentic record of the ritual.[21] Here, too, teaching and research were zealously conducted. To these men the words of Scripture were not an ancient proclamation, but like some recently promulgated order to which all flock eagerly.[22] In its contents they found everything. Law and mystic doctrine, history and prophecy, narrative and parable, warning and consolation, commandment and ideal greeted them in every verse. By constant application of the ancient Charter to current realities they gave their generation a sense of continuity with the past and an assignment for the future.

Therefore, Midrash—that is, the detailed, meticulous exposition of the biblical text that had been carried on from Ezra's days—was now taken up with fresh devotion. Not only was the literal meaning of the Bible investigated; but either exegesis supplied old folkways with scriptural sanction or released new law. The Bible was a divine work. As its interpreters the Rabbis never doubted but that they were raising to the explicit what had remained implicit. When they insisted that the *talio* of Scripture meant something different from what the words themselves would seem to declare,[23] they did not believe that they were inventing a meaning unauthorized by the text. To their humaneness, any other explanation was shocking. In their frame of reference such commentary, even in less dramatic examples, was most natural.[24] Gilbert Murray once observed something similar in the development of Greek religion, and his remarks are difficult to improve upon. "When . . . change does come and is consciously felt we may notice a significant fact about it. It does not announce itself as what it was, a new thing in the world. It professes to be a revival, or rather an emphatic realization, of something very old." And he adds: "This claim of a new thing to be old is, in varying degrees, a common characteristic of great movements. The Reformation professed to be a return to the Bible, the Evangelical movement in England a return to the Gospels, the High Church movement a return to the early church. . . . The tendency is due in part to the almost insuperable difficulty of really inventing a new word to denote a new thing. It is so much easier to take an existing word, especially a famous word with fine associations, and twist it into a new sense. In part, no doubt, it comes from mankind's natural love for these old associations, the fact that nearly all people who are worth much have in them some instinctive spirit of reverence."[25]

The stimulus provided by the activity at Jabneh was immediate as well as vigorous, for in a short while schools sprang up in various cities to which Jabneh scholars had withdrawn. Johanan ben Zakkai himself did not linger on at his newly established center, presumably to make way for a descendant of Hillel, Gamaliel II. At all events, the aged teacher had done his work wisely and well. He had not only found the formula for the preservation of Israel and its historic function, but also the personnel to apply it.

"Towering Pillar, Light of the Universe, Mighty Hammer,"[26] cried Johanan's disciples when they took final leave of their master; and something of his stature, illumination, strength clung to them as they carried on his work. The Sages whom he had ordained were far from alike in upbringing or outlook or temperament. There was Rabbi Eliezer ben Hyrcanus, whose forte, and limitation, was a remarkable memory. There was Rabbi Joshua ben Hananiah whose gentleness and catholicity of spirit reminded one of Hillel. There were others, each with his own distinctive talents and personality, some more or less conservative, some more or less daring; some inclined to sympathize with the Shammaite view, some with the Hillelite. Of course these men did not act in one, fixed pattern on every occasion. Consider, for example, a Sage like Rabbi Tarfon. He was himself wealthy; yet we meet him as a spokesman for the poor.[27] In debate with his colleagues he sounds like a product of the Hillelite group; yet he defends a Shammaite view with extreme vigor.[28] Our sources, unfortunately, are not lavish with biographical detail; but there is enough to make us confident that a full-length portrait of each of these remarkable persons would reveal more than one expression of character and attitude.[29] This is perhaps best evident in the person and career of the Patriarch Gamaliel II, who acted also as new head of the academy at Jabneh.

Johanan's mantle was now on his shoulders, and the days were still full of stress for Israel. The stricken community was hardly permitted to convalesce during the reign of Domitian. Everywhere his hand lay heavy on intellectual life.[30] With brutal severity he exacted the Jew tax; he was not beyond setting spies even in the Rabbinical academies.[31] Whenever he could, therefore, Gamaliel sought to create legislation to relieve the pressure on the people. He put through economic reforms; he enacted *takkanot* to improve relations between Jews and non-Jews; he visited one community after another in order to see for himself how the population was faring.[32] One thing above all he feared, that the endless debate among the Sages—admirable in so far as intellectual alertness and academic liberty were concerned—would leave the people without a unified pattern of conduct. If Rabbi Eliezer was free to *act* according to his interpretation of the law, and Rabbi Joshua according to his lights, what would happen to a folk which at the moment needed a universally acknowledged norm? Gamaliel did not deny that Shammaites, no less than Hillelites, were dedicated to the greater glory of God.[33] But the stage had been reached when controversy and individual practice had to be terminated. Something had to be done to curb the tendency of different scholars' being law unto themselves.

As a result he set himself to establish unity. During his administration the Jabneh academy virtually[34] determined that henceforth Hillelite teachings, with several exceptions, were to be standard law. He went even further. Within the academy he sought to check argumentativeness and silence disputants.[35] He fixed a liturgy and ordered its adoption.[36] He insisted that all scholars submit to the decisions of the High Court at Jabneh.

Was there an element of the highhanded, of the arbitrary to his program? No doubt there was. And the first to revolt were the men who were his colleagues and allegedly his collaborators. His own brother-in-law clashed with him and had to be excommunicated. One might say that the stubbornness of Eliezer is no surprise. But even Joshua ben Hananiah opposed Gamaliel, not once but several times. One incident is worth retelling.[37] Witnesses had appeared before Gamaliel and testified that they had seen the new moon. Gamaliel thereupon announced that a new month had begun and that all were to regulate their calendar accordingly. But it was soon evident that the witnesses had delivered false testimony; in other words, that the calendar fixed by Gamaliel was in error. When one of the Sages called this to the attention of Joshua, the latter approved ignoring the patriarchal order. Gamaliel, however, was not easily resisted; he ordered Joshua publicly to violate the day which in Joshua's reckoning was the Day of Atonement, the most sacred day of the year. A reconciliation was fortunately effected; nevertheless, it was not Gamaliel, but Joshua, who had to yield. Similar incidents only served to sharpen antagonisms. Eventually feelings ran so high that the members of the academy rebelled against their president[38] and voted to appoint another scholar to the office; and as Gamaliel relinquished his post they cried, in the terrifying words of the prophet (Nah. 3:19), "For upon whom hath not thy wickedness passed continually?"[39]

The scholars had their way. They could flock to the academy once again without restraint and with perfect liberty indulge in debate. Whatever else the schools may have been, they were certainly not dull: the ones forbade, the others permitted; these declared something impure, those declared it pure; some decided an object fit while some decided it unfit. To Rabbi Joshua, the academic freedom was a source of cheer in his old age;[40] but he was not alone in this respect. Numerous scholars now convened to register traditions which had not been included in the academy's sessions. Their object was not disunity (it was this which Gamaliel found so difficult to understand); but they feared excessive authority;[41] hence, too, they were anxious to adopt a principle of enormous importance, to wit, that the minority view in a case must not go unrecorded, despite the fact that law is determined by the majority.[42]

Sometime during this period the biblical canon was finally established.[43] About a few books there had been doubt even at an earlier period; about others there were still qualms. In any event, it was now determined which books did and which did not constitute Holy Scripture. The excluded works, as a result, gradually found fewer and fewer readers. They became apocrypha.

The victory of Gamaliel's opponents had at least two results. One was that, except for certain issues determined by the High Court like the one at Jabneh, schools and individual scholars continued to enjoy abundant liberty;[44] and the second was that the material for study was increased. Gamaliel's contemporaries believed that if opinions of Shammai and Hillel were published even when these did not constitute law, future teachers would learn not to insist obdurately on their own views.[45] At the same time, to men engaged in the study of Torah, all traditions were rich sources for further intellectual give-and-take. A copious Torah was what they wanted.

Once their victory was assured, however, they could afford to reconsider their feelings toward Gamaliel. He was, after all, Patriarch and a descendant of Hillel; moreover, he had behaved with exceptional nobility after retirement from his academic office. He had continued to attend sessions, as one Sage among others, and had not remained aloof from the deliberations. The scholars therefore invited him to resume his former duties. To his last days he concerned himself with the needs of his impoverished people; in order to put an end for all time to extravagance at funerals he left word with his kin that upon his own death he was to be buried in simple, inexpensive shrouds.[46] The example became tradition, and one element of conspicuous waste which previously emphasized social cleavages henceforth disappeared. In this manner a stormy career closed, and words wrung from the man during his strife with Rabbi Eliezer may serve as his epitaph: "Master of the universe, to Thee it is manifest that not for my glory, not for the glory of my father's house, but for Thy glory only have I acted, that controversies might not abound in Israel."[47]

6

The year and a half during which Nerva ruled the Roman Empire and the early years of Trajan's reign brought some respite to Palestine. Thanks to the former, rigors associated with the collection of the *fiscus judaicus* were relaxed. Within Palestine some features of organized community life were revived. The commander of the Roman legion stationed in the province was the governor. His seat remained in Caesarea. Jews paid tribute to Rome. A descendant of Hillel was recognized as Patriarch. All strictly Jewish problems were within the jurisdiction of his scholarly court of which he was the chief. The powers of Court and Patriarch were quite extensive; although it is not fully clear how far such powers went, we know that in civil and ceremonial affairs (perhaps in some criminal instances too)[1] Jews submitted to the Patriarch and the Sages as they formerly had to the Ethnarch and his Sanhedrin. To facilitate relations between the house of the Patriarch and Roman officials there was even an academy of "Greek wisdom" under the Patriarch's auspices.[2]

Poverty was still widespread, but an elaborate system of charity was developed to provide for the local indigent, for wayfarers, for the hard pressed even among the neighboring non-Jews.[3] In the large settlements religious services were regularly conducted and Gamaliel's liturgy was employed. Mornings and evenings the *Shema* was recited; and as the Jew repeated the words "Hear, O Israel, the Lord our God, the Lord is one—and thou shalt love the Lord thy God with all thy heart, with all thy soul, and with all thy being," he took upon himself the yoke of the dominion of Heaven.[4] A prayer (*Shemoneh Esre*),[5] edited at Gamaliel's initiative, was recited daily. Its passages are an interesting commentary on the age. For one, a formula against the Nazarenes and schismatics was incorporated; so, too, a petition in behalf of proselytes, along with the pious and Sages, was included. Again, it is interesting to notice that the supplications were all in terms of the community as a whole, that the yearnings for the Temple had not languished, that the climactic note, on which the prayer ended, was one of peace. Readings from Scripture formed an important part of the service. Various social needs and community projects were entrusted to a city council; perhaps there were several such councils, each with its specific obligations.[6] Public baths were maintained; ritual and hygiene thus collaborated to encourage sanitation. Everyone was urged to engage in some craft, to take pride in it, to teach it to his sons. Attached to the synagogues were schools. A highly developed program of public instruction was constantly supervised, for there was a strong sentiment fostered by the Rabbis that learning was no one's monopoly. Mark well the idiom of the verse (Deut. 33:4) the Rabbis were fond of saying, "Moses commanded us a law, an inheritance of the congregation of Jacob." It is not said, an inheritance of priests or Levites or Israelites; it is not the legacy of princes only; it is the possession of the whole house of Jacob.[7] And Rabbi Meir did not hesitate to put the thought into even stronger language. "Whence do we learn that even a heathen who studies Torah is on a par with the High Priest? From the verse (Lev. 18:5) 'Ye shall therefore keep My statutes, and Mine ordinances, which if a man do, he shall live by them.' The text does not read Which if a Priest or Levite or Israelite do; but 'which if a *man* do!' "[8]

Such sentiments and such a program reinforced the influence and authority of the Rabbis. They completely displaced the priests; and Rabbinic leadership was welcome because, unlike priests, these men were recruited from every station and region of society. Among the Rabbis could be found priest and layman, rich and poor, artisan and farmer, laborer and proprietor.[9] Moreover, the contrast between some late High Priests and principal Rabbis could not but be striking. People did not forget how in the last days of the Temple the high priesthood went to the highest bidder.[10] The present public servants more often than not were heard to disparage excessive luxury, were eager to share their lore with as many as possible, forbade remuneration for instruction and judicial action, were foremost in succor and charity. They did demand certain exemptions and privileges for scholars,[11] but scholarship was no caste opportunity, and their frugality was everywhere to behold.

Political events in the meantime grew turbulent. Trajan's military ambition drove him to undertake the conquest of Parthia; while he was engaged in these campaigns Jews in various countries, "as though they had been seized by some terrible spirit of rebellion,"[12] rose in revolt. Whether or not the Jews of Palestine participated in this uprising is not clear. But the inevitable outcome everywhere was bloodshed and disaster; and once again mourning and a reaction against pagan culture.[13]

This struggle, however, was but a preparatory encounter to another war, whose consequences were well-nigh fatal. Perhaps the first reaction to the new emperor, Hadrian (117-38), was not unfavorable.[14] But—though our sources disagree[15]—it seems that from the closing years of Trajan's reign on, Palestine was in ferment. It may be that the Jews had been led to believe by Trajan that they would be permitted to rebuild the Temple; and then the promise was withdrawn. Hadrian's resolution to abandon the ambitious conquests of his predecessor was due most likely to his realization that Rome's strength had passed its meridian; which would be all the more reason to consolidate the empire and to attempt a leveling of cultures: to eliminate practices which irritated his sense of civilized behavior and expressions which seemed to qualify supreme allegiance to the emperor. If so, such rituals as circumcision (why, after all, should a heathen distinguish it from castration?) and such declarations as the *Shema* inevitably offended him. His prohibition of these, however, could mean only one thing to the Jews—an assault on their way of life. While to Hadrian the measures might be no more than an efficient control over Jews, to the Jews they resembled an attempt at the suppression of Judaism. So black was the mood that, were the elementary functions of life subject to reason and absolute control, no new generation would have been brought forth.[16]

War broke out, the like of which even Rome found difficult to cope with. The leader of the revolt was one Simeon; to multitudes he was the Messiah. He came indeed to be known as Bar Kokba, son of the star, after the most distinguished Rabbi of the century had applied the verse (Num. 24:17), "There shall step forth a star out of Jacob," to him. Not everyone shared this view. "Akiba," said one of the Sages to the enthusiastic Rabbi, "grass will have sprouted from your cheeks and the Messiah will not yet have arrived!"[17] Nevertheless, the reproof went practically ignored, and the determined stand of the Jews suggests that the majority saw in Bar Kokba more than a commander.

The war was bitterly fought; it was, to quote the Roman historian, neither "of slight importance nor of brief duration."[18] Excellent forces and strategy were required to defeat the rebels, and on both sides the losses were tremendous. For two years fortune smiled on the Jews; coins were even minted to celebrate the liberation of Jerusalem. But Severus, whom the emperor had called from Britain to conduct the campaign, was resolute. He was determined to smash the resistance at any cost. Finally in 135, with the fall of Bether ("from which not a man escaped"),[19] the war was brought to an end. For Hadrian it proved an expensive victory; in communicating with the Senate, for example, he omitted the regular formula "I and the legions are in health."[20] But for the Jews the defeat was devastating, worse in its results than the war with Titus. Almost all the Jewish settlements in Judea were wiped out.[21] Jerusalem was definitely converted into a pagan city, Jews were forbidden to enter it. Henceforth the city was known as Aelia Capitolina and on the site of the Sanctuary was erected a temple to the Capitoline Jupiter. The teaching and practice of Judaism became a capital crime; martyrdom ceased to be rare. Now it was in fact not only the Jews as a people who had to defend themselves; their religion was under attack. To whom does the verse (Ex. 20:6) "Of them that love Me and keep My commandments" refer? said Rabbi Nathan. To the inhabitants of the land of Israel who give up their lives for the religious commandments. "Why are you being taken to the execution block?" one is asked. "For circumcising my son," he replies. "Why are you being cast into the flames?" another is asked. "For studying Torah," he replies. "Why are you to be crucified?" a third is asked. "For eating unleavened bread [during Passover],"[22] he replies. "Why have you been sentenced to get a hundred lashes?" still another is asked. "For conducting the ceremony of Palms [during the Feast of Booths],"[23] he replies.[24]

Had Hadrian remained much longer on the throne it is extremely doubtful if Palestinian Jewry could have recovered from the blows. Truth to say, for those who had not been slaughtered or sold as slaves or forcibly deported, flight from the country seemed the only rational conduct, and all the pious protests of the Rabbis were helpless against this exodus.[25] Steadily after 135 the number of Jewish settlements, even in Galilee, declined. The refugees to Babylonia were so numerous (and apparently so confident that the Holy Land was doomed) that shortly a nephew of Joshua ben Hananiah attempted to establish a court independent of Palestinian authority.[26]

Two factors prevented total disintegration, one external and the other an inner one. The former was the repeal of Hadrian's edicts by the new emperor and the general change in Roman policy toward the Jews. Moved by the appeals of the Jewish embassy and the intercession of some influential Gentiles, Antoninus Pius revoked many of his predecessor's measures against the Jews,[27] though he still forbade them to receive proselytes or to enter the Holy City. Such prohibitions Rome could not abolish without fear for her imperial prestige and security. On the other hand, the recent war fully revealed that the Jews were anything but easy conquest when they were aroused and that if quiet was to obtain in the province some compromises would have to be made. A measure of self-government, for example, would have to be allowed; indeed, concession on that score might win over the patriarchate sufficiently to encourage the Jews themselves toward moderation. Again, the kind of governor sent to the country had to be such as to inspire at least a measure of respect.[28]

Even more important to recovery, however, was the inner factor. Despite Hadrianic ruthlessness there were still scholars in the land and for them the threat to survival was but a signal for redoubled efforts. On a handful of the ordained among them fell the task of reconstructing Jewish life from ruins. That they proved equal to the hour was a tribute not merely to their own accomplishments, but to the legacy left behind, especially by two Sages of the previous generation; above all, by Rabbi Akiba.

When Rabbi Tarfon contemplated the character of Akiba he could not help thinking of the verse in Job (28:11), "And the thing that is hid bringeth he forth to light."[29] Superlatives came easily to his contemporaries as well as to his later biographers.

Akiba was born in the middle of the first century and for about half his life remained without any education. Not until his child was ready for schooling did Akiba undertake study at all. Yet the man who in his forties first began to learn the alphabet, rose to be the greatest scholar of talmudic Judaism. He sat at the feet of Rabbi Eliezer, of Rabbi Joshua, of Nahum of Gimzo, of Rabbi Tarfon, and then outstripped them all. And the most distinguished teachers of the post-Hadrianic era were his disciples.

Properly to understand the contribution of Akiba, some introductory comments must be made, particularly since these have to do with the substance known as Talmud. As a result of centuries of activity, especially of Johanan ben Zakkai and his disciples, three important fields of study had evolved. One was Midrash, which, as already observed, was highly developed exegesis applied to Scripture. One was Halaka, which means law, but which also meant the accumulation of legal traditions, concise decisions rendered by the Sages without the attendant biblical passages. An example is perhaps in order. "Civil cases are to be tried by three judges," declares the Mishna succinctly.[30] Because the word *Elohim* is used by the Bible three times in describing the procedure to be followed in the case of theft, we know that civil cases must be tried by three judges.[31] Now, this latter form is Midrash, for not only has a halakic view been given, but the biblical texts to support the law have been summoned. The difference is that between research and conclusion (or codification).

Finally, there was the Haggada (or, Agada), which included every conceivable range of thought not covered by the legal. Haggada contained fable, history, epigram, prayer, sermon, meditation, theology, folklore, science—one despairs of enumerating the subject matter in this vast area. There will be other opportunities to refer to these studies. For the moment the short observations may serve as a preface to our immediate subject, Akiba.

To each of these fields Akiba made contributions of first magnitude; the intensified activity and vitality of scholarship in the following generation were largely the result of his work. In the first place, he introduced logical order in the Halaka. Through a systematic arrangement of legal traditions according to subject matter, he did away with the rudimentary and artificial classification according to some mnemonic device. To what might Rabbi Akiba be compared? scholars later used to say. To a laborer who went abroad with his basket, and purchased wheat and barley and spelt and lentils; and then retired to sort out the wheat into one pile, the barley into one pile, the spelt into one pile, and the lentils into one pile—so that each could be found in its proper place.[32]

In the second place, he opened vistas in Midrash which gave the study of Scripture a new lease on life. Not a curlicue, not a peculiarity of the biblical text was devoid of higher meaning to the man. Conjunctions, particles, repetitions were to him sources of most significant implication. Protest as his notable colleague Rabbi Ishmael might, that Torah must be interpreted only by means of established hermeneutic rules, that Hillel's formulae plus a few additional ones were all that was needed, that many peculiarities of Scripture were no more momentous than similar peculiarities in human speech, Akiba persisted along his own course.[33] The course often led him to farfetched interpretations. But often, also, he was brought to profound *aperçus*, to many acute insights into the spirit of Holy Writ—and it was this which he sought. One need only compare, for example, the earlier interpretation of Lev. 15:33 with Rabbi Akiba's to appreciate the man's motivation and objective, for he put an end to the primitive custom of isolating women completely during certain periods.[34] His method thus gave to the Talmud and to Judaism a quality which neither age nor adversity could defeat.

Au fond, this was why Akiba's school of exegesis prevailed over Rabbi Ishmael's. The latter was not without his followers and the fruits of his work were neither unimpressive nor neglected. But it was the Akiba discipline that unfettered mind and imagination in this and succeeding centuries, and gave to dialectic an expanse without which it would have suffocated.

Finally, despite occasional rebukes from colleagues that several interpretations by him were grotesque,[35] we owe to Akiba some of the most felicitous passages in the Haggada. He was apparently interested in philosophical speculation and opposed to any system which, in the slightest, qualified God's transcendent or unique nature. Not even angels, he declared, can behold the glory of God;[36] certainly no being could be compared to Him. As firmly as he was convinced of Providence, so was he emphatic concerning man's freedom of the will.[37] In this teaching he may have been expressing a criticism of the Christian doctrine of man's natural sinfulness and depravity.[38] Every human being, he further held, possessed an element of the divine in himself; consequently, he that sheds the blood of man has committed a crime against God no less than man.[39] A love for Israel filled his heart and in the Song of Songs he saw the poetic expression of the love between God and Israel.[40] His concept of suffering is too ecstatic for paraphrase. "Beloved are sufferings," he said;[41] and as he taught he lived.

For he was seized during the Hadrianic persecutions and after long imprisonment condemned to death by slow torture for obeying God rather than the emperor. His cheerful acceptance of the agony stunned the executioner. "Are you a sorcerer?" he asked Akiba. "No," replied the Sage, "I am not a sorcerer. But I rejoice at the opportunity finally given me to love my God 'with all my life'; hitherto I was able to love Him only 'with all my means' and 'with all my might.'" Thereupon he began to recite the *Shema*, for the time for prayer had come—"Hear, O Israel," he called, "the Lord is our God, the Lord is One!" And on the word "One" he died.[42]

Akiba was not the only martyr of the time; before him, under similar circumstances, his colleague Ishmael met his end. One Sage was sentenced to be burned with the scrolls from which he had taught; another was pierced like a sieve for ordaining scholars so that they might assume spiritual leadership in the next generation.[43] In the folk memory these events left a permanent mark; these men were Israel's truest sons. They had loved Israel in their life, never tired of teaching them, consoling them, emphasizing their distinctive role and obligation in life, training them to qualify as a holy nation, and in the service of the people had now accepted the supreme sacrifice to make known that the Lord God of Israel is King and His dominion is over all.

7

One of the first tasks for the new generation of Sages was the choice of a new center, to achieve for the present what Jabneh had achieved after the destruction of Jerusalem. Thanks to the humaneness of the new emperor, they could once more assemble to consider legislation for the afflicted settlement; and this they did in the Galilean city of Usha, whose inhabitants extended every hospitality to the Synod.[1] Gradually the Rabbis helped the people regain stability and even spiritual life asserted itself. By means of various laws attempts were made to relieve the economic hardships of the survivors and to prevent the land from falling into pagan hands.[2] Akiba's disciples, particularly Meir, Judah ben Ilai, Simeon ben Yohai; the new Patriarch, Simeon ben Gamaliel; numerous other scholars —each in his way reanimated the Torah, and thus made the people rise higher than the flames that sought to consume them.

The metaphor is not original; it is in effect borrowed from the Rabbi who was burned to death with the scrolls he had used for instruction: "The scrolls are aflame, the words take wing!"[3] Study and the amplification of tradition were resumed in defiance of poverty. Nothing could have given a defeated people civilized mind and heart more effectively than the conception that God is worshiped not only by prayer but by study as well; and not only by these but by ethical conduct. The Rabbis therefore did not fail to preach to the populace—even women lingered at the synagogue to hear the sermons, to the occasional annoyance of their husbands;[4] to devote endless energy to the study of subjects which were altogether of a theoretical nature; to create and develop law which would translate into daily behavior the prophetic ideals so sacred to them. A fervent preoccupation with the law distinguished these men, as indeed it had distinguished their forerunners; they were deeply aware that society does not live on quotations alone. Ideals are either concretized by institutions or they become hollow invocations—a saint or two preaches them, a scholar or two delights in them, and the masses by-pass them. There were admittedly laws whose specific relationship to ethics and *amor dei* was not clear even to the Rabbis; neither Scripture nor past teachers had supplied a rationale for them. But that a higher purpose was served by such commandments also, the Rabbis never doubted. What is meant by the verse (Ps. 18:31) "The word of the Lord purifies"? said a third-century teacher. The commandments were given only to purify the hearts of men. For does it really matter to the Holy One blessed be He whether one prepares food one way or another? Or does it matter to Him if one eats ritually unclean or clean foods? Surely it does not. But the commandments were given for one purpose only—to purify the hearts of men.[5]

Halaka, of course, was not the invention of the Rabbis. All one had to do was consult the Bible, particularly the last four books of the Pentateuch, to discover abundant laws governing every aspect of life. Nor was the Pentateuch the exclusive scriptural source. The prohibition of bearing a burden on the Sabbath was recorded in Jeremiah;[6] that buying and selling must not take place on the Sabbath was reported by Nehemiah,[7] and very likely by an eighth-century prophet long before that.[8] And supplementing Scripture were numerous unrecorded ancient *halakot* (plural of Halaka). These were as current as the biblical statutes. Again, in successive generations, when need arose, certain *takkanot* and *gezerot* (preventive measures) had been enacted; and these, too, were part of the common law. In other words, an impressive body of Halaka was already in existence long before Rabbis turned to jurisprudence. The significance of Rabbinic Halaka lies in this: in implementing the teachings of the Torah and the prophets, it followed principles which protected legislation from inflexibility and society from fundamentalism.

Thus,[9] the Sages insisted that the courts of each generation have the right to issue new enactments, even if these should involve overriding the letter of scriptural law, when circumstances call for such amendment. As the Rabbis put it, when the times demand that something be done for the Lord, a provision of the Torah may be made void![10] And whether or not amendment or new legislation was necessary was to be determined by the courts of each age. Therefore, though Scripture had expressly required the testimony of two witnesses for all charges (Deut. 19:15), Rabban

Gamaliel declared that one witness was sufficient to establish that a woman was a widow, that she might remarry.[11]

Further, according to the Rabbis, all law must lead to the improvement of society and public welfare. Hence *takkanot* to lighten the financial burden of the community, *takkanot* which aim at equity rather than strict judgment, *takkanot* in behalf of family welfare, *takkanot* which ensure peace and good will to all men. And because general welfare is the object, each tentative enactment had to be carefully examined to determine whether it could reasonably be fulfilled. "Do not impose anything on the public," the Rabbis often reiterated, "unless the majority can accept it."[12] Farfetched contingencies, burdensome obligations, were to be avoided.

Again, when enactments were antiquated, they were either revoked altogether or superseded by new, more adequate legislation. And as in every well ordered society, repeals and modifications were entrusted to duly constituted authorities. Development was thus saved from individual caprice and change did not degenerate into lawlessness.

Through such principles and others—for example, that the conduct of society must not be rejected by jurists in search of criteria[13]—emerged a profound respect for human nature and a basic moderation in demands. The Rabbis approved of hedges around the law, to be sure, for they knew well enough how thin was the line separating the not quite forbidden from out-and-out transgression. Nevertheless, an undue raising of hedges was strongly frowned upon.[14] One need only review the older Halaka preserved in such works as Jubilees or the code of the sect at Damascus to recognize the leniency of the Sages. Indeed, in later generations this was stock criticism against talmudic law as a whole by those quite familiar with the Halaka. To whom does the verse (Jer. 5:5) apply, "But these had altogether broken the yoke, And burst the bands"? sang a thirteenth-century Karaite poet. To them that subscribe to the law of the Talmud; "lenient law is their desire, not a rigorous command."[15]

One parenthetical comment. To Judaism all of life is a religious experience; since the division between religious and secular does not exist—such a division would have been incomprehensible to the Rabbis—all laws are religious injunctions. This conception the Rabbis derived from Scripture, where God had ordained not only "Thou shalt love thy neighbor as thyself" (Lev. 19:18), but also what foods might and what foods might not be eaten. Such being the case, the Rabbis had to master fields of learning which may strike us as totally foreign to the discipline of worshiping God. To establish the calendar, they had to learn mathematics and astronomy. Various ritual problems, and problems of civil law, compelled them to study elements of botany, of physiology. In the fourth century, in fact, Jerome upbraided Jewish scholars for wasting so much time in the laboratories of physicians![16] Halaka thus produced a curriculum to which nothing human was alien and with which the prophets were saved from disembodiment.

But what happened to the poetic idiom exemplified of old by prophet and psalmist? Were the Rabbis, in their determination to implement prophetic ideals, content to let the lyrical quality perish? The answer to this question is furnished by the Haggada.

The early Palestinian allegorists used to say, "Do you wish to recognize Him at whose word the world came into being? Study Haggada: for thus you come to recognize the Holy One blessed be He, and cleave to His ways."[17] The statement may serve as an expression of the Rabbinic estimate of Haggada. It may also suggest what in the large the province of Haggada was.

First, however, a preliminary word or two. Like the Halaka, the Haggada was no *ex nihilo* creation of the Rabbis. It owed its origin, its vitality and much of its character to the two main sources of all authentic Jewish expression: the Bible and the *folk* lore. And this in turn requires comment.

The Bible furnished Haggada not only with a record of the past; it was the text out of whose substance pious and ethical imagination could construct a universe of its own, a universe where the themes and *dramatis personae* of Scripture have taken on added stature and color. "And they encamped in the wilderness": thus the verse (Ex. 19:2) on Israel as they were to receive the Ten Commandments. Is there any significance to the location? This: Torah was given in public, in the sight of all, in a place free for all. For had Torah been given in the Land of Israel, Israel might have said to the nations of the world, "You have no share in it!" Therefore it was given in the wilderness, in public, in the sight of all, in a place free for all—whoever wishes to receive it may come and receive it.[18]

Or another example. It is not accident, assures us the Haggada, that Moses began as a shepherd. "He was tested through sheep." Our Sages said: Once while Moses was in charge of Jethro's sheep in the wilderness, a lamb ran away from the flock. Though Moses pursued it, he could not overtake it. Suddenly it reached a spring of water, and the lamb halted to drink. When Moses approached he perceived what had occurred; so he turned to the lamb and said, "It was because of thirst that you ran off, and I did not understand! How worn out you must be!" Then he lifted the lamb and carried it back in his arms all the way. Whereupon the Holy One blessed be He exclaimed, "What compassion hast thou shown toward the flock of flesh and blood! This is My oath; that thou shalt be the shepherd for My flock Israel."[19]

The exegetical, the midrashic character of such passages is clear enough; yet it must not deceive us. The conceptions are genuine folklore, though the form into which they have been cast may be academic. That is to say, legendary and imaginative elements flourished in the market places and at the firesides of Israel as elsewhere. What these elements needed was articulation and correlation. This the Rabbis provided; this they were eminently equipped to provide, for out of the people they had come and to the people they always spoke.

As a result of this intimate relationship, even such aspects of the Haggada as the Rabbis did create, became in time the people's currency. Perhaps the best illustration is furnished by the treatise *Abot*; it is the only Rabbinic work to have been incorporated, in entirety, into the Prayer Book. By constant use the saying of Simeon the Righteous, for example, "By three pillars is the world supported: by the Torah, by worship, and by deeds of lovingkindness";[20] or the saying by Antigonus of Soko, "Be not like servants who serve the master for the sake of receiving a reward, but be like servants who serve their master with no expectation of reward, and let the fear of Heaven be upon you";[21] or Hillel's saying, "Love peace and pursue peace, love mankind and bring them nigh to the Torah";[22] or the saying by Rabbi Tarfon, "Time flies, there's work aplenty, the laborers are sluggish, the reward is great, and the Master is urgent";[23] or others—by constant use these reflections became the values of the whole house of Israel.

It is customary to classify Haggada into various categories. Thus one speaks of exegetical and nonexegetical Haggada; historical Haggada, where events in the nation's past, biblical or otherwise, serve as the material for homily or for unadorned moral reflection; religio-ethical Haggada, where every imaginable phase of life is contemplated, where conduct and thought are charged with sanctity; mystical and eschatological Haggada, where every transcendent mystery from the Creator to the end of days excites the mind. It is even possible to represent a mélange of fantastic material as the Haggada of superstition.[24] The road to Xanadu is lined with ruins as well as stately pleasure domes; or, to give a haggadic figure of speech a slightly unusual meaning, the Ark contains the shards of the broken tables of the Commandments no less than those that were left intact.[25] Whatever the literary classification, this is clear: around three basic themes the whole Haggada revolves, and from these—God, Torah and Israel—all the haggadic concepts take direction and to them they look for consummation.

But the direction of these concepts is not along logical or abstract lines. Here again the biblical legacy is manifest. Conceivably one may arrange a theological system out of the varied content of Scripture; but that system is nowhere in the text itself. One may draw up a series of propositions on the basis of the multitudinous injunctions of the Bible; but that series is not provided by the source. So, too, with the Haggada. The thinking it reflects is of an organic rather than an architectural kind.[26] Therefore any effort to prepare a catechism on the basis of its teachings would be fatal. This Israel knew and the Haggada confirmed: that God was a reality, that Torah had been revealed as a rule of life, that Redemption was a hope never to be despaired of. The consequences of these teachings one might draw as he saw fit. And since imagination knows neither frontier nor restraint, the haggadists ranged over heaven and earth delighting in the liberty that permitted them to proclaim what fancy bred, without fear that their similes or wit would be mistaken for dogma.

Everywhere the Haggada was welcome refreshment. The preacher always knew that with it he could recapture the fleeting attention of his audience.[27] While Halaka, like bread, might be the staff of the community's life, Haggada was its wine.[28] And this was no less true in those circles where apocrypha and pseudepigraphal compositions were cherished. It even found its way into the writings of the Church Fathers.[29] It continued to flourish with undiminished originality for several centuries to come; and when from about the fifth century onward the early haggadic sources began to be compiled,[30] one collection after another, one anthology after another was drawn up.

The universality of its appeal may be variously accounted for; yet we shall not be far from the truth if we see that appeal as the result of four qualities. The first was its charm. It was an art totally without affectation, without mannerisms of any sort. It addressed itself to the heart of man with that spontaneity which dissolves every artificiality. It is a fact that the sun, from its dawn until its setting, does not cease its hymn to the Holy One blessed be He. And the proof is not far to find. When Joshua at Gibeon wished to check the sun in its course, he did not exclaim "Sun of Gibeon, halt!" but "Sun of Gibeon, be still!" For so long as the sun moves in its course it sings to the Holy One blessed be He, and as long as it sings it has the strength to continue on its way. The moment it is silenced, it is unable to stir. Therefore Joshua cried out to it, "Be still!" Whereupon the sun said to him, "Dost thou order me to keep quiet?" "Indeed," he replied. "But if I keep quiet," asked the sun, "who will sing the praises of the Holy One blessed be He?" "Be still," ordered Joshua; "I shall sing now!"[31]

Secondly, the Haggada was distinguished by an extraordinary piety, by so intensive a love of God that only in His will did it see peace. Rabbi Judah the Prince used to say, "If thou hast done His will as though it were thy will, thou hast not yet done His will as though it were His will. But if thou hast done His will as though it were not thy will, then hast thou done His will as though it were His will. Is it thy wish not to die? Die; so that thou needst not die! Is it thy wish to live? Do not live; so that thou mayest live! Better is it for thee to die in this world, where against thy will thou diest, than to die in the future to come where, if thou wishest, thou needst not die."[32]

Thirdly, there moved through the Haggada an ethical fervor which never wavered in its conviction that the fulfillment of civilization lay in dedication to the good and true. As the Egyptians met their death in the Red Sea, said Rabbi Johanan, "The ministering angels prepared to sing; and the Holy One blessed be He called out, 'My handiwork is drowning in the sea, and do you wish to sing!' "[33]

Finally, seldom did Israel meet with as tender a love toward them as they met with in the Haggada; and to the bruised nation the words brought a healing and a hope which no brutality could overcloud. What is the meaning of the verse (Ex. 22:5), "He that kindled the fire shall surely make restitution"? asked a Rabbi Isaac. This: "The Holy One blessed be He said, I am under obligation to make restitution for the fire which I kindled. It was I that set Zion afire, as it is said (Lam. 4:11), 'And He hath kindled a fire in Zion, which hath devoured the foundations thereof'; and it is I who shall rebuild it by fire, as it is said (Zech. 2:9), 'For I, saith the Lord, will be unto her a wall of fire round about, and I will be the glory in the midst of her.' "[34]

Halaka and Haggada united to bring to the religion of the Jew ample content. By developing norms of universal conduct, by underscoring a few doctrines which were held to be fundamental, and by sustaining a sensitivity to ethical demands, the Sages could contemplate the destiny of Jews and Judaism in terms quite independent of any immediate political disappointments. The Bar Kokba revolt may have shattered certain political high hopes. Then, again, some intransigents may have been impatient with the majority's readiness to come to terms, on a practical basis, with the "kingdom of wickedness"; to a Simeon ben Yohai, Rome's accomplishments would always stand for harlotry, self-indulgence, greed.[35] No doubt in some quarters despair encouraged the belief that Judaism could not survive.[36] But the faithful leaders prevented such a belief from striking root. The chief centers of spiritual activity might be shifted from the south to Galilee, once little distinguished for Torah; but the tradition continued to be developed.

Indeed, a step was now taken which proved of major importance in Jewish history. Quite literally, the final compilation of the Mishna drew together material which had been current for several centuries and at the same time released new forces for centuries to come. As such, the Mishna marks one of the great terminals and commencements in the long journey of Judaism.

Ever since the days of Hillel and Shammai's disciples efforts had been made to edit the accumulated traditions of the past according to some

הגרגרת(ב). ניקב קרום של מוח(ג). ניקב הלב לבית חללו(ו). נשברה השדרה(ח) ונפסק החוט שלה(י). ניטל הכבד ולא

ר"ע מברטנורה

ו.יש מבלים לרוב. וחזקה כשנפסקה לרחבה הוא דפסולה ברובה. אבל לארכה של קנה. אפילו לא נשתייר בה אלא חוליא אחת למעלה נגד הראש וחוליא אחת למטה סמוך לכנפי הריאה כשרה לפי שכל זמן שהבהמה מושכת צוארה יותר הסדק מתמעט והיא נראה:

ניקב קרום של מוח. ב' קרומים יש למוח העליון דבוק לעצם הגלגולת והב' הסמוך למוח. אם ניקב העליון והשני הסמוך למוח קיים. כשרה. ניקב השני הסמוך למוח אע"פ שהעליון קיים טרפה ואע"פ שלא ניקב העצם: ניקב הלב לבית חללו. שני חללים יש ללב הגדול לצד ימין הבהמה וחלל קטן לצד שמאל אם ניקב הלב במשהו והגיע הנקב לאחד משני אלו החללים טרפה. וכן אם ניקב בשומן שבלב העשוי כעין ביצ והוא קרוי קנה הלב טרפה: נשברה השדרה. חוליות השדרה: ונפסק החוט. כמין חוט לבן יוצא מן המוח ועובר על פני ארך השדרה כולה. וקרום דק מקיף את החוט. ואם נפסק רוב הקיפו של קרום זה ברחבו היינו נפסק החוט וטרפה. ואפי' לא נשברה השדרה. אלא אורחא דמלתא נקט דרוב פסיקת החוט על ידי שבירת השדרה הוא: ניטל הכבד ולא נשתייר הימנו כלום. טרפה. עד שישתייר כזית במקום מרה וכזית במקום שהיא חיה מנה. דהיינו מקום תלייתה שהיא מעורה ודבוקה תחת הכליות ואם

תוספת יו"ט

הר"ב ושבי התנוך ט' היא הבלוטה העבה המחוברת את הטבעות. כמ"ש בפ"ק משנה ג': ניקב הלב לבית חללו. בבאר נקובי לא איצטריך למתני לבית חללו בין דקין ופשיטא דאין נקב חשוב בהם כלל אם לא ניקב לבית חלל. אבל לב שהוא עב ס"ד דאם ניקב בעומק שהוא חשוב נקב. וניטל הלב והריאה והדקין לא איצטריך למתני דבכלל נקובים הוא דאע"ג דבסתמא אמר בגמ' דניטל כבר וניקב טריפה [וכדפי' הר"ב] בכל המי נקובי דתנן פשיטא דכ"ש ניטל. וניקב המרה נמי נראה דכ"ש ניטל דטריפה ומ"מ ניטלה הכבד ולא נשתייר הימנה כלום איצטריך דאפשר להיות דניטל כל הכבד ולא המרה שניטל כל בשר הכבד ונשארה מרה דבוקה בגידי הכבד והסמפונות. והא דתנן גבי ואלו כשרות. ניקב הלב ולא לבית חללו. נ"ל דמהכא לא הוה שמעינן דה"א ה"ה סמוך לבית חללו דסופו לינקב עד בית החלל. והא דקתני ניקב הגרגרת כשרה היינו משום דבעי למתני נסדקה [נפחתה הגלגולת ט' איצטריך סד"א כי קתני ריאה ניקב קרום של מוח בלא פחת גולגלת קאמר וה"ה דכי נפחתה גלגולת בלא קרום טרפה קמ"ל. הר"ן במתני' דלקמן] ונשברה השדרה ולא נפסק החוט שלה איצטריך. דאי מהכא ה"א או הא או הא. אי נמי ה"א דבעי תרתי קא משמע לן דבחוט תלי מלתא. תוס'. והמסס ובית הכוסות. כתב הר"ן לקמן דלאיצטריך סד"א מאי לתון דקתני ריאה נקב מפולש כל שהוא כן. אפי' במקום חבורן טריפה. קמ"ל דכשרה ומאי בחוץ שלא במקום חבורם. ע"כ. אך הר"ב במשנה ז' פרק ב' דכלים כתב דמתניתין דאלו כשרות דלאע"ג דלא איצטריך. רגילות

המגיה

תפארת ישראל · יכין

חושט. טריפה. משום דדרך עורות חושט להתמשך. ועי"ז אפשר שיתרחקו אהדדי הנקבים. ואפילו רחוקים ב' הנקבים בבצורות זמ"ז. עד שאי אפשר שיתרמו אהדדי. אפ"ה טריפה [רט"ז ל"ג סק"ה]. מיהו כל זה בניקבו ע"י חולי. אבל בנתנקב ע"י קוץ. אז אפילו ניקב רק עור הפנימי. טריפה. דחושט אין לו בדיקה מבחוץ. אבל בניקב עור החיצון לבד. יש חילוק. דבניקב בקוץ או מחט לפנינו במקום ידוע. או בניקב ע"י חולי. אז כשר כשיבדוק עור הפנימי כנגד הנקב. אבל כשניקב בקוץ שלא במקום ידוע. אפילו לא נתנקב רק החיצון לבד. טריפה [שם ל"ג ש"ך סק"ז]. ולא עוד אלא אפילו נקרע רק עור הצואר קלת. הוה כשלא במקום ידוע וטריפה. ואפילו מרט רק נוצה א' מהצואר ויצא דם. טריפה מה"ט [ש"ך ל"ג סקי"ד]. מיהו אם יש שחין על העור אפילו של עוף. ישחט בלאו ויבדוק העור במקום הנגד שבשלא ניקב מעל"ע כשר [רט"ז סי' כ"ג סק"ח]. ובהפ"מ אף בהלם בעל מבהמה ויצא דם. או בהתחיל לחתוך העור של בהמה ויצא דם. או אפילו מרט נוצה של עוף ויצא דם. ישחט בלאו ויבדוק העור במקום החתך בשלא ניקב מעל"ע כשר [ש"ך כ"ג סק"כ וכ"א]: ב) שנפסק רוב חללה לרחבה. ושבי התנוך שבגרגרת לאורכה. אינו מבטים לרוב. מיהו כשנסדקה גרגרה לארכה. אז אפילו לא נשתייר רק חוליא א' למעלה וחוליא א' למטה. כשרה. דחוזר ומתרפא. [א:נ בניקבה הקנה למטה ממקום שחיטה במשהו טריפה. וה"ה בב' ספוגים שמתחלקת הקנה בסופה. אחד ללב וא' לכבד. וא' לריאה. כל א' מהן נקיבתן במשהו]. וכל זה בניקב הגרגרת מחמת חולי. או בקוץ בשעה שאחז הגרגרת לבד וניקבה. שידע שלא נגע בוושט. אבל בניקב בקוץ שלא במקום ידוע טריפה. דחיישינן שניקב גם הוושט. ולא גרע מנקרע עור הצואר [ל"ד]: ג) ב' קרומים יש למוח. א' דבוק על המוח עצמו. וא' דבוק בגלגולת בפנים. ובניקב

התחתון נקב מפולש לבד. טריפה. מיהו שלא בהפ"מ אפילו בניקב עליון לבד נמי טריפה מספק [רמ"א והב"ח בסי' ל"א]. וי"א דבניקב העליון לבד אפילו הגלגולת שלם ואפילו בהפ"מ טריפה [ש"ך וט"ז שם]. מיהו אם נפחת הגלגולת וחסר ממנו כסלע. שבשיעורו הלת פחות משליש טפח. טריפה. דסופו לנקוב הקרום. וה"ה נקבים רבים בגלגולת שיש בין כולם חסרון כסלע. מצטרפין. ובעוף כל שניקב הגלגלת וחסר כל שהוא. טריפה מספק שנתנקב הקרום. רק דבעוף דיבשה מהני כשתשהה כ"א ימים שלא תניח בה ביצים. וכשהתחיל להניח ביצים אחר כך. כשרה. משא"כ בעוף המים כשניקב הגלגולת לא מהני שהוי. ונפסים שכשנחסר בגלגולת העוף כפי שעור סלע בבהמה. אז גם בעוף יבשה לא מהני שהוי [שפתי דעת ל' סק"ז]: ד) ג' חללים יש ללב. ובניקב אחד מהן טריפה [סי' מ']. ונקט הכא לבית חללו. אף על גב דבכל נקובי דמתניתין כך היא. ה"ט משום דהלב חפשו עב. ושייך בי' נקב שלא לבית חללו. משא"כ באחריניהו אינו תלוי בהו נקב שלא לבית חללו. מדהיפכוהיקן דק*): ה) ווירבעלזיילע: ו) כמין חוט לבן יוצא מהמוח. ועובר בתוך כל חוליות השדרה. וקרום דק מקיף את החוט. וכשנפסק רוב היקף קרום זה ברחבו. טריפה. אף שלא נשברה השדרה. רק אורחא דמלתא נקט. דרוב פסיקת החוט ע"י שבירת השדרה היא. אבל נשברה השדרה ולא נפסק עור החוט. או שנפסק המוח שבחוט ועורו קיים. כשר. וטריפות חוט השדרה אינו רק עד סי פרשה ג'. ועד בכלל. ומשפי שכשמגיע החוט נגד הירכיים מתחיל להתפלג. להכי בנפסקו ב' חוטי פיצול הראשונים והשניים. טריפה. אבל בנפסקו השלישיים. כשר. דשם כבר הירכיים מעמידין אותה. ואינה מתה. ובעוף כשנשברה שדרתו או נתעקמה. צריך לבדוק החוט עד נגד סוף שכיבת עלם הכנף המחובר לגוף. והיינו נגד שכיבתו מתוך לגוף. ובהפ"מ יש להקל לבלי לבדוק רק

*) עי' פמ"ג יו"ד סימן מ"ם משבצות זהב סק"א ע"ש. (אהבת איתן).

ציונים

ניקב קרום של מות. פיי פס פי כ"ג סמ"ג פס טוש"ע פס סימן ל"א ס"א: ניקב הלב לבית חללו. פיי פס כ"פ סמ"ג פס טוש"ע פס סימן מ' ס"א: נשברה השדרה. פיי פס פ"ט ה"א סמ"ג פס טוש"ע פס סימן ל"ב ס"א: ניטל הכבד. סימן ס"ס פ"א פיי פס פ"ח ה"א סמ"ג פס טוש"ע פס סימן מ"א ס"א

שנויי נוסחאות

נשברה השדרה ונפסק כו'. כד"נ.. נפסק; בכי"ק הסדר (ובסטוה) נפסק החוט שלה. נשברה השדרה עי' בה"ג ופי' רע"ב. ניטל הכבד ולא נשתייר הימנו כלום. כד"נ ובכי"ק ניהלת.. ממנה כלום וב"ה בכי"ק ובכי"מ ובמי"ה ובמכב"ג ד' שונינו ובהוספה (ובכס הימנה..).

תוספות חדשים

פרק ג א ברע"ב ד"ה ניקב הלב ט' שני חללים. כו'. וכ"כ הרמב"ם אבל בטור יורה דעה כתב ג' חללים הגדול באמצע ושני קטנים לכל צד אחד וכ"כ כמה פוסקים וכתב כ"ג בס ריש סי' מ' דבתחלה בס ג' רק אח"כ נכנס החלל הקטן של ימין תוך חלל האמצעי והוא הגדול: (ממהורש"ח ז"ל):

ראשון לציון

פרק ג א הר"ב ד"ה פסוקת הגרגרת כו' אפי' לא נשתייר בה אלא חוליא אחת למעלה כו' פרי"ף והרא"ש והרמב"ם וטור ש"ע י"ד סי' ל"ד סעיף ד' ספקו דלפי' יש"ר כ"ב למעלה ולמטה כשר. לגד נס' הקרותה והמגות מצריך חוליא אחת למעלה וכיי"נ כ"ב דאז"ר כמי כחולין מ"ה ע"א. אבל אנן קי"ל כרי"י דבכ"מ קי"ל כרי" נגד רב ופמ"ש הר"ב לקמן משנה ב' ד"ס או שנסדקה והוא שישתייר כר כל שהוא וקא"ל דכל שהוא לאו דוקא. וסמך הר"ב לקמן על מ"ש הכא: [שם ד"ה ניקב הלב והוי הגחל לצד ימין וס' והרמב"ם כ' בפירוש והגדול לצד שמאל ועי' רש"י]:

אור גדול

פ"ג א במשנה ניקב קרום של מוח. בגמ' (מ"ה א') נתן סימן לקרמא תתאה חייתא דמתנח בת מוחא. וכתב הרמב"ן בחי' דמשמע דמש"ה נתן סימן משום דעליון אינו סקיף המוח. לכאורה מה יענה גבי ריאה דנתן סימן נ"ב. ואפשר דאין כוונת הרמב"ן לדקדק על הא דנתן סימן רק דקשיא לי' מאי סימן הוא זה הא גם קרום העליון סנה בי' מוחא. ואף די"ל כיון דקרום הב' מפסיק לא סקרי סנה ביה עכ"ז נ"ל יותר לפרש משום דאינו סקיף. אמנם ברשב"א בתוה"ב הארוך בית ב' שער ג'. בד' ברלין י"א ע"ב; נראה דדקדק מדנתן סימן דתתאה לחוד טריפה. וא"כ קשיא מובא מה יענה בריאה ואפשר דאין כוונת הרשב"א להוכיח מינה דתתאה לחוד רק דהלכתא כלשון זה וכן דייק מינה העיטור (באות קרום) ובר"אש, אמנם הוא דחוק מאוד בלשון הרשב"א דא"כ אינו ענין להקודם אי תתאה לחוד או עם עילאה יעו"ש. ועפ"י דברי הרמב"ן הנ"ל אפשר לייסב קו' התו"ח דאמאי לא נקיט קרומי המוח כיון דבעינן תרווייהו, ולהנ"ל

A Page from the Mishna
Treatise Hullin, Chapter III
Romm edition, Vilna, 1927

A Discussion of Dietary Laws

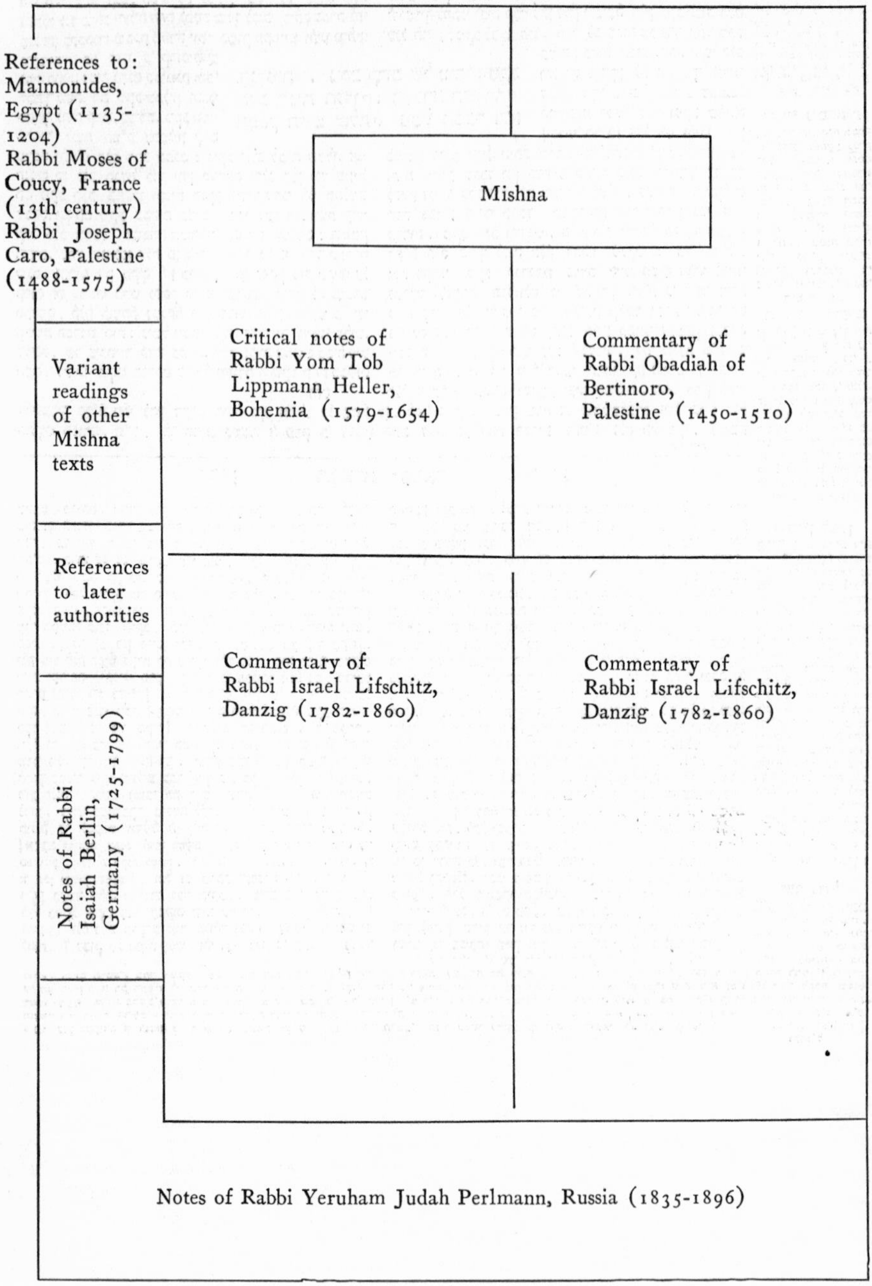

serviceable principle. As we have seen, one of Akiba's chief accomplishments lay in this field—he had organized the Halaka along logical lines; that is, he had arranged a Mishna (literally, review) for students and jurists. His most gifted disciple in the following generation, Meir, had adopted Akiba's Mishna, refined and amplified it, and thereby produced a Mishna of his own. But the fact is that a number of scholars had drawn up such works, each for his own and his academy's use. Frequently traditions which one possessed another lacked. These collections and digests of the orally transmitted law were very valuable; none perhaps recognized this more profoundly than the new Patriarch, Judah the Prince. Hence when he set out to edit a Mishna in his turn, he spared no effort in acquiring the results of previous scholars. And in part, the eminent success that crowned his work was the result of such thoroughness.

There were, however, other reasons as well, not the least of which were Judah's personal attainments and his office. Rabbi Judah—or, as he is generally called, Rabbi, the teacher par excellence—was marked by a devotion to study and a saintliness which could not but impress his contemporaries. That he had inherited wealth or that it came to one in his station little affected his ascetic disposition. "He that accepts the pleasures of this world," he used to say, "shall be deprived of the pleasures of the world to come."[37] Out of his own funds he maintained various impoverished scholars.[38] It was typical of the man to declare, "Much have I learned from my teachers, more from my colleagues, but most from my disciples."[39] And once when he heard a Sage maintain, "He that learns from children is like him that eats unripe grapes and drinks wine out of the vat; while he that learns from the old is like him that eats ripe grapes and drinks wine that has aged," Rabbi retorted, "Look not at the pitcher, but at what is in it! There are new pitchers full of old wine, and old pitchers without even a drop of new wine."[40]

As Patriarch, on the other hand, Rabbi seldom neglected to assert his authority. Notwithstanding occasional criticisms, his powers and influence were unaffected. He had ample cause to feel that the declining community in the Holy Land could not dispense with a strong patriarchate. He was especially jealous for the pre-eminence of Palestine in world Jewry and therefore looked with concern at the rising Babylonian community. From prominent Babylonian teachers who had studied in his academy he withheld full ordination,[41] hoping presumably that the Eastern settlement would continue to depend on Palestine for religious tradition. Nevertheless, this is noteworthy: though he maintained his views with firmness, when he found leading teachers disagreeing with him on some contemplated legislation, or when he knew that the majority opposed him, he would yield and not attempt to force his position on them.

Such transparent honesty and fair-mindedness did as much for Judah's edition of the Mishna as did his skill in arranging the material. Moreover, after he had prepared his draft of the work, he went through it a second time to improve upon it. He was constantly in consultation with collaborating scholars, particularly his associates; what he was anxious to produce was the kind of codex whose quality everyone could respect. The contents were formulated in a felicitous Hebrew, rich in biblical overtones but with a fluid character of its own. Material not immediately essential he excluded; worthy views, however, even if not accepted as established Halaka, he incorporated. Important portions of the older collections were worked into the body of his edition. He divided the whole work into six "orders"; the first, Seeds, dealing with various agricultural problems and ritual laws associated with them; the second, Festivals, treating the halaka connected with the Sabbath and different festivals on the Jewish calendar; the third, Women, on the diverse aspects of marriage and the relations between the sexes; the fourth, Damages, a detailed exposition of civil and criminal law; the fifth, Holy Things, concerning the sacrifices and ritual of the Temple; and finally, Purities, on the difficult laws related to ceremonial impurity. These "orders" in turn he divided into individual treatises, with chapters and appropriate sections. As the first treatise in the entire work he put *Berakot* (Blessings) which treats of prayer for different occasions, and there is hardly any reason to doubt that *Abot* was intended as the final treatise; it was a most fitting peroration to his code.[42] Some minor additions after his death in no way altered the character of Judah's work. The Mishna was the Mishna of Judah the Prince and his academy. And to gauge the degree of its success, only one thing need be observed: not another Mishna has survived. Wherever the Mishna is henceforth spoken of, the reference is to *the* Mishna, the edition prepared by Judah the Prince at the end of the second or beginning of the third century.

So precious had the vast store of traditions become, however, that what Judah felt compelled to omit other scholars hastened to preserve. Thus shortly after the Mishna was completed, compilations of the excluded material appeared. The Tosefta (Supplement), Baraitas (Excluded Traditions), midrashic collections on the last four books of the Pentateuch were redacted by different Sages and transmitted to the academies. But the Mishna retained authority; these additional sources continued to be studied principally for the light they might shed on the content of the great code.

The death of Judah the Prince in 217 closes the great period of the Tannaim, the succession of teachers, particularly from Hillel and Shammai onward, whose labors produced the Mishna and related sources. To overestimate their contribution is more difficult than to underestimate it. Even an inventory of their achievements—the adaptation and implementation of tradition, the canonization and hence preservation of the Holy Scriptures, the guidance of the nation through some of its most hazardous days, the direction of law toward humane purpose, the fixing of a universal standard of religious practice, the democratization of learning—does not tell their whole story. Beams are still not a structure. It is the history of the next generation that fully reveals how firmly the Tannaim builded.

8

There is good reason to believe that because of his position Judah the Prince had enjoyed the acquaintance of one of the Antonine emperors (specifically which one is unknown).[1] If so, the circumstance reflects no more than that the Patriarch may have prevailed upon the emperor to treat Jews no worse than others in the empire. But life for everyone in the empire throughout the third century—or, more accurately, from the reign of Commodus (180-192)—was full of hardship and turmoil. In a sense, the true imperial masters were the soldiers who made and unmade sovereigns; and what the soldiers were after was simply higher pay. "Be of one mind," were the last words of Septimius Severus to his sons, "enrich the soldiers, trouble about nothing else."[2] During the fifty years between 235 and 285, for example, there were twenty-six emperors, only one of whom died a natural death. In turn this necessitated higher and higher taxes for the population: taxes on land and on profits from trades and professions; taxes to support the army and the officials; the head tax; forced labor.[3] On one occasion when a Jewish deputation appealed to the governor to reduce taxes on their fields he retorted that if he could he would tax them for the air they breathed![4] His retort was but a blunt admission of the extremity to which royal aspirants were driven by the insatiable greed of the soldiers. Moreover, the unreasonableness of demands[5] and the irregularity of the taxes drove the people to despair. And the effects of the Hadrianic war on the economic resources of Palestine were still being felt; the grandson of Judah the Prince had to permit Jews to use the oil of Gentiles though this prohibition had been enacted in an earlier period with considerable emphasis.[6] Taxes were so serious a drain on the country's economy that, despite the biblical prohibition (Ex. 23:10 f.; Lev. 25:1 ff.), one of the Sages felt that the people might continue to work in the fields during the sabbatical year.[7] Until Diocletian (284-305) brought some stability to the currency, inflation wrought havoc with wealth; some fields were worth less than the taxes on them![8]

It is true that in 212 Caracalla extended citizenship to all inhabitants of the empire; actually this meant that henceforth everyone was subject to military service,[9] and of course only the rich could buy their release from such obligations. Telling indeed are the words of Judah's son, who succeeded his father as Patriarch: "Beware of the ruling powers, for they befriend a man for their own purposes only; they appear as friends when it is to their advantage, but they do not stand by one when he is hard-pressed."[10] Had the capacities of Alexander Severus (222-235) been equal to his good will and intentions, the empire might have recovered some of its former strength. To the Jews and Christians his reign was certainly "a little help."[11] He adopted as his motto the famous teaching, "Do unto others as thou wouldst have them do unto thee," and ordered it inscribed on his own palace and on public buildings. In his private chapel he kept images of Apollonius, Orpheus, Jesus and Abraham! But he was unable adequately to discipline his army, and in a campaign against the Germans he was killed by his own soldiers.

Three years after Alexander Severus became emperor, a grandson of Judah the Prince, also called Judah (II), became Patriarch. He moved his court from Sepphoris to Tiberias; but although the patriarchate was still an institution to be reckoned with, there were signs that its prestige was on the wane. Since Judah's successors were of even lesser intellectual stature than he, scholars chafed at the patriarchal presumptions. The frequent contrast between their own poverty and the sumptuousness of the Patriarch's household—thanks to contributions pouring in from Jews in every part of the world; the suspicion that incompetent individuals had been appointed judges at a price; the refusal to exempt them from financial obligations toward the support of communal needs; the scholastic mediocrity of Hillel's descendants—such considerations served to make the Sages critical of the patriarchate and speak of it unflatteringly.

Among the various Palestinian scholars of the third century—Haninah, Jannai, Hoshaiah and others—two were especially distinguished, Johanan ben Napeha and Simeon ben Lakish. Johanan had not only studied under some of these men, but had attended sessions at the academy of Judah the Prince. Despite straitened circumstances which eventually induced the Patriarch to fix a pension on him, Johanan devoted almost all his life to study. He was highly regarded by his colleagues; his humaneness attracted the populace to him; and even the Patriarch treated him with a reverence seldom manifested toward other teachers. A contrast to Johanan's mild manner was his colleague and brother-in-law Simeon ben Lakish. Simeon's independence of spirit expressed itself quite as much in his studies as in his relations with his contemporaries. The acumen of this gladiator of Torah was sensational even in his own circle, and it is worthy of record that Simeon taught that the Book of Job was not a historical account, that much of Jewish angelology was an exilic and postexilic phenomenon, that the trustworthiness of certain traditions was open to question.

These were not the only men engaged in the development of the Talmud. There was Eleazar ben Pedat, for example, who later succeeded Johanan as head of the Tiberias academy and who was held in esteem by Babylonian Sages—in part because he had first studied in the East, in part because he developed principles for the understanding of various traditions. Another scholar in the south of Palestine, Joshua ben Levi, was particularly successful in enriching the field of the Haggada. These men, together with their associates, were building on the foundation the Tannaim had laid; they were, in other words, creating the Talmud.[12]

When the Soferim, the lay scribes—in contrast to the exclusive priest scribes—had undertaken to make the teachings of Scripture the norms of every Jew's conduct, a program of study and interpretation had evolved which in every generation strove to perform a dual function. On the one hand, by exegesis Sages attempted (as we have seen) to derive from the biblical record the implications, the large corollaries for each age. On the other hand, Scripture being the revealed Charter, they tried to establish biblical sanction for concepts and institutions which had developed in the life of Israel. Thus Midrash was formed and perfected. When eventually the bulk and exegetical arrangement of the midrashic material proved unwieldy, scholars set about organizing their traditions along more logical and less cumbersome principles. This effort had at last culminated in the Mishna of Judah the Prince and his court. But the Mishna could as little terminate further intellectual activity as the Bible. In the first place, new problems would continue to rise in each period and these would clamor for solution. In the second place, the impulse to correlate the crisp statements of the Mishna with the Bible had not died. Finally, we must not forget that the editing of the Mishna had involved an exclusion of numerous traditions; these were often indispensable for the proper understanding of the Mishna itself. And despite the fact that Rabbi, confronted by a mass of conflicting views, had so arranged his material as to indicate which was authoritative Halaka, there were instances when decision was doubtful. The Mishna, in short, called for commentary; this the Talmud provided. It is, we may say, the elaborate exposition of the Mishna. Hence the men engaged in this task were known as Amoraim, expositors.

Although the Palestinian Amoraim spared no effort in their talmudic activity, they could not regain for the Holy Land its earlier excellence. Already by the next generation the distinguished scholars were either Babylonians or Palestinians who had studied in Babylonian schools. Moreover, there was no blinking at the fact that in the field of the Halaka the Babylonian center was showing deeper insight and greater originality.

Owing to economic and social forces in the Eastern settlement a phase of civil law was expanding which the Palestinians, still almost entirely agricultural, with little major change in their economy, could never have developed. The impressive contribution, for example, of the Palestinian Abbahu was in the Haggada. For a while reforms introduced by Diocletian, in the hope of saving the Roman Empire, may have benefited Palestine too. But the country was hopelessly impoverished—Abbahu's wealth is far from typical. Caesarea, where he lived, as the seat of the imperial governor, enjoyed certain unique economic opportunities. In the country, droughts were frequent and stubborn; when the prayers of well known saints brought no results, people turned desperately to anyone to try his powers.[13] Famine and epidemics were common. The poverty of the Jews was conspicuous, and a vaudevillian could bring down the house with a skit on Jewish beggars: why, the wretches ate even thorns and left nothing for the beasts![14] At the same time, relations between Jews and Samaritans took a turn for the worse, and now the breach between the two was final. With the emperor's abdication civil war again raged; irresistibly the provinces must have suffered. Finally, in 311, Constantine ascended the throne.

The victory of the Cross did not at once spell doom for the Jewish community of the Holy Land; Judaism, for example, continued to be a licit religion even after the Council of Nicea (325) started Christianity off in its career as a state religion; besides, the Christian emperors too were primarily concerned with the collection of taxes and only secondarily with theological fine points. Nevertheless, from 323 on, after Constantine became sole ruler of the empire, but especially during the reign of Constantius, his successor (337-361), the policies adopted and the sentiments expressed testified sufficiently that triumphant Christianity was in no mood to be patient with the members of the *secta nefaria*, as Judaism was now called.[15] That a Christian might on occasion be indebted to Jews for a good deal of his learning made little difference to him. Israel represented a *populum miserum et tamen non esse miserabilem.*[16] Economically, socially, theologically, the fourth- and fifth-century church did what it could to make the Jew an outcast and to pauperize him. Jews were forbidden to proselytize, conversion to Judaism was made punishable by death, under no circumstances were Christian slaves to be owned by Jews, apostasy from Judaism was encouraged, the penalty of death awaited the Jew who cohabited with a Christian. Some of these laws, to be sure, represented nothing new—theoretically. That is just the point, however. Already under Constantius they were being vigorously applied when possible. Perhaps the outbreak and local clashes between Jews and soldiers of the imperial army at Sepphoris in 352 (353) was the result of economic hardships aggravated by depriving Jews of Christian slaves.[17] By 439 Judaism was accepted as so "desperate a sickness" that the emperor (Theodosius II), quoting Hippocrates, almost despaired of finding a cure for it.[18] But he did not neglect to bar Jews from civic dignities and offices, to prohibit them from constructing new synagogues, to decree that Jews active in proselytizing would be punished by death and that their possessions would be confiscated, to insist that onerous public positions and service were to be retained by them. "Let it not appear as if we have accorded the benefit of exemption to these men, detestable in their insolent maneuvering, whom we wish to condemn by the authority of this law."[19]

Such edicts did not demolish the Jewish settlements immediately upon publication, for (in addition to what has already been observed) in the fourth and fifth centuries the legal status of Judaism was still too vivid a precedent entirely to be ignored, and in the fourth century the majority of Palestine's population was not yet completely Christianized. But the edicts fixed the formula, which with sufficient reiteration would become the accepted premise for generations to come. Henceforth the Jew was to be put on the defensive. The only deviation from this rule occurred during the eighteen months when Julian (361-363) attempted to revive pagan civilization. "Though the emperor hated and oppressed the Christians," a fifth-century Palestinian Christian reports,[20] "he manifested benevolence and humanity toward the Jews." What activated the emperor in their favor is not altogether clear. Perhaps he was trying to win the support of world Jewry for his war against Persia.[21] In any event, Julian abolished a number of special taxes which had been levied on the Jews; he even burned the tax records where these accounts were kept. So, too, he ordered the Patriarch to put an end to the collection of funds in behalf of the patriarchate. Finally, he promised to rebuild the Temple at Jerusalem, "which for so many years you have longed to see inhabited";[22] his death, however, prevented the fruition of this project.

But even Julian's tolerance could not restore vigor to the Palestinian center. Comparatively speaking, little enthusiasm was displayed toward Julian's program to rebuild the Temple—and this despite the fact that Messianic hopes were never really abandoned by Israel. A fourth-century Church Father may have been impressed by the stunt of some Jews "to recite all the generations from Adam to Zerubbabel with such accuracy and facility, as if they were simply giving their names."[23] He might also observe a great number of Jews attending synagogue services on certain days, eagerly flocking to the sermons of eloquent preachers.[24] Had he been especially attentive, however, he would have found Jewish communities where even basic prayers were recited in Greek,[25] where Jewish (!) judges had to be coached by Rabbinic teachers in the elements of Jewish law. Indeed a simplified, elementary kind of Talmud was drawn up for the benefit of these ignorant officials.[26]

The stronger the influence of the Christian clergy on the fifth-century emperors the less could violence against synagogues in various parts of the empire be restrained or Jewish rights be protected.[27] Neither could the Patriarchs do much for the community; they were practically resigned to the vanishing of some of their important religious prerogatives. Soon an end was put to their office altogether, which meant that a unifying and stabilizing power now disappeared. Moreover, the Jewish population continued to fall off seriously.[28] The atmosphere, in short, was charged with crisis, and the Sages perceived that again an era was approaching when Judaism, no less than the Jews, would be sorely tried. So long as there were many distinguished scholars, a Patriarch in office, some tolerable relationship with the ruling powers, the folk could receive guidance and hope from its historic leaders. Now, in the steady decline, some alternative had to be discovered to achieve the same results. That alternative proved to be the compilation of a Talmud.

Thus, toward the end of the fourth or the beginning of the fifth century, the Talmud of Palestine—or, as it is called, the Palestinian Talmud—came into being. The compilers availed themselves of whatever work had already been drawn up at various schools in the interpretation of the Mishna. These respective "Talmuds" of generations of scholars they collated to make one Talmud. That the work should suffer from shortcomings was inevitable, for the age and the locale provided neither an abundance of leisure nor peace of mind. For the same reasons, no Talmud was drawn up on the last two divisions of the Mishna, though the interest of the Sages in the subject matter of sacrifices, Temple ritual, ceremonial purity and impurity was as keen as ever. A practical work was the necessity; on it all creative energy had to converge.[29]

The final redaction of the Palestinian Talmud may or may not be related to the abolition of the patriarchate by the emperor in 425, one hundred years after the Council of Nicea. This much, however, is certain: the Holy Land, where for centuries Israel had labored, where the chief institutions—and hence authority—of Jewish tradition rested, now had to relinquish its role to other, more thriving centers. The love and reverence for Zion never diminished; Jewish communities still existed in Palestine; but the actual eminence of another settlement could not be ignored.

9

In one of the front rows of the academy of Judah the Prince sat a young Babylonian scholar whose name was Abba. He had followed the example of one of his uncles and had come to the Holy Land to be close to the source of Jewish learning. At first, possibly, the Palestinians noticed no more than the height of this visitor, for he was rather tall; and they

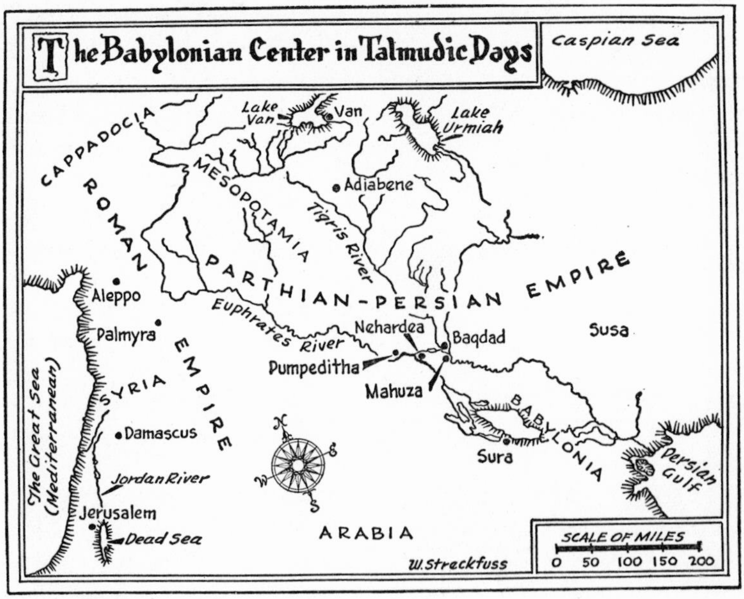
The Babylonian Center in Talmudic Days
Caspian Sea
Lake Van
Van
Lake Urmiah
CAPPADOCIA
MESOPOTAMIA
Adiabene
ROMAN EMPIRE
Tigris River
PARTHIAN-PERSIAN EMPIRE
Aleppo
Euphrates River
Nehardea
Baqdad
Susa
Palmyra
Pumpeditha
Mahuza
SYRIA
BABYLONIA
The Great Sea (Mediterranean)
Damascus
Sura
Persian Gulf
Jordan River
Jerusalem
Dead Sea
ARABIA
W. Streckfuss
SCALE OF MILES
0 50 100 150 200

were probably flattered that he, like others then and formerly, had found only in their country the resources that the sensitive and cultivated Jew required. The time was soon to come, however, when Abba's abilities astonished his classmates. "I can remember," said the most distinguished Palestinian Sage of the third century, "sitting seventeen rows behind Abba at school, and when he engaged Rabbi Judah the Prince in discussion, the words flew like sparks and I could not understand them!"[1]

Abba's diligence and capacity would have been noteworthy in any country and age. Though it was commonly agreed, for example, that the death of Judah the Prince closed the tannaite period, Abba—or, as he came to be known, Rav, the master—was almost accorded the distinction of a Tanna: he could challenge the views of Tannaim whom later Sages were expected to interpret, not oppose.[2] Had he remained in Palestine, however, Rav would have been one more illustrious teacher in Israel. Certainly, even if he could have risen to the leadership of a Palestinian academy, he would have had to contend with the resentment of Palestinian scholars. Happily at this time Babylonia, his native country, was an open plain,[3] a potential which needed a personality such as his. And it was this conjunction of place, time and person which raised Rav to his unique role.

The Jewish settlements in Babylonia were both well and long established. It is sufficient for our purposes to remember that the majority of Jews taken captive by Nebuchadnezzar's forces did not return with Ezra and Nehemiah to their ancestral land. Natural increase, trade, migrations in the course of seven hundred years added to the numbers of these Jews. There were cities in the country—for instance, Nehardea—which were entirely inhabited by Jews. When in the first century B.C.E. Hyrcanus (II) had been taken prisoner by the Parthians, he found a welcome in the Eastern country.[4] At a later date two Jewish brothers succeeded for a while in creating a kingdom of some sort for themselves and their followers.[5] Until the Temple was destroyed, contributions from the Babylonian Jews flowed steadily and liberally. After the Hadrianic revolt Joshua ben Hananiah's nephew, as we have seen,[6] did not consider it impossible to establish a court in Babylonia independent of the authority of the patriarchal institution. By the third century, in other words, Babylonian Jewry was anything but a minor outpost. It could boast of long standing, and this probably made its members touchy about purity of stock.[7] It could point with pride to its organized community life. There were courts, synagogues, schools, communal facilities; Jews filled public and commercial offices; the political representative of the Jews was actually a leading dignitary at the Parthian and Persian courts. He was known as the Exilarch, Resh Galuta, the chief or prince of the Exile; and though several Resh Galutas may have left instructions to be buried in the

Holy Land,[8] their lives and their revenues and their powers hardly made them consider Babylonia as a place of exile. Even prominent scholars felt the Exilarch's power. Rav was imprisoned when he refused to obey the Exilarch's order to legislate in behalf of the public and against the interest of traders.[9] When the royal house was friendly or tolerant, Jewish communities were so self-sufficient as to justify the description of their being a state within a state.

While the majority of Jews were poor, there was practically no field of activity or vocation in which they did not participate. There were laborers and capitalists, professional men and nonskilled workers, farmers and craftsmen, shopkeepers and serfs, cattle dealers and food distributors, producers and exporters, middlemen and peddlers, sailors and clerks. Taxes were very high and Persian law declared that one who could not meet the levies might be enslaved by another who paid for him. Many lost their freedom that way; yet merrymaking was not unknown, especially during holidays. Women enjoyed fine clothes and a rather high status. They married early, ran their households, sometimes even took over important business responsibilities. Polygamy was not usual, because it was expensive and inexpedient. To quote Rav—and he knew what a difficult wife meant—"Do not marry two women; if you do marry two, then take a third!"[10]

Although most Jews engaged in some phase of agriculture, the commercial nature of Babylonian economy and law profoundly affected Jewish life and thought. Provision was now made for such arrangements as purchasing on time. Adult children kept their earnings even when they were supported by their fathers; in an agricultural economy of small landholders this would have been impossible. Of such phenomena Jewish law had to take cognizance. Not that Jewish jurists proceeded to borrow legal instruments from their Persian neighbors.[11] In truth, we know of only one direct appropriation, a certain kind of oath.[12] But the advanced state of commerce within the country inevitably led Jewish scholars to a development of civil law to which their colleagues in Palestine, as already remarked, never attained. The Sages had to respond to needs of their environment; an area of human relationships, where honesty and welfare can either be cultivated or ruined, demanded legislation: what was fair competition, what was fair price, what were fair wages? These and similar questions the Babylonian Amoraim undertook to answer in the light of teachings they had inherited from the Tannaim.

That in each generation they could fruitfully apply themselves to those problems is in large measure due to Rav, as well as to his colleague Samuel, who also had passed some years in the Holy Land. One circumstance especially assisted these men in their scholastic efforts: they now had the Mishna at hand to refer to. Some Babylonian scholars might still prefer to travel to Palestine in order to gather authentic tradition in the land of its origin. But the compilation of Judah the Prince, the Mishna, did make possible Babylonian independence. It was not *necessary* to refer to the Palestinian authorities for information. Hence academies in the East lost much of their former sense of helplessness, acquired self-reliance. Little by little Babylonia was transformed from a region where simply dates could be bought for a farthing to a center where Torah was beloved.[13]

An intensification of the religious and cultural life of Babylonian Jewry began soon after Rav's return. The Exilarch had appointed him an inspector of markets. This gave Rav an opportunity to travel widely through the country and to observe conditions, economic and otherwise. His tours led him to the realization that more than anything the Babylonian Jews needed an extensive program of education. When, however, he was offered the presidency of the academy at Nehardea he refused the honor. The position, he felt, properly belonged to his colleague Samuel, who was a native of the city. Rav himself chose the neglected community of Sura. Here he created a school and a center for Jewish life.

He did not have to wait long for students; these came from many places and in abundant numbers. For the indigent in their midst he provided livelihood. But an advanced academy for professional scholars could not of itself accomplish what Rav desired. He held lectures and sessions in the early spring and fall (known therefore as the Kalla or assembly months) for students who during the remainder of the year worked at various occupations. And for the people at large he reserved the week before the spring and fall festivals. The crowds who attended these lectures were often so numerous that Sura could not provide them all with lodging![14] The program thus thrust greatness on Babylonia. In the next century, for example, the ruling powers charged that enrollment at one of the academies was so large that there was a shortage of manpower for cultivation of the land, that consequently income from taxes suffered.[15] There was little exaggeration, therefore, to the observation of the later homilist: "The Holy One blessed be He has appointed the two academies for the good of Israel. In them day and night are devoted to the study of Torah."[16]

A neglect or ignorance of ritual practice and other aspects of law in the country led Rav to a rigor which under other circumstances would have been unnecessary. Frequently, in fact, his colleague Samuel disagreed with him, despite the awe Rav inspired in him. But Rav's views on ritual and ceremonial questions became authoritative law, Halaka. On the other hand, in the field of civil law Samuel's views prevailed, because he more profoundly grasped the implications of the political and economic aspects of Babylonian life. Two illustrations may suffice. Samuel laid down the principle in *Jewish* law that where religious praxis was not involved, the law of the country in which Jews lived was binding upon Jewish jurists and Jews.[17] This principle has remained in effect ever since. Or, to refer to an incident where Samuel succeeded in influencing Rav to withdraw his opinion: When news reached Babylonia that the Palestinian Patriarch had permitted Jews to use oil grown by non-Jews, Rav at first refused to adopt the reform. Finally Samuel prevailed upon him to yield.[18] How could one insist upon a ceremonial meticulousness of such extremes when Jews were so rooted in a country not their own?

One must not conclude from such instances that Samuel was prepared to take requirements of traditional Jewish practice lightly. This brilliant physician and scientist—he was famous for his accomplishments in medicine and astronomy—could be as much a rigorist as Rav when he felt that occasion called for severity rather than leniency. Samuel can hardly be described as moderate in his pronouncements on questions connected with the relations between the sexes. The widespread levity in his day distressed him as much as it did Rav.[19] The point is, as suggested, that both these men fervently desired to fill the life of Babylonian Jewry with piety and wisdom; neither was content merely to speak in vague generalities about these ideals. Hence, the one in Sura and the other in Nehardea directed schools to raise the educational level of their contemporaries. With their students they carefully analyzed the Mishna and tannaite traditions, tried to understand the reasoning behind the expressions of the earlier Sages, engaged in the development of a Talmud. At the same time, never aloof from the lives of their neighbors or issues of their period, they accented important laws and regulations. Both made contributions to the liturgy, both preached to the folk, both filled public offices. Time, however, proved that Rav's emphasis in some matters and Samuel's in others best responded to the objective both pursued.

The third and fourth centuries in Babylonia did not go by altogether without mishap. Particularly with the victory of the Sassanians in 226 a reaction against all non-Zoroastrians set in. Stimulated by the zealous Magi the monarchs occasionally behaved with fanatical intolerance, in the hope that Persian civilization would thoroughly displace the former Parthian culture. Now Pahlavi was encouraged, and fire worship, and elaborate purification rites. Since the earth must not be defiled, Jews were forbidden to bury their dead; since fire was holy, they were forbidden to kindle lights in their homes on Persian holy days; since the Zoroastrian priests insisted that parts of all slaughtered animals must be offered on their altars, Jews found it almost impossible to eat meats. Not until the fifth century, however, did the menace to Jewish life become serious and prolonged. It was then that a number of persecutions occurred and additional hardships were imposed. Jews were forbidden to observe the Sabbath and their festivals; Zoroastrian dualism took offense at the monotheism that Jews daily proclaimed in the recitation of the *Shema* ("Hear, O Israel, the Lord our God, the Lord is One"); half the Jewish population of Ispahan was put to death on the charge that Jews had slain two Magi; scholars were executed and children forced to accept Zoroastrianism; academies were destroyed. With the triumph of Mazdak communism, which was both economic and social in its import, fresh tribulations appeared, the least of which were the additional taxes.

Until the fifth century, therefore, Jewish life in Babylonia registers an almost uninterrupted crescendo. Distinguished scholars carried on the program begun by Rav and Samuel. After Samuel's death (254), when the Nehardean center was destroyed by invaders, there arose a new academy at Pumbedita which, along with the one at Sura, was destined for a prominent career. Its founder, Judah bar Ezekiel, provided the impetus for advanced casuistry and the most accomplished Sages of the country devoted themselves to it. Making an elephant pass through the needle's eye, as the dialectic was described,[20] had become the fashion. Not all scholars approved of this, by any means. Men like Zera and later Jeremiah, in disgust with the prevailing mode of study, left for Palestine. Even among such as did not abandon their country could be heard protest. But the casuists were riding the wave in the sea of the Talmud. And their activity eventually gave the Talmud which they were producing—the Babylonian Talmud—a quality to excite the minds of generations.

Owing to the fascination which subtle dialectic exercised on the intellects of the time, Pumbedita usually attracted the outstanding scholars until the middle of the fourth century. Here, for example, was Rabbah, rather proud that alone among his colleagues he could tackle difficult treatises on ceremonial purity, never satisfied until he could understand why Scripture said this, why previous scholars said that; a lover of wit who humored his students into the most complicated subjects. Here was Abaye, as brilliant as he was poor; no theoretical contingency, no farfetched possibility was pointless to him. In his acuteness he was matched only by his friend Raba (removed to Mahoza), who prayed for modesty and enjoyed wealth.[21] Delete from the Talmud the "give and take of Abaye and Raba" and large draughts of intellectual day vanish.

All that activity was adding to the bulk of material that demanded assembling and editorial arrangement. This task was welcomed by the Sage who presided at the academy of Sura, Rab Ashi. In him, as earlier in Rabbi Judah the Prince, were combined learning and station, and, again like Rabbi Judah, he undertook the redaction of the traditional lore so that the work of generations might not perish.

Ashi devoted more than fifty years (375-427) to his chief interest. At each of the Kalla sessions the accumulated expositions of a Mishna treatise were examined and put into some order. In this way he could cover practically all of authoritative Jewish tradition, organize the mass of interpretations, and introduce system into what had been carried on in different schools by different generations without uniform plan. Tradition has it that he went through his material not once but twice,[22] devoting each of the semiannual meetings to a different treatise; and no doubt the editorial superiority of the Babylonian to the Palestinian Talmud was in large part due to the opportunity of the Eastern editors to review as well as compile.

The Babylonian Talmud as we now have it—it is frequently referred to simply as the Talmud; due to certain historical factors, it overshadowed the Talmud of Palestine[23]—is not altogether the compilation drawn up by Ashi. Work on the Talmud continued even after his death. Some contribution was evidently made by Rabina II, the last of the Amoraim, who directed Sura during the closing quarter of the fifth century when persecutions and turbulence were fierce. Moreover, in succeeding years at least two generations of scholars (called Saboraim, the Reflective Ones) were engaged in perfecting the work, arranging the discussions therein, at times even adding comments of their own; in short, preparing the Talmud for *its* subsequent interpreters. Perhaps the Saboraim are the ones to have put the Talmud into written form; our sources are a jungle of comments on this period and it is not easy to speak too confidently about the activity of the Saboraim.[24] We shall not go far astray by regarding these Sages as transitional to the next important epoch, even if their role is more significant than it is usually said to be. By the latter part of the sixth century, it is fair to say, the Talmud was completed.

Like the Palestinian Talmud, the Babylonian is an elaborate commentary on the Mishna, and clearly the eastern Sages were not restricted in their conception of exegesis. Frequent contact between the Sages of both countries contributed to a certain similarity of treatment. Differences between the two works, however, do exist. The language of the Palestinian Talmud is Western Aramaic, while Eastern Aramaic is the idiom of the Babylonian. The latter is much more voluminous and diffuse than the former, much more dialectical in approach, reflects a different environment, is more lavish with haggadic portions, extends larger hospitality to popular superstitions.[25] On the first and sixth divisions of the Mishna, with slight exceptions, we have no Talmud from the Babylonian Amoraim.

Here, then, is the Talmud, the work of centuries, a work *sui generis*, containing much that is immediately relative to the Mishna, much that is far removed. To the last editors apparently everything which tradition had preserved seemed precious. One often thinks of these men as curators to whom even the shards of history are treasures. They did not have it in their heart to destroy what they found or what was given over to them. As a result, along with wisdom follies were saved; alongside authoritative

עין משפט נר מצוה

סה א מיי' פכ"ג מהל' סנהדרין הלכה ו סמג לאוין רח טוש"ע ח"מ סי' ז סעיף ו:
סו ב מיי' שם הל' ו טוש"ע שם סעיף ט:
סז ג מיי' פי"ג מהלכות עדות הלכה כ סמג לאוין ריז טוש"ע ח"מ סימן כח סעיף ט:
סח ד מיי' פ"ו מהל' טוען ונטען הל' א טוש"ע ח"מ סימן פא סעיף ח:
סט ה מיי' פי"ו מהל' עדות הלכה ב סמג לאוין ריז טוש"ע ח"מ סי' כח סעיף ט:
ע ו מיי' פ"ח מהלכות סנהדרין הל' ב סמג עשין צז טוש"ע ח"מ סימן יח סעיף א:
עא ז ח מיי' פכ"ג מהל' סנהדרין הלכה ז סמג שם טוש"ע ח"מ סי' יט סעיף א:
עב ט י כ מיי' פי"ג מהל' עדות הל' ב סמג לאוין ריז טוש"ע ח"מ סי' כח סעיף ז:
[גי' ירו' ורי"ף ורא"ש אותן]
[עיין לקמן לה: גרסת רש"י אם אמר הוא אמר לנו וכו' אי"ש פלוני אמר לנו וכו' ע"ש פירושו משום דהוי"ה עד מפי עד]
עג ל מיי' שם הלכה א טוש"ע שם סי' פא סי"ב
עד מ מיי' פ"ו מהלכות טוען ונטען הל' ו סמג עשין צה טוש"ע שם ס"א:
עה נ מיי' שם הלכה ז טוש"ע שם סעיף יא:
עו ס מיי' שם הלכה ט טוש"ע שם סעיף ג:

[מלת ליה ליתא בשאלתות פ' יתרו סי' נג. וכן שכת בקידושין פב: ביום שמת רב יהודה נולד רבא] יבמות קה:

עז ע (מיי' פ"י מהלכות סנהדרין הלכה ח):
עח פ מיי' פי"א שם הלכה ב:

[מ"מ ונראה דליתא צריך שיאמר אתם עדיי]

רבינו חננאל
כל המוסיף גורע עשתי עשרה ווסף ע' ופחת אמה:

הגהות הב"ח
(א) רש"י ד"ה בפניו וכו' עדים מדלא קאמר שמעתם שהודה לו כו' :

קרובים ונתרחקו הוו · שמתה אחותם אשת מר עוקבא: בקבא דקירא אידבקו בכו · בקב של שעוה נדבקתי בכם בתמיה כלומר אני דבוק בכם כלל אלא אתן לא לייתיתן דינא: מיום ראשון ואילך · בטלה שושבינות וכשר להעיד: והוא לא אויב לו יעידנו · דהאי והוא אעד קאי דמעיד שאלא חייב גלות והעד לא אויב לו לרוצח דאי ברוצח הא כתיב (דברים ד) והוא לא שונא לו וקראי אחריני טובא: ולא מבקש רעתו ידינו · דסמיך ליה ושפטו העדה וקאמר ר' יהודה דהאי לא מבקש רעתו אשופטים קאי . ולשון זה מצאתי בברייתא דסיפרי ולא בסיפרי שלנו והוא לא אויב לו העד ולא מבקש רעתו השופט: חד לדיין · דכדיין מודו רבנן דשונא לא ידון דלא מצי חזי ליה זכותא: ואידך · לפסול בדין אחד שני דיינין ששונאין זה את זה:

מתני' מאיימין עליהם · מפרש בגמרא: הוא אמר לי · הלוה אמר לי: לא אמר כלום · דעביד איניש דאמר פלוני עשה בי כדי שלא יחזיקוהו עשיר: הודה לו · שהיו שניהם בפניו להודות נתכוון להיות לו עדים בדבר: שנים אומרים זכאי ואחד אומר חייב זכאי · דכתיב (שמות כג) אחרי רבים להטות: אפילו שנים מחייבין או מזכין והשלישי אומר איני יודע יוסיפו הדיינין · ואע"ג דאי הוה פליג עלייהו הוי בטל במיעוטא כי אמר איני יודע הוי כמי שלא ישב בדין ונמצא הדין בשנים ואין תלתא בעינן: מכניסין אותן · לבעלי דינין ובגמרא פריך הא לא אפקינהו:

גמ' היכי א"ל · לעדים כשמאיימין עליהם: נשיאים ורוח וגשם וגו' · בשביל מתהלל במתת שקר דהיינו מעידי שקר גשמים נעצרים ואפילו כשהשמים מתקשרים בעבים ורוח להוריד גשמים אין הגשם בא: אמר רבא · מאי איכפת להו אם לא ירדו גשמים אמרי בלבם משל הדיוט שב שני הוה כפנא ואבבא אומנא לא חליף על פתח מי שיודע אומנות ובעל מלאכה לא עבר הרעב: מפץ וחרב וגו' איש עונה וגו' · בעון עדות שקר דבר בא ויתיראו שלא ימותו: אאוגרייהו זילי · השוכרים אותם מבזים אותם וקלים הם בעיניו: והושיבו שנים אנשים בני בליעל · גבי נבות היזרעאלי כתיב שועלי המלך היו יועצים לשוכרם והיו קורין אותם בני בליעל: בפניו · משמע בעצמו עדים (א): פטור. ואע"פ ששמעו עדים אתמול שהודה לו הואיל ולא אמר אתם עדיי: משטה אני בך · שוחק הייתי בך בשביל שהיית שואלני מה שלא היה: הכמין · החביא כמו וארב לו (דברים יט) ויכמון ליה: ואין טוענין למסית · המסית חבירו לעבודת כוכבים אין טוענין אותו ב"ד בשבילו טענת זכות אלא אם כן טוענה הוא: ואם לא טען · משטה הייתי בך כשהודיתי אלא אמר לא אתן לך הבא עדים שהלוית לי אין טוענין בשבילו אלא אומרין לו אחרי שהודית לך שלם: ובדיני נפשות · אם יש טענת זכות והוא אינו יודע לטעון טוענין לו: לפי שלא טען · הנחש לא טען הקב"ה בשבילו: ולא תגעו בו · הקב"ה לא הזהירם על הנגיעה ומתוך תוספת גירעו שדחף הנחש את חוה על האילן עד שנגעה בו אמר לה ראי שאין מיתה על הנגיעה אף על האכילה לא תמותי: אמתים · דל אל"ף מהכא קרי ביה (°מתים) ואי שתי מאות אמה כל אותיות שבתורה הברתם כתיבתם במו ועשית ואמרת כאלו כתובה בה"א וכן אתה חסר כמו אותה מלא: עשתי עשרה · דל עיי"ן מהכא הוו להו שתים עשרה:

תורה אור

קרובים ונתרחקו הוו אתו לקמיה לדינא אמר להו פסילנא לכו לדינא אמרו ליה מאי דעתיך כר' יהודה אנן *מייתינן איגרתא ממערבא דאין הלכה כרבי יהודה אמר להו אנו בקבא דקירא אידבקנא בכו דלא קאמינא פסילנא לכו לדינא אלא משום דלא צייתיתו דינא: אוהב זה שושבינו וכו': וכמה אמר ר' אבא אמר רבי ירמיה אמר רב כל שבעת ימי המשתה ורבנן משמיה דרבא אמרי אפילו מיום ראשון ואילך: השונא כל שלא דבר כו': ת"ר °והוא לא אויב לו יעידנו °ולא מבקש רעתו ידינו אשבחן שונא אוהב מנלן קרי ביה הכי והוא לא אויב לו ולא אוהב לו יעידנו ולא מבקש רעתו ולא טובתו ידינו מידי אוהב כתיב אלא סברא הוא אויב מאי טעמא משום דמרחקא דעתיה אוהב נמי מקרבא דעתיה ורבנן האי לא אויב לו ולא מבקש רעתו מאי דרשי ביה חד "לדיין אידך כדתניא אמר רבי יוסי ברבי יהודה והוא לא אויב לו ולא מבקש רעתו "מכאן לשני תלמידי חכמים ששונאין זה את זה שאין יושבין בדין כאחד: **מתני'** "כיצד בודקים את העדים היו מכניסין אותן לחדר ומאיימין עליהן ומוציאין *את כל האדם לחוץ ומשיירין את הגדול שבהן ואומרים לו אמור היאך אתה יודע שזה חייב לזה *אם אמר הוא אמר *לי שאני חייב לו איש פלוני אמר לי שהוא חייב לו לא אמר כלום "עד שיאמר בפנינו הודה לו שהוא חייב לו מאתים זוז "ואחר כך מכניסין את השני ובודקין אותו אם נמצאו דבריהן מכוונין נושאין ונותנין בדבר *שנים "אומרים זכאי ואחד אומר חייב זכאי שנים אומרים חייב ואחד אומר זכאי חייב אחד אומר חייב ואחד אומר זכאי *אפילו שנים מזכין או שנים מחייבין ואחד אומר איני יודע יוסיפו הדיינין *גמרו את הדבר היו מכניסין אותן "הגדול שבדיינין אומר איש פלוני אתה זכאי איש פלוני אתה חייב "ומניין *לכשיצא לא יאמר אני מזכה וחבריי מחייבים אבל מה אעשה שחבירי רבו עלי על זה נאמר (°לא תלך רכיל בעמך ואומר)[א] °הולך רכיל מגלה סוד: **גמ'** היכי אמרי להו אמר רב יהודה "הכי אמרינן להו °נשיאים ורוח וגשם אין איש מתהלל במתת שקר אמר (*ליה) רבא יכלי למימר שב שני הוה כפנא ואבבא אומנא לא חליף אלא אמר רבא "אמרינן להו °מפיץ* וחרב וחץ שנון איש עונה ברעהו עד שקר אמר (*ליה) רב אשי יכלי למימר שב שני *הוה מותנא ואיניש בלא שניה לא שכיב אלא אמר רב אשי אמר לי נתן בר מר זוטרא "אמרינן להו סהדי שקרי אאוגרייהו זילי דכתיב °והושיבו שנים אנשים בני בליעל נגדו ויעידוהו לאמר ברכת אלהים ומלך: אם אמר הוא אמר לי כו' עד שיאמרו בפנינו הודה לו שהוא חייב לו מאתים זוז: מסייע ליה לרב יהודה דאמר רב יהודה אמר רב "צריך שיאמר אתם עדיי איתמר נמי א"ר חייא בר אבא א"ר יוחנן *("מנה לי בידך אמר לו הן למחר אמר לו תנהו לי אמר משטה אני בך פטור) תניא נמי הכי מנה לי בידך אמר לו הן למחר אמר לו תנהו לי אמר לו משטה אני בך פטור ולא עוד אלא "אפילו הכמין לו עדים אחורי גדר ואמר לו מנה לי בידך אמר לו הן רצונך שתודה בפני פלוני ופלוני אמר לו מתיירא אני שמא תכפיני לדין למחר אמר לו תנהו לי אמר לו משטה אני בך פטור ואין טוענין למסית מאן דכר שמיה חסורי מיחסרא והכי קתני "אם לא טען אין טוענין לו "ובדיני נפשות אע"ג דלא טען טוענין לו °ואין טוענין למסית מאי שנא מסית אמר ר' חמא בר חנינא מפירקיה דרבי חייא בר אבא שמיע לי שאני מסית *דרחמנא אמר °לא תחמול ולא תכסה עליו אמר רבי שמואל בר נחמן אמר רבי יונתן מניין שאין טוענין למסית מנחש הקדמוני דא"ר שמלאי הרבה טענות היה לו לנחש לטעון ולא טען ומפני מה לא טען לו הקב"ה לפי שלא טען הוא מאי הוה ליה למימר דברי *הרב ודברי תלמיד דברי מי שומעין דברי הרב שומעין אמר חזקיה מניין שכל המוסיף גורע שנאמר °אמר אלהים לא תאכלו ממנו ולא תגעו בו רב משרשיא אמר מהכא °אמתים וחצי ארכו רב אשי אמר °עשתי עשרה יריעות אמר אביי לא שנו אלא דאמר משטה אני בך אבל אמר

לא

דברי הרב ודברי התלמיד · ואית אם כן כל מסית יפטר עצמו בלואת טענה ויש לומר דדוקא נחש שלא נצטוה שלא להסית ולא נענש אלא לפי שבאת תקלה על ידו אבל מסית שנצטוה שלא להסית כנגלא כשמסית עובר:

מסורת הש"ס

[ר"ה כב: מכות ה:]
[לקמן לו:]
[לעיל כג:]
[לעיל כג: לקמן מג.]
[מ"ק טז: ע"ש]
[ב"ק לג: ע"ש]
[קידושין פב: כרוס]
[לקמן לו: ויבמות לג:]
[קידושין פב: יבמות יח. ב"ק ס.]
[ע"ש מאתים]

הגהות הגר"א
[א] בגמרא (ואומר הולך רכיל מגלה סוד) תא"מ:

A PAGE FROM THE BABYLONIAN TALMUD
Treatise Sanhedrin, 29a
Romm edition, Vilna, 1895

A discussion of methods of examining witnesses and ascertaining the validity of their evidence

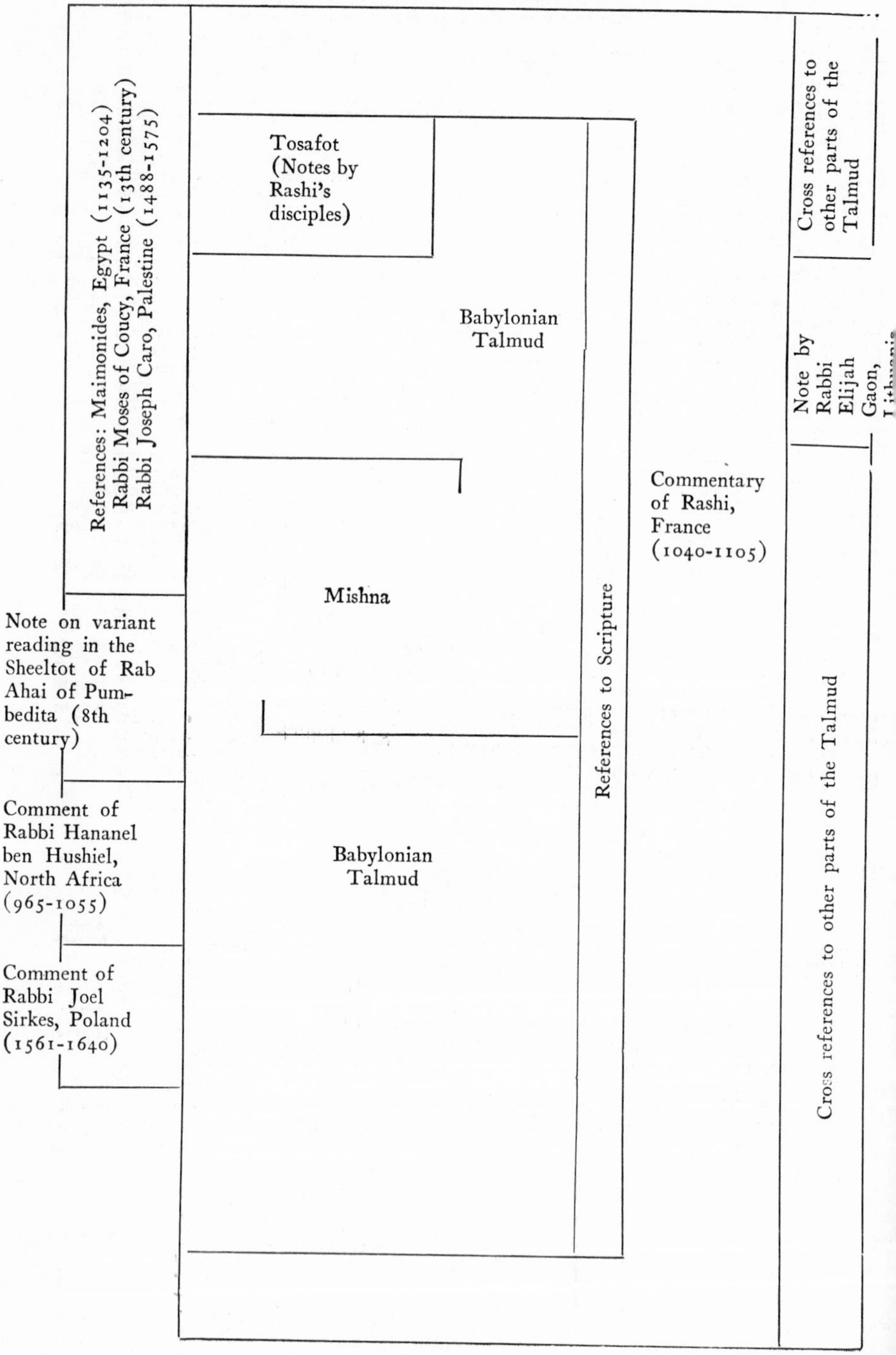

traditions could be discovered individual caprice. A thousand years of Jewish history vis-à-vis the universe re-echo from these folios. Nothing can be more grotesque than to treat the Talmud like an annual report of deacons, where every statement presumably is of official import. It is possible, naturally, to speak of the Talmud as a collection of books; *we* meet it in volumes. But its *creators* did not write books. As soon speak of Percy as the author of the *Reliques*! Even this analogy falls short, for the Talmud is not a lyrical anthology. To speak of it as encyclopedic, on the other hand, is perhaps useful to suggest its catholicity of interests; but the character of its discussions is as unlike an encyclopedia as is a round-table conversation unlike a polished essay. Once one has said that the Talmud is unique, it is futile of course to search for comparisons. It is not a museum, it is not church minutes, it is not an anthology, it is not an encyclopedia. But even stammering efforts to describe it may not be entirely useless. They may warn us of the dangers in applying literary canons from other genres to such a work. And they may refresh the metaphor which the Sages themselves employed when they contemplated the Talmud. To them it was a sea,[26] full of life and action, with deeps and shallows; skill was indispensable to navigate it; but the expanse was wide and the horizon rich and the voyage rewarding. And because the waters never stood still, they never grew stagnant.

10

It is customary to speak of the monarch Noshirwan (531-579) as the most illustrious member of the Sassanian dynasty.[1] His reorganization of the empire, his administration of taxes, the improvements he introduced in irrigation and in the system of communications, and his adoption of a standing army stand in sharp contrast to the chaos during the reigns of his predecessors. But the numerous and frequent wars in which even he engaged were bound to leave their mark. His successor not only had to contend with the Byzantine forces but was faced with an invasion of the Turks. During his reign, the Jews were once again subjected to persecutions; they had little reason, therefore, to regret the revolt of the army against him. The revolt was short lived. But Sassanian Persia was to have little peace in her last sixty years. The war with the Byzantine Empire was particularly disastrous and the period of anarchy that followed saw one pretender after another come to the throne and perish shortly thereafter. By then a new power had made its entrance into world history and it gave the death blow to the Persian Empire.

"Whatever thou hast said regarding the former condition of the Arabs," the last Sassanian emporer was told, "is true. Their food was green lizards; they buried their infant daughters alive; nay, some of them feasted on dead carcasses, and drank blood. . . . But God, in his mercy, has sent us, by a holy prophet, a sacred volume, which teaches us the true faith."[2]

Mohammed was not the first Arab to come in contact with Jews, to hear their tales, to listen to their teachings. Legend as usual has not been inactive in accounting for very early Jewish settlements in Arabia, even as far back as the days of Joshua. This, however, is established: Jews penetrated into the peninsula after the war with Rome in the first century. They were later to be found in Yemen and also in the north. In the latter region, Jewish tribes lived among Bedouins, except for their agricultural occupations,[3] their religion and tradition of learning, hardly distinguishable from their neighbors. Their fascinating names—Kainuka, Nadhir, Kuraiza[4] —are as strange as the sentiments sometimes expressed in their midst. "We are men of the sword," sang one Jewish poet,[5] "and when we draw it we exterminate our enemies."

When people live together influences are reciprocal. And so, while Jews learned Arabic, the Arabs learned Jewish ideas. Whether active propaganda, with the intent to proselytize, was customary, is hard to say. The adoption of Judaism, early in the sixth century, by a king of a half-Sabean, half-Jewish settlement, may have had as much political as religious motivation. Nevertheless, the paganism of pre-Islamic Arabia had already spent itself and Arabs listened eagerly to the new messages that Christianity and Judaism proclaimed. Conversations about the one God, narratives about the biblical patriarchs, solemn ceremonies gradually made their impact. On Mohammed the effect was so strong that he began to hear a "reverberation of bells."[6]

Mohammed's first relationships with Jews were distinctly friendly. He had learned much from such Jews as he had met, and he hoped that they would now agree to learn from him. Was not his religion also a protest against idolatry; did not he, too, admire the biblical heroes; had he not accepted certain Jewish forms of worship, were not ethical injunctions constantly on his lips? He exhorted, he debated, but made no headway. When he grew insistent he was mocked for his ignorance and inconsistencies. This was not calculated to produce good humor in him. What added to the strain was his desperate need of followers, for even among the Arabs he met with little welcome. In 622, in fact, he found it expedient to withdraw to Medina as a result of enmity toward him in his native Mecca. The date is a memorable one (the year of the Hegira) for henceforth the prophet was not without honor and his resentment against the Jews could take concrete form.

Within six years after his arrival in Medina, Mohammed had overcome each of the organized colonies of Jews in the peninsula. He had despaired of converting them and decided that the Arabian peninsula was large enough for one religion only. The victories supplied him with booty and prestige. Two years later Mecca was in his hands. By 631 he felt powerful enough to promulgate his famous Release: All idolators were to embrace either Islam or death. Embassies were sent throughout Arabia and the submission was truly extraordinary. The Arab world knew that it had "to believe in Allah and his prophet Mohammed, to recite the prescribed prayers, to give alms, to make the pilgrimage [to Mecca] and to observe the fast of Ramadhan."[7]

The following year the prophet died and the orthodox caliphate (632-661) began. Roughly speaking, the new leadership faced two problems, one of consolidation and the other of expansion. On the one hand, the new religion had to be deeply rooted in the lives of the Arabs, for their ancient beliefs could not be totally eradicated at one stroke. On the other hand, however, Islam spoke in more than tribal terms. It was a religion with universal implications.[8] Supplementing the theological premises was the pressure of economics. The fertile regions of the north were too attractive a morsel for hard-pressed Bedouins to overlook. Said the Persian general who defended his country against the Arabs, "I have learned that ye were forced to what ye are doing by nothing but the narrow means of livelihood and by poverty."[9] Both these problems, therefore—consolidation and expansion—compelled the representatives of the new faith to think through and formulate the relation of true believers to non-Moslems, infidels. And from the pact attributed to Omar (634-644) we may see quite clearly that, in theory, a large tolerance was out of the question.

Thus, the erection of new houses of worship by non-Moslems was proscribed. Such structures as were already standing could not be repaired, nor might those situated in the Moslem quarter of a town be renewed. The Moslem was to be freely admitted, at all times, into the infidels' church; every form of hospitality was to be extended to him. No prominent display or exercise of other faiths was permitted and under no circumstances were Moslems to be converted to another religion. Conversion to Islam was encouraged. The infidel was forbidden to dress, even part the hair, like a "believer." Riding on saddles, outfitting oneself with sword or arms, wearing silk and cloth sashes round the waist, engraving Arabic inscriptions on jewelry, were privileges limited to the followers of Mohammed. No church or synagogue might tower over a mosque, Jew or Christian had no rights in governing, and in return for protection had to pay a special head tax.

The pact most likely came into being after Omar conquered Christian Syria and Palestine; confronted by competing "universalists" the Arab had to formulate his policy. Had he taken this formula literally—or more precisely, when in certain periods he did take it literally—neither Judaism nor Christianity could have found a place for itself in Mohammedan countries; and let us not forget that eventually the crescent penetrated into Europe! The very fact, however, that in large measure such a policy of intolerance came on the heels, as it were, of a program of expansion, made it often impractical for the Moslem to insist on the terms of his pact. He had to resort to a more workable relationship with the members of other religions. Omar, for example, ordered the expulsion of all Jews and Christians from Arabia. Nevertheless, not only do we later find flourishing Jewish centers in the peninsula, but he permitted the Exilarch to enjoy dignities which were in express contradiction to his pact. Small wonder then that a Jewish visionary could hail "the kingdom of Ishmael" as a salvation and thus allay the fears of his interlocutor.[10]

The history of the first Exilarch under Moslem domination is still blanketed in legend. He was called Bustanai, the story runs, because he was recognized as the child about whom a sinister Persian king had dreamed. In this dream the king had seen himself in a park (*bustan*) furiously cutting down trees and finally prevented from demolishing a last tender shoot. This Josephlike approach to history need not detain us; but the institution of the exilarchate and other phenomena in Jewish life at this point do demand attention.

For it is perfectly clear that, despite the onerous taxation and despite the encroachment of Moslem authorities upon Jewish autonomy, the life of Jews in Mohammedan countries underwent change and often took a turn for the better. In various business ventures we find Jews associated with non-Jews, as partners. Owing to the development of commerce in Babylonia—now called Irak—for decades; owing especially to the devastation of the land as a result of the conflict between the dynasty of the Ommayads and the Abbasids, agriculture proved unprofitable and Jews began more and more to engage in trade. The very expansion of the Moslem empire opened up extraordinary opportunities for commerce. Caravans were now making their way from the Orient to the Occident and back, with goods of all sorts: expensive articles of clothing, bullion, silks, condiments. And the solidarity among Jews in far-flung countries served admirably in the furtherance of foreign trade. Often such traders had to be so long absent from home that the wives protested to the Rabbinical authorities, and Jewish courts finally did not hesitate to forbid husbands to undertake protracted journeys. In the tenth century one even hears of Jewish bankers at the court of a caliph who handled tremendous sums of money, transferred funds over large stretches by means of letters of credit, under duress were capable of advancing 150,000 *dirhams* a month. The influence of these financiers was such that they could effect the dismissal and exile of an Exilarch![11]

Like the Nestorian community, the Jewish settlement was given the opportunity for abundant self-government. In the first place, the Moslems discovered that, occasional defection notwithstanding, the bulk of the people remained loyal to their ancestral faith, and it was the better part of efficiency to have them governed by their own representatives in matters of internal interest. In the second place, such a system facilitated the collection of taxes, particularly outside Irak. This autonomy made the Exilarch quite a powerful figure. When he assumed office elaborate ceremonies were conducted, and everyone was expected to forward gifts. According to the account of a twelfth-century traveler,[12] the Exilarch was something of a potentate. Men had to rise and salute him when he passed by. Mounted on a horse and appareled rather lavishly with silks and turban and gold chain, he attended the caliph's court, "and all the Mohammedan princes who attend the court of the Caliph rise up before him."[13] His authority extended over a considerable range of countries, and in these he appointed rabbis, overseers and other officers. Tribute poured into his treasuries from many lands, and he owned huge estates. "He has," continues our reporter, "a fixed weekly revenue arising from the hospices of the Jews, the markets and the merchants, apart from that which is brought to him from far-off lands."[14] The wealth and distinction of their prince therefore made Jews proud; despite exile, glory had not altogether departed from Judah. Yet the temptation of certain Exilarchs to seize as much power as possible led to clashes with the religious heads of the community; for unlike the Catholicos, the head of the Nestorian community, the Exilarch was not both a political and a religious authority. And since the line between secular and spiritual is not always clearly marked, there were plentiful opportunities for tension.

Along with the economic and political development went a judicial system. Cases where one of the litigants was non-Jewish were tried in the Moslem courts. But where both parties were Jews the Jewish courts insisted that the trials not be taken elsewhere. To enforce their decisions, the judges occasionally appealed to the Moslem authorities! For religious infractions it was not uncommon to administer flagellation. The most effective discipline, however, was the ban, a form of punishment which the medieval Christian or Jew dreaded only less than death. "Let no temple of God be open to Andronicus, Thoas and his followers," pronounced a fifth-century bishop of Ptolemais. "Let every holy house and cloister be closed to them. There is no place in Paradise for the Devil, and if he steals in let him be expelled. I command all citizens and magistrates that they be with him neither under the same roof nor at the same table; and all priests that they neither salute him while living, nor grant him funeral service when dead. . . . And if any one contemns the church of our little city, as though it were needless to respect the poor, let him know that he divides the church which Christ made one. And whether he be deacon, or priest, or bishop, we will hold him as we hold Andronicus, for never will we take the hand or sit at the same table—much less partake of the sacred mysteries—with any one who has aught to do with Andronicus or Thoas."[15]

Similarly a Jewish notice of excommunication: "[When this decree of excommunication reaches you] you will likewise excommunicate him, and make a public announcement that his bread is like the bread of Gentiles, his wine wine of oblation, his fruit untithed, and his books books of sorcerers. And you shall cut off his show-fringes, remove his *mezuzah*, neither eat with him nor take drink with him, [nor include him in the prescribed quorum for services,] nor circumcise his child, nor teach his children Torah in the schools [?], nor bury his deceased relative, nor let him join any of the prescribed or free associations. Pour a cup [of water] after him [as a sign of contempt] and treat him like a Gentile."[16]

The harshness of such a formula made the way of the transgressor hard. To be sure, there were culprits, informers and suchlike, whose crime deserved no less. But the instrument, in the hands of dictatorial authorities, was dangerous and open to abuse. In the tenth century, for example,[17] a conflict between an Exilarch and a famous Rabbi split the Jewish community into two camps. Until reconciliation was achieved the unrestrained issuance of bans alienated neighbor from neighbor.

The most significant development within Jewish life during this period took form in a new institution, the Gaonate. Though related to the academies of Sura and Pumbedita, both in character and in effect it transcended academic features, and its influence was world-wide.

The Gaon (Excellency, an abbreviation of the expression in Ps. 47:5, Excellency of Jacob) presided over a school, a place where students and scholars assemble. But the Gaonate was a good deal more than an academic office. Within the framework of the academy the Gaon enjoyed preeminence, despite the fact that he was often intellectually inferior to other scholars. Most of the Geonim (plural of Gaon) are nothing more than names to us! Like the earlier Palestinian Patriarchs or like the Exilarchs, the Geonim enjoyed their dignity and authority not necessarily because of excellence, but because of family connections. The office was in effect hereditary. Geonim like Exilarchs levied taxes, appointed judges and communal officers for the districts over which they had jurisdiction.[18] What in preceding centuries had been essentially a scholar's forum was now almost literally a Sanhedrin, whose chief not only expressed views but expected his decisions to be enforced, whose personnel's influence was not dependent on talent or erudition, but on established prerogative.

At first the title "Gaon" was attached to the Principal of Sura only, for due to its distinguished history it could lord it over the school of Pumbedita. When funds for the maintenance of the academies arrived from various Jewish communities, unless otherwise earmarked, Sura received two-thirds of the revenue. Not until the tenth century was the distribution equalized, fully a century after Pumbedita had acquired recognition on a par with Sura. At the colorful installation of the Exilarch, the Gaon of Sura took his seat to the right of the prince; the Gaon of Pumbedita sat always on the left. In an interregnum, until a new Exilarch was chosen, it was the Sura Gaon who filled the office. In an exchange of communications between the Geonim, the Gaon of Sura was addressed by his title while the Gaon of Pumbedita was not so honored. Most of the distinguished works indeed come from Sura scholars; not until the latter half of the tenth century could Pumbedita boast of superiority. By then, however, Sura had entered into her final decline; and even Pumbedita had few years of glory ahead. After the death of her Gaon Hai in 1038, Pumbedita ceased to have significance beyond its own locale.

Babylonian Jewry, in other words, had become a community with elaborate machinery for self-government. Parallel with material and social changes arising from the Moslem triumph, an intellectual transformation had come. Inevitably such change affected not only the society of Babylonian Jews, but their estimate of the position they occupied. They were conscious of a new strength; they saw no reason why Jewish settlements everywhere, even in Palestine, should not bow to their authority. In the fourth century, for example, Palestine hardly had the intellectual equal of Abaye the Babylonian. Yet he had been prepared to concede spiritual hegemony to the Holy Land. In the eighth century, on the other hand, a Babylonian scholar settled in Palestine and undertook to teach his hosts the Babylonian Talmud. Its law was for him the only law to be adopted.[19] And in the tenth century the Gaon Sherira announced that the words of the Geonim "are the words of the living God . . . and their learning is verily that which the Lord hath commanded unto Moses. And though they render a decision without accompanying proof, be the matter of little or great import, they are not to be disobeyed: he who departs from one of their words is like him who disputes the Lord and His Torah!"[20]

In short, under the Gaonate Sura and Pumbedita were elevated to a position of importance not limited to the country in which they were established. They served now as spiritual capitals for Jews in many countries. Here the Talmud was studied and taught. But here, too, legal decisions were rendered and the Halaka was fixed. The Palestinians did not meekly yield, nor did they fail to carve out for themselves spiritual spheres of influence. But the relative prosperity of the Eastern settlement, the cumulative excellence of its amoraic period, the vigor of its Gaonate, the geographically strategic position of this center in the capital of the caliphate to which the academies had been transferred by the tenth century, ultimately contributed to the triumph of Babylonian tradition. The

Babylonian Talmud came to be *the* Talmud because of the Geonim; and through their literary and juristic activity its decisions became law.[21]

With the exception of the Gaon Saadia (882-942), Samuel ben Hofni, and possibly of Hai—but he, too, stood on the threshold of an epoch when new voices had become audible—the writings of the Geonim are exclusively in the field of Halaka. The few haggadic reflections we inherit from them hardly deserve to qualify the previous sentence. Moreover, we cannot even pretend to know how they interpreted the fanciful Haggada in the Talmud. Presumably they were little tempted to challenge even the superstition they inherited. Perhaps, too, the rise of schismatics was responsible for the adamant stand the Geonim took when a talmudic passage was under attack. One is apt to be a little unreasonable in the defense of his weakest child. And yet, a note from Hai ought not to be altogether overlooked. "Know," writes this great Rabbi to his correspondent who asked for the meaning of a haggadic passage in the Talmud, "know that we are not, like some others, in the habit of explaining any matter apologetically, in contradiction to the real meaning of him from whom it proceeds. We will therefore expound to thee the opinion of the Tanna, his real meaning and his true purpose, without pledging ourselves for the correctness of the assertion made by him."[22]

Hai, however, wrote poetry, too; and despite his objection to philosophy[23] it is not impossible that he was aware of new influences.[24] Be that as it may, for the cultivation of a variety of literary expression during the Gaonic period, one must look to Palestine. The large compilations of Midrash, the new synagogue poetry, the critical (masoretic) study of Bible make their first appearance in the Holy Land. In Babylonia creative energy concentrated on Halaka.

Furthermore, the form of expression was dominantly of one kind too. We possess a code or two. The oldest work (but not by a Gaon!) of this period, the *Sheeltot*, Discussions, is in the form of discourses, the bulk of which the author, Rab Ahai, filled with extracts from the Babylonian Talmud. But the prevailing literary genre was the responsum, a letter by the Gaon in reply to a question.

The use of epistles for communicating information or instruction was not something altogether unusual. Such exchanges of letters had occurred even in earlier periods.[25] The new station achieved by the academies, however, furnished a stimulus to the development of responsa literature. Or, better still, the ascendancy of the Gaonate was simultaneously both the cause and effect of an increase in responsa literature. From all over questions were submitted to the academies, and the questions covered every phase of life. Sometimes one wanted to know what a passage in the Talmud meant; sometimes litigations arose between Jews in business; problems of marriage and divorce, property rights and taxes, ritual and ethic had to be solved. Precedented and unprecedented issues arose. What was the answer to the question, what was justice, what was the ethical thing to do, what course of action was to be followed, how was one to treat certain schismatics? Questions came in ever-increasing number, at first to Sura and later to Pumbedita too. And the Geonim wrote responses.

During the Kalla months the questions were studied and discussed; when a decision had been reached the Gaon dictated a letter and the responsum was sent off. Most often a decision represented the result of deliberations by the Gaon *and* his colleagues. But not always. He alone, however, signed the letter. The content might or might not be the reflection of the Gaon; but the responsum was his. He might, if he so wished or if he was capable, reply at great length, analyzing the source on which he based his conclusion; again, he might be brief, almost abrupt. The letters sometimes went astray; but many reached their destination. What is more, though many disappeared eventually, a great number were saved. Copies of the correspondence were kept in the academies. (In Cairo, apparently, copies were often kept of letters which had been sent to be forwarded to the Western communities.)[26] Later, about the tenth or eleventh century, many of these letters began to be collected, perhaps first in North Africa. And these remarkable records gave future commentators of the Talmud their first lesson in the interpretation of Israel's second classic.

In their intellectual work then, the Geonim may be described as the first exegetes of the Talmud. And since exegesis is more than mere explanation, since in each epoch new needs arise and new forces operate, the Geonim also developed new Halaka. Their decisions brought stability to many a bewildered community; and at a time when a scattered Jewry might have disintegrated very easily, they supplied the cohesive qualities that kept Jew and Judaism united.

II

The expansion of Islam, as we have seen, was packed with a number of political and economic consequences. Between the political-economic and the spiritual-intellectual, however, the distance is never great. Even the attempt to divide the two sharply from each other may be artificial. The point need not be labored for a modern student; but it will assist him in understanding a phenomenon which might otherwise be perplexing.

There was never a time in Jewish history when in all quarters uniformity or perfect equilibrium prevailed. If there was anything inexact to the reply Rebecca received, it was that within her were only two antagonists. Korah was hardly a partisan of Moses. "And the children of Korah did not die."

The Samaritan schism was undoubtedly a culmination of numerous accumulated dissensions. In the second and first centuries before the Common Era sectarianism was a serious factor to contend with. And so it went in every period.

This is in no way to suggest that a straight line of descent runs from sects of earlier periods to later ones. Such an oversimplification would blur many a distinctive feature. Nevertheless, *mutatis mutandis*, in every age there was a protesting fringe waiting to be drawn up by some powerful circumstances or personality.

Messianic speculation, for example, could always find practitioners, especially in those sections of Jewry where the pursuit of Halaka was neglected. Without it Jews have always seemed to be fulcrumless. In the fifth century there appeared on the island of Crete a mysterious person who convinced the Jewish masses that it was he "who formerly preserved the Israelites by leading them through the Red Sea."[1] He advised them to liquidate their holdings and follow him, one and all, to a mountain overlooking the sea. After a year of exhortation, on an appointed date, he led his followers to the promontory and ordered them to fling themselves into the sea. And many did so!

This occurred in Christian surroundings; but similar spectacles greet us in Moslem countries, where culture no less than politics was in ferment. Along with whatever indigenous echoes excited Jewish imagination, there was ample stimulus from non-Jewish sects—especially in far-off provinces of Persia. "The old Persian Empire," writes Friedlaender,[2] "had for centuries been the battleground of numerous conflicting cultures. The ancient religion of Babylon still exerted its influence, surviving in various sects, such as the Mandeans, and transmitted through other channels. The religion of Zoroaster had reigned supreme for centuries. Persia was the home of Manicheism which, despite all persecutions, still had numerous adherents and spread its powerful influence far beyond the boundaries of Persia. The tenets of Mazdak outlived the destruction of its believers and continued as an important spiritual factor. The Neoplatonic and Gnostic doctrines, [2a] which very early asserted their influence through the medium of the above sects, had been, as it were, personally introduced in the middle of the sixth century through the exiled philosophies of Byzantium. Among these agencies must also be counted the ancient paganism or the so-called Sabeism of Harran, whose adherents were also largely represented in Irak, not to speak of the great Jewish and Christian centers and perhaps Hindu influences. All these variegated elements, often in a modified or mutilated shape, found expression in a motley multitude of Shiitic sects with a weird mixture of all possible doctrines and practices which were artificially harmonized with the official religion by means of allegorical interpretation." This Shiite deposit, he goes on to demonstrate, assisted by the political anarchy of the eighth century, found receptive temperaments in certain Jewish circles.

And so, one Messianic pretender appeared out of some place called Shirin, proclaimed an end to certain established religious forms, urged his followers to abandon their possessions, and promised a miraculous deliverance crowned by a return to the Holy Land. His unhappy end did nothing to discourage another candidate for messiahship, this time at Ispahan about thirty years later. The latter, shrewdly enough, regarded himself merely as the last forerunner of the Messiah, and did not rely completely on miracles, but hoped to make use of an army to get his objective, deliverance from the caliphs. When he disappeared a disciple presented himself to take his place, temporarily; for in typical Shiite fashion, the return of the Prophet was always expected.

In each of these short-lived adventures, there was a strong undercurrent of antitalmudism. But even this was nothing new. Already during the amoraic period there were some who murmured, What good have the Sages ever done us? Exactly what their resentment was directed against is not clear, for even as they disapproved of the law which forbade the eating of ravens, so they objected to the permission to eat dove's meat.[3] Later in some quarters one might encounter Jews who on Passover would recite only biblical passages, refusing to include the Rabbinical homilies connected with this material.[4] It is well to recall what was observed earlier in this study;[5] namely, that though the destruction of the Temple in the first century proved fatal to the Sadducean group, their tendencies, and fragments of their thought persevered in one way or another. Their resistance to a kinetic tradition, their quasi fundamentalism did not altogether meet with rebuff. What was needed was some strong figure in whom inchoate, groping protest could focus; and that individual now stepped forward.

Anan ben David, the story runs, was in line to succeed the Exilarch. Despite his learning and seniority he was passed over in favor of a younger brother, because the Rabbinical authorities feared Anan's imperiousness and unorthodoxy. Whereupon he proclaimed himself counter-Exilarch. This the Mohammedan authorities interpreted as rebellion, since the caliph had confirmed the appointment of the Exilarch; and Anan was imprisoned. In prison he met a famous Mohammedan jurist, Abu Hanifa, who advised him how to win his freedom. Anan was an apt pupil. Once out of jail he assembled his disciples and organized his movement. The great schism had found its spokesman.

Not until the ninth century did the movement get its name Karaism, and by then much that Anan had taught was either modified or abandoned; indeed, by the end of that century a prominent Karaite dared to describe him as the "great fool!"[6] Properly, then, Anan's immediate partisans should be called Ananists, and their teachings Ananism. A unity of purpose, however, runs through the movement from beginning to end, and this it is which determined both its character and momentum.

The movement represented nothing less than a revolt against the Talmud and its authoritative interpreters. Theoretically, for Anan and his circle only Scripture was binding. The biblical text alone, unaccompanied by any part of the tradition that had developed in the course of history, was to constitute the norm for conduct. Consequently, the whole postbiblical legacy was rejected. Back to Scripture, sounded the alarm. And although subsequent Karaites—in a sense even Anan himself!—were to moderate this somewhat, it remained the recurrent justification for a separate movement. "In the written Torah [Scripture] we put our trust," writes a tenth-century Karaite.[7] Had later teachings been approved by God, he continues after a while, would not God have instructed Moses in these? "It is written (Ps. 19:8) 'The law of the Lord is perfect'; what further need can the Mishna fill?"

No sooner, however, had Anan proclaimed his fundamentalism than he had to qualify it. One could as soon abolish tradition as time, and events fully proved that what he intended was the substitution of a Talmud of his own making for the work of generations.[8] Thus began Karaite exegesis; Scripture was expounded and interpreted, frequently by means of the very principles employed by the Rabbis, frequently by means of extended application of those principles. One thing Anan had to avoid, and that was that his conclusions should coincide with the accepted Halaka.[9] As a result he guided himself frequently by older Sadducean example. This, plus what seems to have been a predilection for asceticism, led him to laws distinguished for their rigor, especially where the Sabbath or marriage was concerned. He forbade the enjoyment of light throughout the Sabbath; his followers were not to leave their homes, except for worship, on that day; even on Saturday night cooking was prohibited, lest one wait impatiently for the Sabbath to depart. Forbidden degrees of relationship were so increased that marriage became a serious difficulty. So long as Israel is not in its own land, he ordered that no meats (except deer's meat) were to be eaten. Since it is said (Ex. 15:26), "I am the Lord that healeth thee," medical aid was a violation of the will of God.[10] In determining the calendar, mathematical calculation was to be abandoned; only direct observation of the moon was valid.

The gloom and severity of his code did not always meet with approval. Yet its spirit lingered on among many Karaites. In the development of Karaism, however, more important than his laws was the formula with which he was credited: "Search thoroughly in the Scripture, and do not rely upon my opinion."[11] This message had both its good and bad features.

It sent generations of Karaite scholars back to a careful study of the Bible; and though the Rabbinical circles did not wait for Karaism to underscore biblical scholarship, the polemic that developed added stimulus everywhere to a painstaking study of Scripture. On the other hand, the sanction to every Karaite to be a measure unto himself[12] soon led to division and subdivision within the movement. This may explain, in part, why the Geonim did not at once appreciate the formidable nature of the current schism. And the movement might have disintegrated completely if some powerful successors to Anan had not appeared. When the Arabs, for example, spoke of Karaites as "the companions of Anan and Benjamin (of Nahawend)"[13] they were not altogether off the mark. Benjamin, with his profounder understanding and his milder approach to law, helped consolidate Karaite life. The very fact that he did not fear to adopt a number of Rabbinic ordinances, or that he did not hesitate to accept Rabbinic interpretations of Scripture which Anan had rejected, suggests that Benjamin was not deeply troubled by the independence of the sect, that less of a self-consciousness distracted him. His opponents were simply Rabbanites to him. Neither, of course, in Benjamin, whose intellectual range was wide, nor in his more limited and rather austere follower Daniel al-Kumisi do we reach a crystallization of authority or a recognized legal code. But the writings of these men could form part of the equipment of Karaites as they moved to more favorable centers. A beginning had been made; a literature was being produced, both in Aramaic and in Hebrew; the movement had a distinct identity; it had already included a few forceful personalities. It could afford, therefore, to adopt a more aggressive tone.

With Daniel, but the first period of Karaism closes, and no account of it can be adequate which failed to present men like the learned Qirqisani (tenth century), or the narrow-minded Salmon ben Yeruhim, or the propagandist Sahl ben Masliah, or the philosophical Yusuf al-Basir (eleventh century), or other prominent figures of the movement during later periods in various centers through the death of the amazing Abraham ben Samuel Firkovich (d. 1874). Nevertheless, the principles and certain elements in Karaism clearly suggest why normative Judaism could not adopt such a course. For the antitalmudism was equivalent to a denial of history. We fail utterly to understand the movement if we see in it a form of antinomianism. Not only Anan but almost every Karaite of note was preoccupied with law. What finally petrified Karaism was in truth a combination of factors, not the least of which was its failure to appreciate that talmudic law had been an organic product. No *tour de force* could take its place. Before long Karaite protagonists, too, had to appeal to an inherited corpus of teaching, which, they insisted, was Scripture made explicit. Ironically enough, Kirkisani already tried to establish that Karaism was no recent departure, but a movement whose beginnings were clearly discernible in the time of Simeon the Righteous. An undeveloped historical sense afflicted the schismatics in practically every period. And unlike the Protestant movement—to which Karaism is so often compared; the epithet "Karaite" was in fact flung at the early Protestants—Karaism had no country with which to identify itself; it could not secure the diet to promulgate *cuius regio, eius religio*. When territory is gone, tradition is not expendable. Consequently, though the movement could attack grotesque mystical expression in the Rabbanite camp, though it could set up temporary flourishing settlements in one region or another, though counterattack could occasionally refresh it, though its polemic could be fierce, it could never achieve more than a sectarian status, ultimately dwindling to an insignificant following.

The ultimate fate of the sect, however, is not representative of its state in the tenth century. Then its threat to the unity of Jewish life was serious and the passive opposition of the Geonim was poor strategy. Effective challenge was required, and this was provided by Saadia of Fayyum.

12

With Saadia ben Joseph a new dimension is added to Jewish history. We may seek the climate in which he moved as much as we please; the man towers above every environment with which he was associated. He was born and raised in Egypt, yet his crowning opportunity came to him in Babylonia, and his versatility conjures up scenes of Spain. Saadia Gaon he became, but not another Gaon measures up to him. His independent—a Karaite would say insolent—spirit makes his predecessors and contemporaries seem middling.

All of which is not to say that Saadia owed nothing to the cultural and spiritual currents of his time. The contrary is the case. What made the man unique was that more than any of his Jewish contemporaries he was sensitive to the multitude of stimuli and possibilities in the wealth of material around him. Saadia lived and traveled in Moslem countries, and Arabic civilization in his day could boast of a rich deposit. Owing to a number of foreign influences welcomed by Islam, a tremendous intellectual awakening had taken place. Some of the most important works of antiquity, particularly Aristotle's and Euclid's and Ptolemy's and Galen's, were translated into Arabic. Soon translation led to original reflection in medicine, mathematics, theology, history and belles-lettres. Some of the great achievements in these fields occurred after Saadia's death, but activity was well under way in his day. What is particularly noteworthy is that men of diverse ethnic origins participated in these scientific and literary enterprises.[1] In other words, the awakening attracted and enlisted talent in every quarter and was not merely a sectional enthusiasm. Even Egypt, where Saadia spent the early part of his life, responded to the stir. She had been under Moslem domination since 641, and steadily, Arabic speech and thought and influence penetrated the country. To such a universe Saadia did not remain indifferent.

Nor was Judaism spiritually inert in Egypt. There were flourishing Jewish centers in Alexandria, and later in the new Egyptian capital Fustat. Babylonian Jews who settled in the country under Arabic rule brought along traditions from Sura and Pumbedita. Palestinian Jews, too, came thither, especially after the annexation of the Holy Land by the Egyptian viceroy (878), similarly importing their cultural equipment. Since the Arabic conquest in 636-638, Palestine had shaken herself from the lethargy into which she had been forced; in the eighth century she could once again boast of schools, of poets, of biblical research, of vigorous Midrash study, of a Sanhedrin with a judicial and religious hierarchy. Her émigrés or itinerant natives were not remiss in advocating her customs and traditions. So that, even as there were so-called Babylonian synagogues and congregations in Egypt, so were there Palestinian ones. On a gifted individual such variety and juxtaposition were almost sure to have a quickening effect. And despite our inability to determine the precise nature of Saadia's early education, there are sufficient signs that he drew on both Babylonian and Palestinian sources of inspiration.

Two other circumstances must be included in an account of Jewry in Saadia's time and place. The first is the spread of Karaism; and the other is the decline of the Babylonian academies.

In 928, contrary to precedent, Saadia was appointed Gaon of the academy at Sura. He had none of the family connections that had been well-nigh indispensable to former aspirants. He was not even a native Babylonian. But by the tenth century Sura had only a distinguished past; Yom Tob Kahana, who had served as Gaon since 924,[2] was remembered more for his weaving than for his erudition. After his death there had even been some talk of shutting down this ancient seat of learning altogether. Apparently, then, not everyone who came to Sura[3] gained excellence, even as not every tourist to India accumulated riches.

The new Gaon, however, was not unknown. For a number of years his name had figured prominently in literary and scholarly circles. While still in his native land, at the age of twenty, he put out a Hebrew lexicon and rhyming dictionary; and the note struck is significant. What prompted him to prepare this work, said the young man, was a contemporary need: Jews were rapidly forgetting how to express themselves properly in their own language, in Hebrew. But Saadia's concerns were not restricted to the neglect from which Hebrew prose and poetry suffered. There was the new schism. Shortly thereafter, he issued his first polemic against Anan and

Karaism. And, it may be added parenthetically, this battle against the Karaites he never abandoned. Not only did he publish tracts against them in the ensuing years, but the anti-Karaite theme also recurred in his many works which, at first sight, had nothing to do with the sect as such. Sectarianism in any form undermined the survival of Israel, and the Fayyumite did not intend to be gentle in the offensive against it. Before his appointment to the Gaonate he was to attack the teachings of a Persian-Jewish skeptic as vigorously as he could ridicule fundamentalism.[4] One controversy in particular assumed the character of a *cause célèbre* and brought Saadia useful renown.

While Saadia was in Aleppo news reached him that the Palestinian Gaon, Ben Meir, expected the calendar again to be determined henceforth by the religious authorities of the Holy Land. This ancient and important prerogative had never been cheerfully relinquished by Palestine. Less than a century earlier, even an Exilarch had conceded that, where the calendar was concerned, Babylonia had to submit to the Holy Land. In order to prevent dissensions in Israel, "I, the heads of the academies, the scholars, and all Israel," he declared, "rely on the calendar which has been dispatched by the scholars of Palestine."[5] The Babylonian authorities, therefore, were almost prepared to yield when Saadia took up the defense in their behalf.

A queer, but nonetheless dangerous, controversy developed. Ben Meir insisted that the calculations of the Babylonians were in error. Saadia replied with statements, hardly supported by the sources he invoked,[6] that the Palestinians' claims were baseless. In the meantime, some Jewish communities celebrated festivals according to Ben Meir's calendar, others according to the dates set by the Babylonians. The rift, particularly at a time when Karaism was active, only persuaded Saadia the more that Ben Meir's plans had to be defeated.

Saadia eventually emerged the victor; his campaign no doubt made him enemies, but it won him admirers in the Eastern center. His election to the Gaonate, then, was partly reward for defending Babylonian interests. The Exilarch indeed may have regarded the appointment in such a light,[7] and have hoped to find in Saadia an uncritical champion of everything Babylonian; but he was soon disillusioned. No more than two years elapsed before a quarrel broke out between the new Gaon and his "benefactor"—Saadia refused to sanction an unjust transaction of the Exilarch. Entreaties were of no avail; nor did the subservience of Kohen Zedek, the Gaon of the rival academy at Pumbedita, impress Saadia in the least. When the Exilarch's son appealed to him to approve his father's decision, Saadia replied, "Tell your father that it is written in the Torah (Deut. 1:17) 'Ye shall not respect persons in judgment.' " Persuasion proving useless, threats were attempted; the upshot was that the Exilarch excommunicated Saadia. Thereupon Saadia excommunicated the Exilarch.

For seven years Babylonian Jewry was split into opposing factions, each with protagonists and accusations, neither too fastidious for street brawls. The only good to emerge from this bitter and undignified battle was that Saadia retired[8] to write some of his most important works. Finally, in 937, after the Exilarch once more attempted an impudent judgment, the people were outraged and cried for a reconciliation between the banished Gaon and his enemy. The men were brought together on the eve of Purim and after a touching ceremony embraced. Saadia returned to his post and for five more years directed the activities of his academy. But he was much impaired in health; the struggle he had gone through very likely told upon him; and in 942 he died of melancholia.

We are not done, however, with Saadia's story. The conflicts in which he engaged during his life tell but a part of his extraordinary strength. What, in fact, do they suggest? That at a critical moment in Jewish history—when sects weakened Jewish society, when rivalry between competing centers of Jewry jeopardized authority, when political functionaries of the Jewish community attempted to monopolize all powers of jurisdiction, when the principal spiritual institutions, the Babylonian schools, were languishing—a vigorous personality arose and with his combative talents battled against the disintegrating and overreaching forces in his milieu. This was no slight contribution. And yet for subsequent generations—a very important commentary on Jews and Judaism!—it was Saadia's literary legacy that constituted his chief distinction. Obviously the Gaon and the writer are one person, not a mechanism here revealing an author's conduct, there the conduct of a communal leader. Indeed, if there is anything characteristic of Saadia it is the direction of all his efforts toward one organic result, the integration of Judaism. Earlier—and later—Geonim pursued the same objective, but they lacked Saadia's equipment and perception. They hoped to achieve this integration by focusing exclusively on the Talmud. Saadia would never have denied primacy to the Talmud. But he recognized that Jewish tradition, which talmudic law and lore kept intact, was a larger universe than his contemporaries remembered it to be.

Because of his larger and deeper vision Saadia's labors revolutionized the whole character of Jewish literature, and when later the acute Abraham ibn Ezra called him "the chief spokesman everywhere,"[9] there was nothing unrestrained about the tribute. Maimonides bears similar testimony. "Were it not for Saadia," he writes, "the Torah would almost have disappeared from the midst of Israel; for it was he who made manifest what was obscure therein, made strong what had been weakened."[10] Almost no field of Jewish literature lacked interest for the Gaon, and in many he was the pioneer. He was the first to treat Hebrew grammar and lexicography scientifically. Though he had forerunners in the field of liturgy, notably the Gaon Amram, he was the first to treat the subject with scientific insight. He composed poetry for use in the synagogue and he tried his hand at versification of sundry themes: here he is neither first nor superior. On the other hand, his studies of talmudic methodology and his legal codes are not only the first systematic and critical investigations of the subject, but their influence was almost immediate. He commented on a number of treatises of the Talmud and also on an early mystical work (despite his devotion to rationalism!). In his polemical writings against the Karaites or his opponents he treated various religious and legal problems—to the Karaites, in fact, he became the archenemy. At least five separate works of his are devoted to an analysis of the calendar. As Gaon he composed responsa in both Hebrew and Arabic. He is the first to have translated the Bible into Arabic and to prepare commentaries directly on biblical books. He is the first to have made a systematic examination of the philosophy of Judaism. Put briefly, Saadia is really the first author in Rabbinic tradition. His works are not mere compilations, arrangements or rearrangements of older sources; they are products of original reflection and expression.

Varied as are the literary fields either opened or cultivated by Saadia, they exhibit characteristics which reflect a consistency of outlook. In the first place, the treatises were intended to fill a popular need. This had led him, we saw, to issue his earliest work, the Hebrew dictionary, and the antisectarian tracts. All his other works, however, appeared for the same reason. In his prayer book he omitted reference to authorities as he discussed the laws of worship, since his audience was the folk at large, not the small scholarly circle.[11] When he saw how his generation, ignorant of Hebrew, was forgetting the Bible, he translated it for their benefit. Where mere translation would still leave difficulty, he paraphrased.[12] The philosophical speculations of the age challenged the teachings of traditional Judaism; he undertook in his *Creed and Faith*, therefore, to establish a rational Jewish creed and to demonstrate the soundness of the religious heritage. An oft-quoted passage from the Introduction to this treatise eloquently registers his motivation: "My heart grieved for mankind," he wrote, "and my soul was moved on account of our own people Israel, as I saw in our times many of those who adhere to their faith entertain impure beliefs and unclear ideas; while those who deny the faith boast of their unbelief and triumphantly deride the men of truth, albeit they are themselves in error. I saw men sunk, as it were, in a sea of doubt and overwhelmed by the waves of confusion, and there was no diver to bring them up from the depths and no swimmer to come to their rescue. But as God has granted unto me some knowledge by which I can be useful to them, and endowed me with some ability which I might employ for their benefit, I felt that to help them was my duty and guiding them aright a moral obligation upon me."[13]

In the second place, whatever he had to say was expressed in an orderly, methodical fashion. His codifications of the law, for example, became models for future codifiers. Unfortunately, only fragments of many of Saadia's writings have been preserved, but even these reveal his lucidity of manner and outlook. Before he undertook to treat details, he prepared an introduction to the subject matter as a whole. The very fact, incidentally, that he recognized the purpose and value of introductory discussions is a commentary on his approach to the craft of teaching and writing. His introductions not only outlined the principal ideas of the books, but also furnished him with an opportunity to discuss problems which might occur to a reflective student. Thus in his introductory analysis of the Pentateuch he writes: "The All-Wise purposed in this Book to educate those beings which were gifted with reason and to fashion them for His service. Now, there are three kinds of education, of which one is stronger than the others." There follows an examination of the several types of education, after which comes his summary: "And God has revealed, in this Book which is dedicated to the education of His servants, the three methods . . . He commands piety and prohibits sin; He announces the reward of good actions and the punishment of evil actions; and finally He gives the history of those who lived on earth before us—the salvation of those who have been virtuous and the punishment of those who have been wicked."[14] Nothing even approximating this had happened in Jewish biblical exegesis since Philo.

Finally, a rationalistic spirit dominated all of Saadia's thinking. The Greek philosophic influence of the period is never absent from his works. He had little sympathy with parochial mentality, even within Jewry, which would forbid philosophic inquiry. "It is not conceivable," he wrote,[15] "that honest investigation could have been forbidden us." To him, as to the Mutazillites—the Mohammedan rationalists—there was more than one source of truth, though truth itself was one. A man, for example, says Saadia,[16] might distribute amounts of money to several individuals; if he then wanted to know how much was left in his own hand, he could do one of two things: either he could look into his hand and see at once what remained, or he could add up the amounts which he had given away and subtract the total from the sum with which he had originally started. Whatever the procedure, the result had to be the same; otherwise one of the methods must have been incorrect. So, too, in life, either revelation and reason reached the same conclusion or one of them was unreliable. What raised man higher than the angels was, in fact, that capability and godlike reason with which he had been endowed. What could not the human being accomplish with the aid of his reason! "With his reason man embraces the past and the future; by it he subdues the animals, that they till the ground and carry in its product; by it he is able to draw the water out of the depth of the earth to its surface, nay, by it he even invents hydraulic implements that pump the water automatically; by it he builds lofty palaces, makes magnificent garments and prepares dainty dishes; by it he leads armies, equips military camps and manages the affairs of state, so that men become civilized and orderly; by it he learns the nature of the celestial spheres, the course of the planets, the size of their bodies, their distances from one another, as well as other astronomical matters."[17] Here was a hymn to the mind whose echoes were to reverberate in all the halls of scholasticism as men discovered the secret of an intellectual love of God.

Of Jewish life in the East not much more remains to be told, for after Saadia's death the decline that had set in before his election to the Gaonate merely speeded its pace. Sura was to have only one more personality of any stature, Samuel ben Hofni; Pumbedita was to be directed with distinction by Sherira and Hai.[17a] Intellectually, these men were in Saadia's debt; but, great as the latter two were, they never approached his range, while the former lacked his originality. The academies, now especially Pumbedita, still received requests for information—we owe to Sherira's famous responsum much of the historical information concerning the development of the Talmud and the leadership of the Babylonian academies. But funds for the upkeep of these schools came at rarer intervals and less generously. By the middle of the eleventh century they were out of existence, certainly as far as Jewry outside Babylonia was concerned.

Nor were political circumstances conducive to stability. From the ninth century on, the great Abbasid Empire was being undermined by one dynasty after another. Slave insurrections, a turbulent military, invasions from Central Asia reduced the Bagdad caliphate to impotence. "For two centuries," writes Hitti,[18] "the history of the disintegrating caliphate presents a confused picture of nominal rulers ascending the throne with no power and descending to the grave unregretted. Peace and security, if anywhere, were enjoyed only in those outlying provinces where a governor, practically independent, held the reins with an iron hand."

A few distinguished scholars in North Africa, especially in the prosperous community of Kairwan, continued and contributed to the intellectual tradition, attracted visitors even from remote, virtually legendary, regions,[19] could point occasionally to Jews in the service of the court. Spiritually, "spiced with Torah and wisdom,"[20] they served as heirs to both Babylonian and Palestinian traditions, and their talmudic scholarship was highly regarded. By the tenth century, however, new centers in Europe began to call attention to themselves. Key names were Mayence, Troyes, Rome, Oria, Lucena, Cordova, Granada, Toledo. They were emerging from their derivative period, vigorously assuming a creative independence. The history of the coming centuries was theirs. And by appropriating the talmudic content and tradition they brought to their inhabitants the classic that was to act as code of law and text for comment for the next eight hundred years—and longer.

NOTES

[1] See I Mac. 13:41 f. and 14:25 ff.

[2] See also A. Tcherikower, *Ha-Yehudim Veha-Yevanim,* pp. 256 f.

[3] See also I Mac. 2:51 ff.

[4] Cf. Louis Finkelstein, "Some Examples of the Maccabean Halaka," *Jour. Bibl. Lit.* 1930, pp. 20-42.

[5] Tosefta, Aboda Zara 8: 4; Sanhedrin 56a.

[6] See Acts 15:20.

[7] Our principal source is naturally Josephus, but, as has been observed by every serious historian of this period, we must remember that, the idiom of Josephus notwithstanding, these Palestinian groups or sects or associations were not philosophic schools along Hellenistic lines. For some of the observations in the present summary, particularly in connection with the Sadducees and Pharisees, I have drawn also on Rabbinic sources.

[8] See the discussion and the literature in Emil Schuerer, *Geschichte*[4], II, 651 ff.

[9] War II, 8:14.

[10] See also J. Z. Lauterbach, "Sadducees and Pharisees," in *Studies in Jewish Literature in honor of Kaufmann Kohler*, p. 188.

[[10a] Cf. above Elias J. Bickerman, "The Historical Foundations of Post-biblical Judaism," pp. 109-110.]

[11] See Antt., XIII, 10:6.

[12] Abot of Rabbi Nathan (hereafter cited as ARN), I, ed. S. Schechter, 5, p. 26.

[13] Abot 3:15.

[14] See Mishna Sotah 3:4 and the Talmud 22b; Yerushalmi (hereafter cited as Yer.). Berakot 9:7, 14b, and ARN, pp. 109, 124. Comp. G. F. Moore, *Judaism,* II, pp. 188-195. The various terms in our sources for these false Pharisees are hopelessly obscure and already the talmudic interpretations are no more than conjectures.

[15] See Mishnat R. Eliezer, ed. H. G. Enelow, pp. 225 f. and cf. Sotah 41b f.

[16] See Megillat Taanit, ed. H. Lichtenstein, p. 75 and Mekilta Nezikin 8, ed. Lauterbach, III, p. 67. Cf. Finkelstein, *Pharisees,* II, p. 641.

[17] See the discussion in the Talmud, Sanhedrin 8.

[18] On the other hand see I. Friedlaender in *Jewish Quarterly Review* (hereafter cited as JQR), N.S., IV, pp. 443-448, and more recently G. Alon in *Ziyyon,* III, pp. 300-322, who maintain that the break with the Pharisees came under Alexander Janneus.

[19] I Chron. 22:8 f.

[20] See Tosefta Baba Kamma 7:6 and cf. Mekilta on Ex. 20:25; cf. also Targum Yerushalmi on Ex., *ibid.*

[21] While it is true that Johanan ben Zakkai is the author of this homily, we are told that this was one of his "homer" interpretations, which immediately reminds us of the early allegorists. His statement, to be sure, may very well be original with him, but the view and the feeling registered have much in common with the thought of the passage in I Chron.

[22] Abot 1:7.

[23] See also L. Ginzberg, *Jewish Encyclopedia* (hereafter cited as JE), II, p. 95.

[24] So Josephus (both in War I, 3:1 and Antt. XIII, 11:1); but see Marcus's note in Antt. *ad loc.* (Loeb Classics).

[25] For a detailed discussion see J. Klausner, *Historia Yisraelit,* II, 134 ff.

[26] See Shabbat 14b and Yer. Shabbat 3d, and cf. I. H. Weiss, *Dor Dor Vedoreshav,* (1893), I, 136.

[27] Sotah 22b; see also Josephus, Antt. XIII, 15:5.

[28] Cf. Berakot 48a.

[29] See Taanit 23a.

[30] Ginzberg (JE, I, 360) indeed writes: Now "the Sanhedrin was reorganized according to their [the Pharisees'] wishes. This body had hitherto been, as it were, a 'house of lords,' the members of which belonged to the aristocracy; but it lost all significance when a powerful monarch was at the helm. From this time it became a 'supreme court' for the administration of justice and religious matters, the guidance of which was rightfully placed in the hands of the Pharisees. Thus, the reign of Alexandra marks a most important epoch in the history of Jewish internal government."

[[30a] Cf. below Louis Finkelstein, "The Jewish Religion: Its Beliefs and Practices," p. 1644.]

[31] See Abot 1:8 f.

[32] See Yer. Berakot 7, 11b; Deut. R. 3:3; Rashi in Sanhedrin 44b, catchword *Debayea;* Taanit 3:8.

[33] Cf. Yer. Ketubot 8, 32c (top).

[34] Cf. Shabbat 14b and Yer. Ketubot, *ibid.*; cf. Ginzberg, *Mekomah shel Ha-Halakah,* p. 8.

[35] Yer. Ketubot, *ibid.* See also the note in Moore, *op. cit.*, III, 104.

[36] Josephus, Con. Ap. 1:12. On further expansion of the program by Joshua b. Gamala in the first century, before the destruction of the Temple, see Baba Batra 21a.

[37] Cf. the two accounts by Josephus in War I, 5, and Antt. XIII, 16.

[38] Antt. XIV, 2:1 (Marcus's translation). See also H. Derenbourg, *Essai,* etc., pp. 113 ff.

[39] See, however, the note by Marcus in Antt. XIV, 480 f.

[40] War I, 8:8; Antt. XIV, 7:1. Of course I am referring to the first plundering by Romans. For the plundering by Antiochus IV, cf. War I, 1:1.

[41] This excellent phrase is A. H. M. Jones's (*Cities of the Eastern Roman Provinces,* p. 259).

[42] I Mac. 5:62.

[43] Psalms of Solomon 17:5-12.

[44] That by the next century this was recognized is clearly echoed by

Josephus, who (War II, 16:4) puts the following words into Agrippa's (II) mouth: "There was, to be sure, a time when you should have strained every nerve to keep out the Romans; that was when Pompey invaded this country."

[45] Such a treaty had already been entered into by Judas Maccabeus; cf. I Mac. 8. But see Thackeray's note *d* in War I, 1:4.

[46] ARN 4, p. 22.

[47] Gen. R. 64:9.

[48] See Shabbat 14b and Tosefta Makshirin 3:4; cf. Ginzberg, *op. cit.*, pp. 5 ff.

[49] *Social and Religious History*, I, 132 f. The figures by Jean Juster, *Les Juifs dans l'Empire Romain*, I, 209 f., are almost as high: 6-7 million. Cf. A. Harnack, *Mission and Expansion*, I, 2 ff. In part these large figures are explained by the success of vigorous proselytism. "In 70 A.D., only one million still inhabited Palestine, as against three and one half millions scattered mainly in the Near East and North Africa (Egypt, Asia Minor, Mesopotamia, Persia, Cyrenaica), and also Italy and Byzantium." A. Ruppin, *Jews in the Modern World*, p. 22.

[50] See Ginzberg, *Legends*, VI, 195.

[51] Yoma 71b. See also Josephus, War I, 33:1, on the popularity of the Sages who fomented revolt in Herod's last year.

[52] On the treatment of provincials by Gabinius, see Dio. 39:55 f. (I owe this reference to Marcus's note in Antt. XIV, 5:1), on the *negotiatores* cf. Schalit, *Ha-Mishtar Ha-Romai be-Eretz Yisrael*, p. 35.

[53] See Antt. XIII, 13:2.

[54] See further J. Klausner, *Ha-Bayit Ha-Sheni bi-Gedulato*, pp. 42-159.

[55] See also Tcherikower, *op. cit.*, pp. 255 ff., and V. Aptowitzer in *Livre d'Hommage à la Mémoire de Samuel Poznanski*, pp. 145-169 (Hebrew section).

[56] For example, C. Guignebert, *Jewish World in Time of Jesus*, p. 34.

2

[1] Abot 1:10.

[2] Antt. XVI, 5:4.

[3] See Deut. 17:15. See also Strabo in Antt. XV, 1:2: "For by no torments could they be forced to call him king."

[4] See Antt. XIV, 9:4, and XV, 1:1.

[5] She, too, was finally executed in 28 (?); cf. Antt. XV, 7:8.

[6] War II, 6:2; cf. Antt. XVII, 11:2.

[7] Abot, *ibid.*

[8] *Social and Economic History of the Roman Empire*, p. 6. See also Tcherikower, *op. cit.*, pp. 159 ff.

[9] Antt. XV, 9:1f.; 10:4; XVI, 2:5. Nevertheless, see F. Heichelheim, "Roman Syria," in *Economic Survey of Ancient Rome*, IV, 227.

[10] See Sukkah 51b. The structure, by the way, was not completed until shortly before (62-64 C.E.) the outbreak of the Great War with Rome. See further below, p. 142.

[11] In fact the construction of the Temple may have been undertaken by Herod merely as an emergency measure, to relieve unemployment; for only shortly before he had remitted one-third of the taxes.

[12] Klausner, *op. cit.*, pp. 97 ff., suggests that Herod's foreign policy, his interest in the welfare of Jews in countries outside Palestine, can be explained not only by his desire not to jeopardize possible commercial relations with these settlements and his insatiable ambition to appear as champion of Jews everywhere. There was still another reason. The contributions of these Jews to the Temple treasuries were considerable; to these funds Herod very likely helped himself whenever he was in need; and he sought to maintain the good will of these Jews, says Klausner, so that they would continue to send in their funds to the treasuries over which he no doubt had seized control.

[13] Mekilta R. Simeon, p. 107.

[14] *Ibid.*

[15] Abot 1:15.

[16] Cf. Ginzberg, *Mekomah shel Ha-Halakah*, pp. 41 f.

[17] Yoma 35b.

[18] See Pesahim 70b.

[19] See above, pp. 118 f.

[20] In ARN (both versions), p. 55, this expression is attributed to Hillel. In Abot 5:23 Ben He He is credited with the expression. See W. Bacher, *Agada der Tannaiten*, 1903, I, 8 f.

[21] See Tosefta Sanhedrin 7:11, Sifra, beginning, and ARN (I) 37, p. 110.

[22] Tosefta Pesahim 4:1 f., Pesahim 66a, Yer. Pesahim 33a.

[23] Cf. ARN 15, p. 60.

[24] Shabbat 31a.

[25] See ARN 3, 14 f.

[26] M. Shebiit 10:3. For the form of the *prozbul*, see *ibid.*, 4.

[27] See Keritot 1:7.

[28] See Ginzberg, *op. cit.*, pp. 13 ff. and pp. 23 ff. for one of the best analyses to date of these two schools.

[29] Weiss, *Dor Dor*, I, ch. 19, observes that no less than 316 discussions and statements are preserved from these schools.

[30] See Eduyot 1:4.

[31] Abot 2:6.

[32] See above, p. 128.

3

[1] Note also the speech of Agrippa II (War II, 16:4): "Granted that the Roman ministers are intolerably harsh, it does not follow that all the Romans are unjust to you any more than Caesar; yet it is against them, against him, that you are going to war. It is not by their orders that an oppressive governor comes from them to us, and they cannot see in the west their officers in the east; it is not easy even promptly to hear yonder the news from these parts."

[2] Antt. XVIII, 6:5.

[3] See War II, 9:2 f.; Antt. XVIII, 3:1.

[4] See Antt. XX, 5:1.

[5] "There was no feeling against entertaining a stranger at table among the Jews, although the relation could not well be reversed. And there was the rub." (M. Radin, *Jews Amongst the Greeks and Romans*, p. 185.)

[6] See on this whole subject the relevant references gathered by Juster, *op. cit.*, I, 45-48. Cf. also, more briefly, the discussion by R. Marcus in *Essays on Antisemitism*, ed. K. S. Pinson, pp. 3-24.

[7] Quoted by C. Beard, *Rise of American Civilization*, I, 115 f.

[8] Megillah 6a.

[9] Legatio ad Gaium, 38.

[10] Antt. XVIII, 5:2.

[11] That is why (as historians have repeatedly noted) Josephus has so little to say in his works—directed to non-Jewish readers—of Messianic hopes and movements.

[12] Cf., *e.g.*, Matt. 5:27 f. with the passage on Job in ARN 2, pp. 12 f.

[13] Matt. 5:17 ff. (Moffatt translation).

[14] See Antt. XIX, 7:2 and 8:1.

[15] See Sotah 7:8.

[16] See Tosefta Shabbat 13:2.

[17] Yebamot 1:6.

[18] Abot 1:17. On the identity of this Simeon see Ginzberg, *Tamid*, in Journal of Jewish Lore and Philosophy, p. 288, n. 108.

[19] Abot 1:16.

[20] See Rosh Hashanah 2:5, Yebamot 16:7, Gittin 4:2 f.

[21] See Acts 5:17 ff. for the dramatic account.

[22] So Acts 22:3. Despite Klausner, *From Jesus to Paul*, pp. 309 ff., the matter is still not certain.

[23] Acts 9:4.

[24] Mekilta Pisha 11, I, p. 85.

[25] War II, 13:5. The figure given in Acts (21:38) is 4,000. See also Klausner, *op. cit.*, p. 227.

[26] See War II, 13:6.

[27] Abot 3:2.

[28] ARN (II) 31, p. 67 (on the correct reading cf. Ginzberg in JBL, Vol. 41, p. 134, n. 46).

4

[1] See War II, 19:7 ff.

[2] See Antt. XX, 9:7.

[3] See War II, 17:6.

[4] Cf. Rostovtzeff, *op. cit.*, pp. 429, 568.

[5] With the story in ARN (I) 6, p. 32, cf. War V, 1:4, and Tacitus, Histories, 5:12 (incidentally, version II of ARN 13, p. 31, reads specifically "Sicarii").

[6] See ARN *loc. cit.*, and War VI, 3:3.

[7] See on this subject H. Graetz, *Geschichte* (1905), III, 805-813, and Graetz-Rabinowitz, II, 89-93.

[8] Yoma 9b.

[[8a] Cf. below Ralph Marcus, "Hellenistic Jewish Literature," pp. 1083-1091, *passim.*]

[9] War II, 16:4.

[10] So at least Josephus in several connections (War I, 2; III, 1:2; 5:8; VI, 6:2; VII, 4:2), but cf. Thackeray's note c (referring to Reinach) in War I, 2. Perhaps in part Agrippa's reference, at the beginning of his speech, to so many subdued nations, reflects what may have run through the minds of many Jews. These nations, the Jews may have thought, are probably waiting for an opportune uprising *somewhere* themselves to rise in revolt. And in fact, as Thackeray himself notes, the Gauls did revolt (68) and so did the Batavi (69).

[11] See ARN (I) 4, p. 22 (cf. II, 6, p. 19), and Derenbourg, *op. cit.*, pp. 284 f.; see also Josephus, Life, 6.

[12] For figures see War VI, 9:3, and as Alon (Ziyyon, 1938, Vol. 3, p. 199, n. 38b) writes, "Even if we grant that there is here some exaggeration, nevertheless we must admit that about one third of the Jewish population in the land perished." Cf. Juster, *op. cit.*, I, 211.

[13] See Thackeray's discussion in his Introduction to the War, pp. xxiv f.

[14] ARN 4, p. 24.

[15] See War VII, 10:2.

[16] See War VII, 6:6.

[17] See Tos. Sotah 15:11 f. How profound the mood of despair in some circles was can be gathered also from the speech Josephus "reports" for Eleazar in War VII, 8:6. See also 8:7, "For long since, so it seems, God passed this decree against the whole Jewish race in common, that we must quit this life if we would not use it aright." Surely Josephus (for it is he whom we are listening to) was not alone in such thoughts.

[18] ARN (I) 4, p. 21.

[19] Cf. incidentally Sifre Deut. 352 (beginning), 145a.

[20] Pesahim 57a.

[21] Cf. A. Buechler, *Economic Conditions of Judea after the Destruction of the Second Temple.*

[22] See the series of stories in ARN, ch. 17.

[23] See War VII, 6:6.

[24] Sanhedrin 32b.

[25] See Sukkah 28a.

5

[1] In addition to Sukkah, *ibid.*, see ARN 14, p. 57, and for the proper reading Boaz Cohen, *Mishnah and Tosefta Shabbat*, p. 37, n. 2.

[2] A convenient collection of sayings on and by this sage is to be found in Bacher, *op. cit.*, I, 22-42. See also Alon in *Sefer Klausner*, pp. 154-170.

[3] Sifre Deut. 357, 150a.

[4] See Sotah 9:9.
[5] ARN 4, pp. 22 f.
[6] War IV, 3:2 and 8:1. On what motivated their readmission see Alon in *Ziyyon*, Vol. 3, pp. 189 f.; and see *idem, op. cit.*, p. 203, for a different interpretation of the reasons for the choice of Jabneh by Johanan b. Zakkai.
[7] *Flowering of New England*, p. 15.
[8] Cf. ARN, p. 24.
[9] *Op. cit.*, p. 21.
[10] See Sifre Deut. 41, 60a.
[11] ARN 22, pp. 74 f.
[12] Cf. Yer. Shabbat 16, 15d (bottom).
[13] See for example Sanhedrin 10b-11a.
[14] See Lev. 23-24 and Num. 29:1.
[15] Sounding a musical instrument is forbidden on the Sabbath.
[16] It is interesting to note that a conservative like R. Eliezer later insisted that Johanan b. Zakkai had intended this privilege for Jabneh only, not for other locations.
[17] Rosh Hashanah 4:1 and Talmud *ad loc.* (29b).
[18] Abot 2:8.
[19] See for example Yadayim 4:6.
[20] See for example Pesikta 40a-b.
[21] See Ginzberg, *Tamid: Oldest Treatise of the Mishnah.*
[22] See Sifre Deut. 33, 74a.
[23] See above p. 118 and n. 16 *ad loc.*
[24] For example, Deut. 16:3 was interpreted (see Berakot 1:5) by a scholar to suggest that there is an obligation to recite in the evening service a passage commemorating the redemption from Egyptian bondage (cf. Ginzberg, *Commentary on Palestinian Talmud*, I, 207 f.); he did not feel that he was proposing conduct not contemplated by Scripture.
[25] *Four Stages of Greek Religion*, pp. 57 ff.
[26] ARN 25, p. 79.
[27] See Yadayim 4:3.
[28] See Yebamot 15a.
[29] See the excellent chapters in Vol. II of Weiss's *Dor Dor* on the various sages.
[30] Cf. Teuffel, *History of Roman Literature*, II, 109.
[31] See Sifre on Deut. 33:3; cf. Baba Kamma 38a and Yerushalmi 4b.
[32] See Weiss, *op. cit.*, II, ch. 8, for illustrations and references.
[33] Cf. Yer. Berakot 1, 3b-c.
[34] See Ginzberg, *Commentary*, I, 159 f.
[35] See Sifre Deut. 16, 68b and Berakot 28a.
[36] Cf. Berakot 4:3 and Talmud *ad loc.* (28b); see also Pesahim 10:5.
[37] Cf. Rosh Hashanah 2:8 f.
[38] See Ginzberg, *Commentary*, III, 193 ff.; cf. Ch. Albeck in *Ziyyon*, Vol. 8, p. 166. For the story cf. Berakot 27b f. and Yer. Berakot 4, 7c f.
[39] See Ginzberg, *op. cit.*, III, 176 f.
[40] Cf. ARN 18, pp. 67 f.

[41] See incidentally some pertinent remarks by Ginzberg, *op. cit.*, I, 82 f.

[42] Cf. Eduyot 1:4 ff.

[43] On this subject see H. E. Ryle, *Canon of the Old Testament*, L. Blau in JE, III, s.v. *Bible Canon*, and S. Zeitlin in *Proceedings Amer. Acad. Jewish Research*, 1932, pp. 121 ff.

[44] See the reference above in n. 41.

[45] Cf. Eduyot 1:4.

[46] See Ketubot 8b.

[47] Baba Mezia 59b. See also, by the way, the remark by R. Eleazar b. Zadok in Tosefta Berakot 2:6.

6

[1] See the discussion by Schuerer, *op. cit.*, I, 658 f.; Juster, *op. cit.*, II, 151 f. But cf. Buechler, *Das Synedrion*, p. 46, n. 42.

[2] Cf. S. Lieberman, *Greek in Jewish Palestine*, pp. 1, 20.

[3] See Peah 8:7 ff. and Tosefta Gittin 5:4 f.

[4] Cf. Berakot 2:2.

[5] For the prayer see *Authorized Daily Prayer Book*, pp. 44-53, and cf. I. Abrahams, *Companion*, pp. lv ff. See also I. Elbogen, *Der juedische Gottesdienst* (1913), pp. 250-257, and Moore, *op. cit.*, I, 281-307.

[6] See the discussion by Ginzberg, *op. cit.*, III, 411-428, and more recently Chertoff in JQR, N. S., Vol. 34, pp. 87-98.

[7] Sifre Deut. 48, 84b.

[8] Sanhedrin 59a. See also Moore, *op. cit.*, I, 308-322, II, 239-247.

[9] Cf. also Franz Delitzsch, *Jewish Artisan Life in Time of Christ*, ch. 5. Buechler (*Political and Social Leaders of the Jewish Community of Sepphoris*, ch. 1) is no doubt correct when he points to examples of antagonism to Rabbinic authority. But that this antagonism was general is hard to accept. Our sources certainly leave the impression that for the most part Jews did submit to the authority of the Rabbinic courts.

[10] See Antt. XX, 9:2-4, and cf. Derenbourg, *op. cit.*, pp. 233 f.

[11] See, for example, one of the statements by R. Eleazar in Sanhedrin 92a and cf. Maimonides, Yad, Hilkot Talmud Torah 6:10. In this connection, however, it is well to recall the general attitude (*margela bepumyyehu*) of the Sages at Jabneh; see Berakot 17a.

[12] Eusebius, Ec. Hist. 4:2.

[13] See Sotah 9:14 where instead of Titus read Quietus.

[14] Cf., for example, the Jewish Sybil (V, 46 ff.).

[15] For a discussion of the problem with our sources see Schuerer, *op. cit.*, I, 671 f., who however puts no stock whatsoever in the story (Gen. R. 64:10) that the war was brought on by Hadrian's withdrawal of the permission to rebuild the Temple. "Der historische Werth dieser Legende ist gleich Null." Cf. Juster, *op. cit.*, II, 191 ff. On the Hadrianic policy toward the Jews see now the brilliant study by Lieberman, "Martyrs of Caesarea," *Annuaire de l'Institut de Philologie*, 1939-1944, pp. 424 ff.

[16] Cf. Baba Batra 60b.

[17] Lam. R. 2:2 (ed. Buber, p. 101).

[18] Dio, 69:12.

[19] With this statement of ARN 38, p. 115, cf. the figures given by Dio, 69:13 f.

[20] Dio, *ad loc.*

[21] As Avi-Yonah puts it, "From ancient sources we hear of 75 settlements in Judea, all of which were occupied by Jews. After the destruction of Bether there is not a mention of Jewish settlers in even one of them." *Biyeme Roma Ubizantiyon*, p. 2.

[22] See Ex. 13:6 f.

[23] See Lev. 23:40.

[24] Mekilta Bahodesh 6, II, p. 247.

[25] See for example the statement in the name of R. Simeon b. Eleazar in ARN 26, p. 82. Comp. Tosefta Aboda Zara 4:3 ff.

[26] Cf. Berakot 63a. Furthermore, "There is evidence that he (Nahum) founded the office [of the Exilarchate] during the Hadrianic persecution, when Babylonian Jewry found itself cut off from Palestinian leadership and thus had to look to local leadership." A. D. Goode, "The Exilarchate in the Eastern Caliphate," JQR, XXXI, p. 150.

[27] See Megillat Taanit, ed. Lichtenstein, p. 94, and Rosh Ha-Shanah 19a.

[28] See on this Avi-Yonah, *op. cit.*, pp. 31 ff.

[29] ARN (I) 6, p. 29 (version II reports the tribute in the name of R. Eliezer).

[30] Sanhedrin 1:1.

[31] See Ex. 22:7 f., and Mekilta *ad loc.* (III, 119). Cf. Sanhedrin 3b.

[32] Cf. ARN 18, p. 67.

[33] On this subject see D. Hoffmann, *Zur Einleitung in die halachischen Midraschim.*

[34] See Sifra on the verse (ed. Weiss, 79c).

[35] Cf., for example, Sanhedrin 67b.

[36] See Sifre Num. 103, 27b.

[37] Abot 3:15; see also above, p. 117.

[38] So Ginzberg in his brilliant study in JE, I, s.v. *Akiba.*

[39] Gen. R. 34:14.

[40] See Bacher, *op. cit.*, I, 311 f.

[41] See the story in Sifre Deut. 32, 73b.

[42] Yer. Berakot 9, 14b.

[43] On the subject of the Ten Martyrs see Finkelstein in *Essays and Studies in Memory of Linda Miller.*

7

[1] See Graetz-Rabinowitz, *op. cit.*, II, 264 f., n. 4, and Buechler in *Abhandlungen zur Erinnerung an H. P. Chajes* (Hebrew section), pp. 159-162.

[2] See for example Baba Batra 90b and Mishna Aboda Zara 1:8.

[3] Aboda Zara 18a.

[4] See the story told of R. Meir in Lev. R. 9:9.

[5] Gen. R. 44:1; cf. Mekilta R. Simeon, p. 100, for the thought.

[6] Jer. 17:21 ff.

[7] Neh. 10:32.

[8] Amos 8:5.

[9] On this whole subject see the splendid chapter (7) by Weiss, *op. cit.*, II

[10] Berakot 9:5.

[11] Yebamot 16:7.

[12] Baba Kamma 79b.

[13] Berakot 45a.

[14] Cf. the remark by R. José in ARN (I) 1, p. 5 (cf. II, 1, p. 3).

[15] L. Pinsker, *Likkute Kadmoniyot*, I, 74. The poet is Moses Daroi. On the Karaites, see below, pp. 191 ff.

[16] Prol. ad Oseam, ed. Migne, XXV, 820 (I owe this to Ginzberg, *Students, Scholars and Saints*, p. 44).

[17] Sifre Deut. 49, 85a.

[18] Mekilta Bahodesh 1, II, p. 198. On the proper reading of the text cf. Lieberman, *Shekiin*, p. 73.

[19] Ex. R. 2:2.

[20] Abot 1:2.

[21] *Op. cit.*, 1:3.

[22] *Op. cit.*, 1:12.

[23] *Op. cit.*, 2:15.

[24] The classic work on midrash Haggada is L. Zunz's *Gottesdienstliche Vortraege.*

[25] Baba Batra 14b.

[26] See also M. Kadushin, *Organic Thinking.*

[27] Cf. for example Gen. R. 58:3.

[28] Cf. Sifre Deut. 317, 135b.

[29] See the various instalments of Ginzberg's *Die Haggada bei den Kirchenvaetern.*

[30] That some haggadic collections were already in circulation earlier is clear from statements in the Talmud; see for example Berakot 23a, Yer. Berakot 5, 9a (top), and elsewhere. On the date of Gen. R., regarded as the earliest of haggadic midrashim, see also Albeck, *Einleitung und Register zum Bereschit Rabba*, p. 96.

[31] See Yalkut on Josh. 10:12.

[32] ARN (II) 32, p. 71.

[33] Megillah 10b.

[34] Baba Kamma 60b.

[35] Cf. Shabbat 33b.

[36] Elisha ben Abuyah cannot have been an exception. If there is a uniqueness about him, it is due to his unusual gifts and articulateness, let alone his former prominence.

[37] ARN 28, p. 85. Cf. also the words uttered by him at his death, Ketubot 104a.

[38] Baba Batra, 8a.

[39] Makkot 10a.

[40] Abot 4:20.

[41] Cf. Sanhedrin 5a and Weiss, *op. cit.*, III, 133.

[42] In our editions Abot occurs in the fourth order, most likely as a result of the later general practice to concentrate on the first four orders. That it is placed before Horayot, the last treatise of the fourth order, is no difficulty. Abot has five chapters (the sixth is a later addition) and Horayot has only three; and size played a not unimportant part in the arrangement of treatises within an order: the longer ones were generally put first (see, by the way, Meiri on Abot, Introduction, beginning, where he speaks of Abot being studied *after* Horayot). In the Munich ms. of the Talmud, Abot in fact does come at the end of the Talmud.—I note now that the same view is expressed by Herford in his Introduction to his translation of and commentary on Abot.

8

[1] See also Ginzberg in JE, I, 356 ff. But cf. L. Wallach in JQR, XXXI, pp. 259-286, "The Colloquy of Marcus Aurelius with the Patriarch Judah I," and now Avi-Yonah, *op. cit.*, pp. 28 ff.

[2] Quoted by Rostovtzeff, *History of Ancient World*, II, 306.

[3] Cf. also A. Gulak, "Lesidre Ha-Misim Ha-Romaim Baarez," in *Sefer Magnes*, pp. 97-104.

[4] Spartian, Pescennius Niger, 7:9: "Vos terras vestras levari censitione vultis: ego vero etiam aerem vestrum censere vellem."

[5] Cf. ARN 20, p. 71.

[6] Cf. Aboda Zara 36a.

[7] Cf. Sanhedrin 26a.

[8] Cf. Gulak, *op. cit.*, pp. 103 f. On the inflation, see Heichelheim, "Roman Syria," in *Economic Survey of Ancient Rome*, IV, 219 ff.

[9] See further Rostovtzeff, *Social and Economic History of Roman Empire*, p. 370: "Everybody was now a Roman citizen, and this meant that nobody was such anymore."

[10] Abot 2:3; following Graetz and Bacher that this saying is by Gamaliel, Judah's son.

[11] See also Krauss in JE, I, p. 356.

[12] On these respective Sages see further the relevant chapters in Weiss, *op. cit.*, III.

[13] See Yer. Taanit 1:4, 64b, and cf. Lieberman, *Greek in Jewish Palestine*, pp. 31 ff.

[14] Cf. Lam. R., Introduction, 17; see also on 3:14.

[15] Cf. Laws of Constantine, Oct. 18, 315, in *Theodosiani libri*, ed. Mommsen and Meyer, Vol. I, Pt. II, p. 887.

[16] Jerome, Commentary on Zeph. 1:15 (cited by Schuerer, *op. cit.*, I, 704).

[17] Avi-Yonah, *op. cit.*, p. 124. On the outbreak see now Lieberman, "Palestine in the Third and Fourth Centuries," JQR, XXXVI, 329-370, and the note in JQR, XXXVII, 423 f.

[18] *Theodosiani libri*, Vol. II, Novella III, pp. 8 f.

[19] *Ibid.* (translation by J. Marcus, *The Jew in the Mediaeval World*, p. 6).

[20] See the selection in Marcus, *op. cit.*, p. 9.

[21] See indeed the conclusion of Julian's letter to the Jews.

[22] *Ibid.* On Julian's letter see Levi in *Ziyyon*, VI, 1-32.

[23] Jerome, Ep. ad Titum 3:9 (cited by Krauss, *Jews in Works of Church Fathers*, JQR, 1894, p. 232).

[24] Jerome on Ez. 33:33 (in Krauss, *op. cit.*, p. 234).

[25] Cf. Yer. Sotah 7, 21b.

[26] See Lieberman, *Talmuda shel Kesarin*, and Ginzberg, *Commentary*, Introduction (Hebrew), pp. 81 f.

[27] See further Avi-Yonah, *op. cit.*, pp. 156 f. "Ten times between 393 and 426 orders were issued intended to protect synagogues and to prohibit attacks against Jewish worship."

[28] Avi-Yonah estimates that by the sixth century there were between 150,000 and 200,000 Jews in Palestine, in contrast to the 750,000-800,000 in the land after the Bar Kokbah revolt (*op. cit.*, pp. 175 f.).

[29] See further Ginzberg, *op. cit.*, pp. 114 f.

9

[1] Hullin 137b.

[2] Sanhedrin 83b.

[3] Cf. the expression in Hullin 110a.

[4] Cf. War I, 22:1; Antt. XV, 2:2 ("where there were Jews in great numbers").

[5] Cf. Antt. XVIII, 9.

[6] Cf. above, p. 155.

[7] Cf. Ketubot 28b.

[8] Cf., *e.g.*, Yer. Ketubot 12, 35a (bottom).

[9] Cf. Yer. Baba Batra 5, 15a f.

[10] Pesahim 113a.

[11] See the brief but excellent remarks by Ginzberg, *Commentary*, Introduction, pp. xxiii ff.

[12] *Op. cit.*, p. xxxii.

[13] See Taanit 9b.

[14] Cf. Sukkah 26a.

[15] Cf. Baba Mezia 86a.

[16] Tanhuma Noah 3. The two academies were Sura and Pumbedita. On the latter see below, pp. 179 f.

[17] Baba Batra 55a.

[18] Yer. Aboda Zara 2, 41d. Weiss, *op. cit.*, III, ch. 13 (end), is no doubt correct when he interprets Samuel's view as an effort to preserve the dignity of the Patriarchate; Samuel's sharp words—"If you do not (submit) I shall declare thee a 'rebellious elder'"—certainly express a recognition of the Patriarch's authority. But I feel that the social-economic element played an important part in shaping Samuel's views; and this led him more readily than Rab to accept the Palestinian enactment in this instance.

[19] See on all this (as well as Samuel's proficiency in the sciences) Weiss, *op. cit.*, III, ch. 13.

[20] See Baba Mezia 38b.

[21] On these sages see the relevant chapters in Weiss, *op. cit.*, III.

[22] Cf. Baba Batra 157b.

[23] See Ginzberg, *Commentary*, Introduction (Hebrew), pp. 89 ff.

[24] See on this whole subject the careful work by Julius Kaplan, *The Redaction of the Babylonian Talmud.*

[25] See, however, Lieberman, *Greek in Jewish Palestine*, pp. 110 f.

[26] Cf. Midrash Tehillim on 104:25 (223b). For the expression "sea of the Talmud" cf. Ben Yehuda, *Dictionary*, IV, 2056, col. 1.

10

[1] See Sykes, *History of Persia* (2nd ed.), I, pp. 449 ff.

[2] The Arab ambassadors' address to Yezdigird III (cited by Sykes, *op. cit.*, p. 488).

[3] See H. Hirschfeld, JQR, N.S., Vol. 1, p. 447.

[4] See the articles by Josef Horovitz in *Encyclopedia Judaica*, III, 1024-1027.

[5] Samaual ibn Adiyah (cited by Baron, *Social and Religious History*, I, 310).

[6] El-Bokhari, *Les Traditions Islamiques* (Houdas et Marçais), I, 1 f.: "À certains moments, elle (*i.e.*, la Révélation) m'arrive pareille au tintement d'une clochette, et c'est pour moi la plus pénible." See also n. 1, p. 2.

[7] *Op. cit.*, p. 12.

[8] See on this the study by T. W. Arnold, *The Preaching of Islam.*

[9] Quoted by P. K. Hitti, *History of the Arabs* (1940), p. 144.

[10] See A. Jellinek, *Bet Ha-Midrash*, III, 78.

[11] See for this whole paragraph (and a number of points in the next few pages) J. Mann's study in JQR, N.S., Vols. 7-9, and Walter J. Fischel, "Origin of Banking in Mediaeval Islam," *Journal of Royal Asiatic Society*, April and July, 1943.

[12] Benjamin of Tudela. See his *Itinerary* (ed. Asher), pp. 60 ff. (Hebrew; English trans. pp. 100 ff.). For an earlier account see Nathan the Babylonian in A. Neubauer, *Mediaeval Jewish Chronicles,* 11, 83 ff.

[13] See *Itinerary* in E. N. Adler's *Jewish Travellers,* p. 48.

[14] *Op. cit.*, p. 49.

[15] Cited by H. C. Lea, *Studies in Church History*, pp. 252, 275.

[16] From a responsum of R. Paltoi Gaon (9th cent.) quoted in Asaf, *Ha-Oneshin Ahare Hatimat Ha-Talmud,* p. 49; cf. also Asaf's note *ad loc.*

[17] See below pp. 196-197.

[18] From a responsum of Sherira (reproduced in part by Asaf, *op. cit.*, p. 53) we learn that the Geonim even had "policemen" (monitors) of a sort!

[19] Cf. Ginzberg, *Ginze Schechter,* II, Introduction, p. 6.

[20] *Shaare Zedek,* preface. Cf. also *Shaare Teshubah*, No. 34.

[21] Cf. the remark by Rabad (in Ginzberg, *Geonica*, I, 205): "At the present time we may not explain a Talmud passage other than the Geonim, unless we have irrefutable evidence against their conception of it—which is never the case."

[22] See Levin, *Ozar Ha-Geonim*, IV, 14.

[23] Cf. for example, *op. cit.*, I, Pt. II, 39, bottom. On R. Hai, see the monograph by A. Obadiah in *Sinai*, Vol. 2, pp. 549-591.

[24] Cf. for example his rationalistic discussion in *op. cit.*, I, 130 ff. (in Pt. II, pp. 91 ff.), and Obadiah, *op. cit.*, pp. 562 ff.

[25] See Lauterbach in JE, XI, 240 ff.

[26] I owe this information to Professor Alexander Marx.

11

[1] See the selection in J. Marcus, *op. cit.*, pp. 225 f.

[2] JQR, N.S., I, 200 f.

[[2a] Cf. Below Alexander Altmann, "Judaism and World Philosophy," pp. 964 ff.]

[3] See Sanhedrin, 99b f.

[4] Cf. *Seder R. Amram Gaon* (Warsaw, 1865), 37b-38a. The passage speaks of the Karaites.

[5] See above p. 145.

[6] See Mann, *Texts and Studies*, II, 16; see also the quotation in n. 30, *ibid.*

[7] Salmon ben Yeruhim, *Sefer Milhamot Ha-Shem,* ed. Davidson, pp. 37, lines 45 ff., and 43, lines 75 f.

[8] Cf. the quotation in Pinsker, *Likkute Kadmoniyot*, II, 189, n. 3.

[9] Cf. S. Poznanski in Hastings's *Encyclopedia of Religion and Ethics*, VIII, 662-672.

[10] Even this view is not entirely original. See the story of the sick person whom R. Akiba and R. Ishmael encountered, in Midrash Samuel 4, p. 54. Nevertheless, cf. Buber's n. 7.

[11] Cf. Harkavy's n. 37 in Graetz-Rabinowitz, *op. cit.*, III, 189.

[12] Cf. Sahl ben Masliah (in Pinsker, *op. cit.*, II, 34): "This is to teach us that we are under no obligation to follow in the way of our fathers under every circumstance; rather we are obliged to reflect upon their ways and compare their actions and decisions with the words of the Torah. If we find that the teachings of the one coincide with the teachings of the other, then we must accept and obey (the teachings of our fathers); we must not alter their teachings; we must follow them. But if the teachings of our fathers differ from the Torah, we must reject them, and (ourselves) seek out and investigate and think of the commandments of the Torah."

[13] Quoted by Poznanski, *op. cit.*; see also Pinsker, *op. cit.*, I, 44 f.

12

[1] See Hitti, *op. cit.*, p. 402; and cf. the quotation (*ibid.*) from Ibn Khaldun (14th cent.): "Most of the learned men in Islam were non-Arabians."

[2] A Rabbi Nathan who was appointed to succeed him died before entering office.

[3] See, however, Mann, in *Tarbiz,* V, 159, n. 36.

[4] See Davidson's Introduction to his edition of *Saadia's Polemic against Hiwi Al-Balkhi.*

[5] Mann, *Jews in Egypt and Palestine*, II, 42; cf. I, 52 f.

[6] Cf. the passages cited by Zeitlin in his notes in JQR, N.S., XXX, p. 393.

[7] See Mann in *Tarbiz*, V, 159 ff.

[8] By Saadia's time the Sura academy had been transferred to Bagdad (see above, pp. 187-188). Though Saadia remained in that city, he was simply one more private person, without any official post.

[9] Cf. H. Malter, *Saadia Gaon*, p. 52, and n. *ad loc.*

[10] *Iggeret Teman* (Warsaw, 1927), p. 24. See, indeed, Malter, *op. cit.*, Ch. VII, for the impact and influence of Saadia on later generations.

[11] See Ginzberg's study of Saadia's *Siddur* in JQR, XXX, pp. 326 ff.

[12] Poetically, the paraphrases are sometimes unfortunate!

[13] *Emunot Vedeot*, Josefow, 1885, Introduction, 2, p. 38 (Malter's translation, *op. cit.*, p. 200).

[14] Taken from *The Jewish Anthology* (ed. E. Fleg, trans. M. Samuel), pp. 171 f. See also *Emunot*, Bk. III.

[15] *Emunot*, Introduction, 6, p. 48.

[16] *Op. cit.*, pp. 51 f.

[17] *Op. cit.*, IV, 125 (Malter's translation, pp. 231 f.).

[[17a] Cf. below Abraham S. Halkin "Judeo-Arabic Literature," pp. 1126, 1132.]

[18] *History of the Arabs*, p. 467.

[19] See A. Epstein, *Eldad Ha-Dani*, Introduction.

[20] Quoted by Poznanski, "Anshe Kairwan" in *Harkavy Festschrift*, pp. 175-220.

BRIEF BIBLIOGRAPHY

AVI-YONAH, M., *Biyeme Roma Ubizantiyon*. Jerusalem, 1946.

BACHER, W., *Agada der Tannaiten*. Strassburg, I (1903), II (1890).

———, *Agada der palaestinensischen Amoraeer*. Strassburg, 1892-1899.

DERENBOURG, J., *Essai sur l'Histoire et la Géographie de la Palestine*. Paris, 1867.

FINKELSTEIN, L., *The Pharisees*. Philadelphia, 1938.

FUNK, S., *Die Juden in Babylonien*. Berlin, 1902-1908.

GINZBERG, L., *Geonica*. Vol. I. New York, 1909.

GRAETZ, H., *Geschichte der Juden*. Vols. III-V. Leipzig, 1905-1909.

JUSTER, J., *Les Juifs dans l'Empire Romain*. Paris, 1914.

MANN, J., "The Responsa of the Geonim as Source of Jewish History," in *Jewish Quarterly Review* (New Series), VII-XI, 1916-1921.

MALTER, H., *Saadia Gaon*. Philadelphia, 1921.

MOORE, G. F., *Judaism*. Cambridge, Mass., 1927.

SCHUERER, E., *Geschichte des juedischen Volkes im Zeitalter Jesu Christi*. 4th ed. Leipzig, 1901-1909.

STRACK, H., *Introduction to Talmud and Midrash*. Philadelphia, 1945.

WEISS, I. H., *Dor Dor Vedoreshav*. Vols. I-IV. Berlin, 1924.

CHAPTER 4

THE EUROPEAN AGE IN JEWISH HISTORY
(*to 1648*)

By Cecil Roth

The close of the classical period found the Jews solidly established throughout the Roman Empire in the West as well as in the East. They were to be found already in some numbers (as is clear from abundant literary and archaeological evidences) in Greece, Italy, Spain and throughout Northern Africa, as far as the Pillars of Hercules; there was a sprinkling, at least, in Gaul and the Rhineland; and there is reason to believe that they were settled, too, in Britain and other distant provinces of the empire. Hitherto—above all since the edict of Caracalla (212), which conferred Roman citizenship on all free men—they had lived a fairly ample life, suffering from no legal restriction worthy of note except that they were obliged to pay a special poll tax diverted by Vespasian from the Temple of Jerusalem to that of Jupiter Capitolinus in Rome—the *Fiscus Judaicus*.[1a] There were perhaps some social prejudices against them by reason of their refusal to assimilate (this is indeed reflected in the writings of the classical poets and historians), and like all immigrants they tended to drift into urban callings. But on the whole their status was identical with that of their neighbors and they—indeed, they alone—were specifically exempted by law from the universal obligation of participating in the ceremonies of the state religion.

The Christianization of the Roman Empire in the fourth century, which is generally taken as the watershed between the classical and medieval periods, introduced a drastic change into their circumstances. Legally, they continued to benefit from the unique privilege of religious toleration, as they generally did in most countries until late in the Middle Ages. On the other hand, their status was completely changed. The acerbities that had marked Judeo-Christian polemics during the past two centuries suddenly became translated into state policy; the collapse of paganism left the Jews as the main target of Christian zeal; and everywhere eager neophytes testified to their sincerity by an onslaught on the defenseless unbeliever who was nearest to hand. The church, moreover, considered it desirable to keep the Jews in a position of inferiority, in order to prevent them from exercising what it seemed to consider an undesirable influence on those whose Christianity was still tenuous, as well as to demonstrate for its own purposes that the crime of Calvary was being atoned. This attitude was adopted almost in its entirety by the state. The atmosphere thus changed. Jews were threatened with severe punishment if they interfered with converts to Christianity; they were forbidden to own Christian slaves and, later on, any slaves at all—thus in effect debarring them from being employers of non-Jewish labor, and hence from farming except on the smallest scale; they were ordered under pain of death to desist from seeking proselytes to their faith; intermarriage or cohabitation with a Christian was sternly prohibited; they were not allowed to build new synagogues or to embellish the old; various exemptions and privileges formerly enjoyed were canceled; and in the legislation of the period Judaism was referred to in the most insulting terms, as a "nefarious sect," "sacrilegious gathering" and the like. All this was embodied in 438 in the *Codex Theodosianus*, the basis of later European jurisprudence, thus as it were becoming part of the pattern of the medieval mind.

There was indeed, on the other hand, a positive and favorable side to this policy. Though Judaism was depressed, it was at least tolerated, as a matter of principle and not merely of convenience. Jewish religious assemblies still had the protection of the law, and existing synagogues were not supposed to be disturbed: as under the pagan emperors, Judaism was in fact the only dissenting religion which enjoyed such toleration. This dualism, implicit in the imperial legislation from the fourth century onward, was systematically expounded after the fall of the Western Empire by Pope Gregory the Great (590-604), who simultaneously repressed any attempt on the part of the Jews to exceed the privileges conceded them by the church and state, and at the same time protected them when their limited rights were attacked. "Just as license must not be granted to the Jews to presume to do in their synagogues more than the law permits them," he wrote, in a fundamental passage which continued to be cited by his successors for centuries after, "so they should not suffer curtailment in that which has been conceded to them."

This was the keynote of the official church policy throughout the Middle Ages. But it was not easy for laymen (and even, in many cases, for clerics) to appreciate or much less to maintain the delicate balance. The first centuries after the adoption of Christianity by the Roman emperors witnessed, therefore, a sequence of riots in all parts of the empire, during which synagogues were destroyed and Jews forced into Christianity. The information that we have is sporadic, but it obviously indicates a widespread tendency, especially since the ringleaders were sometimes churchmen of the highest status, such as St. Ambrosius of Milan. Social pressure, theological polemics and the magnetism of a victorious cause also played their part in weakening Jewish cohesion. In these centuries, therefore, many of the great settlements that had once existed under Roman rule were reduced to relative unimportance. The offensive reached its climax in the seventh century. In the Byzantine Empire, Heraclius (610-641) completely prohibited the exercise of Judaism in his dominions and tried to force the Jews into the state religion—a policy sporadically renewed from time to time by his successors. There is, moreover, reason to suspect that he attempted to secure the imitation of his example throughout Europe. The Jews were given the alternative of exile or conversion about this time in Burgundy, in Lombardy and even in France (626). In Spain, the adoption of Catholicism by the Visigothic rulers (after a favorable interlude during which the latter had been supporters of the Arian form of Christianity and, by the same token, relatively tolerant) led to a systematic persecution. Between 616 and the Moslem conquest in 711, the practice of Judaism was generally forbidden throughout the Peninsula, and energetic steps were taken at successive Councils of Toledo, under the guidance of the rulers themselves, to prevent the perpetuation of any sort of Jewish or Judaizing tradition. Thus in the seventh century Jewish life in Europe touched its nadir.

Conditions changed thereafter. The principal factor was perhaps economic. The debacle of the Roman Empire gave the Jews special advantages, as an international element with certain mercantile qualifications which resulted from this fact and from their high degree of literacy (it is to be noted that at an earlier stage in their economic history any propensity in this direction had been conspicuously absent). At the beginning these advantages were shared with others—*e.g.*, the Syrians, who for some time played a vastly more important role in economic life. But the Moslem expansion inevitably changed this. The Mediterranean world was henceforth divided into two mutually exclusive sections—the Romance- (or Greek)-speaking Christian sphere, on the one hand, and the Arabic-speaking Islamic sphere, on the other. The Jew alone had a foot in either camp, could move in all countries with equal or almost equal ease, mastered (if only academically) a tongue which could carry him about everywhere and had reliable connections and agents among his coreligionists in all major centers of trade. Moreover, at this period the former great Jewish reservoir of population in Mesopotamia in the East had for the first time been brought by the Moslem expansion under the same rule and into the same intellectual orbit as the farthest outpost of Europe to the West. The former region was now entering upon a period of economic decline—perhaps through natural desiccation, perhaps through the breakdown of the former methods of agriculture; and the recent political changes had tended to divorce its Jewish population from the soil and concentrate them in the cities. There was in consequence considerable emigration in all directions, northward and eastward as well as westward; but in the long run the latter was infinitely more important. Four main routes, it may be suggested, brought the Jews to Europe at this time. There was the immemorial caravan route from settlement to settlement through Northern Africa, where several important Jewish groups now began to flourish again (including the long-decadent communities in the Nile delta and a learned colony in the new city of Kairouan, which attained a considerable though momentary importance in the ninth and tenth centuries); from the coast of Morocco, it was an easy step across the Strait of Gibraltar into Spain, which alternatively might be reached directly by sea from the Levant. Secondly, there was the expansion from Mesopotamia northward, into Persia and then South Russia, where the Khazar khans, who adopted Judaism at this period (see pages 221-222), naturally welcomed Jewish immigrants. From Palestine, in constant commercial and religious relations with Apulia, an important trade and migration route led to South Italy, and thence up the peninsula via Lucca and over the Alps into France, or ultimately to the Rhineland. Finally, there was the route from Byzantium along the Danube valley into south Germany. Along all these paths Jewish pioneers pressed their way, from township to township and city to city, setting up little communities in every commercial center of importance. The re-establishment of tranquillity in northern Europe under the Carolingians afforded them unprecedented opportunities. Successive emperors highly appreciated the value of their services in the economic sphere, according them for that reason special privileges and protection; and for a time the terms "merchant" and "Jew" were used almost interchangeably in the official documents and charters that they issued.

In addition to the traders, who brought the amenities of Asia and the East to the primitive nobility of the northwest, there were craftsmen as well. Glass, brocades and jewelry of Jewish manufacture were famous; and the Jews were long associated in particular with the dyeing and silk-weaving industries in all Mediterranean countries. A number of them, moreover—especially in the south—settled on the soil, though they were mainly interested in the more specialized branches of agriculture, such as grape and olive growing. It is unfortunate that our records of this period are so scanty, so that we are driven to reconstruct a picture of one of the most important processes in Jewish history from the merest handful of scattered indications and vague allusions—for example, the exaggerated propaganda of Agobard and Amulo, successive archbishops of Lyons in the ninth century and the fathers of medieval anti-Semitism; or the incidental references in Rabbinic literature, which now began to establish itself in western Europe. Whether physical or political conditions were wholly favorable is somewhat dubious. The argument from silence is always dangerous, and various abuses which appear universally later on—

for example, the exposure to licensed mob violence at Eastertide—apparently go back to the Dark Ages. A great deal thus has to be left to conjecture. What is beyond question is that the Jewish population of western Europe, reduced, it seems, to a handful in the seventh century, was enormously reinforced in the eighth and ninth. The same period, therefore, which witnessed the twilight of the surviving Jewish centers in the East, reflected in the decline of the Gaonate,[2a] saw those of the West emerge to robust life. From about the beginning of the tenth century in Spain, of the eleventh in France and western Germany, we have evidence of a numerous, prosperous Jewish population, and firmly established communities in every town of any importance, whose record is from now on continuous. For the next thousand years, Jewish history is, in the main, the history of the Jews in Europe.

It is convenient to pause at this stage to consider the geographical distribution of the Jews throughout the world at this time. There was still a strong nucleus in Mesopotamia, in Syria and Persia, with offshoots in India (whose descendants still maintain their identity) and perhaps, even at this early stage, also in China. The original settlement in Palestine had by now sharply declined, but it had not entirely lost its importance and was, moreover, constantly recruited by pious immigrants, especially after the Moslem conquest had established a somewhat more tolerant rule. Egyptian Jewry, on the other hand, was now very significant, with Cairo as its greatest but by no means its only center; and the chain of Jewish settlements was unbroken all along northern Africa as far as the Atlantic Ocean. How far inland they extended is obscure; but vague rumors circulated from time to time of independent Jewish groups in central Africa, which were naïvely identified with the lost Ten Tribes. (The most famous instance is associated with the circumstantial report made at Kairouan by "Eldad the Danite" in 883.) The dark-skinned Falashas of Abyssinia, presumably descended from proselytes made in a remote age, retain their individuality even now. In what was left of the Byzantine Empire, where Jews had established their earliest settlement in Europe in the first pre-Christian centuries, they had greatly declined as a result of the recurrent intolerance of the later Caesars; the sprinkling still to be found there did thus not have much importance. Italy was the one European country with which the Jewish association has been unbroken from classical times down to the present day, and it had a very great share in the transmission of Jewish learning from East to West. At this period and down to the close of the thirteenth century, the principal communities were situated from Rome southward, the settlement being relatively thick in the Apulian seaports. On the other hand, the trading republics which were now beginning to emerge in the north, such as Venice, were nervous of competition and not only did not tolerate any settlement of

Jews, but even refused to carry their goods and did everything that was possible to drive them out of international trade. The most important community of northern Italy, so far as our information goes, was that of Lucca, but the sources are regrettably defective.

In Spain, the Jewish element was densest in Andalusia and the Moslem south. But Christian principalities had begun to think better of the ferocious intolerance they had shown in the early days of the *Reconquista*, so that already there was a Jewish nucleus in the northern part of the Peninsula as well, destined to become more and more important later on. Jewish litterateurs of the Middle Ages identified Spain with the *Sepharad* of the prophecy of Obadiah (verse 20), where the exiles of Jerusalem had found refuge; and in consequence of this, southern Jewry in general ultimately came to be termed, somewhat loosely, *Sephardim*. The oldest French settlements were in Provence, Narbonne with its "Jewish Prince" (probably no more than the magnifico of the local community) being the most famous at this time. But by now they were outstripped in intellectual vigor if not in number (for regarding this also we have no certain data) by the communities of Champagne and the northeast, already solidly established in many a township such as Troyes, where Rashi was to flourish. Hence, after 1066, some crossed the Channel on the heels of William the Conqueror and settled in England, first in London (always preponderant in Anglo-Jewish life) and then in some provincial centers: the colony was never, however, of great significance. The Jews of Champagne were in close connection with those of the Rhineland, who seem in fact to have been of French origin. Here, already at this period, the communities of Mainz, Cologne and so on were prosperous and famous for their scholarship. Germany was termed by the medieval Rabbis *Ashkenaz* (Gen. 10:3; Jer. 51:27); and hence the term *Ashkenazim*, in contradistinction to *Sephardim*, came to be applied to their descendants, and ultimately to northern Jewry as a whole. Though German Jewish life was strongest in the west, a chain of communities spread along the trade routes eastward and southward. (There is no evidence of any Jewish settlement in the Middle Ages in the Scandinavian countries, where foreign traders were wholly superfluous.) The record of the Jews in Bohemia and Hungary begins from this period, and it is known that they played an important part in commercial intercourse between western and eastern Europe. Poland and the principality of Kiev presumably owed their original communities to direct immigration from the south. In the eighth century, the khan and ruling classes of the independent kingdom of the Khazars in what is now south Russia had adopted Judaism, and were imitated in the course of time by many of the ordinary people; and though this slightly mysterious state met with disaster at the hands of its enemies in the course of the tenth century,[3] the remnant of its population continued, as it seems, to give additional strength to Jewish life in eastern Europe.

The numbers involved were relatively slender. It is certain that what with conversion and oppression, the Jewish population of Europe had very steeply declined since the heyday of the Roman Empire, to a far greater extent than was the case with those among whom they lived, though this was indeed a period of general depopulation. It is computed that there were at this time at the utmost no more than 1,500,000 Jews in the world all told—perhaps no more than half that number. Cities were small, and the Jewish groups, though sometimes not unimportant in relation to the general urban population, were nevertheless utterly insignificant in absolute terms according to modern scales of value. It is probable that throughout the Middle Ages no Jewish community far exceeded two thousand souls in number, while a nucleus of a few hundred was regarded as being of some importance, and perhaps played a great historical role. On the other hand the distribution was far more general (partly as a result of the difficulties of communication and of distribution) than was usually the case at later periods.

Down to an advanced point in the Middle Ages, the Jewish population was divided not unevenly between the Christian and Moslem worlds, probably with a preponderance in favor of the latter. In the areas of Europe subject to the Moslems, the historical process followed much the same lines as in Asia. Once the initial impetus of fanaticism was spent, the rulers showed themselves prepared to extend an almost unlimited toleration to all unbelievers on the payment of a poll tax and the observance of a few none-too-onerous (though sometimes humiliating) regulations. (This policy, essentially a compromise, was based ultimately on the code elaborated in the Christian Empire, which the Moslems had found in vogue when they conquered Syria, but was generally enforced by them a good deal less strictly and was applied against Christians as well.) In Spain there were, moreover, special circumstances—due partly to the presence of a large Christian minority, which made it advisable to ensure the loyalties of the important Jewish group, and partly to the constant intercourse with the contiguous Christian states, which rendered the international outlook and the linguistic qualifications of educated Jews exceptionally valuable.

The first outstanding figure in Spanish Jewish life was Hasdai ibn Shaprut (*c.* 915-970),[4a] body physician and diplomatic adviser of the Caliph Abd er-Rahman III, who entrusted him with several important missions. It was under his auspices that Jewish intellectual life first began to flourish in the Peninsula—apparently with the encouragement of the ruler himself, who was by no means displeased to see the communities of his realm freed from intellectual dependence on the Eastern Caliphate.

Hasdai, moreover, was able to use diplomatic pressure in order to ameliorate the condition of his coreligionists under Christian rule, almost in the spirit of nineteenth-century humanitarianism though in a reverse direction. When forty years after his death Cordoba was captured by the Berber mercenaries and the Caliphate was broken up, the Jewish life formerly centered in that city disintegrated. In the numerous little principalities which now came into being, Jews had exceptional opportunities, however, and in more than one of them Jewish advisers rose to the highest position at court. The outstanding instance was Samuel ibn Nagdela (993-1063), the Beau Ideal of the Spanish Jew—poet, stylist, jurist, talmudist and munificent patron of learning—who became vizier to the king of Granada and governed the affairs of that petty state with conspicuous success from 1020 to his death. At the independent court of Saragossa, Jekutiel ibn Hassan (d. 1039) held a similar status, while other Jews enjoyed lower rank; and toward the end of the century Isaac ibn Albalia (1035-1094) was confidential adviser to the emir of Seville.

This period, from about the year 900 to the middle of the following century, was the golden age of Spanish Jewry. The prominent and wealthy Jewish leaders, like their Moslem neighbors, regarded it as a point of pride to foster learning and to patronize poets; and it was then that the great humanistic tradition of Hebrew scholarship in the Peninsula was established. There was a continuous immigration of savants (and presumably less distinguished individuals as well) from all parts; and Spain attained a predominance in the Jewish world of letters, especially on the humanistic side, which it did not readily relinquish. Politically and socially, life was at its zenith, and it does not seem as though even those regulations which were prescribed by Moslem practice were rigorously enforced.

Prejudice, on the other hand, was by no means submerged. Samuel ibn Nagdela was succeeded in office by his son Joseph, whose less tactful exercise of power resulted in a popular riot, as the result of which he lost his life and the Jews were expelled from the kingdom of Granada as a whole (1066). This did not indeed affect the position of their kinfolk in the neighboring Moslem states, where they continued to flourish for nearly another century. The invasion of the puritan Almoravides from North Africa in 1086 sounded, to be sure, a note of warning, and twenty years later an attempt was made to secure by force the conversion of the learned community of Lucena. Final disaster, however, came only in 1146, when the fanatical Unitarian sect known as Almohades, who had overrun northwestern Africa and brought disaster on the Jewish settlements there, crossed the Straits and made themselves masters of Moslem Spain. Everywhere in their dominions, they insisted on rigid uniformity, and the Jews were compelled either to adopt the dominant faith or else to flee for their lives.

The results of this in Jewish history were incalculable. For something over two centuries, the center of Jewish culture and of Jewish activities outside Mesopotamia had resided in the Moslem areas of northwestern Africa and southwestern Europe, and the future seemed to be firmly tied to the fortunes of the Arabic-speaking world. Henceforth this was no longer the case. There was still a massive center of Jewish life, recruited at this time by fugitives from the west such as the family of Moses Maimonides, in those eastern centers which had so long been associated with the Hebraic tradition—especially in Syria and Egypt. But the most numerous, most influential and most productive portion of the Jewish people was henceforth associated with European life and with the Christian world. In Spain the Moorish tradition and influence long continued; but here, too, they passed away in the end. Literature that had been composed in Arabic so as to reach the widest possible cultured public was ultimately forgotten unless (as was the case with Maimonides's best-known work) it was translated into Hebrew, the one tongue that was accessible to the Jewish masses throughout the world. Jewish history is henceforth bound up for good with what is termed Western civilization.

By this time, unfortunately, a movement had begun which in due course was to revolutionize the life of the Jews in Christian Europe. From the outset, the Jewish, like all other trading settlements (especially those of foreign merchants), had occasionally been exposed to riot and attack, and maltreatment based on religious prejudice was certainly not unknown —especially (as has been indicated above) at Eastertide, with its recurrent memories of the Passion and its poignant, inflammatory ritual. The Crusades, on the other hand, marked the beginning of an unbroken series of murderous outbreaks prompted perhaps in part by economic jealousy, but mainly by religious fanaticism. It seemed to the Crusaders preposterous to journey afar to fight the infidel abroad while leaving behind them untouched the archinfidels of all time, who were actually responsible for the Crucifixion—all the more so if murder might result in canceling their debts or help to equip them for their journey. Accordingly, the First Crusade, of 1096, gave the signal for a series of sanguinary onslaughts on the Jews of the Rhineland—at Speyer, Mainz, Worms, Cologne and many other places which first emerge to the full light of Jewish history in a tragic episode during the spring of that terrible year. Thereafter massacre became the accompaniment of each Crusade, and a regular concomitant of Jewish life in Europe. The Second Crusade, of 1147, was signalized by the spread of the infection to northern France. The Third witnessed a series of outbreaks also in England, where the Jews were solidly established. The massacre at York, on the day preceding Palm Sunday, 1190, became notorious in English as well as in Jewish annals. It was from the period of the Crusades that the Jews became the true Niobe of nations, ever having to bewail the slaughter of helpless children. The ghastly tinge of Jewish history, the perpetual disequilibrium of the Jewish position in the world, the maladjustment of the Jew in European life, all go back in the last analysis to this unhappy time.

The increasing theological odium, reflected in and coupled with an enhanced unpopularity, gave rise, moreover, to a series of malicious charges against the Jews, over and above the usual one of responsibility for the Crucifixion. It was alleged that at Eastertide they made a practice of putting Christian children to death, with every circumstance of cruelty, in ghastly imitation of the Passion of Jesus, or else (a later development) in order to use the blood in their paschal rites: the relics of the victim were frequently believed to perform miracles thereafter, and he was more than once admitted as a matter of course into the number of locally revered saints. The earliest recorded historical instance of such an accusation (though it was not necessarily the first) was that of "Saint" William of Norwich, in 1144. It proved the first of a long series—at Blois in 1171, Paris in 1180, Erfurt in 1199, Fulda and Wolfsheim in 1235, Valréas in 1247, Lincoln in 1255, and so on (to name only a few notorious instances out of very many). Every Eastertide was spent by the Jews in fear and trembling, lest the momentary wandering of some Christian child while he was at play might result in a recurrence of these terrible accusations. They led in very many cases to renewed massacres, some of which were not localized but devastated community after community throughout an entire kingdom or region. It is noteworthy, however, that in barely any case did the alleged martyrdoms receive the official endorsement of the Catholic Church, always intensely objective even in its severity, nor could they stand the test of an objective judicial inquiry.

The recognition of the doctrine of Transubstantiation by the Fourth Lateran Council in 1215 made possible a further series of accusations of ritual outrage of a somewhat different type. It was alleged that the Jews, unrepentant for the greatest of their crimes, endeavored to make the consecrated Host suffer once more from the agonies of the Passion by maltreating or torturing it, undeterred by the miraculous manifestations which their action provoked, such as the shedding of drops of blood. (Probably the appearance of *micrococcus prodigiosus*, a microscopic scarlet organism which sometimes grows on stale foodstuffs, was responsible for this embellishment.) Such an allegation was on the face of it exceptionally ridiculous, for it presupposed a degree of regard for the consecrated elements which was preposterous in a Jew. By now, however, he had come to be regarded widely not as a mere miscreant, but as a deliberate unbeliever, who persisted in denying the verity of what he knew to be true, and consciously battled in fact against the God Whom he purported to worship. Hence, even such a charge was widely believed, and also led to a long series of massacres, some of which devastated entire provinces as well as individual communities. Certain of these alleged episodes are still celebrated each year in the local churches—for example, the famous Brussels case of 1370, or that at Segovia of 1410 which is said to have provoked an earthquake, the devastation caused by which is still pointed out! Thus a Crusade was no longer needed as pretext for an onslaught upon the infidel: other excuses were constantly at hand if they were needed. In the long run, to attack the Jews became what might be termed a reflex action on the part of the populace all over Europe, at any time of domestic ebullition, economic depression or heightened religiosity. To be sure, this was not encouraged by the secular authority, determined to maintain order and, moreover, finding the Jews a useful source of profit; and the local representatives of king and emperor often intervened to protect them or gave them asylum in the royal castles in case of need. The church, too, as an institution, was similarly opposed to violence, its policy with regard to unbelievers being carefully defined. But ultimately it bore a great deal of responsibility, for its constant agitation for humiliation and segregation could not in the long run fail to have sanguinary consequences.

For the ecclesiastical attitude toward the medieval Jew continued to be guided by the principles that had been laid down at the period of the Christianization of the Roman Empire, reconciling (in his case only, it is important to remember) the Latin conception of toleration with the Christian one of religious exclusiveness: he was to be allowed to exist, but in ignominy, as testimony to the punishment of guilt and in order to prevent him from wielding any authority, whether moral or physical (for the one led to the other), over true believers. From the premise it followed that he was to be safeguarded from violence, permitted to practice his religious rites, and not driven to baptism by naked force; and every successive Pope on his accession issued in almost identical terms a protective Bull, beginning with the quotation from Pope Gregory the Great referred to above, *Sicut Judaeis*, etc. (No fewer than twenty-five separate reissues of this are known, from the twelfth to the fifteenth century, and it is possible that some of earlier date have been lost.) Of the negative side, enjoining repression, there was perhaps less need for reminder, as fanatics were always to be found who carried it to and beyond its logical conclusion. Nevertheless, after the Hildebrandine reform of the eleventh century, the Popes periodically warned the faithful against elevating Jews to administrative posts or placing them in positions of authority over Christians. (It is known that the Jewish tax administrators in Spain sometimes exercised important executive powers, and the same was perhaps the case elsewhere.)

In the twelfth century the menacing growth of the Albigensian heresies in southern France compelled the Church to strengthen its organization and to reassert itself at the Third (1179) and especially the Fourth (1215) Lateran Council, under the guidance of Pope Innocent III. Not unnaturally, the offensive was extended from the heretic to the Jew, who was, moreover, suspected (without real justification, though this is more clear today than it was at the time) of deliberately propagating disbelief. The old regulations forbidding him to wield authority over a Christian were reinforced, and henceforth made to cover even domestic services of the most trivial type, as well as functions such as those of bailiff or tax farmer. His association with the soil was further weakened by insisting on the payment of ecclesiastical tithes for any land he owned. An attempt was made to render the legislation against usury comprehensive, by extending it to Jews and driving the Jewish moneylenders out of business. In addition, Jews and Christians were now forbidden to dwell together, thus laying the foundation of the later Ghetto system; and it was ordered that all unbelievers should henceforth be distinguished by a special badge —a regulation taken over from the Moslems, who of course had enforced it against Christians as well.

It proved impossible to secure the immediate enforcement of the entire code. Even in those lands where it was most readily accepted, such as England, the suppression of the practice of usury by Jews was found impracticable or inadvisable, in view of the requirements of the treasury. In Spain, in the interests of the country at large, the regulations regarding the Jewish badge were suspended officially with the Pope's approval, after a very brief experiment, so as to prevent wholesale emigration on the part of the victims. In other lands (not least in Italy, under the Pope's own eye, and even in the Papal States) they were enforced as yet only sporadically. Physical segregation was exceptional, and where practiced was seldom complete; though the Jewish Street (Jewry, Juiverie, Judería, Judengasse, Giudecca, etc.) was an all but universal phenomenon as a social fact. Nevertheless, this codification of the ecclesiastical anti-Jewish regulations marked a turning point in Jewish history. It remained in being, a constant menace, which could be and was enforced whenever reaction triumphed in the state, or a new threat arose for the church; and fanatics and pietists henceforth clamored incessantly, with sporadic success, for its enforcement. The general tendency was to emphasize the Jew's utter separateness, his inferiority, his disfavor in the sight of God and of right-thinking men. The protective Bull, *Sicut Judaeis,* remained to a great degree in the realm of theory; the Lateran anti-Jewish legislation descended into practical politics, and in effect canceled it out.

The conduct of the offensive against the enemies of the Holy Church was now in the hands of the friars—especially those of the Dominican order, zealous propagators of the faith among the heretics and infidels, whose foundation dates back to the same time. It was not long before they began to direct an incessant campaign against the Jews, especially in countries where they were the sole dissidents and there were no heretics or paynims to distract attention. In due course this was more and more elaborately organized. In 1240, the earliest and one of the most notorious of a series of public disputations, in which the Jews were compelled to defend their traditional literature against the charge of blasphemy, or else to justify their nonacceptance of Christianity, took place under the auspices of the king himself in Paris; and the example was frequently followed thereafter. Such episodes were generally the prelude to systematic onslaughts upon Hebrew books—especially the Talmud, which the Popes condemned more than once to the flames, forbidding its study under savage penalties. From the middle of the thirteenth century, Dominican friars began to claim the hospitality of the synagogues for the purpose of delivering conversionist sermons, an abuse regularized and given canonical status by the Papal Bull, *Vineam Soreth*, of 1279. All this emphasized further the degraded status of the Jews, made them even more despicable in the eyes of the ordinary people, and in consequence rendered their physical position even more precarious. The French king, "Saint" Louis IX, following in the path of the German mystical teacher, Meister Eckhart, declared that a sword driven into his side as far as it would go was the only proper argument to use against the Jew. It is true indeed that the natural tendency was the reverse of this. When there was no outside interference, relations between the two elements tended to be far more friendly than religious zealots approved. The Jew adopted the speech, the costume and the social habits of his neighbors so slavishly that the line of demarcation was sometimes blurred. Amicable discussions on matters of faith, feasting and drinking together, and associations not quite so innocent, were common between followers of the divergent faiths. Yet in the course of time, by dint of incessant reiteration from every pulpit week after week and year after year, the propaganda could not fail to have its effect, the results of which are even in the twentieth century uneffaced.

The changed circumstances were accompanied, and in part caused, by a change of economic function. It had been as merchants and as craftsmen that the Jews first came to western Europe; some had indeed settled on the soil, but in the circumstances of their migration (as of any other into inhabited areas) this was none too easy. From about the period of the Crusades, a fundamental alteration took place. These campaigns broke down to some extent the barriers that had formerly existed between land and land. No longer was the eastern shore of the Mediterranean, the meeting place of the routes between Europe and Asia, an unknown territory. The way thither was familiar and well trodden; and merchants followed eagerly on the heels of the fighting men. Moreover, the Italian trading republics, intolerant from the beginning of infidel competition, were now raised to a new pitch of prosperity. On the other hand, if it were easier for the Gentile merchant to travel from country to country, the reverse was the case with the Jew, in view of the growing fanaticism and his enhanced insecurity. Hence he not only lost his advantage, but was placed at a great and increasing handicap. With the development of the craft guild and guild merchant, setting up in effect Christian monopolies both in manufacture and in distribution, he found his former way of life more and more difficult. Simultaneously, the triumph of feudalism and the passing of the independent, free husbandman, coupled with the ecclesiastical insistence on the payment of tithes, dislodged him from his foothold on the soil; and in the end Jews were formally forbidden to own land.

Just at this period, however, the gradual substitution of a money economy for the primitive barter economy gave them a fresh opening. Loans were needed for the payment of feudal dues, for tiding over periods of crisis, for building castles or abbeys, for financing military or other enterprises, or on a smaller scale during interludes of private distress. It was to the merchants or else to a large extent to the church that recourse would naturally be had in such cases, for it was they who had money, the only insuperable requisite in a lender. But for some time past a theological (not, it is important to note, humanitarian) objection had developed in ecclesiastical circles to the institution of interest or "usury"—based partly on an erroneous interpretation of a familiar passage in the teachings of Jesus (Luke 6:35), partly on the doctrines of Aristotle. Slowly this came to be enforced, first against churchmen, and then against the laity. This had the result of suppressing open usury to a great extent. It was thus either driven underground, with the inevitable result of vastly enhanced rates, or left in the hands of those against whom the ecclesiastical prohibition could not so easily be enforced, *i.e.*, the Jews. Thus, from merchants they degenerated (especially so far as northwestern Europe was concerned) into moneylenders—for a time in England, France, Germany and elsewhere, the only officially recognized moneylenders. The arrangement proved generally convenient—to the people, not cut off from a ready supply of credit, as would have been the case had the ecclesiastical prohibition been universally and effectively enforced; to the government, who by dint of merciless taxation relieved the moneylenders of the great proportion of their profits (thus becoming in effect the archusurers of the realm) and therefore stoutly refused to enforce the prohibition in their case; and to some extent to the Jews, thus allowed an outlet for their capital and given leisure for their cherished studies. But a vicious circle developed. In order to pay the overwhelming taxation levied upon them, the Jews were compelled to raise yet further the inevitably high rate of interest which they charged; their enforced rapacity led to resentment and riot; and insecurity raised the rate still higher. More and more the attacks upon them tended to be economic in origin, however much the ostensible pretext was religious. The bonds of indebtedness were among the rioters' first objectives; and in the end an elaborate system of registration was introduced in the interest of the state, so as to ensure that whatever happened the treasury's claims at least would be safe. This was the case especially in England, after the great wave of massacre of 1189-1190; subsequent to this, in fact, the organization of the activities of the Jews, under the control of a special "Jewish Exchequer," became so rigid that it is almost possible to say that moneylending was made into a government monopoly, administered by ostensibly independent Jewish agents who were pitilessly mulcted from time to time. The organization and interests of French and German Jewry were not dissimilar, though in these older, larger and less artificial settlements there was a tendency to somewhat greater variety. In southern Europe, on the other hand, the process of economic degradation made far less headway. Here, notwithstanding the emergence of an upper class of financiers and (in Spain) tax farmers, the Jewish proletariat were craftsmen to the end. In Sicily, we see them engaged in the most exacting manual labor; while farther east, in the Byzantine Empire, the Jewish traveler Benjamin of Tudela found them, about 1170, mainly occupied in the dyeing and silk-weaving industries. It was, on the other hand, the northern European Jew from whom the bulk of modern Jewry is derived, and whom later generations have tended to consider the pattern.

As has been pointed out, even at its most subservient, the state generally refused to collaborate in the church's halfhearted attempt to suppress the practice of usury by the Jew. The reason for this was not theological; it was a question of practical finance. With the perfection of the administrative machinery, more effective methods of exploiting the detested unbelievers had been found, and they had become an integral part of the financial machinery of the state. In England, it is calculated that in the twelfth century they contributed each year about one-seventh of the average royal revenue; in the thirteenth, Henry III extorted from them, by a series of merciless tallages, one quarter of the million marks which he "squandered" on his extravagant building projects. In other countries, the process was similar, if not quite so systematic. An oblique, but for that reason still more burdensome, method of raising revenue was by the remission of interest on Jewish debts, together with a prorogation of the period of payment, either universally or else for individuals, as a special mark of favor. Sometimes, even, the ruler would use his prerogative to cancel the debt outright. This system, which began in England and France in the twelfth century on a small scale, became common in the thirteenth and acquired a hold in fourteenth-century Germany, under

King Wenzel, which made it into an intolerable abuse, sending the rate of interest up still further in dizzy spirals. A frequent procedure when difficulties arose was the arrest of the entire Jewish community of a country—men, women and children—and their incarceration until they had paid the amount demanded from them. This took place time after time in England in the thirteenth century and, less regularly, in France and even in Spain.

The result of these exactions, callously carried out over a long period, was the progressive impoverishment of the Jewish communities. Their operations were now on a smaller and smaller scale, and their utility to the treasury correspondingly decreased. (In England their contribution to the revenue is calculated to have gone down in the course of the thirteenth century from 14½ per cent to only 1 per cent.) Moreover, it was discovered that in the long run their activities might well be prejudicial to the interests of the crown, as the estates pledged to them, which they could not themselves hold, frequently passed into the hands of the church or of the tenants-in-chief and great nobility, whose power was excessively strengthened by this means. Hence there was an increasing tendency during the course of the thirteenth century to prevent them from making loans on the security of real estate. On the other hand, the remarkable expansion in the transmission of revenue to Rome coupled with the growth of the Italian (particularly Florentine) textile trade, based largely upon the purchase of wool in northern Europe, brought about a rapid development in the mechanism of international finance and raised a class of Christian financiers, the scale of whose operations made those carried on by the Jews relatively unimportant. It was to the Christian group henceforth that governments and nobles applied for loans, recourse being made to legal fictions if it was so desired in order to avoid apparent usury. The Jews were thus reduced to what was virtually pawnbroking, and thereby not only lost all importance to the state, but also, as a logical consequence, the protection they had formerly enjoyed. When in 1274 the Council of Lyons summoned Christendom to greater efforts against the sin of usury, there was a readier obedience than hitherto. In the following year, the English Jews were forbidden under heavy penalties by the *Statutum de Judeismo* to follow their previous calling. A brief experiment ensued to force them to adapt themselves to a new way of life, not accompanied, however (as was necessary if it were to succeed), by an attempt to mitigate their social disabilities or to give them greater security. This failing, as was inevitable, in 1290 they were expelled from the country—sixteen thousand of them, according to contemporary estimates, though in fact perhaps the number was not above four thousand.

The process was similar, though not quite so symmetrical, in France, a far greater center of Jewish life and culture. Here sporadic attempts were made to suppress usury from the middle of the thirteenth century onward by the pious St. Louis (1226-1270) and his son Philip the Bold (1270-1285); and the Jews themselves began an experiment at this time at economic rehabilitation, above all in the silk and textile industries. Philip the Fair (1285-1314) was little influenced by reasons of piety, but his rapacity was so excited by the prospects of potential profit that in 1306 he followed the example recently set in England, though in circumstances of unnecessary inhumanity. On July 22, 1306, all the Jews of the country were yet again arrested; and, after being despoiled of all their property, which was taken over by the king (including even their credits—so little was he concerned with the moral obloquy of usury), they were expelled from the country, only a handful remaining (until 1507) in the south under the rule of the Counts of Provence. Twice subsequently—from 1315 to 1322, a particularly bloodstained interlude, and again from 1359 to 1394—small numbers obtained permission to resettle in the country, though specifically as usurers, under conditions that were highly profitable to the crown. This, however, can hardly be considered a renewal of the magnificent tradition of medieval French Jewry, to which Rabbinic culture owes so profound a debt. (It is sufficient to mention in illustration the revered name of the Bible and Talmud commentator Rashi [1040-1105].) For some four centuries thereafter, down to the period of the Revolution, the main current of the history of the Jews of France was interrupted.

The antiusury movement that resulted in the expulsion of the Jews from the centralized monarchies had an opposite effect (partly because of the weakness of national sentiment) in the trading republics, whether of Italy or of Germany. It resulted not only in the elimination of the Jews from the large-scale operations in which they had been useful to the crown, but also in the elimination of the native bourgeoisie from the petty operations in which they had been useful to the cities. In England or in France, no one was left to fill the gap legitimately; and the common people wistfully contrasted the rapacity of the clandestine Christian usurers, into whose hands they then fell, with the relative moderation of the infidel. On the other hand, where there was a greater degree of local autonomy, and there was an infidel reservoir upon which to draw, circumstances were different. Here, therefore, the elimination of the Gentile usurers was counteracted by the systematic utilization of the Jews to serve the needs of the common people. Thus in Germany the function of moneylending, largely in the hands of the clergy before the twelfth century and passing to the citizens and nobility in the thirteenth, became a quasi monopoly of the Jews in the fourteenth.

In Italy, the great trading republics such as Genoa and Venice still rigidly excluded the Jews, from motives of economic jealousy, and up to the thirteenth century their association with north Italy was inconsiderable. From about 1275, however, city after city began to invite wealthy Jewish financiers to come, for a term of years, to open "loan banks" for the benefit of the poor, so as to replace the Tuscans, who had been driven out of business both by the legislation against usury and by the tempting opportunities for operations on a grand scale abroad. It is to this process and to this period that the continuous history of community after community subsequently famous in Jewish annals—Ancona, Ferrara, Padua, Venice, Mantua, Verona and so on—is to be traced.

The degree of local autonomy in Italy and Germany was of itself providential in Jewish history. England and France were indeed at this time the only European countries sufficiently centralized for an anti-Jewish policy to be carried out consistently and universally. Elsewhere, the effects of any similar reaction were local, and often temporary. Thus, when about 1290 a wave of clerically inspired persecution momentarily rid the kingdom of Naples of professing Jews, they were undisturbed in the remainder of Italy. In Germany similarly, though accusations of ritual murder and Host desecrations were more rife than anywhere else, and though massacre attained there a degree of ferocity unknown in any other land, there was never any universal and concerted attempt to rid the entire country simultaneously of the unbelievers by legal process. Hence, though decimated time after time in every region and township, a slender nucleus at least always remained in the country to carry on the tradition. Thus neither the wave of massacre throughout southern Germany in 1298, under the leadership of a certain Rindfleisch; nor those in Alsace, Swabia and Franconia in 1336, at the hands of the *Judenschlaeger* ("Jew-slayers"); nor those which began at Deckendorf in the following year, in consequence of an allegation of desecrating the Host; nor even those in 1348-1349 at the time of the Black Death, when over two hundred communities were exterminated on a charge of spreading the pestilence; nor the destruction of the Austrian communities on a similar pretext in 1431; nor the wave of violence that followed at the heels of the fanatical Franciscan John of Capistrano throughout the eastern provinces after 1450—not even this exaggerated sequence of suffering entirely interrupted the already ancient settlement of the Jews in Germany. The remnant were indeed excluded from one city after another, so that ultimately the only important communities left in the country were those of Frankfort and Worms. To compensate for this, even at the darkest hour independent municipalities and petty nobles continued to offer a strained and far from disinterested hospitality to little groups here and there. Thus the tradition was in fact never entirely broken until our own day. In central and northern Italy a similar inconsistency prevailed from place to place and state to state; and though the history of most communities was disturbed by occasional outbursts of jealousy or pietism, the skeptical, volatile Italian spirit was never able to nurture its resentments for long.

More important by far was the Jewish settlement in Spain. Here, since the disaster that had overtaken the communities under Moslem rule in the twelfth century, the center of Jewish life had been in the central and northern areas, under Christian control (Aragon and Catalonia probably contained at this time the densest Jewish settlement in Europe). The Christian sovereigns had taken over, or even improved upon, the policy of their Moslem predecessors, and for much the same reason. The Jews constituted an important minority in the population which it was wise to conciliate; an element, moreover, which had no foreign allegiances and was therefore to be presumed loyal; and which could furnish the craftsmen and merchants and perhaps the skilled husbandmen who were conspicuously scarce among the Christians. Accordingly, the new rulers used them as colonists in their successive conquests, granting them land, settling them in townships, encouraging them to establish themselves in the cities and guaranteeing their rights in the *fueros*, or local codes. The clerical authorities resented the rights given them, and the populace, too, sometimes protested violently; but though this might lead to momentary reaction, it was as yet never drastic and seldom durable. Moreover, Jewish linguists and physicians were used on diplomatic missions to the Moslem states, and Jewish financial experts were given high employment in the treasury or as tax collectors, with such important executive powers that they were in effect included among the ministers of state.

This policy had reached its zenith under Alfonso VI of Castile (1072-1109) and his grandson Alfonso VII (1126-1157), during whose reign the refugees from Almohadan fanaticism were given generous hospitality in the north. Although conditions were not quite so favorable thereafter, the same general atmosphere conditioned Spanish life for generations to come, and at intervals there would be a sporadic renewal of the former halcyon days under the rule of a broad-minded sovereign. A series of eminent Jewish statesmen, who stood high in the royal favor as financiers and confidential advisers, continued to appear upon the stage at intervals down to the very end, though not infrequently they would meet a tragic fate as a result of the jealousy of rivals or the greed of the ruler. (Typical was the career and the fate of Samuel Abulaffia [d. 1360], at one time treasurer to Pedro the Cruel of Castile.) Thus even at its worst, the condition of the Jews in Spain was better than in any other part of Europe in the Middle Ages. They enjoyed in their *juderías* a high degree of autonomy, not only being allowed to maintain their own courts, as was indeed usual enough, but even being empowered to inflict capital punishment. Above all, their economic degradation made relatively little headway here, for notwithstanding the importance of the Jews in the financial administration and as tax farmers, and the practice of usury by a certain number of them, the backbone of the community continued to be engaged in trade and in handicrafts—especially metalworking and the textile industry in all its branches, in which they had a very important share.

Nevertheless, from the beginning of the thirteenth century, the cumulative effects of the long struggle for Spanish national unity, and the constant stimulus of a perpetual Crusade against the Moslem, began to bring about a serious deterioration in the position of the Spanish Jews. Moreover, the strength of non-Christian faiths in the Peninsula called for special efforts, which in certain circumstances or areas might be directed against them alone. The Dominicans in particular, preoccupied with the propagation and defense of the Holy Catholic faith, conducted an unremitting campaign against them as well as against the Moors. Little by little, the anti-Jewish regulations of the Lateran Councils came to be introduced, though it was recognized that to enforce them all simultaneously would be against the national interest. In 1263, a new tactical experiment was tried, pressure being exerted on the Aragonese communities by staging a public disputation at Barcelona in the presence of the king, at which the apostate friar Pablo Christiani pitted himself against the learned Rabbi Moses ben Nahman ("Ramban" or Nahmanides, 1194-1270). Though the latter more than held his own, this was followed by an attempt to suppress the study of the talmudic literature and to compel the Jews to offer the hospitality of their synagogues for the delivery of conversionist sermons. In 1280, the Jews of Castile were arrested and thrown into prison with the object of extorting an unprecedented levy from them—a commonplace procedure in northern Europe, but hitherto unknown in Spain. A proposal was even made in 1339, during the period of the ascendancy of the upstart Gonzalo Martinez, not only to repeat the process, but to cap it by expelling the Jews, as in England and France. There were occasional instances of physical attack—at Toledo in 1212, at the hands of the Crusaders from beyond the Pyrenees; at the time of the "Shepherds' Crusade" in 1320; in the kingdom of Navarre in 1328; here and there in northern Spain during the Black Death twenty years after; and at the time of the civil war in Castile, in the middle of the fourteenth century, when the Jews suffered for their fidelity to King Pedro. The tendency of a small minority of the upper class to find employment in the financial administration, and thus to become identified with royal rapacity, enhanced the ill-feeling, which was not counterbalanced by the dwindling, though sometimes still important, influence of certain individuals at Court. Yet, whatever the case elsewhere, in Spain the great majority of the Jewish population were craftsmen; and basically the prejudice was religious in character, constantly fostered by the church. Whenever the central administration was weak, this agitation increased. From 1378, notwithstanding all orders to be silent, the lead was taken by Ferrand Martinez, archdeacon of Ecija, whose inflammatory preaching finally resulted in an outbreak of violence in the summer of 1391, which completely overwhelmed the *judería* of Seville. The example spread like wildfire all over the Peninsula, and the attempts made by the civil authorities to restore order proved useless except in the kingdom of Portugal, in Leon and in some parts of Aragon. Elsewhere, hardly a single community was spared.

A phenomenon followed which was unique in the history of the Jews. For the first and only time their morale broke. Very large numbers of persons, seeing no hope for the future, and their convictions undermined by the syncretizing tendencies characteristic of the Hispano-Jewish intelligentsia, saved their lives by submitting to baptism. Their number was reinforced by a constant procession of fresh neophytes who went over to Catholicism under a more or less distant menace of violence, or out of sheer despair, in the following years. They continued to a great extent in their former occupations, especially as taxgatherers; their numbers were too great to make speedy assimilation possible; with the religious bar removed, many pushed their way to high places in the administration and in public life. On the other hand, they were suspected—and in many cases with reason—of scant interest in their new religion, and a secret loyalty to the old one. Hence the religious prejudice that had formerly been so widespread against the Jews was turned into what would today be termed "racial" channels, and was shared by their converted kinfolk, known as *conversos*, or New Christians; or else by an old term of opprobrium, originally signifying "swine," *Marranos*. This problem—a very real one from the point of view of the Catholic Church—was henceforth paramount in Spain, and inevitably hastened the final disaster which was not far distant.

The reinforcement of church discipline under the menace of the Hussite movement at the beginning of the fifteenth century, after the laxity of the period of the Great Schism, proved highly dangerous to what was left of Jewish life throughout Europe. The friars now began a fresh campaign against them—now not only the Dominicans, but also the Franciscans, whose work brought them into close contact with the poor and who, especially in Italy, began to take up for that reason an attitude of uncompromising opposition to the practice of usury. Fray Vicente Ferrer of the former order took the lead in Spain. His religious campaigns throughout the country, backed up by enthusiastic mobs who were whipped into a frenzy by his preaching, resulted in a fresh wave of more or less sincere conversions in and after 1411. His influence was seen, too, in the promulgation of an anti-Jewish code in Castile in 1412, reiterating in almost fantastic detail all the medieval oppressive legislation; in the dramatic religious

Disputation between representatives of Judaism and Christianity—the greatest of the entire series—held at Tortosa in 1413-1414 in the presence of Antipope Benedict XIII; and in a subsequent Bull of the latter forbidding the study of the Talmud. Meanwhile, in Italy (where he had encountered and inspired St. Bernard of Siena) after a visit in 1408 from Vicente Ferrer, the friars began to press for the enforcement of the old legislation against the Jews, especially as regards the wearing of the Jewish badge and segregation in a separate quarter of the cities in which they dwelt; and from the second decade of the fifteenth century this began to be enforced more generally, sometimes accompanied by more extreme restrictions. The Castilian delegation at the Council of Basle demanded fresh anti-Jewish legislation along the usual lines, which was duly enacted at its nineteenth session (September 7, 1434) and echoed in a systematic Bull of Pope Eugenius IV (1442). Though this was not put into execution in Spain, and speedly mitigated in Italy by a further Bull, the friars' agitation continued unremittingly. Bernard of Siena's colleague, John of Capistrano, embodying the reaction against the Hussites, brought disaster in his train wherever he went, from Sicily to the border of Poland, almost succeeded in procuring the expulsion of the Jews from Rome, and later presided over a series of onslaughts in Silesia.

In Italy, in the soft atmosphere of the Renaissance, the agitation subsequently took on a less intimidating aspect, as we shall see. In Spain, on the other hand, the swelling current of national and religious feeling that was to express itself in the conquest of the kingdom of Granada, the last remaining Moslem outpost, kept the anti-Jewish agitation constantly alive. The *juderías* never recovered from the disaster of 1391 and the succeeding years. In some places, such as Barcelona (formerly one of the greatest centers of Jewish life and learning), no community was ever again established on a permanent basis. For those who survived, life was very different. On the whole, it may be said that during the fifteenth century the Spanish Jews were treated with the same harshness that had been usual in other parts of Europe since the thirteenth, though hitherto kept at bay in the Peninsula. Nevertheless, even now they resisted economic debasement; while a few outstanding figures such as the financier-scholar Isaac Abravanel (1437-1508) and the tax farmer Abraham Senior (*c.* 1420-1500) were prominent in the public eye, almost as in the halcyon days. But the professing Jews were not the principal religious preoccupation of zealous Spanish Christians. The growing prominence of the *conversos* in every branch of Spanish life, from the central administration downward, attracted more and more notice, to which their suspected insincerity added a fresh acerbity. They were inveighed against from the pulpits; riots against them became the order of the day; the Dominicans in particular constantly demanded drastic action; and at length in 1478, under the influence of Fray Tomás de Torquemada, Isabella of Castile procured from the Pope a Bull authorizing the establishment of the Inquisition to suppress Judaizing in her dominions and to punish the delinquents.

Its activities began almost immediately, with savage thoroughness, in the first of a long series of autos-da-fé which continued down to the close of the eighteenth century, in the course of which thousands of persons were burned (many of them alive) and hundreds of thousands submitted to lesser punishment for the offense of fidelity to the religion of their fathers. It soon became abundantly clear, however, that there was little prospect of extirpating the Judaizers from Spain while professing Jews remained to teach their brethren, by precept and by example, the practices of their former faith, and the ecclesiastical zealots began to press for their expulsion from the country as the only solution to the problem. Accordingly, almost immediately after the capture of Granada, on March 30, 1492, Ferdinand and Isabella issued a decree of banishment from their dominions, to take effect four months later. The number of persons affected was probably about 150,000, although both contemporary chroniclers and subsequent historians exaggerated it to a fantastic degree. Thus, in the greatest disaster of the Jewish Middle Ages, the oldest and most vital community of western Europe was finally uprooted. So far did this reflect what had come to be (or else subsequently became) the feeling of the Spanish people that even in the nineteenth century the policy of exclusion was maintained.

Of the exiles, the greatest number—nearly two-thirds, as is believed—made their way over the frontier into Portugal, where they were temporarily admitted on the payment of a poll tax. Here, the Spanish example was repeated five years later (1497), when King Manuel desired to conclude a matrimonial alliance with the daughter of the Catholic sovereigns of Spain. The circumstances, however, were different; craft and force were exerted in order to secure the baptism of the Jews prior to and rather than their ejection; and in effect what took place was a forced conversion on a tremendous scale, which filled the country with a vast body of insincere neophytes, the number of exiles being inconsiderable. In Navarre a similar process took place in the following year, though far fewer persons were involved. Thus, though the Iberian Peninsula was cleared of professing Jews, the problem of the Marranos was perpetuated, on a grand scale, with results which were to have a profound influence on local life and on Jewish history for centuries to come.

The Edict of Expulsion of 1492 had extended, not only to the kingdoms of Castile and Aragon, but also to the dependencies of the latter overseas, notwithstanding the fact that the *converso* problem (which was its ostensible pretext) was hardly known there. These included Sardinia and especially Sicily, with the teeming and ancient Jewish communities which had lived there undisturbed since Roman times, and continued throughout the period of Saracen domination. They were mainly artisans and laborers; and the Council of the Realm, in its ineffectual protest against the measure, pointed out how their departure would weaken defense against invaders. Thus anti-Judaism, of the extreme Spanish type, obtained a further foothold in Italy. Shortly after, the French invasion of 1495 and the disturbances that followed all but overwhelmed the Jewish communities of the kingdom of Naples; the process was completed in 1541, after the Spanish conquest, when the Jews were completely and finally ejected.

In the north of Italy, meanwhile, the agitation against them had been continuing—largely through the influence of the "Observantine" Franciscans, with Fra Bernardino of Feltre at their head, who were now pressing for the establishment of public pawnbroking establishments (*monti di pietà*) which would render the Jews superfluous. Their preaching was responsible for a number of riots and sporadic expulsions from one city or the other; and the ritual murder accusation at Trent in 1475, due to Fra Bernardino's personal incitement (one of the few that ultimately received the recognition of the Vatican), had initiated a particularly dangerous interlude. There were, however, other influences at work. This was the heyday of the Renaissance period, and a succession of cultured, polished, luxurious, worldly-wise Popes in Rome regarded the promotion of culture as being as important a part of their function as the forwarding of the religious interests of the Catholic Church. Some of them, moreover, acted primarily as Italian princes, with the future political status of their families at heart. They tended, therefore, from the middle of the fifteenth century onward, to overlook inconvenient details of canon law and to show in addition a wide tolerance for those who were not Catholics. The Jewish loan bankers constituted an integral part of the economic machinery of their dominions, while as broad-minded men of the world they appreciated the conversation of Jewish physicians and others with whom they came into contact. Hence the persecutory regulations that had been elaborated by the fathers of the church, and codified by the Third and Fourth Lateran Councils, were almost entirely neglected by them, or else their observance was reduced to a minimum. The agitation of the friars was therefore consistently neglected, or even discouraged. With this example before their eyes, the other Italian princes—the Medici of Florence, the Estensi of Ferrara, the Gonzaga of Mantua—acted in much the same fashion. Though they were disturbed by occasional interludes of violence or fanaticism—as for example when Savonarola obtained control of Florence in 1497—the Jews mixed with their neighbors and shared in their life to a degree that was almost unexampled. They played a distinct part in certain aspects of the Renaissance, especially as exponents of the Aristotelian philosophy; they mirrored it in their own lives and in their literary activities in the Hebrew tongue; they made important contributions to philosophy, music and the theater; they were familiar figures in many of the Italian courts.

But, notwithstanding the protection of the Popes, they had to face the perpetual antagonism of the friars. Ultimately, in the middle of the sixteenth century, the progress of the Reformation brought about a complete change in the attitude of the former; and this sealed the Jews' fate. They were suspected, though without reason, of sympathizing with the heretics who were undermining the position of the church. The attempt to control the free expression of thought in the Christian world involved their literature as well, the Talmud being burned in 1553, and a rigid censorship of Hebrew works, which applied throughout the Catholic world, being instituted thereafter. This took place at the instigation of Cardinal Caraffa, founder of the Theatine Order, and soul of the Counter-Reformation, who became Pope in 1555 as Paul IV. Almost immediately afterward, he issued the Bull *Cum nimis absurdum*, in which he renewed and enforced down to the last detail all the oppressive medieval Church legislation against the Jews. They were henceforth to be strictly segregated in their own quarter (later known as the Ghetto, in imitation of the existing Jewish district in Venice, located since 1516 in the New Foundry, or *Ghetto Nuovo*, to which the *Ghetto Vecchio* was subsequently added): this was to be surrounded by a high wall and provided with gates, closed at night. They were excluded from the professions, and from all other callings other than dealing in secondhand clothes. They were forbidden to practice medicine among Christians or to employ Christian servants or workmen or to be called by any title of respect. They were forbidden to own real estate. The wearing of the badge of shame was reimposed.

There was nothing fresh about this code. It simply re-enacted, with the addition of one or two unimportant details, the ecclesiastical legislation with regard to the Jews which had been elaborated at the Lateran Councils, demanded vociferously by the friars since the beginning of the fifteenth century, and put into force sporadically here and there—sometimes, though not often, by the Popes themselves—during the past generations. What was new was the systematicness, the ruthlessness and the undeviating fanaticism with which it was applied henceforth over a very wide area. There was a slight alleviation under Pope Pius IV (1559-1565), but reaction triumphed again under Pius V (1566-1572), who expelled the Jews from the smaller places in the Papal States where their moral influence might be more considerable and supervision was more difficult. Thereafter, except under Sixtus V (1585-1590), it may be said that there was hardly any substantial deviation for the next two centuries. Moreover, the papal example was followed throughout Italy—partly as a result of the extension of the States of the Church with the acquisition of the duchies of

Ferrara (1598) and Urbino (1631), partly through undeviating propaganda in the areas that were still independent. By the end of the first third of the seventeenth century, the Ghetto system with all that it implied had finally triumphed in all that part of Italy in which Jews were still allowed to live. They were expelled from the rural centers, thus finally interrupting their already slender association with the countryside. They were immured in narrow, unsanitary, inadequate sections of the cities where they lived. They had to wear the badge of shame, generally in the form of a red or yellow hat, at all times, sometimes even in their own quarter. They were restricted to such occupations as peddling and old-clothes dealing. They frequently had to deplore the loss of their children by forced baptism, which though frowned upon by the church, was recognized as valid once it had happened. They had to attend church from time to time to hear conversionist sermons, generally delivered by apostates, running the gantlet of the mob as they entered. Their literature was submitted to a fantastically severe censorship.

The newly formulated, or rather reformulated, papal policy was obeyed, at least in its general lines, in all those parts of Roman Catholic Europe where Jews still lived. In Germany indeed the external stimulus was hardly necessary, and in fact there was very little difference in so far as their treatment of the Jews was concerned between the Protestant and Catholic areas. At one stage, the prospects had been far more promising; for the original dispute between humanists and obscurantists in Germany, which had merged into the Reformation movement, had grown up out of Johann Reuchlin's championing of the Talmud and Hebrew literature against an attempt made from 1509 onward by the Dominicans, at the instigation of an embittered apostate named Pfefferkorn, to secure their suppression. Indeed, Martin Luther at the outset of his agitation had professed sympathy with the Jews for the way in which they had hitherto been treated by the church, indicating that this was enough in his opinion to blind anyone's eyes. He had apparently hoped that his new approach would command greater appreciation from them, and would result in widespread conversions. When he found himself disappointed in this, he adopted an attitude of uncompromising hostility to them and referred to them in his writings with a bitterness of invective that has hardly any parallel in theological literature. He admonished his followers to destroy their houses, to seize their books, to interdict their worship, to prevent them from practicing medicine or commerce, to close their synagogues, to chase them from Christian lands: it was the current Catholic program, carried to its wildest and most irresponsible extreme.

The electors of Saxony and Brandenburg obediently expelled the Jews from their territories. They were not the only potentates to do so; and in those Protestant areas where Jews were allowed to remain, confinement in the *Judengasse*, the wearing of the badge of shame in the form of a yellow circle over the heart, and the rest of the repressive system inherited from the Middle Ages—together with a few characteristic German complications—was enforced at least as rigidly as in the Roman Catholic districts. Of the latter, the most important were the possessions of the House of Hapsburg, where the treatment of the Jews varied between complete exclusion to a full Ghetto organization on the Italian model. This was the case especially in the kingdom of Bohemia, whose capital, Prague, was famous for its highly organized and populous *Judenstadt*, one of the most important communities left in Europe, and a link culturally, economically and politically between those of the West and those of the East.

On the other hand, the treatment of the Jews was now determined rather more by legal process and rather less by mob outbreaks than had been the case in earlier generations. Even in the sixteenth century, indeed, there were sometimes outrages in the old style—for example in 1510, when in consequence of an accusation of desecrating the Host, there was a judicial massacre at Bernau near Berlin and the Jews were expelled from the Mark of Brandenburg. Yet the long activities of Joselman of Rosheim (1480-1554), who was elected by the communities of Lower Alsace as their civil representative in 1510, introduced a greater semblance of legality. Over an entire generation, we see him traveling about the country, interceding with local authorities and even the emperor, attending anxiously at the Imperial Diets, obtaining favorable edicts and bulls of protection for his coreligionists, trying to contact Martin Luther himself and to secure his intervention at a time of crisis, and generally placing the treatment of the Jews on a legal basis. The more settled era was due to a great extent to his constant exertions.

The new ecclesiastical policy of organized repression initiated in the sixteenth century was practicable only in western and central Europe, with a relatively high economic development, where it had been possible to extrude the Jew from trade though he was still useful (even if not indispensable) in some minor capacities. (It is significant that the reaction coincided with the revolution caused by the great maritime discoveries, which robbed the great trading cities of Italy and Germany of their former international importance and made them eager to find a scapegoat.) In Eastern Europe, economic development was far less advanced and the Jew filled much the same indispensable function as he had five centuries before, as middleman, distributor and economic pioneer. Just as from the ninth century to the eleventh he had been drawn to France and to the Rhineland to fill the economic vacuum there, so from the thirteenth century to the sixteenth great numbers of Jews (as well as Christians) from Germany were attracted for the same purpose to Poland and the adjacent lands under Polish rule, devastated by the recent Tartar invasions. Boleslav the Pious issued a model charter of liberties and protection for them in 1264, which was confirmed and amplified by Casimir IV in 1354. Under the protection of this, large numbers arrived in the country, where they opened up fresh avenues of commerce, and provided a much-needed middle class between the landed proprietors, on the one hand, and the peasantry, on the other. They acted as agents for the landlords; they assisted in the disposal of the produce of the country; they imported textiles and luxuries from abroad, exporting furs and raw materials in return; they were the distributors of merchandise in the villages and towns; they played a very important part in the fairs in which the commerce of the country was centered; their widespread personal and commercial connections abroad gave new vitality to economic life. So important was the part taken by the German Jewish immigrants that they were able to impose their superior culture on the indigenous Jewish elements (perhaps hailing in the first instance from the south, via the Caucasus and Crimea) whom they found on their arrival, already well established and perhaps numerically superior. This had the incidental and in some ways misleading result that the Middle High German language as spoken in the Rhineland (the basis of modern Yiddish) became the Jewish vernacular throughout this area, and that of those who derived from it all over the world.

As a result of the indispensable economic function performed by the Jews in Poland, the ecclesiastical reaction against them failed to make much headway. It was perhaps not for want of desire. Clerical synods of the province clamored for the enforcement of the repressive conciliar legislation. The burghers, jealous of competition, were profoundly antagonistic. There were frequent sanguinary outbreaks in the cities. The German immigrants brought with them their own standards of intolerance. The blood accusation was endemic; and in the middle of the fifteenth century John of Capistrano's visit to Poland as papal legate was accompanied by a resurgence of ill-feeling and was followed by major excesses. But the importance of the Jews was such that they continued to enjoy the favor of the successive sovereigns and the protection of the nobility, whose agents they were; and in the villages where many of the Jews lived they were rarely molested. Hence, notwithstanding occasional darker interludes, and notwithstanding the establishment of Jewish quarters in the Italian or German style in the larger cities, the reaction that overwhelmed the Jews of the rest of Europe during the course of the sixteenth century did not greatly affect Polish Jewry. Their social life was already so aloof (if only because of their use of an alien tongue) as to make them in some ways almost impervious to it. Their intellectual life was on a different and, as a whole, on a vastly superior plane. Their economic position was so important that it could not be challenged. The even balance between Reform and Catholicism during a good part of the sixteenth century automatically eased the position of a confessional minority, as usually happens in such circumstances. The period thus witnessed a constant expansion in Polish Jewry, fresh immigrants continuing to arrive from every part; and by the close of the fifteenth century this was probably the most important section of the entire Jewish world, whether numerically or intellectually. Thanks to the royal protection, the autonomous intercommunal organization, which developed spontaneously in almost every medieval Jewry, attained a remarkable strength. The Rabbinical right to exercise internal jurisdiction was formally recognized by Sigismund Augustus in 1551. The authorization given to the Jewish communities, for reasons of mutual convenience, to apportion their taxation among themselves greatly strengthened the autonomous tendency. The vast importance in Polish economic life of the great fairs—in particular those held in the spring at Lublin and in the summer at Jaroslaw—gave the opportunity for regular conferences of the lay and religious leaders, which became an established institution. As a result there now came into existence the famous Council of the Four Lands or Provinces (Great Poland, Little Poland, Podolia and Volhynia; there was a parallel independent Council also in Lithuania), with its elaborate organization and its quasi-parliamentary powers—the most highly organized autonomous instrument that ever emerged in Diaspora Jewry.

While the bulk of northern European Jewry (colloquially known as "Ashkenazim," from the term applied by the medieval Rabbis to Germany) was then living under Polish rule, the bulk of southern, or "Sephardic," Jewry was concentrated in the eastern Mediterranean. A majority of the exiles from Spain, as we have seen, had gone to encounter a yet more harrowing fate in Portugal, whence however many subsequently escaped to join their brethren overseas. A few thousand found their way to Italy. No other accessible part of Europe being open to them, the rest sought refuge in the Moslem world. Beyond the Strait of Gibraltar, and in northern Africa generally, the traditional Moslem policy applied: a contemptuous and sometimes harsh toleration. A great number of the exiles nevertheless found new homes here, as had indeed been the case ever since the beginning of the Spanish persecutions in 1391. Contemporary chroniclers tell gruesome tales of their experiences, of their sufferings and of the cruelties inflicted upon them. Nevertheless, they were able to establish themselves in large numbers all along the coast and inland as far as Fez. The old quasi-autochthonous communities, which had revived to some extent since the period of the Almohadan persecutions of the twelfth century, were thus greatly reinforced, or even in some cases submerged by the newcomers. With them the latter brought their native Spanish language, their liturgy, their religious customs, and something of the old Spanish literary tradition. It was indeed a hazardous toleration that they enjoyed. From one or two holy cities they were entirely excluded. They were shut up in special quarters of many towns, subjected to rigid sumptuary laws, permitted to dress only in black, not allowed to ride horses, excluded from public office—treated in fact (and this has lasted down to our own day) with the abject contumely that was characteristic of the Moslem world at its least enlightened, with occasional outbursts of unreasoning persecution, systematic spoliation or fanatical fury. On the other hand, affluent merchants, skilled physicians and gifted linguists were sometimes able to attain positions of influence, occasionally even being entrusted as in a happier age with diplomatic missions; and in the sixteenth century any toleration, however radically qualified, was preferable to the policy that obtained in the Christian lands of the Mediterranean.

Farther east, conditions were far more favorable. The Turks, who had captured Constantinople in 1453, were a people of warrior-farmers, for whom city life held no attraction. Hence commerce and manufacture were left to the non-Moslem elements of the population. The loyalty of the Christians, whether Armenians or Greeks, was obviously suspect. It was, therefore, natural for the sultans to encourage other elements; and from the beginning they had extended their favor to the Greek-speaking Jewish communities which they found on their arrival, and encouraged new elements to come from other lands to join these. The expulsion of the Jews from Spain was therefore highly acceptable to them, and Bajazet II extended a cordial welcome to those of the exiles who came to settle under his rule. Not only were the newcomers a useful addition to the loyal population, but they brought with them precisely those arts which were most lacking among the Turks themselves: medical knowledge, skilled handicrafts, the woolen industry, metalworking, glassmaking, the secrets of the manufacture of firearms, the import and export trade, retail trade and distribution, and so on. Hence the immigrants were treated in Turkey with the utmost favor, subject to the payment of the poll tax that was incumbent on all infidels, in accordance with the traditional Moslem code. They settled in all the great cities—particularly Constantinople and Salonica. Salonica soon became a mainly Jewish center, and with its thirty thousand Jews, perhaps the greatest Jewish community of the period. The development of this port into the most important commercial center of the eastern Mediterranean was mainly due to Jewish enterprise; and it acquired a physiognomy that was all its own, reflecting in speech, in costume, in interests and in culture the life of a happier age in Spain. The immigrants from individual countries, or provinces, or even towns grouped themselves in their own congregations, in which local traditions were maintained in all their minutiae: in Salonica, for example, there were some thirty of them, including Aragonese, Castilian, Portuguese, Apulian and Lisbon communities. The Spanish language and outlook which they introduced with them attained a firm foothold—to such an extent that they absorbed the native Jewish elements and those who came from other lands, all alike speaking Spanish before many generations had passed and most following the "Sephardic" liturgical tradition. Though occasionally the janissaries considered the Jews to be fair prey, and although local administrators were not always just, the sultan's favor was unswerving. It extended too, to the refugees from the reaction in Italy and Central Europe, and to the Portuguese New Christians, or Marranos, who down to the end of the sixteenth century constantly escaped to Turkey in vast numbers in order to return to Judaism. On the conquest of Egypt and Palestine in 1517, the same policy was extended to those lands, where hitherto conditions had been somewhat less favorable. Here, too, large numbers of the Spanish exiles settled. In particular, many of them turned their steps to the Holy Land, with its perpetual magnetism for the Jewish mind yet further enhanced (as always) in times of stress. The recent tribulations, which had induced a general conviction that the coming of the Messiah was imminent, proved a further powerful impetus to this mystical urge. In consequence, the Jewish settlement, which had been at a very low ebb since the Tartar invasions of the thirteenth century, was now revived. In view of the restriction upon the number of Jews who might settle in Jerusalem, very many were attracted to Safed in Upper Galilee. Here there grew up a very important Jewish settlement; and it was the center of the neomystical revival[5a] associated with the name of Isaac Luria (1534-1572)—"the Lion of the Cabbala"—which affected Jewish life to probably a greater extent than any other movement since the compilation of the Talmud, imbuing it with a new poetry, but in some cases also with gross superstition. One daring scholar of this period, Jacob Berab (1474-1546), attempted to reassert the spiritual predominance of the Holy Land by reconstituting the Sanhedrin, nonexistent since ancient times, as the prelude to the renewal of the Jewish commonwealth; but vested interests prevented this imaginative step, which at the least would have given Judaism a new cohesion and restored to it the power of orderly development.

The period under consideration in Turkish Jewish history is memorable because of the great part played by Jews in public life. Constantly recruited as they were by fresh immigrants from Italy, or refugee Marranos from Portugal, they constituted one of the few elements in the Ottoman Empire that had a firsthand acquaintance with foreign lands and a knowledge of foreign languages. Their services were therefore used to a very great extent in the conduct of foreign policy, and some of them attained as a result a very remarkable status. Outstanding was the case of the Portuguese João Miguez (*c.* 1515-1579), who arrived in Constantinople in 1554 after amassing a fortune in association with the Marrano financial house of Mendes at Antwerp, adopted as a Jew the name of Joseph Nasi, received in feud the duchy of Naxos (formerly considered the premier duchy in Christendom), and became a favorite of Sultan Selim. Nasi obtained a temporary embargo on French shipping in the Levant in the hope of vindicating his outstanding claims on the French king, secured important financial concessions in connection with the customs and carried on a vast trade, and was permitted to attempt a colonizing experiment at Tiberias in Palestine. He treated with foreign powers in his own name, encouraged the revolt of the Netherlands and promised the insurgents military support, gave Turkish policy a pronounced anti-Venetian bias which resulted in the conquest of Cyprus, and was even, according to report, promised that he would be made king of that island. The defeat of Lepanto resulted in his eclipse. Another Jew, however, the physician Solomon Ashkenazi (1520-1603), obtained the favor of the Grand Vizier Mehemet Sokolli, and because of his wide knowledge of Italy (where he had been born) and Poland (where he had practiced) also attained great influence in Turkish foreign policy, being courted by foreign powers, swaying the election of a new king in Poland, and being sent as ambassador to Venice in 1571. Later other Jews (such as the former Marrano Alvaro Mendes, alias Solomon Abenayish [*c.* 1520-1603] who became Duke of Mytilene and was one of the authors of the Anglo-Turkish alliance against Spain) continued to fill an important role in diplomatic circles in Constantinople. From the accession of Murad III in 1574, the general atmosphere was somewhat less favorable, and the weakening of the central government exposed the outlying Jewish communities particularly to sporadic ill-treatment. Notwithstanding this the general condition of the Jews in the Turkish Empire remained unchanged in essentials down to the end of the old regime.

All this time there had been a continuous emigration from Portugal (where the Inquisition had commenced its activities in 1540) of Marranos descended from those "New Christians" converted by force in 1497, far more prominent and numerous than the corresponding Spanish element. At the beginning the tide of emigration had been directed in great part to Italy—to Ancona, where ferocious proceedings were taken against them in 1555 by Pope Paul IV; to Ferrara, until reaction began in 1581; and thereafter to Venice, and after it was erected into a free port in 1593, to Leghorn. There was also, as has been mentioned, a very considerable influx to Turkey, where the immigrants of this type were soon absorbed completely in the existing communities. Somewhat different in nature was the migration to the great commercial centers of northern Europe. Here the Marranos invariably constituted an important element in the Spanish and Portuguese commercial colonies—especially at Antwerp, where in the second quarter of the sixteenth century the banking house of Mendes attained a foremost position, but also in London, Paris, Bordeaux, Rouen, etc. The public profession of Judaism was permitted as yet in none of these places, and at intervals the colony would be disturbed, whatever circumspection was shown. After the revolt of the Netherlands, conditions changed in Holland, partly as a result of religious and partly of economic forces. From the last decade of the sixteenth century, therefore, the Marranos of Amsterdam were permitted to open a public synagogue. The Spanish and Portuguese community of this place—constantly recruited by refugees from the Peninsula—rapidly attained an outstanding position in the Jewish world; and before long an Ashkenazic congregation was erected at its side by German immigrants, who were quick to take advantage of the new circumstances. A similar process took place in Hamburg, where the establishment of Spanish and Portuguese Jews was formally authorized by the Senate in 1612, after consultation with the Lutheran academies of Frankfort and Jena. These were the spearheads of the new type of Jewish settlement in the Western world, which in the course of the seventeenth and eighteenth centuries completely altered the Jewish scene.

In the first half of the seventeenth century, the Jewish distribution in the world was much as follows: No professing Jews whatsoever lived in Spain, Portugal, England and France (except for the handful in the Avignon and the papal territories of Provence); there was the difference, however, that while crypto-Jews might live without acute danger in the latter lands, in the former they were subjected to perpetual and mortal danger from the Inquisition, as was the case, too, in the Spanish and Portuguese dependencies in America. A similar policy of complete exclusion prevailed in Sicily, Sardinia and the kingdom of Naples, as well as in a few areas (such as the duchy of Milan, a Spanish possession) in north Italy. In the rest of that country, however, there were a number of communities, subjected with the utmost rigor (except at Leghorn) to the Ghetto system: the most important were Rome, Venice, Ancona, Turin, Modena and Ferrara, though the repression was naturally most severe in the Papal States. Over most of Germany, similar conditions obtained, with the reservation, however, that here only a few of the more important cities (Frankfort, Hamburg, Worms and Fuerth being the most noteworthy) as yet permitted Jewish settlements, most of the centers being in small towns or even villages. On the other hand, in Holland, and to some extent in Hamburg as well, a highly cultured community of a new type had by now begun to emerge, eminently European in life and outlook, as the result of Marrano immigration. The Scandinavian countries admitted no Jews, though there were a few in the Germanic provinces of southern Denmark. To the East, however, there were considerable settlements in the Austrian territories—especially Bohemia, with a great community in

Prague; while Poland, at this time covering a very wide area, harbored what was probably the world's greatest agglomeration of Jews. In the Moslem world, there was a fringe of settlements all along North Africa and into Palestine, and very numerous communities all through the Ottoman Empire as far as the Indian Ocean. The vast majority of the erstwhile Spanish Jewry was now concentrated here. A small community in Persia, undisturbed since ancient times, was now entering upon a period of oppression and enforced conversion as the result of the introduction of the Shiite form of Islam as the state religion. So, too, in the Yemen, there was a handful of communities immersed in the Arab environment and almost cut off from the rest of the world. Farther east, isolated settlements had been discovered by travelers in India and China, of slender numerical importance. The bulk of the Jewish people, however, was living in Eastern Europe and the adjacent parts of Asia—the mass of the Ashkenazim under Polish rule, of Sephardim under the Turks, and perhaps evenly divided between the two empires. This equilibrium was to be disturbed by the violent upheaval that was now about to take place.

NOTES

[[1a] Cf. above Judah Goldin, "The Period of the Talmud," pp. 144 ff.]

[[2a] On the institution of the Gaonate and its decline see above *ibid.*, pp. 186 ff. and pp. 200-201.]

[3] The most recent investigations tend to postdate this by some generations.

[[4a] Cf. below Charles Singer, "Science and Judaism," p. 1386.]

[[5a] On the mystical element in Judaism cf. below Chapter 19 by Abraham J. Heschel.]

CHAPTER 5

THE JEWS OF WESTERN EUROPE
(*from 1648*)

By Cecil Roth

The year 1648 was a significant one in Jewish history from many points of view. It saw the first of the outbreaks against eastern European Jewry which ended the golden age of the Polish communities and finally destroyed their tranquillity; with the result that emigration on a vast scale began, and that ultimately the face of world Jewry was entirely changed. The Peace of Westphalia sealed the disintegration of the Holy Roman Empire, and in the petty absolutisms that established themselves on its ruins, new communities began to flourish and Europeanized Jews of a new type to appear, pioneers of the age of emancipation. The independence of Holland, too, was now secured, and the extremely important Marrano settlement that had recently found a refuge there was henceforth safe from disturbance. In England, the execution of Charles I and the establishment of the Commonwealth in this year brought the question of the readmission of the Jews into the sphere of practical politics, and it was then that the slow discussions on the subject began. This was the date, too, of the beginning of the Messianic agitation connected with the name of Sabbatai Zevi, which was to be a landmark in the history of the Jews, especially of the Levant and the Turkish Empire. On the other side of the Atlantic, the Portuguese reconquest of Brazil began to make headway, resulting in the establishment by the Marrano refugees from that country of the earliest Jewish communities in the West Indies and (with tremendous implications for the future) on the North American mainland.[1a] If any precise point of time is to be taken for the beginning of modern Jewish history, no better one presents itself than this fate-fraught year.

In April, 1648, the Cossacks of the Ukraine, under the Bogdan Khmielnitski, rose in revolt against their Polish overlords. The latter's Jewish agents were doubly obnoxious, because of their religion and because of their attachments, as well as because of the administrative and economic abuses of which they were the passive instruments; and there followed a wave of massacre greater probably in scale and in geographical range than anything known in Europe even in the darkest hours of the Middle

Ages. Thereafter, foreign invasions from Russians and Swedes, periodical rebellions, growing resentments, internal disorders and perpetual accusations of ritual crime constantly renewed the horrors of that terrible period. The strength of Polish Jewry was broken, and the first breach made in the walls of what had become the world's great reservoir of Jewish population, as Mesopotamia had been a thousand years before. The whole of Europe began to be overrun by Jewish refugees, whose number was constantly recruited with every further trough of depression or outburst of violence in the Slavonic lands. The tide of emigration has continued, with varying intensity, down to our own day; and it has resulted in a complete redistribution of the Jewish population throughout the world. It is for this reason perhaps the most important episode in the history of the Jews between the fifteenth century and the nineteenth.

The first wave of refugees naturally found their way in great numbers to Germany. Here, during the past hundred years, the Jewish lot had been somewhat less checkered than hitherto, for notwithstanding occasional local outbreaks there had been a temporary cessation of the constant sequence of massacre that had disgraced the Middle Ages. The Thirty Years' War, moreover, besides giving lucrative opportunities to the small traders and hucksters who followed in the wake of the armies, had significant consequences on a major scale for the German Jews, which counterbalanced the results of the incidental disorders that took place here and there. The final debacle of the imperial authority, and the devolutionary process to which this gave rise, resulted in an even more complete lack of consistency than hitherto on the part of the local authorities in their policy. Whereas some of the greater principalities, such as Saxony and Brandenburg, and a majority of the independent city-republics such as Nuremberg, maintained a policy of complete exclusion of the Jews, the lesser states and lordships were inclined to be more tolerant and to admit them, though only perhaps in order to extract from them a maximum of gain. The political fractionalization continued sometimes to a positively ludicrous extent. Thus, for example, in the township of Sugenheim in Franconia there were twelve families of Jews elaborately organized, but divided evenly (six apiece!) between the two rival imperial barons who wielded collaborative authority over that tiny place. Moreover, the complicated political pattern of the country often permitted the Jews to live just outside certain important commercial centers in which they were not allowed to settle permanently, coming in for purposes of business from time to time or even from day to day. Thus the community of Fuerth attained an artificial importance because of its contiguity to ever-intolerant Nuremberg, and that of Deutz because of its nearness to episcopal Cologne. The new settlements tended, moreover, to have a greater security of tenure than in the past. The city of Hildesheim, for example, in which expulsion and readmission had alternated with monotonous regularity at grotesquely short intervals since the fourteenth century, allowed the Jews back for at least the fourth time in 1601, expelled them again in 1609, recalled them shortly after, again expelled them in 1660, but finally permitted them to settle in 1662, after which the record is continuous.

Through such means the area of settlement in Germany, which had been more and more restricted from the period of the Black Death onward, now increased once more. The influx from the east that resulted from the Cossack rising permitted the expansion to be maintained at a rate probably unexampled in German Jewish history hitherto. Though exact data are not available (as is the case with so many of the major phenomena of Jewish history), it is probable that in the following half century the influx was on such a scale as not merely to reinforce, but to all intents and purposes to reconstitute the remnants of the old quasi-autochthonous German Jewry that had survived the medieval persecutions, this continuing to predominate only in certain regions of the south and west of the country. Owing to prevalence of the Yiddish vernacular, however—essentially an archaic form of German with a Hebrew admixture, universally spoken by the Jews throughout central and eastern Europe—the fusion between the two elements was exceptionally easy, rapid and complete.

Little courts were now, moreover, set up all over the country in petty imitation of Versailles, vying with one another in flashy brilliance. They were extravagant in their requirements, and needed a constant supply of money to maintain them. Hence versatile Jews found special opportunities both for the provision and for the expenditure of funds, as financial agents, on the one hand, and as factors and jewelers, on the other. Similarly, as military operations became more specialized, Jews were frequently put in charge of the commissariat and the organization of supplies (this remained a characteristic and highly lucrative calling of the Jewish upper classes throughout Europe, and even in the American colonies, down to the period of the French Revolutionary Wars). For such purposes, Jews considered to possess exceptional abilities and qualifications would frequently be admitted without any restriction whatsoever, even to cities or courts that had previously prided themselves upon their exclusiveness; and they enjoyed in such instances a status and authority equal to that of any Christian subject.

A notorious example was the extravagant, dazzling, dissolute, ruthless but extraordinarily efficient Joseph Oppenheimer, known as "Jew Suess" (1692- or 1698-1738), who for a short time before his disastrous and tragic fall in 1738 was omnipotent at the court of Wuerttemberg; but there were many of his contemporaries, who had a far longer if less sensational career—*e.g.*, his kinsman Samuel Oppenheimer (1635-1703), who financed the Vienna government's military operations during successive campaigns at the close of the seventeenth century; or the great Samson Wertheimer (1658-1724), who supervised the commissariat of the imperial forces with pre-eminent skill during the War of the Spanish Succession. Such "Court Jews," or *Hofjuden* (as they were generally called), and those who gathered round them constituted the nucleus of the community of a different sort from those still huddled in the *Judengassen* of Frankfort or of Worms, being outwardly assimilated to their neighbors (as was necessary if they were to perform their functions in a satisfactory manner) and enjoying a considerable degree of social emancipation. They were not indeed safe against violent revulsions of feeling, and their fall was sometimes catastrophic, as in the case of Jew Suess himself. Similarly, local expulsions continued from time to time, even in the eighteenth century. But they were counterbalanced by the steady expansion in the area of settlement. Thus, for example, the foundation of the Spanish and Portuguese congregation in Hamburg was followed by the infiltration of Ashkenazic Jews, who settled mainly in Altona, just outside the walls, under Danish rule; and this nexus before long became the greatest German Jewish community, as it remained down to the nineteenth century. Similarly, the refugees expelled from Vienna and Lower Austria in 1670, through the influence of an empress of Spanish birth on a ruler of unenlightened piety, were admitted to Brandenburg, so that Berlin took its place before long among the communities of the first rank. That of Vienna, on the other hand, experienced a revival on a smaller scale within a very short time. An inimitable picture of German Jewry at this period, with its hopes and anxieties, its quarrels and its strivings, its teeming *Judengassen* and its scattered village communities, its proletariat of peddlers and its upper stratum of international gem dealers and its quasi nobility of Court Jews (a family alliance with whom was considered a rare privilege) is given in the garrulous memoirs of the Hamburg Jewess, Glueckel of Hameln (1646-1724)—one of the most delightful and most human documents in the entire range of Jewish literature.

The Treaty of Westphalia had established the complete independence of Holland (the United Provinces) and made possible a greater expansion of its Jewish settlement. The influx of Marranos from the Peninsula continued, particularly after the disappointment of the hopes of toleration that had been aroused by the restoration of the native dynasty in Portugal in 1640. Communities were thus established in most of the major cities and some of the smaller country towns. Holland (but especially Amsterdam) thus became a great center of Spanish culture as well as of Jewish life. Inquisitional spies who returned to the Peninsula told with horror of those Spanish and Portuguese whom they had seen there publicly professing the Judaism of their remote ancestors, still bearing in most cases their high-sounding Iberian names and sometimes even flaunting their hidalgo coats of arms. A large literature was published there in Spanish—in part religious, in part secular and sometimes of very high quality: the beginning in fact (outside of Italy) of modern Jewish literature in the languages of Europe. There was a high standard of Jewish as well as of general culture, and an elaborate and very efficient educational organization evolved, capable of training men like Benedict Spinoza. Sometimes, even the Spanish and Portuguese governments employed these polished refugees on important missions, or even as diplomatic agents. Similar oases of Iberian culture, though not perhaps on the same scale, emerged in all the other places where the Marrano exiles found a haven. The Sephardim were followed in increasing number by Ashkenazim, who provided before long a teeming proletariat. By the close of the seventeenth century the Amsterdam community, approaching perhaps ten thousand, was the greatest in western Europe. A similar process, as we shall see, took place at this time in the other lands bordering on the Atlantic seaboard. To what extent the Jews followed, to what extent they initiated, the expansion of trade is still a matter for discussion, as is also the problem of whether the new attitude of tolerance in these areas was in the first instance due to advanced Protestantism or to an appreciation of economic advantage. The complex is not easy to disentangle. What is certain is that in this period, from being (apart from the dense settlement in Central Europe) essentially a Mediterranean people in their Diaspora as they had been in their homeland, the Jews became oceanic and established a firm foothold at the strategic points on the trade routes of the Atlantic. This tendency has continued more and more down to our own day, reaching its culmination in the great transference of Jewish population to America in the past generation.

The period under consideration witnessed the extension of the area of Jewish settlement, in somewhat similar circumstances, to England. There had been a furtive Marrano community in London since the beginning of the sixteenth century, as recent researches have revealed; though there were temporary interruptions during the Catholic reaction under Mary and again (after a period of considerable promise in the reign of Elizabeth) at the beginning of the reign of James I. In 1648, in the first flush of the Puritan Revolution, a remarkable but subsequently forgotten attempt was made to establish in England universal religious toleration, in the widest sense, which would have benefited the Jews as well as other non-Christians; but the times were not ripe for such broad-mindedness. Nevertheless, the change of government, the establishment of the Commonwealth and the Old Testament sympathies of the Puritans, coupled with the revival of foreign trade and the rising tide of Hispanophobia, gave rise to fervid hopes on both sides of the North Sea, among Jewish and Judeophile dreamers alike. In 1655, accordingly, after receiving some encouragement from Whitehall as well as from private individuals in

"Menasseh ben Israel"
Etching by Rembrandt

England, a mystically minded Dutch rabbi of considerable learning named Manasseh ben Israel (1604-1657), well known to Christian theologians everywhere through his Spanish and Latin writings, came over to London as self-appointed delegate of his people to negotiate for their formal readmission to the country. Notwithstanding a cordial welcome in some circles and a highly sympathetic reception by the Lord Protector, Oliver Cromwell, himself, there was widespread criticism of the proposals. A solid body of opposition manifested itself at a conference at Whitehall, of merchants, theologians and others, to whom the problem was submitted for discussion (December, 1655-January, 1656), although the legal experts first consulted pronounced unequivocally that there was no law which excluded the Jews from England. In the end, therefore, Cromwell decided to take no action, while "conniving" at the presence of the Jews in the country and even permitting them informally to conduct worship in accordance with Jewish practices.

When during 1656 the war with Spain seemed to jeopardize the property of those of the Marrano group already settled in the country who were Spanish-born, they considered it to be their best defense to plead that they were in fact refugees from Spain, thus throwing off their disguise. This plea was admitted by the courts. Simultaneously they presented a petition in their Jewish names to the Lord Protector requesting permission in writing to carry on their religious rites undisturbed. Though he did not feel his position strong enough even then to acquiesce, he apparently intimated that he had no objection to their behaving as though the application had been granted, and a synagogue and a cemetery were established. As a result of, rather than despite this informality (for nothing having been done, there was nothing to undo when the reaction came) the settlement survived the Restoration. It received protection from the judiciary when attempts were made to disturb it, and after one of these was recognized in a more formal fashion by the tolerant, or at least religiously indifferent, Charles II, who had as a matter of fact received certain benefits from and made certain promises to some of the Amsterdam Jews during his long exile. Moreover, the informality of the circumstances made it impossible for any special rules to be laid down to regulate the new community. Hence from the very outset it suffered from no restrictions of any great significance additional to those which applied to other dissenters from the established church. It was not even subject, as was invariably the case elsewhere at this time, to special taxation, much less to any Ghetto legislation, such as Manasseh ben Israel presumably would have expected in the first instance; and social equality was thus attainable by the more Anglicized elements from the very outset. What was perhaps more important was the remoter consequence of this; for the same system (or lack of it) extended to the American colonies, where after the Portuguese reconquest of Brazil in the middle of the seventeenth century a few refugees established the first synagogues, with momentous consequences in due course.

As was the case elsewhere, Ashkenazic settlers followed on the heels of the Sephardic pioneers to England, too, profiting from the advantages the latter had won. About 1690 the first "German" synagogue was established in London—subsequently known as the Great Synagogue, and periodically enlarged in order to accommodate the constant influx: a second congregation was established in 1707, and a third in 1761, a fourth in Westminster in or about the same year. In the middle of the eighteenth century, moreover, a number of congregations were established (generally around a nucleus of silversmiths and peddlers) in the provincial trading centers and seaports—*e.g.*, Canterbury (1742), Portsmouth (1747), Birmingham (*c.* 1750), Plymouth (1752), Bristol (1753), Liverpool (1756), though none of these played a part in Jewish life comparable to that of some of the small cities of the Continent. In modern times, in fact, the London community has never comprised less than two-thirds of the Anglo-Jewish population, resulting in a particularly strong tendency to centralization. It is significant that England was probably the only country of western Europe in all parts of which Jews have had unrestricted (or rather unchallenged) rights of settlement during the past three centuries.

Meanwhile, a Jewish community had established itself in Copenhagen, the capital of Denmark, where also Ashkenazim followed on the heels of the Sephardic pioneers. In Sweden, where notwithstanding all blandishments the latter element had been reluctant to settle, restrictions were withdrawn in 1782, when a small Jewish community was founded by immigrants from Germany. (Norway, on the other hand, maintained the policy of exclusion until the second half of the nineteenth century.) There was also a slight infiltration into the present-day Belgium when it passed in 1713 from Spanish to Austrian rule.

France still maintained nominally its exclusive religious policy as it had done since the fourteenth century, but with a mosaic of curious reservations. In Alsace, and in a minor degree in Lorraine, acquired by the French crown during the seventeenth century, there were dense Jewish settlements of the German type, which were allowed to remain undisturbed after the change of rule, though no amelioration was made in their condition. On the other hand, in the southwest, in the ports of Bordeaux and Bayonne (together with some minor places in the neighborhood), Marrano refugees from Spain and Portugal had established themselves in the course of the sixteenth and seventeenth centuries. They long continued to live under a transparent disguise of Catholicism, though neglecting the rites of the church more and more and practicing their Jewish observances with less and less concealment. It was by then patent to all the world that these

"New Christians" were, in fact, Jews; and at length in 1730 formal recognition was extended to them as such. Finally, in the papal territories of Avignon and the Comtat Venaissin there was a long-established Jewish settlement—the last relic of medieval French Jewry, allowed to remain here only without disturbance, under the aegis of the supreme head of the Catholic Church—which in the course of time began to spill out into the surrounding area. All these three elements—the Alsatian, the Marrano, and the *Comtadin*—inevitably had economic and personal connections with Paris, where in the second half of the eighteenth century some of their members were permitted to establish themselves, under strict surveillance. Thus the exclusion that nominally still prevailed in France had become so greatly modified as almost to have lapsed. Spain, Portugal and the kingdom of the Two Sicilies still maintained their stern Catholic policy of exclusion, a contemptuous attempt of 1740-1746 to attract Jewish merchants back to the last-named state being so ringed with restrictions that it inevitably failed. Except for these lands and Holy Russia, the only parts of European lands still closed to the Jews were Norway and certain areas of Germany—pre-eminently Saxony, "the Protestant Russia." Moreover, the Prussian annexations in the middle of the eighteenth century, capped by the successive partitions of Poland at its close, resulted in the transference of relatively great Jewish masses from the eastern to the central European Jewish orbit, greatly reinforcing the numerical strength of German Jewry in particular.

Paradoxically, Italy, the country where hitherto the lot of the Jews had been the happiest, became the most retrograde. The Catholic reaction had finally triumphed in Italy, which, moreover, had entered upon a period of utter economic decadence. The Jewish population that in the Middle Ages had been mainly distributed in the area from Rome southward was concentrated in the north of the country (excluding, however, the duchy of Milan, so long as it remained under Spanish rule, and generally speaking the territories of the Genoese Republic as well). The Jewish communities—the most important of which were in Rome, Venice, Mantua, Modena, Ferrara and Ancona—were strictly confined to their Ghettos, compelled to wear the Jewish badge, driven to listen to conversionist sermons in the churches, closely restricted, except for a handful of merchants, to the most lowly occupations such as dealing in old clothes, subjected to a rigorous literary censorship directed in particular against the Talmud, compelled sometimes to surrender their children to the Church on the pretext that some renegade relative had claimed them or that a drunken ruffian had pretended to baptize them, and treated generally as an insidious menace to their neighbors. It was only in the cities that carried on an important commerce with the Levant, such as Venice and Ancona, that a certain element of the Jewish population was allowed a greater economic, though not social latitude. On the other hand, in order to develop the free port of Leghorn, set up at the end of the sixteenth century, the grand dukes of Tuscany relieved the Jews there of all restrictions, and even went so far as to invite Marranos specifically to settle there, promising them immunity from prosecution on religious grounds. The Jewish colony was thus given a great impetus, in turn contributing outstandingly to the economic prosperity of the city. It became in due course one of the greatest Italian communities, comprising like Rome some five thousand (there was probably no other Italian community which exceeded two thousand in number). For some generations, moreover, it was one of the most important seats of Jewish culture in southern Europe (barely outdone even by Salonica)—a Spanish-speaking oasis, like London or Amsterdam, but in an Italian setting.

The economic structure of the Jewish communities of western Europe was everywhere much the same. At the top there was a small aristocracy (or rather plutocracy) of brokers, financiers, jewelers and wholesale importers, strongest by far among the Sephardim. Below them there was a vast proletariat of working tailors, peddlers, secondhand dealers and old-clothes men. Even in England, where positive restrictions were minimal, the poverty-stricken immigrants could seldom find any other immediate source of livelihood, this process being accentuated by exclusion from the freedom of the City of London and the consequent inability to open retail shops within the City (though not beyond its boundaries); hence by the middle of the century the "Jew peddler" was familiar throughout the English countryside, performing a not unimportant economic function which should not be overlooked. A great proportion of the Jewish population throughout Europe lived below a minimal subsistence level, and it is calculated that in most countries at least one-third were dependent upon the charity of their more affluent brethren.

The appalling conditions in a great part of central and eastern Europe resulted in a general fluidity of population, and constantly disturbed the balance in areas of greater freedom and opportunity. The Ghettos of southern Europe were compelled in the course of the eighteenth century to place an embargo on fresh settlers and to enlist the aid of the secular authorities to exclude the strange poor. In some places there was the curious phenomenon of the arrival of entire bands of Jewish paupers, claiming relief as their right, and actually assaulting the Ghetto if they were not admitted (as happened in 1775 at Lisle in the south of France). In England, the pauper influx in the last quarter of the eighteenth century led to a serious problem of Jewish delinquency, which engaged the serious attention both of the Jewish communities and of the central government, and resulted in a determined attempt to control immigration. It is remarkable how, with the widening of opportunity in the following generation, the problem, in effect the result of an exclusive economic policy, spontaneously disappeared.

The disequilibrium, even in those countries where external conditions were most favorable, was perpetuated by the endemic persecution and consequent penury abroad, resulting in a perpetual influx of penniless and partly demoralized refugees. In Poland, in the eighteenth century, the general economic depression, the succession of petty persecutions and the "Haidamack" massacres, which culminated in 1768, were responsible for the ejaculation of a continuous stream of emigrants to reinforce the communities farther west. In 1758 an appeal was made to the Pope for protection against the unending series of ritual murder accusations which were causing perpetual disturbance, and Cardinal Ganganelli (subsequently Pope Clement XIV) drew up a noble report demonstrating the absurdity of the charge.[2] Nevertheless, there was little intermission in the tragic sequence. In Italy the second half of the eighteenth century witnessed not only an extension of the sequence of forced baptisms, but a widespread general reaction. This was exemplified above all in the *Editto sopra gli ebrei* issued by Pope Pius VI in 1775, which renewed every degradation of the Middle Ages and the Counter-Reformation, with numerous barely credible later embellishments—forbidding, for example, Jews to ride in carriages, or to escort their dead to the grave with the customary dirges, or even to erect tombstones over their remains. (One of the most inhuman documents in the history of mankind, it has been termed.) The lead was followed elsewhere—for example, in the Venetian territories, where the decennial *Ricondotta* issued to the Jewish communities in 1777 (still conditional as it had been two and a half centuries before on the maintenance in the Ghetto of three pawnbroking establishments for the benefit of the poor) deliberately attempted to drive the Jews out of whatever foothold they had gained in the textile industry or any other branch of economic life in a wider sense. The impoverishment and demoralization of the Italian Ghettos was the inevitable consequence of all this. Hence there was a steady emigration from this country as well, the weakest elements being left behind to face the battle of existence and to shoulder the colossal financial burden inherited from a more ample age. It is not to be wondered at under the circumstances if in the course of the eighteenth century several communities, including those of Rome and Venice, were driven into bankruptcy.

Those of Germany (including Alsace) were on the whole in no better state, though there was an increasing degree of great wealth alongside the appalling poverty. The teeming Jewries of eastern Europe were living under conditions of unbelievable misery, many being compelled to contract loans from their Christian neighbors, and even from religious houses, in order to maintain their existence. Except in the handful of communities recently established in the Atlantic seaports, the general picture could hardly have been more deplorable, but even there (as has been mentioned) there was a darker side to the economic and social scene.

Symptomatic of the distress and misery that prevailed at this period was the almost universal allegiance that had been received by Sabbatai Zevi, the seventeenth-century pseudo Messiah,[3a] whose grandiose pretensions and impressive personality were seized upon avidly by his despairing coreligionists in every land without exception. So unwilling indeed were they to surrender their illusions that they continued their credence in him after his apostasy, and even after his death. For many years itinerant preachers (whom there is no need to regard as mere charlatans, as was formerly done), such as Nehemiah Hayun (1650-1730), continued to keep the Jewish world as far afield as London and Berlin in turmoil by their missionary activities in behalf of this curious vagary; the dispute between the rationalistic Jacob Emden (1697-1776) and the crypto-Sabbataian Jonathan Eybeschuetz (1690-1764), later rabbi of Altona, Hamburg and Wandsbeck, not only convulsed Jewish circles, but even invited the intervention of the government; Jacob Frank (1726-1791), the Podolian pseudo Messiah in Zevi's tradition, who had ostensibly apostatized to Christianity, set up his "court" at Offenbach, near Frankfort, almost at the center of European enlightenment, and received the homage of innumerable votaries. Besides these, there were many others, including some of the most eminent rabbinic scholars of the time, who secretly hankered after the curious doctrines of the Sabbataian mystics. It was indeed a species of escapism; there could be no more eloquent commentary than this whole episode upon the depressed condition of the Jewish world.

In some parts at least of northern Europe, anti-Jewish prejudices were not greatly modified, notwithstanding the emergence of the new Jewish type and the dawn of the new age. In 1700 a German anti-Semite named Johann Andreas Eisenmenger published his scurrilous *Entdecktes Judentum* ("Judaism Revealed") which, though banned by the emperor through the influence of the banker Samuel Oppenheimer, was republished in Prussia and has remained a source book of anti-Semitic attacks down to our own day. Frederick the Great's *Generalprivilegium* of 1750 for the Jews of his dominions was a mere regimentation of the former legislation, barely relieved by a single ray of human sympathy, and going so far as to forbid Jewish servants (who were of no special value to the state) to marry and propagate their kind; and the regulations issued at this period in other German states were little different. In England, in 1753, the Pelham government introduced and passed an innocuous measure in the mercantilistic spirit of the time to facilitate the naturalization of foreign-born Jews, as had already been done for the foreign-born Protestants. (It is important to note that this was not, as is generally stated, a measure for the naturalization of the Jews as such; for the native-born were already considered British subjects and enjoyed within certain limitations the rights of their compatriots.) These trivial proposals aroused a tremendous storm throughout the country, partly through the jealousy of the London merchants and partly through the exaggerations of the Opposition, who found in it a useful political weapon. Scores of lampoons, pamphlets, caricatures and ballads were published attacking the measure and exaggerating the consequences that would ensue when Jews would swarm from abroad in uncontrolled hordes and become dominant in the country. Such was the state of popular feeling that in the end the government thought it wisest to withdraw the "Jew Bill," as it was called, before it had been in force for more than a few months. The agitation subsided; but even though not accompanied, strangely enough, by any actual violence, it had been a dangerous portent.[4]

A further notable incident of this period demonstrated both the precariousness of the Jewish position and the growth of European humanitarianism, notwithstanding local setbacks. Maria Theresa, her profound Catholic feeling heightened by reports of the disloyalty of the Alsatian and other Jews during the war with France, determined in 1745 upon the expulsion of their coreligionists from the kingdom of Bohemia—including even the ancient and populous community of Prague, for centuries past one of the most important and best organized in Europe. In consternation, its leaders appealed to their coreligionists abroad, begging them to exert whatever influence they had to avert the crisis. This was possible in the eighteenth century in a new sense, which would have been out of all question hitherto; though indeed philanthropic sentiment was confessedly reinforced by the fear that the expulsion from one land would result in an artificial and highly unwelcome tide of immigration elsewhere. In consequence, when the news was heard, there were protests from all parts of Europe, and the governments of England and Holland in particular ordered their ambassadors to make diplomatic representations in Vienna. These were not entirely successful, as the expulsion was carried into effect, but within a year the edict was withdrawn and the exiles allowed to return. It was a landmark in diplomatic history and a triumph for humanitarian ideas in international relations: though unfortunately the precedent was followed subsequently only in cases where small and weak countries were in question.

In the course of the eighteenth century the deplorable condition of the Jews thus came to be considered a European problem and to engage everywhere the attention of enlightened statesmen and philanthropists. So far as Germany in particular was concerned, it was to some extent brought to the fore by the remarkable career of Moses Mendelssohn (1729-1786) who overcame the disadvantages of his Ghetto background, and without surrendering anything of his Jewish loyalties became one of the foremost

German philosophers, stylists and writers. He and his as yet small handful of associates and followers provided not only a nucleus of agitation, but also an outstanding example of the remarkable potentialities inherent in the Ghetto, and debarred from any useful service to the state. Lessing took him as the model for the central figure of his powerful plea for religious toleration, *Nathan the Wise* (1779); Jews as well as Christians frequented the literary salons established by his wealthy followers and admirers in the Berlin community; the tradition of vernacular literature that was initiated (so far as central Europe at least was concerned) by his independent writings and by his epoch-making translation of the Pentateuch and Psalms removed something of the veil of misunderstanding from Jewish life; the "Court Jews" and "Protected Jews" of a somewhat lower status, who had made their way among the bourgeoisie by reason of their wealth, henceforth began to establish their position among the intelligentsia by reason of their culture; a new ideal of Jewish life became apparent. In 1781 his friend Christian Wilhelm Dohm, invited by Mendelssohn to prepare a memorandum on behalf of the Jews of Alsace for submission to the Royal Council at Versailles, launched an appeal for the emancipation of the Jews in his famous *Ueber die Buergerliche Verbesserung der Juden in Deutschland*. This created a great stir in enlightened circles everywhere, and was widely studied and even translated into foreign tongues; it was, however, concerned more with the pressing problem of exclusion from various elementary human rights than with what was termed "Jewish Emancipation" in a later age. The same tendency was translated into action for the first time by the reforming Emperor Joseph II who, besides abolishing the poll tax and the Jewish badge for the Austrian communities, issued on January 2, 1782, the famous *Toleranzpatent* laying down the principle that the disabilities of the Jews were gradually to be removed and that they were to be encouraged to share in the life of the general population—a complete reversal of the policy that had hitherto obtained in Catholic Europe. The experiment was not in fact very successful, the Jews suspecting with good reason that it was intended to undermine their religious separatism, and their neighbors still demurring to receive them on equal terms, unless they were unusually wealthy. Nevertheless, it aroused a great deal of attention everywhere, and was to some extent imitated, though cautiously, here and there. In the Austrian possessions in Italy, for example, similar regulations were naturally put into force and with a fairly considerable degree of success. Dohm's memorandum had little influence so far as its immediate object was concerned, the royal letters patent of 1784 on behalf of the Jews of Alsace only removing a few especial indignities, such as the *impôt du pied fourchu* which Jews, like animals, hitherto had to pay when they entered a town. They found, however, a native champion in the philanthropic Abbé Gregoire, whose famous prize essay *Sur la régénération physique morale et politique des Juifs*, of 1789, familiarized the new conceptions in France, where they were eagerly welcomed in liberal circles. Meanwhile the American Revolution had introduced the principle of religious equality for the first time into the modern world *de facto*, though to be sure the number of Jews affected was so small that this did not have any great immediate significance.

The traditional prejudices were still so strong as to rob the reformist movement of a great deal of its strength so long as it lacked a powerful external impetus. In Austria the *Toleranzpatent* almost became a dead letter under Joseph II's successors. In Italy various slight ameliorations in the condition of the Jews in Tuscany and elsewhere actually led to rioting. The socially emancipated Jewish aristocracy, whether in Holland, Germany or England, showed a strong tendency to complete their assimilation through the baptismal font; the proletariat, notwithstanding a few minor ameliorations here and there, remained almost unaffected.

The French Revolution, however, forced the issue. The Declaration of the Rights of Man of 1789 had as its logical consequence the complete emancipation of the Jews. This was conceded readily enough, though not automatically, in the case of the sparse and relatively assimilated Sephardic and Avignonese element (January 28, 1790); but the idea of extending similar privileges to the profoundly conservative and aloof masses of Alsace, many of whom still followed the traditional and unpopular Jewish callings, aroused great opposition. It was from this point of view fortunate perhaps that the Revolution centered in Paris, with only a tiny, heterogeneous Jewish settlement, where the popular prejudices were, as it were, academic and the question might therefore be considered almost in an abstract sense. Hence, notwithstanding one or two preliminary rebuffs, it ultimately proved possible for the deputy Dupont to carry a favorable motion through the National Assembly extending equal rights to all Jews without distinction (September 27, 1791).

The principle of Jewish equality was henceforth bound up with the Revolution. It was introduced without any difficulty in 1796 into Holland, where the disabilities hitherto suffered were milder than anywhere else on the Continent, and the Jews were already permitted to share in the life and the interests of their neighbors. Two Jews were elected almost immediately afterward to the National Assembly; and henceforth in Holland, alone in Europe, unqualified religious equality was the rule until 1940, regardless of the changes of government or of the personality of the ruler. The same principle was imposed by the Armies of the Republic in the Rhineland and in Italy, where the destruction of the Ghetto gates automatically followed the French occupation; the abolition of the Ghetto of Venice in 1797 and of Rome in 1810, of Mainz in 1798 and of Frankfort in 1811, were landmarks in the history of the Jewish emancipation. It was imitated by friendly or temporizing governments throughout Germany during the French hegemony, and ultimately even, with only slight reservations, in Prussia as part of the general administrative reforms of 1812 which preceded the War of Liberation. In all these regions the Jews now began to participate in an increasing degree in general life, sometimes filling municipal or local office. Moreover, Jews were conscribed in all the national armies at this time of constant warfare, many becoming officers; thus one of the oldest anti-Jewish prejudices was destroyed and a community of interest and responsibility was recognized in fact, and sealed by community of sacrifice. This was something that no subsequent reaction could easily destroy.

In 1806 Napoleon assembled at Paris a theatrically conceived "Sanhedrin," composed of lay and rabbinical representatives and modeled with somewhat ludicrous antiquarianism on what was believed to be the constitution of the ancient Supreme Council of Palestinian Jewry. Summoned in reality in order to assist in breaking down the last bulwarks of Jewish separatism, it was of little practical importance in fact, notwithstanding its somewhat humiliating declaration of the incumbency on the Jews of all civil responsibilities—a point on which the emperor professed to entertain some doubts, after he passed through Alsace on his way back from Austerlitz. In spite of everything the assembly greatly impressed popular imagination as a symbol of emancipation; and the Jewish communities of the French Empire were now ostentatiously reorganized under governmental auspices, with a symmetrical system of Consistories and a hierarchy of Grand Rabbis, who were expected to assist in organizing their flocks for the good of the Napoleonic state.

After Waterloo the Jews were everywhere affected by the general reaction that set in, the old regime restoring, as a rule, the old code. Nevertheless, there were exceptions. Moreover, the memory of the events of the past generation could not be canceled, nor was it possible to destroy by mere legislative action the community of interest and of outlook that had prevailed during the past years. Before the Revolution, the Jews had appeared to be mysterious aliens; henceforth in most places they were at the most unpopular or merely unfortunate neighbors. Moreover, the *status quo ante* was nowhere restored in all its details. There were some features, such as the enforced wearing of the Jewish badge of shame or yellow hat, which were permitted to lapse even in the most reactionary states, and it was only in certain areas in Italy (in particular the Papal States, the duchy of Modena, the kingdom of Sardinia) that the Ghetto was restored in its former gloom. Jewish shopkeepers, Jewish physicians, Jewish lawyers and Jewish bankers now shared the general outlook and interests of their Christian neighbors, though they might not enjoy all the same rights. Moreover, as the darker aspects of Napoleonic totalitarianism receded into oblivion and it began to figure in retrospect almost as a halcyon period in the eyes of political visionaries, it was impossible to forget that while it lasted the Jews had enjoyed equality. Thus the cause of emancipation—not merely the removal of disabilities—was henceforth a question of practical politics, becoming in due course an integral feature of the liberal and democratic programs everywhere. Moreover, a number of Jews, despairing of the attainment of any sort of amelioration in their status under the current regimes, reactionary in a religious as well as political sense, threw themselves heart and soul into the liberal and revolutionary movements that gathered force. (An outstanding yet typical figure was Gabriel Riesser [1808-1863], a leader in the constitutional struggle in Germany at this period; but there were many more among the lesser leaders and the rank and file, the mention of whose names would fill pages.) In such cases, entry was secured into public life as it were by a trap door; for when success was achieved it was hardly possible for the former agitators and conspirators to exclude from its advantages those who had worked so self-sacrificingly for it in the underground movements.

There was, moreover, a standard of emancipation which could serve as the ideal. Not only were the Jews enjoying full civic rights in the United States of America, where their numbers were increasing with every immigrant ship that put into port at Boston or New York. In Europe, too, religious equality remained a fact in the Low Countries, where the experiment had proved outstandingly successful; and when Belgian independence was established in 1830, it was perpetuated there, somewhat paradoxically, under international guarantee (including that of powers which still indulged in serious discrimination) as a fundamental principle of the constitution. In France emancipation represented a principle with which the restored monarchy did not dare to tamper. In 1817 the time arrived for the expiry of certain economic disabilities imposed by Napoleon by the *Décret Infâme* (as the Jews had termed it) issued at Madrid in 1807 when the findings of the Grand Sanhedrin were implemented, but enforced only in Alsace. Such had been the experience of the past ten years that no one seriously championed their renewal, and after 1831 Jewish ministers of religion also received salaries from the state as did the Catholics and Protestants. (By a curious time lag, however, the special oath in the courts of law *more judaico* remained in force for another few years, though not in its most degrading form.) As for England, the cessation of immigration during the protracted wars had facilitated the development of a native, highly assimilated and socially emancipated Jewish community, which played some part in general life. The brothers Benjamin (1755-1800) and Abraham (1756-1810) Goldsmid had helped to make Pitt's war finance possible by breaking the ring of extortionate loan brokers who had formerly monopolized the treasury issues, and entered into the social circle of the royal dukes, sons of King George III. They were both dead by the time of Waterloo, but the family still continued to be influential; and there were others whose prominence was not much less. Thus in these years an English Jewry, in a somewhat different sense than hitherto, had begun to emerge. But it was not only here that the financial exigencies of the war period, and the prodigious progress of the Industrial Revolution in the succeeding years, favored the emergence of a group of Jewish financiers. The most prominent of these by far was the international house of Rothschild. Their most gifted member, Nathan Meyer Rothschild (1777-1836), who is said to have been the greatest financial genius of all time, had settled in London, where he financed the later stages of the Napoleonic Wars and played a great part in the tremendous economic development of subsequent years; his brother James (1792-1868) in Paris was little less gifted, and surviving him by more than thirty years, continued to dominate the money markets of the world for another generation. Other branches of the firm were established in Vienna, Frankfort and Naples, all shrewdly managed and working in close collaboration with one another. The influence exercised by this house in particular was greater than that of many of the minor powers, and sometimes determined the policy of the major ones. The continued exclusion of the Jews from civil rights thus became not only reactionary, but also in a sense paradoxical.

Nevertheless, the struggle proved to be long and checkered. In Germany, where the old prejudices yielded only slowly and superficially, there were still occasional outbursts of violence in the old style—especially in 1819, to the accompaniment of cries of *Hep! Hep!* (the initials of *Hierosolyma est perdita*, traditionally though not factually the anti-Jewish slogan of the period of the Crusades). In 1818, notwithstanding the deliberations of the Congress of Vienna and the protests of the Concert of Europe, the free cities of Bremen and Luebeck expelled the Jews recently settled there, on the pretext that the rights of settlement granted under the French were no longer binding. Young men of promise and ambition, despairing of being able to make their way as Jews in a hostile world, cynically accepted baptism in increasing numbers, though in many cases (such as those of Ludwig Boerne and Heinrich Heine) continuing to preserve throughout life a nostalgia for the environment of their younger days. For the moment the change of faith was sufficient to remove all discrimination, though (as will be seen) a terrible harvest for the future was thereby sown.

The liberal movement of 1830 brought the question of emancipation forward again as a matter of practical politics, and in some of the short-lived revolutionary governments in Italy emancipation was actually established for a short while, though it was canceled when the old regimes returned. The constitutional movement now being launched, henceforth the problem was generally one of exclusion from civic and political rather than from human rights; this was, however, still the case in certain areas, such as the Papal States, where the medieval Ghetto system was still imposed without the slightest modification of any significance. Nevertheless, though in 1833 full equality was spontaneously reaccorded to the Jews of Hesse Cassel and in 1834 to those of Brunswick, none of the greater German states followed suit for a long while. Hence in the revolutionary movement that swept Europe in 1848 the Jews everywhere took an exceptionally prominent part. In France, Adolphe Crémieux was a member of the Provisional Government; in Germany, several Jews were killed in the street fighting in Berlin, and Gabriel Riesser was a Vice-President of the *Vorparlament* of Frankfort; the heroic March days at Vienna were encouraged by the poet Moritz Hartmann and the journalist Ignaz Kuranda; in Hungary, a Jewish regiment fought under Kossuth; in Italy, Jews were among the followers of Garibaldi, the coadjutors of Mazzini in the Roman Republic and afterward in exile, and disproportionally prominent in the idealistic republic set up under the half-Jew Daniel Manin at Venice. In the reforming fervor of this period, state after state throughout Central Europe granted a liberal constitution. The Austrian and Hungarian Diets carried motions in favor of the full emancipation of the Jews; in Germany the only important fraction that maintained its reactionary policy was Bavaria; in Italy emancipation was everywhere granted completely and without reservation.

A period of reaction followed, however, in which the new constitutions were either withdrawn or else rendered nugatory. In the German states, indeed, the newly won Jewish rights were seldom canceled outright, but in practice they were severely restricted; so that even the degrading oath *more judaico* and the restriction on the number of Jewish marriages and households remained the rule in many parts. Nevertheless, on the balance the liberal movement made slow headway. In France the somewhat feverish financial and industrial development under the Second Empire brought the Jews to terms of complete equality with their neighbors in a sense which was hardly to be reckoned in purely legal terms, and Achille Fould became Minister of Finance in 1849 and again in 1861. In England, where the economic development was on similar though more sober lines, it had proved impossible, owing to the opposition of the House of Lords, to secure the political emancipation of the Jews in 1830 as a logical sequel to that of the Roman Catholics and Nonconformists, although after the Reform Bill of 1832 the new middle-class House of Commons had declared itself unequivocally in favor of it. Other disabilities, however (which in England were never overwhelmingly serious), were progressively removed, to a large extent through the civic ambitions and skillful pertinacity of David Salomons (1797-1873). In 1830 the Jews were first admitted to the freedom of the City of London, and thereby empowered for the first time to open shops for retail trade in the City and to become members of Livery Companies; in 1839 Salomons became the first Jewish sheriff, and ten years later, after long delays and obstructions, the first Jewish alderman, the path being thus opened for his becoming Lord Mayor in 1855. The first Jewish barrister had been admitted in 1833; the first Jewish grand juror in 1835; and a Jew first given an hereditary title when Isaac Lyon Goldsmid was created a baronet in 1841 (the Dutch financier Solomon de Medina had been knighted by William III nearly a hundred and fifty years earlier). Thus, as the nineteenth century approached its meridian, the only important disability remaining for the English Jews was that they could not sit in Parliament (though they had been admitted informally to the franchise, it seems, even in the eighteenth century). In 1847 Baron Lionel de Rothschild, head of the famous banking house, was nominated and elected member of Parliament for the City of London, where he occupied an outstanding position. He was nevertheless unable to take his seat owing to the form of oath "on the true faith of a Christian" which statutorily had to be taken, in those terms, by every member. A series of Relief Bills was passed by the Commons—fourteen in all, in various forms, counting from the beginning—but were mechanically rejected by the strongly Conservative House of Lords. Rothschild resigned his seat, but stood again, and was re-elected time after time—all to no purpose. Meanwhile, Salomons attempted to achieve the same end by direct action, as he had done in municipal politics, and after being elected for Greenwich in 1851 assumed his seat without taking the objectionable oath in statutory form, and both spoke and voted in the debates that resulted from his action. He was nevertheless removed from the House, and heavily penalized. But it was now becoming obvious that a way would have to be found to solve the deadlock between Lords and Commons. In 1858, accordingly, a compromise was reached, a new Jewish Relief Bill being passed which empowered either House to stipulate the form of oath to be administered in special circumstances. Ten years after his election, Rothschild at last took his seat in the Lower House, as the first Jewish member of Parliament; and there was henceforth no reason why a Jew should not become a member of the House of Lords if the sovereign conferred a peerage upon him, which actually happened in the case of Rothschild's son in 1885.

In central Europe, meanwhile, as the new bourgeoisie pushed its way to the fore, the arrested process of emancipation again began to make headway, in accordance with the liberal spirit of the age, once the interlude of reaction was ended. There was full and (as it seemed at the time) final removal of Jewish civic and political disabilities in Baden in 1862, in Saxony in 1868, in Austria and Hungary by the *Ausgleich* of 1868; and it became a fundamental principle of the reorganization of the German states on "modern" principles in these years. When the North German Federation was established in 1869, its constitution embodied a clause which abolished all restrictions of whatever sort due to religious opinions. Two years later, the German Imperial Constitution adopted the same principle, which thus became extended to those few parts of the country which had not yet fallen into line. It seemed to have triumphed for good.

In Italy the abolition of Jewish disabilities had been extracted somewhat reluctantly in Piedmont (the kingdom of Sardinia) in 1848 as a result of the agitation led by the idealistic man of letters Massimo d'Azeglio. However unwillingly granted by the Crown, it was loyally observed; and as Piedmont expanded into the kingdom of Italy by the absorption or conquest of the other Italian states, the same principle was extended step by step throughout the peninsula, as part of the fundamental laws of the state—in Tuscany and the duchy of Modena in 1860, in Venice in 1866 and so on. In 1870, with the capture of Rome and the end of the long-obscurantist temporal rule of the Popes, the process reached its culmination. There was no land in which emancipation was more complete, socially as well as politically; with the result that a rapid disintegration of Jewish communal and religious life began, and Italian Jewry became largely assimilated.

Elsewhere in Europe the process was closely paralleled. In Denmark the handful of Jews had obtained extensive rights in 1814, were admitted to municipal offices in 1837, and achieved full emancipation in 1848. (Only there and in Piedmont were the advances of that year fully preserved.) The handful of Jews in Sweden obtained full civic rights as the result of a series of ordinances beginning in 1853. Two years earlier, the legal exclusion of the Jews from Norway was ended, and in 1891 full emancipation was granted, although the number of persons involved was inconsiderable.

In Switzerland, as late as the middle of the nineteenth century, intolerance was still so extreme that, as in the Middle Ages, most cantons refused to admit Jews even temporarily. This resulted in a diplomatic struggle lasting for many years with England, the United States and especially France, which refused to sign any agreement for commercial reciprocity from the benefits of which some of her subjects would be automatically excluded. One by one, however, the various cantons adopted a more liberal policy, the last geographical exclusion ending in 1866; to be followed by the proclamation of full religious liberty for all inhabitants of the country on the revision of the federal constitution eight years after.

Thus it may be said, by and large, that the third quarter of the nineteenth century saw the achievement of religious liberty throughout central and western Europe—except in Spain, where notwithstanding all efforts the old exclusive policy was in effect unmodified. The year 1870-71 thus marked the grand climacteric of the liberal era in Europe, and with it the climax of the emancipation of the Jews.

Side by side with the change in political circumstances there was a drastic alteration in the Jew's social and economic life, as well as in his general outlook. The progress of assimilation, which had formerly affected only a handful of the upper stratum, was making greater and greater strides. In every country the Jew became fully integrated, in custom, in language and in social habit; the synagogue service tended to conform in external conventions with the accepted standards of the religious life of the country: a vernacular literature sprang up to interpret Judaism to those ignorant of Hebrew; rabbinical seminaries were established to train spiritual leaders in a more modern tradition, the first being opened at Padua in 1829. Frequently, the process went a good deal further, "Reform" (and later on more extreme "Liberal") movements being organized in order to present Judaism in more elaborately assimilated terms, with the concomitant of the weakening or quasi abandonment of the use of Hebrew in religious services and the omission from the revised prayer book of references to a national restoration to Palestine, formerly so passionately craved. Thus, the Jew was presented as an Englishman, Frenchman or German, of the "Jewish" or even, to avoid that despised word, "Mosaic" persuasion. In many cases assimilation went further, culminating in widespread intermarriage and the abandonment of Judaism, whether formally or (in a vastly greater number of cases) informally. Economically, too, the old Jewish distinctiveness was modified, though the proletariat still tended to be engaged in distinctive occupations such as tailoring, and the Jews were more prominent in the distribution of goods than in their production. With the improvement in communications and the consequent expansion of the normal business radius, there was a great proclivity, especially in western Europe, to abandon the small centers that had once been important in Jewish life and to become concentrated in the cities, with the result that everywhere many of the formerly numerous rural and semirural communities were in time entirely abandoned. Later the lure of the cities increased more and more. Whereas in the beginning of the nineteenth century no Jewish community in the world can have exceeded 20,000 inhabitants (there were few that remotely approached this figure) a century and a quarter later one-fifth of all Jews lived in groups exceeding 250,000, and one-quarter in cities the population of which was more than a million. It was true of the Jews as of their neighbors that the city was the graveyard of the countryside; and the diminution of the average size of the family, added to the inroads of intermarriage and assimilation, was so great as to menace western European Jewry with quasi extinction within a measurable period. It was only the constant influx from the teeming Ghettos of Russia and Poland that obscured this intimidating tendency, which, though little realized, was at the beginning of the twentieth century perhaps the most significant fact in Jewish life in other lands.

In order to confront the new circumstances, there was an instinctive readjustment of Jewish life. When in 1840 a ritual murder accusation was brought up in Damascus, a delegation of the English and French Jewish communities was sent to the Levant, headed by the English philanthropist Sir Moses Montefiore (1784-1885) and the French lawyer-politician Adolphe Crémieux (1796-1880) in order to seek redress. This created a tremendous impression at the time. Though the French government, for reasons of prestige, was lukewarm or even antagonistic, the British warmly favored the delegation and gave it all possible support. The episode seemed in a way to symbolize the new phase of life into which Occidental Jewry had entered; and the delegates were greeted everywhere almost dithyrambically on their return, after having secured the release of the accused men, the withdrawal of the charge against them, and an edict from the sultan condemning the ritual murder libel in unequivocal terms. Similar action was taken from time to time subsequently on occasions of this sort, as for example (a notorious instance) when in 1858 the Jewish child Edgardo Mortara was kidnaped in Bologna by the papal government so that he should be brought up as a Christian, on the pretext that his nurse had secretly baptized him some while earlier (not by any means the last instance of this abuse in the states of the Church). Thus, a protracted activity for the assistance of the Jews in "backward" countries was begun by such organizations as the Board of Deputies of British Jews, founded as early as 1760, but previously active only intermittently; and the *Alliance Israélite Universelle*, established by French Jewry in 1860 as an educational and philanthropic organization for work abroad (to be reinforced by similar bodies in other countries, as for example the *Hilfsverein der deutschen Juden*, founded in 1901, and the Anglo-Jewish Association, founded in 1871). Such philanthropic work, which in the end assumed an impressive scale, was to become one of the distinguishing features of the nineteenth century in Jewish life. Moses Montefiore's prodigiously long and active career, on the one side, and, on the other, the French determination to utilize the Jewish philanthropic urge for expansionist purposes (coupled with the exceptional generosity of the French House of Rothschild) set the seal on the supremacy of the communities of these two countries in political work. German Jewry, perhaps conscious of its own weakness in this respect, was left, on the other hand, in almost unchallenged command of the new Jewish learning, the

Juedische Wissenschaft, in which it made a most impressive contribution covering every imaginable facet of Jewish scholarship in the modern sense along the lines laid down by that remarkable pioneer Lepold Zunz (1794-1886).

The Jews had naturally not hesitated to make full use of the opportunities that opened up before them as individuals in this new age: indeed, there were some who regarded it as their duty, in exchange for the emancipation that they had attained. In public life they played their part without reservation in every country. Thus, Adolphe Crémieux was Minister of Justice in France, Eduard Lasker led the National Party in the German Reichstag, Isaac Artom was among the architects of the Italian Risorgimento and the baptized, but nevertheless Jewishly inclined, Benjamin Disraeli, the father of British imperialism in its new sense, became Prime Minister of England. Similarly the modern Socialist movement was founded by Ferdinand Lassalle; while Karl Marx, who was of Jewish parentage though fundamentally and intensely antagonistic to Judaism, became the prophet of communism and one of the most influential figures of the age. The pre-eminence of the English and French branches of the House of Rothschild in finance continued throughout the century. There were several other important Jewish banking houses (especially in Germany), such as those of Bleichroeder, Stern, Seligman, Hirsch, Warburg, Worms, and Erlanger.

So, too, in every other branch of activity.[5] In literature there was, for example, Heinrich Heine, the most eminent German man of letters of the nineteenth century at least, and Georg Brandes, the greatest Danish critic; in music, the name of Felix Mendelssohn was among the very greatest, while Offenbach had many of Wagner's gifts except that of taking himself seriously, and many of the greatest instrumentalists of the time were Jews; in humanitarianism, the Jews took a prominent share in movements as diverse as those for the establishment and maintenance of international peace—a natural Jewish preoccupation (Fried, Bloch), for the teaching of deaf-mutes (Péreire, Prager), for the prevention of cruelty to animals (Gompertz, sponsor of the R.S.P.C.A.); in the visual arts, Pissarro, Liebermann, and Israels, and Modigliani and Epstein later, are a few outstanding names out of very many; in mechanics, Jews were closely associated with the development of the radio, of the telephone, of the automobile, of the airplane. Jewish mathematicians, economists, physicists, astronomers, philosophers, historians, art experts came to the fore everywhere. In medicine the name of Ehrlich is only one out of an entire galaxy, through whose collaboration the sum of human suffering was triumphantly reduced in the course of these years. Jewish jurists codified their countries' laws, Jewish travelers explored unfamiliar parts of the earth's surface, Jewish soldiers attained high rank in the armies of several countries, Jewish philanthropists were responsible for the foundation of many beneficent institutions and the enriching of many public collections. In the course of a single generation, in short, the Jews attempted to catch up and even to overtake their neighbors in all those branches of activity from which they had so long been excluded; and they achieved a fatal degree of success. Above all, in the economic life (now in a fluid state owing to the remarkable developments of the Industrial Revolution and its sequel) their success was perhaps too ostentatious, for the circumstances of their history permitted them to adapt themselves to new conditions with greater speed and success than their neighbors.

The result of all this was the development, *pari passu* with Jewish emancipation and achievement, of bitter feelings of jealousy, above all in those countries precisely where the Jews had shown themselves most vital. Motivated historically in the last instance by the lingering effect of theological prejudice of the Middle Ages (still affecting folklore, literature and religious teaching) it now lacked this quasi justification; for it was directed to a great extent against persons who no longer professed Judaism or had even been formally converted to Christianity. This in turn gave a remarkable impetus to the scientifically untenable but emotionally satisfying racial theories (based in the last instance on the writings of Renan and other cloistered scholars, who were appalled at these developments) that were beginning to spread. The results, which, so far as western Europe was concerned, caused discomfort but little more at the end of the nineteenth century and appeared almost negligible or even ludicrous at the beginning of the twentieth, ended in our own day by the destruction of Jewish life on the continent of Europe, and almost brought Western civilization itself to ruin.

The focus of the infection was Germany, where the participation of the Jews in general life (in what seemed to the outside world at least in a quintessentially Germanic sense) was more complete and more impressive than in almost any other country. Here, accordingly, the emancipation of the Jews, eyed askance by some elements from the outset, was followed by an immediate reaction when its success became apparent. This received a great impetus from the financial crisis of 1873, due to the blundering exaction of a war indemnity from France but blamed automatically, as a matter of course, on the Jewish speculators. Not very threatening at the outset, it suddenly gathered strength in 1879 through the secret backing of Bismarck, who found in it a useful weapon for use against the National Liberal Party founded and led by Jews, which had gone into opposition against him when his antidemocratic bent became apparent, and which he hoped to embarrass and to discredit by this means. Thus fecundated and financed, the movement spread with extraordinary and distressing rapidity throughout Germany. Part of its success was due to the new name "anti-Semitism" (invented by the journalist Wilhelm Marr) under which it was organized—emphasizing "racial" rather than theological antipathies and thus avoiding the charge, which under the circumstances might have been fatal, of perpetuating medieval religious fanaticism. The court preacher Adolph Stoecker put himself at its head, founding the Christian Socialist Workingmen's Union to support it. For the next few years, the movement gathered momentum. It sent a solid block of deputies to the Reichstag, where inflammatory speeches against the Jews were now heard. An Anti-Semitic League was organized and in 1881 presented to the government a petition signed by 250,000 persons demanding their disfranchisement. There was anti-Jewish rioting here and there, in the course of which some synagogues were destroyed. Emancipation notwithstanding, Jews still found themselves excluded from commissions in the army and chairs in the universities, unless they were prepared to abjure their faith. A vast anti-Semitic literature was published, and replied to with more enthusiasm than judgment and in such volume as to tend to publicize rather than mitigate the onslaught. A succession of scandals deprived the movement of something of its strength in the new century, but it remained a powerful organized force, still strongly represented in the Reichstag and the various Diets and obviously with vast reserves of sympathy among the German bourgeoisie.

From Germany the movement spread to the neighboring countries. In Austria-Hungary it found a fertile soil, notwithstanding—or perhaps because of—the remarkable achievements of the Jews in making Vienna one of the intellectual and economic capitals of Europe. Indeed, it was found useful there not only by the minorities who wished to discredit the central government and by the reactionaries, but even by the left wing, who tried to split the Clericalist camp by attacking those in it who were of Jewish extraction. The relapse into obscurantism was such that in 1882 a ritual murder trial was staged in the full medieval tradition at Tisza-Eszlar in Hungary, to be imitated before long in Germany as well. For many years a professed anti-Semitic administration under Karl Lueger controlled Vienna.

In France the new anti-Semitism was introduced on the disastrous collapse in 1882 of the Roman Catholic financial institution, the *Union Générale*, which had been set up in opposition to the Protestant and Jewish banking houses; and it received a powerful impetus four years later when Edouard Drumont published his prodigiously successful *La France Juive*, exaggerating the part that the Jews were playing in French life and alleging that they were deliberately working against the interests of the country. The movement attained an outstanding success when in 1894 a Jewish army officer, Captain Alfred Dreyfus, whose appointment to the General Staff had caused some adverse comment (he was the first Jew to achieve this distinction), was accused of espionage in favor of Germany. He was tried before a court-martial, to the accompaniment of an outburst of wild anti-Jewish agitation in the press and among the public, and was found guilty; he was publicly degraded the following January on the parade ground of the Ecole Militaire and sent to the penal settlement of Devil's Island off French Guiana to serve a sentence of life imprisonment. Subsequently, evidence was presented which showed that the document on which the case against him depended was a forgery by another hand. The sympathy of Emile Zola, the outstanding French man of letters of the time, was aroused, and he published his famous appeal to the French people, *J'accuse,* charging the War Office with a deliberate miscarriage of justice and demanding the reopening of the case. The whole country was divided into two camps, for or against the condemned man. On the one side stood the anti-Semites, the royalists, the clericals and the army, who felt that even if the charge were unjustified it was necessary to persist in it for the sake of the state and of the credit of the armed forces; on the other were the liberals, the republicans and those convinced that justice must be the overwhelming consideration in government. Colonel Henry, of the General Staff, committed fresh forgeries to bolster up the accusation, and took his life when his action was discovered. Nevertheless, it was only in 1899, after a Liberal Ministry had entered into office, that Dreyfus was brought back to France for retrial. A Council of War sitting at Rennes condemned him once more, though reducing the sentence and asserting extenuating circumstances. This was an attempt to secure appeasement rather than justice, as was made clear when the president granted the accused man a free pardon. Later the Court of Appeal quashed the verdict, and Dreyfus's innocence was publicly vindicated. So great had the agitation been, however, and so bitter were the feelings aroused that at one time the episode nearly brought down the Republic, and events half a century later were to show that the feelings aroused at this time were still seething beneath the surface with undiminished violence. Although in France itself the campaign remained physically harmless, generally speaking (this was one of its curious features), it was succeeded by a dangerous outbreak of rioting in the French colony of Algeria, in the course of which a number of lives were lost.

If in western Europe the anti-Semitic movement was on the whole academic, the repercussions in Russia, where German "science" was regarded with the profoundest deference, were of the most deplorable description; and it was not perhaps entirely a coincidence that the terrible series of pogroms that changed the face of Jewry throughout the world broke out at Elisavetgrad on April 27, 1881—two days after the presentation of the mammoth anti-Semitic petition in Berlin to Chancellor Bismarck. The mass emigration from Russia that resulted from this added a helpless, pauper foreign element to the more or less assimilated communities of other European lands. Crowding together for both economic and social reasons in their own quarters, strangers in appearance, language and habits, competing helplessly for any work that was available, they inevitably added to the general anti-Jewish feeling, which now became intensified and complicated by xenophobia. The prohibition of Jewish immigration was one of the demands of the German anti-Semites, and was indeed acted upon with some consistency by the government, which on occasion went so far as to expel recent arrivals. The main tide of Russian emigration was directed, however, to England, where the Jewish population rose from about 60,000 to 160,000 between the years 1880 and 1900. Here, the whole face of Jewish life was transformed in consequence, the process though on a far smaller scale being identical with that which took place during these same years in the United States of America. New communities sprang up or the old ones were reinforced; the Jewish settlements in Leeds (25,000 by the 1930's), Manchester (33,000), Glasgow (15,000), as well as in London (234,000) attained important dimensions; Yiddish literature and journalism were introduced; a Jewish trade-union movement, not without influence on general industrial organization, came into being; the fast disappearing London Ghetto was enormously recruited and took on a new and essentially alien aspect. As in America, the immigrants tended to find employment mainly in the cheap tailoring industry, into which they introduced the new methods of mass production (thereby greatly benefiting the lower classes and helping to bridge the rift between the social life of rich and poor), and to a minor extent in cabinetmaking. As in America, too, they tended at the beginning to crowd together unhealthily and to accept underpaid employment. This, as it happened, coincided with a period of economic depression in England generally. It gave rise in consequence to a widespread anti-alien agitation, which as it developed was not without specific anti-Jewish features—heightened by the prominence and ostentation of some of the members of the new plutocracy, at the other end of the social scale. (There had indeed been mutterings at least of the new anti-Semitism, led by the eminent economist Goldwyn Smith, when the movement had started on the Continent.) At Limerick, in Ireland, a boycott was even organized at this period by an overzealous Catholic priest against the handful of alien Jewish shopkeepers. A Royal Commission on Alien Immigration was set up in 1902-1903, which afforded the opportunity for the fullest possible expression of opposition to the new influx. Its findings exonerated the Jewish immigrants from the more serious accusations of their critics, and specifically championed the continuation of the traditional right of asylum. Nevertheless, the consequent Aliens Immigration Act of 1905 was conceived in a drastic spirit; and henceforth the tide of immigration—though only of the more impecunious elements, as critics hastened to point out—was stemmed.

Yet the impetus of the emancipatory movement of the nineteenth century was by no means exhausted. In the Liberal administration that began to govern England in 1905, professing Jews attained higher rank than they had ever done before, Rufus Isaacs (later Marquess of Reading) becoming Attorney General (1910) and then Lord Chief Justice (1913), and Herbert Samuel being admitted to the Cabinet (1909). The close intimacy between Edward VII and a group of Jews—especially members of the Rothschild and Sassoon families, as well as the Jewish-born Sir Ernest Cassel—was both symbolic of and instrumental toward the final consummation of the process of emancipation in England. It went further here indeed than in any European land other than Italy, where Luigi Luzzatti, eminent economist who "spiritualized the power of gold" by the establishment of co-operatives and People's Banks and who had already served as Minister of the Treasury, was Prime Minister from 1909 to 1911. In France, too, the more intense feelings aroused by the Dreyfus Affair had apparently subsided, and the standing of the Jews in the country was at its highest at this period, particularly in its artistic and intellectual aspects. Even in Germany organized anti-Semitism was apparently on the wane, and in the 1903 elections the strength of the party in the Reichstag, which had once stood at double the number, fell to nine. The election of 1907, it is true, brought the figure up again to the record figure of twenty-five; but it was possible to explain this, and the simultaneous revival of the Christian Socialist Party in Austria, as the result of political maneuvers and of a skillful exploitation of nationalist feelings. Commissions in the army and chairs in the universities were still withheld from professing Jews; but there was no restriction of the sort on those who had been baptized, while Kaiser Wilhelm II counted among his closest intimates men like Albert Ballin, creator of the Hamburg-America Line and of the German merchant marine.

Portugal, where Jews had been living informally since the close of the eighteenth century, abolished religious disabilities on the proclamation of the republic in 1910; while at this time some Spanish statesmen were sentimentally toying with the idea of reinviting to the country the descendants of the exiles of 1492—who still spoke Spanish and preserved forgotten Hispanic traditions in their havens of refuge in North Africa and the Levant. The birth of the anti-Semitic movement, and the ever-succeeding waves of emigration from the Russian Empire in consequence of the recurrent pogroms, had only clouded, not dispelled, the glowing halo of nineteenth-century liberalism; and indeed it was generally considered that the reorganization of the empire of the czars as a parliamentary democracy in the tolerant Western sense was in the long run inevitable. In the British

Empire overseas there was now a community of some importance, mainly British in origin and in organization, in Australia, and another in which the eastern European element was more strongly represented in South Africa, where Jews figured prominently among the "Randlords" who had amassed facile fortunes in the newly found gold and diamond mines; this prominence, however, was in some ways undesirable and did not fail to attract adverse comment. The Canadian community similarly had a rapid development, parallel in many ways to that of the United States. Of the stimulating effect of the influx of eastern European refugees into these lands there can be no question. It took place at a period when the vitality of the communities that had been emancipated in the nineteenth century had begun to flag; and it is significant that Italian Jewry, which was unaffected by the movement of population, was so drastically assimilated.

It seemed at one stage as though the war of 1914-1918 would have completed the retarded process of emancipation where it was still necessary. The Revolution in Russia, it was hoped, would not only bring emancipation to its Jews, but also relieve the pressure on their coreligionists elsewhere; the democratic republics that were to be established on its western confines would of course treat their Jewish population as equals; and with the sweeping away of the old regimes in central Europe, Germanic anti-Semitism, too, would disappear. The alliance between emancipation and the Western democracies seemed to be sealed when the Balfour Declaration was issued, amid the enthusiasm of the Jewish masses. The participation of Jews in public life in England, France and Italy was never so outstanding as in the war and postwar periods, and Sir John Monash, Commander in Chief of the Australian forces in the field, was one only of a number of Jewish generals who fought in the Allied ranks. In Germany, too, some of the traditional anti-Jewish restrictions were now relaxed; and Walter Rathenau in the field of administration, Fritz Haber in science, and Albert Ballin in industry, proved themselves at this time to be among the Reich's most useful children. In all the countries involved in the hostilities, Jews served in the field and suffered heavy casualties, twenty thousand German Jews alone making the supreme sacrifice. (There can be no doubt that the communities were weakened disproportionately as a result of this slaughter—a consideration which has not been taken into adequate account in assessing the contemporary Jewish scene.) At the Peace Conference held in Paris, at which the representatives of Jewish organizations in Europe and America were heard with a degree of deference never before known, an honest attempt was made to secure Jewish rights in central and eastern Europe by a series of Minorities Treaties, generously conceived, but perhaps reflecting more the good intentions than the statecraft of those responsible, and leaving many loopholes for evasion.

On the other hand, the nationalistic feelings always aroused in time of war resulted in every country in a certain degree of anti-Jewish agitation, which left dangerous seeds behind it. The popular equation after 1917 of Jew and Bolshevik, unjustified though it was, made the situation more delicate. In every country of Europe, the egregious *Protocols of the Elders of Zion*, purporting to reveal in a series of fantastic documents mysteriously discovered a Jewish plot to secure the domination of the world, had a considerable circulation and secured credence in circles which were not usually so gullible. Even in England organized anti-Semitism began to show itself to some extent. Meanwhile, the decline in the importance of international banking through the disruption caused by the war, and the consequent weakening of a class that had previously been influential both inside and outside the community; the disaster that overtook the old bourgeoisie in Germany in 1924 during the semifraudulent government inflation; the death in action of many of the natural leaders of the rising generation; the weakening of Jewish allegiances by the calls of the new political ideologies; and the internecine quarrels that resulted from the advance of the ideas of Zionism and Jewish nationalism—all these factors combined to weaken more and more the Jewish powers of resistance and the cohesion that had formerly been marked.

In Germany the traditional anti-Semitism was reinforced by new charges—that Jewish treachery had been responsible for the country's defeat in battle, that they were in complete control of the Weimar Republic, that they were in alliance with the Bolsheviks for the overthrow of Western civilization, that the relatively unimportant influx of eastern European workers and refugees during the war (who indeed had brought about a notable quickening of cultural values) was of such dimensions as to constitute a national menace. The undoubted prominence of the Jews in German cultural life (not to any exceptional degree in politics, however) gave a certain color to the propaganda, but it remained to be shown that it was in any sense undesirable or non-Germanic in character. The agitation against Walter Rathenau, who had been appointed Minister for Reconstruction, culminated in 1922 in his assassination. Numerous anti-Semitic parties came into being, the National Socialist Party founded by Adolf Hitler in 1923 not being the only one which laid the responsibility for all of Germany's ills and grievances upon the Jews. As it turned out, however, it was the most important; and as it gathered strength the anti-Jewish campaign assumed alarming proportions. Once more there was a flood of anti-Jewish publications and an outpouring of anti-Jewish speeches. Assaults on persons of Jewish appearance, the defacing of Jewish public buildings and the desecration of Jewish cemeteries became increasingly common.

When in 1933 the National Socialist Party was borne into office in the trough of a wave of depression, as the result of involved political maneuvers, few persons imagined that it would implement its fantastic anti-Jewish program. But it was in effect the only part of its program that could be carried readily into effect, and moreover provided an easy method of financing a good deal of the rest in its earlier stages. Moreover, by an unhappy fatality, Adolf Hitler was in fact possessed of a blind, unreasoning, all-absorbing mania against the Jews. This was to be responsible in the ensuing years for the greatest tragedy in the history of this or any other people. The initial violence that accompanied the seizure of power by the Nazi Party was followed by the elaboration of a comprehensive anti-Jewish code, preposterously embodying all the medieval restrictions almost without exception, but cunningly enforced by stages so as to acclimatize the idea in the mind of the German people and of the world. Beginning with the extrusion of the Jews from public activities and positions of authority, it rapidly extended so as to cut them off entirely from the life of their neighbors. It applied, moreover, not only to persons professing the Jewish religion, but to all of Jewish birth and even those who were partially of Jewish blood some generations back. The Jews were driven out of the professions, and everything possible was done to organize a boycott of their businesses. In 1935, at the rally of the Nazi Party held at Nuremberg, a new law was announced excluding the Jews in perpetuity from German citizenship and enforcing a number of other restrictive regulations, many of which seemed almost fantastic at the time. Life for Jewish professional men in Germany became impossible; for other Jews appallingly difficult. Some cities even excluded them entirely, as in the Middle Ages. It became obvious that the Age of Emancipation was to be considered only an interlude. German Jewry resumed its history (so at least it seemed: but the actuality was to prove far more terrible) at the point where Moses Mendelssohn had entered it.

The reaction of the Jewish community was memorable. Driven back on its own resources, it reorganized itself in a remarkable fashion. Its children being excluded from the ordinary schools, it built up a fresh educational nexus. No longer allowed to appear at or even to attend public performances, it arranged its own entertainments and theaters. There was a noteworthy intellectual and spiritual revival. How long this could have lasted was doubtful, as it was based upon the dwindling economic resources of a community now forced to be self-contained. In any case it was destined to be violently interrupted. When in March, 1938, Austria was absorbed into the Reich, the process was accompanied by an outburst of incredible brutality against the Jews of Vienna, one of the greatest and most vital Jewish communities of the world (already subjected to discrimination of a more restrained type by the Christian Socialist regime under Dollfuss and Schuschnigg), which scandalized the conscience of

Europe. Synagogues were sacked, communal institutions closed, homes raided, businesses confiscated, rabbis made to perform the most filthy work amid jeering crowds while wearing the symbols of their religion, and delicately nurtured women forced to scrub the pavements with their bare hands. The average number of Jewish deaths rose from under ten to 150 daily. Suicides became appallingly frequent; and the Nazi leaders openly expressed the intention of making the city free of Jews (*Judenrein*) within four years. Yet even this provoked no determined reaction in the conscience of Europe. Thus encouraged, the Nazi government determined to smash what was left of German Jewry. Using the pretext of the assassination of a diplomat in Paris by a young Jew unbalanced by the sufferings of his family, they unleashed an ostensibly spontaneous pogrom throughout Germany on the night of November 9, 1938. Almost every synagogue in the country was destroyed, together with communal centers and institutions. Almost every business house was sacked. Thousands of Jewish homes were raided, tens of thousands of persons were thrown into concentration camps and many were killed. In addition to this a fine of one billion marks (one-third of their property at a generous valuation) was imposed on the Jews of the Reich, they were ordered to transfer their businesses forthwith into "Aryan" hands, and the government solemnly declared its policy to rid the country of all Jews within the shortest possible time. Already since 1933 very large numbers of refugees who saw no future in the land of their birth had done their best to establish themselves elsewhere. The process had been stimulated enormously after the rape of Austria. In 1938 the dam was burst, and throughout the world, in the face of growing restrictions on immigration, commercial jealousies, and the rising tide of xenophobia, hundreds of thousands of central European Jews, many of them literally reduced to beggary, attempted to establish themselves anew. The Hitler annexation of Czechoslovakia in the following year added still further to the flood of human misery, its 350,000 Jews being thrown into the vortex, as were also the smaller groups—at Memel and Danzig—when they came under Nazi influence.

Meanwhile the tide of prejudice had risen menacingly elsewhere. The Nazi propagandists had discovered that the lingering anti-Semitism that could be found or else could be stimulated in all countries constituted a remarkably effective instrument for the extension of sympathy with their views, thus consolidating a pro-German party and preparing the ground for ultimate domination. Vast sums were hence spent on propaganda, the most effective instrument of which was, however, in all probability, the resentment aroused by the presence of masses of refugees. In every country of Europe, Fascist or pseudo-Fascist parties came into being, with antagonism to the Jews as the most important plank in their platforms. In Rumania a declared anti-Semitic government came into power temporarily at the end of 1937 and at once began to enforce restrictive legislation in the German sense. In Hungary, her Jewish population increased by her share in the booty of Czechoslovakia, Judeophobe tendencies had been marked ever since 1918, and had not been checked by the Minorities Treaty.[6] They were now terribly intensified. Even in England consternation was caused by the attempt of the British Union of Fascists, founded by Sir Oswald Mosley, to spread racial and religious prejudice. Conditions were similar in France, Belgium, Holland and other countries.

In Italy, the classic land of Jewish assimilation for the past three-quarters of a century, where some Jews had participated from the beginning in the activities of Fascism, developments were preposterous; for the dwindling handful of some forty thousand Jews, who could fairly be characterized as *italianissimi* in every respect, were ruthlessly offered up on the altar of the Italo-German alliance. At the close of 1938 a code inspired by the Nuremberg laws was suddenly introduced, which punished their eminence as though it were criminal, drove them out of the public life they had long adorned, and forced many to emigrate from the country where their fathers had been settled for twenty centuries. Thus one more was added to the lands of martyrdom, and one more contingent was joined to the never-ending trail of refugees vainly seeking entry into other countries and bringing with them there the seed of their own disaster.

By the middle of 1939 areas that housed upward of 2,500,000 Jews—more than one-quarter of the entire Jewish population of Europe—were thus under the rule or the direct influence of Nazi anti-Semitism. But the cataclysm that began to engulf the world that autumn was to treble the number, and to bring upon them such tribulation as mankind had never before known.[6a]

NOTES

[[1a] Cf. below Anita Libman Lebeson, "The American Jewish Chronicle," p. 449.]

[2] A copy of a new edition of this notable document was presented by the present writer on March 29, 1935, in private audience to Pope Pius XI, whose acceptance of it in effect confirmed his predecessor's pronouncement.

[[3a] Cf. below Walter J. Fischel, "Israel in Iran (A Survey of Judeo-Persian Literature)," pp. 1171-1172.]

[4] John Toland, in his anonymously produced *Reasons for Naturalising the Jews* of 1714 had already put forward a plea for some such measure as this some forty years before. It is important to note that this work, though eminently broad-minded in tone, dealt like the Jew Bill in a practical sense only with the question of facilitating the naturalization of the foreign-born; it had no direct bearing on the broader question of emancipation, as most Jewish historians have erroneously believed and stated. Yet this, too, is significant.

In almost every other country of Europe, the Jews, however long established in the country, were not at this period considered citizens, though at the beginning of the sixteenth century Reuchlin had stoutly maintained that they were.

[5] For more detailed information see *The Jewish Contribution to Civilization* by C. Roth (New York, 1940).

[6] It is noteworthy that the Hungarian Jews had at one time prided themselves on their complete assimilation with their neighbors.

[[6a] See below Bernard D. Weinryb, "East European Jewry (Since the Partitions of Poland, 1772-1795)"; Arieh Tartakower, "The Decline of European Jewry (1933-1953)."]

BIBLIOGRAPHY

Chapters IV and V

There is a rather comprehensive bibliography covering Jewish history in the medieval period, which provides sufficient guidance for the modern period also, appended to the chapter on the Jews in the *Cambridge Medieval History*, Vol. vii. This can be supplemented from the rich material to be found in Salo W. Baron's *Social and Religious History of the Jews* (New York, 1937) and *The Jewish Community* (Philadelphia, 1942). (Cf. also A. S. Freidus, *List of works relating to the history and condition of the Jews in various countries* [New York Public Library, 1914]; and Jacob R. Marcus, *A Brief Introduction to the Bibliography of Modern Jewish History* [Cincinnati, 1935].) There is no need therefore to attempt to make this bibliography comprehensive, but sufficient data will be given to serve as a guide to the American or English reader.

I. GENERAL

GRAETZ, HEINRICH, *Geschichte der Juden von den aeltesten Zeiten bis auf die Gegenwart* (Leipzig, 1897-1911, 2 vols.); English translation ed. Bella Loewy, *History of the Jews* (Philadelphia, 1891-1898, 6 vols.), is abbreviated and unsatisfactory. Notwithstanding the lapse of time, this is still the classical and fundamental history of the Jews on the grand scale.

DUBNOW, SIMON, *Weltgeschichte des juedischen Volkes*. Berlin, 1935-1938, 10 vols. Translated from the Russian.

The Jewish People, Past and Present, The Jewish Encyclopedic Handbooks, Central Yiddish Culture Organization. New York, Vol. I, 1946, Vol. II, 1948, Vol. III, 1952.

MARGOLIS, MAX L., and MARX, ALEXANDER, *A History of the Jewish People.* Philadelphia, 1927.

ROTH, CECIL, *A Short History of the Jewish People* (London, 1948), revised illustrated edition. American edition, abbreviated, *A Bird's Eye View of Jewish History* (Cincinnati, 1936).

There are several other one-volume histories.

ABRAHAMS, ISRAEL, *Jewish Life in the Middle Ages*. New ed. London, 1932.
BARON, SALO W., *The Jewish Community: its History and Structure to the American Revolution.* Philadelphia, 1942.
———, *A Social and Religious History of the Jews*. New York, 1937.
JACOBS, JOSEPH, *Jewish Contributions to Civilization.* Philadelphia, 1919.
KISCH, GUIDO, ed., *Historia Judaica.* New York, 1938-.
MARCUS, JACOB R., *The Jew in the Medieval World; a Source-Book,* 315-1791. Cincinnati, 1940.
MARX, ALEXANDER, *Studies in Jewish History and Booklore.* New York, 1944.
NEWMAN, LOUIS ISRAEL, *Jewish Influence on Christian Reform Movements.* New York, 1925.
ROTH, CECIL, *The Jewish Contribution to Civilization.* London, 1938; New York, 1940.
TRACHTENBERG, JOSHUA, *The Devil and the Jews*. New Haven, London, 1943.

II. CONTEMPORARY JEWISH HISTORY

ELBOGEN, ISMAR, *A Century of Jewish Life* (1840-1940). Philadelphia, 1944.
SACHAR, ABRAM L., *Sufferance is the Badge: The Jew in the Contemporary World.* New York, 1940.

III. THE HISTORY OF THE JEWS IN VARIOUS COUNTRIES

ENGLAND

ADLER, MICHAEL, *Jews of Medieval England.* London, 1939.
JEWISH HISTORICAL SOCIETY OF ENGLAND, *Transactions* and *Miscellanies* from 1895.
ROTH, CECIL, *History of the Jews in England.* New edition, Oxford, 1949.
———, *Magna Bibliotheca Anglo-Judaica.* London, 1937. Provides full guidance for Anglo-Jewish history.
STOKES, H. P., *Studies in Anglo-Jewish History*. Edinburgh, 1913.
WOLF, LUCIEN, *Essays in Jewish History*. London, 1934.

FRANCE

ANCHEL, ROBERT, *Les Juifs de France*. Paris, 1946.
———, *Napoléon et les Juifs*. Paris, 1928.
BERMAN, LÉON, *Histoire des Juifs de France des origines à nos jours*. Paris, 1937.
GROSS, HENRI, *Gallia Judaica*. Paris, 1897.
KAHN, LÉON, *Les Juifs de Paris pendant la Révolution*. Paris, 1898.
POSENER, S., *Adolphe Crémieux*. Paris, 1933-1934; English translation, Philadelphia, 1941.
Revue des Etudes Juives. Paris, 1880-.

HOLLAND AND BELGIUM

BLOOM, HERBERT I., *The Economic Activities of the Jews of Amsterdam in the Seventeenth and Eighteenth Centuries*. Williamsport, 1937.

BRUGMANS, H., and FRANK, A., *Geschiedenis der Joden in Nederland.* 2 vols. Amsterdam, 1939.
ROTH, CECIL, *A Life of Menasseh ben Israel.* Philadelphia, 1934.
ULLMAN, SALOMON, *Etudes sur l'histoire des Juifs en Belgique.* Antwerp, 1927. (And other works.)

ITALY

CASSUTO, UMBERTO, *Gli Ebrei a Firenze nell' età del Rinascimento.* Florence, 1918. Probably the best of all local Jewish histories.
COLORNI, V., *Legge Ebraica e Leggi Locali.* Milan, 1945.
GABRIELI, GIUSEPPE, *Italia Judaica.* Rome, 1924. A bibliography.
ROTH, CECIL, *The History of the Jews of Italy.* Philadelphia, 1946.
VOGELSTEIN, HERMANN, *History of the Jews in Rome.* (Jewish Community Series.) Philadelphia, 1940. Based on his comprehensive German work in collaboration with P. Rieger, *Geschichte der Juden in Rom.* Berlin, 1895-1896.

SPAIN AND PORTUGAL

BAER, FRITZ, *Die Juden im christlichen Spanien.* 2 vols. Berlin, 1929-1936.
———, *haYehudim biSefarad haNozerit* (The Jews in Christian Spain). Jerusalem, 1945.
ISAACS, A. LIONEL, *The Jews of Majorca.* London, 1936.
KATZ, SOLOMON, *The Jews in the Visigothic and Frankish Kingdoms of Spain and Gaul.* Cambridge, Mass., 1937.
MENDES DOS REMEDIOS, JOAQUIM, *Os Judeus em Portugal.* 2 vols. Coimbra, 1895-1928.
NEUMAN, ABRAHAM A., *The Jews in Spain: their social, political and cultural life during the Middle Ages.* Philadelphia, 1942.
ROTH, CECIL, *A History of the Marranos.* Philadelphia, 1932.
Sefarad: Revista de la escuela de Estudios Hebráicos. Madrid, 1941-

GERMANY

ELBOGEN, ISMAR, *Geschichte der Juden in Deutschland.* Berlin, 1935.
ELBOGEN, I., FREIMANN, A., and TYKOCINSKI, H., *Germania Judaica bis 1238.* Breslau, 1934.
Jewish Publication Society: A. Kober, *Cologne* (1940), A. Freimann and Fr. Kracauer, *Frankfort* (1929), M. Grunwald, *Vienna* (1936), R. Strauss *Regensburg and Augsburg* (1939), in Jewish Communities Series, Philadelphia.
LOWENTHAL, MARVIN, *The Jews of Germany.* Philadelphia, 1936.
MARCUS, JACOB R., *The Rise and Destiny of the German Jew.* Cincinnati, 1934.
Zeitschrift fuer Geschichte der Juden in Deutschland. First Series. Brunswick from 1887. Second Series. Berlin from 1938.

(These few volumes must be taken as representative of the vast literature on the history of the Jews in Germany, including many local histories.)

RUSSIA AND POLAND

COHEN, ISRAEL, *History of Jews in Vilna.* Philadelphia, 1943.
DUBNOW, SIMON, *History of the Jews in Russia and Poland.* 3 vols. Philadelphia, 1916-1920.
GREENBERG, LOUIS, *The Jews in Russia.* Vol. I. New Haven, 1944.
———, WISCHNITZER, MARK, ed., *The Jews in Russia.* Vol. II. New Haven, 1951.
LEW, MEYER S., *The Jews of Poland in the Sixteenth Century.* London, 1943.
MEISL, JOSEF, *Geschichte der Juden in Polen und Russland.* 3 vols. Berlin, 1921-1925.

CZECHOSLOVAKIA

BONDY, G., and DVORSKY, F., *Zur Geschichte der Juden in Boehmen, Maehren und Schlesien.* 2 vols. Prague, 1906.
Jahrbuch der Gesellschaft fuer Geschichte der Juden in der Čechoslov Republik, Prague, 1929-.

BYZANTINE EMPIRE, GREECE, TURKEY

EMMANUEL, I. S., *Histoire des Israélites de Salonique.* Vol. I. Paris, 1935.
GALANTE, ABRAHAM, *Histoire des Juifs d'Istanbul.* Istanbul, 1941. The same author has written a large number of other works on the history of the Jews in the Turkish Empire.
ROSANES, SOLOMON A., *History of the Jews in Turkey* (Hebrew). 5 vols. Sofia, 1934-1944. Vol. 6. Jerusalem, 1945.
STARR, JOSHUA, *The Jews in the Byzantine Empire, 641-1204.* Athens, 1939.
———, *Romania.* Paris, 1948.

ISLAMIC WORLD (EXCEPT TURKEY)

EISENBETH, MAURICE, *Les Juifs en Algérie: esquisse historique.* Extrait de Encyclopédie Coloniale et Maritime. Paris, 1937.
HIRSCHBERG, H. Z., *The Jews in Arabia from the Destruction of the Second Temple to the Crusades* (Hebrew). Tel-Aviv, 1946.
MANN, JACOB, *The Jews in Egypt and in Palestine under the Fatimid Caliphs.* 2 vols. London, 1920-1922.
STRAUSS, A., *Toledot Hayehudim bemizraim veSuria tachat Shilton Hamamelukim* (The Jews in Egypt and Syria under the Mamelukes). Jerusalem, 1944.

FAR EAST

KEHIMKAR, H. S., *The History of the Bene-Israel of India.* Tel-Aviv, 1937.
WHITE, WILLIAM CHARLES, *Chinese Jews.* 3 vols. Toronto, 1942.

CHAPTER 6

THE JEWS IN EASTERN EUROPE

(From Ancient Times until the Partitions of Poland, 1772-1795)

By Israel Halpern

The term "Eastern European Jewry," or, briefly, "Eastern Jewry," as commonly used and as it is accepted in Jewish historiography, does not coincide with the present political boundaries of Eastern Europe. The term "Eastern Europe" as commonly used today embraces Soviet Russia and the Soviet-dominated "people's democracies." Indeed, some scholars thus defined in the nineteenth century the geographical limits of Eastern Europe as a historical unit. The term "Eastern Jewry," however, originally embraced only the Jews who dwelt east of Germany, specifically the Jewries of Russia and Poland. It originated in nineteenth-century Germany, in the German Jews' sense of a difference between them and their brethren beyond Germany's eastern frontier. Through common usage the term passed into Jewish historiography. In general historiography the question of Eastern Europe was first raised as a historical problem in the middle of the nineteenth century, soon after the awakening of the Slavic peoples. Since then the problem has often been considered in scholarly literature and even at international historical conferences. The question of Eastern Europe as a *Jewish* historical problem and the geographic limits of this problem has not been clarified, even though certain phenomena seem to demand clarification. For our purpose, it is sufficient to consider the geographical spread of the Yiddish language and the Hasidic movement, as well as the agrarian character of territories resembling Poland and Russia and therefore suggesting a similar status and way of life for their Jewish communities. In a general survey there is obviously no room for detailed elucidation of such phenomena, and without it we certainly need not depart from the commonly accepted boundaries, which are, according to the map of our times, the boundaries of European Russia and postwar Poland.

Even within these limits Eastern Europe occupies a vast area, stretching from the Ural Mountains in the east to the political border of Communist Poland in the west, from the Black Sea and the Caspian Sea in the south to the Barents Sea and the Baltic Sea in the north—an area of more than 3,000,000 square miles. Jewish history in Eastern Europe in the period under consideration—from its beginnings until the end of the eighteenth century—developed in only about one-fourth of this area, principally in Poland, in what are today the Soviet Republics of the Ukraine, White Russia, and Lithuania, and in a section of the Russian Soviet Federated Socialist Republic, principally the Crimea.

I

Jews have been going to Eastern Europe since the period of the Second Temple, at least since the last days of the Temple, from east and west, by divers routes and at various times. They went, naturally, in such numbers and at such times as they found propitious conditions—political, socio-economic, and cultural-religious. A primary condition, of course, was the political organization of Eastern Europe. This process continued for a long time, and it did not encompass the entire area at once, not even the area which was to be the stage of Jewish history. The process began in the south of Russia. Since the seventh century B.C.E. there appeared, side by side, two forms of political organization destined to persist there until approximately the close of the fifteenth century. These were (1) the nomadic empire, and (2) the colonial city-state. The colonial cities were founded on the north shores of the Black Sea and on the shores of the Sea of Azov by emigrants from Miletus and other commercial cities of Asia Minor. At first the colonial centers were bound to or dependent upon the Ionian metropolises, followed by Rome, Byzantium, and, finally, the Italian republics. The nomadic empires were founded on the steppe between the Black Sea and the Caspian Sea by nomadic tribes, the majority of which came from the east—Sarmatians, Khazars, and others, and, finally in the thirteenth century, the Mongols. Only toward the close of the ninth century began the organization of those regions in Eastern Europe which, sooner or later, became large Jewish centers. In the tenth century, Kievian Russia (that centering in Kiev) and the Polish state arose. In the middle of the thirteenth century arose the Lithuanian state, which also included White Russia. Soon after, the state of Muscovy was established.

As we have noted, southern Russia was the first to be organized politically, and there the first Jewish settlement in Eastern Europe was established, in the colonial cities founded on the shores of the Black Sea and the Sea of Azov. This settlement, incidentally, is one of the most ancient in Europe. Among the numerous archaeological relics discovered on the sites of these colonies are many inscriptions entirely or partially of Jewish content. In the oldest, dating from the first century of the common era, the Jews already appear here and there as organized communities, whose beginnings probably preceded the dates of the inscriptions. Obviously, the

Jewish migration to the north of the Black Sea was a part of the general migration from Asia Minor to this region, and also a part of the general expansion of the Jewish Diaspora across the Greco-Roman world. The Jews could not have been among the migrants from Miletus and the other Ionian cities in Asia Minor who founded the settlements on the Black Sea, for as yet there were no Jews in Asia Minor. The Jews did not begin to spread over Asia Minor until the third century, and certainly a considerable time passed before they reached the distant sites on the shore of the Black Sea. Thus it is almost certain that the beginnings of Jewish settlement north of the Black Sea took place sometime during the two centuries before the common era, probably toward the end of the period.

If the existence of the Jewish settlement in this region during the Hellenistic period is still a matter of conjecture, there is certainty regarding the Roman period, and thereafter this region was seemingly never without a Jewish settlement. The Jewish settlement there, like the Greek, apparently was an urban community; in any case, we have no information concerning Jews outside the city walls. To our knowledge, only the local tribes lived outside the colonial cities. These cities supported themselves chiefly as intermediaries between the local tribes and the Mediterranean lands (this included the export of farm produce, fish, and slaves) and some handiwork (for example, pottery and goldware). The Jews were also able to engage in these occupations, just as they were similarly engaged here and there in the Greek Diaspora. It is almost certain that in these cities, too, the Jews generally did not enjoy full civil rights, due to the religious character of the Greco-Roman city, and, in general, were unable to participate either in the election of the city's leaders and officials or in the management of the city's general affairs. The Jews, however, had some religious, legal, and administrative autonomy. The Jews of the city were organized into kehillot, centered around the synagogue which served as a place of prayer, instruction, and judgment. The leadership of the kehilla was in the hands of community leaders who were called *archons* or by other Greek titles. Like all Jews of the Diaspora, and even some of the Jews of Palestine of that period, these Eastern Jews spoke Greek, called themselves by Greek names, and even borrowed Greek forms of communal organization and certain Greek legal forms. Nevertheless, these dispersed Jews knew how to preserve Jewish content, even within the alien forms. An example is their form of freeing non-Jewish slaves by dedicating them to God, shown in an inscription from Panticapaeum (on the western shore of the Kerch Straits). The act of liberation was performed in the synagogue, apparently in the presence of the congregation, and the slave gained complete freedom, except that he was obligated to honor the synagogue and to visit it regularly. Here we have a definite legal form widespread in the pagan Greek world. There the act of liberation took place in the temple, in the form of a fictional sale to one of the gods. However, the slave paid his own redemption price and was only symbolically dedicated to the god; actually he was now a free man. The Jews of Panticapaeum borrowed this legal form from the Greeks and used it, with certain changes. In one case it took place in a temple; in the other, in a synagogue. In the former the slave was sold to a god; in the latter he was brought into the Jewish fold.

The influence of the Jewish religion was felt even outside the Jewish community itself. During the Roman period, aristocratic-military groups stationed in Panticapaeum accepted some tenets of Judaism, such as the belief in One God and Sabbath observance, albeit without renouncing their former beliefs and practices. Many archaeological relics from these groups, inscriptions and graves, have been uncovered in Tanais (on the Azov coast) and in Panticapaeum. Of course, this is not to say that these groups were directly influenced only by their Jewish neighbors. Similar syncretic sects abounded at that time in the Roman world, especially in Asia Minor, and even the groups in Tanais were part of the general movement of religious syncretism which surely came from the southern shore of the Black Sea.

In any case, the Jewish exiles who, in ancient times, settled north of the Black Sea were the first who brought monotheism to Eastern Europe and its first exponents and propagators in this corner of the world. In this lies the special significance of the ancient Jewish colonization of the region from the standpoint of the general religious history of Eastern Europe. Monotheism in its Christian form began to arrive there, as far as we can tell, only after the decline of the Roman Empire, when the region was under Gothic rule. The first clear evidence of the existence of Christianity in these places—a tombstone with a cross—dates from the year 304. From the following century a dim echo of religious tension between the local Jews and the Christian missionaries in this region has reached us.

2

For more than 600 years, Jewish settlement existed only in this one corner of Eastern Europe north of the Black Sea. During all that time in the nomadic empires which arose one after the other in the nearby steppes, there is no mention of a Jewish settlement, although there certainly was economic and cultural contact between the littoral cities and the steppe provinces. The situation began to change at approximately the beginning of the seventh century, when the Khazars assumed control of the steppe region between the Caspian Sea and the Black Sea. The essence of this change was the spread of the Jews and Judaism eastward to the center of the Khazar state on the shore of the Caspian Sea. As is well known, led by the royal house, some Khazars embraced Judaism.

The Khazars had wandered to the south of Russia from central Asia, and settled principally in the steppe which encloses the northern portion of the Caspian Sea. There they established their state. From there they extended their suzerainty over a great number of tribes and settlements in every direction, principally to the north and to the west. Both geographically and politically speaking, the Khazar state was divided into two sections. One was the locale of the settling and wandering of the Khazars themselves. The other, which during the florescence of the Khazar state was the larger section, encompassed areas of settlement and of wandering of other tribes and peoples, which were ruled by their own kings and chieftains, subject to the Khazar khagans. A bond of fealty and dependence existed between these tribes and settlements and their Khazar suzerains. This bond was expressed through payment of tribute to the khagans and through military assistance in time of need. The economic base of the Khazar state was the international trade routes which traversed it.

The Khazars themselves, the ruling class in the state, who gave it their name, were Turks in race and language. Originally they were nomads, but in the course of time they passed from complete nomadism to periodic nomadism, living in cities during the winter and going out to the steppe in the summer. Certain of their religious tenets—belief in a heavenly god alongside a belief in magicians, religious tolerance—ripened them to some extent for the acceptance of monotheism. The spread of the monotheistic religions among the Khazars was also aided by the geographical and political background of their state. Khazaria lay between two great world powers: it bordered Byzantium in the west and the Arabian Caliphate in the south. In the Crimea, whose eastern section lay under Khazar dominion while its western section was under the rule of Byzantium, Jewish and Christian communities, we have noted, had existed for a long time. Consequently, Khazaria from its inception was open to Jewish and Christian influence. When, in the middle of the seventh century, the Arabs reached Transcaucasia, another religious factor—Islam—entered the region. The location of the Khazars on the international trade routes brought merchants from various lands, who passed through Khazaria, and some who settled permanently in the Khazar cities. Even the merchant caravans and colonies were liable to be effective transmitters of religious values in addition to economic values. The three religions worked their influence within the borders of Khazaria to a greater or lesser degree, according to the place and time and the turn of events. The spread of Islam here, as elsewhere, was supported by the political and military strength of the Caliphate. Christianity was similarly backed by the political and military might of Byzantium. The only monotheistic religion backed by no external force was Judaism, and precisely this fact was decisive—the scholars are unanimous on this—in the conversion of the Khazars. The desire to maintain balanced relations with the two neighboring great powers, with Byzantium

1. Baltic Sea
2. District of Pomerania
3. Bydgoszcz
4. District of Poznan
5. Poznan
6. Gniezno
7. Glogau
8. Leszno
9. District of Kalisz
10. Krotoszyn
11. Breslau (Wroclaw)
12. Odra (Oder) River
13. Silesia
14. Hapsburg Empire
15. Danzig (Gdansk)
16. District of Chelmno
17. Torun
18. District of Hohensalza (Inowroclaw)
19. Hohensalza (Inowroclaw)
20. District of Plock
21. Plock
22. Brzesc Kujawski
23. Great Poland
24. Warta River
25. Leczyca
26. District of Leczyca
27. Kalisz
28. District of Sieradz
29. Piotrkow
30. Pilica
31. Olkusz
32. Cracow
33. District of Cracow
34. Niemen River
35. Bug River
36. Vistula River
36a. Mazovia (Mazowsze)
37. District of Rawa
38. Warsaw
39. Region of Wegrow
40. Region of Lublin
41. Radom
42. District of Sandomierz
43. Checiny
44. Opatow
45. Sandomierz
46. Opole
47. Staszow
48. Pinczow
49. Wodzislaw
50. Little Poland (Malopolska)
51. Grodno
52. Tykocin
53. Zabludow
54. Ciechanowiec
55. Wegrow
56. District of Podlasie
57. Brzesc Litewski (on the Bug)
58. District of Lublin
59. Leczna
60. Belzyce
61. Lublin
62. Chelm
63. Zamosc
64. Szczbrzeszyn
65. District of Ruthenia
66. Nine Kehillot
67. Tarnogrod
68. Przeworsk
69. Belz
70. District of Belz
71. Rzeszow
72. Jaroslaw
73. Zolkiew
73a. Lwow (Lemberg)
74. Przemysl
75. Dobromil
76. Russia
77. Province of (Southern) Russia
78. Lesczow
79. Tyszowiec
80. Vilia River (Wilja)
81. Vilna
82. Niemen River
83. Disputed area between Tykocin and Grodno
84. Luboml
85. Kowel
86. Vladimir Vol. (Wolynski)
87. Styr River
88. Luck
89. Horochow
90. Ozierany
91. District of Volhynia
92. Dubno
93. Brody
94. Kremenetz (Krzemieniec)
95. Zloczow
96. Lithuania
97. Sluck
98. Pinsk
99. Pripet River
100. Horyn River
101. Sluck River (Slvcz)
102. Miedzyrzec (Mezretch)
103. Ostrog
104. Rachmanow
105. Konstantynow
106. Miedzyboz
107. Satanow
108. Lanckorona
109. District of Podolia (In 18th century, a separate region)
110. Kamienec
111. Mohilev
112. Dniester River
113. Berezina River
114. Ptycz River
115. Ovruch (Owrucz)
116. Disputed area betwee Volhynia and Pinsk
117. Uzh (Ush) River
118. District of Kiev
119. Teterev River
120. Zhitomir (Zytomierz)
121. Pavlich
122. Vinnitza
123. Nemirov
124. Tulchin
125. District of Bratzlav
126. Bug River
127. Ottoman Empire
128. Dnieper River
129. Sozh River
130. Desna River
131. Kiev
132. Byelaya Tserkov
133. Smyela
134. Uman
135. Muscovite States
136. The Golden Waters
137. Ingul River
138. Ingulets River
139. Dnieper River
140. Black Sea

a. The Jewish Community o the "Four Lands"
b. edited by Israel Halpern equivalents to the original Hebrew generously checke by Shlomo Noble
c. scale
d. kilometers
e. explanations
f. principal kehillot
g. independent (self-governing) kehillot
h. remaining kehillot and settlements
i. cities closed to Jews
j. places of conferences of the "Four Lands"
k. places where fairs were held
l. boundaries of countries
m. boundaries of Poland-Lithuania
n. boundaries of provinces
o. boundaries of lands and regions
p. abbreviations
q. river
r. region
s. province
t. all rights reserved

בית ישראל דד' ארצות
ה'תכ"ז - ה'תקכ"ד (1764 - 1667)
ערך ישראל היילפרין
קנה המידה
250 200 150 100 50 0
קילומטר
ביאורים
קהילות ראשיות
קהילות עומדות ברשות עצמן
שאר קהילות וישובים
ערים אסורות על יהודים
מקומות התועדות דד' ארצות
מקומות של ירידים
גבולות המדינה
גבולות פולין-ליטא
גבולות וויוודויות
גבולות ארצות וגלילות
קיצורים
ווי' = וויוודות , ג' = גליל , נ' = נהר
כל הזכויות שמורות
הים הבאלטי
ארצות הבסבורגים
שלזיה
פולין גדול
פולין קטן
רוסיא
16° 18° 20° 22° 24°
54° 52° 50°

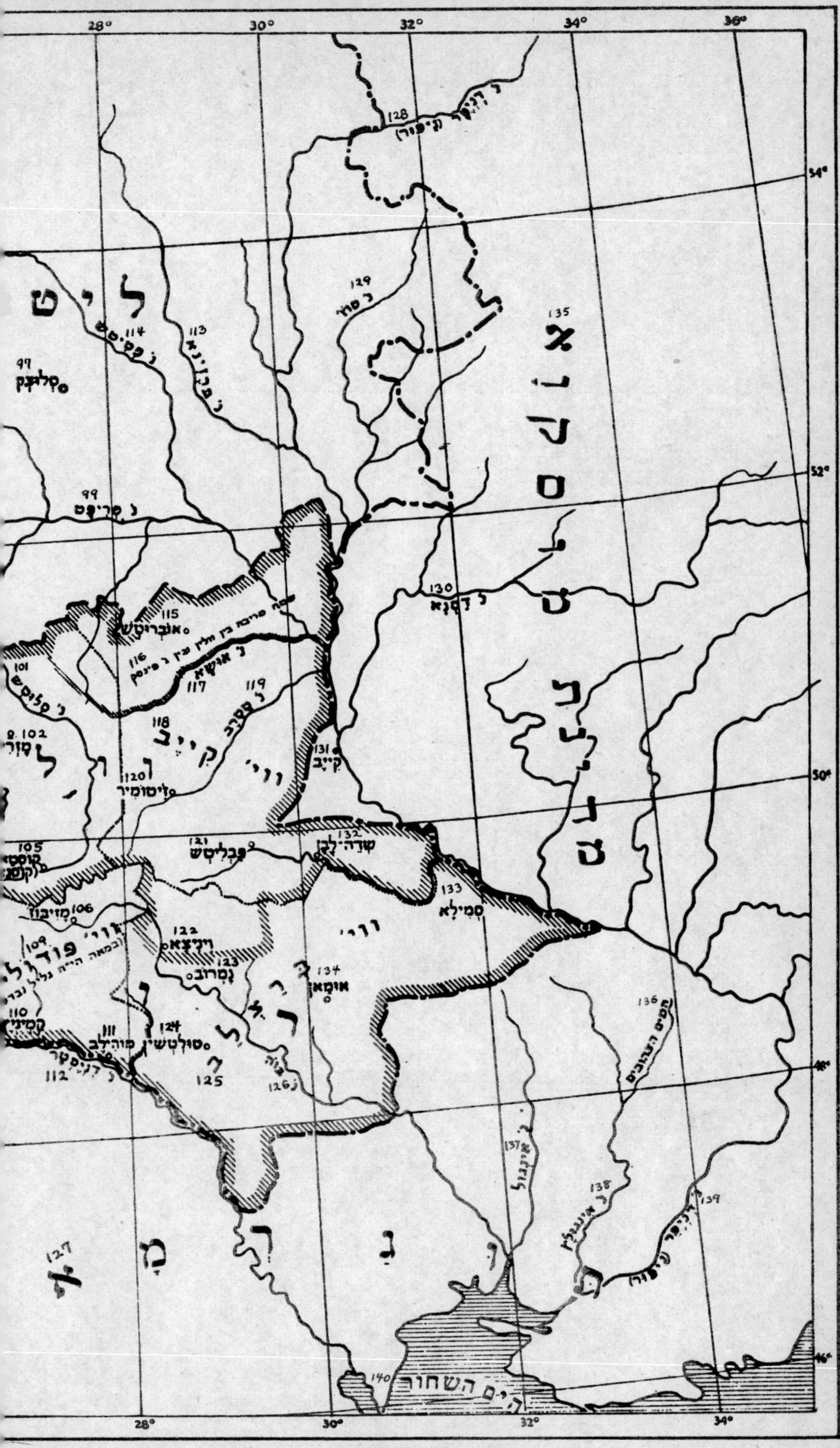

28°
30°
32°
34°
36°
54°
52°
50°
48°
46°
128 נ' דניפר (ניפור)
129 נ' סוז
130 נ' דסנא
131 קייב
132 שדה לבן
133 סמילא
134 אומאן
115 אובריטש
116 נ' אושא
120 זיטומיר
121 פבליטש
122 ויניצא
123 נמרוב
124 סולטשין
112 נ' דניסטר
137 נ' בוג
139 נ' דניפר (ניפור)
140 הים השחור

on one side and the Caliphate on the other, influenced the khan of the Khazars to embrace Judaism, which was politically neutral.

Varying and mutually contradictory data are found in the historical sources and as varying and contradictory opinions are expressed in the historical literature regarding the date of the conversion. According to some scholars, the conversion occurred in the eighth century; other scholars maintain that it was not before the sixties of the ninth century. Soon after the conversion of the royal house, a part of the Khazar people embraced Judaism, principally the nobility who in various ways stood in close relation to the royal court. It is not clear whether the Khazars embraced Judaism *in toto*, or in which tradition, the Rabbinic or the Karaite. In any case, the conversion of the royal house strengthened the authority and the ethical influence of Judaism in the state. Thus for many generations, even after the eclipse of Khazar ascendancy, their proselytization served as a source of encouragement and comfort for the Jews throughout the Diaspora.

In contrast to the life of oppression and degradation in Christendom and Islam, the Jews of Khazaria, even before the conversion, enjoyed the same religious and legal rights as their Moslem and Christian countrymen. The Jewish population increased and became variegated. Immigrants went to Khazaria from Byzantium and from Islam, either because of religious persecution or because of commercial ties. Proselytes joined Khazarian Jewry. Yet, relative to the general population, Khazaria never had a large Jewish settlement. As in the ancient Jewish settlement north of the Black Sea, Khazarian Jewry concentrated mainly in the coastal cities—Itil and Samandar on the Caspian Sea—which were transit stations for the international trade. The very concentration of the Jews in these market towns shows that the economic role of Khazarian Jewry was directly or indirectly connected with the transit trade, which was the general economic base of Khazaria. In both cities the Jews were a minority.

To our knowledge, the conversion of the royal house did not alter the legal status of Judaism or the Jews relative to other religions. All religions and their adherents—pagans included—enjoyed the same measure of religious and legal freedom after the conversion as before. The same geopolitical circumstances which, as we have noted, motivated the khan to embrace Judaism compelled him to maintain a tolerant attitude toward the other religions. Even the inner demographic and political conditions demanded this—the majority of the inhabitants of the Khazar capital, Itil, were Moslems; the majority of the inhabitants of Samandar, the second most important city, were Christians; the security of the state was based upon an army of mercenaries almost entirely composed of Moslems.

No Jewish culture developed in Khazaria, just as, to our knowledge, no Christian, Moslem, or Khazar culture developed.

At about the end of the tenth century, Khazaria collapsed after suffering military defeat at the hands of the Russian Prince Svyatoslav, and the Jewish settlement on the Caspian shore disappeared from view. Some of the Jews assimilated with the non-Jews; others fled or migrated to nearby lands. The center of Jewish settlement in Eastern Europe was transferred to the upper Dnieper to Kiev, the capital city of the Russian prince.

3

In the tenth century, Kiev was already the political and cultural center of the southeastern Russian principalities. In the eleventh century, Kiev became an urban commercial center as well. Even then there was in Kiev a permanent Jewish settlement, occuping a quarter of its own. It appears that some of the Jews were close to government circles; in any case, some were attacked in the insurrection of 1113. The Jews played a considerable role in the foreign trade of Kiev. In Russia at that time there was a special class of merchants who traveled with their merchandise on ships between Russia and Byzantium; these merchants included some Jews. This trade declined at the end of the eleventh century because of the competition of the Italian cities and the Crusades. On the other hand, Kiev's trade connections with the German states were strengthened. The connections persisted through the twelfth century, and the role of the Jews in these commercial contacts was apparently considerable. Central Europe was the outlet for the western trade, and the route led from either Regensburg (Ratisbon) or Prague to Kiev by way of Poland (Cracow)—the same route taken by the Jewish traveler, Petahyah of Regensburg—or by way of Hungary. The merchants who moved on these routes are known in the Hebrew sources as *Holkhei Russia*, "the Russian itinerants," or *Holkhei Derakhim shel Russia*, "the Russian wayfarers"; in Latin sources, *Ruzarii*. Various details concerning the Jewish *Holkhei Russia*, scattered throughout the German halakic literature, combine to give us a picture on the whole similar to that of the itinerant trade of the period. The *Holkhei Russia* traveled in caravans, and caravans of merchants traveling the roads were a common phenomenon, at least until the second half of the thirteenth century. Travel in caravans was then necessary for safety; they were even armed. According to one source, the Jewish caravans included Jewish partners and non-Jewish mercenaries. Mutual security and business partnership were accepted by all commercial caravans, both Jewish and non-Jewish. Regensburg was a manufacturing center and the merchants transported manufactured products (coats among other things) from there to Russia, apparently bringing from Russia slaves, furs, wax, and honey. It should be indicated that they did not buy the merchandise in Germany for sums fixed according to the local market values but took it on consignment, to be paid for according to the selling price in Russia. Even travel risks and inflation or deflation of prices were the responsibility of the seller. The principal profit was made from the sale in Germany of merchandise purchased in Russia with the proceeds from the sale of the Regensburg wares. The *Holkhei Russia* engaged, thus, in export (from Germany) and import (from Russia). In export they served only as agents for the manufacturer and merchant. In import, however, the *Holkhei Russia* were independent merchants, except that they did their business not with their own but with borrowed money.

Cultural ties followed close upon the establishment of economic ties. In a document from Byzantium we read of merchants "from among the elders of the community in Russia" participating in controversy with the Karaites. In another document we learn of a Russian Jew who, in Salonica, heard of "all the splendor of the Land of Israel" and was moved "that he, too, should go to prostrate himself at the holy place." Scholars occasionally came to Russia from Germany with the caravans, and Russian students came to study at the German *yeshibot*. A biblical commentary composed in Russia in 1124 was written in the spirit of German culture, though it contains some Greek explanations of words. There was also cultural intercourse with Babylonia. In the twelfth century, Rabbi Moses of Kiev corresponded on halakic matters with German scholars as well as with the dean of the *yeshiva* in Babylonia. And a Babylonian Karaite book reached Regensburg by way of Russia.

Generally the cultural level of Russian Jewry was then quite low. Kiev was the only community which had a rabbi. A Jewish scholar from Bohemia at the end of the twelfth or early in the thirteenth century points out that in Russia—as in Poland and Hungary—the Jews had no learned men and because of their poverty had to be satisfied with one willing to serve at once as cantor, rabbi, judge, and teacher of their children. The letter of recommendation to this Russian Jew who had been inspired to go to Palestine states that he "knows neither Hebrew nor Greek nor Arabic but only Canaanite (Slavonic) which the people of his homeland speak."

The Russian constitution which was composed in the twelfth century does not mention the Jews. Judaism, however, occupies a place in Russian religious literature. Anti-Judaism is indeed one of the traditional elements in Byzantine theology, whence it certainly carried over into Russian literature. Yet it seems that many attacks against Judaism in the long period of transition from paganism to Christianity did not lack a connection with the realities of their own time as well. Similar to the legendary tradition concerning the Khazar conversion is a Russian tradition that the representatives of three faiths—a German, a Byzantine, and a Jew—one after the other appeared before Prince Vladimir of Kiev and, each according to his own lights, sought to proselytize him. On the other hand, it is said in praise of Theodosius, Abbot of the Pechera monastery in Kiev in the eleventh century, that he was in the habit of going secretly to the Jews late at night to argue with them about Christ. He would reproach them and brand them as godless sinners, in the hope of inciting them to martyr him for his faith. This must mean that the Jews, too, were not altogether passive during that period of religious ferment. The written and oral attack on Judaism certainly did not influence the Christian population in favor of the Jews, then or later.

The Jewish commercial caravans, which, as we have indicated, traveled between Regensburg and Kiev by way of Poland, seemingly left no definite traces along this route. First mention of a permanent Jewish settlement in Cracow, the principal Polish station on the caravan route, was in 1304. To be sure, our first information about Jewish settlements—permanent settlements, that is—within the borders of Poland dates from the twelfth century, but almost all these settlements are located in western Poland, principally in Great Poland and in Silesia, which then belonged to Poland. Coins bearing Hebrew inscriptions have been found in several places in Silesia and in Great Poland. Apparently they were minted in Gniesin (Gniezno on map) and perhaps also in Poznan at the end of the twelfth century or at the beginning of the thirteenth century by Jewish mint farmers. These farmers were undoubtedly immigrants from the west, for there were at the time Jewish coiners and coins bearing Hebrew inscriptions in Western and Central Europe. Jews who for a time owned village property are mentioned in several Silesian documents. This can only mean that Jews used to lend money against such properties, something which was later interdicted. The Jewish settlements in Poland were then small and, as mentioned above, like the Jews of Russia, they possessed little learning.

While there is still no mention of a Jewish settlement on the Caspian Sea, Jewish life in the Crimea persisted. Thus there were Jews on the Black Sea steppes, which since the mid-eleventh century had been controlled by the Comanni tribes. Petahyah of Regensburg, who visited these places in the second half of the twelfth century, met these Jews. They were Karaites. Indeed, even the language which the Karaites of Poland and Lithuania spoke in the centuries until our own time is defined by philologists as Turko-Comanni. Petahyah's account of the Karaites among the Comanni is consequently the earliest information in our possession concerning the Karaites in Eastern Europe. The earliest information we have about the Karaites in Byzantium, whence perhaps they came, dates from the beginning of the twelfth century.

4

Such was the character of Jewish life in Eastern Europe until the invasion of the Mongols in the middle of the thirteenth century. This event, considered epoch-making in the history of Eastern Europe, was felt differently in each of the various lands. From then until the end of the eighteenth century, the Crimean peninsula remained in the possession of the Mongols. The Russian duchies were subjugated for a long period. In time, the northernmost liberated themselves and joined together under the rule of the Duke—later the King—of Moscow. The southeastern duchies never regained their independence and, one by one, became annexed either to Lithuania, which had not been affected by the Mongol invasion, or to Poland, which had been partially affected but quickly recovered. At the end of the fourteenth century, Poland and Lithuania united in a sort of federation, and the bond between them strengthened during the succeeding centuries. For a long period to follow, Jewish history took shape within two national frameworks: the Polish-Lithuanian state and Mongolian Crimea. Prussia and Livonia, the two states founded by orders of German crusaders on the shore of the Baltic Sea at the end of the twelfth and the beginning of the thirteenth century, were barred to Jews. This, more or less, was also the case of Muscovy. Individual Jews were sometimes admitted, diplomats or physicians and sometimes Jewish merchants from abroad. But no substantial Jewish settlement arose there, and subsequently even visits of Jewish merchants were prohibited. The Muscovite authorities remained vigorously and continuously opposed to Jewish settlement. This opposition was later augmented at the end of the fifteenth century among other factors by religious ferment in the priesthood and the aristocracy directed against the established church. Opponents called members of the sect "Judaizers," and their teaching was called "the Judaizing heresy." They rejected the concept of the Trinity, the divinity of Jesus, the use of images, etc. Their literature included translations from the Hebrew philosophical and liturgical literature (Maimonides' *Milot ha-Higayon* and the Festival Prayer Book). Although some Jews had a certain influence on this movement, it is not essentially a part of Jewish history but rather a part of the history of the Christian Church. The actual consequence for the Jews was increased opposition to Jewish settlement in Russia—a policy which persisted in principle almost until the Revolution of 1917.

The Mongols were in Poland only a short time. In 1241, immediately after the conquest of Kiev, they swept toward Hungary by way of Poland, ravaging the south and the central part of the country on their route. Shortly afterward they returned the way they came. Subsequently they forayed from time to time into the frontier districts of Poland and Lithuania. The first raid took place in 1241. Its historical significance does not derive so much from the fact that it was the first of many, or from the slaughter and pillage that attended it, but in its role in bringing about a colonization movement of major dimensions which continued until the end of the fifteenth century. With this movement is linked the rise and florescence of the Polish cities in the closing centuries of the Middle Ages. Historiography knows this movement as "the German colonization" or "the German colonization according to *jus Teutonicum* (German law)," so called because the majority of the new settlers came from Germany, and they —and many of the indigenous urban settlers—organized their lives according to German law, especially the so-called Magdeburg Law.[1a] The movement got under way in the twelfth century, almost one hundred years before the Mongol invasion, but did not gain full momentum until after the invasion. The land was sparsely populated, being covered with forest and marsh and ruined by the civil wars among the princes, the Mongol invasions, and other wars. The conviction grew of the need to rebuild the ruins, settle the wastes, and develop agriculture and urban life—commerce and handicrafts—after the Western pattern. There was not enough population in the land to implement this plan, and foreign settlers were invited. Among the settlers were Dutch, Walloons, Flemings, and Czechs, but the overwhelming majority were Germans. The great demand for settlers in Poland suited Germany's general expansionist aims on political, demographic (excess population), and economic grounds, which were augmented by the political anarchy, the famine, and similar factors. The chief factor was economic: the settlers were promised better living conditions than most of them had enjoyed in their lands of origin. The colonization was administered by agents called *locatores* on the basis of special privileges which defined, among other things, the rights of the settlers and of the agents themselves. It was largely urban colonization. The settlers went to undeveloped areas, where they founded new cities, and to existing settlements, which they developed and reorganized according to the patterns brought with them. At first they settled the western frontier districts, later going also to the east and to Lithuania. German scholars estimate the German settlement in Poland in the Middle Ages in the hundreds of thousands; Polish scholars estimate it in no more than tens of thousands; but it is clear that the German colonization in this period was a decisive factor in the urban development of Poland.

The German colonization figures prominently in Polish Jewish history on several counts:

1. The Jewish immigration to Poland paralleled the German immigration. In certain respects they also complemented each other: together they formed the character of the Polish city. Most Polish cities included two unequal parts: the Christian part, which was usually the larger by far and constituted the city proper, and a small Jewish quarter. The German colony dominated the Christian part of the city; the Jewish colony, of course, established the character of the Jewish quarter and governed it; together, the two colonies constituted the city as a whole.

2. The German Jews were city dwellers, deriving their livelihood from urban occupations. To some extent, thus, the German colonists—by their role in the urban development of Poland—prepared the way for the immigration and absorption of their Jewish compatriots.

3. Along with their *jus municipale,* on the other hand, the German settlers brought the tradition of hatred and Jewish disenfranchisement which in their German cities of origin had marked their relations with the Jews.

4. The German Jews brought to Eastern Europe the organizational forms developed within the framework of the German city. The transplantation of the German municipal pattern to Poland thus made possible a certain continuity in Jewish communal development.

5. The use by the Jews of the German language with the municipal authorities and with German townspeople certainly had some influence on the development of the Yiddish language.

In the eleventh and twelfth centuries, during the urban florescence in Western Europe, the Jews there were considered as important in the settlement and development of the cities. The princes and bishops, eager to see urban development in their domains, invited Jewish and non-Jewish settlers, offering them various privileges. In the famous grant to the Jews in 1084, the Bishop of Speyer wrote: "Desiring to make a town out of the village of Speyer, I thought to raise its dignity many times by getting the Jews to settle there." The situation was much the same in other towns of Germany and of the other lands of Christian Europe—England, France, and northern Spain. When, much later, the process of urban growth got under way in Poland, the Jews once more were considered a desirable element. There were no *locatores,* however, to bring the Jews to Poland as for the non-Jews, nor were the Jews generally allowed to serve as *locatores.* We know of only one Jewish *locator,* a merchant and tax farmer from Lvov (Lemberg), in close relation to the Palace, who in the 1420's founded and colonized several villages. The King had granted him the concession in the hope—expressly stated in the letter of concession—of winning him to Christianity. When the King's hope was frustrated, this Jew under pressure of the Church was forced to sell his rights to the villages he had colonized so that no Jew would be in authority over non-Jews. Nor did the Jews enjoy some of the special concessions granted the German colonists. But the Jews, like the Germans, were granted a charter, which some of them had had in the West.

Jewish immigration and colonization were not organized. The Jews arrived singly or in small groups, for the prospects seemed better than in the West, where they suffered from religious and economic persecution. As persecution mounted in the West, especially in the latter half of the fifteenth century, Jewish immigration to Poland increased. Some immigration also was from the East, principally from the Crimea. With the annexation of Red Russia to Poland and Kievian Russia to Lithuania in the middle of the fourteenth century, a number of Jewish settlements apparently not of Ashkenazic origin were incorporated into Polish Lithuania. Altogether we find traces of Jews in about sixty locales in Polish Lithuania at the end of the Fifteenth century.

Polish Jewry enjoyed legal autonomy based on the privileges given Jews in Central Europe. However, one Jewish colony, the Karaite community at Troki, near Vilna, was granted autonomy based on the Magdeburg Law. Between these two there were various gradations of status, of civil rights in the Christian town, with or without legal autonomy. At the end of the fourteenth century the privileges of Jews in some German countries became the basic general law for the Jews of Poland and Lithuania—Ashkenazic and non-Ashkenazic, Rabbanites and Karaites, except the quarter at Troki already mentioned and isolated Jews here and there. This charter was one of a group granted in the mid-thirteenth century to the Jews of Austria-Bohemia-Moravia-Hungary. The politico-legal principle set down in the charter was that of "Service of the Treasury" or *servitudo camerae*, whereby the Jews were *Kammerknechte*—"Servants of the Treasury." According to this principle the prince was lord-protector of the Jews, their lives and property—he was at liberty to pawn them, sell or banish them, but whoever harmed them in any way was treated as a robber of the treasury; litigation between the Jews could be judged only by the prince or his deputy. The first privilege in Poland was granted in 1264 by Prince Boleslav the Pious (or "the Shy") to the Jews of the Principality of Kalish and apparently also of Poznan. In the course of time, with the territorial dispersion of the Jews of Germany, the charter was extended over all Poland. As it was applied in each place it was modified somewhat, but never fundamentally. Theoretically, and to some extent also in practice, it remained in force—at any rate outside the private domains—until the decline of the Polish Republic.

The king as legislator, however, was not the sole source of Jewish legislation. In the second half of the fifteenth century a new force appeared to assert and spread its legislative sway at the expense of the royal authority: the nobility. The Church had already assumed the authority to enact various regulations concerning the Jews, and the Christians of the towns were already exerting certain influence with respect to the legal status of the Jews, either by pressure on the legislators or by local agreements with their Jewish neighbors.

All these factors, to a greater or lesser extent, directly or indirectly, determined the legal and the practical status of the Jews. The extent of their influence hinged upon the extent of the correlation of interest and balance of power between ruling groups in the state. The princes and kings, in their desire to increase their revenues, to colonize and develop the land, were helped by the Jews among others. Toward this end the Jews were granted a number of basic rights which assured them security of life and property, freedom of worship, and economic freedom. But the interests of the state, as understood by the rulers and expressed in the privileges granted to the Jews, occasionally clashed with the interests of the Church and the other classes. The fundamental aim of the Church with respect to the Jews was to convert them; if that was impossible, to allow them only a wretched, second-class existence. Accordingly, the Polish synods enacted the anti-Jewish restrictions that prevailed in the West. Although these Polish enactments were not as harsh as those in the West, they had more than a minor influence upon the attitude of the masses and the lay legislators. Whenever the lay interests of a powerful class joined to the religious ones, the interested parties succeeded—in practice and often in theory—in determining the living conditions of the Jews. Boleslav of Kalish and Casimir the Great, for example, had allowed the Jews to give real estate mortgages, among other things. This ran counter to the aims of the Church to keep the Jews in a depressed state and to the secular interests of the burghers and of the nobility. This opposition, especially on the part of the nobility as early as the days of Casimir, brought about a prohibition of such loans in a section of the kingdom and, in the following century, throughout the kingdom.

In this instance influence was brought to bear in a legal manner by having the law changed. But the Jews were also subjected to extralegal acts. Although the charters assured the Jews security of life and property, they were attacked from time to time. The first anti-Jewish outbreak, as far as we know, took place in the time of Casimir the Great, who was deemed friendly to the Jews. The wave of outbreaks that accompanied the Black Plague in the middle of the fourteenth century took its toll in Breslau, Kalish, Cracow, and other places. The outbreaks became more frequent and more violent as the fifteenth century progressed, especially in some of the large towns, such as Poznan and Cracow. The direct causes of the outbreaks apparently were accidental: a lost Christian child, some holy wafers that vanished from a church, a fire. Actually, all the outbreaks manifested the same general causes: (1) the rigorous and ongoing battle of the townsfolk against Jewish competition, a battle which intensified as the Jewish population increased; (2) the tradition of hostility of Christians to Jews on the part both of the Church and of various popular movements.

The question of Jewish expulsion appears in Polish political literature as early as the beginning of the fifteenth century. At that time the question was only discussed in theory. At the end of the century it was carried into practice. In 1495, just after the Spanish expulsion, the Jews were banished from the Principality of Lithuania. In that same year they were also banished from Cracow, the capital city, and soon after from Warsaw, which was later to become the capital city. The Jews were allowed to return to Lithuania early in the sixteenth century, but it was long before they were readmitted to Cracow and Warsaw. Henceforth they were frequently banished from one city or another, and more than once they were threatened with total expulsion from the country.

In this period the Jewish struggle for economic survival was already widely ramified. We find Jews engaged in various economic pursuits, in mortgaging, tax farming, commerce, handicrafts, and agriculture.

The German Jews, who as we know expanded their moneylending activities in the final centuries of the Middle Ages, brought their capital and experience to Poland, where they continued to engage in moneylending. Indeed, in the fourteenth and fifteenth centuries the importance of credit in Polish economic life steadily increased, a field in which the Jews played an important role, especially in western and central Poland. They loaned money to members of all classes, from the royalty and nobility down to the peasantry. The number of professional Jewish moneylenders was relatively small, but many Jews engaged in moneylending as a side occupation. It should be noted that among the non-Jewish population, too, the nobility loaned money at interest and the town merchants supplemented their income in the same way.

The Jewish financiers also invested in tax farming. There being no official, regular system for the collection of taxes and tolls and the management of state properties, the various governing bodies farmed out these incomes to private individuals for fixed periods and fixed sums. The Jews had engaged in the farming of state revenues in the West; and despite the opposition of the Church to placing the Jews in such positions over Christians, the Jews tax farmed in Poland. Side by side with the burghers and the nobility, sometimes in partnership with them, Jews engaged in this occupation. Tax farming was not only a financial matter. Until the fourteenth century an *in natura* duty was collected. Subsequently, too, smuggled merchandise was confiscated, half going to the tax collector, half to the farmer. Thus the tax farmers occasionally also had to engage in the marketing of goods.

The Jewish commercial picture in Poland and Lithuania, as we have it from various incidental medieval sources, is diversified. We find a reference to Jewish participation in domestic wholesale and retail trade and in import and export. Jews dealt in domestic and foreign merchandise, in various agricultural products and by-products, and in various types of manufactured goods.

The most profitable branch of commerce was foreign trade, which involved principally transit trade. A number of international trade routes traversed Poland and Lithuania. A trade route from the Italian colonies in the Crimea passed through Lvov and Cracow, where it branched off to

Danzig and Breslau. Several trade routes also reached Danzig from Muscovy by way of Lithuania, and from Hungary by way of Cracow. In addition to these main routes there were several minor ones. We find references to the presence of Jews on almost all the trade routes. They seem to have participated with the Crimea to a considerable extent in the Oriental trade. Indigenous Jews, chiefly from Red Russia and Volhynia, participated in this, as did Jews from the Italian colonies. Competing with the Jews in the Oriental trade were Armenians, Greeks, and Italians; and in the northwestern trade, Armenians, Scots, and, chiefly, Germans (indigenous and foreign). The Jewish merchants in this competition had a distinct handicap. The trade centers—Danzig for the maritime trade, and Cracow and Lvov for the overland trade—tried to restrict the commercial rights of the Jews and succeeded. The various restrictions doubtless affected Jewish commercial development.

The Jews also engaged in various trades, not only in those connected with religious observance, such as baking and the tailoring of ritually approved clothes, but also in weaving, tanning, etc. In several districts of Poland and more in Lithuania, there were Jewish burghers and villagers engaged in various branches of agriculture. The town was still semiagricultural, and among the burghers also were Jews who owned gardens, fields, and pastures. In the eastern districts, especially, the Jews sometimes acquired rural properties as collateral for temporary cultivation, and sometimes, by authority of the prince or king, they even acquired full ownership of the properties. We know some of these property holders by name as wealthy merchants and tax farmers who certainly did not themselves work their properties. We do, however, find occasional references to Jewish tillers of land.

Medieval commerce was characterized by lack of specialization, which was typical, too, of the Eastern European Jewish economy. That is why we have written of the various economic pursuits in which the Jews engaged, rather than of the occupational structure of Jewish society. The Jewish merchant not only dealt in merchandise; he also loaned money at interest, farmed state revenues, etc. Similarly, the moneylender, the tax farmer, and even each tradesman who loaned at interest whatever money he had to spare also engaged in a little commerce on the side. A number of occupations were interrelated by their very nature. A moneylender had to sell forfeited collaterals; if the collateral was rural property, the lender sometimes, for a while at least, became a landholder. The tax farmer had to deal in merchandise acquired in lieu of taxes or in confiscated smuggled goods.

The lack of economic diversification imposed a degree of simplicity and uniformity on Jewish communal life. The picture of Jewish communal organization—as we know it from the texts of the privileges granted Jews in the Middle Ages (no Jewish sources have been preserved)—may be summed up briefly. The Jews were organized into communities which centered around the synagogue and the cemetery. The community elders were its recognized leaders, and the Jew who defied them was liable to fines. The Jewish leaders were authorized to judge civil suits in which both litigants were Jews. Suits involving non-Jews and criminal suits were tried by a judge especially appointed by the government, although the trial had to take place in a synagogue and a verdict to be rendered in consultation with representatives of the Jewish community.

East European Jewish scholars known today not only by name but by their works appear for the first time in the closing centuries of the Middle Ages. Rabbi Abraham the Crimean who had studied in Italy and in the Crimea wrote a commentary on the Pentateuch in the philosophic-rationalist spirit of Maimonides. Rabbi Moses of Kiev studied in Constantinople and lived in Kiev, Lithuania, and, in his last days, in the Crimea. He is the author of a well-known Cabbalistic work. In the Crimea he sought to amalgamate the various Jewish communities in the peninsula. The Mongols then ruled the Crimea. Until the Turkish conquest in 1475, only part of the coast remained the autonomous domain of the Italian Republics of Venice and Genoa, which had established their competing mercantile colonies there. The Jews who lived in the colonies and on the peninsula proper engaged in the service of the Mongol khans in domestic and foreign trade and in handicrafts. The Jewish population was variegated, comprising Karaite and Rabbanite Jews, Jews who had dwelt in the area for many generations, Byzantine, Italian, and even recently arrived Lithuanian Jews. The Jewish population of Poland and Lithuania, too, was still variegated. There were also Karaites and Rabbanites, some Jews who had dwelt there for many generations, Jews who had come from or by way of the Crimea, as well as Jews from the West and Central Europe. Indeed, the Ashkenazic Jews had already put the impress of their culture and language, economic life, and communal organization upon Rabbanite Jewry generally and of their legal status even upon the Karaites.

5

This was the situation at the close of the fifteenth century. In the centuries that follow there are no signs of growth and progress in the old Jewish settlement in the Crimea. On the other hand, the younger Jewish settlement of Poland and Lithuania grew and advanced in every respect, an advancement which continued for about 150 years, until the persecutions of 1648.

First to command attention is the phenomenal increase in the Jewish population and in its expansion over all of Poland. As far as we know, the

Jewish communities were numbered in the dozens at the end of the fifteenth century; on the eve of 1648 they were numbered in the hundreds. The Jewish population of Poland and Lithuania is estimated at the most at 20,000–30,000 at the end of the fifteenth century; on the eve of 1648, in the hundreds of thousands. Yet the burghers had not relented in their struggle against the Jews; indeed they had intensified it. With all the strength they could muster and with the help of the Church, the burghers sought to hinder the Jews economically and territorially, to cut them off from urban sources of livelihood, and to banish them from the towns. In some cases the burghers succeeded in banishing the Jews or in restricting their residence, and in others in cutting them off from substantial sources of livelihood. Yet, individually and in groups, Jews continued to immigrate into Poland. And the immigration was sizable; for by 1648 most of the Jews living in Poland and Lithuania were immigrants or the descendants of immigrants of the past 150 years. How was such a tiny Jewish community able, under such adverse conditions, to absorb such immigration and to grow in such numbers? Indeed, it would have been impossible without the growing political strength and economic activity of the nobility, especially of their upper crust, the magnates.

In the second half of the fifteenth century there was already widespread pressure for urban development of great private estates by founding towns and townlets on them. Shortly thereafter, at the turn and in the course of the sixteenth century, a reorganization of agricultural production took place on these estates. In Poland and other lands east of the Elbe they were put on a *Gutswirtschaft* (goods economy) basis—which persisted until the middle of the nineteenth century—instead of *Grundwirtschaft* (agrarian economy). The increasing demand in the northwest for agricultural products, especially grains, motivated the magnates to turn their estates to large-scale agriculture. The landowner was no longer satisfied with payments of money or produce from his peasant tenants, but, through his growing political power, tied them to his estates as serfs compelled to do *corvée*. In accordance with their interests as producers and consumers, landowners demanded and obtained—even by the end of the fifteenth century—exemption from excise taxes.

In accordance with these interests, furthermore, the high nobility sought to maintain the legal norms of the Middle Ages which restricted the commercial and working rights of the nonburghers, and exerted all its power to abolish or reduce the economic privileges of the towns and of the urban mercantile leagues and trade guilds. This development in several respects directly and indirectly had tremendous influence on the status of the Jews throughout the whole life of the Polish Republic. It opened up to them places of settlement and sources of livelihood on private lands in village and town alike: in the village, on *Gutswirtschaft* in all its facets; in the town, in the private town proper and in the courts of the nobility in the royal town who had freed themselves from the jurisdiction of the municipal authorities (the *Jurydyki*). Thus indirectly—by weakening the political and economic power of the burghers—the Jews were enabled to establish themselves and even to return to the urban sources of livelihood and to the royal towns from which the burghers had always sought to bar Jews. Under certain conditions and within certain limits, the interests of the nobility and of the Jews coincided. Both, according to their strength and in their respective ways, fought the urbanites: the nobility chiefly by political means, the Jews chiefly by economic means. This was no joint war but two parallel battles motivated by diverse interests and by diverse views as to the desirable economic order. The nobility, demanding free enterprise, opposed the monopolistic privileges of the urban guilds and of the towns in general. As producers and consumers, wishing to sell their commodities dearly and buy cheaply, the nobles tried to break the economic hold of the towns. Therefore the nobles needed the Jewish merchant, tax farmer, and even craftsman. The Jews, on the other hand, did not oppose the urban economic order *per se*. Indeed, the kehilla was economically ordered after the urban pattern; the kehillot also enacted regulations in favor of their own members which restricted the economic activity of members of other kehillot; the kehillot boasted certain monopolistic privileges and even secured such privileges for their members vis-à-vis the estates of the nobility. If the Jews sought to undermine the urban order, it was not because of any fundamental opposition to this order but because of the way it discriminated against them. If the Jews migrated to the private town, it was not because its administration was weaker because of its dependence upon the lord, but because its weakness enabled them to live; for there Jews were not discriminated against, at any rate not to the same degree as in the royal towns. If the Jews offered the nobility better prices, it was because only under such conditions could they meet the competition. It was the will to survive which motivated the Jews to undermine the urban order and to use the nobility, just as, for economic reasons, the nobility used them.

The political and economic changes, of course, brought vast changes in the Jewish economy. Jews were now forbidden to farm the royal revenues. The Church, as we have noted, had long since opposed Jewish participation in this activity; now the nobility demanded exclusive rights to tax farming, which, unlike the field of business, they did not consider beneath their dignity and which brought considerable income. The nobility formed the dominant force in the state and were to some extent even the protectors and supporters of the Jews, so the leaders of Polish Jewry, especially in the western and central parts of Poland, tried to discourage their brethren from competing with the nobility by engaging in tax farming. Although here and there, especially in Lithuania, some Jews farmed the royal revenues,

Jewish activity in this branch of farming rapidly dwindled. At the same time Jewish farming of the revenues and estates of the nobility rapidly increased. There were Jews, as well as non-Jews, who thus operated entire estates, but by and large the Jews farmed specific branches of the estates or specific revenues, such as taxes and customs, various crafts, inns, taverns, etc. These occupations flourished in eastern Poland, especially on the Ukrainian steppes, when the tempo of settlement in those regions increased in the mid-sixteenth century. In this manner the Jews participated in various branches of agricultural production—planting, livestock breeding, fishing, and especially in the manufacture of agricultural by-products, such as flour, spirits, potash, etc.—and in their marketing, domestic and foreign.

Agricultural products were the bulk of the Polish export trade. Because the exporters also did most of the importing, it stands to reason that the Jews played a major role in Poland's foreign trade, especially with Western and Northern Europe. Local and foreign Jews participated, too, in the trade with Turkey, the Black Sea colonies, and the south (Moldavia). They also played a significant part in the domestic trade, especially in fairs, in which they enjoyed complete freedom even in the Middle Ages.

The development of Jewish commerce was expedited by the alertness of the Jewish merchant to leap through every breach that developed in the wall of economic restriction. Notable examples are, first, the foothold quickly gained by Jews in the economic activities of the noble class as they developed and increased, and, second, the Jews' particular affinity to fairs. Another most important factor in the development of Jewish commerce was its internal organization. The government of the Christian town zealously protected the interests of the local merchants; yet the merchants organized themselves into guilds for the fulfillment of their social and religious needs and for dealing jointly with their economic problems. The Jewish merchants, on the other hand, were almost completely unorganized in guilds. Apparently they saw no need for it, in view of the general commercial character of the Jewish community, and because the general organization of the Jews also protected Jewish commercial interests. On the one hand, the autonomous Jewish institutions tried to secure, among other things, economic privileges from the kings and the nobility and agreements with the burghers, etc. On the other hand, the Jewish institutions tried to limit and eliminate altogether competition among the Jews themselves in buying, selling, farming, and transport (for example, the renting of wagons to travel to the fairs). The autonomous bodies obtained tax concessions for the Jewish merchant by assisting the Jewish tax farmer by reducing competition. They also saw that honest and fair trading practices were maintained by the Jewish merchants in their dealings both with Jews and with non-Jews. The English minister to Poland stated in 1598, in a report to his government, that almost all Polish commerce was controlled by the Jews. But we lack evidence to fix precisely the extent of Jewish participation in Polish commerce in proportion to the total population.

The development of commerce also brought changes in the money trade. The activities of the Jewish creditor grew and branched into new areas so that his role and his sources changed. The Jewish creditor became a commercial mortgagee. His capital was not necessarily his own or even Jewish capital; a substantial part, often most, of it came from long-term loans from the nobility, monasteries, and wealthy burghers. Middlemen in these affairs were loan brokers, present in every commercial center, whose fees were limited fixed tariffs incorporated in communal and intercommunal ordinances.

The development of Jewish commerce also left its impress upon Jewish handicrafts. Early in the seventeenth century some Jewish merchants began to develop a trade in readymade clothing, using the putting-out system—which characterized early capitalism. These merchants sold the raw material on credit to craftsmen, who, in turn, sewed the garments and sold them back to the credit merchants at a low price. This system made it possible for Jews to enter the garment trades in considerable numbers, for it required almost no investment. The extent of Jewish participation in the fur trade also opened considerable opportunities for Jewish craftsmen. Furthermore, they engaged in practices which were frowned upon by the town guildsmen: Jews went to the homes of customers to solicit orders; they went into the countryside to work for the petty nobility and the farmers. Apparently the Jews also, earlier than other merchants, produced goods specifically to offer them for sale on the market days and at the fairs. The expansion of Jewish handicraft was manifest in the increased number of crafts which Jews plied and in the increased number of Jews plying them. The largest concentration of Jews was in the garment industry, followed by the baked-goods industry. But we find Jews in many sorts of trade, light and heavy. In the first half of the seventeenth century the Jewish craftsmen even began to organize themselves into guilds of their own, similar to the guilds of the Christian craftsmen in the towns. But this movement did not reach its pinnacle until the following century.

The numerical increase and augmented activity of Jews in the estates of the nobility brought about a change in Jews' legal status. Just as the peasantry was feudalized to suit the nobles' needs, they sought legal control of all classes who inhabited their properties. Toward this end the *Sejm* (Polish Parliament) in 1539 passed a law defining the legal status of the Jews inhabiting noble lands. They were made the subjects of their lords, required to pay them taxes and subject only to their jurisdiction. Henceforth the King ceased to be protector of these Jews or to enjoy income from them. According to this law the Jews of Poland were divided into two categories: the King's Jews and private Jews. The former remained under the jurisdiction and protection of the King, while the latter fell under the jurisdiction of their respective lords. The innovation in this law was more theoretical than practical. On the one hand, it was no more than a formal confirmation of a situation which, more or less, already existed. Jews inhabiting private lands were, in fact, already subject to the jurisdiction of their lords. The status of Jews on these properties was, on the whole, no different from the status of others. Jews were, generally speaking, judged according to the pattern which had crystallized over the centuries with respect to the legal status of the Jews of the kingdom. On the other hand, voluntarily or compulsorily, despite the formal waiver, the Jews continued to pay taxes to the King. And the King retained legislative freedom of action with respect to all Jews and continued to give them limited protection, according to the vagaries of royal policy toward the Jews and of the waning royal power. The privileges granted Jews during the period under discussion covered, on the whole, security of life and property, freedom of worship, various degrees of economic freedom, and an increasing degree of internal autonomy.

Our first intimate knowledge of Jewish autonomous organization, at the close of the sixteenth century, shows it well organized and ramified, having gone through a long process of development full of internal and external vicissitudes and struggles. The kehilla, the basis of communal organization, was an association of individuals who dwelt together within the limits of a given city, set its own regulations, maintained a synagogue and a cemetery, its own rabbis and religious judges, and all the other services required by an organized community. The subkehilla, the smaller, outlying settlement, could not maintain all these services and fill its own needs, and therefore had to rely entirely or partly on the nearest kehilla. The governing body of the kehilla, the kahal, included mainly three types of officers: (a) the elders of the kahal, who rotated the office each month, whose function in the Jewish community was the equivalent of town mayor; (b) the *tovim* (aldermen), who gave the heads of the kahal advice and practical assistance; (c) the council. There were also various committees—legal, charity, educational, economic, etc. The leadership was elected by the Jewish community, though only a small percentage participated in the elections. According to prevailing social theory, the communal leaders were considered not the agents or servants of the community but its custodians, and only those of means and class, who were both men of affairs and of learning, were considered qualified to be the communal custodians. Accordingly, the right to vote for communal leadership was not based merely on communal citizenship but also on age, length of habitation in the community, length of participation in communal affairs, and, above all, on economic status and on scholarship—two values accepted by the entire community. As far as we can tell from the few budgets come to hand, the preponderant majority of the expenditures for the members of the community were for welfare, health, and educational needs. Administrative expenses (including salaries for the rabbi and other officials) were low, and the kehilla officers took no salaries. They knew that the communal weal was their responsibility, albeit they did not concern themselves with raising the standard of living of the lower classes. The officials thought that each person had to live according to his means and his class. Accordingly, they allowed no member of the community to stage a festive occasion (wedding, circumcision, etc.), except according to his means. Nor did they allow communal taxes to be imposed upon the members of the community, except according to each man's ability to pay. Indeed, communal revenues were derived largely from direct taxes assessed according to each man's wealth and income. And even some of the royal taxes, such as the poll tax and the real estate tax, while not inherently progressive, were collected on a rather progressive basis, the wealthy and the middle classes covering payments for the poor folk. As in every society, there were of course kehilla leaders who misused their offices, and the moralists were not alone in their protests. But there seems to have been no opposition—at any rate, no organized opposition—to the regime as such, although it denied the majority of the community any influence in the conduct of its affairs. To be sure, there were instances of opposition whose leaders demanded a role in the community administration, but these oppositionists were themselves members of the elite and demanded power on the same basis of economic and scholarly status as those in office. The lower classes, on the other hand, were not ideologically or organizationally consolidated enough to demand any power, although the social differentiation was great.

The kehilla, as we have said, was the basic unit, the cornerstone of Jewish autonomous organization. The kehilla's purview was congruous with the geographical radius of the community and its satellite settlements. From time to time, however, there were problems of internal and external nature which the particular kehilla had not the power to resolve or which concerned all the Jews of the provinces. When the occasion warranted, such matters were dealt with by a council of delegates from the governing kehillot convoked for this purpose. Kehillot, too, were treated according to the system of priorities by which the members of each kehilla were treated: only the large kehillot, important economic, cultural, and religious centers, were considered fit custodians of the common weal. When the need arose, the governing kehillot were organized. The council of the representatives of these kehillot and their rabbis (or the provincial rabbi, when there was one) became the permanent organ of the provincial organization. The representatives of the kehillot who were members of the council, chosen for this task according to an agreed system, were considered the provincial leaders, and together made up the recognized leadership and representative body of the Jewish community of each province. The Kingdom of Poland had four provinces: Great Poland, Little Poland, Red Russia, and, from the the middle of the sixteenth century, Volhynia. Outside Poland proper was the Principality of Lithuania, an autonomous state-province. Regional organizations were established in all these provinces in the sixteenth century, to be sure, not all at the same time. They also differed from each other, according to local conditions which were generally similar but not identical.

Similarly, from time to time internal and external problems arose which the provincial organization could not resolve by itself or which concerned all the Jews of the kingdom. There were annual great fairs at Lublin and Yaroslav to which caravans of Jewish merchants streamed from all the provinces of Poland and Lithuania. With these caravans came Jewish leaders and judges, the former to deal with organizational and administrative problems of their provincial coreligionists, the latter to deal with legal and religious problems. Upon their arrival at the fair, these leaders would convene to deal with matters pertaining to the welfare of the Jews participating in the fair and with matters not pertaining to the fair but which concerned the general welfare of Jewry. The judges from the various provinces would also meet to deal with religio-legal matters, matters of doctrine and principle, as well as practical matters of inter-provincial significance. As the recognition of a community of interests of the Jews of the various provinces grew and crystallized and community of action had to some extent proved itself, the fair councils of the leaders and judges of Poland's three or four provinces merged into the permanent organ of the provincial councils. The judges became the "Judges of the Four Lands"[2a] and the leaders became the "Elders of the Four Lands." Together they were the recognized leadership and representative body of the entire Jewry of the Kingdom of Poland. Lithuanian Jewry had less in common with the Jewries of the Polish provinces. Nevertheless, in the period in question Lithuanian Jewry participated in the activities of the "Four Lands" or at least co-ordinated its activities with theirs.

The "Council of the Four Lands" was the supreme legislative and juridical as well as executive body of Polish Jewry. The religious judges of the Four Lands were the supreme judiciary as well as the supreme legislature in religio-legal matters. The Elders of the Four Lands also performed some juridical tasks—except in money matters, which were considered the exclusive purview of the judges—and served as the legislature in all other matters of Jewish concern. The judges and the leaders separately and jointly, as circumstances required, rendered decisions and promulgated regulations. The legislative activity of the Council of the Four Lands did not, however, prevent the provincial councils, and even the local communities, from issuing local regulations whenever conditions warranted, so long as these regulations did not run counter to the regulations of the general

Council. In the councils and communities alike, decisions were taken by a majority vote, only the repeal of certain regulations occasionally requiring a two-thirds or a unanimous vote. In addition to their legislative and juridical functions the Elders of the Four Lands—like the provincial leaders—also performed executive or administrative functions, principally it appears in the "lands" they represented on the general Council. A modest apparatus was established for administrative purposes, but these officials were concerned primarily with external affairs. There were the *shtadlanim*, who dealt with the rulers and authorities, and the trustes (*neemanim*) who farmed the royal revenues collectable from the Jewish population. This fiscal role gave the supreme organization of the Jewish community a semi-governing character in addition to the moral authority it enjoyed. Its moral authority, incidentally, was recognized outside the borders of Poland, throughout the Ashkenazic cultural sphere and even beyond this sphere, by all Jews who accepted the superiority of Polish Jewish scholarship and even sent their sons to study at Poland's famous *yeshibot*.

This broad autonomy spurred especially the study of Talmud, which was not only a sacred religious work whose study was a religious duty but also a *corpus jure*, a guide to real life. The Talmud and its devotees dominated the public assemblies and kahal deliberations, just as they exercised absolute authority in the educational institutions—the *heder* and the *yeshiva*. The growing differentiation of economic and social life, which from time to time presented the scholars with legal problems, gave considerable impetus to halakic creativity. There developed a whole literature of commentaries and novellae on the Talmud, collections of *responsa* on actual day-to-day Jewish-legal problems, and essays on codes which still serve rabbis as basic legal texts. This literature bears the impress of the Jewish culture in medieval Germany, as does the educational system. In the middle of the sixteenth century some scholars, to be sure, began to refer to the rationalist philosophy of Maimonides and the Spanish scholars. At about the same time, with the onset of the Reformation and the spread of rationalist tendencies in Christian society, there began a free exchange of views between Christians and Jews on matters of religion. This exchange produced anti-Christian essays, as well as attacks on Christians as Judaizers, and attacks on Jews as proselytizers of Christians. One such essay, by a Karaite from the Lithuanian city of Troki, was later translated into several languages and influenced Voltaire. Jewish women and the common folk generally sometimes read secular tales, such as the German stories of knightly deeds which, with some change of content and form, had infiltrated into the Western and then the Polish ghettos. One tale of this genre was published at the end of the sixteenth century in Cracow, which in the latter part of that century had become the most important publishing center of popular literature in the Yiddish language.

All these manifestations of a penchant for rationalist thought, secular literature, and the non-Jewish environment in general, which certainly were not too obvious even in the sixteenth century, subsequently vanished entirely. The popular literature read and created in Poland in the following century—and this literature spread throughout the Yiddish world—was entirely pietistic and moralistic. Alongside the study of Talmud, the study of Cabbala was first firmly entrenched in the middle of the sixteenth century under the spur of Italian and Palestinian influences. By the first half of the seventeenth century, Poland was considered one of the two European centers of Cabbalistic study,[3a] which, through the liturgical, moralistic, and homiletical literature, became popular not only among the scholars but also among the masses. Thus the study of Talmud and Cabbala came to be the spiritual milieu of the Jews.

6

Messianic speculation began to occupy the Cabbalistic circles toward the middle of the seventeenth century. On the basis of a certain statement in the *Zohar* they thought that the Redemption was near; that 1648 was the hoped-for year. That year saw quite the opposite of what had been hoped: 1648 brought the first of a series of catastrophes which inundated Poland and its Jewish settlement.

The first wave was the uprising in the Ukraine in 1648 under the leadership of Bogdan Chmielnitzky, his first war, together with the Tatars, against the Poles. The war was resumed in the following year. In 1651 a third war broke out and in 1652-1653 a fourth. In 1654 the Muscovite forces invaded Poland and in 1655 the Swedes. The successive waves of invasion, beginning with Chmielnitzky's wars, followed naturally upon one another. But for them the Muscovite forces would not have invaded Poland. The Muscovite invasion, in turn, set the stage for the Swedish invasion. Various politico-national, religious, and socioeconomic interests of various nations and within various nations mingled and collided in this maelstrom. Chmielnitzky's onslaughts encompassed chiefly southeastern Poland; the Muscovite assaults wracked the northeastern sector, while the Swedes ruined the western sector. Altogether these waves ravaged the entire Polish-Lithuanian state. Most devastating of all were that of 1648 and the final two.

The Ukrainian insurgents proclaimed a war of extermination against "the nobility, the clergy (Catholic), and the Jews." Social opposition and religious hatred made the Jews a favorite target for the rebel swords. In the final analysis it was the religious factor which proved decisive: no convert was touched, just as no nobleman of the Orthodox communion was touched. The Muscovite forces massacred Jews, expelled them, banished them to the Russian interior, where they were forcibly converted or sold into slavery. And the Muscovites were motivated simply by religious zeal. The Swedes did not single out the Jews; the Polish liberation forces did. Great Poland surrendered to Sweden without a fight. Most of the *Szlachta* as one man accepted the sovereignty of the King of Sweden, and the other classes followed suit. But two religious groups principally were singled out by their contemporaries for accusations of treason: the Arians and the Jews. The Arians were expelled from the land, and after thousands of Jews were slaughtered, they, too, were threatened with banishment. All over Poland and Lithuania the Jews were martyrs for their faith.

Hundreds of Jewish communities and settlements were destroyed and myriads of Jews perished by the sword, famine, and pestilence. Many were taken captive by the Tatars or made a pretense of renouncing their faith. Most of the captives were subsequently ransomed by other European Jewish communities, and the forced converts were permitted to return to the faith of their fathers. Many fled for their lives and went wandering over land and sea, within Poland and beyond its borders, to Hungary, Moldavia, Turkey, Holland, the German states, and to other lands. Some of the refugees became settlers—in Amsterdam, as a matter of fact, there came into being a separate kehilla of Polish and Lithuanian immigrants—and in the course of time the Polish-Ashkenazic version of Jewish culture was implanted there. Some wandered from place to place, finally returning whence they had come. The refugees who roamed the Jewish Diaspora, bringing the evil tidings, by their very appearance roused feelings of Jewish solidarity, moving even distant brethren not only to hasten succor but also to share the severity of exile and the urgency of redemption in the wake of the catastrophes, which were no less than the "birth pangs of the Messiah." This seed planted in Jewish hearts bore fruit in the great Messianic movement which in 1666 encompassed all Jewry, and for a number of generations afterward—until the French Revolution—continued a clandestine existence, with altered form and content.

7

The century after the "deluge," as the period is designated in Polish Jewish history, was a period of progressive deterioration of the Polish state. Urban and rural economy disintegrated. The authority of the central government dwindled and corruption and chaos spread. Social and religious oppression increased. Civil and external warfare constantly haunted the country until, finally, Poland was swallowed up by the neighboring powers. This sealed the destiny of the Polish state, and to a great extent of course also determined the fate of Polish Jewry.

Agricultural production decreased as a result of the wars, and the export of agricultural products—which formerly had occupied a central place in Poland's foreign trade—decreased even further because of Russian competition. The Jews continued to occupy the same relatively important position as before in Poland's domestic and foreign trade. But the general dwindling of commerce spurred the Jews to seek other sources of livelihood, principally in tenant farming and in the crafts. At the same time, the dwindling of urban sources of livelihood led in the royal towns to an intensification of the war against the Jews, a war which received considerable support from the Catholic reaction against the non-Catholics. This war, even apart from the Catholic support, forced the Jews to seek other places. Out of necessity Jews returned to the places and occupations from which they had been uprooted by the upheavals of 1648 and after. Moreover, the stream of Jews to the urban and rural domains of the gentry in the Ukraine and elsewhere gained momentum. In the middle of the eighteenth century most Jews were on noble estates, some 40 per cent of them settled principally in areas originally inhabited by Ukrainians.

Jews inhabiting the noble domains had long been considered "private Jews," dependent upon the good graces or subject to the whims of the landlords. At this period not only did the absolute and relative number of Jews so dependent increase, but their very dependence increased. The landlords, whose income from their estates decreased but whose power grew by virtue of the progressive disintegration of the central authority, intensified their financial and economic exploitation of their Jewish and non-Jewish, urban and rural, subjects. The moral decline of the nobility, furthermore, led to increased oppression and atrocities which could result only from dissipation and disregard for the law.

With the decline of the *Gutswirtschaft*, which never regained its former significance, the gentry derived revenue principally from direct taxes and imposts collected from their subjects, and from monopolistic rights they arrogated to themselves in the production, purchase, and sale of certain products of their estates. Their chief source of income was their monopoly on the manufacture of beer and spirits, Poland's principal industry. All the noble revenues were generally leased, to Jews and non-Jews alike. The Jews, for the most part, entered the alcoholic beverages industry. Some Jewish lessees operated on a large scale, but the majority operated modest taverns and wayside inns. By the middle of the eighteenth century, one-third of Poland's Jewish population, some 250,000, was scattered over the countryside, at an average of approximately two families to the hamlet. The inn performed a vital function in the state of communications of the time. The village tavern was the central socioeconomic and cultural institution of that feudal peasant society. The Jewish lessees were subject to no less, often to more, exploitation than the non-Jewish members of their respective classes. But in farming the revenues of the nobility—and even the remote inn and the little tavern were monopolies for nobles—the Jews perforce served them as tools in the exploitation of the Jewish and non-Jewish subjects in the towns and the non-Jewish subjects in the villages. Thus—as in the period before 1648—the age-old religious antagonism assumed a socioeconomic aspect. This antagonism was expressed with especial vigor in the insurgent movements against the tyranny of the Polish gentry that arose from time to time in the Ukraine and in White Russia and which also affected their Jewish tenants and subjects. The greatest of these movements, a page of blood and tears in Jewish history, erupted in 1768.

The dispersal of the Jewish masses throughout the countryside was also of great cultural significance. The isolated village families could not build and maintain synagogues, support teachers and religious judges, or meet any of the other needs of a Jewish community. A considerable part of the Jewish population dwelt in a backward rural environment without any possibility of educating itself or living a full communal and religious life.

The changes that took place in the Polish-Lithuanian state and in its Jewish sector also influenced Jewish communal organization. With the increasing socioeconomic and cultural differentiation in the Jewish community, the social base of the dominant economic and scholarly aristocracy shrank. The societal base contracted even further with the dispersal of the Jewish population over the noble estates, when the great kehilla which had been the basic unit of Jewish autonomous organization found the majority of its constituency without possibility of influencing the conduct of Jewish affairs because it dwelt beyond the pale of the kehilla, in villages and hamlets. The results were especially evident with respect to the provincial and national organizations. The right to take any part in the election of the heads of the Lithuanian Council in the middle of the eighteenth century did not even extend to 1 per cent of the adult householders. More than 99 per cent of them enjoyed no right to participate either directly or indirectly in elections for this Council. Of these, 93 per cent did not enjoy suffrage because they dwelt outside the five main communities. The situation in Poland was similar.

As the rights enjoyed by the Jewish population dwindled, their debts mounted. Because of the persecutions, the accusations, and all the other troubles visited upon them, all the kehillot and councils were over their heads in debt. Unable to meet the debts, the governing bodies saw need to change the tax system heretofore collected principally on the basis of assets and net income. Additional direct and indirect excise taxes were accordingly collected on gross income and on victuals, taxes which the poor folk also had to pay and which hit them especially hard. This further undermined the authority of the Jewish governing bodies and led to protest and defiance, sometimes in organized form. The oppositionist manifestations in the kehillot were given further impetus by, among other things, the growth of the Jewish working class, which in the middle of the eighteenth century constituted approximately one-fourth of the total Jewish population. Following the example of their Christian counterparts, the Jewish craftsmen organized themselves into guilds to meet their special social, economic, and religious needs. More than once, as an organized force—independently or in conjunction with other forces—they took a stand against the existing kehilla regime. The sole *raison d'être* of the Jewish autonomous institutions was their tax-collecting function. This function also gave the institutions political and police power, in addition to the moral authority they enjoyed from the Jewish-legal point of view. As the central governmental authority disintegrated, the central Jewish communal authority also disintegrated to the extent that its power derived from the former. To the extent that the Polish-Lithuanian state disintegrated into a collection of all sorts of petty and major domains—each noble holding in town or village becoming an independent domain—the authority of the Jewish governing bodies waned. Their power and authority vis-à-vis the Jews on the noble estates disintegrated, and, as we have noted, most of the Jews then dwelt on such estates. The decline of the internal and external authority of the Jewish governing bodies hindered them in their task for the central government—the collection from the Jews of the royal taxes. Their impotence to carry out this function, together with other factors, finally led, in 1764, to the dissolution of the Councils in Poland and Lithuania.

On this bleak landscape of internal and external upheaval there glimmered, blazed, and died, from time to time, Messianic expectations; heralds and prophets of Redemption appeared and vanished. The Sabbataian movement[4a] in its various ramifications took hold especially in Podolia, which adjoined Turkey, the center of the movement. In Podolia and its environs—even in some remoter regions—secret Sabbataian societies persisted until they were revealed, and encountered the vigorous and bitter opposition of traditional Judaism. About one hundred years after Sabbatai Zevi forcibly embraced Islam, many Polish Sabbataians followed suit and, for appearance' sake, adopted an alien faith in the belief that this was the path that had to be traveled to the Final Jewish Redemption.

At the time of this crisis in Jewish life on the two frontiers of Poland, in Podolia itself and in Lithuania, a spiritual renaissance developed. It is linked with two names: Rabbi Elijah of Vilna and Rabbi Israel of Miedzybos. The first bequeathed to posterity a rich literary legacy, inaugurated a new method in the study of Torah, and developed a following of illustrious scholars. The second left no literary legacy; but he taught a new approach to faith, to the service of God, and launched a great religious movement which persists to this day.

Neither Rabbi Elijah nor Rabbi Israel occupied a rabbinical office. Both were considered Hasidim. Rabbi Elijah was popularly called "Hasid," in addition to the title "Gaon" which he had earned by virtue of his outstanding scholarship. Rabbi Israel, too, was considered a Hasid by his disciples and admirers, albeit the common folk dubbed him "*Baal Shem Tob*"[5a]—"Master of the Good Name"—because he issued charms to those who requested them. The term hasid (as well as "zaddik"), as it crystallized in the earlier pietistic-moralistic literature, refers to a man who lives a solitary, ascetic life dedicated entirely to the service of God—in study and prayer, deed and meditation. Rabbi Elijah was such a hasid. Rabbi Israel personified a new type of hasid: constant dedication to God not through asceticism and withdrawal from human society, but by participation in life, by the enjoyment of worldly pleasures. These he invested with spiritual meaning, thus transforming them into a way and a means to the service of God. This way of Hasidism—piety—appealed to the masses. Whoever wanted to walk this path was already a hasid. Whoever thus attained to the supreme level became a "servant of God," "the whole man," "the leader of the generation." It was this type that was destined to be called the "zaddik," and to become a central institution in the new movement, the center of the Hasidic community. The masses flocked to this new idea. The antihierarchical tendency which marked the beginnings of the Hasidic movement, as it had marked the Sabbataian movement, served Hasidism in its battle against its adversaries, the religious and administrative leaders of the kehillot, in so far as they had not yet been won over to Hasidism. Several years after the death of the *Baal Shem Tob* the first partition of Poland took place. But neither the new borders nor the old could contain this religious revivalist movement. It crashed all barriers and very quickly inundated the entire German-cultural, Yiddish-speaking world.

Even as the flood of Hasidism swept along, in seeped, then burst, from the West the *Haskala* movement.[6a] The struggle between Hasidism, which was an internal development, and *Haskala*, which entered Jewish life from without, is beyond the scope of this paper. This struggle is one of the crucial phases in the dawn of the modern period in Jewish history.

NOTES

[[1a] See below Abraham Menes, "Patterns of Jewish Scholarship in Eastern Europe," p. 393.]

[[2a] See *ibid.*, p. 391.]

[[3a] See below *ibid.*, p. 395; also Itzhak Ben-Zvi, "Eretz Yisrael under Ottoman Rule, 1517-1917," pp. 627 ff.; Abraham J. Heschel, "The Mystical Element in Judaism"; Yudel Mark, "Yiddish Literature."]

[[4a] See Ben-Zvi, *op. cit.*, pp. 605 ff., 629 ff.]

[5a See below Menes, *op. cit.;* Arieh Tartakower, "The Decline of European Jewry (1933-1953)"; Ben-Zvi, *op. cit.*]

[6a See below Bernard D. Weinryb, "East European Jewry (Since the Partitions of Poland, 1772-1795)"; Menes, *op. cit.*; Ben Zion Dinur, "The Historical Foundations of the Rebirth of Israel"; Hillel Bavli, "The Modern Renaissance of Hebrew Literature"; Mark, *op. cit.*]

BIBLIOGRAPHY

BALABAN, M., *The History of the Frankist Movement* (in Hebrew). Vols. I-II. Tel-Aviv, 1934-1935.

———, *The History of the Jews in Lwow in the Seventeenth and Eighteenth Centuries* (in Polish). Lvov, 1906.

———, *The History of the Jews of Cracow and Casimierz.* Vols. I-II. Cracow, 1931-1936.

BERLIN, I., *The Historic Destiny of the Jewish People in Russian Government Territories* (in Russian). St. Petersburg, 1919.

BERSHADSKY, S. A., *The Jews of Lithuania* (in Russian). St. Petersburg, 1883.

DUBNOW, S., *The History of Hasidism* (in Hebrew). Vol. I. Tel-Aviv, 1930.

———, *History of the Jews in Russia and Poland.* Vol. I. Philadelphia, 1916.

———, *The State Records, or the Records of the Council of the Leading Kehillot in the State of Lithuania* (in Hebrew). Berlin, 1925.

DUNLOP, D. M., *The History of the Jewish Khazars.* Princeton, 1954.

FRANK, A. N., *The Jews and the Burghers in Poland* (in Hebrew). Warsaw, 1921.

GELBER, N. M., *The History of the Jews of Brod* (in Hebrew). Jerusalem, 1955.

GURLAND, H. I., *Persecutions of the Jews* (in Hebrew). Vols. I-VI. 1892-1897.

HALPERN, I. (ed.), *The Jews in Poland* (in Hebrew). Vols. I-II. Jerusalem, 1948-1953.

———, *Acta congressus generalis Judaeorum Regni Poloniae* (1580-1764). Jerusalem, 1948.

HORODETZKY, S. A., *Three Centuries of Polish Jewry* (in Hebrew). Tel-Aviv, 1945.

KLAUSNER, I., *Vilna in the Time of the Gaon* (in Hebrew). Jerusalem, 1942.

MAHLER, R., *The History of the Jews in Poland* (in Hebrew). Merhaviah, 1946.

POLLAK, A. N., *Khazaria: The History of a Jewish Kingdom in Europe* (in Hebrew). Tel-Aviv, 1951.

SCHIPPER, I., *The Cultural History of the Polish Jews in the Middle Ages* (in Yiddish). Warsaw, 1926.

———, *The History of Jewish Commerce in Polish Lands* (in Polish). Warsaw, 1937.

SCHORR, M., *The Legal Status and the Internal Legislation of the Jews in Poland* (in German). Berlin-Vienna, 1917.

WEINRYB, D., *Studies in the Economic and Social History of Polish Jewry* (in Hebrew). Jerusalem, 1939.

———, *Texts and Studies in the Communal History of Polish Jewry*. New York, 1950.

This is merely a list of books of a general and selective nature. The chapter is based chiefly on research by the author, only part of it published.

CHAPTER 7

EAST EUROPEAN JEWRY

(Since the Partitions of Poland, 1772-1795)

By Bernard D. Weinryb

Eastern Europe, reaching approximately from the Baltic to the Black Sea and from east of the Oder and the Carpathian Mountains to the Urals and the Asiatic mainland, was backward in comparison with Western Europe. For most of the nineteenth century it was a region populated in the main by peasants, most of them serfs up to the second half of the century, and some small artisans and workers. Material civilization, industrialization, and technical knowledge from the West were slow to penetrate the East. The ideas of enlightenment, liberalism, democracy, romanticism, nationalism, socialism, and later anti-Semitism and Fascism, in all their variations, also developed somewhat tardily in the East. Belated, too, were the results of the revolutionary tendencies (1831, 1848) and the modernization of the state.

The population in most of this vast area lacked ethnic and/or religious unity. Each part of the area was inhabited by a conglomeration of different nationalities and denominations: Ukrainians, Poles, Jews, Germans, some Armenians, White Russians, Russians, and in the south also Greeks, Tatars, Rumanians, and some other groups. And with regard to religion, Catholics struggled against Greek Orthodox or Greek Catholics, and they all had to cope with Protestants and some smaller religious groups.

In the era of rising nationalism, wars, revolutions, and intergroup tensions ran high. These tensions were superimposed upon the political events: the partition of Poland among her neighbors, expansionist politics and the rivalries of these neighbors, the declining power of the Ottoman Empire, the struggle of the suppressed groups for independence, the rise of the Balkan States, the reshaping of the map of Eastern Europe after World War I, the impact of both World Wars.

Socially, the abolition of serfdom in 1848 and in the 1860's gave the peasants freedom without providing them with sufficient land. It intensified the struggle between peasants and landowners and combined with the rising natural growth to accelerate the movement toward urbanization and the large waves of overseas emigration. In the cities the incoming peasant population constituted the proletariat and the lower rungs of the middle class seeking better status and higher positions in society. The nationalist aspirations amplified the social tensions created in the cities, and political chauvinism took an economic turn. Meanwhile the spread of industrial capitalism, though slow, brought changes in the whole socioeconomic fabric, creating new and annulling old sources of income, uprooting millions, and causing social disorganization.

Between times of deepening crisis—or parallel with them—there were years or decades of heightening hopes for political or social freedom and elevation, for renaissance of national cultures, for improving prospects for human brotherhood, equality, and co-operation.

Against this background of world and local events—and subject to all these influences—the fate of the Jews in this region was shaped. The lines of their development ran more or less parallel with or were reactions to the trends in Eastern Europe generally. As a result of all this, changes were wrought in the composition of the Jewish group, in its "geography," character, structure, and content. There were fluctuations in population size, in political-legal standing, occupational and economic status, social structure, group cohesiveness, religious and traditional adherence, cultural and literary creativeness, and organizational affiliations. There were times of persecution, danger, and threats to physical existence—the epoch of Nicholas I in Russia, the pogroms at the end of the nineteenth and beginning of the twentieth century, persecutions in Rumania, World War I and the pogroms immediately following it, and the Nazi attempt at annihilation. There were also disruptive forces working against cultural and group survival—enforced and "free" conversion and assimilation, developments in Soviet Russia after World War I, and in the satellites in recent years. But there were at the same time external and internal forces which made for survival and progress despite frequent setbacks.

One may observe a number of almost contradictory trends and developments. In terms of population there was a great increase throughout almost the entire period. This slackened somewhat in the pre-World War II decades, with big losses during the war resulting from Nazi annihilation policies. But in the preceding century and a half, East European Jewry had expanded tremendously. From about 1,000,000 in the last quarter of the eighteenth century (Polish Jewry being at that time almost identical with East European Jewry) it grew to 5,500,000 a century later—peopling Russia and Rumania—and about 7,000,000 at the end of the 1930's. East European Jews also "colonized" the United States of America, Canada, Argentina, Brazil, and other Latin American countries, as well as South Africa and Palestine, settling millions of Jews in those countries. Similarly they had a fructifying influence on West European Jewry by repeated infusions of new blood and fresh minds.

The rapid natural growth in a time of changing economic structure accelerated the population pressure upon the means of making a living, increasing poverty, on the one hand, and occupational diversification, on the other. Largely a mass of occupationally slightly differentiated small traders, innkeepers, craftsmen, and middlemen, living in backward areas at the beginning of the nineteenth century, East European Jews underwent a considerable restratification process. They penetrated into manufacturing, large-scale business, banking, the liberal professions, and, to a lesser degree, agriculture. They formed a labor class, and then proceeded, in part, to move from this group into middle-class occupations.

Socially they were transformed from a largely static, traditionally bound society, with deep roots in the townlets and villages, into a highly urbanized group. The old compulsory kehilla and its affiliated societies (*hevrot*) were partially supplanted by a modernized institution and by a number of parties, labor movements, and other modern organizations—which again declined in the post-World War II period.

Politically the East European Jews led a hard, unceasing struggle against expulsions and discrimination, and for civic equality—a struggle which seemed to have reached its goal at the end of World War I. But the subsequent years saw about half of East European Jewry subjected to the Communists' new order and, in due course, cut off from world Jewry. The rest of the East European Jews suffered from the extreme nationalist chauvinism in the succession states and a sharply rising tide of anti-Semitism.

Culturally, the trends were varied, running sometimes parallel, at other times supplanting each other or merging. At the end of the eighteenth century East European Jewry was a slightly differentiated mass, whose unity had not been greatly undermined by the Frankist schism, the Hasidism-Mitnagdim controversy and strife, by some social cleavages and stratification developing within the Jewish communities, or by the beginnings of migration. During the ensuing century and a half the Jewish mass was subjected to upheavals, revolutions, and manifold cultural trends which penetrated into the backward area of Eastern Europe—cosmopolitan enlightenment, nationalism and struggle for independence by subjected nationalities, socialism, scientific research and inquiry. The reaction was differentiation and division, ranging from a tenacious clinging to the old cultural patterns and beliefs to a tendency toward complete assimilation and submergence. Between these two extremes lay all stages of compromise—slight modernization of Jewish education and study, "Judaization" of general external trends and their adaptation to the needs and circumstances of the Jewish group, secular or semisecular Jewish trends.

There came into being the *Haskala*,[1a] Zionist and Diaspora nationalist trends, Jewish socialism of varying shades, as well as modern orthodox trends. Modern Yiddish and Hebrew literatures and secular or semisecular cultures developed, and modernized Jewish school systems and learning arose. These movements have had different destinies. While the Yiddish trend has been on the decline for the past decade or so, modern Hebrew, the creation of East European Jewry, has become entrenched in the new State of Israel and is bound to undergo transformations with the changing character of the Jewish population there.

1. FROM THE POLISH PARTITIONS (1772-1795) TO WORLD WAR I

The dismemberment of the Polish Kingdom (1772-1795) broke up the more or less homogeneous Polish Jewry, numbering a little less than 1,000,000, and placed the Jews within three different spheres of influence, each opening its own avenue of development and path to migration. Thus the Polish partitions furthered the process of Jewish division and change.

The partition of the country was a slow process, and a long time elapsed before its impact was felt. The partitioning was accomplished in three stages (1772, 1793, and 1795), taking about a quarter of a century, and then nearly a quarter of a century more passed before the borders were fixed. These borders then remained generally the same until World War I.

At the time of the first partition (1772) the northeastern part of Poland —White Russia—went to Russia, the southwestern parts (Galicia) to Austria, and parts of western Poland to Prussia. Poland lost about one-quarter of her territory and one-fifth of her population. The rest, some 150,000 square miles, with a population of 7,000,000, remained a Polish state. In 1793 Russia and Prussia enlarged their Polish possessions considerably, dividing about a half of Poland among themselves; and 1795 saw the three neighbors participating in the spoils, with the largest parts going to Prussia and Russia. But before long Napoleon appeared on the scene as the arbiter of Europe and again changed the map of Eastern Europe. After Napoleon's victory at Jena in 1806 and the Peace of Tilsit (July, 1807), a semi-independent Duchy of Warsaw was carved out of the portion which had belonged to Prussia since 1793. This state, enlarged in 1809 by formerly Polish parts taken from Austria, existed up to Napoleon's defeat in Russia. At the Congress of Vienna (1815) the political map was again redrawn. Austria kept Galicia; Prussia received Thorn and surroundings, which united with its other Polish territories to form the Grand Duchy of Posen; a small free state of Cracow lasted until 1846, being later absorbed by Austria into Galicia. Russia had most of the spoils of the first and second partitions incorporated in the provinces of southern and western Russia, while the central part of Poland, consisting of most of the Duchy of Warsaw, became the so-called Kingdom of Poland, a semiautonomous political structure attached to Russia with the Czar as king until it subsequently became a Russian province (after 1831).

The first partition brought about one-third of Polish Jewry, amounting at that time to nearly 750,000, under the rule of Austria, Russia, and Prussia—the great majority under Austria. The second and third partitions divided some 800,000 Jews among Austria, Prussia, and Russia. The Duchy of Warsaw, in 1808, had 205,000 Jews, and their numbers increased in the following year. And when the Kingdom of Poland was established it included 212, 996 Jews (1816).

Meanwhile, during the half-century following the first partition, changes were taking place in Jewish settlement in Eastern Europe. Since about 1770 a constant stream of emigration to the east, particularly to the neo-Russian provinces in the south, had been flowing from southern Poland, while another stream wended its way from Galicia to Hungary as a result of the expulsions and banning of Jews from innkeeping. Further thousands of Jews were expelled from Prussia's part of Poland, and they, apparently with other Jews of Galicia and Poland, wandered to the northern provinces.

Of the countries absorbing Poland and with it East European Jewry, Russia had had no Jews since the expulsion in 1744, Prussia had had a small Jewish population, and in Austria the number of the newly acquired Jews surpassed the existing Jewish population. A new "Jewish problem" was created in all three countries.

These states were ruled as absolute monarchies and by what were known as enlightened despots (Frederick II of Prussia, Joseph II of Austria, Catherine II of Russia), prepared, from time to time, to introduce certain innovations and to enforce them ruthlessly. With regard to the Jewish question, Prussia and Austria, like most German states during the seventeenth and eighteenth centuries, had developed the policy of dividing the Jews into the rich and useful and the poor and useless or harmful. The first group was accorded privileges and given "protection" of varying degrees in accordance with their usefulness and ability to pay; and efforts were made to get rid of the second group, or to limit their numbers and occupational opportunities. Russia had had no practice in handling the Jewish question. All three states were, like Poland, distinctly agricultural, with the gentry exercising the greatest influence upon the government, though the feudal order was in varying stages of decline. In all three states the tensions between the peasant-serf and the landlord were increasing under the impact of a changing situation and growing population. The landlords, in their "natural" desire to pin the misery of the serfs on somebody other than themselves, were ready, at least officially, to accuse the Jewish innkeeper, middleman, and peddler of causing all the evils. A similar situation prevailed in the nineteenth century in Rumania.

By the end of the eighteenth century additional pressures came to the fore. Under the influence of economic ideas prevailing at that time—such as those of the physiocrats and of Adam Smith—agriculture and manufacturing were regarded as the most useful occupations. With the beginning of modernization of the state, assimilation of the Jews, adjustment to the general population, and cessation of communal self-government and inherited mode of life were demanded. These reforms were either looked upon as the conditions for granting equality or were, in part, enforced by the power of the state, or both.

In all three states policies regarding the newly acquired Jews were generally similar. They included institution of a "pale of settlement" in all three countries; refusal to let the former Polish Jews move into the interior of Prussia, Austria, or Russia; differentiation between the few rich or assimilated Jews and the mass of poor ones, whose numbers it was sought to limit by restrictions on marriage, high marriage taxes, and even by expulsions; removing Jews from the villages and drastically curtailing their business contact with the village population; attempts, often well meant but badly executed, to transfer them to new occupations, mainly to agriculture, and to increase the "usefulness" of the Jews by increasing their taxes and instituting new ones. Later, in the first half of the nineteenth century, with the growing modernization of the state and the tendencies toward democracy and emancipation, the principle of division into rich-useful and poor-useless Jews was transferred to the practice of graded emancipation, of conferring equality upon the former and (in the beginning) of denying it to the latter. In Russia similar steps were followed, except that at first there was vacillation between putting Jews on equal footing with other city dwellers and keeping them in the same status as in Poland. Expulsion from villages and removal from occupations connected with the village were practiced much longer in the Russian than in the Austrian and Prussian portions of Poland—in the first half and even in the last decades of the nineteenth century and, to some extent, up to World War I. Again, modernization of the state brought in its wake emancipation for the Jews in Posen by the middle of the nineteenth century, in Galicia in the 1860's, while in Russia the modernization made slow progress and Jewish emancipation did not become a reality before the Revolution of 1917.

There are many other similarities in treatment of the Jews in all these countries, with Russia and Russian Poland again lagging behind (to some extent learning from or imitating the others). Examples are the introduction of military service (Galicia 1788, Russia 1827, Poland 1843), intended, in part, to change Jewish behavior, as did the opening of secular schools for Jews—maintained out of special Jewish taxes—and the attempt to enforce attendance. The same intentions prompted the efforts to change Jewish attire and external appearance, the prohibition of Hebrew and Yiddish in documents and commercial papers (Galicia 1789, Russia 1804, 1835). In each of these states there was also contradiction. On the one hand the desire on the part of the state to limit the power and rights of Jewish self-government—the Kehilla—or to close it (Posen 1797, Galicia 1789, Russia 1795, 1799, 1844, Poland 1821). On the other hand, endowing in practice the newly created substitute organization with authority, the state used it to raise taxes from Jews, and to enforce military service or other specific laws concerning Jews. Similarly, the enforcing or instituting of specific taxation (i.e., on *kosher* meat, Friday night candles) was bound to increase rather than lessen Jewish separateness. In this, too, Russia began, or continued, these practices later than the others.

In the last decades of the nineteenth century the growth of nationalism, chauvinism, and modern anti-Semitism in Europe had an impact upon the Jewish situation in all three states, as did the increasing tendency to settle issues by stirring up the masses and "arousing their ire." The attempts toward assimilation of the Jews, to make them resemble others and to integrate them in the general society, gave way to the idea of eliminating them from that society and curbing their activity. Again the difference between Russia (and Rumania) and the other states was mainly a matter of degree. Instead of discrimination there was in Russia government action; instead of "excesses" and small pogroms there were full-scale pogroms with heavy destruction of life and property.

Common to all three states was also the apparent contradiction between the central government, instituting reforms by decree, and the local officials, hampering or boycotting the execution of these laws and regulations, either because of their own prejudices or interests, their knowledge of the factual situation on the spot, disbelief in the possibility of changing the Jew, or their different national attitudes (such as those of the Poles in Galicia and Russian Poland).

In broader issues and in political matters, too, the Polish population, or its leadership, in Galicia and Russian Poland thought the Jews would support Polish national demands, with some Poles even advocating Jewish emancipation. They were opposed to Jewish nationalism and the appearance of the Jews at elections as a group with their own demands and programs: Galicia, for example, forbade the registration of Yiddish as a mother tongue (census, 1910), and opposed the Zionist slate for the Vienna parliament in 1911; a similar situation developed in Russian Poland at the elections to the Russian Duma. There were attempts to build up a "genuine" Polish middle class and eliminate the Jews from city life. Discrimination against Jews on the part of local government, run or influenced by Poles, sometimes went beyond the legal limitations set by the central government.

The reactions of the Jews to political and economic pressures, to anti-Semitic tendencies, to intergroup tensions, and to growing nationalistic trends were somewhat alike in all three states, although varied from region to region—to some extent paralleling the varying density of the Jewish population, and the opportunities open to Jews in other parts of the respective country. In the province of Posen, with its small Jewish population, dispersion into the rest of Germany (after 1848) served as a "safety valve," while those Jews who remained in Posen could be absorbed into the German cultural sphere. In Russia and Poland the density, compactness, and size of the Jewish population, numbering millions, the backwardness of the region and the lack of opportunities "to move out," made the Jews "stand up and fight" both in terms of a struggle for existence on the spot and the creation of cultural, socioeconomic, and political organizations. A great many Jews clung tenaciously to the traditional forms and content, and made efforts to continue the old way of life and to cultivate the *Shtetel* culture. The large emigration to Western Europe and overseas absorbed only the natural increase.

Galicia and Rumania, which also had dense Jewish populations, though numbered in the hundreds of thousands instead of millions, fell somewhere between the province of Posen and Russia in terms of achievement and modernization of Jewish life and of preserving the old traditional way of life.

Prussian Province of Posen. In the part of Poland which went to Prussia there was, in 1772, only a small group of Jews, numbering about 15,000. But as a result of Prussia's acquisitions in the last two partitions, the number of Jews increased to about 200,000 by the end of the century. In the Duchy of Posen, created in 1815 after most of the Polish provinces went to Russia, there were 51,951 Jews.

Prussia attempted at first to rule the annexed Polish provinces in the spirit of the Prussian *Judenreglement* of 1750, designed to keep the number of Jews low. An order of 1772 specified that only Jews with a capital of 1,000 reichsthaler or more could remain in the country; the rest (dubbed *Betteljuden*—Beggar Jews or paupers) were to be expelled. The Prussian officials in personal contact with the Jews, however, recognized that only very few could qualify to stay, and persuaded the King to modify the order. Nevertheless, thousands of Jews were actually driven out during the first years and even later.

The second and third partitions of Poland brought to Prussia a Jewish population twelve to fifteen times that of the former Prussian Polish possessions, and about four times that of Prussia itself. The Jews constituted more than one-quarter of the city population; in some cities they even were a majority. In the task of absorbing the vast Polish lands, the bureaucracy considered the Jewish element somewhat more reliable than the Poles. It also seemed that by improving the Jewish status in the cities the strength of the existing Polish order could be undermined. The policy and practice of the government in the newly acquired provinces (now named New East

Prussia and South Prussia) wavered between strict measures limiting the number of Jews and their occupational activity, and cancellation of the old anti-Jewish privileges of some Polish cities (*de non tolerandis Judaeis*) and of the guilds. A decree of 1793 limited the marrying age of Jewish males to twenty-five and granted permission to marry only to those who had a certain amount of capital or knew a craft; attempts were made to expel Jews from villages. On the other hand, Jews were admitted a little later into hitherto *Judenrein* cities and towns, Polish guilds were requested to accept them, and Jews were induced to avail themselves of general education.

Most of these orders found their codification in the regulations of 1797 (*Generaljudenreglement*) conferring the right to reside in the region and promising "protection" to all Jews who were in the territory at the time of the occupation and had permanent employment. The same ruling forbade Jewish men to marry before the age of twenty-five, raised the special taxes for Jews, and limited the autonomy of the Kehilla to religious affairs, thus making the Jews subject to the general courts in civil matters. It also prescribed that the rabbi must know German or Polish, and made these languages obligatory in all schools for Jews maintained by the state. Moneylending was forbidden, trading rights limited, and the village Jews given the right to sell only agricultural implements. Jews were encouraged to learn crafts, to become agriculturists—for which purpose lands were promised them—and to build factories.

But there was a disparity between legal attitudes and practice. Most of the stipulations were difficult, if not impossible, to carry out. The poverty of the Jews, their established mode of life, the backwardness of the country generally, served as barriers to social change. The number of "protected" Jews was small (in Lissa in 1798 but 18 per cent of the Jews). The idea of agricultural colonization was abandoned in 1803 after some attempts had been made and a flood of projects generated; Jews were only reluctantly admitted to the cities formerly closed to them, and most of the guilds remained virtually inaccessible. The Jewish Kehilla carried on its previous functions, to some extent because the state found it a convenient vehicle for collecting the high Jewish taxes. The type of rabbi remained generally as of old. Schools for Jewish children with teachers paid by the state failed to open, while the old type *heder* and Beth Hamidrash remained unchanged.

Whatever German influence was felt emanated mostly from the small group of German Jewish bankers, merchants, and professionals who settled in Warsaw and some other places during the Prussian occupation.

When, following the downfall of Napoleon, Prussian dominance over the Posen region (a part of former Polish territories) was renewed, there was in the semiautonomous Grand Duchy of Posen a heritage of two legal practices, that of Prussia before 1806, and that of the Duchy of Warsaw where the promised Jewish rights had been suspended in 1808.

The population of the Grand Duchy of Posen (779,000 in 1815) consisted of about 50 per cent Poles, 40 per cent Germans, and 7 per cent Jews. But the Jews comprised an important factor in the economic life of the cities and in the city of Posen itself, where they held about a two-thirds share in trade, industry, and banking, and about one-third in crafts.

In the ensuing struggle of the Germans and Poles the Jew was caught between the pro-German forces and those favoring maintenance of the region's Polish character. The Prussian government or its officials attempted to help Jews assimilate to German culture by introducing compulsory education, trying to modernize the *heder*, and promising civil rights to those who became Germanized. The decree of June 1, 1833, gives the Jewish community organization the status of a public law corporation, setting up the regulations for election of elders and administration. The Jews themselves were divided into two groups: the naturalized and the tolerated. Those with a knowledge of German, owners of a factory or house or a considerable amount of capital, were able to become naturalized. The "tolerated" Jews were limited with regard to their domicile rights and occupations (forbidden to live or peddle in villages or to sell beverages, or to engage in trade), their marriage age (twenty-four years at least), and movement throughout the country.

The number of Jews eligible for naturalization was small (535 in the city of Posen in 1834 out of a Jewish population of about 6,000). The prospect of naturalization failed to induce many Jews to assimilate culturally with the Germans. Most of the Jews in the smaller towns, like a great many in Posen itself, continued to adhere to the Jewish tradition. Only the small group of wealthier and better educated Jews was attracted by German culture. In 1847, for instance, only 25 per cent of the Jewish children of school age in Posen, and 20 per cent in Bromberg, attended general schools. But during the 1840's hundreds of Jews became naturalized, for the most part because the Prussian bureaucrats hoped to maintain the German majority in the city councils with the help of the Jewish voters. (In 1843 about 20 per cent had been naturalized.)

These efforts by German officials coincided with the inclination of some Jews to accept German culture. Only a very small proportion of the "enlightened" Jews were ready to side with the Polish nationalists. When in 1848 a group of Cracow Jews called upon those of Posen to identify themselves with the Poles, the latter—or their mouthpiece—replied that they had always "felt with Germany" (*Orient*, May 22, 1848). Thus they were suspect in the eyes of those Poles who wished to cultivate Polish national consciousness and political activity. During the insurrection of 1848, Jews were attacked in some places by patriotic Poles. After the insurrection the specific semiautonomous status of the Grand Duchy of Posen was annulled and it became a Prussian province. Thereafter Jews enjoyed citizenship, like Prussian Jews, although the local authorities in some localities discriminated against them and refused them participation in the elections to the city councils.

From then on the Jews played a still larger role in the struggle between the Germanizing and the Polonizing forces. With some exceptions, the Jews, who in the meantime had become attached to German culture through the general schools, identified themselves and were identified with the Germans.

The rise of Polish nationalism, and the nationalists' attempts at economic self-defense through a system of co-operatives, banks, and other enterprises, had an anti-Jewish bent, while growing anti-Semitism among the German population did not fail to have its impact upon the Jewish population. As a result there ensued a constant migration, first from the smaller towns to the larger cities, leading to a transfer from local trade to banking, industry, and professions, and later to Prussia, particularly Berlin and Breslau, and America. Since the second half of the nineteenth century, the proportion of Jews in the population had constantly declined and, since the last quarter, their absolute numbers had decreased, too. The Jewish population fell from 76,757 (5.7 per cent) in 1849 to 26,512 (1.26 per cent) in 1910. In Prussia —in Berlin, Breslau, and other German cities—Posen Jews formed a considerable proportion of the Jewish population. Most of those remaining in Posen left for Germany after World War I, when the province was transferred to the newly resurrected Poland. No more than a few thousand Jews remained in the Province of Posen.

Galicia. Through the first partition Austria gained from Poland a territory with more than 2,000,000 inhabitants. The third partition added the provinces of Cracow and Lublin with over 1,000,000. But in 1809 a considerable part of the former Polish territories was taken by Napoleon and incorporated into the Duchy of Warsaw. Another part, the Tarnopol region, went to Russia (to be returned in 1813).

Galicia—the name given by Austria to the territory acquired from Poland —was stabilized after the Congress of Vienna. It comprised 77,000 square kilometers with a population of 3,500,000. For some time another territory —Bukovina, which Austria acquired in 1786 from Turkey—was administratively connected with Galicia (1786-1790, 1817-1848), but became a separate administrative unit in 1848.

When Galicia was occupied by Austria in 1772 it had between 150,000 and 220,000 Jews (the statistics and censuses are unreliable), of whom about one-third lived in villages. In the cities and towns the Jews and Germans constituted the principal commercial and artisan elements. The main characteristics of the Austrian rule were those of a bureaucratic police administration moderated somewhat by the reforms of Joseph II (1780-1790).

Austria started out with measures concerning the Jews similar, if not identical, to those of Prussia, i.e., reduction of the Jewish population through partial expulsion and limited marriage rights, increase of taxes, limitation of Jewish economic activity in the villages. But, unlike Prussia, Austria began imposing residence restrictions on Jews or renewing the old Polish limitations, permitting them to live only in certain parts of some cities and towns or having cities and towns entirely closed to them, curtailing their movement from city to city, and forbidding Jewish artisans to work for non-Jews.

The Polish head tax—now renamed "toleration tax"—was first doubled, later multiplied several times. Especially high taxes on marriage licenses, on dwellings, on synagogues, were instituted; a tax on *kosher* meat, formerly paid to the Kehilla, was introduced in 1784, and another tax on Friday night candles in 1797. All these taxes were doubled and tripled in due time, and strict compulsory collection introduced. Thus a married Jewish woman had to pay a tax on two Sabbath candles every Friday, even though she did not have the means to buy the candles themselves. To all these "regular" taxes were added many special ones (1800, 1801-1804).

During the short rule of Joseph II, an enlightened despot who had some good intentions but achieved poor results, experiments were made to lessen "the harmfulness of the Jews." These efforts ranged from the order of 1784 removing Jews from innkeeping, the sale of liquor, farming of taxes, and similar occupations to the introduction of military service in 1788, obligating Jews to acquire family names, opening schools for Jewish children, inducing Jews to become agriculturists by granting them land and some financial support, and extending the Austrian "Edict of Toleration" of 1782 to Galicia in 1789. This edict for Galicia, officially regarded as a document promulgating legal treatment of Jews on an equal footing with others, was intended to regulate all walks of Jewish life. To a great extent it was a summary of the various decrees with some additions, such as the introduction of elementary and high schools for Jews, whose certificate of graduation was made a prerequisite for obtaining a marriage license. The Kehilla and the rabbis were shorn of their rights and limited to religious matters. Jews were forbidden to employ non-Jewish help, to send money to Palestine, to use documents written in Hebrew or Yiddish. Galician Jews were not permitted to move to Vienna, where they were allowed only a temporary stay of fourteen days, for which they had to pay a special tax. In some Galician cities, Lvov, for instance, Jews were allowed to live, as of old, only in certain streets, in a "ghetto."

The government in Galicia was a government by men and not by laws; the actual situation of the Jews was, in the subsequent decades, decided by the whims of the bureaucracy, made up chiefly of Germans and Germanized Czechs. These officials are characterized by a Polish historian as "representing the worst element of the monarchy, consisting chiefly of people with an inferior education . . . morally weak and anxious for an easy and rapid career," having no knowledge of the country. Their lack of knowledge of the Jewish situation was coupled with disregard for Jews and with the anti-Jewish influences and pressures emanating from the other groups in Galicia —Poles, Ukrainians, and Germans.

The revolution of 1848 brought fundamental changes in Galicia: social distinction between the estates, differentiation of taxes, and the serfdom of the peasants disappeared. The special Jewish taxes also were canceled. The constitution of March, 1849, conferred full equality upon the Jews in Austria, and hence also upon those in Galicia. About two years later, in the wave of reaction sweeping Austria, this constitution was canceled. Thus the way was opened for local government and bureaucrats to discriminate against Jews on the assumption that Jewish rights had also been canceled. The confused legal situation was aggravated by the fact that Galicia became semiautonomous after 1848, with Austria wavering between granting full autonomy to her provinces and a centralizing policy of Germanization. An order of 1853 again put into force the legal limitations on the acquisition of real estate by Jews which had existed prior to 1848.

The members of the city councils and the burghers of Cracow and Lvov (Lemberg) fought tooth and nail against permitting Jews to move from the ghetto, and had their way. As late as 1858, Count Goluchowski, the governor of Galicia, confirmed the right of Lvov to keep the Jews within the ghetto. Likewise some other towns guarded their privileges of *de non tolerandis Judaeis*. The local Diet (*Sejm*), in existence in Galicia since 1861, passed resolutions which excluded any Jew from becoming the mayor of a city and set a quota for the number of Jewish councilmen. But little by little the Jews did acquire rights. In the 1850's legal limitations on Jews in the liberal professions were removed. In 1859 the restrictions on marriage were annulled, and a year later Jews were permitted to buy—with certain exceptions—landed property and to exercise all crafts. In 1867 Jews were granted the right to acquire houses in any part of Cracow and Lvov, as well as in other towns, or in the sections hitherto "out of bounds" for them. This was the year in which the new Austrian constitution proclaimed full equality for all citizens of the Empire. Since Galicia could not remain an exception, the Galician Diet was forced to pass resolutions in 1868 giving Jews full equality in the province.

Official emancipation, however, did not eliminate possibilities of administrative discrimination. After 1866 the administration in Galicia became wholly Polish and three years later the Polish language became obligatory both in administration and the judiciary. The Poles demanded far broader autonomy—legislative authority for the Galician Diet. Failing to achieve it, they shifted from political romanticism to economic positivism, improvement of agriculture, opening of credit banks, and organization of co-operative stores in town and village, and, in 1883, of the important organization "National Trade." These methods were also employed by the Ruthenes (Ukrainians), constituting some 43 per cent of the population of Eastern Galicia (1910), in their struggle against dominance by the Poles. All this meant not only the elimination of many Jews from their economic positions but also that the patriotic and nationalistic slogans and propaganda which developed around these institutions were a sharp thrust against the Jews—the more so since this was the time of growing anti-Semitism in Europe, including Austria, and its rise in Galicia.

Around 1880 some of the Polish press began a campaign to boycott Jewish commerce and develop an indigenous Polish middle class. About a decade later a "Christian Social Party" was founded which, in imitation of the German Christian Social Party in Austria led by the anti-Semitic Mayor of Vienna Karl Lueger, openly sponsored active anti-Semitism and total boycott of Jews. At the same time, about the turn of the century (1897), the National Democrats separated from the Democrats and formed an all-Polish extreme nationalist, anti-Semitic party. There were also anti-Jewish pogroms—in 1897, excesses by railway workers in Chodorov in which one Jew was killed, and a year later a few pogroms in Western Galician cities. More important than the pogroms themselves was the fact that the leader of the Christian Social Movement, a Catholic clergyman, openly assumed moral responsibility for what he termed "the effervescence of the people's ire," and an important Catholic daily, *Glos Narodu* (*The Voice of the People*), aligned itself with the anti-Jewish feelings, propagating the elimination of Jews from economic life.

In such an atmosphere there was more than a little discrimination. In government offices, in the Universities of Cracow and Lvov, the proportion of Jews was a good deal smaller than their percentage in the population. In 1910, when the government monopoly on salt was introduced, hundreds of Jews lost their livelihood, and a year later thousands more were eliminated when their "concessions" to sell liquor were withdrawn and given to Poles. Discrimination was also practiced in elective offices and government service also was banned; when the elections to the Galician Diet were to be held in 1861, local Polish government wanted to exclude Jews entirely. The central authorities in Vienna, however, accorded them these rights, but their participation was limited to three to five deputies (2 to 3 per cent). In the election to the parliament in Vienna the number of Jewish deputies was far below their proportion in the population. This discrimination combined with other factors to bring a change of mind among Jews.

In general, from the second half of the nineteenth century, Jews tended more and more to ally themselves both politically and culturally with the Poles, who, with the Jews, constituted the chief element in the cities, whereas the Ruthenes were mostly concentrated in the villages.

This orientation toward the Poles had come both from the assimilated Jewish intellectuals and wealthy group and from the Orthodox group. The latter was ready to support the Polish conservatives to gain concessions concerning the *heder*, the Kehilla, and other religious matters. For this purpose the rabbi of Cracow, Shimeon Schreiber (1821-1883), who in 1879 was elected deputy to the Austrian parliament, joined forces with the "Belzer rabbi," Jehoshua Rokach, and founded an organization, Machzikey Hadath (Supporters of the Faith). In the elections to the Parliament in Vienna many Jews voted for the Polish list, and the few Jewish deputies in Vienna joined the Polish Parliamentary Club (not so the Ruthenes).

Only a few attempts were made in Eastern Galicia to align Jews politically with the Ruthenes. By the end of the 1860's an association was founded there, Shomer Israel (Defenders of Israel), oriented toward the Austrian liberals and the Ruthenes. And in 1873 a Ruthene-Jewish bloc for the parliamentary elections sent three Jewish deputies to Vienna.

The political situation in Galicia at the turn of the century, coupled with the economic misery of the Jewish masses and growing nationalistic tendencies, were instrumental in causing a partial turning away from the Polish orientation. In 1890, for instance, one of the protagonists of Polish assimilation, Herman Feldstein, accused the Poles of malice against Jews and attempts to eliminate them from trade and government service. A few years later similar disappointment with and criticism of the Polish ruling clique was heard from the young Jewish groups which earlier had favored complete assimilation with the Poles. This disappointment and critical stand were influenced by, and at the same time exerted an influence upon, the rising tide of Jewish nationalist, Zionist, and Socialist tendencies. And these, together with developing Jewish organizations, were in favor of the creation of a new, Jewish-minded political orientation. Thus in 1907, in the elections to the Vienna parliament, Jews from Galicia elected nine deputies—three of them Zionists—who subsequently joined with the Jewish deputy from Bukovina to form a Jewish Parliamentary Club in Vienna, apparently the first in Jewish history. The Poles and the Polish ruling groups, however, resented the separation of the Jews and made desperate efforts to retain Jewish support. The Polish rulers attempted in this way to force the Jews to help them maintain their small numerical margin over the Ruthenes (46:43 per cent). Thus in 1910, at the time of the census, the Jews were forbidden to list Yiddish as their mother tongue. A year later falsifications and terror (in Drohobicze twenty Jews were killed) helped to defeat the Zionist slate for elections to the Viennese parliament.

Russia and Russian Poland harbored the bulk of East European Jews. The existence of Russian Jewry is largely an outcome of the Polish partitions. White Russia was acquired during the first partition of 1772. During the second partition Russia annexed the region of Minsk in the north, Volhynia, a part of Kiev province, and Podolia in the south. During the third partition Russia acquired Lithuania. All these provinces, including the regions of Courland and Bialystok, which were acquired later, were incorporated into Russia proper, whereas Central Poland (over three-quarters of the Duchy of Warsaw) after 1815 formed the so-called Congress Poland or Russian Poland (until 1830 the Kingdom of Poland with a special constitution). From there the Jews spread out and peopled the southern parts of Russia, the Black Sea coast, as well as Bessarabia, all annexed from Turkey. Small groups of Jews also penetrated into the interior of Russia.

From the outset Russian policy toward the Jews was vacillating and contradictory, often reversing itself and moving simultaneously in different directions. The government policy was directed against Jewish separatism, but refused most of the time to permit entry into Russian society without conversion. The government sought to destroy the exclusiveness of the Jews and, as in Prussia and Austria, tended to "grade" the Jews, piling disabilities upon the "useless" or "harmful" ones but without making many concessions to the "useful" ones. The policies themselves, enforced by sheer force, met with mostly passive, but tenacious, opposition from the Jews, and were sidetracked by the bureaucrats (in return for bribes or for other reasons), or were from the beginning double-faced. Again later, in the last decades of the century, Jews were blamed for their exclusiveness and separatism, while at the same time laws were designed to keep them out of general high schools and universities.

After the occupation of White Russia (1772), the Russian governor general promised the tens of thousands of Jews living there "the enjoyment of all those liberties which they possess at present" and a share in the favor of the Empress "so long as they . . . shall live in due obedience as faithful subjects."

At first the Kehilla retained its jurisdictional powers of the Polish times, thereby setting the Jews as a group apart in the cities and towns. But in 1783, Jews were granted rights similar to those of the non-Jewish merchants and burghers, namely, to elect and be elected to town councils and municipal courts. This met with opposition from the non-Jewish townspeople and the local administration. The Jews' own organization, the Kehilla, on the other hand, subsequently lost much of its power as a result of this ostensible equality (1786, 1795, 1799). In other directions, too, there were similar two-sided developments.

Officially the Jews were assured of equal treatment "without distinction of religion or nationality," denying the validity of the old Polish discriminatory laws against the Jews. But under pressure, as a result of administrative practices later sanctioned by the central authorities, anti-Jewish tendencies of the Senate and the general trend toward reaction in the last years of Catherine II led to a pattern not unlike that of the treatment of former Polish Jews in Prussia and Austria.

Taxes were at first set low, but in 1794 it was stipulated that Jews in the cities had to pay double the tax paid by non-Jews. Pressure by merchants in Moscow who feared Jewish competition led to orders (in 1790 and 1791, reinforced in 1794) which forbade Jews to live in the interior Russian cities, thus creating the Pale of Settlement, consisting of the former Polish territories with the addition of certain other regions. Again the governor of White Russia started on his own in the beginning of the 1780's to eliminate Jews from villages by forbidding the gentry to lease the inns to them. Local authorities were frequently arbitrarily expelling Jews from villages. The central government in St. Petersburg (today Leningrad) declared the governor's orders illegal, but a decade later (1795) another order sanctioned these practices by advising that the village Jews should be transferred to the towns, or, in other words, expelled from the villages. From then on the problem of the village Jew did not cease to plague the Jews and the Russian administration, aggravated during famine, revolt of serfs, or other upheavals. In attempts at solution, inquiries were made among representatives of the gentry in the last years of the eighteenth century. Their opinions as well as the proposals of the self-styled specialist in Jewish matters, the Russian poet and minister Gabriel Derzhavin (1743-1816) were followed by the Jewish Statute of 1804, which provided among other things for expulsion of the Jews from the villages. Next came postponements of expulsion in 1808, 1812, and expulsion from villages in White Russia in 1823-1825 and from the rural settlements near the border. Then followed, over half a century later, the May Laws of 1882 forbidding Jews to settle anew in villages—and the subsequent expulsions of those who settled "illegally."

The statute "Concerning the organization of the Jew" issued in December, 1804, was the first comprehensive piece of Russian legislation dealing with Jews. But it was a compilation of different sources: the "opinions" solicited from the gentry of the region and from high officials, Derzhavin's proposal, various memoranda and schemes submitted by Jews and non-Jews during the last years of the Polish state, the work of a special Russian committee whose membership changed in the course of time, and the influence of the Prussian legislation. The deputies of the large Jewish communities, called in 1803 to St. Petersburg, and the Kehillot, who were asked to suggest ways and means of enforcing the clauses of the proposed statute requested postponement of the proposed limitations for twenty years.

The varied, often contradictory propositions and traces of existing practice combined in the statute negative and positive approaches. It permitted Jewish children to attend all types of general school, and Jews were allowed to open their own secular schools, in which either Russian, Polish, or German was to be obligatory; after six years all documents and commercial papers were to be executed in one of these three languages, the knowledge of which should become obligatory for rabbis and those who held an elective office either in a municipality or in a Kehilla. Jews were permitted to buy or rent land for agricultural settlement—freeing the settlers from taxes for five to ten years. A certain amount of government land was promised free for Jewish settlement. The existing Pale of Settlement was reaffirmed, but Jewish manufacturers, artisans, and merchants were granted permission to sojourn temporarily, under certain conditions, in the interior Russian regions, including the capitals (Moscow and St. Petersburg). The statute confirmed the existing rights to participate in local self-government and the limited jurisdiction of the Kehilla, confined to religious matters, forbidding the use of the ban (*Herem*). Beginning with 1807-1808 Jews were forbidden to sell liquor, to run taverns, or even to live in villages.

As the time for expulsion from the villages neared, its implementation was spread over three years. But after the expulsion began it proved impossible to carry out—only a few hundred Jewish families were able to find land and funds to turn to agriculture—so it was again postponed and then stopped in 1812, in part under the impact of the impending conflict with Napoleon.

After the war and the Congress of Vienna (1815), the reactionary tendencies of the Metternich era and the Holy Alliance had their effect upon Russia, although this became most evident later in the reign of Nicholas I (1825-1855). Contradictory approaches continued to mark the policy toward Jews. In 1818, on the initiative of the government, a permanent Jewish advisory body—Deputation of the Jewish People—consisting of elected deputies of the Jewish communities, was organized. In the same year Alexander I (1801-1825) gave the impression that he was inclined to take the initiative in leading the states united in the Holy Alliance to grant Jews equality. At the Congress of Monarchs in Aix-la-Chapelle, he listened attentively to the proposals of Lewis Way, a representative of the London Bible Society, that Russia should emancipate the Jews in her dominion and induce Prussia and Austria to do the same. Way had been invited earlier to Russia to study the Jewish problem on the spot. Alexander I, turned Way's memorandum and plans over to the diplomats participating in the Congress, who managed to dispose of it with a general phrase. The

Deputation of the Jewish People in Russia itself remained impotent, able to serve only as a lobbying group, or through personal contact with high officials sometimes to avert some minor pressures from the Jews. It was dissolved in 1825. Government plans to reform Jewish conditions through comprehensive legislation with the help of Jewish representatives came to nothing. The "Committee for the Amelioration of the Jews," called into being in 1823, did not complete its work until some years after the Deputation went out of business. And the Committee itself was apparently founded —according to its testimony a few years later—with the intention of finding ways and means for "the reduction of the number of Jews in the monarchy."

Instead of being a period in which the Jewish situation improved, in actual fact these were years of renewed legislative and administrative measures *against* Jews. In 1820, Jews were forbidden to employ non-Jewish domestics. A year earlier new limitations had been introduced on the dealings of Jews with the landowners in the villages, and in the subsequent years—in White Russia in connection with a famine—the order to expel the Jews from the villages was renewed (in 1823-1824 for expulsion from villages in White Russia, in 1825 to expel Jews from villages near the frontier). There was also a ritual murder trial toward the end of Alexander I's reign (at Velizh in the province of Vitebsk in 1823) the effects of which were felt in years to come, in the time of Nicholas I.

The main policies during the thirty-year reign of Nicholas I (1825-1855) took a similar direction: the intention was to change the Jews, to destroy their exclusiveness, to fuse them with the rest of the population, to segregate the "useless" ones and heap oppression upon them without making substantial concessions to the other Jews. Interspersed among these measures were limitations and restrictions designed either to reduce the alleged harmfulness of the Jews or to allay Russian suspicions concerning the possibility of their harmfulness. Nicholas I in Russia occasionally borrowed from the past policies of Prussia and Austria. But Nicholas, autocrat and military despot that he was, tried to achieve these ends by more coercion, brutal force, and punitive policies, with complete disregard for their effect upon the Jews or for their reactions. Despite all the force and military rigor, the policies were inconsistent, which to a certain extent nullified their impact, at least in so far as the Russian government's intentions were concerned.

The first decisive act in connection with the Jews was the introduction of military service in 1827. Service in the Russian army at that time lasted twenty-five years. Among the motives for subjecting Jews to military service was the desire to decrease the Jewish population, to force Jews to choose "a useful occupation"—those were partly exempt from military service—and "that it will move them most effectively to change their religion." For this purpose the draftees should preferably be young—between twelve and twenty-five—and thus more likely "to abandon their superstitions."

At the same time the members of each Jewish community were made mutually responsible for supplying the required number of draftees, and the community organization, the Kehilla (or specially elected trustees), could press into service anyone it decided upon, which gave the organization maintaining the separation of the Jews more power than ever.

This trend was continued through subsequent legislation. The Statute of 1835 was intended among other things to make the Kehilla subservient to the state by imposing new duties such as to enforce government regulations in connection with the Jews and to make it responsible for their taxes. In reality, this made it a more powerful factor in Jewish life. Even when in 1844 the Kehilla organization was abolished because it was an "important element obstructing Jewish assimilation with the Christian population," the Jews of each community remained mutually responsible for the number of recruits and the taxes of the Jews. Officially, these duties were to be undertaken by special boards of trustees and tax collectors; actually, they were fulfilled by the same Kehilla as before, minus its legal autonomy but enforced by factual power. However, the power or abuse of power exerted by the official Kehilla up to 1844, and later the unofficial one—the system of hired "catchers" for assembling the quota of recruits or their substitutes, the young children who were to be raised to become soldiers, the method of farming out and collecting Jewish taxes, particularly the meat tax—demoralized internal Jewish relations.

In the seventeen years between the introduction of military service for Jews and the abolishing of the Kehilla, a number of restrictive orders were issued. Among them were expulsion from the villages of the province of Grodno and from the city of Kiev (1827), from some port cities at the Black Sea and partially from Courland (1829), and from villages in the Kiev province (1830). The Statute of 1835 codified these and other limitations; forbade marriage before the age of eighteen for males and sixteen for females, and the use of Hebrew in documents and commercial papers. At the same time some privileges were provided for those turning toward agriculture, among other things, freedom from military service. There followed (1836) the introduction of strict censorship on Jewish books and the closing down of most of the Jewish printing shops, with the intention of eliminating the Hasidic literature and eradicating the "prejudices fostered by the Talmud."

The same intent, influenced by the Prussian example, was behind the effort to establish Jewish secular schools and two rabbinical institutes intended to reduce Jewish separatism. This was preceded by the appointment of Max Lilienthal (1815-1882) in 1841 as a special official of the Ministry of Education to bring the idea of secular schools closer to the Jewish population and to convince them of the benevolent intentions of the government. (Lilienthal left in 1845 for the United States, where he became a leading Reform rabbi.)

The desire to have its good intentions trusted by the Jews did not deter the government from issuing an order (in 1843) expelling them from a fifty-verst (some thirty miles) stretch along its borders with the West, a threat to hundreds of thousands which aroused Jews all over Europe. A few years later a number of new measures were introduced with the purpose of "correcting the Jews": in 1850, increasing the responsibility for delivery of Jewish recruits and prohibiting traditional Jewish attire and earlocks; in 1851, married Jewish women were forbidden to follow tradition by shaving their heads, and "useless" Jews were segregated to subject them to more oppression and a higher quota in the draft.

The military debacle in the Crimean War and the death of Nicholas I brought a partial change in the Russian government. Alexander II (1855-1881) embarked on a system of reforms—emancipation of the peasants, in 1861 and 1864, change in the military service, establishment of local self-government. The road to a constitutional government was believed open. These and other measures speeded up the pace of economic development in industry, railroad building, and business. New opportunities opened for Jews. Parallel with these trends went the lifting of some restrictions. The idea of changing the Jews and fusing them into the general population remained, but the approach was reversed. Instead of heaping disabilities upon the "useless" Jews, the useful ones were given some privileges, somewhat in line with the Prussian tactic a generation earlier. (The military obligation of juveniles was ended in 1856, in line with a change in the whole system of military service.) Certain selected groups were allowed to move into and settle in the interior of Russia (in 1859, the first-category businessmen; in 1861, Jews with full university education; in 1865, artisans). Limitations on Jewish domicile in parts of former Polish cities (Vilna, Zhitomir) were abolished. Jews were allowed to become members of the bar, and were granted broader rights in provincial self-government (1864).

Yet the use of force, although in indirect manner, was not entirely shelved. In order to extricate the Jews from their exclusiveness, it was planned to abolish the Jewish *heder* and to cause the old-type rabbi to disappear. An order of 1855 declared that after twenty years each teacher (*melamed*) or rabbi must be a graduate of one of the existing government-sponsored rabbinical institutes, or of other institutes of higher learning. In the following years supervision of the *heder* was begun and the introduction of the modern type of rabbi ordered. However, after constant resistance by the Jews, the government in the 1870's gave up the idea of closing the *heder*.

By that time an entire change in policy was already in the making. Both the economic upswing and the epoch of reforms were short-lived. The emancipation of the peasants freed them from bondage, but did not give them enough land and capital to enable them to stand on their own. Impoverishment of the peasants already became evident at the end of the

1860's, and was aggravated by the falling grain prices in the 1870's. The shrinking local market had an impact both on the general economic development and on the Jewish trader and artisan.

Again the worsening situation of the peasants, and the dismal living conditions of those who swelled the ranks of the city proletariat, constituted good soil for the growth of the revolutionary movement. This, in turn, set the stage for emergence of a reactionary trend also nurtured by other factors, such as the growth of Russian nationalism, expressed by the Slavophiles and in part generated by the Russification policy in the former Polish provinces after 1864. All this spelled a growing negative approach toward the minorities and the Jews, an attitude further developed by the influences from Western Europe—increasing chauvinistic nationalism and its parallel, anti-Semitism.

The economic position some Jews had achieved was regarded with envy and suspicion. The charges of Jewish economic domination and exploitation of the non-Jews, advanced in the wake of anti-Jewish propaganda, were adopted to serve also as "explanation" of the 1871 pogrom in Odessa, the first pogrom against Jews. These charges were coupled with another accusation—the old "sin" of separateness which Russian policies had been laboring for more than half a century to break. There emerged the myth of a secret Jewish shadow government—the Kehilla—out to rule the world in conjunction with the "Jewish World Government," the *Alliance Israélite Universelle* (founded in Paris in 1860). These attitudes, pronounced in the press and other publications, had an impact upon the higher rungs of Russian bureaucracy, who in the 1870's were pondering the "Jewish question," but had little practical significance before the following epoch.

The assassination of Alexander II on March 1, 1881, brought into the open the reactionary forces which had been gaining a hold on the Russian administration for a number of years. Constantine Pobedonostzev (1827-1907), procurator-general of the Holy Synod (the highest administration of the Greek Orthodox Church), a fanatic reactionary and advocate of a police state guided by the Church, with his clique became the most influential force in the state. Autocratic power was proclaimed by Alexander III (1881-1894) as his guiding principle. In mid-April, 1881, the first pogrom against Jews following the assassination of Alexander II was launched (Elizavethograd, southern Russia), followed by a series of others, and in the spring and summer of the same year more than one hundred Jewish localities suffered. Then, in December, 1881, came the pogrom in Warsaw, and again in the spring of 1882 a pogrom in Balta in southern Russia. Pogroms became from that time on a feature of Russian-Jewish relations repeated over and over again (1883, 1884, 1891, 1897, 1899, and at the beginning of the twentieth century).

Meanwhile, after a brief period of vacillation, Russian government circles—and the Czar himself—put forth the theory that the pogroms resulted from the Russian population's hatred of the Jews because of their "economic domination" and their exploitation of the original population. The conclusion was that the government must "shield the Russian population against this harmful Jewish activity." The policy of eliminating the Jews from economic and political life replaced the former ideas of integration and fusing the Jews with the Russian population. Most of the legislation which followed was an elaboration of this approach, leading toward curbing the Jews.

The "Temporary Laws" of May 31, 1882, forbade Jews to settle anew in the villages or to own real estate outside the urban areas, and gave the village communities the right to oust by a resolution those already settled. Then came expulsions of illegal Jews from the interior of Russia—from St. Petersburg, Moscow, Kiev, and elsewhere—followed by the eviction of about half the Jews from Moscow (1891). Still earlier (1887) a *numerus clausus* or "percentage norm" was established for the admission of Jews to secondary schools and universities. In 1889 the admission of Jews to the bar was temporarily halted, and in 1890 Jews were barred from participation in local self-government. The situation was not changed by the majority report of the government commission under the chairmanship of Count Pahlen (the Pahlen Commission was appointed in 1883 for revision of the current laws concerning Jews), which in 1888 opposed the repressive policy, stressing that the "system of repressive and discriminatory measures must give way to a graduated system of emancipatory and equalizing laws."

The government of Alexander III and that of his successor, Nicholas II (1894-1917), continued the same practices, making Jewish life subject to ministerial decrees, secret circulars, arbitrary administrative decisions, or interpretations of the courts. There was only a brief respite after the manifesto of October, 1905, when it seemed for a while that the revolutionary trends had finally forced a change in the Russian system of government. This manifesto was preceded by years of mounting revolutionary forces and increasing efforts by the bureaucracy and reactionary groups to counteract the revolutionary movement, not only by suppression and executions, but also by agitation against the Jews. Instigation to pogroms was used to divert popular attention. There were pogroms in Kishinev and Mohilev in 1903; agitation against Jews, accusing them of helping the enemy, during the Russo-Japanese War; some pogroms at the end of 1904; and in October, 1905, at the height of the revolutionary tide. Police, high government officials, and other "defenders of the monarchy" were among those who prepared the sweeping wave of pogroms in October, 1905 (about fifty in one week), and again in the following year.

The October manifesto of the Czar (1905), promising freedom of speech and assembly, instituted the Duma (parliament) with some legislative powers, to which Jews had full rights to elect and be elected. The Jews succeeded in sending twelve Jewish deputies to the first Duma in 1906 and there were many liberal non-Jewish deputies who took up the Jewish cause particularly by exposing the role of the bureaucracy in the pogroms. But the Duma itself was short-lived. Soon in June, 1907, came the counterrevolution. The subsequent Dumas were devoid of any influence. The new "doctored" election laws minimized the participation of the Jews. After 1907 the growing reaction both within and outside the Duma canceled any hope for improvement of the Jewish situation.

The old restrictions—some not applied since 1905—were renewed, new ones added, and in the last prewar years, 1911-1913, came the blood libel the famous Beilis trial in which liberal forces rallied to the Jewish cause as some had done in the case of pogroms and legal oppression.

Outside the country, too, public opinion was aroused by these events in Russia. The press, the English Parliament, the American Congress and State Department, more than once espoused the cause of the Russian Jews in debate, resolution, or diplomatic correspondence. The United States had also, since the end of the nineteenth century, been involved in a diplomatic dispute with the Russian government concerning discrimination against American Jews, to whom Russia denied entry visas. This controversy went through a variety of stages and finally led to the cancellation of the American-Russian Commercial Treaty in 1912.

Russian Poland. The legal situation of the Jews in Russian Poland in the last half-century of the Russian rule differed only slightly from that of Russia itself. What differences there were stemmed from earlier specific situations and from the Polish-Jewish-Russian relations.

This region, in which close to 1,500,000 Jews lived before World War I, was created as a political unit at the Congress of Vienna (1815) and united with Russia under a single sovereign. The Polish Kingdom (popularly called Congress Poland) comprised over three-quarters of the former Duchy of Warsaw. The Kingdom was at first, in contrast with Russia itself, a constitutional monarchy. The constitution was to a great extent patterned upon that of the Duchy of Warsaw (1807-1812), which, being a creation of Napoleon, was in turn based on the French system. In connection with Jews the Duchy of Warsaw, after accepting its constitution in 1807, published a decree (1808) patterned upon Napoleon's "infamous" decree of March 17, 1808, postponing for ten years the Jews' enjoyment of the rights implied in the constitution. Meanwhile the short-lived Polish state maintained the old Polish disabilities, excluding Jews from sections of cities, as well as following the pattern laid down by Prussia—amplifying Jewish taxation and, in 1812, forbidding Jews to produce or sell liquor. Enforcement of this order was postponed because of the Franco-Russian war.

The new Kingdom (1815) inherited from the Duchy of Warsaw not only the 213,000 Jews but also the restrictions of the Jews and the attitudes of the Polish ruling group, who in internal and economic matters had broad autonomy in the old-new state. The administration, most of the legislature, and the army were Polish, while the Czar's brother, the Grand Duke Constantine (1779-1831), served as Commander in Chief, semiofficially assuming greater powers. Nicholas Novosilitzev (1762-1838), as the Czar's Commissioner to the Polish government, was functioning, unofficially, as the Czar's watchdog. An intrigant by nature and always in need of funds, he was from time to time ready to throw his weight in favor of Jews for a price or so as to weaken the Polish order. Constantine was no friend of the Jews. In addition he sought to attach himself to Poland by marrying a Polish woman in 1820; thus he became connected with the ultra-Catholic camp and was not inclined to take up the case of the Jews against the Poles.

The latter, with the exception of a very small group of liberals, were imbued with an anti-Jewish bias—although divided on practical approaches toward the Jewish question, ranging from those who demanded removal or severe curtailment of Jews to those who believed in the possibility of "improving" them. From this hostile attitude evolved a policy which combined most of the negative aspects of Russia, Austria, and Prussia in their respective parts of the former Polish territory, superimposed upon the fear that the Jews, by multiplying, would turn the country into a "Jewish Poland." Ritual murder trials in 1815-1816 had to be stopped by orders from St. Petersburg.

In the economic field the attempts to remove Jews from the liquor trade were continued. The law of 1812 was vetoed by the Czar, but the Poles achieved most of their aims by levying a high fee on stores selling beverages. The settlement of Jews in agriculture was left to the wealthy Jews —settlement of twenty-five Jewish families on the land was a prerequisite for permission to acquire an estate. (The law was issued at the time of the Duchy of Warsaw.) A number of cities and towns continued barred to Jews; in some others, including Warsaw, they were allowed only in a limited number of streets; sojourners in the capital had to pay a daily impost which entitled them to stay for a limited number of days; "Jewish separateness" was attacked by abolition of the Kehilla in 1821 and its replacement by synagogue boards whose jurisdiction was limited to religious matters. The same end was sought through attempts to found secular Jewish schools and a government-sponsored rabbinical school in 1826, by instituting a censorship on Jewish religious literature, and by prohibiting importation of Jewish books from abroad.

After the uprising of 1830-1831, Poland lost much of its autonomy, but part of the administration remained unchanged. The general trend was toward integration of Poland into the Russian empire and the Jewish situation was somewhat equalized with that of Russia, although Polish officials found a way to express their bias in their treatment of Jewish groups. On the other hand, the Russian bureaucracy sometimes attempted to win the Jews to Russia's side through minor concessions. The Viceroy Paskevitch (up to 1856) tried to play one group in Poland against the other, and so he made attempts to attract the Jews to the Russian camp.

Military service for Jews (introduced in 1843) and the decree forbidding the wearing of Jewish attire were handled somewhat more mildly in Poland than in Russia.

During the first years of the reforms of Alexander II, attempts were made by Russia to win over the Poles through a number of concessions. Marquis Alexander Wielopolski became for a while (1861 and 1862-1863) head of the Polish civil government. Among the reforms he introduced was emancipation of the Jews, opening for them the cities and towns, or those parts which were still closed, annulling special taxes, allowing them to acquire landed property, and granting some other rights. The ensuing short-lived Polish revolutionary government granted full rights to the Jews.

Following the suppression of the uprising, Poland became an integral part of the Russian empire, with Russification policies taking hold after 1867. The restrictive legislation against Jews in Russia from the 1880's on was generally applicable to Poland, with some exceptions (the May Laws forbidding Jews to settle in villages, for instance). Nor was Russian Poland free from pogroms, although their number was small.

However, the anti-Jewish trend which grew in Russia in the last quarter of the nineteenth century had another aspect in Poland. After collapse of the uprising in 1863 a positivist realistic trend took hold of the Poles, emphasizing constructive development of the economy. The general upswing of the economy in Russia and the opening of the Russian market offered great opportunities for economic growth. Jews made the most of these new possibilities, as well as of the right granted them to settle in all cities and towns. In banking, commerce, and industry the influence of Jews grew considerably. Commerce with Russia, opening the wide Russian market for the products of Polish industry, was carried on chiefly by Russian Jews who settled in Poland after the 1880's.

The growing anti-Jewish trend in Europe and Russia since the 1870's found a good background in Poland for anti-Semitic propaganda. The Jew was considered a dangerous competitor by the Polish middle class and the gentry who moved to the cities when impoverished by confiscation of their estates after the uprising of 1863 or after the land reform of 1864. The economic struggle was inflamed by nationalist slogans and ideologies. As in Russia, separatism was blamed upon the Jews, and the hope of assimilating them was abandoned. But elimination of Jews from economic life was demanded in Poland for the purpose of Polonization, while the "Litvaks" —Russian Jews who had settled in Poland—were blamed both for their

Russification and for spreading Jewish nationalism or building a "second Judea" on Polish soil.

The National Democratic Party which came into being in 1897 was in Poland, as in Galicia, thoroughly anti-Semitic. It aimed to "free Poland from Jewish influence." In the elections to the Duma, party members spread anti-Jewish propaganda and in the Russian Duma itself, under the leadership of Roman Dmowski, they supported the anti-Jewish policies of the Russian rightist reactionary groups.

In Poland a boycott was organized against purchases from Jews. This was strengthened after the elections to the fourth Duma (1912). The Jews in Warsaw, numbering about 200,000, could have elected a Jew as representative. But to avoid offending the Poles by sending a Jewish deputy from the Polish capital, there was general willingness to vote for a Pole on condition that he should not be an anti-Semite. The Poles, however, designated a representative of the National Democrats, an anti-Semitic candidate. The Jews then voted for Eugen Jagiello, a Social Democrat, who was elected. The rightist Polish circles, particularly the National Democrats, regarded this "mixing of the Jews" in "national elections" as a declaration of war against the Poles. As a result anti-Jewish propaganda was intensified, and the slogan "There is no room for two nations" in Poland was formulated. The boycott was greatly increased.

Impact on Jews. During the century and a half before World War I, the Jews of Eastern Europe reached their highest peak of natural growth, underwent various transformations, adapted themselves to the changing socio-economic structure; but preserved essentially their substance, their religion, culture, individuality, separateness, and cohesiveness. Living in compact concentrated masses, forming majorities in most of the small towns—in fact, often constituting the entire town, with the non-Jews living for the most part on the outskirts—and occupying sections of their own in the big cities, the Jews could continue to live their own traditional life, paying scant attention to the changing political structure of the country, or to the policies of the state.

The main contact with the non-Jewish world came in the process of earning a living—in business, industry, crafts. For the most part there was a distinction between the Jewish relation to non-Jews in business and in private. The business relationship was cultivated and developed. But in private life, within his family, on the Sabbaths and holidays, in his synagogues and prayer and study houses, and in "his streets," the Jew lived a life distinct from the business atmosphere and from his non-Jewish neighbor. The bulk of Russian-Polish (and Galician) Jews remained for the whole period an entity, living its own life, and in Poland-Galicia clinging mostly to the different Hasidic trends. The impact of the various experiments and oppression made by the three states were, of course, felt in a physical sense. Jewish families were stricken with sorrow when their young children were snatched away and sent off to an unknown fate. Jews expelled from villages or cities lost their homes and their livelihood. But, spiritually, this was mostly on the fringe of Jewish existence. The Jews tried to ward it off by tenaciously clinging to their own, by showing a stubborn front, by the belief that the restrictive laws and persecution were a punishment for their sins, which again led them to still stricter adherence to their traditions and institutions. High Russian officials, according to Lilienthal, regarded this tenacity of the Jewish community as more effective than the Polish uprising, since it was impossible to "overcome it with bayonets."

In practice the Jews, both as a group and as individuals, fought government measures by bribing Russian officials, by making personal contacts, by lobbying, by arousing public opinion, or by trying to forestall oncoming events. For instance, when it became known in Russia in the 1830's that the government was to institute a minimum age for marriage (the statute of 1835), Jews married off their small children of grade-school age. (This period is known as the *behalah*.) Other means of circumventing the government included paying fines for failure to obey the laws, and boycotting the government schools.

To be sure, all these developments took their toll of the Jews. The oppressions and deprivations led to much suffering, while curtailment of Jewish economic activity contributed greatly to the growth of poverty among Jews. By imposing upon the Kehilla the power and obligation to deliver the quota of Jewish draftees, Nicholas I forced the Jewish community to hunt for young children and adults alike, helped to demoralize the institution, and enabled men of doubtful morality to gain influence in Jewish society, further antagonizing the Jewish masses against their qualified leaders, the elders. But none of this broke the group cohesion. Poverty among East European Jews in the nineteenth century was apparently no greater than in the eighteenth century and certainly less than among the peasantry, the bulk of the non-Jewish population of the region. Only very small groups of Jews, the Enlightened (*Maskilim*),[2a] and a few of the more wealthy were ready to co-operate in various degrees with the government. The small group of the Enlightened of the first half of the nineteenth century, in their hopeless struggle to modernize Jewish life, put exaggerated hope in the power of the state. They supported—or even suggested—the annulment of the Kehilla, introduction of strict censorship on religious literature, and compulsory general education, and they regarded military service as a step leading to Jewish equality. Again, a few of the rich and assimilated were ready to help assimilate the rest of the Jews or took seriously the idea of grading the Jews into the "useful" and "useless," requesting privileges from the government for the "better Jews."

The masses of the people were prepared—or forced—to make adjustments for the most part in connection with their economic life. There were serious attempts by thousands of Jewish families to transfer to agriculture (in Russian Poland in the 1840's thousands of Jewish families and in Russia a few hundred families settled on the land in 1809-1810, and a few thousand in the 1840's). Many thousands sought work, in the 1840's to 1850's, as unskilled laborers in building roads, bridging rivers, or in similar projects. There was also, beginning in the 1840's—at first in small numbers—emigration to Western Europe and overseas, which increased in the subsequent periods in proportion to the growth of the Jewish population, mounting pressures, and economic distress.

Emigration accelerated under these circumstances, despite the opposition of Jewish notables and intellectuals in Russia and elsewhere who feared that an exodus would jeopardize the chances of attaining equality. And every wave of emigration increased the mobility of the Jews in Eastern Europe, created a psychosis favoring emigration, brought larger groups in contact with foreign countries, and thus inspired further emigration. The number of Jewish emigrants began to rise by the end of 1860's in connection with the famine in the northwestern regions, and continued at the rate of a few thousand yearly during the next decade.

A further impetus was given by the pogroms and May Laws of the 1880's. The exodus was directed principally toward the United States, with some groups dreaming of establishing a state there populated by Jews. Beginning with some 5,000 to 6,000 in 1881, the Jewish emigration to America doubled in the following year, increased to over 32,000 by 1887, and reached over 51,000 in 1891. In the decade 1904-1914 the average annual number of Jewish immigrants from Eastern Europe passed the 100,000 mark and in 1906, 1907, and 1914 it reached almost 150,000. All in all, during the years between 1880 and 1914, about 2,000,000 East European Jews arrived in the United States, with an additional few hundred thousand spreading over Germany, England, South Africa, Palestine, Canada, and the Latin American countries.

By that time, in the last three or four decades before World War I, wider circles in Russia and Poland were being brought into contact with general culture and were more strongly influenced by phenomena outside their own circle. Rising Polish nationalism, in both its manifestations—stirring up national hopes and breaking into anti-Semitism—had an impact upon growing Jewish nationalism. The revolutionary movement again gave Jews opportunity, as individuals or in groups, to express their reaction toward mounting oppression.

Passive resistance through tenacity and group coherence paved the way among some Jews—the large masses remained mostly concerned with their own traditions—to a more active struggle, ranging from self-defense against pogroms, fostering Hebrew and Yiddish culture, ideas of building their own state, or reconstructing Jewish life on the spot to participation in th Socialist movement, forming their own organization (see the particular below in the section on cultural and communal developments) to take par in the political struggle of the liberal or Socialist groups, or to carry o their own political struggle. Most of this activity came to the fore durin the Russian Revolution of 1905-1906 and afterward.

In the elections to the Duma and in the Duma itself, the Jews led a active political struggle for their rights and exposed the pogrom tactic of the reactionary forces. In Russian Poland the Jews refused to be in timidated by the Polish nationalists, refusing to allow them to monopoliz the election of the deputies, or to agree that an anti-Semite should represen Warsaw (1912). In Galicia about half the Jews—as a demonstration o their national group coherence—registered Yiddish as their mother tongu (1910), despite the law forbidding it and the threat of a fine.

Both the anti-Jewish trends and the active struggle of the Jews for thei civil, political, and group rights were to become more intense during an after World War I.

2. THE INTERWAR YEARS

Soon after the outbreak of World War I (August 1, 1914), Galicia Bukovina, Russian Poland, Lithuania—areas with dense Jewish population —became the theater of military operations, with armies of both sides mov ing back and forth, and Russian commanders taking "hostages" from Jew and bribes for "protection" from pillaging and killing by Russian Cossacks The prewar anti-Semitic tensions were intensified and led to trumped-u charges that the Jews were spying and helping the Germans. The Russia High Command officially accused Jews of assisting the enemy and set ou to deport those near the front. Thus about 500,000 Jews were sent to Russi during the winter of 1914-1915, many at short notice and under the wors possible conditions. Again from Galicia tens of thousands of Jews fled t the interior of Austria.

During the summer and fall of 1915 the Austro-German troops occupie Congress Poland and a great part of the Russian northwestern regions Two almost contradictory tendencies developed. On the one hand, Jew were plagued by semiforced labor, strict regimentation in the economi field, rationing, requisitions, dismantling of factories, seizure of raw ma terials and scrap, which spelled unemployment, hunger, epidemics, and th growth of speculation and smuggling, with some connivance of the occupa tion officials themselves. On the other hand, the years of the Austro-Germa occupation were a period of intensive Jewish cultural, political, and organ izational activity. The proclamation of the German High Comman (printed in Hebrew and Yiddish), that our armies "bring you [equal rights and freedom," permission to publish Hebrew and Yiddish newspapers and periodicals (forbidden by the Russians in July, 1915), the use of Jewish officers as liaison between the occupation authorities and the Jews, and the official or semiofficial sanctioning of most institutional activity, released pent-up Jewish energy. The modern Yiddish and Hebrew school system, "*Vilnaer trouppe*," economic institutions, party activities in Lithuania and Poland, either began or developed considerably during this occupation.

On the other side of the front, in Russia, there was also lively activity, particularly after the March, 1917, Revolution and the granting of full emancipation. Pent-up energy burst out, seeking outlets. A country-wide Russian-Jewish assembly was prepared. This was, however, curtailed and later entirely suppressed after the Bolshevik October Revolution (1917), while growing Jewish autonomy and social and cultural activity in the Ukraine were swamped in a sea of blood by the hundreds of pogroms carried out by Ukrainians and various anti-Soviet troops during the Civil War. When both the war and the "small wars" following it had ended, the political set up and the "Jewish political map" in Eastern Europe included about 2,500,000 East European Jews in Soviet Russia and almost 3,000,000 in Poland, resurrected by restoration of most of the parts which had been under Prussian, Austrian, and Russian domination. The newly created Baltic States—Estonia, Latvia, Lithuania—had a Jewish population of about 250,000. In the south, Rumania acquired Bukovina (102,900 Jews) and Bessarabia (228,000 Jews), thus almost doubling the Rumanian Jewish community.

World War I and its aftermath shattered the unity of the Jews' East European center, and initiated fundamental transformations and changes. The war and the subsequent pogroms and struggles cost East European Jewry some 500,000 casualties, killed and wounded in the pogroms and on the battlefield, or dead in epidemics. It meant also a breakdown of the patriarchal way of life of the *shtetel*, of the old time Hasidic-conservative mode of life, and the spread of secularism as a result of the uprootings and the new conditions evolving among the youth.

The changed political and social settings of East European Jewry after World War I called for adjustment to the new states with their varied political and social orders and economic realities. On the one hand, there was Soviet Russia with its state economy and elimination of free enterprise and middle men. On the other hand, there were the succession states with the growing trend toward state enterprise and strict control of commerce and industry, and the tendency to build up a middle class from the majority, thereby eliminating the Jews. This was over and above the national and social conflicts which became pronounced in all states of Eastern Europe. At the same time the succession states—and with them the Jews—were faced with the hard task of readjusting their economies, which had formerly been linked with those of the parent empires.

In general two conflicting trends manifested themselves in Eastern Europe in the years following the Armistice of 1918. On the one hand, there was a strengthening of liberal reformist and revolutionary tendencies, of the effort to improve the social and economic order, to further the ideas of justice and freedom, and to prevent future wars. These trends were counterbalanced, on the other hand, by chauvinistic and reactionary bents emanating from the scramble for war "loot," the propensities in the new states (and their attempts) to grab more territory from their neighbors. Tension between classes increased: groups whose influence and possessions had been reduced by the vagaries of war, inflation, or by the postwar changes refused to reconcile themselves to the new situation; others, who had retained their positions or acquired new ones, often reached out to strengthen them. The peasantry, previously static and apparently little aware of politics, was aroused in the course of the war and in military service and also by the ideas of land distribution, and fell easy prey to all sorts of propaganda and slogans. Throngs moved to the cities, increasing tensions there already augmented by the economic crises and recurrent unemployment. Emigration abroad, particularly to the United States, which had served as a safety valve for more than a generation, was drastically curtailed by the new quota system. In the 1930's the effects of the deepening world economic crisis and the rise of Nazi totalitarian power stimulated totalitarian tendencies in East European states.

These trends were naturally reflected in the position of the Jews, among whom both the aspirations and disappointments were also discernible. The Treaty of Versailles and the Russian Revolution brought equality to all Jews in Eastern Europe. Minority rights founded on international treaties were granted to Jews, along with other minorities, in the succession states. In Soviet Russia a "Communist edition" of minority rights was introduced in connection with the Soviet nationality policy. At the same time the reactionary postwar trends resulted in a combined onslaught against democracy and Jewish equality, characterized at first by assaults against Jews and discrimination, and later by curtailment of their rights.

The disturbances of the war, the loosening of the "old moorings" during the war years, the freedom of activity and the hopes generated by the social message which was at first connected with the revolutions, achievement of equal rights, the minority treaties and the Balfour Declaration, "split the atom," releasing the concentrated Jewish energy into political, cultural, communal, organizational, and to some extent economic fields. Increasing poverty marred these developments in part. However, Jews in Eastern Europe reached their zenith in the interwar period. Like their newly created "enclaves"—groups of Russian Jewish refugees in Germany;

the third, fourth, and some of the fifth *Aliyah* in Palestine; intelligentsia immigrants in the United States and other countries—they developed a dynamic activity, creating new avenues of Jewish group living or fructifying old ones.

Soviet Russia. Soviet Russia's internal policy since the Communists came into power in October, 1917, has been a chain of contradictions and inconsistencies studded with purges, resulting in part from the discrepancies between Marxian theory of cosmopolitan Communism based on industrial labor, and the realities of an agricultural country with many national and ethnic groups. For practical reasons the Soviets had to assure all nationalities full freedom of development of their national cultures, and the state became based on autonomous national units. The national renaissance of the various nationalities inevitably bred nationalistic anticentralist tendencies. The formula put forth by Stalin in 1925 that the culture should be Socialist in content and nationalist in form, limiting nationalist aspirations to language only, changed very little in practice. In the eyes of the ruling group in Soviet Russia the elite of the various nationalities and their cultures became a menace to the unity of the party and country. Many attempts to "denationalize" these cultures and to "weed" out the nationalist "heresy"—and the heretics—followed.

There were similar developments regarding the Jews. According to Communist dogma, Jews are not a nation and equality before the law will solve their problems, while anti-Semitism was termed a counterpart of the capitalist order and counterrevolutionary, hence bound to disappear with the Revolution. The facts seemed to contradict these theories.

Of the 2,500,000 Jews remaining in Soviet Russia after the repatriations and emigration of the first years of Soviet rule, 75 to 80 per cent lived in western Russia, in the Ukraine and White Russia, leaving only a small proportion in the rest of the country, including the Oriental Jews in Asia. Jewish occupational and social structure was typical of the Pale of Settlement; an urbanized group with only a small percentage of industrial workers, they were mostly occupied in commerce as middlemen and artisans. They lived in compact masses. As a group they had their own communal structure, lived to a great extent apart from the non-Jewish population, used their own language (Yiddish), and were steeped in their own religious or secularized culture.

Economically the years of civil war, pogroms, and military Communism (1918-1922) were years of destruction, starvation, confiscation, and socialization.[3a] Jewish property, shops, and enterprises were destroyed in the wake of the Civil War, and those that remained were confiscated by the Communist authorities. After a short breathing spell during the N.E.P. (New Economic Policy, 1922-1925), private trade and shops were suppressed and liquidated. Artisans lacked raw materials, while the consumers of their goods, the peasants, were themselves under economic and political pressure and ceased to be customers. The great majority of the Jewish population became "declassed"; there was an increase in every sort of *Luftmensch,* those seeking to earn something by smuggling, buying, and selling whenever and wherever they could despite the death penalty for "speculators," while other Jews were simply in great need.

Nor was the relation of Jew to non-Jew without complications. Anti-Semitism, which increased considerably during the Civil War, may as a result of official suppression have gone underground for a short time, but it reappeared beginning with the mid-1920's, in the factory, in the Communist youth organizations, among intellectuals; even discrimination by the administrative machinery was observable.

Jewish Communists were few in number and had originally very little influence on "the Jewish street." On the other hand, during the years of civil war and pogroms by the various anti-Communist forces, a certain amount of sympathy for the Soviets began to be felt among Jews, because only the Communist forces offered security. The task which the Communist government set itself in connection with the Jews was: "Bring Socialism into the Jewish street"; in other words, communize Jewish society and solve the economic problems by integrating the Jews into the new economy.

Communization of Jewish life was begun through (1) dissolution of the existing Jewish community organization, party structure, and school system, and (2) supplanting them by Communist organizations. In January, 1918, a Commissariat for Jewish National Affairs (or Jewish Commissariat—in Russian *Evkom* for short) was established as a section of the People's Commissariat for National Affairs under Stalin. In the same year Jewish Sections of the Communist Party (Yevsektzya) were founded "to establish the dictatorship of the proletariat on the Jewish street." One year later all Jewish communities were dissolved. Social welfare agencies were taken over by the government, while most religious institutions were confiscated. Religious observance was permitted but frowned upon, religious functionaries were deprived of political rights, religious instruction of children under eighteen years of age was forbidden, the *heder* and *yeshiva* became illegal, and the Hebrew language and Zionism were first tolerated and later banned. A number of voluntary organizations, such as ORT, or those affiliated internationally, such as ICA, were left, or their institutional machinery was preserved to be operated under orders of the government or the Jewish Sections.

A further task, the elimination and absorption of the Jewish parties or Jewish Socialist parties, was accomplished in 1919-1921 by the Jewish Sections. Through pressure for "unity," Jewish Socialist parties (Bund, Socialist-Zionists, and others) were maneuvered and induced to join as special semiautonomous groups, shortly thereafter to be integrated into the Jewish Sections. The function of the Commissariat for Jewish Affairs and the Yevsektzya might have ended there—the Commissariat actually lost its value and was closed in 1924. But the process of dissolving the old order and of establishing themselves in the Jewish street meant for the Communists also handling daily necessities of Jewish life, management of the existing—or confiscated—Jewish institutions and sometimes creating for this purpose new institutional frameworks. For propaganda purposes a Yiddish newspaper was issued beginning with 1918, and a net of Yiddish periodicals soon developed.

The government applied its minority policy, recognition of minority languages, to the Jews. In the former Pale of Settlement Yiddish became one of the fully, or partially, recognized languages (in White Russia in 1920 on a par with White Russian and Russian, later of lesser importance). Jewish municipal soviets in village and town, Jewish divisions of courts, were organized. A school system was developed, distinctively Jewish national by Communist definition (national in form), although religion was banned, Hebrew soon eliminated, and Jewish history limited to the history of class struggle among Jews. In the Ukraine and White Russia one-third or more of the Jewish school population by the middle of the 1920's attended the Yiddish schools. Along with the schools—primary and secondary—came teacher training institutes, or Yiddish departments of general institutes, two research institutes of "Jewish Proletarian Culture" (in Minsk and Kiev), a Jewish department in Odessa University, a net of Yiddish theaters (in 1933-1934 there were eighteen), a number of Yiddish periodicals, and government presses were issuing a few hundred Yiddish titles each year. All this activity benefited from the prestige and the budget of the state, and helped to draw in many formerly non-Communist Jewish intellectuals, who in turn strengthened nationalist leanings bound to emanate from these activities.

This was in conflict with the antinational political tasks of the Jewish Communists. They, for their part, became enmeshed in a tangle of disputes and bureaucratic rivalries, resulting both from the inconsistencies of the task of building a proletarian Jewish culture and from the conflicting demands of Soviet policies. The Jewish Communists, like some non-Jewish ones having to deal with Jewish problems, were insecure especially regarding the extent to which the Soviet government policy on nationalities applied to the Jews, who did not have a territory of their own. A "normalization" of the Jewish situation, a territorial autonomy for the Jews, seemed to be the solution. By the middle of the 1920's the idea of Jewish statehood in Soviet Russia, of settling large Jewish masses in a contiguous territory and thus achieving autonomous Jewish statehood, was promulgated. Some regarded the autonomous Jewish territory as a center for the Jews in the rest of Russia (taking a leaf from Ahad Ha-Am). Official motivations were varied, ranging from "dealing a deadly blow to Zionism" to winning over the petty bourgeois Jewish masses in Russia and abroad. The Yevsektzya, at its conference in 1926, came out officially in favor of such a Jewish republic. (It soon was silenced and dissolved in 1930.)

The Communist Jewish state idea was connected with the problem of Jewish integration into the economy, or rather the agricultural phase of such integration. Before the war the Jewish agricultural population in Russia was very small, being in part a remnant of the Jewish colonies founded in the south in the first half of the nineteenth century. During the Civil War most of them were destroyed. But in the first years of Communist domination, many Jews from the *shtetel* in White Russia and the Ukraine sought to escape hunger and unemployment by agriculture on the peripheries of the small towns. By 1923 the Jewish farm population surpassed that of the prewar years. From 1924 on, the Soviet government actively sponsored Jewish agricultural settlement both by granting land and by giving some material assistance, while the bulk of the funds came from the Joint Distribution Committee, which organized a special section for this purpose (Agro-Joint—American Jewish Joint Agricultural Corporation). The Jewish farm population tripled during 1923-1928; the area under cultivation grew about four times. The Soviet government in 1924 established a special agency on the highest governmental level, the Komzet (Commission for the Rural Placement of Jewish Toilers), which was to co-ordinate the resettlement of Jews on the land. A plan soon emerged (1925) which called for the transfer of 100,000 Jewish families to agriculture.

One of the main centers of Jewish agricultural colonization was the Crimea, a thinly populated steppe region, where because of changed conditions and famine the cultivated area dropped by about a half in the first postwar years. The Crimea was at first intended to become an area of concentrated Jewish settlement and to constitute a Jewish territorial unit. The plan, however, met with opposition from the local population, and so after 1928 Biro-Bidjan, a remote Far Eastern area, was assigned the task of assuring the Jews of "the survival of their nationality." Biro-Bidjan was in 1934 declared a Jewish autonomous province, but Jews there remained a small minority. Despite efforts at recruitment, Jewish immigration continued to be minimal, both because of the hardships of settlement in that remote province and of shifting emphasis—in Russia and among the Jews—from agriculture to industry.

Toward the end of the 1920's, under the Five-Year Plan (1929-1934), which emphasized industrial development and the resultant increased demand for manpower, possibilities for Jews to engage in productive labor opened in Soviet Russia. From the beginning of the 1920's Jewish organizations such as ORT, J.D.C., and ICA, as well as some government agencies, opened or reopened trade schools and training courses for Jews in crafts, transferring them after 1924 into training for industry. Beginning with 1926, the governments of White Russia and the Ukraine formulated plans for the training of Jewish youth in industry. In connection with the Five-Year Plan, arrangements went forward to absorb a few hundred thousand Jewish workers and to train 150,000 Jewish juveniles. Although the plans only partially materialized and in a number of cases Jews met with anti-Semitic abuse and even discrimination, many found their way into the large public works outside the Pale of Settlement and into public service.

All in all, the number of Jews outside the Pale of Settlement (mainly those who were absorbed in the economy) almost doubled during the inter-war years, while those inside the Pale declined somewhat. Incomplete, and none too reliable, figures indicate that the process of industrialization and proletarianization made great strides. The number of Jewish salary and wage earners grew from 394,000 in 1926 to about 1,400,000 in 1939, forming 71.2 per cent of all gainfully employed Jews.

But by that time—the end of the 1930's—the situation of the Jews had changed considerably. The inconsistencies and conflicting trends of Soviet policies, the contradictions between the minority policy and the cosmopolitan centralism, as well as other factors, had ripened struggles against "nationalism" and small and large purges followed. The Jewish Sections were closed in 1930. Purges and "self-confessions" took their toll among Jewish intellectuals and leadership active on the Jewish scene. Most of them disappeared. The Jewish content of Jewish schools, periodicals, and research institutes was more and more watered down and *gleichgeschaltet*. The Yiddish schools, press, and publications numerically declined from the middle of the 1930's, a number of them being closed down. Meanwhile the continuous struggle against nationalist heresy and "chauvinism," the increasing suspicion of the West among the Soviet leadership, and the charge of contacts with the West in most of the Jewish purges raised a barrier between Soviet Russian Jewry and world Jewry which led to separation of the two groups.

In Russia itself anti-Semitism was again on the rise. Neither instigated nor supported but rather suppressed by the government, anti-Jewish tendencies remained alive in the population, appearing in the open from time to time. At the end of the 1920's the government took up the fight against these tendencies. They seemed to decline—or went underground—during the 1930's, to reappear at the end of that decade. The purges destroyed most of the "old guard" Communists who had a tradition of cosmopolitanism. Some among the younger cadres which then found their way into the administration and leadership brought with them a bent toward Russian nationalism and prejudices against Jews which became pronounced during the subsequent years of war and invasion.

Poland and the Baltic States. Poland, resurrected from the ruins of the old Russian, Austro-Hungarian, and German empires, had a Jewish population (1921) of 2,854,364 (10.5 per cent of the total population); and of the three Baltic States, Lithuania had 150,000 Jews (7.1 per cent), Latvia 93,479 in 1935 (4.8 per cent), and Estonia 4,000 (0.4 per cent). In each of these countries the proportion of the minorities was high (Poland about 35 per cent, Latvia 25 per cent). These countries either signed—the Polish state not too willingly—minorities treaties with the Allied and Associated Powers at Versailles or made declarations to the same effect. In addition to guaranteeing the civil and political equality of the minorities and safeguarding their rights as citizens, the treaties (or declarations) also proclaimed the right of each minority to use its own language both in private and in public, and to establish its own schools (with public funds), as well as charitable, religious, and social institutions. Provision was also made for the rights of the Jews to observe their Sabbath (Article 11 of Polish treaty). The same principles of civil and political equality and of group rights for a minority were included in the constitutions of each of these states (the Polish constitution of March 17, 1921; Lithuanian of May 12, 1922).

But these liberal tendencies either failed to materialize or were swept away by the aggressive nationalism and the trends toward dictatorship which developed in all these countries (Pilsudski's 1926 *coup d'état* in Poland, the dictatorship in Lithuania, in 1934 Karlis Ulimanis's *coup d'état* in Latvia and Konstantin Paet's in Estonia), and were later semiofficially reversed under the impact of rising Nazism.

The timing of the reversal and the differences in intensity of the anti-Jewish measures were dictated by local conditions. Poland, with her tradition of nationalist struggle, was nurturing a dream of greatness, based on militarism and chauvinism, and was touchy about any minorities and especially about the Jews. Even prior to independence, in Galicia and Russian Poland a growing middle class was fighting against Jewish concentration in commerce and industry. Indeed, Poland's independence was inaugurated by anti-Jewish outbreaks in different places and by excesses of the military —such as throwing Jews from moving trains; shooting Jews in Vilna, Pinsk (1919), and other places; interning Jewish volunteers; accusing Jews of spying during the Russo-Polish war of 1920 and shooting some without trial. The echo of these excesses led foreign states to send observers to Poland (England and the United States).

From the beginning, violations of the Minorities Treaty and constitution were not infrequent. Although obligated by the treaty to declare as citizens all inhabitants within Poland's boundaries, the government denied citizenship to thousands of Jews by making it subject to presentation of certain documents which many had lost irretrievably in the course of the war. The government took six years to issue an instruction to facilitate the acquisition of citizenship. And it took the government ten years after the promulgation of the constitution of March 17, 1921, which affirmed equal rights, to abolish administratively the Czarist discriminatory laws against the Jews in the formerly Russian parts of Poland. Discrimination prevailed, however, all the time in civil service—with gradual dismissal in Galicia of those Jews "inherited" from Austria, an unofficial *numerus clausus* for Jews in the universities, and use of discriminatory taxation and credit by the government to help diminish the range of Jewish economic activity.

Meanwhile increasing government control of economic life resulted in elimination of many Jews, for instance, through introduction of monopolies for match and tobacco production, the sale of salt, and the export of lumber. Liquor licenses were issued mainly to non-Jews. The Anti-Shechita Law of April 17, 1936, deprived large numbers of Jews of their livelihood, as did a law for the regulation of the cattle and meat trade two years later. But at that time, in the second half of the 1930's, anti-Semitism became the official policy of the government, following the death of Pilsudski in 1935, although no laws were promulgated to revoke Jewish equality officially. The Prime Minister, however, in 1936 justified the economic struggle against the Jews; local and unofficial restrictions multiplied. Demands for the Polonization of commerce and mass emigration of the Jews were included in the program of the OZON Government Party (Camp of National Unification).

All this created a setting for the picketing of Jewish stores, for excesses and pogroms against Jews organized by the National Democrats, for "ghetto benches" in the universities and "Aryan paragraphs" adopted by the bar association.

The Kehilla, envisaged by most of the Jewish parties as becoming an all-embracing institution of Jewish autonomy, was instead narrowed by the statute of 1927. The government, playing the ultrareligious groups against the secularists, gained the support of the former for the statute which assured the predominantly religious character of the Kehilla, thus denying it any function in other walks of life. In education the government did little to fulfill its obligation under the Minorities Treaty, which entitled the Jews to their own primary schools supported with a proportional share of state and municipal funds. Small, inadequate sums were at first granted to Hebrew and Yiddish schools by several municipalities, but even this aid was withdrawn later. The government did open primary schools for Jews, organized to eliminate the Saturday session usual in Poland and to set aside a few hours a week for instruction in the Jewish religion. Later the government began to close these special schools and to transfer the

Jewish children to regular primary schools. In 1934 the Polish government renounced unilaterally the Minorities Treaty and no longer acknowledged the obligation to do for the Jews even the little it had before.

Quite different, at first, were the government policies toward the Jews in the Baltic States. Lithuania, a thoroughly agricultural country, in the beginning lacked intellectual and middle-class elements from the majority group. Some leading Jews participated in the very creation of the state and its negotiations with outside powers. In Latvia there was a Social Democratic majority in parliament until the *coup d'état* of 1934; this party supported Jewish rights.

In a declaration of August 5, 1919, Lithuania made an offer to the Committee of Jewish Delegations at the Versailles Conference to grant equal rights as well as minority rights to the Jews. An official declaration to this effect was made by Lithuania to the Council of the League of Nations on May 12, 1922, and included in the state constitution. Even earlier, in 1919, an organized Jewish community was established with jurisdiction over culture, education, and welfare, as well as religious affairs. The structure of the recognized Jewish community consisted of a national council and local branches, maintained by state budget, which financed the network of elementary and secondary schools with Hebrew or Yiddish as the language of instruction. About four-fifths of the Jewish children attended these schools in 1935-1936. Yiddish was recognized as one of the official languages of the state. Supervision of the school network and the other Jewish institutions was the duty of a minister for Jewish affairs, a member of the Cabinet, and his staff, whose political activities were controlled by the elected Jewish Council.

In Latvia there was no special ministry for Jewish affairs, but nevertheless Jews, like other minorities, enjoyed broad autonomy in education. The schools were maintained by the state in proportion to the number of each minority. The administration of these school systems was in the hands of a special department of the Ministry of Education, the head of which was assigned by the respective minority deputies in parliament. Almost all Jewish children attended the Hebrew or Yiddish schools (86 per cent in 1934-1935). In some parts of the country where Jews formed a conspicuous part of the general population, Yiddish was granted some rights in municipal government.

The tiny Jewish community in Estonia enjoyed (along with other minorities) the broadest measure of self-government. The Jewish community began to function in 1925-1926, organized in a central council and local communities which had the right to raise taxes. Jewish education and other cultural functions came under its autonomous jurisdiction.

Most of these benefits, however, were not long lasting. The Christian Democratic government in Lithuania, under the influence of the Catholic clergy, curtailed in 1924 the power of the Jewish Kehilla. The right to raise taxes for communal purposes was annulled. Instead, the old "synagogue councils" of Czarist times were reintroduced. Yiddish, along with other minority languages, lost its position in municipal administration in 1925, which made Lithuanian the only official language. The system of Jewish education, the varied types of Hebrew and Yiddish schools, continued to function even after the semi-Fascist dictatorship had been established (in 1926). But in the 1930's state subventions to some schools were cut.

By that time the policies of the government and the agitation by Christian Democrats and the Catholic urban population for elimination of the Jews from city occupations were already in full swing. Through its taxation, credit, and licensing policies the government encouraged the growth of a non-Jewish middle class, while by supporting the credit and consumer co-operative it made the peasant independent of the Jewish middleman. Again, the growing measure of state economy interfered with Jewish business. Timber export, as well as some other businesses, either became government enterprises or were transferred to a semipublic corporation (interurban bus service in 1938, for instance) and thus passed out of Jewish hands. Only a few Jews were admitted to civil service, and in the 1930's most of them were dismissed. At that time limitations on admission of Jews to medical school were set. Then also the organization of Lithuanian business and artisan elements (*Versilininkaj*) founded in 1930 was developing lively agitation for boycotting Jews under such slogans as "Lithuania for the Lithuanians," "Buy from your own." In 1938-1939 plans to eliminate Jews from commerce and industry were formulated by this organization and the government promised support. There were also minor excesses and hooliganism in some towns and villages (in 1935, 1938-1939), although these never reached the same measure as in Poland.

Latvia began with a considerable non-Jewish urban middle class, but its efforts to eliminate Jews were thwarted by the democratic government. However, it did not go so far as to appoint Jews to civil service. The *coup d'état* of 1934 brought to power the Peasants' Union, composed of well-to-do farmers, which became the dominant group in the state. The dictator, Ulimanis, was not especially anti-Semitic, but he was attempting to create a "Lettish Latvia." His dictatorship liquidated Jewish cultural autonomy along with other minority rights. Both Ulimanis and the Peasants' Union were imbued with the idea of eliminating minority groups from economic life. The economic laws passed in subsequent years made of Latvia a corporate state of the Fascist brand, with the state economy predominating. Although the minority schools remained, the minority departments of the Ministry of Education were liquidated. The Jewish schools were turned over to the supervision of Agudas Israel (the ultra-Orthodox party), which tried to convert them into Orthodox institutions. In the wake of the nationalization policies, Jewish-owned enterprises were taken over by the state. Export of butter and other agricultural products was concentrated in special corporations. Administrative bureaus were busy eliminating Jews from industrial and financial positions, while Jewish students were barred from professional schools. Jewish doctors in city health departments were dismissed.

The Jews themselves reacted to these developments in many ways. Stirred by the ideals of liberation amid the nationalities of Eastern Europe emanating from the struggle for freedom, and aroused by the opportunity to participate in a democratic political setup, Jews in Eastern Europe attempted at first to insure their rights through parliamentary means. In the first postwar years, before the rise of authoritarian government, when parliaments in the new states had some power, the Jewish deputies—those who represented the Jewish group rather than those who merely happened to be Jews ethnically—developed lively parliamentary activity. They tried to influence legislation in favor of the Jews, or to prevent the passing of anti-Jewish laws. They also used the parliamentary rostrum to arouse public opinion, both in the country and abroad, against the wrongs being done to the Jews.

Another avenue of activity was lobbying to intervene with high officials in individual cases of discrimination against Jews. Such action was originally despised, for it amounted to conversion of rights to which the Jews were entitled into favors which might or might not be granted, but in the course of time this became a vital function. After all, the Jewish deputies did not have a great deal of power, and their effectiveness was still further reduced as the parliaments lost influence. This shifting emphasis in activity resulted in the increasing popularity of certain individuals or groups, opening the way for the governments to play them against other Jews and thus to disrupt Jewish unity.

Within the framework of the short-lived democracy in Lithuania, and also in Latvia, the Jewish deputies had developed lively pro-Jewish activity. In Latvia the proportional representation of the Jewish minority in parliament and other public bodies nullified many of the attempts by non-Jewish groups to eliminate Jewish competition in the country's economy. In parliament and many municipal councils Jews formed united fronts and coalitions with various political factions and thus assured support for their constituency. But even in Latvia personal intervention became the most effective means of redress for the Jews. This constituted the background for the rise of Mordecai Dubin, the leader of Agudas Israel, who was at home in every government office and frequently rendered assistance without thought of remuneration. The authoritarian government which came to power in 1934 then played Dubin (and the Agudas Israel) against the other parties and made him, so to speak, the sole "representative" of the

Jews. In Poland both private intervention and the attempt of the government to play personalities or groups against each other were still more prevalent.

Despite the large Jewish population, political action by the Jewish parliamentary representation was thwarted again and again by the ultranationalists of the Polish rightist parties, who questioned the right of the Jews (and other minorities) to have any say in the destiny of the country. In the first general election in Poland eleven Jewish deputies were seated in the *Sejm* (Diet). They represented most of the Jewish parties, from the Orthodox Agudas Israel to the Poale Zion. They formed a "Free Association of the Jewish Representatives" which, while the Polish Constitution was being written (1919-1920), fought to assure full equality for the Jews.

At first the anti-Semitic deputies tried to prevent them from speaking in the Diet, but this tactic was abandoned a year later. For the next elections (1922) the Jews formed a united front with the other minorities—Ukrainians, White Russians, and Germans—and succeeded in winning a considerable number of seats. Thirty-five Jewish deputies and twelve senators were elected and they all—with one exception—were united in the "Jewish Club" of the Diet. The possibility of gaining influence by forming united fronts with other groups was, however, nipped in the bud by the nationalists and anti-Semites, who intimidated the other minority groups. The first Polish President (Narutowicz), elected with the help of the minorities and the "Jewish Club," was dubbed "the Jewish President" and assassinated two days after his inauguration.

The government, for its part, tried to weaken the minority bloc by drawing away the Ukrainians and White Russians through promises which, incidentally, were never fulfilled.

Only once, at the time of the Pilsudski *coup d'état* (May, 1926), was the Jewish Parliamentary Club looked upon as a force to be reckoned with. While the fighting was going on in the Warsaw streets, the chairman of the Jewish Parliamentary Club was approached by one of Pilsudski's lieutenants seeking elucidation of the Jewish demands. The main points (annulment of Jewish disabilities, curbing of anti-Semitic propaganda, support of Jewish cultural needs) were then formulated in one of the secret command posts and later made public in an official declaration in the Diet by the new Prime Minister. The following two years were politically the best in the history of the Jews in the new Poland. The extreme anti-Jewish propaganda was silenced; discrimination largely disappeared; many concessions were made to Jewish schools.

But at the next elections (1928) the administration, through chicanery and falsification, prevented the minority bloc—and the Jews—from gaining a considerable number of seats. The Pilsudski regime then ceased to be a government of "benevolent dictatorship." It began the attempts to destroy the existing parties, forming a "Nonparty Bloc of Co-operation with the Government," and ultimately suppressed the opposition of the center and left. The Jewish front was split by promises which lured the Association of Jewish Merchants, Agudas Israel, and the "Folkists" to join the government bloc. The following decade saw the entrenchment of the dictatorship and dissolution of the parties by force. Jewish parliamentary representation declined to a minimum, with the bulk of the Jewish parties, and the non-Jewish opposition parties, boycotting the government-managed "elections." All that the few remaining Jewish representatives could do was concentrate even more than before on personal intervention in individual cases, a task which became ever more futile in view of the increasingly authoritarian and anti-Semitic trend. The dissatisfaction of Jewish voters with those groups who played ball with the government, despite its anti-Jewish bent, became pronounced in the elections to municipalities and Kehillot held in 1938-1939. The Socialist "Bund," which had consistently opposed the government, gained a considerable number of Jewish votes, entirely out of proportion to its strength in Jewish society, or with votes previously held.

In their struggle against the economic impasse the Jews were able to show more initiative and self-reliance than in the political struggle. Economic changes were made imperative by a number of factors: disruption of trade with Russia and, in part, with Germany, inflation, economic crisis and unemployment in the 1930's. At the same time, because of quotas and other limitations in the overseas countries, emigration played only a small role in solving the problems of the growing population. Against 40,000-50,000 Jewish youth coming of age annually in Poland and demanding jobs, only 16,000-17,000 could leave the country. In Lithuania there were 2,000-3,000 new candidates each year for jobs against 1,000 emigrants annually. Anti-Semitic pressures, boycotts, and discrimination increased the urgency of the need for these changes.

Both institutional and private facilities were employed by the Jews to alleviate the situation. Jewish economic associations—of merchants, artisans, trade unions—used political pressure and organized institutions for self-help. Discrimination in credit by government banks and lack of sufficient funds were among the chief problems encountered by Jewish merchants and artisans. To defend their economic positions Jews established—often with the help of J.D.C. and other organizations—their own co-operative credit banks and loan societies. The Union of Jewish People's Banks in Lithuania had eighty-five member banks in 1939, a few of them operating on a large scale. In Poland in the last prewar year there were 700 Jewish co-operative people's banks and societies, with a membership of over 100,000. And individual Jews—industrialists, merchants, salesmen, artisans, and workers—often tried on their own to find new ways to carry on their business or work, or to make a fresh start. Many Jewish textile manufacturers and their agents succeeded in finding new outlets (after the Russian market was closed) for their products in China, India, the Balkans, Hungary, and even in England and France, while German manufacturers in Poland had to close down for lack of a market. Throughout most of the interwar years Jewish merchants "discovered" new articles for export—eggs, meat, feathers, geese, etc.—and found a market for them, until government-supported corporations, or co-operatives, took over and eliminated the Jews.

The new generation and those who had been thrown out of the professions and trades tried to make their way into industry and handicrafts, into the lowest-paid jobs, or organized new types of production. Some new small industries were developed and Jews tried to find work there, for the most part as unskilled laborers. In these smaller establishments there were no organized groups of non-Jewish workers to keep the Jews out. Small enterprises were not subject to supervision by the government and one could compete through lowering wages or lengthening the working hours, or both. Similarly, homework, despite its attendant evils, was expanded.

After World War I, Rumania more than doubled its territory and almost doubled its population by acquiring Transylvania, Bessarabia, and Bukovina. The Jewish population, too, more than doubled. (In 1930 there were 756,930 Jews, 4.2 per cent of the population.) Transylvania, since 1868 a part of Hungary, was settled (aside from a small group of Sephardic Jews who arrived earlier) by Jews from Galicia and Rumania. Bukovina, since 1774 Austrian territory, was settled mostly by Galician Jews. Bessarabia, Russian territory since 1816 with a short intermission, was settled mostly by Russian Jews.

Rumania adhered, despite treaties and obligations, to her accepted tradition of depriving Jews of citizenship. In order to prevent legal evasions, the makers of the postwar agreements inserted in the Minority Treaty signed by Rumania on September 4, 1920, a clear obligation "to recognize as Rumanian nationals, *ipso facto* and without the requirement of any formality, Jews inhabiting any Rumanian territory who do not possess another nationality." Still the constitution of March 28, 1923, granted naturalization only to Jews living in the Old Kingdom. A year later a naturalization law was passed for the new provinces, making citizenship subject to proof of continuous residence in one locality for a number of years before 1918 and giving to anyone the right to protest during a limited time against a grant of citizenship. In 1936 this right to protest citizenship was extended to all naturalizations since 1924, giving the administration legal possibility to deprive tens of thousands of Jews in the new provinces of their citizenship. Two years later, at the time of the short-lived government of Octavian Goga, a "Revision of Citizenship Decree" (January 21, 1938) was promulgated which stripped more than a third of all Jews of their citizenship. Discrimination against Jews in the civil services, the professions, and in general economic life was more prevalent in Rumania than in other East European states. So, too, were overt anti-Jewish manifestations.

In the 1930's the economic crisis gripping the country, the efforts of King Carol II to establish a personal rule at the expense of the traditional parties, and the impact of Hitler's rise to power in Germany combined to bring to the fore the Nazilike organization of the Iron Guard and other extremely chauvinistic groups. Fanatical adherents of the Greek Orthodox Church and rabidly anti-Semitic as they were, they poisoned public opinion with anti-Jewish propaganda and demands to eliminate the Jews and preserve "Rumania for the Rumanians." There followed—officially or semi-officially—restrictions in the professions, elimination of Jews from Rumanian newspapers and from the Rumanian stage, exclusion from the sale of alcoholic beverages, attempts to imitate the Nuremberg Laws by forbidding Jews to employ non-Jewish females under forty years of age. Local authorities frequently issued more drastic regulations, such as prohibition of Yiddish in public or forbidding Jews who had lost citizenship to work in a factory, business enterprise, or artisan's shop.

3. World War II and After

The Nazi attack on Poland on September 1, 1939, precipitated fundamental changes in the political and social structure of Eastern Europe which left a great part of the region virtually devoid of Jews.

First came the division of Poland between Germany and Soviet Russia, after the German Wehrmacht had in a few days swept the Polish army away. Eastern Poland was entered on September 17, and in the next few days occupied by the Soviet army. Soviet Russia also absorbed the Baltic States and incorporated them into the U.S.S.R. as autonomous republics, after having officially, if briefly, guarded their independence—even turning over the Vilna region to Lithuania—and being satisfied at first with the establishment of military bases. In the south, Soviet Russia obtained (summer, 1940) northern Bukovina and Bessarabia from Rumania, with a Jewish population of about 300,000. Then came Nazi Germany's attack on Russia (June 22, 1941), which brought the Nazi war machine to the gates of Moscow after having subjugated all of Poland, the Baltic States, all of western Russia and beyond. In the south, in Rumania, the Fascist military dictatorship of Ion Antonescu in partnership with the Nazis recaptured Bukovina and Bessarabia, together with a part of southern Russia. The Jews of the whole East European region, over 6,000,000, were subject to a policy of annihilation which finally reduced their numbers to about one-third.

At first, in September, 1939, about 2,000,000 Jews came under Nazi domination in western Poland, while about 1,250,000 were to be found in the eastern and southeastern parts occupied by Soviet troops. This population was swelled by about 250,000-300,000 Jews who reached eastern Poland as they fled from the sections occupied by Nazis. These 1,500,000 or so Jews in eastern Poland, as well as the 250,000-300,000 Jews in the Baltic States and a similar number in Bukovina-Bessarabia, in the brief period of about a year and a half went through various stages of Sovietization, such as destruction of Jewish community organization and of the Jewish parties, liquidation of different types of Jewish schools, and the rise of the Communist Yiddish school. The Jews of this region, particularly the refugees from western Poland, were subjected to a series of deportations during 1940-1941, the last of which began in June, 1941, on the eve of the German-Russian war. About 250,000 or more Jews were deported to the far outlying regions of northern Russia, Siberia, and central Asia. Thousands of Jews were also deported from the Baltic States and from Bukovina and Bessarabia.

When the German attack on Soviet Russia was launched on June 22, 1941, about 3,500,000 Jews in eastern Poland, the Baltic States, western Russia, Bukovina, and Bessarabia were immediately in danger. The unexpectedness of the attack, the confusion in the first days of the war, the haphazard evacuation of western Russia, hampered evacuation or flight by larger numbers of Jews. Only from the Ukraine, which was occupied some weeks later, and from regions deeper in the interior of Russia, such as the Crimea or Caucasus, was a considerable number of Jews either evacuated or able to flee. From Bessarabia and Bukovina, too, tens of thousands of Jews reached the interior of Russia. All in all, the Nazis, in 1941, became masters over an additional 2,000,000-2,500,000 Jews, whose extermination was begun without delay.

A special task force for the purpose of annihilating the Jews was assigned to the army invading Russia. Ruthless execution of whole Jewish communities ensued and had repercussions on the treatment of the Jews in western Poland under the Nazi yoke since September, 1939. In general, the Nazi destruction of East European Jewry was accomplished in three stages.

1. The first months of occupation of Poland were marked by anti-Jewish decrees and regulations, looting of Jewish property, pogroms, shootings, burnings, rape. Violence, though encouraged from above, was more or less unorganized or organized only locally.

2. The ghetto period (1940-1941), when most Jews of western Poland were herded into a number of ghettos, ended with the outbreak of the German-Russian war.

3. The period of planned mass extermination began in mid-1941 in eastern, previously Soviet-occupied Poland, and half a year later in the

western areas of Poland which had been occupied by the Germans in September, 1939.

Most of the 3,000,000 Polish Jews, the 250,000 in the Baltic States, and a part of those in western Russia were massacred by special detachments of the Nazi army or gassed in the death camps of Auschwitz, Treblinka, Majdanek, Chelmno, Belzec, Sobibor; the rest were worked to death, starved, or murdered in other camps and ghettos. Only a small part found its way into either general or Jewish partisan groups, or into hideouts, or survived in the camps after the swift march of the Allied armies thwarted plans for last-minute annihilation.

The local population, or at least parts of it, in one way or another generally co-operated with the Nazis in annihilating the Jews. Inhabitants of Lithuania and Latvia began killing Jews even before the arrival of the Nazis, and shared with them the spoils of the Jewish wealth, acquired Jewish property from the Nazis, or otherwise appropriated it. Only small groups of the non-Jewish population were ready to help the Jews—often for a price—although the organized political underground was often ready to aid them. The anti-Semitic sentiments which held sway before the war found overt outlet under the impact of Nazi propaganda. This annihilation of Polish-Lithuanian-Russian Jewry was paralleled in Rumania by pogroms and bloody riots staged by the military led by Ion Antonescu, by the Iron Guard and other groups, and the destruction of almost three-quarters of the Jews of Bukovina and Bessarabia followed their conquest by Rumanian and Nazi troops.

The Jews themselves, intimidated by the Nazi might, isolated in the ghettos, fooled about possibilities of survival, refused to believe the inevitable—the fact that they were to be annihilated—and offered little resistance. Only in the later years, when the Nazi annihilation tactics became clear, were there heroic struggles in some ghettos in Poland and in some death camps, of which the uprisings in the Warsaw Ghetto (1943) and in Bialystok are the best known.

At the time of liberation some 50,000 Jews were found in Poland. In Rumania most of the Jews in the Old Kingdom survived, while of the 300,000 in Bukovina and Bessarabia only a small percentage remained. Of Russian Jewry there remained 2,000,000 or a little more—estimates being uncertain—besides the 300,000 or more Jewish deportees, refugees, or forced laborers from Poland and Rumania who survived in the outlying regions of Russia the rigors of exile, forced labor, starvation, and epidemics. Most of these Jews were later repatriated to their home countries.

After the war Soviet Russia reverted more or less to the 1939-1940 boundaries. She retained the Baltic States, eastern Poland—with some minor digressions—and northern Bukovina and Bessarabia. Poland was compensated by a shift westward, by Silesia, about two-thirds of East Prussia, Pomerania, and a small part of eastern Brandenburg taken from Germany, in accordance with the decisions of the Yalta Conference of February, 1945, reiterated at the Conference in Potsdam. Most of the German population of this area of 39,986 square miles was expelled.

Both Poland and Rumania, falling within Soviet Russia's sphere of influence, before long became satellites. During the first postwar years they had coalition governments with the small group of Communists playing an important role, thanks to the presence of the Red Army in the country. Civil rights, free elections, minority rights, were guaranteed. But in the years up to 1948 and 1949 pressures, maneuvers, faked elections, intervention from Moscow, and some purges put the Communist Party in full control. Most of the other parties were either eliminated, forced to unite with the Communists, or turned into puppets. Thus all of Eastern Europe was, in a brief period, molded to one sociopolitical system whose basic policies were directed from Moscow. The remnants of East European Jewry were once again, about a century and a half after the Polish partitions, in a more or less unified system, although certain divergencies between one country and another were observable.

There was in all the countries of Eastern Europe the curious phenomenon of anti-Semitism surviving the Jews. And there was at first a revival of Jewish hopes, activity, and cultural life, disintegrating later, with differences in degree between one country and another. Also from the two satellites, Poland and Rumania, there was, for a time, emigration abroad—mainly to Palestine-Israel—while Soviet Russian Jewry became hermetically locked up within the country.

Increased tensions and strains of war, occupation, the impact of Nazi anti-Jewish propaganda, as well as the growth of nationalist sentiments in reaction to war and occupation, led to an upsurge of anti-Semitism in all of Eastern Europe, in the Russian interior as well as at the front lines. Stereotyped accusations were reiterated: that Jews evaded military service, were speculators, war profiteers, killers of Christ. Anti-Semitism also made itself felt in many partisan detachments under Soviet control, operating behind the German lines, although there were some groups who defended Jews.

These anti-Jewish feelings and attitudes did not die down with the end of the war. In the Ukraine liberation was followed by a flare-up of anti-Semitism. Returning Jews were received with animosity. And in Poland and Rumania anti-Semitism was even more rampant after the war. Many of the non-Jews had collaborated with the Nazis in their treatment of Jews, had acquired or stolen Jewish property, had benefited in some other way from what the Jews left behind when they fled, or had taken their stores, market places, and apartments. These people regarded the reappearance of the Jews as a personal menace, and were certainly opposed to any restitution. Reactionaries, chauvinists, nationalists, the Church—that is, a great part of the population—blamed the "Jewish Bolsheviks" for annexation of their territory by the Soviets, the harsh treatment meted out by the Red Army, and the new regime itself, in which some Jews occupied important positions and followed orders from Moscow. Anti-Semitism became an expression of nationalist defiance, and served as a weapon in the struggle for power. Boycott, robbery, murder, pogroms, arson, and attacks launched from hideouts were means employed in this struggle. Some individuals penetrated into the lower echelons of the government and the Communist (or pro-Communist) Party, and there thwarted the central government, which intended fair treatment of Jews, or even helped the pogromists. In Rumania the problem of citizenship continued to plague the Jews for a number of years.

In spite of all these developments, a renaissance of Jewish life was stimulated by the general rise of nationalist trends, by the hopes nurtured during the black hours of war and Nazi dominance, by the heightened national consciousness of the survivors, and by the sense of compulsion or duty to reconstruct the ruins of Jewish life.

In Soviet Russia this began while the war was still in progress, in line with the general reversal of Soviet policy concerning the minorities during the war. Fostering of nationalist feelings, appeals to patriotism, were employed to bolster the nationalities' resistance against the common enemy. In April, 1942, a Jewish Anti-Fascist Committee was organized and began to issue a Yiddish periodical (*Einigkeit—Unity*) thrice weekly. Soviet Russia had been devoid of any Jewish organization since 1930, when the remnants of the Yevsektzya were liquidated. Komzet, which was a general institution dealing with Jewish problems, went out of existence in 1938 and no Yiddish periodical had existed—outside of Biro-Bidjan—since before the war.

Although the Jewish Anti-Fascist Committee was principally a tool for Soviet Russia's propaganda abroad, enlisting support of world Jewry, it served to a certain extent as a rallying point for Jewish intellectuals and others who were eager to turn it into an organization dealing with Jewish problems. It also served as contact with world Jewry. This was continued during the first postwar years, during which Soviet Russia's attitude toward Zionism changed from hostility to neutrality and later to support of the Jewish demands in the United Nations (1947) concerning Palestine. When the Jewish State was established on May 14, 1948, Soviet Russia immediately recognized it *de jure*.[4a]

This period, 1947-1948, marks the peak reached by East European Jews in the postwar years. In Poland, after the repatriations and the exodus following the pogrom in Kielce (1946), the Jewish population had been more or less stabilized at a little under 100,000, about half of whom lived in Lower Silesia. Economically they had made a comeback attributable to the general recovery of the country, to their own efforts, and to the support received from J.D.C. and other overseas sources. A net of Jewish co-operatives had grown up, helping to stabilize Jewish economic life. Two central Jewish organizations, the Central Committee for Polish Jews and the Union of Religious Communities, were active representative bodies of Polish Jewry, supervising a whole network of schools (Hebrew, Yiddish, religious), children's homes, congregations, and welfare institutions, which again were in part subsidized by the J.D.C. Most of the Jewish prewar parties and groups were active, issuing periodicals and other publications, and showing considerable vitality. Jewish national consciousness, shared in part by the Jewish Communists, ran high during the rise of the State of Israel and its struggle against the Arabs.

The economic recovery of the Jews in Rumania lagged far behind that of Polish Jewry. The economic collapse of 1947, the devaluation of the lei, made things difficult both for employees and independent shopkeepers alike. However, the community organization of old Rumania was reconstructed, local communities were revived, and by 1946 the J.D.C. shifted from direct individual assistance to reconstructive aid with the help of the community organizations. Jewish schools and welfare institutions were developing, Jewish parties and groups were active, although under heavy pressure from the Communists.

But 1948 marked a change in Soviet policies—and those of the satellites—in many directions. The Tito heresy in the Cominform, the cold war in the making, and the growing division from the West hastened the completion of the Sovietization of the satellites. With regard to the Jewish question, a return to denationalization, suppression of Jewish nationalist tendencies, and anti-Zionism were conceived.

This was heralded by Ilya Ehrenburg in an article published in *Pravda* and *Einigkeit* in September, 1948, denying the existence of a Jewish nation; condemning Jewish nationalism; dubbing Israel a bourgeois state, a tool of Anglo-American capital, ineffective in solving the Jewish problem; and suggesting that the solution was rather in the Communist order of the Soviet Union. By the end of 1948 the Anti-Fascist Committee in Russia was dissolved, *Einigkeit* was suppressed, and the Jewish writers were either then or a little later arrested and most of them killed or deported. In the same year the settlement of Jews in Biro-Bidjan was under pressure, followed by a purge there the next year. From then up to the death of Stalin (March 5, 1953) followed a number of anti-Semitic or anti-Jewish acts: the disappearance of all Yiddish writers, deportation of Jews from western Russia to Siberia, recall to Russia of Jewish officers serving with the army in Germany, apparent discrimination against Jews in certain government services (foreign affairs and foreign trade), anti-Semitic overtones in the campaign against "cosmopolitans" in literature and art launched in 1949. Then, at the beginning of 1953, came the "doctors' plot," arrest of doctors in Moscow, mostly Jews, on charges of having murdered Soviet leaders on the orders of J.D.C. (The doctors were released about a month after Stalin's death, with the admission that this had been a frame-up and the evidence falsified.)

The same period marks a change in the Jewish situation in the satellites. The Jewish Communists began, like the Communist Party generally, to espouse class struggle, antinationalism, the supremacy of Soviet Russia, and to fight Zionism, Jewish nationalism, Jewish "cultural particularism," "Jewish separatism." The governments of the satellites were transformed into Communist dictatorships. The Jewish Communists, who since the end of the war had been trying under the slogan of "unity" to dominate Jewish community life, now set out to control it, and were of course supported—or instructed—by the government and the Communist Party. Before long most Jewish institutions and parties, and their publications, disappeared.

There was some difference in method in the various countries. In Rumania Zionist parties were silenced with the help of the police force and arrests. In Poland the government gave Zionists (and nationalists) permission to emigrate to Israel, on the understanding that their offices were to close down. Rumania also deported Jews twice: in 1949 those born in Bessarabia and Bukovina to Russia, and in 1952 middle-class, unproductive Jews to labor camps. Jewish welfare institutions and Yiddish schools were nationalized (the Hebrew schools closed) and forced to "unite" with the Communists. Such Jewish institutions as the Central Jewish Committee in Poland and the Jewish Writers' Association were dissolved. The Jewish cooperatives were "aryanized" by introducing an overwhelming number of non-Jewish members, and by making them part and parcel of the Polish cooperatives. Most of the Jewish periodicals and publications were discontinued, leaving in Poland one Yiddish weekly published by the Communist Party, *Folkshtime*, and a few others. Their content generally resembled that of the Polish Communist periodicals, in addition to some diatribes against Jewish nationalism, Zionism, Israel, and Jewish Fascists. The activities of the Jewish congregations were limited and their over-all organization became a bloodless "Union of Congregations of Mosaic Faith."

There remained in Poland, with its 30,000-40,000 Jews, a Jewish Social-Cultural Union which at first undertook to combat any expression of Jewishness and make the Jews "participate in building a Communist Poland."

In Rumania there remained the Federation of the Union of Jewish Communities, which, since 1948, had been under Communist leadership, and the Jewish Democratic Committee—in the first postwar year a united front of Communists, Social Democrats, and left-wing Zionists, later a purely Communist organ—which made the fight against Zionism and Jewish nationalism its main task, as did also its two periodicals, *Viata Noua* (*New Life*) and *Ikuf Bleter*. Contact with world Jewry was severed in both countries and the activities of J.D.C., ORT, OSE (World Union for the Protectors of the Health of the Jews), and other foreign Jewish organizations banned.

At the present time (second half of 1955) a more lenient policy toward Jews and Jewishness seems to be developing in Soviet Russia and the satellites, in line with the general "New Look." Official publications have warned against spreading anti-Semitism, while there are some signs that the hostile attitude of the Soviet government toward Yiddish has been relaxed. Zionists have been released from jail in Rumania and allowed, together with some other Zionists, to proceed to Israel.

Nevertheless, the picture is a sorry one. The remnants of East European Jewry—numbering about 2,000,000—are partially under political pressure, forcibly isolated from world Jewry. Robbed of their communal organization, again forced to adjust to a new sociopolitical system, and subjected to Communist assimilation, they are bereft of all that sustained former generations in time of stress, and are in peril of losing even the final support of the Jews throughout history—the religious and national core of their culture and their faith.

Notes

[[1a] See above Israel Halpern, "The Jews in Eastern Europe (From Ancient Times until the Partitions of Poland, 1772-1795)"; below, Abraham Menes, "Patterns of Jewish Scholarship in Eastern Europe"; Ben Zion Dinur, "The Historical Foundations of the Rebirth of Israel"; Hillel Bavli, "The Modern Renaissance of Hebrew Literature"; Yudel Mark, "Yiddish Literature."]

[[2a] See below Arieh Tartakower, "The Decline of European Jewry (1933-1953)"; Mark, *op. cit.*]

[[3a] See below Tartakower, *op. cit.*, p. 434.]

[[4a] See below Oscar I. Janowsky, "The Rise of the State of Israel."]

Bibliography

The selected bibliography listed below is arranged according to the subdivisions of the essay. Many items listed for one section, however, contain also materials about the next. The bibliography is limited in scope and lists a minimum number of titles, in so far as possible in English. Further bibliography is to be found in most of the books included, and particularly in Dubnow, Elbogen, and Salo W. Baron's *A Social and Religious History of the Jews,* Vol. III (New York, 1937), and his *Bibliography of Jewish Social Studies, 1938-39* (New York, 1941).

A partial review of historical literature on East European Jewry is to be found in E. Tscherikower's "*Di Yidishe historishe Wissenshaft in mizrech Europe*" [Jewish Historiography in Eastern Europe], *Yivo-Bleter,* I (1931), pp. 97-113, and Ph. Friedman's "Polish-Jewish Historiography Between the Two Wars 1918-1939," *Jewish Social Studies* (1949), pp. 373-408.

I

BALABAN, MAJER, *Dzieje Żydow w Galicyi i w Rzeczypospolitei Krakowskiej 1772-1868*. Lvov, 1914.

———, *Dzieje Żydow w Krakowie i na Kazimierzu*. Vol. II. Cracow, 1935.

BRESLAUER, BERNHARD, *Die Auswanderung der Juden aus der Provinz Posen (Denkschrift des Verbandes der Deutschen Juden)*. Berlin, 1909.

Cambridge History of Poland, The. Vol. II. Edited by W. F. Reddaway and others. Cambridge, 1951.

Di Yidn in Polin. New York, 1946.

DUBNOW, SIMON, *History of the Jews in Russia and Poland*. Vols. I-III. Translated by I. Friedlander. Philadelphia, 1916-1920.

———, *Die Neueste Geschichte des Jued. Volkes*. Vols. I-III. Berlin, 1920.

———, *Weltgeschichte des Juedischen Volkes*. Vols. VIII-X. Berlin, 1930.

———, *Divrey Yemey am Olam*. Vols. VIII-X. Tel-Aviv, 1936-1940.

ELBOGEN, ISMAR, *A Century of Jewish Life*. Philadelphia, 1944.

FRIEDMANN, PHILIP, *Die Galizischen Juden im Kampfe um ihre Gleichberechtigung 1848-1868*. Frankfort on the Main, 1929.

GELBER, N. M., "*Koroth Hayehudim be-Polin mi-Reshith Halukata vaad milchemeth Haolam Hashniya*," *Beth Yisrael Bapolin*, I (Jerusalem, 1948), pp. 110-127.

GESSEN, YULII, *Istoriya Yevreyskogo Naroda v Rossii* [*History of the Jewish People in Russia*]. Vols. I-II. Petrograd, 1916.

GREENBERG, LOUIS, *The Jews in Russia*. Vols. I-II. New Haven, 1944, 1951.

HEPPNER, A., and HERZBERG, J., *Aus Vergangenheit und Gegenwart der Juden und der juedischen Gemeinden in d. Provinz Posen*. Koschmin-Bromberg-Breslau, 1904.

Istoriya Evreyskago Naroda [*History of the Jewish People*]. Vol. XI. Moscow, 1914.

LEVITATS, ISAAC, *The Jewish Community in Russia 1772-1844*. New York, 1943.

MAHLER, RAPHAEL, *Divrey Yemey Yisrael, Doroth Achronim*, I, 2. Merchaviya, 1954.

RAISIN, JACOB, *The Haskalah Movement in Russia*. Philadelphia, 1913.

SHATZKY, JACOB, *Di Geshikhte fun Yidn in Varshe*. Vols. 1-3. New York, 1947-1953.

SILBERGLEIT, HEINRICH, *Die Bevoelkerungs-und Berufsverhaeltnisse der Juden im Deutschen Reich*. Vol. I. Berlin, 1930.

WEINRYB, B., *Neueste Wirtschaftsgeschichte der Juden in Russland und Polen*. Breslau, 1934.

———, "*Yehudey Polin mi-chutz Lapolin*," *Beth Yisrael Bapolin*. Vol. II. Jerusalem, 1954, pp. 185-217.

———, "East European Immigration to the United States," *The Jewish Quarterly Review*, Tercentenary Issue, XLV (1955), pp. 497-528.

2

Dubnow, S. M. *Divrey Yemey am Olam*. Vol. XI. Tel-Aviv, 1940.

Hartglass, A., "*Milchemeth Yehudey Polin al Zechuyotehem Haezrachiyoth VaHaleumiyoth,*" *Beth Yisrael Bapolin,* I (Jerusalem, 1948), pp. 128-151.

Janowsky, Oscar I., *The Jews and Minority Rights 1898 to 1919*. New York, 1933.

Joseph, Samuel, *Jewish Immigration to the United States from 1881 to 1910*. New York, 1914.

Lazerson, Max M., "The Jewish Minorities in the Baltic Countries," *Jewish Social Studies,* III (1941), pp. 273-284.

Lestschinsky, Jacob, *Dos Sovetishe Identum*. New York, 1941.

———, "The Economic Struggle of the Jews in Independent Lithuania," *Jewish Social Studies,* VIII (1946), pp. 267-296.

Segal, Simon, *The New Poland and the Jews*. New York, 1938.

Weinryb, Bernard D., *Jewish Emancipation under Attack*. New York, 1942.

———, "Jews in Central Europe," *Journal of Central European Affairs,* VI (April, 1946), pp. 43-77.

———, *Jewish Vocational Education*. New York, 1948.

Zinger, L. G., *Dos Banayte Folk*. Moscow, 1941.

Żydzi w Polsce Odrodronej. Edited by Schiper, I., Tartakower, A. Vols. I-II. Warsaw, 1933-1934.

3

Apenszlak, Jacob, *The Black Book of Polish Jewry*. New York, 1943.

Lestschinsky, Jacob, *Crisis, Catastrophe and Survival*. New York, 1948.

Meyer, Peter; Weinryb, B. D.; and others, *The Jews in the Soviet Satellites*. Syracuse, 1953.

Reitlinger, Gerald, *The Final Solution*. London, 1953.

Schwarz, Solomon M., *The Jews in the Soviet Union*. Syracuse, 1951.

CHAPTER 8

PATTERNS OF JEWISH SCHOLARSHIP IN EASTERN EUROPE

By Abraham Menes

Introduction

Jewish history in the past 1,000 years has been, primarily, a history of Jewish life in Europe. There were, as indicated in previous chapters, a number of Jewish settlements there much earlier, even as far back as the time of the Second Temple. Their role in Jewish life as a whole was, however, quite modest. Up until the tenth century Jewish history mainly hinged on the large Jewish centers of the East: Palestine, Egypt, and Babylonia.

The general decline of the Roman Empire from the third century on led also to a decline of the Jewish settlements in the countries under Roman rule. The status of the Jewish population in the Roman world, including Palestine, became particularly difficult after the triumph of the Church during the reign of Constantine (beginning of the fourth century). The center of gravity of Jewish life gradually shifted eastward (to the countries of the Persian Empire), primarily to Babylonia. For the next seven hundred years the Babylonian academies played a leading role in the spiritual history of the Jews, and the Babylonian Talmud became increasingly respected and followed in Jewish settlements the world over.

Babylonia preserved the heritage of Palestine. The large settlement in the east managed to develop a distinctive and rich cultural life unparalleled in any other community in the Diaspora. The fact that Babylonian and Palestinian Jews spoke the same language (Aramaic), despite certain dialectal divergences, undoubtedly played an important role in the successful and complete maintenance of continuity in Jewish cultural life.

After the beginning of Arab-Islam expansion in the seventh century, the Jewish communities in Mesopotamia became a center of emigration. Babylonian Jews settled in Palestine, North Africa, and a number of localities in Europe. The decline of the Bagdad Caliphate, which began in the ninth century, and the continuous disturbances in the country, increased the stream of Jewish emigration from east to west. At the same time, the revival of the urban centers of Western Europe created favorable conditions for Jewish immigration. Before long the Jewish communities in Western Europe had established themselves. Babylonia no longer played the role of a spiritual center, and the beginning of the eleventh century can, without doubt, be considered the beginning of the European or Western era in Jewish history.

Until the end of the Middle Ages the West European communities were the most prominent in the Jewish world. After the expulsion from Spain (1492), the center of gravity of Jewish life shifted eastward, and the sixteenth century brings us to the East European era in Jewish history.

General conditions in Western Europe were very different from those in Babylonia. The Jews in Europe were mainly an urban element. They were less concentrated and therefore felt the pressures of the non-Jewish surroundings more acutely. There was another important difference. The language of everyday life and the language of study were, in Babylonia, one and the same: Aramaic. (This condition changed slowly after the rise of Islam.) Moreover, it was not too difficult for the student who knew Aramaic to learn to understand a Hebrew text. In Europe, on the other hand, a split was created between the language of everyday life and that of study. The student had to overcome the considerable difficulties of studying texts in language that was totally unfamiliar. Of course, translations could have been used, as in Egypt during Hellenistic times, when the Bible was translated into Greek. The new communities in Europe, however, held on to the Babylonian tradition. True, Palestinian and Babylonian Jews had also, to some extent, made use of an Aramaic translation of the Bible. The Bible in Hebrew, however, continued as the foundation of Jewish education. This particular Babylonian tradition—under much more exacting conditions—was now adopted by the Jewish settlements in Europe.

The development in Europe itself was not uniform. The differences between the Sephardim (the Jews in Spain) and the Ashkenazim (the communities in northern France and Germany) were particularly important. While Spain was almost completely under Arab rule (from the eighth to the twelfth centuries), the Jewish community there was very strongly influenced by the then blossoming Arabic culture. A considerable number of learned Sephardim held their own with the times, even as far as secular knowledge was concerned, being well versed in scientific and philosophical literature in Arabic. Thus there was close spiritual contact between Jews and the non-Jewish environment. The state of the Ashkenazic communities was very different. The Church did everything in its power to maintain the division between Jews and non-Jews. At best the Jews were "tolerated." The Ashkenazim were, therefore, to a lesser extent "men of the world," and secluded themselves more within the confines of Judaism. The study of the Talmud assumed a central position; talmudic law reigned over the totality of Jewish life. The well-known Ashkenazic authority, Rabbi Jacob ben Asher, who early in the fourteenth century moved from Germany to Spain with his father, Rabbi Asher ben Jehiel, characterized the difference between the Ashkenazim and Sephardim as follows: "The custom of the former was to observe the commandments and to like them. . . . It was also the custom in Ashkenaz for the leaders in the community to be the first in observance . . . which is not the case in Sepharad. . . ."[1]

Small wonder, then, that while Maimonides began his *Mishne Tora* with a religio-philosophical introduction explaining and proving the principles of the existence and the oneness of the Creator, Rabbi Jacob ben Asher, on the other hand, began the first part of his *Arbaa Turim* with the order of procedure to be followed upon rising in the morning. The Sephardic thinkers began with the question, "What must a Jew know?" The Ashkenazic asked, "What must a Jew do?"

The Ashkenazic Jews were secure in their faith, and were not in need of a *Guide to the Perplexed*, such as Maimonides attempted to create for the doubters of his time. Education in the Ashkenazic communities was, first and foremost, aimed at teaching deeds, at the raising of generations of Jews who would be ready to offer maximum resistance in times of overwhelming temptation. Surely this was also the aim of education among the Sephardim. In the Ashkenazic communities, however, the notion of Torah and Commandments was the exclusive content of Jewish education and the main theme of Jewish life. The Ashkenazic Jew was therefore better prepared in times of trial, and during periods of danger the number of Jews who left their faith was incomparably smaller in the Ashkenazic communities than had been the case in Spain.

THE JEWISH COMMUNITY IN POLAND

The Jewish settlements of Eastern Europe also have a history of some two thousand years. Until the close of the Middle Ages, however, the Jewish communities in the Slavic countries were far from the mainstream of Jewish life. After the Crusades, when Jewish emigration from Western Europe increased, this gradually changed. In a controlled and regimented economy, characteristic of the end of the Middle Ages, the status of the Jews in Western Europe became more and more precarious.

The battle of the guilds of Christian artisans and merchants against the competition of the "foreigners" became steadily more acute, and the hatred of Jews continually rose. In 1290, the Jews were expelled from England. Shortly thereafter, in 1306, the large Jewish community in France met with the same fate. During the fourteenth and fifteenth centuries the majority of Jewish communities in the German countries was destroyed. The tragic chain of persecutions and catastrophes culminated at the close of the fifteenth century (1492) with the downfall of the proud and creative community in Spain.

The expulsion from Spain was a particularly great shock to the Jewish world, representing the greatest crisis in Jewish history since the destruction of the Second Temple. The large Jewish communities in Western Europe as a whole ceased to exist.[1a] Thousands upon thousands died the death of martyrs, while others were forced, at least nominally, to give up the religion of their parents. Even of those who managed to survive, even of those who had the opportunity to emigrate, only a fraction achieved their goal. A considerable number of the exiles died en route. Fortunately, the gates of several countries remained open to Jewish refugees. The large majority of those who had escaped from Spain and Portugal found new homes in the provinces of the then powerful Ottoman Empire (Turkey), while Poland became the most important haven for the refugees from Germany. The road of Jewish migration now went from west to east. The exiles received hospitable treatment precisely in those countries that were least developed economically and where there was dire need for an urban population.

At the beginning of the sixteenth century, the Sephardim doubtless still were pre-eminent in the Jewish world. With the passage of time, this role of the Sephardic communities in Jewish life as a whole steadily diminished. The refugees from Spain and Portugal had not found appropriate conditions for normal continued development.

A very different fate was in store for the Jewish community of Poland, where refugees from the German persecutions found an opportunity to become integrated into a rising economy. The cities were only beginning to develop, and there was more than enough place for Jewish work and Jewish initiative. Poland and the other Slavic countries were, it is true, still very poor compared to Western Europe. However, the general trend was upward. This explains the optimism prevalent among the Jews in Poland. In this respect a letter by Rabbi Moses Isserles (*c.* 1525-1572), the famous rabbi and head of the Cracow *Yeshiva*, to a student traveling to Germany in search of a rabbinical position, proves instructive. When the young scholar quickly returned to Poland, the Rabbi of Cracow wrote him:

> I was happy to learn that you have safely returned, although I had hoped that you would remain to become a rabbi and guide in one of the communities. But perhaps a piece of dry bread and a tranquil life in our countries . . . where their hatred toward us is not as great as in Germany, is better, after all. If it could only stay this way until the Messiah's arrival.[2]

Since the golden age of Jewish life in Babylonia, Jews had not felt as much at home in a country as they now did in Poland. The general situation of the Jewish population with regard to security of life and property was incomparably better than in the German countries. The Polish Jew felt greater security because he was fully integrated into the economic life of the country. Jews were represented in the most varied branches of commerce and crafts, both in the cities and in the villages. And the more differentiated and ramified the Jewish economy became, the more compact the Jewish communities, the more the Jews lived together as a separate group. In the seventeenth and eighteenth centuries Poland already had numerous cities and towns in which Jews were a majority of the total population. For this reason the Jew felt more secure with respect to his own future and the fate of his children. The East European Jew lived hopefully. Even during difficult times he rarely despaired: with God's help one would find a solution; as long as one lived among Jews one would not be abandoned! This optimism created appropriate conditions not only for the flowering of Torah study in the sixteenth century but also for the development of a ramified network of Jewish autonomous institutions in the form of local communal and social organizations, culminating in the central organization for Jewish autonomy, the *Vaad arba arazot* (Council of the Four Lands).[2a]

The path of Torah and of Commandments in the Ashkenazic version attained its greatest development in Poland. Jews felt relatively freer there, and relations with the non-Jewish population were much friendlier than in the German lands. At the same time, Jews lived more among their own kind, and the Jewish world was a separate world. Only in Poland did Judeo-German become the Yiddish language, while the remnants of an older Jewish population that had been settled there for hundreds of years and had spoken a Slavic language were also gradually assimilated to the Ashkenazic newcomers and began speaking Yiddish. The Jews in Poland usually lived in separate sections of the cities. There was, however, no trace of a ghetto life, as in many communities of Western Europe. The Jew in Eastern Europe thus had more opportunity to be a Jew at home and a Jew outside his home: "The Jews here did not know what being ashamed of Jewishness meant. . . . It did not even occur to them that their non-Jewish neighbors might laugh at them."[3]

A special role was played by the synagogue (Yiddish, *bes-medresh;* Hebrew, *bet hamidrash*). One can say, without exaggeration, that a considerable portion of the Jews spent more of their time in the synagogue than in the market place. It was in the synagogue that the Jew began his day, and it was there that he said his prayers, met his friends, and occupied himself with public affairs. There were synagogues whose doors were never closed: night and day men studied and prayed. They studied both alone and in groups. There was a widespread custom of "appointments" (Hebrew, *keviot*), according to which each man pledged himself to study an appointed page of the Talmud, a chapter of the Mishna, a portion of the Pentateuch, etc., each day. Merchants would frequently take along a book while on the road, to be able to keep up with the daily portion. Rabbi

Abraham Danzig, the author of *Hayye Adam*, who remained a merchant until the last years of his life, wrote about himself as follows:

> And the merchants will bear witness that it was always my custom to take along copies of the Talmud, Bible, and Mishna with me on the road, and that even during trade fairs I would study one and a half pages of the Talmud, in addition to the Mishna, every day.

Should a merchant have to miss his daily lesson, he would "repay" his debt on his return home. There were also some who would learn a certain section of the Talmud by heart and repeat it on the road, lest they violate the Commandment to study, even when they had no books with them. Collective study was also very popular. The talmudic sentence, "Learning is achieved only in company" (*Berakot*, 63), was always highly thought of, and it was not particularly difficult to find friends with whom to study in the cities and towns of Eastern Europe. Indeed, the Jewish communities were full of study societies. In a description of the small town of Kroz in 1887, nine study societies were listed. Among them the Talmud Society, which was "full of scholars well-versed in the Law," occupied the highest prestige position. The town of Kroz at that time had a total of 200 Jewish families. Yet this small, poor town supported by its own means as many as ten male teachers, two women (who probably taught girls), a rabbi, two slaughterers (of *kosher* cattle), three sextons, and—what is perhaps exceptionally important to note—two bookbinders. (It was customary then to buy books unbound. Moreover, from time to time sacred books were rebound, particularly in the synagogue, where they were used a good deal.) In addition there were, of course, also a considerable number of scholars who studied alone, both at home and in the synagogues.

In his autobiographical work, *Shloyme Reb Khayims* the well-known Yiddish and Hebrew writer, Mendel Moieher Sforim,[3a] gives a description of the synagogue in his native town of Kapulye:

> The synagogue is full of householders and young married men who are engaged in study, and also of *yeshiva* students and men from other towns who have abandoned their wives and children . . . as they receive charitable board. Every evening, between afternoon and evening prayers, artisans and others in the crowd gather around separate tables to catch a "good word" from the reciters: at one table of the Midrash, at another of *En Yakob*, at a third *posuk* [Bible], at a fourth *Hobat ha-Lebabot* and similar philosophical and edifying books.[4]

THE YESHIBOT IN POLAND IN THE SIXTEENTH AND SEVENTEENTH CENTURIES

The founder of the Polish system of study was Rabbi Jacob Polak (*c.* 1460-1530), the *Baal ha-Hilukim*. Rabbi Jacob was educated in Germany;

he was, however, not satisfied with contemporary methods of studying the Law. The persecutions at the end of the Middle Ages had led to a decline in talmudic learning. The Jew no longer had the peace of mind necessary for profound study. Because there was little time for studying for its own sake, efforts were made to study at least the fundamentals, so that one would know the laws covering everyday conduct. Even the great scholars in Germany at the end of the Middle Ages felt they were living in an orphaned generation. They therefore saw as their objective the preservation of the heritage bequeathed them by previous generations. It was a time for collecting rather than for creating. And there was good reason behind this, for the French-German period had introduced into Jewish life the profoundest changes since the completion of the Talmud. On the other hand, there was peril in this concentration on practical problems and on local customs. The practical needs varied from country to country, and each community had its own customs. There was therefore increased danger of atomization in the Jewish world. Moreover, a deep spiritual crisis had been created by the expulsions and the migrations. Would it be possible, it was asked with anxiety, to preserve the unity of the Jewish people in such difficult times?

Rabbi Jacob Polak saw the answer to this problem in a novel way of studying the Law. There must be a return to the tradition of the *yeshibot* in France and Germany as they had functioned during the time of Rashi and the *Baale ha-Tosefot* (eleventh to twelfth centuries), and that involved a *return to the Talmud*. The function of the *yeshibot* must be not only to educate rabbis able to consult an authority in interpreting a law, but above all to raise a generation of scholars who could find their own way through the maze of the Talmud. Thus it would be possible to introduce more unity in the way of life of the various Jewish communities.

Rabbi Solomon Luria, one of the greatest scholars in sixteenth-century Poland, motivated the necessity for a return to the Talmud as follows:

> And the Torah became not two doctrines, but 613 of them; everyone built his own platform—the Sephardi justifying the Sephardic books, while the Zarfatim [the French] their own, each one choosing his own, just as each people has its own language and considers the Law a family heirloom. But this is the wrong means to the wrong end. For since the days of Rabina and Rab Ashi no one has the authority to make judgments like one of the Gaonim or Aharonim [Latin scholars] unless these opinions can be demonstrably based on the Babylonian or Palestinian Talmud or on the Tosafot—where the Talmud is not decisive.[5]

The central idea was: one people, one Law. A return to the source of the Law, i.e., to the Talmud, was essential. This, however, was far from a simple task. The Halakic literature that was collected in the Mishna and in the Talmud had taken several centuries to create, and is a meeting place of authorities of various eras and of various schools. In addition, the Talmud lacks clear-cut organization. A great many laws are scattered throughout its six orders, and only one who is thoroughly versed in talmudic literature knows where to look for a given legal text. It was therefore necessary to teach students to think independently, to be able to compare one legal text with another, and—above all—to understand the spirit of the text. This could best be achieved, according to the great scholars of Poland, by the dialectic method (*pilpul*), because "dialectics reveal the spirit of things." It was this new method of study which Rabbi Jacob Polak introduced in his *yeshiva* in Cracow.

The dialectic method evoked great dissatisfaction from a number of scholars of the day. Modern historians of Jewish life in Eastern Europe also often speak contemptuously of it. Without doubt, the dialectic method can be misleading; it can become a game of questions and answers. It should, on the other hand, be remembered that it was the old method of the legal texts themselves. It was precisely this old and now renewed dialectic method that endowed Rabbi Jacob's *yeshiva* with such extraordinary prestige, and which enabled the upsurge of scholarship in Poland.

Rabbi Shalom Shakna, a student of Rabbi Jacob, continued the tradition of his teacher. His *yeshiva* in Lublin attracted students "from the ends of the earth." Among them were such scholars as Rabbi Moses Isserles and Rabbi Hayyim ben Bezaleel, brother of the Maharal of Prague. It is important to note that neither Rabbi Jacob Polak nor Rabbi Shalom Shakna left any written works. That this was not accidental we know from the testimony of the son of Rabbi Shalom Shakna, who wrote in a letter to Rabbi Moses Isserles:

> On my word of honor, many scholars and I asked him to compile his decisions. His reply, because of his great piety and modesty, which was unparalleled in the world, was: I know that in the future people would base their judgments on my writings; I don't want the world to rely on me. And for this reason, too, his teacher, Rabbi Jacob Polak, did not write any book. Nor did these scholars make copies of any of their responsa to be sent abroad, for the same reason.[6]

Rabbi Jacob Polak and his pupil, Rabbi Shalom Shakna, thus remained true to their method of study. Their aim was to raise a generation of scholars who could pass legal judgments according to their own interpretations of talmudic texts. In this way the spirit of the great *yeshibot* of Babylonia was reborn in Poland. The study of the Law became the outlet for all the spiritual energies of the Jewish community in Poland. In the Law the scholar sought the answer to all questions relating to life, and in the Law he found joy, consolation, and encouragement. Those who could not devote themselves to study did all in their power to help others to do so. The greatest joy was for one's children to become scholars, or to take a scholar as son-in-law. An entire people lived for scholarship; each, according to his own means, studied the Law. Jews the world over, therefore, admired the Jewish community in Poland. The well known mystic, Aaron Berechiah of Modena, Italy (died 1639), cites in the Introduction to his *Seder Ashmoret ha-Boker* the testimony of a "dependable man" about the "Ashkenazic communities in Poland: where the entire community consists of holy persons. There they are engaged in the discussions and argumentations of Abayye and Raba, and they do not rest night or day." And this certainly was not mere exaggeration. The Law here became the property of the entire people. Thanks to the relatively rich religious literature in Yiddish, e.g., the *Tsene-rene* (the so-called "women's Bible," first published about 1600), the *Kab ha-Yashar* (1706), etc., women also became partners in the Law. Suffice it to record the fact that up until 1732 as many as thirty-four editions of the *Tsene-rene* appeared. Yiddish in Poland, incidentally, was unrelated to the language of the country, contrary to the case in Germany. Thus the Jews in Eastern Europe became trilingual. Polish (or another Slavic language) was spoken to non-Jewish neighbors; Yiddish was the language of the home and the synagogue; while Hebrew was the language of the Law and of prayer. Yiddish, in time, absorbed more and more words of Hebrew origin, and also a good deal of the sacred atmosphere of the *heder*, synagogue, and *yeshiva*.

Study of the Talmud with children was started very early—usually at eight or nine, and often even earlier than that. At thirteen to fourteen a student was expected to be able to study a page of the Talmud "on his own." That meant that he ought to find his way through a relatively complicated talmudic text without the help of his teacher. There were a number of rabbis and scholars who believed that the method of study in Poland and in the Ashkenazic communities in general was not proper, who pointed rather to the example of the Sephardic communities, where much more time was devoted to the Bible and to Hebrew grammar. One of the sharpest critics of the Polish Ashkenazic system of education was the Maharal of Prague. How could one begin, he asked, to teach the Talmud to a child of six or seven? The methods of the past must be restored: "In the early generations they set limits and periods to educating a boy in a natural way: at five he was taught the Bible, at ten—the Mishna, at fifteen—the Talmud. And it is harmful to give a boy a heavier load than he can naturally lift."[7]

Mere erudition and false dialectics were too much pursued, and the result that was achieved, complained the famous rabbi of Prague, was just the opposite: little of what he learned was retained by the pupil, who, at the end, would abandon his studies altogether. The Maharal wrote a good deal on the necessity of improving the education of the young, and on the method of teaching, in general. He also addressed the communities of Poland and the Ukraine on these matters. He did not, however, find any response to his plans. There were very important reasons for this.

The Jews in Poland were "Talmud Jews." Their ramified system of administrative autonomy offered favorable opportunities for the practical application of talmudic law. Moreover, it should be borne in mind that the world of the Bible was far removed from the realities of Jewish life in the sixteenth century. A large portion of the Biblical injunctions could not be observed under Diaspora conditions. On the other hand, many new customs and laws which are not mentioned in the Bible had been gradually introduced. For example, the Bible offers very little on prayers and benedictions. The same holds true for laws related to family life and to commerce. All of this is, however, given elaborate treatment in the talmudic literature. One of the defenders of the Polish method of education, Rabbi Solomon of Mezritsh, in fact, pointed to the practical importance of the Talmud as a subject of study.

Even a bit of the Talmud will do more to produce piety than a great deal of other study, and consequently it has been said that the Talmud is great, because it leads to action, and it also leads to insight into all the sacred and philosophical books. . . . But the Bible students, upon my soul, do not even know the ritual of putting on *tephillin* as required.[8]

It should also be remembered that Jews in Poland were largely simple working people, artisans, and poor tradesmen. Allowing a child to study until the age of thirteen or fourteen was a great economic strain. To accept the Maharal's plans for reform would, in effect, have led most of the students to leave the *heder* with very little knowledge. The alternative method of beginning the Talmud as early as at the age of eight or nine had the great advantage of offering the pupil the key to the entire Jewish literature. Those who could handle a page of the Talmud could easily manage a chapter of the Bible, but not vice versa. Actually, for the student of the Talmud the door was open to everything written in Hebrew and Aramaic. The study of the Talmud put the young student on his own. This was the greatest merit of the Polish way of studying.

Moreover, the study of the Talmud gave the student exceptional intellectual satisfaction. Most of the students in the *yeshibot* did not aspire to be rabbis. The cities and towns of Eastern Europe were, as we have seen, full of learned householders, who studied not only for the sake of studying, i.e., to fulfill the commandment to study, but because they actually felt an urge to study. They sang their studies; they sang them fervently, and felt transported to a higher world. There was a certain enchantment to studying a page of the Talmud. The great poet Hayyim Nahman Bialik in an autobiographical note described, in classic fashion, the uplift of the soul experienced by the student of the Talmud:

At midnight I was sitting alone in the synagogue, as always, and I was completely absorbed in the Talmud. The fierce snowstorm that night drove even the last two or three stragglers from the synagogue to their homes earlier than usual, and I was left alone. . . . On nights like these I would suddenly be seized by a spasm of diligence and piety, and would dive in completely, with all my 248 limbs and five senses, into the sea of the Talmud, and immersed in it up to my neck, I would descend down to its depths, and my soul would be filled with nameless delights unlike anything else. These were wonderous hours of an uplifted soul, of ecstasy, of barriers and curtains transcended. Study turned to prayer. Its rules became songs to me.[9]

The Talmud is notable for allowing the student many possibilities for searching and for thinking. Herein lies a basic difference between the Bible and the Talmud. In studying the Bible the student is confronted with the word of God; "the written Law" thus does not admit any discussion, only differences of interpretation. The Talmud—"the oral Law"—on the other hand, confronts the student with human beings—great men, to be sure, Tannaim and Amoraim, but only men. The Talmud not only enables the student to interpret the Law but also to introduce innovations. The creators of the Talmud brought the Law down from heaven to earth, and presented it to man. The fact that the Talmud offers many differences of opinion has been particularly exciting to the imaginations of young students, for this meant that one could choose between one opinion and another, and, furthermore, that everyone had a chance to be creative. And if there could have been several schools of thought in the *yeshibot* of Sura and Nehardea, the same might then be applied to the *yeshibot* of Cracow and Lublin. It is therefore not surprising that the scholars felt so fully at home in the world of the legal texts. It was only necessary to learn the art of "swimming in the sea of the Talmud." For this reason the study of the Talmud was particularly capable of introducing so much life and movement into the minds and hearts of the students.

However, even study of the Law in Poland could not remain merely an oral process. The introduction of printing in the middle of the fifteenth century, which doubtless greatly stimulated the dissemination of the study of the Law in Poland, at the same time served as a stimulus for a number of scholars to put their talmudic innovations into writing. The Jewish population of Poland had grown substantially, as had the number of students within and outside of the *yeshibot*. A need was therefore felt for new compilations, and particularly for a summation of talmudic law.

This task was taken up by Rabbi Solomon Luria (also known by the initials Maharshal or Rashal, 1510-1573), who was one of the greatest scholars of the sixteenth century. His work *Yam shel Shlomo* is an attempt to treat talmudic law systematically, not in the form of a codex such as Maimonides' *Mishne Tora*, but as an exhaustive commentary on the talmudic text. The Maharshal felt that it was not enough merely to list the final decisions; that definitive solutions were not always possible, and authorities had, from time to time, fallen into error. Therefore, he felt, the scholar must be given opportunity to rely on his own wisdom in interpreting the talmudic sources, although, of course, he must be cognizant of what other scholars had thought on these matters. This gigantic task, however, was too much for even so great a scholar as Rabbi Solomon Luria. The vast and courageous undertaking of the Maharshal, unequaled in Polish rabbinical literature, was never completed.

At the beginning of the sixteenth century appeared the first printed editions of the Talmud. (Individual sections had been published even earlier.) Many errors crept into these printed editions, both from mistakes in the manuscripts and printers' errors. Rabbi Solomon Luria therefore felt it necessary, in the first place, to investigate the talmudic text. His commentary *Hokmat Shlomo*, which is included in all larger editions of the Talmud, was the result of this difficult and strenuous critical work. The commentaries and novellae of Rabbi Samuel Eliezer Edels (Maharsha, 1555-1631) and Rabbi Meir of Lublin (Maharam, 1558-1616) are usually published together with *Hokmat Shlomo*. Both the Maharam and the Maharsha dwelled at length on the explanation of the difficult passages in Tosafot. In their commentaries on the Talmud, the Maharsha and the Maharam were little concerned with practical legal problems. The commentaries were not meant for rabbis but rather for students. In time the commentaries of the Polish scholars (the Maharshal, the Maharsha, and the Maharam) came to occupy a position in the *yeshibot* similar to that of the commentaries of the Tosafists.

It was, however, impossible to do without a systematization of the legal texts in the form of a codex. This applied not only to Poland, but to the Jewish world in general. After all, 1,000 years had passed since the Babylonian Talmud had been completed. Over the years, profound changes had taken place in Jewish life. A number of new regulations and customs had been introduced, and it was, in effect, no longer possible for even the great scholars to pass legal judgments on the basis of the Talmud alone. In the *yeshibot* it was therefore also necessary to study the post-talmudic authorities. Even these authorities, however, were no longer suited to the times, especially as there were many differences of opinion among them and "doctrines without number" were arising.

The task of introducing unity and organization into the legal material that had accumulated in the West European era was shouldered by the Sephardic scholar Rabbi Joseph Karo (1488-1575). Of Spanish or Portuguese origin, he went to Turkey as a child, along with his family and many other exiles. Later he settled in Safed, then an important center for scholarship and, incidentally, the place where the famous Sephardic scholar, Rabbi Jacob Berab, had attempted the creation of a Sanhedrin. At this time Sephardim still played the leading role in the spiritual life of the Jews. Poland was already an important center of learning, but the Polish scholars had not yet done much writing. At that time Rabbi Joseph Karo began writing his commentary, entitled *Bet Yosef*, on the *Turim*, the code of Rabbi Jacob ben Asher. In fact it was more than a mere commentary; in his introduction to *Bet Yosef* he explained his purpose, as follows:

> As time went on, we were thrown from and dispersed from vessel to vessel, and many heavy trials and tribulations descended upon us. The Law became not two Laws, but doctrines without number, because of the many existing books that explain its judgments and regulations. . . . In view of this, I conceived the idea of compiling a book which would include all the customary regulations, with an explanation of their origin and their derivation from the *Gemara* along with the discussions of the post-talmudic authorities.

On the basis of *Bet Yosef*, the Sephardic scholar then drew up a condensation of the Laws entitled *Shulhan Aruk* (*The Set Table*). The *Shulhan Aruk* was, initially, intended as an auxiliary book for handy reference by those unable to look up the laws in primary sources. As it developed, however, this was precisely the kind of book that was needed by his generation.

The *Bet Yosef* was sharply opposed by the Polish scholars, mainly because the author showed preference for the Sephardic tradition. (There were also some scholars who felt that a new authority was not necessary.) It was for this reason that Rabbi Moses Isserles (Rama), rabbi and director of the *yeshiva* in Cracow, wrote his work, *Darke Moshe*, likewise in the form of a commentary to the *Turim*, in which he defended the Ashkenazic tradition. Later, after the *Shulhan Aruk* had appeared, the Rama became even more aware of the necessity of allowing the Ashkenazic authorities to be heard, in view of the fact that the *Shulhan Aruk* merely listed laws without their justification and without their sources. The Rabbi of Cracow then wrote his *Mappa* (*Tablecloth*) for *The Set Table* of the Sephardic authority.

In this way the *Shulhan Aruk* became a joint work, in which both the Sephardic and Ashkenazic traditions were properly represented. This fact did much to help raise the prestige of the new authority. On the other hand, an authority without the justifications and without references to talmudic sources was not enough for the East European scholars. Eventually, in the first half of the seventeenth century, commentaries to the *Shulhan Aruk* were prepared by some of the most prominent Polish scholars. Thanks to these commentaries, the so-called *Nose Kelim*, the *Shulhan Aruk* became the recognized and accepted authority in the Jewish world.

THE 1648-1649 MASSACRES AND THE SPIRITUAL CRISIS

At the beginning of the seventeenth century Poland had achieved its pinnacle of power and influence. Internally, however, signs of decline were beginning to appear. The rebellion of the Cossacks in the Ukraine in 1648 made its internal weakness evident to the world, and Poland never recovered after that. Unfortunately, as is often the case during revolutions and wars, the Jews were exposed to particular suffering also during the Cossack uprising. A wave of terrible pogroms swept the country. Hundreds of Jewish communities were destroyed and tens of thousands of Jews martyred. Not quite five years after the pogrom of 1648-1649, the invasion of Byelorussia and Lithuania by the Russian armies began, again accompanied by a series of pogroms. In 1656, during the Swedish-Polish War, a number of Jewish communities were destroyed by Polish forces. To make things worse, the general poverty and the epidemics sweeping the country threw the Jewish population into despair and helplessness. Rabbi Nathan ben Moses Hannover, author of *Yeven Metzulah* (1653), ends his description of the 1648-1649 persecutions, as follows: "To this day there is in Poland devastation and hunger and great pestilence throughout the land, and other common troubles in addition. In the evening they say: If it were only morning, and in the morning they say: Would that it were evening."

The destruction in Poland shocked the entire Jewish world. Over one-third of the Jewish population was wiped out; tens of thousands of families were dismembered: parents lost their children, children their parents. Not quite 200,000 Jews remained in Poland. A large number of the communities were destroyed; the entire settlement was impoverished. It is not surprising that mystical messianic moods gained strength at this time. After so tragically experiencing the pains of the Messiah, the birth pangs of salvation, it was not difficult to believe that the Redeemer was about to arrive.

The uprising and wars ruined the entire country. The process of economic and political decline ended, at the close of the eighteenth century, with the total collapse of the Polish state. And the worse the situation became in Poland generally, the more difficult and insecure became the situation of the Jews. Persecutions and pogroms became frequent, and the competitive war by Christian townsmen more acute. Even so-called protectors and friends—the state officials and the gentry—made things worse for the Jews by pressing more and more money from them at every opportunity. The Jew had to pay for everything: not only for a trading or artisan's license, but even for the right to be a Jew. When a community was in need of a rabbi, it was necessary to offer an appropriate "gift" to the local squire or governor. Feelings of helplessness were heightened by the general reign of anarchy and corruption, and it was no longer possible to study in a peaceful atmosphere.

After the great national disaster, the Jew in Poland was dejected. His thoughts turned to theological problems and to the fate of the Jewish people. The old books were examined more deeply, with an eye to determining the date of salvation, the time when all troubles would cease.

The trend toward mysticism and asceticism increased, while the approach to life became more stringent. "How can I forget the destruction of the Temple and of the sacred sheep who died a martyr's death?" cried out a mystic of those days. "May God, blessed be He, say 'enough!'" In this atmosphere the Cabbala of Rabbi Isaac Luria (1534-1572), with its doctrine of *tikkun*, met with the strongest response. The Sabbatai Zevi movement likewise had a great following, and even after this messianic pretender had accepted the Mohammedan religion (1666), many remained faithful to him. Secret societies of his followers, who continued to wait for the return of their messiah, continued to function in Poland for two or three generations.

To be sure, these were only small groups; yet the messianic tensions enveloped much larger numbers. The legal tradition based on the talmudic texts taught the people how to live in the Diaspora, and how to preserve its Jewishness there. This, however, was no longer sufficient. Many asked: How much longer could one wait? Hence the reaction against the implied pro-Diaspora nature, so to speak, of the talmudic texts. It is not enough merely to wait for the Messiah. The students of Rabbi Isaac Luria were taught that each generation can bring on salvation, if only it desires it with all its heart. Repentance, fasting, and an entire system of mystical rituals can help hasten the time of salvation. For this reason the mystics were disgruntled at the overemphasis on personal problems and the lack of concern for the anguish of the Divine Presence in exile. They felt it to be the mission of man to do all in his power to hasten salvation.

In 1699 Rabbi Judah Hasid of Siedlce (or Szydlow) set out from Poland to Palestine.[9a] A considerable number of his followers—men, women, and children—went with him. This was the first case of mass migration from Eastern Europe to Palestine. A strict ascetic and a great preacher, Rabbi Judah called upon his people to repent, pray, and fast because the time of Redemption was at hand. Rabbi Hayyim Malak, who did not think highly of Rabbi Judah's ascetic doctrine, nevertheless joined this group gone forth to meet the Anointed King. With this we now approach the second stage in messianic mysticism.

From time immemorial, militant messianic movements have been critical of the Commandments. There is a well-known dictum in the Talmud which says, "Commandments will be void in the future world." Naturally, this is no more than theory: when the Messiah arrives, man will become morally pure and the strict discipline of Commandments will no longer be necessary. There were, however, messianic visionaries who felt that the "burden of Law and Commandments" should be cast off immediately. This, incidentally, was simpler than casting off the burden of the Diaspora. The messianic expectations provoked profound spiritual unrest, and people tended to accept extreme doctrines, particularly in view of the fact that the messianic dream was generally tied in with the longing for *temporal prestige, for power and splender*. It was a protest against resigned acceptance of life in the Diaspora and therefore, to a certain degree, also against Talmudic law.

It is no coincidence that the regal behavior of Sabbatai Zevi greatly impressed his followers. Delegates from Poland who met him reported enthusiastically "on the reverence, and the abundance of silver and gold, and the regal clothes which he would wear every day, and the large crowds who came there, and the honors which the Gentiles bestowed on him."[10] Not surprisingly, the idealized figure of the Anointed King overshadowed the authority of scholars, and even of the sacred books. Moreover, the messianic mystics often referred to the authority of direct divine revelations in the form of prophecy or divine inspiration, and therefore needed no moral support from the rabbis.

For the first time Polish Jewry encountered sharp opposition, in principle, to the whole pattern of talmudic law and the authority of the rabbis. The ideological crisis took on serious dimensions because the central institution of Jewish autonomy, the *Vaad arba arazot*, for a long time the pride and joy of the Jewish community in Poland, had gone through a long process of continuous decline as a result of general developments in the country. The same holds true for the local institutions of Jewish autonomy. The communities could no longer manage on their small budgets during the difficult times when persecutions were rampant. The more necessary it became to use ransom money to escape persecution and libel, the deeper the communities sank into debt, and the heavier became their tax burden. At the same time, the general rule of anarchy in the country led very often to the selection of unqualified persons as the heads of the communal organizations. The only point in their favor was that they were on good terms with the gentry and government officials. Moreover, the moral prestige of the rabbinate fell. The rabbi was, in many cases, helpless. It was difficult for him to pass over the wrongs in silence, and equally difficult to oppose them. Arguments occurred frequently in the communal organizations from time to time—even between the community leaders and the rabbis.

In 1764 the Polish government completely abolished the central organization for Jewish autonomy, the Council of the Four Lands, and the Council of Lithuania. Less than eight years later came the first partition of Poland.

It was the messianic adventurer, Jacob Frank (1726-1791), who openly declared war on the Talmud. His followers called themselves "countertalmudists" or "Zoharists." Copies of the Talmud were burned at the order of the Kamenets Bishop Dembowski after the tragic dispute between the Frankists and the rabbis of Kamenets (Podolia) in 1757. It was no longer possible for the Frankists to remain a Jewish sect, and in 1759 Frank and a number of his followers adopted Catholicism. It is, nevertheless, important to note that for several generations the Frankist families, though nominally

Catholic, continued to marry within their own group and to observe the Frankist tradition.

In the Frankist movement anti-Talmudism assumed extreme forms. The mere fact that the crude and ignorant Jacob Frank was able to enchant men superior to him culturally is symptomatic of the profound confusion in Jewish life. This messianic adventurer symbolized, in grotesque form, the protest against generations of strict, ascetic piety, of fasts and repentance, of mourning and mortification. The Frankist movement went so far as to create an ideology of "Gentileness" (paganism). The Jews, it was felt, must become like other peoples, emphasizing the pleasures and interests of this world rather than the hereafter. Despite the fact that Frank and some of his followers adopted Catholicism, he tried to retain a certain independence. He called his doctrine the faith of Edom. By this he meant not the Christian faith, but rather the Christian secularity, the splendors of statehood, military might, wealth, and all worldly pleasures. Frank had visions of a Jewish state, not in Palestine, but in an autonomous region of Poland. This striving for the pleasures of the world in the Frankist movement at times led to forms of moral irresponsibility and depravity. "I have come," he declared to his followers, "to nullify all faiths and all mores, and my intention is to bring life into the world." He particularly protested against Jewish concentration on books. The time has come, he taught his followers, for the Jews to become a military nation. Children six years of age should be taught military craft. Jews should begin to follow in the footsteps of Esau, because "even the Resurrection will be by the sword, and it will be appropriate that women, too, bear arms."

Jewish community life had been shaken to its very roots, and the individual Jew felt lonely and abandoned. Hence this strong longing for leadership, for a messianic personality.

RABBI ISRAEL BAAL SHEM TOB AND THE GAON OF VILNA

A search began for a new approach, rather than for a renewal of the old patterns of Jewish tradition. The search was not for a new Law, but for new things within the Law, for new reformulations of old truths. Never before were Jews in Poland so in need of undaunted thinkers and spiritual guides. Fortunately, there were such teachers and guides. In the southern districts of Poland, where spiritual unrest had enveloped the broadest masses, Rabbi Israel baal Shem Tob[10a] (Besht, *c.* 1700-1760), founder of the Hasidic movement, again found an approach to the people; at about the same time, in the northern region of Poland, Rabbi Elijah ben Rabbi Solomon (the Gaon of Vilna, 1720-1797) redirected the people onto the road of the Law.

Neither the Besht nor the Gaon were associated with the traditional institutions of Jewish community life. They were neither rabbis nor leaders in communal affairs. No organization or institution backed them; but precisely because of this, their influence on their own generation and on generations to come was extraordinary.

In various ways and employing different methods the Besht and the Gaon managed to give a new look to Jewish tradition. Both were messianic visionaries, strongly influenced by the mysticism of salvation; both made the attempt to migrate to Palestine: "however, they were prevented by heaven because their generation was not worthy of it."

To understand the development of the Jewish communities in Eastern Europe during the eighteenth and nineteenth centuries, it is essential to consider the Jewish *shtetel* (small town). At the same time that the situation in larger communities was continually worsening, the number of Jews in Poland as a whole greatly increased, especially in the villages and small towns. This fact changed radically the whole face of East European Jewry and created the appropriate conditions for a renaissance of Jewish cultural life.

In Western Europe the centuries-long battle of Christian burghers against Jews had culminated in their expulsion from England, France, and Spain and the destruction of the majority of Jewish communities in Germany. In Poland, too, the battle against the Jews was fought with particular venom in those cities where Christian craftsmen and tradesmen were organized in guilds, and where, following the German model, the "Magdeburg Laws"[11a] were in effect. The Christian guilds fought for their monopolistic privileges, and in some cities managed to bar entry to Jews as early as the fifteenth and sixteenth centuries (*Privilegium de non tolerandis Judaeis*). On the other hand, there were many private markets and trading points in Poland that had been founded by the gentry, and where Christian craftsmen and tradesmen could not claim old privileges and reserved rights. In many cases these private market places had actually been established by Jews, naturally with the approval of the gentry, for whom these private towns were a source of income. Here greater opportunities for work and economic initiative were open to the Jews. For the first time in their history, Jews tried to establish their own towns in Europe. They were able to succeed in Eastern Europe because the larger urban centers were, at the time, completely incapable of satisfying the demands of the poorest consumer—the peasant. This explains the rise of the small towns in the eighteenth century.

For the very same reasons, many Jewish merchants and craftsmen left the cities for the villages. It is remarkable that Jews often felt more secure in village communities than in large cities. At the close of the eighteenth century, about 80 per cent of the Jewish population in Poland lived in small towns and villages.[12a]

The *shtetel* gradually became the center of Jewish spiritual life. The old centers of learning, such as Lublin, Cracow, and Lemberg, continuously lost their importance. The great centers of learning in the nineteenth century were associated with the names of such small communities as Volozhin, Mir, Eyshishok, Slobodka, Telz, etc. Similarly, the centers of Hasidism were almost exclusively in small towns: Mezhbizh, Lyubavitsh, Ger, Talne, etc. In a large number of towns Jews comprised a majority of the population and were the only craftsmen and tradesmen. Thus the Jew enjoyed more freedom and security precisely in the smaller towns. Relations with non-Jewish neighbors were generally friendly, and embittered competition between the guilds and the Jews was lacking.

As is well known, the *shtetel* has been given an exceptional place in modern Yiddish and Hebrew literature. This is no mere coincidence. It is hardly possible for us, today, to appreciate the role played by the *shtetel* in East European Jewish life. The situation of the village Jews, on the other hand, was more difficult. Although relations with the peasant population were generally friendly, Jewish villagers often suffered from the whims of the gentry, on whom they were totally dependent for their livelihood. It was particularly hard to give children a proper Jewish education in the village. Nevertheless, the village contributed much to Jewish cultural life in Eastern Europe.

Rabbi Israel baal Shem Tob lived in the Ukraine and Galicia, where the number of village Jews was particularly large. The Baal Shem Tob himself lived in a village for a long time. There, in the southern regions of old Poland, the influence of the messianic adventurers and the opposition to talmudic law were still strong. It is therefore understandable that the Jewish villager felt especially lonely there. It was in the Ukrainian village that the founder of Hasidism discovered the individual Jew living in tragic solitude and spiritual helplessness. In the small towns, on the other hand, Jews lived together, and the Divine Presence was with them. The *shtetel* had a rabbi, a synagogue, and people could study and pray together. Pressures emanating from the outside world were not felt as keenly. But in the villages, could a single Jewish family, without a praying quorum, without a synagogue, preserve its Jewishness?

Of course it could, Rabbi Israel replied. "The entire earth is full of His glory." God is omnipresent, and can be served everywhere. In this way the Besht introduced the Divine Presence, as it were, right into the Jewish villager's home: no matter where a man happens to be, he is never alone; everywhere and at all times the Presence is with him.

Thus ancient Jewish monotheism received new emphasis. Jews understood the meaning of "the entire earth is full of His glory" very clearly. The belief in a single God, the Creator of the universe, supplied them with the strength to withstand the greatest of temptations offered by life in the Diaspora, because wherever they migrated the Divine Presence was with them. At the same time, however, Jewish tradition continually emphasized the immense difference between the world of impurity and the sacred world, between the world of evil and the world of justice. The ascetic mystics went further still. They constantly called upon man to wage war against the powers of impurity, in order to redeem the Jewish people from living in the Diaspora and the Divine Presence from its exile. The mystics argued that precisely because the Divine Presence is with the Jews in the Diaspora it is their duty to mourn, since the sorrow of the people in their wanderings is compounded by the sorrow of the Divine Presence.

This was too much of a burden for the simple man. The Besht believed that it was impossible and also unnecessary to burden him with so much sorrow. On the contrary, the way to serve God is through joy and faith, and there are grounds for joy and faith. We are never alone. God is also with us in our solitude, even in the Diaspora. There is therefore no cause to despair. God will not foresake His people.

The author of *Seder ha-Dorot he-Hadash* formulated the difference between Rabbi Isaac Luria's Cabbala[13a] and the Besht's doctrine, as follows:

> All that Rabbi Isaac revealed pertains to heaven, beyond the uppermost sphere, and it is not every mind that is capable of comprehending these lofty matters. But the Besht revealed the Divinity here on earth, especially in earthly man, who has no limb and no power that is not clothed with the Divine Power contained and concealed in him. And of all the things that exist in the world, there is literally none that is removed from the Divine Power.

There is therefore no absolute line between evil and good: "Evil is the chair on which rests the good," for nothing can happen without Divine Providence: "And this is the secret of the dictum, 'And Thou givest life to all'—that even when man commits a sin, God forbid, even then Divine Providence is with him. And this, as it were, is the exile of Shekinah [Divine Presence]."[14]

Clearly Hasidism could not assume the ascetic approach to life on earth. The Besht taught that sorrow, indeed, causes man to stray from the Jewish path. God can be served through simple, everyday deeds, even through conversation and social customs. A Hasidic leader stated that even when two Hasidim clink glasses, it is as if they were engaged in studying a page of the Talmud.

Sharp polemics against scholars and rabbis are frequently found in the older Hasidic literature. Not study, but prayer, was first in importance in the Hasidic movement. "God sees the heart," is a central motif in the doctrine of the Besht and his followers. The right intention is the main thing. Hasidic folk literature is replete with stories of untutored men who did not even know their prayers. In their own mute tongue, they poured out their hearts to their Father in heaven. And the helpless, unlearned man's silent prayer was better received by God, blessed be He, than the prayer of the greatest scholar, because "God sees the heart."

This brings us to that tendency in the early period of the Hasidic movement which was in opposition to the prevalent rabbinic tradition. Hasidism brought about a re-evaluation of traditional Jewish values. It is mainly a question of emphasis. Hasidism did not negate learning, nor was there any direct argument with the pattern of the Commandments. Rather, special emphasis was laid upon intention, prayer, and on serving God in joy.

> Weeping is very bad. For man should serve [God] in joy. But if the tears are those of joy, then weeping is very good. And let not man burden his deeds with excessive pedantry, for it is the intention of [Evil] Inclination to make man worry that his actions are insufficient in order to bring him to sorrow, and sorrow is a great obstacle to the service of the Creator, blessed be He. And even he who has stumbled into sin ought not to be too sorrowful, for his devotion will be nullified; let him be sorrowful over the sin, but rejoice in the Creator, blessed be He, precisely because his repentance is complete.[15]

Hasidism also created a new type of leader; in this respect it was greatly influenced by the prevalent longing for a messianic figure, an intermediary between man and his Creator. Talmudic law had replaced the crown of Priesthood by the crown of Learning, the rabbi functioning mainly as a learned man to whom questions were referred. Contrariwise, the *rebe* or the *zaddik* (saintly man) is not only a teacher and guide; he is in the category of a priest (or even of a high priest), who brings requests made by the plain folk to the heavenly Father. The *rebe's* court is in the category of the Temple and the *rebe's* table is in that of its altar.

The *zaddik* is the focus of the Hasidic community. Hasidic leadership is founded on the principles of authority and heredity. Hasidism teaches that the *zaddik* cannot be approached with ordinary human measures; even when it appears that the *zaddik* committed some sin, no evil should be thought of him. Even his sinfulness may have profound meaning. For it is written, "Seven times the saint falls; yet he rises."

Consequently, visiting the *zaddik* takes on great importance. It is comparable to undertaking a pilgrimage to Jerusalem. *To a certain degree* the *zaddik*, thus, also replaces the sacred book. One of the students of Rabbi Dov Ber of Mezritsh once said, "I did not visit the preacher of Mezritsh to study the Law with him, but to observe how he tied his shoelaces." Every movement of the *zaddik* is of the greatest significance. His entire conduct, even in simple day-to-day living, is worthy of study.

The road of Hasidism was full of perils, especially after Hasidim began isolating themselves, creating their own *shtiblekh* (prayer houses), and replacing the Ashkenazic with the Sephardic tradition of prayers. It is not surprising, therefore, that the most prominent rabbis and scholars of that time showed concern. They were fearful lest the Besht's methods lead to a new schism in the Jewish world. The Gaon of Vilna headed the Opponents of Hasidism (Mitnagdim).[15a] At the end of the eighteenth century, sharp and embittered conflicts raged. After long-drawn-out quarrels, a *rapprochement* was achieved between the two parties at the beginning of the nineteenth century, and the pattern of Law and Commandments remained accepted by both Hasidim and their opponents. The efforts of the Gaon and his students to restore the status of learning had its effects on the Hasidic world.

According to a widely held view, the rise of Hasidism was principally a result of social conflicts within the Jewish community in Poland. The protests of the wronged masses against the leadership of the rabbis and the wealthy members in communal organizations and in Jewish life generally are alleged to have received their expression in Hasidism. There is a grain of truth to this. On the other hand, one should be wary of exaggerations. As noted earlier, the Gaon of Vilna was associated neither with the institution of the rabbinate nor, to be sure, with the leaders of the communal organizations. It is also worth mentioning that the Gaon's doctrine was well and widely received in impoverished Lithuania, while the doctrine of Hasidism found its following among the more well-to-do Ukrainian villagers and townsmen. The conflict between Hasidism and its opposition was first and foremost an ideological one, although social factors undoubtedly played some role, too.

The tendency of Hasidism to create separate prayer houses and its polemics against scholars, which naturally led to a denigration of learning, caused the Gaon the greatest anxiety. While the Besht was so concerned with the problems of the individual, the Gaon concentrated more on the group as a whole. The Besht focused on the Jew in the Diaspora, while the Gaon was deeply concerned with the fate of Jewishness in the Diaspora. Both were actually striving toward a single goal, although their methods diverged. The Besht attempted to bring the Divine Presence down to earth; the Gaon, on the contrary, tried to raise man to heaven. The way of achieving this, according to the Gaon, was not through weakening but, on the contrary, through strengthening the talmudic legal tradition. With an eye on the classic era of scholarship in Poland, the Gaon called for a *return to the Talmud*. At the same time, however, the strong influence of messianic mysticism can be observed in the writings of the Gaon and his followers. The longing for the unification of the people made itself felt with particular strength. Messianic tensions are given further expression in the Gaon's method of studying the Law. *One people, one Law* meant to him *an undivided people and an undivided Law.* The Law must therefore embody all that the people have created over the many generations. No part of the Law may be deleted, since the totality of the Law and the totality of the people are one and the same thing. Consequently, the Gaon and his followers studied not only those subjects related to the Commandments that could be observed in the Diaspora but also paid particular attention to those parts of the Mishna and Talmud (including the Palestinian Talmud) that are exclusively concerned with the Commandments pertaining to the Holy Land. The Law and the Commandments are the path to redemption and restoration, and as long as the Law is in exile the people of the Law will be in exile and the world will be in exile, too.

To observe the Law in its entirety, however, clearly implies abiding by the talmudic ruling, "the Law is no longer in heaven." The Law was given to man and it is his duty and his privilege to study, interpret, and amend it. This can only come about through great effort. Every attempt at making innovations in the Law through direct revelation can lead astray. Therein lies the danger of coining a new Law which might break away from the existing tradition.

Stories about people who had the privilege of studying the Law with angels are frequent in Hasidic literature. The Gaon and his followers likewise believed that angels sometimes visited man to reveal secrets of the Law. Yet this possibility did not hold particular interest for the great anti-Hasidic scholar.

One of the most prominent disciples of the Gaon reported the following extraordinary tale about his master:

> I heard from the saintly man himself that many times there came to his door numerous heralds from heaven, asking and praying for permission to transmit to him secrets of the Law without any effort. . . . And he said . . . I don't want my understanding of the Law of the Lord to be based on any contrivances whatsoever. My eyes are raised to Him; let Him reveal to me whatever He wants, and impart to me my portion of the Law with the effort which I have given it, with all my strength. . . . But I have no desire for insights conveyed by angels and heralds and heavenly masters of the Law over which I have not labored nor cogitated.[16]

The Gaon definitely harbored no ambitions for creating a new philosophy of Judaism. Nor did he ever formulate his doctrine in systematic fashion. On the other hand, on the basis of his own works and of the various biographical notes in his disciples' works, it is possible to delineate in its general characteristics his approach to the problems of the Law and the Commandments.

The Gaon's doctrine represents a synthesis of Jewish thought from Biblical times to his own day, with the exception of the philosophical inquiries of Maimonides and of several other philosophical thinkers to which he did not subscribe. He did, on the other hand, include the Cabbala along with the mystical deliberations of Rabbi Isaac Luria. The secret of man, the Gaon taught, is that he was created in God's image. His disciple, Rabbi Hayyim of Volozhin, gave a particularly detailed treatment of the subject of the secret of man in the first chapter of his *Nefesh he-Hayyim.*

The subject of "God's image," he explained, belongs among the "highest things in the world." We cannot take these words literally, since it is explicitly stated, "What likeness will you compare unto Him?" (Isaiah 40: 18). The true meaning is entirely different. The Creator made man a partner to the world's continued existence: "Because by his good deeds, words, and thoughts, he gives reality and potency to many powers and sacred upper spheres . . . and, on the contrary, God forbid, by his evil deeds, words, and thoughts he immeasurably damages, heaven forbid, many powers and sacred upper spheres."

The Law and the Commandments are the instruments by which man becomes partners with the Creator in the process of creating and supporting the world. The Law and the Commandments are also the roads to restoration and perfection. No one can, therefore, ask, "What can I achieve by my acts and what difference does it make what I do?"

> And this is the Law of man: Let no man of Israel think, heaven forbid, "What am I, and what power do I possess to achieve anything in the world with my lowly deeds?" Rather, let him understand and know and resolve in his mind that every detail of his deeds and words and thoughts are not lost at any time, God forbid. And how numerous are his deeds and how great and lofty in that each rises to its [sacred] roots to have an impact in the heights above, in the clarities of the upper light.[17]

The responsibility of man, of every man, is therefore very great, and great demands must be put on man. It is no mean task to be the partner of the Creator, to bear God's image in oneself. It is a great honor, a difficult mission, and a tremendous responsibility.

The Gaon and his disciples therefore have another attitude toward the problems of intention and deeds. Of course intention is very important, but it is not everything.

> And although it is man's thought that ascends upward to cleave to his root, it is not thought which is the essence, but deed which is the essence in our serving [God], and a good thought attaches itself to the deed. . . . Because just as a man cannot get up on the upper rungs of the ladder if he misses the lower steps, so, too, it is the duty of us, men, whose houses in our lifetime are in the world, to fulfill the deeds. The more sincerely one performs the deeds, the better it is.[18]

The anti-Hasidic thinkers understood the meaning of intention, of the principle that "God sees the heart," very well. They were aware, however, of the immense pitfalls of mere intentions, of good wishes that are not accompanied by deeds. They felt, therefore, that men should be judged not only by their intentions but also by their deeds.

In the Gaon's doctrine there is therefore no place at all for the *zaddik* for an intermediary between man and the Creator. Every man is rather in the category of a *zaddik*. God did not create any superhumans. The privilege of being a human being, and of fulfilling the functions God has appointed for man, should more than suffice.

Rabbi Hayyim of Volozhin also strongly argued against the Hasidic interpretation of the principle, "The earth is filled with His glory," as if there was no evil on earth. Unfortunately, forces of evil do exist, and man must wage war against them. Man is not merely a partner to the creation and preservation of the world; he is also a partner to the creation of both heaven and hell: "The truth is that the future world is made by man himself, who, by his deeds, expands and enlarges and perfects a portion for himself . . . and the point of the penalty of Hell, too, is that the sin itself is the penalty."[19]

The Gaon and his disciples also were in favor of serving God in joy. Can there, however, be a greater joy than that of studying the Law and observing the Commandments? Moreover, the Gaon was afraid that the road taken by Hasidism would lead to contempt for the Law. Man, after all, has so much to do in the world and so little time in which to do it. This concern led the Gaon to a strict, ascetic approach to life. It is the ascetism of the pioneer who knows he has much to accomplish during the short period that he is ordained to spend in the *world of deeds*, and must therefore be very sparing with his time, which is his greatest treasure. It is told that, before his death, the Gaon placed his *sisit* in his hands, burst into tears, and said, "How difficult it is to part with the world of deeds, where man, by observing so simple a Commandment as the wearing of *sisit* earns the privilege of seeing the Divine Presence. How shall we achieve this level in the world of souls?"[20]

It is clear from this that the Gaon's longing for redemption was not related to the idea that "the Commandments would be nullified in the future." What, then, is the purpose of life without the Commandments? The problem of statehood likewise held little interest for him. The Gaon waited for redemption so that Jews, once freed from the yoke of the Diaspora, would be able to devote themselves more to the Law and the Commandments, so that they would grow firmer as Jews, and more saintly. The purpose of salvation is the perfection of the world and of the Law, and the road to salvation is the road of the Law.

VOLOZHIN

The first partition of Poland took place in 1772. Not long thereafter Poland ceased to exist as an independent state (1795). Russia received the largest portion of land and population, and for more than a century, until the First World War, the history of Jewish life in Eastern Europe is mainly associated with the large Jewish settlement in the Czarist empire.

The Jewish settlement in Russia took over the Polish and Lithuanian heritage. The first sproutings of the Jewish Enlightenment (*Haskala*)[20a] began to appear in Eastern Europe at the threshold of the nineteenth century. The secular tendencies of the Enlightenment were often supported by the Czarist government, which, however, had another purpose in mind, namely, assimilation. In spite of this, the nineteenth century brought with it a remarkable revival of traditional learning. The founding of the large *yeshiva* in Volozhin played a very large role in this.

The most important task now was to *revive the prestige of learning*. East European Jews never ceased studying, even in the most difficult times. The problem was, however, as we have already seen, the position of learning in the scale of moral values.

A life based on studying the Law was always difficult. The *yeshiva* students were mostly young sons of poor parents, and the community organizations had to assume responsibility for them. Widespread was the custom of "eating days" (*esn teg*). Every day of the week the student would eat in a different house. In most cases, the communities also had to assume the salary of the head of the *yeshiva*, and this was often more difficult than arranging eating days for the pupils. The purchase of necessary books for *yeshibot* and synagogues represented a particularly large expenditure. A set of the Talmud cost a small fortune (about $3,000 at current rates). The fact that learning had lost much of its earlier prestige made its support difficult, as the need for special efforts to preserve the *yeshibot* was not felt strongly. In his last chapter of *Nefesh he-Hayyim*, Rabbi Hayyim of Volozhin complained:

> And now in the present generations . . . many people concentrate their studies, on most days, on books of devotion and edification, saying that it is of the essence for every man in his world to be concerned with them always. . . . And I saw, with my own eyes, in a certain region that this had become so widespread among them that most synagogues had only edifying books in abundance, but not a single complete Talmud was in them. . . . Should this continue, it may come to pass, heaven forbid, that there will be no scholar any more, and then what is going to happen to Learning?

The disciple of the Gaon felt that the time was ripe for searching the answer to the question, "What will happen to our Learning?" The great prestige of his master helped him greatly, but it was in no small measure to his own credit that the Volozhin *Yeshiva*, founded in 1802, rapidly became a center of learning for all of Russia.

It is not an exaggeration to state that the Volozhin *Yeshiva* marks the beginning of a new epoch in the history of learning in Lithuania and

Poland. The mere fact that the *yeshiva* was founded not in Vilna, capital of Lithuania, but in a small town, little known until then, is characteristic, and undoubtedly was intentional. In the small towns Jewish life was freer; outside pressures and influences were felt less poignantly. Furthermore, in the small town the *yeshiva* could make itself felt. It became the pride of the town. In the large city of Vilna the *yeshiva* could not have occupied so prominent a position.

The main task was, after all, to raise the prestige of learning and of the scholars. Rabbi Hayyim therefore immediately abolished the old custom of eating days. Pupils received assistance directly from the *yeshiva* treasury. It was a very modest amount, but the social position of the *yeshiva* students was greatly enhanced by the changed system. The *yeshiva* was totally independent of the town in a financial sense, and was actually a source of income to the town. In Volozhin the student was no longer called "*yeshiva* boy" (*yeshive bokher*) but "*yeshiva* man." The mere change in name is representative of the new pattern of scholarship.

Volozhin revived the tradition of learning for learning's sake. The *yeshiva* man was not preparing for the rabbinate; his ambition was, rather, to be a scholar. The methods of study were established with this in mind. No differentiation was made between those sections of the Talmud that had practical value for contemporary times and those that dealt mainly with the Commandments applicable to the Holy Land. In Volozhin the entire Talmud was studied, page by page, from the beginning, *Berakot*, to the end of *Niddak*, day after day excepting the Sabbath, the holidays, and the ninth of *Ab*. The daily lesson was a kind of "daily sacrifice."[21]

The study of the Law here became a kind of service, like the divine service in the Temple of old. In the Volozhin Temple of Learning men studied night and day, even during the Sabbath and holiday nights. The sound of study was continuous all twenty-four hours of the day.

In Volozhin it became clear what the prestige and love of learning could mean. This explains the extraordinary influence of Volozhin and the other great *yeshibot* in Lithuania. Even the admirers of the Enlightenment, who often criticized the old forms of Jewish life so carpingly, felt it their duty to offer wholehearted recognition to the students in the *yeshibot*. It was not only the diligence of the *yeshiva* men that was so impressive but also their passionate desire for knowledge, their desire to immerse themselves in study and to seek truth—characteristics which called forth feelings of reverence among writers such as Peretz Smolenski, Judah Loeb Gordon, Hayyim Nahman Bialik, etc.

At the death of the founder of Volozhin, the leadership of the *yeshiva* went to his son, Rabbi Isaac of Volozhin, who possessed his father's positive traits. After his demise, in turn, the leadership passed on to his sons-in-law. In this way a dynasty was established, which continued to the last days of Volozhin.

It should not be imagined that giving the daily lecture in this Temple of Learning, filled with accomplished scholars, was an easy task. For this reason the directorship of the *yeshiva* was often handed down not from father to son, but rather from father-in-law to son-in-law. To choose a scholar as son-in-law was at times simpler than to raise a son to be an outstanding scholar, worthy of the directorship in a *yeshiva* such as Volozhin.

Volozhin reached its peak in the size of its student body and in prestige under the leadership of Rabbi Naftali Zevi Judah Berlin (known also as Nzib, 1817-1892), son-in-law of Rabbi Isaac of Volozhin. For forty years he headed the largest Jewish center of learning in the nineteenth century. The number of students exceeded 400; they came from various countries. The Nzib carried on the tradition of the Gaon and of Rabbi Hayyim of Volozhin. In the first place, he always emphasized the importance of "toiling" as one studies. In his lectures he put particular store by "immediate" comprehension of the problem. The lecture was given every day but Saturday, from 12:30 to 2 P.M., three times a week by the director of the *yeshiva* and three times by his deputy, who was also customarily a member of the Volozhin dynasty. In the 1880's Rabbi Hayyim Soloveytshik (later rabbi of Brisk, known also as Rabbi Hayyim of Brisk) was deputy director. His lectures were particularly popular. Rabbi Hayyim's method of teaching was distinguished by his logical analysis of the legal texts. Great weight was placed, in Volozhin, on independent work by the student. Even attendance at the lectures was optional. There were no formal examinations. The head of the *yeshiva* occasionally interviewed the students or joined them in their studies, thus deriving a good idea as to their achievements. Moreover, there were no separate divisions or classes, although the differences among students, both with respect to age and knowledge, were considerable. Despite differences, the spirit of a single *yeshiva* family prevailed. The custom of studying together in teams of two was widespread. At times a younger student would seek out an older *yeshiva* man and compensate him for his tutorship. This was a small source of income for the older students. Larger groups used to get together for "conversational study." Usually they discussed the director's lecture, and this gave them opportunity for dialectic exercises, for original observations, and for clarifying certain matters that had remained obscure.

In this fashion each student studied alone and yet all studied together. Each *yeshiva* man depended primarily on himself, on his own abilities and his own diligence; at the same time all were imbued with the spirit of the *yeshiva*, of complete spiritual partnership. And the partnership extended to material things as well. They helped one another. The *yeshiva* men had their own "Society for the Support of Scholarship," whose function was to help students in times of need, and a "Student Loan Fund." The main responsibility for the maintenance of the *yeshiva*, however, lodged with the director of the *yeshiva*, and the responsibility was great indeed.

Fund-raising emissaries from Volozhin traveled all over Russia, while contributions came from other European countries as well. In the 1880's, the United States contributed relatively substantial sums for the great *yeshiva* in Russia.

Some of the *yeshiva* men came from wealthy families, and were not in need of support. These, however, represented a relatively small minority. Most students had to resort to the stipend of the *yeshiva* treasury, between half a ruble and a ruble a week. Thus the life of scholarship in Volozhin was also rather difficult. Most of the students had to be satisfied with "bread and tea for breakfast and supper, bread and some warm dish for luncheon, and meat once a week—on the Sabbath." The budget of a *yeshiva* man amounted only to 1.50 rubles a week. Of this, about 30 to 40 kopeks went for rent. Ordinarily two or three *yeshiva* men shared a room. A student did not even dream of the luxury of having a room to himself. The student's landlady also took care of buying and preparing his food.

The trends of the times, however, also found their way to Volozhin. There were *yeshiva* men who would leaf through a *Haskala* book or a Hebrew newspaper. The Hebrew press of that day often discussed the question of introducing secular subjects and Russian-language instruction into Volozhin and other *yeshibot*. In the 1880's, after the south-Russian pogroms, the "Lovers of Zion" movement met with strong response from the students of Volozhin. The secret society "Nes Ziona" (A Banner Toward Zion) was founded, and counted among its members a number of the most prominent *yeshiva* men. The very existence of such a group, basically secular in its nature, tended to weaken the internal discipline of the *yeshiva*, even though the director himself favored efforts for settling the Holy Land.

External pressures, particularly the government's decision to introduce Russian as obligatory, also added to this tendency at the time. The *yeshiva* administration finally was forced to submit. Secular subjects were, however, not included in the *yeshiva's* regular program of study. A teacher was hired, a separate room assigned him, and those students who wanted to study Russian were able to. The number of *yeshiva* men who attended his courses was very small. Naturally this did not satisfy the government. In the winter of 1892 the police suddenly appeared on the scene. They forced all the students to evacuate the *yeshiva* building, and ordered them to leave Volozhin within three days.

For several years the *yeshiva* was closed. When it reopened (in 1895), Rabbi Berlin was no longer alive, and the renewed *yeshiva* never regained its former prestige.

The Volozhin *Yeshiva* existed for almost 140 years. Founded in 1802, shortly after Poland had disintegrated, it closed in 1939, at the outbreak of the Second World War. Throughout its existence, the Volozhin *yeshiva* observed times of prosperity and times of decline. Until 1892, Volozhin had been the most prominent center of Jewish learning. From all corners of Russia and from many Jewish communities in other lands, young Jewish scholars were drawn to the source of learning. But even later, when the *Musar yeshibot* of Rabbi Israel Salanter's school occupied first place, the name of the Volozhin *yeshiva* was sanctified and beloved by the entire Jewish world.

THE YESHIBOT IN MIR AND EYSHISHOK

The large *yeshibot* of Mir and Eyshishok had also been founded at the start of the nineteenth century. The Mir *Yeshiva* was set up like Volozhin, yet did not enjoy the same prestige and was poorer financially. Some of the poorer students had to resort to eating days, while it was even more common to eat the Sabbath meal at the home of a benefactor. In the second half of the nineteenth century, when Rabbi Hayyim Leyb Tiktinski headed the Mir *yeshiva,* about three hundred students were studying there. His lectures were outstanding for their simplicity and lucidity. His strong point was his "immediate comprehension" without dialectics. "Anyone who wants to understand a page of the Talmud," said Rabbi Israel Salanter, "ought to hear a lecture given by Rabbi Hayyim Leyb." A new era began in Mir in 1900, when Rabbi Elijah Barukh Kamay became its director. In 1907 Rabbi Eliezer Judah Finkel, the son-in-law of Rabbi Kamay, became deputy director. Mir achieved the height of its success in the period between the two World Wars, when it occupied first place among the *yeshibot* of Poland. (See pages 415-422 on the *Musar yeshibot.*)

The *yeshiva* in Eyshishok, a small town in impoverished Lithuania, needs a chapter in itself. Little was known about Eyshishok, and for the simple reason that Eyshishok sent no fund raisers abroad, although its great scholars made it worthy of a place among the great *yeshibot* of the world. This small town in Lithuania supported over one hundred students, unmarried boys and particularly young men preparing for the rabbinate, by its own modest means, and very respectably at that.

The *yeshiva* in Eyshishok also managed to preserve the dignity of learning and of the students in its unique and modest way. The tradition of the Gaon of Vilna and his disciples influenced this *yeshiva* as much as it had that of Volozhin. The students did not go out for meals to local townspeople. In Eyshishok the townspeople brought the meals to the students.

In the proclamation *Ez Pri,* issued by Rabbi Israel Salanter and other leading personalities in 1881, for the purpose of arousing the public to establish and support *yeshibot,* Eyshishok was set up as an example:

> Why do you not emulate in piety the small town of Eyshishok, where they have taken it upon themselves—rich and poor alike—not to eat their bread

themselves unless they have first given food to the students of the Law who sit there before the Lord; in joy they bring their food, like the first crops, each one at a specified time, to his house of study.

In addition to food for the students, the townsmen also took care of the other expenses of the *yeshiva:* fuel, light, books, and all other needs. This was the concern of special societies, and the sums that they collected were relatively large. It is therefore not surprising that this poor town in Lithuania became the symbol of "love of learning."

THE SMALLER AND MEDIUM-SIZED YESHIBOT

The number of students able to travel to the large *yeshibot* was relatively small. The greater number of students were in the smaller and medium-sized *yeshibot,* which, although lesser known, nevertheless played no lesser role than the large *yeshibot* in the diffusion of scholarship in Eastern Europe.

The smaller and medium-sized *yeshibot* employed no fund raisers, and it was therefore necessary to collect on the spot the funds necessary to support the institutions of learning. Consequently, it was impossible to renounce the old system of eating days. Of course it was difficult for the young students, often no more than children, to live away from home and to eat at unfamiliar tables. We must remember, however, that eating days were common until the beginning of the twentieth century. The student who was enjoying an eating day at a strange house knew very well that at his own parents' table there also sat an out-of-town student, enjoying a similar privilege, and therefore had no feelings of degradation. Those householders who offered eating days to students usually knew how to preserve the students' sense of pride.

In the smaller *yeshibot* most of the students were local boys and men. Parents of means would, in many cases, pay the tuition of their sons. In the medium-sized *yeshibot* the number of out-of-town students was considerable, and here poverty was much more obvious. The well-known Yiddish and Hebrew writer, Mendel Meicher Sforim, in his memoirs, *Shloyme Reb Khayims,* offers the following description of the *yeshiva* in Slutsk, where he studied in the late forties of the past century:

One of the cities in Lithuania which God has blessed with a *yeshiva* is a certain city called S——k. No other thing does it possess, aside from the *yeshiva* which is known far and wide, to give it a mark of distinction and a name in the world. . . . Its professors are common people, needy teachers, even if they are called "directors of *yeshibot*"; the students there—poor boys, without a groshn [penny] to their name, who mostly hike to school on foot, empty-handed and bare. No sooner does the student cast off his bundle—some two old patched shirts and a pair of mended socks that have been worn through, brought from home—than the city assumes the burden of caring for this out-of-towner, supporting him in every possible way, despite its own impoverished circumstances and the claims of its own paupers upon it. The poorest man is prepared to share such food as he may have, for the sake of scholarship.[22]

There were smaller and medium-sized *yeshibot* in many communities in Lithuania, and also in a number of communities in Poland and the Ukraine. There were also *yeshibot* supported by individual synagogues, societies, or even by individuals. In Vilna, for example, at the close of the past century, there was a *yeshiva* in the butchers' synagogue where about eighty students studied. Another such *yeshiva* existed in the furriers' synagogue of Minsk.

In the memoirs of Israel Isser Katsovitsh we find the following description of the Minsk *yeshiva:*

> Our *yeshiva* was built and supported by furriers, i.e., by poor people. . . . The head of our *yeshiva* has a yard-goods store. The store is run by his wife. He is in the shop only for a few hours, and devotes all of his time to studying alone and to teaching. All week he studies with us, the *yeshiva* students, and on Saturday with the furriers. . . .[23]

The founders of the well known *yeshiva* in the Ramayles Synagogue in Vilna also were simple artisans. In the forties of the past century such prominent personalities as Rabbi Israel Salanter and Rabbi Mordecai Meltzer headed it. Most of the students had eating days assigned to them. Those students who were short an eating day received bread and a warm dish at the *yeshiva.* In the nineties these conditions even led to a strike of students, who complained that they were not getting enough bread.

THE SYNAGOGUE STUDENTS

It is very likely that the large majority of young students in Eastern Europe belonged to the category of so-called synagogue students (*kloyznikes*). The entire system of scholarship was founded on the principle of "independent study." Even the large *yeshibot* could not have existed, from the financial point of view, but for the method of independent work on the part of the students; therefore generally there was no division into classes according to age or previous knowledge. All the students heard the same lecture; all studied the same section— although they were completely free to study additional sections—and each one tried to achieve as much as his powers allowed. Thus even so large a *yeshiva* as the one in Volozhin was able to manage with only two directors.

Ordinarily, independent study was begun at the age of thirteen or fourteen. Parents of means, however, used to keep a teacher for their children even after this. Very poor but capable children sometimes started on their own even before their thirteenth year because their parents did not have the means to pay for tuition.

If the young student did not travel to a *yeshiva*, he might take up study in a synagogue—sometimes in his home town—where there were books aplenty and where he also had opportunity for "conversational study," to discuss things with friends of his age or with older scholars. The well known scholar and author, Simeon Bernfeld, for example, tells of his father:

> My father began his studies with his maternal grandfather, Rabbi Zev Hirsh. Thereafter he may have had another teacher who tutored him until he was eleven. From then on he sat in the synagogue of his native town and studied on his own. The frequenters of the synagogue loved this upright boy who was very industrious and worked hard at his studies. For this reason they helped him with all their means, but my father studied primarily on his own.[24]

No less characteristic is the education of the great thinker, Ahad Ha-Am (Asher Ginzberg), who came from a rather well-to-do family, his father being a pious Hasid, a merchant in the Ukraine. When young Ginzberg reached the age of twelve, his family moved to a village where, in the solitude of rural life, Ahad Ha-Am spent his school years.

> Coming to the village far from other children and the amusements of childhood, my soul came to long for learning. I spent night and day on the Talmud and subsequent authorities, at first with the help of a teacher and later, when I was fifteen, on my own. My labors bore fruit in a remarkable way. . . Along with this, I applied myself to Hebrew grammar and the Bible and I also read chapters in the philosophical books of the Sephardim, but all these readings were scattered and random, a bit here and a bit there, without instruction or assistance.[25]

This, incidentally, had been the method of study for generations. Personalities such as Rabbi Israel baal Shem Tob, the Gaon of Vilna, and Solomon Maimon had never studied in a *yeshiva* at all. Early in their lives they had set out to study independently. This was made possible by a system of education which helped even the very young student to work on his own.

There were, of course, also dangers in this system of independent study. Not every student is capable at the age of thirteen or fourteen of finding his way independently through the sea of the Talmud. There were, as a result, a considerable number of failures. Not all who started out became scholars. All things considered, however, the method of studying independently was actually the only one possible in view of the economic level of the Jewish population in Eastern Europe.

Ordinarily a young boy would seek out a synagogue where there were other students, young and old. Many cities and towns had a large synagogue or study house which served as a center of learning. Older scholars and younger men who lived and studied at their parents-in-laws' expense, would engage in discussions, and the younger boys would listen and interrupt with questions or individual opinions. Frequently the young boys would study in groups of two or three, which was more congenial and enabled them to converse on scholarly subjects.

The custom of studying in a synagogue or study house was particularly widespread in Poland, where there were relatively few *yeshibot*. Polish synagogues and study houses were filled with students, and although there was no set discipline for the students who worked independently, the sound of study was usually heard in the synagogues and the study houses from early morning on.

At 5 A.M. on a frosty winter day, when the city of Warsaw was still engrossed in slumber, hundreds of young men were already seated around tables in the study houses of Ger, Ostrowce, Sochaczow, and Radzyn, engaged in the study of the Law. This was the early morning lesson before prayers. The best preparation for prayers, it was said in these study houses, is a page of the Talmud.[26]

In the synagogues and study houses of Poland there were large numbers of young married men who boarded with their in-laws. The younger boys were also mainly from the locality. The reverse was true in Lithuania, where it was customary to travel to another city for one's studies. Among the synagogue students in Lithuania there were many out-of-towners, young boys and also married men, so-called *prushim*. In a description of the tiny town of Kapule in the middle of the past century, we read:

The Kapule synagogue served at the same time as a college, where young boys . . . supplemented their knowledge of the Talmud and the later authorities. In addition to the local boys, there also studied in the Kapule synagogue young married and unmarried out-of-towners. The inhabitants of Kapule treated these newcomers, with their tremendous thirst for study, very hospitably. No sooner did such a boy appear in the synagogue, carrying a walking stick in his hand and a bundle on his shoulders, than everyone surrounded him, greeted him, and immediately began supplying him with eating days. . . . Food—he had; books and candles—all that his heart desired; a royal shelter—the synagogue; a bed and pillow—he had no need of, since he slept on a bench with his coat as his pillow.[27]

There were several synagogues and study houses with a long tradition of learning, such as, for example, the Gaon's study house in Vilna. Except for the Sabbath meals, those students did not resort to eating days. The synagogue used to supply them with very modest financial assistance.

Independent study in a synagogue had the great advantage of allowing the student freedom to consult various books in the fields of Cabbala, philosophy, etc. He was able, himself, to decide on the order of his studies; and his knowledge, provided that he possessed the proper ability and diligence, was often more extensive than the knowledge of the students in the *yeshibot*. A large portion of the *yeshiva* students, incidentally, had earlier been synagogue students for varying periods of time. There were also cases where a young student would purposely choose a desolate synagogue so that he could be alone more, and study and think independently. This independence placed a certain stamp on the life and thinking of the *yeshiva* boys and synagogue students. In Yiddish and Hebrew literature we still hear, from time to time, the echo of such years of loneliness and isolation. The following autobiographical note by Bialik about his synagogue years (before he went to Volozhin) proves instructive in this respect:

> When I was thirteen, I passed from the jurisdiction of the teachers to my own, and began to study in the synagogue alone. Alone—because I was the only boy in the whole suburb who sat and studied in the synagogue except for the *dayyan* [rabbi's assistant], who bent over the Torah and prayers until midday. Otherwise there was no teacher there. This solitary sitting in the synagogue became one of the most important channels of influence on my spiritual development, and on my inner world. Alone with my old and new thoughts, my doubts and suppressed meditations, I sat there many days, near the bookcase, interrupting my study to sink into a mass of dreams and visions, contemplating relations and calculating the structure of the world, seeking meaning for myself and humanity.[28]

In this creative loneliness many other young students worked out their relations to themselves and to the world. These ruminations and reckonings not infrequently led to tangential courses. It was precisely among the synagogue students that the Enlightenment found many enthusiastic followers. The ideological crisis that arose, even in a center of learning such as Volozhin, was felt even more keenly among the scattered synagogue students. Once again it became necessary to introduce novelty into the pattern of study, so that the student might be able to resist the currents of secularity which were becoming ever stronger. This task was taken up by Rabbi Israel Salanter Lipkin (1810-1883), founder of the Musar (Ethical) Movement.

THE MUSAR MOVEMENT

The nineteenth century was, for the Jews in Russia and in Europe in general, a period of spiritual searchings. Until the second half of the eighteenth century, Jews in Europe, and above all in Eastern Europe, had lived completely in a world of their own. There were very few opportunities for social contacts and cultural exchanges between Jews and non-Jews. For this reason the Jewish "apartness" was not obvious. The rise of a capitalistic economy, the great French Revolution, the gradual introduction of universal military service and universal education, introduced profound changes in this respect. The problem of integrating the Jewish population into the general social, political, and spiritual life of the land was posed. More favorable conditions tended to further such an integration. The modern bourgeois culture strongly appealed to the Jewish intelligentsia. The Jewish student always had had tremendous respect for reason, and because of this he was enchanted by the modern, thoroughly rationalistic, culture.

The Enlightenment in Europe was replete with optimism and faith in man, and it was this faith in man that was also characteristic of the Jewish Enlightenment movement. Not only did men feel drawn to the rich world outside, but there was also a profound belief that the world keeps improving, and it was felt to be the duty of young men to get to know the world and to be in closer touch with it. Sproutings of the Enlightenment were found in Eastern Europe as early as the end of the eighteenth century; however, it was not until the nineteenth century that it became an important factor in Jewish life.

The center of the Enlightenment in Lithuania was Vilna. In the early forties Rabbi Israel Salanter reached Vilna, where he became the head of the *yeshiva* in Ramayles Synagogue. Here the founder of the Musar movement discovered more than the Enlightenment. In 1847 the Czarist government opened a rabbinical school in Vilna, whose function it was to educate "progressive" rabbis. Since the young man heading the Ramayles *Yeshiva* was held in great esteem in Enlightened circles, he was offered the directorship of the rabbinical school. Rabbi Israel, however, categorically refused, and when the offer was made official by the government, he left Vilna.

Rabbi Israel was no less aware of the ways of the world than any of the naïve and optimistic Enlightened men who did not see the true motivation behind the Czarist policy of "civilizing" the Jews. Rabbi Israel also took into account the problems of the new era; yet he at the same time realized the great perils connected with the trends of the Enlightenment and reform.

There were a number of religious leaders who, in principle, were opposed to secular education. Yet the first question that required answering was: Is it possible to manage to offer both a general and a Jewish education to children in the relatively short time they spend in *heder* and *yeshiva?* Even more serious was another problem: experience taught that general education often led away from the traditional path of Jewishness. It was difficult to find a harmonious adjustment between tradition and modern secular culture, and Rabbi Israel also was unable to find the harmonious solution, although he did look for it. Thus throughout all of the nineteenth century there was no *rapprochement* between the rising stream of secular culture and religious Jewishness in Eastern Europe.

The strong impression made by the Enlightenment on *yeshiva* yout can be explained, to a large extent, by its *new* approach to the world an to contemporary problems. After going through a popular book on natura science, the young student often saw new vistas opening before him. H became aware of a *new* world, a large, bright, and beautiful world. Com pared to this, Jewish life seemed old, perhaps too old. For this reason a *ne* approach to Jewish life, a *new* interpretation of Jewish philosophy, as Rabb Israel put it, was so important. To the slogan of the Enlightenment, "Kno the world," Rabbi Israel replied, "Know yourself; comprehend the mean ing of Jewishness"; and he also tried to demonstrate that there was, indeed something to know and to understand in Jewishness.

The Enlightenment was naïvely optimistic. It believed in man and wa hardly aware of his evil inclinations. For this reason, men of the Enlighten ment held knowledge in great esteem and set great store by education. O the contrary, Rabbi Israel felt it important to stress the role of the huma will, of actions, because "the distance between knowledge and actions i even greater than the distance between knowledge and ignorance." Th same idea was expressed in another aphorism, frequently quoted in Musa circles in the name of Rabbi Israel: "If only the greatest did what th littlest knows."

It is not too easy to control the deeper powers that operate within u taught the founder of the Musar movement. Nature constantly drags ma downhill, and only by very strenuous efforts can he gradually overcom his evil inclination and attain good habits. All of life is a continuous struggl with oneself. "Life is a ladder. One either goes up or down; one cann stop in the middle." Therefore the greatest sin is casual action and living Just as the Gaon, less than a century earlier, had strongly emphasized th necessity of effort in study, Rabbi Israel emphasized the importance o effort in attaining good habits. Man must work on himself, and know hin self and the world, because "Every man is a Musar book [edifying book] and all the world is a house of Musar."

Rabbi Israel especially emphasized the responsibilities of the leaders. H did not think much of the quiet and hidden saints who seclude themselve from the hubbub of the world. In our days, he said, it is the duty of th higher type of man to take part in the concerns of the generation. And i we see men leaving the path of the Law, it is our fault. *We* will have t answer for this, because *we*, the teachers and guides of the people, have n done our duty. There is even a connection between Jewish communiti of various countries. "All Jews are responsible for each other," and Rab Israel formulated this mutual responsibility in classic form: "If people go sip in the Kovno synagogue, the Sabbath is desecrated in Paris." Cons quently, the leaders upon whom such weighty responsibilities rest mu also have a good deal of courage. When he was once asked why he ha not accepted the offer to direct the rabbinical school, he replied that the education of rabbis called for a very special approach.

We see from experience, from daily events, that if a rabbi receives an inquiry from a poor man, he hastens to issue a decision, even in the middle of his meal. He makes an effort and properly consults authoritative books, and seeks grounds for a favorable answer. But if an inquiry comes to him from a rich man, he makes no corresponding effort to find the best solution. However, among doctors one knows the opposite from experience. When he is summoned to a rich patient, he hastens to run to him to treat him with extreme devotion, whereas he does not hurry so much to a poor patient, and tries to avoid visiting him.[29]

The reason for this, explained Rabbi Israel, is simple. From his youth onward, the rabbi studies for the study's sake, so that the morality of the Law becomes ingrained in his nature; while the doctor does not study medicine at first as a mission, but rather as a skill that is to bring him a respectable and sizable income. The doctor therefore apportions his work according to the income he can count on. The rabbinical position, however, cannot be properly fulfilled unless the rabbi is permeated with the idea of a mission and pursues his path regardless of all obstacles. If we want to educate rabbis to become worthy of being leaders of their generation, it is necessary to conform to the *yeshiva* tradition. Rabbi Israel was once asked whether preparation for the rabbinate could be considered study for its own sake. His response was that there could be no better example of this than studying the Law in order to become worthy of a position as responsible as that of rabbi. The student had to realize, however, that the path of the rabbinate is difficult. Not everyone could be pleased, and a spiritual leader of a community ought not to feel intimidated by opposition. "A rabbi that is not threatened by expulsion from town," Rabbi Israel once said, "is no rabbi; and if he is, in fact, driven out, he is no man."

There are certain similarities, as has rightly been pointed out by some, between Hasidism and Musar; but even greater are the differences between these two movements. It is therefore a mistake to call the Musar movement the Lithuanian form of Hasidism. On the contrary, a distinguishing feature of the Musar movement is the great demands it placed on man. "I cannot understand," Rabbi Israel once said, "how a Jew can so much as move without the Talmud." For the observance of all matters in human relations it was necessary to know the appropriate laws. This is why the Musar movement never became a folk movement, despite Rabbi Israel's great efforts to disseminate the Musar doctrine among plain folk.

The founder of the movement also realized that merely studying the Law was hardly enough. And this held true for the study of Musar works as well. Merely by reading an edifying book or listening to a moralizing sermon, one could not improve oneself, "for distant is the road between knowledge and action, between words and deeds, as distant as the heaven from the earth." The main question for Rabbi Israel was, therefore, how to study ethics. How could one achieve the gradual transformation of the purified words of Musar into good deeds and good habits? How could the study of ethics be made to help Jews turn into better people?

First of all, *ethics must be studied regularly every day*. Just as a Jew has set hours for prayers and for study, so, too, must he find time for edification. Rabbi Israel was once asked, "What should a person do who can hardly manage an hour a day for study? Ought he to study ethics or a page of the Talmud?" Rabbi Israel answered that he ought to study ethics, for he would then realize that he had more than the one hour to devote to study. Furthermore, Rabbi Israel taught that the study of ethics was everyone's duty, from the greatest scholar down to the simplest man.

In the second place, *ethics must be studied with fervor*. Man's heart is locked and good words do not always find their way to the human mind. One must therefore study so that one is aroused and shaken to the depths of one's soul. Rabbi Isaac Blazer, a disciple of Rabbi Israel, added that one should note the effects of music, which has the power to evoke the strongest emotions in us, of both joy and sadness. Similarly, the edifying words should be said in such a manner as to arouse man and lead him to repentance and self-evaluation.

The third rule is *repetition*. The main task of studying ethics is to reach the stage where correct moral behavior becomes habit, a part of human nature. It is therefore important to repeat the same ethical dictum again and again to engrave it ever more deeply on the soul. The founder of the Musar movement used to refer to the well-known talmudic legend about Rabbi Akiba in this connection. Until he reached the age of forty, it is told, Rabbi Akiba was an ignorant man. Once, while standing near a well, he noticed a hole in a stone below. To his question, "Who made the hole in the stone?" he was given the answer, "The drops of water that continually fell onto it." Rabbi Akiba then said that if soft water had the power to pierce through stone, then surely the words of the Law would be able to penetrate his heart. And he began studying the Law.

Likewise, the words of edification will not fail in their effect if man will continually allow them to work on him. Each individual impression alone is weak, to be sure, but in time they strengthen one another and become inscribed in one's heart. Only through continual repetition do the main ideas of ethics become a part of human nature.

The fourth rule of the Musar doctrine is to *study ethics together*. In a group it is easier to find strength and overcome Evil Inclination. Many rabbis and scholars of the day strongly doubted the wisdom of collective study. Musar had become a movement. Separate Musar circles were founded and the question was posed: Is this a new sect? May it not, God forbid, lead to schisms in Jewish life? If someone wants to study ethics alone there can be no objections; but collectively? Rabbi Israel Salanter, however, insisted on the importance of creating a movement for Musar. Like the Law, ethics is not merely a matter for individuals. Hence a way of arousing the public to the study of ethics must be found.

The Musar movement, too, distinguished itself by its profound faith in man. Of course, Rabbi Israel was far from harboring the naïve view that man is, by nature, good. He believed, however, that each man had the ways and means of achieving a higher stage. Rabbi Israel warned, in particular, against fatalistic approaches to the matter of human sinfulness:

> Let man not say: what God has made cannot be changed; the Lord, blessed be He, has implanted in me the power of evil, and how can I hope to root it out? This is not the way things are. Human powers are capable of suppression and change. Just as our eyes see animals in nature which man has the power to conquer and to impose his will on, to make them harmless and domesticate them . . . so, too, man has it within himself to conquer his evil nature, to prevent it from escaping from human control, and to change his nature for the better through study and practice.[30]

The Musar movement of Rabbi Israel Salanter was for a select group. It was difficult for busy and overtired people to spend so much time on introspection and on delving into the Law. On the other hand, the Musar movement had its greatest influence in the circles of the young students where the Enlightenment had introduced so much anxiety and doubt. The mere fact that Musar called for profound study, that it was a complete doctrine in itself, helped spread it as a subject of study in the *yeshibot*. The men of Musar were not overwhelmed by the wide world, and therefore had the power to stand up to it. They realized that all the material affluence of modern civilization could not compensate for the moral failings of man. The richer our cultural life became, the more confused the individual felt. Rabbi Israel therefore taught his disciples always to keep man in mind, to understand the individual and to help him in his tribulations and gropings.

THE MUSAR YESHIBOT

At the end of the seventies, on the initiative of Rabbi Israel Salanter and Rabbi Isaac Elchanan Spektor (the famous rabbi of Kovno), there was founded in Kovno the *Kolel ha-Perushim*, a center for married students from other towns, to give young married scholars the opportunity to prepare for a rabbinical career. In 1880 Rabbi Isaac Blazer, former rabbi of St. Petersburg and one of the most prominent students of Rabbi Israel Salanter, was appointed manager of the newly established center of learning. In 1881 Rabbi Eliezer Gordon, a disciple of Rabbi Israel, became rabbi in Telz (Kovno province). He became head of the *yeshiva,* which had been founded there several years before, and under his leadership the name Telz became increasingly well known and recognized in the *yeshiva* world. At about the same time, the foundations were laid in Slobodka, a suburb of Kovno, for the later famous Musar *Yeshiva Keneset Yisrael.* Lithuania proper (actually the area of Kovno) now became the most important center of learning in Russia. Many of Rabbi Israel Salanter's friends and disciples lived in Lithuania, so a wide field for Musar activities now opened. With this, the stormy period of the Musar movement in the *yeshibot* was launched.

The Musar doctrine in the first place armed the young student with a philosophy of Jewishness. It raised his own self-respect and his esteem for the Law. And it was precisely this pride of the men of Musar, their belief that they had rediscovered the light of the Law, that was of such great consequence for the revitalization of the *yeshibot.* The *yeshibot* needed Musar even more than the movement needed them.

The pride of the men of Musar and their aggressive method in attempting to disseminate their doctrine, however, caused rabbis and scholars to voice protests. Among the opponents of militant Musar was such an authority as Rabbi Isaac Elchanan Spektor. Sharp quarrels ensued. Rabbi Isaac Blazer was ultimately forced to resign from his post in the *Kolel ha-Perushim.* In the meantime, however, the men of Musar had managed to establish their positions firmly in the *yeshibot.* The leadership of the Musar movement was now taken over by Slobodka.

The founder of the *Yeshiva Keneset Yisrael* in Slobodka was Rabbi Note Hirsh Finkel, an original thinker and an excellent organizer with a profound insight into human nature. Rabbi Finkel had all the characteristics necessary for a teacher and guide of young people with great intellectual demands and ambitions. He was not the head of a *yeshiva,* but merely a supervisor. For forty-odd years he was, however, the heart and soul of Slobodka, and his influence went far beyond the boundaries of this suburb. He was middle-aged when *yeshiva* students began calling him "the old man," and it was under the name of "the old man of Slobodka" that he was known in the *yeshiva* world.

Rabbi Note Hirsh was a disciple of Rabbi Simha Zisl Broyde of Kelem, which held a very special position in the Musar movement. Rabbi Simha Zisl was one of the oldest and most beloved disciples of Rabbi Israel Salanter, and the first to attempt, in systematic fashion, to apply the Musar doctrine to the field of education.

Man must study all his life. Man must work at self-improvement all his life. These are the central motifs of Rabbi Simha Zisl's pedagogic doctrine. What a man studies in his youth is insufficient. No matter how thorough his education at that time, there are many things that cannot be understood by the young student, and this is particularly the case of the Commandments regarding man's relations with his fellows. As a consequence we go through life with the same childish notions that we acquired in our youth. Therefore it is imperative that the mature person begin studying anew, as if he were confronting the world for the first time. Above all, however, a man must study hard to understand himself:

> Man lives with his body and his soul all his life as he eats and drinks and sleeps, and does not make a single step without himself, and he knows all his own deeds, his private thoughts, his joys and his sorrows, and he is a partner to his own secret and he cannot separate one hand from another, even for an instant. . . . And after all this he does not know himself on as much as a single point, unless he is a very wise man, who has toiled and labored at it.[31]

Rabbi Simha Zisl liked to say that each man is a Musar book, and it is not at all a simple matter to understand the book called man. The trouble is, however, that we are generally too indolent to make any mental efforts. Our first task is therefore to learn to think: "Not to let a single day pass without practice in thinking, for this is the key to wisdom and the preface to all powers, and that is man." And to think means to be able to concentrate on a specific point, and not permit thoughts to wander to unrelated subjects.

Rabbi Simha Zisl's Talmud Torah in Kelem, which was in the beginning an educational institution for younger students, became in the eighties a Musar *yeshiva* on a higher plane. It was attended mainly by students who aspired to greater perfection in Musar. A number of Rabbi Simha Zisl's students later headed the large *yeshibot* in Lithuania. Kelem thus strongly influenced the entire Musar movement. On the other hand, the pedagogic method of Rabbi Simha Zisl was not completely suited to the *yeshibot*. The *yeshiva* students were accustomed to more freedom, more independence. Of course, they also needed assistance and guidance; yet they were not prepared to turn the *yeshiva* into a *heder*, even a *heder* along the ideal lines of the Talmud Torah in Kelem.

Rabbi Note Hirsh Finkel, founder of the Slobodka *Yeshiva Keneset Yisrael*, therefore had to find his own solution. Slobodka preserved, to the utmost, the principle of the scholar's independence, and it was precisely the study of Musar that enhanced the student's faith in his own powers. Other large *yeshibot* in time copied the example set by *Keneset Yisrael*. They introduced the study of Musar, and the teacher of Musar, the *mashgiah*, took on an increasingly prominent position in the life of the *yeshiva*.

In Slobodka Musar was studied each day, half an hour before evening prayers. It was the daily hour for stocktaking. Each student was able to select the Musar work of his choice, and each made his own self-reckoning.

Saturday, at twilight, they studied even more earnestly, making their accounts for the entire week. The Sabbath-eve longings, the twilight mood that always came over the Jew when the sacred Sabbath was departing, when his "additional soul" was leaving him, were underscored even more strongly here through the earnest stocktaking.

> Every day between afternoon and evening prayers, not to speak of Sabbath at twilight, the *yeshiva* resembles a ship about to sink. The holy Sabbath is departing; everyone wants to preserve the tranquillity a little longer. But darkness looms ever closer. Shadows become longer, and more crowded together. The week is approaching. No light can yet be lit. To peruse a book is impossible. This is the time when each man is engaged in thinking edifying thoughts. One bemoans his sins in a loud voice . . . one beats his desk with his hand . . . in order to chase away evil thoughts, and another is carried away on wings by thoughts. . . .
>
> And after evening prayers, all recite, in a chorus of tears, the Psalm *Maskil le-David* [Ps. 142]. One man recites, employing such a heart-rending melody that stones are caused to move from their place. The entire group repeats after him in unison, woefully and in tears. Everyone moans. . . .
>
> Suddenly, there appears on the scene, from among the crowd, "the old man." He performs the end of Sabbath ceremony with utmost sweetness. The atmosphere becomes less dense, and more pleasant. He hastens from bench to bench, wishing everyone an intense *gutvokh* [good week].[32]

The Musar movement held the guiding teacher in great esteem. For this reason the Musar discourses on colloquy by the supervisor were not considered any less important by the students than the lectures given by the head of the *yeshiva*. The purpose of the Musar discourses was mainly to teach the student to consider more deeply problems that at first sight appear simple. The supervisor therefore often reverted to the same matter again and again, to clarify the various aspects of a Musar problem, and to demonstrate that there is much to learn.

The idea of the dignity of man occupied a central position in the school of "the old man" of Slobodka. He taught that man is not merely a book; he is a subject for profound study. This is the meaning of the dictum: Respect for man comes before the Law. "The Law was not given to man as a command and admonition, but it reveals itself through man's personality. . . ." And if we study and understand man, we will understand the Law the better. We must therefore try to reach the point where we are worthy of the name man, and then we will also be worthy of studying the Law.

Man is the crown of God's creation. Hence the importance of preserving the honor and dignity of man. We must watch our conduct lest our acts put the species of man to shame. Self-respect, and therefore the utmost responsibility for one's actions, was an especially important issue in the Slobodka school.

The laws of the Torah, "the old man" taught, are mainly concerned with preserving man's dignity. It is a mistake, for example, to believe that the benedictions we make when we have enjoyed something in the world are a toll that man owes the Creator for his pleasures. The true meaning of the benedictions is very different. They are God's gift to man to help him realize the beauty and splendor of God's world.

The ways of the world are such that man is only surprised by new things. As soon as he becomes accustomed to something, he loses the pleasure of its enjoyment. Man should, however, view the world each day as if it were created on that day. Each day he should admire anew the greatness and beauty of God's creation. The benedictions were given man so that he might approach the world each day as if he were newborn, as if he were enjoying the creation of God, blessed be He, for the first time in his life.

The following Musar discussion by "the old man" on reverence and joy is characteristic of the Slobodka school. It is usually held that fear of God and joy are two concepts that are mutually exclusive. People think that he who lives in fear does not enjoy himself, and he who is happy has no fears. But this is erroneous. The Law teaches us that fear and joy are not entirely different matters. On the contrary, the fear of God includes happiness over God's Law and His Commandments. Man cannot become God-fearing unless he can become joyous over God's Law. We find proof of this in the Commandment of "the second tithe." The Law admonished our parents to take along their tithes to Jerusalem and to consume them there, so that they might become God-fearing in Jerusalem. It might then appear that Jews used to come to Jerusalem worried, sad, and frightened because of their fear of God. Actually, just the reverse is true. In the Law itself it is written that when one arrives in Jerusalem for a holiday, one should be joyous, and Jerusalem itself is called the "joy of the world."

The doctrine of "the old man" was far from asceticism. Slobodka did not deny the world. The Commandments were not given to enslave man but, on the contrary, to elevate and purify him. The world was created for man, and the Law was given to man. "And if man is lacking something, the Law, too, is lacking."

All of this concerns the individual and not the group. The men of Musar, as we have seen earlier, generally devoted much thought to the problems of the individual. Rabbi Jeruham Lvovits, head of the great Mir *Yeshiva* and one of the most prominent thinkers the Musar movement produced, paid particularly great attention to the matter of the individual versus the group.

Why did God command the Jews to be counted in the desert? Because he wanted to set apart, answered Rabbi Jeruham, *each individual, each individual with his own name and with his own concerns*. Through the process of counting, each individual making up the group became a personality in his own right, and not merely part of a whole. The Torah, likewise, was given on Mt. Sinai, not only to the group, but to each individual separately; "for each individual received the holy Torah with his interpretation."

In general, it is wrong to give the group one's main consideration. Man is shamed when the Divine Image is reduced to a group. Man was created to be an individual, a personality in his own right. This may be conceit, but a necessary conceit. Man's modesty must not go to such extremes that he totally disappears into the group. "Man needs to be an individual unto himself." Each individual is a world of his own. For this reason the Law so strictly prescribed all Jews to share alike the taxes for the *Ohel Moed* (the tent of meeting). "The rich man shall not exceed and the poor man not fall short of half a shekel." It would have been highly unfair to have allowed the rich man to offer more than half a shekel. This would have meant, after all, that the rich man had a larger share in the House of God. A group of rich people might even have offered to take on the entire expense of the tent of meeting, on condition that it be in their name. Rather, each individual had an equal share in the tent of meeting and an equal share in the community of Israel.

A unique path was taken by Novaredok (Nowogródek). Rabbi Joseph Yozel Hurvits, founder of the Novaredok *yeshiva*, belonged to the first group of scholars in the "Center for Married Students" in Kovno. While he was studying in Kovno, his wife died, and Rabbi Joseph Yozel cut himself off from the world completely. He lived isolated for almost two years, neither leaving his room nor allowing anyone to enter. Rabbi Joseph Yozel was a man of Musar, however, and he realized that his isolation from the world was but a preparation for a higher stage when he would take on the mission of spreading his ideas throughout the Jewish world.

Rabbi Joseph Yozel belonged to the extreme pioneering ascetic wing of the Musar movement. The first and most important task, he believed, must be the dissemination of learning, the founding of *yeshibot* which would raise a generation of scholars with the necessary courage and power to negate the world and oppose the streams of the Enlightenment. After several attempts in various cities, he founded the *yeshiva* of Novaredok in 1896, and within a short time it became one of the most prominent centers of scholarship and Musar in Eastern Europe.

Novaredok was ascetic and militant. The world can be changed, if only one really wants it changed. The students of Novaredok frequently repeated the dictum: "All the world says that if you can't [go] over, you must [go] under; Rabbi Joseph Yozel says that if you can't [go] over, you must [go] over." The following Musar aphorisms of Rabbi Joseph Yozel emphasize the same ideas. "I never ask if it is possible; I ask only if it is necessary. If there is no path, I will blaze one."

The human personality occupies a foremost position in Musar philosophy, including the Novaredok school. Rabbi Joseph Yozel's approach is stated with particular clarity in the first chapter of his work *Madregat ha-Adam*. How did it happen, asks the author, that Adam defied God's injunction and ate of the Tree of Knowledge? Was it only due to weakness, because he was unable to resist Evil Inclination? That is an error, answers Rabbi Joseph Yozel. Eating of the Tree of Knowledge was not the beginning of sinfulness, but the beginning of our human culture; it was man's first attempt to raise himself to a higher level, an attempt that was unsuccessful. In the Garden of Eden Adam was in the category of an angel: "He knew evil and recognized it, and in spite of this he did not do anything but good." He did not even have the desire to do any evil. However, there was one important difference between him and an angel. The first man was given a choice: "If he wished he could cease being an angel, and if he wished to live a life of decision-making and not the life of an angel—it was up to him. . . . This depended on eating of the Tree of Knowledge. If he wanted to live the life of an angel, without any danger to his spiritual properties, then he must take care not to eat of the Tree of Knowledge. But if he wished to choose a life of decision-making, if he wanted the passions and desires to awaken in him so that he would have the possibility of combating and conquering them—then he should eat of the Tree of Knowledge." The first man did not want to remain in angelic state because he wanted to be free to choose between Good and Evil. The privilege of freedom, to be sure, is associated with great perils, since man can rise ever higher only if he is willing to take the risk of sinking ever lower. Adam was not disturbed by the danger, and he ate of the Tree of Knowledge. This was when man's wars against the powers of Sin and Evil began.

This remarkably original and, in fact, revolutionary explanation of the story of Adam offers us the key to the Novaredok school. "Man is the only creature in the world," Rabbi Joseph taught his disciples, "who can commit sins; therein lies his greatness."

Therefore all of man's life is a war. His function is to rise ever higher. And if man, for his part, does all that is necessary and possible, he need not be anxious whether he will succeed. Hence the problems of hope and faith have a particularly important role in the Novaredok doctrine. Man must never lose faith in himself, and Rabbi Joseph Yozel of Novaredok cites Maimonides on this: "All men are worthy of being as saintly as Moses or as evil as Jeroboam."

The Novaredok doctrine therefore also held that the world could be changed. "In order to remedy the present situation we have to begin by the building of *yeshibot* on dependable foundations, and from them the world will gradually be built." The *yeshiva* students are therefore under particular obligation to concern themselves with the group. In the last chapter of *Madregat ha-Adam* Rabbi Joseph Yozel appeals to the "public workers" (by this he meant scholars in general, and particularly his own students), as follows:

> Therefore, anyone who has the power to establish learning must not remain aloof. Let him not love restfulness, but gather his strength for wandering from place to place and for founding places of learning and piety. For who will be to blame for the low state of learning and piety? Only the workers who had the possibility of establishing it and of trusting that God would fulfil their wishes.

Can individuals change the world? Certainly, answered Rabbi Joseph Yozel: "Every worker, if only he abandons his family and devotes his strength on behalf of the Truth, can as an individual exert an influence on the whole world. . . . Above all, let the individual be an individual and not look behind him to see if the multitude is following; but let him stand firm on the point of Truth and the multitude will follow."

Rabbi Joseph Yozel's words were properly received by his disciples. The expansion of Novaredok began even before the First World War. During the war years, when the Novaredok *yeshiva* moved to Gomel, Rabbi Joseph Yozel founded *yeshibot* in Kiev, Kharkov, and a number of other cities. In 1920 Rabbi Joseph Yozel died in Kiev. Because of the Soviet persecutions, his disciples were forced to leave Russia. This is when the era of Novaredok's great expansion began. Between the two World Wars over seventy "Bet Joseph" *yeshibot* named for him, with a student body of about 4,000, were founded in Latvia and Poland. Among the *yeshibot* in Poland that merit mention were those in Bialystok, Warsaw, Mezritsh, and Pinsk. The dynamic development of the "Bet Joseph" *yeshibot* is unequalled in the history of the *yeshibot* over the past three centuries.

The doctrine of "the dignity of man," in its various nuances, strengthened the students' belief in themselves and in Jewish tradition. The philosophy of understanding and grasping the Law through efforts at first understanding man, understanding oneself, became the philosophy of the Musar *yeshibot*.

BETWEEN THE TWO WORLD WARS

Between the two World Wars the number of students in the East European *yeshibot* grew considerably. The *yeshibot* drew scholars away from the synagogue houses of study. The economic status of the students in the *yeshibot* was better than that of the students in the synagogues. The old custom of eating days was no longer appropriate to the times. It also became more difficult to study alone after secular trends had so strongly influenced all of Jewish life. Consequently, this was a time for traveling away from home to study. The number of students in the *yeshibot* grew, and along with this the budgets of the large centers of learning also increased in size. A considerable portion of the income came from America, partly via the Joint Distribution Committee, but mostly through independent campaigns for the *yeshibot*.

Since the end of the nineteenth century, since the rise of the great political organizations such as the Zionist movement, the Bund, and so on, Jewish life in Eastern Europe became more organized and centralized. In 1912 the Agudas Israel, the organization for the strictly traditional sector in the Jewish world, was founded in Katowice. The rise of political parties played an important role in the reorganization of the entire educational system in Eastern Europe. The private *heder* all but disappeared. A large number of religious schools for girls (the Bet Jacob schools) were now created; a program of secular studies was introduced in the boys' schools. In 1929 the Agudas Israel founded a central body called Horev which took over the administration of the religious schools, including the *yeshibot*. In the northeastern provinces of Poland, however, where there were centers of learning with long traditions, such as Volozhin, Mir, and Radin, there already existed an organization called the *Vaad ha-Yeshibot* in Vilna, which had been founded in 1924 on the initiative of Rabbi Israel Meir Hacohen, author of *Hafez Hayyim*, and the Vilna rabbi, Hayyim Ozer Grodzenski.

In the Hasidic world, as well, the significance of the *yeshibot* was now better appreciated. And the importance of the rule, "Learning cannot be acquired except collectively," became more evident. In 1897 the Tomeke Temimim *yeshiva* was founded in Lyubavitsh. Shortly thereafter a number of additional Tomeke Temimim *yeshibot* were created in various cities in Russia. After World War I the Lyubavitsh *yeshibot* in Russia continued their work for many years despite Soviet persecution. Between the two World Wars several Tomeke Temimim *yeshibot* were founded in Latvia, Lithuania, and Poland. A good deal of attention was devoted to the study of Hasidism in these institutions. In general the method of study was almost the same as in the Lithuanian *yeshibot*.

Among the large *yeshibot* in Poland, several deserve special mention: *Yeshiva* Hakme Lublin, founded by Rabbi Meir Shapiro; the Metivta in Warsaw; and the Keter Tora *yeshibot*, founded by the Rebe of Radomsk. The number of *yeshibot* in Warsaw and throughout Poland in general increased considerably after the First World War, although in Hasidic regions the number of students in the synagogues and study houses even between the two World Wars was still very considerable. The large Musar *yeshibot* were mainly concentrated in the northeastern provinces of Poland. Of these, the *yeshibot* in the following cities and towns should be mentioned: Mir, Kamieniec, Kletsk, Radin, Grodno, Baranowicze, Lomza, and Bialystok. Tiny Lithuania also managed to preserve its honorable place in the world of the *yeshibot*: Slobodka, Telz, Ponevezh, and Kelem remained important centers of Talmudic study and of Musar up until the catastrophe in Europe.

In all, the *yeshibot* in Poland, Lithuania, and Latvia had a student body of about 25,000. In many *yeshibot* the system of dividing students into classes according to their knowledge had been introduced. On the other hand, the principle of independence was now also preserved to a great extent, both with respect to the study of the Talmud and Musar and to life in the *yeshiva* in general. In the larger *yeshibot* the students had their own mutual aid societies for loans to the needy, and for help to the sick. In several *yeshibot* there were "committees for conversational study" and for Musar.

The tragic years of World War II saw the destruction of the *yeshibot* in Eastern Europe. Only very small remnants of the *yeshiva* teachers and students managed to escape. And the enormous spiritual strength of the *yeshibot* is revealed in the fact that wherever rescued leaders and students have turned up—be it Western Europe, America, or Israel—they have once again built centers of learning that continue the great traditions of Eastern Europe.

NOTES

[1] *Tur Orah Hayyim,* 5585, sec. *Rosh ha-Shanah.*

[[1a] See above Bernard D. Weinryb, "East European Jewry (Since the Partitions of Poland, 1772-1795)."]

[2] *Responsa of Rabbi Moses Isserles,* 95.

[[2a] See above Israel Halpern, "The Jews in Eastern Europe (From Ancient Times until the Partitions of Poland, 1772-1795)," pp. 298 f.]

[3] Jacob Lifshits, *Zikron Yaakob,* Vol. I, Kaunas, 1924-1930, p. 71.

[[3a] See above Hillel Bavli, "The Modern Renaissance of Hebrew Literature"; Yudel Mark, "Yiddish Literature."]

[4] Mendele Moicher Sforim, *Shloyme Reb Khayims,* Warsaw, 1928, ch. 2.

[5] Quoted after Hayyim Tschernovits, *Toledot ha-Posekim,* Vol. III, New York, 5708, p. 6.

[6] Rabbi Isserles, *op. cit.,* par. 25.

[7] Quoted after Simhah Assaf, *Mekorot le-Toledot ha-Hinuk be-Yisrael,* Tel-Aviv and Jerusalem, Vol. I, 5685-5703, par. 46.

[8] *Ibid.,* Vol. IV, p. 43.

[9] F. Lahover, *Toledot ha-Sifrut ha-Ivrit ha-Hadashah,* Tel-Aviv, Vol. IV, 5708, p. 47.

[[9a] See below Itzhak Ben-Zvi, "Eretz Yisrael under Ottoman Rule, 1517-1917."]

[10] Quoted after Gershom Shalom, "*Ha-Tenuah ha-Shabetait be-Polin,*" in *Bet Yisrael be-Polin,* Jerusalem, 5714, Vol. II, p. 43.

[[10a] See Halpern, *op. cit.;* below Arieh Tartakower, "The Decline of European Jewry (1933-1953)"; Ben-Zvi, *op. cit.*]

[11a See Halpern, *op. cit.*, pp. 295 ff.]

[12a See Tartakower, *op. cit.*]

[13a See below Ben-Zvi, *op. cit.;* Abraham J. Heschel, "The Mystical Element in Judaism."]

14 *Degel Mahaneh Efraim*, sec. *Ki Teze.*

15 *Tzvaat ha-Ribash, Lemberg*, 1860, 3.

[15a See Tartakower, *op. cit.*, p. 431; Ben-Zvi, *op. cit.*, pp. 657-659, 679.]

16 Introduction to the *Biur ha-Gra al Sifra de-Zeniuta.*

17 *Nefesh he-Hayyim*, Part I, ch. 4.

18 Introduction by Rabbi Hayyim Volozhiner to the *Biurha-Gra* on the *Shulhan Aruk.*

19 *Nefesh he-Hayyim*, Part I, ch. 12.

20 *Aliot Eliyahu*, end.

[20a See Halpern, *op. cit.;* Weinryb, *op. cit.;* below Ben Zion Dinur, "The Historical Foundations of the Rebirth of Israel"; Bavli, *op. cit.;* Mark *op. cit.*]

21 Rabbi Meir Berlin, *Fun Volozhin biz Yerusholayim*, New York, 1933, p. 25.

22 *Sforim, op. cit.*, Part II, p. 29.

23 Abraham Isser Katsovitsh, *Zekhtsik yor lebn*, pp. 83-84.

24 Simeon Bernfeld, "*Zikronot*," in *Reshumot*, Vol. IV, p. 149.

25 *Kol Kitbe Ahad Ha-Am*, Jerusalem, 5707, p. 467.

26 A. Zamba, "*Shtiblakh bevarshe*," in *Mosedot Torah be-Eropah*, New York, 1956, p. 356.

27 A. Paperne, *Zikhroynes*, Warsaw, 1923, pp. 16-18.

28 Lahover, *op. cit.*, Vol. IV, p. 47.

29 Dov Kats, *Tenuat ha-Musar*, Vol. I, Tel-Aviv, 5706-5716, p. 148.

30 Isaac Blazer, *Or Yisrael*, Vilna, 5660, p. 80.

31 Kats, *op. cit.*, Vol. II.

32 M. Gerts, *Musernikes*, Riga, 1936.

BRIEF BIBLIOGRAPHY

ASSAF, SIMHAH, *Mekorot le-Toledot he-Hinuk be-Yisrael.* Vols. I-IV. Tel-Aviv and Jerusalem, 5685-5703.

BERLIN, MEIR, *Fun Volozhin biz Yerusholayim.* Vols. I-II. New York, 1933.

Bet Yisrael be-Polin. Vol. II. Jerusalem, 5714.

BLAZER, ISAAC, *Or Yisrael.* Vilna, 5660.

CARLEBACH, ESRIEL, "*Mussar*," in *Jahrbuch der juedisch-literarischen Gesellschaft*, Vol. XXII. Frankfort-am-Main, 1931-1932.

DUBNOW, SHIMON, *Toledot ha-Hasidut.* Vols. I-III. Tel-Aviv, 5690.

GINZBERG, LOUIS, *Students, Scholars and Saints.* Philadelphia, 1928.

GLENN, MENAHEM G., *Israel Salanter.* New York, 1953.

HORODETSKI, SH. A., *He-Hasidut ve-ha-Hasidim.* Vols. I-IV. Jerusalem, 5683.

———, *Lekorot ha-Rabbanut.* Warsaw, 1914.

KATS, DOV, *Tenuat ha-Mussar*. Vols. I-III. Tel-Aviv, 5706-5716.
LIFSHITS, JACOB, *Zikhron Yaakob*. Vols. I-III. Kaunas, 1924-1930.
Lite. New York, 1951.
MAIMON, Y. L., *Sefer ha-Gra*. Jerusalem, 5714.
Mosedot Torah be-Eropah. New York, 1956.
OVSAY, JOSHUA, *Maamarim ve-Reshimot*. New York, 5707.
SCHARFSTEIN, ZEVI, *Toledot ha-Hinnuk be-Yisrael be-Dorot ha-Aharonim*. Vols. I-III. New York, 5705-5709.
Sefer ha-Yobel li-Kebod Rabbenu ha-Gaon R. Shimon Yehudah ha-Kohen Shkop Shelita. Vilna, 5696.
Sefer ha-Zikkaron shel ha-Yeshibah ha-Gedolah "Keneset bet Ishak," be-Kamenets de-Lite (Polin). Warsaw, 5698.
TSCHERNOVITS, HAYYIM (RAV TSAIR), *Toledot ha-Posekim*, Part III. New York, 5708.
ZAVIN, SHELOMO YOSEF, *Ishim ve-Shitot*. Tel-Aviv, 5712.

CHAPTER 9

THE DECLINE OF EUROPEAN JEWRY (1933-1953)

By Arieh Tartakower

The Balance Sheet of Extermination

There are few events in Jewish history which in their tragic significance could reasonably be compared with those in Europe in the past twenty years. The destruction of the first and the second Jewish states in ancient times and the expulsion of the Jews from Spain in the Middle Ages apparently might disprove this statement; but as far as figures are concerned, even they become comparatively insignificant. Hundreds of thousands were involved then; the fate of millions was and to a rather considerable degree is being decided—in the negative—in this contemporary destruction. Significantly enough, this unique process of decline is being concluded today in the same country in which it started thirty-five years ago. Russian Jewry was the first and seems to be at present (beginning of 1953) the last link of this chain of disaster; in the middle there were several others, comprising such Jewish communities as the German, Polish, Lithuanian, and finally almost all those in Europe, with exceptions which can be enumerated on one set of fingers. The impact of those terrific blows shattered a world 1,500 years in the building, almost half of known Jewish history in terms of time, and incomparably more in terms of human endurance and of creative spirit.

The following table, giving the available data about the Jewish population in the countries of Europe in 1900, 1933, 1946, and 1952, may serve as the best introduction to this whole subject.[1]

A few words may be needed to explain why the four data were chosen and the meaning of the various figures.

The year 1900 means more than simply the beginning of a century. It is no less significant as the conclusion of a century, probably the best in Jewish history in all respects, certainly the best from the demographic point of view. It also is significant as a year when, because of the census in Russia (1897) and in Austria-Hungary (1900), the two countries including three-quarters of the world's Jewish population, more figures were available about this population than at any other period in Jewish history. The year

TABLE I

The Jewish Population of Europe

Country	1900	1933	1946	1952	Per cent in 1952 compared with 1933
Russia (including Asiatic part)	5,600,000	3,021,000	1,800,000	2,000,000	66.5
Austria-Hungary	1,866,800	—	—	—	—
Poland	—	3,113,000	200,000	35,000	1.1
Rumania	269,000	728,000	360,000	225,000	30.9
Germany	567,900	503,700	85,000[a]	30,000	5.9
Hungary	—	444,500	150,000	80,000	17.9
Czechoslovakia	—	356,800	50,000	18,000	5.1
Great Britain	150,000	280,000	400,000	450,000	160.7
France	80,000	260,000	180,000	250,000	96.1
Lithuania	—	155,100	—[b]	—[b]	—
Holland	90,000	102,000	30,000	25,000	24.6
Latvia	—	93,400	—[b]	—[b]	—
Greece	—[c]	72,700	10,500	6,500	8.9
Yugoslavia	—[c]	68,000	10,000	6,500	9.5
European Turkey	150,000	51,000	50,000	30,000	58.8
Belgium	—[d]	50,000	25,000	35,000	70.0
Italy	38,000	48,300	35,000	32,000	66.3
Bulgaria	28,000	47,800	46,000	6,000	12.5
Switzerland	12,000	17,900	35,000[a]	19,000	106.1
Sweden	—[e]	—[e]	22,000[a]	13,000	—
Other countries	48,300	45,800	19,800	31,770	69.3
Total	8,900,000	9,459,000	3,508,300	3,292,770	34.7
Percentage of the Jewish population of the world	80.9	57.8	32.8	27.4	

[a] Including displaced persons.

[b] The remnants of the Jewish population of Lithuania and Latvia are included in the population of the U.S.S.R.

[c] Greece and Yugoslavia do not appear in the column for 1900 because the Jewish population of Greece was at that time less than 10,000, whereas Yugoslavia did not exist as a separate state; the population of Serbia was less than 10,000.

[d] The Jewish population of Belgium at the beginning of the century was less than 10,000.

[e] The Jewish population of Sweden at the beginning of the century was less than 10,000; it was less than 10,000 also in 1933.

1933 for the Jewish population meant the end of a development which began with the French Revolution and brought Jews equal rights in Europe with all their consequences. It means at the same time the beginning of the catastrophe which within ten years reduced European Jewry to almost one-third of what it had been before. The year 1946 was the first more or less normal year after the inferno of the Nazi domination in Europe; and the year 1952 brings us up to the present chapter, although the development, as will be shown later, is far from concluded.

The first look at the table immediately shows a crisis hardly ever known in such proportions in human history. The Jewish population of Europe grew in the thirty-three years from 1900 to the establishment of the Nazi regime in Germany, but the increase was rather slow (no more than 8 per cent), incomparably less than the growth of the entire Jewish population of the world (almost 50 per cent at that period), not to speak of the former century, when the Jewish people grew almost fourfold within 100 years. Accordingly, at the beginning of the century four-fifths of the Jewish population of the world lived in Europe, but not much more than one half resided there thirty-three years later. This development was the result, on one hand, of the great stream of Jewish emigration from Europe, which subtracted at least 2,000,000 at that period and added to other continents (especially to America), and, on the other hand, of the falling rate of natural increase not only in Western Europe, where this process began in the second half of the past century, but in Eastern Europe as well.[2] However this trend of development, significant as it may have been at that time, does not mean very much when compared with what happened afterward. In the short period of thirteen years from 1933 to 1946, European Jewry dwindled from 9,500,000 to 3,500,000, representing no more than one-third of the Jewish population of the world. The reasons for this phenomenon are too well known to need much explanation. No more than a fraction of the 6,000,000 who disappeared, around 500,000, were emigrants, especially German and Austrian Jews who managed to escape before the outbreak of World War II; all others were killed by the Germans and their accomplices during the war years. However, even after the collapse of Nazi Germany the gradual disappearance of European Jewry continued. In the seven years following the end of the war their number decreased again by more than 300,000, and today they are no more than one-fourth of the Jewish population of the world. This time it is mainly emigration which accounts for the reduction of the figures; hundreds of thousands left Eastern and Middle Europe, especially for Israel and for the United States; and hundreds of thousands more would have left or are only too anxious to leave, were there legal means of emigration to those countries. This, then, may be considered as showing the trend of development in the years to come; no increase of Europe's Jewish population can possibly be foreseen; on the other hand, further reduction can be considered as virtually certain (unless, if as at present seems improbable, the existing regime in Eastern Europe will modify its policy), in which case the number of European Jewry may eventually dwindle away to a handful of a few hundreds of thousands.

However, the over-all figures quoted so far, significant as they are, are not sufficient to describe the existing situation. It may be more convenient from this particular point of view to study the figures for each country separately. We shall then easily find out first the fundamental difference between Eastern and Western Europe. Whereas in the West figures of the Jewish population, with but few exceptions, did not fall sharply and in a few cases (Great Britain, Sweden, Switzerland) the population actually even increased,[3] the situation in Eastern and Middle Europe is quite different. The example of Poland, whose Jewish population dwindled to not much more than 1 per cent when compared with 1933, may be enlightening enough; and if anything can be still worse than that, it is the case of Lithuania and Latvia, whose Jewish population practically ceased to exist. But no less significant are the figures for Germany, Czechoslovakia, Austria, Greece, and Yugoslavia; in all those countries the Jewish population dropped to a fraction of what it had been before the Nazi onslaught. (The case of Bulgaria is of a different nature, for its Jewish population did not suffer much in the war years and the great reduction of figures in the past few years is the result solely of emigration to Israel.)[4] Neither should the seemingly different situation in the U.S.S.R. give rise to any illusion. If the decrease of the Jewish population there is not much more than one-third compared with 1933, it is not because the Soviet Jews suffered less than their coreligionists in other Nazi-occupied territories. Actually the number of Soviet Jews was not 3,000,000 when Nazi Germany declared war on Russia, but almost twice as much. In the meantime the Soviet government had incorporated into its territory the eastern provinces of Poland, with a Jewish population of at least 1,500,000, including the refugees from the Nazi-occupied western provinces, as well as the Baltic States and former Rumanian Bessarabia, with another 500,000 Jews. In reality not one but two-thirds of the Jewish population of the U.S.S.R. were killed by the Nazis during the years of occupation.

This, then, is the balance sheet in figures. Within a few years European Jewry dropped both in absolute numbers and, when compared with the Jewish population in the world, to almost one-third of what it had been at the beginning of the century; and in many countries the reduction reached proportions close to practical disappearance. This process is far from being concluded, and the Jewish evacuation of Europe may under certain conditions be only a question of time.

2. The Meaning of the Decline

The fact that the European era in Jewish history may for all practical purposes be concluded cannot, however, be evaluated merely from the viewpoint of figures. European Jewry is incomparably more than a demographic factor. It is, or rather was, in the first place a unique cultural phenomenon. The history of European Jewry is a history of the Jewish creative genius with which hardly anything can reasonably be compared, except the period of the Bible and of the Talmud. What Spanish Jewry did in the Middle Ages, or German, Russian, and Polish Jewry in the following generations, stands unparalleled in the Jewish history of the past 1,500 years. Nothing of this kind could—at least not so far—be achieved in any other part of the world. Both the American and Palestinian (today Israeli) Jewish cultures were built by European Jewish emigrants, and they are responsible for the most significant achievements; compared with them the original creative work (i.e., work done by persons native to the new countries) does not yet mean very much. This of course has little, if anything, to do with any inborn abilities of the Jews of Europe; it was to an overwhelming degree the result of the specific atmosphere born in the course of generations, in which Jewishness and Jewish creative effort appeared as something self-intelligible; even the man in the street, the half-illiterate artisan, and the beggar became imbued with this spirit.[6] During generations and centuries—in Eastern Europe almost up to the very end—religious tradition was both the basis and the content of Jewish life. God was always with man and He decided the course of developments. The story of the Jewish *balegole* (Hebrew *baal agalah,* owner of a carriage, a famous type in the Jewish little town of Eastern Europe), who greased the wheels of his carriage while carrying phylacteries on his head and praying to God, is almost symbolic for that period. From this sanctification of daily life arose a religious culture unique in human history. But no less significant was the half-secular *Wissenschaft des Judentums* in Germany and the worldly culture of Eastern Europe, both in Hebrew and in Yiddish.[7] Just as the praying owner of a carriage became the symbol of past generations, so later did the Jewish *treger* porter of Vilna, sitting with a big cord around his waist reading the Hebrew paper, especially its literary and political sections. The first was symbolic of the atmosphere from which arose traditional Jewish culture, and the second, while different, nevertheless in its essence was closely connected with the former and gave birth both to modern Jewish literature and to virtually all the great movements of the Jewish renaissance. With the disappearance of both symbols the Jewish people is faced with a vacuum for which no replacement has been found so far, not even in Israel despite its grandiose potential force and its actual achievements.

But this is not only a problem of spirit and of literary achievement. It is a problem of a Jewish way of life, created through long generations of common thinking and common suffering, unique in the social life of mankind. The Jewish *shtetel* (little town) of Eastern Europe,[8] or the Jewish sections in modern cities; Jewish family life with its highest morality and the treasure of its habits; Jewish philanthropic institutions, strangely combining their business practices with principles of highest mercy;[9] the world of the Hasidim, Mitnagdim, and Maskilim,[10] of the *Batlonim,*[11] of the *Talmidei Hakomim,*[12] and many, many others, each so specifically Jewish that there are no words for translation; the deep, positive attitude to life, with great natural increase as its consequence, so characteristic for Jewry in Eastern Europe—all this disappeared with European Jewry and with it disappeared a great, probably most characteristic, part of Jewish life.

One thing remains to be stressed again. Not all countries of Europe suffered to the same extent in the years of Nazi domination, but some of them (even in Middle and Eastern Europe) lost only part of their Jewish population, whereas in others the Jewish communities were virtually wiped out. As tragedy within tragedy appears the fact that the spiritually strongest Jewish communities were altogether destroyed, whereas others suffered less. Nothing, or almost nothing, remained of Lithuanian, Polish, or Bessarabian Jewry; incomparably larger was the number of survivors from among the Hungarian or Bulgarian or Old Rumanian Jews. Even within the limits of one country the development ran a similar course, as in the case of Rumania already mentioned. The Jewish population of Bessarabia and Bukovina, outstanding in its contribution toward Jewish culture and social life, was practically eliminated; what remained of Rumanian Jewry was the population of Regat (Old Rumania), whose record is incomparably less significant. The same thing happened in Russia. The 3,000,000 Jews exterminated there were mainly from the former Polish provinces, White Russia and the Ukraine, where Jewish life had preserved much of its intensity even at the period of its sovietization; whereas the 2,000,000 spared were to a considerable degree from the Great Russian and Asiatic provinces of the U.S.S.R., Jews already strongly assimilated and whose Jewish content of life was insignificant. The decline of European Jewry is, therefore, much more pronounced than it may appear when only statistics are taken into consideration.

3. THE GREAT DIVISION

So far the chapter has evaluated what has happened in the years of disaster. But there are still Jews in Europe, 3,250,000, more than one-fourth of the Jewish population in the world. What about them? What is their situation? What are their problems? What are their chances of survival?

It is not only today that such questions are being discussed. When the war was nearing its end and immediately afterward, both Jewish scholars and Jewish social workers busied themselves investigating what was left after the inferno and what possibly could be done to enable the survivors to start a new life. However, the problems as they appeared then and the methods of solution then discussed were of a quite different character than at present. Very few doubted that Jewish rehabilitation in Europe was possible, although there was no place for illusion as to the proportion in which this could be done when compared with the prewar situation. The main problems seemed to be the undermined health of the Jewish population and especially of the children, and that contact between the Jewish and non-Jewish population had virtually ceased to exist during Nazi occupation of Europe. The re-establishment of Jewish positions in commerce and in free professions seemed doubtful under such conditions. As against that appeared the important possibility of new contact with the Jewish community of the U.S.S.R., through means found during the war years, so that a unified Jewish policy throughout Europe was no longer considered fantasy.[13]

All those plans and ideas are at present no more than water under the bridge in view of events in the past few years. Developed in centuries of persecution, the Jews' astounding ability to recover from blows was apparent in the present case, too, despite the magnitude of the disaster. The number physically or mentally broken by the horrors of the period seems considerably less than was originally feared; to a certain degree this may be the result also of the efficient protection of health organized immediately after the war. On the other hand, the economic reintegration of European Jews went on rather smoothly in the Western countries, where the Nazi occupation did not succeed in poisoning the atmosphere and severing relations between the Jews and their neighbors; whereas in Eastern Europe the establishment of the new Socialist regimes opened the way for absorption of the Jews into the general economy, along lines similar to those in the Soviet Union. But at the same time this very process, coupled with the growing tension between the Western democracies and the Soviet bloc, abolished hope of Jewish co-operation in all countries of Europe. With the idea of One World disappeared also the idea of one Jewish world. Not only is Soviet Jewry today incomparably more separated from other parts of the Jewish people than ever before, but that has occurred with regard to Jews in other countries of the Soviet bloc. To speak today about one European Jewry would be utterly unrealistic. A short while ago contact with at least the Jewish population in the People's Democracies still seemed possible to a certain degree; however, developments in the past few years, and the ever growing anti-Israel and even anti-Jewish propaganda in those countries, apparently put an end to such hopes and made the full sovietization of those Jewish groups only a matter of time.

No unified presentation of the problems of European Jewry is, therefore, possible today. Whatever is being discussed has necessarily to take into consideration this fundamental division into two sections, deep and apparently hopelessly apart, as hardly before in Jewish history.

However, before attempting to evaluate the situation in those two distinct parts, one additional remark may still be appropriate referring to both. The hope that Jewish life in Europe might be restored after the war was far from being shared by all parts of the Jewish population or even by the majority. On the contrary, almost immediately hundreds of thousands saw in emigration the only possible solution of their problems. This was the situation especially with regard to the displaced Jewish population in the camps of Germany, Austria, and Italy, whose number—considerable from the very beginning—grew with the influx of new masses of refugees from Poland and other countries of Eastern Europe. Repatriation of this army of 250,000 could hardly be considered, for very few, if any, were inclined to return to places soaked with the blood of their closest relatives and to populations as anti-Semitic as ever before, if not more so. Only emigration overseas, especially to Palestine, could solve the problem and did so after a certain period.[14] It was not only displaced persons in the technical sense who tried to get out of Europe. The number of candidates for emigration was at least twice as large as the number of D.P.'s from the very beginning, especially in Eastern Europe. This soon appeared, for instance, at the inquiry held by the Anglo-American Committee on Palestine, when the majority of the Jewish population in many countries expressed a desire to leave as soon as possible,[15] and shortly afterward all who possibly could, did so. In this way the Jewish population of Bulgaria dwindled to one-tenth of what it had been before, of the remnants of Polish Jewry four-fifths left the country, Czechoslovakian Jewry dropped to less than half, and the same without doubt would have happened in Rumania and Hungary, were the Jews there free to leave. In Western Europe the emigration tendencies were also strong from the very beginning. Not only did the Jewish D.P.'s in countries such as Switzerland or Sweden soon go overseas, but they were joined by considerable groups from other countries, such as France, Belgium, and Holland. The reasons for emigration may have been different than in Eastern Europe; the driving force was not anti-Semitism or reluctance to remain under a Communist regime, but rather future insecurity especially in view of the world political situation. But the results nevertheless remain the same or almost the same in both cases.

This, then, leads us to the second general remark before taking up separately the affairs in the two parts of Europe. Not only has the number of the Jews today dwindled to one-third of what it had been before the war, and not only has this downward trend continued, but the psychological situation of this remnant Jewish community can best be described as that of people who know, or rather who feel, that they are on the verge of disappearance. The Jews of Europe in former years were considered and considered themselves as the very center of Jewish life. This accounted for their leading position in virtually all Jewish activities and even in the relief work done for them by their more fortunate brethren in America. The status of European Jews was the result not only of their numerical strength, but to no lesser degree of their great cultural tradition and of their power of initiative. All this seems to be a thing of the past. It is sufficient to see the European representatives at the various Jewish conferences of the past few years to have a rather exact picture of the existing situation. With a few exceptions the Jewish communities of Europe may be considered stagnant or even declining, not only in the numerical but also in the moral sense of this word, which adds even more to the tragedy of destruction.

4. JEWISH FATE AND FUTURE IN EASTERN EUROPE

So far we have discussed the few phenomena in common. But apart from them hardly any comparison can be ventured today between the Jewish communities in the Soviet bloc and those in Western Europe. Numerically the Jews of Western Europe are less than one-fourth of what was left on that continent, but spiritually and morally their importance is incomparably bigger than that of their coreligionists in Eastern Europe.

The East European Jewish community, comprising, apart from the small splinter groups in Greece, Yugoslavia and Finland, the entire Jewry of the Soviet bloc, around 2,500,000 souls, can be considered as virtually doomed from the cultural and spiritual, today perhaps even from the political, point of view. But not so economically. The situation, paradoxically enough, is strictly opposite to what it had been at the beginning of the century and—apart from the U.S.S.R. itself—continued to be until the outbreak of the past war. Then the main problem of European Jewry was economic—desperate struggle against mass poverty hardly ever had reached such proportions in Jewish history. But at the same time a tremendous creative force existed in all fields of Jewish culture, almost automatically giving East European Jewry its leading role in Jewish life. Yet the political situation was very difficult and remained so, although the difficulties today are of a quite different nature. At present an economic problem hardly exists for Jews in the U.S.S.R. and is gradually disappearing also in other countries of the Soviet bloc. The Soviet Union after a series of efforts solved the problem of Jewish poverty, originally even aggravated by Soviet economic and social policy. Hundreds of thousands of Jews found place in the process of industrialization initiated at the end of the 1920's, others were absorbed by the great administrative machinery and by free professions, so that no significant number of destitute Jews remained in that country.[16] This great example is being followed today in other countries of the Soviet bloc, although the difficulties there are incomparably greater and the problem is still far from solution, especially in Hungary and in Rumania. On the other hand, even before the past war the great effort to build in the U.S.S.R. a new Jewish culture in place of the one declared bourgeois and counterrevolutionary because of its religious, Hebrew, and Zionist foundations broke down to a considerable degree. The idea of a culture "national in form and Socialist in content," as the slogan of the Soviet government says, based mainly on Yiddish in its Soviet version, could hardly find sympathy among the masses of the Jewish population, who preferred Russian assimilation to this poor and superficial Yiddish culture. Russian, therefore, became more and more the language of the Jewish population, the number of children in Jewish schools decreased from year to year, Jewish literature and the Jewish press dwindled, and mass indifference took the place of the great Jewish initiative and vitality of the former period. The linguistic and cultural assimilation was also stimulated by the growing integration of the Jews into the economic life of the country and by their daily contact with the non-Jewish population. All this, coupled with the liquidation of Jewish institutions, especially in the field of philanthropy and social work, practically sealed the cultural fate of the Jewish population of the U.S.S.R. even before the past war. Whatever remained of Jewish culture was suppressed by the anti-Jewish policy initiated at the end of 1948, whose results included closing all Jewish schools and other cultural institutions, abolishing the few still existing Jewish papers, and deporting the leading Jewish writers. Cultural annihilation describes the fate of Russian Jewry at present.[17]

With this cultural decline of Soviet Jewry a second phenomenon is closely associated, namely, the falling birth rate of the Jews of the U.S.S.R. In strange contrast to the beginning of the century, when the Russian Jewish community was outstanding in its natural increase (a birth rate of over 35 per 1,000 population), at present it figures last among the various population groups of the U.S.S.R. The Jewish birth rate in the 1920's dropped to 24.6 per 1,000, and the annual birth rate of children per 1,000 women aged twenty to forty-four was 515 among Russian Jews, barely sufficient for replacement and incomparably lower than among other sections of the population (White Russians 949, Ukrainians 860, Russians 830, Poles 734). Soviet government policy, intent upon stimulating the natural increase of the population, remained in this respect without noteworthy influence upon the Jews. Jewish dispersion throughout the huge territory, cultural assimilation and the vastly increased number of mixed marriages as its consequence—all contributed toward depressing the Jewish birth rate to a minimum.[18]

The situation may not be as clear for the time being in other countries of the Soviet bloc, at least not in all of them. There are countries whose Jewish population underwent a rapid process of cultural assimilation even before the past war, so that the new regime only strengthened the existing trend: Hungary, Czechoslovakia (especially the Czech part of the country), and Rumania (in its present borders) may be quoted as examples. On the other hand, the small Jewish community of Poland managed to preserve, particularly in the first years after the war, much of its former vitality. Strongly organized from the very beginning and successful even in re-establishing the Union of Jewish Religious Communities, the Polish Jews also developed significant economic as well as cultural activities. A net of over 300 co-operatives of production, organized practically overnight, played a decisive role in introducing the Jewish population into the new economy of the country. At the same time Jewish schools with both Hebrew and Yiddish as languages of instruction were established; Jewish periodicals and even scholarly magazines began to appear; Jewish public opinion took strong interest in whatever happened in Jewish life in Poland and in other countries. However, this period ended rather soon with the growing role of the Jewish Communists in the general social life. Jewish co-operatives were declared open to non-Jews and lost their specifically Jewish character. Jewish institutions were gradually taken over by the government and underwent a process of rapid assimilation, and the atmosphere of indifference so characteristic for present Jewish life in the U.S.S.R. apparently prevails also in Poland. Left, at least for the time being, are a certain number of Jewish schools with Yiddish as language of instruction, a few papers devoted mainly to Communist and anti-Zionist propaganda (there is, however, still one scholarly historical magazine), and a publication society for books, conducted, of course, in a strictly Communist spirit.

It may also be worth while to stress that religious life in Poland (as well as in other countries of the Soviet bloc) remains, at least theoretically, free and plays a certain role in preserving Jewish cultural identity. However, in this case, too, assimilation seems to be merely a question of time. The development of affairs in the U.S.S.R. will probably be repeated in satellite countries with the process of their growing integration into the Soviet system, especially should the new anti-Jewish policy be followed by them —and there are many signs pointing to such a development in the near future.[19]

This political problem remains to be explained here because it certainly represents the most striking phenomenon in Jewish life in the Soviet bloc today. Originally the establishment of the Soviet regime brought Russian Jewry not only abolition of all anti-Jewish restrictions and full equality of rights (actually this was done by the first democratic government of Prince Lvov, established after the outbreak of the Revolution in 1917) but also a decided and merciless fight against anti-Semitism, declared a crime by the Soviet authorities. More than that, in continuation of its policy of full equality of national rights and opportunities to be granted to all parts of the population, the regime went so far as to recognize the principle of a Jewish national autonomy and even of an autonomous region to be established in the province of Biro-Bidjan. This was one of the most significant achievements in the political history of the Diaspora. However, the postwar years brought a sudden change of this policy, actually its reverse. Not only were Jewish cultural rights practically abolished, but an anti-Jewish policy was begun, expressed first in the gradual elimination of Jews from all responsible positions in the political administration of the country; then in mass arrests because of "cosmopolitan" views, which suddenly became a crime; in publication of the former Jewish names of those convicted; and finally even in deportation of Jews from certain western border provinces. As a link in this chain of events, in January, 1953, came the arrest and trial of several leading Jewish physicians, accused of having served American imperialism by causing with premeditation the death of the Soviet political leader Andrei Zhdanov a few years before.

It is not easy to find the exact reasons for this new policy, which certainly cannot be explained as indicating a new course in the U.S.S.R., toward national minorities; the general line favoring the cultural development of the various nationalities is being continued. Apparently the Jews are discriminated against not for racial reasons, but because they are not trusted, as happened a few years before with the Volga Germans and the Tatars. In the hysteria caused by ever-growing tensions in their relations with the Western world and by fear of war, the Soviet authorities decided to eliminate all those parts of the population which might possibly become dangerous because of their actual or potential contact with the West. The Soviet Jews are considered members of a nation whose majority lives in the Western countries, so these Jews are looked upon with suspicion, for which no remedy can under present conditions possibly be found. A second reason for Soviet distrust of the Jews is the considerable number of them with cosmopolitan tendencies—a fact welcomed in the U.S.S.R. only a few years ago but now considered hardly less than a crime; not cosmopolitanism but Soviet nationalism becomes the highest virtue as one of the fundamental conditions of preparedness in case of war. And last but not least there remains the old anti-Zionist, at present also the anti-Israel, tendency of the Soviet government, discarded only for a short period in 1947-1948, when the Soviets hoped that for the price of their support of the idea of a Jewish national home they would win a potential ally in the Near East. The very moment this hope disappeared, the old hatred came again to the fore and again complicates the situation. The Soviet Jews apparently are suspected of love of Zion, despite their ever-growing cultural assimilation.[20]

Whatever the real reasons for this new policy, its dangers for Soviet Jewry are obvious. Not only does it mean cultural annihilation, as mentioned before, but it may endanger the very physical existence of the Jews in the case of mass deportations and forced labor, far from unusual in the Soviet Union. The great anxiety over the fate of the Soviet Jews among the world Jewish population is, therefore, intelligible. This was the psychological basis for the idea of evacuating the Russian Jewish population with the agreement of the Soviet authorities. The assumption is that, having a choice between mass deportation or eliminating the Jews by emigration, the authorities, especially when pressed by world public opinion, might still decide for the second eventuality. Whether and to what degree this at present rather fantastic assumption might become reality remains to be seen. The attitude of the Soviet authorities is far from encouraging.[21]

So much for Soviet Jewry. The course in the other countries seems for the time being somewhat different. In territories where before the war mass anti-Semitism and anti-Jewish discrimination were typical, the new regime followed the early example of the Soviet authorities, proclaiming both full equality of rights for the Jews and fighting against anti-Semitism. The problem at present is whether these governments will also follow the later anti-Jewish policy of the Soviet Union. With the sole exception of Czechoslovakia, no visible signs of change have appeared so far (beginning of 1953). The anti-Zionist propaganda continues, but without ousting Jews from responsible positions or by other anti-Jewish acts. Contrary to the situation in the U.S.S.R., the People's Democracies never hermetically closed their borders to Jewish emigration to Israel, although emigration in general is forbidden. With the exception of Hungary, rather significant emigration occurred from all these lands, in the case of Bulgaria a virtual mass evacuation, as indicated above. However, another grave problem faces the Jewish communities of those countries, especially in Hungary, Poland, and Rumania—the danger of a violent underground anti-Semitism. Anti-Semitism, although suppressed by the new regime, not only failed to disappear, but on the contrary grew even stronger, and Jews are being accused as leaders of the regime, hated by a considerable part of the population. The fear of the authorities' iron hand precludes for the time being outward manifestation of these feelings; but should the power of the regime decrease for any reason, the Jewish population may easily become the first and foremost victim of disturbances and may even be doomed. In this case, too, the only possible solution may be emigration. However, a violent campaign against the idea of Jewish emigration to Israel has long been conducted by the Jewish Communists, who succeeded in a few cases in influencing government policy. The situation became even more delicate because of the anti-Zionist and anti-Israel policy of the Soviet bloc, on orders apparently from Moscow.[21a] Whether in such circumstances a continuation of Jewish emigration in noteworthy proportions will be possible remains to be seen; just as, on the other hand, it is difficult to foresee whether in view of the growing separation of those countries from the Western world it may still be possible to preserve at least a minimum of contact with their Jewish population, thus strengthening its Jewish consciousness and preventing a cultural fate similar to that of Russian Jewry. The prospects in both respects are unfortunately far from bright.

5. THE WESTERN SECTOR: THE STRUGGLE FOR SURVIVAL

As against this dismal picture of the Jewish communities in Eastern Europe whose chances of survival, if any, are very limited, the position of

West European Jewry seems incomparably more encouraging. The world of democracy, in which they are living, is a sufficient guarantee of freedom for man and freedom for development of spiritual forces. At the same time all those communities are connected with the Jewish people all over the world and especially in Israel, which seems to be the strongest possible basis for their survival. This is not only because of the existing legal situation, important as it may be when compared with the situation in Eastern Europe. No less significant is the inner preparedness of the Jewish population for co-operation with world Jewry. The situation has not always seemed so favorable in this respect as today. In the years before the war Western Europe was a stronghold of Jewish assimilation, not only in the cultural but also in the political sense of the word. Nowhere were Jews so deeply rooted in the life of their countries as in Italy, in France, or in England; and nowhere was assimilation as militant as among certain Jewish groups in those countries. German Jewry alone may have surpassed them in both respects, but in the last years before the war it was already broken, physically and spiritually, and its tradition was taken over by the West European Jewish communities. However, the situation today is different from what it was in the prewar years. Both external and internal factors contributed toward very significant changes. The Jewish problem, which hardly existed in those countries in past generations, suddenly appeared under the impact of the events in Germany. The non-Jewish population became aware of the problem and considerable numbers were influenced by the violent anti-Semitic propaganda, which of course left its imprint on the psychology of the Jews in those countries. Assimilation is no longer self-intelligible today, as it was twenty or thirty years ago; and with its decreasing strength disappeared also the indifference to Jewish affairs which formerly prevailed in large sections of the Jewish population in Western Europe. This may be the result also of another half-conscious reasoning. With the extermination of 6,000,000 Jews, the great majority of them East Europeans, the numerical significance of the West European Jewish communities grew considerably. No longer a small minority in Jewish life, their proportion grew to almost one-fourth of European and one-fifteenth of world Jewry, and with it grew their responsibility for the fate of Jews throughout the world and willingness to participate in building their present and future.

So much for the positive phenomena. But the negative ones ought not to be ignored. West European Jewry as a whole may have become more interested and more active in Jewish affairs; but at the same time the very groups whose Jewish consciousness had formerly been the deepest are slowly disappearing. Contrary to the situation in Eastern Europe, West European Jewry before the war was far from one monolithic group. A great distance—both social and psychological—separated the old Jewish inhabitants of those countries from the immigrants arrived from Eastern Europe at the beginning of the century or in the period between the two wars. The majority of the first were thoroughly assimilated and indifferent to Jewish affairs, whereas the second group preserved much of its Jewish culture and vitality. There was also a third group, German Jewish refugees who mostly arrived in the thirties and separated both from the autochthon and from the East European Jewish population, although psychologically gravitating closer toward the native Western Jews. This division into two or even three sections, although to a certain degree still existing, lost much of its significance both because of the revived Jewish interest of the old Jewish community and the reduced influence of the immigrant population. Considerable numbers of the newcomers were exterminated during the years of Nazi occupation, the first and foremost victims of the ferocious anti-Jewish policy; many left for Israel in the past few years; and those who remained, as is also the case with several thousand immigrants who arrived after the war, are incomparably less active than they were before, especially in the field of culture and education. This decline of East European influence is felt in the first place in Great Britain, where the once teeming center of Whitechapel in London, with its Jewish language and Jewish traditional life, with its papers and clubs and theaters, is slowly disappearing, although British Jewry as such tries to preserve its identity and even to strengthen its position in the current Jewish world of today.[22] The same is more or less the case in other countries. The Jewish center of Paris still remains, but it also has lost much of its importance.[23] And so the increased activity of the Jews of Western Europe and their efficient organization (in certain cases perhaps even overorganization) are not always accompanied by increased Jewish content, a situation which does not augur well for the future.

Apart from that, there is a second disturbing phenomenon. Although the numerical significance of West European Jewry as a whole grew considerably because of the reasons mentioned, the size of the Jewish communities in most of those countries is very limited. Except in Great Britain and France, the Jewish population is no more than a few tens of thousands or even a few thousands in a given place, which makes difficult preservation of Jewish identity; and the high assimilating power of the surrounding culture complicates the situation even more. It may still be possible for the handful of Jews in Bulgaria, Yugoslavia, or Greece to retain their Jewishness, although even there the situation is far from easy; but in countries such as Sweden or Switzerland or Denmark, there is almost no hope left for the long run. No danger whatsoever exists there, nor may be expected from the authorities or public opinion in those countries; forced renunciation of language or culture can hardly be conceived in the West European democracies; but what cannot and will not be achieved by administrative pressure results from sheer force of the general culture. And against such a force no efficient method of protection can easily be imagined.

This may be considered the fundamental problem in the life of West European Jewry. Economic rehabilitation—unnecessary in countries such as Great Britain, Sweden, or Switzerland, which were never occupied by the Germans—went smoothly and the standard of life is as high as before the war; even immigrant poverty in places such as London or Paris is slowly disappearing. Neither does any noteworthy political problem exist for the Jewish communities in those countries. Anti-Semitism, revived in a few of them by Nazi propaganda and by German occupation, dwindled again and is without importance at present. So the West European Jewish problem boils down to that of Jewish cultural survival. There exists a certain similarity in this respect to the East European Jewish communities, but at the same time also a fundamental difference. In both cases Jewish survival is what matters, and in both cases the situation may be desperately difficult at present. In Eastern Europe the difficulties were brought about by political factors, which in the case of the Soviet Union and perhaps also the other countries of the Soviet bloc may undermine the very existence of the Jewish communities even in a physical sense. However, the problem of West European Jews is strictly cultural. It may thus sound paradoxical at first, but is nevertheless correct, to say that from this particular point of view the situation in Eastern Europe may be more encouraging than in the West. In the countries of the Soviet bloc a change of the regime or even a modification of its present policy may have an immediate positive influence in the field of culture, whereas nothing of this kind can reasonably be expected in Western Europe. Only by strengthening considerably contact with Israel and with other sections of Jewry, and by a great work of Jewish education, can a solution, if any, of this problem be found. The possibility is also not excluded that the philosophy of biculturism, at present developing especially in the United States, may influence the situation in Western Europe, despite the rather considerable difference of conditions. Should more Jews decide that living in one civilization does not solve the problem, individually or for the Jewish community, perhaps a new generation may combine its Western civilization with the old Jewish tradition and with the creative spirit of Israel, and a way may be found out of the present impasse.

Whether and in which form this problem of West European Jewry, and also the grave problems of the Jewish communities in Eastern Europe, can be solved remains to be seen. The outlook in both cases is far from encouraging. But even with the most favorable assumption, not much can be expected from those remnants of the old glory. It remains for others, especially for American Jewry and for the Jewry of Israel,[23a] to continue the great tradition of the past and to develop further the eternal spiritual forces of the Jewish people.

NOTES

[1] Figures for 1900 quoted in this table are taken mainly from the *American Jewish Year Book,* especially volumes for the years 5662 (1901-1902) and 5663 (1902-1903). The column for 1933 is based on data quoted by Arthur Ruppin in his article "The Jewish Population of the World," in *The Jewish People, Past and Present,* Vol. I, New York, 1946, pp. 348-360. Figures for 1946 are quoted mainly from the two publications of the Institute of Jewish Affairs in New York, *Statistics of Jewish Casualties During Axis Domination,* New York, 1945 (mimeographed), and *Hitler's Ten Years War on the Jews,* New York, 1943. A few figures were corrected so as to take into consideration certain events following immediately the end of the war, for instance, re-emigration of Polish Jewish refugees from the U.S.S.R., and data were added for countries not quoted in those two publications. Figures for 1952 are the author's estimates based on all available sources. Countries which did not exist as independent states at the beginning of the century are not quoted in the column for 1900. All countries are of course considered within their borders in the respective years, which in several cases (Russia, Rumania, Germany, Turkey, Bulgaria) accounts for the rather considerable differences of figures between 1900 and 1933. Only countries with a Jewish population of 10,000 and more are quoted specifically; all others are included in the group of "Other countries." Exception was made only in cases where the Jewish population, originally more than 10,000, dropped consequently below this figure.

[2] On the falling rate of natural increase of European Jews, see L. Hersch, "Jewish Population Trends in Europe," in *The Jewish People, Past and Present,* Vol. II, New York, 1948, pp. 1-24. (Only English sources are quoted here and afterward; sources in other languages are quoted merely when of special significance.)

[3] It may still be advisable to indicate that if the figures in the West European countries remained without great modification, this does not always prove that the Jewish population of those countries escaped suffering in the war years. The inferno of Nazi occupation was felt there no less than in Eastern Europe, and considerable parts of the population were wiped out; but the figures nevertheless went up again in the past few years because of a new Jewish immigration. This is the case especially of France, whose Jewish population dropped from 260,000 in 1933 to 180,000 in 1946, but increased afterward to 235,000; or of Belgium, with a Jewish population of no more than 25,000 in 1946 as against 50,000 in 1933, but again with 42,000 in 1952; Jewish immigrants mainly from Eastern Europe filled the gap.

[4] About the fate of Bulgarian Jewry, see I. Cohen, "Jews of Bulgaria," *Congress Weekly,* New York, March 12, 1951.

[5] The best source books in English about German Jewry are Jacob Rader Marcus, *The Rise and Destiny of the German Jew,* Cincinnati, 1934, and Marvin Lowenthal, *The Jews of Germany; a Story of Sixteen Centuries,* Philadelphia, 1936. See also Ismar Elbogen, *A Century of Jewish Life,* Phila-

delphia, 1944. About Russian Jewry, see especially Simon Dubnov, *History of the Jews in Russia and Poland,* 3 vols., Philadelphia, 1916-1920. About the economic and cultural achievements of Polish Jewry, see *The Black Book of Polish Jewry,* Jacob Apenszlak, ed., New York, 1943, Part Two, pp. 249-316.

[6] See the impressive description of this atmosphere in Abraham Joshua Heschel, *The Earth is the Lord's,* New York, 1950.

[7] In addition to the preceding chapter in this volume, good analysis of European Jewish culture in its various aspects is to be found in the extensive article of Abraham Menes, "The Eastern European Period in Jewish History," *Universal Encyclopedia,* The Jews, Volume 4, New York, 1950, pp. 275-430 (Yiddish). On the deep Jewish roots in Europe, see Cecil Roth, "The Jew as a European," presidential address delivered before the Jewish Historical Society of England, January 11, 1938; see also his Chapter 4 in the present volume, "The European Age in Jewish History."

[8] The *shtetel* with its typical atmosphere, frequently described in both Hebrew and Yiddish literature, in the past few years found its way also into the field of sociology. See especially the two articles of Theodor Bienenstock, "Social Life and Authority in the East European Jewish Shtetel Community," *Southwestern Journal of Anthropology,* Autumn, 1950, pp. 238-254; "Anti-authoritarian Attitude in the Eastern European Shtetel Community," *American Journal of Sociology,* September, 1951, pp. 150-158; also Mark Zborowski and Elizabeth Herzog, *Life is with People; The Jewish Little-Town of Eastern Europe,* New York, 1952.

[9] About the sociology of Jewish traditional philanthropy, see Boris D. Bogen, *Jewish Philanthropy,* New York, 1917; and the article by N. F. Joffe, "The Dynamics of Benefice among East European Jews," *Social Forces,* University of North Carolina, March, 1949, pp. 238-247; see also my article, "This, Too, Is a Remnant of the Past" (Toward a Sociology of Jewish Poverty), *Bitzaron,* October, 1949, pp. 1-16 (Hebrew).

[10] On the Hasidim and Maskilim, see below Yudel Mark, "Yiddish Literature" [as well as above Israel Halpern, "The Jews in Eastern Europe (From Ancient Times until the Partitions of Poland, 1772-1795)"; Bernard D. Weinryb, "East European Jewry (Since the Partitions of Poland, 1772-1795)"; Abraham Menes, "Patterns of Jewish Scholarship in Eastern Europe"; below Itzhak Ben-Zvi, "Eretz Yisrael under Ottoman Rule, 1517-1917"].

[11] Like all the other descriptive words mentioned here, perhaps even more than they, the term *batlan* can hardly be translated. It means a man whose life from the normal economic point of view can be considered rather useless, but nevertheless is full with Jewish wisdom and with seeking the way to God. About this unique, probably most characteristic, type in Jewish life, see Theodor H. Gaster, "The Passing of the Batlan," *Commentary,* February, 1952, pp. 142-146.

[12] *Talmidei Hakomim* means learned people who devote most of their time to study of Jewish traditional culture and who are recognized both as experts and as scholars in this particular field.

[13] About plans for Jewish rehabilitation in Europe, see the author's contribution, "European Jewry, 1939-1945," ch. 6 in the first and second editions

of this volume. Of the books and articles devoted to this question still of interest today, the following deserve to be mentioned: Zorach Warhaftig, *Relief and Rehabilitation,* New York, 1944; Nehemiah Robinson, *Indemnification and Reparation, Jewish Aspects,* New York, 1944, and "The Jews in The Postwar Period," *Journal of Educational Sociology,* January, 1945 (Special Issue). [See Weinryb, *op. cit.,* pp. 350 ff.]

[14] About the problem of Jewish displaced persons after the war and its solution, see especially Zorach Warhaftig, *Uprooted. Jewish Refugees and Displaced Persons After Liberation,* New York, 1946; and the pamphlet of Kurt R. Grossmann, *The Jewish D.P. Problem. Its Origin, Scope and Liquidation,* New York, 1951. A full description of the problem of Jewish refugees is to be found in Arieh Tartakower and Kurt R. Grossmann, *The Jewish Refugee,* New York, 1944.

[15] See *Anglo-American Committee of Inquiry, Report to the United States Government and His Majesty's Government in the United Kingdom,* Lausanne, April 20, 1946, published by the Department of State, Washington, 1946.

[16] The best description of the absorption of the Jewish population into the Soviet economy in connection with the industrialization of the country is to be found in the book of the Soviet Jewish statistician L. Singer, *The Rejuvenated Nation,* Moscow, 1940 (Yiddish). In English, see Solomon M. Schwarz, *The Jews in the Soviet Union,* Syracuse University Press, 1951, Part I, ch. XII, "Agrarianization and Industrialization," pp. 160-173. [See Weinryb, *op. cit.,* p. 351.]

[17] About the cultural disintegration of Soviet Jewry, see Jacob Lestschinsky, "Jewish Expression in the U.S.S.R.," *Jewish Frontier,* December, 1948; see also my article, "Destruction Through Liberation" (Remarks about Sociology of Russian Jewry), *Davar Annual,* Tel-Aviv, 1952, pp. 111-123 (Hebrew).

[18] See figures about this development and its explanation in my article, "Fundamental Problems of Jewish Demography Today," *Hebrew Union College, Seventy-Fifth Anniversary Publication, 1875-1950,* Cincinnati, 1953, Part II, pp. 649-678.

[19] About the Jewish life in the People's Democracies, see especially the two articles, Nathan Reich, "Jewish Life in the Russian Satellites: The Prospects for Recovery under Totalitarianism," *Commentary,* April, 1949, pp. 328-334; and "Jewish Fate and Future in Eastern Europe," *Zion,* Jerusalem, Vol. II, Nos. 5-7, August, 1951. See also American Jewish Committee, Library of Information, *Jews behind the Iron Curtain,* New York, 1952. About the Jewish communities of Hungary and Rumania, see the two publications of the Institute of Jewish Affairs in New York, *The Jews of Hungary; Survey of Their History and Postwar Situation,* 1952; and *Rumanian Jewry in the Postwar Period,* 1952.

[20] About the development of Soviet anti-Semitism and its reasons, see especially the book of Schwarz already mentioned, Part Two, "Anti-Semitism in the U.S.S.R.," pp. 241-380. See also the open letter of Hayim Greenberg to the Soviet Ambassador to the United States, "What Is Happening to Soviet Jewry," published in the *Jewish Frontier,* February, 1951.

[21] About the idea and the prospects of a Jewish evacuation from the U.S.S.R., see my "Let My People Go—Russian Version," *Hadoar,* New York, November 2, 1951 (Hebrew).

[[21a] See below Oscar I. Janowsky, "The Rise of the State of Israel," pp. 756 ff.]

[22] About these vital problems of Jewish life in England, see a series in the monthly *The Jewish Forum,* which appeared in London during 1945-1946, especially the three articles, Cecil Roth, "The Anglo Jewish tradition," November, 1945; I. Fishman, "Jewish Education in Great Britain," November, 1945; J. Webber, "The Present Position of Anglo Jewry," October, 1946. See also the article by Joseph Leftwich, "A Son of Anglo-Jewry Speaks," *The Menorah Journal,* New York, Winter, 1950.

[23] About the problems of French Jewry, see the book Michel Roblin, *Les Juifs de Paris; demographie, economie, culture, Ouvrage publié avec le concours du Centre National de la Recherche Scientifique,* Paris, 1952; see also the two articles, M. Shtrigler, "Is There a Future for French Jewry?", *Zukunft,* New York, September, 1951 (Yiddish); J. Fink, "French Jewry is Seeking a Way to Return," *Hadoar,* New York, August 11, 1950 (Hebrew).

[[23a] See Janowsky, *op. cit.*]

CHAPTER 10

THE AMERICAN JEWISH CHRONICLE

By Anita Libman Lebeson

American Jewish history begins with the Exodus of 1492. In March of that year there occurred a major catastrophe known as the Edict of Expulsion. Within a few months the Jews of Spain were ordered to liquidate their affairs and to dispose of their possessions.[1a] While Columbus was outfitting his ships, the Jews of Spain, stunned by calamity, were mournfully packing their belongings. They bequeathed their cemeteries to the nearby towns so that the cherished graves of their ancestors would be safe from desecration. Over the green mounds there arose poignant cries of anguish as men and women and children parted from the hallowed ground that held their past and their cherished memories. They fasted and wept and left their beloved Spain on the anniversary of the destruction of the Temple in Jerusalem. And at dawn of the following morning, August 3, 1492, Columbus sailed from Palos. The ships of weeping exiles passed the ships adventure-bound.

The destinies of the exiles and the discoverers were curiously intertwined. For well over a century Jewish scholars, scientists, cartographers, cosmographers, mathematicians and travelers had labored to pave the way for the drama that was being acted out on the high seas in the year of miracles. Mobile adventurers and sedentary scholars had given the fruit of their talents that the oceans might be spanned and the terrors of fear and superstition dispelled. At Majorca there was a famous school of Jewish scientists. From there Master Jacob was summoned by Prince Henry the Navigator to direct the Academy of Navigation at Sagres. The maps of Cresques lo Juheu were the most famous in the world. John II of Portugal called together a Junta of mathematicians and astronomers to codify the latest scientific information. A member of this Junta, Master Joseph, a Jew, was sent to Guinea in 1485 to test out the theories that these research scholars had developed and the system of calculating latitude by measuring the height of the sun at noon. This mathematical Junta of experts relied largely on the famous pioneering work, the *Almanach Perpetuum* of a great Jewish scholar, Abraham Zacuto. Abraham Zacuto and his pupil and disciple and translator, Joseph Vizinho, were at the apex.

There were many, many others. Mecia de Viladestes, *juif cosmographe.* Gabriel de Vallsecha, whose map became famous because it was used by Americus Vespucius. There was Pedro Nunes, author of *Dos Crepusculos.* Little wonder that La Roncière, eminent French scholar of the Bibliothèque Nationale, refers to Jewish scholars as "the bedrock of the great discoveries, from the voyage around Africa to the discovery of the New World."[1]

The close and intimate collaboration of Columbus and the Jews is an old story. Recent studies by eminent scholars have added to our knowledge. It is not enough to point out that Jews were among those present at the moment of discovery. Theirs was a role of creative participation. The mariners who accompanied Columbus were no strangers to the portolani, the astrolabes and the weather charts of Jewish scientists.[2, 2a] The moot question of the derivation of Columbus is still unresolved. There is no question, however, about some of the men who accompanied him. One historian, Henri Harrisse, categorically states: "D'abord se trouvaient sur les caravelles de Colomb un grande nombre de Juifs . . ." Of the eighty-seven names of crew members identified by one scholar, there are many names which appeared on the Inquisition lists. Some of these names are familiar: Luis de Torres, linguist; Alonso de la Calle, named for Jew's Lane which was his address; Rodrigo Sanchez; Maestre Bernal, ship's surgeon; Dr. Marco, surgeon. They were members of every crew. For among the *degradados*, men with a prison record, there were relapsed Jews who were impressed as seamen. And Columbus, who so delighted in befuddling his contemporaries, was the hero of a song which contained the lines—

Quexoso del amirante
este español judaizante.

The historic voyage, begun on the ninth day of Ab ended on Hoshana Rabbah, the twenty-first day of Tishri, a day of rejoicing during the Sukkot festival when the Temple was bedecked with twigs of willow and the altar reverently and joyously adorned. The Expulsion had fallen on a day of mourning. The Discovery was made on a day of rejoicing. Was there ever a better omen in history? The landfall was marked by thanksgiving. Then Columbus called two men to his side—Rodrigo Descoredo and Rodrigo Sanchez. Solemnly he bade them to bear witness to his discovery. Now emissaries were chosen to serve as envoys to the newly discovered land. They were Luis de Torres and Rodrigo de Jerez. And it is recorded further that Luis de Torres tried both Hebrew and Arabic on the stalwart redskins—but to no avail. Luis made an important agricultural discovery of a certain grain called "maiz." "And so was introduced to the white man a plant which has since become, from the standpoint of total production, the second most important food plant in the world."[3]

Columbus duly reported his discoveries. He wrote detailed letters to two Jews who had assisted him when, poverty-stricken and discouraged, he was prepared to abandon all hope of finding a sponsor for his dream. The letters to Gabriel Sanchez and Luis de Santangel are the priceless records of the dawn of American history. On his way back to Spain Columbus was perforce driven to seek refuge in Portugal. The Jews of Portugal had seen the handwriting on the wall. They were living under the threat of immediate expulsion. They heard the momentous news, which Columbus brought back, with bated breath. Was there sanctuary for the Jews and Marranos on the western shores of the great Atlantic Ocean? The Portuguese were spurred to undertake voyages of their own. Vasco da Gama was chosen to head an expedition to the Indies. Then Abraham Zacuto, noted Jewish astronomer, was called in to furnish the needed scientific information. Zacuto in the presence of the entire crew briefed the navigators.[4] On this eastward voyage, like the westward one just completed by Columbus, there were *degradados* and New Christians among the personnel. Soon after they set out adventuring they captured a seasoned navigator, a Polish Jew named Gaspar Judeo (later called Gaspar da Gama in tribute to his chief) who became Vasco da Gama's right-hand man. So it came to pass that Gaspar Judeo became the first Jew in South American history. For when Vasco da Gama returned to Portugal in August of 1499 from the Indies, a new voyage was under way—this time to the westward. Pedro Álvares Cabral was chosen to head a thirteen-ship armada. Twelve hundred men had been assembled to man the ships. Gaspar Judeo was appointed as one of the two official interpreters. But unofficially this seasoned sailor was to serve as both adviser and navigator. He had earned a reputation as a man of parts. Gaspar Judeo had on the expedition some coreligionists to whom if he chose he could speak Hebrew. Cabral's Brazilian landfall took place in April of 1500. Of the *degradados* in the various crews, some jumped ship and others were left behind.

Now there began a period of exploration, discovery and settlement in which the Jews played an active role. Spain was well launched. Portugal entered the race for a western empire. The treaty of Tordesillas drawn up in 1494 divided the spheres of influence of the two nations. Portugal shrouded her preparations and her accounts of the voyages in a fog of secrecy and mystery. Out of that fog prominent men have now emerged, rescued from oblivion by Prestage and Greenlee and other scholars.[5] Foremost of Brazilian pioneers was a wealthy New Christian of Lisbon whom the king called "*cavaleiro de nosa casa*"—Fernando de Loronha or Fernão Noronha. A man of action, charming, personable, likable, was this Marrano who remained at heart a loyal Jew. Loronha now called together a group of fellow converts and proposed a bold plan—a voyage of their own to the New World. He bought a ship and renamed it the *Judea*. He discovered a harbor in southern Brazil and named it Cananea. Is there any doubt where his innermost thoughts lay? Or of his allegiance to his ancient religion? In addition to the *Judea*, Loronha owned four other vessels. An agreement involving exploration and settlements in the new land was now drawn up between King Manuel and Loronha. "And the King of Portugal leased lands which were discovered for him to certain New Christians . . ." reads the record of this transaction. These settlers undertook "to discover each year three hundred leagues." They further agreed to erect a fort on their land and to remain there for at least three years. Loronha paid handsomely for this concession. The expedition had a famous man along, one of its leaders was Americus Vespucius whose name is now attached to all the land comprising the Western Hemisphere. There is one eminent scholar, Dr. William B. Greenlee, who suggests that if that honor was a reward for exploring the coast of Brazil, it was to Loronha that the credit may well belong and "his name rather than that of Vespucci might have been placed on the early maps of America."[6]

Fernando Loronha had to be content with an island off the coast of Brazil which to this day bears his name. The initial Loronha voyage was made in 1501-1502. The following year, twenty-four New Christian settlers built a fort, the first in Brazil, and named it Cape Frio.

The American Jewish chronicle has ancient roots.[7]

The Holy Office of the Inquisition was seeking out its victims. Frantically the victims and the hunted sought means of escape and a place of refuge. Jews took to caravels and barcos in relatively large numbers. They were quick to throw off their crypto-Jewish role. The Inquisition lost no time in setting up branch offices in the New World. Business in *conversos* was booming. In 1537 the "Inquisitors of the Indies" were so swamped that they had to appeal for papal help. In South America, in the West Indies, in Mexico, even in the far-off Philippine Islands, there is a long and blood-stained record of early pioneering by Jews, of Jewish martyrdom. But the numbers of Jewish pioneers swelled and the refugees from the Inquisition and the displaced persons who owed their status to the Edicts of Expulsion would not be deterred from seeking sanctuary. From the first there were men from lands other than the Iberian Peninsula. Gaspar Judeo had many successors. The tendency to describe Jewish immigration to the Western Hemisphere in terms of strata and waves is, like all generalizations and oversimplifications, an erroneous practice. No matter what land a man came from, the common denominators at work were the same. Social rejection and social hostility, persecution and expulsion are leveling agents.

There was occupational diversity. Jews owned large sugar plantations. They cultivated tobacco. They exported Brazilian dyewood. In the vicinity of Bahia there were some two hundred Jewish-owned sugar mills at the end of the first eventful century of Brazilian history.[8] Even far to the north, it was Juan Sanchez of Saragossa, a secret Jew, who had a monopoly on trade in the land that Columbus had discovered. Gradually in addition to the planter class there developed in Jewish society of the New World the merchant and the financier, the farmer and the artisan. *Loronhaland* prospered and as the news trickled back more and more crypto-Jews joined their kinsmen. Men and goods flowed steadily across the ocean. In addition to dyewood, there was a brisk transoceanic trade in marmalade and wheat, in salted meats and felt hats and sugar. Raw materials poured into the ports of Europe and the finished products were carried back to Brazil and other colonies. Scholars and grammarians, physicians and poets were transplanted on the barcos and the caravels that breasted the waters of the vast ocean. Side by side with accelerated economic and industrial development there grew up dynamic cultural patterns whose activities centered around the "esnoga," as the synagogue was popularly called. The marrying and the feasting, the mourning and the fasting were centered there. Group discipline and group folkways stemmed from the religious life of the transplanted Jewish communities. It was the social agency through which the Jewish group met the impact of life in a new setting and through which it imposed the attitudes Jews were expected to adopt toward their government and their Christian neighbors.

In the larger sense the life and the tempo of a transplanted Jewish community derived its pattern from the government. Under comparatively friendly nations, Jewish settlers prospered. Under hostile rule, their activities were circumscribed and their individual lives soon began to resemble, in insecurity and in nagging anxiety, the life they had left behind in Europe. As old hostilities and aggressions were transplanted from Europe to America, Jews had often under Spanish or Portuguese regimes to go into hiding again. Native Americans became crypto-Jews. Under the Dutch and under the English it was another story. When the Dutch gained a foothold in Brazil, there was rejoicing in Jewish hearts and homes. Then the thriving Amsterdam Jewry sent settlers of stature and eminence to the Brazilian colonies. But when the Portuguese recaptured Recife in 1654 evil times befell its Jews. Five thousand Jewish colonists left Recife. Some under the leadership of the scholar Aboab went back to Holland. Others found a haven in Dutch Guiana. Still others wended their way northward to New Amsterdam. There began a new chapter in the New World Chronicle.

Between 1621, when Elias Legardo came to Virginia, and 1654, when the *Peartree* brought Jacob Barsimson to New Amsterdam, there were scattered Jewish settlers along the north Atlantic seaboard. But the group from Brazil was the first to migrate as a unit composed of families.

For the new settlers were "big and little." They could not pay for their passage and were in financial straits from the start. They had been promised pecuniary help from their kinsmen in Holland who knew of the misfortunes that had dogged them. But it came too late. So David Israel, Moses Ambrosius and Asser Levy were thrown into debtor's jail. To Peter Stuyvesant and some of his associates the mere presence of these "godless rascals" was an affront. But to have them "healthy but poor" was adding insult to injury. However, despite vigorous protests and heated complaints that these Jewish immigrants be expelled, the directors of the Dutch West India Company, with an eye to their profits and their business relations with wealthy Amsterdam Jews, allowed them to remain. They advised the irascible Stuyvesant to ignore the Jews. But the Jews would not and could not be ignored. In 1655 they petitioned for the right to buy "a burying place for their nation." They secured trading privileges. They won the right to bear arms. Jews won a permanent place for themselves and remained.

In the spring of 1658 the residents of Newport witnessed the arrival of fifteen Jewish families. It was a village then dating back to 1639 when William Coddington and a handful of settlers chose that beautiful harbor for their home. In 1646 the first ship was built and launched there. When the Jewish settlers came from Holland, they brought with them, along with their household goods, the rites of the Masonic Order. In the house of Mordecai Campanal the first three degrees of the order were administered. Soon there were enough Jewish residents in Newport to have a street called *Jew's Street.* Nor was Newport unique in having Jewish residents. In nearby Boston, in 1674, Rowland Gideon's name appeared on its first tax list. Later he and a partner named Barruch sued a man for £100 and in invoking justice pleaded that the same law be applied for the Israelite as for any sojourner in the land. This was not always the rule. The Maryland Toleration Act of 1649 provided that no person who professed belief in Jesus Christ should be molested, which did not protect non-Christians.

To the south it was said that "the Jews so swarm" as to be a menace to the English. There was active trade between South Carolina and Barbados, where Jewish settlers could be found. When John Locke drew up a constitution for the Carolinas, he carefully inserted a clause for the protection of "Jews, heathens and other dissenters." Nor was Locke the only one to raise his voice for toleration. Roger Williams wrote a pamphlet in 1649 titled *The Bloudy Tenent of Persecution . . .*, which included a plea for the Jews.

Hebraism and Puritanism had much in common.[8a] Jews and their influence were in the minds of the earliest settlers on the Atlantic seaboard. The Old Testament was a living tradition in the homes of New Eng-

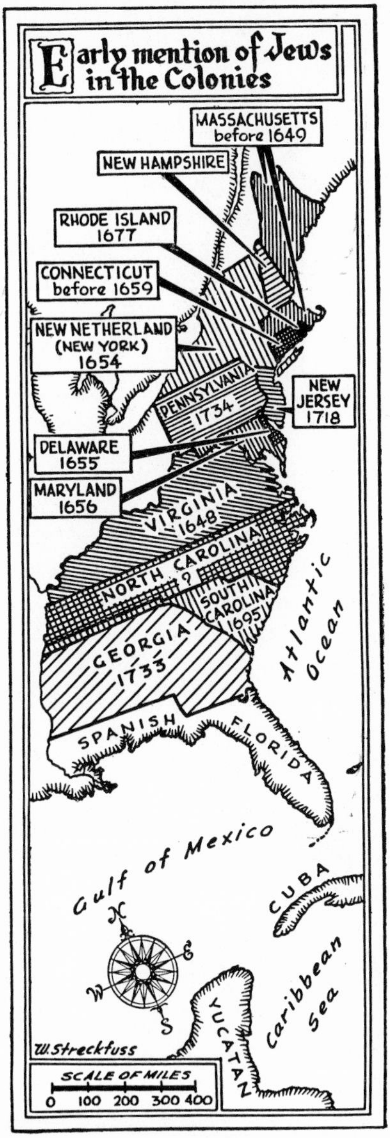
Early mention of Jews in the Colonies
MASSACHUSETTS before 1649
NEW HAMPSHIRE
RHODE ISLAND 1677
CONNECTICUT before 1659
NEW NETHERLAND (NEW YORK) 1654
PENNSYLVANIA 1734
NEW JERSEY 1718
DELAWARE 1655
MARYLAND 1656
VIRGINIA 1648
NORTH CAROLINA ?
SOUTH CAROLINA 1695
GEORGIA 1733
SPANISH FLORIDA
Atlantic Ocean
Gulf of Mexico
CUBA
YUCATAN
Caribbean Sea
N
E
W
S
W. Streckfuss
SCALE OF MILES
0 100 200 300 400

landers. Prophets, major and minor, had their namesakes in almost every home. Hebrew was looked upon as a key to the sacred Scriptures. It was early included in the Harvard curriculum. The Restoration of Jews to England was followed with the greatest interest. The legend identifying American Indians with the Ten Lost Tribes of Israel found ready acceptance. A code of laws adopted in 1634 was called "Draft of the Model of Moses, his Judicials." In 1658, Plymouth adopted the Jewish code as a model. Increase and Cotton Mather preached and wrote about Jews, always with an eye to their conversion and absorption. The *Bay Psalm Book* was the first book to be published in the English colonies. Jews were prayed for, appealed to, preached over. In Connecticut, as in other New England colonies, Jews were expelled and fined for Sabbatarian conflicts. In New York, where the English had supplanted the Dutch, the Jews were tolerated in the quiet profession of their religion, but as late as 1684 a Charter of Liberties and Privileges limited its benefits to those who professed Christianity. Nevertheless, Jewish pioneers in America pursued their course with unyielding tenacity. Gradually there emerged patterns of Jewish communal life. There developed areas of intercolonial communication between the scattered groups of Jewish settlers.

Soon the seaboard was conquered. Through virgin forests, over mountain passes, along arterial rivers, in wagons and boats and barges, on horseback or afoot, intrepid Jews, along with their Christian neighbors, pursued the course of inevitable expansion. In an ox train of eleven families that reached Easton, Pennsylvania, Meyer and Rachel Hart were among those present. Joseph Simon was in Lancaster before the town was laid out. He was followed by Dr. Isaac Cohen from Hamburg, who came "to practice physic and the art of healing." The eighteenth century found many Jews throughout the colony of Pennsylvania. Philadelphia was the hub and there were prosperous Jewish merchants who led lives of leisure in settings that were gay and opulent. German Jews were becoming more numerous. The Gratz family reached the apex of the pre-Revolutionary social pyramid. A generation of native American Jews had grown up in New York and in Newport and in Philadelphia. Their portraits were painted by Gilbert Stuart and other artists of note. Their sons were often sent abroad or tutored by specialists at home. They had large estates. They owned ships and imported brocades and laces and velvets from Europe for their personal adornment.

The last seaboard colony to be settled was Georgia. In 1732, James Oglethorpe gathered some English debtors, collected funds from charitably disposed individuals and started a colony. Three Jewish members of a committee for collecting funds for Georgia diverted some of the money for the transporting of twelve families of German Jews for whom they chartered a ship. The trustees were indignant. At the same time about forty Portuguese Jews of some means decided to migrate to Georgia. To the sponsors of Georgia there was no difference between the two groups. They could not distinguish between the Sephardim and Ashkenazim.[8b] There were loud and angry protests. "Georgia will soon become a Jewish colony," wrote one unhappy complainant. But Oglethorpe, unlike Stuyvesant, was impressed by the thrift and industry of the Jewish settlers. The Jews remained. They bought land. They introduced viniculture. They helped develop the silk industry. Dr. Nunez earned the gratitude of the settlers by his unselfish devotion to the sick of the new colony. New names were added to the roster of early Jewish pioneers—Sheftall, Machado, Nunez, De Lyon, Olivera. While to the north names like Gratz and Franks and Levy and Simon and Salomon soon merited respect and attention.

Inland trade expanded. Boats laden with merchandise sailed the Ohio to the Mississippi. Vast landholdings were acquired by Jews. Many partnerships with Christians were entered into. Jewish settlers and entrepreneurs carried on trade with the Indians, tilled land, planted vineyards, sailed ships, established many new industries vital to colonial economy. The United Company of Spermaceti Candlers was but one vital industry brought to America by Jews. The Rivera family had learned the art of candlemaking in Spain and had cherished the skills they knew and had transplanted them. Jacob Rodrigues Rivera opened the first factory in Newport. It soon supplied candles to all the colonies and many lands abroad. In 1761 a syndicate of Spermaceti Candlers was established. Among the Jewish firms which belonged to that select group were Aaron Lopez, Moses Lopez, Naphthali Hart and Company, and J. Rivera and Company. But they were not all rich. Analysis of the occupational diversity proves their versatility as well as their differences in income levels. So among Jewish freemen as early as 1687 we find chandlers and perukemakers, butchers, watchmakers and vendue-masters. On the eve of the Revolution they ranged from mendicants to merchant princes, from unskilled laborers to physicians, from peddlers to shipowners. Jewish shipowners signed the Non-Importation Resolutions and when hostilities began readily turned their ships over to the patriot cause. There were but few Tories among them.

In the Revolutionary War Jews fought with courage, yet with a dignified insistence on their peculiar needs. In 1776 a Jewish soldier petitioned to be excused from the performance of military duties on the Sabbath. His request was granted subject to his performance of "his full tour of duty" at other times. We know that men considered it a point of honor to observe their dietary laws. Some Jews carried special knives for the ritual slaughter of animals. Others abstained from eating pork; among them Reuben Etting, who enlisted in Baltimore as soon as the news of

Lexington had reached him. He was captured by the British. His captors, learning that he was Jewish, gave him only pork to eat. His fellow prisoners kept him alive by sharing their food with him. But he gradually starved and died shortly after he was exchanged.

There were soldiers in the ranks and officers. There were financiers and victualers. Women smuggled supplies and food to captured patriots. Men gave freely of their lives and of their possessions. It was their war. The members of the Congregation Shearith Israel saw their rabbi, Gershom Mendes Seixas,[8d] depart with the Scrolls and ceremonials and candlesticks rather than let them fall into Tory hands. Colonel Nathan Bush described the Battle of Long Island of 1776, which began in a watermelon patch. In his plan to defend New York, Major General Lee submitted to General Washington the use of the Jewish cemetery for the locating of a strategic battery. Philip Moses Russell, surgeon's mate of the 2nd Virginia Regiment, starved with the rest of the men at Valley Forge. In the Virginia ranks were many Jewish soldiers as well as a Captain Jacob Cohen. Francis Salvador of South Carolina was the first casualty of the Revolution for his colony. When in July of 1776 news came that the British fleet was steaming toward harbor, Salvador "forthwith mounted his horse, and galloped to Major Andrew Williamson's residence, twenty-eight miles from thence." It was in this campaign that Salvador lost his life.

To the north in Newport, Aaron Lopez sacrificed his ships and goods with a willing heart. The Pinto brothers of Connecticut left Yale College to enlist. Two of the brothers were wounded in defending New Haven from the enemy. William Pinto, a third brother, noted for his beautiful penmanship, was asked to transcribe the Declaration of Independence for President Daggett of Yale. Their parents, Jacob and Thankful Pinto, could point with legitimate pride to the record of their sons in the Revolution. David Salisbury Franks was one of the most noted Jewish patriots. He served under Benedict Arnold at West Point. When Arnold's treason was discovered, Franks wrote to General Washington demanding a thorough inquiry into his own record, which was investigated and proved completely without blemish. In 1781 Robert Morris sent Franks as confidential messenger to John Jay at Madrid and to Benjamin Franklin at Paris. George Washington lived in the home of Colonel Isaac Franks. The "Calendar of Gratz Papers," the more than three thousand items in the Sheftall papers, the *Letterbook* of Haym Salomon, could literally fill volumes. In three years there were recorded seventy-five transactions between Robert Morris and Haym Salomon.

That is the record, condensed, of the Jews in the Revolutionary War. There were three Seixas brothers who were captains in the War of 1812. There was Major Mordecai Myers who saved two hundred soldiers and marines from wrecked ships off Sacket's Harbor and who was severely wounded later at the battle of Chrysler's Farm. There was Isaac de Young who fought in many major engagements, becoming a close friend of General Winfield Scott. Judah Touro, distinguished for his many philanthropies, fought under General Andrew Jackson and incurred serious wounds.

Commodore Uriah P. Levy, soldier, humanitarian and ardent champion of Jewish rights, rose to prominence in the navy. In the Texan War of Independence, there are Jewish records of superb heroism. There were thousands of Jews on both sides in the War Between the States. A young soldier wounded seven times and promoted on the battlefield. A young lieutenant killed while rallying his company, the colors of his regiment falling from his lifeless hands. Leopold Karpeles, color sergeant of the 59th Infantry Regiment, was awarded the Congressional Medal of Honor for saving a part of the Union Army during the disastrous retreat of the Battle of the Wilderness. A sixteen-year-old boy, Benjamin P. Levy, saved the steamer *Express* when attacked by a Confederate gunboat. There was Private David Obranski, whose heroic exploits at the Battles of Shiloh and Vicksburg earned him the Congressional Medal of Honor. Dr. Jonathan Phineas Horwitz was the Civil War chief of the United States Bureau of Medicine and Surgery. He was responsible for the plans that led to the building of the Naval Hospital in Philadelphia. He discharged his duties as a medical officer with such humanity and such dispatch that he was commended at the close of the war by a unanimous vote of Congress. And so the record unrolls with honored names inscribed in the imperishable archives of the American nation. From "the fighting Jew," Sam Dreben, of World War I, to the nineteen-year-old private of the 743rd Tank Battalion in World War II who, like Paul Revere, rode alone at night through the snow-banked passes of the Ardennes to round up his regiment during the Battle of the Bulge—to be cited posthumously for valor—it is a treasured legacy for all Americans to cherish.

The Revolution and the Declaration of Independence, the Constitution and the Bill of Rights were dearly earned. Ideologies born of the revolutions in America and in France opened new social vistas. The American Jew was integrated. It was his land. He had fought for it and members of his group had died for it. The patriots whose monuments dot our land were his friends and intimates. Thomas Jefferson was more than a name. Some Jews knew him. More were aware of his noble principles. Religious toleration was one of the cornerstones of his philosophy. In his own state, Virginia, the religious issue was put to the test in 1776. In that year a Constitutional Convention met to draw up a constitution for the state of Virginia. Heated debate surrounded the provisions concerned with toleration. Madison opposed the use of the word "toleration." Freedom of worship was a right inherent to all mankind, he insisted. It was the Jeffersonian doctrine. It triumphed. In 1779, Thomas Jefferson introduced a bill for the establishing of religious freedom in Virginia. It was a broad program within whose framework people of every faith were safe. Its enactment in 1785 was a momentous forward step in the history of religious emancipation. The first land outside the United States where its influence was felt was France. "The Virginia Act for religious freedom has been received with infinite approbation," Jefferson wrote to Madison in 1786, calling attention to the fact that the French Encyclopedists had inserted it into their epoch-making work.

Jews were vocal in their insistence on equality. Wherever disqualifying laws operated they were indefatigable in behalf of their removal. So in 1797, Barnard Gratz and his son-in-law, Solomon Etting, were hard at work in Maryland to change the existing law. William Pinkney drew up the *Jew Bill*, which would have made it possible for Maryland Jews to hold office. It failed, but the fight went on. In 1818 the Jews of Maryland were fortunate in getting another champion to carry on their fight. Thomas Kennedy, who knew well and associated with many Jews in Baltimore, ardently advocated the *Jew Bill*. He was ably assisted by Colonel Worthington, who urged passage of the bill because of the many Jewish officers who had contributed to the Revolution "who were nearly all cut off and destroyed early in the war." A compromise measure was finally adopted by Maryland in 1825. In North Carolina, despite a disqualifying clause, Jacob Henry was twice elected to the state legislature. But it took many years and much hard work, including the impassioned editorials of Isaac Leeser, to secure a clause in the new state constitution of 1868 which removed all civil disabilities. In New Hampshire civil disabilities directed against Jews and Catholics were on the statute books until 1876. The Board of Delegates of American Israelites, organized in 1859, was from the first an agency of vigilance alert to every infraction of rights of Jews, an avowed advocate of equality, an eager and zealous guardian for maintaining the position and status of Jews in America and abroad.

Estimates of numbers of Jews in America have always been haphazard. At the opening of the nineteenth century there were some three thousand known Jews in the United States. By 1802 the Ashkenazic group of Philadelphia founded the Congregation Rodeph Shalom. By 1847 one authority stated that their numbers had grown to fifty thousand. There was no hard and fast distinction between them on the basis of origin, as has generally been assumed. It is true that by and large the Sephardim preferred to have their sons and daughters marry within their circle. Yet they welcomed and often favored the accretions to their society which "intermarriage" brought. Haym Salomon had no trouble in wooing and wedding a daughter of a Sephardic family. The favorite son-in-law of

Rabbi Gershom Mendes Seixas was Israel Baer Kursheedt, an immigrant from Germany.[9] If the division be drawn, then it may be drawn with greater justification between the native American Jew and the one of foreign birth. In the letters and diaries, in the journals and scrapbooks of the nineteenth century there emerges a subtle psychological difference in the ideas and attitudes of the native Jew which separates him from the ideologies of the transplanted Jew. Often and with justice, the teachers and rabbis and editors who came to America called attention to the fact that in their religious observances the native Jews of each area partook of the color of the Christian ideology which was geographically nearest them. None more astute than Isaac M. Wise, who said that "there were Episcopalian Jews in New York, Quaker Jews in Philadelphia, Huguenot Jews in Charleston . . . everywhere according to the prevailing sect." Isaac Leeser, beloved editor of the *Occident*, stanch defender of Orthodoxy, on the other hand, charged the Reform group with deliberately seeking to set up in America "a new system which is to be acceptable to gentiles."

The economic activities of Jewish settlers in the early and middle years of the nineteenth century are manifold. There were the hawkers and walkers, the lowly peddlers who began with the few commodities they could carry on their backs. After a while, when success rewarded their industry, they progressed to the horse-and-wagon stage. Then—happy day—a little store in a small community. At first a solitary existence with living quarters back of the store or above it. Then, with growing prosperity, the merchant would send for his family, for his friends. Gradually a little community evolved and with it a form of social organization. A place to worship. A place to bury the dead. Group life to meet recreational needs. Mutual assistance or benevolent societies to distribute the burdens of caring for the indigent and the sick. An emergency fund for the use of mendicant Jews—for that was always the simplest solution, to send them journeying to another community. A fund for widows and orphans and for the dowries of poor girls. In addition to the itinerant peddler and merchant there were artisans and craftsmen. Skilled and unskilled workers were found in every community. There were men who bought and sold land and men who tilled the soil. There were men who operated barges for the dispatching of merchandise. There were millers and innkeepers and hoop-skirt manufacturers and vintners. There were physicians and professors, who taught in the medical schools in addition to having a private practice. There were brokers and financiers. There were journalists and artists and musicians and teachers in Jewish schools and academies which often served on a nonsectarian basis although nominally owned by Jews. The occupational pyramid followed largely the pattern of the greater community. The "elite" were few.

The home life of the Jewish family, on the other hand, had much to differentiate it from the home life of the Christian family. Countless writers of all faiths have testified to the sense of immigrant unity, the closeness of parents and siblings. For this there were many reasons. Whatever sense of strangeness, of isolation and cultural difference was felt outside the home, which constituted the phenomenon of "social distance" from one's non-Jewish neighbors, fell away when the individual returned home to his own. The host culture of the greater community had its own customs and holidays and calendar rhythms. The little immigrant group knew another set of calendar observances. Physicians and social workers who worked in the developing urban communities where crowding and poverty and lack of sanitation bred disease, have commented on the relative freedom from epidemic diseases in Jewish homes. This was attributed to the weekly scrubbing and cleaning, the bathing and the change of clothes that preceded the Sabbath. The periodic housecleanings before Passover and the High Holy Days and other festivals also ensured a measure of cleanliness which favored health. On the psychological side there were also important and significant practices which were salutary. The transformation of a poor, insecure, awkward immigrant into a dignified patriarch on Friday evening and Saturday was a morale-building practice which fortified him for the long days of menial tasks and degrading rounds when both poverty and lack of linguistic skills made the immigrant the butt of jokes and the target of the buffoon. Religious services at home and in the synagogue were a subtle tonic which supported flagging morale. They renewed tattered spirits and rebuilt shattered moods.

It was largely as an urban people that the Jews of America became established. The problems of urbanization were therefore increasingly their problems. This tendency to live in cities may have been a self-protective measure. For where were the descendants of the Jewish planters? Some had remained spinsters and bachelors. Others had intermarried, like members of the Mordecai and the Gratz families, and had by a process of social osmosis gradually been absorbed by their Christian in-laws. Those who remained Jews were jealous of their rights and of their cultural and religious survival. Dearly won and fought for, they cherished their status of equality. From the precarious days of Asser Levy, the battling butcher of New Amsterdam, the fight was waged unceasingly. In 1805 the members of the Congregation Shearith Israel sued Caleb Vandenburg for falsely affixing a seal on meat which resembled the one used by them to denote that it was acceptable in Jewish homes. In 1816 a Pennsylvania Jew won exemption from the Sunday statute. In 1831 the right of a Jewish witness to be excused from testifying was conceded at the discretion of the court. In 1834, Harriet Martineau was deeply impressed with the superior status of Jews in the United States and launched a vigorous campaign to secure for them the same rights in England. From Mikve Israel in Philadelphia to Bevis Marks in London was but a step. It was the French Jew, Adolphe Crémieux, speaking at an antislavery convention in London in 1840 who voiced the great truth that "All liberties are united. All persecutions are associated." Jews learned that to wage war for their own rights was not enough. The fight for freedom and for emancipation was soon to merge with the great issue that was before the United States—the Abolitionist issue. We learn from the *Allgemeine Zeitung des Judentums* that as early as 1838 a Jewish planter of Jamaica celebrated Queen Victoria's accession to the throne of England by freeing his slaves on Coronation Day. He was the first to take the step. Rabbi Bernhard Felsenthal was to write one day in *Die Juden und die Sclaverei* that the majority of American Jews were antislavery in sentiment. He was right. For the majority was in the north, composed of the poor and the insecure. By and large the economic status and geographic location of the Jews determined their ideologies. On the slavery issue many Jews hedged. Others were inscrutable. Some salved conscience by freeing their slaves on their deathbed or posthumously. Others emancipated their personal servants during their lifetime. Still others launched into the campaign to free all slaves with an impetuosity and an abandon which earned for them the contempt of some and the endorsement of other Americans. Ernestine Rose, a Polish Jewess, campaigned for emancipation with such zeal that she was called "Queen of the Platforms." The *Liberator* saluted this eager radical for her courage and her daring. Freely did Ernestine Rose ascribe her ardor to the fact that she was "a daughter of . . . the downtrodden and persecuted people called the Jews." Moritz Pinner was an associate and coworker of Wendell Phillips, William Lloyd Garrison and many others. As editor of the outspoken abolition paper, the *Kansas Post*, as one of the men who distributed that incendiary book, *The Impending Crisis*, as delegate to the National Republican Convention that nominated Lincoln, Pinner was nationally known. Lincoln sought to reward him by a consular post. He chose to enlist in the Union Army instead. Soon many other immigrant Jews joined the Abolitionist crusade. The conscience of American Jews was stirred and prodded from the pulpit. There was Rabbi Felsenthal, who went from Madison, Indiana, to Chicago, to write and to preach against slavery. There was David Einhorn, who had to flee an angry mob because of his antislavery views. August Bondi was an associate of John Brown. With other immigrants from Germany, Bohemia and Russia, Jews took part in the forays that were the preludes to war. Undeterred by flying bullets these men were in the thick of it, their spirits high. *"Sof odem moves,"* said one of the Jewish associates of John Brown—"man is born to die"—shrugging his shoulders at danger. Another immigrant, Isidor Bush, rallied his countrymen of every faith about him by pleading that they must all unite to put down slavery. Sabato Morais, too, dared to urge a cause which was far from popular in his congregation. From 1851 on he was the unyielding foe of slavery. His "burning sermons" continued in spite of the mutterings and the averted heads of the wealthy and the influential. The logic of freedom was inexorable.

For a generation, from 1859 to 1878, the Board of Delegates of American Israelites was the sensitive sounding-board of American Jewish citizens. It was a sentinel alert for signs of infringement of Jewish rights. The organization grew out of a long-felt need. As far back as 1840, when the evil known as the "Damascus Affair"[9a] had befallen them, Jews felt the need for concerted action to protect group interests. On September 4, 1840, the Jews of Richmond had petitioned our State Department for intervention in behalf of their persecuted coreligionists in the East. It was one meeting of many. Ten years later scattered meetings all over the land were decrying discrimination in Switzerland. Rabbi Isaac M. Wise and other Jewish leaders tried vigorously to rally American public opinion. The Jewish press, too, entered the arena. Jewish rights were vigorously asserted. Discrimination and persecution were stubbornly assailed.

With accretion in numbers, Jews now had a number of their own publications edited by men of outstanding ability. These periodicals are our windows to the past.

American Jewish journalism had its birth in 1823 when the *Jew* first saw light of day. Its purpose was to keep the Jews of America safe from the blandishments of Christian missionaries. It lasted a scant two years. *Israel's Herold* was the abortive effort of Isidor Bush to transplant the brave new ideologies of revolutionary Europe to America. It was short-lived. The first major weekly of Jewish interest was the *Asmonean* founded by Robert Lyon. In its pages luminaries like Isaac M. Wise and Max Lilienthal found a channel for the expression of opinion. Here dogma and fantasy found free play. Its editor could claim for his paper, from 1849 on, a wide and nonsectarian audience. According to his somewhat bombastic claim, it was "the Organ of the 200,000 Jews of America" and of many Unitarians and Christian immigrants from Germany as well. This editorial exaggeration did not detract from the usefulness of the *Asmonean*. From its inception it continued to rally American Jews to forget their differences, to stand together as Jews, to fight against intolerance no matter where found. Robert Lyon deplored Jewish "cliquism." He sought to unite the disparate groups. He advocated such communal institutions as hospitals and organized philanthropy. He pleaded for idealism and deplored all forms of skepticism. He clung tenaciously to the rock of Maimonidean Judaism and rejoiced in all signs of its renaissance in America. It is a sprightly paper whose pages still arouse reader interest. Nevertheless, the dean of American Jewish journalism was the gifted and energetic Isaac Leeser, who came to Richmond from Germany at the age of eighteen. In

1843 he founded the *Occident and American Jewish Advocate*. For twenty-five years he continued to serve as its editor, lending to it all the zeal and energy, lavishing on it all the love and care that other men devote to their families.

In the pages of the *Occident* the times are recorded. It is a glistening mirror for posterity, reflecting deed and thought. Here we trace the ideas that stirred the men and women of another generation. We follow the growth of congregations and their auxiliary schools. We note the development of hospitals and homes for the indigent and aged and provisions for the care of orphans. Scattered congregations come to know each other. School curricula in various parts of the country are described. Here are news items of Jews in many parts of the world. Palestine is a topic of frequent occurrence. Pleas are made to look upon that ancient land as more than a dumping ground for the poor and the aged. Race prejudice is analyzed and ways of meeting it are discussed. Jewish authors are encouraged. Because of this editorial hospitality, Grace Aguilar and others became household names in many an American Jewish home. Current events are woven through the fabric of its pages. Names dear to all Americans are introduced. So in 1865 the Jews of America are taught "How to Mourn" in connection with the death of their martyred President. The beauties of the Hebrew language are extolled. Fads and fancies like spiritualism are noted and decried. Readers of the *Occident* are urged to read more Jewish authors and to support a Jewish Publication Society. The need for a Jewish College is emphasized again and again. The contemporary Jewish press is welcomed and encouraged. Every means is exerted to prevent Jews straying from the fold. Religious and social pressure is exerted on those marginal groups of Jewish society which are the first to merge with the host culture. The editor and his contributors are "lovers of ancient usages." All modern trends are viewed with suspicion as leading to intermarriage and eventual extinction. The *Occident* is a listening post. It is alert to sound the alarm when Jewish rights are invaded. Should a Thanksgiving Proclamation specify that America is a Christian nation, should a public official overstep the bounds of propriety, should missionary zeal make inroads into the ranks of our children—the *Occident* vigorously protests the violation and heatedly insists on remedial measures.

Those rival editors whose opinions are at variance with Leeser's are viewed with a jaundiced eye. Leeser warns the Jewish journalistic fraternity to remember that "no editor writing in America should forget the comities of life." He needs to remind himself of that from time to time, when the heat of controversy over *Minhag America* as introduced by Isaac M. Wise seems likely to tear the social fabric of Jewish life in two. Restraint is a virtue which he, too, must needs practice. Yet for him Judaism remains a discipline which rests on three concepts—conformity, ceremony, orthodoxy. Still the inevitability of social change frustrates the fundamentalist crusader. As his days draw to a close, Isaac Leeser launches his "darling project"—Maimonides College. This in addition to the sponsorship of the Hebrew Education Society of Philadelphia and the Board of Delegates of American Israelites. Isaac Leeser became the provost or president of the college.[10] On the faculty were Aaron S. Bettelheim, Marcus M. Jastrow and the wise and gentle and scholarly Sabato Morais. The load was too much for one man. Isaac Leeser lived but three short months as head of this beloved project. He died in 1868 and so in 1873 did Maimonides College.

In Isaac M. Wise, Isaac Leeser had found an adversary worthy of his own doughty talents and genius. For Wise was the spearhead of the Reform movement in America. The story of the growth and development of the Reform movement, from its native roots in Charleston to the transplanted ones in Cincinnati and elsewhere, is told elsewhere in this volume.[10a] But the social implications of this dichotomy in Jewish life are significant and persist to our day.

In order to understand the psychological and sociological aspects of this rift in American Jewish life, we must go back to trace the beginnings of these ideologies. We must be aware of the types of immigrants who came to America in their European frame of reference and in terms of their goals in America. Basically all migratory patterns include two motives—(1) the escape pattern; (2) the magnet pattern. An appraisal of the chronicle of Jews in America demonstrates that, while certain geographic and economic trends predominated at various periods of our history, there was at no time in American history a clear-cut stratification based only on geographic origins. If anything, separation was economic in origin. Jews, owing to their dispersion and to their perennial troubles, have always been a highly mobile people. Economic and political hazards which created insecurity acted as a spur to their social mobility. But wealth was everywhere the social yardstick. Wealthy Jews had early evolved a simple pattern of philanthropy. This was to facilitate the emigration of the newcomer and the poor. This was true in the more established communities in Europe. Dutch Jews of Sephardic origin were reluctant to accept Polish Jews who flocked to Holland for sanctuary. Even great east European scholars were treated as menials and then encouraged to migrate. The first Jewish settlers of Georgia were twelve families of German Jews who had made their way to London and who were hustled out of the country to the new colony by a committee of three gentlemen, acting for the Sephardim of England—Salvador, Baron Suasso and DaCosta.

All immigrants have the same objectives—a way of life free of hampering laws and restrictions, economic security, and a chance to live according to self-determined patterns. These tendencies are seen in Europe, in America. Persecution and the Inquisition drove Jews from the Iberian Peninsula to all parts of Europe and to all parts of the New World. The Revolution in France and its impetus toward emancipation next gave to the Jews of Europe contacts previously denied them. Mendelssohn, Lessing and Dohm were eloquent spokesmen for an enlightened attitude toward Jews. A psychological revolution in Jewish circles was the work of Mendelssohn, of Wessely.[10b] For they brought the wider knowledge of the great community to the isolated Jewish population of central Europe. Language barriers were surmounted and schooling revised. Mendelssohn brought the message of a reconciliation between loyalty to Judaism and a permissive attitude toward the acquisition of knowledge that was freely available to non-Jews. The fruits of freedom once tasted were never voluntarily relinquished. When the reaction and counterrevolution set in, emigration to America was the solution of countless central European migrants. That is why the numbers of Jews in America swelled and expanded. Many of the new immigrants were literally fellow travelers of noted Christian refugees from reaction. It was to be expected that their first efforts at acculturation in America were to be parallel to those of their enlightened non-Jewish associates. *Minhag America* was the answer. It was the bridge, so thought its founders, between two cultures. It was the practice of Judaism according to an evolving pattern based on interaction and integration in American life.

The Reform movement sought to transplant from Europe to America the cultural phenomena involved in the Enlightenment movement. It had a vigorous, enthusiastic, scholarly leadership. It had a broad program. Surveying the American scene with realism, these transplanted men—Lilienthal, Wise, Einhorn, Adler, Felsenthal, Hirsch—felt that Orthodoxy was to blame for loss of Jews to Judaism. They blamed outworn ceremonials, indifference and intermarriage. The reforms they proposed were designed to shorten the services, to reinterpret some of the outworn beliefs, to lay aside "unmeaning forms as outworn garments." Whatever their objectives, they divided American Jews into two divergent camps. Looking back over the years it is possible to see that the difficulties might have been overcome through compromise and evolution. Certainly Isaac Leeser, that gallant and stouthearted fighter for Orthodoxy, yielded at some points. For he insisted that compromise was possible. The personal contacts between him and Isaac M. Wise were, despite every handicap, stimulating and rewarding. The two men found that they had much in common. Both were concerned with making the synagogue a dynamic center of Jewish life. Both wanted a union of all factions and joined in the creation of the Board of Delegates of American Israelites, which after Leeser's death merged with the Union of American Hebrew Congregations. Both wanted a Jewish College. Leeser founded one and died. Wise founded one and lived to see it become a great training school for the Reform rabbinate—Hebrew Union College.

Stratification in Jewish life became a reality. The immigrants from Germany had had time to grow roots in America. Along the economic front they had prospered. They enjoyed all the liberties that had been hard won by the men of earlier generations—tested in the courts and tried on the battlefields. When the hour of the inevitable conflict struck and the Union was in danger, these earlier Jewish settlers had unhesitatingly plunged into the fray. Civilians became soldiers overnight. Men who were still baffled by the intricacies of the English language enlisted for combat service, emerged as seasoned veterans who had earned their right to live and vote as Americans. And while some men fought as soldiers, others, jealous of their human rights, fought against every form of discrimination. The exclusion of Jews from the chaplaincy during the Civil War brought protests from the Jewish press until the matter was rectified. When in 1862 Grant and his subordinates issued orders culminating in the infamous Order No. 11 expelling all Jews from the territories over which he had jurisdiction, a storm of protest arose in which outraged Jews and their Christian friends equally participated. Cesar Kaskel and a Jewish delegation called on Abraham Lincoln urging him to intervene, pointing out that the Jews have again sought protection in "Abraham's bosom." Lincoln revoked the offending orders. When he died the Jews of America mourned him as a father. In New York City alone seven thousand Jews marched in a solemn procession and in historic Shearith Israel, on the Sabbath following Lincoln's assassination, the Sephardic prayer for the dead was recited for the first time for one not of the Jewish faith.[11]

When Grant became President in 1869, the persecution of Jews in Rumania was the nightmare of their coreligionists the world over. Simon Wolf, who was a close friend of Grant, persuaded him to call a special Cabinet meeting to consider their plight as well as the expulsion of Jews from Russian Bessarabia. Heading our State Department was the eminent statesman, Hamilton Fish, whose exertions in behalf of the victims of persecution upheld that department's historic, humanitarian tradition. Grant's appointment of Benjamin Franklin Peixotto as consul to Rumania was token of his earnest desire to see justice done. Peixotto, son of a distinguished Jewish doctor, president of the Supreme Lodge of the B'nai B'rith, humanitarian and philanthropist, not only kept the United States informed about the bloody outrages but was instrumental in securing the calling of three International Jewish Conferences. Simon Wolf and A. S. Solomons next took up the cudgels for the victims of persecution in Russia. Again Americans were fortunate in their Secretary of State, W. M. Evarts, whose state papers are eloquent in their insistence on "the liberal sentiments of this government" and America's unyielding adherence to the principles of religious toleration. Later T. F. Bayard, John Hay, Elihu Root upheld the established American tradition. On this issue—that of universal application of justice and egalitarian principles—American Jews presented a solid front.

Each generation has its voice. Each crisis finds its spokesman. American Jewry during the middle years of the nineteenth century had spoken through Isaac Leeser. Then it found a new and a passionate pleader. In the year that Isaac Leeser founded the Hebrew Education Society, 1849, Emma Lazarus was born. Her life ended when The Jewish Theological Seminary of America was one year old, 1887. Her brief lifetime spanned two eras of Jewish life in America. Emma Lazarus spoke for two worlds. She was a native of America. What she believed in was what the Jews of America had wrought. She stood like a mourner at the bier of murdered Jews of Europe. She expressed their universal needs in *Songs of a Semite*:

> Freedom to love the law that Moses brought,
> To sing the songs of David, and to think
> The thoughts Gabirol to Spinoza taught.
> Freedom to dig the common earth, to drink
> The universal air—for this they sought
> Refuge o'er wave and continent . . .

To the victims of persecution in Russia, Emma and her sister Josephine held out eager hands in warmest welcome. "Day long I brooded upon the Passion of Israel . . . And always the patient, resolute martyr face arose in silent rebuke and defiance," wrote Josephine Lazarus. "Give me your tired, your poor, your huddled masses yearning to breathe free," Emma sang in "The New Colossus." In the *Century Magazine* and in the *American Hebrew*, Emma set forth her new philosophy of a renascent Judaism which insisted on the dignity of the individual, on the abolition of every form of discrimination, overt and covert, on absolute equality, on justice instead of pity. But that was not all. This far-seeing Jewess became an ardent disciple of George Eliot. She saw in the rebirth of Zion and in the creation of a Jewish state for the victims of persecution, a goal to which she was determined to devote the rest of her life. "I am fully persuaded," she wrote, "that all suggested solutions other than this of the Jewish problem are but temporary palliatives." There were great Americans who applauded her words. Ralph Waldo Emerson and John Burroughs and Clarence Stedman were among those who encouraged her. It was a problem of worldwide importance which had to be faced for humanity's sake.

The streets of New York and other Atlantic seaboard cities were thronged with newcomers. Abject poverty dogged their footsteps. Privation was their constant shadow. Papers and magazines began to "view with alarm" the onrushing tide of immigrants. Every new outburst of pogroms and persecution sent "hordes of destitute emigrants here." In one year, 1892, 45 per cent of the transplanted migrants needed financial assistance. The United Hebrew Charities had 23,571 clients out of a total of 52,000 who came in that year. The nightschools were crowded. And the little children thronged the public schools and the Hebrew schools. There were sounds of children practicing scales. High young voices were learning the Preamble to the Constitution and the Gettysburg Address. Patient older pupils were spelling out with work-grimed fingers the alphabet of the new freedom. The Hyman Kaplans were declaiming in thick accents the words of *America* and *The Star-Spangled Banner*. Yet always there were native Americans whose hearts beat in unison with their transplanted kinsmen. Others, viewing Jews as outsiders, soon found that the immigrant's score had a credit as well as a debit side. So George F. Parker, writing in the *Forum* in 1893 on "What Immigrants Contribute to Industry," said: "The Jewish influx from Russia has recently been unnaturally large, as the result of serious complications at home. But these people are not paupers or dependents. They are anxious for work, intelligent, quick to learn our language, and promise, in the fullness of time, to become useful additions to our population."

After the Lazarus sisters came Nina Morais and Lillian Wald and Henrietta Szold to teach the immigrants and write about them and plead their cause. Yet these foreigners brought their own leaders with them also. Young men and women of vision and education they were, who had tasted the adventure of underground resistance to czarist tyranny, who had cut their teeth on Karl Marx and whetted their intellects on Adam Smith and Ricardo. These men and women began a campaign to educate and elevate and unionize those who were sorely exploited and badly pushed around in the land of freedom and the home of opportunity.

From 1881 until 1943, when the designation "Hebrew" was ordered deleted by Earl G. Harrison, Commissioner of the Immigration and Naturalization Service of the Department of Justice, there were 2,499,154 Jewish immigrants admitted to the United States.[12, 12a] This figure is impressive. Yet it does not represent the full extent of migration to the Western Hemisphere. Statistical data, particularly for South America, are inadequate and far from exhaustive. Between 1901 and 1944, 132,970 European Jews entered Canada. This was a total of 2.22 per cent of its total number of immigrants within that span of years. Between 1901 and 1945, 50,943 Jews entered Brazil; 19,555 settled in Uruguay; 208,678 became settlers in Argentina.[13] Like their predecessors who accompanied Gaspar

Judeo and Fernão Noronha, they brought few tangible assets. But they were rich in cultural heritage.

One of their poets, Morris Rosenfeld, lyrically voiced their uncertainties. It was their theme song on the eve of the twentieth century. It is appropriate to many Jews now!

> We only are desolate. Earth, cold and stern,
> Begrudges us fiercely the home that we found.
> We journey, but no one awaits our return.
> O, tell us I pray of you, whither we are bound.[14, 14a]

They were vocal. They were articulate. They were literate. They published books and periodicals in Hebrew and in Yiddish. Since 1871, some 125 Hebrew periodicals have been published in America. A number of Yiddish and Anglo-Jewish papers have had Hebrew supplements.[15] The Yiddish press in America dates back to 1880 and to the founding of *Die Juedische Post*. A rival weekly was begun in 1885. The *Jewish Daily Forward* was established twelve years later. Its vigorous editor, Abraham Cahan, a man of parts, was typical of the transplanted leaders whom the immigrant Jews brought with them. As a labor leader, as a Socialist, his editorial policy shaped the thinking and determined the behavior at the ballot box of thousands of immigrant Jews.

There were many familiar names introduced to Yiddish readers whose works of poetry and philosophy and fantasy were heatedly discussed over the tall glasses of strong tea fortified with lemon and preserves. Israel Leibush Peretz, Sholem Aleichem, Simeon Frug, Abraham Goldfaden, David Pinski, Abraham Reisen. The alphabet was canvassed from Abramowitz to Zangwill.[15a]

Hebrew had preceded Yiddish in America. In 1870 *Hatzofeh Baaretz Hahadashah* made its debut in New York. It lasted for six years. *Haleumi*, advocate of the *Hovevei Zion* managed to last for three years. *Haibri* ran for a decade. *Hadoar* was more sturdy than several other publications, for it was established in 1921 and still flourishes.

As their English vocabularies were enlarged and their interests became more diverse, as their incomes expanded and their homes moved to the outer fringes of areas of dense concentration, later immigrants, like their native American cousins, had access to various periodicals appealing to women, to children, to diverse geographic localities and to specialized interests. There was *Helpful Thoughts* edited by Julia Richman and Rebekah Kohut. The *American Jewess* made its bow between 1895 and 1899. *Young Israel* was the vehicle for reaching the small fry from 1871. From San Francisco, where Jews had their own periodical since 1855, through the great Mississippi Valley, this tide of Jewish journalism flowed, reaching its zenith, of course, in New York.

While in the halls of learning American scholars were debating a new doctrine enunciated by one of their number, Frederick Jackson Turner, who had proclaimed the passing of the American frontier, the new knowledge was subtly changing the lives of immigrants. A new era in American history had begun. The vast domain of land into which immigrants of preceding generations had dipped so recklessly had gradually become exhausted. In the last decade of the nineteenth century, the great reservoir of free land had dried up. It was just at this moment, when the passing of "the good old days" was being recorded, that Russian Jews entered the scene. Henry James took a long look at the gabardined stranger and his aristocratic nostrils twitched in disgust. "There is no swarming like that of Israel when once Israel has got a start," he wrote after a visit to the congested New York section where they lived. But other Americans rushed to the defense of the Jews. *Harper's Weekly* interpreted the immigrant to America, deplored "race-patriotism," chauvinism and jingoism. In 1902 an editorial writer in that liberal publication wrote: "As for that dream of Anglo-Saxon Empire, it is a cheap and vulgar hallucination . . ." As if to prove him right, the Jews out of dire poverty reaped a harvest of cultural riches.

It was a new age in many ways. America was becoming aware of the Jew and of his contribution. It was but a little more than half a century from the days when Emma Lazarus unobtrusively discussed "the Jewish problem" to the days when the front page of every metropolitan daily in the land carried stories about Jews in America and in the lands across the sea. In America the crescendo of philo-Semitic voices was often drowned by the rasping shouts of hate. It is true that in the United States both trends had long been discernible. Philo-Semitism in America had ancient roots. From the earliest days of pioneering and settlement men and women of Christian faith have not only befriended the Jew but have given him their fellowship as equals. The classic example is the close and abiding friendship between Ezra Stiles, who became president of Yale, and Rabbi Carigal of Hebron in Palestine, who visited Newport. There was the American publisher, David Longworth, who from 1797 to 1821 published many books, carefully expunging prejudicial paragraphs. The State Department has a noble tradition, from the first Secretary of State, Thomas Jefferson, through many a great successor.

There was an army of special pleaders among American writers who urged *Justice to the Jew*, like Madison Peters. There were editors like Lyman Abbott and Norman Hapgood, whose periodicals were the means of refuting lies and disseminating truth. For every *anti-image* which the rabble-rouser tried to foist on a gullible and uncritical public, there were those who collected facts and told them. Social scientists studied group tensions, analyzed the factors involved in "social distance," discussed the pros and cons of "consciousness of kind." It took lies and forgeries whicl had been proved false in Europe, like the *Protocols of the Elders o Zion*,[15b] but a short time to germinate and spread in America. The quot system, tentatively introduced and quietly administered, blossomed like weed for all to see. A correspondent writing from Hull House in Chicag to the editor of the *Nation* sadly asked ". . . is Americanism a hollov sham?" In 1936 the editors of *Fortune* defined anti-Semitism as "the delib erately incited phobia which has produced the social and economic an sometimes physical pogroms of modern Germany just as it produced th murderous pogroms of Czarist Russia." It reached the inescapable con clusion that in America anti-Semitism is "feeble." The impact on the rank and-file American may have been slight, but on the youth of America' Jewish population it laid a heavy hand. Boys and girls unprepared at hom or in synagogue for the cold blasts of hostility and social aversion, for th impact of discrimination and exclusion, knew not how to face or meet th problem. This was an evil that led to positive countermeasures by the Jew of America.

What were they? What steps were taken to affirm the truth? How wer the rising generations prepared to do battle with the enemy who thoug small in numbers was strident and vocal and abusive, as harmful as capsule of deadly germs? Some of the remedial measures came fron aroused Christians. Working independently or in groups they girded them selves with facts and figures and exposed the hatemongers wherever the were found. The Jews of America did not rely upon their non-Jewis friends alone. They organized. They studied the problem in every aspect The demands on the Jews of America were becoming increasingly great As the numbers of Jews of Europe were reduced by the Nazi criminals the problems in America multiplied. Between 1939 and 1946 the numbe of Jews was reduced from 16,000,000 to some 11,000,000.[16] Those wh survived became that tragic remnant designated as "displaced persons. The saving of that remnant of Israel was one additional task whicl devolved upon America's Jews. Material sustenance, moral leadershi preservation of Jewish learning—all this and more was to come from th American reservoir. The Jews of America were ready. They had grown i numbers and in moral stature.

On the eve of the twentieth century it was estimated that there wer half a million Jews in the United States. Between 1899 and 1930 ther were 1,905,561 Jews admitted to this country.[17]

Upon the shoulders of immigrants and on their children there fell th task of meeting a twofold problem—first, that created by their own tran planting to America and, second, that caused by outside forces which wer an inherent part of the American scene. As early as 1906 the America Jewish Committee was formed. The Kishinev massacres had been th spark. But the group of men who met under the chairmanship of Judge Mayer Sulzberger of Philadelphia addressed themselves to national as well as international problems that were urgently in need of solution. Within a decade the scope of the Committee was enlarged and provision made for proportionate representation and a larger membership. In one hundred and ninety-eight urban areas with a Jewish population of one thousand or more, members were chosen to grapple with many issues. The Committee was active in counterpropaganda and in securing the retraction of falsehoods disseminated by the *Dearborn Independent*. When the base lie of "ritual murder" was perpetrated at Massena, New York, in 1928, the American Jewish Committee exposed it. It co-operated with a number of other Jewish groups in vigorous, forthright insistence on equality and fair play. Among the leaders it has attracted were men like Louis Marshall, Jacob H. Schiff, Oscar S. Straus, Felix M. Warburg, Cyrus Adler, Julius Rosenwald, and Sol M. Stroock. In 1909 the then-active New York Kehillah was allowed representation in the American Jewish Committee. One of the great achievements of the Committee was its sponsorship of the American Jewish Relief Committee, out of which was actually created the Joint Distribution Committee. In many ways the program of the American Jewish Committee parallels that of the Board of Delegates of American Israelites.

One of the basic influences in American Jewish life was the rise of the Zionist movement. Since 1896 under the leadership of Theodor Herzl, Zionism had come to embody an active program for the redemption of Palestine and its resettlement by Jews. The concept was not new. The Earl of Shaftesbury had advocated the returning of the ancient biblical land to the people who had given the Bible to the world. That was in 1842. George Eliot had nursed the dream and given it to the world in *Daniel Deronda*. The English mystic, Laurence Oliphant, had persuaded powerful and influential friends to back a project of Jewish resettlement in Palestine. He journeyed to Palestine and selected Gilead as the center of his colonization project. But it was deep in the heart of the Russian Ghetto that the dreams of countless men and women, the yearning of centuries, crystallized into a more enduring program. That flame was brought to America. It found an answering spark in the heart of Emma Lazarus and a number of native American Jews. In Theodor Herzl the movement had a spokesman and a prophet. As in England, so were there Christian Zionists in America. A Protestant clergyman of Chicago, the Reverend William E. Blackstone, drew up a petition which was sent to President Benjamin Harrison. It advocated the consideration of the status of Jews and their "claims to Palestine as their ancient home." Among those who signed the Reverend Mr. Blackstone's petition were Americans of prominence such as Chief Justice Fuller, Cardinal Gibbons, John D. Rockefeller, J. Pierpont Morgan, Russell Sage.

Between such men and the little transplanted group from Russia who called themselves "Lovers of Zion," the *Hovevei Zion*, who even before the days of Herzl had propagated their dream of Palestine—there was a wide gulf. Yet ideas know no boundaries. The movement gathered momentum and gained friends. Sometimes great moral reverses, like the Dreyfus Affair in France, focused attention on the unhappy plight of Jews. At other times a speech, an article in a periodical, a poem or a song won converts. Sometimes the partisan lines were clearly drawn. The Reform movement rejected Zionism. The East European Jews nurtured it. The subject was debated in Jewish and general periodicals. The *Arena*, the *Fortnightly Review*, *Harper's Weekly*, *Century* and many other periodicals aroused reader interest by discussing the issue. In 1905 one writer boasted in the *Jewish Quarterly Review* that he was not a follower of "the Zionist heresy." Had he not been preceded by Rabbi Isaac M. Wise at a meeting of the Central Conference of American Rabbis in Montreal in 1897 when he repudiated in no uncertain terms the concept and philosophy, the dream and objectives of Zionism? Had not Rabbi David Philipson declared before the Union of American Hebrew Congregations: "We are unalterably opposed to political Zionism"?

But Zionism soon made inroads into the ranks of its opponents, picking up adherents in the halls of plenty and even in the citadels of the Reform group—even among the scions of German and Bohemian Jews whence had come the strongest opposition and the most active disdain. For the timid and reluctant, there was reassurance in counting the names of the great and the noted, like Louis D. Brandeis, whose conversion to Zionism was the greatest blessing that American Zionists could receive. For those who hesitated because of possible conflicts with American ideologies, always the nightmare of the Reform movement and the bedrock of its opposition, there was comfort in the doctrine of cultural pluralism advocated by noted Americans like Norman Hapgood, who in espousing Zionism wrote that it was consistent with Americanism, adding "Uniformity is the curse of democracy. Diversity is its ideal."

Out of the ranks of native Americans great Zionist leaders emerged. In addition to Brandeis, Henrietta Szold, Judah L. Magnes and a host of others rose up to assume leadership in America and in Palestine.

Little societies had sprung up all over America. Richard Gottheil and Stephen S. Wise together laid the foundations of the Federation of American Zionists in New York. Out of the Middle West men like Bernhard Felsenthal joined the ranks. From Baltimore there came leadership and guidance from Dr. Aaron Friedenwald and Rabbi Benjamin Szold. Then a new generation of younger men rose up in American

Israel to carry on the work so nobly begun. Historically inportant events transpired which accelerated the impetus of American Zionism. On the second of November in 1917, in the midst of World War I, a historic letter was mailed from the British Foreign Office to Lord Rothschild stating that the British government viewed with favor the establishment of a Jewish National Home in Palestine. It was signed by Arthur James Balfour. But behind the declaration there was the tacit consent of Woodrow Wilson and of the French government. Congress declared itself in favor of the Balfour Declaration and President Harding approved the Congressional Resolution on September 21, 1922. The development of Zionism in America has grown apace.[17a]

Just as the Russian Jew introduced Zionism to America, so did he begin an agrarian movement here.

At the turn of the century, in the year 1900, the Jewish Agricultural and Industrial Aid Society was incorporated in New York. But there had been earlier attempts to found agricultural colonies in America. When the first victims from the Russian nightmare began to arrive in the eighteen-eighties, the Hebrew Immigrant Aid Society bought a tract of eleven hundred acres. There on poor barren stretches of land, working under every conceivable handicap, erstwhile urban workers turned to the soil. Four colonies were established that supplemented their agrarian economy with small factories operating during the winter months. Dairying and canning and truck gardening and viniculture were, however, the major activities of Alliance and Carmel and Woodbine and Rosenhayn. In 1891 Baron de Hirsch gave a vast sum of money, £493,000, for the use of Russian Jewish immigrants in the United States. With these funds an agricultural school was established at Woodbine, New Jersey, and numerous scholarships were endowed. The Jewish Agricultural and Industrial Aid Society was created jointly by the Baron de Hirsch Fund and the Jewish Colonization Association. The process of cultural adaptation was phenomenal considering the centuries of separation from the soil. By 1909 there were more than three thousand families tilling the soil. A contributor to the *Arena* in that year estimated that there were 30,000 Jews engaged in farming in thirty-four states of the United States.

Agricultural societies were established to guide and advise inexperienced workers. Some of their own men rose from the ranks to confer prestige and scholarship, to bring their gifts not only to the Jews engaged in agriculture, but to all tillers of the soil. Such a man was David Lubin, an immigrant from Galicia, founder of the International Agricultural Institute. His youth was spent on the East Side of New York. He crossed the continent with a mule team after the Civil War, became a fruit farmer in the Sacramento Valley, joined the Grange, formed farmers' co-operatives. Applying stern discipline and unyielding idealism to his life and work, his name became synonymous with ethical economics in agriculture. "Lubinism" was officially endorsed by the Republican Party of California. Fifty-five Philadelphia clergymen formed a "Lubin Club." His ideas had spanned the American continent. Next he gave them to the world. He died in Rome. Twenty-five years after his death, seventy nations sent representatives to his tomb in Rome to pay homage to one who had all of his life practiced the philosophy that it was the mission of the Jew to lead the world into the pathways of justice and economic fair play.

In the ranks of labor, too, there were leaders of vision and idealism whose efforts benefited all workers of all creeds and all origins. From the docks to the areas of economic competition was but a short step. But it was an important one. For men like Samuel Gompers, Sidney Hillman, David Dubinsky—it was the step that led to leadership of the exploited and the underprivileged, to the creation of unions, to the promulgation of a dynamic philosophy and an integrated way of life. It was in keeping with the Jewish tradition. From the days of Abraham Galanti, a sixteenth-century employer who set up a pattern for fair dealing in labor relations, to the meeting of the Central Conference of American Rabbis, who again and again adopted resolutions favoring a decent standard of living for workers—the record has been consistent. In these occupations men who believed in social justice dedicated their lives to ameliorating the evils that would otherwise have blotted out all hope, all future, all chance of survival.

To the careful student of society the organic structure of Jewish life in America is too complex for brief summary. This is also true of the economic and social scene.[18a]

A noted sociologist, Jacob Lestschinsky, writing on "The Economic Development of the Jews in the United States,"[19 19a] states: "There are, unfortunately, no official data on the occupational distribution of the Jewish population in America. The census questionnaire does not contain any questions on nationality or religion. Hence the following figures are only approximations. They are based on unofficial investigations in various small, medium-sized and large Jewish communities and on estimates often arrived at indirectly . . . We must utilize such data because no more authentic statistics are available." Caution is the watchword with careful writers in the social sciences. This applies to every segment of Jewish life in America. In *Recent Social Trends*, published in 1933, we find the following statement applying to denominational membership:

> Strictly comparable figures for Jewish congregations are not available because this denomination recently expanded its definition of a "member" until its membership figures are now virtually population estimates. On this new basis, the total number of Jews, including infants and children as well as adults, is reported to be approximately 4,000,000. From this figure it is conservative to estimate that Jewish church members do not constitute more than a twentieth of the nation's total church membership.[20]

Mathematical approximations are deceptive and often misleading. Intensive surveys made in limited urban areas may, however, serve as guideposts to interpretation if enough scientific safeguards are used as controls. Fortunately such studies are being made and their findings are published. A decade after the publication of *Recent Social Trends*, the Conference on Jewish Relations published its excellent report titled *Jewish Population Studies*. Dr. Sophia M. Robison ably edited a symposium in which demographic analyses were made in conformity with the best scientific practices. The results growing out of prevailing conditions compelled "statisticians interested in getting accurate and detailed demographic data . . . to resort to . . . various devices . . ."[21] The major "devices" include a series of studies on Yom Kippur absences, a method which has glaring shortcomings. A series of analyses of death rates also were attempted. Finally the method of statistical sampling was invoked.

All these methods have the same pitfalls. Dr. Robison concludes on a discouraging note:

> Any comparison of the various techniques of estimating the Jewish population raises the question of how to define the designation "Jew." In the Chicago study a Jew is one whose death certificate indicates that he was buried by an undertaking firm whose business it is to conduct Jewish burials. In the Detroit study a Jew is one who has a Jewish name. In the other reports Jews are defined as persons born of Jewish parents or of mixed marriages, who are members of Jewish communal and religious organizations, and as those who when interviewed were willing to be identified as Jewish by "race" or religion. It is clear that this last category excludes from the count those Jews by birth who are unaffiliated with Jewish organizations, but who would be considered Jewish by non-Jews, as well as those born of Jewish parents but not identifiable as Jewish.[22]

Illusive as are the "facts" when culled from census and school and synagogue, they are simple when compared with all data involving such designations as are concerned with social status, with relative importance attached to various trades and occupations, with "social distance" based on these factors. We may safely assume that, being predominantly urban, the same general observations may be made of Jewish as of non-Jewish urban residents. We may also focus the spotlight on obvious groupings, on major deviations from the "norm." As the great reservoir of land was absorbed, urban concentration became more marked for the nation as a whole. The bulk of Jewish migrants came here after the passing of the American frontier. Concentration in cities was determined therefore not only by the immigrants themselves, but by the general situation. Opportunities for employment were limited by available places of residence, by linguistic limitations, by vacancies to be filled in close proximity to the areas of debarkation, by previous occupation, by economic stratification of earlier

Jewish settlers. Factory work was the first step. By 1900 East European Jews began to make a gradual transition from the factory to trade and commerce.[23] In 1937 it was estimated that 28.8 per cent of the Jewish population were owners and 71.2 per cent were employees. This, when compared with the non-Jewish population, shows differences. For among non-Jews the owners were 11.7 per cent, employees 88.3. Among gainfully employed in the Robison study the following figures are indicative of patterns of economic and occupational organization:[24]

City	Number of Jews gainfully occupied	Per cent occupied in: Professions	Trade	Manufacturing	All others
Trenton	3,061	12.3	59.0	13.3	15.4
Passaic	4,370	12.3	43.2	22.5	22.0
Pittsburgh	25,000	9.5	60.4	13.8	16.3
Chicago	(No data available)	8.5	44.4	35.5	11.6
New London	597	13.7	54.5	16.2	15.6
Norwich	620	9.4	50.8	22.7	17.1
Stamford	1,540	12.5	52.4	15.0	20.1
New Orleans	2,590	12.5	48.6	14.5	24.4

City	Number of Jews gainfully occupied	Per cent occupied as: Professionals	Proprietors, managers and officials	Clerks and kindred workers	Skilled workers	Semi-skilled workers	Unskilled workers	All others
Buffalo	6,081	14.3	25.9	35.6	16.3	3.0	3.2	1.7
Detroit	29,300	7.6	26.8	39.1	8.9	14.8	2.8	...
San Francisco	13,400	11.4	30.8	40.2	5.6	9.4	0.6	2.0
Pittsburgh	25,000	10.8	22.3	42.7	9.9	1.4	2.3	10.6

The editors of *Fortune* in 1936 made a thorough study of economic and occupational trends titled *Jews in America*. Their first major conclusion was "that there is no basis whatever for the suggestion that Jews monopolize United States business and industry."[25] The bulk of America's Jews, like its non-Jewish population, are workers employed and unemployed, skilled and unskilled. Jews "do not run to banking."[26] They have "a subordinate place in finance" and "an even more inconspicuous place in heavy industry."[27] "But the clothing business is the spectacular and outstanding exception to the statement that Jewish industrial interests are generally in the minority."[28] In the main "Jews are most frequently to be found in those reaches of industry where manufacturer and merchant meet."[29]

He may be a small factor in the total American scene, but the American Jew is beset with world problems. Since 1933 he has had to provide for the "displaced persons." He has had to prepare the way for future homes in Palestine for those made homeless by the war. Upon his shoulders, willy-nilly, has fallen the mantle of leadership of world Jewry. He has had to develop the methods and provide the means.[30]

Ameliorative social services among the Jews have always been both national and international in scope. The American Jewish Joint Distribution Committee founded in 1914 has functioned in eighty-five overseas areas. By 1942 more than one hundred million dollars had been spent for relief and rehabilitation. In 1939 the United Jewish Appeal co-ordinated the fund-raising campaign. On the domestic scene the highest standards of administrative social work have won from their colleagues in social work both respect and recognition. Case-work standards are high. Community organization is well administered. Hospitals and sanatoria, homes for the aged and the handicapped, foster-home care for children, as well as institutional care, are planned with utmost care. Agencies too numerous to mention, each with a specialized field of interest, carry out specific functions in the community.

Overseas relief and rehabilitation in 1946 necessitated the campaign for $100,000,000 to be apportioned among the Joint Distribution Committee, the United Palestine Appeal, and the National Refugee Service.[31, 31a] The Joint Distribution Committee has performed a herculean service in emergency relief, economic rehabilitation and social service extended to children, migrants, displaced persons and deportees. This program has been world-wide, operating in Europe, Africa, China and South America. Other organizations also are global in scope and plan. The World ORT Union with a history of sixty-six years of realistic planning and accomplishment in retraining men and women for useful occupations, has continued its heroic task of readjusting the victims of war by providing them with new and wanted skills. In 1945 the World ORT Union was instrumental in offering a program, which was accepted, to establish workshops and training courses in the displaced-person camps.[32] Another organization deriving its major strength in the United States is the Hebrew Sheltering and Immigrant Aid Society, known as HIAS, which has since 1887 served as an agency to assist individuals who wish to migrate. It has extended subsidies and advice. It has undertaken large-scale plans designed to facilitate resettlement. It has maintained temporary hostels and shelters for migrating Jews—a vital service when social mobility is the major problem for a large segment of Jews.

An interesting instance of the development of an institution to meet a special situation occurred in connection with the disaster of the First World War. In August, 1914, a resolution was adopted by a Zionist Conference, calling for the creation of a representative assembly of American Jews to take such action as might be deemed appropriate with regard to Jewish problems in any country. While at first various groups opposed the establishment of such an assembly, gradually the difficulties were overcome, and in the end, a delegation was sent to the Peace Conference in Versailles on behalf of the American Jewish Congress, which represented virtually all organized American Jews.

Among the members of this delegation were Julian W. Mack, Stephen S. Wise, Louis Marshall, Jacob De Haas, and Bernard L. Levinthal. Cyrus Adler joined the delegation as representative of the American Jewish Committee. The delegation co-operated effectively with similar Jewish groups, coming from other countries, so that there was greater agreement and understanding among the delegates than might have been expected in view of the diversity of origin and opinion on general matters.

Undoubtedly, the presence of these eminent Jews at the Peace Conference, and their influence on provisions for the protection of minority groups in the newly constituted states of Central Europe was of historical significance. The activity leading to the establishment of the delegation, and the work of the delegation, gave American Jews a sense of responsibility they had never before had for their brethren.

As we look backward along the road that Jews in America have traveled, certain facts emerge with clarity.

Jews have been in the Western Hemisphere from its first contact with Europeans. From the first there was occupational diversity and geographic scattering. Some of the very earliest settlers in America and the last immigrants came here in family units. Only in the nineteenth-century migrations of the middle years was there a noticeable single-man pattern of mobility. The family has always been the vehicle for the transmitting of Jewish folkways and mores. As soon as numbers permitted, the Jewish group purchased a burial ground and established a religious center. From the first there was an insistence on civic and religious equality. There has been a high sense of moral responsibility for the widow and orphan and the indigent. Stratification has been more largely constituted along economic levels than based on geographic origin until the 1880's. The coming of great masses of impoverished East European Jews just after the first major schism in American Jewish life through the establishing of the Reform movement, tended to separate the American Jewish population on the basis of a threefold pattern: (1) economic differences; (2) religious separation; (3) geographic origin.

The roster of the elite from the point of view of achievement is too long to mention. Jews have held responsible public offices, including appointments to the Supreme Court. They have held positions of public trust and have served in Congress and as governors of their states and in state legislative assemblies. They have held professorships in the great universities. They have risen to eminence in the professions of medicine and law. They have enriched the literature of the land. They have held posts on the leading newspapers and have advanced the development of radio. They have written many of the ballads and much of the music since 1900. They have become columnists, editors, novelists, newspaper owners.

The alphabet of Jewish accomplishment ranges from the academic field to Zionism. The list is long and honorable. To mention some is to affront others equally gifted.

But also there have been the little folk, the toilers in the factories, the small storekeepers, the salesmen and stenographers—the farmers and the laborers. And out of the needs of the multitudes there have arisen social vision and social planning, advocacy of public health and housing, insistence on equal opportunity, on fair employment practices, on collective bargaining.

To meet urgent needs, philanthropists like Judah Touro and Julius Rosenwald have dispensed largess. Social service techniques have been perfected. Social legislation has been promoted. The Council of Jewish Federations and Welfare Funds, the National Conference of Jewish Social Welfare have interpreted Jewish social service philosophy and administration. Labor unions have set up and administered departments of social welfare. Private agencies, federations and societies have supplemented with money and volunteers many neglected fields.

Much remains to be added. Great gaps in the story must await the fuller and more leisurely telling. What is a Jew? How set up a definition which encompasses both reluctant adherent and ardent devotee? Who is to sit in judgment, separating the sheep from the goats? What of the perennial "Jewish Problem"? In one of his notable addresses, titled "The Jewish Problem, and How to Solve it,"[33] Justice Brandeis said: "The sole bulwark against demoralization is to develop in each new generation of Jews in America the sense of *noblesse oblige* . . . That spirit can best be developed by actively participating in some way in furthering the ideals of the Jewish renaissance. . ." Perhaps here lies both the definition of the problem and its solution.

The Jewish chronicle of America is rich and colorful. Each pilgrim who crossed the Atlantic received sanctuary. Yet he did not come empty handed. For bearing his gifts, his skills, his talents, his genius, he freely and gladly offered them to the land of his adoption. His children and his children's children have continued to cherish and to serve the land that is their beloved home.

NOTES

The writer has dispensed with many additional note references in the interest of brevity. However, attention should be called to the fact that full footnote citations appear in her book, *Pilgrim People* (New York, 1950).

[[1a] Cf. above Cecil Roth, "The European Age in Jewish History (to 1648), pp. 237 ff.]

[1] Jules T. E. Hamy, *Portolan Charts of the XVth, XVIth, and XVIIth centuries* (New York, 1912); Edward L. Stevenson, *Early Spanish Cartography of the New World, with Special Reference to the Wolfenbuettel-Spanish Map and the Work of Diego Ribero* (Worcester, 1909), and *Portolan Charts; Their Origin and Characteristics* (New York, 1911); George H. T. Kimble, *Geography in the Middle Ages* (London, 1938), 185; Francisco de Borja P.M.A. Sousa Holstein, *A Escola de Sagres as Tradições do Infante D. Henrique* (Lisbon, 1877), 34-35; see also article "Maps," *Encyclopaedia Britannica* (11th ed.) xvii; Kimble, *op. cit.*; "Atlas Catalan de Charles V, par Cresques le Juif." Photostat in the Edward E. Ayer Collection, from the original in the Bibliothèque Nationale, Paris, Ge CC54; Jules T. E. Hamy, "Jaffuda Cresques (Jaime Ribes). "Commentaires sur Quelques Documents . . . Publiés par D. Miguel Bonet sur ce Géographe Juif Catalan," *Bulletin Géographie Historique et descriptive, Année 1897,* No. 3 (1898), 381-388. See also Jules T. E. Hamy, *Cresques, lo Juheu; Note Sur un Géographe Juif Catalan de la Fin du XIV Siècle* (Angers), 189 ff.; Charles G.M.B. de La Roncière, *La Découverte de l'Afrique au Moyen Age, Cartographes et Explorateurs* (3 vols., Cairo, 1924-1927), I, 128-129; Hamy, "Jaffuda Cresques," *op. cit.* In this monograph Hamy confuses Abraham with Jehuda Cresques, 381 ff.; João de Barros, *Da Asia,* 13 parts in 24 vols. (Lisbon, 1777-1788), Decada I, Livro I, Cap. XVI, 133. The entire chapter is most pertinent to our subject.

[2] Morales Correa, *Clasificación cartográfica* (Gaea, Buenos Aires, 1938), VI, 227-274, in *Bibliographie Géographique Internationale,* 1928, vol. 48, 16; *Atlas composé de Cartes des XIV, XV, XVI, XVII siècles pour la plupart inédites . . .*, (Paris, 1841); also M. Jomard, *Les Monuments de la Géographie . . .* ; Konrad Kretschmer, *Die italienischen Portolane des Mittelalters* (Berlin, 1909), Karte des Meca (*sic*) (Viladestes, 1413), 126-127; "Karte des Gabriel de Valsequa," 133; see also "Die mittelalterlichen Seekarten," 34-49; Gonzalo de Reparaz, "Els Mapes Catalans de la Bibliothèque Nationale de Paris," *Estudis Universitaris Catalans* (Barcelona, 1928), XIII, 218 ff.

[[2a] Cf. below Charles Singer, "Science and Judaism," pp. 1401 ff.]

[3] See United States Department of Agriculture. Agricultural Research Administration, Bureau of Agricultural and Industrial Chemistry, September, 1943, "Corn, Its Products and Uses," for this significant tribute to Luis de Torres and to his companion as discoverers of the uses of this vital grain.

[4] Luiz de Camões, *The Lusiad* (Fanshawe translation) (Cambridge, 1940),

cantos 23 and 25, 152-153; Gaspar Corrêa, *Lendas da India* (4 vols., Lisbon, 1858), 23 ff. Chap. V deals with the years 1497 ff.; see also Cantera Burgos, *Abraham Zacut, Siglo XV* (Madrid, s.a.), and his *El Judio Salmantino Abraham Zacut, Notas para la Historia de Astronomía* . . . (Madrid, s.a.) 69; Abel Fontoura da Costa, "L'Almanach Perpetuum de Zacut," *IIIe Congrès International d'Histoire des Sciences, Actes, Conférences et Communications* (Lisbon, 1936), 137-146. Also his *A Marinharia dos Descobrimentos.*

[5] The writer has been materially assisted in uncovering the record of Jewish participation in Brazilian history by Dr. William Brooks Greenlee, trustee of the Newberry Library, whose generous help and direction it is a privilege to acknowledge.

[6] William B. Greenlee, *The Voyage of Pedro Álvares Cabral to Brazil and India* (London, 1938), published by Hakluyt Society; also his articles titled "A Descriptive Bibliography of the History of Portugal," *Hispanic American Historical Review,* XX (1940), 491-516; "The First Half Century of Brazilian History," *Mid-America,* n.s. XIV (1943), 91-120; "The Background of Brazilian History," *Americas,* II (1945), 151-164; "The Captaincy of the Second Portuguese Voyage to Brazil, 1501-1502," *Americas,* II (1945), 3-12, should be consulted by the reader. In addition, the writer had access to the Greenlee Collection in the Newberry Library and to his manuscript notebooks.

[7] Portugal. Agencia geral das Colonias, *Os Sete Unicos Documentos de 1500, conservados em Lisbôa, referentes à viagem de Pedro Álvares Cabral* (Lisbon, 1940); Thomaz O. Marcondes de Souza, *O Descobrimento da América e a Suposta Prioridade dos Portuguêses* (São Paulo, 1944); Solidonio Leite, *Da Influencia do Elemento Judaico no Descobrimento e Commercio do Brasil (seculos XVI e XVII)* (Rio de Janeiro, 1938). The writer has had this valuable thesis translated in full; Joseph F. Lafitau, *Histoire des découvertes et conquestes des Portugais dans le Nouveau monde* (4 vols., Paris, 1736), I, 157. See also the Anonymous Narrative in Greenlee, *The Voyage of Pedro Álvares Cabral, op. cit.,* 60; *Alguns Documentos do Archivo Nacional da Torre do Tombo, acerca das Navegações e Conquistas Portuguezas* (Lisbon, 1892), 459; there are several references to the activities of Loronha and to his association with the enterprises involving Brazil in *Centenario do Descobrimento da America, op. cit.* For additional Noronha references see *Alguns Documentos, op. cit.,* 408, 458-460; Gaspar Corrêa, *Lendas da India* (4 vols., Lisbon, 1858), II, 134; Armando Cortesão, *op. cit.,* I, 144; *Os Judeus na História do Brasil, op. cit.,* 10; *História da Cólonizacão Portuguesa do Brasil, op. cit.,* II, 294, 324-330; Joannes de Laet, *Iaerlijck verhael van de verrichtinghen der geoctroyeerde West-Indische compagnie (1624-1626)* ('s Gravenhage 1931-1937), 73-74, 104, 148-151, 161; Marcondes de Souza, *op. cit.,* 89; Francisco M. de Mello, *Espanáforas de Vária História Portuguesa* (Coimbra, 1931); Arthur P. Newton, *The Great Age of Discovery* (London, 1932), 65; Alfonso Toro *(ed.), Los Judios en la Nueva España: Selección de Documentos del Siglo XVI* (Mexico, 1932); Francisco A. Varnhagen, *Examen de Quelques Points de l'Histoire Géographique du Brésil* (Paris, 1858), see map opposite p. 706.

[8] See *Concerning Latin American Culture* (Columbia University Press,

New York, 1940), p. 86. "... most of the traders engaged in the importation of slaves and in the exportation of sugar were Sephardic Jews . . ." Gilberto Freyre in *Masters and Slaves,* p. 24 ff., discusses the role of New Christians [Sephardic Jews] in the development and ownership of sugar mills. See also Freyre's *Brazil.* Also *Universal Jewish Encyclopedia.*

[[8a] Cf. below Moshe Davis, "Jewish Religious Life and Institutions in America (A Historical Study)," pp. 489-490.]

[[8b] Cf. above Cecil Roth, *op. cit.*, p. 221.]

[[8c] Cf. below Davis, *op. cit.*, pp. 490-491.]

[9] American Jewish Historical Society *Publications,* 35, 189-205.

[[9a] Cf. above Roth, "The Jews of Western Europe (from 1648)," p. 271.]

[10] *Occident,* Vol. 25, p. 598.

[[10a] Cf. below the chapter by Moshe Davis, *loc. cit.*]

[[10b] Cf. above Roth, *op. cit.*, pp. 261-262.]

[11] For this section see *Occident and American Jewish Advocate,* XXVI vols., 1843-1868, *passim.* See also *Asmonean, A Family Journal of Commerce, Politics, Religion, and Literature, Devoted to the Interests of American Israelites,* XVIII vols., 1849-1858.

[12] *The American Jewish Year Book,* 1946-1947, vol. 48, pp. 610 ff.

[[12a] For immigration figures cf. also below, Jacob Lestschinsky, "Jewish Migrations, 1840-1956," *passim.*]

[13] *The American Jewish Year Book, op. cit.*, pp. 614-616.

[14] M. Rosenfeld, "On the Ocean," 1899, *Jewish Quarterly Review,* 1899-1900, XII, 91.

[[14a] Cf. below Yudel Mark, "Yiddish Literature," pp. 1210 ff.]

[15] Moshe Starkman, "The Yiddish Press—75 Years Old," *Congress Weekly,* March 2, 1945.

[[15a] Cf. below Mark, *op. cit.*, pp. 1210 ff.]

[[15b] Cf. above Roth, *op. cit.*, p. 279.]

[16] *American Jewish Year Book,* 1946-1947, Vol. 48, p. 603.

[17] Maurice R. Davie, *World Immigration* (New York, 1939), pp. 135-145.

[[17a] Cf. below Davis, *op. cit.*, p. 526.]

[18] Nathan Goldberg, *Jewish Review,* Vol. 3, No. 2, July, 1945.

[[18a] For some economic and social statistics on American Jewry, see below Uriah Zevi Engelman, "Sources of Jewish Statistics," Simon Kuznets, "Economic Structure and Life of the Jews," and Nathan Glazer, "Social Characteristics of American Jews."]

[19] Jacob Lestschinsky, "The Economic Development of the Jews in the United States," *The Jewish People: Past and Present,* I, 396.

[[19a] See Lestschinsky, *op. cit.*, Glazer, *op. cit.*]

[20] C. Luther Fry, with the assistance of Mary Frost Jessup, "Changes in Religious Organizations," *Recent Social Trends in the United States,* 1933, p. 1024.

[21] Sophia M. Robison (*ed.*), *Jewish Population Studies* (New York 1943), p. 2.

[22] *Ibid*, p. 184.

[23] Lestschinsky, *op. cit.*, p. 397.

[24] Robison, *op. cit.*, p. 189.

[25] By the editors of *Fortune*, *Jews in America* (New York, 1936), p. 24.

[26] *Jews in America*, p. 39.

[27] *Ibid.*, p. 42.

[28] *Ibid.*, p. 50.

[29] *Ibid.*, p. 52.

[30] See H. L. Lurie, "Social Welfare," in *American Jewish Year Book*, 1946-1947, pp. 157 ff.

[31] Geraldine Rosenfield, "Overseas Relief and Rehabilitation," *American Jewish Year Book*, 1946-1947, p. 202.

[[31a] Cf. below Israel S. Chipkin, "Judaism and Social Welfare," pp. 1043 ff.]

[32] Rosenfield, *op. cit.*, p. 214.

[33] A. T. Mason, *Brandeis, A Free Man's Life* (New York, 1946), pp. 448-449.

BIBLIOGRAPHY

On the geography and cartography of the European Age of Explorations see the following works:

Atlas composé de Cartes des XIV, XV, XVI, XVII siècles pour la plupart inédites . . . Paris, 1841.

BARROS, JOÃO DE, *Da Asia.* 13 parts in 24 vols. Lisbon. 1777-1788.

CORREA, MORALES, *Clasificación cartográfica.* Buenos Aires, 1938, Vol. VI.

Encyclopaedia Britannica. "Maps." 14th ed. New York, 1936.

HAMY, JULES T. E., *Cresques, lo Juheu; Note Sur un Géographe Juif Catalan de la Fin du XIV Siècle.* Angers, n.d., [189-?].

———, "Jaffuda Cresques (Jaime Ribes). Commentaires sur Quelques Documents . . . Publiés par D. Miguel Bonet sur ce Géographe Juif Catalan," in *Bulletin de Géographie Historique et descriptive,* 1897. No. 3, Paris, 1898.

———, *Portolan Charts of the XVth, XVIth, and XVIIth centuries.* New York, 1912.

HOLSTEIN, FRANCISCO DE BORJA P.M.A. SOUSA, *A Escola de Sagres as Tradições do Infante D. Henrique.* Lisbon, 1877.

JOMARD, M., *Les Monuments de la Géographie.* Paris, 1862.

KIMBLE, GEORGE H. T., "Atlas Catalan de Charles V, par Cresques le Juif." Photostat in the Edward E. Ayer Collection, from the original in the Bibliothèque Nationale, Paris, Ge CC54.

———, *Geography in the Middle Ages.* London, 1938.

KRETSCHMER, KONRAD, *Die italienischen Portolane des Mittelalters.* Berlin, 1909.

NEWTON, ARTHUR P., *The Great Age of Discovery.* London, 1932.

REPARAZ, GONZALO DE. "Els Mapes Catalans de la Bibliothèque Nationale de Paris," in *Estudis Universitaris Catalans*. Barcelona, 1928. Vol. XIII.

LA RONCIÈRE, CHARLES G. M. B. DE, *La Découverte de l'Afrique au Moyen Age, Cartographes et Explorateurs*, 3 vols. Cairo, 1924-1927.

STEVENSON, EDWARD L. *Early Spanish Cartography of the New World, with Special Reference to the Wolfenbuettel-Spanish Map and the Work of Diego Ribero*. Worcester, 1909.

———, *Portolan Charts; Their Origin and Characteristics*. New York, 1911.

On the Portuguese explorations, especially of the New World, see the following works:

Alguns Documentos do Archivo Nacional da Torre do Tombo, acerca das Navegações e Conquistas Portuguezas. Lisbon, 1892.

CAMÕES, LUIZ DE, *The Lusiad* (Fanshawe translation). Cambridge, 1940.

CANTERA BURGOS, FRANCISCO, *Abraham Zacut, Siglo XV*. Madrid [1935].

———, *El Judio Salmantino Abraham Zacut, Notas para la Historia de Astronomía en la España Medieval*, Publicado en La Revista De La Academia De Ciencias, XXVIII, 12 de la 2ª Serie, Madrid, s.a.

CORRÊA, GASPAR, *Lendas da India*. 4 vols. Lisbon, 1858.

FONTOURA, ABEL DA COSTA, *A Marinharia dos Descobrimentos*. Lisbon, 1934.

———, "L'Almanach Perpetuum de Zacut," in *IIIe Congrès International d'Histoire des Sciences, Actes, Conférences et Communications*. Lisbon, 1936.

GREENLEE, WILLIAM B., "A Descriptive Bibliography of the History of Portugal," in *Hispanic American Historical Review*, Vol. XX, 1940.

———, "The Background of Brazilian History," in *Americas*, Vol. II. Washington, 1945.

———, "The Captaincy of the Second Portuguese Voyage to Brazil, 1501-1502," in *Americas, op. cit.*

———, "The First Half Century of Brazilian History," in *Mid-America*, n.s. xiv. Chicago, 1943.

———, *The Voyage of Pedro Álvares Cabral to Brazil and India*. London, 1938.

LAET, JOANNES DE, *Iaerlijck verhael van de verrichtinghen der geoctroyeerde West-Indische compagnie (1624-1626)*. 's Gravenhage, 1931-1937.

LAFITU, JOSEPH F., *Histoire des découvertes et conquestes des Portugais dans le Nouveau monde*. 4 vols. Paris, 1736.

LEITE, SOLIDONIO, *Da Influencia do Elemento Judaico no Descobrimento e Commercio do Brasil (seculos XVI e XVII)*. Rio de Janeiro, 1938.

MELLO, FRANCISCO M. DE, *Espanáforas de Vária História Portuguesa*. Coimbra, 1931.

PORTUGAL, AGENCIA GERAL DAS COLONIAS, *Os Sete Unicos Documentos de 1500, conservados em Lisboa, referentes à viagem de Pedro Álvares Cabral*. Lisbon, 1940.

SOUZA, THOMAZ O. MARCONDES DE, *O Descobrimento da América e a Suposta Prioridade dos Portuguêses*. São Paulo, 1944.

TORO, ALFONSO (*ed.*), *Los Judios en la Nueva España: Selección de Documentos del Siglo XVI*. Mexico, 1932.

VARNHAGEN, FRANCISCO A., *Examen de Quelques Points de l'Histoire Géographique du Brésil*. Paris, 1858.

American Jewish Historical Society *Publications,* Vol. 35. New York, 1939.

The American Jewish Year Book, Vol. 48. Philadelphia, 1947.

Asmonean, A Family Journal of Commerce, Politics, Religion and Literature, Devoted to the Interests of American Israelites. New York, 1849-1858.

DAVIE, MAURICE R., *World Immigration*. New York, 1939.

EDITORS OF FORTUNE, *Jews in America*. New York, 1936.

FRY, C. LUTHER, AND JESSUP, MARY FROST, "Changes in Religious Organizations," in *Recent Social Trends in the United States*. New York and London, 1933.

GOLDBERG, NATHAN, "Occupational Patterns of American Jews," in *Jewish Review,* Vol. 3, July, 1945.

LESTSCHINSKY, JACOB, "The Economic Development of the Jews in the United States," in *The Jewish People: Past and Present*. Vol. I. New York, 1946.

LURIE, H. L., "Social Welfare," in *American Jewish Year Book,* 1946-1947.

MASON, ALPHEUS THOMAS, *Brandeis, A Free Man's Life*. New York, 1946.

Occident and American Jewish Advocate. Philadelphia, 1843-1868.

ROBISON, SOPHIA M. (*ed.*), *Jewish Population Studies*. New York, 1943.

ROSENFELD, M. "On the Ocean," *Jewish Quarterly Review,* Vol. 12. London, 1899-1900.

ROSENFIELD, GERALDINE, "Overseas Relief and Rehabilitation," in *American Jewish Year Book, op. cit.*

STARKMAN, MOSHE, "The Yiddish Press—75 Years Old," in *Congress Weekly*. March 2, 1945.

UNITED STATES DEPARTMENT OF AGRICULTURE. Agricultural Research Administration. "Corn, Its Products and Uses." Washington, September, 1943.

WALKER, SYDNOR H., "Privately Supported Social Work," in *Recent Social Trends in the United States, op. cit.*

CHAPTER II

JEWISH RELIGIOUS LIFE AND INSTITUTIONS IN AMERICA

(A Historical Study)

By Moshe Davis

Introduction

The essential factor in American history was the migration of some sixty million Europeans to the Western Hemisphere during the past four centuries. The meaning of American civilization lies in the ideals and motivations which prompted these immigrants to come to the New World, the influences of the American natural environment upon them, and the adjustment of their traditions and culture to the new way of life. The history of the Jews in the United States, like that of any other group in America, must be studied in the light of the forces that molded the character and civilization of the American people.

The Jews, like their fellow immigrants, sought complete integration into the American pattern. They contributed freely and fully to the American enterprise; they benefited greatly. In one major respect, however, the Jews were different from the other peoples of European origins. They insisted not only on maintaining and practicing their religious tradition, but they also continued to maintain a special relationship to their fellow Jews throughout the world. Although the Jews identified their future and the future of their children with that of America, they were also part of *Kelal Israel*, or Catholic Israel, and therefore shared in the destiny of the Jewish people and its faith.

This striving for social integration and religio-cultural identity within the framework of American democratic society is the unique quality of American Jewish history and its central theme. It can be traced most effectively in the history of Jewish religious life and institutions in the United States.

Ever since the earliest settlements of Jews on this continent, one question concerned them as a religious group more than any other: what shall be the nature of Judaism in America? In colonial times, when there were in the United States but a handful of congregations, similar in design and purpose, the answer seemed comparatively clear and simple. During the nineteenth century and until World War I, as American Jewry increased greatly, and as the patterns of belief and observance varied in the widest degrees, contradictions and confusions multiplied. Religious leaders proposed conflicting formulas of social and religious adaptation and created movements to implement their views. These movements vied with one another for the support of American Jewry—this against a background of continuing waves of immigration and unprecedented changes on the American and Jewish scenes.

Yet, early in the twentieth century, despite the inner contradictions and confusions, American Judaism began to take distinctive shape and form. After World War I, international responsibilities hastened the process of maturity. American Jewry rose to world Jewish leadership. In May, 1948, the historic declaration of independence proclaiming the republic of Israel brought into sharper focus the need to define the character of American Judaism and, more specifically, the exact relationship between American Jewry and Jewry in the new state. The religious groups had an answer which was deeply rooted in Jewish tradition. This answer emphasized American Jewry's undivided allegiance to the United States, its duty to sustain maximum Jewish life and expression in this country, as well as its obligation to help build the republic of Israel as the vital spiritual center of Judaism.

This essay surveys the history of Jewish religious life, thought, and institutions in the United States in relation to the American Jewish experience as a whole.

I

JEWISH RELIGIOUS LIFE IN COLONIAL TIMES, 1654-1800

Already during the colonial period steps were being taken and thoughts expressed which were to have a singular effect on American Jews and Judaism. It is significant that all kinds of people—fundamentalist and separatist, deist and theist—searched the Bible for guidance in their daily lives; that in Massachusetts was a town called Salem (*Shalom*, peace); that a Pennsylvania Quaker went by the name of Israel Israel; that William Bradford, colonial governor of Plymouth Colony, should manifest an abiding love for the Hebrew language in his *History of Plymouth Plantation*. Even more significant, perhaps, was the proposal by Benjamin Franklin, Thomas Jefferson, and John Adams, that the theme of the Exodus be adopted for the seal of the United States of America. It seems as though these men hoped to engrave on the minds of every American in every generation the scene of "Pharaoh sitting in an open chariot, a crown on his head and a sword in his hand, passing through the dividing waters of the Red Sea in pursuit of the Israelites; with rays from a pillar of fire beaming on Moses, who is represented as standing on the shore extending his hand over the sea . . ." The legend on the seal reads: "Rebellion to tyrants is obedience to God." The statute of Jacob was to feed the spirit of the law of the American people.[1]

The character of the religious life of American Jewry in the pre- and post-Revolutionary years can best be portrayed by a description of the leading religious personality of the period, Gershom Mendez Seixas, and of Jewish synagogal life in the Sephardic community of his time.

Seixas was the first native American *hazzan*. He was born in New York in 1745. In 1768, at the age of twenty-three, when Congregation Shearith Israel issued its call for a new *hazzan,* Seixas was elected for the period of his "Decent and Good Behavior" at a salary of eighty pounds per year, in addition to firewood and other perquisites.[2] His task, as was the wont in those days, was all inclusive. He was preacher, reader, teacher, and community servant. The pedagogic assignments were carefully detailed by his congregation. He was to teach his students to read Hebrew, and enable them to translate portions of the prayer book and Bible; moreover, he was to furnish convenient quarters for a classroom, and assume final responsibility at the religious services for the conduct of lads under the age of thirteen.

On the outbreak of the War for Independence, Jews like others in the country were divided over the issue of rebellion. In Shearith Israel one could meet Tory, as well as patriot. But Seixas used every influence he had to win his congregation's sympathy and support for the American cause. When Lord Howe brought his British army to Long Island and was about to approach New York, Seixas chose to shut down the synagogue rather than serve under occupation. Immediately prior to the capture of the city, he gathered his flock and held a farewell service. He thought this was perhaps the last service before the Ark in the Mill Street synagogue. Every object of worship in the synagogue, the scrolls of the Law, the tablets, the prayer books, and the candlesticks, he took with him, and fled to Stratford, Connecticut, to the safety of the American lines. The synagogue, barren of its appurtenances, was used on occasion by the Tories, and its sanctity was carefully guarded by the British.

The stream of American refugees wound its way to Philadelphia. Many of the former Shearith Israel congregants settled in the mother city of the Revolution. The handful of original Philadelphia Jewish residents grew to a considerable number, as the Jews of all occupied cities, including Newport and Savannah, arrived. Mikveh Israel, the congregation that was formerly without a home of its own, soon had a reader and a building. The dedication ceremonies, held in 1782, just before the end of the Revolutionary War, were attended by many distinguished Christian patriots; special prayers were offered on behalf of the Continental Congress and the commander in chief, George Washington.

Seixas became famous as the patriot Jewish minister of the Revolution. His zeal for the revolutionary cause was expressed in prayer, in sermon, and in action. The *Pennsylvania Gazette* of July 9, 1788, carries an account of the extraordinary demonstration in Philadelphia to celebrate the ratification of the Federal Constitution. In the parade, the correspondent writes, marched "the clergy of different Christian denominations with the rabbi of the Jews walking arm in arm." American legend tells of fourteen ministers invited to attend the inauguration of Washington, and Seixas is said to have been one of them.

In 1784, after the evacuation of New York by the British, Seixas and the Congregation Shearith Israel were reunited, the synagogue rededicated, and his former activities resumed. He continued to serve his congregation until his death in 1816. He introduced Pinto's translation of the Hebrew prayer book,[3] published in 1766, the first work of its kind ever issued in America, and containing the prayers for the Sabbath and High Holy Days, in order to meet the need of the members of the congregation who lacked a Jewish education. As Pastor, Seixas felt the need for a special society to aid in the relief of the sick and the burial of the dead. He therefore founded the Hebra Hesed v'Emet (Society of Loving-kindness and Truth) in 1802.

Seixas was one of the first American preachers to deliver regular Thanksgiving sermons. As spokesman of the Jewish community and as an American patriot, he was invited to preach in the churches of the city. One of his most important addresses was delivered in historic St. Paul's Church in 1800. Special honor came to him when he was appointed a member of the board of trustees of Columbia College, and his name is in its charter as one of the original incorporators. Through the War of 1812 and until his death, Seixas continued his fervant work in the vineyard of the Lord. He was the forerunner of a new type of spiritual leader, created by the needs of American Jewish life—student, preacher, teacher, pastor, and community servant.

Six Jewish congregations sent greetings to President George Washington. They were, in the order of their establishment: New York (1655); Newport, Rhode Island (1658); Savannah, Georgia (1733); Philadelphia, Pennsylvania (1740); Charleston, South Carolina (1749); and Richmond, Virginia (1790).[4] Though the Jews were primarily settled in seaport cities and busily engaged in commerce and trade, Jewish life maintained its traditional character. Religious life and practices were traditional in every respect. The house of worship was a house of assembly and also a school; the order of the service was in accordance with the ancient Spanish *minhag* and was observed in all of its minutiae; members of the congregation were subject to community opinion; community sanction derived from a central authority.

The Jewish population is variously estimated as having reached between twenty-five hundred and three thousand in the first decade of the nineteenth century. The majority were of Sephardic stock: Spanish, Portuguese, and Dutch. The number of German Jews, however, was considerable, far larger than the impression given us by historians of the past generation, who enjoyed dividing American Jewish history into three sharply defined periods of immigration.

The chief of the community, in law and in substance, was the *parnas*. He and his associates supervised every aspect of congregational life. Their control was supreme and autocratic. The *parnas* set the schedule of hours for the services, distributed the "honors," and authorized the performance of wedding ceremonies. This prerogative, preserved in many Sephardic congregations to this day, was accepted also by most of the Ashkenazic synagogues in the nineteenth century. As late as 1862, Dr. Morris Raphall, the rabbi of Congregation B'nai Jeshurun, was compelled, in accordance with his congregation's ruling, to request permission from the *parnas* to officiate at the wedding of his own daughter! The *parnas's* duties included rendering opinions on ritual law and supervising all congregational needs. For Passover, matzot were prepared under the auspices of the congregation and the price was set sufficiently above cost to ensure adequate income for free distribution of matzot to the needy. The *shohet* was engaged by the congregation, and all kosher food was issued under synagogue supervision and sanction. Unlimited authority was granted to the *parnas* in the punishment of the unaffiliated and religiously wayward. The files of Rodeph Shalom Congregation, Philadelphia, for 1810 (first congregation of German Jews, established in 1802) state:

> This Committee, after much deliberation, found it advisable, that when a married Yahudi, with family, comes to live in the State of Pennsylvania, such Yahudi be allowed to remain in this state 6 mos. and should during this time declare himself willing to join Rodeph Shalom. When such a family has in the eyes of the cong. been found well behaving and when it should, may God forbid, be in need or trouble, then the cong. should come to its help. But in case the family has not declared itself as desiring to affiliate itself with us, no help should be forthcoming to it.[5]

Shearith Israel warned transgressors that

> whosoever . . . continues to act contrary to our Holy Law by breaking any of the principles command will not be deem'd a member of our Congregation, have none of the Mitzote of the Sinagoge Conferred on him & when Dead will not be buried according to the manner of our breathren.[6]

These stringent regulations already indicate the beginnings of community disintegration and laxity in observance. This became more serious as the Jewish community spread beyond the confines of its original small area of settlement. Demographic change was the barometer of the weakening of religious influence. In the early period, however, major offenses were rare. There were no doubt many minor infractions, the penalty for which was a petty fine. But there was no redress for one who intermarried and thus deserted Judaism.

Except for Seixas, the *hazzan* was most often a lay member of the congregation, a man with a pleasant voice and smattering acquaintance with Hebrew, who served as reader and teacher to the young. On occasion he would preach. Most frequently a distinguished member of the congregation assumed the responsibilities of preaching or delivering the address. Second to the *hazzan* was a *shammash*, who served as a combination superintendent, secretary, and beadle: it was his duty to "call the Yechidimz that they may assemble togeathere at the usuall hours."[7]

Frequently Christian members of the community visited at Jewish services. Ezra Stiles (1727-1795), later president of Yale, was a frequent visitor at the Newport synagogue in the days of his own ministry in that city. Another visitor, the Swedish traveler Peter Kalm (1716-1779) who came to America in 1748, offers us a description of a Jewish community in action as seen through Christian eyes:

> During my residence at *New York,* this time and in the next two years, I was frequently in company with Jews. I was informed among other things, that these people never boiled any meat for themselves on Saturday, but that they always did it the day before; and that in winter they kept a fire during the whole Saturday. They commonly eat no pork; yet I have been told by several men of credit, that many of them (especially among the young Jews) when traveling, did not make the least difficulty about eating this, or any other meat that was put before them; even though they were in company with Christians. I was in their synagogue last evening for the first time, and this day at noon I visited it again, and each time I was put in a particular seat which was set apart for strangers or Christians. A young *Rabbi* read the divine service, which was partly in Hebrew, and partly in the Rabinical dialect. Both men and women were dressed entirely in the *English* fashion; the former had all of them their hats on, and did not once take them off during service. The galleries, I observed, were appropriated to the ladies, while the men sat below. During prayers the men spread a white cloth over their heads; which perhaps is to represent sackcloth. But I observed that the wealthier sort of people had a much richer cloth than the poorer ones. Many of the men had Hebrew books, in which they sang and read alternately. The *Rabbi* stood in the middle of the synagogue, and read with his face turned towards the east; he spoke however so fast as to make it almost impossible for anyone to understand what he said.[8]

That not all young Jewish men when away from home transgressed the religious precepts may be adduced from extant letters and records. One, for example, records that

Hart Jacobs, of the Jewish Religion, having signified to this Committee that it is inconsistent with his religious profession to perform military duty on Friday nights, being part of the Jewish Sabbath, it is

Ordered, That he be exempted from Military duty on that night of the week, to be subject, nevertheless, to the performance of his full tour of duty on other nights.[9]

The architecture of the colonial synagogue was in a style typical of the period. The first New York synagogue, which was built on Mill Street in 1730, and remained the center of worship for all New York Jewry until 1825, was a structure but thirty-five feet square and twenty-one feet high. The oldest example of colonial synagogal architecture, still in existence, is the Jeshuat Israel Synagogue at Newport, Rhode Island. (On March 5, 1946, this was declared a national American shrine.) Newport was visited by George Washington on August 17, 1790. At this time the congregation sent him greetings, and his reply is the oft-quoted historic letter which, among other things declares, "It is now no more that toleration is spoken of as if it was by the indulgence of one class of people that another enjoyed the exercise of their inherent natural rights. For happily the Government of the United States, which gives to bigotry no sanction, to persecution no assistance, requires only that they who live under its protection, should demean themselves as good citizens, in giving it on all occasions their effectual support."[10] The cornerstone of the synagogue was laid on August 1, 1759. On December 2, 1763, corresponding to the first day of Hanukkah of the year 5523, the synagogue was dedicated, as Ezra Stiles says in his *Diary*, "in a Edifice, the most perfect of the Temple kind perhaps in America, & splendidly illuminated, could not but raise in the Mind a faint Idea of the Majesty & Grandeur of the Ancient Jewish Worship mentioned in Scripture."[11]

In traditional Jewish manner, great attention was devoted to the education of the young. The school was the core of society. In the years prior to the advent of public education, those children who had any schooling at all received both their general and their religious education from private tutors. The congregations realized the need for a more effective educational system. The most advanced school, the Yeshibat Minhat Areb, was conducted under the auspices of Congregation Shearith Israel. From its beginnings in 1731 until 1800, it was run along lines characteristic of all other schools within the colonial educational system. Full and final responsibility for the school was vested in the congregational board. They arranged curricular standards and requirements. In addition to English and Hebrew, students were taught Spanish; general courses were given in arithmetic, spelling, and literature. Classes were conducted the year round, daily from nine to five with an intermission period of two hours. The cost of maintenance was covered by tuition fees and community sub-

Touro Synagogue

Congregation Jeshuat Israel
Newport, Rhode Island
Founded 1658

his photograph of the south- corner, the Ionic columns ›ort the women's gallery, Co- hian columns support the ceil- the reading desk is in the er.

In this view of the east wall a southeast corner, the Ark is clos Above it are the Ten Comma ments. The two ancient can labra are in front of the A On the balustrade are four cand sticks (gift of Enoch Ly 1766) and lectern.

vention. The children of the poor were admitted without charge. At the beginning of the nineteenth century the school was given the same grant-in-aid that the state advanced to religious schools of other denominations. The affluent retained private instructors or sent their children to private schools, conducted by Christian teachers; others sent their children abroad.[12]

Social service aid also was controlled by the religious authorities. The conditions of the Dutch West India Company, qualifying the admission of the Jews to New Amsterdam, "provided, that the indigent among them shall not become a burthen on the Company or the public, but maintain'd at the expense of the Jewish nation."[13] This promise was zealously fulfilled even beyond the expectation of Peter Stuyvesant and others of his ilk. The widow and the orphan, the halt and the blind, the feeble and the indigent found their source of relief in the synagogue.

The minute books of Congregation Shearith Israel fully reveal how taxing "*Sedaca*" was. Records of specific cases spanning the full range of social disabilities are included. Itinerants were aided in their journey; "sufficiencies for lodging and boarding the sick" were dispensed; the poor were not denied their daily bread; ". . . if application be again made for Moses Hart to allow him a Loaf of Bread per day if he wants it." The constitution of the congregation required the reading of its section on charity procedures twice a year both in Portuguese and in English:

> If any poor person should happen to come to this place and should want the assistance of the Sinagog the Parnaz is hereby impowered to allow every poor person for his maintainance the sum of Eight Shillings pr Week and no more Not Exceeding the term of twelve weeks. And the Parnaz is also to use his utmost endeavours to despatch them to sum othere place as soon as Possible assisting them with necessarys, for their Voyage, that is for a single person fourty Shillings, but if it be a family then the parnaz shall call his assistance and consult with them both for their maintainance whilst ashore and also for their necessarys when they depart; those poor of this Congregation that shall apply for Sedaca [charity] shall be assisted with as much as the Parnaz and his assistants shall think fitt.[14]

At the close of the colonial period there was a small, compact and united Jewish community, firm in the tradition of their fathers, at home in the land of their adoption, and partners in the creation of its greatness.

2

Growth of the Jewish Community, 1800-1840

The first German Jewish congregation was organized in 1802. And in the hundred years which followed, American Jewry grew from a comparatively simple congregation of some 2,500 concentrated on the Atlantic seaboard to a complex community of approximately 1,050,000 reaching to the farthermost points on the continent.

Every sign in the American adventure pointed westward: the Louisiana Purchase, expansion beyond the Mississippi basin, the conquest of the west. In his book, *The Epic of America*, James Truslow Adams appropriately entitles the chapter on the twenties and thirties of the nineteenth century, "The Sun Rises in the West." By 1830 the "men of the western waters" beyond the Alleghenies constituted one-third of the American population. The imprint of settlers' boots paved new roads. American industrialists in the east attempted to stop the exodus. They failed.

During the first four decades of the nineteenth century the Jewish population multiplied fivefold. Isaac Harby writing in the *North American Review*, placed the number at 6,000 in 1826. In 1840, the *American Almanac* raised the figure to 15,000. The *Publications of the American Jewish Historical Society* are sprinkled with accounts of plans for local colonization. The motives of the initiators were varied; they included speculation, promotion, and even conversion. In one superdramatic incident —the dream of bringing Noah's Ark to an American Ararat—its impresario, the dreamer, journalist, and alcalde, Mordecai Manuel Noah, claimed that the future of the entire Jewish people was at stake. These plans to colonize the Jews in America, heralded by advertisements, pamphlets, and European agents, lured many an innocent soul in quest of the "golden bough." The European unrest caused by the Napoleonic Wars was a further incentive to the emigration of Jews from Central Europe.

The new arrivals moved westward in the American train; Gratzburg and Aaronsburgh were two stopovers on the western route. Jewish communities were slowly formed along a typical pattern; the steps in the operation became almost mechanical. A concrete example is Cincinnati, the city that was destined to play a leading role in the history of American Judaism.

Joseph Jonas of Exeter, England, arrived in Cincinnati in 1817. Among his other gifts, Jonas evidently possessed a keen sense of history, for he bequeathed to posterity his memoirs, replete with important historical information. The economic potentialities of the Ohio Valley attracted Jonas. He traveled westward, against all sound advice, the first Jew to be seen in those parts. People traveled many miles to view this object of curiosity. One old Quaker woman said to him: "Art Thou a Jew? Thou art one of God's chosen people. Wilt thou let me examine thee?" As she turned him round about, she remarked, "Well, thou art no different to other people."[15]

In 1819 a trio of English Jews joined him; then came another handful. Within five years, in 1824, a congregation was established and named, simply, Bene Israel. The synagogue required assistance. Letters were dispatched to England, Barbados, and older sister congregations in America: ". . . a few years before nothing was heard but the howling of wild beasts and the more hideous cry of savage man. It is worthy of remark that there is not a congregation within 500 miles of this city . . . and we are well informed that had we a Synagogue here, hundreds from that City who now know nothing of their religion would frequently attend here during holidays." Until 1830 only English Jews resided in Cincinnati. Then the German Jews poured in. In 1836, the Bene Israel dedicated their house of God.[16]

In short, the record of American Jewish history in these early years of the nineteenth century not only indicates that the Ashkenazic Jews fanned out into the American hinterland; but, more profoundly, the record reflects how deeply American Israel was involved in the expansion of America. From these two primary forces—the westward expansion of America and the German Jewish immigration—there emerged several ancillary factors which slowly weakened the uniform congregational structure. They are, in order: the preponderance of Ashkenazic over Sephardic Jewry,[17] the waning of synagogal authority, and the beginnings of Reform.

The problem of "authority" has always constituted one of the most fascinating and complicated chapters in the Jewish spiritual odyssey. In America the problem was all the more interesting because the two contesting mother countries, England and Holland, exerted a powerful influence on American culture. During the greater part of the nineteenth century, America was firmly tied to the skirts of the mother continent. One lived in America but Europe was "home." In each important legal question, the congregations referred to their chief rabbi, for American Jewry lacked qualified scholars and rabbis who could interpret ritual law. The authority sitting in London was accepted as the final word by all English Ashkenazic synagogues in America. As late as 1837, Congregation B'nai Jeshurun, for example, paid an annual half shekel to the chief rabbi, as the minutes of the congregation reveal.[18]

While in such matters as the pronunciation of Hebrew there may have been differences, and the minor details of custom and ceremony were performed with varying emphases, the forms of synagogal organization were not altered. In this respect, the American Sephardic congregational tradition prevailed. Shearith Israel was the model for the new Ashkenazic synagogues. The *parnas* retained all his powers, synagogue attendance was declared compulsory, the recalcitrant and obstreperous were duly fined. Once the new congregations were established and the stringencies of personal feuds reduced, the most amicable relations existed between them. A helping hand was extended in times of need. Properly enough, Harmon

Hendricks, then *parnas* of Shearith Israel, contributed generously to the seceding congregation, B'nai Jeshurun. The respective Sephardic and Ashkenazic synagogues continued to accept members of the other group into their fold.

This relationship was more than an expression of amenities. In the deeper realm of religious life, in theology and in fundamental practice, the Sephardim and Ashkenazim were of one thought. The shade of difference was infinitesimal in comparison with the wide area of common interest. Both Sephardim and Ashkenazim sought to uphold the Torah through the institution of the synagogue. All hands were joined to ward off the onrushing forces of assimilation and communal disintegration. With one voice they proclaimed the inviolability of the Sabbath. With equal determination they joined to ban the faithless. They were also pained when they saw that the synagogue was slowly but surely being dislodged from its central position in Jewish life.

The battle over the centrality of the synagogue was not lost without a serious attempt to meet the growing needs of the expanding community. In 1828, Shearith Israel established a Hebrew Benevolent Society as part of the congregation's functions. However, as the push toward decentralization became stronger, the synagogue simply could not meet the pressing social needs of the heterogeneous and undisciplined community. Sixteen years later, when German Jews were to establish a social agency, they organized the German Hebrew Benevolent Society apart from the synagogue. That very decade saw the founding of the largest international Jewish order, B'nai B'rith (1843), to be followed by the orders B'nai Israel (1853) and B'nai Abraham (1859). Slowly the Jews were weaned away from the synagogue as their central communal institution. The fraternal orders, which began as supplementary agencies to the synagogue, were to become their chief competitors.

The school, the very heart of the congregational system, also spread its wings in trial flight. The first Sunday school, which was organized in Philadelphia in 1838 by Rebecca Gratz (1781-1869), assumed a communal rather than a congregational character. Similar schools were shortly introduced in Charleston, Richmond, Cincinnati, and New York.

The real challenge to the uniformity which characterized the synagogue came from a totally unanticipated source: the challenge came from within. The first signs of Reform Judaism appeared in Charleston in 1824. After a brief period of existence, this attempt disappeared and seemingly left no trace. Twenty years later, however, Reform flowered once again; this time to remain permanently in the garden of American Judaism.

History cannot be controlled by logic. It was in a sedate Sephardic congregation, Beth Elohim, not a German synagogue, that Reform Judaism was first planted in America. A group of forty-seven members, led by Isaac Harby (1788-1828) and David N. Carvalho (1784-1860), influenced by the developments in Hamburg and repelled by the perfunctory order of their own congregational affairs, appealed for a modification of their service. They asked what seems in retrospect to be very little: a shorter, more intelligible, and more decorous service. They requested that some prayers be read in English as well as in Hebrew and that the rabbi offer a commentary on the portion of the week. The heads of the community refused to depart from their accustomed practice. In protest, twelve of the more determined members in the group resigned and established the Reformed Society of Israelites. Within the short space of two years their number grew to fifty. Their long range purpose soon became apparent. They published a new prayer book, introduced the organ, and announced reforms in Jewish practice in order to adapt Judaism to the "situation of an enlightened world." Despite these serious preparations, the project failed and the money that had been donated for the proposed building was returned to the contributors. This sudden dissolution was not the last chapter in the story of Charleston Reform. It was but the first attempt. As a footnote to the development of Reform in Charleston, it is interesting to observe with David Philipson that the practice of establishing "Reform-Vereine" for the purpose of propagating Reform sentiment in the community and then organizing a congregation was adopted by other groups as well. Such societies served as the basic units of congregations Har Sinai in Baltimore, Emanu-El in New York, Keneseth Israel in Philadelphia, and Sinai in Chicago.

At the end of this period, in 1840, American Jewry entered a new stage in its development. The dynamism of American life had released powerful forces. America and its Jews were on the move. Now centrifugal forces gained sway. The older methods of fines and bans lost their punitive powers. Disaffection and spiritual corrosion could not be met with declarations and resolutions. Intermarriage, Jewish ignorance, and above all, the paralyzing indifference to the destiny of Judaism thoroughly upset Jewish religious institutional life. In the Colonial period, a Jew was zealously controlled from birth to death by the synagogue. Now a Jew could live or die as a Jew without regard for that control.

3

NEW JEWISH RELIGIOUS TRENDS, 1840-1869

The hundred years from 1840 to 1940 marked the greatest period of migration in all human history. The political, social, and industrial revolutions in Germany, and the resultant agrarian crisis in the forties of the nineteenth century, compelled large portions of the population to emigrate to western countries, particularly the United States. The appeal of Leopold

Kompert (1822-1886), the German Jewish novelist and political writer, that all Jews of Central Europe emigrate to America, was answered in deed by tens of thousands of his fellow religionists. In eight years (1840-1848), the estimated Jewish population figures in America jumped from fifteen to fifty thousand.

These statistics of Jewish increase serve but as an index to the formidable spiritual complications that now beset American Judaism. Fortunately, the enveloping crisis brought forth elements for its own cure. Fresh forces arose. They injected a vitalism which gave the sagging religious life a new spirit and a new heart. The most prominent participants in this revival were Isaac Leeser and Isaac Mayer Wise.

"To learn and to teach, to observe, and to do." This is the legend Isaac Leeser (1806-1868) selected for the masthead of his new magazine, the *Occident and American Jewish Advocate*. It serves as a clue to the life, character, and activities of this pioneer in Jewish religious life in America.[19]

Leeser pioneered in every conceivable field of Jewish endeavor. He is credited with being the first *hazzan* to introduce the English sermon as a permanent part of the Sabbath service. He translated the Sephardic and Ashkenazic prayer books into English. In the field of publications his name is imprinted on the flyleaf of virtually every important Jewish religious text that appeared in his generation, including children's spelling books, catechisms, and supplementary liturgical volumes. He was the first to produce a volume on Eretz Yisrael, the English translation of the famous geography of Rabbi Joseph Schwarz, *A Descriptive Geography and Brief Historical Sketch of Palestine*. The climax of his literary career was his translation of the Bible into English, a translation which for the first time replaced the King James version in Jewish schools and homes. Until the appearance of the Jewish Publication Society translation in 1917, Leeser's edition served as the Jewish home Bible in all English-speaking countries in the world.

Isaac Mayer Wise (1819-1900) was rabbi, student, editor and administrator *par excellence*. The history of American Judaism will ever remember him as master architect of Reform religious institutions. In his autobiography, Isaac Mayer Wise, the man with the penetrating eyes and the spectacles on his forehead (whose portrait is fixed in the heart and imagination of American Israel), wrote: "The reforming spirit was innate in me; it was my foremost characteristic."[20]

Wise the reformer was not an iconoclast. He had many orthodoxies. Denying the central position of Eretz Yisrael in the future of world Israel, he substituted America in its place; declaring modernism as his child, he insisted that biblical critics keep hands off the sacred and ancient text; rejecting talmudic authority, he nevertheless created a new authority of rabbis; rejecting aspects of ceremonial law, he believed with a firm

Isaac Mayer Wise
1819-1900

Solomon Schechter
1847-1915

faith that Judaism was the theosophy of mankind; disgruntled with the absence of lay leadership in religious life, he created the Union of American Hebrew Congregations. Wise's successes were unquestionably due to his accent on the positive task. As Professor Samuel S. Cohon chooses to describe him, Wise was the "foremost leader of Constructive Reform in America."

Leeser and Wise, who were to join forces only to separate, were the respective founders of the two contending movements in American Judaism in the nineteenth century—Historical, or Conservative Judaism; and Progressive, or Reform Judaism. Both men attracted to themselves devoted associates who helped establish their policies of action. The goal was the same: the adjustment of Jews and Judaism to the American scene. The anarchy in American Jewish religious life was inherent in its very system of organization. Throughout the Western Hemisphere, from Canada to the West Indies, congregational independence held sway. The principle of the separatists, who abandoned Elizabethan England because they repudiated the idea of a national church, was the rule in America; and, thought Leeser, this system as it applied to Jewish life could serve only further to decentralize the synagogue. Congregational absolutism led to dishonorable competition and stubborn isolationism even between sister congregations in one city. Leeser began to speak of *Kelal Israel*—the United Synagogue. He was the first to use the idiom "Catholic Israel" in the exact connotation and frame of reference that Schechter so effectively employed in the twentieth century.

Leeser formulated a program of action. Citizen of the United States and ardent advocate of its democratic principles, he thought along American constitutional lines. He devised a federated synagogue plan which would guarantee congregational autonomy. The proposed union was to deal with transcongregational problems: religious issues, education, publications, community representation, etc. The union would not seek to interfere in any manner with the local *minhag*, order of service, or language of prayer. As early as 1841, Leeser met with Louis Salomon, *hazzan* of the Rodeph Shalom Congregation, and together they issued a joint proposal. The full details of this program, as elaborated by the leaders of the three Philadelphia congregations—Mikveh Israel, Rodeph Shalom, and Beth Israel—and published in the *Occident*, make up a document of historic importance in the development of American Jewish communal organization.[21] A call was issued for a national assembly. Leeser was rebuffed. Union was declared unfeasible. The plan was premature.

Leeser turned to other tactics. If the solution to congregational anarchy was not to come from reorganization, why not reform from within? With careful and self-critical step, he outlined the procedures: pruning the service of unnecessary encumbrances, introduction of novel ceremonies, incorporation of English readings, and production of a religious literature.

To the reformers these efforts seemed trivial. The American synagogue, they insisted, would not fulfil its potentialities unless a more radical revision of the traditional service were instituted. Reform forces were growing in number and their program of action began to take shape.

In November, 1845, Max Lilienthal (1815-1882), then just thirty, arrived in the United States. Though a young man, his fame preceded him, for he came from Russia where for five years he had served on the staff of Count Uwaroff, imperial minister of education. This newcomer to the ranks of American Reform played a leading role in the growth of that movement. Although in his introductory sermons Lilienthal declared himself to be a traditionalist, he later veered to the moderate reformism of Isaac Mayer Wise.

It was Max Lilienthal who introduced the custom of confirmation into the United States. The festival of Shabuot, 1846, is the date of the first ceremony of confirmation, which later came to be observed in Orthodox and Conservative, as well as Reform, synagogues. Lilienthal carries the additional distinction of being the president of the first rabbinical association in America. Wise had been in Albany scarcely a month when he joined with Lilienthal, Dr. Hermann Felsenheld and Rabbi Kohlmeyer to organize an ecclesiastical court, a *Bet Din.* Lilienthal was chosen president and Wise served as secretary. But three rabbis gathered at the initial meeting held April 18, 1847. Nevertheless, the small gathering had a lasting effect. They declared their purpose was to offer "beneficial service to the Jewish congregations of America," and "not to assume any hierarchical authority, but to act only in advisory capacity." The agenda of the conference called for preparation of a catechism and biblical history for Jewish schools. These plans did not materialize.

The more important assignment given at that time to Wise was ultimately accomplished. It was at this meeting that Wise proposed his *Minhag America.* The very name is indicative of the spirit with which Wise and his associates conceived the future of American Judaism. They (like the traditional groups) declared their faith in America as a permanent home for Israel. However, in place of the prevailing liturgies in American congregations, the Sephardic and Ashkenazic *minhagim*, they intended to substitute an American rite. Characteristic of Wise's approach was his insistence that the new prayer book be issued under the imprimatur of an accredited rabbinical body. He prepared his manuscript subject to its being considered at the following meeting. That meeting was never held. He placed the text aside until a proper authority of rabbis would be constituted.[22]

The service book could wait, but other synagogal reforms could not. Upon his return to Albany, Wise set to work. As yet no one, either in

Europe or in America, had ventured to impose the reforms proposed by Abraham Geiger, as early as 1837, for the "religious emancipation of the Jewish woman." Geiger's important essay *"Die Stellung des weiblichen Geschlechtes in dem Judenthume unserer Zeit"* (The Position of Woman in the Judaism of our Time),[23] remained a theoretical statement as far as European Judaism was concerned. It was Wise who initiated the practice of mixed choir and family pews in American Jewish religious life. Then came the issue over the use of an organ at religious services. In 1846, the organ dispute reached the Court of Errors and Appeals in the state of South Carolina. In time organ music was to be heard in all Reform congregations throughout the land and in many Conservative congregations.

These differences of opinion did not sever the bond between the men of the Historical and Reform schools. Differences existed, but lines of opposition were not yet formed. On the contrary, the growing differences made both groups ever more anxious to seek an area of compromise. The amorphous mass of indifferent Jews concerned them more than rabbinical polemics. Reform was moderate and Historical Judaism alert. All minds searched for a formula.

Suddenly Isaac Mayer Wise wrote to Leeser. He prepared an article for publication in the *Occident* in which he endorsed Leeser's activities on behalf of a national religious federation. The two captains rallied their parties and issued a call of assembly for 1849. Eight congregations responded favorably. Nevertheless, they sought a large representation of at least twenty participants. Once again New York City was the determining factor. Wise took the organizing lead. Temple Emanu-El, fearful lest common effort with the traditionalists would impede the growth of Reform, demurred. Wise lashed out in characteristic manner. He challenged Emanu-El's integrity. Not the greater interests of Judaism, but autocratic congregational independence compelled Emanu-El's refusal to co-operate, he wrote. Recriminations only aggravated difficulties. The lone New York support of Shaaray Tefila, synagogue of Samuel Myer Isaacs (1804-1878), stanch friend of Leeser, was small consolation. The champions laid down their arms for a brief respite before they began the next round in the battle for unity.

A third impassioned attempt was made. In 1855, largely through the tireless efforts of Isaac M. Wise, a gathering predominantly of Reform elements was assembled in Cleveland with the symbolic motto *Shalom al Yisroel* (Peace in Israel). Leeser, who was apprised of the constituent delegates, was wary of participating unless his condition, that all discussions be premised on the authority of tradition, be accepted. The eastern contingent of reformers absented themselves for a contrary reason. They were unhappy with the moderation of Wise and Lilienthal. Thus, it was largely a midwestern moderate Reform-oriented group that convened in Cleveland. Wise was so concerned with "Union in Israel" that he was prepared to meet Leeser more than half way. He was convinced, as his later writings reveal, that once all the elements in Judaism would function co-operatively, Reform, which in his opinion was weighted with truth, would inevitably triumph.

Leeser returned from the meeting in Cleveland with the wreath of victory. Even the rightists in the Historical school, those who had counseled abstention, agreed that Leeser had been vindicated. What lasting good might have come to American Judaism had Leeser and Wise stood firmly together! But they did not remain united. The wind of wrath blew strongest from the eastern Reform camp. David Einhorn led the opposition. "Who authorized you," the reformers scorned, "to make alliances with the Orthodox and their talmudic ideas?"[24] Further rebuke came from the house of Reform in Germany. Rabbis Ludwig Philippson (1811-1889) and Leopold Stein (1810-1882) admonished their former *Liebling*, Wise, for his treachery, and gave full support to Einhorn. Wise was bitterly discouraged by this opposition. The simmerings of doubt and challenge directed against his leadership now developed into a full-fledged revolt. New personalities had emerged on the Reform scene in America. They were to be reckoned with.

Foremost among the eastern Reform wing was David Einhorn (1809-1879), who came to America in 1855. Einhorn had already benefited from his experience in the German Reform movement. His native talents and especially his oratorical ability won him an established place on the central dais of American Reform. Einhorn summarized his philosophy of Judaism in one sentence: "Like man himself, the child of God, the divine law has a perishable body and imperishable spirit." Idealistic German philosophy was at the root of his thinking. He was convinced that the permanent ideas of Judaism could find their truest expression only in the German language. Second only to the doctrine of God, Einhorn stressed the priestly mission of Israel as the hope of humanity's salvation. He published the magazine "Sinai" a monthly in German, from 1856 to 1862.

Bernhard Felsenthal (1822-1908), who arrived in America in 1854, was known for his independent views and scholarly attainments. Later he was to be one of the founders of the American Zionist movement. From 1858 on, even before he became rabbi, first of Sinai Congregation and later of Zion Congregation in Chicago, he was a leading spokesman for congregational union, but urged that individual synagogues maintain their autonomy. In March, 1859, the pamphlet, *Kol Kore Bamidbar, ueber juedische Reform* (A Voice in the Wilderness), in which he preached his doctrine, established the new arrival as an important and dominating spirit.

Following Einhorn and Felsenthal came Samuel Adler (1809-1891) who arrived from Alzey in 1857. He, too, had participated in the early deliberations of the German Reform movement. Adler served at Temple Emanu-El in New York for nineteen years and consistently called for a crystallized Reform position.

In 1866, Samuel Hirsch (1815-1889) assumed the Keneseth Israel pulpit in Philadelphia. He was soon recognized as the philosopher of extreme Reform. Hirsch's wide influence had been felt even earlier from abroad. Now his scholarly support in America was added to the struggle for theological reorientation. Hirsch was bound to the Hegelian system and regarded history as the divine process of revelation. Differing from his master, however, he developed the conception of Judaism as *Lehre*. Torah is not "law" but *Lehre*, doctrine. These doctrines were revealed to Israel through the prophets, and Israel was chosen to exemplify *Lehre* before the entire world.

Wise read the handwriting clearly. American Judaism was in a state of confusion. His dream of an all inclusive synod had to be postponed, if not forgotten. The reality of the moment required a stabilization of the Reform position. There were two groups in Reform, fairly well distributed in the East and the West. The well defined program of the German school was transplanted to America, while the more moderate and adaptable program of pragmatic Reform was losing its hold. Strategy called for concentration on the advancement of the Reform position and co-ordination of its high command.

In the ranks of the Historical school, the identical cell splitting took place. Only the reasons and personalities varied. The rightists in the group were soon aided by Wise himself. The *Minhag America* appeared, and it reflected his writing and thinking. Prayers for the return to Eretz Yisrael, the rebuilding of the Temple in Jerusalem, the restoration of the sacrificial system and the restoration of the Davidic dynasty were all eliminated. Bernard Illowy (1814-1871) submitted a bill of particulars explaining why he, Wise, should be placed under ban.[25]

Leeser was stunned. The appearance of the *Minhag America* completely shattered his hopes. It demonstrated the true position of Wise, Lilienthal, and their like minded associates. The Cleveland Conference was wasted. Disappointment was transmuted to open warfare. Reform, Leeser claimed, was bankrupt. Its synagogues were empty, its memberships static, and the religious feeling of its congregants dissipated. So-called Reform was only a paring of the candle ends.

Leeser then reached the very conclusions for the Historical school that Wise had formulated for Reform Judaism. If an all-inclusive synod was impossible, the obvious alternative was a union of traditionalists.

But as in the case of Reform, immediate unification of the Historical school was frustrated from within. The Historical school in America included a number of adherents who were as estranged from the rightist elements in the traditionalist grouping as they were from the extreme of German Reform. They had greatest affinity with the moderate reformism of Wise and Lilienthal and actually went beyond them in proposals to modify Jewish practice. The chief exponents of moderate reformism in the ranks of the Historical school were Benjamin Szold and Marcus Jastrow.

Benjamin Szold (1829-1902) received his advanced Jewish training at the Breslau Juedisch-Theologisches Seminar, where, under the influence of Zacharias Frankel (1801-1875), Heinrich Graetz (1817-1891), and Jacob Bernays (1824-1881), he prepared for his calling as rabbi and teacher in Israel. In 1859, Szold settled in Baltimore, serving Congregation Oheb Shalom for forty-seven years with distinction, integrity and affection.

Marcus Jastrow (1829-1903) was dedicated to the rabbinical service in his early youth. He received an excellent training in Rabbinics. Under the influence of Professor Graetz, Jastrow assumed a post in Warsaw, where his modernism and liberalism combined with his traditional bearing, reflected much credit on the young rabbi. In 1866 he accepted the call of Congregation Rodeph Shalom in Philadelphia. Jastrow's arrival in the United States was marked with pomp and circumstance. The rabbis of the city readily deferred to his learning and scholarship, and turned to him in all matters of interpretation of Jewish law. Jastrow soon discovered a kindred soul in Szold, with whom he shared a common platform of thought and action. Szold and Jastrow attempted to clarify their position which, despite their reforming practice and their interest in Wise's work, kept them well within the ranks of Historical Judaism when the final test came.

"Judaism," Szold wrote to Wise in German, "has two fundamental principles; one is mobile, the other is static. Only through the fusion of both elements will we discover the golden mean."[26] The purpose of Reform is to vitalize the precepts, not to force their abrogation. Development does not come in spurts through radical change in the elimination of ancient usage, but rather in adapting the *Mitzvot* to the spirit of the times.

As early as 1864, Szold prepared the original edition of the *Abodat Israel* in Hebrew with German translation for use in his congregation. The following year he found it necessary to issue a Hebrew and English edition. In 1871 a second edition of the Hebrew and German prayer book appeared, revised by Marcus Jastrow and Henry Hochheimer (1818-1912). The latter was a left wing colleague of Szold and Jastrow in the Historical school, an authority on classical German literature, and rabbi of the Nidche Israel Congregation in Baltimore. The prayer book became exceedingly popular in many of the German congregations. In 1873

Jastrow published his Hebrew and English edition of the *Abodat Israel*, which subsequently gained popularity as the *Minhag Jastrow*.

Despite many theological disagreements, all the rabbis, Reform or Conservative or Orthodox, felt strongly that Judaism represented more than worship and ritual practice. In the nineteenth century it was the recognized duty of the rabbi to function as a *religious* leader in every area of Jewish service, despite the specialized nonreligious auspices under which he served. In this manner the rabbis endowed with religious spirit and instruction all communal agencies in which they served. The foundation stones of Jewish institutional life—education, social service, defense of Jewish rights, overseas relief, Palestine aid, and democratic action—were hewn from the quarry of religious inspiration and leadership.

In the field of education, the Jews had a special stake in the victory of the free public school system in American education, for the private schools were pervaded by Christian belief and practice. Even the most punctilious religious care of the Jewish child at home could not weather the emotional associations and habits imbibed in a strong Christian religious culture and environment. Until the complete acceptance of the public school, there was but one corrective to the existing Christian private schools—Jewish private schools. An example of the type of school established in this period was the boarding school opened by Max Lilienthal in 1849. He had the undivided support of all Jewish religious groups. The full curriculum, as announced in the *Occident*, included both religious and secular studies.[27]

The advocates of public education, led by Henry Barnard (1811-1900) and Horace Mann (1796-1859), triumphed. State after state adopted formal laws. In the wake of this important change in the texture of American life, for which they, too, had labored, Jewish religious leaders were compelled to build a new structure of Jewish education. All day schools were on the wane. As a result, the supplementary Jewish school system for Sunday and weekday afternoons was created.

The Sunday school rapidly became part of the American Jewish way of life. However, as time went by, the hollowness of a curriculum based on a one-hour instruction period per week became shockingly apparent. Rote recitation of catechisms was not Jewish education. And what of Bible, Hebrew, and prayers? That which ostensibly seemed so excellent a contribution to Jewish life (was it not created in the image of the Protestant Sunday-school system and as such integral to the American pattern?), became a sham and delusion which undermined any possible effort for intensive Jewish living. A flickering effort was made by the leaders of the Historical School in the direction of building a congregational supplementary school system. In word, Leeser, Szold, and Jastrow stressed the inadequacy of Sunday-school education. However, their action was not equal to their promises and the results were unrewarding.

However, in the realm of higher Jewish education their approach was more vigorous. Although the obstacles were overwhelming, the initiators brooked no compromise, accepted their several defeats with equanimity, and ultimately emerged victorious. In a series of leading articles entitled "Education for the Ministry," published in the *Occident* in 1847, Isaac Leeser projected a plan for the training of a native ministry and teachers' corps in a higher school of general and Jewish education. The Hebrew Education Society of Philadelphia responded to his appeal, applied for a charter, and received permission to create such an institution in the state of Pennsylvania. Isaac Mayer Wise echoed Leeser's call with a proposal to establish the Zion Collegiate Institute. After announcing his plan in 1854 in the *Asmonean*, a New York Anglo-Jewish weekly, Wise launched a series of supporting societies in several cities on behalf of his new venture. For a variety of reasons, chiefly indifference and petty jealousies, Wise's project was rejected after a brief and dismal start.

The next to raise the theme of higher Jewish education was a group of young men in Baltimore. Banded together in an association of Hebrew literary societies, they called for the establishment of a National Hebrew College. In 1866, Benjamin Franklin Peixotto (1834-1890), grand master of the B'nai B'rith, proposed the establishment of an American Jewish university. He planned to finance the school through a per capita volunteer tax of ten dollars from the general membership. The heavy response of silence crushed his high hopes.

A final drive was made to overcome indifference. In 1864, toward the end of his days, Isaac Leeser rallied the forces of Historical Judaism and established the Maimonides College in Philadelphia—on the strength of the original charter granted to the Hebrew Education Society authorizing the granting of degrees "in divinity and other subjects." The Board of Delegates of American Israelites agreed to support the new institution. Marcus Jastrow and Sabato Morais, among the rabbis, and Mayer Sulzberger (1843-1923) and Moses A. Dropsie (1821-1905), representing the laity, supported Leeser's noble attempt. A curriculum including all the subjects necessary to a college of Jewish studies was published. The opening of classes was announced for October, 1867.

The college constantly faced a struggle to exist. Until his dying day, Leeser held the reins. He was replaced by Marcus Jastrow. Matters went from bad to worse. The Board of Delegates slowly withdrew support. In 1873, after a valiant struggle, the doors of Maimonides College were closed. Four students had been graduated, the first four men in America to receive specialized training for Jewish service.

The cause of Jewish education was advanced further by the establishment of the first Jewish publication society. The agency through which

Leeser hoped to solve the problem of an acute shortage of literary material, was born quite by accident. Two friends of Leeser turned to him for a rare book. They were prepared to spend a goodly sum to acquire the volume. Leeser nonchalantly suggested that they reprint the edition. They agreed. Thus in 1845 a new organization came into being.[28] Leeser issued a prospectus which included a plan for publications, memberships, and distribution. Gathering its funds, penny by penny, the American Jewish Publication Society managed to maintain itself for five years until a fire broke out in the buildings where the plates and stocks of books were stored. The flames consumed the books and the society. A score of years were to pass before Isaac M. Wise gathered the courage to propose the re-establishment of this vital organization. The second American Jewish Publication Society was incorporated in 1872, but it, too, had a short life, ceasing publication in 1875.

As the Jewish population grew in numbers, specialized social agencies were required to meet the problems of the sick, the infirm and the aged. The first philanthropic institution, the orphan house in Charleston, had been established in 1801. Here and there, as the need arose, additional homes were built. The German inflow accelerated the process and provided, as in the case of education, a compelling challenge to social initiative. In this program of social work, the role of the religious institutions and personnel was paradoxical. While the human and material resources for the development of Jewish social agencies came in greatest measure from the synagogue, corporate control was vested in a nonsynagogal body which ultimately divested itself of the compelling influence of the synagogue. This was a departure of great consequence.

Jewish hospitals were a primary concern. In many cases the dying were furtively baptized by hyperzealous nuns in order "to save them from the hands of Satan and to assure them a place in Paradise." Missionizing Christianity was the reason given for the establishment of the first Jewish hospitals in Cincinnati, Philadelphia and Baltimore, respectively.

As regards the organization of charity service, the rabbis quickly realized that direct personal gifts compromised both donor and recipient. Isaac Leeser called attention to flagrant iniquities and urged the formation of a central agency which could regulate and report income and disbursements to the entire community and which would be subject to community surveillance and counsel. Out of this idea the United Hebrew Charities of Philadelphia was formed in 1869.

Aid to European Jews was restricted in these years to those who sought the haven of American shores. The Jewish communities on the mother continent were self-sufficient. From time to time reports were received from distant places—from China, India and North Africa—concerning the activities of Christian missionaries among the impoverished Jewish communities. Very little, however, was done by the organized American Jewish community to act on these reports.

Support of Eretz Yisrael was always forthcoming. In 1832 a Hebrah Terumat ha-Kodesh (Society for Offerings of the Sanctuary) was formed under the chairmanship of Israel Baer Kursheedt (1766-1852) with the specific purpose of collecting annual membership contributions for Palestine Jewry. The revolutions of 1848-1849, which unbalanced community life in Europe and consequently forced European Jews to curtail their support to Eretz Yisrael, compelled the Jews in Palestine to cast about for alternative sources of income. They turned to American Jewry. A thorough housecleaning was necessary in the affairs of Eretz Yisrael philanthropic effort. Samuel Myer Isaacs assumed the task. In 1853 the North American Relief Society for the indigent Jews in Jerusalem, Palestine, was organized with Isaacs as treasurer. To this association, Judah Touro (1775-1854) left a bequest of $10,000 with an annual income of $700. The pages of Isaacs' *Jewish Messenger* are replete with information about the cause and continued appeals for community support. While he did not wish to withhold aid when needed, Isaacs protested against useless and demoralizing charities. He called for a working community in Palestine. Leeser went further. He spoke of the possibilities of an agricultural economy. In 1853 Leeser upheld the hands of Moses Sachs of Palestine to found such a settlement in Jaffa and accepted the chairmanship of the American committee. In addition, Isaacs appeared before the Board of Delegates and prevailed upon them to grant an extensive subsidy to the new agricultural school established in Jaffa by the Alliance Israélite Universelle.[29]

In the mid-nineteenth century, the central issue of group discrimination was not based on racial or national differences but on specious religious argument. To speak of nineteenth century America as a secular country is a myth. Church and state were perhaps constitutionally divided, but the Christian spirit penetrated deep into the character of the American people and into every phase of American social life. One of the sharply debated questions that reflected itself in the public mind and deed was: Is the United States a Christian country? The Jews had to face the question and its implications. The influences of this continued belief that America was a Christian nation were exceedingly subtle. This was particularly important in so far as both the general and the Jewish educational systems were affected. The question of Bible teaching in the public school (in its Christian translation and commentary) has recurred again and again in American educational theory, but at no time before had the problem been so acute as in the period under discussion.

A second area in which the Jews had to overcome discrimination was that of Sunday law legislation. Every piece of discriminatory legislation had to be pulled up root and branch. Slowly, but steadily, the legislatures of New York, Maine, New Hampshire and Vermont granted to Jews who "keep the seventh day as the holy day" the right to engage in business on the "Christian Sabbath." The change in law as regards Jewish rights was but one aspect of the general trend toward greater religious freedom and understanding among the various faiths. It became increasingly apparent that restrictive religious laws had no place in the democratic tradition.

Other illustrations of the overbearing influence of the dominant faiths on American life were the official public statements, particularly the Thanksgiving proclamations. It had become good American political practice for the governors and President of the United States to issue annual declarations announcing the Thanksgiving festival. These proclamations most of them unwittingly, yet others with deliberate denominational conviction, were couched in Christian religious phraseology. On one occasion, in 1849, when Hamilton Fish, the governor of New York State, confused his private Christian belief with his public office, ten Jewish congregations in New York called off the specially announced Thanksgiving service in protest.

If the Jews were successful in combatting discrimination in the United States, it was primarily due to the fundamental democratic precepts of the country. In Europe, and in North Africa, the tradition of universal freedom did not prevail. Prejudice and bigotry reared their heads in a series of three international incidents: the Damascus, Swiss, and Mortara affairs. The Damascus blood libel (1840) brought American Jewry to its feet; it was the beginning of the organizational awakening of American Israel. The Swiss regulations (1855) were even more humiliating, for in a proposed commercial treaty the attempt was made to draw the line between American citizens of the Christian faith and those of Jewish origin. The third incident that inflamed American Jewry was the kidnaping of the Mortara child in 1858, and his enforced conversion to Catholicism.[29a]

The troubles of the hour produced a formula of hope. The Board of Delegates of American Israelites was brought into being by the spontaneous combustion of the Mortara incident, although in a profound sense, the board was the capstone of congregational, lay, and rabbinic efforts over the hardworking decades. It was the first attempt to organize American Israel on a congregational basis for the total interests of American Jewry. Apart from the later attempt by Isaac M. Wise through the formation of the Union of American Hebrew Congregations, religiously oriented Jewry was never again in the position to assemble a supervisory body of such proportions and design for the affairs of American and world Israel. The Board of Delegates had no intention of creating a hierarchy or of interfering in the affairs of local congregations. Its areas of action were sevenfold: education, statistics, Jewish law court, strengthening of charity organizations, information exchange, relations with international Jewry, and defense of Jewish rights. This was an ambitious program; and though little was achieved toward its realization, some lasting contributions were made.

One of the important acts of the Board was the influence it exerted to establish a Jewish chaplaincy in the armed forces of the United States. The Acts of Congress approved July 21 and August 3, 1861, calling for the chaplaincy in the Union Army, read: "The chaplain appointed by the vote of the field officers and company commanders, must be a regular ordained minister of some Christian denomination." As a result of continued effort on the part of the Board, the section II regulation was amended to read:

> . . . That no person shall be appointed a chaplain in the United States army who is not a regularly ordained minister of some religious denomination, and who does not present testimonials of his present good standing as such minister, with a recommendation for his appointment as an army chaplain from some authorized ecclesiastical body, or not less than five accredited ministers belonging to said religious denomination.[30]

The precedent for the Jewish Chaplaincy was firmly established.

The picture of American Jewish religious thought and action in the formative period would be incomplete without understanding the contemporary Jewish religious view of American society and destiny. To these immigrants, America was not a haven, but a hope; not a refuge, but a dream. Even the traditionalists, who did not equate America with Zion, and Washington with Jerusalem (as did Wise, Einhorn, and the Reform leaders), felt that America was the land where justice and righteousness would emerge triumphant. The profound identification with the American spirit was reflected in the concentrated, almost wearying efforts, emotionally and linguistically, on Americanization. For the Jews, the transfer was more than a change in geography. The entire Western European experience was to be exchanged for the spiritual climate of the Anglo-Saxon world, and the religious tradition of the Orient was to be merged with Occidental values.

4

DIVISION IN AMERICAN JUDAISM, 1869-1886

The year 1869 was the beginning of the great divide in American Jewish religious history. Philadelphia was the scene of the first independent Reform conference. During the two preceding years, the pages of the *Israelite* regularly carried Wise's refrain for a meeting. Eighteen congregations had responded to the call, when David Einhorn and

Samuel Hirsch stole a march upon Wise and called a conference in Philadelphia. Wise participated; Hirsch was host and chairman of the sessions; but the spirit of Einhorn permeated the resolutions. Wise's star dimmed at this conference. His *magnum opus*, the *Minhag America*, was not accepted as the American prayer book. The personal opposition to him was formidable. Ignoring the expressed agreement to convene the following assembly in Philadelphia, Wise called the convention to Cleveland in 1870, with the avowed purpose of considering suggestions for, and modifications of, his prayer book. Thirteen rabbis constituted the western wing of the Reform camp. Their final resolutions differed from that of the eastern segment only in the names of the signers. Being unified in counsel, the western rabbis were better prepared to meet their eastern colleagues. They returned for further deliberations. Einhorn avoided the contest of strength. Wise, anxious to seal the final decision in his favor, called a third conference in Cincinnati in 1871. Twenty-seven delegates appeared, the majority of them representing western congregations. The agenda included discussions on education, publications, and itinerant preachers. The most important decision was the confirmation of Wise's proposals to found the Union of American Hebrew Congregations and the Hebrew Union College. In 1873, this Union was organized by Wise with an initial membership of twenty-eight congregations located in the Midwest and South. The first president was Moritz Loth. Its purposes were to establish a seminary, to stimulate popular Jewish education, to organize new congregations, and to provide such other institutions as Judaism would require.

Despite the inevitable clash of personalities, the paltry differences in emphasis, and the underdeveloped organizational structure, Reform Judaism was the foremost movement on the American Jewish horizon. In contrast, the forces of Historical Judaism were anemic. Leeser's sharp and clear voice was silenced forever. Szold, Jastrow, and Hochheimer were straddling, so to speak. The numbers dwindled. Sabato Morais (1823-1897) and Samuel M. Isaacs held the fort alone.

Had this weakness of the Historical school continued but a few years more, the very nature of American Judaism would probably have been formed, unalterably, in the mold of Reform. A series of external and internal factors prevented this from happening: the return of Szold and Jastrow to the group now rallying about Morais and Isaacs, the enlistment of younger men in the ranks, the steady trickle of Eastern European immigration, and the establishment of the *American Hebrew*.

Szold, Jastrow, and Hochheimer found increasing reason to be disappointed with the extremism of many Reformers. The irresponsible slurs upon basic Jewish precepts, such as those on the Sabbath and *kashrut*, violated their beliefs. They proclaimed publicly their disavowal.

The newer spirits who served to refresh the Historical school were

Frederick de Sola Mendes (1850-1927), who served first as assistant and later as successor to S. M. Isaacs in the Congregation Shaaray Tefila of New York; Aaron Wise (1844-1896), who was called originally to Congregation Beth Elohim in Brooklyn and then, after two years, succeeded to the post of rabbi at Congregation Rodeph Shalom in New York; Henry Pereira Mendes (1852-1937), younger brother of Frederick de Sola Mendes, who was invited to the pulpit of Congregation Shearith Israel and remained its *hazzan* until his retirement in 1927. These men not only contributed their own powers, but also brought the added strength of their important congregations.

The Russian-Polish immigration that began to be significant in the seventies gave increased strength to the Historical school. In time, these immigrants formed a separate Orthodox movement. At first, however, they served as opponents of the reformists and provided a wider base for the Historical school. An Orthodox congregation had been established in Buffalo as early as 1848. The first synagogue of Russo-Polish extraction formed in New York in 1852, was the Beth Hamidrash; in Boston, the first Russo-Polish synagogue was Beth Abraham, established in 1873. The largest settlements were in New York. It is estimated that as early as 1872 there existed twenty-nine synagogues of the Orthodox Eastern European *minhag* in New York City. However, fair sized representations were soon to be found in Philadelphia, Boston, and Baltimore, on the east coast; in Chicago, and in dozens of other cities as far west as California. In 1874 an Orthodox weekly, *Die Yiddishe Gazette*, began to appear, and in 1885 its founder, Kasriel H. Sarasohn (1835-1905), commenced the publication of the first Yiddish daily in New York, the *Yiddishes Tageblatt*.

The establishment of the *American Hebrew* in 1879 as a weekly was a fourth factor in the revival of the Historical school. The initiator and leading spirit behind the magazine was Frederick de Sola Mendes, who had formerly been the editor of the short lived *Independent Hebrew*. Although the news was impartially presented, the editorial policy was clearly that of Historical Judaism. This was reflected not only in the leading articles and editorial statements but even in the advertisements; the sponsors of *trefa* food or restaurants were not permitted advertising space.

In aggregate, these compelling factors reduced the fears of extinction from the Historical school and induced that group to co-operate as equal partners with the reformists in all community efforts. During the period 1840-1870 co-operation between the two contending religious factions had been based on the hope of each that the other would be *ideologically* absorbed in an eventual all American-Jewish organization. On the other hand, co-operation in the years 1870-1886 was based on the recognition that opposition was permanent. At the same time, each group hoped that the other would be organizationally absorbed in some future congregational union.

The communal structure of American Israel was undergoing rapid change. The census of 1870 reported a count of 189 Jewish religious organizations, 152 edifices, and 73,265 sittings, an increase from 77 synagogues with a total seating capacity of 34,412 as calculated in the 1860 census. For an understanding of the extent of Jewish settlement, it is important to note that, in the 1870 tally, the states of Arkansas, Colorado, Iowa, Kansas, Maine, Michigan, North Carolina, Tennessee, Texas and West Virginia reported congregations for the first time. Religious statistics under governmental auspices were gathered in 1880. Unfortunately, they were never published. However, a census was made of the Jews under the jurisdiction of the Union of American Hebrew Congregations and the Board of Delegates of American Israelites during the years 1875-1878. The totals indicated increases to 270 congregations and 50,000 communicants.[31]

Co-operation was manifest in every phase of communal endeavor, while the field of education preoccupied the religious leadership. The communal Sunday school gave way to the congregational Sunday school. Each synagogue developed its own unit. The midweek supplementary school system continued its slow growth. The strongest support for the "Hebrew Free School" movement which started in 1872 in New York came from the traditionalists. The reformists looked askance at this type of Jewish education. All hands, however, joined in the establishment of several Jewish vocational schools for orphans and immigrant children. The serious lack of proper Jewish school texts continued to plague the authorities. In order to meet the requirement for printed matter, teachers would use Christian textbooks replacing the name of the central figure in the Christian faith, with that of God. Even foremost scholars, recognizing this serious need for proper material, took time to prepare educational texts for children.

The greatest educational lack was qualified teachers. Strenuous efforts were made to establish the indispensable training school for teachers. Two projects were in progress simultaneously, in the East and in the West, both under Reform auspices. The trustees of Temple Emanu-El had provided ample funds for such a purpose. They elaborated their original plan of creating an "Emanu-El Theological Seminary Society," as it was known two decades earlier, and sought to establish an "American Hebrew College" in New York. Their brochure announced both secular and Jewish courses on a college level. Rabbis Samuel Adler and David Einhorn supported this plan. The school was actually launched, increased funds were made available, and a preparatory department begun. Unfortunately, the energies soon gave out and the venture lapsed. In lieu of the total program, a portion of the funds was allocated to send gifted students abroad. Two of these young men were Felix Adler (1851-1933) and Bernard Drachman (1861-1945), neither of whom returned to the fold of Reform Judaism.

The first permanent rabbinic institution was the Hebrew Union College established by Isaac M. Wise in Cincinnati in 1875. He had almost given up all hope of seeing his dream come true. In 1873, dejected at his failure in Cincinnati, he agreed to accept the call of Congregation Anshe Chesed in New York. His Cincinnati congregants were appalled. They succeeded in retaining him, only after a promise that they would support his school. The institution, as conceived by the founders, was not to be narrow or limited in outlook; it was to serve the total needs of American Israel. From its very inception, the catholicity of Jewish interests was stressed. Indeed, in the first announcement of Moritz Loth (1832-1913), president of Wise's congregation, the traditionalists were conscientiously considered. The eastern congregations were not invited to the founding sessions. The Historical school was adequately represented. Marcus Jastrow participated in the deliberations; Lewis N. Dembitz (1833-1907), a leading lawyer and protagonist of Historical Judaism in the Middle West, was elected secretary of the sessions; Sabato Morais was a member of the committee of examiners.

October 3, 1875, was the historic day of opening. The rabbinic motto, "the study of Torah is equivalent to all other duties," was adopted by the institution. Work at the school began in earnest. In 1875 the library, apart from a few textbooks, contained but a set of the Talmud and Midrash Rabbah. One year later, Wise reported, the library contained 154 volumes. The house of books had to be built. A faculty had to be created. A student body had to be enlisted. And all this Wise accomplished with prodigious effort and perspicacity. In 1883 the first class was graduated. They were four: Israel Aaron (1859-1912), Henry Berkowitz (1857-1924), Joseph Krauskopf (1858-1923), and David Philipson.

The Board of Delegates played a progressively diminishing role. Marcus Jastrow, sensing that in the decline of the Board's power the Historical school would suffer further loss of influence, devoted himself for a time to its reorganization. Mayer Sulzberger (1843-1923) proposed a new constitution for the Board which was as ingenious as it was impractical. The attempt at an artificial revival of the organization was reminiscent of Herbert Spencer's warning that "a government agency originally formed to discharge a function is apt to reach a stage at which its self-sustention becomes the primary thing and the function to be performed by it, the secondary thing." Sulzberger soon realized the artificiality of his program, and became the chief proponent for the absorption of the Board into the Union of American Hebrew Congregations, particularly since the Reform group now controlled the policies of the Board as well. In 1876 two subcommittees representing the Board and Union, respectively, were appointed to consider possibilities. In 1879 the merger was consummated and the Board became a standing committee of the Union. A gala conference was called in which 118 congregations (of an estimated 200 invited) participated. The all American-Jewish congregational organization was in the hands of Reform leadership.

Along with all other American theologians, Jewish religious thinkers had to face the challenge of the new and revolutionary theories in science, philosophy and religion. Fundamental tenets of supernaturally revealed religion were shaken. The writings and speeches of Asa Gray (1810-1888) at Harvard and of John Fiske's (1842-1901) *Outlines of Cosmic Philosophy*, were but the frontal assault in America on the certainties of the age. The universities became the centers of the new thought. One of the foremost thinkers of the period, William T. Harris (1835-1909), who founded the *Journal of Speculative Philosophy* in 1867 in St. Louis, encouraged a younger group of American scholars including Josiah Royce (1855-1916), Charles S. Peirce (1839-1914), and William James (1842-1910). Everyone was intent on finding the solution to the riddle of the universe; philosopher, scientist and religionist in turn each insisted that his was the only solution.

Skepticism had its effect on Jewish institutional life, too. In 1873, Felix Adler (son of Rabbi Samuel Adler) who had originally been trained for the rabbinate, returned from his studies at Heidelberg, found his philosophic ideal in conflict with the Jewish faith, and established in 1876 the Society for Ethical Culture. In this movement moral and ethical purposes were considered independent of all religious orientation or ritualistic practice. Adler did not conceive his group to be a talking society. He proposed the creation of institutions, particularly of an educational character. The movement spread throughout the United States and even abroad.

The inner need to defend the faith and the sincere desire to discuss that which united them, brought the rabbinic leaders together in newly formed ministers' associations. It was Dr. Gustav Gottheil (1827-1903) who inspired the formation of the first New York Local Board of Jewish Ministers, or as it was good humoredly titled, "The Big Six"—Gottheil, Kohler, Adolph Huebsch (1830-1884), Henry S. Jacobs (1827-1893), and the two Mendes brothers. Soon the New York group was expanded to include the Jewish ministers of the Atlantic seaboard. Semiannual conferences were held. Of these Gottheil said, paraphrasing the familiar verse in Psalms: "Behold how goodly and how pleasant it is if we can get the brethren merely to sit together."

Despite such meetings, the real lines of division between the Reform and Historical schools remained. They were drawn largely in the areas of Jewish practice. The groups were inexorably divided on questions of synagogue ritual, Eretz Yisrael, Sunday or Historical Sabbath, Hebrew and *kashrut*. However, in certain areas of ritual practice, the Historical school incorporated various moderate reforms. The Western European concept of synagogue decorum became normative in all their congregations. Special instructions were issued on the method of folding the *tallit* after services, uninhibited frivolity on Simhat Torah was condemned, many prayers were read rather than chanted, the *piyuttim* were deleted, the names of those called up to the Torah were not announced by the *baal kore*, and sections of the service were read in English. The left-wing congregations of the Historical school went further. They introduced mixed pews and the organ. The *American Hebrew* was neutral on the organ question, for within the Historical school opinion was divided. There was no equivocation as to the mixed choir. The Reform group was chastised. It was an effrontery to the spirit of worship, the *American Hebrew* wrote, to select Christians as leaders of the service.

As a result of the Russian pogroms, the ancient hope for Zion took on fresh meaning. The Historical school's ardent devotion to Eretz Yisrael in contradistinction to Reform's negativism was a second factor of division between two groups. The Reform position was on record in the Philadelphia conference of 1869.[32] With minor exceptions, the entire Reform rabbinate and laity continued to maintain this position.

The third issue between Reform and the Historical school arose over the Sabbath. The issue was not a result of the conflict of tradition with scientific thought; it was the result of other circumstances, essentially practical and not speculative. The majority of Jews, particularly the younger generation, were above all preoccupied with the pressure for a livelihood; and it was not an easy matter to find employment and at the same time refrain from work on Saturday, the traditional Sabbath day. No wonder then that Synagogues on the Sabbath were soon empty and that observances continued to decline. It may be said that the traditionalists took the view that while the Sabbath was made for man, Israel was made for the Sabbath—in other words, that the Jewish Sabbath could not be shifted to another day. The reformists on the other hand were prepared to make some accommodations.

One fact is highlighted in the speeches, articles, and papers on the Sabbath question. The reformists were not, as they are so often accused of being, committed to the elimination of the historical Sabbath. The responsible leadership was appalled at the radical twist that fate and time forced upon their ideas. Their error was grievous only in their unrealistic compromise, not in the sincerity of their motives. The Historical school was prepared to suffer temporary failure and unpopularity, but refused to yield on fundamental tenets.

Said the Reform leaders: men need a living religion and to get this they need "a living day of worship." Einhorn's unsuccessful attempt in 1854 to establish a Sunday service was recalled. The leaders of the movement for the Sunday service were Kaufmann Kohler, then of Sinai Congregation in Chicago, and Samuel Hirsch of Philadelphia. Isaac M. Wise was unalterably opposed to any compromise with the biblical Sabbath. Under the impress of Kohler's inaugural Sunday sermon, *Das neue Wissen und der alte Glaube* (The New Knowledge and the Old Faith), delivered January 18, 1874, the Sinai Congregation made the radical departure from Jewish tradition which, it is true, had been advocated by such Reform leaders abroad as Holdheim, Formstrecher, Philippson, and Geiger for some forty years, but was first translated into practice in America.

Samuel Hirsch represented the extreme view. He proposed that Sunday, the civil day of rest, should be Judaized as a real Sabbath day. Kohler's approach was of another character. In a sermon entitled "Sabbath Observance and Sunday Lectures" delivered December 27, 1879, he set forth his views:

> I sincerely and heartily support all efforts in behalf of restoring our Sabbath to its pristine glory, and wish I could prevail on all the members of my congregation to join the Sabbath Observance Association just now started. But I think the only successful beginning can alone be made at home. *The Jewish household must have the Sabbath revived in all its attractive lustre and sweetness. The Friday evening family reunions with all their melodious strains of song and joy must be restored as means of cultivating piety and devotion. . . .*
>
> . . . And if, thus, the Friday evening will sound the silver trumpet of liberty and joy to herald the day of God, while Jewish Sunday lessons will work like scouts and skirmishers in disarming and routing rampant atheism all along the line, the walls of Jericho will fall, the victory will be ours.

It was during these years that the practice of convening the congregation for late services on Friday was instituted in many Reform congregations. Congregation Adath Jeshurun in Philadelphia, which was slowly moving into the Reform camp, instituted late Friday evening services in 1883, thus becoming the first congregation in Philadelphia to hold such services. Of the two attempts, the Friday and Sunday services, the latter won immediate popularity. Yet gradually the former, by virtue of its relation in time and spirit to the Sabbath day, has pre-empted the position of the Sunday Sabbath even in Reform congregations.

This very truth the Historical school felt instinctively. It was to be expected that the right wing of the Historical school would be outraged by this new phase of Reform. It was unanticipated, however, that a left-winger such as Szold would come to the forefront and assume command of the counter-Reform battle on this very issue. In a passionate address,

Der Sabbat, he ruled that all who violated the Sabbath profaned the entire Torah.

The attitude toward the Hebrew language in America (as in every country in every generation) was a further token of devotion to traditional values. Einhorn's *siddur*, the *Olat Tamid*, ignored the Hebrew text almost entirely; the text indeed, symbolically enough, was laid out to be read from left to right.

But the breaking point in Reform-Traditionalist relations came over *kashrut*. For the Reformists *kashrut* was a primitive barbarism and its upholders "kitchen Jews." Isaac M. Wise heaped derision upon the heads of those who would maintain the laws and practices of *kashrut*.

Jastrow challenged Wise's authority. He precipitated a series of resignations from the Union by influencing his congregation, Rodeph Shalom of Philadelphia, to withdraw from the Union. De Sola Mendes's congregation Shaaray Tefila, resigned from the Union. Szold, although he petitioned his Baltimore Synagogue to take similar action, was not successful in his endeavor.

The year 1885 may be taken as the date when the hope to unite American Israel was definitely abandoned and separate groups—Reform, Conservative, and Orthodox—came into being. Three events tell the tale. In the spring, the Historical group hailed Alexander Kohut as its leader; in the fall, Kaufmann Kohler convened the Pittsburgh conference; and in the winter, Sabato Morais became president of the Jewish Theological Seminary Association.

Alexander Kohut (1842-1894), surnamed "the Mighty Hammer," combined in himself a passion for scholarship and community action. His record of achievement in Hungary included important scholarly works, exciting rabbinical experience, and participation in liberal movements. No sooner had he arrived in New York as successor to Dr. Huebsch at Congregation Ahavath Chesed, than he declared his full alliance with the Historical school.

The Kohut-Kohler controversy, which soon broke out, became the "talk of the town." The phrases were chiseled, the ideas clear, the tones gentlemanly but none the less firm. And the antagonists were worthy of each other. Kohler presented his philosophy of Judaism in a series of six lectures which he called "Backwards or Forward." He regarded Mosaic-Rabbinical Judaism as retrospective and backwards; Reform Judaism as prospective and forward looking. He contested Kohut's belief in revelation as well as his emphasis on the observance of all the ceremonies of Judaism, and he vehemently opposed the restoration of the Jewish state with its sacrificial institutions. The Kohut-Kohler debate accelerated the final development of a specifically Reform group. After consultations with Isaac

M. Wise and Samuel Hirsch, Kohler issued a call for a conference to be held in Pittsburgh from November 16-18, 1885, "for the purpose of discussing the present state of American Judaism, its pending issues and its requirements, and of uniting upon such plans and practical measures as seem demanded by the hour."[33]

Nineteen rabbis met in Pittsburgh. Wise was elected chairman, but Kohler was the leading militant spirit behind the sessions. He had prepared the draft of a statement which, edited and modified, was to become the famous Pittsburgh Platform—the standard document of classic American Reform. In eight paragraphs, the current Reform theology—on the God-idea, Bible, Mosaic legislation, *kashrut* and priesthood, nationalism, Jewish mission, immortality, and social justice—was succinctly formulated.

Over every one of the statements there was violent debate. Kohler declared the platform to be the "declaration of Jewish independence." His critics rhetorically asked, "Independence from what?" and answered, "Independence from Judaism." Ismar Elbogen (1874-1943) in his analysis of the Pittsburgh statement, described it as "a peculiar document which can only be understood on the basis of contemporary intellectual currents. Nothing was said of faith or piety; the advantages of Judaism over other religions were mentioned, but not clarified. It was not a *Confessio Judaica* but a homage to the latest European school of thought in science, in the history of religion and particularly of the religious evolution of Israel. The laymen did not get much out of this platform; they did not learn what to believe and what to do, but only what not to believe and not to do."[34]

Not only the later historian, but even devoted contemporary reformists, did not consider the declaration binding. Dr. Gottheil castigated the platform. The program as such was never endorsed by the Central Conference of American Rabbis organized four years later; Isaac M. Wise, in defense of his college and its curriculum, forthrightly stated that the platform, the Union, and the College were not of one mind. In a straightforward disavowal he wrote in the *American Israelite* of December 4, 1885:

> But who can tell what that Pittsburgh Conference had to do with the Union of American Hebrew Congregations? . . . The Union consists of congregations and their elected representatives, and the Conference consisted of Rabbis who went there voluntarily and without the advice or appointment of their respective congregations. That Union, according to its Constitution, is entirely secular, takes no cognizance whatever of theological questions, and the Conference discussed theological questions exclusively. That Union consists of a hundred and odd congregations, while in Pittsburgh only eighteen Rabbis were present, not all of whom are at the head of congregations belonging to that Union.

Two weeks later he wrote in the same publication:

The enactments, resolutions or proceedings of the Pittsburgh Rabbinical Conference, or of any other Conference, except the Council of the Union of American Hebrew Congregations, have nothing in the world to do with the course of studies or the methods of teaching adopted in the Hebrew Union College. The Hebrew Union College . . . remains the honest seat of Jewish learning—and no drilling institution for opinionated candidates—to educate competent scholars of free and unbiased minds . . . men who can draw their information from the original Jewish sources and think for themselves.

Nevertheless, the alarm had been sounded. Sabato Morais turned to his associates in the Historical school—left, center, and right—and urged that the reply to the Pittsburgh platform be delivered in action, not words. What had been in his mind since the closing of Maimonides College, and had been postponed because of the united attitude toward the Hebrew Union College, now emerged in specific form. Morais wrote to Congregation Shearith Israel in New York calling upon its board to take the lead in the establishment of a new seminary actively counter-Reform and dedicated to the "knowledge and practice of historical Judaism."

Morais was a pillar of strength and determination. He urged, cajoled, disturbed, encouraged, and inspired his coworkers in the building of the Seminary. He referred to the Seminary as "my Benjamin—the son of my old age." Alexander Kohut and State Senator Joseph Blumenthal (1834-1901) upheld his hands. It was Kohut who influenced his friend to name the new institution The Jewish Theological Seminary rather than the Orthodox Seminary as Morais proposed. Kohut's intuition was correct, for in the name, as in the development of the institution, Kohut sought to establish the tradition of historic Judaism, rejecting denominationalism and partisanship and embracing *Kelal Yisrael*. Historical Judaism, he maintained, is not a movement or a party—it is Judaism. This thought was knit into the fabric of the constitution and by-laws of the Jewish Theological Seminary Association, which states in article II:

The purpose of this Association being the preservation in America of the knowledge and practice of historical Judaism as ordained in the Law of Moses (*Torat Moshe*) and expounded by the prophets (*Nebiim*) and sages (*Hakamim*) of Israel in Biblical and Talmudical writings, it proposes in furtherance of its general aim the following specific objects:

1. The establishment and maintenance of a Jewish Theological Seminary for the training of Rabbis and teachers.
2. The attainment of such cognate purposes as may upon occasion be deemed appropriate.

The dedication exercises were held in Lyric Hall, January 2, 1887, after a year of preparation and planning. That very week an advertisement appeared in the newspapers with the single-line announcement that preparatory classes were being conducted at the Congregation Shearith Israel. Eight students were registered in the first class, one of whom, Joseph H. Hertz (1872-1946), rose to international prominence as chief rabbi of the British Empire.

With the dedication speeches over, the struggle for survival began in earnest. The faculty was selected, the student body was increased, and classes were moved to larger quarters in Cooper Union. Historical Judaism had permanently launched its first independent institution in America.

5

THREE JEWISH RELIGIOUS GROUPS: REFORM, CONSERVATIVE, ORTHODOX, 1886-1902

The years until the turn of the century were devoted by both Reform and Historical Judaism to clarification, intensification, and expansion of their respective emphases and institutions. Each group sought to erect its citadel on three pillars: a rabbinical school, a union of congregations, and a conference of rabbis. First to achieve this triad was the Reform movement.

The organization of the Central Conference of American Rabbis in Detroit on July 9, 1889, celebrated Isaac M. Wise's seventieth birthday year. The purpose of the new organization was to maintain and perpetuate a union of all American rabbis, to publish a yearbook of proceedings, and to establish a fund for the support of superannuated ministers. Perhaps the most important declaration made at the conference, which linked the new organization to the Reform movement in Europe, was "That the proceedings of all the modern Rabbinical Conferences from that held in Braunschweig in 1844, and including all like assemblages held since, shall be taken as a basis for the work of this Conference." The Conference instantly became the legislative body of Reform Judaism, for it was resolved that at its annual meetings decisions would be taken in "all matters appertaining to Judaism, its literature and its welfare."[35] Nineteen members were present in Pittsburgh; one hundred joined the Conference. Isaac M. Wise served as president until his death.

The Historical school was faced with the additional task of creating a congregational base and an assembly of rabbis. The leaders attempted to solve their problem indirectly. Hoping to gain a large mass following by a coalition with the Orthodox, who showed vital signs of organization, a movement was encouraged, led by H. Pereira Mendes and Bernard Drachman of the Seminary and supported by Cyrus Adler (1863-1940) and Max Cohen (1853-1941). They wished to create a union of Orthodox congregations which would accept the Seminary as its own rabbinical school and the rabbis associated with it as coworkers in a traditional federation. An orthodox union would probably have been established in the normal course of events. The attempted alliance, however, was premature and had two major effects on Jewish religious history in America: the more rapid development of official Orthodoxy and the diversion of effort from Historical or Conservative, Judaism's immediate object of creating its own institutions.

Chaos and confusion prevailed in the internal life of American Orthodoxy. Small celled congregations came into existence suddenly and in almost as short a time split up. This seemed to go on endlessly. The chief attraction of the Orthodox synagogue was its cantor, and only in rare cases the spiritual leader; the Hebrew classes were conducted in dingy unsanitary stores and cellars; the sale of religious objects was abused; *kashrut* was mismanaged.

The first attempt at formal organization of the Orthodox congregations had taken place in 1879. Representatives of twenty-six congregations met to found a Board of Delegates of Orthodox Hebrew Congregations. They planned to invite a chief rabbi from abroad who would set their house in order. The attempt failed for want of a proper candidate. Nine years were to pass before further action was initiated. Chief Rabbi Jacob Joseph (1848-1902), distinguished scholar of Vilna, consented to come to America. The tragedy that befell him and the shame and disgrace that resulted to the community were a painful reflection of the scandalous state of affairs. The salary of the rabbi was to be gathered from the tax that was attached to kosher meat. Despite severe warnings by friends among the Reformists and Conservatives, not to finance the office of the rabbinate through kosher food income, the Orthodox association insisted on its plan. The direst predictions were unhappily realized; the association was dissolved and the idea of an Orthodox chief rabbinate shattered on the rocks of irresponsibility.

Other Orthodox ventures had more fortunate results. The aspiration to establish a higher institution of learning in keeping with the high traditions of the European *yeshibot*, became a reality. The development and progress of Yeshiva University is a wholesome chapter in American education. The Rabbi Isaac Elchanan Theological Seminary, known by its Hebrew name, *Yeshivat Rabbenu Yitzchak Elchanan*, was founded in 1896. The new Orthodox seminary was named in memory of Rabbi Isaac Elchanan Spektor (1817-1896), the Lithuanian scholar and saint, who had passed away in the months preceding the founding of the institution. Its patrons properly claimed the distinction for their school as being the first higher Yeshiva to be established on the continent of North America.

The purpose of the Yeshiva differed from that of the other two seminaries in that it did not consider the training of students for the rabbinical calling its primary task. *Torah Lishmah* was its object—the study of Torah for its own sake. In the miniature *Bet Ha-Midrash* at 156 Henry Street,

New York, was a group of young men who had already begun their Talmud studies in Europe. They were supported by a weekly stipend ranging from $2.50 to $4; the "supervisor," or one-man faculty, was Rabbi Benjamin Aronowitz (1864-1945); the course of study consisted exclusively of the Talmud and related rabbinic literature. Such were the Yeshiva's beginnings. Today it is a university, in addition to a school of rabbinic studies.

A call for an Orthodox Jewish Congregational Union was issued in Hebrew and in English. Of the thirteen signers to this document only two were of the official Orthodox camp; the other eleven were members of the Jewish Theological Seminary's faculty and board. The address was also that of the Seminary. One hundred delegates attended the founding convention on June 8, 1898. H. Pereira Mendes was elected president.

Steps were taken to implement the new program. At the second biennial convention, Mendes, as president, was in a position to render a favorable report. It was soon obvious, however, that Conservative Judaism's major purpose in helping to found the federation was to be vitiated. If any group was to capture the Orthodox Union, the West European faction would be the last. The clash was not in religious orientation; it was in spiritual backgrounds and cultural proclivities. A variety of obstacles, seemingly conquerable in individual relations, but impassable in the aggregate, separated the two groups: the differing attitudes toward form and behavior during the service; the latent "snobbism" of the *Westjuden*, the insular attitude of the Russian Jew toward the American environment; the deep love of the East European Jew for Yiddish, and the manifest disdain of Yiddish by the others. These deeper and virtually unexpressed disparities were symbolized in two words which the respective groups used for Jewish study: *Lernen* (learning) and *Juedische Wissenschaft* (the science of Judaism). The East Europeans scorned the baggage of Western civilization; the Western oriented Jews considered such knowledge their passport to civilization.

Antipathies, suspicions and basic differences came to the fore. The Jewish Theological Seminary was the target. At first, in deference to the respected H. Pereira Mendes, a resolution was passed in support of both the Conservative and the Orthodox Seminaries. At a later assembly, a resolution was passed with Mendes himself in the chair, to repudiate the authority of The Jewish Theological Seminary's graduates as rabbis in Israel. Inevitably, the Conservative group returned to its own needs and responsibilities. Yet, out of the unsuccessful effort at union a strong third party in American Judaism was born.

The immediate requirements of American Jewry in the religious and educational realms brought co-operation between the three parties on limited objectives. The nonexistence of a teaching profession was the result, not the cause, of the infantilism in Jewish educational efforts. Adolescents and other volunteers taught in the Sunday schools; few professional teachers were qualified either pedagogically or temperamentally to educate the American school child. A minority voice in Jewish institutional life had always proclaimed the high priority of teacher-training institutions. It may be recalled that the Hebrew Union College proposed to establish such a department. Kohut, in his early conversations with Morais, attempted to persuade him that the teachers' college should take precedence over other departments in the order of Conservative institutions.

In 1893, Congregation Mikveh Israel fell heir to a bequest from Hyman Gratz (1776-1857). The will stipulated that an institution be established "for the education of Jews residing in the city and country of Philadelphia." Subject to legal sanction, Gratz Mordecai (1849-1902), a grandnephew of Hyman Gratz, hoped to establish a Jewish university in America. He corresponded with the presidents of Columbia, Harvard, and Cornell. The exchange of letters to be found in the unpublished correspondence of Sabato Morais at Dropsie College is in itself an interesting commentary on the prevailing attitudes of American college presidents toward Jewish universities. In brief, Mordecai was counseled that the results would not be advantageous to the Jewish position. Sabato Morais, rabbi of the congregation, was violently opposed to the inquiry and the trend of thought it reflected. He wished to establish the long awaited teacher training school. In a series of communications to Doctor Solomon Solis-Cohen (1857-1948) he expressed these views candidly. Morais's position won out. Classes at Gratz College began in 1897. Rabbi Henry M. Speaker (1868-1935) was principal; Arthur A. Dembitz (1870-1940), instructor in history; and Isaac Husik (1876-1939), instructor in Hebrew and Bible. Moses A. Dropsie (1821-1905) served as chairman of the Board of Trustees. Gratz College was established as the first American Jewish teachers' college.

The settlement activities in Eretz Yisrael continued apace. Conservative and Orthodox circles supported every wholesome venture in the Holy Land; the reformists continued to echo Gustavus Poznanski's refrain, "America is our Zion, Washington our Jerusalem." Orthodoxy supplied the mass following to the "Lovers of Zion" and the "Seekers of Zion" movements; the Conservatives contributed active leaders such as Jastrow, Szold, H. Pereira Mendes, Solomon Solis-Cohen and Lewis N. Dembitz. In 1894, Szold was instrumental in founding in his home city of Baltimore the first Zionist group in America.

Then came the book that shook the Jewish world. Theodor Herzl's (1860-1904) *Der Judenstaat* (1896). *Hibbat Zion* became political Zionism. American Judaism was drawn into international Jewish affairs. And the reformists decided to attack. Emil G. Hirsch (1851-1923) made invidious comparisons between the ancient Temple sacrifices and the Chicago slaughterhouses. Kaufmann Kohler wrote that "The Zionists cry: 'Back to Judea!' shows a degeneracy, a demoralization, a Katzenjammer sentiment . . ."; Wise termed the dream of ages Ziomania. For half a century, the philosophy of Reform, as expressed in the creeds of Philadelphia and Pittsburgh, had devastating effect on the development of Zionism.

Not all reformists were in the anti-Zionist camp. Bernhard Felsenthal, Maximilian Heller (1860-1929), Gustav Gottheil, and the younger men, Stephen S. Wise and Richard Gottheil (1862-1936), helped establish the American Federation of Zionists. But, for the while, anti-Zionism remained the most prominent note in Reform circles.

The Conservatives, despite their wariness as to the impact of a purely political movement on Judaism, rallied about the Zionists' banner. They, too, had their surprising exceptions. Frederick de Sola Mendes stressed the impracticability of colonizing a country which included the holy places of three contending faiths. Sabato Morais expounded against the secularist antireligious Zionist spokesmen and leaders. Both men, however, supported every activity of a constructive nature in Eretz Yisrael. Most of the Conservatives saw in political Zionism a means to an end: not only the reclamation of the Jewish people, but, in the spirit of Herzl's classic formulation, the return of the Jews to Judaism.

The census of 1890 established for the first and only time the existence of two bodies within what the officials termed the "Jewish Church." They divided all their information into two sections: Orthodox and Reform. The more strictly religious problems that confronted American Israel in the years 1886-1902 were in a sense variations on a familiar theme. Debate continued on *kashrut* control, "mushroom" synagogues, the use of English in the service, Reform-Traditionalist relationships, religious activities among the immigrant groups, and the problem of the unaffiliated. And in smaller circles arguments flew pro and con over the Sunday service and prayer book proposals (in the Reform ranks) and on the synod question (among the Conservatives).

With the establishment of the creedal principle in Reform Judaism all barriers of ceremonial law had disappeared; the phrase "eternal truths" had sanctioned all excesses made in its name—even the transfer of the Sabbath to Sunday. Now for the first time such radicalism became less self-confident. The very holiday celebration which was called at the Chicago Sinai Congregation to commemorate the introduction of Sunday services twenty-five years earlier offered evidence of the serious misgivings of even such intrepid reformers as Hirsch and Kohler. At these exercises, Rabbi Moses J. Gries (1868-1918), reiterated the Sunday-Sabbath plea:

"This is the evil of two Sabbaths, blessed with two we are cursed with having none." Hirsch had other things to say to a congregation which ignored the Sunday service as they had formerly ignored the Sabbath service.

I can understand the difficulties which beset congregational participation in the services on the traditional Sabbath, and if I had the fortune of being the minister of a congregation with a Saturday service, never would my lips open to chide the members for their indifference manifested by their non-attendance . . . but a congregation that has a Sunday service has no excuse for empty pews. Every empty pew is a monument to hypocrisy. It points to a pretense, and it calls as such for a rebuke. . . .

I plead for honesty to the cause. You have chosen Sunday; not I. You proclaimed it the day of our worship, not I. Therefore we must show by the deed that it is our day. Prove that you are in terrible earnest. There can be no excuse for absence from the self-appointed service hour. Charity meetings are no excuse. Other business is no excuse . . .

We must have a temple filled with our own members unless we wish to stand before the world as pretenders . . . Empty pews do not spread the message; neither do the wooden backs and all the beautifully upholstered seats.

It was Kaufmann Kohler, however, chief advocate of the Sunday service and the initiator of the idea in that very Sinai Congregation, who suggested that the attempt to shift the Jewish Sabbath day to Sunday was unwarranted.

During these years, the Reform movement succeeded in publishing a uniform prayer book for its constituency. This was the climax of Wise's importuning since his first call for a *Minhag America*. At the organizational session of the Central Conference of American Rabbis in 1889, Wise had urged the immediate establishment of a committee to prepare a uniform prayer book. He deemed it a vital necessity in order to end the uninhibited individual prayer book production that catered to a wide variety of congregational tastes. Two years later, the subject was formally considered. A committee prepared a text. In 1894 the volume was ratified. The completed version of the Union Prayer Book was satisfactory to all shades of Reform opinion and represented the consummation of Reform thought on synagogue ritual and practice. After Part II was adopted, Kohler could proudly state that in the new ritual Einhorn and Wise dwell together in the historical past and the living present.[36]

The synod proposal was to be debated furiously twice more in American religious life before it was to be abandoned, by the Conservative school in the fading nineties and by the Reform wing in the early years of the new century. Two new forces were represented in the discussion among the Conservatives: Solomon Schechter (1847-1915) and the young Henrietta Szold (1860-1945). Writing from England on December 26, 1898, Schechter said:

On the whole, I think, Synods, unless confined to purely administrative affairs, are useless and even harmful . . .

Besides that, I think no man is capable of representing other men in matters spiritual.

Synods have also a tendency to create among us certain sacerdotalism which is quite foreign to the Jewish spirit.[37]

Borrowing her title "Catholic Israel," a term which Schechter had popularized, Miss Szold subjected the synod proposal to a thorough-searching analysis in an essay which identified her in thought as in action with the Conservative movement.[38]

As the American Jewish community continued to grow, cultural institutions of great importance were developed in which the religious leadership served on the strength of individual gifts rather than as representatives of organized religious groups. These developments included the incipient Hebrew and Yiddish literary movements, the permanent establishment of the Jewish Publication Society of America (1888), the founding of the American Jewish Historical Society (1892), and the recognized participation of the Jews in the World's Columbian Exposition at Chicago (1893). Last in order but perhaps foremost in significance came the rooting of Jewish scholarship on the American continent.

Until the mid-nineteenth century there was no American Jewish scholarship to speak of; in the second part of the century, such scholarship was to be found only among the learned rabbis who came from abroad. Benjamin Szold published his *Hebrew Commentary to the Book of Job* (1886), and occasional articles on the Bible; much of this work remained in manuscript form. Marcus Jastrow might be said to have benefited from his ill health, for he thus found the leisure from other duties to prepare his *magnum opus, A Dictionary of the Targumin, the Talmud Babli and Yerushalmi, and the Midrashic Literature* (1903), the first important rabbinic work in English. Alexander Kohut completed his monumental *Aruch Completum* (1889), which is so dramatically described by Rebekah Kohut.[39]

Jewish scholarship was firmly established in American soil through the various seminaries. These became, in addition to training schools for rabbis, citadels of learning and centers of study for scholars. The rabbinical schools attracted men of international standing who magnetically opened new frontiers for American Judaism. The Hebrew Union College in its formative years included Moses Mielziner (1828-1903), first full time professor at the College, whose special field was Talmud. He wrote an *Introduction to the Talmud*, in which he included a section on "Outlines of Talmudical Ethics" (1894). At the College were also Gotthard Deutsch (1859-1921), gifted student of Heinrich Graetz, whose archives of rare history sources in the Hebrew Union College Library contain a veritable mine of information; Max Leopold Margolis (1866-1932), philologist and Bible student, later to become the editor of the Jewish Publication Society translation of the Bible; Casper Levias (1860-1934), Semitist; Moses Buttenwieser (1862-1939), Bible scholar and critic; and, at the end of the century, Henry Malter (*c.* 1864-1925), leading scholar of Judeo-Arabic literature and medieval philosophy. At first the Hebrew Union College had an advantage over the later organized Jewish Theological Seminary and Yeshiva. Soon, however, the two younger institutions, had no less distinguished men on their respective faculties.

In these years, too, still another opportunity began to present itself to scholars of Judaism. American universities began to invite them to their Semitic, religion and history departments. In 1886 a chair in Semitics was endowed at Columbia University, and was filled by Richard J. H. Gottheil (1862-1936); Cyrus Adler, the first student in America to receive a higher degree in Semitics, was appointed to that department at the Johns Hopkins University in 1887; in 1892, Morris Jastrow, Jr. (1861-1921), began to teach Semitic languages at the University of Pennsylvania; in the same year Emil G. Hirsch was called to the chair of Rabbinic literature and Jewish philosophy at the University of Chicago; in 1902, William Rosenau (1865-1943) was appointed to the Johns Hopkins University department of Semitics.

This was a beginning—admittedly belated and faltering, but a beginning nonetheless. Two new plans for the rapid development of scholarship in America were proposed by Isidore Singer (1859-1939), later editor of the *Jewish Encyclopedia*, and the resourceful Cyrus Adler. Dr. Singer suggested a Jewish University of Theology, History and Literature. Dr. Adler had another plan. "We have Mss. and some books at Columbia College, the Library of the Jewish Theological Seminary, the Leeser Library in Philadelphia, the Cohen Library in Baltimore, the Library of the Hebrew Union College, and the Sutro Library in California. But," he pleaded, "who would think of comparing all of them together with any of the better libraries in England, Germany, Italy or Austria?"[40] In his limpid mind, Adler charted a course of action. He proposed therefore the establishment of a Jewish academy in America for the advancement of scholarship. This academy was to collect a great library, publish the fruits of scientific research, arrange meetings of learned societies, and above all encourage, stimulate and support young and gifted scholars to devote of their time and talent to Jewish research. Adler suggested that a fund of a half million dollars (an enormous sum for those times) would be required to launch this venture. But neither an individual nor a communal Maecenas appeared to support his project. Adler's suggestion, though enthusiastically received in limited circles, was premature. Once again scholarship was being treated as though it were a luxury and not a prime necessity of Judaism.

As the liberal and expansive nineteenth century gave way to the new era, America looked forward to the literal fulfillment of Isaiah's prophecy, "That the government may be increased, And of peace there be no end" (Is. 9:6). All the inhabitants of the great American continent shared in the dream of such a future; and the Jews were no exception. Internally American Judaism was faced with division of opinion. Despite mutual reproach, fundamentally the religious groupings were in search of the same solution. As Mayer Sulzberger wrote to Schechter, "Orthodoxy, reform, conservatism, all have been found to be names, and it is no bad thing to be uncomprehended in or by any of them. He who has scholarship, talent, and enthusiasm may be more appreciated for the first time in our history than he who leads a party."[41]

Organizational impasses were surmounted. Isaac M. Wise was succeeded by Kaufmann Kohler at the Hebrew Union College. The Seminary, after some years of extremely doubtful prospects, suddenly took on new life. Both schools had spurned a suggested amalgamation; each group had confidence in its own future. Orthodoxy, too, supplied with an ever-flowing stream of immigrants, felt secure and hopeful. As in the dream which Joseph interpreted, religious life and institutions became a vine of three branches, and, as it was budding, its blossoms shot forth. Would the clusters bring forth ripe grapes? That was the question.

6

IDEOLOGICAL CLARIFICATION AND EMPHASIS ON LEARNING, 1902-1919

In the very developments of the new century were concealed those events that, in their unfolding, brought to American Jewry the material, numerical and, in the dream of a few, the spiritual hegemony of world Israel. From 1900 to 1912 ten million immigrants came to the shores of the United States, of whom approximately one million were Jews. The centrality of America in the orbit of Jewish world affairs, first perceived by the historically sensitive and confirmed by events, strengthened the hands of religious leaders as they prepared for American Judaism's great role. On the horizon, new leaders appeared, each devoted to the fulfillment of the philosophy of life for which he stood. Their achievements are organically incorporated in the institutions they helped to create. Such was the case with Jacob H. Schiff (1847-1920). He was the unelected head of his people, respected by all alike—religious and secularist, learned and illiterate, fourth- or first-generation American—for he transcended all party lines. As Jacob Schiff grew older in the service of American Israel, two younger men, Louis Marshall (1856-1929) and Felix M. Warburg (1871-1937), continued his tradition.

Reform's first major decision was the selection of its new leader. After

Wise's death, Professors Mielziner and Deutsch served as acting presidents of the Hebrew Union College. It was, however, the devout and scholarly Kaufmann Kohler who was called to the presidency. At the age of sixty, when most men place their mantle on younger shoulders, Koehler, fondly named "the Battler," began to build the College on the three-pillared philosophy of Revelation, Reform, and America, or God, Progress, and the Democratic Spirit.

Scholarship was the nerve center of the College. Kohler fashioned the faculty and the student body in his own image. With the twofold purpose of raising the teaching standards and encouraging academic pursuits, Kohler added to the faculty Julian Morgenstern, gifted Bible scholar and later his successor in the presidency of the College; Jacob Z. Lauterbach (1873-1942), talmudic scholar and associate of Kohler in the *Jewish Encyclopedia;* and David Neumark (1866-1924), philosopher and Hebraist, who despite Kohler's earlier objections succeeded in introducing the techniques of modern Hebrew into the curriculum.

Kohler was the exemplar of industry. He continued to work for the *Jewish Encyclopedia*, producing in total some three hundred articles; his *Jewish Theology*, originally published in German in 1910, appeared in English translation in 1918; during his retirement he published a volume *Heaven and Hell in Comparative Religion* on the occasion of the Dante anniversary in 1923; *The Origins of the Synagogue and the Church* appeared posthumously in 1929. The latter two books represented the fruits of his labors during the busy presidential years.

Physical growth accompanied scholarly development. The movement to acquire a new home for the Hebrew Union College began in 1905, and in 1913 the college and library buildings were dedicated on their present site. The library is a monument to the foresight and assiduity of Adolph S. Oko (1883-1944), who served as its director from 1905 to 1938.

In 1909, as a direct result of the establishment by Jacob H. Schiff of a fund of $100,000, the interest of which was to be equally divided between the Hebrew Union College and the Seminary for use of their respective teachers' institutes, a teacher-training department was established at the College. Because there was no significant Reform congregational school system, students could not be developed for the institute, and those who might have chosen teaching as a calling saw in it no future. In lieu of formal classes, extension lectures for Sunday-school teachers and limited-period institutes were arranged, particularly in the smaller cities of the country.

The Union of American Hebrew Congregations continued to expand its program. A department on circuit preaching was established to provide opportunities for religious instruction and service to the smaller communities. Holiday sermons were published for congregations without rabbis. In 1905 this committee was expanded into a full Department of Synagogue and School Extension. In 1913 the Union merged the local sisterhoods into a national women's auxiliary under the name of National Federation of Temple Sisterhoods with an initial charter membership of forty-nine groups.

Despite these externals of organizational expansion, the Reform movement was stunted in its growth: and this for a variety of reasons. Numbers were not in its favor. The mass of Jewish immigrants were East European. In the first decade of the century eighty-seven per cent of the recent arrivals settled in the east, while only eight per cent moved on to the central states. The center of Reform, being located in a midwestern city, was thus far away from the heart of the American Jewish community. Then again, socially, the membership of Reform congregations was comfortable and staid, having little in common with the recent immigrants. Nor did Reform theology respond to the needs or idioms of the large masses of Jews. Reform did not reckon with traditional associations, the deep and ancient love for Eretz Yisrael, the ceremonial of home and synagogue. The carefully documented records of the annual conventions of the Central Conference reveal how, consistently, the choice was always on the side of classic Reform doctrine. Nationalists and ceremonialists were quickly outvoted; the overwhelming majority sought to fulfill the prophecies and declarations of Reform. It must be emphasized, however, that despite the fervent antitraditionalism and antinationalism, the intention was not to break away from the main stream of Judaism; a party, yes; but not a schism. The specific cases in point are those of creed, synod, Zionism, and religious ceremonialism.

In 1903, Max L. Margolis (1866-1932), under the distinct influence of Protestant theology and higher criticism, attempted to influence the Reform movement to accept a formal creed on an ecclesiastical basis. His report to the Central Conference, "The Theological Aspect of Reformed Judaism"[42] was a departure from classic Reform lines and included his suggested creed under the four headings of Theology (and Cosmology), Anthropology, Psychology, and Ecclesiology. Margolis's plea for an ecclesia was rejected on the basis of counterreports submitted by Rabbis Felsenthal, Marcus Friedlander (1866-1944), Max Heller (1860-1929), and Kohler. The principle of the opposition was Reform's determination to disagree with Orthodoxy, but not to dissociate Reform from the Synagogue of Israel. As Kohler stated: ". . . nor will it [Reform] be checked by the champions of conservatism whose power appears to be in the ascendancy at present, but we shall ever insist on being in full continuity with the Judaism of the past."[43]

Zionism almost proved to be the splintering rod of Reform Judaism at all times. The old guard repeated the standard clichés and fulminated vociferously at any suggested watering down of the universalistic mission of Reform. Against this position two valiant spirits arose and contributed to the reshaping of Reform Judaism. These were Stephen S. Wise and Judah L. Magnes. The young Wise had been one of the first to answer Herzl's call. He became, as it were, Zionism incarnate, everywhere in America, troubling the placid and self-confident souls. Wise, Magnes, Richard Gottheil, and their elders—Gustav Gottheil, Felsenthal, and Heller—were the *Nachshonites* of an imposing movement against a well nigh overwhelming opposition.

Stephen Wise was also critical of the congregational structure of Reform Judaism. In 1906, after a spirited exchange of letters with the board of Temple Emanu-El, which had invited him to become its rabbi, he spurned their invitation on the issue of a free pulpit. He came to New York and established the Free Synagogue, in which the pulpit was to be free of all restraint. The congregation was to be supported by voluntary contributions; both the pew system and class distinctions were abolished, and greater democracy was introduced in synagogue organization.

Judah Magnes had additional charges against Reform. He found its doctrine and ritual to be a spiritual wasteland. Magnes had accepted the call to Emanu-El only to quit its pulpit and that of Reform Judaism altogether on the Passover of 1910. His dramatic plea for a "return to the sources of Judaism" was but the climax of a long bill of particulars which he had expressed earlier both publicly and privately. Magnes urged that Reform Judaism could be saved from oblivion only if there were a reformation of Reform Judaism. He sought contact with the living Jewish people—its Torah, language, custom, ceremony, and observance. He demanded a proper Jewish educational system, adult classes, the return to the *Bar Mitzva*, the reduction of congregational dues so that the lower income groups could afford to join a congregation, and the use of the traditional *siddur*.

In the stability and security of Reform Judaism, these gusts of wind did not affect the main line of its action. On the Zionist issue antinationalism held sway. And so, too, Reform stood pat on ceremonial and ritual issues, apparently unaware that its classical position was no longer adequate.

Waves of immigration, the ascendancy of the Conservative movement, the emptying of pews and the consequent de-Judaization of the young, the Balfour Declaration and a cataclysmic war—these historic factors seemingly did not affect the official Reform position. Toward the end of the period, after World War I, the first signs of Reform's response to the changing times became noticeable.

The Conservative movement and the Seminary had the unparalleled opportunity of undergoing a complete metamorphosis. The positive historical tradition was promulgated and the counter-Reform program de-emphasized; the limited faculty was replaced by a unique group of scholars; the financial structure was thoroughly rebuilt through the creation of a new board of directors, including Jacob H. Schiff, Louis Marshall, Mayer Sulzberger, and Leonard Lewisohn (1847-1902); the new head of the institution was the peerless Solomon Schechter. Chiefly responsible for the entire reorganization was Cyrus Adler, devoted student of Sabato Morais, who would not permit his master's foremost contribution to American Judaism to disintegrate. The uniqueness of Adler's achievement was the alliance he formed between a board almost completely Reform and a faculty unswervingly devoted to traditional Judaism. This was possible because of the extraordinary caliber of the lay leaders who felt that only a traditional school could function effectively among the new immigrants.

Center of all eyes and hope of all hearts was the Rumanian-born, German-trained, British professor, American-destined Shneur Zalman Schechter. Virtually every person of importance claimed some influence on Schechter's decision to come to America; he was the most wooed Jewish scholar in modern times. Dramatized by his fortunate Genizah find, *hasid*, Zionist, and anti-reformist, master of style and gifted scholar, Schechter was what Conservative Judaism needed as a leader and a symbol.

In his inaugural address, delivered on November 20, 1902, Schechter proclaimed the goals of the re-created Seminary. Unity must be forged out of the diversities in Jewish community life; such unity would be realized through the training of a native ministry; Jewish scholarship was to be the chief altar in the temple of Judaism. "Judaism is absolutely incompatible with the abandonment of the Torah"; the Seminary stands for historical and traditional Judaism, for, "we cannot create halting places at will. We must either remain faithful to history or go the way of all flesh . . ."[44]

Schechter's first and most formidable task was to create a faculty worthy of his dream and representative of his thought. The ultimate success with which his efforts were crowned is represented not only in the rare individuals whom he brought to the Seminary, but in their collective strength. The faculty selected by Schechter is perhaps his greatest contribution to American Judaism, for as a body they were unrivaled. Their international standing established the Seminary as a central pillar of Jewish scholarship in America.

Louis Ginzberg, dean of Jewish scholars and pathfinder in every field of Judaica, was considered by Schechter even prior to his arrival in America. Professor Ginzberg's extraordinary learning, catholicity of knowledge and unswerving devotion to scholarly pursuits, quickly established him as, next to Schechter, the central figure of the faculty. After a thorough search in Europe in the summer of 1903, Schechter announced his selection of Dr. Alexander Marx for the chair of history and Dr. Israel Friedlaender (1876-1920) as professor of biblical literature and exegesis. Little did he suspect that in Dr. Marx he had invited not only a historian and bibliographer who was to achieve distinction second to none, but also the builder of the world's greatest Jewish library. Dr. Friedlaender, promising young docent at the University of Strasbourg, became in his short span of years a brilliant teacher, an exponent of Zionism, and the leader of American Jewish youth. In his martyr death, American Judaism lost one of its leading spokesmen.

Joseph Mayer Asher (1872-1909), English-born rabbi of Congregation B'nai Jeshurun, was appointed professor of homiletics. The faculty was completed with the addition of the gifted Israel Davidson (1870-1939), who rapidly rose to prominence as the world authority in medieval Hebrew literature.

The second department to be launched was the library. Mayer Sulzberger, to whom Professor Ginzberg repeatedly refers as the "outstanding Jew produced in America," was the library's greatest benefactor. It was Sulzberger's unique collection that served as the nucleus of the new library. "To compass the high ends for which we strive, the library must satisfy the needs of the few choice spirits as abundantly as it provides for those of ordinary scholars," Mayer Sulzberger said at the dedication of the Seminary library in 1902. By identifying himself completely and overwhelmingly with this purpose, Professor Marx, at once master and servant, has created what the men assembled at the opening ceremonies could neither anticipate nor dream of.

The Teachers Institute, which was to inaugurate a religious educational movement, was the third link in the chain of Seminary institutions. The young Mordecai M. Kaplan, European-born and American-trained graduate of the Seminary in whom Schechter had detected "a power so inspiring and stimulating," was invited to become the principal of the new institution. Kaplan threw himself into the task with originality of approach and breadth of action. The growth of the Institute and of its later auxiliary, the Seminary College of Jewish Studies (for the training of lay leaders), to the status of the foremost Jewish collegiate institution in the country was due to the efforts and amazing vision of Dr. Kaplan and the faculty he later assembled: Joseph Bragin (1875-1932), principal of the Hebrew High School of New York; Professor Zevi Scharfstein, leading American Jewish pedagogue, distinguished Hebraist and author of pedagogic textbooks used throughout the world, and Professor Morris D. Levine, who wrote his enduring volumes on the tablets of his students' hearts.

These institutions under way, Schechter and his colleagues turned to the task of developing a conservative movement in American Judaism. This was manifest in their attitudes toward scholarship; Torah and *mitzvot*, Zionism, and the American center. Schechter's favorite plea was that a community as practical as America stood in dire need of a few men who had the courage to be impractical—impractical in the material sense of the word. For scholarship was not divorced from life; it was the only force that could save American Judaism.

In contrast with the majority of the board, the Seminary faculty represented a united force of active Zionists. The adherence of the Conservative wing of Judaism to the official Zionist movement, as opposed to the antizionism of the Reform rabbinate and as differentiated from the Orthodox Mizrachi position, gave to the center Zionist Organization of America its greatest strength. Schechter's decisive statement of 1906, coming at a time when it meant a public debate in the *New York Times* with Jacob H. Schiff, was an extraordinary declaration. In his Zionism, Schechter repeated the Jewish pledge of ages: "Zionism was, and still is, the most cherished dream I was worthy of having." However, the Zionism of the Conservative movement, while it stressed the national factor in Israel's history, did not relegate the religious character of that history to a secondary position. Louis Ginzberg who had identified himself immediately with Herzl's call and had written one of his first essays, *Het Zionisme*, in Dutch, and who together with Friedlaender had voted "no" on the Uganda proposal while all other Americans had voted favorably, stressed the great danger that faced Judaism if its religious elements were ignored. Foreseeing the possibilities of a later development of a philosophy negating the Diaspora, he warned that an exclusive nationalist Zionist viewpoint would cut Diaspora Judaism off from its future. If Judaism is equivalent to nationalism, then only those who will reside in the Jewish state will be Jews. Moreover, he held that Jewish nationalism is not an abstract concept; its very essence is religious. "For us who adhere to historical Judaism, Jewish nationalism without religion would be a tree without fruit, Jewish religion without Jewish nationalism would be a tree without roots."[45]

This point of view expressed itself in a new formula: Diaspora plus Palestine. Granted that a wholesome Jewish life could be obtained in Eretz Yisrael by the Jewish resettlement of the Holy Land, could, however, a wholesome Jewish life be established in America? Conservatives responded with an unqualified, Yes. The building in America of a dominant center of Judaism was a cardinal plank in the program of Conservative Judaism. This was especially well expressed by Israel Friedlaender in his remarkable essay, "The Problems of Judaism in America."[46]

With scholarship, Torah and *mitzvot*, Zionist-Hebraism, and the American center as the dynamic constants of the Conservative movement, it became necessary to find a task force which, in addition to the Seminary, could make these ideals active in the life of the Jews in America. A younger generation of graduates had grown up. They rallied about their teachers; they brought their own congregants and students in February, 1913, to New York. This was the founding assembly of the United Synagogue of America.

The purpose of the new organization was defined as follows:

The advancement of the cause of Judaism in America and the maintenance of Jewish tradition in its historical continuity; to assert and establish loyalty to the Torah and its historical exposition; to further the observance of the Sabbath and the Dietary Laws; to preserve in the service the reference to Israel's past and the hopes for Israel's restoration; to maintain the traditional character of the liturgy, with Hebrew as the language of prayer; to foster Jewish religious life in the home, as expressed in traditional observances; to encourage the establishment of Jewish religious schools, in the curricula of which the study of the Hebrew language and literature shall be given a prominent place, both as the key to the true understanding of Judaism, and as a bond holding together the scattered communities of Israel throughout the world. It shall be the aim of the United Synagogue of America, while not indorsing the innovations introduced by any of its constituent bodies, to embrace all elements essentially loyal to traditional Judaism and in sympathy with the purposes outlined above.[47]

The Seminary and the Rabbinical Assembly had co-operated in the establishment of its action group. Under a joint committee, the Central Administrative Committee, representing the three branches of the organized movement, and under the presidency first of Schechter and then of Adler, Conservative Judaism went out among the people. In November, 1915, Solomon Schechter passed away in the midst of his labors.

Cyrus Adler became acting president of the Seminary and, in time, president. He had already become the head of the United Synagogue. Professor Louis Ginzberg became the scholarly leader of the movement. Both men had serious problems to cope with, for the inner perplexities and inconsistencies that had been passed over in the rush of organization and expansion now were increasing rather than disappearing. An umbrella ideology was agreeable in the abstract; in its application to contemporary problems and events interpretations varied. A definitive stand had to be taken on the approach to Jewish law and *mitzvot*, the Jewish Homeland, and the American Jewish Congress. The last two issues were hammered out to majority satisfaction. A definite position on the adjustment of Jewish law and observance has yet to be taken.

The major characteristics of Orthodoxy in America during the early part of the twentieth century were these: transplantation of type, decentralization, and spiritual insulation. Nor could the characteristics have been otherwise. Groups of immigrants, establishing miniatures of their old country in some corner of a metropolis, huddled together into *hebrot*, painted a sign, and organized themselves as a congregation in exile—exile from Kasrilevke. Shortly thereafter their religious functionaries, the *rabbonim*, *melamdim*, *shohetim*, and *mohalim*, arrived with the training, viewpoint and spiritual armor of East European Judaism. This was in full effect a transplantation of culture.

If energies were squandered and hopes dashed in the effort to implant Orthodox belief and practice in America, it was due in additional measure to the stubborn refusal of Orthodoxy to reckon with the facts of American life and thought in the twentieth century—the very life indeed of their children born and raised in the new world. Orthodox parents still liked to pretend that the East European pattern of culture could be native to America, too. And when the rabbi of Slusk came to America and appeared at a public meeting of the Union of Orthodox Jewish Congregations, he chastised the assemblage for having emigrated to this *trefa* land.

The history of Orthodoxy in America since 1900 is the development of an Orthodox rabbinate and laity who were as anxious as their predecessors to transmit the ancient heritage but who proceeded in a spirit and language which took the contemporary American trends and ideals into account. This transfer of leadership from the Agudath Ha-Rabbanim to the Rabbinical Council of America, from the basement synagogues to Young Israel and to Hapoel Hamizrachi, from the "rented store" schools to the United Yeshivot, did not happen overnight. Three decades were to pass before it became clear that Orthodoxy could flourish on American soil.

The patterns of Reform and Conservative religious institutional life had their counterpart in the Orthodox party: higher institutions of learning, a lay organization, and a rabbinical association. Latest in formation (1902), the Union of Orthodox Rabbis of the United States and Canada (the Agudath Ha-Rabbanim) was first in strength.

The initial call came from the West. The former plan to establish an American *Bet Din* of three learned Russian rabbis, was found to be impractical. Rabbis Judah Leib Levin (1862-1926) of Detroit and Asher Lippman Zarchy (1862-1932) of Louisville sent a circular letter to ten of their colleagues in Cincinnati, Chicago, St. Louis, New York, Boston, Pittsburgh, Philadelphia, Omaha, and Denver, under the title *Et La-asot* (Time for Action). The second step was taken in Boston when a group of Orthodox rabbis attending the Zionist convention gathered to prepare a tentative constitution. The leaders of the group were the veteran Rabbi Moses Z. (Ramaz) Margolies (1851-1936), chief rabbi of Boston and later rabbi of Congregation Kehilath Jeshurun of New York City, who had come to America in 1889, and Rabbi Bernard Louis Levinthal (1864-1952), who arrived in America in 1891 and resided in Philadelphia during his long and fruitful career as the revered head of Orthodoxy in that city.

The newly formed union was short lived. After four years of disappointment a second call was issued, once again from the western Orthodox rabbis: Rabbis Abraham Lesser (1834-1925) and Sander Lifshitz (1846-1915) of Cincinnati, Rabbi Zarchy of Louisville and Rabbi Isaac E. Neustadt (1869-1913) of Indianapolis. Was it due to the fact that these men, situated in the nest of Reform Judaism, were disturbed by the heavy inroads which Reform had made among their people? A guide to the promptings of this western group may be discovered in their heartrending appeal for the slumberers to awaken, urging as the prerequisite of an active Orthodoxy "the training of ordained rabbis, teachers and preachers who have mastered the English language and who will be fit to wage combat against the forces of reform."[48]

At the seventh convention, Rabbi Levinthal, in his opening address, pleaded that the organization "take to heart the needs of the Yeshivat Rabbenu Yitzchak Elchanan, from which Judaism may be rebuilt in America." The Agudath Ha-Rabbanim did intensify its efforts on behalf of the Yeshiva. A double purpose was served. Not only was the Yeshiva reinforced as a nursery for future teachers of Orthodoxy, but, in the concrete and constructive effort to build institutions, the Agudath Ha-Rabbanim itself took on life.

The recognition that the older, European way of Jewish life was not the path to the future, first came to the students of the Yeshiva. They sought to prepare themselves more effectively for service in the American scene, and therefore arranged their secular studies in local colleges. The directors of the Yeshiva violently opposed this practice. In 1908, an assembly of rabbis met to adjudicate the difference between the authorities and the students. The students won. They were granted permission to continue with their general studies until such time as the Yeshiva itself could organize courses under its own administration. The acceptance of higher education as compatible with rabbinic integrity was the first important step that American Orthodoxy took toward winning a position of equality with the other religious parties in American Judaism. In addition, the Yeshiva, unlike the other rabbinical seminaries and in keeping with the tradition of European *yeshibot*, did not limit its student body to those preparing for the rabbinate, but rather encouraged students who might later pursue other professions, including business careers, to master Jewish knowledge. This change of approach placed the Yeshiva in an advantageous position, for it made possible the training of an intensely devoted Orthodox lay leadership. Amalgamation between the Rabbi Isaac Elchanan Theological Seminary and the Yeshiva Etz Chaim in 1915 led to greater strength. To cap these constructive factors, the new institution elected Dr. Bernard Revel (1885-1940) as *Rosh Ha-Yeshiva* and president of the combined institutions. Thus was inaugurated an era of consolidation and expansion which was climaxed by the incorporation of Yeshiva University as the first Jewish university in America.

Dr. Revel was born in Kovno in 1885. After his arrival in America in 1906, Dr. Revel pursued studies at Dropsie College, where he received his Ph.D. degree. He keenly understood the need for relating the Jewish tradition to American community life. His firm organizing hand was felt immediately. Through the establishment in 1915 of the first Yeshiva high school, the Etz Chaim Talmudical Academy, where both secular and general studies were taught under the same roof, he blazed a new trail in Orthodox education. As the First World War came to a close, Orthodoxy had laid the foundation for a higher educational institution of historic proportions.

A second Orthodox rabbinical school, which was in its infancy at the turn of the century, was organized in the Midwest in 1916, the Beth Midrash Le Rabbonim of Chicago. This seminary grew out of a small group of students who were taught Talmud in a private *heder* in 1895, later called the Yeshiva Etz Chaim. The student body consisted in the main of young immigrants who received regular weekly stipends (as was customary in European *yeshibot*) in order to be free to continue their full-time talmudic studies.

The activities of the Orthodox group were based on the opposing premises of negation and affirmation. The Reform, Conservative, and secularist theories of survival were vigorously condemned; the fields of education, ceremonial, and ritual observance, European aid, and Zionism were actively cultivated. Greater rewards accompanied the constructive efforts. First and foremost was the precept "And thou shalt teach them diligently." The schools were in a sorry state. At an early convention of the Union of Orthodox Jewish Congregations, it was stated that the Christian mission schools on the East Side "take the place of those schools which we have neglected to provide." In the first decade of the century, matters took a turn for the better. Communal Talmud Torahs were built and supported largely by local Orthodox parents. These schools offered a condensed version of the subjects of the European *heder*. The schools prospered and were effective in attracting devoted and gifted teachers. Children of the poor were given free instruction. In 1903 the Yeshivat Jacob Joseph on the lower East Side of New York was founded with facilities for one thousand children. The Agudath Ha-Rabbanim called for the rapid multiplication of such effort. They were anxious to found adequate elementary schools in the rural areas and to conduct classes in Talmud and Midrash for the adolescents. The national Yeshiva Ketanah movement for the establishment of all day schools, as the effective solution to the problems of Jewish education, was not yet in existence. In 1918 there were only four such schools in New York City.

Most effort was concentrated on ritual and ceremonial matters, particularly Sabbath observance and *kashrut*. One of the first and most important achievements of the Union of Orthodox Jewish Congregations was the establishment in 1905 of the Jewish Sabbath Alliance of America, whose object was to promote "the observance of the Holy Sabbath in every possible way." Recognizing that Sabbath observance has "in many places . . . become the exception rather than the rule," the Alliance endeavored to restore the sanctity of the traditional holy day in a variety of ways—by means of propaganda, political or legislative activity, securing employment service for Sabbath observers, and so on. For several years, a monthly organ, the *Sabbath Journal*, was published in English, Yiddish, and Hebrew. The Alliance frequently appeared in the legislative halls of many states to secure desired legislation; it was instrumental in defeating a bill in the New York state legislature which would have prohibited the sale of all articles of food on Sunday. Some seventy thousand Sabbath observers, including grocers, butchers, clothiers, tailors, laundrymen, watch repairers, shoemakers, standkeepers, pushcart peddlers, and other merchants, arrested for work done on Sunday, were defended in the courts; Alliance representatives appeared before Christian Sunday Associations explaining the Jewish Sabbath view; an employment bureau was opened to bring together Sabbath-observing employer and employee; successful intercession on behalf of public service employees gave them the opportunity to observe Saturdays and holy days. In these efforts the Alliance was aided by many individuals, primarily among the Orthodox, but also from the Conservative and Reform ranks. Louis Marshall was one of their most active counselors. An interesting development occurred in labor circles when, in 1910, a special section of the cloak and skirts union formed a Sabbath observing chapter. They appealed to the Agudath Ha-Rabbanim to help them enlarge their membership.

The control of *kashrut* fell into the domain of the Orthodox. For some unknown reason, certainly not because they were less concerned, the Conservatives defaulted completely. The results, though not entirely due to the inadequacies of the Orthodox, were truly discouraging. New York State aid, for example, was forthcoming, and the Agudath Ha-Rabbanim were effective in gaining that aid. Nevertheless, the variety of excesses against the law and spirit of Judaism rendered the observance of *kashrut* a challenge to the basic fidelity of many observant Jews.

The supervision of *mohalim* was another illustration of how the maladministration of religious duties ofttimes drives even its most ardent devotees away from observance. In this case, the state medical laws took control of the situation. The Orthodox were keenly aware of these indignities to religious life; the proceedings of their conferences include unabashed statements of the repugnant state of affairs. Fundamentally, the evil arose from the fragmentization of Jewish religious life. The Reform paid no heed; the Conservatives defaulted; the Orthodox alone were helpless.

In the area of overseas relief Orthodoxy displayed superior imagination and originality. Impatient with the general relief agencies because of their neglect of religious institutions, the Central Jewish Relief Committee and Ezrath Torah Fund were organized. The original purpose of the Committee was to bring aid and succor to the European *yeshivot*, their rabbis and students, as well as to all religious functionaries during World War I. But because of the great need for relief for all Jewish sufferers from affliction, the Committee's plans were expanded to meet developing emergencies. The Ezrath Torah Fund fulfilled the original functions of the Committee. Some of the world famous *yeshivot*—Mir, Slobodka, Lomza, Telz and Slonim—were saved from total extinction through the efforts of this fund. The work that was executed under the chairmanship of Rabbi Israel Rosenberg was not limited to European *yeshiva* relief but was also extended to the religious institutions in Eretz Yisrael.

The separation of American Jewry's communal, social and cultural affairs from the control of organized religious bodies, was complete early in the new century. The last effort to bring together an American Jewish Congress under religious auspices was the attempt of the Union of American Hebrew Congregations. It did not succeed. Henceforth religious organizations were reduced to the same status as all other national organizations in the representative councils of American Israel. The responsibilities for world Israel suddenly became so heavy, the activities so intensified, and the need for leadership so urgent, that the religious parties welcomed the new alignment.

The Kishinev pogroms shook American Jewry out of its parochialism. Emil G. Hirsch, rabid antinationalist, cried out under the stress and agony of the pogroms, "I am now a Zionist." American Jews, who had not sent one dollar to aid their distressed brethren overseas in any nationally organized manner until 1905, hastily dispatched $1,250,000 through the office of the National Committee for the Relief of Sufferers by Russian Massacres. The Galveston movement expended a million dollars for the more effective settlement of immigrants in the American hinterland; national Jewish agitation started for the organization of an American Jewish congress or assembly; in November, 1906, the American Jewish Committee was founded "to prevent the infraction of the civil and religious rights of Jews, in any part of the world . . . [to] alleviate the consequences of persecution and to afford relief from calamities affecting Jews, wherever they may occur . . ."

In its attempt to effect a better internal organization of American Jewry, the Jewish community of New York City tried the experiment of establishing a Kehilla which would not merely represent one party in Judaism, but include all Jews who believed in a Jewish future, even though they differed considerably as to what form that future should take. The Kehilla was started because of false allegations regarding the percentage of criminality among Jews, but it did not succeed. Some of its branches, such as the Bureau of Jewish Education and the Federation of Jewish Philanthropies, survived as independent agencies. Nevertheless the Kehilla was a sign of the times. An advisory council of seventy, representing every walk of Jewish life—religion, *Landsmannschaften*, philanthropy, and labor, etc.—began to learn how to work together.

The Americanization of the immigrants was a serious problem, although not half so serious as was the social maladjustment of their children. This was true for all ethnic groups. The children lived in two worlds, at home in a world of their parents, and outside in an American universe of discourse. The Jewish parents worked out their own salvation. Yiddish cultural activities enjoyed extraordinary developments. Channels of communication such as the press, stage and club organizations, served as instruments for Americanization. But neither the synagogue nor Yiddish culture seemed to be the way to the heart of Jewish youth. To solve the cultural, social and recreational problems of the juvenile, the Young Men's Hebrew Association was reconstructed. The model "Y" was the famous 92nd Street building which was established in 1900 by Jacob H. Schiff. In 1905, the Center movement was given financial stability when it was granted full community support, through the intercession of Schiff, who contended that "there is absolutely no reason . . . why larger provision should be made for the orphan than for the religious education and moral care of the juvenile." The movement expanded rapidly. In 1910 five regional Y.M.H.A.'s were in existence; in 1913, at a special conference, the Council of Young Men's Hebrew Associations and Kindred Associations was created.

The organization was founded, the need was great, but the specific program for the "religious education and moral care" of Jewish youth was wanting. Although the Y.M.H.A. called itself by a name adapted from the existing Christian organization, it did not adopt the same purpose. The Y.M.C.A. was a religious movement among the unchurched with the avowed purpose of propagandizing for Christian religious interests. The Y.M.H.A. was recreational, social, and at best, cultural—certainly not religious. This problem of Jewish program content plagued the sponsors since the earliest days. Professor Mordecai M. Kaplan, who among the religious leaders is probably the foremost protagonist of the Center movement, wrote to Felix M. Warburg, then president of the Y.M.H.A. Council, on November 1, 1913:

In my opinion, all Young Men's Hebrew Association work, which at present is still to a large extent a mere fumbling in the dark, would be rendered more definite and effective, if ranged about a religious, rather than a purely social or philanthropic ideal. By this I mean, that, instead of confining ourselves to holding out such distractions as might compete successfully with the dangerous distractions that tempt young men, we should seek to stimulate in them a positive enthusiasm for Judaism. Entertainments, the pool room and the gymnasium may serve as a temporary means of keeping young men away from the gambling dens and worse places. But a Young Men's Hebrew Association should not content itself with evoking anything less than the very highest manhood of which the young men are capable. The fact is that ignorance due to a lack of youthful training has been the cause for religion appearing to many of our young men a negligible factor in their lives. It is this very defect in their training that a Young Men's Hebrew Association should strive to eliminate . . .

It must be borne in mind, however, that it is futile to expect Young Men's Hebrew Associations to adopt this course without leaders who unite in themselves the qualifications of social worker as well as those of the religious worker. That there are no such leaders at the present time is due to the fact that the Young Men's Hebrew Association movement has only begun to assume the proportions necessary to call them forth. Instead, however, of leaving it to chance for these leaders to arise, it were advisable that the National Young Men's Hebrew Association get into touch with the two Seminaries in this country, which prepare men for the ministry, and urge them to encourage some of their students to prepare themselves for a career of Y.M.H.A. leadership. This might be brought about by having those students who have a leaning for social work, take up in addition to their regular Rabbinic course, such post-graduate studies in the University as have a bearing upon practical social work. With the problem of leaders solved the rest would be sure to follow.

Had this sound advice not been neglected in practice by both Synagogue and Center authorities, Jewish religious life would have benefited exceedingly, the Center movement might not have been regarded as a competitor of the Synagogue and, most important, we probably would have gained a generation which would have been trained in the moral and religious spirit envisaged by the founders of the Center movement and their successors.

A new type of institution of higher Jewish learning, the first post-graduate Jewish institution in the world devoted exclusively to scientific research, was created in 1907 through the bequest of Moses Aaron Dropsie. He directed in his will that "there be established and maintained in the City of Philadelphia, a college for the promotion of and instruction in the Hebrew and cognate languages and their respective literatures and in the Rabbinical learning and literature." According to Cyrus Adler, the first president of the Dropsie College for Hebrew and Cognate Learning, the idea occurred independently to the boards of the Seminary and of the Dropsie College that the cause of Jewish learning might be best served if a consolidation could be effected. A plan was considered for the establishment of a Jewish university which would combine the faculties and facilities of the Seminary, the Gratz College, and the new foundation. However, the time was not propitious, and instead the first nonsectarian higher academy of learning was brought into being. The original faculty included Henry Malter and Max L. Margolis, who left their posts at the Hebrew Union College; Jacob Hoschander (1874-1933) was added a year later; and, in 1913, Benzion Halper (1884-1924). In the same year, a history department was established and Abraham A. Neuman, who was later to become the president of the college, was chosen as professor of history. The *Jewish Quarterly Review*, which had been issued in England for twenty years under the editorship of Israel Abrahams and Claude G. Montefiore, was re-established at Dropsie College in 1910 by Dr. Adler in association with Schechter. After Schechter's death, Adler continued the editorial responsibilities alone.

Learning was a great cohesive force. Men of all schools of thought worked together to produce major contributions which could only have been made collectively. The *Jewish Encyclopedia* (1901-1906) was a landmark of scholarship. Under the leadership of Isidore Singer and the editorship of Joseph Jacobs a whole array of pre-eminent figures in Jewish learning combined to produce a twelve-volume work which has until this date (1948) remained unrivaled. In 1917 the long awaited authoritative Jewish translation of the Bible into English was presented to the American public. This first American Jewish edition of the Bible since Leeser's translation was supervised by an editorial board including Adler, Jacobs, Kohler, David Philipson, Schechter and Dr. Samuel Shulman, with Dr. Margolis as editor in chief.

The Orthodox rabbis and scholars continued in their tradition of publishing commentaries and insights on talmudic texts. In 1919, after years of patient effort, the full text of the Talmud Babli was issued for the first time in America under the vigilant auspices of the Agudath Ha-Rabbanim. Through this effort they were enabled partly to repay their martyr teachers and dispersed fellow students of the European *yeshibot*. Hundreds of sets were sent as gifts to the *yeshibot* in Lithuania, Poland and other places, where the centers of learning had been destroyed and the holy texts consumed by the ravages of war.

World War I was the first great test of American Israel's strength and mercy. The Joint Distribution Committee combined the efforts of the Central Jewish Relief Committee (organized by the Orthodox), the American Jewish Relief Committee (organized by the American Jewish Committee), and the People's Relief Committee (organized by labor groups). The new agency brought comfort and aid to millions of Jews caught in the net of devastation.

On April 6, 1917, America declared war. On April 9, 1917, seven national Jewish organizations convened and called for the creation of the Jewish Welfare Board. Before the war was ended, nine additional organizations had joined the Jewish Welfare Board. The newly created instrument was to serve as the organized Jewish voice to the men in service and as the official representative to the government on behalf of Jewish religious activities; moreover, the Board was to provide for the social and religious needs of the men in the armed forces of the United States at training base, military front or hospital. The responsibilities were overwhelming, for there was no precedent to guide Jewish action.

During the Civil War, four Jewish hospital chaplains had been appointed. Army organization did not call for Jewish regimental chaplains to serve with the battle troops. Consequently, at the outbreak of World War I, the legal question of chaplaincy appointments in other areas of service was not clear. Dr. Cyrus Adler, the first chairman of the Committee on Chaplains, met with Secretary Newton D. Baker to draft the legal formula that would qualify appointment of chaplains of denominations not represented at that time in the armed forces. The first Jewish chaplain to be appointed was Rabbi Elkan C. Voorsanger. He had enlisted in the service, was sent overseas, became a sergeant in the Medical Corps, and then, when the law was changed to allow the appointment of Jewish chaplains, was commissioned by appointment of General Pershing overseas. Twenty-three Jewish chaplains served during the war; twenty-two in the army and one in the navy. Dr. David de Sola Pool, then president of the New York Board of Jewish Ministers, became active aide to Dr. Adler and finally succeeded him as chairman of the committee. There were very special problems to solve. One of these had to do with the insigne, which in the army was the shepherd's crook. A special Jewish insigne was authorized in Washington. When Chaplain David Goldberg, the only Jewish naval chaplain in World War I, requested the authorities to change the insigne from the shepherd's crook to the star of David, he was informed by the Bureau of Navigation that "this star constitutes part of an insignia used by the Army" (the Sixth Army used it). Other problems which had to be faced were the preparation of an abridged Bible and a prayer book. Edited by Adler, Drachman, and Rosenau, the prayer book was published as an abridged traditional *siddur* with footnotes indicating the Union Prayer Book variations.

The war had taken a heavy toll of Jewish lives. European Jewish communities were in shambles. Yet out of the horror came a promise, the promise of the Balfour Declaration. American Israel, having suddenly grown into the responsibility of leadership, began its role in the rebuilding of the mother communities overseas, and in helping to establish Eretz Yisrael as the Jewish homeland.

7

AMERICA, A CENTER OF WORLD JUDAISM, 1919-1939

World War I altered the face of Europe; it changed the heart of America. In a series of laws passed during the years 1921, 1924, and 1929, America ended her former liberal immigration policy. President Wilson, who vetoed two restrictive immigration bills, asked of the American conscience: "Has not every ship that has pointed her prow westward borne hither the hopes of generation after generation of the oppressed of other lands?" The legislative voice in Washington responded in effect: America is no longer the Promised Land. It is the land of splendid isolation.

The changes in the immigration policy of the United States transformed the internal structure of the American Jewish community. Within two decades, American Jewry was preponderantly native American. The children of former immigrants rose to affluence and station in the rapidly expanding economy. A survey of Jewish occupational distribution shows that the white collar workers among the Jews exceeded the number in manual trades. In the natural course of events, these special and economic factors reflected themselves in Jewish communal life.

As the period of immigration came to an abrupt close, second generation American Jews became predominant in the leadership of all religious groups. Ever since the days of Leeser and Wise, progressive Jewish leadership had urged the training of a native ministry and teaching service. With immigration arrested, it became difficult to import rabbis and teachers.[49] A native born rabbinate therefore assumed religious responsibilities of the hour. Symbolically, the two new appointees to the presidencies of the Jewish Theological Seminary and the Hebrew Union College—Cyrus Adler and Julian Morgenstern—were both born and educated in America.

The emergence of an American trained and American centered religious leadership brought with it the development of new outlooks on Judaism and different interpretations of the special tasks which confronted the religious groups. While the leaders of the former generation saw as their central objective the building of strong and well knit independent religious parties and institutions, the leadership of the new generation sought, in addition, spiritual hegemony over all American Israel. This desire to create an indigenous American pattern for all American Jewry which would be predominantly Reform, Orthodox, or Conservative (depending on the particular designer of the pattern) is the special characteristic of

American Jewish religious history in the decades between the two world wars. Each group shaped its thought and action toward the ultimate goal of becoming, not as formerly, the major party in American Judaism, but American Judaism itself; the others ultimately would be assimilated into the new and main stream of American Judaism.

The desire to influence the religious character of American Judaism is reflected in the dissatisfaction of the rising generation with the adjectives of their respective group names. Reform Judaism at varying times called itself Progressive Judaism, Historical Judaism, and Liberal Judaism.[50] Orthodox Jewry was also unhappy with that description. For a period, the term "Torah-true Judaism," based on the Germanic compound *Torah-treu*, gained wide popularity; the official statements of the Yeshiva College and its authorities preferred the name, Traditional Judaism. The Conservatives were dissatisfied with their name (except for the active anti-Reform period in their history), and they used terms like Historical, Traditional, and Conservative interchangeably. Many preferred to drop the adjective altogether.

A second characteristic of this period was the refusal of the religious leadership to confine its role to that of the pastorate in American Jewish life. Reform leaders began to speak of relating their movement to the totality of American Jewish life; Orthodoxy sought to place all communal enterprises under the influence of Torah ideals; Conservative Judaism proclaimed that the synagogue should be the center of all Jewish activities.

This striving for an all embracing program was expressed in the first instance through an intensification of congregational activities and efforts. Memberships were increased, new departments established, personnel augmented. It was soon apparent, however, that the religiously unaffiliated were eagerly courted by each of the organized Jewish religious groups. The drive for possession was on. Each religious group planned to capture larger numbers for its special platform, and soon discovered that theological arguments and sectarian philosophies seemed irrelevant in broad areas of the Jewish community. Rivalry for primacy only led to further misunderstanding and confusion, particularly on the local scene. The American Jew did not comprehend the ideological differences which divided religious spokesmen. Native Jewish community life was primitive; a generation of de-Judaized Jews had grown up on American soil; to children, who did not learn about Judaism in Jewish schools, was presented a Judaism based on misconceptions and misinterpretations from the general world. Consequently, even when many Jews later did return to Jewish life, as a result of the Hitler catastrophe, they identified themselves principally with Jews, rather than with Judaism. This fact had to be faced by all Jewish religious groups. In the early years of the century, Jewish leaders had to meet the problem of Americanization; now it was the opposite problem: assimilation.

In their competition with each other all the religious groups soon discovered that each was emphasizing the same ideals for a healthy Jewish life in America: learning, scholarship, traditional values and ceremonials, the influence of Eretz Yisrael, ethical and social objectives.

The chapter heading for the history of Reform Judaism in these decades may well be entitled *Heshbon Ha-Nefesh* (Spiritual Re-evaluation). Reform had drifted from the people. The events that led to the Columbus platform in 1937 were signs of the return.

Julian Morgenstern was elected president of the Hebrew Union College in 1921. Under his direction, the school grew in strength and scope. Intensely engaged in biblical scholarship all the days of his busy presidential years, Morgenstern came to symbolize the combination of modern American Jewish scholar-administrator. He conceived the Hebrew Union College to be the focal institution in American Judaism and consecrated himself to this purpose. New faculty appointments were made.[51] Courses were added to the curriculum: religious education, pastoral psychology, Jewish music, and American Jewish history. A younger group of scholars, many of them graduates of the college, were invited to join the faculty.[52] Qualified students were encouraged to pursue postgraduate research work in international capitals of learning, and exchange lectureships with Christian theological seminaries were established. In 1924 the college began the publication of the *Hebrew Union College Annual*, the only scholarly publication of its kind in America. It has appeared regularly since the first issue.

During these years the library of the college grew to magnificent proportions including some 125,000 books and pamphlets, 3,000 manuscripts, 10,000 Jewish art and ceremonial objects, and about 130 incunabula. The Teachers Institute, after conducting summer sessions from 1926 to 1936, resumed its earlier practice of arranging special seminar meetings in local cities.[53] One of Morgenstern's most significant contributions was the establishment of a college-in-exile during the years of the Hitler regime. Foremost scholars, who might otherwise never have survived the world cataclysm, were saved to continue in Cincinnati their fruitful work.

Morgenstern always possessed a passionate faith in American Reform Judaism as the only philosophy of Judaism which adjusted itself consciously and sympathetically to modern life. As he continued in office, he came to believe that all three religious groups in America would ultimately be one, and in the final union, he foresaw the principles of American Reform as dominant. The differentia between Judaism and other American social units, he predicted, would be essentially theological. National elements in Judaism would be reduced to a minimum, but a consciousness of membership in the world Jewish community would prevail. The Jewish people will think of itself as a distinct, chosen people with a destiny to fulfil God's revelation, and American Israel would then be the *Ebed Adonai,* the servant of the Almighty.

To the ranks of Reform Judaism was added a second higher institution of learning when the Jewish Institute of Religion was established in New York in 1922. The new rabbinical school was a symbol of the bold and free spirit which America and the world came to know in the personality of Stephen S. Wise. From the very beginning, both in the selection of faculty and student body, the Institute fully lived up to its declared purpose of creating a school where "the different constructions of Judaism and of Jewish life, orthodox, conservative, liberal, radical Zionist, and non-Zionist, are expounded to the students in courses given by men representing different points of view." A four story building was erected by the Free Synagogue for the combined use of the Synagogue and the Institute. Originally the faculty consisted of Jewish and Christian guest lecturers. Dr. Wise soon succeeded in creating a permanent faculty.[54] In a brief span of years, largely through the indomitable efforts of its president, the Institute rose to an important position in higher Jewish academic circles through its library, lectureships, publications, and scores of graduates prepared for leadership in the rabbinate, Jewish education, and other areas of community service.

Wise's attempt to bring greater unity into American Judaism by training a rabbinate at a common center, despite individual differences in religious orientation, did not materialize in practice. Dedicated as "the only inter-denominational school for the training of rabbis in America," the Institute virtually became a New York Reform college, for most of the graduates, inspired by the thought and deed of the founder-president, affiliated themselves with the Central Conference of American Rabbis. Only a small group later chose to join the Rabbinical Assembly of America. As the work of the Institute progressed, and as the thesis of its trans-sectarianism proved untenable in the pattern of American Jewish religious life, a merger between the Cincinnati and New York schools became eminently desirable for both institutions.[55] In the full score of Reform Judaism's development, the Jewish Institute of Religion represents the accents of community, international Jewish solidarity, and Zionism-Hebraism, so sadly lacking in classic Reform's formulation.

In the meantime, the work of the Union of American Hebrew Congregations continued apace. The National Federation of Temple Sisterhoods had been organized in 1913; ten years later the National Federation of Temple Brotherhoods was created "to stimulate interest in Jewish worship, Jewish studies, social service and other kindred activities." The work of the Jewish Chautauqua Society advanced considerably. Lectures on Judaism and Jewish problems were assigned to hundreds of colleges throughout the United States and Canada. A union of temple youth groups, the National Federation of Temple Youth, was established in 1939. Regional departments of the Union were organized in 1931 to secure greater co-operation between the isolated settlements and the larger communities, as well as to raise the standards of Jewish education in the smaller towns. The Union functioned through a series of commissions, most of them in co-operation with the Central Conference of American Rabbis. The former Tract Commission became the Commission on Information about Judaism. It published a series of studies on a wide variety of historical and contemporary subjects. The reorganized Commission on Jewish Education (1923) and the newly created Joint Committee on Ceremonies (1936) represented revolutionary departures in Reform activities. In 1926, the Union, wishing to extend the influence of Reform Judaism to other countries, founded the World Union for Progressive Judaism. The new organization, however, was seriously resisted in Europe and therefore made little headway.

The beginning of ideological evaluation is stocktaking. In 1931 the Commission on Research of the Union, under the directorship of Abraham N. Franzblau, supervised "a survey of the homes of members of Reform Congregations affiliated with the Union of American Hebrew Congregations in the eleven cities of the United States which have a Jewish population of over fifty thousand."[56] This study disclosed the great lag between the *avant garde* leaders and their congregational constituents. It did indicate, however, the loyalties and attachments to Judaism of the affiliated membership, and the basis upon which a convinced leadership could build a more intensive synagogue program.

The forum and the tribunal for the developing Reform movement were the annual conventions of the Central Conference of American Rabbis. The volumes of proceedings of the Conference include symposia, scholarly papers, and resolutions reflecting the profound changes that came over Reform Judaism. Reform leaders must recognize, Dr. Samuel Schulman once said, that Reform was a revolutionary movement and, like all revolutionary movements, it went too far. "Reform Congregations continue the process of reforming," Dr. Solomon B. Freehof wrote in a similar vein, "They do not hesitate to change not only the practices of Orthodoxy but even the earlier practices of Reform itself." Thus did the highest and most effective form of criticism, self-criticism, emanate from the leadership. Retreat from earlier Reform attitudes toward education, worship, Jewish practice and ceremony, and Eretz Yisrael was demanded. It was a battle in which the very foundations of the movement rocked. After steady and unceasing struggle, the intensivists emerged victorious.

In 1923 the Commission on Education brought Emanuel Gamoran to

Cincinnati. Within two decades, Gamoran, a Zionist and Hebraist, who fully understood the inherent values of Jewish ceremony and observance in Jewish tradition, helped chart a new approach to the education of the young. His program of educational action included the intensification of Jewish life, the introduction of Jewish practice into the home, straightforward propaganda for the increased use of Hebrew in the curriculum, the development of weekday instruction in the Reform school system and the higher priority rating of Jewish education in the schedule of Reform organizational activities. These views were slowly and democratically impressed on the main line of rabbinic and lay Reform leaders. In time, because of the high caliber of his work and extraordinary standards of book production, the texts that Gamoran prepared were used in many Orthodox and Conservative schools. History texts, for example, were produced under the guiding principle that no religious party should be offended by their contents. In such progressive manner did Reform educational methodology reflect the deeper stirrings in the movement.

The accepted forms of the Reform prayer service were more emotionally rooted. Little was done until the criticism against the Union Prayer Book became an organized and formal complaint. In a special symposium held in 1930, the inadequacies of the Union Prayer Book were scored. Professor Bettan warned that "The Jew does not pray philosophy"; Professor Cohon stressed that the prayer book must speak to the hearts of all worshippers; Dr. Freehof called for a Union Prayer Anthology. Some asked for more Hebrew in the services; others for the re-identification of American Israel with the dream of Eretz Yisrael. Everyone urged greater congregational participation in the service.[57] Out of the welter of criticism and suggestions, another committee was appointed to prepare a basic revision of the prayer book.[58]

The Committee on Ceremonies was more practical. It embarked upon a program of Jewish ceremonial revival. The *kiddush*, the lighting of the candles, the traditional Sabbath melodies were reinstated; Hanukkah and Purim, virtually nonexistent in Reform practice, were introduced; the public *Seder* gave new communal meaning to the Passover; the *Shofar* was heard again at the High Holy Day service; Sukkot was re-established as a consecration festival.

From synagogue, to school, to home. The following quotation from an official report by Rabbi Jacob D. Schwarz reflects the complete turnabout from the earlier days of deceremonialization in Reform practice:

> If, as we believe, the perpetuation and advancement of Judaism depend on the cultivation of Jewish life, the revival of ceremonies cannot stop with synagogue and school. It must penetrate the home, to make the home again the sanctuary of Jewish faith and practice. The traditional home was made Jewish by a regimen of prayer and song and ceremony and consecrated living. It

will become Jewish again when Jewish observance, nurtured in synagogue and in Religious School, takes root and flourishes there within the family circle. When the rabbis took steps to replace, through the medium of the synagogue and all its agencies, ceremonies discarded in the home, their ultimate objective was a revival in the home. By teaching the children and by presenting ceremonial object lessons, as it were, in the synagogue, they hoped to restore the spirit of knowledge and understanding that was so woefully lacking and to create an appreciation of symbolism and a desire for ceremony that would make home observance not only possible but also devoutly wished.

Some results are already apparent. Through the children the Jewish holidays have become more intimate and are being brought back in some measure to the home. Hanukkah candles put in the hands of the children have kept the home lights burning; the school Seder has encouraged the restoration of the home Seder, as has the public Seder in general. The introduction of Sabbath songs and ceremonies in the synagogue has brought closer their revival in the home. Sukkot symbolism, exemplified by the table Sukkah and other decorative motifs, is adapting itself anew to the home. Congregations are beginning officially to urge upon their congregants the restoration of the Jewish home observance and are furnishing suggestions and materials to that end. Thus, the synagogue has become the instrument and the home the objective for the revival of ceremonies in these modern days.[59]

The road to unity on the Palestine issue was paved on the floor of the annual conventions. In 1935 the classic anti-Zionist formula was discarded and the famous neutrality clause adopted in its stead. The final reading was as follows:

> Whereas, at certain foregoing conventions of the Central Conference of American Rabbis, resolutions have been adopted in opposition to Zionism, and. . .
>
> Whereas, we are persuaded that acceptance or rejection of the Zionist program should be left to the determination of the individual members of the Conference themselves, therefore
>
> Be It Resolved, That the Central Conference of American Rabbis takes no official stand on the subject of Zionism, and be it further
>
> Resolved, That in keeping with its oft-announced intentions, the Central Conference of American Rabbis will continue to co-operate in the upbuilding of Palestine, and in the economic, cultural, and particularly spiritual tasks confronting the growing and evolving Jewish community there.[60]

The time had come for a new official platform. At Columbus, Ohio, on May 27, 1937, fifty-two years after the Pittsburgh platform had been adopted, a new set of guiding principles of Reform Judaism was formulated. Under three main divisions—Judaism and its foundations, ethics, and religious practice—the debates and discussions of two decades were crystallized into a compromise program.[61]

There was much unhappiness on the right and on the left with the

Columbus declaration.[61a] To those who now became an organized minority, this was the beginning of the end; to the victors, it was but a temporary respite in the battle for greater intensification of Judaism. During the following decade, the intensivists achieved victory. Reform Judaism redefined its entire program in accordance with the objectives foreshadowed in the period of *Heshbon Ha-Nefesh*.

Orthodoxy in this period in America was passing through a stage of transition—transition in methodology and techniques, not in basic belief or ritual practice. The European-trained, Yiddish-speaking rabbinate and their American-schooled, English-speaking associates worked in separate camps, but preached the same doctrine of the supernatural revelation of the written and oral law and the scrupulous observance of the commandments of the Torah, as interpreted in the Talmud and codified in the *Shulhan Aruk*. In the course of events, disagreements developed in substance as well as in form.

For Orthodox Jews the Rabbi Isaac Elchanan Theological Seminary met the demands of the modern American scene with creative force. In 1928 the pathfinding decision to incorporate a fully equipped American college under Orthodox auspices, was carried through. The establishment of the Yeshiva College was duly authorized by an amendment in the charter of the Rabbi Isaac Elchanan Theological Seminary, and in September, 1928, the college was opened in temporary quarters at the Jewish Center in New York with a mixed faculty of Jewish and Christian scholars. It fulfilled the dual purpose of raising a Jewishly trained laity in America and offering Orthodox rabbis a fine secular education.

The entrance of the Yeshiva into the field of general education was but one of the important tasks which this pioneering institution had assumed for itself under the presidency of Dr. Revel. In 1921 the Teachers Institute, which had been founded four years earlier by the Mizrachi Organization of America as the first teacher training institution established under Orthodox auspices in the world, was incorporated as a regular department of the Yeshiva. Pinkhas Churgin became dean of the Institute. In 1937 as an outgrowth of graduate courses first offered in 1935, the Yeshiva Graduate School was formally opened. Eminent Jewish scholars were brought to these faculties.[62]

The financing of this program was a tremendous undertaking for the modest means of Orthodox Jewry and its constituencies. Not only were funds unavailable; the entire project was jeered at in many sanctimonious quarters. Promises of aid were no sooner made than they were promptly forgotten. Dr. Revel and his associates continued in a spirit of enthusiasm and courage. In December, 1924, a building fund for the Yeshiva College was launched; in May, 1927, the cornerstone of the new institution was laid on a site at Amsterdam Avenue and 186th Street; in December, 1928, the new structure which had been reared was finally dedicated.[63]

The Yeshiva soon embarked upon a series of scholarly publications. The *Scripta Mathematica*, a quarterly journal devoted to the philosophy, history, and expository treatment of mathematics, appeared in September, 1932, and has subsequently earned an international reputation for its excellence. In 1934 Dr. Churgin founded the semiannual *Horeb*, a magazine devoted to Jewish history and Hebrew literature.[64]

Higher Jewish education made further headway under Orthodox auspices in the Midwest. After much struggle and indecision, the Beth Ha-Medrash La-Torah, the Hebrew Theological College, was established in Chicago in 1921 for the purpose of preparing Orthodox rabbis, teachers, and lay leaders. The curriculum provided a four year prerabbinical (high school) course to be followed by a seven-year rabbinical training course. While attending the rabbinical school, the student was required to take general studies leading to a college degree. The final three years were to be devoted entirely to rabbinic studies. In 1922 Rabbi Saul Silber (1881-1946), spiritual leader of the Anshe Sholom Congregation in Chicago, was elected president, an office he held until the time of his death; Rabbi Jacob Greenberg became the dean.[65] The college attracted a student body primarily from Chicago and the Midwest, but included young scholars from other parts of the country as well. Scholarships and dormitory facilities were provided. Within a decade the school population grew to some 450 students, of whom 125 prepared for the rabbinate. The others were registered in preparatory or teachers' courses. The first class was graduated in 1925; in 1938 a library fund drive was completed; in September, 1940, the Teachers' Institute of the College was officially established. As the graduates of the high school and college entered into the many walks of Jewish lay and professional service throughout the country, it was demonstrated that Orthodoxy had established a firm center of higher Jewish learning in the Midwest.[66] Shortly, the young American-trained graduates of both the eastern and midwestern Orthodox rabbinical schools, were to join hands and bring their two alumni associations into one national rabbinic body. Other alumni, who preferred to associate themselves with the Conservative movement, entered the ranks of the Rabbinical Assembly of America.

The lay organization from which Orthodoxy in America derived its chief strength remained the Union of Orthodox Jewish Congregations of America. A chain of affiliates was soon established corresponding to the varying age levels and interest groups of the movement. The Women's Branch (founded 1923), consisting of the sisterhoods of the congregations, organized and sponsored a Hebrew teachers' training school for girls, the Ha-Banot clubs for adolescent girls and the Jewish University Club, for

Orthodox college youth. The National Union of Orthodox Jewish Youth completed the organizational framework.

The Union and its agencies embarked on a program of expansion and intensification. The established forms of American organizational procedure were adopted. However, one of the singular attempts of the Union which transcended strict religious party lines was the effort to standardize *kashrut* endorsement and supervision. The conflict over *kashrut* was so uncontrolled that the Union felt compelled to enter the field officially in order to protect the interests and good name of Judaism. A special Rabbinical Council was appointed with Dr. Leo Jung as chairman. In its capacity of rabbinic advisory board to the Union, it was the Council's duty to render decisions upon questions of Jewish law and to raise the standards of *kashrut* enforcement throughout the country. The Union established a policy of limiting the costs of rabbinic supervision to a minimum.[67] One of the most important acts passed by the Rabbinical Council under the administration of Dr. Jung was the condemnation of *heksherim* (endorsements) granted by individuals without regard for the social consequences involved. Vested interests were fought off. In many instances, these questions were brought before the bar of legal state opinion. The Council even appeared before the Supreme Court of Ottawa in an important decision. In 1934 as part of this trend, Governor Herbert H. Lehman established the Division of Kosher Law Enforcement as a section of the Bureau of Food Control under the New York State Department of Agriculture and Markets. It was in this year that the New York legislature first appropriated funds for the implementation of the law which had been on the books since 1922. These efforts on the part of the Union while extremely worthy in each individual case, did not succeed in solving the profounder problems of *kashrut* observance in America. But they did establish a precedent of communal interest, control and sanction.

The Union was not the only lay organization that functioned on behalf of Orthodox Jewry. Orthodoxy in America had segments of rightists, centrists and liberals. In the thirties, for example, largely as a result of increased immigration from Poland, Germany and Central Europe, the neo-Hasidic, Agudas Israel, and German congregational movements found new sources of strength. The Hasidic movement was considered a strange plant in American soil even by many of its own most ardent devotees. While its numbers increased slightly, it did not show signs of becoming part of the American Jewish milieu. Among the first of the Hasidic rabbis to establish the order and service of the Hasidic movement in America after World War I was Rabbi Joshua Heschel Rabinowitz (1860-1938), known as the Monastrishtcher Rabbi, and author of numerous works on Hasidism. He was one of the founders of the Union of Grand Rabbis of the United States and Canada (organized in 1928). The influence of these men was confined and limited to special small coteries. In March, 1940, the Lubavitcher Rabbi, Joseph Isaac Schneersohn, came to America with his family and entourage. The impact of this personality on the educational system of the Orthodox was phenomenal. Day schools and *yeshibot* were established in sections of the land where such efforts were formerly inconceivable. It is interesting to note that many of the Yiddishist and Hebraist culturalists found an intrinsic emotional and aesthetic appeal in this Hasidic movement.

A more remarkable resurgence in the ranks of Orthodox Jewry was the growth of the Sephardic community in America. Although many a nineteenth century writer predicted their extinction, the Sephardic Jews have recently come into a new pulsating community life. At the turn of the century, a trickle of immigration, chiefly from the Middle East and the Balkans, forecast the renewal of Sephardic congregational life in the United States. The majority of Sephardim settled in New York City; others dispersed among the larger cities of the country. In New York they found the lower East Side and Harlem most congenial, for they shared the limited economic lot of other immigrant groups. In religious life they were completely isolated from their Ashkenazic brethren, speaking neither English nor Yiddish. During this period the Sephardic newcomers were as disorganized on their limited scale as were their East European brethren on a larger one. The basis of organization was the city of origin. In 1912 the first attempt to organize the various groups resulted in the formation of the Federation of Oriental Jews of America, whose purpose was the creation of "a forum where communal problems are discussed and presented to the Oriental Community for solution." These problems related to Americanization, immigration, employment, and social welfare. But the Federation ultimately ceased functioning because of the indifference of its members.

A second attempt at organization was made in 1924. Almost all the Ladino-speaking groups were united into the Sephardic Jewish community of New York. The organization conducted a community center in Harlem which included a synagogue, a Talmud Torah, a youth program, and adult social services. It also sponsored two schools in the Bronx where the Sephardim were beginning to settle, and a Talmud Torah on the East Side. The depression wiped out all these centralized efforts and the community was dissolved once again. But the groundwork had been laid for a renewal of activity which took place on an unprecedented scale after the arrival, during World War II, of Dr. Nissim J. Ovadia (1890-1942), former chief rabbi of the Sephardic community of Vienna and Paris.[68]

Far more indicative of the fundamental transformation which American Orthodoxy was undergoing, was the growth of the Young Israel movement, which in its act of incorporation in 1926 declared as its purpose, "To awaken a love for orthodox Judaism and the Jewish people within the hearts of American Jewish youth." The Young Israel movement began in 1912 as an effort on the part of young people to establish, within traditional Judaism, surroundings where the disheartening aspects of the East Side synagogues would be eliminated. The movement was inspired and activated by Israel Friedlaender, Judah Magnes and Mordecai M. Kaplan. At first the group was gathered together for Friday night lectures. Then, in 1915, it established a model synagogue in one of the rooms of the Educational Alliance. Religious services were held "with the dignified practice of proper decorum, and with the added interests of congregational singing, abolition of commercialism, delivery of sermons in English, and a synopsis of the weekly portion or *sidra*." Social activities for youth were an important part of their program. In a very short time, as the original membership began to move away from the lower East Side, similar organizations were formed in other sections of the city. Before long an important national movement was under way. In 1922 a Council of Young Israel was formed to centralize the various activities and to serve as the authoritative body of the entire movement. At this meeting, the bond of relationship with the founding leaders was broken and the Young Israel identified itself completely with the Orthodox group. In 1939 about thirty-five synagogues were associated in the National Council. The well rounded program of Young Israel's activities in the fields of Sabbath observance, Zionism, youth and adult education, defense of Jewish rights, synagogal activities, *kashrut* enforcement, and social activities, fully reflects the efforts made by the organization to bring the older and newer generations of Orthodoxy together and to create an indigenous American Orthodoxy for the youth of America.

The gradual replacement of the European *rabbanim* with an American-trained rabbinate, completed the cycle of change in American Orthodoxy. A new type of Orthodox rabbi grew out of the American experience. While the younger men sought a unified front with the Agudath Ha-Rabbanim in questions of Jewish ideology and national Jewish policy, they found it impossible to work within the ranks of the older group. They therefore determined to form a separate organization. The Rabbinical Council of America grew out of a union in 1935 between the original Council (which was organized in 1923 as the advisory arm of the Union of Orthodox Jewish Congregations) and the Rabbinical Association of the Rabbi Isaac Elchanan Theological Seminary, the alumni body of the Yeshiva. The new organization opened its membership rolls to all duly ordained Orthodox rabbis who had *Semika* from a recognized Yeshiva or from two recognized authoritative Orthodox rabbis, in addition to one year of service in the active Orthodox rabbinate. In 1936 the graduates of the Hebrew Theological College in Chicago organized their own alumni association. Further consolidation was thought desirable, and the amalgamation between the eastern and western rabbinical bodies was arranged in 1942.[69] With the establishment of an authorized American trained, national Orthodox rabbinical association, native American Orthodoxy came of age.

The records of the Agudath Ha-Rabbanim reveal how little the group understood the social forces that were radically changing the American scene. Nevertheless the efforts of this group produced excellent results (considering its limited energies) in matters relating to European relief and intercession. The *yeshivot* and religious institutions in Europe were its special interest. In 1924 when word came from Lithuania that the government had passed discriminatory legislation against the Jews which resulted in the enforced closing of religious institutions, the Agudath Ha-Rabbanim influenced important political action in Washington. With the beginning of the Nazi regime and the conquest of Europe, the specially created Vaad Ha-Hatzala (Committee for Rescue) carried on vigorous and, in many cases, highly successful, efforts for immediate relief, escape, and support of Jewish victims. This aspect of Orthodoxy's history is a noble and as yet unwritten chapter of devotion and sacrifice.[70]

In the overall picture of Orthodox influence and achievement, the Mizrachi Organization of America has a special place. The Zionist members of the Reform movement joined either the centrist Zionist Organization of America or the Poale Zion (Workers of Zion). The Conservatives in largest numbers entered the Zionist Organization of America; some of their members joined the Poale Zion or the Mizrachi Organization. The Orthodox, however, built their own movement which organically represented both their religious and Zionist beliefs. The Mizrachi Organization was supported and financed almost exclusively by the various Orthodox agencies. The Orthodox rabbis and lay leaders formed the parent organization; the sisterhood members joined the Mizrachi Women's Organization; and the young people became affiliated with the junior groups. Several delegations of the antipolitical-Zionist Agudas Israel movement visited the United States. They founded an American wing of the movement, with their established purpose: "To solve in the spirit of the Torah all problems which confront Jewry from time to time in Eretz Yisrael and the Diaspora." But they made small impression on the broad masses of American Orthodoxy.[71] From the very beginning, in order to avoid an internal rift, the Agudath Ha-Rabbanim officially endorsed both the Agudas Israel and Mizrachi organizations. The heart of the people, however, was with political Zionist action. Thus the work of Mizrachi flourished.[72] The organic relationship between Mizrachi and American Orthodoxy had beneficial results on American Jewish life, particularly in Jewish education. Unlike the other political Zionist parties, Mizrachi embarked on an intensive program of educational effort in America, in addition to its propaganda and fund-raising work for Palestine.

In 1938 the Orthodox movement developed the United Yeshivos Foundation which, in the light of subsequent events, played a telling role in the advancement of Orthodox life and institutions. In very short time the educational structures of the Conservative and Reform movements also felt the impact of this intensive educational system. The Foundation was organized in the midst of the most depressing crisis in the history of the *yeshiva* movement. After a long list of failures in the attempt to coordinate *yeshiva* schools, a Central Board of Yeshiva Education was formed. This board concentrated on the raising of standards and unification of curricula in the *yeshiva* schools. Then a secular Yeshiva Board of Education was organized which served as liaison with the New York State Board of Regents in Albany. Within a comparatively brief period of eight years (1938-1946), the *yeshiva* parochial school movement grew from fourteen schools with an approximate enrollment of 4,000 students to eighty-four day schools with an enrollment of 17,500. These figures of increase do not represent the profounder development. As one of their spokesmen put it: "One of the main aims of the United Yeshivos Foundation was to bring out the *yeshiva* movement from the ghetto to the broad American avenue. This we achieved fully. The idea of the *yeshiva* parochial school has taken root in American soil. . . ."[73]

As the younger American Orthodox elements assumed control and responsibility for the destiny of American Orthodoxy, they began to appraise their problem realistically. Could they arrest the progressive dwindling of their numbers? Could they create an "Orthodox Jewish Front" which could speak authoritatively on behalf of a united and integrated American Orthodoxy? Could they meet the challenge of other Jewish religious groups who had formulated a program of adjustment to modern conditions and particularly to the American scene? Could they train the coming generation in the belief and practice of the ritual laws, as expressly formulated in the legal codes? These were the crucial questions which the new Orthodox rabbinic, lay and congregational leadership had to answer as a new era in Jewish history dawned upon American Jewry. Despite the imperfections they knew had to be reckoned with in their movement and approach, the Orthodox leaders believed that the survival of American Judaism depended on unification in the spirit of Orthodoxy.

During this period, the Conservative movement was the most rapidly developing religious group in American Judaism. Scores of new congregations affiliated with the United Synagogue; a constant stream of students turned from the Orthodox preparatory *yeshibot* to study at the Seminary's rabbinical school. American Israel clearly required a synagogue program which was traditional in thought and practice, modern in its recognition of the validity of change, Zionist in orientation, and Hebraic in spirit.

Cyrus Adler, who became acting president of the Seminary after the death of Schechter, was elected president in 1924. He served in office until his death in 1940. In his interpretation of Conservative Judaism, Adler reasserted the Leeser formula of an adjectiveless Judaism; in community relationships, he endeavored to transcend all factionalism; although he was head of two higher institutions of learning and many kindred societies he nevertheless refused to use his vast influence in other associations for his own institutional purposes. As a leader and administrator of rare gifts, Adler's guidance was sought by American Israel in many official capacities. But his outlook was fundamentally spiritual and his conception of Judaism essentially religious. Adler's doctrine of active faith, stated as early as 1894, helped him remain staunch in his views even when he stood as a minority of one:

> I will continue to hold my banner aloft. I find myself born—aye, born—into a people and a religion. The preservation of my people must be for a purpose, for God does nothing without a purpose. His reasons are unfathomable to me, but on my own reason I place little dependence; test it where I will it fails me. The simple, the ultimate in every direction is sealed to me. It is as difficult to understand matter as mind. The courses of the planets are no harder to explain than the growth of a blade of grass. Therefore am I willing to remain a link in the great chain. What has been preserved for four thousand years was not saved that I should overthrow it. My people have survived the prehistoric paganism, the Babylonian polytheism, the aesthetic Hellenism, the sagacious Romanism, at once the blandishments and persecutions of the Church; and it will survive the modern dilettantism and the current materialism, holding aloft the traditional Jewish ideals inflexibly until the world shall become capable of recognizing their worth.[73*]

During Adler's incumbency, the Seminary continued to maintain the scholarly integrity for which it had already gained international renown. Additional faculty members were required to teach the expanding student body.[74] The Seminary Library, containing about 117,000 printed books and pamphlets, and about 7,800 manuscripts, became the largest and finest collection of Hebraica and Judaica in the world. Because of its growing importance and the need for a special board to manage its treasures, the library was chartered in 1924 as a separate corporation.

The Museum of Jewish Ceremonial Objects of the Seminary was opened in 1931 as an adjunct to the library, under the direction of Professor Alexander Marx. Its growth was enhanced in 1939 through the addition of the notable collection of Dr. H. G. Friedman. Later, through the gift of Mrs. Warburg, the Museum became a separate department of the Seminary and moved to expansive quarters in the former home of Mr. and

Mrs. Felix M. (Frieda Schiff) Warburg at 92nd Street and Fifth Avenue.[75]

The Teachers Institute expanded considerably. In response to the petition of the Jewish youth educational institutions in New York, the extension department of the Institute was formed in 1921, called the Israel Friedlaender Classes, with the purpose of offering Jewish youth nonprofessional Jewish training. The motto selected for the Friedlaender Classes was *Torah Lishmah* (study for its own sake). Under the direction of its founder and guiding spirit, Israel S. Chipkin, the school soon became a model for similar ventures in adult Jewish education throughout the country.[76] In 1929 the Seminary College of Jewish Studies was created as the academic department of the Teachers Institute. The Seminary outgrew the Schiff building on 123rd Street, and moved to its present quarters at 122nd Street and Broadway. It was the climax of a half century of vision, tireless effort, and devotion.

In this period the Conservative movement also enlarged the scope of its activities in the congregations. The United Synagogue was considered by Dr. Schechter as "the greatest bequest that I shall leave to American Israel." Without a strong and vibrant congregational base, Conservatism would have remained an academy, not a movement. Within two decades, some 400 congregations were affiliated with the national organization; the National Women's League had been established in 1917; the Young People's League in 1921; the National Federation of Jewish Men's Clubs in 1929. In addition to these strictly organizational activities, the United Synagogue pioneered in religious educational programs for Boy Scout camps, in cultural centers at universities, and in pedagogic curricula for the congregational school.[77]

One of the most significant trends in the Conservative congregational system was the development of the synagogue-center movement. Professor Kaplan had inspired and founded the first such institution in New York City in 1918. "The Jewish Center" as developed by Kaplan, represented the institutional integration of religion, education, and recreation based on the traditional threefold function of the synagogue as a place of worship, study, and fellowship.[78] The second synagogue-center was the Brooklyn Jewish Center, of which Israel H. Levinthal became the spiritual leader. "Institutional synagogues" with the similar purpose of providing a full and varied program of Jewish activities under congregational auspices, were later developed by the Orthodox. In line with its effort to develop this type of synagogue movement as the pattern for the future, the magazine established by the United Synagogue in 1940 was named *The Synagogue Center*.

An important undertaking of the United Synagogue, was the building and support of a synagogue-center in Jerusalem. This project was designed to render for the Jews of Jerusalem the same services as those of the synagogue-center in America. Moreover, it was intended as a vital bridge between Conservative Jewry in the United States and the rapidly growing Yishuv. The Jerusalem Center was auspiciously dedicated by Dr. Levinthal in 1926, in the presence of Chief Rabbi Kook, Nahum Sokolow, Menahem M. Ussishkin, and other Eretz Yisrael leaders. Unfortunately, the plans were not completed, and the deed to the land was given to the Jewish National Fund. The lapse of the United Synagogue's interest in this center project is all the more lamented, for the Yishuv in Eretz Yisrael had no notion of Jewish traditional religious life other than East European Orthodoxy, and the Center would have given Conservative Judaism an opportunity to be of great service to the developing spiritual life of Eretz Yisrael.

The third sphere of expansion in the Conservative movement was the Rabbinical Assembly of The Jewish Theological Seminary, originally organized as an alumni body of the Seminary. In 1919 it changed its name to the Rabbinical Assembly of America, and in so doing, it also redefined its scope and purpose. Membership was opened to graduates of other rabbinical seminaries in America and abroad, who wished to identify themselves with the Conservative group. In the threefold division of responsibilities within the movement, the Rabbinical Assembly became, in consultation with the other two agencies, the legislative body. The Assembly was described as the motive power of Conservative Judaism. In its attempt to evolve a specific program of action, the Assembly was perforce required to come to grips with its philosophy of Judaism in relation to the daily problems of Jewish life in America and most particularly, with those in the field of Jewish ritual and practice.

The unresolved, recurring question at every convention was: what is Conservative Judaism? Many, like Cyrus Adler and Louis Ginzberg, contended that the adjective "Conservative" should be eliminated; some leading alumni, including Solomon Goldman and David Aronson, maintained that the term should be more specific and definitive. All Conservative Jews accepted the formula that Judaism is a changing and developing religion. The difference of opinion revolved about the procedures for implementing "the changing and developing" aspects of Judaism. The advocates of the theory of obsolescence argued that Catholic Israel will itself determine what laws are to be abrogated and what laws retained in the permanent system of Judaism. Others, who could not suffer the steady disintegration of Jewish legal sanction, proposed immediate collective revision of the ritual law. A third group counseled that both these viewpoints be incorporated into an organic Judaism, for "these and these are the words of the living God."

The predominant group in the Rabbinical Assembly shared the views of Professor Ginzberg. The Committee on Jewish Law was especially influenced by his learning and advice. Ginzberg's attitude toward the interpretation of Jewish practice was fully expressed on many occasions. In an address delivered at the United Synagogue convention on the theme of "Judaism and Modern Thought," Professor Ginzberg stressed the view that private judgment cannot be held up against the collective judgment of *Kelal Israel*. He was not unaware of the gravity of the problems that confronted modern congregations, including: the organ question, seating of men and women together, the use of electricity on the Sabbath, membership rights for a Jew married out of the faith. Nevertheless, he warned:

> Tampering with the laws and regulations of the Talmud harbors great danger. It is very easy to discard them but extremely difficult to put something better, yes, something else, in their place. And who are the men today that could take the place of the great saints and religious geniuses of the Talmudic times? They may have had their shortcomings, but they were those of their times while their virtues were their own; our shortcomings are our own; our virtues those of our times. . . .
>
> . . . It is, however, the Synagogue one and indivisible from which we may hope for the solution of our difficulties, but not the synagogues.
>
> The Synagogue is the essential, but the synagogues are accidental. It is one of the most grievous misfortunes of modern Jewry that many are found who are willing to sacrifice the essentials for the sake of the accidental. If, indeed, the Synagogue is to remain a genteel and fashionable communion for the rich and happy, as it has been in some measure in modern times, then it may indulge in any incongruity or monstrosity for any length of time; but if the Synagogue is to be as it has been in our glorious past; if it is to be real and to encounter the realities of human life; need, sickness, pain, affliction, sin, doubt, despair; if it is to match the great ills, which it was sent to the world to overcome; it must express the religious soul of Israel and not the vagaries of those who are tossed about with every wind of thought that may chance to blow from the cave of Aeolus.[79]

Although the law committee of the Rabbinical Assembly deliberated and voted its decisions in the spirit of this judgment, in effect every effort was made to keep congregations within the Conservative fold, even if they deviated in individual practices. This precedent had been established by Schechter. Inquiring congregants were told that the law did not sanction instituting mixed pews or an organ, yet those changes alone were not sufficient reason for any individual to withdraw from the congregation. A festival prayer book was issued by the United Synagogue in two versions. One was prepared for those congregations wishing to change the traditional petition for the return of the sacrificial order; the official version, on the other hand, retained the historical prayer service in every detail. Thorough study was made by Louis M. Epstein (1887-1949) of the *Agunah* problem, and a procedure completely within the legal tradition was adopted by the Rabbinical Assembly in regard to this vexing problem.[80] However, because of the outcry which was raised by the Orthodox rabbinate against this procedure, the Rabbinical Assembly withdrew from its established position.

In opposition to this prevailing school of thought in Conservative Judaism, there developed another school of opinion, of which Professor Kaplan was the focal personality. As early as 1915, Kaplan had launched an attack on the working hypothesis of the Conservative movement and its arch concept, Historical Judaism. Subsequently, other independent forces rose to challenge the official majority viewpoint. Chief among them was Solomon Goldman, rabbi of the Anshe Emet Congregation in Chicago, who formulated his interpretation in a series of addresses and articles later published in his volume, *A Rabbi Takes Stock*. He felt that "Jewish laws, customs and ceremonies must be searchingly studied. Many of them we will find obsolete—these we must lose no time in discarding if we hope to continue Jewish communal life. Many practices, however, we will have to retain because of their group binding value."[81]

It was Dr. Kaplan, however, who succeeded in consolidating the opposing forces into an organized group. He attracted to himself disciples and supporters for whom he became spokesman and ideologist. His closest associates among the members of the Assembly in this effort were Ira Eisenstein, Eugene Kohn, and Milton Steinberg (1903-1950). Kaplan presented his philosophy in his *Judaism As A Civilization* (1934), and became the founder of the Reconstructionist movement. Within a few years, he and his associates produced many volumes and brochures explaining the theory of their movement. The program of Reconstructionism was later graphically represented in a seal on the cover of the Reconstructionist magazine (established 1935). The explanation of the seal follows:

> The form is that of a wheel. The hub of the wheel is Palestine, the center of Jewish civilization from which all the dynamic forces of Judaism radiate. Religion, culture and ethics are the spokes by which the vital influence of Palestine affects and stimulates Jewish life everywhere and enables it to make its contribution to the civilization of mankind. The wheel has an inner and an outer rim. The inner rim represents the Jewish community that even in the dispersion, maintains its contact with the Jewish civilization rooted in Palestine, by the spiritual bonds of religion, ethics and culture. The outer rim is the general community, for us the community of America, with which the Jewish civilization as lived by the Jewish community maintains contact at every point. The seal thus symbolizes the whole philosophy of the Reconstructionist movement.[82]

As regards Jewish practice, Kaplan was prepared, if necessary, to depart from traditional observances. He urged the development of new ceremonial patterns in keeping with the facts of Jewish living in modern times. He did not seek to freeze Jewish practice into a new code. Rather did he hope for the development of guides for ritual practice which would release new creative forces in the entire realm of religious life and experience.

During the early years of the movement, the Reconstructionists had to determine whether they would become a separate religious party or serve as a catalytic school of thought in American Judaism, permitting the individual Reconstructionist members to maintain their former institutional affiliations. They chose to remain a transparty school of thought. This decision became confused in the public mind as the Reconstructionist Foundation continued to publish religious works of a distinctive theology by the foremost exponents of the movement.[83] They are, therefore, frequently referred to as a fourth religious party in American Judaism. The example set by the Reconstructionist members of the Rabbinical Assembly, continuing to work within the framework of Conservative Judaism, had a salutary effect on the entire movement. It revealed the great wisdom of the minority in not confusing the part for the whole; it also revealed the commensurate wisdom of the majority in not using numbers to crush opposition and eliminate differences. Professor Kaplan, granted freedom to continue with his independent thinking, teaching and studies at the Seminary, even by those who disagreed most radically with him, devoted his talents, in collaboration with his colleagues, to the further intensification and consolidation of the Conservative movement and its institutions. As a result of this reintegration with the Seminary, there later developed the concept of expanding the Seminary into a University of Judaism.

Many of the younger alumni, while they were deeply impressed by Kaplan's analyses and interpretation, could not accept his whole program of Reconstruction. Many strenuously objected, for instance, to his ideas about ritual. Two groups were in the process of crystallization in the late thirties. The first group was led by a succession of presidents of the Rabbinical Assembly, Louis M. Levitsky, Robert Gordis and Israel M. Goldman. They demanded unequivocal formulation of Conservative Judaism *vis-à-vis* Reform and Orthodox Judaism, the adaptation of Jewish law to contemporary needs within the legal framework of traditional Judaism, and the development of a philosophy and literature which would establish Conservative Judaism as an aggressive ideological movement in American Israel. While they thoroughly disapproved of the radical changes of the Reconstructionists in the area of ritual practice, they were also unhappy with the temper of inaction represented in the Seminary faculty. They prodded the Rabbinical Assembly into decisive action. This group soon became the predominant voice in the counsels of the Rabbinical Assembly.[84] The chief exponents of the second group were Max Kadushin and Simon

Greenberg. They consistently underplayed the adjective, Conservative, and opposed all trends leading to the definitive reformulation of Conservative Judaism. In taking this position, they did not regard themselves as evading the problems of modern Judaism. Quite the contrary. They were most emphatic that the complexity, the fluidity, the organic character of life, and the imponderables of human affairs, defy in the present state of the Jewish world, any specific pattern of formal legislation. Any formulation of new guides could not possibly include the variety of practices which mark the lives of individual Jews and congregations. What then is their program for Conservative Judaism? To interpret the specific situation in Jewish life in terms of its organic relationship to the totality of the Jewish tradition, with a sympathetic understanding of the needs and demands of the changing times. This was what Schechter meant by the "positive-historic" approach of Catholic Israel. This point of view was developed in the writings of Dr. Kadushin; it was further extended and propounded in the councils of the Rabbinical Assembly by Dr. Greenberg.[85]

These deep stirrings within the Conservative movement did not lead to a splintering of forces, as was originally feared. While the points of difference were noted, the comprehensive body of common belief was also clarified. As early as 1927, when the first signs of the intellectual ferment began to take shape, Dr. Finkelstein, in a symposium called, "The Things That Unite Us," analyzed the cohesive elements of Conservative Judaism: the conception of God; the attitude toward the Torah; the attitude toward change in ceremonial; the attitudes toward Israel, Palestine and the Hebrew language; the Seminary.[86] In his discussion of the crucial question in Conservative Judaism, the attitude toward change in ceremonial law, Dr. Finkelstein wrote:

> . . . the purpose that fills the minds of all of us is to maintain the Torah. None proposes to yield the marriage law or the Sabbath; the most rash among us have suggested only the abrogation of some customs, ceremonies and prohibitions that have arisen in the course of time, and of which the value is no longer evident to all. After all, Resh Lakish did say "Sometimes the transgression of part of the law is the saving of the whole of it." There is all the difference in the world between proposing a change in a single law for the sake of saving the Torah and disregarding the whole of the Torah.
>
> Still, it cannot be denied that the attitude of permitting changes in the usage of Israel by individual congregations and rabbis is untraditional and revolutionary. . . .
>
> As to the proposed innovations and new interpretations, there is none of us so bigoted as to refuse to cooperate with those who are attempting them, provided always that the ultimate purpose of the change is to strengthen the attachment of Israel to the whole of the Torah, and that it does not defeat its own end by striking at the fundamentals of Judaism.[87]

While the interpretations of each particular element in Dr. Finkelstein's analysis of Conservative Judaism's "consciousness of unity" may have varied, the constellation as a whole was overwhelmingly accepted by the entire movement. This was the uniqueness and underlying unity of Conservative Judaism as interpreted and bequeathed by Schechter, advanced by Adler and intensified by Finkelstein. As the Conservative movement rapidly expanded under the unifying influence and guidance of Dr. Finkelstein, the newly elected head of the Seminary, it demonstrated that the broad base of Conservative Judaism had within itself the power to build constructively while adjusting at the same time to the diversities within its ranks.

In addition to the Reform, Orthodox and Conservative movements, in the post World War I period other agencies developed whose contributions to the spiritual welfare of American Jewry were of lasting benefit. As the Jews became rooted in the large American cities, they had need for organized citywide sponsorship and supervision of their educational and cultural activities. The national religious institutions were neither prepared nor disposed to establish the necessary boards of Jewish education, libraries and colleges of Jewish studies, so vital to local Jewish life; while the local congregations of the various groups could not find a basis for co-operative effort. For a time a cultural vacuum was created. Soon community organization on a trans-religious-cultural basis began to fill the void. A new trend was discerned: the growth and subsequent communalization of educational institutions under metropolitan auspices.

Boards or bureaus of Jewish Education were established in Pittsburgh, Boston, Detroit, New York, Baltimore, and Chicago. Teacher training institutions were created under Educational Bureau auspices in Baltimore (Baltimore Hebrew College and Teachers Training School founded 1918), Chicago (College of Jewish Studies organized in 1924), and Boston (Hebrew Teachers College chartered in 1927). The Herzliah Hebrew Teachers Institute in New York City began to function in 1921.

In the area of elementary Jewish education, metropolitan boards of education went beyond their administrative and supervisory functions and assumed responsibility for the operation and direction of a communal Talmud Torah school system. For a time, this system seemed destined to become the established pattern throughout the country. Before long, however, the place and purpose of the communal Talmud Torah system was contested by a rapidly developing congregational school system. The individual congregation was zealous for the loyalty of its children; the rabbi and the congregational board refused to relinquish their privilege to train the children of their members. They further insisted on the right of direct religious indoctrination.

The conflict between the congregational and communal education viewpoints halted the progress of the Bureau of Jewish Education movement. Indeed, for a considerable time, the entire field of Jewish education was injured, for the roof of one educational system was taken off, before the foundations of another system had been built. In the premature transition from a communal to congregational school program, many losses were suffered. The enrollment fell, the cost per child increased, classes were smaller, the teaching less proficient, and supervision not as readily available. The leaders of both opinions searched for a solution. The rabbis and congregations recognized their educational shortcomings. They were ready to participate in a communal board of education with the provision that they could be free to conduct their schools in accordance with their own interpretations of Jewish life. The educators also were prepared to revamp their program. They reckoned with the changes which had come over Jewish life. They realized that the congregation would probably be the basic educational unit in the future Jewish educational structure. It would therefore be the function of the communal agency to advise, counsel and aid the congregational school to realize its own objectives.

Another indication of the general trend to develop local foci of culture and scholarship in the major cities of America and to spread Jewish education into the broader reaches of the community, was the establishment of chairs of Jewish learning and special collections of Judaica in the great universities. Jewish scholarship in America, with the outstanding exception of the Dropsie College, seemed heretofore to be the exclusive concern of the various national rabbinical seminaries. Now it was slowly being spread into the broader reaches of the community through independent and specially created agencies. The Nathan Littauer chair in Jewish literature and philosophy was endowed at Harvard in 1925 and the Miller Foundation for Jewish history, literature and institutions was endowed at Columbia in 1929. Notable collections of Judaica and Hebraica had already found their way into the Jewish Division of the New York Public Library and the Semitic Division of the Library of Congress. Famous collections of Jewish scholars were acquired by the libraries of Harvard University, the University of Texas, Columbia University, and the College of the City of New York, while the Sutro Library in San Francisco opened a valuable collection on the west coast. The Alexander Kohut Memorial Foundation created a large Jewish scientific library at Yale University and published a considerable number of scholarly works. The American Academy for Jewish Research was organized in 1920, providing opportunities for scholarly discussion and publication. The Yiddish Scientific Institute (YIVO) established in 1925 with its center in Vilna, Poland, transferred its possessions and center of activity to New York City in 1940.

On the campus proper, in addition to the effective work of the Menorah Society (founded 1906) and Avukah (founded 1925), the National Hillel

Foundation movement was launched under the sponsorship of B'nai B'rith. It is of especial interest that the Hillel movement, although supported by a national fraternal organization, adopted the techniques of student organization devised by various Christian denominations. It therefore assumed a religio-cultural-social character. From the very beginning, the Hillel Foundations were led by rabbis and scholars. The first Foundation was established at the University of Illinois in 1923, by a newly ordained rabbi, Benjamin Frankel. In 1933 Dr. Abram L. Sachar became director of the national Hillel Foundations. Under his brilliant organizational hand, Hillel became a part of the American university tradition and, in association with the names of Wesley and Newman, the spiritual values of the historic Western religions were integrated into American university life.

The steady growth of opportunity for intensifying Jewish religious life in America and the rapid advance of the organized religious groups called for the creation of an agency where matters of common interest could be considered and clarified. This purpose was already accomplished on the local level through the extension of the various boards of Jewish ministers in every major city or region of the United States. Reform, Conservative and Orthodox colleagues met to discuss the questions of common concern and action. On the national level, the Synagogue Council of America was organized in 1926. It included representation from the three unions of congregations and the three rabbinic bodies for the purpose of "speaking and acting unitedly in furthering such religious interests as the constituent organizations in the Council have in common."

The declared primary purpose of the Synagogue Council was to strengthen Judaism in America by making the Synagogue "the center of Jewish spiritual influence." Unfortunately, the Council was not very successful in achieving this aim. Technically, this failure might be explained by the veto agreement which nullified any decision that did not receive unanimous support. But the fundamental reason was the fact that the major areas of Jewish activity in cultural and spiritual affairs were pre-empted by communal and national nonsynagogal and religious bodies—all were jealous of their prior jurisdictional rights. The Synagogue Council was therefore compelled to develop only those projects that would neither duplicate nor conflict with the older established institutions. However, some significant steps were taken. In 1929 the Council issued a pronouncement and joined with other groups in opposing the adoption of any system of calendar reform that would interfere with the fixity of the Sabbath. The Council was responsible for arranging the Jewish exhibits at the Sesquicentennial Exhibition in Philadelphia (1926), at the Chicago World's Fair (1936), and at the New York World's Fair (1939-1940); it became the representative of the Jewish religious group in the interfaith program of the National Conference of Christians and Jews, and co-operated in similar interfaith projects with the Federal Council of the Churches of Christ in America and the National Catholic Welfare Conference. Surveys were made of Jewish and Christian religious textbooks for suggested revision of those portions not consonant with proper respect for other faiths. Other studies were made of proselyting activities among Jews, and representation was made before the appropriate Christian bodies.

One of the most important and fruitful areas of religious activity developed during this period by all the groups was in the realm of social action. In the latter part of the nineteenth and early twentieth centuries, the American religious groups were compelled to face the issues of the changing economic order particularly as it affected the conflict between capital and labor. The religious ethic had to be translated into action; social justice meant nothing if it did not mean social reform. In the struggle for these reforms, labor found strong friends not only among the social workers and intellectuals, but also among the clergy.

The American rabbinate responded to the social challenge with understanding and vigor. The Reform rabbis especially applied themselves to a constructive evaluation of religious social vision in the machine age. The religious lay and rabbinic associations expressed themselves on social issues in a variety of ways: committee reports and official resolutions adopted at conventions; social justice platforms or "creeds" summarizing agreements reached over a period of years; prayers and devotions, either as regular or supplementary readings in the prayer book; special services, appeals and public meetings for the underprivileged and victims of social unrighteousness; investigations and impartial arbitration in industrial conflicts; intercession with employers and government officials. In the action phase of this work, the rabbinate usually participated jointly with Catholic and Protestant welfare and social groups.[88]

The determination of the American rabbinate to become involved in the immediate problems of minimum wage, working hours, rights to organize, unemployment insurance and other contemporary social issues, strengthened the position of religion and religious leadership in their constant struggle for the betterment of mankind.[89]

With the outbreak of World War II the Jewish religious community was united as never before. A half million young Jewish men and women were destined to serve in the armed forces of the United States all over the globe. Their spiritual needs had to be taken care of. This was the task of the American rabbinate. The National Jewish Welfare Board was once again authorized by the War and Navy Departments to endorse Jewish chaplains. A Special Committee on Army and Navy Religious Activities (CANRA) was organized on which all the Jewish religious groups were represented.[90] The rabbinical groups immediately recognized the full authority of the Jewish Welfare Board, although they reserved judgment as to the wisdom of the initial decision to place the control of chaplaincy endorsements and religious program in the agency of a non-synagogal body.[91] Each rabbinical organization supervised the work within its own group. More than half the rabbis of the country volunteered for service. The seminaries, like the other professional schools in American university life, accelerated their classes and virtually became, on a volunteer basis, schools for the training of chaplains. The new young wartime graduates, if eligible, enlisted in the service, and if ineligible, replaced older graduates who were thus freed to leave their congregations for the duration of the war to serve as chaplains. By September 2, 1945, when the Japanese surrendered, 309 rabbis had been commissioned chaplains. According to Philip Bernstein, wartime director of CANRA, these constituted two-thirds of the eligible qualified rabbis of the country and probably the highest percentage of any religious group in the land to be commissioned chaplains.[92] A model of working harmony was achieved. Liturgical materials, literature and responsa were created for all Jewish personnel in service.[93] It was agreed that no material would be used which might influence religious practice in the postwar period. The individual chaplains were free to work out their own solutions to special problems. Yet most of the chaplains, irrespective of group affiliation, arrived at the same conclusions. The accepted decision that the denominational loyalties and personal religious predilections of the chaplains must be subordinated to the needs of the Jewish G.I., "led to more observance of tradition by the Reform, a liberalization of the Orthodox and an expansion of Conservatism, which seemed to characterize the general pattern that evolved under military conditions."[94] Out of the meetings and deliberations on behalf of a common objective during the critical war period a mood of co-operation was created and a desire for even greater association of interests in other areas of Jewish religious endeavor. This feeling was shared by rabbis in the field, congregations in the community, and national officers and seminary authorities.[95] Joint meetings of rabbinic bodies were considered. The Reform and Conservative groups had set the pace. They conducted a joint convention in 1943. A joint committee, composed of the representatives of all the rabbinical bodies, lay organizations, and seminaries, was convened in 1946 to work out a standard for relationship between rabbi and congregation. The Synagogue Council of America was reinforced in scope and administration, and embarked on an expanded program as the co-ordinate agency and spokesman of the religious groups.

The war had compelled amalgamated religious activity. Other forces operative in general and Jewish life, also were leading to collaborative effort. It is premature to attempt a systematic description and appraisal of these forces. At most, they may be considered as trends which are helping to create a basic and underlying unity in American Judaism. The most significant are: the identification of the religious groups in a new conception of higher Jewish education; their firm desire to remain rooted in American society and, in co-operation with other faiths and intellectual forces, to strengthen the spiritual foundations of American tradition and experience; their complete and fervent enlistment in the struggle to establish the Republic of Israel.

The tendency of the theological schools to expand into universities was not accidental; it was the natural culmination of their earlier decision to serve the totality of Jewish interests. American life and the Jewish community within it had changed radically since 1920. The temper of the time called for new techniques to introduce Jewish ideals and values into the stream of Jewish consciousness. Interpretation of Judaism on both the highest intellectual and popular mass levels was of vital importance.

Scholars, rabbis and teachers were not the only individuals who could influence Jewish life. Social workers, communal workers, artists and lay leaders trained in Judaism, were other key people who could exercise decisive influence upon American Jewry. A chasm of disregard, born out of unfamiliarity, separated the two groups of social engineers. A program of joint training and collective undertakings, could bring the two separate camps together. Moreover, if all these powerful forces could be coalesced into a religious leadership dedicated to the conservation and advancement of Jewish life itself, then a new future would await the Jewish community in America.

The Yeshiva, Hebrew Union College and Seminary almost simultaneously launched a series of new schools in these various fields of endeavor, each developing differently in accordance with its special emphases.[96] In every instance the rabbinical school was to remain the heart and core of the expanded institution. The very plan of including schools of education, community service, social work, and creative arts as coordinate schools of a theological seminary, although it intensified institutional loyalties, broadened the horizons of the religious groups, lessened the tensions of denominationalism and helped bring them closer to one another in thought and spirit.

A second major influence for basic unity among the religious groups was their shared determination to go beyond the realms of Jewish activity and to participate actively in interdenominational efforts for the solution of problems of group tension and group adjustments in America. In the local communities, the rabbinate participated with the ministers of other faiths as co-sponsors of significant undertakings, such as Thanksgiving celebrations and other national observances. The goodwill movement soon became part of local American community vernacular. In an effort to transpose the formalistic expression of pious intentions between the various American faiths into a positive program of religious fellowship and understanding, the National Conference of Christians and Jews (organized in 1928), engaged in a series of important projects. One of its chief contributions was the annual celebration of Brotherhood Week which promises to become a national institution, between the anniversaries of Lincoln and Washington in February. In order to create an academic center for authoritative dissemination of information about the Jewish faith, the Hebrew Union College called together Institutes on Judaism in various cities throughout the country for the clarification of Jewish thought and practices.

The very need which gave rise to these activities reflected the basic weaknesses in the American democratic structure. The American dream, conceived by the Founding Fathers, of establishing a society in which the human being could achieve full emancipation, was vanishing. The profound religious precepts which were the very essence of the American society-in-creation were being slowly disassociated from American society-in-action. The growing cynicism and amorality of government was the unhappy result. American religious leaders began to probe the root evil, and the Jewish religious groups wished to contribute to the reintegration of religious ideas into the thought-fabric of American democracy. The seminaries planned their specific programs in the areas of learning and scholarship; the rabbinical and lay associations in social action. Dr. Finkelstein evolved a pattern of action as a possible solution to this vexing problem. In 1939, speaking at the founding meeting of the Conference on Science, Philosophy and Religion (organized in 1940), he urged American scholars of all disciplines to attempt a new form of intellectual integration. He stressed that, "the true relation of democratic ideas and institutions to religious traditions, the historical indebtedness of science to monastic and rabbinical schools, and the vindication of traditional ethics in our growing economic and political confusion have been consistently overlooked. The various religious traditions may, without sacrifice of their integrity, recognize analogous values in their faiths. The totality of science, philosophy and religion can become a pluralistic but well regulated universe of thought."[97] In the spirit of this interpretation of the deeper issues in American democracy, the Seminary established its Institute for Religious Studies (later called The Institute for Religious and Social Studies) in 1938. In the very same spirit, Dr. Nelson Glueck, as he discussed his plans for a far reaching expansion program at the Hebrew Union College, declared that "the universal spiritual values of religion must be made a part of our higher education." He felt that if America is to solve its deepest spiritual problems, then teacher and educator must stand shoulder to shoulder with men of religion working together toward the achievement of humanity's highest ideals.[98] The ever widening perspective of the Jewish religious groups with regard to their responsibilities in America's spiritual crisis, enlarged the area of the shared common problem and opened new vistas for collaborative efforts in the strengthening of the foundations of American democracy.

A third overwhelmingly vital force for the consolidation of Jewish life in America, was the historic effort on behalf of Eretz Yisrael leading to the United Nations decision of November 29, 1947, and the declaration of Jewish independence in the new born State of Israel on May 15, 1948. The interrelationship between American Jewry and the Yishuv in Eretz Yisrael since the earliest days of Haim Carregal's visit to America, is one of the most interesting chapters in modern Jewish history. American Jewry, destined to become one of the greatest and most influential Jewish communities in all history, never forgot Jerusalem. The prayer for the rebuilding of the Holy Land, though for a time and in limited circles removed from its lips, was never removed from its heart. The martyrdom in death of six million Jews during the war and the martyrdom in life, after the war, of the remnant that was saved, made the immediate realization of the Zionist program for Jewish independence a crucial necessity. During the most intensive and difficult phases of the struggle for international recognition, the organized congregations in American Israel were completely and readily available for any action on behalf of the Yishuv. As an increasing majority of the Reform rabbinate and congregations joined with the other Zionist forces, the American Synagogue stood in the vanguard of the supreme effort to redeem Zion.

Perhaps necessarily, the birth of the new state was accompanied with great travail. Although recognized as a *de facto* state by the enlightened nations of the world, including the United States, the new Republic of Israel was forced to wage war for its right to freedom and independence.

A century ago, in September, 1848, Isaac Leeser, in a dream of Zion established, described the vision of the ages to which the contemporary Israel stands consecrated:

> If our religion flourishes, if our state is triumphant, it need not be at the expense and tears of others; we hope for a kingdom of peace, for a spread of divine truth, to be accomplished without the agency of the sword, or political tyranny. It is mercy which is to rule; it is blissful peace which is to conquer. We are to be the pioneers of the regeneration of man. . . .[99]

Whether these forces are the precursors to a greater unity in American Judaism or whether they are the temporary aftergrowth of a war and enforced co-operation, is a query which will only be answered in the fullness of time. There are many unresolved questions, within and without the religious community structure, which will have a decisive influence on the specific directions of religious life in the second half of the twentieth century. Will the vigorous leadership now at the head of the religious groups, while pursuing a program of expansion and intensification of their own institutions, seek isolation, co-operation or integration among themselves? Will the rabbinate in the cities and smaller communities insist on increased denominationalism in the accepted pattern of three distinct party and organizational divisions in American Judaism? Is a federated synagogue plan feasible in America? If so, will it permit of a variety of religious expression while amalgamating the separate national bodies? What will be the influence of the newly conceived Jewish center program on the synagogue? What will be the future of the American Zionist movements as they necessarily abandon political activity and seek an intrinsic Hebraic centered program of activity? Will the immediate relationships between the non-synagogal national movements (Zionist, philanthropic, fraternal, and defense) be complementary to or competitive with the synagogue? Can American Jewry be trained to respond as graciously and liberally to long range religious and cultural enterprises as it has responded in the past to the demands of philanthropic, relief and Zionist activity? What will be the permanent influences of the Republic of Israel on the religious life and practice of American Judaism?

These are the questions and counter-questions, the doubts and the hopes of the great Jewish settlement in America as it stands on the threshold of its newest and most important test of world Jewish leadership. In the chronicle of human events, America has become the greatest center of Diaspora Jewry, the partner with Eretz Yisrael in the rebuilding of world Judaism. As, in the years to come, the cultivation of the Holy Land and its spirit will be the sacred task of the people in Israel, so will it be the consecrated duty of American Jewry to nurture the spirit and practice of Judaism in America. This is the promise of our generation.

NOTES

[1] Oscar S. Straus, *The Origin of Republican Form of Government in the United States of America* (2nd ed., rev.; New York and London, 1926), p. 140. See also Abraham A. Neuman, *Relation of the Hebrew Scriptures to American Institutions* (New York, [1938]), especially pp. 11-16, where his interpretation and parallels of Puritan institutions and the community organization of the Jewish *kahal* are particularly interesting.

[2] *Publications of the American Jewish Historical Society* [PAJHS] *(The Lyons Collection,* I), No. 21 (1913), p. 101.

[3] *Prayers for Shabbath, Rosh-Hashanah, and Kippur, or the Sabbath, the beginning of the Year, and the Day of Atonement; with the Amidah and Musaph of the Moadim, or Solemn Seasons, according to the Order of the*

Spanish and Portuguese Jews, translated by Isaac Pinto (New York, 5526 [1766]).

[4] Joshua Trachtenberg, *Consider the Years* (Easton, Pa., 1944), p. 317, n. 1. See also Rudolf Glanz, "The First Twenty-five Jewish Communities in the United States," *YIVO Bleter*, XXVI (September-October, 1945), pp. 37-49.

[5] Edward Davis, *The History of Rodeph Shalom Congregation, Philadelphia, 1802-1926* (Philadelphia, 1926), pp. 27-28.

[6] PAJHS, No. 21, p. 74.

[7] *Ibid.*, p. 4.

[8] Peter Kalm, *Travels into North America,* translated into English by John Reinhold Forster (Warrington, England, 1770), I, pp. 245-246.

[9] PAJHS, No. 10 (1902), p. 163.

[10] Morris A. Gutstein, *The Story of the Jews of Newport* (New York, 1936), pp. 212-213.

[11] Franklin Bowditch Dexter, ed., *The Literary Diary of Ezra Stiles* (New York, 1901), I, p. 6. n.

[12] PAJHS, No. 21, p. 14; Alexander M. Dushkin, *Jewish Education in New York City* (New York, 1918), pp. 40 ff., 449 ff.; Hyman B. Grinstein, "Studies in the History of Jewish Education in New York City (1728-1860)," *The Jewish Review,* II, No. 1 (April 1, 1944), pp. 41-42. See also Hyman B. Grinstein, *The Rise of the Jewish Community of New York, 1654-1860* (Philadelphia, 1945), pp. 228-230.

[13] PAJHS, No. 21, p. 180.

[14] *Ibid.*, pp. 2-3.

[15] David Philipson, "The Jewish Pioneers of the Ohio Valley," PAJHS, No. 8, p. 45.

[16] *The Occident and American Jewish Advocate*, I, No. 11 (February, 1844), pp. 547-550; II, No. 1 (April, 1844), pp. 29-31. See also Anita Libman Lebeson, *Jewish Pioneers in America, 1492-1848* (New York, 1931), pp. 263-264.

[17] Jacques J. Lyons and Abraham de Sola, *A Jewish Calendar for Fifty Years* (Montreal, 1854), pp. 148-165. This list of new congregations strikingly demonstrates the shift from Sephardic to Ashkenazic influence.

[18] Israel Goldstein, *A Century of Judaism in New York* (New York, 1930), p. 77.

[19] The most comprehensive essay is that of Henry Englander, "Isaac Leeser," *Yearbook, Central Conference of American Rabbis,* XXVIII (1918), pp. 213-252. See also Moshe Davis, "Isaac Leeser, Builder of American Judaism," *Hadoar,* XXI, Nos. 7 and 8 (December 13 and 20, 1940) (in Hebrew).

[20] Isaac Mayer Wise has been well served by a virtual library of biographies, essays, and evaluations. The best single volume is his autobiography, *Reminiscences,* translated from the German and edited by David Philipson (Cincinnati, 1901).

[21] *Occident,* III, No. 4 (July, 1845), pp. 169-176; No. 5 (August, 1845), pp. 217-227.

[22] David Philipson, *Max Lilienthal* (New York, 1915), pp. 54-56; *Occi-*

dent, IV, No. 11 (February, 1847), pp. 554-555; V, No. 2 (May, 1847), pp. 109-111.

[23] *Wissenschaftliche Zeitschrift fuer juedische Theologie*, III (1837), pp. 1-14.

[24] Philipson, *op. cit.*, pp. 76-78; *Occident*, XIII, No. 8 (November, 1855), pp. 407-414.

[25] *Occident*, XIII, No. 8 (November, 1855), pp. 414-417.

[26] *Israelite*, VI, No. 21 (November 25, 1859), p. 165.

[27] *Occident*, VIII, No. 8 (November, 1850), pp. 424-426; IX, No. 2 (May, 1851), pp. 104-105. See also Grinstein, "Studies in the History of Jewish Education in New York City (1728-1860)," *The Jewish Review*, pp. 47 ff.

[28] *Constitution and By-laws of the American Jewish Publication Society* (founded on the 9th of Heshvan, 5606), adopted at Philadelphia, on Sunday, November, 30, 1845, Kislev 1, 5606.

[29] See Salo W. Baron and Jeanette Baron, "Palestinian Messengers in America, 1849-1879," *Jewish Social Studies*, V, No. 2, pp. 115-162; No. 3, pp. 225-292.

[[29a] Cf. above Cecil Roth, "The Jews of Western Europe (from 1648)," p. 271.]

[30] *Occident*, XX, No. 5 (August, 1862), pp. 212-215. See also Bertram W. Korn, "Jewish Chaplains During the Civil War," *American Jewish Archives*, I, No. 1 (June, 1948), pp. 6-22.

[31] Uriah Z. Engelman, "Jewish Statistics in the U.S. Census of Religious Bodies (1850-1936)," *Jewish Social Studies*, IX, No. 2 (April, 1947), pp. 130-134.

[32] See Joseph Krauskopf, "Fifty Years of Judaism in America," *American Jews' Annual*, IV (Cincinnati, 1888), pp. 65-95.

[33] *American Israelite*, XXXII, No. 19 (November 6, 1885), p. 4.

[34] Ismar Elbogen, *A Century of Jewish Life* (Philadelphia, 1944), pp. 344-345.

[35] *Yearbook of the Central Conference of American Rabbis, 5651—1890-91*, I (Cincinnati, 1891), pp. 4-5.

[36] *Ibid.*, IV (1895), p. 87.

[37] *American Hebrew*, LXIV, No. 11 (January 13, 1899), p. 372.

[38] *Ibid.*, LXV, No. 1 (May 5, 1899), pp. 9-11; No. 2 (May 12, 1899), pp. 45-49.

[39] Rebekah Kohut, *My Portion* (New York, 1925), pp. 91-92, 126-127, 135-139, 143-145, 160-165.

[40] *American Hebrew* LVI, No. 6 (December 14, 1894), p. 181.

[41] Norman Bentwich, *Solomon Schechter* (Philadelphia, 1938), p. 169.

[42] *Yearbook*, CCAR, XIII (1904), pp. 185-308.

[43] *Ibid.*, XV (1905), p. 101.

[44] Solomon Schechter, "The Charter of the Seminary," *Seminary Addresses and Other Papers* (Cincinnati, 1915), pp. 9-33.

[45] *The United Synagogue of America, Sixth Annual Report* (New York, 1919), p. 21.

[46] *Jewish Comment,* XXVIII, No. 2 (December 25, 1908), pp. 193-195, 204-205; No. 13 (January 1, 1909), pp. 219-220, 223.

[47] *The United Synagogue of America, Fourth Annual Report* (New York, 1917), pp. 9-10.

[48] *The Jubilee Volume of the Union of Orthodox Rabbis of the United States and Canada* [in Hebrew], (New York, 1928), pp. 134-136.

[49] In 1937 the number of Jewish congregations in the country was about 3,700: approximately 3,000 Orthodox congregations with a membership of about 250,000; approximately 350 Conservative congregations with a membership of about 75,000; approximately 300 Reform synagogues with a membership of about 65,000. A closer analysis of these statistics reveals that the greatest number of Orthodox congregations were tiny units, a fraction of which was served by rabbis. In sum, the total estimated congregational membership based on family affiliations was about 1,500,000 individual Jews which represented less than one-third of the Jews in the United States at the estimated 1937 calculation of 4,770,647. The statistics are based on the United States Census of Religious Bodies report of 1937.

[50] The latter description seemed to have the widest acceptance. In 1943 the official magazine established by the Union of American Hebrew Congregations and the Central Conference of American Rabbis was called *Liberal Judaism.*

[51] Jacob Mann (1888-1940), historian and scholar of the Genizah; Zevi H. W. Diesendruck (1890-1940), philosopher and Hebraist; Abraham Z. Idelsohn (1882-1938), musicologist. Jacob R. Marcus, who had been an instructor in Bible and Rabbinics, was appointed assistant professor (and later, professor) of Jewish history.

[52] Israel Bettan, homiletics and Midrash; Samuel S. Cohon, Jewish theology; Abraham Cronbach, Jewish social studies; Sheldon H. Blank, Bible; Nelson Glueck, Bible and archaeology. In 1947, Dr. Glueck succeeded Dr. Morgenstern as president of the College.

[53] In 1946 the College decided to establish a School of Religious Education in New York City. The Union of American Hebrew Congregations joined in the support and administration of the school, and in January, 1947, classes were held for the first time at the Community House of Congregation Emanu-El. Abraham N. Franzblau was named dean.

[54] Among the scholars who served on the faculty were: Salo W. Baron, history; Sidney E. Goldstein, social studies; Julian J. Obermann, Bible and Semitic philosophy; Ralph Marcus (1900-1957), Bible and Hellenistic literature; Henry Slonimsky, philosophy; Shalom Spiegel, Hebrew language and literature; Nisson Touroff (1877-1953), psychology and education; Chaim Tchernowitz (1870-1949), Talmud; Harry A. Wolfson, Jewish philosophy.

[55] This merger was formally consummated in June, 1948, and the combined institution was called the Hebrew Union College-Institute of Religion.

[56] *Reform Judaism in the Large Cities* (1931).

[57] *Yearbook,* CCAR, XL (1930), pp. 251-303.

[58] Vol. I of the newly revised edition of *The Union Prayerbook,* was published in 1940; vol. II in 1945.

[59] "From the Synagogue" (issued in mimeographed form by the Union of American Hebrew Congregations, April, 1937).

[60] *Yearbook*, CCAR, XLV (1935), p. 103.

[61] Guiding Principles of Reform Judaism (adopted by the Central Conference of American Rabbis, at Columbus, Ohio, May 27, 1937).

[[61a] For full text, cf. below Louis Finkelstein, "The Jewish Religion: Its Beliefs and Practices," pp. 1756 ff.]

[62] Solomon Polachek (1877-1928), Moses Soloveitchik (1877-1941) and Julius Kaplan (1884-1939), in Talmud Solomon Zeitlin, in history; Pinkhas Churgin, in Bible and history; Joshua Finkel, in Semitic languages; Jekuthiel Ginsburg (1889-1957), in mathematics; Samuel K. Mirsky, in Rabbinics; Samuel Belkin, in Hellenistic literature; Leo Jung, in ethics; Joseph H. Lookstein, in sociology, and Joseph Soloveitchik in philosophy. In June, 1943, Dr. Belkin was elected president of the Yeshiva. For a statement of his views on the role of Yeshiva University, see *The Inauguration of Samuel Belkin* (New York, 1944), pp. 31-37.

[63] For a survey treatment of the history of Yeshiva College, see Jacob I. Hartstein, "Yeshiva University: Growth of Rabbi Isaac Elchanan Theological Seminary," *American Jewish Year Book,* 5707 (1946-1947), XLVIII (Philadelphia, 1946), pp. 73-84.

[64] *Talpioth,* a quarterly in Hebrew dedicated to Jewish law and ethics, began publication in September, 1943, under the editorship of Samuel K. Mirsky.

[65] The faculty included such figures as Meyer Waxman, author of the four volume, *A History of Jewish Literature,* and Samuel I. Feigin (1893-1950), orientalist.

[66] Other *yeshibot* for higher learning were established. The most important were the Mesifta Torah Va-Daat, the Mesifta Chaim Berlin, the Yeshiva Rabbi Israel Meir Ha-Cohen, the Mesifta Tifferes Yerushalaim, and the Yeshiva of the Lubavitscher Rabbi. *Yeshibot* in other parts of the country were: the Yeshiva Ner Israel in Baltimore and the Rabbinical College of Telshe, in Cleveland. Famous European *yeshibot* which established schools in America were the Mirer Yeshiva and the Lomze Yeshiva; schools for exiled scholars were also established in Spring Valley, New York, and Lakewood, New Jersey.

[67] The nationally known Ⓤ symbol soon offered the food manufacturer a regular method of indicating to the consumer that the product had rabbinic endorsement.

[68] The new organization, named the Central Sephardic Jewish Community of America, was organized in 1941. It issues a quarterly bulletin called *The Sephardi,* the first number of which appeared in September, 1943. The Union of Sephardic Congregations (organized in 1929, David de Sola Pool, president) did not confine its interests to the needs of the Sephardim in the United States. It serves the world Sephardic community and co-operates in America with the Central Sephardic Jewish Community.

[69] *Proceedings of the Seventh Annual Convention of the Rabbinical Council of America* (1942), pp. 46-47.

[70] After World War II, the special status of the Union of Orthodox Rabbis in this field of endeavor was officially recognized by the American Jewish

Joint Distribution Committee. An agreement was signed in July, 1947, between Rabbi Israel Rosenberg, chairman of the presidium of the Union, and Edward M. M. Warburg, J. D. C. Chairman, which provided "that those programs of the J. D. C. specifically devoted to the rehabilitation and advancement of Orthodox Jewish life in Europe will be conducted with the advice and counsel of the chief elements of Jewish Orthodoxy in America."

[71] For a statement of the Agudas Israel program, see *Agudist Essays* (London, 1944); and Jacob Rosenheim, *Agudist World Problems,* an address delivered to the convention of Agudas Israel of America, in Baltimore on August 23, 1941.

[72] In 1922 Hapoel Ha-Mizrachi was founded as a worldwide religious labor movement, as an affiliate of the Mizrachi, with the motto of *Torah Va-Avodah* (Torah and Labor). In America, Hapoel Ha-Mizrachi is the senior organization of the Torah Va-Avodah movement, with branches in various cities. Its Halutz department is known as the Halutz Ha-Mizrachi, and its youth movement is known as Zeirei Ha-Mizrachi. An independent youth organization, Ha-Shomer Ha-Dati, was also organized (1934) with the specific aim of *Kibbutziut* (collectivization). In July, 1947, the first religious collective of American halutzim was established at Ein Hanatziv in the valley of Bet Shaan, by this group.

[73] For a fuller statement of the growth of the *yeshiva* parochial movement, see *Yeshiva Review* (April, 1941), published by the United Yeshivos Foundation. For a rationale of the all-day school, see Jacob I. Hartstein, "The Yeshivah as an American Institution," *Jewish Education,* XVIII, No. 2, (March, 1947), pp. 26-29. Other national Orthodox agencies who are determined to introduce the *yeshiva* movement, through their financial aid, into every community with a sizable Jewish population, are the Yeshivah Tomchei Temimim, the Mizrachi, and the Torah Umesorah Organizations.

[73*] Joseph H. Hertz, (ed.), *A Book of Jewish Thoughts* (London, 1920), p. 4.

[74] Jacob Hoschander (1874-1933), Bible; Louis Finkelstein, theology; Boaz Cohen, Talmud; Alexander Sperber, H. L. Ginsberg, Robert Gordis, Bible; Simon Greenberg, education; Max Arzt, practical theology. At the beginning of World War II, as the lanes to and from Palestine were being closed, Saul Lieberman, world renowned Talmudist, began his association with the Seminary as professor of Palestinian literature and institutions. In 1937 Dr. Finkelstein was appointed Provost of the Seminary, and in 1940 he succeeded Dr. Adler as president of the institution. In 1947 Dr. Greenberg became Provost.

[75] At that time, 1947, Stephen S. Kayser was appointed Curator.

[76] In 1942 the name of the Classes was changed to the Seminary School of Jewish Studies and Dr. Louis M. Levitsky was appointed Director.

[77] Samuel M. Cohen (1886-1945) was the first Executive Director of the United Synagogue. He served from 1917-1945. In 1946 Albert I. Gordon was appointed as Director.

[78] "The Jewish Center," *American Hebrew,* LI, No. 20 (March 22, 1918), pp. 529-531.

79 "Judaism and Modern Thought," *United Synagogue Recorder*, II, No. 4 (October, 1922), pp. 2-4.

80 *The Problem of the Agunah,* A Statement by the Rabbinical Assembly of the Jewish Theological Seminary of America (New York, 1936).

81 Solomon Goldman, *A Rabbi Takes Stock* (New York, 1931), p. 19.

82 *The Reconstructionist*, XI, No. 1 (February 23, 1945), p. 15.

83 See *Sabbath Prayer Book* (New York, 1945), especially the Introduction, xvii-xxx.

84 The most important expression of their point of view is the publication of an official Prayer Book under the joint sponsorship of the Rabbinical Assembly and the United Synagogue, *Sabbath and Festival Prayer Book* (New York, 1946). Also see, Robert Gordis, "A Jewish Prayer Book for the Modern Age," *Conservative Judaism* II, No. 1 (October, 1945), and "The Tasks Before Us," *ibid.*, I, No. 1 (January, 1945).

85 For Dr. Kadushin, see *Organic Judaism* (New York, 1938). For Dr. Greenberg, see "Evaluating the Mitzvot," *Bulletin of the Rabbinical Assembly,* V, No. 1, (New York, June, 1942), pp. 9-18.

86 *Proceedings of the Twenty-Seventh Annual Conference of the Rabbinical Assembly of the Jewish Theological Seminary of America* (1927), pp. 42-66.

87 *Ibid.*, pp. 48-49.

88 See Abraham Cronbach, "The Social Outlook of Modern Judaism," *Popular Studies in Judaism,* No. 25, published by The Union of American Hebrew Congregations.

89 See *Yearbook* CCAR, XXVIII (1918), pp. 101-104; XXXVIII (1928), pp. 73-97; XLVII (1937), pp. 114-125; "Pronouncement of the Rabbinical Assembly of America on Social Justice," adopted July 5, 1934, *Proceedings of the Rabbinical Assembly,* V (1939), pp. 156-164; the Union of Orthodox Jewish Congregations of America, at a conference in New York in April, 1936, set up a permanent committee for social justice.

90 David de Sola Pool was Chairman, Barnett P. Brickner (Reform), Chairman of the Administrative Committee, Louis M. Levitsky (Conservative), Chairman of the Executive Committee, and Joseph H. Lookstein (Orthodox), Vice-Chairman of the Executive Committee.

91 All considerations of the change of auspices were postponed until the end of the war. In 1947 as an act of deference to the will of the Association of Jewish Chaplains, the Jewish Welfare Board created a Division of Religious Activities under its general supervision and administrative control. All the religious groups are represented, and they have full authority in the determination and implementation of policy. Solomon S. Freehof was appointed chairman; Aryeh Lev, director.

92 "Jewish Chaplains in World War II," *American Jewish Year Book,* 5706, (1945-1946), vol. 47 (Philadelphia, 1945), pp. 173-178.

93 See *Responsa in War Time* (New York, 1947), published by the Division of Religious Activities, National Jewish Welfare Board.

94 Philip Bernstein, *op. cit.*, pp. 174-175.

[95] At the first national convention of the chaplains' association, the following resolution was unanimously passed:

"We Chaplains who served in this last war, alumni of the three major rabbinic seminaries, and representative of the Orthodox, Conservative and Reform religious ideologies within American Judaism unanimously affirm that the mutuality, fellowship, and conradeship which united us in our common service of God and country proved a most enriching spiritual experience which we aim to apply in our civilian ministry. To expand and extend the blessings of this creative fellowship so that it may embrace other facets of Jewish life, we urge upon the three rabbinic bodies to project plans for their respective national conventions in a manner that would provide, once every three years, a simultaneous session for the three bodies."

Proceedings of the First National Convention (New York, 1947), p. 26.

[96] In February, 1945, Dr. Kaplan, speaking at a convocation of the Seminary, called for its development into a university of Judaism; the following year the Seminary did establish a University of Judaism in Los Angeles as its West Coast Branch. In November, 1945, the Yeshiva announced its change to university status. See Samuel Belkin, *Yeshiva University—Its Purpose and Philosophy* (New York, 1948). While the Hebrew Union College did not announce a formal change of name, its plan of growth as outlined by Dr. Glueck in his inaugural year, 1947-1948, probably will bring the college into a similar scheme.

[97] "The Aims of the Conference," *Science, Philosophy and Religion* (New York, 1941), pp. 11-19.

[98] *New York Times* (March 14, 1948).

[99] "The Past and Future," *Occident,* VI, No. 6 (September, 1848), pp. 275-285.

Selected Bibliography

ADLER, CYRUS, *I Have Considered the Days*. Philadelphia, 1943.

———, *Jacob H. Schiff. His Life and Letters*. 2 vols. New York, 1928.

———, *Lectures, Selected Papers, Addresses*. Philadelphia, 1933.

———, "Louis Marshall: A Biographical Sketch." Reprinted from *American Jewish Year Book*, Vol. 42. New York, 1931.

———, (ed.), *The Jewish Theological Seminary of America*. Semicentennial Volume. New York, 1939.

———, and Margolith, Aaron M., *With Firmness In The Right: American Diplomatic Action Affecting Jews, 1840-1945*. New York, 1946.

ADLER, SAMUEL (Chairman of the Editorial Committee), *Protokolle der Rabbiner-Conferenz abgehalten zu Philadelphia vom 3. bis 6. November 1869*. New York, 1870.

AGUS, JACOB B., *Modern Philosophies of Judaism*. New York, 1941.

BARON, SALO W., *A Social and Religious History of the Jews*. Vol. II., pp. 164-462. New York, 1937.

———, and Baron, Jeanette, "Palestinian Messengers in America, 1849-1879," in *Jewish Social Studies,* V, Nos. 2 and 3, April and July, 1943.

BENTWICH, NORMAN, *Solomon Schechter*. Philadelphia, 1938.

COHON, SAMUEL S., "The Theology of the Union Prayer Book." Reprinted from *Central Conference of American Rabbis Yearbook*. Vol. XXXVIII, p. 245. Cincinnati, 1928.

———, *What We Jews Believe*. Department of Synagogue and School Extension of the Union of American Hebrew Congregations. Cincinnati, 1931.

COWEN, PHILIP, *Memories of an American Jew*. New York, 1932.

DALY, CHARLES P. (M. J. Kohler, ed.), *The Settlement of the Jews in North America*. New York, 1893.

DAVIDSON, GABRIEL, *Our Jewish Farmers*. New York, 1943.

DRACHMAN, BERNARD, *The Unfailing Light*. Rabbinical Council of America. New York, 1948.

DUSHKIN, ALEXANDER M., *Jewish Education in New York City*. New York, 1918.

EINHORN, DAVID, *Selected Sermons and Addresses*. New York, 1911.

David Einhorn Memorial Volume, ed. by Kaufmann Kohler. New York, 1914

EISENSTEIN, J. D., "The History of the First Russian-American Jewish Congregation." *Publications of the American Jewish Historical Society*, No. 9, pp. 63-74. Baltimore, 1901.

ELBOGEN, ISMAR, "Alexander Kohut," *American Jewish Year Book*. XLIV, pp. 73-80. Philadelphia, 1942-1943.

———, *American Jewish Scholarship: A Survey*. New York, 1943.

———, *A Century of Jewish Life*. (Translated by Moses Hadas.) Philadelphia, 1944.

ELIASSOF, HERMAN, *German American Jews*. 1915.

ELZAS, BARNETT A., *The Jews of South Carolina* (From Earliest Times to the Present Day). Philadelphia, 1905.

FELSENTHAL, EMMA, *Bernard Felsenthal, Teacher in Israel*. London and New York, 1944.

Fifty Years of Social Service. The History of the United Hebrew Charities of the City of New York (Jewish Social Service Association). New York, 1926.

(Editors of) Fortune Magazine. *Jews in America*. New York, 1936.

FINK, REUBEN (ed.), *America and Palestine*. New York, 1945.

FREEHOF, SOLOMON B., *Reform Jewish Practice and Its Rabbinic Background*. Cincinnati, 1944.

FRIEDLAENDER, ISRAEL, *Past and Present*. Cincinnati, 1919.

FRIEDMAN, LEE M., *Jewish Pioneers and Patriots*. Philadelphia, 1942.

GAMORAN, EMANUEL, *Changing Conceptions in Jewish Education*. New York, 1924.

GINZBERG, LOUIS, *Students, Scholars and Saints*. Philadelphia, 1928.

GOLDSTEIN, ISRAEL, *A Century of Judaism in New York*. New York, 1930.

GOODMAN, ABRAM VOSSEN, *American Overture*. Philadelphia, 1947.

GORDIS, ROBERT, *Conservative Judaism*. New York, 1945.

GRINSTEIN, HYMAN B., *The Rise of the Jewish Community in New York 1654-1860*. Philadelphia, 1945.

GUP, S. M., "Currents in Jewish Religious Thought and Life in America in the Twentieth Century." Reprinted from *Central Conference of American Rabbis Yearbook*, XLI, 1931.

GUTSTEIN, MORRIS A., *The Story of the Jews of Newport: 1658-1908*. New York, 1936.

HELLER, JAMES G., *As Yesterday When it is Past*. Cincinnati, 1942.

HIRSCH, EMIL G., *My Religion*. New York, 1925.

———, *Twenty Discourses*. Reprinted from Reform Advocate. New York, n.d.

JANOWSKY, OSCAR I. (ed.), *The American Jew*. New York, 1942.

———, *The J.W.B. Survey*. New York, 1948.

JUNG, LEO (ed.), *The Jewish Library*. First Series. New York, 1928.

———, *The Jewish Library*. Second Series. New York, 1930.

———, *The Jewish Library*. Third Series. New York, 1934.

KALLEN, HORACE M., *Judaism At Bay*. New York, 1932.

KAPLAN, MORDECAI M. (ed.), *The Jewish Reconstructionist Papers*. New York, 1936.

———, *Judaism as a Civilization*. New York, 1934.

———, *Judaism in Transition*. New York, 1936.

———, *The Future of the American Jew*. New York, 1948.

KARPF, HYMAN J., *Jewish Community Organization in the United States*. New York, 1939.

KOHLER, KAUFMANN, *Backwards or Forward?* New York, 1885.

———, *Hebrew Union College and Other Addresses*. Cincinnati, 1916.

———, *Jewish Theology*. New York, 1918.

———, "Personal Reminiscences of My Early Life." Reprinted from *Hebrew Union College Monthly*, May, 1918. Cincinnati, 1918.

———, *Studies, Addresses and Personal Papers*. New York, 1931.

KOHN, EUGENE, *The Future of Judaism in America*. New York, 1934.

KOHUT, ALEXANDER, *Ethics of the Fathers*. (Translated into English by Max Cohen and edited by B. Elzas). New York, 1920.

KOHUT, REBEKAH, *My Portion*. New York, 1925.

LEBESON, ANITA L., *Jewish Pioneers in America: 1492-1848*. New York, 1931.

LEVINGER, LEE J., *A Jewish Chaplain in France*. New York, 1921.

LEVINTHAL, ISRAEL HERBERT, *Judaism, An Analysis and An Interpretation*. New York, 1935.

LEVY, BERYL H., *Reform Judaism in America*. New York, 1933.

LIPSKY, LOUIS, *Thirty Years of American Zionism*. (Vol. I. of *Selected Works*) New York, 1927.

MARCUS, JACOB R., *The Americanization of Isaac Mayer Wise*. Cincinnati, 1931.

MARX, ALEXANDER, *Essays in Jewish Biography*. Philadelphia, 1947, pp. 223-298.

MAY, MAX B., *Isaac Mayer Wise*. New York and London, 1916.

MIELZINER, ELLA M. F., *Moses Mielziner* (1828-1903). With a reprint of his *Slavery among the Ancient Hebrews and Other Works*. New York, 1931.

MOISE, L. C., *Biography of Isaac Harby*. Sumter, S.C., 1931.

MORAIS, HENRY SAMUEL, *Eminent Israelites of the Nineteenth Century*. Philadelphia, 1880.

———, *The Jews of Philadelphia*. Philadelphia, 1894.

NEUMAN, ABRAHAM A., *Cyrus Adler*. New York, 1942.

PHILIPSON, DAVID, *Max Lilienthal, American Rabbi: Life and Writings*. New York, 1915.

———, *My Life as an American Jew*. Cincinnati, 1937-1938.

———, *The Reform Movement in Judaism*. New York, 1931.

Reform Judaism in the Large Cities, A Survey. Union of American Hebrew Congregations. Cincinnati, 1931.

ROSENAU, WILLIAM, *Benjamin Szold*. Baltimore, 1902.

SCHACHNER, NATHAN, *The Price of Liberty*. New York, 1948.

SCHECHTER, SOLOMON, *Seminary Addresses and other Papers*. Cincinnati, 1915.

———, *Studies in Judaism*. First Series. Philadelphia, 1896.

———, *Studies in Judaism*. Second Series. Philadelphia, 1908.

———, (Alexander Marx and Frank I. Schechter, eds.), *Studies in Judaism*. Third Series. Philadelphia, 1924.

SOLIS-COHEN, SOLOMON, *Judaism and Science, with Other Addresses and Papers*. Philadelphia, 1940.

———, "Mayer Sulzberger." In *Addresses Delivered in Memory of Mayer Sulzberger*. Pp. 24-55. Philadelphia, 1924.

STEINBERG, MILTON, *A Partisan Guide to the Jewish Problem*. New York, 1945.

STILES, EZRA, *The Literary Diary of Ezra Stiles*. (ed. by F. B. Dexter). New York, 1901.

STRAUS, OSCAR, *The Origin of Republican Form of Government in the United States*. New York, 1901.

TRACHTENBERG, JOSHUA, *Consider the Years*. Easton, Pa., 1944.

TSCHERIKOWER, E., *History of the Jewish Labor Movement in the United States* (Yiddish). 2 vols. New York, 1943, 1945.

WILANSKY, DENA, *Sinai to Cincinnati—Isaac M. Wise, Founder of Reform in America*. New York, 1937.

WISE, ISAAC MAYER (David Philipson, ed.), *Reminiscences*, Cincinnati, 1901.

———, (David Philipson and Louis Grossman, eds.), *Selected Writings*.

WISE, STEPHEN S., *As I See It*. New York, 1945.

WOLF, SIMON, *The American Jew as Patriot, Soldier and Citizen*. Philadelphia, 1895.

ZEITLIN, JOSEPH, *Disciples of the Wise*. New York, 1945.

CHAPTER 12

THE HISTORICAL FOUNDATIONS OF THE REBIRTH OF ISRAEL

By Ben Zion Dinur*

I

By the term "rebirth of Israel" I do not mean to imply merely its rebirth as a state, or even those basic factors which constitute this political rebirth. There are those who date this political rebirth from November 29, 1947, the day of the United Nations' decision to partition Palestine and establish in one of the partitioned areas a Jewish State; and there are others who date it from the Declaration of the fifth of *Iyar*, 5708 (May 14, 1948), concerning the establishment of the State of Israel. To the first of these two events, or to both together, are attached the subsequent Arab invasions and the Jewish victories which culminated in armistice agreements with the Arab states, and the recognition by the international community of nations of Israel's independence, which found its full expression in the admittance of Israel to the United Nations.[1a] And there are those who add the awakening of multitudes of Jews in the Diaspora and the Ingathering of the Exiles—two events which manifested the recognition of the State of Israel on the part of the Jewish people—as being at least a partial fulfillment of the hopes of many generations for Redemption and deliverance.

However, these significant events, if taken by themselves, do not at all reveal the true essence of the rebirth of Israel, for they are only the expression and revelation of this rebirth. Its essence lies in an altogether different factor, namely, in the emergence of a large Jewish settlement in the country, a settlement which struck roots in the land and built an independent economy tied to the land and its natural characteristics; which established a new unified and consolidated Jewish society; which revived the Hebrew language, and invested the life of the community with renewed national-territorial-cultural foundations; and which showed ability to govern its own affairs, to set its own life in order, and to protect itself against its enemies.

Seventy-two years ago, approximately 22,000 to 24,000 Jews lived in

* This paper was originally delivered as a lecture in Hebrew at The Jewish Theological Seminary of America, on October 3, 1954. The English translation is by Rabbi Herman Potok.

Israel, the vast majority in the four cities which were called "Four Lands": Jerusalem, Hebron, Tiberius, and Safed. A very small minority lived in tiny communities in the coastal cities of Jaffa, Haifa, Acre, and Gaza. In a few other cities, such as Shefaram and Shechem, there were also a few Jewish families. The majority of this Jewish settlement was without economic roots, lived on monetary donations from abroad, and played virtually no part in the economy of the land or in its meager productivity, being only consumers. Even from a demographic point of view, this was not a settlement of wage earners, for an unusually large percentage were old men and women. The settlement was not consolidated; it was divided into communities and *Landsmanshaften*, each a world in itself. The settlers did not constitute an entity *per se*. They were divided into groups according to their places of origin, and generally maintained past ties, spoke different languages, and were distinct not only as citizens of different countries but also in ways of life. The Jewish settlers were far from modern culture and seemed to be remnants of an historical phenomenon concentrated in a distant corner on the edge of the vast expanse of Jewish existence.

This essay deals essentially with the sixty-five years, 1882-1947. During the thirty-two years between the first settlement and the First World War, the *Yishuv* (the settlement of Jews in the Land of Israel) multiplied three and a half times (to 84,000 persons), and the number of settled communities grew from eight to fifty-four, forty-four of them agricultural. The proportion of the Jewish population to the total increased from approximately 4.5 per cent to 12 per cent. Within the *Yishuv* itself, the proportion of Jews settled in villages rose to 14 per cent.

During the thirty-three years which followed (1914-1947) the *Yishuv* increased more than seven and a half times (to 643,000). The number of communities and settlements rose to 330, 302 of them agricultural; the proportion of the Jewish to the total population rose to 33 per cent, and the proportion of Jews settled in villages rose to 25.6 per cent (165,000). At the beginning of the Jewish resettlement, the proportion of Jews in the *Yishuv* to Jews in the rest of the world was 0.18 per cent; in 1947, it was approximately 6.3 per cent. Though the *Yishuv* possessed only 7 per cent of the total land of Palestine (within the boundaries of the "national home") it succeeded in establishing an independent economy which constituted a separate economic unit and which fixed permanently the nature and character of the country. The proportion of Jewish settlements to that of all other settlements was 27.3 per cent; and though the proportion of grain products raised by Jews was not more than 8 per cent, in other fields of agriculture their proportions were high: 25 per cent in greens, 50 per cent in citrus, 89 per cent in fodder and herbage. The Jewish share in industry and trades, which began to play a significant role in the country's economy, was about 84 per cent, or—according to the value of industrial production and the number of people gainfully employed in it —about 88 per cent.

All of this economic and communal upbuilding was done by the Jews themselves: with their labor and their money, with their organizational ability, and with the strength of their ideals. They formed an independent economic entity in the country, as well as an organized unit of people who toiled zealously to build up the country and promote the development of the *Yishuv,* to better their lives, to raise their standard of living and their social status, to meet the colonization requirements of the *Yishuv,* and to protect it against the outside forces always conspiring against it.

The *Yishuv* also succeeded in consolidating itself culturally. It not only established a complete system of education, from kindergarten to the Technion and the University, which encompassed almost the entire *Yishuv,* but remarkably it also succeeded in unifying itself through the Hebrew language. The Hebrew language became the living language of the masses, the language of the educational system, of the culture, the learning, and the science—and also the *official language* of the people.

All these events together constitute *the rebirth of Israel.* Only on the basis of these fundamental factors did the United Nations decide to establish a Jewish State in a portion of the Land of Israel. The fundamental importance of the *Yishuv* in the creation of the State was made fully apparent with the Declaration of Independence and revealed itself in the War of Independence, and the nations of the world took full cognizance of it when they decided to admit Israel to the United Nations.

In other words, the political rebirth of Israel is a direct result of the the resettlement of Israel in its own land: within sixty-five years there arose a Jewish settlement, whose progress, growth, and expansion embodied and interwove elements which brought about its crystallization as a seedling people and a fledgling state, and thus made it the bearer of Israeli independence. This growth and expansion of the *Yishuv* is deliberately called "the resettlement of Israel in its own land," because this term expresses fully the unique historical character of the formation of the new settlement.

2

I shall try first to explain the meaning of my definition of the rebirth of Israel, and then to establish its veracity: the term "historical foundations" denotes those forces and elements operative in the formation of the *Yishuv* that resulted from the endeavors of previous generations. During the formation of the *Yishuv* such historical factors already existed.

The formation of the *Yishuv,* its growth to the status of a seedling people and bearer of Israeli independence, is undoubtedly one of the most remarkable chapters not only in the history of the Jewish people but in the history of civilization. The essence of this phenomenon can best be defined and understood by describing the formation of the new settlement as "the resettlement of Israel in its own land." The term "settlement" in Hebrew denotes permanent settlement in a specific land, identification with it, and self-rule. It implies not merely settlement but permanent settlement born out of a realization of continuous possession, of ownership. Because of this, settlement, in the language of the Bible, is always used in terms of a family, a tribe, or a nation. "Settlement" then has, as an essential part of its meaning, a taking hold which contains something of permanence, of duration, of the will to own and control. Every act of settlement has within itself an element of the eternal.

The formation of the *Yishuv* was not merely a socioeconomic process—not merely the result of the fact that Jews, suffering in the places where they dwelt, decided to emigrate from the countries of their fathers to where living conditions were better, where there was greater security and opportunity to earn a livelihood. The formation of the *Yishuv* was also the result of political, social, spiritual, and moral processes.

The true significance of the resettlement was that the acquisition of the soil was intimately tied to a complete renewal of social and psychological experiences. This resettlement in the homeland could be accomplished only through laying bare the basic instincts which bind man to the soil and which are hidden in the recesses of his being, and through their renewal as a primary force in the crystallization of a society and in the emergence of a people. It is understandable that this renewal was, by its very nature, bound to influence, to a great degree, both the individual who had already settled in the country and the new society which arose there. In this process of resettlement there was naturally embodied a great human drive for the spiritual renewal of the individual, both through his intimate relationship to nature and to labor and also through his relationship to other individuals and to the community in everyday living.

The human drive embodied in and arising from this process was inherent in men and women permeated with a sense of mission on behalf of the entire Jewish people. They regarded themselves and their endeavors, their efforts and their self-renewal, as an expression of generations of yearning, of the collective will of the Jewish people revealed and renewed in all its manifestations through the desire to return to Zion; they regarded themselves as the messengers of a people returned to its homeland. This aim of the resettlement achieved remarkably clear manifestation in every major and minor act associated with it. One need only recount the names of the groups and organizations established to acquire soil and promote immigration, or the names of the settlements: *Dabber 'el bnai Yis-*

rael veyisau (Speak unto the children of Israel, that they go forward—Exodus 14:15), *Bet yaakob leku venelku* (O house of Jacob, come ye, and let us go—Isaiah 2:5), *Shearit Yisrael* (Remnant of Israel), *Mikveh Yisrael* (Ingathering of Israel), *Tehiat Yisrael* (Revival of Israel), *Petah Tikvah* (Door of Hope), and *Rosh Pinah* (Cornerstone), *Zion* and *Rishon le-Zion* (First of Zion), *Ezra ve* (and) *Nehemiah, Yesud la-maaleh* (Beginning of the Homecoming), and *Halutze Yesud ha-maaleh* (Pioneer of the Homecoming—Ezra 7:9).

The names of the settlements and the organizations were symbolic and expressed the true nature of the "resettlement of Israel in its own land" inherent in them. In these names, as in the entire movement that began to stream toward Israel, were embodied the historical, national, and political aims of *Aliyah* (immigration) to Israel. This was understood by the immigrants, by the Jews generally, by the Turks and Arabs. The immigration was infused with a recognition of historical continuity, a recognition which grew gradually more intense as the resettlement progressed. *Eretz Yisrael* (the Land of Israel) was without unified administration, being divided by the Turks into a number of districts (Damascus, Beirut, and Jerusalem); and its Jewish population had already begun to send its children abroad because there was no possibility of economic sustenance for them at home. Yet unity of purpose in Jewish immigration and resettlement was achieved only through the power of recognition of Jewish historical destiny and the will of *all the Jewish people.*

This was clear to the Turks and Arabs. The Turkish government forbade entry into Israel, and from the 1880's until World War I its attitude was apparent: namely, to oppose the immigration and settlement of Jews there. Turkey claimed complete readiness to encourage Jewish settlement in any of her regions except Israel, and did all in her power to impede the development of the *Yishuv.* Rauf-al-Rauf, the Turkish governor of Jerusalem, was a bitter opponent of Jewish resettlement because he detected in it the vigor of a people resettling in its homeland, and he was tireless in his persistent efforts to mobilize in opposition both the Turkish government and the Arab populace.

The Jewish resettlement, unrelated to the demands of local conditions, and opposed by the government, necessitated extraordinary efforts, perseverance, efficiency, and administrative skill. It was infused with energy stemming from every segment of the Jewish people, from every historical factor of past generations. The settlers themselves were from different places: Hungary (*Petah Tikvah*), Russia (*Rishon le-Zion*), Lithuania (*Ekron*), Poland (*Yesud ha-maaleh*), Rumania (*Rosh Pinah* and *Zichron Yaakob* [Memorial to Jacob]) and Bulgaria (*Hartov* [Good Mountain]). And Jews from the entire Diaspora took an interest in the settlers' fortunes and supported them. To illustrate: Sigmund Zimmel, a Jew from

Berlin who was a devoted adherent of the Lovers of Zion movement in Russia, went to Baron Rothschild to enlist his help for settlements in Upper Galilee (*Yesud ha-maaleh* and *Rosh Pinah*) which had been founded by Jews from Poland and Rumania. The Baron said: "Aren't you impressed by the remarkable fact that a Prussian Jew comes at the request of Russian Jews to a Parisian Jew to enlist his aid for Rumanian and Polish Jews living in Israel?"

Indeed, the entire resettlement was accompanied by and dependent upon the combined endeavor of all Jews, as well as their organizational, financial, and political efforts. Neither the means nor the methods are of importance in this context. It is, however, a fact that Jewish lawyers of Spanish descent who had lived in Turkey and in Asia Minor and settled in Israel purchased land there with moneys acquired from Jews of Russia, Lithuania, Rumania, and other countries, together with funds from Baron Rothschild and Baron de Hirsch (from the Jewish Colonization Organization) and others, and acquired title in the names of Jews who were citizens of Germany, France, England, and Turkey. It is again a fact that the interventions with the Turkish government on behalf of Jewish resettlement were based on the possibilities and realities of general Jewish life at that time: leaders of *Alliance Israelite Universelle*, rabbis and lay leaders, lawyers from Russia (Rosenfeld, Kalmanovitz), a member of the British Parliament (Montagu), an ambassador from the United States (Oscar S. Straus), a professor from Hungary (Arminius Vambery), and many others. The associations and organizations which preached Jewish emigration, which collected money for resettlement, and which were preoccupied with its problems, derived their organizational structures and methods of operation from Jewish groups in every part of the world, from charitable and mutual aid organizations, from corporate groups, *Haskala* groups, youth groups, clandestine societies, fraternities, and revolutionary societies. The general Jewish reality also is indicated in the names of the organizations for land acquisition: for example, *Menuhah Venahala*, *Dorshe Zion*, *Agudat ha-elef*, up to the various *ahuzot* (estates) and the setting up of urban *Shekunot* (quarters) in the cities of *Eretz Israel*. In other words, the actual establishment and crystallization of the *Yishuv* were made possible by the nature of the process of which it was the result.

3

This fact is customarily expressed in somewhat simpler terms: the fact is constantly stressed that the land was one to which people "went up" (*Aliyah*), not one to which people merely immigrated, and it was particularly this concept which enabled the builders of the *Yishuv* to achieve and carry the responsibility of independence.

To be sure, among the motives for *Aliyah* were also common factors which forced great masses of Jews to abandon the lands of their abode and to seek for themselves a new "birthplace"—such factors as the pogroms in Russia, the persecutions in Rumania, the anti-Semitism in Germany, Austria, and Western Europe, and others. But of greater significance was the fact that decisive in the choice of Israel as the place for Jewish settlement was the longing for a resettlement of Israel in its own land.

During this period there were successive waves of immigration, and in every wave there was a substantial core of immigrants that had always felt themselves to be inhabitants of the Land of Israel. These men and women longed for a truly Jewish community, striving for and living a completely Hebrew cultural life. This desire to be a people dwelling in its own land, a people working its own earth, comprising the majority of the land's citizens and its constructive labor, gave direction and purpose to their immigration. These men and women knew the country well, though their knowledge came from the tradition, from literature, from legend; they recognized and remembered the names of its rivers and streams, hills and valleys, cities and villages. Before they emigrated, many had a clearer picture of the ways and paths of the land and the streets of Jerusalem than of the ways and cities of the countries in which they were born. In other words, *Aliyah* implies that these settlers carried within themselves both the Jewish community and the Jewish State, even while in the Diaspora.

Of no lesser importance was the fact that the *Aliyah* by its very nature brought to the land a vision of a new kind of Jew. Each of the immigration waves was composed of volunteers going to the aid of the Jewish people, of pioneers imbued with profound, collective, national feelings toward future tribulations. Each immigration wave was, therefore, a clarion call to young and fresh talents, who by their longing to build a path into the future were transformed from individuals into a mass movement. Thus every immigration wave eventually expressed a readiness for sacrifice, for acceptance of the yoke of responsibility for the future. And all of this with due consideration for the present, prompt reaction to developing events, and a vision of the distant future. All these are the basic factors in the creation of a society, any society.

Every wave of immigration brought those who knew Israel well, although neither they nor generations before them had trod upon it. Not an ordinary geographical area, but *The* Land, the Promised Land of the dream and the vision, of legends and miracles, of glory and splendor. To be sure, the immigrants encountered miserable living conditions. But while they were fully aware of the hardships of daily life, they were never reconciled to them. The present was not accepted as permanent fact, as a necessary condition of affairs, but was regarded as temporary, a transient reality, which the *Aliyah* would dissipate. The essential meaning of every

Aliyah was the transformation of existing factors and the building of new factors conforming to *Aliyah* and to the spiritual nature of the immigrant. With this inner strength the *Aliyah* built the *Yishuv* and laid the foundations for a "fledgling state."

It is only through such an understanding of the situation that it is possible to comprehend the way the new Jewish community was formed. This extreme contradiction between the spiritual nature of the *Aliyah* and the reality naturally created an inner tension which by its very nature could not long endure. At first the entire *Aliyah* considered itself one unit, and the individual identified himself with the general, total undertaking, his very personality fluctuating with every forward or backward step in the building of the land, as though it were his own personal, intimate concern. However, eventually as a result of numbing tension, of wearying tumult, and of a fatigue which finally possessed a whole generation, individuals came naturally to identify the undertaking with themselves. After ten to fifteen harassing years, the members of each *Aliyah* began to regard themselves as the core of the entire undertaking, and measured its progress by the degree to which they themselves had achieved a firm foundation in the Land.

This phenomenon was an established part of every *Aliyah*, but the reverses were always followed by advances. The *Yishuv* was constantly refreshed through the successive waves of immigration. New stirrings of the Exile resulting from echoes of disaster spread throughout the Diaspora, launching new waves of immigration and further building and pioneering, readiness for sacrifice, yearning for the homeland, agitation for a firm rooting there, and a sense of mission. These factors strengthened the efforts to create a new society. They built settlements, formed groups, united divergent feelings; and, because the tension never abated, the conditions necessary for the upbuilding of Israel served also to knit together the different parts of the Jewish people which, under other conditions, could never have been united. And so with *Aliyah* after *Aliyah* and layer after layer, the new Jewish settlement gradually developed, a settlement of the people dwelling in Zion. This was the great historic mission of the second *Aliyah*, the third *Aliyah*, and every subsequent *Aliyah*. Every wave of immigration brought fine building blocks and elements which acted as magnets, drawing toward themselves the basic elements of previous waves. In this way the various social bases for the independence of Israel were steadily enlarged.

4

Both the immigration waves and the "self-mobilization" of the Jewish "social factors" in aid of resettlement testify to the existence of resources within the people which, by their nature, served as an impetus for action; these resources were as if destined to bring about Jewish resettlement in the homeland. To be sure, the immigration waves were limited in scope and the intertwining of the "Jewish social factors" with the progress of the resettlement was extremely slow; it was only by degrees that broader sections of the "Jewish world" were joined to this development.

But, on the other hand, already revealed in the early history of the Lovers of Zion movement—easily understood as the "rebellion against the Exile"—was a power to penetrate all the widespread segments of the Jewish people, a persistence and continuity of action, and a stubborn clinging to past accomplishments. These traits testified to a profound reawakening of a people, in which were renewed and revealed such primary and essential factors as land, language, and social cohesion.

Even before the actual resettlement, a desire for the covenant with the land was renewed in the hearts of the people—not only because this covenant already existed but because it was (as stated above) a basic factor in Jewish life.

Many are inclined to claim that, in part, this "covenant" was not significant, not a fundamental frame of reference, and not something basic to present reality. Everywhere Jews prayed for "dew and rain," for "wind and rains"—in conformity with the climate of Israel—ate of the fruit of the land on the fifteenth of *Shebat*, and made Jerusalem the focus of all their joyous and mournful holidays. Yet some state that this "covenant" was merely an intense, imaginary longing tied to dreams of Redemption, to a vision of the future: beyond actual attainment, at most a matter of the spirit, with no temporal foundation in the Land itself.

But this concept overlooks the significant historic fact that the desire for resettlement was strong throughout the generations, that the struggle for the establishment and maintenance of the *Yishuv* continued through all the generations, and that at all times and from all Jewish communities those groups that included a maximum of Jewish living had streamed to Israel. The extreme elements—those who would not come to terms with the Exile, those who tried to hasten the day of decision—were attracted to the Holy Land, "to stand" (as one living in the ninth century put it) in the gate, because "if they seek mercy, it is incumbent upon those who incurred the anger to stand at the gates of the palace of the King Who was angry at His sons, therefore they go to His home to seek mercy." The age-old *Yishuv* in its persistent clinging to the land was objectively and partly consciously the emissary of the people destined to prepare the way for Redemption. This was true of the eighth and ninth centuries, of the time of the Mourners of Zion, and of the Messianic movements; also of the time of Judah Ha-Levi, Maimonides, and Nahmanides; of the emigration from Germany at the end of the thirteenth century; and of the expulsion from Spain, the emigration to Safed, and the immigration of the extremely pious and ascetic Jews (Hasidim and Perushim) at the end of the eighteenth and beginning of the nineteenth century; and this was true also of the immigration of the devout Jews and the pupils of Chatham Sofer from Hungary. The whole concept was expressed by a *Haskala* poet, Adam Ha-Kohen, in his poem about the old *Yishuv*, written approximately 110 years ago.

It should also be noted that the Land of Israel and the settlement there was a magnetic attraction and not only from an abstract point of view. The *Yishuv* continually sent forth messengers, preachers, and propagandists, who fanned the flame and who may be considered, as it were, the "guardians of the covenant" with the land, from the time of the messengers of Zion up to the eighteenth and nineteenth centuries and the later voices crying out for *Aliyah* until today. There was also an entire literature, with unique characteristics and motifs, which testified to this love of Zion and Jerusalem." It is sufficient to mention the letters from those living in Israel to those in the Exile which, from the nineteenth century until the present day, filled the Jewish press (both that published in Hebrew and that published in other languages) with word which upheld and strengthened the living tie with the Land.

Who responded? Those who because of their social status were moved to emigrate, those who would be reared most thoroughly in the Jewish tradition; and these characteristics were frequently combined.

"Exile" and "Redemption" are not merely abstract ideological concepts which varied from generation to generation with changes in the outlook and understanding, in the beliefs and opinions, of Jews. "Exile" and "Redemption" are systems of concepts and social perceptions which absorb the experience of generations, the experience of the misfortunes of Exile and the trials of Redemption. All of traditional, mystical Jewish thought is suffused with these historical experiences. Those elements of the people (not many, to be sure) which were moved by this tradition of constant search for ways of Redemption, fulfillment, and spiritual activity were always ready to go to the Land of Israel.

This was true also of later generations. Not only from the ranks of the Messianic movements, from the various offshoots of Sabbateanism which constantly stimulated the search for ways of Redemption, but also from the ranks of Hasidism and the followers of Elijah Gaon, and others, came those who spurred the return to Israel. Their immigration was dependent upon varying ideologies, but the common factor was the longing for a way of life in which the boundaries between the sacred and the profane would be dissolved through the sanctification of the profane. For all such immigrants the Land of Israel was an anteroom where the Jew could prepare himself for his lofty destiny. This historic element acted as a causative factor in molding the *Yishuv*. The *Aliyah* to the Land of Israel was regarded by every immigrant not merely as a geographical change but as a further step toward the attainment of human perfection.

5[2a]

The period of the *Haskala* and the Emancipation apparently uprooted the Jew from the world of the past. The slogan of the *Haskala* was, "Be aware of your time and your place," and the aim of the Emancipation was to infuse a sense of permanence and stability in the land of the Jew's birth. One well-known nineteenth-century German Jew expressed this in a uniquely grotesque manner in his address on the Ninth Day of Ab when he urged gratitude for the destruction of the Temple and the subsequent Exile because, as a result, he and others of his generation were privileged to be subjects of the Prussian king. However, not all Jews shared this feeling. We can easily believe the testimony of another member of that German generation who complained that he was constantly receiving letters from young Jews concerning news from Israel and the immigration of Jews, all of the letters filled with justifiable yearnings "to find at least a tiny spot on earth where one can feel himself completely free." The existence of this feeling and its enduring influence was one of the causes of the bitter polemics of some groups of German Reform Jews who sought to alter, or (to be accurate) to restrict the emphasis on the Land of Israel in the Jewish religion.

The Hebrew language, its vitality and scope, were far stronger and more deeply rooted than is customarily assumed, even during the period when linguistic identification was thought necessary for the political, legal, and social equality of Jews in the Diaspora. And even in that period, though suffering a staggering cultural and linguistic decline, on the one hand, and severe restrictions upon their Jewish creativity, on the other, a segment of the Jews nurtured longings for full Jewish cultural, political, and social independence.

The tension between those who furthered Hebrew and those who furthered other studies is illustrated by Mendele Moicher Sforim (pen name of Shalom Jacob Abramowitsch). At first glance, Mendele's introduction to his story "My Horse," and the story concerning "the Jewish boy who lost his sanity as a result of examinations in Russian literature," appear to be criticism of those Russian educational techniques and standards which permitted the expression in ridiculous terms of the legends and early poetry of Russia. But actually from an experiential viewpoint Mendele is showing the psychological rebellion of the Jewish youth who, against his will, was taken from his own spiritual world to an entirely new world. One hundred and ten years ago there existed in Odessa a school, under the guidance of the *Maskil* Beezalel Stern, in which modern Hebrew literature was studied. Among the teachers was Simha Pinsker, and among the subjects were the writings of Samuel David Luzzatto, Isaac Baer Levenson, and the like, along with those of the newer Hebrew poets. In private corrrespondence and correspondence found in newspapers from the 1850's and 1860's, there is ample testimony to the way education was deprived of modern Hebrew elements and the distress this caused in the hearts of individuals, many echoes being preserved in Jewish literature.

The elegy of Isaac Ichal on the decline of the Hebrew language in Germany, *The History of the Pioneer* by Isaac Erter with his dreams of the revival of Hebrew, and the dirge of J. L. Gordon in his poem "For Whom Do I Labor?", all express the sadness of those who constantly experienced the "covenant of the generations" both culturally and traditionally, and whose souls at the same time yearned for a completely new way of life. Also in this circle there arose the individual immigrants who gave new form and quality to the re-establishment of Israel.

It is no accident that the immigration in the 1890's and at the turn of the century was from Russia, at a time when the Russian literature and Russian Jewish schools put pressure upon Jewish education, even in the villages of the Pale of Settlement. The novel *Against the Stream* by Isaiah Bershadski gives only a meager picture of this background. The influence of the Emancipation was not limited to those localities where Jews enjoyed equality, but was also felt where Jews had not as yet achieved legal and civil rights. Even in those countries Jews participated in the struggle for general cultural and political freedom, and to that extent participated in the general life of the state and its society. If Moses Hess was the first Jew in the West who sensed the restrictions placed by the realities of the Exile upon the social creativity of the Jewish group, thousands and tens of thousands sensed it in the East. Paradoxically, the effort to rebuild society generally and the depth of the current social ferment made many Jews aware of the Jewish reality for the first time, and stirred them to readiness for future events.

6

But perhaps the most significant factor in the rebirth of Israel was the independent nature which characterized the new settlement. Independence is never achieved save through independence. Historical experience taught the Jews that it was impossible to maintain inner independence unless their inner lives were free. The words of Hillel, "If I be not for myself who shall be for me?" which Pinsker proclaimed as a slogan of the Love of Zion movement, contained profound political wisdom, and were not only a theoretical truth but also a fundamental guiding force in all the endeavors to which the Zionist movement was dedicated. A high Turkish official, Rauf-al-Rauf, expressed his opposition to the Jewish resettlement: "The Jews enter the land, acquire properties, build settlements, establish schools, all as though there were no Turkish government, as though the land were already in their possession. Is there really no need," he queried, "to ask us, to have us join their program? Has the Land of Israel already been taken from us and given to the Jews?" Rauf-al-Rauf understood the true political significance of the Jewish efforts far better than did the Jewish statesmen and savants who mocked the attempts of the Lovers of Zion to nullify the political *status quo*.

This independence was prevalent in the *Aliyah*, in the resettlement, and in the *Haganah;* and to all these the past experiences of Jewish life were applied. To the area of economic life the Jews in Israel transferred all the experience acquired in the countries where they had lived. From the very beginning of the resettlement they established their own self-government; set up councils and executive committees, land registries, courts of law, and ordinances; founded kindergartens, elementary schools, high schools; and opened schools of education and higher learning. All of this they accomplished by themselves.

Out of inner deliberations and discussions and without any interference on the part of government, they utilized both their individual and collective experience, and thereby constantly renewed their social creativity, which for the first time was being given opportunity for full expression and implementation.

This was plain with the *Haganah*. The people did not rely solely on the government for security, but learned to fall back on their own experience and utilized that of Jewish soldiers who had served in the armies of various countries and in various wars—the Franco-Prussian War, the Russo-Turkish War, the Russo-Japanese War, the First World War, the Russian Civil War, and the revolutionary underground. In this way they established means for their own protection, in this way the *Shomer* (the Jewish Militia) was organized, and in this way—from their own experiences—the *Haganah*, a national underground army, was made up of tens of thousands of disciplined volunteers. In this way factories and war industries were established underground. In this way an "illegal" navy was created which transported "illegal" immigrants, and a system of secret air transit was organized to bring additional immigrants. Jews who had fought in the Second World War with the Allied Armies, with the United States Air Force, in Britain, North Africa, and so on, took part in all these efforts. And all around them widespread segments of the people mobilized and grouped together—particularly after the destruction of European Jewry.

To sum up: the political rebirth of Israel is the very essence of Jewish history. She absorbed into herself the experiences and activities of generations, the covenant of generations. She renewed the covenant with the Land out of a longing, through the creation of a new community, to develop the covenant of Man into a World Covenant.

NOTES

[1a See below Oscar I. Janowsky, "The Rise of the State of Israel."]

[2a See above Israel Halpern, "The Jews in Eastern Europe (From Ancient Times until the Partitions of Poland, 1772-1795)"; Bernard D. Weinryb, "East European Jewry (Since the Partitions of Poland, 1772-1795)"; Abraham Menes, "Patterns of Jewish Scholarship in Eastern Europe"; below Hillel Bavli, "The Modern Renaissance of Hebrew Literature"; Yudel Mark, "Yiddish Literature."]

CHAPTER 13

ERETZ YISRAEL UNDER OTTOMAN RULE, 1517-1917

By Itzhak Ben-Zvi

From the Jewish point of view the period of Turkish rule differed greatly from that of the Mamelukes which preceded it. As the reign of the Mamelukes drew toward a close, the Jewish communities in Palestine were declining steadily. The sporadic influx of Jewish immigration from the east and west, quickly absorbed into the tiny Palestinian community, proved unable to re-invigorate the *Yishuv* (the Palestinian Jewish community). Counterbalanced by an excess of current Jewish emigration, the spiritual and material condition of the community deteriorated and presented a picture of steady disintegration.

The instability of the Mameluke regime and its attitude toward Jews were not designed to attract the Spanish exiles, victims of Moslem and Christian persecution for many generations. However, the most recent developments had been initiated by the church and by a Christian regime. The general expulsion forced Spanish Jewry to seek refuge in other lands, particularly in those where they hoped to find economic security and religious freedom. The so-called "Western" lands—that is, North Africa—were nearest to Spain, and for lack of any alternative that is where the exiles went. But even there they found no rest. Many found safe harbor in Turkey, where Sultan Bayazid welcomed their immigration which concentrated in the cities of the Balkans and Asia Minor. Only a few went to Egypt and Palestine, then under Mameluke domination.

It was surely the misfortune of the *Yishuv* and of the Spanish exiles that their expulsion came about fifty years before the conquest of Palestine and Syria by the armies of Sultan Selim. It is tempting to speculate what the *Yishuv* might have become had this conquest preceded the expulsion of the 300,000 Jews from the Iberian Peninsula. Tens of thousands of those who found haven in Turkey and Morocco might instead have settled in Judea and Galilee, the energy they invested in the establishment of new communities in Turkey—in Salonica, Constantinople, Izmir, Adrianople, etc.—might have gone into the upbuilding of Jerusalem, the reclamation of Galilee, and the development of the Lake Kinneret region. But Palestine was under Mameluke rule, and there was little contact between Europe, on the one hand, and Palestine and Egypt, on the other. At the same time, the Jews found conditions in Turkey favorable to the re-establishment of their communal life, and there they struck roots. When the Turks conquered Palestine, few of the Jewish immigrants were inspired to uproot themselves once more to go to the Holy Land.

Yet an incipient movement of immigration was discernible immediately after the Ottoman conquest of Palestine. The movement which began in Turkey, embraced but a small fraction of the Spanish exiles who came by thousands rather than tens of thousands. But even this trickle was sufficient to advance and consolidate the *Yishuv*, in a manner unparalleled for many centuries. This "mass" immigration continued for two or three generations, till the end of the sixteenth century. It brought to Palestine the children and grandchildren of the Spanish and Portuguese exiles, immigrants from various sections of the Ottoman empire and North Africa—Jews and Marranos—and also immigrants from Italy and the Germanic states. The movement which began in the sixteenth century continued by waves for more than two centuries after the Spanish expulsion, bringing to the shores of Palestine entirely new elements which changed the face of the *Yishuv* demographically, spiritually, and economically. Among them were men and women of enterprise and energy, laborers, craftsmen, merchants and scholars. Many of them were filled with Messianic enthusiasm and the yearning for Redemption. They brought with them the talents, initiative, experience, and capital necessary for developing industry and trade. They founded institutions of learning, established factories, and generally revealed horizons unknown to the "*Musta'rabim*," the Jews who had lived in the land since before the Arab conquest and had never gone into exile. The newcomers also conducted successful experiments in fishing, especially on Lake Kinneret, and established plantations and small farm settlements in Lower Galilee and the hills of Upper Galilee.

There was also a spurt of activity in the spiritual sphere. Outstanding scholars appeared in Jerusalem and Safed, and the land became a religious and spiritual center whose light illumined the farthest corners of the Diaspora. In the larger towns Jewry began to organize itself along new lines, similar to the advanced communities of Spain. The rule of Mameluke-appointed "Elders" was replaced by a more democratic communal organization with autonomy of jurisdiction. The problem of valid rabbinic ordination arose, and new communal institutions, among them many academies for the study of halakic and mystical lore, were founded.

To be sure, the Ottoman regime did not encourage or direct the immigration, but neither did it hinder in any way. The three great Sultans, Selim I (1512-1520), Suleiman the Magnificent (1520-1566), and Selim II (1566-1575), did not interfere with Jewish immigration or with the affairs of the *Yishuv*, which, like the Christian minorities throughout Turkey, enjoyed autonomy, but unlike the Christians suffered relatively little discrimination, so that from time to time some of its members attained high government office.

In the present essay I do not wish to describe merely the "passive" fate of the Jews of Palestine, but rather propose to examine the active, and creative social functioning of a stateless people in its historic homeland. The main factor in the new rise of the *Yishuv* was immigration, inspired by a national and religious renascence and by the continuity of the ties that bound Diaspora Jewry to their homeland from which they had been banished many generations before. The period under discussion was marked by an unprecedented, vigorous effort to repopulate Palestine with Jews. The desire to return to the Holy Land was not collective; it was the personal desire of numerous individuals. Yet this immigration was the prime factor that determined the destiny of the *Yishuv* and the character of the land during the Ottoman period, as in every other period. As the tide of immigration rose the *Yishuv* gained strength, and as also the tide ebbed and ceased, the *Yishuv* correspondingly diminished and degenerated. Yet the period is also characterized by a remarkable economic endeavor. Many immigrants sought to develop commerce by exploiting their contacts in West and East, and by establishing new trades, industries, and even agriculture with the talent and experience they had acquired in the Diaspora, especially in such advanced areas as the Iberian Peninsula from which they had been banished only a generation earlier.

Finally there was the development of spiritual and cultural life which stemmed from the desire to establish Palestine once more as the center of the nation, and to lead there an independent life. Rabbinical courts were appointed, educational and social welfare institutions were founded, and judicial bodies were established to promulgate authoritative communal legislation, enforced by common consent. A Hebrew printing press, the first in the Middle East, was established in Safed. Especially noteworthy is one of the first attempts at self-defense by the *Yishuv*—the erection in Safed of a Jewish citadel against marauders.

This situation, which prevailed during most of the first century after the Ottoman conquest, changed completely during the reign of Murad III (1575-1595). In the wake of the internal and external wars which ravaged the Asiatic part of the empire in particular, public order as well as the economy deteriorated and finally collapsed. Both life and property, especially that of the recent immigrants, were at the mercy of predatory officials. It was then—during the third and fourth generations after the Spanish expulsion—that immigration ceased almost completely. The *Yishuv* quickly regressed to its state under the Mameluke rule prior to the Turkish conquest.

The deterioration of the Jewish situation throughout Eastern Europe in the seventeenth century brought further hardship to the *Yishuv*. The aid which had flowed from the Diaspora ceased as a result of persecution and pogroms, and immigration came to a standstill. Instead there began a slow but steady emigration from Palestine to Egypt and Constantinople and to other cities of Asia Minor and the Balkans.

The end of the seventeenth century witnessed a new renascence inspired by one of the greatest Messianic movements in Jewish history. The movement which arose in the latter half of the seventeenth century among Turkish Jewry left its mark on many subsequent generations. Centering around a young cabbalist by name of Sabbatai Zevi,[1a] it drew considerably upon the Lurianic Cabbala of Safed and proclaimed a redemption that would be effected by mystical means. The results of this movement, whose motto was the redemption of the Jewish people, were the very opposite of its high hopes: it turned into a false messianism and not only failed to effect any radical reform in Jewish life or bring about the unification of the various elements of Jewry, but actually led to a degeneration of Jewish life, to apostasy, dissension, and despair, and even to a collapse of the economic position which the Jews of the Turkish empire had achieved in Turkey proper and in Egypt, Syria, and Palestine.

True, in the wake of the Sabbataian movement and impelled by the hope of supernatural redemption which it had inspired, there came to Palestine small groups of immigrants from Poland, Italy, Morocco, and other Mediterranean lands. But unlike the Spanish exiles in the early years of the Ottoman conquest, few of these immigrants struck roots in the country. The Sabbataian immigration differed from previous ones both in composition and size, and the episode ended in a stampede of the Sabbataians out of the country.

But once more "the strength of Israel did not lie" (I Samuel 15:29). When the messianic illusion had spent itself in the mid-eighteenth century, immigration to Palestine of those who hoped for redemption by natural means recommenced, and new settlement attempts were made. The activities of Rabbi Hayim Abulafia and his disciples in Tiberias, Rabbi Solomon Abbadi at Kfar Yasif, and Rabbi Hayim ben Ater and his group in Jerusalem, all in the early eighteenth century, are well known. They were followed by the "first Hasidim" and the disciples of the Baal Shem Tob from Poland and Russia, who settled in Galilee; and then, early in the nineteenth century, by the disciples of the Gaon of Vilna, who were the first Jews to go to Jerusalem after the destruction of the Ashkenazic community there about a century earlier. This movement marked the dawn of a new era, characterized by a slow but steady and systematic growth of the *Yishuv* which continued up to the days of Hibbat Zion and political Zionism and which culminated with the War of Liberation, and the establishment of the State of Israel.

Jerusalem at the Time of Rabbi Obadiah and the Nagid Rabbi Isaac Shulel

Toward the end of the Mameluke reign, the Jewish community of Jerusalem was impoverished by the heavy taxes collected by the community elders under pressure from the Mameluke officials. The burdensome poll tax was levied on the community as a whole rather than on its individual members. In the mid-fifteenth century it was raised to 400 ducats annually, over and above the wine tax of fifty ducats paid the governor of the city. Many of the more wealthy men and scholars opposed the current system of taxation as particularly unfavorable to them and began to leave the city. Among those who left was Jonathan Hakohen Shulel, who was later Nagid (head of Jewry) in Egypt. Rabbi Obadiah of Bertinoro, Italy, blamed the exodus on the notorious behavior of the community elders, but a contemporary traveler does not confirm his charges. There were certainly also other reasons for the exodus, and Rabbi Obadiah himself admits that except for the poll tax the elders levied no taxes on him (as a scholar), and in the first year did not collect even that.

A major cause of the exodus of the wealthy was undoubtedly the manner of tax collection. The government made the community leaders responsible for the poll tax. The amount was not prorated according to population, and when the population decreased the government continued to demand the full amount. The government appointed a "Vice Nagid" of Jerusalem, Rabbi Meshullam ben Menahem of Volterra. He, in turn, appointed five "Sheikh al-Yahud," or "Jewish Elders," whom he authorized to use every means they saw fit to collect the taxes.

This rule of Jewish Elders aggravated the situation. As the exodus of the wealthy Jerusalemites continued, the full burden of the taxes fell on those who remained, most of them poor. By the 1480's the Jewish community of Jerusalem had fallen low indeed. As early as 1481 Rabbi Meshullam counted only 250 householders in the city. This traveler while singing the praises of the Holy Land emphasized the depression that wracked it.

Rabbi Obadiah, who arrived from Italy seven years after Rabbi Meshullam, paints a depressing portrait of the decline of the *Yishuv:*

> Most of Jerusalem is desolate and in ruins; needless to say that the city has no wall. The population, I am told, numbers some 4,000 householders, but of the Jews, only seventy householders of the poorest class remain, without a source of livelihood. There is scarcely a soul with enough to eat and one who has bread for a year is considered rich. For every man there are seven aged and forsaken widows of the Ashkenazic, Sephardic, and many other communities.

Rabbi Obadiah arrived in Jerusalem in a year of famine, but he was impressed by the beauty of the city: "Amid all the ruins and desolation of

Jerusalem there are four long and beautiful bazaars, at the end of the Zion quarter, such as I have never before seen. They are all covered with cupolas and contain wares of every kind. Each occupying a separate area: the merchant's bazaar, the spice bazaar, the vegetable bazaar, and the cooked food and bread bazaar." Prices continued to rise, but the famine was soon followed by a period of plenty.

The collective poll tax was abolished in the time of Rabbi Obadiah, and payment was put on an individual basis by the Mameluke sultan. "This was a great reform in Jerusalem," Rabbi Obadiah wrote. Yet there was little improvement of the general situation of the Jewish community. The restrictions imposed by Islamic law, *e.g.*, the prohibition of building a new synagogue except to replace one that had already existed before the Arab conquest, remained in force. Jews were not even permitted to build or repair private houses or courts without a special permit that could be obtained only by bribes.

From time to time Jews were accused of transgressing Moslem law by causing Moslems to drink wine. These accusations provided the city officials with further opportunities to extort money from the Jews and impose fines on them. The Jews were forced to borrow from Moslems, at usurious rates, and when in due course, Jews could not pay, all their property was confiscated. Impoverished by the exorbitant taxes and by the methods of collection employed by the Elders, many Jews were compelled to sell their belongings. The Elders themselves sold the community's property and sacred objects, and in that way some antique Torah Scrolls were sold to Christians, who resold them in Europe. In Jerusalem, according to local ordinance, the estate of anyone who died without a direct heir became community property to be administered by the Elders, who claimed that they used it for repaying public debts, such as those contracted for the building of a synagogue. The community, however, generally suspected the Elders of appropriating the money for themselves after pacifying the creditors and the officials by letting them share in the spoils.

In the end the strenuous efforts of Rabbi Obadiah brought about an improvement. Jerusalem recovered its former reputation, and once more the city began to attract immigrants, especially from the Spanish and Portuguese refugees. Within seven years the population doubled and trebled, and by 1496 it numbered some 1,600 souls.

Jerusalem also enjoyed a spiritual revival, and before long the Holy *Yeshiva* was re-established. From a letter sent in 1504 by the scholars of Safed to the heads of the Jerusalem *Yeshiva*, we learn that the former recognized the primacy of Jerusalem, and the fact that the law goes forth from Zion. The Jerusalem scholars had rendered a decision concerning the Sabbatical Year without consulting their colleagues in Safed. The latter, though feeling slighted, yet admitted: "Indeed we shall be called the priests of the Lord, and you are found written among the living in Jerusalem (Is. 4:3); you are in the van of the battle of the Lord, servants in His habitation, and His portion and His inheritance. The bread of holiness is the lot of each of you," but protested that consideration should also be given to the opinions of "the fledgling sheep of the holy community of Safed that is in Upper Galilee," for "we are not men of no account."

The communal reform continued after the death of Rabbi Obadiah (*c.* 1500) until the Ottoman conquest. The text of the new regulations has been preserved for us by Rabbi Moses Bassola of Mantua (1522), who copied them from a bulletin board of the Jerusalem synagogue. One of the most important reforms, designed to encourage scholarship, exempted professional scholars, even those who were well-to-do, from all taxes except the poll tax. Disputes between the community and scholars claiming exemptions could not be judged in Jerusalem but had to be brought before the Nagid in Egypt. The reform, promulgated toward the end of the Mameluke period, remained in force also under Ottoman rule.

The author of the measure appears to have been the Nagid, Rabbi Isaac Hakohen Shulel, in 1509. It was signed by the four Jewish communities in Jerusalem: *Musta'rabic*, Sephardic, North African, and Ashkenazic. This ordinance, clearly intended to attract scholars from the Diaspora to Jerusalem and to make it into a center of learning, was confirmed many times in the course of the sixteenth century and after. All ordinances of a communal nature during this period were promulgated by the Rabbis and leaders of the community, subject to the confirmation of the Nagid and his rabbinical court in Egypt.

From the reports of Rabbi Bassola (1522), it appears that the general condition of Jewish Jerusalem improved somewhat after the Spanish expulsion. One of the city's four bazaars was occupied by Jews, most of them spice merchants. Rabbi Bassola mentions three gates by Mt. Zion, of which one was controlled by Jews: "A Jew guards it [the gate in the wall]—opening and closing it." The city had one synagogue, but the community comprised four subcommunities: the Ashkenazic, which numbered fifteen families, descendants of the Ashkenazim who had lived there since the time of Nahmanides and who were later joined by other European immigrants (at that time Italian Jews were still considered Ashkenazim); Sephardim, *i.e.*, the Spanish and Portuguese exiles—who constituted the majority; the North African immigrants, known as "the Westerners"; and the *Musta'rabim* or "Morescos," descendants of the ancient inhabitants of the country who had never gone into exile. All four groups were represented among the judges and scholars of the community and occasionally disputes arose among them concerning religious customs, questions of liturgy, and the like. Before the conquest, the *Musta'rabim* were the dominant group.

By then the community of Jerusalem numbered about 300 families, in addition to more than 150 widows who were exempt from tax. Some 200 souls lived off public charity, provided by the community through special funds sent for this purpose from Turkey, Egypt, and other lands of the Diaspora. After Rabbi Obadiah's death, the community was headed by the Nagid, Rabbi Isaac Hakohen Shulel, a North African who went to Palestine via Egypt. The Ottoman record of the affairs of the Jewish community in 1525-1526 lists a population of 199 bachelors only, but we may assume that this "census" did not cover all of Jewish Jerusalem.

The Early Exiles in Safed

Let us now turn from Jerusalem to Galilee, and particularly to Safed, which at that time had the largest population of all Palestinian cities.

Rabbi Joseph de Montagna, an Italian immigrant who visited Safed in 1481, reported that it was "a fine community, with 300 householders including those of the surrounding villages which are within its limits." Kfar Kana (near Nazareth) then had some "seventy worthy householders, especially one named Isaac, who is a learned man." In both places the heads and the rabbinic judges of the community showed respect for scholarship and urged Rabbi Joseph to stay, promising him exemption from taxation.

A more detailed picture is given by an anonymous traveler, a disciple of Rabbi Obadiah, who visited Safed in 1495. According to his report:

> The land is good and rich and the water is excellent. In very truth, I saw men much older than sixty or seventy years, including one old man of 130, and he was still in the prime of life . . . The holy community numbers some 300 householders, and most of the Jews keep shops with spices, cheese, oil, legumes and fruit. I have heard that such a shop with a capital of twenty-five ducats can provide a livelihood for five people. Food is cheap, and the head of the community is Rabbi Perez Colombo . . . He was gracious to us, praising us and asking us to stay with him, offering to teach us for twelve ducats annually each if we wished to settle there. The community provides his needs, I forget the sum. However he keeps a food shop for a living.

This traveler mentions the Jewish settlement at Kfar Kana only in passing. Because of the dangerous roads in the Jezreel region, his brother remained behind to guard the effects of the caravan; we may surely assume that it was in a Jewish settlement that he was left. Also Rabbi Obadiah, who states that he never visited Galilee, reports having heard that "the Jews of Safed, Kfar Kana, and everywhere in Galilee dwell in peace and security, and they do not suffer at the hands of the Arabs, most of them, though, are poor, putting up in the villages, peddling from door to door and in the countryside to seek their bread."

The campaign of the leaders of the Safed community to attract scholars was successful. In 1504, only a few years after the visit of the anonymous traveler, Safed already harbored a group of scholars who would sign the aforementioned letter of protest to Jerusalem in connection with the Sabbatical Year. Rabbi Perez, still alive at the time, was not among the signatories, but on the other hand we find new names, among which that of Rabbi Joseph ben Abraham al-Saracosti (of Saragossa), the teacher of Rabbi David ibn Abi Zimra (Radbas). Several of the signatories were *Musta'rabim* and some were North Africans, but most were Spanish and Portuguese exiles. To be sure, the holiness of the land had attracted many Jews from Spain even before the final expulsion, especially the Marranos, who came to Jerusalem and Hebron to do penance for their past lives. Rabbi Obadiah observed that half the Jews of Hebron were of Marrano stock; there were some in Jerusalem also, but most had fled the city because of their treatment by the Elders. Of his students, Rabbi Obadiah singles out "two Sephardic students who study with [him] regularly." Some of the Sephardic scholars who had left Jerusalem may well have gone to Safed.

Indeed, as already noted, the scholars of Safed did not consider themselves inferior to the scholars of Jerusalem, or as "men of no account." For the fixing of the Sabbatical Year they relied chiefly on "the testimonies of our elders and sages concerning the custom of our region." This was not merely a theoretical dispute, but a practical issue for the Jewish farmers in the Galilean villages, about whom more will be said presently.

More details about the Galilean settlements of which Rabbi Obadiah had heard, can be gleaned from reports written several years after the Ottoman conquest.

While the Jews of Jerusalem were not affected by the Ottoman invasion, those of Safed suffered heavily. The retreating Mameluke forces attacked them and the Arabs of the surrounding villages used the opportunity to set upon the Jews and despoil them. They abandoned everything and fled for their lives to hide in the fields. The Jews of Egypt sent them clothing and more than 3,000 gold florins. Rabbi Nissan Biba, who organized the aid, went to Safed to help rehabilitate the victims. By the time Rabbi Bassola arrived in Safed five years after the conquest, the flourishing city showed no signs that it had been sacked but recently.

The Ottoman conquest did not affect the size or composition of Jewish Safed. This is attested by the government roll of taxpayers which was prepared in 1525-1526 and which mentions four Jewish quarters:

Musta'rabim Quarter		130	householders
Frank	"	40	"
Portuguese	"	21	"
North African	"	33	"
Total		224	"

Bearing in mind that the roster of inhabitants was not always drawn up very carefully, that the first census had been far from accurate, and that the numbers mentioned by the various travelers were only estimates, we find that all the numbers roughly agree, especially if we take into account that the roll did not list the bachelors. This number did not change for a long time, no doubt because natural decrease was offset from time to time by incoming Spanish exiles. The immigration of Spanish exiles to Safed reached its peak after the Ottoman conquest.

The Galilean Villages

There was no material change in the situation of the Galilean villages from the end of Mameluke rule to the period under review. The two sources already referred to enable us to understand better the character of these settlements.

1. *Ein Zeitun.* Rabbi Bassola found some forty Morescan (that is, *Musta'rabim*) householders when he visited there. The government roll listed forty-two. The village *Waqf* had a property of 400 olive trees in memory of Rabbi Judah bar Ilai and his son Rabbi José. It may be inferred from this that Jews owned land, and certainly that they tended these trees.

2. *Biriya* had an old Jewish community, though Rabbi Bassola did not mention it. This is evident from the similarity of some local customs to those of Ein Zeitun—both differing from the Sephardic custom in such matters as the Torah reading on the two days of Purim. The government roll listed nineteen families.

3. At *Alma,* north of Ras el Ahmar, there was a Jewish agricultural settlement of fifteen families.

4. Rabbi Bassola mentioned the presence of Jews at *Bukiah.* The government roll listed thirty-three Jewish families there. Another settlement existed at nearby *Ein Tiraya.*

5. Forty families are mentioned as living at *Kfar Kana;* the government roll listed fifty. Rabbi Bassola decribed this place as a market town which brought "great profit to the Jews."

6. *Kfar Hananiah* (Kfar Anan) was then the site of a Jewish settlement of thirty families, comprising largely Morescan *Kohanim,* who were most certainly farmers. The government roll listed only fourteen families.

7. *Kfar Yasif* (1525-1535), near Acre, certainly had a Jewish settlement. Rabbi Bassola did not mention it and the first census did not include Jews, but the census of 1535-1539 mentioned ten Jewish householders. The village was mentioned in contemporary *responsa.* Rabbi Moses the Judge, head of the Safed *yeshiva,* in 1507-1509 was a student at Kfar Yasif.

8. From the Constantinople archives we know of Jewish settlements at *Shefaram* and *Kabul* at the foot of Mt. Carmel. The government roll of

1525-1526 listed three Jewish families at Shefaram, while the census of 1533-1539 listed ten householders. The first census listed no Jews at Kabul, but five families were registered in the second roll.

The existence of a rural population clearly indicates why the question of the Sabbatical Year was of such practical importance in Galilee. Rabbis Obadiah and Bassola mentioned peddlers and merchants who toured the Galilean villages. It is almost certain that the villagers raised everything they needed, and that the merchants operated supplementary farms in addition to their produce businesses. The growth of this rural population in the sixteenth century kept the problem acute even after 1504, and caused scholars to re-examine it from time to time.

Let us now review some of the smaller settlements, outside Galilee.

Other Settlements

At the time of the Crusades and during the Mameluke era, there were several Jewish settlements along the southern coast of Palestine, such as Rafiah, Gaza, and Ashkelon. However, by the time of the Ottoman invasion only the Gaza settlement remained, though no mention of it was made by Rabbi Bassola. The Jews of Gaza apparently supported themselves mainly by trading with the Egyptians, though several were landowners. The Turkish invasion did not affect them adversely, for they certainly did not side with the Mamelukes. The government roll listed ninety-five Jewish and twenty-five Samaritan families.

The Jewish community of Gaza dated back to the time of the Second Temple and is mentioned in the Talmud; its uninterrupted continuity throughout the Arab and Mameluke eras is further attested by the ancient "*Minhag* Gaza custom." In 1481, toward the end of the Mameluke era, Rabbi Meshullam praised the city's natural setting and its produce, and noted that only the Jews engaged in wine production. According to him, Gaza had some sixty Jewish and four Samaritan householders. He mentioned the beautiful little synagogue and named some of the local scholars who extended their hospitality to him. Rabbi Obadiah, who visited Gaza seven years after Rabbi Meshullam, reported that the head of the community was an Ashkenazi, Rabbi Moses of Prague, who had escaped from the persecution of the Mameluke-appointed Jewish Elders in Jerusalem. Rabbi Meshullam also reported that some of the Gaza Jews engaged in farming. The Jewish community of Gaza and the small Samaritan community persisted for about another 300 years until the Napoleonic era.

There are no adequate data on the Jewish community in *Jaffa* during the Mameluke period, though we have some information on the Samaritan community. *Caesarea* had a sparse Jewish settlement which traded with the villagers and the mountain dwellers. There was a more important and better established settlement at Hebron, city of the Patriarchs. It numbered some twenty families at the time of Rabbi Obadiah and only ten in 1522, but the ancient synagogue attests the permanency of this settlement. The register of 1525-1526 listed no Jews in Hebron. *Nablus* had about a dozen Jewish families before the conquest, all *Musta'rabim*, as well as a synagogue, though the first Ottoman census listed no Jews, or even Samaritans, in the city. We might also mention here the twenty Jewish families living in Sidon, near Beirut, in the Lebanon.

The Conquest

The conquest of Palestine in 1517 by Sultan Selim was welcomed with enthusiasm by the Jews as it seemed to spell hope for the improvement of their lot and of the general condition of the land. The friendly attitude of the Turkish rulers to the Spanish exiles seemed to justify the hope that the annexation of Palestine to Turkey would raise Palestinian Jewry from the depth to which it had fallen under Mameluke rule to the status enjoyed by Jews throughout the Ottoman empire. It also created an opportunity for strengthening the *Yishuv* by a more vigorous influx of Spanish exiles.

The Jews of Palestine could not openly express their attitude to the Ottoman invasion while they yet lived in terror of their Egyptian rulers. But the Jews of Turkey saw a good augury for all Jewry in the conquest of Palestine by Sultan Selim. A chronicler of the period writes: "And a mighty king shall rule them,"—the word "mighty" [whose numerical value in Hebrew is 77] signifies the conquest of Palestine in the year five thousand two hundred and *seventy-seven* [-1516/7 C.E.], whereas the letters of the Hebrew word for "shall rule" are the same as those constituting the name "Selim." There were Jews in Selim's army, some of high rank, such as the physician Moses Hamon. It may be assumed that the presence of Jews in the Ottoman army was ignored neither by the Jews of Palestine nor by the Arabs, who used this as an excuse to incite the Mamelukes against the Jews in Egypt proper, and—at a later period —also in several Palestinian cities.

The Egyptians accused the Jews of pro-Turkish sympathies, and the masses, incited by the Mamelukes, marched on the Jewish quarter of Cairo to sack it. But in what is perhaps the first example of Jewish self-defense in the Orient in modern times, the Jews of Cairo put up an armed resistance for several days and finally drove off the mob.

The Turkish conquest of Palestine at last opened the gates for a large-scale immigration of Spanish exiles. However, in the twenty-five years between the Spanish expulsion and the conquest, the exiles had already settled too well in Salonica, Constantinople, and other Turkish cities. Very probably many would have gone directly to Palestine, had not political frontiers prevented them. But then at least they were all united under one flag with the Jews of Syria, Palestine, and Egypt, and one great Ottoman Jewry was created. Security in Palestine improved, sea travel became safe, and a new, chiefly Spanish-Portuguese immigration began to arrive. The Sephardim re-invigorated the old *Yishuv* that had subsisted in Palestine since the time of the Crusades and even since the first Arab conquest, and stamped their character upon it. The immigrants brought with them new spiritual and material energies, outstanding scholars and leaders, and commercial talents which created an economic prosperity that lasted for several generations. The immigrants concentrated in Safed and Jerusalem, but also settled in other areas of the country. It is certain that not only Sephardim but also Ashkenazim from Central Europe and Poland and Jews from Italy and North Africa again began to settle in Palestine.

HOPES OF REDEMPTION

In Judea and Samaria

The Turkish conquest aroused new hope for the *Yishuv,* hope which directed the steps of the Spanish exiles to Zion. This hope was epitomized in the visions of Rabbi Abraham ben Eliezer Halevi, one of the first Spanish immigrants who had already settled in Palestine in the Mameluke period. He arrived in Palestine, via Greece, Turkey, and Egypt, at the same time that Rabbi Isaac Shulel came from Egypt or perhaps slightly earlier. There is definite documentary evidence that Rabbi Abraham lived in Jerusalem from 1516 to 1528.

Rabbi Abraham Halevi was famous as a scholar and author before he went to Palestine. In Jerusalem, where he was at once admitted into the circle of leading scholars, he found hearts receptive to his message of "repentance" in preparation for the final Redemption. By his enthusiastic activity he infused into the people the expectation of imminent redemption. His writings, which also contain important historical information on the period, give a clear picture of the mood and yearnings of his generation. Rabbi Abraham saw Christianity as the enemy of Judaism and counted heavily on the defeat of Christianity and the victory of Islam. In the downfall of Byzantium and the capture of Constantinople by the Ottomans in 1453 he saw the harbingers of redemption, and expansion of the Ottoman empire in the time of Selim I seemed to augur the imminent collapse of "the kingdom of Edom." Rabbi Abraham's commentary on *The Prophecy of the Child Nahman ben Pinhas* of the village of Biram, an apocalypse written just before Selim's conquest of Palestine, is full of prophecies concerning the "End," the visitations that would take place in 1522, 1524, or 1525, and the appearance of the Messiah in 1530 or 1531. When the first dates passed without event, Rabbi Abraham, in a letter of 1525, tried to rationalize: "It may well be that redemption came in 1524, though it is not yet known to us. How so? My heart tells me that the children of Reuben and of several other tribes left their places in that year and that some of their brethren were delivered by them."

We also know of steps taken by the members of the Jerusalem *Yeshiva* to prepare themselves for the final Redemption. They fixed vigils for penitence and the study of Cabbala: Rabbi Isaac Shulel, too, seems to have participated in these mystical preparations. Rumors spread concerning miraculous occurrences, such as the collapse of pillars in the Dome of the Rock and the skewing of the crescent on the roof of the Dome. Letters were dispatched from Jerusalem to the Ten Tribes and to the Sons of Moses who had waged victorious war against "Prester John" and were now preparing to conquer Palestine by storm. These rumors, which spread in the countries nearby, fanned the desire to immigrate to Palestine from Egypt and other neighboring lands to behold the imminent Ingathering of the Exiles and final Redemption.

Among prophets of Redemption there were also some who expected the spectacular downfall of Moslem rule. Quite naturally the spokesman of this version was a Jew hailing from a Moslem country. In 1523 David Reubeni visited Palestine and told of the existence of the "Lost Tribes of Israel" beyond the Mountains of Kush. He had with him a plan for the liberation of Palestine by a confederation of the Tribes with the rulers of Europe. At the same time the Portuguese Marrano, Solomon Molkho, appeared and preached his own version of apocalypse. According to some reports, Molkho passed through Damascus, Safed, and Jerusalem in 1525, enthusiastically proclaiming that Redemption would come in 1540. These two heralds made a profound impression on the Jews of Safed and Jerusalem, many of whom began to repent and to prepare themselves by ascetic exercises for the coming Redemption. However, Rabbi Levi ibn Habib (Ralbah), the Rabbi of Jerusalem, a veteran of bitter experience in the lands of the Inquisition, called all these fantastic messages "the tidings of fools" and fought them vigorously.

Rabbi Levi, mainly remembered for his opposition to the renewal of ordination, was born in 1484 in Zamora, Spain. In his youth he experienced the Expulsion and the Portuguese Inquisition, and at the age of fourteen he arrived in Salonica with his father, Rabbi Jacob ben Habib (author of *Ein yaakob*). Rabbi Levi soon won distinction among the scholars of Salonica, where he became the head of the *yeshiva* of the Castilian community. In 1525 he went to Jerusalem where he soon succeeded Rabbi Isaac Shulel as Chief Rabbi. Rabbi Jacob concerned himself not only with the spiritual affairs of the community but was also active in improving difficult material conditions. He fought the established practice whereby the Elders seized the estates of those who died without heirs in Palestine, and decreed that all wills must be witnessed by a recognized rabbinical judge.

The impact of the growing immigration to Palestine was already felt. The immigrants concentrated in Safed and Jerusalem, but as a result of the different conditions obtaining in the two cities it was not the ancient and holy city Jerusalem but the young Safed that was developed by the immigrants and became the flourishing metropolis of the incoming exiles for fifty years and more.

In the early years of the Ottoman conquest the Jews were still harried by the various local authorities and by the Arab inhabitants. In a letter to Italy a writer of that period complains of high prices and of the sufferings of the Jews at the hands of their Arab neighbors.

For all its ruin and desolation the land rejoices now, but many are the false accusations they have brought against us this year so that we thought they would drive us from the land, but for the mercy of heaven. In any case this Holy Community paid 3,000 florins in three days to appease the lords of the land. A destitute community such as this cannot afford such payments, for the poverty is great. But they all borrowed at interest from the wealthy Ishmaelites, and the interest consumed them from day to day until our brethren in Egypt helped with 600 florins. In Damascus they also offered to help a little, for they have also suffered, having paid 8,000 florins to the lord of the land. The Egyptians also paid 3,000. All this happened this year.

This is the first reference during the Ottoman period to loans obtained by the Jews, at high interest from their Moslem neighbors. The Jews of Egypt and Damascus were themselves in difficulties and could help their Jerusalem brethren but little this time. But according to Rabbi Moses ben Joseph di Trani, their help later increased: "For all the Holy Communities that send money to Jerusalem know that in addition to what is distributed among the scholars and the poor, they also cover whatever losses are incurred by the community, for the inhabitants of Jerusalem are unable to pay more than the annual land tax, and the other losses which they cover from the money from abroad. For if they did not do so no one would want to settle in the city."

The Jerusalem community, its scholars, and its *yeshibot* were in especially straitened circumstances. The women who worked at embroidery earned one asper per week, but this was not enough to buy even a loaf of barley bread. The little trading that was possible was limited mainly to the sale of clothing and pepper, and was in the hands of the well-to-do. The rest of the populace kept small shops or were itinerant peddlers. There were some who plied an illegal trade in saffron, which was a government monopoly. Rabbi Elijah Mizrahi (Reem) of Constantinople in a *responsum*, describes a "guild" of the Jerusalem clothing and pepper merchants: he mentions that the merchants had called a meeting at the synagogue, to hear the complaints of the shopkeepers against the peddlers who, they said, were hurting their business by hawking from door to door among the Moslems. It was agreed strictly to prohibit this practice for economic as well as security and national reasons.

For they realize that with this agreement they will avert many perils and evils which might otherwise befall, and they have seen that the gentile rulers have forbidden the Jews of larger communities than this to engage in door-to-door peddling. *It is better that we control ourselves than await the repressions and restrictions that come upon us.* And we have heard that the Holy Community of Hebron has dealt thus, and to this all our community agrees.

Among the business restrictions imposed upon the Jews mention must be made of the ban on the sale of wine to Moslems. Though their religion forbade the drinking of wine, many of them drank; the demand produced the corresponding supply and many Jews and Christians willing to cater to them. The government reacted vigorously, imposing heavy fines on the sale of wine, and prohibiting the use of wine even to Jews for a period. Wine being essential to Jews for ritual purposes, the prohibition was considered a major calamity warranting a public fast. Jews who had brought money with them and could not invest it in business lent it to Moslems, Christians, and even Jews. Rabbi Obadiah of Bertinoro mentions that he lent 100 ducats at 10 per cent interest to communities and individuals, according to a special "dispensation." Some kept their wealth outside the country and had the dividends sent to them. Rabbi Obadiah mentions that he had an income from a deposit he had left in Italy. Apparently this was also the practice of other scholars who did not wish to engage in business.

Rabbi Levi ben Habib, in his *Kuntras ha-Semikah,* described the miserable state of the Jerusalem scholars early in the sixteenth century: "Not only do the scholars of Jerusalem not eat delicacies, but they eat bitterness and woe, and whoever is fortunate enough to be able to afford to buy the head or intestines of a sheep or goat, or even a fowl, for the Sabbath and festivals accounts himself as having gone forth from the house of bondage to freedom and as having sat in the seat of the mighty."

It is not surprising, therefore, that Rabbi Jacob Berab failed in his effort to settle in Jerusalem. On the other hand, we know of the determination of the Jerusalemites to remain there even under the most difficult circumstances. In an account of Jerusalem life at the time of Rabbi Isaac Shulel we read: "A certain person vowed not to leave Jerusalem until he had spent his last penny. As his funds ran out he began to fear that in the end he might not even have enough money to leave Jerusalem and so would have to go begging. He therefore asked to have his vow annulled and the Nagid so ordered." The peculiar difficulties of Jerusalem were due in part to the hostility of the local authorities who did more to sabotage the development of the Jewish community, *e.g.*, the expansion of its *yeshibot*, the ordination of spiritual leaders, than was the case in the rural areas. The case of Rabbi David ibn Abi Zimra who came from Egypt in 1554 may serve as a good example. Upon assuming the leadership of the Jerusalem community, he encountered the opposition of the Pasha, who refused to recognize his authority and harassed Radbaz at every turn. Finally he was forced to leave Jerusalem and went to Safed. In this Jerusalem atmosphere there was little incentive for the establishment of *yeshibot* and certainly no attraction for outside scholars and students. It seems that the hostility of the authorities finally also drove from Jerusalem most of the wealthy men, who went to friendlier environments in northern Palestine. Public order and security in the city and its vicinity also left much to be desired, and in the *responsa* of that period we find many references to the murder of Jewish travelers. In one incident three merchants, making the rounds of the villages, were robbed and murdered by their Arab muleteers. Raphael, the son of Rabbi Moses Castro, was slain en route from Jerusalem to Gaza.

The reforms of Suleiman the Magnificent brought some improvement. In 1536-1542 he erected the great wall which still surrounds the Old City of Jerusalem. He built a reservoir and repaired the city's aqueducts and cisterns, so that a regular and sufficient water supply was assured. Life in general became easier. These improvements no doubt made the city more attractive and the population increased, though to a lesser degree than in Upper Galilee.

The official census of 1525-1526, as we have noted, listed 199 Jewish householders in Jerusalem. In another register, drawn up in 1533-1539, we find the following figures:

	Householders	*Bachelors*	*Total*
Sharaf Quarter	85	9	94
Maslah "	43	4	47
Raisha "	96	6	102
	224	19	243

totalling about 1,200-1,300 souls.

In 1553-1554 an increase to some 1,800 souls, *i.e.* about 50 per cent, is recorded:

	Householders	*Bachelors*	*Total*
Jerusalem (quarter not specified)	107	3	110
Maslah Quarter	79	3	82
Raisha "	138	7	145
	324	13 (plus one feeble-minded)	337 (plus one feeble-minded)

In 1586, under the tyrannical rule of the governor of Jerusalem Abu Seifin (Master of the Two Swords), the ancient synagogue (restored when Nahmanides arrived in Palestine and named after him), was confiscated from the Jews after 320 years in their possession. Already in the days of the Mamelukes, Moslem fanatics had sought unsuccessfully to gain possession of the edifice. In the time of Abu Seifin it was made into a warehouse, never to be returned to the Jews.

Even in the difficult years of the sixteenth century, Jerusalem attracted many pilgrims who came to pray at the holy places in and around it. The principal destination of the visitors was the Western Wall (the so-called "Wailing Wall"), of which the Talmud said that "the Divine Presence did not depart from it" even when the Temple was destroyed. Second to it was King David's tomb on Mt. Zion, and there were also Rachel's Tomb on the Bethlehem Road; the tombs of the prophets Samuel, Haggai, Zachariah, and Malachi around Jerusalem, the tomb of the Prophetess Hulda; the Pillar of Absalom, the Bet Hahofshit at the foot of the Mount of Olives, and many more. Occasionally a pilgrim would remain in the land and even urge his compatriots in the Diaspora to join him. In this manner the Oriental, Italian, and Ashkenazic communities were augmented by new settlers. During the sixteenth century the principal Sephardic community of Jerusalem was joined by an Ashkenazic (as indicated above, the term usually included also the Italian Jews), and a North African community, as well as by the *Musta'rabic* community, whose "forefathers never went into exile."

The Karaite community in Jerusalem, which had come from Hebron, remained unique in Palestine. The Karaites concentrated around the ancient cave which figures in the history of Anan, founder of the sect, and which served them for several centuries as a prayer place. Near the cave was what is known to this day as the Courtyard of the Karaites. They also erected a communal dwelling which was supported by contributions from Karaites in Damascus, Egypt, Constantinople, the Crimea, and Mesopotamia.

Most of the old Jewish settlements in Judea had been abandoned and only Hebron and Gaza had permanent Jewish communities. Hebron, the city of the Patriarchs, had maintained its small community since the reign of the Mamelukes.

In the middle of the sixteenth century Rabbi Malkiel Ashkenazi settled in Hebron, where he bought from the Karaites their ancient courtyard fortified by stone walls and a safe retreat in times of danger. The "Jews' Street" of Hebron was, as a matter of fact, a compound surrounded by stone houses; this ancient "ghetto" of Hebron was not abandoned until the massacre of 1929.

During the sixteenth century Hebron was not only a center for pilgrims who came to pray at the tomb of the Patriarchs, in the Cave of Makhpelah, but also the site of a modest settlement where a number of outstanding rabbis and scholars from Safed and Jerusalem sought solitude. Among these was Rabbi Elijah de Vidas, a disciple of Rabbi Isaac Luria (Ari) and author of the ascetic moralist work *Reshit Hokhmah.* He died in 1578, and pilgrims used to pray at his tomb until recently when Hebron became part of the kingdom of Jordan. There is no inscription on his or on any Jewish tombstone in Hebron. According to local Jewish tradition this is a burial custom peculiar to Hebron. Its real origin seems to have been the desire to protect the tombstones against the vandalism of local Moslem fanatics who would not brook any sign of equality in life or in death between "infidels" and "believers," and defaced all tombstones bearing Hebrew inscriptions.

Another great Safed scholar who settled in Hebron during this period was Rabbi Menahem ben Moses Bavli, author of *Taamei ha-Mitzvot* (Lublin, 1571). His arrival in 1546 seems to have been related to the movement for the restoration of Jewish life in Hebron, in which the scholars of Safed played a part. In the preface to his book Rabbi Menahem wrote that he was assigning the proceeds from its sale "to Hebron, to repair the devastation and build up the ruins."

Among the next generations of scholars to come to Hebron was Rabbi Solomon Adani, author of *Mlekhet Shlomo*, a commentary on the Mishna. Rabbi Solomon was born in Yemen in 1567. When he was four years old his parents immigrated to Safed, but soon afterward moved to Jerusalem. When he was fifteen years old his father died and Solomon entered the *yeshiva* of Rabbi Hayim Vital from Calabrese; at the age of nineteen Solomon studied under Rabbi Bezalel Ashkenazi. Several years later Solomon moved to Hebron, where he wrote his commentary on the Mishna. In the preface he mentioned the names of other scholars then living in Hebron and his *responsa* indicate that the Jews of Hebron also engaged in business and plied various crafts.

The Spanish-Portuguese immigration also strengthened the Jewish community of Gaza. Mention has already been made of a contract drawn up in Gaza in the year 1495 and brought to Rabbi Jacob of Trijal, an outstanding Spanish scholar who settled in Jerusalem. In 1553-1559, ninety-eight householders were registered in Gaza; in 1548-1549 there were 116 householders and five bachelors. However by 1555 the number had decreased to only eighty-one householders. The Jews of Gaza engaged mainly in commerce, which flourished at this crossroads of the caravan route to Egypt. There were also a number of planters, especially viniculturists.

There were several isolated groups in Samaria. A small community of Jews lived beside a Samaritan community in Nablus (Shekhem), and there is a passing reference to Jews in Ein Ganim. Caesarea, which in the time of Benjamin of Tudela harbored a large Jewish community, is also mentioned only in passing by contemporary sources.

It was chiefly the annual procession of pilgrims passing through Nablus from Upper Galilee to Jerusalem which kept a sparse Jewish settlement alive in Nablus for many generations. Another source of sustenance was the local holy places: the tombs of Joseph, of Eleazar the son of Aaron and father of Phineas on the Hill of Phineas at Avertah near Nablus, and of Joshua at Kfar Haris. Six years after the Ottoman conquest Rabbi Bassola found in Nablus a Morescan community of twelve householders, with a synagogue of its own. The official census of 1533-1539 lists seventy-one householders. Thirty-four Nablus Jews perished in the earthquake of 1546, and it is likely that some emigrated from the town, for the register of 1548-1549 lists only thirty-six householders and five bachelors.

Safed's Golden Age

The chief factor in the growth and flourishing of Jewish Safed was the stream of Spanish exiles which at this time began to reach the city. Jerusalem's economic blight and the despotism of the authorities there lowered the pre-eminence of that city during this period. Even the yearning for Redemption and the expectation of the Messiah ceased to be linked with Jerusalem. Jewish activity moved to Galilee and the community in Safed grew as commercial opportunities were opened. Fruit, wheat, sheep, and wool were exported to Damascus and to Turkey's European provinces, and Safed merchants imported from Constantinople, Syria, and other maritime lands goods to fill local needs and to supply the army. Ships laden with cargo regularly put in at Beirut and Tripoli and, later on, at Sidon, Acre, and Haifa.

Set in fertile country, Safed was surrounded by many agricultural villages. In 1549 a wall was built to protect the city against enemies and marauders. By then there were twelve or thirteen Jewish settlements in Galilee, three urban and the others rural, which were in close contact with settlements in Syria and the Lebanon. There were also normal and regular relations with the urban and rural Arabs of the vicinity.

The new immigrants were no longer exclusively the aged wanting to live out their years in the Holy Land or pilgrims, but also wealthy merchants with widespread interests. Among them were some slave traders. One source tells of an Egyptian Jew who traded eighty-five male and female slaves in addition to sugar, rice, and paper, in Tripoli for other merchandise which he sent back to Egypt. Another merchant brought gems and spices to Safed.

The immigrant merchants adjusted well to life in Palestine, engaging in wholesale and retail trade and in itinerant peddling. Many became money brokers, dealing especially in gold and silver. They had a special market place called the Caga Bazaar. The coin of the realm was the florin, sometimes called the "Shulal florin," after the Nagid Shulal who had been master of the mint in Egypt, the "Sultanic florin," etc. The brokers used to "fix the rate of exchange according to the business value of the florins, whose general value was approximately one silver piece more than when purchased from a broker. The Sultanic florin was then worth in Safed thirty-nine aspers and forty in business." The brokers also engaged hired help.

There was also a special farmer's bazaar with spice, cheese, oil, legume, fruit, and grocery shops. Local agriculture largely consisted of planting, especially viniculture and wine manufacture.

Another huge bazaar specialized in clothing and indigo linen. In addition to the large wholesale wool and clothing shops and warehouses, this bazaar also had sewing, weaving, dyeing, and tailoring workshops. Similar shops existed undoubtedly for the other Safed craftsmen. The city also had "coffeehouses" which remained open well into the night. Night watchmen, "bazaar police," guarded the shops against burglars. Fulling mills were established whose brand, "Batan," was famous everywhere. They also supplied uniforms to the army in Syria, Damascus, and Northern Syria. This brand was in great demand in the important markets of Turkey, Salonica, Smyrna, Constantinople, Wallachia, Alexandria, and even in such a flourishing commercial city as Venice. One fulling mill, belonging to Rabbi Judah Abulafia, stood at the foot of the mountain on which the city is situated. Once a year Turkish ships brought the wool to Trabulus or Sidon; its color was usually red, and "Futur" trousers and surtouts were manufactured from it. Rabbis and scholars were also engaged in the clothing industry so as to avoid dependence upon public funds.

Safed was the best protected city in Palestine. From the wall, built by Suleiman the Magnificent in 1549, Turkish soldiers guarded against raids by tribes from the neighboring villages. Apparently even this did not afford the Jews complete security, for at some time before 1586 they built themselves a "khan," a fortified compound. The community heads delegated Rabbi Moses Bibas to buy up the plots around the city "heights," probably the site of the army citadel. The permission of the central government needed for the building of the khan was not easily obtained and only after the site was presented to the Pasha was permission granted to build the khan as *Waqf* property. The khan, constructed in the middle of the sixteenth century and known as Khan al-Basha (the Pasha's Khan), consisted of many houses and shops and several warehouses built around a large court, with a large balcony ringing the houses on the outside. Every night the gates were locked and special night watchmen guarded the area. The hundred-odd Jewish families in the court felt safe from marauders, who did not dare to attack it. Nor did the Jews bother to lock their shops inside the court, relying on the guards and the wall gates. The khan served the

Jews as a haven for about a century. Evliya Chelebi wrote of some 1,000 Jews living in the "Caravanserai," by which he certainly meant this khan. Some of the khan residents also kept shops in the bazaar outside.

Though at the time the Jews of Safed lived secure from marauders and robbers, they were occasionally visited by other disasters: famine, locusts, and particularly epidemics were frequent in the unsanitary and congested dwellings. In 1523-1525 there was a serious epidemic, followed by others in 1533, 1550, 1563, 1572 (when Rabbi Isaac Luria died), and 1594.

During these epidemics the Jews often left Safed for the surrounding villages and mountains, especially seeking places inhabited by other Jews and sometimes staying away from the city for half a year or longer. We know of instances when they fled to Ein Zeitun, Biriya, Pekiin, Tiraya, etc., as well as to Arab villages in which the Jews had some hold, such as Meron, Shefaram, etc. Occasionally the refugees stayed on in the villages, which thus grew in proportion to the ruin of the towns.

At the end of the sixteenth century, public order and security throughout the country deteriorated, especially in the north. We have no data on actual oppression by the Turkish authorities in Safed before the closing decades of the century. Jewish life was still secure during the reigns of Suleiman the Magnificent (1520-1566) and his son Selim II (1566-1574). There were Jews in influential positions at court, and Safed reached the pinnacle of its development. But with the death of Selim II, the local situation worsened and the Safed community had to apply to the influential Jews of Constantinople for protection against depredations and persecution by the local authorities. Moreover, the Bedouin and semisavage Druse tribes had begun to set their eyes on the rich stores of prosperous Safed; in 1567 they pillaged the city and many Jews fled to the hills and villages.

In 1576 the Jews of Safed sent a petition to Constantinople accusing Mohammed, governor of the city, of torturing some of the more wealthy Jews and trumping up charges against them to extort money. In addition to the governor, a number of officials, including one Jew, one night watchman, and some interpreters, were accused of oppressive acts. In July of that year the regional satrap of Damascus, whose jurisdiction included Safed, was instructed to investigate the charges thoroughly, and the governor of Safed was ordered to dismiss the accused officials and to protect the Jews of the town. But the weak central government was not always able to control the local governors, who had begun to usurp more and more power to the point of ignoring orders from Constantinople. Thus the decline of Safed set in, though a permanent Jewish settlement, including some outstanding scholars, remained in the city.

The immigration to Palestine in one great wave of so many outstanding rabbis and scholars and their settlement in Safed was a phenomenon unique in Jewish history. Nothing like it had occurred in Jewish life since the closing of the Talmud. Clearly this unprecedented immigration was no mere coincidence. The Spanish expulsion had left an indelible impression on the Jewish soul and given new impetus to the hopes of Redemption; at the same time conquest of Palestine by Turkey, now ruling over many countries and the Mediterranean Sea, brought the Land closer to the Jewish population centers of Europe. No wonder that a number of rabbis and scholars conceived the idea of establishing anew in the Holy Land a religious and spiritual center which would serve as a "beginning of Redemption" and prepare the ground for it. Thus it was not long before Safed became the spiritual center of the Jewish people.

Safed's Chief Rabbi during its golden age was Rabbi Jacob Berab, who arrived there in 1524. For twenty-four years its leading scholar, he founded a great *yeshiva* which strengthened the other institutions of learning as well, attracting scholars by the hundreds from many lands. He personally saw to their sustenance and freed them from the oppressive tax burden. But Rabbi Berab did not content himself with the advancement of scholarship. He devoutly believed that the advent of the Messiah would follow the return to Zion, and in his desire to hasten Redemption he conceived the idea of restoring the ancient Jewish institution of rabbinic ordination. This rite would re-establish the full legal authority of rabbinical courts by once more empowering them to judge criminal cases and impose fines and physical punishment, as in the days of the Nesiim and the Sanhedrin.

One of his chief objectives was to exempt the Marranos, who had been forced to renounce Judaism, from Divine retribution by imposing upon them the alternative punishment of lashes provided by the law but which only a properly ordained rabbinical court was authorized to carry out. By administering this penance, he thought, the Marranos would consider themselves once more bona fide Jews, and their sins would be forgiven. Rabbi Berab meant to realize his scheme by means of the authority vested in the Palestine rabbinate which was entitled—according to Maimonides—to renew ordination by unanimous consent. The original ordination had been officially abolished by Roman decree early in the Byzantine era, though there is reason to believe that it was restored at various times up to the end of the eleventh century, such as in the period of the Palestine Geonim, the heads of the *yeshibot* at Tiberias and Jerusalem.

Five factors motivated Rabbi Berab to seek the renewal of ordination. First, the aforementioned desire to have a rabbinical court authorized to impose "stripes" on penitent Marranos and thus free them from "cutting off" by Heaven; second, only a rabbinic authority vested with full legal powers could ensure the communal peace by rendering binding decisions in cases of basic differences of opinion; third, the need of concentrating in a central supreme body the power to issue authoritative religious decisions; fourth, the establishment of a civil judiciary; and last, the preparation of the generation for the Final Redemption, which, as Rabbi Berab saw it, could come only after an ordained rabbinical court had been established, according to Maimonides's interpretation of Isaiah I: 26-27: "And I will restore thy judges as at the first, and thy counselors as at the beginning . . . Zion shall be redeemed with justice." The last motive apparently was the crucial one, for the ingathering of the exiles would not be complete without the creation of a properly ordained judiciary. Just as exile did not follow immediately on the destruction of statehood but came after the abolition of the Nassi's office and the destruction of the last vestiges of political sovereignty, so also Redemption would come about gradually, the first stage being the re-establishment of an autonomous judiciary.

Rabbi Berab began to implement his program in 1536. After discussing the question for two years with the scholars of Safed and receiving their consent, Rabbi Berab, in 1538, called an assembly of Safed's twenty-five outstanding rabbis. The assembly formally approved the renewal of ordination and ordained their master, Rabbi Berab, who was thereby automatically entitled to confer ordination upon others.

Rabbi Levi ben Habib (Ralbah), Chief Rabbi of Jerusalem and one of the greatest scholars of the time, vigorously opposed the renewal of ordination, not only on personal or theoretical but also on political grounds. It was his view that Rabbi Berab's legal arguments on behalf of the renewal of ordination were inadequate, and that his own ordination by the scholars of Safed had no validity. Ralbah entered into sharp polemic with Rabbi Berab, arguing that the establishment of an ordained rabbinic court would lead to a great schism, as in the time of the controversy between Rabbi Aaron ben Meir and Saadia Gaon, particularly as it would raise questions about fixing the calendar and festivals through direct observation of the moon. Ralbah also feared that the step might be considered a subversive act by the Turkish government and would ultimately lead to repressive measures. Rabbi Berab would thus achieve quite the opposite of what he intended. No doubt Ralbah and the Jerusalem rabbinate also felt that Rabbi Berab's initiative had hurt their prestige, in as much as Safed had established itself as the spiritual center of Jewry whereas it behooved Jerusalem to be the seat of the Sanhedrin.

The opposition of the Jerusalem rabbinate was too powerful for Safed to withstand. The Jerusalem scholars maintained that the renewal of ordination required the unanimous approval of all the scholars of Palestine, and lacking such approval the Safed ordination was not valid. The opposition gained ground even in Safed, where a number of the original proponents of ordination apparently withdrew their support. Quarrels broke out among the scholars of Safed, leading to calumnious accusations and finally to the collapse of this daring attempt to create an organizational and political instrument which might, with more luck, have developed into a unifying political force in Jewish Palestine and might have created an important spiritual center for all Jewry.

Rabbi Berab had to flee to Damascus, apparently because of calumnious charges. But before he left Palestine he managed to accomplish what Rabbi Judah ben Baba did for his time—ordination of four of his students: Rabbi Joseph Karo, author of the *Shulhan Aruk;* the great jurist Rabbi Moses di Trani (Mabit); Rabbi Abraham Shalom; and Rabbi Israel di Curial. These, in turn, later ordained some of their students in Safed, such as Rabbi Moses Alsheikh, Rabbi Moses Galante, Rabbi Hayim Vital (the cabbalist and disciple of Rabbi Isaac Luria), Rabbi Eliezer Azikri, Rabbi Hiyya Rofeh, Rabbi Jacob Abulafia, and Rabbi Yomtov Zahalon. Thus ordination continued for at least three generations. Rabbi Berab returned to Safed from Damascus and soon after, in 1545, he died. He was succeeded by his disciple, the great codifier, Rabbi Joseph Karo, who presided over the Safed rabbinate for some thirty years.

Rabbi Karo had been one of the Spanish exiles in Turkey. Even while in Adrianople his fame as a scholar spread and he served as head of the academy there. In Adrianople he began his great commentary, *Bet Joseph,* on the code of Rabbi Jacob ben Asher, thoroughly analyzing the sources and stages of development of every halakh and summing up with a final ruling. Rabbi Karo's second great work, a summary of the earlier one, was entitled *Shulhan Aruk.* This compendium of Jewish law, arranged in brief sections divided into paragraphs, was acclaimed and accepted by Jewry in both Moslem and Christian countries, and has since served as the code of Jewish law and a practical reference work for rabbi and intelligent layman alike. Rabbi Karo wrote several other works, including *Kessef Mishneh,* a commentary on the code of Maimonides, and *Maggid Mesharim,* a mystical diary containing the revelations of a celestial mentor.

Upon Rabbi Karo's death in 1575, Rabbi Moses di Trani (Mabit) became Chief Rabbi of Safed. Born in 1505, Rabbi Moses was one of the outstanding jurists of his time and his *responsa* are among the best-known halakic works. He died in 1580.

Other Safed scholars who left their impress upon Jewish life everywhere were Rabbi Solomon Halevi Alkabez, poet, cabbalist, and author of commentaries on parts of the Bible (*e.g., Manot ha-Levi,* 1585; *Shoresh Yishai,* 1561), today mainly remembered for his song, *Lekha Dodi,* which forms part of the Jewish Sabbath Eve service; his pupil, friend, and brother-in-law, the great cabbalist, Rabbi Moses Cordovero, author of *Pardes Rimonim;* Rabbi David ibn Abi Zimra, a famous halakic authority; the preacher Rabbi Moses Alsheikh; and the cabbalist and moralist, Rabbi Eliezer Azikri, author of *Sefer Haredim.* Their writings and legal rulings are considered authoritative to this day.

All the time an unremitting struggle continued to exempt religious functionaries and professional scholars from taxation. From time to time the local rabbis issued statements and resolutions urging the exemption of scholars from all taxes and levies. One such statement was issued by the rabbinic court of the Nagid Rabbi Isaac Shulel in 1509, during the Mameluke period; another in 1548; another is dated *Tishri*, 1585; another, issued seven months later, in *Iyar*, 1586, declared that no taxes were to be imposed on scholars, "without discrimination between poor and wealthy men of Torah, whose occupation is the Torah—all shall be free of the obligation." More statements were issued in 1593, in 1596, two in 1625, and again in 1648. The frequent repetition of the sanctions indicates constant opposition to the exemption.

An excellent illustration of the nature of this dispute is the fact that many outstanding rabbis and communal leaders were successful businessmen. Rabbi Jacob Berab had large commercial interests, and one source tells of his buying spices from two merchants in 1528 to the value of 970 florins. Rabbi Moses Negrin, author of *Mlekhet Abodat ha-Kodesh*, sold 200 florins worth of merchandise to Rabbi Judah of Brusa. A document of 1539 shows that Rabbi Isaac Luria (Ari) himself made a sale of pepper to the value of 150 Venetian gold florins. Rabbi Leon de Modena relates, on the authority of emissaries from Safed, that Rabbi Luria used to spend most of his day at business, and three days before his death settled accounts with everyone, saying to them: "I forgive you, and if any of you have been cheated, come forward and we will pay." Moses Galante, an ordained rabbi, member of the rabbinical court and head of the *yeshiva* in Safed, was a clothing manufacturer, employing many seamsters, weavers, tailors, and dyers. An interesting exception is provided by Rabbi David ibn Abi Zimra who himself was a wealthy merchant but in view of the poverty of Jerusalemites abolished the exemption from half the tax and required the Jerusalem scholars to pay the full amount.

Moreover Safed was not only a center of Torah, renowned for its *yeshibot* and for its scholars whose contributions occupy a permanent place in rabbinic literature. Its chief fame is in the field of Cabbala,[2a] which brought forth its richest fruit in Safed. The natural setting of the city and its proximity to Meron—the residence of Rabbi Simeon ben Yohai, to whom tradition ascribes the authorship of the *Zohar*—inspired cabbalistic creativity nourished, moreover, by messianic yearning. Mysticism quickly began to flourish in the places where the first Spanish exiles settled. After the eschatological agitation caused by David Reubeni's appearance in Palestine in 1523, the writings of the Jerusalem cabbalist Abraham Halevi, and the enthusiastic preaching of the proselyte Solomon Molkho (1525), there followed a period of reflection and study. Rabbi Moses Cordovero, whose speculative system was already accepted among the Safed cabbalists before the arrival of Rabbi Isaac Luria, died in 1570. Then "the lion came forth from his lair." Rabbi Isaac Luria Ashkenazi,[3] a native of Jerusalem, laid the foundations of a new cabbalistic cosmology. Some of the outstanding scholars of Safed, including some great halakists, joined his circle, receiving his doctrine through his long-time disciple Rabbi Hayim Vital. Rabbi Luria revealed his doctrines directly only to Rabbi Vital, allowing him to transmit them to but a few other disciples. This circle of disciples, known as "the Lion's Whelps," put the stamp of mysticism also on the interpretation of the Law. The fame of the Sacred Lion and his system spread throughout the Diaspora, chiefly through Palestinian emissaries who visited the Diaspora communities, and from everywhere Jews streamed to Safed to learn the Lurianic mysteries. Those who believed (on the basis of the phrase in Genesis 49:10, ". . . until Shiloh[4] come,") that the Final Redemption would come in the year 5335 (1574-1575) expected Rabbi Luria to be the herald of Redemption. But his death in 1572 blighted their hopes.

The spiritual renaissance in Safed brought an awakening of the poetic genius in the hearts of Safed's sages. Mention has already been made of Solomon Halevi Alkabez, whose moving *Lekha Dodi*, expressing yearning for Redemption and for Israel's exaltation from its degradation, has become one of the most popular liturgical poems of all time. Other poets arose and continued the great tradition of Hebrew poetry which had originated in Spain. The greatest poet of the period, Israel Najera (born in Damascus in 1555, died in Gaza in 1625), wrote both religious and secular poetry. Many of his religious hymns and songs, which were published in a volume called *Zemirot Yisrael* (Safed, 1585; Venice, 1600), have been incorporated in the prayer book, and to this day are sung not only in the synagogue but also at all kinds of private gatherings to musical accompaniment. Rabbi Luria, too, wrote poems in Aramaic, the language of the *Zohar*, and they are recited or sung at the Sabbath meals. Rabbi Eliezer Azikri, mentioned above, also composed religious poems full of love of the Holy Land.

Safed's spiritual importance in the mid-sixteenth century increased with its economic and commercial prosperity. Tradition has it that 290 fully qualified rabbis were congregated in Safed under the leadership of Rabbi Joseph Karo, to whose final verdicts all would consent. The *yeshibot* of Safed attracted students from throughout the Diaspora. The Yemenite traveler, Zechariah Alzahri, described one *yeshiva* where "approximately 200 precious and talented students sit on benches as the master sits in the chair and expounds the subject." Toward the end of the "golden age" a printing house, the first in Palestine, was established. Founded in 1577 by Eliezer and Abraham Ashkenazi, it published six books of high technical quality in the ten years of its existence.

The unique concentration of scholars, *yeshiva* teachers, and masters of the Law and Cabbala made Safed, after the Spanish expulsion, the most important Jewish center in the world. Its growth was connected with the view prevailing at the time that the re-establishment of a center of study and law in Galilee would be a prelude to Redemption. The Sanhedrin was therefore intended to create a supreme judicial body whose jurisdiction would be accepted by all the Jews of the world, and at the same time to advance both rural and urban colonization and to lay the groundwork for administrative autonomy, similar to the earlier attempts of Donna Gracia and Don Joseph Nasi. Only when it became clear that the generation was not fit to realize these ideals, did Messianism assume a more mystical character and attempts to hasten Redemption resorted to more "supernatural" techniques, such as the permutation and combination of "Holy (*i.e.*, Divine) Names." This cabbalistic Messianism reached its climax and end in the latter half of the seventeenth century with the appearance of Sabbatai Zevi.

The Galilean Villages and the Rebuilding of Tiberias

As we have noted, the Jews of Upper Galilee dwelt amid Arab villages, which they visited occasionally to buy milk, cheese, wool, wheat, etc., and in which they sometimes settled as shopkeepers, peddlers, smiths, tailors, etc., and as physicians. Some hawked their wares in the villages, returning home for the Sabbath. Others rented shops in the villages or amid the Bedouins, returning home only for the festivals. Some peddlers settled in the villages with their families and took up farming in partnership with their neighbors or bought land which they leased to tenant farmers.

A unique factor drawing the Jews to the villages was the pilgrimages. Galilee was full of sacred sites linked to the memory of the prophets of old, the talmudic Sages, and great men of later periods, and the Jews have never broken the time-honored tradition of visiting such holy places.

Pilgrimages became more frequent during the flowering age of Cabbala. Rabbi Moses Cordovero and Rabbi Isaac Luria visited remote villages such as Meron, Shefaram, Ashbera, Gishcala, Biram, which no longer had any permanent Jewish inhabitants, merely traditions of ancient Jewish habitation.

Before passing in review some of the villages in which Jews settled as farmers, we should remind ourselves that in Safed proper there were some landowners who engaged in farming. Documents of the years 1597-1599 mention Rabbi Moses Dayan, who "went out to the villages to collect the honey of his bees, and once went to harvest his wine and oil and fresh ears." A generation later, we hear of Rabbi Jacob Gavioso of Safed who toured the villages and Jewish settlements to exhort the Jews to observe the Commandments and to circumcise their sons.

Among the villages in which Jews dwelt at that time are Maon, near

Tiberias, Yaquq, Banias and Eglon in Transjordan. But Galilee in the sixteenth century and after had not only single Jewish families scattered among the Arab peasant population but also consolidated village communities.

The village of Pekiin and its Jewish peasants are first mentioned in 1522, in the travel memoirs of Rabbi Moses Bassola, but it was well established before the Ottoman conquest. References to the Jews of Pekiin in the *responsa* of the period attest that they were peasants of *Musta'rabi* stock, that is, of those who had dwelt in Palestine prior to the Ottoman conquest. They tilled the soil and grew mulberry trees and other plants. The registers of 1555-1556 and 1572-1573 list forty-five Jewish householders there. Of the ancient Jewish settlements Pekiin is the only one to have survived to this day.

Near Pekiin was Ein Tiraya, whose Jewish population was only transient.

Kfar Yasif, near Acre, had an ancient Jewish settlement apparently not destroyed until the Ottoman period. We know that a student of Rabbi Moses di Trani was from Kfar Yasif, and we have evidence from the late sixteenth century of the existence of a rabbinical court there. According to the government census the population dropped from twenty-nine householders in 1555-1556 to eighteen in 1572-1573. As far as we know the Jews of the village were craftsmen, merchants, and farmers.

Two other village settlements that existed throughout the sixteenth century are Alma and Kfar Hananiah.

Alma, north of Safed, was inhabited by *Musta'rabim*, and there is reason to believe that it also had an agricultural settlement. Alma is mentioned by Rabbi Bassola and in the *responsa* of Rabbi Yomtov Zahalon to Rabbi Moses Galante at the end of the sixteenth century, but was one of the smaller communities. In 1555-1556, eight householders were registered there, and three in 1572-1573. Several old Pekiin families bear the name "Almani," attesting their origin in Alma.

Kfar Hananiah is still officially known as Anan. Rabbi Bassola's reference to the Jewish settlers there indicates that they were farmers. The registers list eighteen families. A synagogue stood in the village throughout the sixteenth century and the Jewish settlement there was still mentioned at the end of the century.

There was an old Jewish settlement in the Druse village of Jilas. This settlement, whose existence has escaped the notice of scholars, was first mentioned by Rabbi Tanhum Yerushalmi in 1388, in the Mameluke period, and apparently again by Rabbi Moses di Trani in the sixteenth century. But it was expressly mentioned in the rolls of the sixteenth century, which are in the Turkish Government Archives. In 1555-1556, and again in 1572-1573, there were nine Jewish taxpayers in Jilas. The existence of this settlement in an agricultural village which was not a business center indicates that the Jews of Jilas were farmers.

Of the Jewish settlement at Kabul, about five miles northeast of Shefaram, little was known from the registers. We learn only that it was established after 1525, that in 1533 five of its twelve families were Jewish, and that in 1555-1556 fifteen of its twenty-six taxpayers were Jews.

We have mentioned that already in the Mameluke period Kfar Kana (between Nazareth and Tiberias), near which tradition places the tomb of the Prophet Jonah, had a sizable Jewish settlement. According to official statistics, in the 1540's fifty-two of its 147 families were Jewish. In 1555-1556 we find an increase to sixty-five householders, ten bachelors, and one feeble-minded; but in that same register we find 375 non-Jewish householders and forty-nine bachelors. The ratio of Jews to non-Jews increased in the 1572-1573 census: seventy-seven Jewish householders to 313 non-Jewish families and two bachelors. A Spanish Franciscan monk wrote in 1553-1555 that "many Spanish Jews" lived there.

The antiquity of the Jewish rural settlements is further attested by some of their old customs which antedate the Spanish influx, mentioned by a contemporary, Rabbi Issachar Shushan, in his book *Tikkun Issachar*. Rabbi Joseph Karo lived for a while in Biriya, where on 2 *Elul*, 5315 (1555), he completed *Orah Hayyim*, one of the volumes of his *Shulhan Aruk*. In 1599-1601 a *yeshiva* stood in Ein Zeitun which was founded by Rabbi Moses ben Makhir, author of *Seder ha-Yom*. The very fact that this *yeshiva* sent an emissary abroad indicates its size and importance. The emissary was Rabbi Moses ben Makhir's son-in-law, Rabbi Solomon bar Nahmias Mor David. He visited Italy in 1595, and several documents list the donations he received from Italian Jewish communities.

In the congregational ledger of Casale Monferrato there is an entry for 13 *Tebet*, 5359 (1599 C.E.) as follows:

Just as we heard, so we saw . . . from scribes and books brought by a faithful representative. To his constituents . . . the Honorable, the Teacher, Rab Solomon Mor David, may he be kept by his Rock and Redeemer, the hardship and need of the group of sages . . . who are in a quarter of Safed, may it be speedily rebuilt and re-established in our days, (*i.e.*) in Ein Zeitun. At their head is the Honorable, the Teacher, Rab Moses ben Makhir. . . . They contributed ten ducats of silver from Milan annually for three consecutive years to further the institution of study (*hesger*) at the above mentioned Ein Zeitun.

In another document these words are stated about the *yeshiva:*

Worthy students and attentive members whom the perfect sage, the Honorable, the Teacher, Rab Moses ben Makhir made balanced and perfected, he and his court and the council of the wise members of the *yeshiva* for diligent study of the sages, which is in the institution of learning, new, yet filled with most ancient (vintage) of Torah and of man by their study and joy which is a light to them in Zion, Ein Zeitun within the boundary of Safed, may it be speedily rebuilt and re-established in our days.

These two settlements (Biriya and Ein Zeitun) probably served the Jews of Safed as a refuge in times of persecution and other troubles which were but infrequent in that period. It is worthy of note that while the tax rolls of 1555-1556 list fifty-two Jewish householders and one blind man at Ein Zeitun and sixteen householders and one bachelor at Biriya, there is no mention of them in the register of 1572-1573. We may assume that the Ottoman records in such instances are not reliable, for the populace surely used to deceive the census taker to evade taxes.

Jewish agriculture, then, existed in the period before the Ottoman conquest and expanded with the arrival of the Spanish exiles. This is not to say that there was no Jewish agriculture even before this, but rather that the Jewish farmers did not strictly observe the laws which relate to life in the Land of Israel. It should be noted that at that time there were no outstanding scholars in Palestine to teach the relevant laws and supervise their observance; the Jewish peasants themselves do not seem to have been very strict. But as soon as the great halakists arrived, they turned their attention to agricultural laws and proclaimed a Sabbatical Year in 5264 (1503-1504) according to the reckoning of Maimonides (as against Rashi's reckoning), a reckoning followed to this day.

The Spanish exiles did not go only to the cities and settled areas. Many of those energetic, enterprising men wanted to colonize the wastes. Some Portuguese refugees seem to have settled at Zaida, Khorazin, etc., on the shores of Lake Kinneret, where they engaged in fishing. Others settled in the ruins of Tiberias. A Christian tourist in 1549 found a tiny Jewish community in Tiberias eking out a precarious existence.

At that time Donna Gracia apparently prepared to settle in Palestine. She was especially interested in Tiberias, and since the city was in ruins she wanted to rebuild it so that she might live there. Her son-in-law, Don Joseph Nasi, undertook this task, adding his own dream of a flourishing Jewry in Tiberias, free from tyranny, and living its own life unhampered by hostile and autocratic rulers. Both probably also hoped to settle there fugitives from the Inquisition. Don Joseph therefore used his influence at Court to obtain the Sultan's permission to settle Jews in Tiberias in exchange for an annual payment of 1,000 ducats. It is not certain when the project got under way, but it seems to have been before 1565, the year to which the rebuilding of Tiberias is generally assigned. It seems that as soon as news of the project spread, some Jews decided to settle there immediately without waiting for the completion of the building operation. A visitor of 1561 related that he found in Tiberias an embryonic Jewish settlement with several scholars and a synagogue.

Although the influence of the Nasi family at the Court in Constantinople was well known, the implementation of their plan did not proceed altogether smoothly. The Christians, who had an old church in Tiberias, feared that it would be affected by Don Joseph's development plan, one going so far as to state that Don Joseph planned to populate Tiberias with "serpents" even more dangerous than those which inhabited the city's ruins. When the Papal representative in Palestine was at Constantinople, he protested against the plan and was assured by the Grand Vizier that it would not be carried out. But upon the death of the Grand Vizier in 1561 Don Joseph received from Suleiman the Magnificent the grant of Tiberias and seven neighboring villages. The grant also bore the signatures of Crown Prince Selim II and of Murad, the Sultan's grandson. According to the historian Joseph Hakohen, Suleiman appointed Don Joseph "prince and chief over them." Apparently the city was leased to him in exchange for a fixed annual tax which he was to pay the Sultan. The Turkish government thereby assured itself not only a fixed annual income but also the likely florescence of the entire desolate region when skilled and clever Jews had settled there.

Actually it seems that Don Joseph hoped to turn the area into a great Jewish spiritual and economic center, and his plans were certainly general knowledge. The Turkish government did not interfere in the internal affairs of the inhabitants of Tiberias, satisfying itself with the collection of the annual tax through Don Joseph.

Don Joseph's many affairs did not permit him to leave Constantinople personally to supervise the rebuilding of Tiberias. He therefore sent his agent, Joseph ibn Ardit, who before his departure was received with great honor by the Sultan. Suleiman fixed his salary at sixty pieces of silver per day. Ibn Ardit, who was also given the status of a Turkish government emissary, received from the Sultan a firman and letters to the Governor of Safed and the Pasha of Damascus directing them to give him full co-operation.

The date of ibn Ardit's arrival in Tiberias is still subject to debate, but 1563 seems to be the most probable. His first task was to assure the security of Tiberias by building a wall. Laborers were sent from Safed and Damascus and the work proceeded smoothly. But once more obstacles arose. The Papal representative applied to the Grand Vizier Ali Hashman, Rustem Pasha's successor. News of the building at Tiberias reached a nearby sheikh, who knew the talmudic saying that from Tiberias "they are destined to be redeemed." He started a rumor that he had found an ancient scripture stating that if the Jews rebuilt Tiberias, Islam would perish. When the Arab laborers heard the rumor they abandoned their work. The intervention of the Pasha of Damascus was needed to make resumption of the work possible. Ibn Ardit went to see him and the Pasha assigned a complement of soldiers to him and punished the dissidents.

At the end of 1564 the wall, almost a mile long, was completed. It was then possible to proceed with rebuilding the city proper. Some inhabitants cleared away the ruins and moved into the existing buildings; others erected new structures on old foundations. The ancient synagogue in which Rabbi Simeon ben Yohai was said to have prayed, was rehabilitated. Donna Gracia apparently requested that a home be built for her near the hot springs, and according to one traveler this was a great event for the Jews of the area. But she never seems to have reached Tiberias.

There is no doubt that the rehabilitation of Tiberias brought an influx of Jews from Safed and environs, certainly rich enough in halakists and scholars, to provide the new city with the spiritual forces it needed. It is known that Rabbi Eliezer ben Yohai came to Tiberias from Safed. The Yemenite traveler, Zechariah Aldahri, the date of whose visit to Palestine is still uncertain, spoke highly of the scholars of Tiberias and its *yeshiva*. Some historians still doubt whether this visit can be assigned to the year 1562, although the date is given by the traveler himself. He again spoke of Tiberias after his return to Yemen, when Rabbi Abraham, an emissary from the Tiberias *yeshiva*, visited Sanaa in 1579. In book twenty-three of his *Sefer ha-Musar*, in describing his first visit, he speaks of the city's notables, who "sit in the synagogue by the city wall. . . . When I arrived, I saw elders and notables, the glory of Jewry, masters of Scripture and Talmud, including masters of both theoretical and practical Cabbala. And when I beheld them I was inspired with awe, for I am but a fledgling compared to them."

In book twenty-four he told of the visit of the *yeshiva* emissary. (One theory has it that this was Rabbi Abraham bar Isaac Ashkenazi, who in 1572 in Safed founded with his brother the first printing press in Palestine.) He quoted the emissary as follows: "Know that our *yeshiva* exists from olden days, with seventy scholars whose needs were provided by a noble lady doing God's work from Constantinople, great among women and close to the Palace . . . [she was a] good advocate for us until she was summoned to the celestial academy. Now our academy is destitute and our hope is lost." He added that the *yeshiva* was badly off in all respects and that emissaries had to be dispatched to Turkey, Egypt, Mesopotamia, Italy, etc. The Yemenite poet cites the text of the letter which the emissary had brought with him, signed by the heads of the Tiberias community, "first the great sage Our Master Rabbi Samuel Hakohen, Rabbi Jacob Halevi, Rabbi Moses Gedaliah, Rabbi Abraham Gabriel, and Rabbi Abraham, their Rock preserve them." The Tiberias sages are ". . . sages from Spain. All hearts tremble at their word."

With Donna Gracia's death Don Joseph's great interest in Tiberias apparently waned, and he turned his attention to the development of his duchy in the Aegean Islands. The economy of Tiberias was not yet stabilized and it remained unsettled until Don Joseph's death in 1579. "The Tiberias project was not a failure, but its great hopes were not fulfilled."

Not long afterward a new savior appeared for Tiberias in the person of Don Solomon ben Yaish, formerly known as the Marrano Alvaro Mendez. In 1585 he reached Turkey, where he became Grand Commissioner of the Ottoman Empire and for fifteen years, until his death in 1603, directed the Sublime Porte's foreign affairs. The Sultan made him Duke of Mytilene, an island off Greece. Don Solomon became interested in the colonization of Palestine as soon as he reached Constantinople, no doubt under the sway of the Messianic dreams current among the Marranos.

Don Solomon turned his attention to the redevelopment of Tiberias. Sultan Murad gave him the grant of the city. Don Solomon sent to Tiberias his son, Jacob ben Yaish, who built many homes and a beautiful castle there. According to his father's testimony, Jacob studied Torah and Cabbala and was much loved even by the Arabs, but was a poor businessman and administrator.

Thus the Jewish settlement in Tiberias survived for several generations after Don Joseph Nasi's death. It was still there in the time of Rabbi Isaiah Halevi Hurwitz, who in 1624 went to Safed and then, because of the persecution of ibn Farukh, moved to Tiberias, remaining there until his death.

Stagnation and Decline

Safed and Tiberias

The indifference of the regime to the security of the inhabitants, as well as to sanitary conditions, resulted in occasional severe epidemics, which led to the dispersal of the population. Eveliya Chelebi, the famous Turkish traveler (1649), reported a mass exodus of Jews from Safed in his time; but in all likelihood he referred to a flight from persecution and anti-Jewish disturbances rather than to a regular exodus. Some fled to nearby towns and villages, and some as far as Sidon, Beirut, Damascus, and Egypt. But the Galilean refugees concentrated mainly in Jerusalem, strengthening the Jewish community there.

The various disasters that visited Galilean Jewry diminished the most important Jewish population center, Safed. The economic situation worsened; the trade routes lay idle; the famous textile and clothing industry almost completely died out. Spiritual life, too, deteriorated. The academies were empty, the printing press closed (1587), the sages and their disciples fled and none came to replace them.

Early in the seventeenth century Safed enjoyed a brief revival of its former glory. The cabbalist Solomon Meinsterl of Dresnitz, Moravia, thirsting to drink at the wellspring of mysticism, arrived in Safed in the fall of 1602. In his letters he painted a vivid picture of the spiritual and general condition of Safed in the period 1603-1609: "I found . . . a great city of God, a city full of wisdom, with almost 300 great rabbis all rich in piety and deeds, with eighteen *yeshibot*, twenty-one synagogues, and a huge study house where almost 300 boys and young men are taught by twenty teachers, at no charge, for there are wealthy men in Constantinople who pay the teachers and clothe them every year." He mentioned the sermons of Rabbi Isaac Luria's disciples, Moses Galante, Massod Sagi Nahor, Solomon Maaravi (Ohanna), etc., and described visits near Safed to the tombs of the great. He also mentioned the synagogues—in ruins even in his time—at Biriya, Ein Zeitun, and Meron, "which contain numerous Torah Scrolls in the Arks, which the Ishmaelites treat with great reverence, keeping the keys, tending them, and lighting the candles before the Arks, none daring to touch the Torah Scrolls. Sometimes we go to those villages and offer long prayers, according to the requirement of the hour." Thus it was only shortly before Meinsterl's arrival that the villages had been emptied of Jews, and in his time synagogues containing Torah Scrolls still stood there.

Meinsterl emphasized that there was peace in the land, that the Arabs treated the Jewish sanctuaries with respect, never disturbing Jews as they went out in prayer shawls and phylacteries to pray in the fields or at their holy places. But his description was apparently intended for external "propaganda," for other contemporary sources spoke of the "exile" which the Jews of Safed were suffering at the hands of both their rulers and their neighbors. In 1586-1587 the assault took place in which the printing press was wrecked, and letters of the period also spoke of other persecutions.

A letter of 1604 to Rabbi Hayim Quansino described Safed as still being "a beautiful city," with twelve synagogues and sixteen houses of study for children, young men, and advanced scholars, a home in which 120 invalids and scholars who did not work for a living were cared for and which provided a livelihood for fifty outsiders and maintained about 1,200 destitute people. The Jewish community paid the government an annual tax of 3,500 florins.

This description is doubtless exaggerated. During the revolts of Jumblatt and Fakhr-al-Din of the Ma'n dynasty, the ruler of the Lebanon who controlled northern and central Palestine in 1603-1607, Druse invaders and the local Arab peasants added to the devastation wrought in the northern section of the country by drought and locust (1599) and epidemic (1602). Safed was desolate from 1599 to 1601, and shortly after its revival came another plague which drove its inhabitants to the villages, especially Pekiin, which had a Jewish agricultural settlement. In 1604 the Druses and in 1613 the neighboring Arabs sacked the city. In 1621 Rabbi Joshua Handali was among the first to enter Safed to rebuild the Jewish settlement there.

As the toll of nature and government persecution mounted in Safed, many emissaries began to leave the city to visit parts of the Diaspora, from the last decade of the sixteenth century onward. These emissaries included such outstanding scholars as Rabbis Moses Alsheikh, Yomtov Zahalon, and Joseph di Trani.

Rabbi Moses Alsheikh, author of famous homiletic commentaries on the Bible, left after 1590 for Syria, Persia, and Turkey. His campaign on behalf of Safed was typical of the preacher: he proclaimed the duty of the Diaspora to share the burden of rebuilding the city of scholarship, and issued a tract, *Hazut Kashah,* in which he described the city's plight and made his demands on the wealthy Jews of the Diaspora.

In Venice a center, headed by the city's spiritual and financial leaders, was established for the collection of funds for the Safed community. In October, 1600, they wrote to the communities of Germany, Poland, and Russia, apprising them of the city's plight and of a ship bearing wool and money for Safed that had sunk en route to Palestine from Constantinople.

In March, 1601, the heads of Venetian Jewry decided to collect an annual levy of one-quarter of a ducat from every member of the Jewish community who paid the communal tax, and proposed the same impost to other communities.

The substantial assistance rendered Safed by Constantinople Jewry (mentioned above) continued past this period. Rabbi Elijah ibn Hayim of Constantinople wrote: "We are again this year concerning ourselves with the plight of the people of Safed and are collecting contributions from our men of means to send them wheat."

Rabbi Yomtov Zahalon (b. 1558) and Rabbi Joseph di Trani (b. 1568), both natives of Safed, went to Egypt and Constantinople. Rabbi Joseph traveled with Rabbi Abraham Shalom in 1599. His mission accomplished, Rabbi Joseph settled in Constantinople, where he became the head of a *yeshiva* established for him by the sons of the wealthy Abraham ben Yaish.

Other emissaries went to North Africa, Italy, and Germany. In 1601 Rabbi Abraham Ekron visited Worms, and in 1604 Rabbi Yehiel Ashkenazi and Rabbi Solomon ibn Zur were in Algeria. One of the notable emissaries to Italy was Rabbi Yedidiah, son of Rabbi Moses Galante. The Italian community in Safed sent emissaries of its own, and in 1610 Rabbi Joseph Hayim went to Italy.

The deterioration of Safed's security and economy which, as we have noted, also led to its spiritual decline, caused the incipient German immigration to turn to Jerusalem. Rabbi Isaiah Halevi Hurwitz (Shalah), author of *Shne Luhot ha-Brit* (abbreviated as *Shelah*), who arrived in Palestine early in the winter of 1621, declined an invitation to settle in Safed and continued on to Jerusalem, "for the Ashkenazic community in Jerusalem is double that of Safed and grows every day . . . they dwell behind walls, unlike Safed . . . where there are great depredations, for they dwell in an area that is open on all sides."

To be sure, a Jewish settlement existed in Safed throughout this period, and suffered no unusual catastrophes such as the persecutions of ibn Farukh in Jerusalem, but Safed no longer had the vitality of the community of only a generation earlier. Life was a great struggle and the Jews were at the mercy of their Arab and Turkish overlords. In 1628 the Druses attacked Safed. Mulhim, brother of Fakhr-al-Din, took the city and plundered the Jews, many of whom fled for their lives. In 1633 the Pasha of Damascus routed Fakhr-al-Din and again Safed felt the heavy hand of a conqueror. After Mulhim's defeat the Jews returned to Safed, once more under Turkish rule, but again they did not long enjoy peace.

In 1656 the Druses destroyed successively the Jewish communities of Safed and Tiberias. During the fighting between the heirs of Fakhr-al-Din, both factions took turns plundering the Jews of Safed. Many fled to other parts of the country and the Safed Jewish community was in effect dead. When Tiberias was razed in about 1660, some refugees went to Safed, but it never regained its former stature.

Tiberias was much worse off than Safed, continuing a wretched existence early in the seventeenth century, and Rabbi Hayim Vital mentions the Tiberias synagogue in which Rabbi Luria had prayed. Rabbi Isaiah Hurwitz lived out his last years in Tiberias and prayed in that same synagogue. "Not a Jew remained in 1669, for the inhabitants had fled from the Arabs (the Bedouins), abandoning their homes and taking with them whatever they could conveniently carry." Jewish Tiberias was still in ruins until 1740, according to the book *Zimrat ha-Aret* published in that year: "It is now seventy years that she lies waste and desolate, without her children, without synagogue or study house, without inhabitants at all, the *Kaddish* not having been heard in her since the day she was destroyed."

Jerusalem: Persecutions and Disasters

When Jerusalem began to suffer depredation and persecution toward the end of the sixteenth century, the city had already surpassed Safed as a spiritual center. In 1586, as we have noted, the 320 year old Nahmanides Synagogue was wrested from the Jews, never to be returned, and soon they began to leave Jerusalem en masse. Nonetheless the spiritual situation of the city apparently still gave some hope for the future. In 1587 Rabbi Bezalel Ashkenazi gave a letter to Rabbi Isaac Shikhmi, an emissary from Jerusalem to Italy, stating that "the synagogue indeed remains closed," but "the land is filled with Torah as it has not been for many years, for there is a Talmud Torah with more than 100 youngsters . . . and a house of study where they study day and night. . . . And a synagogue . . . may it be speedily reopened . . . for the great judge of the Holy City and all the judges have written to the Palace . . . wherefore we know that His Majesty's word will come that Jerusalem be rebuilt . . . and all this was accomplished at great expense."

Rabbi Bezalel Ashkenazi's optimism was vain, for the synagogue was never returned to the Jews. He instituted several reforms, however, including one whereby one-sixth of the funds raised by the Ashkenazic emissaries was allocated to the Sephardic "*kollel Yerushalayim*." In this way his hope to spread Torah through the Jerusalem *Yeshiva* was realized. When he died this financial arrangement was rejected by the Ashkenazic community. Rabbi Ashkenazi himself presided over the Jerusalem *Yeshiva*, and one of his disciples was Rabbi Solomon Adani, author of the commentary on the Mishna, *Mlekhet Shlomo*. Rabbi Bezalel died in Jerusalem a few years after his arrival there, between 1591 and 1594.

The Ashkenazic community at that time could boast of a number of outstanding scholars, headed by Rabbi Ephraim Fisch, son-in-law of Rabbi Solomon Luria, and including Rabbi Simon Annesburg of Frankfort on the Main (who arrived in 1589), Rabbi Simon Bak (1584), Rabbi Uri Feibush and Rabbi Tevlin, who later went as emissaries to Germany.

The Jerusalem community surmounted its difficulties, and the bulk of the emigration of this period from Turkey, North Africa, Italy, and Germany went to Jerusalem rather than to Galilee. Immigration from North Africa and Italy increased particularly, and Jerusalem had separate North African and Italian community organizations. A letter of 1630, signed by thirteen North African scholars, stated that "the North Africans comprise the bulk of the poor" of Jerusalem. We learn of the large Italian immigration from an immigrant's letter of 1625. Jerusalem then had parnassim (community wardens), the physician Jacob ben Amram, Isaac Gaon, and David Shneour, of whom two were certainly Italians. From time to time large groups of pilgrims contributed substantially to the communal institutions and the *yeshibot*, and dispensed much charity among the poor. The anonymous author of the famous letter, *Hurvot Yerushalayim* (Ruins of Jerusalem), describes the city's florescence:

More of our people now inhabit the city of Our God than have dwelt there since Israel was exiled from its land, for daily many Jews come to settle there, in addition to the pilgrims who come to pray to Him Who stands beyond our wall, to behold the pleasantness of God . . . and they give generously for the strengthening of Jerusalem. And the news is abroad that we dwell in peace and security, and the streets are filled with children, and from Zion comes forth knowledge and wisdom . . . to all the world . . . it abounds in study houses open to all who would come and do holy work, and its leaders support the scholars and needy, providing each his needs . . .

When Rabbi Isaiah Hurwitz went to Palestine from Prague in 1622, as noted above, he did not want to settle anywhere but in Jerusalem. For only there could he find a flourishing community of 500 Sephardic families as well as an Ashkenazic community of 500, twice the size of the Ashkenazic community of Safed. He noted that there were many great scholars in Jerusalem, and that the entire populace dwelt in one court, walled off against bandits and marauders. The Jews of Jerusalem "are increasing by the very hundreds and erecting huge structures. We account all this as tokens of Redemption."

The magnitude of the immigration from the various centers of the Diaspora led to the re-enactment in 1623 of the prescript "to create no new division within the Holy Community, its Rock preserve it, nor of the wardens who tend to the city's needs, except for the already existing Ashkenazic community, and not to write a disparaging word about our holy communities." This was directed at the North African, *Musta'rabic,* and Italian communities. The Ashkenazim, however, were permitted to organize themselves separately and to send their own emissaries abroad. The prescript was signed by eleven scholars and communal leaders, and aptly illustrates the growth of the Ashkenazic community at the time of Rabbi Isaiah Hurwitz's arrival. The Ashkenazic community's demand for full autonomy in dealing with the affairs of the new Ashkenazic settlers seems to have given rise to the fear that the other communities would follow suit; hence the special provisions of the prescript.

Two years later disaster struck. In 1625 Mohammed ibn Farukh (apparently of the Farukhides), a wealthy Nablus tyrant, bought the Pashalik of Jerusalem. His reign was one of the blackest periods in the city's history. His avarice and tyranny did not spare the Jews of Jerusalem: plundering them, imprisoning their leaders and notables, imposing onerous levies, so that they were forced in the end to borrow 50,000 kurush at an annual interest of 10,000 kurush to avoid imprisonment and slaughter by ibn Farukh.

After ibn Farukh

In 1625, after ibn Farukh entered the city, an Italian Jew living in Jerusalem wrote to his son at Carpi, Italy, that the Jews had "to wear Turkish garb" or risk death. "They are overburdened with debts and in need of mercy." He urged that the Jews of the Diaspora extend hospitality to the emissaries from Jerusalem and tender them all possible help. There were two synagogues in Jerusalem, "which from morning to evening and from midnight to morning are never silent." Study sessions took place in the synagogues and sessions of prayer for deliverance, and the congregants also "sat on the ground bemoaning the destruction of Jerusalem." He mentioned a small congregation of Karaites, "numbering almost twenty," who dress "like the Jews but do not mingle with them." The Ashkenazic community, smaller than the Sephardic, was headed by two Sephardim.

The community numbered some 2,000 souls, and it was agreed that the Ashkenazim were to cover one-fourth of the communal budget and the Sephardim the balance. He lauded the customs of the Jerusalem community and its wardens, "whose reputation is good . . . beyond suspicion."

The *responsa* of the period tell us much of the treatment of the Jews of Jerusalem by the authorities, who oppressed the Jews, extorted money from them, and believed every slander about them. The accused were mercilessly punished, their money confiscated, and they themselves imprisoned. If a victim could not pay ransom, the whole community was penalized, and the warden was required to pay huge sums to the governor on behalf of the Jewish community. This happened again and again during the period, forcing Jews to leave the city, until in 1663 most of them had gone to Ramleh, abandoning their property in Jerusalem.

Nature, too, took its toll. An English clergyman told of a drought and famine in 1637. When the Turks saw their prayers unanswered, they thought they were being punished by Allah for allowing the Jews to live with them, and threatened to put the Jews to the sword if rain did not fall within three days. The Jews proclaimed a fast and on the third morning gathered at the tomb of Zechariah on the Mount of Olives, where they prayed till noon. In the afternoon the sky became overcast and a heavy rain began to fall, overflowing the reservoirs. The clergyman added this was proof that there is none to help the Jews but their God in Heaven, implying that it was a religious obligation to support the Jews of Jerusalem.

SABBATAI ZEVI

After the death of Rabbi Isaac Luria, his mystical doctrine spread rapidly among all the classes of Jewry, which was weary with the travails of exile and longing for deliverance. Rabbi Luria had ordered that his teaching be kept secret; his main disciple, Rabbi Hayim Vital, in fact strove to keep it within an esoteric circle. Nevertheless, Lurianic cabbalism spread from the limited conventicles in Safed through Palestine and thence to Italy, North Africa, Turkey, Poland, and the other lands of the Diaspora.

Rabbi Luria's disciples and their students, including Rabbi Joseph ibn Tabul—rival of Rabbi Hayim Vital—Rabbi Israel Saruk of Italy, and others, propagated his cabbalistic system. Rabbi Jacob Zemah, a Portuguese Marrano who had returned to Judaism in Salonica at the age of thirty-five, was especially active as a propagandist of Lurianic mysticism. He went to Safed to study, then to Damascus (1633) where he was initiated into Lurianic Cabbala by Rabbi Hayim Vital's son Rabbi Samuel Vital. In Jerusalem Rabbi Jacob Zemah discovered a manuscript of Rabbi Hayim Vital's last and final exposition of the Lurianic doctrine kept secret until then, and founded a school for the study of Cabbala, which then became known in wider circles. Diaspora Jewry, and even more so that of Palestine, were then steeped in fantastic expectations of a miraculous, supernatural redemption to be effected by cabbalistic means. With the decline of Jewish Safed at the close of the sixteenth century, Hebron and Jerusalem became the centers of Cabbala, and thus the climate was created in Jerusalem, too, for expectation of a supernatural redemption.

The preceding section described the major disaster that struck Jerusalem in the first half of the seventeenth century. But persecution of the Jews did not cease with ibn Farukh's fall. Various sources indicate that in 1643 the Governor of Jerusalem imposed on the Jewish community a tax which it could not pay. He threatened dire punishment and took some of the community notables as hostages. The community had to seek outside help and dispatched emissaries to Turkey, Italy, Morocco, Holland, Hamburg, and as far as Persia and India. One of the emissaries, Rabbi Barukh Gad, dissipated the funds he collected and in 1646 wrote back fanciful tales of a visit to the land beyond the River Sambatyon where the "Lost Ten Tribes" and the "Children of Moses" dwelt. The Jerusalemites doubted the veracity of Gad's letter and at first suppressed it. But in 1657 they appended the fanciful report to their requests for help from the Diaspora, in the vain hope of inspiring their coreligionists.

Sabbatai Zevi reached Jerusalem in 1662, after Safed and Tiberias had been sacked by the Druses: Tiberias lay waste and only a handful of Safed's former inhabitants had returned after its destruction. Almost the whole of Palestine Jewry was concentrated in Jerusalem, Hebron, and Gaza, but it was a generation bereft of great sages. In 1663 the governor of Jerusalem imposed a heavy tribute on the Jews of the city, forcing most of them including the leading scholars to flee to Ramleh. The young ascetic "scholar" from Smyrna, whose mortifications and fervent prayers at the tombs of the holy men of old, attracted common folk and scholars alike, soon won many enthusiastic followers. Sabbatai Zevi's standing seems to have been such that the community sent him on an errand of mercy to Egypt. He traveled via Hebron and Gaza where he met Nathan Benjamin ben Elisha Hayim Ashkenazi, who later became his "prophet." In Egypt Sabbatai Zevi was received with great honor as the emissary of Jerusalem by Joseph Raphael Chelebi, a wealthy and generous man close to the Viceroy of Egypt. Chelebi was also a scholar and greatly under the influence of the cabbalists (his teacher had been Rabbi Samuel Vital). Sabbatai Zevi who had already made his acquaintance on his way from Smyrna to Jerusalem, now "revealed" to him that he was the Davidic Messiah, and Chelebi gave him 4,000 kurush (a tremendous sum in those days, worth more than 1,000 florins) for the poor of Jerusalem. Sabbatai Zevi did not deliver the money but spent it on his followers. As a result, the heads of the community excommunicated him after his return to Jerusalem. When he refused to submit, they reported him to the governor and Sabbatai Zevi was forced to flee to Gaza, whence he returned to Smyrna. Nathan of Gaza retaliated by proclaiming that henceforth Gaza, and not Jerusalem, was the Holy City. The Sabbataian movement in Palestine did not die out with Sabbatai Zevi's flight, but its end came with the news of his apostasy in *Elul*, 1666. The unbridgeable contradiction between the ideal image of "the Anointed One of the God of Jacob" and Sabbatai Zevi, the apostate to Islam, put an end to the fata morgana of messianic enthusiasm.

The appearance of Sabbatai Zevi wrought irreparable havoc with the moral, social, and economic life of Jewish Jerusalem. The bitter dissension he created rent the community and prevented any concerted effort to improve the general condition of the community and its institutions. Even the emissaries dispatched to raise funds in the Diaspora spent less time on their missions than in disseminating all kinds of rumors concerning the appearance of the false messiah.

In the Countryside

Hebron frequently served as a haven for Jerusalemites forced to flee oppression, epidemics, and other disasters. Early in the seventeenth century a number of Jerusalemites fled there from persecution by ibn Farukh. But there was never a self-sustaining economy in Hebron. Some of Luria's outstanding disciples found safe harbor there during the seventeenth century, including Rabbi Elijah di Vidas, author of *Reshit Hokhmah;* Rabbi Solomon Adani, author of *Mlekhet Shlomo;* Rabbi Abraham Azulay, author of *Hesed le-Abraham;* Rabbi Isaac ibn Arha and his son Rabbi Eliezer ibn Arha; and, much later, Rabbi Hayim Abulafia, a descendant of Rabbi Jacob Berab. Rabbi Abulafia, a contemporary and uncompromising opponent of Sabbatai Zevi, was forced to leave Hebron when the Sabbataians trumped up false accusations against him. Other noteworthy scholars who lived in Hebron included Zerahiah Gotha, author of *Zerah Yaakob* (whose manuscript is lost); Isaac Nissim ibn Jamil; Abraham Gidlaya; and Judah Habiliyo.

There were Ashkenazim among the Jews who settled in Hebron in the seventeenth century. The Karaite community established there a century earlier had ceased to exist and the Rabbanite Jews had bought the Karaite communal property, including their synagogue. The Karaite travelers of the mid-seventeenth century, Samuel ben David and Moses Hayerushalmi, found no Karaites in Hebron and prayed in the Jewish synagogue. Although Hebron numbered few Jews, they were not spared the oppression or the natural disasters suffered by their brethren in Jerusalem and Safed. Abraham Azulay, in the introduction to his *Hesed le-Abraham*, tells of the epidemic which raged in Hebron in 1619.

It was chiefly Italian Jewry who came to the aid of Hebron. Fund-raising centers existed in Verona and Venice, and the Aboab family in particular took special interest in Hebron. Even before 1640 Samuel Aboab used to send money to Hebron through Italian merchants at Aleppo, the funds being received by the wardens of Jerusalem, who transmitted them to Hebron. The Rabbi of Hebron at the time was Eliezer ibn Arha, who was assisted by Abraham Azulay and Hezekiah Aboab of the Italian Aboabs.

At that time a major campaign in Hebron's behalf was conducted by Rabbi Meir Rofe, a native of Safed who had moved to Hebron in his youth. He went to Italy, Holland, and France to raise money, which he sent to Samuel Aboab in Venice, who forwarded it to Hebron in the way already mentioned.

Rabbi Rofe completed his mission in mid-1652, and Samuel Aboab, in a letter to the Hebron community, praised him highly: "Due to his untiring efforts in these parts, though in constant danger, the sum of money he gathered was greater than expected." Rabbi Rofe also founded two *yeshibot* in Hebron. The *Yeshiva Hesed le-Abraham* which he established on his return from his fund-raising mission, existed for several generations as the center of Jewish communal life in Hebron.

In the time of Sabbatai Zevi, when Nathan of Gaza was spreading the "messianic" tidings, the members of *Hesed le-Abraham* wrote to Abraham Pereira in Italy that "henceforth they would no longer need his donations but wish that he would join them to behold the pleasantness of the Lord." According to one source, most of the Hebron scholars had become adherents of Sabbatai Zevi and continued to believe in him even after his apostasy.

While Rabbi Rofe was travelling in Europe, Hebron sent another emissary, Hiyia Dayan, on a mission to North Africa. In a letter handed to him in 1661, the heads of the Hebron community bemoaned the city's plight, their subjection to the local sheikhs, and the constant feuding among the local Arab tribes. In 1660, when Hebron was invaded by locusts, the Arabs attacked the Jewish quarter, looted the synagogue, and exacted a heavy tribute from the Jews to allow them to stay in the city.

The Jewish settlement in Gaza, which flourished in the sixteenth century, lasted into the seventeenth. From time to time the city was filled with refugees from persecution in Hebron and Jerusalem. Gaza had less exacting rulers and in times of epidemic Gaza's ample orchards and gardens sustained the stricken Hebronite and Jerusalemite refugees. From time to time even refugees from Safed and Tiberias came to Gaza, some staying to found a *yeshiva,* thus strengthening the city's spiritual life. We also find reports that the Jews of Gaza tried to enlarge the permanent Jewish settlement.

The newcomers to Gaza included merchants and businessmen who knew how to exploit the city's location on the highway connecting Syria and

Egypt. They also established commercial ties with the desert tribes, as the Jews of Safed had done with the Arabs of Galilee and Transjordan.

The head of Gaza's rabbinical court at the close of the sixteenth century was Rabbi Isaac ibn Arha, a disciple of Rabbi Luria and associate of Rabbi Moses di Trani in Safed. Rabbi Isaac moved from Safed to Gaza during an epidemic and died there *c.* 1600. He was followed to Gaza by his son, Rabbi Eliezer ibn Arha, who apparently headed the community till 1619, when he moved to Hebron. During this period Abraham Azulay came to Gaza, where he wrote his *Baalei Brit Abraham.* He was followed by Israel Najera, the renowned poet who headed the community until his death. Mention has already been made of the book *Zemirot Yisrael*, a collection of his songs which are sung at weddings and other family and community gatherings. His religious poetry is found in various prayer books. His son, Moses Najera, succeeded him, and in turn was succeeded by his son, Jacob, an ardent Sabbataian.

In this period a significant event brought fame to Gaza: Sabbatai Zevi passed through it once or twice on his travels between Palestine and Egypt; it was there that he met Nathan, his apostle and prophet. A contemporary wrote: "And it came to pass when he entered Gaza that the Prophet Nathan proclaimed aloud: 'This is the savior of Israel, the Anointed One of the God of Jacob. Israel has no other redeemer, and it is of this one that all the prophets prophesied.' "

According to Professor Gershom Scholem, Nathan was the driving force behind the Sabbataian movement and the creator of its ideology. For our purpose here it suffices to note that it was in Gaza, a city of gardens and orchards on the Mediterranean coast, and steeped in traditions of Samson and his feats, that Sabbatai Zevi dreamed his dreams and Nathan proclaimed his visions of redemption by the new messiah, composed his main prophecy, and wrote epistles to the Diaspora containing the messianic tidings. It was also in Gaza that Sabbatai Zevi achieved quite unexpectedly what he had vainly sought in Jerusalem—recognition by scholars. Abraham Nathan of Gaza was a scholar who had studied in the *yeshibot* of Jerusalem, and the son-in-law of one of Gaza's wealthy men, Samuel Lisbona. There was no one in Gaza bold enough to oppose Nathan or the "renowned rabbi and cabbalist" from Smyrna.

Gaza became the propaganda center of the new messianic movement. It was from there that Nathan dispatched his epistles and proclamations concerning the revelation of Sabbatai Zevi, and called upon all Jewish communities to fast and repent. The Jews of the Diaspora were bidden to Palestine to behold the face of the messianic king, and to accept the yoke of his kingdom. In one of his letters describing the birthpangs of the messianic age, Nathan also praised the excellence of Gaza and its Jews, saying, "None will be spared the pre-messianic travails save the inhabitants of Gaza, where the head of the government [Sabbatai Zevi] lives, for 'Gaza' signifies 'the might of God.' "

With the end of the seventeenth century, the decline of Jewish Gaza set in. The small Jewish settlement in Nablus continued to exist and was even augmented by some Jerusalemites who fled the oppression of ibn Farukh. Samuel ben David, the Karaite traveler, reported (1640) finding twelve Jewish householders and a synagogue in Nablus, as well as ten Samaritan householders. Samaritan scribes record a series of persecutions by the governors of the city which forced a number to flee to Gaza and Jaffa. Moses Yerushalmi, another Karaite traveler, wrote (1656) that a "rabbanite" Jew took him to pray at the tombs of Joseph in Nablus, of Joshua and Caleb at Kfar Haris, of Eleazar son of Aaron at the Hill of Phineas, and of Ithamar son of Aaron at Avertah. When Abraham Yarak, rabbi of Casale, wanted to emigrate to Palestine in 1660, he asked Samuel Aboab about a good place to settle. In addition to the well-known towns, Aboab mentioned newly settled areas, "such as Nablus and Lydda and vicinity." The poll tax roll of 1690-1691 lists thirty-four Jewish taxpayers in Nablus and none in Lydda or Ramleh.

With the decline of Jewish life in Galilee, most of the agricultural settlements there, except Pekiin and Kfar Yasif, Alma, Kfar Hananiah, Kfar Kana, Kabul, Jilas, etc., were liquidated. In the *responsa* of the period we find references to Jewish merchants and peddlers among the Arabs of Upper Galilee. These references appear mainly in connection with testimonies regarding the murder of peddlers by Bedouins or Arab villagers.

Jerusalem at the End of the Seventeenth Century

With the further decline of Safed as a center of Torah, the importance of Jerusalem rose again. Immigrants began to stream to Jerusalem, which soon numbered many scholars among its citizens. One of the most active in advancing the spiritual life of Jerusalem was Rabbi Jacob Hagiz, a native of Fez, Morocco, who had spent his youth in Verona, Italy. An outstanding pedagogue, he devoted himself primarily to Jewish education. In Italy he succeeded in influencing the wealthy Vega family of Leghorn to found a large house of study in Jerusalem which would both serve scholarship and relieve the community's plight.

The *yeshiva*, *Bet Jacob*, was established when Rabbi Hagiz reached Jerusalem in 1658. He instituted a new system of study, concentrated the finest scholars in the *yeshiva*, and attracted many young students who were trained for the rabbinate and later served communities in Palestine and the Diaspora. The scholars were assigned two tasks: some dealt with "the needs of the city and the entire Diaspora, answering questions that came to them from remote places outside" Palestine, and the rest conducted classes. The *yeshiva* also had a synagogue and a meeting hall which was the center of communal and rabbinic activity.

By producing the future leaders of Jerusalem, the *yeshiva* exerted a decisive influence on the development of the community. The period was one of the most fertile in rabbinic literature, and the works it produced still serve as basic texts in Jewish law. The *yeshiva* was renowned throughout the Diaspora and its authority was accepted everywhere.

Contemporary sources give us a detailed picture of the community at the end of the seventeenth century. There were "some 300 householders, almost 1,200 souls," most of them poor folk who lived off communal funds and the city's *yeshibot*, and some men of means who lived on the income from businesses and investments outside Palestine. These well-to-do men had to pay the communal tax and a special levy to the Sultan's treasury, each according to his means; payments ranged from twelve to seventy lions annually. The community needed 5,000-6,000 lions annually. Each householder paid only 400 lions annually until communal expenses rose in 1698 and their annual participation was increased to 1,200. If we compare the budget of the Jerusalem community to those of Hebron and Safed, we find that Jerusalem was the largest Jewish community in the land. According to Rabbi Mordecai Malki, Rabbi Hagiz's father-in-law, Hebron needed only 1,000 lions annually for its regular budget, but debts had increased its requirements to 2,000. Safed need more than 2,000.

The community raised about 850 lions, about 15 per cent of its total expenses, from individual taxes (400), from the income of the Rabbi Johanan ben Zakkai Synagogue (about 300), and from the meat tax (about 150). The balance must have been covered by funds raised by emissaries in the Diaspora or by the regular contributions of some Diaspora communities. But the income from the Diaspora was not always sufficient, and the community sometimes had to borrow money from the Moslems, at high interest, which put a severe strain on community resources.

RENEWED IMMIGRATION IN THE EIGHTEENTH CENTURY AND THE DISSOLUTION OF THE ASHKENAZIC COMMUNITY OF JERUSALEM

As a result of the Ottoman defeats in Europe at the end of the seventeenth century, the local sheikhs and "feudal lords" in Syria and Palestine increasingly encroached upon the central government and seized control of various areas. At the beginning of the eighteenth century they led revolts in Jerusalem and later in northern Palestine and other parts of the country.

The great revolt broke out in 1703, when the Sultan's agent came to collect the money due the royal treasury. The land tax was sometimes farmed out to local officials, who sought to collect more than the regular sum and used every delay in payment as a pretext for further extortion.

The Sultan's money had to be turned over every spring to a pasha who came from Constantinople, but the local officials never failed to defy him when they thought themselves strong enough. They would seal the city gates and refuse to admit him and his escort. The pasha's forces did not dare to violate the sanctity of Jerusalem by using arms against the rebels, and the Jerusalemites were thus able to hold out for long periods. The revolt of 1703 lasted till 1706, when a pasha was sent from Constantinople with a larger complement of soldiers. He besieged the city, and finally took it by storm.

It is no surprise that under the unbridled rule of greed and cruelty, the Jews were frequently victimized by the Moslems, and that the Jewish situation was frequently unbearable. Often they dared not even show their faces in the street and many had to hide in caves. Naturally the elders and leaders of the community were considered personal sureties for the payment of taxes and levies by every single Jew and often had to hide for their lives. With the elders taken as hostages for ransom or else going into hiding, no normal leadership was possible and the community was bound, in the long run, to disintegrate. We learn from Jewish sources of a debate among the elders whether to allow themselves to be taken or to remain hidden from the authorities and informers. It was finally agreed that whenever an elder suffered over a communal matter, communal funds were to be spent in ransoming him. Frequently elders were seized upon their emergence from concealment and huge sums had to be spent in ransoming them. It is known, for example, that one of the communal leaders, Rabbi Meyhuas ben Samuel, was forced to pay 146 Turkish gold coins.

The communal debt mounted as the interest on loans from the Arabs rose as high as 40 per cent, and was added to the principal, which thus increased geometrically. As the Jews were not allowed to work and there was no commerce in Palestine, the economic situation of Jewish Jerusalem became hopeless. In the end the elders, the wealthy men, and most of the scholars emigrated from the country, leaving behind only the indigent who had no money to be extorted. New immigration was impossible and most of the sources of help in the Diaspora dried up. Within three or four years, Jewish communal life in Jerusalem, bereft of leadership, disintegrated completely.

Radically new ways and means had to be found to assure the survival of the community of Jerusalem. Their coreligionists in Constantinople, to whom an appeal was made to use their influence at Court, finally saved the situation. They did not stop at temporary measures but sought to put the aid to Jerusalem on a new basis.

A permanent committee consisting of seven influential members was organized in Constantinople, the "Constantinople Committee of Elders and Honorary Wardens of the Holy Land." The committee was supplemented by a rabbinic committee, which included the most outstanding rabbis of Constantinople, and supervised and advised the officials. The chief obstacle—the debt of the Jews of Jerusalem to the Moslem moneylenders—was eliminated by a successful intervention at the Palace, and as a result the Sultan issued a firman ordering the creditors to fix the sum of the debt to be defrayed by the Jews of Constantinople.

The Constantinople Committee in effect took over the management of the Jerusalem community and sent an official there to administer communal affairs. To prevent future complications with creditors, the Committee imposed certain taxes and restrictions on the Jerusalemites: Jewish creditors could not collect their debts from the community council until the debt to the Arabs had been paid in full; every gift or will made in Jerusalem had to be approved by the Elders; and there was to be no private selling of gravestones, so that the community might realize the full income from this source. The Committee also assumed control over all fund raisers for Palestine in the Diaspora. Emissaries were sent to Yemen, Egypt, Syria, Mesopotamia, Persia, and all the cities of Turkey to organize the collection of the tax and to establish special funds in all those places.

A new era dawned for Jewish Jerusalem. With the help of the Constantinople Committee, the community was reorganized on a firm foundation, and a new florescence of Jewish life in the city made possible.

The influx of scholars to Jerusalem gathered strength and brought talmudists and cabbalists from all parts of the Turkish empire, as well as Italy and North Africa. Among the outstanding events of the period was the arrival in Jerusalem of Rabbi Hayim ibn Atar of Sali and his group. Setting out from Sali in Morocco, Rabbi Hayim and his thirty followers traveled through Italy, where he organized committees to support the *yeshiva* he planned to establish in Jerusalem. He was joined by several Italian students, and, after many vicissitudes, reached Jerusalem. In 1742 the *yeshiva*, *Midrash Keneset Yisrael*, was established and produced some outstanding scholars.

At that time a unique *yeshiva*, *Bethel*, was established by Gedaliah Hayun, a wealthy cabbalist from Constantinople. The *yeshiva* was to serve as a center of cabbalistic study and prayer according to the teachings of Rabbi Isaac Luria. Among the members of the *yeshiva* were Rabbi Sar Shalom Sharabi, the renowned Yemenite cabbalist, and Rabbi Abraham Gershon of Kutower, the Baal Shem Tob's brother-in-law. The *yeshiva* formed a spiritual brotherhood, numbering more than thirty cabbalists who divided equally among themselves all the religious Commandments they performed and the merits accruing from them. In addition to Rabbi Sharabi the group included such outstanding scholars as Rabbi Israel Jacob Algazi, his son Yomtov, who was later Chief Rabbi of Jerusalem, and Rabbi Hayim Joseph David Azulay (Hida).

In the wake of the immigrant scholars and merchants followed the masses of pilgrims from Turkey who went to pray at the tombs of the holy men. Group after group gathered in Constantinople harbor, especially in the month of *Elul* and during the festival periods, to sail for the Holy Land. The Constantinople Committee organized the journeys and chartered the ships to bring the pilgrims to the port of Jaffa. It became the custom for every Turkish Jew who could afford it to visit the Holy Land at least once in his lifetime. Thanks to these pilgrimages, the bonds between the Jews of Palestine and the Diaspora were strengthened.

The pilgrimages of the wealthy Jews of Turkey and Italy were described in detail by Moses Yerushalmi, who lived in Jerusalem in 1768. They were organized frequently and in large groups, the favorite time being before the Festival of *Shabuot*, when a number of ships bearing wealthy Diaspora Jews put in at Jaffa. Moses himself served as guide for the pilgrim caravans, and he reported that these wealthy men spent 100 to 300 ducats. Each brought along several attendants: one to prepare his coffee, a butcher, one to take care of his tobacco, another to tend his hookah, and a secretary to record descriptions of the holy places. Moses served at once as coffee maker and secretary. He reported that, where necessary, the pilgrims would also donate money for the repair or beautification of the holy places.

In addition to the organized immigration from Turkey, there was immigration from other parts of the Moslem world, especially North Africa. Unlike the Turkish immigrants, who were able to support themselves or who could count on regular assistance, the North Africans were indigent.

For all the external and internal obstacles in the path of the immigrants, the population of Jerusalem grew in the second quarter of the eighteenth century. The authorities in Jerusalem, wishing to obstruct this trend, once more began to harry the Jews. In a letter of 1741 the scholars of Jerusalem reported to the Diaspora communities that the city's population had increased to 10,000. The increase, however, brought on fresh persecution.

One of the severest blows was the ban in 1782 on the burial of Jewish dead on the Mount of Olives. The ban was annuled upon payment of a huge bribe to the governors of the city, "for it is many years since we bought a plot of land for a burial place on the Mount of Olives and we have buried hundreds and thousands of rabbis and scholars, their memory be a blessing for life in the world to come, and it is for these that our eyes darkened when wicked men [*i.e.*, the Moslem oppressors] rose up against us . . . who consider it a transgression to have the dead of Israel buried there . . . and they disturbed the last rest of the dead of Israel. . . . And the mourning was great throughout the House of Israel. . . . How could we bear to behold this great evil? Therefore we had to annul their decree by the payment of a huge sum to all the mighty of the land."

The second half of the century was marked by epidemics, droughts, and the severe earthquake of 1760, which, however, caused no casualties in Jerusalem. In 1757 150 children perished in a smallpox epidemic. In 1772 during the revolt of Ali Bey, there was a prolonged drought. A truce was called to allow shipment of provisions to Jerusalem, but prices were inflated and there was famine. In 1787 another drought was again followed by famine. Once snow fell for about five successive days—the heaviest snowfall known to the sources of that period—and the synagogue established by those from Istanbul collapsed. The inhabitants of the city could not leave their homes even to bury those who had perished in the storm.

To sum up: the eighteenth century witnessed a unique endeavor to reorganize Jewish communal life in Jerusalem, to put its economy on solid foundations and to strengthen its spiritual life, so that it might become a great center for world Jewry. Both the Constantinople Committee and the Jews of Jerusalem made valiant efforts to this end, but external events often threatened to put all their efforts to naught, and more than once Jewish Jerusalem seemed about to relapse to its state at the beginning of the century. No doubt Jerusalem was a religious and scholastic center, and in the first decades of the century most of the immigrants to Palestine went thither. But economic and security factors halted the advance of Jewish Jerusalem, and by the end of the eighteenth century immigration once more turned chiefly to Galilee.

The Aftermath of the Sabbataian Movement

One of the most interesting phenomena at the beginning of the eighteenth century was the great movement of "repentance" that inspired the immigration to the Holy Land of the group headed by Rabbi Judah Hasid and Rabbi Hayim Malak. Not one of Rabbi Malak's contemporaries doubted that this *malak ra* ("wicked angel") was a fanatical Sabbataian belonging to the radical wing of the movement, one of the "thorns" which even moderate Sabbataians felt had to be extirpated from the Lord's vineyard. More recently reliable evidence has been discovered that Rabbi Judah, too, was a Sabbataian, although of the moderate wing which unlike Rabbi Hayim did not go to the length of maintaining that since the "Messiah" had come, the Law and the Commandments were abrogated.

Here we are concerned with the movement only in its bearing on the revival of immigration to Palestine. Toward this end Rabbi Judah joined forces with Rabbi Malak. The two attracted a large following of men, women, and children, including such scholars as Rabbi Jacob of Vilna, Rabbi Kalonymos, Rabbi Nathan Notte of Mannheim, and Rabbi Isaiah Hasid of Zbaraz. In 1700 Rabbi Judah and his devotees went on an extensive and successful "revival" tour of Poland, Moravia, and Hungary, where Rabbi Judah, dressed in white, preached the imminent advent of the Redeemer. Samuel Oppenheim, the wealthy Viennese money broker, supplied them with means to continue their journey. Some of the Hasidim traveled with Rabbi Malak via Constantinople, and the rest went via Venice with Rabbi Judah. The groups reached Jerusalem in October, 1700, and settled in a compound acquired for them at Rabbi Judah's request.

Before the arrival of this group Jerusalem numbered 1,200 Jews, including about 200 Ashkenazim. The head of the Ashkenazic community was Rabbi Moses Hakohen, in whose time the community groaned under the burden of its debts to its Moslem neighbors, which mounted steadily as interest was added to the principal. In 1688-1692 Rabbi Hakohen was abroad collecting money to pay off the debt. With the help of the wealthy Jews of Constantinople and Egypt an agreement was reached with the Moslem creditors whereby interest was not added to the total debt and only the principal was to be paid off in regular installments. The first installment of 80,000 lions was paid before 1707. When the Jews could not pay the next installment, the Arab moneylenders set fire to the synagogue, which was destroyed with the Torah Scrolls and everything else in it.

The current view that the Ashkenazic community of Jerusalem ceased to exist when the synagogue was burned in 1721, and was not restored till 1816, is erroneous. It is true that every Ashkenazic Jew was in danger of being taken hostage for the payment of the community's debts. The garb, custom and mannerism of the Ashkenazim sufficiently distinguished them from their Sephardic coreligionists to make Ashkenazim an easy mark for the Arabs, and the Ashkenazim therefore had to disguise themselves as Sephardim. But we should not infer that Ashkenazic immigration halted altogether; it only waned and most of the immigrants went to Safed or Tiberias. Even in 1742 Rabbi Abraham Ishmael Hai Sanguinetti, one of Rabbi Hayim ibn Atar's group, wrote to his father that twenty Ashkenazim had arrived in Safed. Other sources also attest the presence of Ashkenazim in Jerusalem. In the early years after the destruction of their synagogue the Ashkenazim might well have been cautious about appearing in public. But within twenty-five years the situation had improved, and we know of an Ashkenazic community of some fifty souls. The Ashkenazim carried on despite constant fear of the city's tyrannical rulers, who had all the Jews of Jerusalem at their mercy.

The first to try to re-organize Ashkenazic communal life in Jerusalem was the aforementioned Rabbi Abraham Gershon of Kotower who went to Palestine with his family *c.* 1746. He settled in Hebron, but six years later moved to Jerusalem. At first he did not appear as an Ashkenazi but dressed as a Sephardic *hakam* (rabbi). In 1748 he wrote to his brother-in-law, the Baal Shem Tob, that the Ashkenazic scholars, with the consent of the Sephardim, had entreated him to become their head.

The Palestine immigration of Rabbi Judah Hasid and his group was followed in 1702, just after the collapse of his plans, by the arrival of a similar Italian group, consisting of Rabbi Abraham Rovigo and Rabbi Mordecai Ashkenazi and their followers. Compared with Rabbi Judah Hasid, Rabbi Abraham was certainly the greater scholar and cabbalist, but less inspiring a preacher and leader. He was a disciple of Rabbi Moses Zacuto and a friend of Rabbi Benjamin Hakohen of Reggio. A wealthy and generous man, Rabbi Abraham had always opened his house to scholars and Palestinian emissaries, and he maintained a *yeshiva*. He decided to go to Palestine specifically to establish a new center for the study of the Law and Cabbala. Rabbi Mordecai Delattes, a member of the group, described the journey in a letter to his family in Italy. The whole group, about twenty people, all apparently traveled at Rabbi Abraham's expense. In his *yeshiva* in Jerusalem Rabbi Abraham accepted scholars for study and prayer, among them, characteristically enough, the last of Rabbi Judah Hasid's disciples —his son-in-law Isaiah, Nathan Notte of Mannheim, and Jacob of Vilna— this may serve as further evidence of Rabbi Abraham's link with the crypto-Sabbataians of Rabbi Judah's wing and the arrival of Rovigo's group may, therefore, be viewed as a continuation of the immigration of Rabbi Judah Hasid and his group.

Hebron, Gaza, Nablus

The attempt of the Safed cabbalists to develop Hebron proved abortive. The Jews continued to concentrate in the one compound there. Oppression by the rulers of Hebron and frequent epidemics caused many Jews to flee the city, chiefly to Gaza—with which they had close relations since the trade routes between Gaza and Hebron were always open, and to the extent that Jews were allowed to engage in commerce, they had done so with Gaza, a coastal city which received merchandise from Egypt and other sources.

The peculiar situation of Hebron Jewry prevented it from organizing an autonomous communal life, and it had to be supported by the Jerusalem community and sometimes by the Safed community.

For Hebron the Sabbataian movement spelled economic and spiritual decline, as well as internal strife which caused many Jews to leave the city. Government persecution and natural disaster took a further toll.

We hear of frequent wars between the governors and the sheikhs; of constantly changing regimes; of the governors' victimization of the Jews through exorbitant taxes and threats to destroy the synagogue and cemetery. As a result, Jewish Hebron had a budget far out of proportion to its size. Raphael Mordecai Malkhi (d. 1702) reported that the community required about 2,000 riyals annually, or about 1,000 riyals if the burden of debt were eased, while Safed needed more than 2,000 riyals. According to Rabbi Gedaliah of Semiatic, who arrived in 1700 with Rabbi Judah Hasid, Jewish Hebron numbered about forty householders. He also confirmed that all the Jews lived in a single compound.

The letters of the period indicate that for a long time there was no improvement in the plight of Jewish Hebron. The heads of the community reported that in 1717 the communal debt had risen to 12,000 riyals, and in 1727 to 19,000 piezas; to this amount 20 per cent interest must be added.

The internal disorders among the Bedouin tribes of the vicinity also affected the Jewish community. In 1724 a three-year war broke out, and in 1727 the heads of the Hebron community wrote:

The wars that have afflicted this city for the past three years have split the city into two factions. We, situated in the center, are liable to violent death at every moment, for the lead bullets fly back and forth, most of them falling into our compound, and a number of Jews have narrowly averted death. Moreover, the various factions now threaten to plunder our court and burn some Torah Scrolls and to throw the court to the mercy of the soldiers, and we have had to pay a bribe to the military commanders of 3,000 piezas at 30 per cent interest.

We have already described the restoration of Jerusalem by the Constantinople Committee. Soon the other sacred cities, too, were to benefit from this type of endeavor. In 1733 the Jerusalem cabbalist, Rabbi Gedaliah Hayun, went on behalf of Hebron to Constantinople, where a "Hebron Committee" was organized, parallel to the older Eretz Yisrael (*i.e.*, Jerusalem) committee. The new committee also saw as its prime task the organization of the payment of the debt, and a special emissary was sent to Hebron for that purpose.

Already in 1729 the Constantinople Committee sent 20,000 zlotys to Hebron in part payment of the debt, which then stood at 46,000 kurush. But the amount was spent on current expenses and the peril from the creditors did not abate.

The new Hebron Committee then assumed management of the relief activities and earmarked most of the funds for liquidation of the debt. The Jews of Hebron continued to live in difficult circumstances. Two of their outstanding emissaries who went on successful fund-raising missions to the Diaspora and who made a deep impression on Diaspora Jewry should be mentioned here: Rabbi Hayim Joseph David Azulay (Hida) and Rabbi Hayim Joseph Karigal. Rabbi Azulay, one of the greatest scholars and most impressive personalities of his time, went twice to Western Europe, in 1753 and in 1773. He left a detailed account of his journeys in his diary, *Maagal Tob*. Rabbi Karigal went to Egypt, Syria, Mesopotamia, and Turkey in 1754, at the age of twenty-one; in 1757 he visited Europe, whence he returned to Hebron seven years later; and in 1768 he went on a prolonged journey to Europe, the West Indies (Jamaica), and Philadelphia (1772), New York City, and Newport, Rhode Island. In 1773 he left Newport for Surinam, going thence to Barbados, where he became Rabbi of the Nidhei Israel congregation and where he died in 1777. [Details of Rabbi Karigal's visit to America are known from the diary of Ezra Stiles, later president of Yale University.]

From a document of 1765 we know that the threat of expulsion continued to hover over the Jews of Hebron also in the second half of the eighteenth century. The debt reached 25,000 piezas, in addition to interest of 15 per cent. The Jewish population had grown to 200.

The Jews of Hebron suffered heavily during the revolt of Ali Bey and the Russo-Turkish war of 1773. The inflation of food prices brought on famine, as the Jews had no money to feed their families and support from the Diaspora ceased when the war barred tourists and pilgrims for eight years.

In 1773, upon the intervention of the Hebron Committee, Sultan Abdul Hamid I issued a special order directing Arab creditors to reach agreement with the Jews, fixing the amount of debt and the terms of payment. The amount was interest free. But whenever the Jews could not meet an installment, their creditors severely harassed them and imprisoned the heads of the community. This continued through the eighteenth and into the early nineteenth century. In 1775 the Moslems accused the Jews of Hebron of murdering the son of "the great Sheikh, the King of the land" and throwing the corpse into a sewer. "The Sheikh . . . confined all the Jews, including women and children, in one place to wreak vengeance" (and it was only miraculously that they were spared).

In 1780 Hebron numbered 300 Jews, an increase of some 100 in fifteen years. In 1782 the heads of the community were again imprisoned when a debt installment was not paid. Both famine and inflation raged from 1783-1788. Debts mounted and by 1788 40,000 florins were due for interest alone.

By 1798 the debt had risen 120,000 kurush—80,000 to the Arabs of Hebron and 40,000 to the neighboring villages. Once more the Sultan, upon the intervention of the Hebron Committee, issued a firman canceling the interest on the debt and obligating the Jews to pay off the debt at 10,000 kurush annually, of which the Hebron Committee undertook to defray 8,000.

Our first information about the presence of Jews in Gaza in the eighteenth century is contained in some notes in a manuscript of the Jerusalem physician and warden, Raphael Mordecai Malkhi, apparently written by his son, Ezra Malkhi. The scribe stated that he was writing in Gaza in 1711, and he may well have been Rabbi of Gaza. Another reference to Gaza is found in the travel journal of Rabbi Hayim Joseph David Azulay (Hida). In January, 1754, en route to Egypt on a fund-raising mission for Hebron, Rabbi Azulay arrived in Gaza and had to wait more than fifty days for a caravan to Egypt.

When Napoleon's army reached Gaza in 1799 the community disintegrated, and by 1811 all the Jews had fled to Hebron and Jerusalem.

There is little information about Nablus (Shekhem) in the eighteenth century. Nehemiah Hiya Hayun, of Sabbataian fame, lived there in 1698-1702, and we may assume that there was a small Jewish community. Apparently Nablus had no rabbi or rabbinical court, for prior to 1749 cases regarding marriage and divorce had to come before the rabbinical court in Jerusalem, and the Jerusalem rabbis had to send to Nablus "to learn the facts from the Shekhemites." Rabbi Joseph Sofer mentioned the Jewish community of Nablus in 1760.

Apparently an effort was subsequently made to re-establish Jewish communal life in Nablus, for we have the text of an ordinance promulgated by the Jerusalem scholars requiring all who wanted to pray at the holy places in Nablus to pay "four lions, a donation of every man and woman for the settlement of the aforementioned Holy City."

In speaking to Ezra Stiles about the Palestinian synagogues in 1773, Rabbi Karigal mentioned a small synagogue in Nablus.

However, it appears that the effort to resettle Nablus failed and only a few solitary Jews remained in the city.

IMMIGRATION IN THE EIGHTEENTH CENTURY

Pilgrimages to Palestine were popular in wide circles of Diaspora Jewry, especially in Turkey during the eighteenth century. We have already mentioned the journey of Rabbi Hayim Abulafia with a large group from Turkey to rebuild Tiberias, and the groups organized in Italy and North Africa by Rabbi Hayim ibn Atar.

Turning now to the Ashkenazic immigration—chiefly to Galilee—during this period we wrote that a member of Rabbi ibn Atar's group mentioned twenty Ashkenazim who intended to settle in Safed. He gave no details other than their country of origin. It may be assumed that this group was no isolated phenomenon, but that immigrants—of whom all trace has been lost—also came from Poland and the other East European lands then torn by revolt and civil war.

We know, for example, of the immigration of Rabbi Abraham Gershon of Kutower to Hebron and of Rabbi Eleazar Rokeah of Brod, author of *Maaseh Rokeah,* to Safed and then to Jerusalem (1740). And there is a tradition that the Baal Shem Tob himself set out for Palestine and reached Constantinople, whence, for some unknown reason, he returned to Europe.[5]

These immigrants are held by some scholars to continue the movement begun by Rabbi Judah Hasid; and indeed names of descendants of his followers appear in letters sent during this period from Jerusalem to the Diaspora. It may well be that the Baal Shem Tob[5a] and his brother-in-law, Rabbi Abraham Gershon, intended to establish a Hasidic center in the Holy Land.

Shortly after Rabbi Gershon's death in 1759, Rabbi Joseph Sofer of Beresteczko went to Palestine, followed in 1764 by a large group led by Rabbi Simhah of Salasitz (near Brod), author of *Tales of the Galilee.* With Rabbi Simhah were two outstanding disciples of the Baal Shem Tob, Rabbi Nahman of Horodenka (whose son married the daughter of the Baal Shem Tob) and Rabbi Menahem Mendel of Premiszlan. Rabbi Nahman, comrade and disciple of the Baal Shem Tob, died in Tiberias (*c.* 1780). Rabbi Menahem survived him, but both lived to see an influx of Hasidim from Lithuania and the Ukraine.

Some of these immigrants wished to hasten the advent of Redemption by the mystical methods of the Baal Shem Tob, others according to the Cabbala of Rabbi Isaac Luria. The "First Hasidim" to come in groups from Lithuania, White Russia, and the Ukraine at the end of the eighteenth century, however, had a more practical and "political" objective: they hoped to create in Palestine a new center of Hasidism, a spiritual center which would raise the prestige of the Diaspora Hasidim and strengthen them against their opponents, who had taken the offensive.

A similar attempt on a much larger scale had been successfully made in the eighteenth century, when in 1777, the Hasidim of Lithuania and White Russia, followers of the Baal Shem Tob led by Rabbis Menahem Mendel of Vitebsk, Abraham of Kolisk, and Israel of Polachek, made another attempt.

Rabbi Judah Hasid's effort was restricted to his group. When it failed, it was never revived. The immigration of the disciples of the Baal Shem Tob, on the other hand, was a continuous mass immigration. It even snatched success from failure by becoming a kind of vanguard of the later Ashkenazic immigration and of what is now called the "Old *Yishuv.*"

We have already noted that after Rabbi Judah Hasid's failure, the Ashkenazic community of Jerusalem disintegrated almost completely and the Sabbataian remnants of his group dispersed. The situation remained static for almost a century. Rabbi Gershon had great difficulty in settling in Jerusalem, and but a few Jews remained in Hebron. Tiberias only began to be rebuilt. Some of the Ashkenazim began the move to Safed, which was, in fact the only city in Palestine which remained an overt center of Ashkenazic communal life after the failure of 1720. The historical significance of the Hasidic immigration, therefore, consists—in addition to the strengthening of Safed itself—in the establishment of new Ashkenazic settlements in areas, reaching as far as Pekiin, especially Tiberias, which hitherto had known virtually no Ashkenazim. Moreover this immigration served as the first pioneering link in a chain of immigrations by the disciples of the Baal Shem Tob and the Gaon of Vilna, which laid the foundations of the "Old Ashkenazic *Yishuv*" of the nineteenth century. This also prepared the ground for the "New *Yishuv*" which began in the latter half of the nineteenth century, originating largely in Germany, Russia, and Poland.

The tiny Ashkenazic community adjusted well to the Sephardic majority in language, dress, custom, and manner, insisting only upon retaining the Ashkenazic mode of prayer and autonomous community organization. Even the remnants of Rabbi Judah Hasid's group became assimilated with the Sephardic majority of Jerusalem; and the Ashkenazim of Safed, Tiberias, and Hebron so adjusted to the Sephardic majority that almost all differences between the two groups vanished.

As the Ashkenazic immigration proceeded it was swelled by disciples of the Baal Shem Tob and the Gaon of Vilna, both still alive and apparently approving. This was not, however, a "systematic" immigration, and it was not until seventeen years after the death of the Baal Shem Tob and twelve to fourteen years after that of the Gaon that the Hasidic and Mitnagdic immigrations, respectively, assumed major proportions.

Outstanding disciples of the Gaon who went to Palestine in his lifetime included Rabbi Hayim bar Hayim of Vilna and Rabbi Azriel of Shklov (1770-1772). The Gaon himself set out for Palestine, but for some unknown reason interrupted his journey and returned home.

On the fifth of *Elul*, 1777, the first group of Hasidim arrived and, for reasons already explained, unable to stay in Jerusalem, settled in Safed. The group, headed by Rabbi Menahem Mendel of Vitebsk, comprised more than 300 men, women, and children from Lithuania, Volhynia, the Ukraine, and Wallachia. Their ecstasy upon arrival in the Holy Land quickly gave way to disappointment as they began to suffer want. Indeed, immediately they arrived they turned for assistance to their coreligionists in their places of origin. Rabbi Menahem sent Israel Polotzker to the Diaspora to raise funds. The "Prince" Barukh Zunana helped the emissaries to raise 3,000 lions in Constantinople, of which 2,000 went for payment of a tribute to the governor of Safed, 750 to their families in Safed, and 250 for their own travel expenses. Rabbi Menahem continued to rule from Safed his Hasidim in the Diaspora by appointing not a successor but an "assistant," Rabbi Shneour Zalman of Liadi (who later founded the Lubavitch Hasidic dynasty). Others who helped Rabbi Menahem to keep Diaspora Hasidism from disintegrating and who materially assisted the Hasidim in Palestine were Rabbi Levi Isaac of Berdichev, the Rabbi of Shipitovka, and the Rabbi of Nesvisz. They strictly prohibited the diversion to any other cause of funds raised for Palestine. The emissaries established a fund for the settlement of Palestine, which was of great help to new immigrants. Rabbi Menahem, on his part, sent epistles of encouragement to his followers in the Diaspora, in which he also urged them to do their best for the strengthening of the Palestine *Yishuv*.

In Safed the Hasidim encountered the opposition of the Ashkenazic Mitnagdim who had preceded them. The Mitnagdim were joined by the local Sephardim, whom Rabbi Menahem described as "utterly evil men, believers in Sabbatai Zevi, and led by the evil Leib Sokolier." The Hasidim also mentioned "the Rabbi of Lvov" as one of their tormentors. As a result of this strife the Hasidim had to leave Safed and went to Tiberias or to Pekiin. In Tiberias at last they found peace, and Rabbi Menahem founded a religious center with the help of his followers in the Diaspora. In 1788 he died and was succeeded by Rabbi Abraham Hakohen of Kalisk, who headed the Hasidim until he died in 1810. After his death several disasters, including severe epidemics, ravaged Galilee, and Jerusalem regained ascendancy. At this time the disciples of the Gaon of Vilna, opponents of Hasidism, began to reach Palestine in larger numbers. Although their ultimate destination was Jerusalem, they first went to Safed. They did, in fact, with great self-sacrifice, succeed in striking roots in Jerusalem, and put their stamp on the Ashkenazic immigration of the seventy years between the revival of the Ashkenazic *Yishuv* and the beginning of the Zionist immigration.

The Resettlement of Galilee

Hayim Abulafia, Rabbi of Smyrna (who was born in Hebron, lived in Jerusalem, and for a time was Rabbi of Safed), was a master of the Law and of Cabbala. But he won his place in history by his role in the restoration of Jewish Tiberias, which had stood desolate for some eighty years. Notwithstanding his advanced age, he planned and carried out—along the lines of Don Joseph Nasi's project—the rebuilding of the city in which generations earlier his ancestors had served as spiritual leaders.

According to his son-in-law, Rabbi Jacob Berab, Rabbi Abulafia was invited by the Bedouin Sheikh Zahir al-Omar, the ruler of Galilee, to resettle Tiberias. We know Zahir as a man of great foresight who devoted himself to development of his dominion and who highly regarded the Jews. Thus, just as he had encouraged the Greek Cypriote settlers near Acre, he wrote to Rabbi Abulafia: "Come and inherit the land of Tiberias, seeing that it is the land of your fathers."

Rabbi Abulafia reached Tiberias in 1740. The Sheikh received him with great honor, dressing him in clothes as precious as royal garb, and the rabbi received everything that he requested of the Sheikh. During two years (1740 and 1741) he built houses and courts for the Jews and a beautiful and splendid synagogue without equal in all of Eretz Yisrael. He also built a fine bathhouse, shops for bazaar day, and a press for sesame oil, and he began to construct roads. He ordered the planting of the fields and orchards. The love of the rulers for the rabbi mounted every day. "The people of Tiberias are all healthy and happy, for the land is free from all fear." Here was the beginning of a serious attempt to establish a new settlement on a sound economic basis—on commerce, crafts, and industry—not only an urban but also a rural settlement.

It is clear that Rabbi Abulafia and his group did not view the rebuilding of Tiberias as just a useful activity but as the beginning of an "ingathering of the exiles" for the resettlement of Palestine, and that he sought to repair the wall that protected the Jewish quarter. We have no further details on this venture, but according to another source the Constantinople rabbinate initiated this attempt to rebuild Tiberias. Be that as it may, it was Rabbi Hayim Abulafia who implemented the plan and linked his fate with the fate of Jewish Tiberias.

We know him as a devoted pastor of his flock and a political personality who blazed a new trail for the Jewish resettlement of Palestine through friendly relations with the indigenous leaders. He was helped by Sheikh Zahir and remained true to him. When a violent dispute broke out between Zahir and the Turkish authorities in Damascus, Rabbi Abulafia stanchly supported Zahir at great risk to himself and the Jewish community. He respected Zahir's ability and believed that Zahir would continue to support Jewish immigration as he had in the past and as he had supported other non-Moslem immigration.

Another example of Zahir's positive attitude to Jewish colonization was the restoration of the Jewish agricultural settlement at Kfar Yasif, near Acre. Here Rabbi Solomon Abbadi, author of *Shaarei Rahamim*, a less outstanding personality than Rabbi Abulafia, also played a role. Kfar Yasif had existed for many generations. In 1741 Rabbi Abraham Hai Ishmael Sanguinetti and his associates, who had reached Palestine with Rabbi Hayim ibn Atar, visited Kfar Yasif. But it had been gutted by siege and by invading troops. Rabbi Abbadi restored it as an agricultural settlement which existed till the mid-nineteenth century.

A tradition in Shefaram had it that the village was resettled with the aid of Rabbi Hayim Abulafia. In any case the missionary Schultz attested that in 1754, when he visited Kfar Yasif, he asked to see the rabbi and was told that he was not at home but had gone to Shefaram. Apparently the Shefaram colony grew, especially after Osman, Zahir's son, built a fortress there in 1768. We also know of a "Western" rabbi who settled in Shefaram, where he completed a rabbinic book in 1773. Buckingham, in 1816, also attested the presence of Jews in Shefaram. David Hillels, who visited the village in 1825, reported the presence of twenty Jewish farming families, natives of Palestine. He added that they had a small synagogue and that there was a large Jewish cemetery in the area. Judith Montefiore in her memoirs also referred to Shefaram as a Jewish agricultural settlement.

The Jews of Shefaram, like those of Kfar Yasif and Pekiin, were a farming community, and an agricultural or semiagricultural settlement existed there all during the nineteenth century and till the outbreak of World

War I. The revival of Jewish colonization there belongs to the period of the restoration of Tiberias, a period when the idea of rebuilding Palestine by natural means was born.

Jewish colonization was also strengthened at Pekiin, the oldest continuous Jewish agricultural settlement, which had survived many vicissitudes. It received an infusion of new blood and strengthened its bonds with the other settlements in Zahir al-Omar's time. The name "Pekiin" appears for the first time in the days of Rabbi Hayim Abulafia, in a letter by Rabbi Sanguinetti. In 1760 Rabbi Joseph Sofer settled in Pekiin, where he died, and in 1765 Rabbi Simhah of Salasitz visited it. Rabbi Simhah mentioned the existence of a Jewish farming colony there of an estimated fifty families. This is the only one of the old Jewish agricultural settlements which has persisted to our day [1958].

While the lot of Jewish Tiberias improved under Zahir, Safed suffered at the hands of his son Ali. Zahir derived little pleasure from his sons, among whom he apportioned his dominion. One revolted, unsuccessfully, against him; after defeating him Zahir became reconciled with him. The sons were, on the whole, not as foresighted or capable as their father. They were concerned only with their private affairs, and the many wars in which they were involved, in which Bedouin tribes and the Druses also participated, took a heavy toll of the land. In this period Jewish Safed was depleted by depredation and extortion.

Safed suffered not only at human hands but also from frequent locust invasions, famines, epidemics, and earthquakes. In 1722-1723 there was a famine and in 1728 an epidemic. In 1728 the governor of Safed forbade the Jews to bury their dead in their old cemetery and threatened to destroy the existing tombs, on the ground that the property had not been lawfully acquired. By paying a heavy bribe, the Jews secured annulment of the decree.

According to a document of 1727, the Jewish population of Safed had increased considerably by that year. "The city was resettled and its ruins rebuilt," but this merely increased the burden of the community council. Most of the immigrants had little or no means of subsistence and became public charges. "Expenditures for charity and for the scholars increased tenfold." The increase in the population also led the local governors to make greater demands upon the Jews. Extortion did not cease, and in a letter of 1736 the leaders of Safed repeated, "Our calamity has increased because of the force of the oppressor; and straitness has silenced us." The debt reached 10,000 kurush, and 15,000 by 1767. In that year the Jewish tax farmer was arrested: "A Jew who had bought the taxes of this city was seized" and the community had to defray his debt.

Two severe earthquakes in 1760 (described by Rabbi Joseph Sofer in his *Edut Biyehosaf*) destroyed the houses and synagogues. These disasters and the wars made life impossible in Safed. In 1742 Rabbi Hayim Abulafia wrote in a letter to Italy that "every day, for our many sins, life becomes increasingly bitter for them, each trouble surpassing the former . . . because of the plotters, instigators, slanderers, thieves, and particularly inflation."

Early in 1743 there was an epidemic in which "some Jews perished." In 1778 there was a locust invasion, and Rabbi Israel Polotzker wrote in a letter that he found Safed in ruins and its Jewish inhabitants "in flight, so that the place was left desolate for lack of inhabitants. . . . Food is very dear because of the many wars and the locusts. . . ."

The economic and cultural situation of the Jews of Safed did not improve until the last decade of the eighteenth century with the end of the civil wars. The community grew and its leaders succeeded in obtaining a firman canceling all past debts.

Acre's revival as an important economic and administrative center is linked to the activity of Zahir al-Omar. Acre was important both as a port and as a fortress, which Zahir rebuilt. One of the most important cities in Palestine, Acre played an important commercial role also in a later period, in the time of Ahmad al-Jazzar.

With Acre's reflorescence Jews began to settle in the city and its environs, several dozen families in the city proper. We know that Zahir, who had invited Greek Cypriotes to Acre, also encouraged the settlement of Jews there. It was in his time that Rabbi Moses Hayim Luzzatto (Ramhal) came to Acre. There he soon died in an epidemic and was buried at Kfar Yasif.

After Zahir's defeat the area was taken over by a Turkish administration, Acre falling to the jurisdiction of the Wali of Damascus. Ahmad al-Jazzar, a freed Bosnian slave, was appointed governor of Acre. Quite naturally some Jewish merchants went from Damascus to Acre to do business.

Among the latter was the Mu'allim Hayim Parhi, whom al-Jazzar invited to serve as his financial counselor. Hayim Parhi used his great influence with the government for the betterment of the Jews, and defended them against decrees and extortions by local rulers. Parhi was very influential in all state affairs, not only in al-Jazzar's time but also in the time of his successors, Suleiman Pasha and Abdullah Pasha, for a period of some forty years, on into the nineteenth century. Ahmad was known as a ruthless tyrant, and in one outburst ordered one of Parhi's eyes plucked out and the tip of his nose cut off. Afterward the two men became reconciled and Parhi returned to al-Jazzar's service.

When al-Jazzar died in 1804, Parhi remained in the service of Suleiman, helping him to become governor of Acre, for which Suleiman rewarded him in turn. Suleiman died young, in 1818, and Parhi sought to acquire the governorship for his pupil, Suleiman's orphan, Abdullah. But Abdullah, in a fit of wrath, ordered his benefactor slain on August 24, 1820, his body cast into the sea, and his property confiscated.

Parhi's brothers, important men in Damascus, would not let his death go unavenged and they pressed the Sublime Porte to put an end to Suleiman's tyranny. According to the author of *Tebuot ha-Aretz*, they organized a punitive expedition which besieged Acre for fourteen months. Finally Abdullah smuggled some assassins into the camp of the besiegers who poisoned Solomon Parhi, Hayim's eldest brother. With his death the punitive expedition disintegrated and Abdullah wreaked vengeance on the Jews of Safed.

Napoleon wanted to conquer Egypt, Palestine, and Syria, not only to expand the French empire but also to open new markets, smash the British mercantile hegemony of the Mediterranean and India, and turn them into French spheres of influence. Palestine was an important point in Napoleon's strategy; knowing the attachment of Diaspora Jewry to its ancestral homeland, he interested himself in Jewish history and, to exploit the influence of the Jews of Egypt and other places, brought Jewish soldiers on his campaign in the Orient.

At first Napoleon hoped that Ahmad al-Jazzar, being of Bosnian origin, would join him against the Sultan. But being soon convinced that al-Jazzar was unreliable, Napoleon decided to conquer Palestine, to consolidate his conquest of Egypt and thus assure provisions for his armies. His objective was not Jerusalem, first in the minds of the Crusaders, but the strategic points on the route to Constantinople. But he encountered stiff resistance by the Turks, and his army advanced only slowly, coming to a standstill for several weeks before mounting the attack on Acre. The Jews of Acre, led by Hayim Parhi, sided with the Turks. Napoleon thought that if he could enlist Parhi, the French would be able to take the fortified port and proceed with his plans. Toward this end he sent emissaries to Parhi. In the hope of winning over all the Jews of the East, Napoleon hit upon the plan of proclaiming a Jewish State, and on June 22, 1798, called on the Jews to renew their independence. Apparently there were African Jews in his army who fought valiantly. It is said that when he had conquered Jaffa, a delegation of Jews came to him and told of the Messianic hopes which they pinned on his victory.

On April 14, 1799, a French force led by Kléber won a decisive victory at Mt. Tabor. Napoleon then hoped the Jews would join him, and on April 20 issued a proclamation calling on the Jews of Asia and Africa to rally to his flag for "the restoration of ancient Jerusalem." We know from contemporary sources that many Jews did enlist in Napoleon's army, but we have no certain evidence concerning the formation of a Jewish brigade that was to capture Jerusalem.

The news of Napoleon's proclamations quickly spread throughout Palestine and the neighboring lands, and, as may be expected in the Orient, in greatly exaggerated form. The Moslems, suspecting the Jews of Jerusalem of favoring Napoleon, began to harry them with renewed vigor.

ON THE THRESHOLD OF A NEW ERA: THE NINETEENTH CENTURY

The Domestic and External Political Situation

The Ottoman Empire reached its nadir in the nineteenth century, and the weakness of its domestic civil administration, its military establishment, and its conduct of international affairs was exposed to the sight of the world. This weakness was rooted in developments during the seventeenth century, but did not become obvious until the end of the eighteenth century. Selim III (1789-1807) failed in his attempts to modernize his army and administration after the European pattern, especially the French, and was assassinated by his opponents.

The clouds over the Sultan's Court and the Sublime Porte darkened. The rulers of Europe began to intervene in the internal affairs of the Ottoman Empire which they regarded as "the Sick Man on the Bosphorus" whose days were numbered. Austria already started to express herself thus in the eighteenth century, and her attitude was shared early in the nineteenth century by Russia and France. Some politicians thought they saw signs that Turkey might rally and surmount the crisis that threatened to engulf her. In 1844 Lord Palmerston, British Foreign Secretary, in a letter to the British ambassador at Constantinople took exception to the general view that the Turkish Empire was on the brink of collapse, pointing to Turkey's latent ability to confute all calculations based on comparison with other states. But the nineteenth century, and the twentieth until the peace treaties at Sèvres (1920) and Lausanne (1923), were marked by the dismemberment of Turkey as one by one the non-Turkish European provinces of the Empire, and finally also the Asiatic provinces, broke away and became independent states.

Strategic, political, and religious factors raised Palestine (and all of Syria) to international importance during this period. After the Crusades, and especially after their annexation to the Ottoman Empire, Palestine and Syria became outlying provinces of little importance to their masters in Constantinople. The revolts of Fakh-al-Din the Druse, Zahir al-Omar the Bedouin, and Ahmad al-Jazzar the Albanian, who dreamed of widening their spheres of influence and aggrandizing their private coffers from taxes in those lands, were not important enough to disturb the Sublime Porte, which regarded them as minor pests.

The Courts of Europe had been only casually interested in Palestine, on account of the Christian holy places. The interest of France, which developed the idea of "capitulations," was primarily economic, her religious interest having begun to wane in the mid-eighteenth century.

In 1824 the Arab peasants of Jerusalem and its vicinity rebelled against a tax increase imposed by the new governor of Damascus, Mustafa Pasha. According to a Jewish source the small Jewish community was required to pay, in addition to the usual taxes, a sum of 100,000 piasters, *i.e.*, more than half the total annual income of the Jerusalem community. According to a Christian source the Greek Orthodox community of Jerusalem was so poor that the sacred articles of its church were pawned to a Jew (Anjel) for 50,000 piasters, but the Pasha would not relent and demanded the full sum due him from the Greek Orthodox community. When the Pasha left the city in the spring of 1825, the revolt spread and the Arabs drove the Turks and Albanians from the city. In the month of *Tishri*, 1826, Sultan Mahmud II had to order Abdullah, the governor of Acre, to take Jerusalem and restore it to the Wali of Damascus. Abdullah camped on the Mount of Olives and after two weeks of bombardment took Jerusalem on the day of *Simhat Torah*. He then invited the Wali of Damascus to send an occupying force.

In October, 1831, Ibrahim Pasha, Mohammed Ali's son, invaded Palestine by land and sea. The Egyptian forces took Jaffa without a fight, and generally met little resistance until they reached Acre. There Abdullah Pasha and his garrison held Ibrahim at bay until May, 1832.

Constantinople did not hasten to Abdullah's aid, apparently wishing to give Ibrahim time to weaken him and thus be rid of two dangerous pashas at once. But once again Constantinople miscalculated. After Mohammed Ali's army had conquered Acre and taken Abdullah prisoner, the Egyptian advance could not be halted. The Egyptians took Syria, penetrated to Konieh in Anatolia, and threatened Constantinople. Only the threats of Russia and Great Britain stemmed Mohammed Ali's advance and saved the tottering throne of Sultan Mahmud II.

In the autumn of 1831 the Egyptian legions began to move in the direction of Palestine. Abdullah's vizier of the sector of "Gaza, Ramleh, Lydda, Hebron, and Jaffa" quickly informed his master that the Egyptians had reached el-Arish, and that a rumor had spread that they were turning toward Gaza. The Egyptians were led by Ibrahim Pasha and did not encounter much resistance until they reached the walls of Acre, where they were stopped for a half a year.

The Egyptian conquerors were careful not to antagonize the populace. At first they retained the Moslem officials of Jaffa and Jerusalem who had been appointed by Abdullah, and only later began to replace them with members of families newly risen to power, such as the Abd el-Hadi family of Nablus and the Kasm family of Jerusalem. To serve beside the regional civil governors they appointed military governors. Sherif Bey (later Pasha) was appointed governor of Syria. Ibrahim Pasha was not satisfied to make only administrative changes but tried to revolutionize the society itself. He rejected support by the sheikhs of the Abu Ghosh family and even imprisoned as a rebel one who had disobeyed his orders. The rift widened after the revolt of 1834, and Jabr Abu Ghosh, the Jerusalem commissioner, was ousted from office.

Ibrahim abolished the administrative taxes and the collection of tolls from the devout and pilgrims, and tried to substitute a system of regular government wages for the old system whereby the officials lived off whatever they could extract from the indigenous populations.

The liberal attitude of the Egyptian regime to the non-Moslems was manifested in the permission granted the Jewish community to repair the four synagogues known as the Elijah the Prophet, the Rabbi Johanan ben Zakkai, the Istanbul, and the Middle Synagogues. Permission was granted, moreover, to replace a wooden beam in one of these synagogues with a rock dome, although it seems that technically the synagogues were allowed only to be restored to their *status quo*. According to a Christian writer, the repairs cost 1,000,000 piasters.

Notwithstanding these reforms intended to raise the economic, social, and cultural level of the land, and vigorous, sincere efforts to maintain public order, most of the populace was hostile to Mohammed Ali's regime. We have noted that in the spring of 1834 the Arab peasants in Palestine revolted, taking Jerusalem, Tiberias, and Safed, and besieging Jaffa and Acre. Ibrahim Pasha had to send to Egypt for help in quelling the insurrection. Its direct cause was the military conscription of Moslems. The sheikhs and the other feudal lords who would not surrender their prerogatives or accept Ibrahim Pasha's administration incited the Moslem populace against him, pointing to him as an "infidel" for his liberality toward the Christians.

When the Egyptians came to "restore order" in the hotbeds of revolt, they did not distinguish between Jew and non-Jew, innocent and guilty, but gave their troops free rein to pillage and slaughter. In Hebron, for example, it was the Jews who suffered most when the conquering Egyptian soldiers set upon the populace.

In Jerusalem the Jews suffered only a few casualties, and in Tiberias averted disaster by surrendering all their wealth as a bribe. Safed, which at the beginning of the century still occupied first place in Jewish Palestine, felt the full fury of the Egyptians. According to reliable sources (to be discussed later), there were 4,000 Jews in Safed at the beginning of the century. By the 1820's or 1830's, the Jewish community had dwindled.

The Egyptian forces retreated with the intervention of the European powers on Turkey's behalf. At the end of October, after the conquest of Lebanon, Acre fell after a bombardment by British and Turkish naval forces. The fortress, which Napoleon could not conquer and which Ibrahim had besieged for seven months, now fell after a joint sea offensive and the fate of Palestine was decided. One by one the tribes surrendered to Turkey, whose armies took all the cities and villages unopposed. At the end of December the shattered remnants of the huge Egyptian army reached the Egyptian border and the Turkish army reoccupied all Palestine. According to a contemporary Jewish historian, "Constantinople has risen."

On November 11, 1840, the Turks installed in Jerusalem a fourteen-member council to attend to the welfare of the Jerusalem populace. The council included Hawaja Runa (Aaron), commissioner for the Jewish community, and one Joseph, commissioner for the "Frank" (apparently the Latin) community.

That year the Jews of Jerusalem requested permission to pave the area before the Wailing Wall. Their request was denied at the order of Mohammed Sherif Pasha (issued on May 27, 1840), when it was learned that the area adjoined the wall of the Haram esh-Sherif and the Mosque el-Buraq and belonged to Abu Madin, the custodian of ecclesiastical property. However, the Jews were allowed to continue to visit the wall.

Between Oppressors

Although Napoleon abandoned his plan to conquer Palestine, the Turks continued to suspect the Jews of having conspired with him. The early years of the nineteenth century were difficult for the Jews of Jerusalem, and Turkish suspicion brought fresh oppression with them. Not only the governor but his assistants, his military commanders and their troops, used every opportunity to exploit the Jews. In addition to the regular poll and land taxes they were compelled to pay a "government aid" tax, festival taxes, and a monthly tax.

In 1825 the Arab peasants of Jerusalem revolted and violent fighting raged between them and the army of Mustafa, the new Pasha of Damascus. In retaliation the Pasha imposed numerous new levies on the populace. The revolt was sketched above, but we should add here that the Jews, who did not participate in the revolt, yet suffered no less than the rebels. They were assessed 100,000 lions, more than half the annual income of the Jerusalem Jewish community, in addition to their regular taxes. News of the outrageous taxes imposed by the Pasha, the revolts against him, and the action of the inhabitants of Jerusalem in seizing control of the city from the Turks and Albanians, reached Sultan Mahmud II; and he ordered Abdullah Pasha, the governor of Acre, to lead a large force to Jerusalem, occupy the city, and punish the rebels. He marched on Jerusalem in *Tishri*, 1826. Unable to enter because the inhabitants had sealed the gates, he camped on the Mount of Olives and from there bombarded the city. Many Jewish houses were struck, but miraculously there were no Jewish casualties. Two weeks later the rebels surrendered, and Abdullah entered Jerusalem.

Although many emissaries went to the Diaspora, the funds that reached Jerusalem did not cover the community's debts and ordinary needs. Not all Diaspora communities responded generously to the fund appeals, some complaining that the expenses of the emissaries were excessive, being enough to "build castles of gold and silver." We have a detailed accounting, however, of the community's needs, income, and expenditure in the book *Tub Yerushalayim*, by Isaac Parhi, the communal treasurer.

There were in Jerusalem during this period four funds which had existed for many years: the scholar's fund, the poor fund, the sick fund, and the orphan girls' fund.

In addition to the regular stipends from their *yeshibot*, the students and scholars of Jerusalem, twice a year—before Passover and before *Sukkot*—received special grants from the scholar's fund. The administrators of the fund also helped scholars to support their families. The fund expended an average of 12,000 kurush annually and was replenished by 10 per cent of the amounts raised by the emissaries and by memorial gifts from the wealthy.

The poor fund provided Jerusalem's numerous native poor and indigent pilgrims with food every Sabbath, fuel in winter, and special food for Passover. The fund was replenished by a regular tax paid by all who received annual contributions from the Diaspora according to the ratio of one para for every kurush received (forty paras equaled one kurush). Every Friday the wardens would go from house to house collecting loaves of bread for the poor, and before Passover they made a special fund collection.

The sick fund aided the ailing and their families, paying the doctors, buying the medicines, and, when occasion arose, paying burial expenses. The fund was reimbursed by the relatives of the deceased to the extent of forty kurush by wealthy relatives and twenty-five by those of the middle class.

The orphan girls' fund supported the orphan girls, provided for their education, and helped to marry them off. The fund was replenished by selling gifts of clothing of deceased members of the community.

The finances of Jerusalem had three major sources: the funds raised by the emissaries, the estates of deceased, and the tax paid by individuals who received money from abroad. The chief source, according to Isaac Parhi, was the money raised by the emissaries. He defended the Jerusalemites against the charge of becoming rich on the contributions of the Diaspora, by arguing that the charges were based on the erroneous calculation that the regions covered by the emissaries—Turkey, North Africa, and the Arabic lands—sent 50,000 kurush each, while Western Europe sent 100,000 kurush, so that the community received according to the statistics of the inquisitors, a total of 250,000 kurush. Actually, claimed Parhi, the emissaries were sent out only once every three or four years, and half their income went to defray their wages and expenses. At the same time the needs of the community were great. Most of the income did not go to the Jews of Jerusalem at all, but to the governors and officials as bribes to avert fresh persecution and allow the community to live. There was also the heavy burden of interest on outstanding debts, in addition to the maintenance of a huge number of aged, widows, and orphans. Moreover, there were always some indigent among the immigrants who continued to arrive from various lands. Parhi listed the places of origin of these newcomers: "For the most part there is not one ship from Constantinople or Salonica, etc., that does not bear at least ten needy men and women, in addition to those who come from Aleppo, Damascus, Babylon, and the Aegean cities, etc., and every day the expenses mount." It was difficult for the Jews to engage in labor or crafts and only few succeeded. Parhi enumerated some of the other needs provided for by the community: support of scholars, orphans and widows, education of children, Passover supplies, shrouds for the dead, graves and tombstones for the poor, etc.

In spite of many and unceasing tribulations, the community decided to rehabilitate their old synagogues, which had long since begun to crumble. At first the Jews were denied the special permit which, under Moslem law, members of non-Moslem religions had to obtain, but when the Egyptians conquered Palestine the heads of the community renewed their request, and in 1835 permission was granted. The community then found it could not afford to undertake the necessary repairs, but decided that it must begin lest the permission be revoked and great expense required to secure it again. Forthwith fund-raising emissaries were sent to the Diaspora and in August, 1835, the work began.

At the same time that the repair of the old Sephardic synagogue in Jerusalem was begun, the Ashkenazim received permission to restore the ruins of their old synagogue, named after Rabbi Judah Hasid. The Ashkenazim began to establish themselves again in Jerusalem in 1817, with the arrival of Rabbi Menahem Mendel of Shklov, disciple of the Gaon of Vilna. He founded a large Ashkenazic nucleus in the city and secured a firman canceling the debts of the Ashkenazim and allowing them to build an open residential quarter. But these efforts (to be described later in greater detail) did not bear fruit, for external reasons, until the regime of the Egyptian Ibrahim Pasha.

Already in 1820 Rabbi Solomon Pah had been sent to Constantinople to obtain a firman canceling the old debts of the Ashkenazim and thereby legally establishing their right to live openly in Jerusalem. But the Arab families, contending that the Ashkenazim owed huge sums to their ancestors, would not surrender their claim to the Ashkenazic ruins. It was not until 1824 that the Ashkenazim succeeded in obtaining a *fetwa* from the Kadi of Jerusalem canceling their old debts. Just as the Ashkenazim began to clear away the ruins and prepared to build, Mohammed Ali of Egypt conquered Palestine and negotiations had to be undertaken anew. In 1836 Rabbi Abraham Solomon Zalman Zoref went to Egypt for this purpose. With the help of the European powers, who saw the Jews as a means of expanding European influence by the acquisition of capitulations, Rabbi Zoref succeeded in obtaining a firman ordering the creditors to reach a compromise with their Ashkenazic debtors.

On 19 *Elul*, 1836, one year after the Sephardim had begun to dismantle their synagogue in order to repair it, the Ashkenazim started to clear away the debris from their ruins. Four and one-half months later, on the New Moon of *Shebat*, 1837, the *Menahem Zion* (Comforter of Zion) synagogue was dedicated.

When the Ashkenazic community proved capable of receiving the refugees from the great earthquake of 1837 in Galilee, Jerusalem became the center of Ashkenazic life in Palestine until the beginning of the modern Zionist era.

Fresh impetus to the rebuilding of Jerusalem was given by Sir Moses Montefiore's visit to Palestine. His rare love of Palestine and the Jewish religion brought him to Palestine seven times so that he might become acquainted at first hand with conditions there and seek ways of bettering them. He sent regular contributions to the cities and towns of the Holy Land from his own wealth, as well as from funds he raised. He planned the establishment of public institutions and economic projects in Palestine and was particularly interested in the advancement of agriculture.

Sir Moses first visited Palestine with his wife Judith in 1827. While his purpose was to become acquainted with the Holy Land, he lavished money on educational and charitable institutions. He began to initiate projects during their second visit, in 1839. He instructed his secretary, Eliezer Halevi, to compile a detailed roster of all the Jews in Palestine. Ostensibly this roster was to serve as a basis for carrying out various projects for the amelioration of the condition of Palestine Jewry; actually, it merely served for the distribution of alms.

From this roster we know that 83.3 per cent of the Jewish population of Jerusalem were Sephardim, the balance Ashkenazim; of the 16.7 per cent Ashkenazim, 14.2 per cent were *perushim,* 1.4 per cent Hasidim, while 1.1 per cent belonged to the Dutch and Hungarian congregations. We also know that the Sephardim came from Anatolia, the Balkans, Syria, Iraq, Algeria, Morocco, Persia, Kurdistan, etc., and that Sephardic immigration reached its peak in 1829 (during the Balkan wars and when Ibrahim Pasha of Egypt ruled Palestine).

According to Montefiore's roster, eighty of Jerusalem's Sephardim and seven Ashkenazim were brokers, money-changers, peddlers, and dealers in livestock, cheese, wine, and books. Other professions included weavers, tailors, porters, muleteers, bakers, butchers, barbers, mill workers, carpenters, metalworkers, smiths, bookbinders, household workers, hatters, masons, a cobbler, a watchmaker, and several "physicians."

After the destruction of the Safed community, Jerusalem was the center of Jewish life in Palestine, with a population of 2,943, or 46 per cent of the total Jewish population of Palestine. Of these 2,450 were Sephardim and Orientals, and 493 Ashkenazim. The Ashkenazim were divided into three groups, thirty-four of Dutch and Hungarian origin, forty-one Hasidim, and 418 of miscellaneous European origin, while the Sephardim and Orientals were united in one organization. The ratio of Jews in Jerusalem to Jews in the rest of Palestine remained fairly constant until after World War I. Thus in 1914, Jerusalem's 45,000 Jews comprised 45 per cent of the country's Jewish population. After the Balfour Declaration, when Palestine became a British mandate and the Third *Aliyah* got under way, the Jewish population of all of Palestine increased tenfold while that of Jerusalem a little more than doubled (to 100,000).

Montefiore's second visit to Palestine was at a time of relative quiet, at the height of Egypt's withdrawal. In Syria, on the other hand, this was the period of the Damascus blood libel (1840), which inspired the Jerusalem blood libel of 1847. But the glimmerings of national awakening which appeared among world Jewry in Ibrahim Pasha's day did not fade. No new colonization endeavors were undertaken in Montefiore's time, but the idea of a natural return to Zion remained alive. To be sure, this period, which saw the liberation of Greece and the establishment of Egyptian independence under Mohammed Ali, was politically unpropitious for the realization of the Jewish national idea within the borders of Ottoman Turkey, which discountenanced all national movements. Yet it was in this period that the Zionist idea, even before any Zionist movement had come into being, began to win friends among outstanding non-Jewish writers and statesmen. In Great Britain especially there were voices declaring the restoration of the Jews to Zion as the sole solution to the Jewish problem.

This period also marked the beginning of the intervention of foreign consuls in Turkey on behalf of the Jews. The British consuls (James Finn and others) were especially sympathetic to the Jewish aspirations to resettle their ancestral homeland. Some had missionary objectives in mind, hoping by their sympathy and support to win the Jews to Christianity. Others, however, took the Jews under their protection out of a genuine and altruistic desire to expedite the return to Zion.

The period before the Crimean War saw not only the beginning of a new immigration but also basic changes in the status and composition of the Jewish population of Palestine. Enjoying the protection of the European powers, their numbers increased. Whereas in the fifteen years after Turkey reconquered the land from Egypt the population grew but little (by 6,500 according to Montefiore, 10,600 according to Fraenkel), the increase was much more considerable in the twenty years after the Crimean War.

More important than the quantitative increase was the improvement in quality and the great economic progress. Let us compare the record prepared by Montefiore with the record of the emissaries of 1876.

In 1839 eighty Sephardim and seven Ashkenazim engaged in commerce; in 1877, 241 Sephardim and 215 Ashkenazim. In 1839 there were 257 householders engaged in labor and the crafts, 229 Sephardim and twenty-eight Ashkenazim; in 1877, 390 Sephardim and 579 Ashkenazim—*i.e.*, a fourfold increase. In 1839 there were 289 Sephardim and 118 Ashkenazim in the religious callings; in 1877, 290 Sephardim and 255 Ashkenazim, including adult *yeshiva* students. With this marked increase in gainful employment there grew a desire to cast off the life of doles and dependence upon the charity of wealthy benefactors. In memoranda submitted to Montefiore, the leaders of the *Yishuv* spoke of the need to develop new sources of livelihood by providing technical and agricultural training. Primary stress was laid on the education of children and the need to train them in profitable trades. The first to concern themselves with this were the missionaries, who, while their philanthropic endeavors among the Jews had an ulterior motive, also provided medical services, aid to the poor, and some assistance in agriculture. Inverting a famous phrase from the book *Kuzari:* "Their deeds were good albeit their intentions were not." There was an increasing desire among the Jews to be rid of missionaries and their benefactions.

Montefiore founded a number of charitable institutions and aid funds, which due to poor management were short-lived. Later in 1855 Fraenkel founded the Eliza von Laemel School, and in 1864 the Evelina de Rothschild School was founded.

There was also a radical innovation in urban housing. Up to this time most of the houses in which the Jews lived and a number of synagogues were rented from their Arab neighbors, whom the Jews constantly feared. It required great courage to move outside the city walls, whose gates were sealed every night with iron bolts, to an area open to bandits and robbers. This is precisely what the Jews did; they began to build themselves new living quarters outside the Old City.

The first quarter *extra muros* was Mishkenot Shaananim (1856, Tura Houses, and later Yemin Moshe), built by Montefiore. In 1869 Nahlat Shibah was founded, in 1873 Meah Shearim and Even Yisrael, in 1875 Bet Jacob and Mishkenot Yisrael. New quarters continued to spring up on the northern, western, and southern sides of the Old City, until the vast majority of the Jews of Jerusalem were living outside the walls.

The building crafts flourished as never before and Jews became masons, stonecutters, and bricklayers, trades entirely new to them which now provided livelihood for hundreds of families. The Jews also introduced stagecoach travel from quarter to quarter, thus pioneering in urban transportation.

New welfare institutions were established in addition to the old dole institutions. Alongside the old Sephardic and Ashkenazic religious schools modern schools were founded, such as the Laemel School (teaching in German); the Evelina de Rothschild School (teaching in English); and the *Alliance Israélite Universelle* agricultural school at Petah Tikvah (1870) and elementary school in Jerusalem (1882) (teaching in French). Homes for orphans and the aged were founded, dispensaries, clinics, and hospitals, enabling the Jewish population to free itself once and for all from the charity of the missionaries.

With this material growth and progress came the need for the printed word. The first printing press was founded in Jerusalem by a Jew, Israel Bak, who established it there in 1842—with Montefiore's help—after his press had been wrecked in Safed during the revolt of the Arab peasants in 1834 and again in the great earthquake of 1837. Soon both Jews and European Christians brought additional presses to Jerusalem and this new trade became firmly rooted. With the presses the first newspapers began to appear (*Halevanon Yehudah Viyerushalyim*, etc.) not to mention religious books, scholarly and homiletical works, prayer books, announcements, brochures and pamphlets of charity institutions, and the like. Jews also pioneered in Palestinography. One of the world's first scientific studies of Palestine geography, history, and nature was *Tebuot ha-Aretz*, published in Jerusalem in 1845 by Joseph Schwarz. Other outstanding Palestinographers were Hayim Horowitz, author of *Hibbat Yerushalayim*, and somewhat later A. M. Luncz.

Judea and Samaria

Jewish Hebron continued a precarious existence well on into the nineteenth century, unable to keep pace with the new developments elsewhere in Palestine. Only now and then would an odd individual coming with the great streams of immigration from Turkey, North Africa, Russia, and Poland settle in Hebron.

In 1819, as a result of the widening rift between the Hasidim of Rabbi Abraham Hakohen (who went from Kalisk in White Russia to Tiberias) and the Habad Hasidim (the followers of Rabbi Shneour Zalman of Liadi, who in Russia was the leader of the endeavors on behalf of the Hasidim in Galilee), fifteen Habad families (fifty-six souls) moved from Galilee to Hebron. There they established themselves as a separate community, sending emissaries of their own to the Diaspora. The Habad community in Hebron grew as the immigration from Russia increased.

During the war of Ibrahim Pasha, when the Arabs of Hebron revolted against the Egyptians, the Jews of Hebron suffered more than any other Jewish community in the land. Ibrahim Pasha ordered his troops ruthlessly to suppress the revolt, and, when they attacked the city with permission to plunder and slaughter at will, they did not distinguish between the Arabs and the Jews, who had no part in the rebellion.

This calamity united the Hebron Sephardim and the Habad Hasidim, and in 1834 they jointly sent Rabbi Nathan Amram to seek aid in Western Europe for Jewish Hebron.

The community did not fully recover until Rabbi Elijah Mani arrived in the city in 1858. Going to Jerusalem from Bagdad in 1856, he quickly became famous for his scholarship and piety, and was received as one of the master cabbalists at the Bethel *Yeshiva*. At Hebron he immediately began devoting himself to the advancement of Jewish communal life. He founded the Bet Jacob *Yeshiva* and synagogue, turning Hebron into a center of scholarship for youth. When Moses Pereira, the Rabbi of Hebron, died in 1865, the Hebronites asked Rabbi Mani to become their leader. He did not immediately accept, for that year a plague had stricken Hebron and he was busy administering aid to the victims; but when the plague passed he accepted, on condition that he receive no salary. Communal life was reorganized and Jews from Oriental lands began to immigrate in large numbers to Hebron. In 1872, during a drought, Rabbi Mani went abroad and obtained substantial aid for the Jews of Hebron. Another time he went to raise money to buy the Cave of Makhpelah. He was also active in promoting agricultural colonization in the Hebron environs, writing to Sir Moses Montefiore and Rabbi Judah Alcalay about the plots of land around Hebron which ought to be purchased from the Arabs for colonization and cultivation by Jews.

A major figure in the advancement of the *Yishuv* generally and of Jewish Hebron in particular was Rabbi Hayim Hezekiah Medini, author of *Sdei Hemed*, the eighteen-volume halakic encyclopedia. A native of Jerusalem, he served for thirty-three years as the Rabbi of Khersobazaar in the Crimea, where he revolutionized Crimean Jewish life. In 1899 he returned to Palestine and in 1901 settled in Hebron.

Gaza had a sparse and poor Jewish settlement after 1799, when Napoleon took the city. In 1811 the Jews left Gaza altogether for Hebron and Jerusalem. The old Hebronites related that when the Gazaites reached Hebron they brought along the doors of the old synagogue in Gaza and affixed them to the old synagogue in Hebron. The doors, which existed until the destruction of Jewish Hebron in 1929, were decorated with the Star of David and other carvings.

Some Jews returned to Gaza to trade, and by 1860 a number of them were living there. According to A. M. Luncz, who organized the Jewish community in Gaza after 1870, among the first new settlers were two Moroccan Jews who bought the durrah (millet) crops that grew around Gaza. Ten years later a Jewish government official from Damascus settled in Gaza with his family, and five years later a Moroccan family. But the major Jewish colonization in the area took place further north, at Gedera and Beer Tuviah, which were administratively and economically linked to Gaza.

The Jewish population of Gaza grew slowly. According to Luncz, Gaza had seventy-five Jews in the 1890's, increasing during the decade preceding World War I to 200; more than half were Moroccans, two Yemenites, and the rest Sephardim and Ashkenazim.

The Jews of Gaza were economically well off. They dealt chiefly in durrah and barley bought from wholesale merchants for export to beer brewers. Gaza was famous for barley, and ships put in regularly at its port to load grain for beer manufacturers.

At the beginning of World War I the Jewish subjects of England and France were banished from Gaza, and when the battle reached the city gates the rest of the Jewish inhabitants were banished.

In Samaria, the old Jewish community at Nablus continued to exist. The attempt in 1760 to strengthen this settlement failed, but early in the nineteenth century the Jewish population there increased. In 1832 Rabbi David Hillels visited Nablus and found "about ten native Jewish families who have a small synagogue." The following year Rabbi Mendel of Kamenitz reported that there were "two *minyanim* of Sephardim and one *minyan* of Ashkenazim." There is no doubt, however, that the Jewish population of Nablus increased during this year. Nablus was hard hit by the earthquake of 24 *Shevat*, 1837. According to Rabbi Israel of Shklov, "houses and all the shops collapsed and approximately sixty souls perished." In Montefiore's census of 1839, there were twenty-five Jewish families—or seventy-five souls—in Nablus. Only two families were native to Nablus, the majority originating from Aleppo and Damascus and some from Jerusalem, Mesopotamia, Yemen, Rhodes, Constantinople, Sarajevo, and the West. Some were merchants but the balance were handicraftsmen: smiths, cobblers, woodchoppers, and one tailor.

According to Montefiore's census of 1866 there were twelve Jewish families—or sixty-two souls—in Nablus, of whom four were merchants and eight cobblers, smiths, a silk worker, and a watchmaker, all living in great want. Seven youngsters studied at the school located in the town synagogue.

With the rise of the modern *Yishuv*, these small communities disintegrated, dispersing largely to Jaffa and Jerusalem. In 1895 Luncz counted 120 souls in Nablus, and in the report of 1896-1897 of the General Council we find: "For the strengthening of the *Yishuv* in the other Holy Cities: for the wages of a ritual slaughterer and to aid the inhabitants of the Holy City of Nablus—490.20 kurush; to help the inhabitants of Jericho in their straits—1,045.10 kurush."

No new Jewish colonies were established in the vicinity of Nablus, and the younger generation of the city saw no future there. Little by little they left Nablus, until in 1896 only fifty Jews remained. Three or four years later Luncz counted thirty-one, and when I visited the city in 1908 I found not a single Jew. But for a few tombstones which had survived the vandalism of the local Arabs, not a trace was left of this 700-year-old Jewish ghetto.

Except for several individuals who remained in Gaza and Jaffa, the Samaritan community, formerly represented in all the cities and towns of the country—especially the coastal cities—then concentrated in Nablus. In 1842, after the rout of the Egyptian army, the Arabs of Nablus began to persecute the Samaritans on the grounds that they had no religion. Chief Rabbi Hayim Abraham Gaguine saved them by certifying that they believed in One God and in the Pentateuch.

The Jewish community of Ramleh did not become firmly established until the nineteenth century. Previously it was mainly a stopping place for travelers to Jerusalem from the port of Jaffa, who had to spend the night in Ramleh en route.

The Sephardic community of Jerusalem bought a building in Ramleh to serve as a wayside inn for pilgrims. It may be assumed that this house also served as a center for Jewish refugees in Ramleh.

Jewish colonization of Ramleh began with the establishment of the agricultural colonies. David Yudelowitz wrote in 1886 that a number of Jews had just gone to settle in Ramleh, heretofore without Jewish settlement. The new settlers included a number of carpenters and metalworkers who came with the help of Nissim Bechar, at whose school in Jerusalem they had learned their trades, and were then earning a comfortable livelihood.

Ramleh remained static after World War I, when the Third *Aliyah* began to stream to Palestine. In the first census under the British Mandate in 1922, thirty-five Jews were recorded in Ramleh, 5,837 Moslems, and 1,440 Christians. But by 1931 the city had five Jews, 8,156 Moslems, 2,184 Christians, and two Druses, the remainder of the Jews having fled the city during the riots of 1929.

With the establishment of the State of Israel and the conquest of Ramleh by the Israel Defense Forces, many immigrants and refugees made their home in Ramleh and it became a Jewish city.

The destruction of Jaffa by Napoleon on March 3, 1799, on his march north from Gaza has already been mentioned. Mohammed Abu Nabbut, a vassal of Jazzar Pasha, rebuilt the city early in the nineteenth century. He built the harbor and the market place, and soon vineyards and orchards again abounded in the area.

The fact that Jaffa served as a transit station for the immigrants and pilgrims to Palestine aroused the special interest of Turkish Jewry, who made up the majority of the pilgrims. In 1820 Isaiah Ajiman, treasurer to the chief of the Janissaries in Constantinople, went to Jerusalem. When he saw the Jews' distress at having to lodge in a Christian house upon arrival in Palestine, he bought a compound in Jaffa for an inn for Jewish pilgrims and tourists.

The Jewish settlement at Jaffa was said to be established in 1838 by a group of Moroccan immigrants. But Sir Moses Montefiore's census of 1839 —immediately after the arrival of the North Africans—proved conclusively that there was a Jewish colony in Jaffa when this immigration arrived. In addition to the North African Jews, a minority, there were in Jaffa Jews from the Turkish Empire (the majority from Constantinople, Smyrna, Salonica, Bosnia), Egypt (Damietta), Bulgaria (Sofia), Yemen, one from Russia, and several natives of Palestine (Acre and Jerusalem).

Most were merchants and handicraftsmen—tailors, tinsmiths, glaziers, and laborers—among whom were a *hakam* (Sephardic rabbi) and a teacher. Most were young, but there were several aged among them, and one had been in Palestine for twenty-six years.

Jewish Jaffa started to flourish after 1857, when the Crimean War ended. Christian pilgrims from abroad began to pass through Jaffa on their way to the holy places. At this time, too, commerce expanded in Jerusalem and many Jerusalemites moved to Jaffa. One was Sir Hayim Amazlag, formerly of Gibraltar, who with several partners opened a commercial establishment in Jaffa, where after some years he was appointed British vice-consul. Twelve years later a group of Jerusalem Ashkenazim founded the first Ashkenazic community in Jaffa. This grew very slowly until the first great wave of Russian and Polish immigration arrived simultaneously with the First *Aliyah* of the *Hovevei Zion*.[6a] The growth of Jaffa thus is closely linked with the idea of agricultural colonization and with the colonization of Judea.

In 1888 Neveh Zedek and in 1890 Neveh Shalom were built, two Jewish quarters which served as the nucleus of the new Jaffa and in 1909 of the newly founded city of Tel-Aviv.

In Northern Palestine

The series of disasters that struck the cities of Galilee precluded the strengthening and expansion of their Jewish communities. But after recovering from the earthquake of 1759 and its aftermath of revolts and pillaging, the Jewish populations of Safed and Tiberias began to increase and the arrival of the Hasidim and the disciples of the Gaon of Vilna breathed new life into them. Fortunately for the Hasidim, the governor of Acre, who had jurisdiction over Safed, did not hinder their immigration, for he saw it as a means of rebuilding and developing Safed and of replenishing his coffers. Indeed, he helped the immigrants build homes for themselves on the ruins.

In 1808, several years later than the Hasidim, their opponents the Mitnagdim, the disciples of the Gaon of Vilna, arrived. Before we consider this group, let us review the general situation of Jewish Safed.

The rulers' attitude toward the Jews was always dictated by self-interest. The arrival of the Jews was welcomed for their salutary effect upon the economy of the city. But this did not prevent the rulers from using every pretext to extort money from the Jews.

Plague and famine broke out in 1793 and the Jewish community had to borrow heavily to pay the taxes and tribute and to feed the poor. In a letter the Jewish leaders of Safed wrote that the debt had reached 50,000 kurush besides the exorbitant interest and the huge annual tax they had to pay the imperial treasury. The situation progressively deteriorated, and in 1795 they wrote: "The despot has levied upon us the enormous sum of more than 23,000 kurush . . . and the communities of our Holy City, may she be rebuilt, have had to get the funds from cruel gentiles at exorbitant interest." Five years later Safed was sacked.

This was a period of shifting power and growing anarchy and chaos. Sources of income dwindled. The sages of Safed also mentioned a new difficulty, the Jews of the vicinity who had suffered during the upheavals had moved into the city "to live off the public fund and soup kitchen." The explorer John Lewis Burckhardt speaks of the sack of Safed by the "Turks" after the French withdrawal from Galilee in 1799. But in 1810 Burckhardt reported the existence of 150 Jewish houses in the city, one-quarter of its structures.

In the winter of 1812 a cholera epidemic broke out and most of the Jews fled to the countryside, many never to return. Thus two factors were responsible for the decline of Jewish life in Upper Galilee generally and in the regions of Safed and Tiberias particularly: civil disorder, and the destruction of sources of income.

Standing faithfully beside the Jews of Safed through all their vicissitudes was the Mu'allim Hayim Parhi, mentioned above as the treasurer of the governor of Acre. Parhi also provided his brethren with financial aid. But when he was slain in Acre in August, 1820, at the order of Abdullah Pasha, their plight worsened still further. In 1826 the sages wrote of Safed: "Since the death of [Hayim Parhi] her travails have increased." Locusts and drought once more afflicted Safed, and by 1826 the Jewish communal debt had reached 300,000 kurush.

The first earthquake struck in 1822. In 1825 and 1833 houses collapsed from heavy rainfalls. In 1834 was the second earthquake. This was followed on 4 *Sivan*, 1834, by the revolt of the Arab peasants of the Safed region against Ibrahim Pasha. Upon reaching Safed they set upon the Jews, whom they plundered for thirty-three days.

Hardest hit by the great earthquake of January 1, 1837, were Nablus, Tiberias, Safed, and some thirty villages in Upper Galilee. The greatest tragedy occurred at Safed, where, according to Hebrew sources, some 2,000 Jews perished. Rabbi Israel of Shklov reported that 200 Mitnagdim alone perished, in addition to many Hasidim and most of the Sephardim. Not all the bodies were recovered, so that the exact number of victims has never been established.

In the summer of 1838 the Druses revolted against Ibrahim Pasha, and once more the Jews were the scapegoat. The Moslems joined the Druses in repeating the slaughter and plunder of 1834.

Let us now return to Safed's Mitnagdic community from its founding until its transfer to Jerusalem. The first group of disciples of the Gaon of Vilna, led by Rabbi Menahem Mendel of Shklov, arrived in Palestine in 1808. They first settled in Tiberias. When they saw, however, that their adversaries, the Hasidim, who had settled there thirty-one years earlier, were well entrenched in their positions in Tiberias, the Mitnagdim moved to Safed. There they were well received by the community, which was predominantly Sephardic. The following year the outstanding disciple of the Gaon of Vilna, Rabbi Saadiah (son of Rabbi Nathan Notte of Vilna), and Rabbi Nathan Notte (son of Rabbi Menahem Mendel of Shklov) led another group to Palestine. In *Tishri*, 1810, Rabbi Hayim (son of Rabbi Tuviah Katz) and Rabbi Israel (son of Rabbi Samuel of Shklov) arrived in Safed at the head of a third group. All told, some 150 souls arrived in the first year of the Mitnagdic immigration, and they continued to arrive until, by 1837, they numbered 420.

Rabbi Israel of Shklov reached Safed in *Tishri*. Several months later, at the urging of Rabbi Menahem, he went to Lithuania and Poland on a mission. "It behooves you," the leader of the Mitnagdim told him, "to sally forth to our land to lay foundations amid the sacred mountains." The written message he was given to take along was a "tiding" of the new community which had been established in Safed and of the Redemption sure to come through the resettlement of the land of Israel.

In 1816, when Rabbi Menahem Mendel moved to Jerusalem with several families, Rabbi Israel was his obvious successor as head of the Mitnagdim in Galilee. A brilliant leader, he worked tirelessly and successfully for the material and spiritual welfare of his flock and the advancement of scholarship.

He, too, moved to Jerusalem following the earthquake of 1839, and with him the Mitnagdic center in Palestine was transferred from Galilee to Jerusalem. He died that year on 9 *Sivan*, during a visit to Tiberias.

After Ibrahim Pasha's withdrawal to Egypt and the restoration of Palestine to Turkish rule, the wars in Galilee ceased. But persecution of the Jews by their Arab neighbors and by the officials did not abate. Documents prove that the Jews complained to the authorities in Beirut, Sidon, Tripoli, and Acre, who responded favorably. But their orders were either disobeyed or obeyed only for a brief period, for persecution continued.

Tiberias shared the fate of Safed.

At the end of the eighteenth century the city's situation improved somewhat. In 1798, in a letter to their emissary, Rabbi Moses Majar, the leaders of the Tiberias community wrote of the persecutions and of the communal debt which had reached 20,000 lions, stressing at the same time the constructive work (building schools, enlarging the Jewish quarter, etc.) on which they were engaged.

Early in the nineteenth century the situation deteriorated again. Already in 1802 Rabbi Joseph ibn Samoon, an emissary from Tiberias, gave a depressing description of the city's lot, to the Jews of Cochin, India. Neither did the situation improve with the death of Jazzar Pasha in 1804, and in 1806 the Jews of Tiberias still found themselves in the same plight. On the other hand, they suffered relatively little during the peasant uprising of 1834 against Ibrahim Pasha because they succeeded in bribing the rebels.

The great earthquake of 24 *Tebet*, 1837, shook Tiberias. The damage was not as great as in Safed, but, according to one estimate, 700 Tiberian Jews perished and many houses were wrecked.

These calamities dampened the spirits of the Tiberians, but the community held fast because the tomb of Rabbi Meir Baal Haness ("the Wonder Worker") was in their midst. Jews throughout the Diaspora sent regular contributions in memory of Rabbi Meir and from these the Jews of Tiberias supported themselves. Moreover, Tiberias drew many pilgrims from the West and from Syria and Mesopotamia, as well as tourists and invalids seeking cure at the hot springs.

As the nineteenth century progressed, Tiberias recovered and began to grow again. In 1843 the city numbered eighty Sephardic and fifty Ashkenazic families, or 650 individuals. When Fraenkel visited the city in 1848 the population had increased to 1,514, of whom 881 were Ashkenazim. Of the 300 heads of families, only nineteen were gainfully employed, the balance living off the dole. In 1868 British explorers counted 900 adult male Jews in Tiberias. In 1887 Schumacher counted 2,045 Jews. Luncz, in 1895, counted 3,200 and in 1908, 7,000! But the Turkish census of 1911 recorded 3,389 Ottoman Jews. In 1922 there were 4,427 Jews in Tiberias, 63 7 per cent of the population. In 1931, 5,381 Jews comprised 62.5 per cent of the population.

These figures indicate that the prospects of growth were better in the capital of Lower Galilee than in that of Upper Galilee. In the early 1900's more new colonies were founded around Tiberias than in the Safed region.

Those around Tiberias included Kfar Tabor, Yabnial, Beit Gan, Milhamieh, Sejera, Mizpah, and Sharona; Kinneret and Bitania, founded by the Jewish Colonization Association and the Palestine Colonization Association; Kinneret and Deganiah, the two *kibbutzim* founded on Jewish National Fund land; and Havat Migdal and Poriah, founded by the Palestine Office, the Jewish National Fund, and private settlers. It was not until the period of World War I that a new factor made Safed the center of new settlement activity—the Palestine Labor Fund of the Labor Zionist movement. These new settlements included Kfar Giladi, Tel Hai, Ayelet Hashahar, and Mahanayim. Obviously all the settlements of Lower Galilee were closely linked to Tiberias, which thereby acquired the character of a predominantly Jewish city.

Jewish life in Acre was insignificant and less permanent. At times it flourished briefly, but more often dwindled completely. In its halcyon days, as in the time of Hayim Parhi, Acre had Jewish merchants and Jewish officials, and Jewish life then centered around Parhi's home. Parhi, for a time "kingmaker" and virtual ruler of the land, was able to defend the Jews against the depredations of the authorities and to ameliorate their lot. But inevitably he also had enemies, and was killed, as indicated before, by Abdullah Pasha, whom he had raised from childhood and placed on the throne.

Joseph Schwarz, mentioned above as author of *Tebuot ha-Aretz*, related that Parhi's brothers, bent on revenge, obtained a *fetwa* from Sultan Mahmud II in Constantinople and hired Suleiman Pasha of Damascus and Mustafa Pasha of Aleppo to march against Abdullah. The forces of the pashas, with whom the Parhi brothers marched, crossed the Jordan and swept through Abdullah's domain, appointing their own governors as they went. But they were unable to take the citadel of Acre. It has already been mentioned that Suleiman had Solomon Parhi, the eldest brother and leader of the expedition, poisoned in the camp near Acre, and paid the two pashas to return home. Until Ibrahim Pasha captured it in 1823, Abdullah ruled Acre, then fled to Constantinople, where he died a pauper.

Acre returned to Turkish jurisdiction when the Turks reconquered Palestine from the Egyptians. In the interim, Jewish life had begun to develop in Haifa and Jaffa. Acre, unable to compete with them, was gradually depleted of its Jewish population, and during most of the nineteenth century there were in Acre none but a few isolated paupers.

New Horizons

Religious and national historical factors turned the interest of European Jewry to Palestine and its resettlement. But the advancement of the *Yishuv* depended on outside material and political factors over which the law had little control.

The political forces were an auxiliary rather than a direct factor in the renewal of colonization in the ancestral homeland. Formerly, because of the civil disturbances and the attitude of the authorities, it had been difficult for the Jews to consolidate their colonization of the land. However, the interest of the Western powers in Palestine, and the presence there of many of their Jewish subjects who enjoyed special privileges under the capitulations system, greatly encouraged the establishment of a permanent agricultural community.

Early in the nineteenth century Jews had already settled in villages and tilled the soil (albeit only a few who dwelt in Moslem surroundings); there were also the descendants of the old Jewish "peasantry" who continued the agricultural tradition of their forebears. Our sources show Jewish farming communities in Pekiin, Shefaram, Kfar Yasif, and Lebanon. Documents of the time of the great plague which swept Galilee in 1812 tell of the flight of Jews from the plague area not only to Jewish settlements but also to Arab villages with which they had enjoyed friendly commercial relations, buying grain, milk, cheese, fruit, etc., and selling products manufactured in the cities or imported from abroad. At the time these Arab centers had no old Jewish settlements. But now and then Jewish families visited Arab villages for months at a time, which may have helped to create in the Jews an affinity to rural life and to prepare them psychologically for the agricultural attempts to come.

Thus, during the plague, most of the refugees went to live at Ramish, about half a mile northwest of Biram and half a mile southwest of Ein Ebel, and the rest to other Arab villages, such as Gishcala, Daltun, Hamissa, Meron, Kfar Yasif, and perhaps also to Abu Susa near Safed and Hazavieh in Lebanon.

During the reign of Mohammed Ali a significant effort, lasting about two years, was made by Israel Bak, from just after the earthquake of 1837 until the final battles between Ibrahim Pasha and the Sultan's armies in 1839. A practical man with a deep faith that the land could be rebuilt by the efforts of its own sons, he engaged in practical endeavors to pioneer in industry and in agriculture—with his own hands and his own money. Upon arriving in Safed in 1832, he tried to establish a printing press, but failed because of the disasters already described. Then Bak went to Ibrahim Pasha, who was living in Acre, and asked for a plot of land to cultivate. Ibrahim granted him the abandoned Druse village of Jermak, on top of the mountain known as Atzmon. Bak moved to Jermak after the earthquake of 1837, built houses there, planted gardens, and sowed fields. According to one source, five Ashkenazic families lived in Jermak at the time, engaging in viniculture.

The chief impetus to the establishment of Jews in agriculture came from the visits to Palestine of Sir Moses Montefiore and his wife. In his diary notes of his visit, Sir Moses wrote that in Safed he became convinced that the Jews there wished to free themselves from their economic plight and turn to agriculture. He also told of several Jews who had leased land near Safed which they cultivated in partnership with the Moslems, but were unable to make progress because of lack of funds to buy implements.

Montefiore believed that Mohammed Ali would not respond negatively if he understood that Jewish agricultural endeavor would benefit the government and the imperial treasury. Montefiore noted in his diary that he would like "to meet the Pasha of Egypt at Alexandria to ask him to protect the Jews of the Holy Land, especially the inhabitants of Safed and Tiberias who are always liable to pillage and slaughter . . . to repair the ruins of Tiberias . . . to permit the Jews to lease fields and vineyards for fifty years on condition that the lessees be exempt from all taxes and imposts except the rent."

The outcome of his audience with the Pasha was not very encouraging. Mohammed Ali told Montefiore that he viewed with favor the plan to settle Jews in Palestine and Syria, and to develop agriculture and commerce by means of modern methods and the international commercial ties to be established with Montefiore's assistance. He also promised to give Montefiore his reply and his approval in writing, but never did. Eliezer Halevi, Montefiore's secretary, who was present at the audience, reported: "I was convinced from his [the Pasha's] words that the proposal to found Jewish settlements in the Holy Land and in Syria had caused him to fear that the Jews intended to establish a new state in their ancestral homeland."

Various proposals were submitted to Montefiore in Palestine. In 1839 Mordecai Zoref (one of the forebears of the Solomon family) of Jerusalem proposed the establishment of a Jewish colony in Judea, near Ramleh. The heads of the Safed and Jerusalem communities submitted a series of memoranda containing proposals for Jewish farm settlements. One memorandum submitted by "the representatives of the Sephardic community and the Ashkenazic community of the Holy City of Safed, may she be rebuilt speedily in our days," declared that the Jews "were most eager to eat their bread by tilling the soil or to be shepherds, although they have had no previous experience in this." They asked Montefiore "to purchase or rent for them arable soil to plant vineyards or olive trees. Also to engage in animal husbandry or an allied occupation, so that they might hope to eat the bread of their own toil."

The aspirations and requests of the leaders of the *Yishuv* with respect to agricultural colonization mark a significant turning point in the mood of the *Yishuv* at the end of the third decade of the nineteenth century. The predicament in which the *Yishuv* found itself in the wake of the various human and natural calamities, and its insecurity amid the hostile Arab settlements, gave rise to the first Hibbat Zion idea fifty years before the birth of the movement in Russia. Substantial segments of the *Yishuv*, who lived in the slough of idleness, of beggary, and of dependence upon the benevolence of Diaspora philanthropists, sought land where they might be secure and where they could support themselves by normal means. They wanted to found independent settlements which would provide them with the fruits of their own toil and also enable them to defend themselves against hostile neighbors. It was this concept which prompted the leaders of the *Yishuv* to address such a request to the aristocratic Montefiore, who had come to see their travail and seek amelioration.

Montefiore took their appeal to heart. When he returned to England he developed a plan for the renting of 200 villages in Galilee to be settled by Jews, and submitted the idea to Mohammed Ali. To finance his plan Montefiore intended to establish a bank with a capital of £1,000,000. But as we have noted, Mohammed Ali delayed his reply, soon the Egyptians were driven from Palestine, and all the negotiations proved futile.

Montefiore did not abandon his plan. It seemed to him that the new situation called for slower, more cautious steps, and he began to map the establishment of agricultural schools where European instructors would teach modern European methods of agriculture.

But this noble Jew's great plan did not materialize. In addition to adverse political factors, the Jews of Palestine were not psychologically or technically ready for the required struggle. They knew Montefiore as a man whose heart was open to every Jew in Palestine and, rather than toil for their living, they relied on his generosity without sufficiant desire for economic independence and willingness to work hard. Yet Montefiore's efforts continued for a long time, serving as the basis for the new Jewish agriculture which came with the rise of Zionism.

A great reawakening of interest ultimately affected not only the Jews of the Diaspora but also Christians and some Christian governments. British lay Christian and government circles were especially moved by the thought of restoring the Jews to Palestine, and in 5600 (1839-1840), the year in which Rabbi Judah Alcalay predicted the Messianic Redemption, some practical efforts were made in this direction.

Two Scottish missionaries who in 1839 were sent to Palestine, Turkey, Wallachia, etc., told in their travel journals of conversations with Wallachian Jews from whom they heard of Rabbi Judah Bibas of Corfu. He was then visiting various Jewish communities preaching self-help and demanding that the Jews study science and worldly knowledge, and "learn the military arts and wrest Palestine from the Turks under the leadership of the Messiah just as the Greeks took their own land from them." Later they met Rabbi Bibas: "Immediately he began to speak of the condition of the Promised Land. . . . He thought that the collections for the Holy Land ought to be given up, and that the Jews there ought to be obliged to work even were it by the bayonet. Sir Moses Montefiore's plan of purchasing land for them in Palestine, he considered useless, as long as there is no security for property there."

Rabbi Bibas made a great impact where he spoke, and he certainly paved the way and created a favorable climate of opinion for the great "revivalists" who followed him, including his disciple, Rabbi Alcalay.

He was a Sephardic rabbi at Semlin on the Danube who dedicated his entire life to the ideal of a Jewish return to Palestine. He traveled up and down Europe—to Vienna and Berlin, Paris and London—rousing Jews to action and winning adherents to his idea. He also published several books expounding the duty to go to Palestine and rebuild it. In his travels, he succeeded in rallying round him rabbis, intellectuals, and wealthy men, and to implement his idea he founded the *Hebrat Yishub Eretz Yisrael* (Palestine Colonization Society).

His program embraced all the aspects of national liberation: the redemption and colonization of Palestine, securing labor and economic positions, security measures, problems of language and culture—in fact, all the questions and matters with which his teacher Rabbi Bibas had dealt before him.

The interest of Diaspora Jewry in the resettlement of Palestine, motivated by religious and national historical factors, had never ceased. Never had Jews ceased to believe in and hope for the miraculous Final Redemption which would restore them to their ancestral homeland. Nor had immigration and pilgrimage to the Holy Land ceased. But the advancement of the *Yishuv* and the rate of immigration from Eastern Europe depended on various objective political factors. First among them was the discriminatory treatment by the Christian states of their Jewish subjects, especially in Czarist Russia, where anti-Jewish enactments led to pogroms, resulting in mass exodus of Jews. On the positive side came the national awakening of the Greeks, Serbs, Bulgars, and other small nations of the Turkish Empire which achieved independence in the nineteenth century. Their example inspired some of the fine Jewish spirits of the time. The first to expound Jewish renaissance and national independence in Palestine was Moses Hess, in his *Rom und Jerusalem, die letzte Nationalitaets frage* (Leipzig, 1862). He wrote (pp. 149-150):

... Are not things being prepared there and roads leveled, and is not the road of civilization being built in the desert in the form of the Suez Canal works and the railroad which will connect Asia and Europe? They are not thinking at present of the restoration of our people. But you know the proverb, "Man proposes and God disposes." Just as in the West they once searched for a road to India, and incidentally discovered a new world, so will our lost fatherland be rediscovered on the road to India and China that is now being built in the Orient. Do you still doubt that France will help the Jews to found colonies which may extend from Suez to Jerusalem, and from the banks of the Jordan to the coast of the Mediterranean? Then pray read the work which appeared shortly after the massacres in Syria, by the famous publisher, Dentu, under the title *The New Oriental Problem.* The author hardly wrote it at the request of the French government, but acted in accordance with the spirit of the French nation when he urged our brethren, not on religious grounds, but from purely political and humanitarian motives, to restore their ancient state.

Some twenty years before Pinsker's *Autoemanzipation* Rabbi Zvi Kalischer of Thorn, Prussia, called upon Jews to redeem the soil of Palestine. In 1860 he published his book *Derishat Zion,* in which he argued the need to buy huge stretches of land in Palestine and to found colonies in preparation for the coming of the Messiah. He tried to interest rabbis and wealthy men in his program; but except for his success in inducing the *Alliance Israélite Universelle* to found the Mikveh Israel Agricultural School, his program did not materialize. The first *halutzim*—the Biluim, the founders of the first modern colonies—did not come until the early 1880's.

As we have noted, immigration to Palestine took place largely under the protection of foreign powers. The growing urban settlement of this period (actually only a continuation of the old immigration) must be distinguished from the agricultural colonization of Hibbat Zion of the period of Abdul Hamid, which was an altogether unprecedented phenomenon. This colonization was possible not only because of the particular condition of Palestine and Turkey but also—and primarily—as a direct consequence of the Jewish situation in the Diaspora, especially in Eastern Europe, and above all in Russia, Rumania, and Austria.

The urban colonization, which had continued almost uninterruptedly over the centuries, was sustained largely by the Jews of the Turkish Empire and the other Arab lands. This maintained the Sephardic-Oriental character of the *Yishuv* during the first three centuries of Ottoman rule. Sephardic Jewry kept alive the intimate and integral bond of Jewry with the land of Israel, with Jewish tradition, and to a great extent also with Hebrew as a living language. Indeed, it is the Sephardic pronunciation of Hebrew that is accepted today.

The *Yishuv* was still largely Sephardic-Oriental in the mid-nineteenth century. It was only after the Crimean War and the introduction of the capitulations system in the Turkish Empire that the picture changed. Immigration from Eastern Europe began to exceed that from the Islamic lands. Ultimately the entire character of immigration and the composition of the *Yishuv* changed when the Jews of Russia, Rumania, and Galicia began to stream into Palestine in the Hibbat Zion immigration of the early 1880's.

At first these immigrants were under the wings of Great Britain, which protected not only her own Jewish subjects but also—at their request—those of the East European lands then persecuting the Jews and little concerned about those who had emigrated to Palestine. But soon Russia, Rumania, and Austria-Hungary began to evince interest in their Jewish subjects and to take them under their protection. Thus the foreign Jews came to enjoy more privileges than their Ottoman brethren and still more than Christian Ottoman subjects. Nevertheless the foreign Jews in the Turkish Empire were considered merely protected "*hamayah*" who benefited from privileges denied their brethren the "*re'eya*" or Ottoman subjects who were dependent on the grace of their rulers.

The anti-Jewish outbreaks in the early 1880's in Czarist Russia were the chief impetus to the great East European immigration of this period. Out of these disturbances were born *Am Olam*—the movement for the evacuation of the Diaspora, and *Bilu*—the "back to Zion" movement. The latter turned eastward, to the ancestral homeland, and the former turned westward seeking across the Atlantic Ocean rest for the eternal wanderer. With Pinsker's *Autoemanzipation* and with the inception of *Hibbat Zion*, the longing for Zion crystallized into an organized, national, political movement, *Hovevei Zion*—the Zionist movement.

Bilu, the first *halutz* immigration, actually comprised only a minor portion of the First *Aliyah*.[7a] But it was Bilu that gave this immigration its meaning. The first *Aliyah*, which continued all through the closing years of the nineteenth century, infused new life into the old *Yishuv*, that is, the urban *Yishuv* which was concentrated in the "Four Holy Cities"—Jerusalem, Hebron, Safed, and Tiberias.

At the same time this immigration founded two new urban settlements, not counted among the "Holy Cities," but to play a crucial role in the development of the modern *Yishuv*. These were the two Mediterranean cities of Haifa and Jaffa. The importance of this period consists, however, in the laying of the foundations of the new agricultural *Yishuv* which put its impress on the entire modern *Yishuv* as the first since the Expulsion to succeed in striking roots in the soil of the homeland.

In 1903-1904 came the Second *Aliyah*, which accomplished the "conquest of labor" and of self-defense.

As we have noted, the immigration to the cities had never ceased, and went mainly to Jerusalem. In the time of Montefiore the residents of the Old City had already ventured outside the city walls and started to build new residential quarters, which grew until by the end of the nineteenth century there were sixty. The productive character of the urban *Yishuv* gradually improved until, from depending chiefly on the dole and outside support, it came to live on its own labor, handicrafts, commerce, and some industry. The building trades grew (as we have seen) and Jews became active in crafts they had not known in the Diaspora—masonry, stonecutting and other aspects of building and transportation, carpentry, locksmithing, etc. At the same time the institutions of the old *Yishuv* increased and expanded—the *yeshibot* and synagogues, the philanthropic and welfare institutions. Thus new horizons gradually opened for further colonization.

According to Luncz, there were 28,112 Jews in Jerusalem in 1895, and 50,000 Jews in 1905 out of a total population of 75,000. Baedecker's figures in 1912 are a little lower—45,000 Jews out of a total of 70,000.

These new immigrants strengthened the urban *Yishuv*, but beyond that established agricultural villages and settlements, making the waste land flower. The early settlers found barren ground, and the urban *Yishuv*, still living chiefly on charity, were of no aid or encouragement. Nevertheless, stanch of faith and will, they went out to reclaim the land. The people were aroused, albeit not as quickly as the first *halutzim* had hoped. One by one, individuals, then groups, followed in the footsteps of these *halutzim* to give their energy and means to the building begun by the preceding generation. That generation had been marked by the efforts of Baron Edmond de Rothschild whose remains were interred at Zikhron Ya'akov, which, with Ekron, he had bought and named after his father. The colonization efforts which Rothschild had supported continued after his death, and today there are forty-five settlements founded with his help.

In 1915, at the close of the Ottoman era, the Jews owned 420,000 dunams (105,000 acres), of which 16,400 dunams belonged to the Jewish National Fund. On the eve of World War I there were almost 100,000 Jews in Palestine, of whom 12,000 lived in the agricultural settlements.

The Second *Aliyah* was able to surpass the First *Aliyah* in ability, initiative, and endurance because of changes already introduced. The new generation merged the idea of personal with that of national fulfillment, and saw the happy fruits of its labor on its own soil.

Mood and circumstance were both propitious for a syncretic political-practical Zionism. Herzl appeared with his *Judenstaat*, the Zionist Congress was founded, and the institutions of the Zionist Organization were established. A landless and defenseless minority transformed itself into a nation striking roots in its homeland and preparing to cast off alien domination. It became "a state in the making," and from the "state in the making" or "national home," it erected the State of Israel.

The vision of the great seers of Israel in the nineteenth century of a Jewish spiritual and material renaissance and of the redemption of the homeland from its conquerors, not by entreaty, but by strength of will and by faith in Israel as the chosen people and in the future foretold by the Prophets of Israel, ceased to be mere fantasy.

In 5708 (1947-1948), fifty years after Herzl dreamed his dream of Jewish statehood, the army of Israel went out to defend and restore to its rightful owners the land promised Abraham and his seed.[8a] Vision became reality. Israel, firmly established, awaits the Ingathering of the Exiles.

NOTES

[[1a] See above Israel Halpern, "The Jews in Eastern Europe (From Ancient Times until the Partitions of Poland, 1772-1795)."]

[[2a] See above Halpern, *op. cit.;* Abraham Menes, "Patterns of Jewish Scholarship in Eastern Europe"; below Abraham J. Heschel, "The Mystical Element in Judaism."]

[3] The Hebrew word *ha-Ari* ("the Lion") consists of the initial letters of the words "*ha-Elohi* (the Godly) Ashkenazic Rabbi Itzhak."

[4] The numerical value of the Hebrew word *Shiloh* is 335. The name of a city in biblical Palestine, the meaning of "*Shiloh*" in this context is obscure and a great deal of Messianic speculation has been built around this phrase in Jacob's blessing to his son Judah (Gen. 49:10).

[5] In the book *Vetzivah ha-Kohen* by Rabbi Aaron Samuel Hakohen (pp. 29-30), originally published in 1823 and recently reissued by the Foundation for the Publication of Works of Morality and Hasidism (*ha-Mosad le-Hozaat Sifrei Mussar Vehassidut*) in Jerusalem, there appears the following tale concerning the author's ancestor, Rabbi Naftali Katz, author of *Semikat Hakamin,* who died in Constantinople, in 1729 on his way to Palestine:

> "The Holy Baal Shem Tob yearned all his life to meet the author of *Or ha-Hayyim* (Rabbi Hayim ibn Atar), who had settled in Jerusalem, for Heaven revealed to him that if they met, they would succeed in bringing about the Redemption. In the winter of 5513 (1753-1754) he left Miedzyboz . . . for Jerusalem. . . . After many vicissitudes he reached Constantinople, where he went to pray at the grave of Rabbi Naftali . . . that night Rabbi Naftali appeared to the Baal Shem Tob in a dream and told him that if he did not immediately return home he would meet the same end as he (Rabbi Naftali) and die in an alien land and never under any circumstance see Jerusalem."

[[5a] See Halpern, *op. cit.;* Menes, *op. cit.;* above Arieh Tartakower, "The Decline of European Jewry (1933-1953)."]

[[6a] See below Walter J. Fischel, "Israel in Iran (A Survey of Judeo-Persian Literature)," pp. 1177-1178.]

[[7a] See above Ben Zion Dinur, "The Historical Foundations of the Rebirth of Israel"; below Jacob Lestchinsky, "Jewish Migrations, 1840-1956."]

[[8a] See below Oscar I. Janowsky, "The Rise of the State of Israel."]

CHAPTER 14

THE RISE OF THE STATE OF ISRAEL

By Oscar I. Janowsky*

1. Introductory

The proclamation of the State of Israel on May 14, 1948, was at once the culmination of earlier developments and the beginning of a new era. A climax was reached in the building of the Jewish National Home, foreign rule was terminated, and the Jews of Israel assumed governmental powers. But the fundamental aims of the preceding period—Jewish immigration, land settlement and economic development, national regeneration and cultural unity—remained substantially unaltered. In large measure, too, the same agencies, men, and political groupings continued to provide leadership. The changes wrought by independence were most significant, but the stabilizing factor of continuity must not be ignored.

Origins of the State of Israel[1a]

The Jews or Hebrews have been identified with Palestine—the Land of Israel—since patriarchal beginnings. For some 500 or 600 years, the entire Hebrew people dwelt in the Land of Israel. Between the eighth and sixth centuries B.C.E., the Diaspora developed, and increasing numbers of Jews lived outside the homeland. But Palestine remained the center of Jewish life during the Second Commonwealth, and throughout that long period Jews in varying numbers continued to return to Palestine from the Diaspora. Even after the Romans sacked Jerusalem and burned the Second Temple in 70 C.E., the Jews of Palestine enjoyed a limited autonomy and continued to exert religious and cultural leadership over the Jews of foreign lands. After the fourth century C.E., persecution sapped the strength of Palestine Jewry and the population dwindled, but the idea persisted that the Jews and the Land of Israel were indissolubly linked to one another. Throughout the Middle Ages, and in modern times, too, small groups of Jews felt the need to "Return to Zion," and came to live in the Holy Land or at least to be buried in hallowed ground.

* I am indebted to Dr. Oskar K. Rabinowicz for suggestions covering the entire chapter, and to the Honorable Haim Cohen of Israel for comments on the section dealing with "Development of State and Government." This acknowledgment, however, does not involve delegation of responsibility.

The lure of Palestine for the Jews endured through the long centuries of dispersion. The land was remembered as the cradle of early peoplehood. There the Jews had been welded into what we call today a nation. National triumphs and catastrophes, perpetuated in religious lore, remained associated with the country. Above all, the religious and literary genius of the Jews had blossomed in the Land of Israel, and it ever remained as the spiritual haven. In prayer and poetic yearning, in synagogue art and group imagery, the Land of Israel symbolized at once the glory of bygone days and the hope of redemption as a people.

This set the stage for the Zionist movement of the late nineteenth and early twentieth centuries. The impulse came from within the Jewish group, primarily in Eastern Europe, where a cultural revival fostered national consciousness. The nationalist ferment among the submerged peoples of the area likewise affected the Jews, and the external pressures of anti-Semitism added a compulsive urge to return to Palestine and rebuild the old homeland. During the 1880's, groups of pioneers began to settle in Palestine, and an organized movement developed to encourage and sustain the settlers.

Theodor Herzl gave dynamic leadership to the incipient Zionist movement. A Zionist Congress was held in Basle, Switzerland, in 1897, and a Zionist Organization was established with the aim of creating "for the Jewish people a home in Palestine secured by public law." An administrative apparatus was set up, an official journal founded, financial instruments established, and Herzl launched diplomatic and personal negotiations which brought Zionism to the attention of governments and public opinion. Herzl's activities were cut short by untimely death, but the Zionist movement endured. Jewish immigration to Palestine continued and by 1914 there were some 85,000 Jews in the country.

The First World War proved decisive in the history of Zionism. On November 2, 1917, the British government issued the Balfour Declaration, pledging to facilitate "the establishment in Palestine of a national home for the Jewish People." Soon thereafter the British conquered the country and, when the war was over, Palestine was administered as a Mandate under the League of Nations, with the United Kingdom as Mandatory or trustee. The Balfour pledge was incorporated in the terms of the Mandate, which recognized "the historical connection of the Jewish people with Palestine" and the right to reconstitute "their national home in that country." Britain was to encourage the immigration and close settlement of Jews on the land; Hebrew (as well as English and Arabic) was to be an official language; and a "Jewish Agency" was to assist and co-operate with the British in the building of the Jewish National Home. The approval of the terms of the Mandate by the Council of the League of Nations gave international sanction to the ideal of a Jewish National Home in Palestine.

These triumphs of Zionism appeared decisive, but they proved insufficient for the realization of a viable Jewish National Home. The fundamental need was large-scale Jewish immigration, which depended on extensive economic development. The latter, however, required governmental powers which the Jews did not possess.

The British wielded the powers of government, but their primary objective was to advance imperial interests rather than Jewish national aspirations. Imperial interests required peace and stability in the Middle East with tractable native populations and governments. If the National Home could be built with Arab acquiescence, British good will would, no doubt, have been assured. But the Arabs opposed the National Home and resorted to rioting and bloodshed. Since suppression threatened to alienate the native population, the British sought to placate the Arabs by restraining Jewish efforts.

The commitments of the Balfour Declaration and the Mandate included safeguards for the Arabs, and the British attempted to steer a course which they regarded as just to both peoples. However, as the Arab-Jewish conflict sharpened, that course veered away from the requirements of the Jewish National Home. The emphasis shifted, and the demands of the Arabs began to outweigh in British policy the positive injunctions to further the Jewish National Home.

The Arabs proved the most formidable obstacle. Their leadership was imbued with the spirit of nationalism, and the masses were aroused to resist Jewish immigration and the entire idea of the National Home. The Jews argued that economic development increased the capacity of the country to absorb Jewish immigration without harm to the Arabs, and they adduced evidence that the latter profited from Jewish efforts. All to no effect. The Arab leadership repeatedly fomented violence, which taxed British patience, not so much with Arab resistance as with Jewish dynamism, which they came to regard as the cause of their difficulties.

In 1936, Arab riots broke out again and soon assumed the character of a national revolt. And in the late 1930's, world events predisposed the British to sacrifice the National Home to real or presumed imperial interests. The challenges of Hitler and Mussolini induced a policy of appeasement in Europe, in the Mediterranean, and in the Middle East. The Arabs, too, were to be appeased by the White Paper of 1939. The latter limited Jewish immigration to a total of 75,000 between 1939-1944, and thereafter the Jewish National Home was to be shut tight even against Jewish refugees, unless the Arabs approved. This was followed by drastic restrictions on land sales to Jews which barred further acquisition of land in 95 per cent of the area of Palestine. In the end, the Arabs were not appeased, but these measures committed the British to the scuttling of the Jewish National Home.

The Second World War taxed the statesmanship of Palestine Jewish leadership. They had no choice but to rally to the support of Britain, for the Nazis were the supreme enemy. However, the brutal enforcement of the White Paper of 1939 led to defiance. When the victims of Nazi terror perished for want of asylum, and when hapless refugees were turned away from the National Home, Palestine Jewry was bitterly resentful. Some elements resorted to terrorism, but among the Jewish population as a whole national discipline held. A threefold policy was evolved: co-operation in fighting the war was offered the British government; illegal immigration was encouraged in defiance of the British authorities; and the desire for a National Home hardened into a demand for statehood.[1]

The Building of the Jewish National Home

The Jews were obliged to expend much effort in defending their policies, in presenting evidence before the numerous British commissions of inquiry, and in pleading their cause in Palestine, England, and elsewhere. But their best energies were devoted to constructive work and, despite all hindrances, remarkable progress was made in the building of the Jewish National Home.

The work of building was guided by various agencies, some of which had the support of non-Zionists. But the most important were the instruments of the world Zionist movement. The leading body was the Zionist Organization, or the Jewish Agency (after 1929), which had the right under the Mandate of advising and co-operating with the British authorities on matters affecting the National Home. It mobilized the support of Jews and others, negotiated with the British, and represented the cause of the National Home before the organs of the League of Nations. The Palestine Executive of this body set up administrative departments which dealt with immigration, agricultural settlement, trade and industry, labor, education, health, and other functions.

The *Keren Hayesod* and the Jewish National Fund were the chief financial instruments. The former raised over £P18,000,000 between 1920-1946 (59 per cent in the United States), and figured in the financing of almost every important effort relating to the building of the National Home. The Jewish National Fund purchased land as the "possession of the Jewish people"; in 1945-1946, it held over 213,000 acres—about 44 per cent of all land owned by Jews.

Numerous other agencies co-operated in the development of the National Home. Baron Edmond de Rothschild of Paris had generously supported the early agricultural settlements, and in the 1920's the Palestine Jewish Colonization Association (PICA) took over his holdings and continued his work. By 1945, the Rothschild and PICA activities had resulted in the acquisition of about 123,000 acres and the founding or support of some forty settlements.

Hadassah, the Women's Zionist Organization of America, concentrated its efforts on public health and medical service, in which it became a major influence in the country. It maintained hospitals and clinics; pioneered in child welfare, nurses' training, preventive medicine, and the care of the tubercular; and co-operated in antimalaria and other health efforts. The Women's International Zionist Organization (WIZO) engaged mainly in the training of pioneer women in agricultural, vocational, and home-making functions.

Business organizations worked with private capital independently of the Zionist bodies. One example was the Palestine Economic Corporation, which participated in financing large undertakings, such as the Palestine Potash Company and the Palestine Electric Corporation. Finally, Palestine Jewry developed numerous agencies, notably the *Histadrut* or General Federation of Labor, which shared in the work of building, and profoundly affected the character of the Jewish National Home. During 1917-1945, the Jews brought into Palestine about £P154,000,000, of which about 29 per cent was secured by "national" and philanthropic agencies, and close to 71 per cent was imported and invested as private capital or brought by immigrants who settled in the country.[2] The Jewish investment in Palestine in thought, energy, and financial means was prodigious, and the achievement was worthy of the effort.

Population Growth and Economic Development. In 1882, when modern Jewish immigration to Palestine began, the Jews were an insignificant minority of some 24,000 who lived on sufferance. During the following sixty-six years, about 550,000 Jews settled in the country; and in 1948, the *Yishuv* was a self-reliant community of about 650,000,[3] imbued with national purpose, conscious of its aims, and determined to see to their realization.

Settlement on the land absorbed the best energies of the Jewish public bodies because Jews had long been city dwellers lacking experience in agricultural work. Land was purchased at high prices, mainly from large and absentee landowners, costly reclamation work was undertaken, and the pioneers were trained in modern methods of cultivation. In 1882, Jews were in possession of less than 6,200 acres; by 1946, some 446,000 acres had been acquired—barely 7 per cent of the country's area, or about 12 per cent, if the Negev is excluded. From five Jewish agricultural settlements in 1882, with a population of about 500, the number of settlements had grown to some 293 by 1948, with a population of about 110,000. When the Mandate came to an end, more than 16 per cent of the Jewish population lived in rural settlements and supplied close to one-half the food supply of the Jewish population of the country.[4]

Urban and industrial growth was equally marked. In 1948, the Jews of Jerusalem (102,000) were about two-thirds of the city's population. Haifa's Jews increased from some 3,000 in 1914 to 66,000 in 1944-1945 (55 per cent of the population). And Tel-Aviv, founded in 1909 as a suburb of Jaffa, became by 1948 an "all-Jewish city" of about 190,000.

Industry in the modern sense was barely known in Palestine before the First World War. Twenty-five years later, industry was an important factor in the economy of the country, and local needs and military requirements during the Second World War accelerated the trend toward industrialization. A few figures will reveal the extent of growth. In 1925, some 536 Jewish industrial establishments (exclusive of handicrafts) operated with less than 5,000 in personnel, about £P1,517,000 in capital investment, and horsepower of 5,733. In 1946, the corresponding figures were as follows: number of establishments, 2,500; personnel, 47,000; value of annual output, £P44,000,000; capital investment (1943), £P20,523,000; horsepower, 167,532. And it was Jewish immigration and the application of Jewish enterprise and capital which effected this radical expansion of industry.[5]

Domestic commerce and foreign trade likewise grew at a rapid rate. During 1923-1945, imports increased eightfold and, while exports lagged far behind imports, the *rate* of increase of exports was nearly twice that of imports. The balance of trade was consistently unfavorable, but the percentage of imports covered by exports rose markedly: in 1923, exports were less than 29 per cent of imports, but by 1945 fully 50 per cent of imports were balanced by exports. And the deficits in foreign trade were covered by capital imports of immigrants, the tourist trade, remittances from abroad, and funds secured by the Zionist agencies. A careful comparative study of the economies of the Middle Eastern countries led Alfred Bonné, Professor of Economics at the Hebrew University, to conclude that "Palestine is the only country presenting, mainly in its Jewish sector, the picture of an economy approaching that of the developed communities of the West."[6]

Distinctive Features of the Jewish National Home. Economic expansion was not uncommon in underdeveloped countries after the First World War. What made Palestine unique was the national and social setting in which the economy functioned. The National Home was not built on cheap labor, its architects were not dominated by the urge for profits, and the financial backers were motivated by national idealism or philanthropy rather than by gain. There was experimentation with co-operative institutions and a widespread conviction that social stability and change must rest on respect for human personality, individual freedom, and democratic processes.[7]

The dominating ideal was national rebirth, and *halutziut*, or dedicated pioneering, the means of its realization. The Hebrew language was revived, so that in 1948 over 75 per cent of Palestine Jewry above two years of age spoke Hebrew, and over 93 per cent of all children aged two to fourteen employed it as their vernacular.[8] The traditional Jewish faith in education was reflected in a far-flung voluntary system which imparted some elementary education to about 90 per cent of the Jewish children, and which expended in 1944-1945 nearly four times the Palestine government's education budget. The Hebrew University and the Haifa Institute of Technology were founded when the National Home was little more than a hope and a half-promise. Adult education in the form of evening courses, lectures, and tours brought knowledge to the isolated settlements as well as the urban centers. And Hebrew culture, the press, the theater, music, and the plastic arts were developed to a high level in two generations by a heterogeneous immigrant population.[9]

Advanced health and welfare services were a distinctive feature of the Jewish National Home. The work of Hadassah has been noted. In addition, Palestine Jewry maintained health organizations, among which *Kupat Holim* (the Sick Benefit Fund of the *Histadrut*) was the most important. The latter was a co-operative welfare agency which was established in 1912 with an initial membership of 150 and grew so rapidly that by 1945 it was serving about 46 per cent of the Jewish population of Palestine. This voluntary agency, and several additional smaller mutual aid associations, performed the functions of health insurance. Members received hospital and medical services, medicines, convalescent facilities, maternity aid, and sickness benefit allowances. The insurance funds were composed of contributions from workers and employers, but the Palestine government furnished neither subsidy nor administrative aid.

The results of Jewish health work were evident in the vital statistics. The death rate among Jews fell from an annual average of 13.70 per thousand during 1922-1925 to 8.08 per thousand during 1936-1940. Infant mortality among Jews was 132.11 per thousand in 1925 and 35.80 in 1945. And the influence of Jewish health measures reached the entire population of Palestine, including the non-Jews.[10]

The unique feature of the Jewish National Home was the social idealism which inspired large segments of the Jewish population. Physical labor—self-labor and toil especially on the land—was idealized as the preferred means of restoring the land and reclaiming the people.[11] Novel forms of group living were evolved in the collective settlements (the *kvutzot* and *kibbutzim*), in which property and income, production and distribution, were socialized. And this was done without compulsion, because human needs rather than preconceived doctrines determined social evolution. Those who preferred less pervasive forms of co-operative living fashioned the Workers Smallholders' Settlement (*Moshav Ovdim*) and the Collective Smallholders' Settlement (*Moshav Shitufi*), which combined individualized family living with varying degrees of collective production, or joined middle-class settlements, where co-operation was limited to joint purchasing, marketing, water supply, and the like. In 1945-1946, there were about 140 *kibbutzim* and *kvutzot* with a population exceeding 40,000; some sixty-two *moshavei ovdim* (population over 17,000), and nine *moshavim shitufiyim* (population close to 900).

The co-operative movement extended also to urban industries, trade, and services. *Tnuvah,* the most successful of the marketing co-operatives, was occupied with the domestic sale of agricultural produce. The export of citrus fruit was handled mainly by co-operatives. Jewish motorized transportation was almost wholely organized co-operatively. Co-operatives were popular in homebuilding, irrigation and water supply, in credit and banking. In 1945, when the Jews numbered less than 600,000, they maintained about 1,000 co-operative societies, with a combined membership of some 350,000 and total resources in excess of £P32,000,000.[12]

The *Histadrut* (General Federation of Jewish Labor) represented most of the elements affected by labor idealism. It was not the only Jewish labor organization, but by far the most important one. Organized in 1920 with an initial membership of 4,400, it grew rapidly, and after 1930 embraced over two-thirds of all gainfully employed Jews.

The *Histadrut* was one of the unique institutions developed in the Jewish National Home. It was a labor organization which included industrial and farm workers, the skilled and unskilled, wage earners, co-operative farmers, "white-collar" workers, and members of the liberal professions. The usual trade union efforts relating to organization, bargaining, and labor conflicts occupied its attention, and it won important concessions in collective bargaining, regulation of employment, insurance against industrial accidents, paid vacations, separation allowances, and the like. However, its functions went far beyond those normally associated with labor organizations.

Through co-operative self-help measures, the *Histadrut* sought to alleviate the effects of illness, old age, and unemployment. *Kupat Holim* (the Sick Benefit Fund) has been mentioned. An unemployment fund was used as a reserve for periods of depression, and assistance was provided for the aged, the invalid, and the dependent. Moreover, the *Histadrut* was involved in the ownership and management of units of production, marketing, transportation, banking, and other economic activities. Finally, it engaged in far-reaching educational and cultural services, conducting a network of schools and sponsoring adult education, book publishing and a labor press, artistic ventures connected with the theater and music, and recreational and sport organizations. Through these and other efforts, the *Histadrut* profoundly affected the character of the Jewish National Home.[13]

Democracy, too, was a distinctive feature of the Jewish National Home. The atmosphere of Jewish Palestine was democratic. Equality was a working principle of social relationships; respect for human personality and for individual differences prevailed; above all, freedom to differ and to express varying points of view was maintained. And voluntarism rather than compulsion governed political, social, and economic life. Jewish Palestine was not a utopia, but diverse elements were able to work together in relative peace in the building of the Jewish National Home.

Development of the Jewish Community

Palestine Jewry was a composite of immigrant groups differing in language, religious observance, social doctrine, and political orientation. But the overwhelming majority felt a sense of community which transcended factional loyalties and responded readily to efforts at representative unity. The first efforts in that direction were voluntary: in 1920 an Elected Assembly was chosen and it designated a National Council (*Vaad Leumi*) which pressed for government recognition. This was achieved under the Religious Communities Organization Ordinance (1926), which sanctioned a considerable measure of semiautonomous government.

Four elections were held for the Elected Assembly during the period of British rule—in 1920, 1925, 1931, and 1944—and each was contested by various parties and factions. The *Mapai* (the Palestine Labor Party) was predominant throughout, controlling 35 to over 50 per cent of the seats in the Elected Assemblies.[14] Other important parties were the middle-class groups, such as the General Zionists and Zionist Revisionists, the *Mizrachi*, and groupings of Oriental Jews.

The Elected Assembly and National Council served primarily as organs of Jewish public opinion, representing the Jewish point of view before the British administration, commissions of inquiry, and the Mandates Commission of the League of Nations. However, during the 1930's, the administrative functions of the National Council increased steadily as it assumed supervisory and financial responsibilities in education, culture, health, and welfare.

The Arabs and the Building of the Jewish National Home

The Jewish National Home was built in the midst of an Arab majority which was inevitably affected by the far-reaching changes. That the Arab population, or at least its leadership, was hostile has been noted, but this hostility was not the result of harmful economic or social effects suffered by the Arabs. On the contrary, they profited, at least materially, from the coming of the Jews.

The Jews bought all but an insignificant fraction of the land they acquired, and the exorbitant prices paid by them[15] enriched the Arabs. Except for some 317 families, Arab cultivators did not become landless as a result of direct land sales to Jews.[16] The Arab death rate and infant mortality declined, and the Arab population of Palestine grew more rapidly than in neighboring countries. Jewish medical and health facilities helped the Arabs, and banks and mortgage companies were available to them. They were encouraged by the example of the Jews to improve farming methods, develop industry, organize co-operatives, combat usury. Their wages were higher, agricultural productivity greater, and per capita national income larger than in neighboring Arab lands.[17]

Moreover, Jews made repeated attempts to promote understanding and co-operation with the Arabs. The *Histadrut* helped in the organization of Arab labor and in the attainment of better working conditions. In the middle 1920's, the "*Brit Shalom*" group, in the early 1940's the "*Ihud*" group, and especially the League for Arab-Jewish Rapprochement, all worked for co-operation. These elements were not numerous, but they included prominent Zionist leaders who exerted considerable influence.[18]

However, the differences between Arabs and Jews were too fundamental to be bridged by these efforts. Estrangement deepened and the two peoples constituted separate and self-contained communities. By the end of the Second World War, the Jews were a vigorous community with a dynamic economy and effective political leadership. The Arabs, too, were organized, determined, and militant. A quarter-century of conflict had reached a critical stage, and decisive events were in the making.

2. From National Home to Sovereign State

After the Second World War

The Second World War brought on an uneasy truce between Palestine Jewry and the British. Official Jewish leadership, represented by the Jewish Agency, was centered in Palestine, with David Ben-Gurion as the dominant personality. Its basic position was opposition, not to British rule, but to the policy of the White Paper of 1939—a subtle distinction but an important one. The rescue of Jews from certain death at the hands of the Nazis was the central issue, and when the British refused to tolerate the infiltration of refugees, they met with defiance. So far as official Jewish leadership was concerned, this defiance was limited to illegal immigration; in other matters affecting the war, the British had the co-operation of the *Yishuv*. However, dissident elements were straining against this Jewish policy, and to clarify this factor a glance backward is necessary.

During the Arab revolt of the late 1930's, the *Haganah* (Jewish defense units), an arm of the Jewish Agency, was under restraining orders not to engage in retaliatory terror against the Arabs. The policy was to co-operate with the British, and some 19,000 Jews were enlisted as auxiliary police. The Revisionists, however, organized in 1937 the *Irgun Zvai Leumi* (National Military Organization), which took punitive measures against the Arabs and promoted illegal immigration, employing violence when necessary. By 1938, the *Haganah*, too, was encouraging illegal immigration, and when the White Paper was issued in 1939, its co-operation with the British lapsed. The *Haganah* avoided clashes with the British, but it, too, defied the immigration law. The British retaliated by dismissing and disarming Jewish auxiliaries, and by resorting to mass arrests, collective fines, and elaborate searches for arms. The *Haganah* persisted in the policy of restraint (*Havlagah*), but the reply of the *Irgun* was guerrilla war upon the British.

During the Second World War even the *Irgun* co-operated for a time with the British, but this led to a secession from its ranks and the appearance of the Fighters For Freedom (the Sternists), who continued to employ terror against the Mandatory power. The vigorous reaction of the British, who did not distinguish between degrees of opposition, led to a renewal of *Irgun* terrorism. By 1944, the *Irgun* and the Sternists were in open revolt.

When the World War came to an end in Europe on May 8, 1945, all elements in Palestine were consolidating their positions for the final struggle. The Arab States had become allies by declaring war on Germany and Japan the preceding February, and they had formed the League of Arab States, which warned against any compromise on the issue of Jewish immigration. The Palestine Arabs, too, demanded that the White Paper be enforced.

The mood of the masses of Palestine Jews was one of anxious hope that the policy of the White Paper would be abandoned. This hope was not entirely baseless. The British admitted to Palestine the illegal immigrants who had been interned at Mauritius. A Labor government came to power in London in July, 1945, and the British Labor Party had been emphatically pro-Zionist. The feeling of horror which gripped the world when the enormity of Nazi crimes against the Jews stood revealed encouraged the Jews to believe that the gates of Palestine would not be closed to the remnant which had been snatched from the gas chambers. The White Paper policy could not endure!

In these circumstances the Jewish Agency pursued a twofold policy: it appealed to the humanitarian impulses of public opinion, especially in the United States, to reinforce the demand for the admission of refugees to Palestine; and it defied the White Paper by organizing and promoting illegal immigration. The effect was to focus attention on the dramatic issue of refugee settlement. The survivors of the Nazi extermination camps had no homes to return to, and no state offered them asylum. The Jewish National Home appeared to be the proper place for them.

This policy appeared promising. European governments no longer hindered the movement of Jews toward Palestine, as they had done during the war. American public opinion was aroused: members of Congress and state governors appealed to the President on behalf of the Jews; and later, in

December, 1945, both houses of Congress passed a resolution favoring free Jewish immigration into Palestine and the development of the country as a democratic commonwealth.

In August, 1945, President Truman requested the British government to admit 100,000 refugees (displaced Jews) to Palestine.[19] This embarrassed the British, because the fundamental problems were ignored and the issue narrowed to the moral and humanitarian plea of salvaging victims of brutal persecution. But the admission of 100,000 Jews would mean the violation of the White Paper and a radical departure from accepted policy. This the Labor government was not prepared to do.

Like its predecessors, the Labor government hoped to hold the Middle East with the aid of the Arabs. It therefore agreed to admit no more than 1,500 Jews a month, but to ease the tension it proposed that an Anglo-American Committee of Inquiry examine the entire situation. Apparently it was hoped thus to set the humanitarian problem into its complex political framework. The committee's report appeared in April, 1946, and it recommended, among other measures, the admission of 100,000 refugees to Palestine, the removal of restrictions on land sales, economic development, and the suppression of terrorism and violence.[20] This meant the repudiation of the White Paper, and the Arab States responded immediately by threatening violence. The British government decided to delay action, pending further negotiations with the American government. The White Paper remained British policy.

The delays and disappointments lashed Palestine Jewry to fury. Many months had passed since the end of the war, and the hapless victims of the Nazis still languished in camps. The methods of diplomacy had been tried and powerful friends had interceded, but the British government held fast to the White Paper policy and showed no signs of relenting. To all appearances, the Arab threats of violence were more effectual than the policy of restraint of the Jewish Agency. As hopes for a peaceful solution and faith in moderation withered, violence became inevitable.

The appeal of the terrorist methods of the *Irgun* gained ground. Apparently its appraisal of British intentions had been more realistic. The Jewish Agency still tried to distinguish between disaffection and rebellion, between defiance of and resistance to the White Paper and open warfare on the British administration. It tried to avoid bloodshed by directing *Haganah* attacks not against British personnel but against barriers to illegal immigration. But the failure of diplomacy to achieve results in London, and the indiscriminate reprisals of the military in Palestine, caused some members of the Jewish Agency to waver, especially since it was becoming increasingly difficult to restrain certain leaders of the *Haganah*. The Jewish Agency therefore authorized from time to time co-operation with the *Irgun* in local raids on British installations which hampered illegal immigration.

When the British government declined to admit 100,000 Jews, as recommended by the Anglo-American Committee, the *Haganah* decided on a demonstration of force, in the hope of influencing the British and probably also to reassure the *Yishuv* so that leadership would not fall into the hands of the extremists. In June, 1946, the *Haganah* attacked vital communications, blowing up strategic bridges on the borders and damaging the railway workshops. The British retaliated with mass arrests, including leaders of the Jewish Agency and National Council, widespread house searches for arms, and other repressive measures. This only encouraged the extremists, and in July the Government Offices in the King David Hotel in Jerusalem were demolished by the *Irgun*, with the loss of nearly 100 British, Arab, and Jewish lives. The *Yishuv* was shocked by this outrage, and the Jewish Agency denounced it as a "dastardly crime." Shortly thereafter, condemning other activities of the *Irgun*, the Agency announced that it would root out terrorism.

Skillful leadership on the part of the British might have isolated the terrorists, but the military authorities of Palestine ignored the declaration of the Jewish Agency and met the challenge by reprisals upon the entire *Yishuv*. Tel-Aviv was isolated for several days, a curfew was imposed on all Palestine Jews, many thousands were interrogated, hundreds detained, and the Military Courts imposed death sentences on terrorists. The British security forces became a veritable army of occupation.

The temper of the military was symbolized by an order issued by the commanding general against fraternization with Jews. He condemned the entire Jewish community of Palestine, placed all Jewish homes and business establishments out of bounds, forbade "any intercourse with any Jew," and concluded by assuring the troops that they would thus "be punishing the Jews in a way the race dislikes more than any, by striking at their pockets and showing our contempt for them."

The Jews, not yet recognized as ripe for practical statecraft, were more fortunate in their spokesman than the experienced and stately British Empire. In October, 1947, when bitterness against the British had become even more intense, Ben-Gurion said to the Elected Assembly in Jerusalem,

> We have not absolved the Labor Party of its pledges, nor will we, but we shall not entreat it to carry out a new policy against both inclination and ability. Well and good—the British wash their hands of us and depart! Go in peace, we say: we can manage—and at once—if you will just let us be.[21]

The British government in London was not as reckless as the military in Palestine, but it, too, was determined not to yield to Jewish pressure, diplomatic or activist. It sanctioned the deportation of illegal immigrants to Cyprus, which began in August, 1946. This intensified violence which was met with further repression.

About the same time, the so-called Morrison Plan proposed the division of Palestine into Arab and Jewish provinces, with the British in effective control.[22] It was rejected by Arabs and Jews and also by President Truman. Further negotiations with Arabs and Jews followed, but no solution could be found.

By the beginning of 1947, the Palestine conflict had reached deadlock not only as between Arabs and Jews but for the British as well. The Arabs were adamant against any compromise. Jewish opposition in Palestine could not be liquidated without bloody repression, and world opinion would not tolerate that. And American public opinion, unequivocally expressed by President Truman, pressed for action on the admission of refugees. Harassed and impotent, the British Government announced on February 25, 1947, that it would submit the Palestine problem to the United Nations.

It must be noted that this decision did not mean the abandonment of the Mandate. Apparently the aim was to convince the United Nations and world opinion of the soundness of British policy. Assured that the Mandate was unworkable, and that chaos would ensue if they withdrew, the British appear to have expected little more than futile debates in the United Nations, and a new mandate from that body to govern Palestine without the troublesome provisions for Jewish immigration, the Jewish Agency, and the National Home. From present available evidence, one can only assume this conclusion, but the assumption appears warranted by subsequent British actions. At all events, the British remained in Palestine.

Palestine Before the United Nations

The General Assembly met and, after extensive discussions, adopted a resolution on May 15, 1947, constituting the United Nations Special Committee on Palestine (UNSCOP) to investigate the problem and present proposals for a solution. The committee's report, submitted at the end of August, unanimously recommended that the British Mandate be terminated as soon as practicable; that Palestine achieve independence after a short transitional period; that the economic unity of Palestine be preserved; and that in the interval between the end of the Mandate and independence, the governing authorities in Palestine should be responsible to the United Nations. Other recommendations dealt with the Holy Places, the displaced Jews, and with the need for a peaceful transition to independence and democratic government in Palestine thereafter.

On the basic question of Palestine's future, the eleven members of the committee were divided. A majority of seven members proposed partition into an Arab state, a Jewish state, a special regime for the city of Jerusalem under United Nations control, and economic union. A minority of three favored a federal state, with Jerusalem as its capital and autonomous Arab and Jewish provinces. One member abstained from voting on either plan.

The General Assembly convened in September, 1947, and after lengthy debates in committees and in full session adopted the partition plan by a vote of thirty-three to thirteen (with ten absentions) on November 29, 1947. The United States, the Soviet Union, and France voted for partition; the United Kingdom abstained. In approving the partition plan, the General Assembly added two significant provisions, namely: a United Nations Palestine Commission of five states was established to implement the decision, and the Security Council was asked to provide for the enforcement of partition.[23]

The Jews accepted partition. The leadership of the Palestine Arabs defied the United Nations and determined to resist. And the Arab States threatened invasion of Palestine. Under these circumstances, successful and reasonably peaceful implementation might have been achieved if the Palestine Commission had been able to effect a gradual and orderly transfer of authority from the Mandatory power to the Arab and Jewish States; if the Security Council had taken an unequivocal and forceful stand against open warfare; and, above all, if the British government had co-operated or at least refrained from hindering the process of orderly partition. None of these conditions obtained.

The Palestine Commission sought to arrange for the establishment of Arab and Jewish Provisional Councils of Government and for a progressive transfer of administrative authority to itself by taking over areas as the British evacuated them. It planned to supervise the Provisional Councils during the transitional period following the termination of the Mandate, to control military forces, to maintain essential public services, to protect the Holy Places, to delimit frontiers, to divide government assets, and to make preparatory arrangements for economic union. The British government, however, announced that it would co-operate only in a solution acceptable to Arabs and Jews. Since partition did not meet this condition, it declared that the Mandate would be terminated on May 15, 1948, and its troops evacuated in stages soon thereafter.

Moreover, the Palestine Commission was informed that Britain would remain in full control until the end of the Mandate, and that there would be no piecemeal or gradual transfer of authority. While it remained the Mandatory power, Britain refused to facilitate the delimiting of frontiers, the establishment of Provisional Government Councils, the organization of armed militias, or the transfer of any administrative personnel to the Commission. In fact, the Commission was not authorized to enter Palestine until two weeks before the end of the Mandate. Without consulting the Commission, the British also proceeded to dispose of government assets. They blocked sterling balances and excluded Palestine from the sterling area. Such measures invited chaos.

While the United Nations was grappling with the problem, the situation in Palestine deteriorated rapidly. Illegal immigrants continued to arrive and, when apprehended, were forcibly transferred and interned in Cyprus. Terrorism by Jews and reprisals by the military became endemic. A climax was reached in July, 1947, when the ship *Exodus*, with over 4,000 illegal immigrants, was intercepted. The refugees were sent back to France, where they had embarked, and when they refused to leave the ships they were taken to Germany and forcibly interned in a displaced persons' camp.

The partition resolution passed by the General Assembly called on the Mandatory power to evacuate, not later than February 1, 1948, a port and hinterland in the territory of the projected Jewish state in order to facilitate substantial Jewish immigration. The British government declined to comply.

The passage of the partition resolution by the General Assembly was the signal for open fighting between Arabs and Jews in Palestine, and early in 1948 armed Arab bands entered the country from Syria and Transjordan. Casualties were counted in the thousands, and the British either could not or would not maintain law and order, for which they were solely responsible, as they refused to allow the Palestine Commission to intervene.

The Arab States, too, were arming for invasion, and there is no record of any efforts on the part of the British to dissuade or restrain them. In fact, the British continued to supply arms to Arab states in accord with treaty obligations, while they imposed and enforced an embargo on Palestine. And they refused to permit the formation of a Jewish militia. The Arabs could not but conclude that the British would welcome action in defiance of the partition resolution of the United Nations.

Had the Security Council taken a determined stand, open warfare might have been avoided. But the Security Council took no action for nearly three months, and when it did take up the question toward the end of February, 1948, it was evident that the policy of the British had had its effect. After prolonged discussions, a resolution presented by the United States delegation was adopted, calling for another session of the General Assembly to reconsider the question.

The Assembly convened on April 16, 1948, and its committees debated at length a United States proposal for a temporary trusteeship for Palestine until a permanent solution could be found. In the end, this idea failed because the Arabs favored it only if it meant the total abandonment of a Jewish state, the Jews rejected it, and no state other than the United States was prepared to provide armed contingents for its enforcement. On May 14, 1948, this tragic fumbling reached a dramatic denouement. While the Assembly was in plenary session it was announced that the State of Israel had been proclaimed and that the United States had granted it *de facto* recognition. The Assembly then resolved that the Security Council appoint a Mediator to seek peace for Palestine.[24]

The War of Independence

What is known in Israel as the War of Independence began immediately after the adoption of the partition resolution by the General Assembly on November 29, 1947, and ended with the Israel-Syrian armistice on July 20, 1949. It consisted of two distinct phases, marked off by the termination of the Mandate at midnight on May 14, 1948. During the first phase, the British were responsible for law and order, but desultory fighting punctuated the entire period. The Palestine Arabs attacked immediately after the adoption of the partition resolution and were soon joined by irregulars from across the borders. Isolated Jewish settlements were attacked, attempts were made to block vital roads, and fighting flared up in the cities of mixed population, including Jerusalem. After the middle of February, the entire country was affected. Arabs and Jews clashed, vantage points were seized, and truces arranged by the opposing forces, while the British did little to stay bloodshed. In fact, the Arab Legion, a well-armed Transjordan force commanded by British officers, became involved shortly before the termination of the Mandate.

By May 14, 1948, when the State of Israel was proclaimed, the Jews held Haifa, Jaffa, Safed, and Tiberias, most of the roads had been cleared, and numerous Arab villages in the Jewish sector of the country had been occupied. In Jerusalem there was a stalemate: the Arabs held most of the Old City, within the walls; the Jews held most of the New City; but, while some of the surrounding Arab strong points had been taken and supplies pushed through, the road to the coast was blocked and the Jews of Jerusalem were under siege. One thing was clear when the first phase of the war ended—the Jews more than held their own against the Palestine Arabs and the irregulars from across the borders.

The second phase began on May 15, 1948. The Arab States—Egypt, Transjordan, Iraq, Syria, and Lebanon, with auxiliaries from Saudi Arabia and Yemen—invaded Palestine with high expectations of a quick and easy victory. But the Jews, far from being overwhelmed, made notable gains. The north held against the Syrians and Acre (Acco) was taken. The Arab Legion seized the Old City of Jerusalem and cut the coastal road, but the Jews built a new road—the "Road of Valor"—and relieved the New City. The Egyptians were ineffective in the south.

It was the turn of the United Nations to bring the fighting to an end. On May 20, 1948, Count Folke Bernadotte of Sweden was appointed Mediator to help restore peace to Palestine. About the same time, the United States proposed that the Security Council order a cease-fire with a clear threat of sanctions against the recalcitrant party. Israel favored and the Arab States opposed such action. The Soviet Union and France supported the resolution, but the United Kingdom rejected it, and it failed to pass. Instead a mild resolution was adopted calling on Israel and the Arab States to arrange a cease fire. Israel agreed, but the Arab States refused.

On May 29, 1948, a United Kingdom resolution was adopted, calling for a four-week truce and warning that noncompliance would lead to the consideration of enforcement action by the Security Council. This had the desired effect and Bernadotte, the Mediator, succeeded in establishing a four-week truce, beginning on June 11, 1948.

Before the truce expired on July 9, the Mediator and the Security Council requested both parties to extend it. Israel made a favorable reply, but the Arab States refused and fighting was renewed, with Israel scoring further gains. The Council thereupon ordered a cease-fire, indicating that noncompliance would lead to the consideration of sanctions. On July 18, 1948, the second truce went into effect without a time limit.

Clashes continued to occur during 1948-1949, but the truce was invariably restored by the Mediator, supported by Security Council warnings to the adversaries. The Mediator, Bernadotte, was assassinated by Jewish terrorists on September 17, 1948, and the American, Ralph J. Bunche, became Acting Mediator. It was the latter who succeeded in negotiating the armistice agreements between Israel and Egypt (February 24, 1949), Lebanon (March 23, 1949), Transjordan (April 3, 1949), and Syria (July 20, 1949). Demarcation lines were set and Mixed Armistice Commissions, in each case with a chairman from the staff of the United Nations, were appointed to deal with infractions. The agreements were therefore under the supervision of the United Nations.[25]

In sanctioning the armistice agreements, the United Nations recognized the reality of the partition of Palestine. But the partition was the issue of war and not of the conciliatory efforts of the world organization. The United Nations Special Committee on Palestine had proposed a division based mainly on the distribution of population, and had awarded about 3,600 square miles to the Arab state and about 6,400 square miles to the Jewish state. And its proposals for economic union had held out the hope of a viable economy for both Arabs and Jews. The partition resolution of the General Assembly (November 29, 1947) had made some revisions, so that the Arab state was to receive about 4,300 square miles and the Jewish state about 5,700 square miles.[26] The Jews had accepted the change, keeping the door open to a peaceful solution and economic union.

However, the Arabs rejected the proposals for a peaceful settlement and resorted to war, while the British refused to co-operate in the implementation of the decisions of the United Nations. The war and the armistice agreements resulted in the occupation by Israel of territory including Acre, Lydda, Ramleh, Beersheba, and Nazareth, extending its area to about 7,000 square miles. The rest of Palestine was divided: Egypt held the

Gaza strip, and Transjordan seized the remainder despite protests from the other Arab States. In addition, the Jerusalem enclave, which was to have been internationalized, was held in part by Israel and in part by Jordan in defiance of the United Nations.

At this writing, [Spring, 1958] the armistice agreements define the uneasy relation between Israel and the Arab States because the attempts to achieve a political settlement have failed.

Bernadotte, the Mediator, had proposed modifications of the partition plan which abandoned the idea of economic union of the Arab and Jewish states, and which, Israel claimed, would have reduced its territory to some 2,100 square miles.[27] The Arabs were quite willing to receive the additional territory, but they refused to accept the State of Israel which was part of the Mediator's plan. Rejected by both parties, the plan was dropped.

In December, 1948, the General Assembly established the United Nations Conciliation Commission to assist Israel and the Arab States in achieving a final settlement through direct negotiation. No mention was made of the original partition resolution.

The Conciliation Commission made repeated efforts to find the basis for a settlement. Negotiations were held in Lausanne, Switzerland, during 1949 and subsequently at New York, Geneva, and Paris. But the Arab States and Israel could not be brought together in face-to-face negotiations. On the basic issues, too, no agreement could be reached. Israel sought an over-all peace settlement; the Arab States preferred to deal with individual issues, especially with that of the Arab refugees who had fled during the war. On this issue, Israel was ready to readmit a limited number of the refugees as an integral part of a peace settlement, but the Arab States would not agree even in principle to the settlement of refugees in other lands. As to Jerusalem, Israel agreed to international control of the Holy Places but not of the entire part of Jerusalem which it held. The Arab States, not including Jordan, accepted in principle an international regime for Jerusalem, but Transjordan, which held the Old City, rejected the idea. The same deadlock held on the question of boundaries. The Arab States, which had rejected the original partition plan, now sought to secure the cession of the additional territories seized by Israel, but it was not clear that they would accept that as a final settlement. Israel insisted on its *de facto* boundaries.[28]

Thus the Palestine situation remained and remains unsettled to this day. No peace with the Arab States has been achieved, and the armistice agreements define a *de facto* situation. In Jerusalem, too, Israel and Jordan hold their respective segments without the approval of the United Nations. However, Israel was admitted to membership in the United Nations on May 11, 1949, and by that time it had been recognized by fifty-four of the states of the world.[29]

The Flight of the Arabs

The flight of the Arabs from Israel remains to be considered—a startling development which has affected profoundly the State of Israel and the entire Middle East. This phenomenon of mass hysteria may never be fully explained, but available evidence warrants a number of conclusions, or at least reasoned assumptions.

War obviously involves killing, but in modern times the idea of "civilized" warfare has been evolved. This means that combatants may be killed but not tortured or mutilated, and that the civilian or noncombatant population must be protected against outrage, pillage, or murder. Every war has produced its crop of charges of atrocities, particularly against civilians, and some of the charges have undoubtedly been true.

In Palestine, it was especially difficult to wage "civilized" warfare. There was a legacy of bitterness and violence and a tradition of murder and mutilation even of the innocent, as in the Hebron atrocities in the riots of 1929, when more than sixty devout and nonpolitical Jews—men, women, and children—were done to death. Moreover, when disciplined armies are involved, the reckless elements can be held in check, but during the last weeks of the Mandate, Palestine was in a state of anarchy. The British had not permitted the Palestine Commission to supervise the establishment and functioning of Arab and Jewish militias. Fighting was conducted by small bands, some of which could not be controlled. Finally, during the early months of 1948, Arab-Jewish hostilities consisted of raids, reprisals, ambushes along the roads, and other guerrilla tactics. In that situation, the distinction between combatants and noncombatants became as blurred and tenuous as the difference between legitimate military operations and atrocities. When Arabs ambushed a bus and killed its occupants; when the Jews staged a commando raid at night on a village which harbored foreign irregulars; or when a member of either party threw a bomb: were these legitimate measures or atrocities? Charges and countercharges therefore filled the air.

Then came in rapid succession two shocking acts of terror. On April 9, 1948, a band of the *Irgun* attacked Deir Yassin (a village on the outskirts of Jerusalem which had not permitted foreign Arab infiltrators to use it as a base of operations) and massacred some 250 Arab men, women, and children. The Arab response was quick and sharp: on April 13, 1948, a convoy from Jerusalem to the Hadassah hospital and Hebrew University on Mt. Scopus was attacked and seventy-seven doctors, nurses, teachers, and students were massacred. These atrocities quickened the sense of insecurity into panic.

By January, 1948, Arabs in considerable numbers had begun leaving cities such as Haifa and Jaffa. In April, when hostilities were intensified, whole villages were evacuated. But after the massacres of Deir Yassin and the Hadassah-Hebrew University convoy, panic and total flight accompanied occupation by enemy forces. The number of Jews in Arab areas was small—only about 7,000 eventually left. The Arab exodus was a mass flight of hundreds of thousands.

The two massacres, particularly that of Deir Yassin, must therefore be designated a cause of the flight of the Arabs. But it was not the only cause. There is evidence that the Arab leaders stimulated, if they did not actually order, the exodus. An eyewitness learned from Arabs fleeing Tiberias in April that their leaders had ordered them to leave and that they would soon return. The same writer concluded from what he saw in Haifa that the exodus of the Arab civilians was the policy of the Arab leaders.

Apparently the Arab leaders, especially those of the Arab States, expected a lightning war and a quick victory. Evacuation of the Arabs from war areas was considered desirable to allow guerrilla and regular forces greater freedom of action and to arouse war passions in neighboring Arab States. The Arab leaders therefore encouraged fear and panic and, at the same time, gave assurances of a speedy return home. It is significant that 80 per cent of the Moslems and only 50 per cent of the Christian Arabs fled the country.

One conclusion appears incontrovertible. The mass flight of the Arabs came as a surprise to the Jews. Early in April, 1948, before the massacre of Deir Yassin, Ben-Gurion was speculating on the reasons for the flight of Arabs. During the latter part of the month, when the Jews took Haifa, the Jews pleaded with the Arab leaders not to encourage flight, and the *Haganah* distributed leaflets assuring the Arabs equal treatment.[30] As the initial shock passed, however, the Jews ceased to discourage the exodus and even welcomed it.

The State of Israel: Geographical Features

The new state that emerged from the war is a narrow strip on the southeastern coast of the Mediterranean Sea extending irregularly for 260 miles from the borders of Lebanon and Syria in the north to Egypt and the Gulf of Aqaba in the south. It is bounded by 590 miles of hostile Arab borders which cut deep into the heart of Israel. North of Tel-Aviv, the country is only twelve miles wide, and at Elat only nine miles; its greatest width is south of Beersheba—seventy miles. The Mediterranean alone affords free access to the outside world, but even there the Gaza strip of some 125 square miles is under Egyptian occupation.

The total area of Israel is about 8,050 square miles, somewhat smaller than the State of Massachusetts. The Coastal Plain runs along the Mediterranean and extends in varying depths into the interior, and most of Israel's population lives in this region. Eastward the mountains range from Galilee to Sinai, with fertile valleys, notably the Valley of Jezreel, affording good agricultural land for settlement. The Jordan Valley is mostly below sea level. The Negev comprises about half the area of the country. Desert and steppe land until recently, Israel has begun the cultivation of the northern portions, and its potential in minerals and oil holds promise of economic viability for the young state.

The climate in the north and west is of the Mediterranean variety, with warm summers and mild winters. The Jordan Valley, however, is hot and humid in the summer, and the hot days and cool nights of the Negev are reminiscent of the desert. Rainfall is ample in the north and generally also in central Israel. The Negev, however, is dry, and agricultural development in that area depends on piping water from the north. The water resources of the country as a whole are limited. The Jordan River flows for 73 of its 158 miles in Israeli territory, and the Yarkon and Kishon are relatively small rivers. Lake Kinneret (Lake Tiberias) is a large body of fresh water, but the Dead Sea, although rich in minerals, is too salty for agricultural irrigation.

3. THE FIRST DECADE OF ISRAEL: 1948-1958

The Ben-Gurion Era

No single individual has had so profound an influence on the development of Israel as David Ben-Gurion. He was a dominant influence in the molding of the labor movement of Palestine; he led Palestine Jewry during the last decade of the Mandate; he headed the Provisional Government and was the driving force in the War of Independence; his views were a determining factor in the fashioning of the new state and government; and, except for an interval when he voluntarily retired, he has been the unchallenged leader since the establishment of the state.

Ben-Gurion was born in Poland in 1886 and arrived in Palestine in 1906. He received a traditional Jewish education and private instruction in general subjects and languages. For a time, he studied law at the University of Constantinople, and at the age of fifty-five he learned ancient Greek in order to read the classics in the original.

During his formative years in Palestine, Ben-Gurion worked as an agricultural laborer, and participated in the early efforts at trade union organization, self-defense, and co-operative settlement. He was quickly recognized as the leader of the Poale-Zion Party of Palestine, and played a prominent role in the founding of the *Histadrut*, which he served as General Secretary from 1921 to 1933. During the First World War, he helped organize the Jewish Legion and himself served under its colors. And throughout these hectic years, he traveled widely, lectured, and wrote extensively.

By the middle 1930's, Ben-Gurion had attained top leadership in Zionist counsels. In 1933, he was elected to the Executive of the World Zionist Organization, and he became its chairman as well as the chairman of the Jewish Agency Executive in Palestine; these positions made him the effective leader of the Zionist movement. He was the moving spirit behind the adoption of the "Biltmore Program" (1942), which called for a Jewish Commonwealth in Palestine, unlimited Jewish immigration, and the formation of a Jewish army. Before the various commissions of inquiry, too, he represented the Jewish cause with force and dignity.

Ben-Gurion is richly endowed with the qualities of leadership. Possessed of deep insight and extensive knowledge, he has applied both to the furtherance of a clear-visioned objective—the creation of a secure and prosperous Jewish state, based on a society of workers and rendered viable by economic development with the aid of modern science and the support of world Jewry. Jewish immigration and dedicated pioneering (*Halutziut*) have been and remain the basic principles which he has championed with fervid eloquence and obstinate devotion.

Ben-Gurion does not argue premises but posits them as self-evident truths, and he speaks with contagious conviction. But he is no doctrinaire. He can appraise opposing viewpoints and balance social and economic ideals against the unyielding facts of a situation. This realism enables him to compromise in order to achieve the attainable.

Ben-Gurion's achievements are due in no small measure to his unflagging vitality and indomitable courage and determination. And these qualities have found expression not only in defiance of the enemy but also in the stern suppression of evil within his own camp. Finally, although at times impatient and self-assured, he is immune to the temptation of this age to impose doctrinaire ideals by violence. His conception of unity is not enforced totalitarian conformity, but co-operation cemented by democratic processes and the rule of law.[31]

Development of State and Government

The State of Israel (*Medinat Yisrael*) was proclaimed on May 14, 1948, when Ben-Gurion read the Declaration of Independence at a meeting of the Council of the People held in the Tel-Aviv Museum. The government and administration were fashioned gradually in successive stages.

It was noted above that the Jews had developed quasi-governmental autonomous institutions during the period of the Mandate—the Elected Assembly with its National Council (*Vaad Leumi*) and the Palestine Executive of the Jewish Agency. These bodies formed the nucleus of the first Jewish national administration. In November, 1947, a Joint Emergency Committee was set up, and during the following four months it took measures to counteract the creeping chaos which resulted from the disintegration of the British administration. Provision was made for the conservation of food and fuel supplies, for hospital facilities, a broadcasting system, a police force, and similar services; mobilization of persons of military age was begun; and plans were made for the future state. In March, 1948, the Emergency Committee was superseded by a more representative agency. The National Council (*Vaad Leumi*) was reorganized to represent all elements in the Jewish population and reconstituted as the Council of the People—a body of thirty-seven, including the fourteen members of the Executive of the National Council, the twelve members of the Palestine Executive of the Jewish Agency, and eleven deputies of parties and groups not heretofore represented. The new Council, and the executive of thirteen (known as the Administration of the People) which it designated, conducted Jewish affairs until the end of the Mandate. It was the Council of the People which proclaimed the State of Israel.

With the establishment of Israel, the Council of the People became the Provisional State Council, with Chaim Weizmann as President, and the Administration of the People became the Provisional Government, with David Ben-Gurion as Prime Minister. The Provisional Council and Government, which functioned until February 14, 1949, discharged all affairs of state. Its first legislative act was to repeal the legal provisions which had restricted Jewish immigration and land transfers to Jews! Beyond that, it declared in force the existing law, the courts, and the local governments, unless modified by the constituted authorities.

The Provisional Government directed the war, provided for internal security, adopted budgets and imposed taxes, set up administrative agencies and a civil service. It facilitated immigration and took a census of the population of the country (November 8, 1948). It appointed a special committee which approved a draft constitution for submission to the Constituent Assembly. Finally, the Provisional Government made all the legal and administrative arrangements for national elections to the Constituent Assembly, which were held on January 25, 1949. The Constituent Assembly —the *Knesset*—met on February 14, 1949, and inaugurated a permanent government. Chaim Weizmann was elected President of Israel and David Ben-Gurion became Prime Minister of a coalition government.[32]

SYSTEM OF GOVERNMENT

Israel is a democratic parliamentary republic. The Proclamation of Independence declared that the State of Israel ". . . will be based on the principles of liberty, justice and peace as conceived by the Prophets of Israel; will uphold the full social and political equality of all its citizens, without distinction of religion, race or sex; will guarantee freedom of religion, conscience, education and culture. . . ." At this writing, no formal Bill of Rights has been adopted, although the first Cabinet's program, which was approved by the *Knesset* in March, 1949, included as fundamental principles equality of rights and duties for all, including women, freedom of expression, of religious observance, of education and culture, and labor rights in significant detail.[33] Moreover, the safeguards of the Mandatory regime have remained in force, and new legislation has decreed full equality for women and the abolition of corporal punishment and of the death penalty for murder. In actual practice, the principles of democracy, the rule of law, human rights, and fundamental freedoms have prevailed. Representative government based on popular elections and majority rule has functioned effectively. Above all, the rights to differ and to express differing views in speech, assembly, and publication have been observed. The status of the Arab minority will be discussed subsequently.

Israel has no formal written constitution in the sense of a fundamental law which requires, as in the United States, a special process of amendment and which limits the powers of the organs of government. Steps were taken to formulate a written constitution: under the Provisional Government a draft with elaborate provisions for fundamental human rights was prepared and submitted to the First *Knesset*.[34] But it was decided after lengthy debates to allow constitutional law to evolve gradually. The compelling motivations against a formal, written constitution appear to have been the desire to allow the government freedom of action during the formative fluid period, and the practical difficulty of harmonizing the demands of the orthodox elements with those of the anti-clericals. Individual constitutional laws were therefore enacted, equal in legal authority to other laws and subject to change by the ordinary process of legislation.

The structure of government embraces the usual executive, legislative, and judicial branches, with a President, a parliament, a cabinet, and a system of courts. The President is the titular head of the state, who enjoys great public esteem but whose functions are mainly ceremonial and formal. His powers are limited. He convenes the *Knesset*, calls on the outstanding party leader to form a government, and receives the resignation of a cabinet which has lost the confidence of the *Knesset*. He may dissolve the *Knesset* when no new cabinet can be formed.

The President signs all bills passed by the *Knesset*, but he has no veto power over legislation. He signs treaties after ratification by the *Knesset*. He receives diplomatic representatives from foreign powers and names Israel's diplomats and consular agents, but the appointments are first approved by a cabinet minister. All his important official acts require the countersignature of a cabinet minister. He does have two significant discretionary powers. He may pardon offenders and reduce punishments, and he has the authority to consult with leaders of various parties before designating one to attempt to form a cabinet.

The President is elected by a majority vote and secret ballot of the *Knesset* for a term of five years. The first President was Chaim Weizmann, a distinguished scientist, the central figure in the negotiations which secured the Balfour Declaration, and the outstanding leader of the Zionist movement during the period of the Mandate. He was elected on February 16, 1949, and died on November 9, 1952. His successor, chosen on December 8, 1952, and re-elected on October 30, 1957, is Yitzhak Ben-Zvi,[34a] who shared in the building of the National Home as pioneer in self-defense, scholar, leader of the *Histadrut* and, for more than a decade, Chairman of the National Council.

The *Knesset* is the supreme agency of government. It is a one-chamber parliament of 120 members, whose powers are not limited either by formal constitution or by presidential veto or by Supreme Court. It is answerable only to the people, who elect it for a term of four years by direct, equal, and secret ballot, and proportional representation.

As a legislative body, the *Knesset* has functioned after the manner of the British House of Commons, with bills introduced by the government, scrutinized in committees, debated in full session, and passed by majority vote. Debates are limited by allotting time to each party in accord with its representation in the *Knesset*, and filibustering is thus eliminated.

The *Knesset* exercises extensive controls over the executive. The cabinet or government is responsible to it: it cannot be formed without the support of a majority of the *Knesset* and must resign when it fails to command the latter's confidence. The *Knesset* also ratifies treaties, and it supervises the administration of government departments. Ministers and other officials are required to appear before *Knesset* committees and to report on their activities, and special committees conduct searching investigations when necessary. Interpolations or questions are addressed to ministers and their replies are presented to the *Knesset*. Finally, control of the budget reinforces the power of the *Knesset* over the government and administration.

Special provision has been made for close and continuous scrutiny of state financial and economic activities under the aegis of the *Knesset*. A State Comptroller, named by the President on the recommendation of a committee of the *Knesset*, audits accounts and reports to the Finance Committee of the *Knesset* on the legality, economy, and efficiency of the government bodies under his supervision. And it is specially stipulated that the State Comptroller is responsible to the *Knesset* and not dependent upon the government.

The *Knesset* has proved an efficient and effective parliament. Informal in dress and appearance, it has conducted affairs with proper decorum and has shown an independent spirit toward the government.

The cabinet or government is the functioning executive body. The Prime Minister, a member of the *Knesset*, is charged by the President with the responsibility of forming a government, and he negotiates with party leaders on the choice of his colleagues, who may or may not be members of the *Knesset*. When approved by the *Knesset* through a vote of confidence, the government is constituted.

The principles of responsibility and unity govern the cabinet system. Responsibility involves accountability to the *Knesset* and dependence on the confidence of the latter. Unity means collective responsibility of the cabinet: once a decision is made by majority vote, all its members are expected to support it, and open opposition to a cabinet proposal cannot be voiced or indicated except by express permission of a majority of the cabinet. The cabinet system of Israel rests on the coalition of political parties.

The administrative departments of the government follow the pattern of all governments, with several exceptions. There are ministries of defense, foreign affairs, finance, commerce and industry, agriculture, labor, interior, justice, health, social welfare, education and culture, communications, and posts. There is a ministry of police, and the special needs of the country have prompted the establishment of ministries of development and of religious affairs. In addition, the Prime Minister's Office embraces important administrative units, with total personnel exceeding that of a number of the ministries. Among these are the Civil Service Commission, the Central Bureau of Statistics, the Scientific Research Council and institutes of specialized research, the Atomic Energy Commission, broadcasting and press services, a technical assistance liaison office, state archives, and the Government Tourist Corporation.[35]

The judicial branch of the government comprises religious as well as civil courts. The hierarchy of civil courts includes four Municipal and seventeen Magistrates' Courts (including two Juvenile Courts) with minor civil and criminal jurisdiction; three District Courts which hear appeals from the lower tribunals and serve as courts of first instance in major civil and criminal cases; and the highest court of the land—the Supreme Court of seven justices, a president, and a deputy president. The Supreme Court cannot declare unconstitutional laws passed by the *Knesset*, but it can invalidate administrative actions or interpretations of statutes which it regards as contrary to the "rule of law."

The Rabbinical Courts exercise exclusive jurisdiction in marriage and divorce, while in other matters of personal status, such as alimony, probate, and succession, they may act when all parties consent. The ecclesiastical courts of the Christian communities have exclusive authority in marriage, divorce, alimony, and confirmation of wills, and they may judge other matters of personal status with the consent of the parties. The Moslem courts have exclusive jurisdiction in all matters of personal status. The Jews have recourse in these matters to Rabbinical Courts and the Moslems and Christians to religious courts of their respective communities. There are also tribunals for special types of cases, such as rents, profiteering and speculation, and national insurance, and tribal courts for the Bedouins.

The independence of the judiciary is assured by special safeguards against political appointments and by tenure subject only to good behavior. The civil judges and those of the Rabbinical Courts are appointed by the President on the recommendation of Appointments Committees consisting of judges of the Supreme Court, ministers of the government, members of the *Knesset*, and representatives of the Israel Bar Association. The judges of the Moslem and Christian Religious Courts are appointed by the Minister of Religious Affairs in consultation with their respective communities.

The body of law administered by the courts consists of enactments of the *Knesset* and laws inherited from the previous regimes. The latter include Ottoman survivals especially in private and land law, legal provisions which obtained under the Mandate, English common law and equity, rabbinical law, and religious law of the Moslem and Christian communities.[36]

Local government,[37] initiated cautiously during the period of the Mandate, has been extended and democratized since the establishment of the state. Property qualifications for voting have been abolished. The franchise has been extended to women in all local elections. And mayors and vice-mayors, appointed under the British regime, are now elected by the local representative bodies.

At the end of 1956, a total of 154 local authorities were functioning, and their jurisdiction covered about 90 per cent of the population of the country. There were twenty Municipalities of varying sizes, with a population of over 1,065,000; eighty-six Local Councils, with some 335,000 people; and forty-eight Regional Councils, embracing nearly 650 agricultural settlements and about 215,000 people. All these bodies are elected directly by their constituents, but they operate under the close and confining supervision of the Ministry of the Interior.

The functions of the local authorities embrace education and culture, health and sanitation, water works, housing, and other local needs, with special attention devoted to the absorption of new immigrants. The Regional Councils pool the efforts of the villages in public works, antimalaria measures, drainage, and major water works. However, the competence of the local authorities has not as yet been fully defined, and there is considerable variation in the services performed even by the large municipalities. Nor is there a clear division of function between them and the central government. To remedy these and other deficiencies, the Minister of the Interior has appointed an advisory Local Government Council which will, no doubt, assist in the preparation of appropriate legislation.

PARTIES, PARLIAMENTS, AND CABINETS

Political Parties: Since the establishment of Israel, and before that, too, Ben-Gurion's leadership has been exerted through the Israel Labor Party, because political parties are the decisive influence in the government and they permeate all public life in Israel. Local government, trade union affairs, agricultural settlements, co-operative agencies, and numerous other activities reflect party differentiation, and practically every political party conducts some social, economic, or cultural institutions, including youth movements, theaters, athletic clubs, and housing projects. Politics and partisanship are, therefore, never dormant, and ideological loyalties create an atmosphere of intense and zealous rivalry. The clash of economic interests and of social and religious philosophies is reinforced in Israel by the fact that economic, social, and cultural institutions are newly fashioned and susceptible of being molded; that the state itself and the governmental apparatus have not yet achieved permanent form. Hence the anxious desire of every party to attain power in order to stamp its image and ideals on the country and its people.

The present system of government, structured as it is on party loyalties, both reflects the influence of the latter and serves to strengthen their hold on public affairs. Elections to the *Knesset* are based on a system of proportional representation, whereby the citizen votes for a party list rather than an individual. The lists of candidates, up to 120 (the total membership of the *Knesset*), are prepared and numbered in descending order of preference by the central bodies of the parties, and seats in parliament are allocated in accordance with the proportion of votes won by each party list. If a member of the *Knesset* dies or resigns, he is replaced not by the successful candidate in a by-election but by the next name in the order of preference on the party list. Thus a member of parliament represents his party and not a specific constituency. The members of a coalition cabinet, too, are chosen in interparty negotiation, and it is the party rather than the Prime Minister which designates its representatives in the government. As a result, the composition of the *Knesset* and the cabinet as well as programs and policies are controlled by the party organizations.

Israel is a multiparty state, and every one of the Jewish political parties had its origin or early development during the period of the Mandate. The parties reflect the composite character of the population. Emigrants from many lands, the Jews have brought with them differing cultural backgrounds, religious orientations, political conceptions, and social ideals. Many of the European immigrants had made doctrinal commitments and stanch party affiliations in their native lands, and slogans, programs, even party names, were transplanted to the new homeland. The result was a plethora of parties and groupings during the period of the Mandate, and these have persisted under the new state.

The parties represent differences in social doctrine, religious loyalties, economic status, national objectives, and geographical origin. However, these divisive factors are not all-embracing, because some of the parties include subgroups with diverse subsidiary interests. For example, the religious parties are at one in opposing the secular state, but elements within these parties differ on the question of private versus co-operative enterprise. Therefore, the common practice of arranging parties in a political spectrum ranging from right to left or from conservative to radical coloration could be misleading. In the interest of clarity, the most important parties of Israel will be grouped according to the major emphases of their ideologies and programs.

Labor or Socialist objectives are the fundamental tenets of several political parties. The most important and the dominant party in Israel is the *Mapai*, or the Israel Labor Party, which originated in a merger in 1930 of several factions: the *Poale Zion*, a Zionist-Socialist group largely Marxist in orientation; a non-Marxist Zionist-Socialist element, known as the *Hapoel Hatzair* (Young Worker); and an organization of agricultural workers. The philosophy of the Israel Labor Party is social-democratic, but it seeks to attain the Socialist goal primarily through the co-operative ownership of the means of production and distribution rather than through their nationalization. Symbolized by the policies of its leader, Ben-Gurion, and by the achievements of the *Histadrut*, the program of the Israel Labor Party favors political and social democracy and a planned economy which includes state-controlled private enterprise. In foreign policy, it is oriented toward the Western democracies, without definite commitment to the Eastern or Western blocs.

Mapam, or the United Workers Party, was founded in 1948 when three left-wing Socialist elements joined forces. The constituent elements were the *Left Poale Zion*, a strictly Marxist faction which favored Zionism but emphasized the class struggle; another group—*Hashomer Hatzair* (The Young Watchman)—which combined militant socialism with Zionist pioneering; and leftist elements (*Ahdut Haavoda-Poale Zion*), which had seceded from the *Mapai*. The adherents of *Mapam*, like those of *Mapai*, had long labored in the Zionist pioneering movement and in the building of collective and co-operative settlements, and they had been in the forefront of the struggle for independence.

The *Mapam* program, seeking to combine Zionism with Marxism, favors a united Socialist Labor Front, the rapid socialization of the economy, and co-operation with Arab labor. In foreign policy, it has vacillated between a pro-Soviet position and neutralism.

Mapam has proved an unstable union of leftist forces, with the pro-Soviet orientation the chief cause of discord. As a result, the strength and influence of the party have declined. Several of its *Knesset* representatives have gone over to the Communists or to *Mapai*. Others have seceded to form an independent faction—*Ahdut Haavoda-Poale Zion*—which favors neutralism in foreign policy and is outspokenly critical of the Soviet Union.

At the extreme left of the Socialist movement is the Communist Party, a small but vociferous group which echoes faithfully the line dictated by the foreign policy of the Soviet Union.

The "Religious Bloc" has consisted of four parties—The *Agudat Israel* and *Poale Agudat Israel*, and the *Mizrahi* and *Hapoel Hamizrahi*. The *Agudat Israel* represents the uncompromising Orthodox elements which, before the rise of Israel, frowned on Zionist ideology, opposed the Hebrew movement, and held aloof from the organized Jewish community. Since the establishment of the state, it has co-operated in forming various governments, but it still sets its face sternly against all forms of modernism, including woman suffrage. Its positive policy aims to maintain and further strict adherence to Orthodox ritual and traditional religious lore.

The *Mizrahi* has been a religious party within the Zionist movement and it has participated in Jewish national and communal institutions. It is less intransigent than the *Agudat Israel*, accepting woman suffrage, for example, as a concession to the mood of the times. It strives to develop Jewish national life in the spirit of religious tradition.

The *Poale Agudat Israel* and *Hapoel Hamizrahi* are the labor offshoots of the parent parties. Sharing the religious views of the latter, they differ on economic policy: whereas the parent parties favor private enterprise, the labor groups have turned to co-operative endeavors. In 1956, the *Mizrahi* and *Hapoel Hamizrahi* merged into a single party.

Middle-class interests are represented by two strong parties and several minor factions. The General Zionists embrace the secularist and non-Socialist segments of the Jewish population who seek to develop Israel without the constraints of class conflict, social doctrines, or religious-clerical controls. This party played a leading role in the building of the Jewish National Home, and some of the foremost figures in Zionism, including Chaim Weizmann, came from its ranks. In part, its influence has been due to the paramount role played by middle-class elements in the Zionist organizations of various countries, and consequently also in the World Zionist Organization.

The General Zionist Party favors private enterprise with a minimum of government or party interference, and the abandonment of state encouragement of collectivism. It calls for the elimination of party influence in education, public health, labor exchanges, and other national functions. It is oriented toward the Western democracies in foreign policy.

The *Herut* (Freedom) Party is an outgrowth of the Zionist Revisionists and the *Irgun* elements of the Mandate period. Its program, which calls for "a self-supporting national economy, based on initiative, free competition and increased productivity," is strongly anticollectivist and, like the General Zionists, it opposes party influence in education and the social services. Its distinguishing characteristic is the maximalist national position:

it seeks the "reunion of the land of Israel," that is, the inclusion of all of Palestine in the State of Israel.

In addition, there are various minor parties or splinters. The Progressives are an offshoot of the General Zionists who favor co-operation with the moderate labor parties. The *Sephardim* and Yemenites have attempted, with diminishing success, to organize Oriental Jews. Finally, several Arab parties have won seats in the *Knesset* and, although neither Socialist nor prolabor in orientation, they have generally supported the Mapai Party.[38]

Parliaments: Three national elections have been held since the establishment of Israel. The Constituent Assembly—the First *Knesset*—was elected on January 25, 1949. By the end of 1950, the *Knesset* majority which supported the coalition government began to founder over religious issues, and early in the following year Ben-Gurion precipitated general elections, which were held on July 30, 1951. The Second *Knesset* lasted the full term of four years, and on July 26, 1955, the Third *Knesset* was elected.

The table (page 722) presents comparative figures on the three elections —the popular vote and its distribution among the parties, the percentage of citizen participation, and the party strength in each *Knesset*. These figures and the general conduct of the elections suggest a number of conclusions.[39]

First and foremost, the elections reveal that Israel is a functioning democracy, that the vote is taken seriously, and that the electorate is mature enough to shun violence and rely on the ballot to effect desired changes. All the elections have been peaceful, democratic, and free of corrupt manipulation, and the percentage of popular participation has been high—nearly 87 per cent of the eligible voters in 1949, over 75 per cent in 1951, and close to 83 per cent in 1955. This is most significant because the electorate doubled between 1949 and 1955, and large numbers of the new immigrants had never voted before and could hardly have been expected to share effectively in democratic processes. Apparently faith in democratic elections is deep enough in Israel to permeate the masses of politically primitive new arrivals. In this respect at least, large numbers of the new immigration have been assimilated.

The multiplicity of parties has remained a characteristic feature of Israeli elections: twenty-one parties and factions took part in the elections of 1949, and twelve secured seats in the *Knesset*; seventeen party lists contested each of the subsequent elections, and representation in the *Knesset* was secured by fifteen parties in 1951 and by twelve in 1955. However, closer examination will reveal that only six or eight parties really matter, and that splinter groups tend to disappear. In 1949, nine splinter groups polled a combined total of less than 5 per cent of the vote, and three others won only one seat each. Furthermore, nine Jewish splinter parties of 1949 failed to appear in 1951, and two new factions that submitted lists in 1951 failed to elect any candidate to the *Knesset*. The decline of splinter groups

Table I

Elections to the Knesset

	1st Election, January 25, 1949			2nd Election, July 30, 1951			3rd Election, July 26, 1955		
	Votes	% of Total	Members	Votes	% of Total	Members	Votes	% of Total	Members
Mapai	155,274	35.7	46	256,456	37.3	45	274,735	32.2	40
Mapam	64,018	14.7	19	86,096	12.5	15	62,401	7.3	9
Ahdut Haavoda-Poale Zion	—	—	—	—	—	—	69,475	8.2	10
General Zionist	22,861	5.2	7	111,394	16.2	20	87.099	10.2	13
Hapoel Hamizrahi [a]				46,347	6.8	8	77,936 (with Mizrahi)	9.1	11
Mizrahi [a]				10,383	1.5	2			
Agudat Israel (a)	52,982 (four parties together)	12.2	16	13,799	2.0	3	39,836 (with Poale Agudat Israel)	4.7	6
Poale Agudat Israel (a)				11,194	1.6	2			
Herut	49,782	11.5	14	45,651	6.6	8	107,190	12.6	15
Israel Communist Party	15,148	3.5	4	27,334	4.0	5	38,492	4.5	6
Progressives	17,786	4.1	5	22,171	3.2	4	37,661	4.4	5
Israel Arab Democrats	7,387	1.7	2	16,370	2.4	3	15,475	1.8	2
Sephardic Oriental Communities	15,287	3.5	4	12,002	1.8	2	6,994	0.8	—
Progress and Work (Arab)	—	—	—	8,067	1.2	1	12,511	1.5	2
Yemenites	4,399	1.0	1	7,965	1.2	1	2,448	0.3	—
Agriculture and Development (Arab)	—	—	—	7,851	1.1	1	9,791	1.1	1
Fighters (Lohamim)	5,363	1.2	1	—	—	—	—	—	—
WIZO	5,173	1.2	1	—	—	—	—	—	—
Other Jewish tickets	13,198	3.4	—	4,413	0.6	—	16,133	1.9	—
Other Arab tickets	6,026	1.3	—	—	—	—	4,484	0.5	—
Eligible voters		506,567			924,885			1,057,795	
Total voting		440,095			695,007			876,085	
Canceled votes		5,411			7,515			22,866	
Voting participation		86.9%			75.4%			82.8%	

[a] These four parties presented one list, the "United Religious Bloc," at the 1949 election; they ran on separate lists in the election for the 2nd *Knesset* (7/30/51); and in the 3rd *Knesset* election, the religious parties ran on two lists, one including the *Mizrahi* and *Hapoel Hamizrahi*, and the other the *Agudat Israel* and the *Poale Agudat Israel.*

has been accelerated by the election law of 1951, which denied representation to any party which polled less than 1 per cent of the valid votes cast. One can detect a tendency toward the consolidation of parties along ideological lines, but the present *Knesset* (elected in 1955) still includes three independent labor parties, two religious blocs, and three Arab splinter parties with little, if any, ideological differences.

The election of 1951 indicated a trend toward the more moderate parties: *Mapam* declined, while *Mapai* increased its percentage of total votes; and the General Zionists emerged as the second party in the *Knesset*, with *Herut* reduced to a fraction. The 1955 election, however, appears to have reversed this trend. *Herut* nearly doubled its proportionate following and the General Zionists lost heavily. *Mapam's* decline continued, but *Mapai* lost, too, and the total non-*Mapai* (leftist) labor strength increased. Whether this connotes a trend toward the extremes of the right and left, it is difficult to say. In all likelihood, the election of 1955 registered the disappointment of the new immigrants with the hardships and insecurities of life in Israel, and also general impatience with the government's moderation in the face of border provocation, and with its reliance on the West when the latter was barely friendly. At all events, *Mapai* emerged from every election as the preponderant party in the *Knesset*, with one-third or more of the seats.

Cabinets or Governments. The governments (cabinets) of Israel have been coalitions, reflecting the multiparty composition of the *Knesset*. The Provisional Government (May 15, 1948–March 10, 1949) included all of the important parties (*Mapai*, *Mapam*, Religious Front, General Zionists, Progressives, and *Sephardim*) except the Revisionists or *Herut*. After the election of the First *Knesset*, however, Ben-Gurion formed a less unwieldy government of *Mapai* and the Religious Front, with representation also of the Progressives and the *Sephardim*. This coalition of the secularist *Mapai* and the clerically-oriented Religious Front created tensions and cabinet crises, but it was repeatedly reconstituted and held together until December, 1952—close to four years. *Mapai* made a number of concessions in religious matters and the Religious Front supported the basic economic and political policies of the Prime Minister and his party.

The success of the General Zionists in the election of 1951, when they emerged as the second largest party in the *Knesset*, foreshadowed a radical shift in the parliamentary and cabinet coalition. The *Mapai* and the General Zionists were both moderate parties, albeit with rival labor and middle-class philosophies and programs. If a compromise could be effected on basic policies, government stability would be immeasurably enhanced, because the two parties commanded a clear majority in the *Knesset*.

The attempt was made, with the understanding that practical measures rather than theory would be stressed, especially economic development to absorb the new immigrants. In December, 1952, a *Mapai*-General Zionists government was formed, with the co-operation also of *Hapoel Hamizrahi* and the Progressives. This coalition held despite secondary crises until June, 1955, when the General Zionists withdrew from the government.

During this period, a momentous change occurred when Ben-Gurion resigned from the government and withdrew from public life (December 7, 1953). Leadership in the government was assumed by Moshe Sharett, an outstanding figure in the *Histadrut* and *Mapai*, a skillful negotiator, head of the Political Department of the Jewish Agency during the period of the Mandate, and the foremost Israeli diplomat who had served as Foreign Minister since the establishment of the state. However, Ben-Gurion's retirement was temporary. He returned as Foreign Minister in February, 1955, and on November 3, 1955, succeeded Sharett as Prime Minister.

The return of Ben-Gurion to power ushered in a third major shift in the composition of the government coalition. The General Zionists had withdrawn in June, 1955, just prior to the election of that year. Their defeat at the polls eliminated them from consideration as a compelling factor in a cabinet coalition. The new government therefore reflected the labor-liberal majority of the Third *Knesset*. It consisted of a five-party coalition: the three labor parties—*Mapai*, *Mapam*, and *Ahdut Haavodah*; the combined *Mizrahi-Hapoel Hamizrahi*; and the Progressives. This has proved a stable combination and, at this writing, it still constitutes the government of Israel. In January, 1958, a crisis developed when one of the parties revealed to the press an important matter under consideration by the cabinet. The Prime Minister, and hence the cabinet, resigned, but it was soon reconstituted, after a firm commitment of all five parties that the secrecy of cabinet deliberations and collective responsibility would be preserved, and that the coalition would hold until the election of 1959.[40]

Coalition cabinets based on a multiplicity of parties are notoriously unstable, as is evidenced by the French Third and Fourth Republics. The Israeli cabinet system, however, has been astonishingly stable. There have been eight or nine major cabinet changes between 1948 and 1958, but only once (in 1951) did a government fall because of an adverse vote in the *Knesset*. The changes have been due mainly to such formal factors as the election of a new *Knesset*, the choice of a new President, and the withdrawal of a Prime Minister. The significant shifts have been three, and each has resulted from a national election: the election of the First *Knesset* resulted in the *Mapai*-Religious Front coalition; the Second *Knesset* produced the *Mapai*-General Zionist bloc; and the Third *Knesset* yielded the labor-liberal government. To be sure, the cabinets have been uneasy coalitions, with all too frequent flare-ups and crises, but that is the nature of peacetime coalitions everywhere. In fact, even where the two-party system prevails, as in England, minor crises are not uncommon when a government lacks an overpowering leader.

Several factors have contributed to the relative stability of the Israeli government. First, the preponderant strength of *Mapai*, with one-third or more mandates in every *Knesset*, has made it the anchor of every cabinet. The predominant influence of Ben-Gurion has served as a stabilizing force, and the usual carry-over of most ministers into reorganized cabinets has enhanced the continuity of policy. Finally, the rigorous discipline of Israeli parties has curbed irresponsible action by individual members of the *Knesset*.

The press of Israel has devoted much attention to the question of parties and coalitions, and Ben-Gurion himself has deplored the fragmentation of the electorate. However, for Israel coalitions are not an unmixed evil. The burden of a Prime Minister would, no doubt, be eased by the solid support of a majority party. But where, as in Israel, differences are ideologically motivated, a two-party system might result in irreconcilable conflicts. Coalitions which make compromises imperative tend to soften differences, thus contributing to national unity. A case in point is the fact that even the unyielding and unco-operative *Agudat Israel* was held in line by participation in the government.

POLITICAL AND SOCIAL REFORMS

During the first decade of independence, the issues which have agitated the public in Israel and occupied the attention of government and parliament have dealt with the consolidation of state institutions and agencies and with the fundamental problems of mass immigration, security, national unity, and economic prosperity. The policies relating to immigration, economic development, the furtherance of welfare, and foreign affairs will be dealt with subsequently. Here the major political and social reforms will be outlined.

The fundamental laws relating to the structure and functions of government—the so-called "small" or "minor" constitution—have been discussed in the preceding section. The system of taxation was reorganized, customs and excise duties were regulated, the effort was made to curb profiteering, and necessary modifications in the law and in legal procedure were introduced, including the abolition of the death penalty, except for treason and for Nazi collaborators. In addition, provision was made for coinage; for the flag, emblem, and seal of Israel and similar appointments of statehood; for passports, visas, and other matters governing relations with foreign countries. Especially important was the Nationality Law of 1952, which declared that Israeli nationality might be acquired through birth, residence, naturalization, and "return," the latter referring to immigrating Jews who were endowed with the "right of *Aliyah*."[41]

The National Defense Army. Apart from the Arab attack, the most formidable challenge to the new State of Israel came from within, and it centered in the issue of a single and disciplined national army. In May, 1948, the Provisional Government issued an ordinance establishing a "Defense Army of Israel," and forbidding the maintenance of "any armed forces outside the Defense Army of Israel." The *Irgun* complied, but with reservations: its members joined the government forces and some of its arms were surrendered; the *Irgun* command, however, was maintained and independent efforts continued to import arms from abroad. In June, 1948, after the first truce had come into effect, the ship *Altalena* arrived off Tel-Aviv with a consignment of arms for the *Irgun,* and the demand that the *Irgun* yield the ship to the government met with defiance. Regarding this as rebellion, Ben-Gurion had the ship wrecked by gunfire and the *Irgun* organization outlawed.

This must have been one of the most difficult decisions in Ben-Gurion's career. The arms and the military personnel of the *Irgun* were desperately needed, for the truce was temporary and the Arab States were preparing for renewed attack. He realized, however, that the *Irgun* challenge was the greater menace, threatening civil war and the loss of the respect of foreign powers for the new state. And this incident affords a superlative illustration of Ben-Gurion's qualities of leadership—the ability to identify and concentrate on the basic issue, the courage to make a difficult decision, and the determination and daring to see it through regardless of immediate consequences.[42]

Another fundamental decision was made about that time, again at the behest of Ben-Gurion. In the early days of the war, the *Palmach* was the pride of Israel's defense. It was a tough and spirited striking force, drawn mainly from the *kibbutzim* and held together by self-discipline and comradeship in arms. Some of the leaders wished to preserve that element as a separate military elite, but Ben-Gurion firmly opposed the plan, and his view prevailed despite the serious opposition of high officers. The forces were reorganized as a national army on the usual model prevailing in democratic countries. Conscription was introduced for able-bodied men and unmarried women, and formal discipline enforced with ranks, officers' quarters, and differential rates of pay. The notion of an ideological elite among the defense forces was abandoned.[43]

National System of Education. During the period of the Mandate there was no compulsory education in Palestine, even on the elementary level, and the Jews maintained and supported a network of schools on an autonomous basis. However, the Jewish schools varied widely in curriculum and orientation, with religious emphasis and labor ideals the chief differentiating factors. The religious schools of the *Agudat Israel* were entirely independent, and the nationally motivated schools were divided into three types or "trends." The General schools taught (along with the secular subjects) the Bible as national literature and as the repository of national tradition and ideals, but they were regarded as "secular" schools because, as a rule, they did not seek to instill in the children the urgency of religious belief or observance. The *Mizrahi* schools emphasized religious instruction, without neglecting the elementary branches. And the Labor schools, situated mainly in the co-operative settlements, underscored the ideals of labor and included work in field or shop as part of the curriculum.

The establishment of Israel rendered imperative the co-ordination of the schools into a national system of education, but the government proceeded with caution. In September, 1949, compulsory and free elementary education was decreed for all children five to fourteen years of age, and for adolescents, aged fourteen to eighteen, who did not complete their elementary education. Provision was made for local rates to cover educational budgets, and responsibility for regular attendance was lodged with employers (of adolescents) as well as with parents. The trends were recognized by law, and parents were empowered to designate the type of school to be attended by their children.

The trends were not an artificial improvisation but an outgrowth of the heterogeneous character of the Jewish population. During the period of the Mandate, when voluntary effort characterized Jewish education, division along religious and party lines was unavoidable; but once the state assumed responsibility for elementary education, the trends became an anachronism. They were costly, necessitating two or more schools in a locality where one could meet essential needs. They perpetuated partisan indoctrination when national unity was essential. And they occasioned unseemly and harmful competition for the children, especially of the immigrant camps, which in turn threatened the stability of cabinets.

The reform was achieved in August, 1953, when the State Education Law was passed. The General, *Mizrahi*, and Labor trends were eliminated, and partisan administrative control as well as selection and training of teachers lapsed. The setting of standards and supervision was vested in the Ministry of Education, which has discharged this function in co-operation with local authorities.

However, the objective has been unity rather than strict uniformity, and provision has been made for differences. The standard curriculum of the elementary schools allows for variations in the subjects taught up to 25 per cent of school time. Private schools, too, are permitted to function outside the state system, provided basic standards are met to the satisfaction of the Ministry of Education. These concessions have afforded the legal basis for the continued existence of the schools of the ultra-Orthodox *Agudat Israel*, the most troublesome obstacle to educational unity. Such of these schools as accept three-quarters of the standard curriculum receive a state subsidy, and the remainder are allowed to function independently as private schools. The *Agudat Israel* schools include only a small fraction of the school population (about 4 per cent). For the country as a whole, partisan schooling has begun to give way to a national system of elementary education.[44]

Religion and the State. The American ideal of the separation of church and state does not obtain in Israel, where historical precedent and current conditions have created distinctive needs and imposed religious functions upon the state. The British Mandatory administration and all preceding regimes in Palestine were involved in religious affairs, of which one example was the application of religious law in matters of personal status. The immigration into Israel of masses of devout Oriental Jews called for state aid in matters affecting religion no less than in economic and social requirements. The Moslem, Christian, and Druse minorities required state attention. Finally, the dependence of the government upon the religious parties resulted in concessions which extended state concern with religion.

In Israel, the religious courts are an integral part of the judiciary. Religious Councils deal with public services of a religious nature on the local level, and the state budget assists in providing synagogues for public worship. Non-*kosher* food is banned in the Army messes and in related state institutions. Orthodox women subject to military conscription may be exempted on religious grounds. And the Ministry of Religious Affairs performs administrative and fiscal functions. It administers the moneys paid out of state funds for religious needs and supervises the administration of the religious courts and of other state agencies entrusted with matters involving religion.[45]

In general, it may be said that religion is part of the function of the state in Israel and that religion has figured prominently in politics. However, the attempt has been made to preserve freedom of conscience and freedom of religious observance and nonobservance. The state provides for the citizens who desire a religious way of life, but it does not seek to impose religious observance on nonbelievers. In fact, a large part of the population, including many of the leading officials, are nonobservant in the Orthodox sense of the word. Yet, in some respects, Orthodox practice is imposed on all Jews. Marriage and divorce, for example, are legal only when performed by the recognized Orthodox functionaries.

Women's Rights. In the Middle East, the emancipation of women has been retarded by religion, which has sanctioned their inferior status. During the period of the Mandate, the British authorities made no serious effort to advance women's rights, but the government of Israel has boldly promoted the legal equality of the sexes, despite the vigorous opposition of religious fundamentalists. The right to vote has been extended to women, and civil office is open to them. Under the Equality of Women's Rights Law (1951), women have full power to own and dispose of property, even after marriage, and to effectuate any legal transaction. Discrimination against women in the guardianship of minor children has been eliminated. The conditions for the acquisition of Israeli nationality apply equally to men and women. Equal pay for equal work has been decreed. Even the laws of marriage and divorce have been modified to deprive man of his time-honored privileged position. Child marriage is prohibited, as is the divorce of a woman against her will, unless authorized by a court. And polygamy is a criminal offense.[46]

Israel and World Jewry. Before the establishment of the State of Israel, the building of Palestine had been furthered through the co-operative efforts of the local Jewish population and of large segments of the Jewish communities of various countries. And the Jewish Agency, with consultative power under the British Mandate, served to co-ordinate Jewish constructive efforts. Since political authority was then wielded by the British, and since Jewish activities were in the main of a voluntary nature, the role of the Jewish Agency was acceptable to the Jews, if not always to the British. The rise of Israel, however, rendered necessary a clarification of the relationship of the Jewish Agency to the new state, and this was provided in 1952 by a law which defined the status and functions of the World Zionist Organization and Jewish Agency.

The law states that Israel is "the creation of the entire Jewish people"; that its gates are open to Jewish immigration, and that the World Zionist Organization-Jewish Agency will continue as before to concern itself with immigration and with settlement and absorption projects. Specifically, the State of Israel has recognized the World Zionist Organization "as the authorized agency which will continue to operate in the State of Israel for the development and settlement of the country, the absorption of immigrants from the Diaspora and the co-ordination of the activities in Israel of Jewish institutions and organizations active in those fields."[47]

From this and other laws it is clear that governmental power resides in the constituted authorities which are duly elected by the people of Israel. Jews of other countries are not citizens of Israel unless they choose to migrate thither. Active Zionists, too, are not Israeli nationals unless they settle in that country. However, Jews of other countries who desire to aid in the development of Israel have a function which the State of Israel has recognized. That function is to co-operate in the work of immigration, settlement, and progress of the country so that the immigrants may be properly absorbed. To be sure, the people of Israel, and the State too, expect all Jews to assist immigration and to co-operate in the building of the country. But Israel cannot and does not wield any authority over Jews of other lands. Such assistance as is rendered is entirely voluntary.

In one area—that of religious and cultural life—the Jews of various countries have a close and intimate bond with the Jewish people of Israel. They share with them the fundamentals of religion, a language, over three millennia of Jewish history, customs, ceremonies, and folkways. But this relationship, too, is purely voluntary. The state and people of Israel have no compulsive authority, even in the religious and spiritual sense, over Jews of other countries.

Israel's Population—Policies and Problems

The machinery of government which has been described is fundamentally a means for the attainment of desired ends and, like all peoples, the Israelis have sought to achieve domestic unity, economic prosperity, and national security. Considering the limited resources of the country and the circumstances surrounding the establishment of the state, these objectives would have been most difficult of attainment even for a settled and stable population. The immigration policy pursued by Israel has rendered infinitely more formidable the obstacles to unity and prosperity, if not to security. That policy has been called the "Ingathering of the Exiles."

THE "INGATHERING"[48]

Mass immigration and its effects have dominated government policy and public life in Israel since the establishment of the state. Immigration into Palestine had been the key to the building of the Jewish National Home from the very beginnings of the Zionist movement and, during the entire period of the Mandate, it had been the paramount issue that divided Jews, Arabs, and British. The admission and absorption of immigrants had become a passion with the Jews, and desperate efforts had been made to bring refugees into the country in the face of obstacles that appeared insurmountable. Once independence endowed the Jews with governmental authority, the gates were thrown wide open, beckoning to all to come and share in the building of the new homeland.

The Declaration of Independence announced that "the State of Israel will be open to the immigration of Jews from all countries of their dispersion." The Law of the Return of July 5, 1950, proclaimed *Aliyah* (immigration of Jews for settlement in Israel) as a right: "Every Jew has the right to come to this country as a settler." And this principle, accepted as an axiom, echoed and re-echoed from the rostrum of the *Knesset*, the press, the radio, and public and private utterances throughout the land. The ringing words of Ben-Gurion in the *Knesset* were characteristic of the mood of the Jews of Israel:

> It was for this [mass immigration—the Ingathering of the Exiles] that the State was established, and it is by virtue of this alone that it will stand.[49]

The chief reasons for this passion for immigration are twofold. Many of the Israelis themselves endured homelessness and persecution, and they have felt keenly for their brethren who have languished in refugee camps or lived on sufferance in the midst of unfriendly majorities. In addition, immigration has been regarded as a means of self-preservation. A small people in the midst of vast and hostile Arab populations, the Israelis have feared the overwhelming force of numbers. An increase in the Jewish population enhances the sense of security.

At times the zeal for immigration leads to extravagant hopes that all Jews will settle in Israel, and even to impatience with those who are content to remain in their present homelands. However, sober reality has prevailed, certainly among the leaders, and most Israelis understand that the Jewish masses of the United States, and of other countries, too, do not regard themselves as "exiles" and do not feel the need to migrate to Israel. They even recognize that "at all times *Aliyah* has been a product of Jewish anguish"; that persecution and insecurity as well as vision have motivated emigration of Jews from their native lands. The emphasis of the Ingathering has been upon the Jewish communities which really have suffered "exile" in the sense of insecurity or inferior status. And with respect to these, the policy has been to transport them to Israel en masse, even when Israel is not fully ready to absorb them.[50]

The achievement of the Ingathering has been startling—in many respects, unparalleled in the story of organized human migration. With a Jewish population of about 650,000 at the time of the establishment of the state, Israel has had the dauntless courage to bring into the country nearly 900,000 immigrants in less than ten years! And about 685,000 of the latter arrived in the first three years and eight months of independence! The table (page 732) presents the annual immigration totals.[51, 51a]

It is evident from this table that mass immigration continued from the rise of the State of Israel until close to the end of 1951. And during that brief period of about three and one-half years, the most troublesome of the Jewish refugee problems were liquidated. The words "Jews" and "refugees" had become practically synonyms as a result of Nazi terror, and the Western world had been unable or unwilling to provide asylum for the masses of desperate human beings. At the close of the Second World War, the condition of the survivors of the Nazi extermination camps aroused a sense of horror and widespread sympathy for the victims, but that, too, fell short of a solution: large numbers continued to languish in camps with little hope for the future. The State of Israel welcomed the hapless beings, not grudgingly but eagerly, and the displaced persons' camps were quickly emptied of Jews, except for the small "hard core" cases who could not or would not be moved. The Jews ceased to figure as a major refugee problem in Western Europe.

TABLE II

Annual Immigration Since May 15, 1948

Year	Immigration
1948 (May 15-December 31)	101,825
1949	239,424
1950	169,720
1951	174,014
1952	23,408
1953	10,388
1954	17,485
1955	36,327
1956	54,996
1957	71,100
Total	898,687

Cyprus had become a refugee center where the British had interned illegal Jewish immigrants to Palestine. By February 10, 1949, the last Jews had been transported to Israel and the camps closed with festivities in which even the British participated. The surviving Balkan Jews, notably those of Bulgaria, had emerged from the war and the accompanying Nazi savagery destitute and broken in health. The large majority found homes in Israel. The masses of Polish and Rumanian Jews had perished at the hands of the Nazis, and the survivors found their erstwhile homelands intolerable. Those who were allowed to emigrate were transported to Israel.

The Moslem countries of the Middle East and North Africa were reservoirs of refugees. The war between Arabs and Jews in Palestine naturally exposed local Jewish communities in Arab lands to persecution. But that was only the culmination of deeper forces of hostility. For centuries, Jews had been tolerated but despised in Moslem lands because of their difference in religion. In Yemen, for example, medieval conditions had prevailed, with Jews not only relegated to an inferior status but also subjected to gross and humiliating discrimination and intermittent persecution, including ritual murder charges and mob violence. The effects of nationalism in Moslem lands had likewise resulted in economic deterioration for the Jews and in mounting political and legal insecurity. Finally, Nazi-Fascist propaganda, and in some cases anti-Jewish legislation, despoiled the Jews and endangered their lives. Thus, massacres occurred in Libya during 1945, before the Palestine situation became acute. A mass refugee problem was building up, when Israel came to the rescue.

There was a dramatic quality about the Ingathering from the Moslem lands. The Jews of Yemen (some 45,000) and of Iraq (about 123,000) were brought in by airlift, popularly known as "Operation Magic Carpet" and "Operation Ali Baba." This gave the refugees a sense of dignity and human worth. Although totally beggared, they were not just human debris, discarded by their native lands and unwanted elsewhere. They had a sense of belonging, of being wanted and welcomed. They were returning "home."

In many an instance the Ingathering removed practically the entire Jewish population of an area, thus sweeping clean the festering remains of age-old Jewish problems. Practically all the Jews of Yemen, of Iraq, of Libya, and of other countries were transported to Israel. There was an atmosphere of finality about Ingathering. Israel claimed for its own the Jews who were "unwelcome guests" (a Nazi phrase) in certain lands.[52]

However, mass immigration created overwhelming problems in Israel. The cost of transporting destitute multitudes to Israel was high; that of settling and rehabilitating them all but prohibitive. A modification in policy therefore ensued. The ideal of the Ingathering remained, and families or individuals who came of their own accord were assisted. But publicly financed mass immigration was curtailed and limited to such Jewish communities as were subject to pressure or attack. The result was a sharp decline in immigration during 1952-1954. By the middle of 1954, mass immigration was again resumed in response to the urgency of the North African situation, where the national revolt against French rule increased Jewish insecurity.

The economic, social, and cultural absorption of nearly 900,000 persons in less than a decade, and by a community which numbered initially only 650,000 Jews, would have been a formidable undertaking even under the most favorable conditions. In Israel this effort has been made in the face of unyielding obstacles and discouraging perplexities. The resources of the country have been relatively meager. The borders have been continuously disturbed by latent or active hostilities. Constructive economic measures have been hampered by legal restraints, regional boycott, and naked force. And the human material of the new immigration has added a host of special problems.

A brief comparison of the new immigration with that of the Mandate period will reveal the magnitude of the task of settlement and absorption. During the entire period of the British administration, about 484,000 Jewish immigrants arrived in Palestine, whereas nearly 900,000 immigrants were admitted from May, 1948, to the end of 1957. Immigration during the Mandate period was severely limited by a strict definition of the economic absorptive capacity of Palestine. Under the new state, the immediate absorptive capacity of the country has been disregarded: masses of immigrants have been transported to Israel and then the means have been sought to absorb them. Furthermore, prior to 1948 immigration was highly selective; that is, persons with some means were admitted, and those without means were in the main young persons with good employment potential, who received training in economic skills as well as in the Hebrew language and national ideals. The new immigrants have been either destitute displaced persons or Jews who have been obliged to leave property and belongings in their native lands. They have arrived in Israel without capital, without a knowledge of the language, the country, or the national values of their new homeland, and many have been lacking in education and culture, in the modern sense of the words. A large segment of the old immigration was imbued with social idealism, with a passion for labor, especially manual labor; among the masses of new immigrants, work and work standards have not been held in high esteem.[53] The hundreds of thousands who have swept into Israel since the establishment of the state became consumers even before they set foot on Israeli soil. Their participation in production has been a gradual process.

The territorial origin of the immigrants is of considerable importance. Prior to the establishment of Israel (1919-1948), close to nine-tenths of the Jewish immigrants hailed from Europe or other "Western" countries, with Asia and North Africa supplying only about 10 per cent of the total. Since May, 1948, however, a majority of the newcomers have been of Asian or African origin. Invidious comparisons respecting countries of origin are, of course, inadmissible and unsound. But the sociocultural character of the new immigration has complicated the problems of adjustment to the new environment. Lack of technical training, indifference to sanitation and health hygiene, the prevalence of infectious diseases, illiteracy, and a heritage of substandard living in slum areas—these and other difficulties have had to be met and mastered in order to preserve the social, economic, and cultural standards of Israel.

Finally, in transporting to Israel the entire Jewish communities of several Moslem countries, the Ingathering has added to the burdens of the young state. With proper planning, the young and vigorous could be trained to take their place among the gainfully employed in a relatively short time. But along with that element have come also the aged and infirm, the handicapped and the diseased, the mentally and socially maladjusted, the young children and those past middle age whose economic productive capacity has been problematical or long delayed. This is evident in the age distribution of the Israeli population. The census of November, 1948, showed a child population (under 15 years of age) of 28.5 per cent; at the close of 1956, it was 34.2 per cent of the Jews of Israel. In 1948, the component of the Jewish population over 45 years of age was 18.8 per cent of the total; at the end of 1956, it was 23 per cent. The population element which held the greatest promise of economic productivity, that is, the fifteen–forty-four age group, composed of 52.7 per cent of the Jewish population in 1948, and only 42.8 per cent in 1956. And there were other, less obvious considerations. For example, a considerable proportion of the women of the old immigration was gainfully employed, especially in the rural areas, whereas the immigrants from Moslem lands were not accustomed to gainful employment away from home.

In a word, the settlement and absorption of the new immigration have been a colossal undertaking. Many have had to be trained or retrained for gainful employment. Housing has had to be provided for hundreds of thousands, and schooling for a large child population. Medical needs have mounted, health services have been strained, and special efforts have been necessary to acquaint the newcomers with elementary hygiene and sanitation.

The measures taken to cope with the problems of mass immigration have been numerous and varied, but only the main features of the effort can here be outlined. During and immediately after the War of Independence, the immigrants remained in reception camps until housing and employment could be found for them. This was obviously unsatisfactory because the newcomers remained idle and dependent, with little opportunity to help themselves.

In the summer of 1950, the *Maabara* system was introduced. A *Maabara* (plural, *Maabarot*) was a transitional settlement with temporary housing and employment, and the immigrants resident therein were in considerable measure dependent upon their own resources. Some of the *Maabarot* were entirely temporary, set up in an area because of the availability of employment. Others were planned to evolve into permanent settlements as the land or industries were developed to absorb the immigrants. In such cases, the temporary housing was gradually replaced by permanent dwellings. During 1954, still another method—the "Ship to Farm" form of settlement—was inaugurated. Villages were laid out, homes furnished, schools and clinics built, and immigrants taken to the settlements immediately on arrival, where they worked under the supervision of instructors.

However, one must not assume that the process of absorption has worked smoothly. Inevitably, there have been complications, hardships, disappointments, and improvisations. For example, tent settlements are hardly satisfactory in the winter season, and torrential rains have created emergencies which have required the removal of immigrants to better shelter. Yet, somehow, the situation has been kept in hand, and the vast majority of the immigrants have found homes in Israel. The visitor to Israel during the past decade could see the dreary reception camps and the hardly less unsatisfactory *Maabarot*. But he could also see numerous new villages and permanent housing dotting the countryside, with the remains of the temporary settlements still bearing witness to the rapid progress achieved.

The essential point is that the immigrants have not been left to shift for themselves, as has been the practice in many countries of immigration. The government of Israel has sought to guide the process of absorption, and the settled population has endured austerity and hardship to ease the lot of the newcomers. World Jewry has helped generously with funds, for the cost has been stupendous. It has been estimated that, on the average, the cost of transporting and settling an immigrant has amounted to about $3,000.

The result of the Ingathering is evident in the growth of Israel's population. On May 14, 1948, the Jewish population was estimated at 650,000. An incomplete census taken on November 8, 1948, recorded 716,000 Jews and 69,000 non-Jews, in a total of 785,000. By the end of 1957, the population of Israel had grown to 1,975,954, and this total included 1,672,741 Jews and 213,213 non-Jews.[54] The non-Jewish minority, mainly Arabic, calls for special analysis.

THE MINORITY POPULATION

The minority population of Israel consists predominantly of Arabic-speaking Moslems and Christians, with a small group of Druses situated in Galilee and on Mt. Carmel. For convenience, the entire minority population will be referred to as "Arabs."

The census of November 8, 1948, which recorded only 69,000 non-Jews, did not include the Arabs of western Galilee, the Beersheba areas, and the villages of the Sharon. The inclusion of these districts increased the initial Arab population of the new state to an estimated 120,000 at the end of 1948. One year later the Arabs numbered about 160,000, and at the end of 1957 their population was 213,213. The increase was due largely to the Family Reunion Scheme, which allowed relatives to rejoin families, and to infiltrators who returned clandestinely and settled down.

The essence of minority rights relates to the acquisition of nationality; constitutional equality; actual nondiscrimination in political, economic, and social opportunities; and the sharing of social services. In areas of mixed national groupings, special rights affecting religion, language, and culture are likewise of supreme importance if minorities are not to be forcibly denationalized.

As has been noted, nationality is acquired in Israel by birth, residence, naturalization, or immigration. The condition of birth applies equally to Arabs and Jews. Residence has been established by national registration instituted in 1949 or by legal entry prior to July 14, 1952. This has no doubt involved some difficulty for Arabs, but over 90 per cent of the Arabs resident in Israel have acquired Israeli nationality. Immigration does give preferential treatment to Jews: under the Law of the Return, immigrant Jews acquire Israeli nationality automatically, whereas Arab immigration is discouraged and those who do return to Israel must undergo a process of naturalization.

Legal equality has been proclaimed for all regardless of "religion, race, or sex," and this has been implemented in the functioning of democratic government and in the operation of the social services.

At the end of the War of Independence, some 35,000 Israeli Arabs could not return to their homes because these were outside the borders of Israel, because the villages had been settled by Jewish immigrants, or because the government held the area for security reasons or for large-scale development. In such cases, provision has been made for compensation in land or in cash, and the claimants have had recourse to judicial settlement when necessary. At the time of writing, some 80 per cent of the Arab agriculturists own their farms, and agricultural methods and yields have improved markedly as a result of government assistance, including irrigation, loans, and instruction in modern cultivation. Agricultural machinery is being introduced, crops have been diversified, and new crops such as tobacco, cotton, and sugar have been encouraged, and the output per acre has increased. The *Histadrut* and the Ministry of Labor have assisted in the formation of co-operatives, and some thirty-two agricultural marketing co-operatives and twenty-five co-operative wholesale associations function in the Arab villages. These measures and the ready market for farm produce have brought prosperity to the Arab peasants.

The Arabs in industry and in service occupations have profited from the labor legislation which applies equally to all: the work day is limited and a weekly day of rest and paid holidays are enforced. National insurance, too, covers Arabs as well as Jews. Equal pay for equal work obtains for Arabs and Jews in government jobs and public institutions as well as in the Jewish farm communities which employ Arab labor and in the *Histadrut* industrial undertakings. In private industry, the unskilled Arab laborer is at a disadvantage, but the *Histadrut* efforts to unionize the Arab workers have resulted in wage increases which have narrowed the differential in scales of pay.

The government has made loans to Arabs engaged in the fishing industry. Emergency public works and labor exchanges in Arab areas have been provided to care for the unemployed. Roads have been built around Arab villages and towns. Water works have been constructed, as at Nazareth, which now, for the first time in its long history, has water piped into the homes. Vocational training facilities have been set up and government loans advanced to Arabs to enable them to acquire industrial and agricultural skills. The effort has even been made to assist Arabs through evening courses to qualify for the Civil Service.

The health and welfare services of the country are available to and utilized by the Arabs. The government has made grants-in-aid for the maintenance of clinics by Arab local authorities, and it has established a visiting nursing service and mobile medical units for villages without clinics. Anti-malaria work has been extended to all Arab areas, and courses have been organized to train Arab personnel in nursing and sanitation. As a result, the Arab death rate and infant mortality have declined.

Arab education has undergone remarkable progress. Under the British Mandate, 454 Arab schools (in 1946) were maintained for a population of over a million. With the development of the new state, and especially with the enactment of compulsory education, educational facilities have multiplied. In 1957, there were some 103 Arab villages and eight towns inhabited in whole or in part by Arabs. These were served by 115 Arab state primary schools with 1,064 classes for a population of about 213,000, and a considerable number of the schools are in villages which formerly had none.

The growth in Arab education since the establishment of the state is especially significant. In 1949, only 56 Arab schools functioned with 186 teachers and some 7,400 pupils, whereas in 1957 the 115 schools had 835 teachers (including 243 women) and 28,267 pupils. The over-all percentage of Arab school-age children attending school, which was 48 per cent during the period of the Mandate, has risen to over 70 per cent of the settled Arab population. The state has also taken steps to improve the qualifications of Arab teachers. Special in-service and refresher courses have been given, and the higher educational institutions of Israel have, of course, been available to the Arabs. In 1956, an Arab Teachers Training College was opened in Jaffa.

The Arabs have participated in the public life of Israel. Men, and women too, have voted in parliamentary elections in surprisingly high percentages: 79.3 per cent of the qualified voters in the election of 1949, 85.5 per cent in 1951, and 91.2 per cent in 1955. And every *Knesset* has had Arab deputies—three in the First *Knesset*, eight in the Second, and eight in the Third. The Arab vote has been divided between independent Arab splinter parties and the general parties of the country. In the election of 1955, close to one-half (about 48 per cent) of the Arab votes were cast for three Arab factions, which elected a total of five deputies. The latter generally voted with *Mapai*, which polled in addition close to 14 per cent of the Arab votes. The predominant party of Israel thus had the support of about two-thirds of the Arab electorate. About 15 per cent of the Arabs voted Communist, and *Mapam* and the General Zionists received appreciable support.

Some progress has also been made in local government among the Arabs. This has been especially difficult because of the lack of experience of the latter in self-government and because of the fear that local government would entail taxation. Under the British Mandate, elementary education and local services had been provided free of charge, and taxation had been minimal. Family feuds have likewise militated against united local efforts. However, local government is functioning in the two all-Arab towns, and some sixteen Arab local councils have been set up. In all, about 40 per cent of the Arab minority have been involved in some measure of local self-government. The Arabs vote eagerly: in elections in 1955 to five local authorities, about 94 per cent of the qualified voters cast ballots. Some of the councils have concerned themselves with water and sewage systems, roads, and electricity and telephone services. But the government has had to supply most of the necessary budgets through loans and grants-in-aid.

The Arabs also enjoy national-cultural rights. The special religious courts with jurisdiction over matters of personal status (marriage, divorce, custody of children, wills, etc.) have been mentioned. In addition, the Arabic language has official status. It is the language of instruction in the state-supported Arab schools, and it is freely used by Arabs in public life. Arabs employ their language in the *Knesset* and its committees and their addresses are immediately translated into Hebrew. Similarly Hebrew speeches in the *Knesset*, simultaneously translated into Arabic, are heard by the Arab members through earphones. At committee meetings, an interpreter sits beside an Arab member and whispers a running translation of the discussion. Proposed legislation, the agenda of meetings, and the main clauses of the budget are available in advance in Arabic translation. The *Official Gazette*, which contains the laws and ordinances of the state, appears in Arabic as well as Hebrew, and in Arab districts official notices appear in Arabic. Finally, coins, banknotes, postage stamps, and the like carry Arabic along with the Hebrew inscriptions.

However, one important disability remains to be noted. Military government has prevailed in certain Arab areas, especially along the borders, with restrictions on freedom of movement, night curfews, and other security regulations. The stringency of the controls has varied with the tension resulting from the activities of armed infiltrators. However, a noticeable relaxation has been evident. During 1957, Druses and Arabs serving in the army were allowed freedom of movement in border areas, and intervillage travel restrictions in Galilee were relaxed for the general Arab population. At one time, there were forty-six "closed areas" in Galilee, but these have been reduced to strictly border regions which affect perhaps 10 per cent of the Arab population of Galilee. In the Negev, too, travel restrictions have been eased.

In summary, it may be said that the Jewish majority and Arab minority have eyed each other with suspicion and even hostility. The Arabs have suffered an unprecedented upheaval, physically and psychologically. War destruction and dislocations have brought economic ruin to many. Family units have been severed; old parties, associations, newspapers, and leaders have vanished; and the entire social fabric has distintegrated. The shock of military defeat and reduction to the status of a minority has been overwhelming. Loyalties of kinship and fears of reprisals, too, have predisposed Arabs to co-operate with infiltrators in acts of sabotage. This has engendered fear and suspicion in the Jewish majority, and security restrictions have further estranged the Arabs.

The Arab States have fanned the smoldering hostility from without, and the Communists have exploited Arab grievances within Israel. The center of Communist strength is in the Arab city of Nazareth. A third of the party membership and party vote is reputed to be Arab, and as much as 35 per cent of the Arab urban vote went to the Communists in 1955. (It was about 15 per cent of the total Arab vote.) All of this is a reflection of Arab hostility to the State of Israel.

Yet the extent of co-operation and accommodation has been most impressive. The policies of the government have brought economic prosperity to the Arabs, educational progress, improvement in health, and social betterment. The major grievances are the Arab refugees, reduction in status to that of a minority, preferential treatment of Jews in immigration, and security restrictions. The progress made in majority-minority relations during the past ten years has been considerable, but permanent harmonious co-operation will depend on a solution of the refugee problem and on peace with the Arab States.[55]

The Welfare State

The term "welfare state" is generally employed to describe the trend of the twentieth century for the state to become actively involved in the functioning of the economic system in order to ensure maximum economic and social security. Previously the ideal had been "free enterprise," which precluded state intervention and state controls of the economy. The free functioning of economic "laws" had been regarded as the best assurance of general prosperity, and hence of individual security. The maladjustments resulting from industrialization and the disruptive effects of two world wars have rendered necessary state intervention. In some countries, state controls have destroyed democratic liberties, but the Western democracies have attempted to combine varying forms of state control of the economy, and even state planning, with political democracy. Israel, too, has sought to fashion a democratic welfare state.

The ideal of the welfare state is deeply rooted in Israel. It permeated all of the major efforts in the building of the Jewish National Home during and prior to the period of the Mandate. Formerly, however, it found expression in the voluntary activities of the Jews, who did not wield governmental power. With the rise of Israel, social security and welfare have become state functions.

The welfare state is evidenced in Israel by the assumption of state and government responsibility for the economic welfare and social and cultural progress of the people. It is sustained by a passion for equality among large sections of the population and a conviction that full employment and a "living wage," health facilities, rest and leisure, education and culture, are human rights; that advanced levels in social services and standard of living must be maintained, if necessary even in defiance of adverse economic realities. The means employed for the realization of the ideal have been direct involvement of the government in economic affairs through ownership or control; planned settlement of the immigrants and planned economic, social, and cultural development; the control of housing; social security legislation and relief and rehabilitation; and measures for health, welfare, education, and culture.

LAND AND LABOR

Land is nationally owned or administered, except for about 10 per cent of the total area remaining in private possession.[56] The rest is held by the state or the Jewish National Fund or the Custodian of Abandoned Property, and parcels are assigned on long-term lease to groups, institutions, or individuals. Private enterprise in agriculture and especially in industry is permitted and even encouraged, but it is subject to government regulation. Moreover, a large segment of the economy—industry, commerce, communication, transport, and finance—is directly controlled by the state through public corporations which are to a considerable extent state-financed and in which management is frequently shared by the government. The government is thus the largest employer and investor, and in addition the *Histadrut* controls at least 20 per cent of the economy through its far-flung enterprises.[57]

In an uncontrolled economy, wages are conditioned by the productivity of labor, but in Israel wage policy is determined largely by the tradition of social idealism and by labor organization, especially of the *Histadrut*. There is, of course, a differential in wages between the skilled and unskilled, but the effort has been made to achieve a single wage scale for particular jobs, even for the untrained Arabs and immigrants. And provision has been made for cost-of-living allowances, seniority rights, paid vacations, and social services.

Special legislation has been enacted setting up machinery for the settlement of labor disputes, without curtailment of the right to strike, and collective agreements in labor relations are encouraged and must be registered with the Ministry of Labor. A state inspection service has been set up and charged with the supervision and promotion of labor safety and vocational hygiene and welfare.

A comprehensive scheme of social security insurance was projected as soon as the United Nations Assembly approved the establishment of a

Jewish State. The first phase was enacted by the National Insurance Law of 1953, which made provision for old age and survivors' benefits, maternity grants, and insurance against industrial accidents. This compulsory insurance covers all inhabitants between the ages of eighteen and sixty-seven, the salaried, self-employed, and nonemployed as well as wage earners. The insurance fund is composed of contributions by employers and employees, with a subsidy from the state treasury. Old age pensions are paid generally at sixty-five for men and sixty for women, but there is encouragement to continue working for an additional five-year period. The pensions are related to the cost-of-living index, so that a rise in prices does not undermine the value of the benefits.

Maternity insurance not only provides the usual payments but also serves as a stimulus for proper medical care. Benefits may be denied for employment outside the home against the advice of a physician, or for noncompliance with medical instructions. Since delivery in hospitals or maternity clinics is directly related to the payment of benefits, 95 per cent of Jewish women utilize such facilities, and even Arab mothers increasingly turn to hospitals and clinics for delivery.

Apart from maternity, the employment of women is regulated by law. The Minister of Labor is empowered to prohibit or restrict their employment in certain industries, and night work is forbidden, save in stated exceptional cases.[58]

National health and unemployment insurance has not as yet been introduced because of financial stringency. But health needs are met by the voluntary insurance schemes, especially the Sick Fund of the *Histadrut*. The unemployed, too, have not been disregarded. The government attempts to estimate in advance anticipated unemployment and provides public works programs to absorb them.

HOUSING

The housing and settlement of immigrants quickly became the government's responsibility, and the latter has also built homes for war veterans and civil servants. In addition, the government has co-operated in low cost housing schemes for the settled population, and it has made loans to housing companies to stimulate building. Since the establishment of Israel, the government has built or assisted in the building of about two-thirds of all housing units. The *Histadrut* and political parties have also subsidized housing projects for their adherents.

Private ownership and construction of housing is permitted but strictly controlled. Tenants of residential and business premises are protected against eviction or arbitrary rise in rentals, and even the state is subject to the same restrictions with regard to its tenants as private owners of property.[59]

RELIEF AND REHABILITATION

Relief and rehabilitation have received a great deal of government attention, with major emphasis upon wounded or handicapped veterans and their families. Provision is made for hospitalization, medical care, convalescence, education and retraining, and housing and pension payments for the seriously disabled.

Mass immigration has imported mass misery, and the government has made an effort to alleviate distress. The Ministry of Public Welfare has maintained the necessary agencies in the *Maabarot*, and it has subsidized over 150 bureaus of local authorities to the extent of 20-90 per cent of their budgets. The assistance has taken the form of material support, medical aid and hospitalization, placement in institutions of the aged, children and mental cases, and counseling in family problems. The effort has been made to train the blind and handicapped for gainful employment, and to rehabilitate physically and mentally defective children and neglected youth. Insurance has been provided for the aged, including those of the minorities, with the government contributing 25 per cent of the cost.

Nongovernment agencies have greatly reinforced the efforts of the government. The Jewish Agency and the *Histadrut* have borne a large share of the burden. Hadassah has continued its extensive medical services, and it has launched a family health program near Jerusalem which combines medical, health, and social service facilities. The Women's International Zionist Organization (WIZO) has rendered valuable aid. And Malben (agency for the care of handicapped immigrants), founded and financed by the American Joint Distribution Committee, has maintained special centers for the handicapped who can do some useful work, as well as institutions for the aged, the chronically ill and disabled, and the mentally afflicted.

The shortage of trained social workers has been a serious handicap, but measures have been taken to cope with the problem. A Social Welfare Institute functions in Jerusalem under the joint supervision of the government and the Hebrew University, and a Social Welfare School is maintained by the Tel-Aviv Municipality with the aid of a government subvention.[60]

PUBLIC HEALTH

The achievements in public health have been truly phenomenal. When the Mandate came to an end, Palestine Jewry enjoyed through voluntary health services standards of health, life expectancy, and an infant mortality rate which compared favorably with the Western world. The mass immigration threatened to undermine these health standards. Many immigrants from the displaced persons' camps and especially from Oriental lands were chronic cases or permanently disabled, needing hospitalization. Typhus, typhoid, diphtheria, filariasis, trachoma, malaria, and other diseases were endemic in the Arab areas of emigration. Yet so effective have been the health measures of Israel that no major epidemic has occurred. The tubercular have been hospitalized, and the incidence of other diseases sharply reduced.

The voluntary agencies have continued their admirable health services, nominally under the supervision of the Ministry of Health. *Kupat Holim*, the Sick Fund of the *Histadrut*, has expanded its facilities, so that it serves about two-thirds of the population. With a budget twice that of the Ministry of Health, it functions in some 600 localities, and maintains fourteen hospitals, fourteen convalescent homes, and over 900 clinics staffed by about 7,800 professional workers, including 1,400 physicians and over 2,200 nurses. The *Kupat Holim* and four smaller sick funds provide voluntary health insurance for about 75 per cent of the population.

Hadassah, the pioneer in health work in Palestine since 1918, has remained a primary influence in Israel. Its medical facilities are paramount in the Jerusalem area, and it has led the way in experimenting with mental health, occupational therapy, and preventive medicine. It has devoted much attention to medical education, co-operating with the Hebrew University in the establishment of the first medical school in the country. Its community health work, mentioned above, is a pioneering venture which supplies at one center preventive medicine and social services as well as curative facilities.

The work of Malben, founded by the American Joint Distribution Committee in 1950, has been noted. Its special sphere of interest has been the handicapped immigrant, with emphasis on the tubercular. Some 18,000 tuberculosis cases have been treated, and extensive rehabilitation has restored many to economic usefulness. Sheltered workshops have been set up for cured tuberculosis patients as well as for the physically handicapped. Malben also maintains homes for some 3,000 aged and indigent invalids. Finally, the *Magen David Adom* (the equivalent of the Red Cross) operates over forty branches and first-aid stations, conducts a blood bank and ambulance service, and campaigns for accident prevention.

The government has supplemented the efforts of the private agencies in all fields of public health, and it has concentrated attention on antimalaria work, sanitation and food hygiene, the control of epidemics through testing and quarantine, the expansion of hospital facilities and public health laboratories, and mother and child care.

The progress achieved by the combined efforts of the government and private agencies can be indicated here only by a few illustrative figures. The number of hospitals has increased from 63 in 1948 to 100 (at the end of 1955); hospital beds from 4,600 to over 12,200, of which 37 per cent are maintained by the government. In 1955, Israel had 3.1 beds in general hospitals per 1,000 population, compared with 5.1 in the United States and 1.2 in Egypt. Mother-and-child-care stations have grown rapidly: at the end of 1954, there were 375; by the end of 1956, the number had increased to 485. The number of licensed physicians was 3,957 (over 20 per cent women) at the end of 1956—the highest proportion of doctors to the population of any country in the world. The proportion of dentists was one per 2,025 inhabitants, again one of the highest in the world. There is a shortage of nurses, but the ratio of 3.3 per 1,000 population is higher than in Norway, Sweden, Poland, and even the United States.

The effects of medical and health work are reflected in the vital statistics of Israel. The birth rate in 1955 was 27.2 per 1,000 among the Jews and 42.78 among the Arabs. (It was 24.9 in the United States, and 44.8 in Egypt.) The crude death rate was 5.77 for the Jews and 8.01 for the Arabs. (In the United States it was 8.2, and in Egypt 19.3.) Life expectancy at birth for the Jewish population has risen from 65.2 years in 1949 to 69.4 for males and 72.1 for females in 1955. The latter figures were close to those of the United States, but in Egypt life expectancy was 35.6 for males and 41.5 for females.

Infant mortality, a good index of public health, affords the best evidence of the successful effort to maintain health standards. In 1947, the last year of the British Mandate, the infant mortality rate among Jews was 29.2 per 1,000 live births. In 1949 the rate leaped to 51.75, but by 1955 it was down to 32.5 for the entire population. (In the United States the rate was 26.6, and in Egypt 128.6.) A breakdown of the Israeli figure for 1955 indicates future possibilities. In the *kibbutzim*, the infant mortality rate was only 18.7, the lowest in the world. In the *Maabarot* and rural settlements, it was high—45.3 per 1,000—but this represented a sharp decline from 1950.[61]

At the time of the establishment of Israel, the health conditions among the Jewish population had risen to a high level as a result of a quarter-century of intensive voluntary effort. Mass immigration from substandard areas threatened retrogression, but energetic measures have obviated the danger. The health of the new arrivals has been improved and the high standards of the settled population maintained. The task has been prodigious and commands further effort, but Israel has remained a health oasis in the bleak Middle East.

EDUCATION AND HEBREW CULTURE

The educational problems posed by mass immigration have been hardly less challenging than those of health. The enactment of compulsory and free elementary education in 1949 and the fashioning of a unified national system of education in 1953 have been noted. These measures have resulted in four categories of schools, namely Jewish State and State-Religious Schools, Jewish Independent (or Unofficial or Recognized) Schools, and Arab Schools. The elementary school enrollment in 1957 was as follows:[62]

	Hebrew Schools			Arab-Primary	Grand
Total	*State*	*State-Religious*	*Independent*	Schools	Total
285,796	196,178	71,082	18,536	24,659	310,455

Of the total primary school population, 68.6 per cent attend State Schools, 24.8 per cent attend State-Religious Schools, 6.6 per cent attend Independent Schools.

The above figures do not include the children who attend preschool kindergartens, and Christian missionary schools, which are not under government supervision. Furthermore, some 11,800 pupils attend continuation classes. If these are added, the preschool, elementary school, and continuation school population is at least 400,000.

Secondary education is less satisfactory because it is neither free nor compulsory, and because many parents depend upon the supplementary earnings of adolescents. In 1957, the enrollment in academic secondary schools was about 26,000. About one-third of the secondary school pupils receive scholarships or grants, and the government also provides subsidies for teaching equipment and other purposes.

In addition to normal academic education, Israel also provides specialized instruction for relatively large numbers of students. Close to 3,000 students attend high school evening classes. Trade and agricultural schools include 11,000 or 12,000 pupils, and close to 5,000 students are in special schools and classes for the handicapped.

The majority of Israeli schools are coeducational. The elementary curriculum covers eight years and the secondary school four years of intensive study. In addition to the common branches, the course of study includes physical education, agricultural and prevocational work, nature study, arts and crafts, and English. Arabic is taught in 116 Hebrew primary and secondary schools and continuation classes.

The teacher problem has become acute because of mass immigration and because of the lack of qualified Arab teachers. In 1957, there were 4,601 full-time and 9,450 part-time teachers, and the shortage was estimated at 10-15 per cent. To meet the need, over 3,200 students were in training in 1957 in more than twenty-five teachers' colleges and courses, and in addition the School of Education of the Hebrew University has provided specialized and advanced instruction for teachers and other educational personnel.

Higher education and research are maintained on an advanced level in Israel. The Hebrew University is the central institution of higher learning in the country, with an enrollment of 4,373 graduate and undergraduate students (1957-1958), an academic staff of 756, and courses of study and research embracing the humanities, the natural and social sciences, medicine, dentistry and pharmacy, law, agriculture, education, and librarianship. Its standards of scholarship, the renown of members of its faculty, and the high quality of its productive research have won recognition for the Hebrew University as one of the great centers of learning in the world. The state contributes materially to its maintenance budget and the University, in turn, has been a vital factor in the economic and cultural development of the country. The campus on Mt. Scopus became inaccessible after the War of Independence, but the faculty and students carried on in improvised quarters under the most perplexing difficulties. This courage has been rewarded, and a new campus, constructed at Giv'at Ram in Jerusalem, was officially opened in May, 1958. The new campus is already becoming one of the foremost cultural centers of the country.

The Israel Institute of Technology (*Technion*), situated at Technion City on Mt. Carmel, has won an enviable reputation as a school of engineering, architecture, aeronautics, and applied science. Its staff of 427 is engaged in the instruction of 2,021 students (1956-1957) and in extensive research. *Technion* also provides varied facilities for laboratory testing.

The Weizmann Institute of Science at Rehovot has functioned under that name since 1949. It is devoted mainly to advanced research in applied mathematics, nuclear physics, electronics, optics, and the chemical and biological sciences. Its staff of 500 workers includes 150 scientists, some of whom are widely known in scientific circles. The Prime Minister's Office also contains a Scientific Research Council and an Atomic Energy Commission, as mentioned above. The former consists of the leading scientists and engineers and it serves as the consultant body to the government in matters affecting public health and the development and utilization of the country's resources. In recent years, two other universities have been founded, namely, the Bar-Ilan University at Ramat Gan and the Tel-Aviv University, which is developing under the guidance of the Hebrew University. Finally, a large number of talmudic academies devote themselves to religious studies.

Archaeology is pursued systematically in Israel under the supervision of the Department of Antiquities. The latter directs the diggings in co-operation with the Hebrew University and the Israel Exploration Society, and finds are widely discussed in the press and by the general public. During 1956-1957, some forty excavations were in progress in various parts of the country and a partial survey was made of the Sinai Peninsula.

Israel's cultural life is rich and varied, and the government plays a leading role in its advancement. Adult education has received special attention because of the keen desire for learning among all classes of the population, and also because of its efficacy in facilitating the cultural absorption of the new immigrants. The Ministry of Education and Culture organizes thousands of meetings with cultural content each year. Hundreds of lectures (some 900 in 1956-1957) are given under the auspices of the Hebrew University. And other agencies, notably the *Histadrut*, bring popular education to the remotest settlements.

The study of the Hebrew language is central in adult education. The revival of Hebrew was one of the great achievements of the Jewish National Home, and in 1948 over 75 per cent of all Jews above two years of age spoke Hebrew, while more than 93 per cent of all Jewish children aged two to fourteen employed it as their vernacular. The new immigration, however, necessitated renewed efforts because relatively few of the newcomers had command of the language. Of the adult immigrants of 1948-1949, only 0.4 per cent employed Hebrew in daily life, and only about 16 per cent could speak, read, and write Hebrew. As a result, the percentage of Hebrew-speaking Jews in the Israeli population fell sharply: at the end of 1950, less than 60 per cent of those over two years of age and only about 80 per cent of the children between two and fourteen spoke Hebrew. The central and local governments and private organizations have therefore worked strenuously to spread knowledge of the language even as new waves of immigrants have poured into the country. Short-term courses in Hebrew, given to thousands each year, have proved especially effective.

The Ministry of Education and Culture also maintains a Hebrew Language Academy which continues the work of the Hebrew Language Council (*Vaad Halashon*) of the pre-state era. This body decides on questions of grammar, terminology, and other matters affecting the use of Hebrew in daily speech, scholarship, and science, and its publications include a quarterly for language research and popular pamphlets.

Libraries are widespread and popular. The most important by far is the Jewish National and University Library, which had amassed a valuable collection of 500,000 volumes on Mt. Scopus. When the bulk of that collection became inaccessible, the work of replenishment began anew, and persevering efforts have assembled some 450,000 volumes, which will soon be housed in a new library building. In addition, there are some 700 libraries of varying size and degrees of specialization. Even immigrant settlements have been provided with basic libraries. Archives, too, are well organized and regulated by law. There are state archives, Zionist and historical archives, labor archives, military archives, archives of Middle East Jewish communities, and collections relating to personalities such as Weizmann, Jabotinsky, and others.

Books are read avidly in Israel. About 1,000 titles appear every year, three-quarters of them original works in fiction, poetry, and scholarship, and the remainder translations. A twenty-volume *Hebrew Encyclopedia*, now in process of publication, has over 40,000 subscribers. The Bialik Foundation publishes works of lasting value in literature, art, and science, the Rabbi Kook Foundation concentrates on religious literature, and inexpensive paperback books are issued by the *Histadrut* and by others in relatively large editions.

The Jewish population of Israel supports twenty-three daily newspapers, fifteen of them in Hebrew and the remainder in a half-dozen foreign languages. Some 290 periodicals, including fifty government publications, appear in the country, and devote themselves to literature, art, economics, law, youth, etc.

The arts, too, have a wide following in Israel. The Israel Philharmonic Orchestra, founded by Bronislaw Huberman, gives 135 concerts annually, which are attended by some 19,000 subscribers, and special concerts attract additional numbers. The State Broadcasting Company, the Defense Forces, and the city of Haifa have their own orchestras, and a Music Festival is held every year during Passover at Ein Gev on Lake Kinneret. There are also conservatories, choirs, and chamber music, folk, and ballet groups. The government encourages these activities and takes special pains to further the study of music in the schools.

The theater has achieved a high artistic level. Four co-operative repertory companies—*Habimah*, *Ohel* (a workers' theater of the *Histadrut*), the Chamber Theater, and the *Zira* Theater—gave some 2,500 performances in 1955-1956 before audiences which totaled over 1,000,000. Tel-Aviv is the center of these companies, but performances are given throughout the country and especially in the co-operative settlements. The latter have their own amateur theatricals as well, and so do the schools, the army, and other groups. A special group arranges performances in the immigrant camps.

Arts and crafts are taught in several schools, notably the Bezalel Art School of Jerusalem, founded in 1906. Painters of note have settled in the country, and their works have been exhibited in New York and Paris as well as Israel. The new immigrants have brought art skills in design, embroidery, and jewelry, and the government as well as private organizations have encouraged the preservation and continued practice of these crafts.

Sports are popular in Israel, and the major political groupings have their sports affiliates. But co-operation is achieved through the Israel Amateur Sports Federation, which works with the Ministry of Education and Culture in planning the sports curriculum of educational institutions and in encouraging training and competitive events.[63]

THE CO-OPERATIVE MOVEMENT

The active concern of the Israeli government with economic, social, and cultural life has not discouraged individual or group initiative. On the contrary, the spirit of self-help and voluntarism, deeply rooted among the Jewish pioneers of the country, has gained in range and influence. This is well illustrated by the co-operative movement.

The collective and co-operative agricultural settlements and their urban counterparts developed before 1948 have been outlined in the introductory pages. These and similar group efforts have continued both because of the momentum of the immediate past and because the forces which produced co-operative forms of living—social idealism, the passion for Jewish immigration, the need to absorb the immigrants, and the requirements of defense in a hostile environment—have been and are still at work. However, modifications have appeared in response to changed conditions. Through the Ministry of Labor, the government has furnished continuous supervision of the work of co-operatives. It has promoted education in co-operative administration, assumed the tasks of research and statistical tabulation, and has aided in the settlement of interco-operative disputes. All co-operatives have joined in a General Cooperative Council which serves as an advisory body to the government. The new type of immigration has likewise necessitated compromises in co-operative living.

At the end of 1956, the number of active co-operatives was 2,508, with a membership of some 750,000, which embraced more than one-third of the population of the country. Of this total, about 78 per cent were working-class societies, and three-quarters of the latter were affiliated with the *Histadrut*. It should be noted, however, that more than 20 per cent of the co-operatives are middle-class and other nonworking-class undertakings. As much as one-fifth of the entire economy of the country is organized co-operatively, and in specialized fields the influence is far greater. For example, co-operatives account for about 90 per cent of citrus exports and for the distribution of about 73 per cent of Israel's agricultural produce. Almost all urban and interurban bus transport is in the hands of co-operatives.

More than one-third of all co-operatives (850) are concerned with agriculture. They embrace the collective and co-operative settlements, marketing and processing agencies, and societies for irrigation, mutual insurance, and other agricultural purposes. Co-operation in housing is widespread, with 484 societies; 297 are engaged in industrial production, services, and transportation; 403 are devoted to provident and pension funds; and the remainder deal with credit, mutual assistance, savings, and miscellaneous functions.

The collective agricultural settlements were a distinctive feature of the Jewish National Home before independence was achieved. Since the establishment of Israel, the number of these settlements has increased, as indicated in the following table.[64]

TABLE III

Growth of Collective and Semi-Collective Agricultural Settlements

Type of Settlement	1946 Number	1946 Population	1956 Number	1956 Population
Kibbutz and *Kvutzah*	140 (in 1945)	over 40,000	223	81,300
Workers Smallholders' Settlement (*Moshav Ovdim*)	62	17,099	101	93,000
Immigrant Smallholders' Settlement (*Moshav Olim*)	—	—	182	
Collective Smallholders' Settlement (*Moshav Shitufi*)	9	878	20	3,082

However, the pressures of mass immigration and the shortage of trained manpower have resulted in modifications which have compromised the original ideals of co-operative living. Some of the *kibbutzim* have been obliged to employ hired labor, mainly in construction and in industrial enterprises. The chief difficulty has been with the immigrant settlements. The new immigrants have had no understanding of the ideas and forms of the co-operative, and many have demanded immediate payment for work done. The result has been an ingenious improvisation for the gradual enlightenment of the newcomers. The older *moshavim* have established a special company which supervises the work of the immigrant settlers and pays the latter in wages and a share of the profits. In the first stages, the company absorbs losses, but gradually the new settlers are taught to share in the losses as well as profits. Leadership in these settlements has been provided by experienced members of collectives who have left comfortable homes and pleasant associations and volunteered for the arduous tasks of training the new immigrants.[65]

The collective and co-operative movement has permeated all Israel, but fundamentally it has been a product of the same forces which fashioned the labor movement, notably the *Histadrut*. Some labor elements have championed co-operation as an ideal, as the antithesis to competition, and as the beginnings of a new society in which private enterprise would disappear, and with it the profit motive and "exploitation."

However, the development of the co-operative movement warrants the conclusion that the co-operative commonwealth has been a secondary consideration. The primary purpose of all Jewish efforts in Palestine has been first the building of the Jewish National Home, and more recently the consolidation of the state. And in the process of building, abstract ideals and preconceived doctrines have yielded to the necessities of promoting immigration and facilitating land settlement and urban development in order to absorb the newcomers. The co-operative movement has been for some persons an end, a feature of the ideal society of the future. But more emphatically, it has been a means—an effective method of building the commonwealth.

The welfare state is often confused with the regimentation of totalitarian regimes. Since government plays an active role in economic, social, and cultural life in both types of social and political organization, the analogy is drawn. But it ends abruptly. The essence of totalitarianism is compulsion, regimentation, and the denial of the right to differ. In Israel, however, democratic processes prevail, differences are freely expressed, and voluntarism permeates the entire social and cultural pattern of life. The state supervises and works with voluntary associations, but it neither destroys nor dominates them.

Economic Growth

The Ingathering and the welfare-state policies were undertaken in defiance of economic realities. The known natural resources of Israel in 1948 were meager indeed.[66] Agricultural expansion was dependent upon irrigation, which in turn required costly development of the none too plentiful water resources of the country. The major Dead Sea works, which constituted the only exploitation of mineral resources prior to 1948, were occupied and destroyed by the Arabs during the War of Independence. The development of large-scale industry was hampered by deficiencies in industrial raw materials and by lack of coal for the generation of power. If economic considerations had prevailed, the Ingathering would not have been undertaken and the welfare state would not have endured.

Noneconomic factors have motivated basic Israeli policies,[67] as they did formerly the building of the Jewish National Home. Jewish homelessness and persecution and the requirements of national security have produced the bold and almost reckless policy of unrestricted immigration. Social idealism and a powerful labor movement have emphasized social welfare in economic development, so that the wage scale has not been determined solely by labor productivity and agricultural or industrial progress has not been measured exclusively by its profitability. In brief, national and social ideals have fashioned the fundamental objectives of Israeli policies, and the economy has been employed as a purposive instrument for their realization.

STAGES IN ECONOMIC POLICY

Three stages are well marked in the economic development of Israel, and the volume of immigration has been the cardinal factor in each. Mass immigration and extensive but mainly improvised economic activity marked the period from the establishment of the state in May, 1948, to the end of 1951. This was followed by the New Economic Policy during 1952-1954, which achieved greater economic stability. Since 1955 the country has been grappling with conditions and problems similar to those of the first period but not as acute.

During the first three years and eight months of independence (May, 1948 to the end of 1951), about 685,000 Jewish immigrants arrived in Israel—a total exceeding the entire Jewish population of May, 1948. The economic absorption of such a mass, and of the considerable proportion of the older immigrants who were only partly rooted productively in the economy,[68] would have been difficult even under normal conditions and favorable circumstances, neither of which obtained in Israel. The War of Independence, fought during this period, strained the economy of the country, and the failure to achieve peace settlements with the Arab States necessitated further outlays for defense. Boycott by the Arab States likewise affected the Israeli economy adversely by cutting off markets and sources of supply. Finally, the new immigrants were untrained manpower which could not be used with economic efficiency even when employed.

The Israelis attacked these formidable problems with zeal and determination. Between May, 1948, and 1951 the number of agricultural settlements nearly doubled, and the total cultivated area more than doubled, while the irrigated area increased by more than one-third. Large sums were spent in the building of some 168,000 rooms, mainly as housing units for immigrants. The output of electricity, as well as the amount supplied for industrial purposes, more than doubled. Basic industries were established, industrial machinery imported, roads built, and natural resources surveyed and studied for effective utilization. And special legislation was enacted to attract foreign capital. The Law for the Encouragement of Capital Investment (1950) offered exemption from property and local taxes for at least the first five years of an undertaking; it allowed special concessions in matters affecting depreciation and income tax rates; and it held out the opportunity for nonresidents to withdraw annually in foreign currency a maximum of 10 per cent of the investment.[69]

However, the strains of settling masses of immigrants, liquidating a war, building up defense forces, and promoting extensive development projects were too much for Israel's economy. The weaknesses showed especially in inflation and in an unfavorable balance of trade.

The immigrants became consumers as soon as they arrived in Israel, because they had to be supplied with a minimum of food, clothing, and shelter. But the majority arrived without means and did not immediately share in the production of goods. This created an increased demand for the available supply of commodities. Large defense expenditures likewise increased purchasing power without adding to the supply of consumer goods. The long-range program of economic development added to the pressure upon the goods desired for current consumption. Finally, unbalanced budgets, deficit spending, the issue of Treasury Bills, and the expansion of credit created a spiral of inflation, with increased prices, costs, and wages and a decline in the value of the Israeli pound.

The pattern of foreign trade was equally discouraging. Military equipment and economic development were dependent upon foreign sources of supply, and considerable quantities of consumer goods had to be imported to provide for the increased population. But purchasing power at home and inflation curtailed even the meager exports of the country, so that during 1949-1951 exports amounted to only 11 or 12 per cent of the value of imports, and the annual trade deficits increased steadily, reaching a total of some $333,000,000 in 1951. During this period the government attempted to check inflation by means of rationing, price controls, and other direct administrative measures. But these efforts were nullified by black-market operations and by waning public confidence, especially after clothing and footwear rationing was introduced in the summer of 1950. The drought of the following winter aggravated the situation, threatening collapse of the entire currency and price structure.[70] A change in policy became imperative.

The New Economic Policy is generally associated with the official devaluation of the Israeli pound on February 13, 1952. In fact, however, it was more far-reaching, and some of the measures were adopted as early as the spring of the preceding year. The New Economic Policy gradually abandoned direct controls such as rationing and sought to curb inflation and improve the balance of payments by indirect means. The issue of Treasury Bills was stopped and the attempt was made to balance the regular state budget. Credit was restricted and consumption curtailed through the reduction of purchasing power. Basic wages were frozen, except when justified by higher productivity, and a compulsory development loan was levied. These measures helped to reduce imports, and a special exchange rate served to stimulate exports. Above all, immigration dropped from over 174,000 in 1951 to less than 24,000 in 1952, some 10,000 in 1953, and about 17,500 in 1954.

The effects of the New Economic Policy were evident in increased agricultural and industrial production and in the development of local raw materials. Average daily unemployment fell sharply during 1954. The foreign trade deficit fell from $333,000,000 in 1951 to some $198,000,000 in 1954. Greater stability in prices and costs was achieved during 1954, and public confidence was restored.[71]

In 1955, however, noneconomic factors again disturbed the trend toward economic stability. Mass immigration reappeared as a result of disturbances in North Africa. Military expenditures mounted to meet the threat of the arms agreement of Egypt with the Soviet and its satellites in September, 1955, and the Sinai campaign of October-November, 1956, further strained the Israeli economy. Dependence on foreign imports again increased and greater purchasing power intensified inflationary pressures.

ECONOMIC ACHIEVEMENTS

The recurring difficulties have not discouraged the Israeli government or people. Economic planning, building, and development have been pursued with vigor and the achievements since independence have been most impressive, not only in quantitative growth but also in dynamic planning which has discovered hitherto unknown resources, increased the fertility and yield of the soil, and attacked desert and swamp through bold irrigation projects.

Self-sufficiency in agriculture may be a future hope, but the progress made since 1948 has been remarkable. The cultivated area has increased from some 412,000 acres (1,650,000 dunam) in 1948 to about 950,000 acres (3,825,000 dunam) in 1957. The irrigated area has more than tripled, and agricultural machinery has multiplied. The number of tractors, for example, increased from 681 in 1948 to 4,700 in 1956, and that of combines from 261 to 896. As a result, agricultural production has nearly tripled, although only 17 to 18 per cent of the labor force has been employed in agriculture, afforestation, and fisheries. It has been estimated that all local requirements in milk, eggs, poultry, vegetables, and potatoes are now met by Israeli agriculture, and that it supplies two-thirds of the country's food needs.[72]

Water and reclamation are the keys to agricultural development in Israel. From 1948 to 1956 water consumption for agricultural purposes increased more than threefold. In 1955 a sixty-six-inch pipe line went into operation, carrying water from the Yarkon River, north of Tel-Aviv, to the Negev. Other pipe lines are under construction, but the realization of the elaborate Jordan River development plan has been delayed because of Arab obstruction. The draining of the 15,000 acres of swamp land in the Huleh area, north of Lake Kinneret, was completed in 1957.

Industrial development has had to cope with serious obstacles. For example, the Dead Sea potash works were destroyed by the Arabs, and rehabilitation required not only a new plant but a new road from Beersheba to Sodom (the south end of the Dead Sea). Operations, resumed toward the end of 1953, did not really get under way until 1955-1956. Furthermore, industrial raw materials have had to be imported, except for some food products, fertilizers, and the cement, glass, and ceramics industries.

However, progress has been made despite the difficulties. New establishments have been built for the production of steel, pipes, tires and other rubber goods, electrical appliances, paper products, fertilizers, automobile assembly, radios, and other articles. The labor force engaged in industry, mining, and quarrying reached about 125,000 in November, 1955, and the annual output has increased consistently, tripling between 1948-1956. The relative concentration in the various fields of industry is revealed in the following figures on industrial production in 1956: food processing industries, about 24 per cent of the total industrial production; metals and textiles, 12 to 14 per cent each; stone and cement, about 10 per cent; wood, chemicals, clothing, and footwear, 6 to 7 per cent each; printing and paper, mining and minerals, electrical appliances, motor vehicles, machinery, and diamond cutting and polishing, about 2 to 4 per cent each; and rubber products and leather goods, less than 2 per cent each.[73]

Construction, especially for housing, is a major industry. Between 1949 and 1956, over 150,000 housing units comprising more than 460,000 rooms were built. Notable progress has also been registered in transportation and communication, vital for Israel's economy. The railroad system was disrupted by the war and passenger service was not restored until 1950. Since 1948, railway mileage in operation has increased about two and one half times, including an extension to Beersheba. The road network and motorized transportation have been expanded. Civil aviation has grown. The merchant marine has increased from ten to thirty vessels between 1948-1957, and the tonnage from about 14,000 to 136,000. The port of Haifa and the facilities at Tel-Aviv–Jaffa have been modernized and improved, and work has begun on the development of Elat, on the Gulf of Aqaba, as a major port.

Industrial expansion will be vitally affected by the planned exploration and development of natural resources, especially in the Negev. Oil, discovered at Heletz in September, 1955, is already providing about 5 per cent of the country's needs.[74] Phosphates, copper, ceramic clay, and glass sand have been found in large quantities, and exploitation is under way or in preparation. Some iron has beeen discovered in Upper Galilee, and there are indications that the Negev contains other minerals. Notable progress has also been made with industrial crops, such as cotton.[75]

ECONOMIC PROBLEMS

The economic progress of Israel has been striking, but serious problems remain, with the trade gap between imports and exports the most baffling. The table (page 757) summarizes the balance of trade in American dollars.[76]

These figures show that Israel has had a trade deficit since its establishment as a state, and that, after a steady rise in the annual deficit through 1951, it declined considerably from 1951 through 1954. Since 1955, however, the deficit has been rising again, chiefly because of renewed mass immigration and the threat of Egyptian and Syrian arms purchases.

Closer analysis will reveal that Israel has made significant progress in

TABLE IV

Balance of Trade, 1949-1956
(in millions of dollars)

Year	Imports	Exports	Trade Deficit (Excess of Imports over Exports)	Exports as % of Imports
1949	253.1	29.7	223.4	11.7
1950	298.8	36.9	261.9	12.3
1951	379.8	46.8	333.0	12.3
1952	321.1	44.4	276.7	13.8
1953	281.2	59.7	221.5	21.2
1954	286.5	88.1	198.4	30.8
1955	325.0	90.2	234.8	27.8
1956	364.0	107.2	256.7	29.5

its trade balance. Between 1949 and 1956 imports increased by about 44 per cent, but exports multiplied more than two and one-half times. In 1949, exports covered only 11.7 per cent of imports; in 1956, they covered 29.5 per cent of imports. Equally significant has been the change in the nature of the imports and exports. Whereas consumer goods accounted for about one-third of all imports in 1949, they constituted less than one-sixth of the imports of 1956; and raw materials, which were about one-third of the imports of 1949, increased to about one-half in 1956. Exports, too, have undergone a change. Citrus fruit, which provided 63 per cent of all exports in 1949, constituted only 39 per cent of the exports of 1956, although the value of the amount exported doubled. At the same time, the export of industrial products, including diamonds, increased from about 26 per cent to about 52 per cent of total exports.

The annual trade deficits have been covered by American government grants-in-aid and technical assistance, German reparations payments, Israel government bond sales abroad, private foreign investment, and private foreign philanthropy.[77] For a new and underdeveloped country, foreign trade deficits and even indebtedness are neither unusual nor alarming, so long as capital is available from external sources. However, dependence on foreign aid is risky, and Israel has been seeking (with considerable promise, as has been noted) to achieve greater balance in its international trade.

Other economic problems relate to the relative paucity of natural resources, the occupational structure and utilization of manpower, the need of foreign capital to finance development, and the Arab boycott. The planned exploration and development of mineral resources has been mentioned, and the success achieved in raising 30 per cent of the country's cotton needs and 28 per cent of sugar beet requirements holds the promise that the resource base can be expanded.

The manpower problem is largely but not wholly the result of unselective immigration. The distribution of the civilian labor force is given in the following table.[77a]

TABLE V

Distribution of Civilian Labor Force in Percentages[78]

Branch of Economy	% of Total November, 1955	June, 1956
Agriculture, forestry, and fisheries	17.6	17.7
Industry, mining, and quarrying	21.5	20.9
Construction and public works	9.3	8.3
Electricity, gas, water, and sanitary services	2.0	2.9
Commerce, banking, and insurance	13.5	12.5
Transportation, storage, and communication	6.6	6.4
Government and public services	21.2	23.2
Personal and recreational services	8.3	8.1
Total	100.0	100.0

It is evident from this table that a low proportion of the labor force is engaged in essential production, especially in agriculture and industry. In part this is due to the lack of training of the immigrant population, which government efforts have not yet been able to overcome, and to the lack of funds for the expansion of productive industries. Intensive training and concentration on production for export remain basic needs for the future.

Finally, stabilization of the Israeli economy requires increased investment from internal sources and a reduction of the gap between exports and imports. The arbitrary reduction of imports would reduce living standards, and the diversion of funds from public services to investment would entail the sacrifice of the ideal of the welfare state. The alternative to such drastic remedies lies in the ability of Israel to secure funds from external sources until resources can be developed and manpower trained.[79]

In summary, it may be said that the economic progress of Israel depends not only on the development of the country but actually upon the creation of essential resources and an effective labor and managerial force. Materials, men, money, and markets are the basic needs. Arable land must be created through irrigation. Potentially available minerals must be found and exploited, and industrial raw materials grown and developed. Managerial skill must be acquired and the mass of immigrants trained into an effective labor force. Savings and foreign capital are necessary for investment, and the cost of production of Israeli goods must be low enough to compete in world markets. And Israel requires peace and security, so that money and manpower will not be diverted to military preparedness and war.

International Relations

Israel's international relations began auspiciously enough. The United States and the Soviet Union were among the first to accord recognition to the new state, and both voted for its admission to the United Nations. Relations with Britain improved rapidly, France was cordial, and diplomatic contacts were soon established with a large majority of the lesser states of the world. Israel was ready to play the role of a small but enlightened state and to make its contribution to international co-operation.

ISRAEL AND THE UNITED NATIONS

Within the United Nations, Israel has participated in the General Assembly and its committees as well as in the Specialized Agencies which deal with world health, education and culture, agriculture, labor, economic and technical assistance, and other matters. It has also made a good record in the ratification of international conventions, including the declaration on compulsory jurisdiction of the International Court of Justice and the Genocide Convention. In 1952, an international symposium on desert research was held in Jerusalem under the auspices of the United Nations Educational, Scientific and Cultural Organization (Unesco). And in the following year, Israel was honored by the election of its representative as a vice-president of the United Nations General Assembly.[80]

On broad international questions, Israel has sought to pursue an independent policy and to keep clear of involvement in the conflict between the Soviet Union and the Western democracies. Characterized successively as "neutrality," "nonidentification," and "independent," this foreign policy has attempted to preserve freedom of judgment and action, without automatic commitments in orientation toward East or West, and without permanent political alignment with either bloc. In this spirit, Israel recognized the People's Republic of China, which the Soviet Union favored, and supported United Nations action against North Korean aggression, which was sponsored by the United States and the West.[81]

However, the early eagerness of Israel to share actively in the efforts of the United Nations to promote international co-operation has waned. The inability of the United Nations to effect a peace settlement in the Middle East has discouraged the Israeli government and people. And the repeated charges directed against Israel have compromised its position in the world organization and compelled concentration of its energies on the defense of its policies. The result has been a progressive withdrawal from active sponsorship of proposals and resolutions that have come before the General Assembly and its committees.

The unresolved issue of Jerusalem has remained an embarrassment to Israel. The General Assembly Resolution of November 29, 1947, had provided for an international regime. The Conciliation Commission, too, favored a form of internationalization, and, while its plan was discarded, a majority of the General Assembly resolved in December, 1949, in favor of internationalization. The Arab States had originally rejected the partition resolution of the General Assembly, including the proposed international regime for Jerusalem, and they had resorted to force in defiance of the United Nations. Subsequently, when Jordan had seized the Old City of Jerusalem, it had refused to accept internationalization.

Israel proposed "functional internationalization," that is, an international regime for the Holy Places but not international government for the entire territory of Jerusalem. In December, 1949, after the General Assembly had declared in favor of an international regime, Israel moved the *Knesset* and the ministries to Jerusalem, and in July, 1953, the Foreign Ministry, too, was lodged in the New City of Jerusalem as the nation's capital.

The General Assembly considered the question again in 1950, but the necessary majority could not be secured either for a proposal relating to the Holy Places or for internationalization. In 1952, another motion reaffirming internationalization failed of adoption.

The issue has thus remained deadlocked. It is significant that the General Assembly has declined to reaffirm internationalization, but in principle the resolution of December, 1949, remains in force. Both Israel and Jordan have failed to comply with that resolution, while the other Arab States have supported internationalization, apparently as a means of embarrassing Israel. It is Israel's view that the issue of Jerusalem no longer centers in the Holy Places, which are located, with few exceptions, in Jordan, but rather in the eagerness of certain governments to placate the Arab States in their quarrel with Israel.[82]

The problem of the Arab refugees has likewise served to compromise Israel's international position. It has been a matter of continuing concern for the United Nations, and funds have had to be raised for the maintenance of the mass of uprooted humanity. All disinterested states would like to see the troublesome problem liquidated, and repatriation has appeared to many as the simplest solution. Israel has argued that the flight of the Arabs was the issue of the fighting which the Arab States had precipitated; that Arab leadership directed or encouraged the exodus; that extensive repatriation in the climate of Arab hostility would undermine its very existence. Proposals have been made for the resettlement of the bulk of the refugees with international financial assistance. But the Arab States have opposed resettlement, and they have made effective use both of the problem and of individual refugees in their protracted conflict with Israel.[83]

ENMITY OF THE ARAB STATES

The Arab States have presented the most formidable obstacle to the consolidation of Israel's international position. They have refused to recognize the existence of Israel and their hostility has hardened into a determination to destroy the new state. To this end, they have pursued a policy of encirclement, noncommunication, economic boycott, and harassment along the borders and in the United Nations.

All of Israel's land frontiers border on Arab territory. These have been sealed off against trade and travel, and even foreigners cannot normally proceed to or from Israel by way of an adjoining Arab state. The Arab States have refused visas to travelers holding a visa for Israel. The effort was made to deny entry into an Arab state to anyone who had or was about to visit Israel, and when Premier U Nu of Burma did visit Israel in 1955, he was obliged to cancel a projected call in Cairo.

The Arabs have refused to have any intercourse with Israel, not only in direct negotiation (except for the Armistice Supervision Commissions) but also in the regional agencies of the United Nations. Several of the Specialized Agencies, including the World Health Organization and the Food and Agricultural Organization, maintain regional offices in Egypt or Lebanon, and the latter have denied access to these institutions to Israeli representatives. The Arabs have also declined to participate in any conference, seminar, or educational institute held under international auspices anywhere in the Eastern Mediterranean if Israel is included. The acquiescence of the international bodies has resulted in the exclusion of Israel from United Nations regional activities. Similarly, the Arabs were successful in barring Israel from the Asian-African Conference at Bandung, Indonesia, in 1955.[84]

The boycott has hampered water development projects. Obstacles were interposed in the drainage of the Huleh swamps, which delayed the completion of the project. It, and the unwillingness of the Arabs to relate water development to refugee settlement, have been important factors in bringing to a halt elaborate irrigation plans for the Jordan River Valley. International financial aid, particularly from the United States, would have benefited the Arabs as well as Israel, but after an auspicious beginning the project has languished.[85]

The Arab boycott of Israel has cut off all direct trade relations and sought to influence foreign firms and governments to shun Israel or face in their turn exclusion from Arab lands. Ships calling at Israeli ports have been blacklisted and denied trade facilities or services in Arab ports. Goods consigned to Israel have been seized. All commercial aircraft serving Israel have been forbidden to fly over Arab territory. Business firms which maintain branches in Israel have been threatened with boycott, and the boycott propaganda has reached out to Jewish firms of neutral countries, regardless of their trade relations or lack of relations with Israel. Saudi Arabia has directed that no Jewish personnel be included among the American forces at the Dhahran air base, and the American government has acquiesced. Israel has contended that the acquiescence of governments in the restrictive measures which affect their nationals and trade has encouraged the Arabs in the far-reaching boycott, which it regards as a menace to peace and hence a violation at least of the spirit of the United Nations charter. It is a fact that when the Arab threats have been ignored or challenged, they have proved hollow. In 1952, when West Germany and Israel were negotiating a reparations settlement, the Arab States threatened Germany with a boycott, but the latter disregarded the propaganda without serious consequences. Similarly, a warning was issued to the airlines in 1954 that they would be barred from Arab countries if any of their planes touched Israel. An effective protest disposed of this threat.

The blockade of Israel has been extended to the Suez Canal and the Gulf of Aqaba. The Constantinople Convention of 1888 clearly stipulates that free passage be allowed all ships through the Suez Canal, even in wartime. But the Canal has been barred not only to all Israeli ships but also to goods consigned to Israel and defined unilaterally by Egypt as contraband. Israel took the matter to the Security Council, which censured the action of Egypt as "unjustified interference with the rights of nations . . ." but the latter has persevered in its policy. In 1954, the Security Council again considered a resolution expressing grave concern over Egypt's failure to heed its previous decision, but the negative vote of the Soviet Union precluded any further action. At the same time, a Soviet veto prevented any decision on the blockade of the Gulf of Aqaba.[86]

Armed clashes along the borders of Israel have proved even more damaging to Israel's foreign relations, and they have, of course, contributed to tension and disturbance in the Middle East. The Armistice Agreements have constituted the legal basis of interstate relations, and Mixed Armistice Commissions have been charged with supervision. An armistice is a temporary condition which generally bridges the gap between war and peace. When it extends over a long period without a peace settlement, conflict is inevitable. Since no peace has been negotiated, the Armistice Agreements have remained in force to the present.

In such a situation, suspicion, anxiety, and misunderstanding would produce border clashes, even if hostility were minimal. On the Israeli borders, the presence of refugees and the enmity of the Arab governments have created a maximum of distrust and conflict. "Infiltrators" have penetrated Israel in small bands and perpetrated theft, sabotage, and murder. Moreover, trained and armed commando units, known as *fedayeen*, have operated chiefly from bases in Gaza and Sinai, attacking border patrols, mining roads, wrecking houses, and engaging in other forms of sabotage. The result has been thousands of charges and countercharges, many of which have been investigated by the Mixed Armistice Commissions. But the latter have been able to do little more than hand down findings in favor of one or the other of the parties. The outrages have continued.

Israel's policy has been to resort to raids in force as reprisal and deterrent. The most serious raid occurred in October, 1953, after the gruesome murder of a Jewish woman and her two children. The Jordanian village, Kibya, was attacked and some fifty-three men, women, and children were killed. The action came before the Security Council and Israel argued that the raid was the result of provocation and border harassment; that hundreds of its citizens, including women and children, had been killed by Arab marauders with the connivance and assistance of the Arab States; that the alternative would be private action by Israeli irregulars. But the Security Council severely censured Israel. Israel was clearly at a disadvantage. Small bands of "infiltrators" or *fedayeen* are difficult to apprehend or to identify with official Arab authorities. They can be disowned and classed as irresponsible irregulars. Moreover, the murder of a few Israeli civilians at a time lacks dramatic appeal. A raid in force, however, involves the constituted authorities, and the innocence of the victims is accentuated. Since Kibya, Israeli reprisals have been directed against military posts and bases, but legally reprisals cannot be tolerated by agencies of the United Nations.[87]

The root of the evil has been the continuance of a precarious armistice and the inability to achieve a peace settlement. And this, in turn, has been largely due to the divided world in which "East" and "West" have sought to use the Middle East in their struggle for power.

THE "EAST-WEST" CONFLICT

The Arab States have been courted by both the Western powers and the Soviet Union. Western Europe is dependent on the oil supplies of the Middle East, and huge investments in oil properties have won the Arabs powerful friends.[88] Moreover, the United States and Great Britain have sought to enlist the Arab States in defensive alliances for the containment of the Soviet Union. Finally, Arab bases are considered essential for the West in the struggle with the Soviets.

The United States has been friendly to Israel and quite generous with economic aid, and Britain and France as well as the United States have sought to maintain stability in the Middle East. On May 25, 1950, the three powers made a declaration opposing an arms race in the region and "the use of force or the threat of force between any of the states in that area."[89] However, the use of the Dhahran airport as an American base was secured from Saudi Arabia in 1951, and the Bagdad Pact of 1955 has depended on Arab States. These have involved the strengthening of the military potential of the latter, and the exclusion of Israel from the defensive alliances of the Middle East has resulted in its isolation. Israel has protested against the arms build-up of the Arab States, and it has sought an effective guarantee of its frontiers. These pleas have remained unanswered.[90]

The Soviet Union has become increasingly hostile to Israel. During 1952-1953, and especially after the infamous Jewish doctors' case, Soviet policy became blatantly anti-Israel and even anti-Semitic, and since then the Arab States have had strong Soviet support against Israel in the United Nations. But it would be an oversimplification to ascribe this development to anti-Semitism.

The Soviet Union has always been hostile to Zionism, but its foreign policy is determined not by ideological considerations but by the exigencies of power politics. It has carved out a sphere of influence in Eastern Europe, in which it brooks no outside interference, but it has recognized no such limitations upon itself beyond its sphere of influence, and it has especially sought to penetrate the Middle East. It favored the establishment of Israel and the termination of the Mandate in order to dislodge the British from Palestine, but Israel could not serve the purposes of Soviet designs upon the Middle East. Israel's early policy of nonidentification with the East or West was not in keeping with the character of a faithful satellite, and its position against aggression in Korea showed that its inclinations were toward the West. Moreover, the Arabs were more numerous, and their sense of grievance against the West could be more easily exploited. The Soviet Union has therefore become the champion of the Arabs against Israel.[91]

By 1955, Israel found itself almost completely isolated. The United States and Great Britain were committed to the Bagdad Pact, from which Israel was excluded. The Soviet Union was openly pro-Arab. And the United Nations, which had approved the establishment of a Jewish State, brought the Palestine war to a close, and admitted Israel into the international organization, was proving unequal to the task of effecting a peace settlement or of preventing economic warfare. Moreover, the Arabs were using the United Nations as a forum for attacks and denunciations of Israel, which it regarded as unjustified. Border attacks and harassments, it felt, were balanced by fine legal formulas rather than viewed as the inevitable consequence of the latent state of war which the Arabs perpetuated. Finally, the maneuvering of the Great Powers created the feeling that Israel was a pawn in a power conflict and might be sacrificed on the altar of appeasement. A mood of pessimism gripped the country, and both people and government reached the conclusion that they could look for assistance neither to the Western democracies nor the United Nations; that they must rely on their own strength to achieve security.[92] The arms deal between Egypt and Czechoslovakia turned this pessimism into bitterness. The Arabs were about to secure the means of making good their threats, and they were freed from the moderating pressures of the West. Israel felt in mortal peril.

THE SINAI CAMPAIGN

During 1955-1956 arms from the Soviet bloc enabled Egypt to effect a military build-up in the Sinai Desert, and by the fall of 1956 a unified military command was formed with Jordan and Syria. Israel regarded these measures as directed against itself, and on October 29, 1956, its army struck and soon cleared the Egyptian forces out of the Gaza strip and Sinai, at the same time lifting the blockade in the Gulf of Aqaba. For their own reasons, British and French forces attacked the Suez Canal area. United Nations action, and United States and Soviet pressure, resulted in the withdrawal of all forces from the occupied areas, but the Sinai campaign had important results for Israel. The Egyptian military preparations in the Sinai Desert were disrupted. A United Nations Emergency Force was established along the Israel-Egyptian border and in the Gulf of Aqaba, which put an end to the *fedayeen* raids and the blockade of the port of Elat. Israel was no longer isolated in the United Nations. And it served notice that it would not submit passively to armed attack or to partition of the Munich variety.[93]

However, the basic issues remain and the Arab States are even more unyielding. Israel is still surrounded by hostile neighbors, and its efforts to build a viable welfare state are still thwarted by isolation in the Middle East and by the threat of world conflict between the Soviet bloc and the West.

NOTES

[1] The most thorough and comprehensive study of Palestine under the British Mandate is *Palestine: A Study of Jewish, Arab and British Policies,* 2 vols., New Haven, 1947. This study was made by I. B. Berkson with the assistance of a group of scholars. It was sponsored by the Esco Foundation for Palestine. J. C. Hurewitz, *The Struggle for Palestine,* New York, 1950, is a thorough scholarly study, and P. L. Hanna, *British Policy in Palestine,* Washington, 1942, is a well-documented account of political developments. On the history of Zionism and its chief leaders, see N. Sokolow, *History of Zionism, 1600-1918,* 2 vols., London, 1919; I. Cohen, *The Zionist Movement,* New York, 1946; J. De Haas, *Theodor Herzl: A Biographical Study,* 2 vols., Chicago, 1927; C. Weizmann, *Trial and Error,* London, 1949. A penetrating analysis of the latter work is given in O. K. Rabinowicz, *Fifty Years of Zionism,* London, 1952. See the texts of the following: The Balfour Declaration, in Great Britain, *Zionism* (Foreign Office

Handbook, No. 162), London, 1920, p. 44; the Mandate for Palestine, in Great Britain, Colonial Office, *Mandate for Palestine* (Cmd. 1785), London, December, 1922; the White Paper of 1939, in Great Britain, Colonial Office, *Palestine Statement of Policy,* May, 1939 (Cmd. 6019), London, 1939; the Land Transfer Regulations, in Great Britain, Colonial Office, *Palestine Land Transfer Regulations,* February, 1940 (Cmd. 6180), London, 1940.

[[1a] See above Ben Zion Dinur, "The Historical Foundations of the Rebirth of Israel"; Itzhak Ben-Zvi, "Eretz Yisrael under Ottoman Rule, 1517-1917."]

[2] A. Ulitzur, *Two Decades of Keren Hayesod: A Survey of Facts and Figures, 1921-1940,* Jerusalem, 1940, especially pp. 26-27; Hadassah Medical Organization, *Twenty Years of Medical Service to Palestine, 1918-1938,* Jerusalem, 1939, pp. 13-62. D. Gurevich and A. Gertz, *Statistical Handbook of Jewish Palestine, 1947,* Jerusalem, 1947, is an invaluable collection of statistical information. See pp. 192-193, 344, 366-367, 369, 375, 427.

[3] See *The Hebrew Encyclopedia* (Hebrew), Vol. VI, Jerusalem, 1957, p. 671. Allowance has been made for some 60,000 who emigrated.

[4] See *Palestine Review,* January, 1945, p. 161; *Statistical Handbook of Jewish Palestine,* pp. 140, 142, 155, 435; *Palestine: A Study of Jewish, Arab and British Policies,* Vol. I, p. 368, Vol. II, pp. 691-692, 1052; Government of Israel, *Government Yearbook,* 1952, pp. 305, 327; *The Hebrew Encyclopedia,* Vol. VI, p. 837. For a general discussion of agricultural settlement, see A. Ruppin, *Three Decades of Palestine,* Jerusalem, 1936.

[5] See *Statistical Handbook of Jewish Palestine,* pp. 48, 206-209, 220-223; A. Bonné, *State and Economics in the Middle East,* 2nd ed., London, 1955, pp. 302-303; A. Revusky, *Jews in Palestine,* New York, 1945, chs. VI, VIII; *The Hebrew Encyclopedia,* Vol. VI, pp. 898-902; *Government Yearbook,* 1950, p. 241.

[6] Bonné, *op. cit.,* p. 222. On the development of trade, see also *Statistical Handbook of Jewish Palestine,* pp. 233-239 ff., 254-259.

[7] An extended analysis of these factors will be presented in the author's projected work on Israel.

[8] See *The Hebrew Encyclopedia,* Vol. VI, p. 676.

[9] See *Statistical Handbook of Jewish Palestine,* pp. 334-341; *Palestine: A Study of Jewish, Arab and British Policies,* Vol. I, pp. 321-324, Vol. II, pp. 698-704. An extensive account of the development of the arts is given in *The Hebrew Encyclopedia,* Vol. VI, pp. 1070-1129.

[10] See *Statistical Handbook of Jewish Palestine,* pp. 84-85, 344-351; *Palestine: A Study of Jewish, Arab and British Policies,* Vol. II, pp. 667 ff.

[11] A symbol of labor idealism was Aaron David Gordon (1856-1922), whose writings were published in Hebrew in five volumes. A selection is available in English in his *Selected Essays,* New York, 1938. See, for example, pp. 247-253.

[12] There is an extensive literature on the collective and co-operative movements. See, for example, H. Viteles, "The Cooperative Movement," *The Annals of the American Academy of Political and Social Science,* November, 1932 (Palestine issue), pp. 127-138; *idem,* "The Cooperative Movement in

Israel," *The Hebrew Encyclopedia,* Vol. VI, pp. 943-951; *idem,* "Communitarian Rural Settlements in Palestine," *Year Book of Agricultural Cooperation, 1939,* London, 1939, pp. 133-153; A. Ben-Shalom, *Deep Furrows,* New York, 1937; G. Baratz and others, *A Village on the Jordan,* London, 1954; E. Samuel, *Handbook of the Jewish Communal Villages in Palestine,* 2nd Eng. ed., Jerusalem, 1945; H. F. Infield, *Cooperative Living in Palestine,* New York, 1944; *Statistical Handbook of Jewish Palestine,* pp. 64-65, 178, 406-410.

[13] On social insurance and co-operative activities of *Histadrut,* see I. Kanievsky, *Social Policy and Social Insurance in Palestine* (submitted to 30th Conference of ILO, Geneva, 1947), Tel-Aviv, 1947, ch. VI; General Federation of Jewish Labour in Palestine, *Memorandum Submitted to the Anglo-American Commission of Inquiry,* Tel-Aviv, March, 1946 (mimeographed), pp. 68-74; S. Kurland, *Cooperative Palestine: The Story of the Histadrut,* New York, 1947, Part 3. On *Histadrut* membership, compare the *Histadrut* Executive Committee, *The Histadrut During 1945-1948, Summary Report* (Hebrew), Tel-Aviv, 1949, pp. 392-393; *Memorandum Submitted to the Anglo-American Commission of Inquiry,* p. 9; and *Statistical Handbook of Jewish Palestine,* p. 290.

[14] See M. Burstein, *Self-Government of the Jews in Palestine Since 1900,* Tel-Aviv, 1934, chs. IV-VII; *The Hebrew Encyclopedia,* Vol. VI, pp. 538-540.

[15] For the prices of land, see *The Hebrew Encyclopedia,* Vol. VI, pp. 822-823.

[16] This figure is for the end of 1936. On the "displaced Arabs," see Lewis French, *Reports on Agricultural Development and Land Settlement in Palestine,* Jerusalem, 1931-1932, pp. 59-60 ff.; Great Britain, Colonial Office, *Palestine Report, 1936* (Colonial No. 129), London, 1937, p. 90; *Palestine: A Study of Jewish, Arab and British Policies,* Vol. II, pp. 717-718.

[17] See Bonné, *op. cit.,* p. 304; *idem, The Economic Development of the Middle East,* New York, 1945, p. 126; *idem, Statistical Handbook of Middle Eastern Countries,* Jerusalem, 1944, pp. 59, 119; and *Memorandum Submitted to the Anglo-American Commission of Inquiry,* pp. 21-27, 60-65, 76-77.

[18] For a discussion of Arab-Jewish relations and the idea of binationalism, see *Palestine: A Study of Jewish, Arab and British Policies,* Vol. I, pp. 562-593; Vol. II, pp 1015-1020, 1099-1104, 1158-1177. See also O. I. Janowsky, "Zionism Today: A Clarification," *The Menorah Journal,* October-December, 1943, pp. 227-258.

[19] The text of President Truman's letter to Prime Minister Attlee is in *The Department of State Bulletin,* November 18, 1945, pp. 790-791. For Concurrent Resolution 44, see *Congressional Record,* 79th Congress, First Session, December 17, 1945.

[20] Department of State, *Anglo-American Committee of Inquiry: Report, April 20, 1946,* Washington, 1946, pp. 1-12.

[21] General Barker's order is quoted in J. Kimche, *Seven Fallen Pillars: The Middle East, 1945-1952,* New York, 1953, pp. 42-43. The British government justified Barker's instructions but dissociated itself from "the actual terms" of the letter. See *Parliamentary Debates,* House of Commons, Vol.

426, No. 188, p. 963. Ben-Gurion's quotation is from D. Ben-Gurion, *Rebirth and Destiny of Israel,* New York, 1954, p. 217. For summaries of policies of the *Haganah, Irgun,* and Sternists, and relations among them, see H. Sacher, *Israel: The Establishment of a State,* New York, 1952, pp. 181-194; M. Pearlman, *The Army of Israel,* New York, 1950, ch. 8; B. Litvinoff, *Ben-Gurion of Israel,* New York, 1954, pp. 143-146 and ch. 7, *passim; The Hebrew Encyclopedia,* Vol. VI, pp. 553-562. For the *Irgun* view of the King David Hotel attack, see M. Beigin, *The Revolt: Story of the Irgun,* New York, 1951, ch. XV.

[22] See Great Britain, Colonial Office, *Proposals for the Future of Palestine* (Cmd. 7044), London, 1947, pp. 2-8.

[23] United Nations Special Committee on Palestine, *Report to the General Assembly,* U.N. Doc. A/364, especially pp. 42-65; United Nations, *Official Records of the Second Session of the General Assembly,* Vol. II, November 29, 1947, pp. 1424-1425. For the debates, see pp. 1310-1428. For a detailed analysis, see J. Robinson, *Palestine and the United Nations,* Washington, 1947, chs. IV–XVI.

[24] J. Garcia-Granados, *The Birth of Israel,* New York, 1948, Ch. 25, especially p. 287. For the discussions in the Security Council, beginning with February 24, 1948, and in the General Assembly, see United Nations, Security Council, *Official Records,* 3rd Year, Nos. 16-51, 57-58, 65-67, 69; United Nations, *Official Records of the Second Special Session of the General Assembly,* Vol. I, April 19–May 14, 1948, pp. 9-47. D. Horowitz, *State in the Making,* New York, 1953, pp. 297-304, conveys the dramatic quality and tension of the final vote on the partition resolution. The same author reveals (pp. 232-235) the uncompromising attitude of Azzam Pasha, leader and Secretary-General of the Arab League. L. L. Leonard, "The United Nations and Palestine," *International Conciliation,* October, 1949, pp. 603-786, is an excellent study of United Nations efforts.

[25] Summaries of the military operations are given in Pearlman, *op. cit.,* chs. 9-21; E. O'Ballance, *The Arab-Israeli War, 1948,* London, 1956; *The Hebrew Encyclopedia,* Vol. VI, pp. 569-594. The atmosphere of the period is caught in H. Levin, *I Saw the Battle of Jerusalem,* New York, 1950. The texts of the armistice agreements are in United Nations, Security Council, *Official Records,* Docs. S/1264 (Egyptian-Israeli Armistice, 24 February, 1949); S/1296 (Israeli-Lebanese Armistice, 23 March, 1949); S/1302 (Jordan-Israel Armistice, 3 April, 1949); S/1353 (Israeli-Syrian Armistice, 20 July, 1949). For a juridical analysis of the agreements, see S. Rosenne, *Israel's Armistice Agreements with the Arab States,* Tel-Aviv, 1951. An interesting comment on the United Nations Conciliation Commission is given in J. G. McDonald, *My Mission in Israel, 1948-1951,* New York, 1951, pp. 174-180 ff.

[26] Leonard, *op. cit.,* pp. 737-738, 740.

[27] Great Britain, Foreign Office, *Progress Report of the United Nations Mediator on Palestine* (Cmd. 7530), London, 1948. For a summary of Bernadotte's proposals, see F. Bernadotte, *To Jerusalem,* London, 1951, pp. 235-244.

[28] See United Nations, Conciliation Commission for Palestine, *First Prog-*

ress Report, Doc. A/819, March 15, 1949; *Second Progress Report,* Doc. A/838, April 19, 1949; *Third Progress Report,* Doc. A/927, June 21, 1949; and subsequent reports.

[29] Carnegie Endowment for International Peace, *Israel and the United Nations* (report of a Study Group set up by the Hebrew University of Jerusalem), New York, 1956, p. 50.

[30] See Kimche, *op. cit.*, pp. 209-210, 227-232; Ben-Gurion, *op. cit.*, pp. 228, 237; photostat copies of a British officer's reports, in Pearlman, *op. cit.*, pp. 116-117; Levin, *op. cit.*, pp. 90 ff. Quotations from Arab sources are given in Government of Israel, *The Arabs in Israel,* New York, 1955, pp. 9-12, and extensive excerpts from Arab works are given in Hebrew translation in S. Sabagh (trans.), *Be'eynei Oyev* (*Through the Eyes of the Enemy*), Tel-Aviv, 1954. See epecially pp. 22-24, 32-33, 48-49, 52.

[31] Litvinoff, *op. cit.*, is a full-length scholarly biography. See also the penetrating account of M. Syrkin, "Ben-Gurion at Seventy," *Jewish Frontier,* December, 1956, pp. 9-12. Selected addresses are available in English in Ben-Gurion, *op. cit.*

[32] On the Provisional Government, see Law and Administration Ordinance, May 21, 1948; Courts (Transitional Provisions) Ordinance, June 30, 1948; and Transition Law, February 16, 1949, in *Laws of the State of Israel,* Vol. I, pp. 7-11, 23-25; Vol. III, pp. 3-4. See also Government of Israel, *Government Yearbook,* 5710 (Hebrew), Tel-Aviv, 1950, pp. 3-10; *The Israel Yearbook, 1950-1951,* pp. 49, 197-198 ff.

[33] For the text, see *Government Yearbook,* 1950, pp. 50 ff. See also *ibid.*, 1956, p. 31.

[34] The text of the Draft Constitution is given in J. Ben-Jacob, *The Rise of Israel,* New York, 1949, pp. 200-217; in J. Dunner, *The Republic of Israel,* New York, 1950, pp. 249-259; in *The New York Times,* December 10, 1948. For the debates in the *Knesset,* see *Divrei Haknesset,* 1st *Knesset,* 113th-117th Sessions, February 7, 13, 14, 20, 1950, pp. 725-746, 766-784, 794-804, 808-828. Ben-Gurion's address on the question of a constitution is available in English in Ben-Gurion, *op. cit.*, pp. 363-380.

[[34a] Author of the preceding chapter.]

[35] For the system of government and legal structure, see Transition Law of 1949; State Comptroller Law, May 24, 1949; State President (Tenure) Law, December 5, 1951; *Knesset* Immunity Laws, 1951-1952; in *Laws of the State of Israel,* Vol. III, pp. 23-26; Vol. V, pp. 149-152; Vol. VI, pp. 4-6, 45-47; M. Rosetti, "Israel's Parliament," *Parliamentary Affairs,* Vol. VIII (Autumn, 1955), pp. 445-452.

Summary accounts are given in *The Hebrew Encyclopedia,* Vol. VI, pp. 623-633; N. Bentwich, *Israel,* New York, 1952, pp. 94 ff; M. H. Bernstein, *The Politics of Israel,* Princeton, 1957, ch. V, and especially ch. VI on the Civil Service; G. de Gaury, *The New State of Israel,* New York, 1952, *passim;* J. Dunner, *The Republic of Israel,* New York, 1950, ch. VIII; H. Lehrman, *Israel:The Beginning and Tomorrow,* New York, 1951, pp. 12-56; O. Kraines, *Israel: The Emergence of a New Nation,* Washington, 1954, pp. 1-37; S.

Rosenne, *The Constitutional and Legal System of Israel,* New York, 1957, pp. 17-38; L. F. R. Williams, *The State of Israel,* London, 1957, ch. IX.

[36] On the legal structure, see especially *The Hebrew Encyclopedia,* Vol. VI, pp. 633-665; *Government Yearbook,* 5717 (1956), pp. 311-332; B. Akzin, "Codification in a New State," *The American Journal of Comparative Law,* Vol. V, No. 1, pp. 44-77; Y. L. Kohn, "The Emerging Constitution of Israel," in M. Davis (ed.), *Israel: Its Role in Civilization,* New York, 1956, pp. 130-145; Rosenne, *op. cit.,* pp. 1-16.

[37] For the legislation on local government, see *Laws of the State of Israel,* Vol. IV, pp. 177-178; Vol. VI, pp. 21, 63-72; Vol. VII, p. 131; Vol. IX, pp. 54-60. See also *Government Yearbook,* 5716 (1955), pp. 436-438; 5717 (1956), pp. 300-302; and the appropriate sections under "Ministry of the Interior" in the preceding yearbooks. See also R. Shaffar, "Local Government in Israel," in *The Israel Yearbook,* 1952-1953, pp. 319-363; M. Kalir, "Local Government," *ibid.,* 1957, pp. 237-247. Bernstein, *op. cit.,* ch. 12, contains an appraisal based on close study and personal observation.

[38] The salient points of party platforms are given in *The Israel Yearbook,* 1952-1953, pp. 97-101; 1957, pp. 17-24. For a penetrating analysis, see B. Akzin, "The Role of Parties in Israeli Democracy," *The Journal of Politics,* Vol. 17, 1955, pp. 507-545. See also de Gaury, *op. cit.,* pp. 76-90; M. Roshwald, "Political Parties and Social Classes in Israel," *Social Research,* Summer, 1956, pp. 199-218. A good summary of parties during the Mandate period is given in Revusky, *op. cit.,* pp. 194-208.

[39] Central Bureau of Statistics, *Totz'ot Habhirot* (Election Results, 1955), Special Series, No. 51, Jerusalem, August, 1956, Tables I-V, pp. 3-7.

[40] Good accounts of the functioning of the *Knesset* and of cabinet crises are given in *Government Yearbook,* 5711 (1950), pp. 59-65; *ibid.,* 5713 (1952), pp. 51-56; *ibid.,* 5714 (1953-1954), pp. 55-61; *ibid.,* 5715 (1954), pp. 13–21; *ibid.,* 5716 (1955), pp. 16-17 ff.; *ibid.,* 5717 (1956), pp. 35-37 ff.; *ibid.,* 5718 (1957), pp. 51-58; *The Israel Yearbook,* 1950-1951, pp. 65-76; *ibid.,* 1957, pp. 13-17. The cabinet crisis of 1951 affords a good example of Israeli parliamentary government. See *Divrei Haknesset,* 1st *Knesset,* 225th-227th Sessions, February 12-14, 1951, pp. 1037-1110. For the cabinet crisis of January, 1958, see *ibid.,* January 7, 1958, pp. 563-591.

[41] For the Nationality Law, April 8, 1952, see *Laws of the State of Israel,* Vol. VI, pp. 50-53; and for the abolition of the death penalty, *ibid.,* Vol. VIII, p. 63. For other laws dealing with currency, coinage, customs, passports, etc., see *ibid.,* Vol. I, pp. 13, 30-34, 43-44; Vol. II, pp. 58-59, 92-93; Vol. III, pp. 26-27; Vol. VI, pp. 76-77, 159-162.

[42] On the *Altalena* incident, compare Ben-Gurion, *op. cit.,* pp. 251-260, and Beigin, *op. cit.,* chs. XI–XII. The vital importance of national discipline at that time is illustrated in McDonald, *op. cit.,* pp. 17-18.

[43] See Defense Army of Israel Ordinance, May, 1948; Defense Service Law, September, 1949; Defense Service (Amendment) Law, February, 1950; and Reserve Service (Compensation) Law, in *Laws of the State of Israel,* Vol. I, pp. 15-16; Vol. III, pp. 112-118; Vol. IV, pp. 62-64; Vol. VI, pp. 27-32.

[44] See *Laws of the State of Israel,* Vol. III, pp. 125-131 (Compulsory

Education Law, September, 1949); Vol. IV, pp. 91-92, 184-185 (amendments of 1950); Vol. VII, pp. 113-119 (State Education Law, August, 1953).

[45] *See Laws of the State of Israel,* Vol. I, p. 18 (Days of Rest Ordinance, June, 1948); Vol. II, p. 37 (Kasher Food for Soldiers Ordinance, November, 1948); Vol. III, pp. 66-67 (Jewish Religious Services Budget Law, August, 1949); p. 116 (Art. 11 [d] of Defense Service Law, September, 1949); Vol. VII, p. 137 (Art. 8 of National Service Law, August, 1953). On the structure and functions of the Ministry of Religious Affairs, see appropriate sections in *Government Yearbooks,* especially 1950, pp. 188-192, and 1956, pp. 365-371. For a general discussion, see E. Samuel, *Problems of Government in the State of Israel,* Jerusalem, 1956, ch. 8.

[46] See *Laws of the State of Israel,* Vol. IV, pp. 158-159 (Marriage Age Law, August, 1950); Vol. V, pp. 171-172 (Women's Equal Rights Law, July, 1951).

[47] See *Laws of the State of Israel,* Vol. VII, pp. 3-4 (World Zionist Organization-Jewish Agency [Status] Law, December, 1952).

[48] There is a vast literature on the Ingathering, of which only some salient items can be noted. See Law of the Return, July, 1950, in *Laws of the State of Israel,* Vol. IV, p. 114. Examples of official policy are available in the government programs; see *Government Yearbook,* 1950, pp. 50-51 ff.; *ibid.,* 1956, pp. 25-27 ff. The *Government Yearbooks* also provide annual summaries on "Immigration and Absorption." See also appropriate sections in the *Israel Yearbooks.* The best analysis of the demographic aspects of the Ingathering is R. Bachi, "Demography," *The Hebrew Encyclopedia,* Vol. VI, pp. 665-707. For the position of the major political parties, see Note 38 above. L. Eshkol, "How to Absorb 100,000 Immigrants," *The Jerusalem Post,* July 4, 1957, illustrates the more recent preoccupation with mass immigration.

[49] For debates on the need for and significance of the Ingathering, see *Divrei Haknesset,* 1st *Knesset,* 19th, 25th-26th, 28th-29th, Sessions, March 30, 1949, April 26-27, 1949, May 3, 11, 1949, pp. 266-275, 399-404, 409-458, 470-477, 486-500. See also Ben-Gurion, *op. cit.,* pp. 346 ff., 360-361, 386-388, 427-428, 468-471, 492, 495-496.

[50] See, for example, *ibid.,* pp. 347, 396, 468, 470.

[51] The latest figures available at the time of writing are in Government of Israel, Central Bureau of Statistics, *Statistical Monthly of Israel* (Hebrew), Part I, February, 1958, p. 160.

[[51a] See below Jacob Lestschinsky, "Jewish Migrations, 1840-1956."]

[52] J. Schechtman, "The End of Galut Yemen," *Jewish Affairs,* February 1, 1950, pp. 3-33, is a very good illustration of the Ingathering from one Moslem country and of the conditions that made it necessary. For a popular, human-interest account, see S. Barer, *The Magic Carpet,* New York, 1952. The *JDC Review* contains valuable information on conditions in Moslem and other refugee lands and on mass emigration to Israel. See, for example, the issues of April, 1948, pp. 13–14, 21-22; May, 1948, pp. 29, 32-33; September-October, 1948, pp. 61-63; May, 1949, pp. 13-24; July, 1949, pp. 25-26, 32-34.

[53] A careful survey, however, has revealed that the new immigrant has,

on the whole, adjusted himself better to work and the industrial situation than to the general community. See "Cultural Assimilation and Tensions in Israel," *International Social Science Bulletin* (UNESCO), Vol. VIII, No. 1, 1956, pp. 7-123. See also R. Patai, *Israel Between East and West,* Philadelphia, 1953, especially chs. 7, 10, 11.

[54] *Statistical Monthly of Israel* (Hebrew), Part I, February, 1958, p. 157. See also *Government Yearbook,* 5711 (1950), p. 358.

[55] On the Arab minority, see Land Acquisition (Validation of Acts and Compensation) Law, March, 1953, in *Laws of the State of Israel,* Vol. VII, pp. 43-45; G. T. Renner, "Arab Education in the Near East," *Middle Eastern Affairs,* August–September, 1950, pp. 215-224; J. L. Benor, "Arab Education in Israel," *ibid.*, pp. 224-229; *ibid.*, June-July, 1950, pp. 199-200; S. D. Goitein, "The Arab Schools in Israel Revisited," *ibid.*, October, 1952, pp. 272-275; M. Piamenta, "Arabic in the *Knesset,*" *ibid.*, February, 1955, pp. 45-47; A. Zidon, *Haknesset* (Hebrew), Tel-Aviv, 1950, pp. 83-84. For the distribution of the Arab vote in the election of 1955, see *The Hebrew Encyclopedia,* Vol. VI, p. 714. Good summaries of the condition of the Arabs are given in Government of Israel, *The Arabs in Israel,* New York, 1955; D. Peretz, "The Arab Minority of Israel," *The Middle East Journal,* Spring, 1954, pp. 139-154; Bernstein, *op. cit.*, pp. 68-69, 85-86, 298-302; Williams, *op. cit.*, ch. X. See also sections under Ministries of Interior and of Religious Affairs in *Government Yearbooks,* especially 1957, for statistics on education and culture.

[56] *The Hebrew Encyclopedia,* Vol. VI, pp. 819-820.

[57] Bernstein, *op. cit.*, p. 229.

[58] See *Laws of the State of Israel,* Vol. V, pp. 125-133 (Hours of Work and Rest Law, May, 1951); Vol. VIII, pp. 4-35 (National Insurance Law, November, 1953), 175-182 (Labour Inspection [organization] Law, September, 1954); *Government Yearbook,* 5718 (1957), pp. 450-459 (Settlement of Labour Disputes Law, February, 1957, and Collective Agreement Law, February, 1957); see also P. B. Nortman, "Working Conditions and Social Security in Israel," *Middle Eastern Affairs,* May, 1951, pp. 167-179.

[59] See *Laws of the State of Israel,* Vol. VIII, pp. 75-89 (Tenants' Protection Law, April, 1954); Vol. IX, pp. 172-183 (Tenants' Protection Law, July, 1955).

[60] See *Government Yearbook,* 5718 (1957), pp. 383-388; Bernstein, *op. cit.*, pp. 334-338.

[61] On health conditions, see *Government Yearbooks,* especially 5717 (1956), pp. 284-295; 5718 (1957), pp. 181-190; *The Hebrew Encyclopedia,* Vol. VI, pp. 717-728.

[62] *Government Yearbook,* 5718 (1957), pp. 172-173.

[63] On education and culture, see *Government Yearbooks,* especially 5718 (1957), pp. 172-199; *The Israel Yearbooks,* especially 1957, pp. 201-235. *The Hebrew Encyclopedia,* Vol. VI, pp. 675-679, 983-1129, contains detailed information on education, culture, and especially the arts. H. Gamzu, "The Israel Theatre," *Middle Eastern Affairs,* May, 1952, pp. 150-154; E. Silberner, "Libraries in Israel," *ibid.*, March, 1955, pp. 78-83. For a thorough study of the revival of Hebrew, see R. Bachi, "A Statistical Analysis of the

Revival of Hebrew in Israel," *Scripta Hierosolymitana,* Vol. III, Jerusalem, 1956, pp. 179-247. For the development of higher education, see M. Spiegel and others, *The Hebrew University of Jerusalem,* Jerusalem, 1950; L. Levensohn, *Vision and Fulfillment,* New York, 1950; S. Livny, "Technion—Israel Institute of Technology," *Middle Eastern Affairs,* June-July, 1956, pp. 222-227. On archaeology and excavations, see *Israel Exploration Journal,* published in Jerusalem.

[64] This table is based on State of Israel, Ministry of Labour, *Cooperative Societies in Israel, 1956,* Jerusalem, 1957, pp. 11, 13, 15, and on the listing of all Jewish settlements and their social structure in 1946, in *Statistical Handbook of Jewish Palestine, op. cit.,* pp. 411-426.

[65] On the co-operative movement, see *Cooperative Societies in Israel, 1956,* pp. 3-31; Viteles, in *Scripta Hierosolymitana,* pp. 53-103; S. N. Eisenstadt, "The Social Conditions of the Development of Voluntary Association—A Case Study of Israel," *ibid.,* pp. 104-125; Y. Talmon-Garber, "Differentiation in Collective Settlements," *ibid.,* pp. 153-178. On recent developments in the collectives, see United Nations, *Monograph On Community Settlements and Report of the Survey Mission on Community Organization and Development in Israel,* February, 1954; M. E. Spiro, *Kibbutz: Venture in Utopia,* Cambridge, Mass., 1956; M. Weingarten, *Life in a Kibbutz,* New York, 1955.

[66] See C. Tadmor, "Natural Resources of Israel," *Middle Eastern Affairs,* May, 1954, pp. 154-158; *The Israel Yearbook,* 1950-1951, pp. 79-80.

[67] Bernstein, *op. cit.,* chs. 7-9, presents a realistic analysis of Israel's economy. See also D. Horowitz, "Fundamental Trends in Israel's Economy," *Middle Eastern Affairs,* May, 1952, p. 139.

[68] E. Levy, *Israel Economic Survey, 1953-1954,* Jerusalem, 1955, p. 12.

[69] *Laws of the State of Israel,* Vol. IV, pp. 93-100 (Encouragement of Capital Investments Law, 1950). For the achievements to the end of 1951, compare address of Prime Minister in *Divrei Haknesset,* 2nd *Knesset,* 55th Session, February 13, 1952, pp. 1315-1321, with *Statistical Abstract of Israel, 1956-1957,* pp. 65, 98, and with Levy, *op. cit.,* pp. 17-18.

[70] P. Hartal, "Changes in Living Standards in Israel," *Middle Eastern Affairs,* February, 1953, pp. 37-50; D. Patinkin, "Monetary and Price Developments in Israel: 1949-1953," *Scripta Hierosolymitana,* Vol. III, pp. 25-27; *Statistical Abstract of Israel, 1956-1957,* p. 159.

[71] On the New Economic Policy and its effects, see Levy, *op. cit.,* pp. 18-24 ff., 55 ff.; Patinkin, *op. cit.,* pp. 28 ff.; *Middle Eastern Affairs,* March, 1952, p. 98; August-September, 1952, p. 260; December, 1952, p. 404; January, 1953, p. 32; May, 1953, p. 198; June-July, 1954, p. 244; December, 1954, pp. 406-407.

[72] See *Statistical Abstract of Israel, 1956–1957,* pp. 64, 65, 81, 82, 185; Levy, *op. cit.,* pp. 84 ff.; *Israel: 10 Years of Progress, 1948-1958,* pp. 18-20. On water development, see G. G. Stevens, "The Jordan River Valley," *International Conciliation,"* January, 1956, pp. 227-283; *Israel Digest,* May 11, 1956, pp. 1-2; *Middle Eastern Affairs,* August-September, 1955, p. 287.

[73] See *Bank of Israel Bulletin,* No. 7, Jerusalem, 1958, p. 57.

[74] American Israel Corporation, *16th Annual Report,* 1957, p. 9.

[75] On developments in industry and transportation, see *Statistical Abstract*

of Israel, 1956-1957, pp. 91-94,98-99, 108-109, 111-113, 116 ff.; United Nations, *Economic Developments in the Middle East, 1955-1956,* New York, 1957, pp. 32-35; Levy, *op. cit.*, pp. 98-118; M. Orion, "Transportation in Israel," *Middle Eastern Affairs,* May, 1953, pp. 172-179; January, 1950, p. 30; April, 1950, p. 129; November, 1950, pp. 338-339; November, 1955, pp. 355-357; May, 1956, p. 204; February, 1957, p. 86; American Israel Corporation, *Annual Report, 1956,* pp. 4-10. On Israel's national income, see *Bank of Israel Bulletin,* p. 20; Bernstein, *op. cit.*, p. 208.

[76] *Statistical Abstract of Israel, 1956-1957,* p. 159. Compare *Bank of Israel Bulletin,* p. 53, and Bernstein, *op. cit.*, p. 219. The table presents the latest figures of the Central Bureau of Statistics, which has recalculated previous data at the single rate of exchange of £I. 1.800=$1. For a detailed analysis of the composition of imports and exports, see L. H. and M. D. Keyserling, *Speeding Israel's Progress,* New York, 1957, pp. 37-42.

[77] For an excellent summary of foreign sources of capital, see Bernstein, *op. cit.*, pp. 211-219. On American aid and its effects, see *Israel Economic Forum,* Vol. VII, November, 1955, pp. 10-29; B. W. McDaniel, "American Technical Assistance and Economic Aid in Israel," *Middle Eastern Affairs,* October, 1955, pp. 303-318; "Facts and Figures: United States Aid to the Middle East, 1945–1957," *ibid.*, November, 1957, pp. 385-390.

[[77a] See Lestschinsky, *op. cit.*]

[78] *Statistical Abstract of Israel, 1956-1957,* p. 185.

[79] See D. Horowitz, *Kalkalat Israel* (*Israel's Economy*), Tel-Aviv, 1958, pp. 385-399, for analysis of income and standard of living. On the problems of manpower, see E. Ginzberg, *Manpower Utilization in Israel,* Tel-Aviv, August, 1953 (Report to the Government of Israel), pp. 1-47; *idem, Second Report on Manpower Utilization in Israel,* Tel-Aviv, June, 1956, pp. 1-45. On development of natural resources, see Levy, *op. cit.*, pp. 87, 120-124. Good accounts of basic economic problems are given in Bernstein, *op. cit.*, pp. 185-192; D. Horowitz, "The Economic Problems of Israel," *Middle Eastern Affairs,* November, 1956, pp. 373-377.

[80] See *Government Yearbook,* 5713 (1952), pp. 124-125; 150-159; *ibid.*, 5715 (1954), p. 132; B. Akzin, *New States and International Organizations,* Paris, 1955, pp. 49, 67 ff., 84-88; *Government Yearbook,* 5713 (1952), pp. 124-125.

[81] See, for example, addresses of Foreign Minister Sharett in the *Knesset, Divrei Haknesset,* 1st *Knesset,* 103rd Session, January 4, 1950, pp. 429–430 ff.; 161st Session, July 4, 1950, pp. 2057-2058; W. Eytan, "Israel's Foreign Policy and International Relations," *Middle Eastern Affairs,* May, 1951, pp. 155-160; *Israel and the United Nations,* pp. 182-187. This report of a study group set up by the Hebrew University of Jerusalem contains an excellent summary of Israel's attitude on various questions that have come before the United Nations.

[82] W. Eytan, *The First Ten Years: A Diplomatic History of Israel,* New York, 1958, p. 84; ch. 4, *passim;* M. Sharett, address in *Knesset, Divrei Haknesset,* 1st *Knesset,* 101st Session, January 2, 1950, pp. 375-380; A. Eban, *Voice of Israel,* New York, 1957, pp. 31-33, 45-61; *Government Yearbook,* 5711 (1950), pp. 143-145. On United Nations proposals and resolutions, see

United Nations, General Assembly, *Official Records,* Plenary Meetings, 4th Session, December 9, 1949, pp. 606-607; 5th Session, December 15, 1950, p. 684; 7th Session, December 18, 1952, p. 413; *ibid., Resolutions,* 4th Session, September 20–December 10, 1949, p. 25; *ibid.,* 5th Session, Supplement No. 9 (Doc. A/1286), and Supplement No. 18 (A/1367/Rev. 1), pp. 10-11. For Israel's position, see *ibid.,* Plenary Meetings, 4th Session, pp. 598-602. See also P. Mohn, "Jerusalem and the United Nations," *International Conciliation,* October, 1950, pp. 425-471.

[83] For Israel's position on the refugee problem, see Eban, *op. cit.,* pp. 33-37, 216-237 (statements of Ambassador Eban before General Assembly on May 5, 1949, and November 18, 1955); Eytan, *op. cit.,* ch. 6.

[84] See Akzin, *op. cit.,* pp. 135-137.

[85] See G. G. Stevens, "The Jordan River Valley," *International Conciliation,* January, 1956, pp. 227-283; D. A. Schmidt, "Prospects for a Solution of the Jordan Valley Dispute," *Middle Eastern Affairs,* January, 1955, pp. 1-12; *Israel and the United Nations,* pp. 105-107.

[86] United Nations, Security Council, *Official Records,* 558th Meeting, September 1, 1951, pp. 1-3; *ibid.,* 664th Meeting, March 29, 1954, pp. 12 ff. See also *Government Yearbook,* 5713 (1952), p. 127; *ibid.,* 5714 (1953-1954), p. 150; *ibid.,* 5715 (1954), p. 125; *ibid.,* 5716 (1955), pp. 184-185; Eban, *op. cit.,* pp. 255-275 (address before the Security Council, October 13, 1956); Eytan, *op. cit.,* pp. 88-104; B. Shwadran, "Egypt Before the Security Council," *Middle Eastern Affairs,* December, 1951, pp. 383-400; E. Ereli, "The Bat Galim Case before the Security Council," *ibid.,* April, 1955, pp. 108-117.

[87] See United Nations, Security Council, *Official Records,* 642nd Meeting, November 24, 1953, p. 21; *Government Yearbook,* 5713 (1952), p. 126; *ibid.,* 5714 (1953-1954), pp. 149-150; *ibid.,* 5715 (1954), pp. 123-155; *ibid.,* 5716 (1955), pp. 180-186; *ibid.,* 5717 (1956), pp. 237-239 ff.; Eytan, *op. cit.,* pp. 104-117; M. Dayan, "Israel's Border and Security Problems," *Foreign Affairs,* January, 1955, pp. 1-18; B. Shwadran, "Israel-Jordan Border Tension," *Middle Eastern Affairs,* December, 1953, pp. 385-401; M. Pearlman, "Bagdad-Gaza-Bandung," *ibid.,* May, 1955, pp. 145-149. For a pro-Arab view on border clashes, see E. H. Hutchison, *Violent Truce: A Military Observer Looks at the Arab-Israeli Conflict, 1951-1955,* New York, 1956, *passim.*

[88] B. Shwadran, *The Middle East, Oil, and the Great Powers,* New York, 1955, presents a thorough and well-documented account of the role of oil in Middle East power politics.

[89] For the text of the Three Power Declaration, see *Middle Eastern Affairs,* June-July, 1950, p. 173.

[90] See address of Foreign Minister Sharett in *Divrei Haknesset,* 2nd *Knesset,* 496th Session, November 15, 1954, pp. 64-66 ff.

[91] See *Government Yearbook,* 5714 (1953-1954), p. 155; *ibid.,* 5716 (1955), pp. 181-184; *ibid.,* 5717 (1956), pp. 239-240, 249-250; Eytan, *op. cit.,* ch. 7; D. J. Dallin, "Soviet Policy in the Middle East," *Middle Eastern Affairs,* November, 1955, pp. 337-344; I. London, "Evolution of the U.S.S.R.'s Policy in Middle East, 1950-1956," *ibid.,* May, 1956, pp. 169-178, and Soviet policy statements, pp. 188-195.

[92] See *Israel and the United Nations,* pp. 289-294.

[93] On the Suez-Sinai crisis, see United Nations, General Assembly, *Official Records,* First Emergency Special Session, *Resolutions,* pp. 2-4, and debates in *ibid., Plenary Meetings,* First Emergency Special Session, November 1-10, 1956, *passim; ibid.,* Eleventh Session, November 12, 1956–March 8, 1957, *Resolutions,* pp. 61-62, and debates in *ibid., Plenary Meetings, passim.* See also *Government Yearbook,* 5718 (1957), pp. 247-251 ff.; *Divrei Haknesset,* 3rd *Knesset,* 228th Session, January 23, 1957, pp. 826-829 ff. (Premier Ben-Gurion's address); Eban, *op. cit.,* pp. 276-292 (Address before General Assembly, November 1, 1956). The exchange of notes between President Eisenhower and Prime Minister Ben-Gurion, and between Premier Bulganin and the latter, are given in *Middle Eastern Affairs,* January, 1957, pp. 13-16. The radio-television address of President Eisenhower, February 20, 1957, is given, in *ibid.,* April, 1957, pp. 139-143. On the lifting of the Aqaba blockade, see P. A. Porter, *The Gulf of Aqaba: An International Waterway,* Washington, 1957, pp. 1-18.

BRIEF BIBLIOGRAPHY

AKZIN, BENJAMIN, *New States and International Organization.* Paris (UNESCO), 1955.

BACHI, ROBERTO (ed.), *Scripta Hierosolymitana.* Vol. III (Studies in Economic and Social Sciences). Jerusalem, 1956.

BARATZ, G., and others, *A New Way of Life: The Collective Settlements of Israel.* London, 1949.

BARATZ, JOSEPH, *A Village by the Jordan.* London, 1954.

BARER, SHLOMO, *The Magic Carpet.* New York, 1952.

BEIGIN, MENACHEM, *The Revolt: Story of the Irgun.* New York, 1951.

BEIN, ALEX, *Theodor Herzl.* Philadelphia, 1941.

BEN-GURION, DAVID, *Rebirth and Destiny of Israel.* New York, 1954.

BEN-JACOB, J., *The Rise of Israel.* New York, 1949.

BEN-SHALOM, A., *Deep Furrows.* New York, 1937.

BENTWICH, NORMAN, *Israel.* New York, 1952.

BERNADOTTE, F., *To Jerusalem.* London, 1951.

BERNSTEIN, MARVER H., *The Politics of Israel.* Princeton, 1957.

BONNÉ, ALFRED, *State and Economics in the Middle East.* 2nd ed. London, 1955.

BURSTEIN, MOSHE, *Self-Government of the Jews in Palestine Since 1900.* Tel-Aviv, 1934.

COHEN, ISRAEL (ed.), *The Rebirth of Israel.* London, 1952.

———, *A Short History of Zionism.* London, 1951.

———, *The Zionist Movement.* New York, 1946.

CROSSMAN, RICHARD, *Palestine Mission.* New York, 1947.

CRUM, BARTLEY C., *Behind the Silken Curtain.* New York, 1947.

DAGAN, PERETZ, *Pillars of Israel Economy.* Tel-Aviv, 1955.

DAVIS, HELEN MILLER, *Constitutions, Electoral Laws, Treaties of States in the Near and Middle East.* Rev. ed. Durham, 1953.

DAVIS, M. (ed.), *Israel: Its Role in Civilization.* New York, 1956.

DE GAURY, GERALD, *The New State of Israel*. New York, 1952.
DE HAAS, J., *Theodor Herzl: A Biographical Study*. 2 Vols. Chicago, 1927.
DUNNER, JOSEPH, *The Republic of Israel*. New York, 1950.
EBAN, ABBA, *Voice of Israel*. New York, 1957.
EISENSTADT, S. N., *The Absorption of Immigrants*. London, 1954.
ELATH, ELIAHU, *Israel and Her Neighbors*. New York, 1957.
Esco Foundation for Palestine, *Palestine: A Study of Jewish, Arab and British Policies*. 2 Vols. New Haven, 1947.
EYTAN, WALTER, *The First Ten Years: A Diplomatic History of Israel*. New York, 1958.
FRANKENSTEIN, CARL (ed.), *Between Past and Future: Essays and Studies on Aspects of Immigrant Absorption in Israel*. Jerusalem, 1953.
GAMZU, HAIM, *Painting and Sculpture in Israel*. Tel-Aviv, 1951.
GARCIA-GRANADOS, JOSÉ, *The Birth of Israel*. New York, 1948.
General Federation of Jewish Labour in Palestine, *Memorandum Submitted to the Anglo-American Commission of Inquiry*. Tel-Aviv, March, 1946. Mimeographed.
GINZBERG, ELI, *Manpower Utilization in Israel*. Tel-Aviv, 1953.
———, *Second Report on Manpower Utilization in Israel*. Tel-Aviv, 1956.
GORDON, A. D., *Selected Essays*. New York, 1938.
Great Britain, Colonial Office, *Mandate for Palestine*, Cmd. 1785. London, 1922.
———, *Palestine Land Transfer Regulations*, Cmd. 6180. London, 1940.
———, *Palestine Partition Commission Report*, Cmd. 5854 (Woodhead Report). London, 1938.
———, *Palestine Royal Commission Report*, Cmd. 5479 (Peel Report). London, 1937.
———, *Palestine Statement of Policy*, Cmd. 6019 (White Paper of 1939). London, 1939.
———, *Reports on the Administration of Palestine and Transjordan*. London, 1920-1938.
GROSSMAN, KURT R., *Germany's Moral Debt: The German-Israel Agreement*. Washington, 1954.
GRUBER, RUTH, *Israel To-day*. New York, 1958.
GRUSHKA, THEODORE (ed.), *The Health Services of Israel*. Jerusalem, 1952.
GUREVICH, D., and GERTZ, A., *Statistical Handbook of Jewish Palestine, 1947*. Jerusalem, 1947.
Hadassah Medical Organization, *Twenty Years of Medical Service to Palestine, 1918-1938*. Jerusalem, 1939.
HALKIN, S., *Modern Hebrew Literature*. New York, 1950.
HANNA, PAUL L., *British Policy in Palestine*. Washington, 1942.
Hebrew Encyclopedia, The. Vol. VI. Jerusalem, 1957.
HOROWITZ, DAVID, *Kalkalat Israel*. Tel-Aviv, 1958.
———, *State in the Making*. New York, 1953.
HUEBNER, T., and VOSS, C. H., *This Is Israel*. New York, 1956.
HUREWITZ, J. C., *Diplomacy in the Near and Middle East*. Vol. II. Princeton, 1956.

———, *The Struggle for Palestine*. New York, 1950.
HUTCHISON, E. H., *Violent Truce: A Military Observer Looks at the Arab-Israeli Conflict, 1951-1955*. New York, 1956.
HYAMSON, ALBERT M., *Palestine Under the Mandate, 1920-1948*. London, 1950.
Israel, Government of, *Cooperative Societies in Israel, 1956*. Jerusalem, 1957.
———, *Divrei Haknesset* (Official Records of the *Knesset* in Hebrew). Jerusalem, February 14, 1949, to date.
———, *Government Yearbook*. Jerusalem, 1950-1957.
———, *Iton Rishmi, Moetzet Hamedinah Hazmanit* (Records of the Provisional State Council). Tel-Aviv, May 16, 1948–February 10, 1949.
———, *Laws of the State of Israel* (Official English translation). Jerusalem, Vols. 1-9. This series thus far includes laws enacted during 1948-1956. For subsequent legislation, see *Reshumot, Sepher Hahukkim*.
———, *Statistical Abstract of Israel*. Jerusalem, 1949/1950–1956/1957.
Israel and the United Nations (report of a Study Group set up by The Hebrew University of Jerusalem; prepared for the Carnegie Endowment for International Peace). New York, 1956.
Israel Economist, The: Annual. Jerusalem, 1949/1950–1956/1957.
Israel Yearbook, The. Tel-Aviv, 1950-1951 to 1957.
KALLEN, H. M., *Utopians at Bay*. New York, 1958.
KANIEVSKY, I., *Social Policy and Social Insurance in Palestine*. Tel-Aviv, 1947.
KIMCHE, JON, *Seven Fallen Pillars: The Middle East, 1945-1952*. New York, 1953.
KRAINES, OSCAR, *Israel: The Emergence of a New Nation*. Washington, D. C., 1954.
KURLAND, S., *Cooperative Palestine: The Story of the Histadrut*. New York, 1947.
LAQUEUR, WALTER Z., *Communism and Nationalism in the Middle East*. New York, 1956.
LEHRMAN, HAL, *Israel: The Beginning and Tomorrow*. New York, 1951.
LEVENSOHN, L., *Vision and Fulfillment*. New York, 1950.
LEVIN, HARRY, *I Saw the Battle of Jerusalem*. New York, 1950.
LEVY, EMANUEL, *Israel Economic Survey, 1953-1954*. Jerusalem, 1955.
LITVINOFF, BARNET, *Ben-Gurion of Israel*. New York, 1954.
MCDONALD, JAMES G., *My Mission in Israel, 1948-1951*. New York, 1951.
NATHAN, ROBERT; GASS, OSCAR; and CREAMER, D., *Palestine: Problem and Promise*. Washington, 1956.
O'BALLANCE, EDGAR, *The Arab-Israeli War, 1948*. London, 1956.
PATAI, RAPHAEL, *Israel Between East and West*. Philadelphia, 1953.
PEARLMAN, MOSHE, *The Army of Israel*. New York, 1950.
PERETZ, DON, *Israel and the Arab Refugees*. 2 Vols. New York, 1955. Mimeographed.
RABINOWICZ, OSKAR K., *Fifty Years of Zionism*. London, 1952.
———, Herzl, *Architect of the Balfour Declaration*. New York, 1958.
RACKMAN, EMANUEL, *Israel's Emerging Constitution, 1948-1951*. New York, 1955.
REVUSKY, ABRAHAM, *Jews in Palestine*. New York, 1945.

ROBINSON, JACOB, *Palestine and the United Nations*. Washington, 1947.
ROSENNE, SHABTAI, *Israel's Armistice Agreements with the Arab States*. Tel-Aviv, 1951.
ROYAL INSTITUTE OF INTERNATIONAL AFFAIRS, *Great Britain and Palestine, 1915-1945*. London, 1946.
RUPPIN, A., *Three Decades of Palestine*. Jerusalem, 1936.
SABAGH, S., (transl.) *Be'eynei Oyev* (Through the Eyes of the Enemy). Tel-Aviv, 1954.
SACHER, HARRY, *Israel: The Establishment of a State*. New York, 1952.
SAMUEL, EDWIN, *Handbook of the Jewish Communal Villages in Palestine*. Jerusalem, 1945.
———, *Problems of Government in the State of Israel*. Jerusalem, 1956.
SCHECHTMAN, JOSEPH B., *The Arab Refugee Problem*, New York, 1952.
SHWADRAN, BENJAMIN, *The Middle East, Oil and the Great Powers*. New York, 1955.
SOKOLOW, N., *History of Zionism, 1600-1918*. 2 Vols. London, 1919.
SPEISER, E. A., *The United States and the Near East*. Cambridge, Mass., 1950.
SPIEGEL, M., and others, *The Hebrew University of Jerusalem, 1925-1950*. Jerusalem, 1950.
SPIEGEL, S., *Hebrew Reborn*. New York, 1930.
SPIRO, M. E., *Kibbutz: Venture in Utopia*. Cambridge, Mass., 1956.
SYRKIN, MARIE, *Way of Valor, A Biography of Golda Myerson*. New York, 1955.
TAUBER, E., *Molding Society to Man: Israel's New Adventure in Cooperation*. New York, 1955.
ULITZUR, A., *Two Decades of Keren Hayesod (A Survey of Facts and Figures, 1921-1940)*. Jerusalem, 1940.
UNITED NATIONS, General Assembly. *Official Records*.
———, Security Council. *Official Records*.
———, *Monograph on Community Settlements and Report of the Survey Mission on Community Organization and Development in Israel*. United Nations, 1954.
———, Conciliation Commission for Palestine. *Progress Reports*, 1949 ff.
———, Department of Economic and Social Affairs. *Economic Developments in the Middle East* (varying titles), 1949/1950–1955/1956. New York, 1951-1957.
———, Special Committee on Palestine. *Report to the General Assembly*, U.N. Doc. A/364.
United States, Department of State, *Anglo-American Committee of Inquiry: Report, April 20, 1946*. Washington, D.C., 1946.
WEIZMANN, CHAIM, *Trial and Error*. London, 1949.
WALLENROD, REUBEN, *The Literature of Modern Israel*. New York, 1956.
WEINGARTEN, MURRAY, *Life in a Kibbutz*. New York, 1955.
WILLIAMS, L. F. RUSHBROOK, *The State of Israel*. London, 1957.
UNESCO, *International Social Science Bulletin*, Vol. VIII, No. 1. Paris, 1956.
ZIDON, ASHER, *Haknesset*. Tel-Aviv, 1950.

II

THE ROLE OF JUDAISM IN CIVILIZATION

CHAPTER 15

THE BIBLE AS A CULTURAL MONUMENT

By Robert Gordis

I. Attitudes Toward the Bible—Old and New

The observation made almost two centuries ago by Voltaire that "*La Bible est plus célèbre que connue*" is as true today as ever before. Many factors have conspired to produce this unfortunate situation, some superficial, others more fundamental. Many a prospective reader is deterred by the form in which the Bible is generally presented—the columns closely printed, the verses numbered as in a catalogue, with no distinction indicated between prose and poetry, between genealogical tables and exalted poetic utterances. A more basic hindrance to the widespread appreciation of the Bible today is, strangely enough, the veneration in which it is held as the Word of God. As a result, most readers turn to it with more devoutness than alertness and expect to be edified rather than stimulated by its contents.

The most important factor, however, leading to the neglect of the Book of Books in modern times is the confusion prevalent in men's attitude toward the Bible. In this respect, as in so many others, our age is a period of transition, with "one world dying, another powerless to be born." Two conceptions are to be met with today, one steadily losing ground, the other possessing implications as yet imperfectly understood. These contemporary attitudes reflect two stages in the development of Western thought.

For the greater part of its history, until the eighteenth century, Western civilization approached the Bible dogmatically through the theory of verbal inspiration. For nearly two millennia the Bible was regarded as the repository of God's messages to the human race, literal transcripts of His will revealed to worthy men through the ages. The role of the biblical authors was fundamentally passive. Their distinction lay in their moral and spiritual greatness, which made them worthy of receiving the Divine Revelation. Thus, in dealing with the closing verses of Deuteronomy, which describe the death and burial of Moses, the Talmud declares: "The Holy One, blessed be He, was dictating and Moses was writing with a tear."[1]

As will be noted below, this conception of the literal inspiration of the Bible began undergoing reinterpretation as soon as it was subjected to scrutiny by talmudists, theologians and philosophers. But for the masses of the people it remained the regnant view. In large measure it has retained its hold upon devout believers in both Judaism and Christianity to the present day.

This attitude has several important implications. If Scripture is a literal transcript of God's Word, everything in it is of equal importance. As Maimonides quite rightly insisted, the genealogies of Esau in Genesis are no less sacred than the Ten Commandments or the *Shema*.

Moreover, everything within it is forever binding, being an emanation of the Eternal. Hence, many centuries after the composition of the Bible, the Puritans could adopt the Old Testament as the basis of their polity in the New World without the slightest doubt as to its relevance to their problems. At the same time, without any sense of anachronism, they could validate the burning of the witches in Salem by a reference to Ex. 22:17 which declares: "Thou shalt not suffer a witch to live."

The drawbacks inherent in this second implication were largely overcome in Judaism because of a third. Since the Bible is the Word of God, every apparently unimportant word and insignificant incident must have a deeper meaning. In order that the true intent of the Bible be revealed, the text is therefore in need of interpretation. Thus there developed various schools of biblical interpretation, which sought to reveal this hidden meaning of the text by finding important implications in the repetition of words and phrases, and by drawing deductions from each particle and copula, often from each syllable. The imposing development of the Talmud rests upon this method of textual interpretation. Given the premise, the conclusion was inescapably logical—a message coming directly from the Divine could have nothing accidental or superfluous, either in its content or in its form.

Whatever our attitude toward this approach to the Bible, it should be noted that the modern world owes it an incalculable debt, all too often ignored. In the first instance, it meant that the Bible remained a living and evolving law, keeping pace with new conditions and growing insights. Thus, to cite a few instances at random, almost two thousand years ago the rabbis had, by a process of biblical interpretation, virtually eliminated capital punishment, in spite of its frequent mention in the Pentateuch, and interpreted "an eye for an eye" to mean monetary compensation for damages. Similarly, talmudic law abolished the execution of "a stubborn and rebellious son," enjoined in Scripture (Deut. 21:18-21). It also modified the biblical prohibition of interest in order to meet the needs of commercial credit in an advanced society. Particularly noteworthy is the extension of the rights of women beyond the narrow limits of the ancient

Orient. This was accomplished very simply. All the biblical passages which speak of a *na'arah*, or "girl," as being in the power of her father, who could sell her into slavery or marriage, were referred to a girl between the ages of twelve and twelve and a half! Before that age, she was a *ketanah*, or a "minor," and entitled to special protection. Above that age she was a *bogeret*, or "mature" woman and hence free from the *patria potestas*.

Moreover, this conception of the verbal inspiration of the Bible is to be credited with the creation of a fascinating literature in its own right. The vast nonlegal material in the Talmud and in the independent compilations of the Midrash called the Haggada[2a] consists of ethics, legends and folk wisdom of incomparable value and scope. Most of this literature takes the form of interpretations of biblical passages.

This conception of the literal inspiration of Scripture not only produced an evolving law and a rich ethical and religious literature. It also made possible the creation of religious philosophy in Judaism and in Christianity. In two periods, the traditional religion of the Western world came into contact with Greek philosophy. The first was at the beginning of the Common Era, when Alexandria was the cultural center of the world. The second came some eight or nine hundred years later. First in Bagdad and then in Spain, Arab scholars and thinkers, together with their Jewish confrères, were engaged in preserving and expounding the writings of the Greek philosophers, which were neglected and forgotten in Christian Europe. In addition, new discoveries in mathematics and the sciences were enriching and modifying the ideas to be found in these philosophic classics. From this vast and far-flung intellectual activity, there emerged a world view greatly at variance with traditional concepts found in the Bible.

The conflict was resolved by the allegorical interpretation of Scripture, which had been previously utilized with great skill by Philo of Alexandria in the first century. A great line of philosophically trained thinkers arose during the Middle Ages, who interpreted the biblical text so as to bring it into harmony with the "modern" thought of their age. In the process they broadened immeasurably the horizons of traditional religion, besides making many fruitful contributions to philosophy. It is paradoxical but true that the apparently naïve conception of the Bible as the direct dictation of God was the basis for the great medieval philosophical systems of Saadia, Maimonides, Crescas, and their associates.[3a]

The most important debt owing to this dogmatic attitude still remains to be noted: to it we owe the preservation of the Bible. At a time when the great classics of Greek and Latin literature were being neglected and in many instances lost in the West, the Bible was being preserved with loving care, both in the Hebrew original by Jewish scribes and in the Greek and Latin translations by Christian monks. The achievement of these Hebrew scribes, called *masoretes* or "preservers of tradition," has not been sufficiently appreciated. These nameless scribes copied the Sacred Book with meticulous and loving care. Carefully they noted every letter and every detail of spelling, accentuation and musical notation, in order to prevent errors or changes in the text which they had received from earlier ages. They did not hesitate to count the letters and verses in each book, and noted every exceptional form in spelling or usage. The extent of their veneration for the Bible can be judged by their observation that the middle word of the entire Pentateuch was *darash* in Lev. 10:16 and that the middle letter of the entire Bible was the *yod* in the word *bayyir* in Jer. 6:7!

The development of talmudic law, the creation of the religio-ethical literature of the Rabbis, and the growth of medieval Jewish philosophy, as well as the physical preservation of the Bible, all rested upon the theory of literal inspiration. But the detailed study and analysis of the biblical text led to a recognition that there were differences within the Bible which could be explained only in terms of the human factor. The prophets and poets of the Bible were not mere passive vessels for the Divine, or their messages would have been identical in form and content. They were active participants in the process of Revelation, reflecting or refracting the Divine Light in accordance with the depth of their insight and their spiritual capacity. Thus the Talmud noted the differences in the theophanies described by the prophets Isaiah and Ezekiel. It explained that Isaiah's simple and majestic vision of God (ch. 6) was like the reaction of a city dweller accustomed to the proximity of the royal court, while Ezekiel's circumstantial and elaborate picture of the heavenly chariot (2:8) reflected the attitude of a rustic dazzled by the unwonted spectacle of royal splendor.[4] Similarly, Moses' pre-eminence over the later prophets was graphically expressed by comparing him to a stargazer with a clear telescope while they had blurred instruments of vision.[5]

The talmudic Sages could not overlook the obvious fact that, while the Torah and the prophets seemed to be citing the words of the Deity ("The Lord spake to Moses saying," "Thus saith the Lord"), there were other books in the Bible which made no such claim and were obviously human in origin. The beloved Book of Psalms consisted of hymns addressed by men to their Maker. Job was a flaming protest against the apparent miscarriage of justice in Divine Government. The Book of Esther does not so much as mention the Divine Name.

Hence, it was recognized early that there were different levels of inspiration in the Bible. The highest was represented by the Torah, the second by the Prophets, and the lowest by the Hagiographa. This distinction became a principle of talmudic jurisprudence: "Matters of Law [Torah] are not deducible from other biblical books."[6] Similarly in its provisions for the handling and exchange of scrolls of the Torah and the

ומקדשי תיראו. לא יכנס לו במקלו ובמנעלו ובאפונדתו ובאבק שעל רגליו ואף על פי שאני מזהירכם על המקדש את שבתותי תשמרו אין בנין בית המקדש דוחה שבת: אל תפנו אל האבות. אזהרה לבעל אוב וידעוני. בעל אוב זה פיתום המדבר משחיו: וידעוני. המכניס עצם חיה ששמה ידוע לתוך פיו והעצם מדבר: אל תבקשו. להיות עסוקים בם שאם תבקשו בם אתם מטמאים לפני ואני מתעב אתכם: אני ה' אלהיכם. דעו את מי אתם מחליפין במי: מפני שיבה תקום. יכול זקן אשמאי ת"ל זקן אין זקן אלא שקנה חכמה: והדרת פני זקן. איזהו הדור לא ישב במקומו ולא יסתור את דבריו יכול יעצים עיניו כמי שלא ראהו לכך נאמר ויראת מאלהיך שהרי דבר זה מסור ללב ללבו של עושהו שאין מכיר בו אלא הוא וכל דבר המסור ללב נאמר בו ויראת מאלהיך: לא תונו. אונאת דברים לא תאמר לו אמש היית עובד עבודה זרה ועכשיו אתה בא ללמוד תורה שנתנה מפי הגבורה: כי גרים הייתם. מום שבך אל תאמר לחבירך: אני ה' אלהיכם. אלהיך ואלהיו אני: לא תעשו עול במשפט. אם לדין הרי כבר נאמר לא תעשו עול במשפט ומהו משפט השני כאן היא המדה והמשקל והמשורה מלמד שהמודד נקרא דיין שאם שקר במדה הרי הוא כמקלקל את הדין וקרוי עול שנוי ומשוקץ חרם ותועבה וגורם לחמשה דברים האמורים בדיין מטמא את הארץ ומחלל את השם ומסלק את השכינה ומפיל את ישראל בחרב ומגלה אותם מארצם: במדה. זו מדת הארץ: במשקל. כמשמעו: ובמשורה. היא מדת הלח והיבש: אבני צדק. הם המשקולות ששוקלין כנגדן: איפה. היא מדת היבש: הין. זו היא מדת הלח: אשר הוצאתי אתכם. על מנת כן. דבר אחר אני הבחנתי במצרים בין טפה של בכור לטפה שאינה של בכור ואני הנאמן ליפרע ממי שטומן משקלותיו במלח להונות את הבריות שאין מכירין בהם: ואל בני ישראל תאמר. ענשין על האזהרות: מות יומת. בבית דין ואם אין כח בבית דין עם הארץ מסייעין אותן: עם הארץ. עם שבגינו נבראת הארץ שעתידין לירש את הארץ על ידי מצות הללו: אתן את פני. פנאי שלי פונה אני מכל עסקי ועוסק בו: באיש. ולא בצבור שאין כל הצבור נכרתין: כי מזרעו נתן למולך. לפי שנאמר מעביר בנו ובתו באש בן בנו ובן בתו מנין תלמוד לומר כי מזרעו נתן למולך זרע פסול מנין תלמוד לומר בתתו מזרעו למולך: למען טמא את מקדשי. את כנסת ישראל שהיא מקודשת לי כלשון ולא יחלל את מקדשי: אם העלם יעלימו. אם העלימו בדבר אחד סוף שיעלימו בדברים הרבה אם העלימה סנהדרי קטנה סוף שיעלימו סנהדרי גדולה: ובמשפחתו. אר"ש וכי משפחה מה חטאה אלא ללמדך שאין לך משפחה שיש בה מוכס שאין כולן מוכסין שכולן מחפין עליו: והכרתי אותו. למה נאמר לפי שנ' במשפחה יכול יהיו כל המשפחה בהכרת תלמוד לומר אותו אותו בהכרת ולא כל המשפחה בהכרת אלא ביסורין:

וטעם להזכיר את שבתותי תשמורו בעבור המת שאין אבל בשבת. וטעם ומקדשי תיראו על הכהן הגדול שלא יהיה כשאר האבלי' וכן אזהרה על כל אנשי המקדש. וטעם אני יי' שאם לא יראו ממקדשו ויתנו לו כבוד יענישם. וטעם להזכיר האובות וידענים בעבור המת וכן כתוב בישעיה בעד החיים אל המתים: האובות. מגזרת וכאובות חדשים כי הם עיקר זאת האומנות והידעוני. מגזרת דעת שיבקשו לדעת העתידות וריקי מוח אמרו לולי שהאובות אמת גם כן דרך הכשוף לא אסרם הכתוב ואני אומר הפך דבריהם כי הכתוב לא אסר האמת רק השקר והשוא האלילים והפסילים ולולי שאין רצוני להאריך הייתי מבאר דבר בעלת אוב בראיות גמורות. וטעם אל תפנו לידע האומנות. וטעם אל תבקשו לשאול כשואל. וטעם אני יי' אלהיכם שלא תבקשו כי אם השם לבדו והנה הזכיר לטמאה כי נפש הפוך והמבקש טמאה היא כי איננה דבקה בשם. וטעם להזכיר מפני שיבה תקום. בעבור המת כי הזקן קרוב למית כי גופו כמת נחשב והנה טעמו כל זקן וכל איש שיבה. וטעם ויראת מאלהיך שיענישך בימי הזקנה: וכי יגור אתך גר. הזכירו אחר הזקן והטעם כאשר הזהרתיך לכבד הזקן הישראלי בעבור שאין לו כח כך אזהירך על הגר שאתה גדול ממנו או בעבור שאין לו כח שהוא בארצך ברשותך: ואהבת לו. מפורש. וטעם לא תעשו עול בעבור הגר כטעם ושפטתם צדק בין איש ובין אחיו ובין גרו וכן במדה שלא תעשה מרמה במדת האמות גם האמות משתנות ויתכן להיות פי' כמשפט הידוע בארץ: מאזני צדק אבני צדק. פירוש במשקל. איפת צדק. כיבש: והין צדק. בלח פי' במשורה. וטעם אני יי' אלהיכם אשר הוצאתי אתכם בעבור שהזכיר כי גרים הייתם בארץ מצרים על כן אתם חייבי' לשמור חקותי ומשפטי בלבבכם ועשיתם אותם. וטעם אני יי' שתרדפו אחרי החקות שמתתי בכם כי כלם צדק. וטעם וידבר יי' אל משה לאמר בעבור כי אלה המצות חיוב על כל ישר' ואין גר עמם על כן כתוב בתחלה אל כל עדת ישר' ועתה יחל להזכיר עונש הזנות על כל מי שהוא דר בארץ ישראל אזרח או גר תושב והחל מהקשה שבכלם והוא אשר יתן מזרעו למולך והטעם לשבב עם עובדת ע"ז. וטעם עם הארץ ארץ שהוא דר בה אזרח או גר וזה בפרהסיא: ואני אתן את פני באיש ההוא. אם היה בסתר ויש כי טעמו להכרית זרעו: למען טמא את מקדשי. שהוא בתוך ארץ ישראל: ולחלל את שם קדשי. שישמעו הגוים והיה נראה לנו כי טעם באבן שם המין כמו ויהי לי שור וחמור ודברי הקבלה נכונים והם אמת. ויאמר רבי יונה המדקדק הספרדי נ"ע כי פי' ובמשפחתו הדומה אליו ומי הביאנו בצרה הזאת רק פי' כמשמעו כי עם הארץ יעלימו עיניהם בעבור שהם ממשפחתו. וטעם

האבת ו' וחס' בליש' וסימ' בסדור אלה כסעי גבי פסו' ויונו באבת: וכי יגור אתך ב' וסימ' ועשה פסח ליי'. גר בארצכם: כאזרח ג' קמצין וסימ' כאזרח מכם. כאזרח בבני ישראל. ומתערה כאזרח רענן: במשפט ח' דגשים וסימ' לא תעשו עול במשפט. וחברו. ויגבה יי' צבאות. על כן לא יקומו רשעים. ודרך ענוים.

אֶת־שַׁבְּתֹתַי תִּשְׁמֹרוּ וּמִקְדָּשִׁי תִּירָאוּ אֲנִי יְהוָה׃ אַל־תִּפְנוּ אֶל־הָאֹבֹת וְאֶל־הַיִּדְּעֹנִים אַל־תְּבַקְשׁוּ לְטָמְאָה בָהֶם אֲנִי יְהוָה אֱלֹהֵיכֶם׃ מִפְּנֵי שֵׂיבָה תָּקוּם וְהָדַרְתָּ פְּנֵי זָקֵן וְיָרֵאתָ מֵּאֱלֹהֶיךָ אֲנִי יְהוָה׃ ס וְכִי־יָגוּר אִתְּךָ גֵּר בְּאַרְצְכֶם לֹא תוֹנוּ אֹתוֹ׃ כְּאֶזְרָח מִכֶּם יִהְיֶה לָכֶם הַגֵּר ׀ הַגָּר אִתְּכֶם וְאָהַבְתָּ לוֹ כָּמוֹךָ כִּי־גֵרִים הֱיִיתֶם בְּאֶרֶץ מִצְרָיִם אֲנִי יְהוָה אֱלֹהֵיכֶם׃ לֹא־תַעֲשׂוּ עָוֶל בַּמִּשְׁפָּט בַּמִּדָּה בַּמִּשְׁקָל וּבַמְּשׂוּרָה׃ מֹאזְנֵי צֶדֶק אַבְנֵי־צֶדֶק אֵיפַת צֶדֶק וְהִין צֶדֶק יִהְיֶה לָכֶם אֲנִי יְהוָה אֱלֹהֵיכֶם אֲשֶׁר־הוֹצֵאתִי אֶתְכֶם מֵאֶרֶץ מִצְרָיִם׃ וּשְׁמַרְתֶּם אֶת־כָּל־חֻקֹּתַי וְאֶת־כָּל־מִשְׁפָּטַי וַעֲשִׂיתֶם אֹתָם אֲנִי יְהוָה׃ פ

וַיְדַבֵּר יְהוָה אֶל־מֹשֶׁה לֵּאמֹר׃ וְאֶל־בְּנֵי יִשְׂרָאֵל תֹּאמַר אִישׁ אִישׁ מִבְּנֵי יִשְׂרָאֵל וּמִן־הַגֵּר ׀ הַגָּר בְּיִשְׂרָאֵל אֲשֶׁר יִתֵּן מִזַּרְעוֹ לַמֹּלֶךְ מוֹת יוּמָת עַם הָאָרֶץ יִרְגְּמֻהוּ בָאָבֶן׃ וַאֲנִי אֶתֵּן אֶת־פָּנַי בָּאִישׁ הַהוּא וְהִכְרַתִּי אֹתוֹ מִקֶּרֶב עַמּוֹ כִּי מִזַּרְעוֹ נָתַן לַמֹּלֶךְ לְמַעַן טַמֵּא אֶת־מִקְדָּשִׁי וּלְחַלֵּל אֶת־שֵׁם קָדְשִׁי׃ וְאִם הַעְלֵם יַעְלִימוּ עַם הָאָרֶץ אֶת־עֵינֵיהֶם מִן־הָאִישׁ הַהוּא בְּתִתּוֹ מִזַּרְעוֹ לַמֹּלֶךְ לְבִלְתִּי הָמִית אֹתוֹ׃ וְשַׂמְתִּי אֲנִי אֶת־פָּנַי בָּאִישׁ הַהוּא וּבְמִשְׁפַּחְתּוֹ וְהִכְרַתִּי אֹתוֹ

יָת יוֹמֵי שַׁבַּיָּא דִּילִי תִּטְּרוּן וּלְבֵית מַקְדְּשִׁי תְּהוֹן דָּחֲלִין אֲנָא יְיָ׃ לָא תִתְפְּנוּן בָּתַר בִּדִין וּזְכוּרוּ לָא תִתְבְּעוּן לְאִסְתַּאָבָא בְהוֹן אֲנָא יְיָ אֱלָהֲכוֹן׃ מִן קֳדָם דְּסָבַר בְּאוֹרָיְתָא תְּקוּם וּתְהַדַּר אַפֵּי סָבָא וְתִדְחַל מֵאֱלָהָךְ אֲנָא יְיָ׃ וַאֲרֵי יִתְגַּיַּר עִמְּכוֹן גִּיּוֹרָא בְּאַרְעֲכוֹן לָא תוֹנוּן יָתֵיהּ׃ כִּיצִּיבָא מִנְּכוֹן יְהֵי לְכוֹן גִּיּוֹרָא דְּיִתְגַּיַּר עִמְּכוֹן וְתִרְחַם לֵיהּ כְּוָתָךְ אֲרֵי דַּיָּרִין הֲוֵיתוּן בְּאַרְעָא דְמִצְרָיִם אֲנָא יְיָ אֱלָהֲכוֹן׃ לָא תַעְבְּדוּן שְׁקַר בְּדִין בְּמִשְׁחֲתָא בְּמַתְקָלָא וּבִמְכִילְתָּא׃ מֹאזְנָוָן דִּקְשׁוֹט מַתְקָלִין דִּקְשׁוֹט מְכִילָן דִּקְשׁוֹט וְהִינִין דִּקְשׁוֹט יְהוֹן לְכוֹן אֲנָא יְיָ אֱלָהֲכוֹן דִּי אַפֵּקִית יָתְכוֹן מֵאַרְעָא דְמִצְרָיִם׃ וְתִטְּרוּן יָת כָּל קְיָמַי וְיָת כָּל דִּינַי וְתַעְבְּדוּן יָתְהוֹן אֲנָא יְיָ׃

וּמַלֵּיל יְיָ עִם מֹשֶׁה לְמֵימָר׃ וְלִבְנֵי יִשְׂרָאֵל תֵּימַר גְּבַר גְּבַר מִבְּנֵי יִשְׂרָאֵל וּמִן גִּיּוֹרַיָּא דְּיִתְגַּיְּרוּן בְּיִשְׂרָאֵל דְּיִתֵּן מִזַּרְעֵיהּ לְמֹלֶךְ אִתְקְטָלָא יִתְקְטֵל עַמָּא בֵּית יִשְׂרָאֵל יִרְגְּמֻנֵּיהּ בְּאַבְנָא׃ וַאֲנָא אֶתֵּן יָת רוּגְזִי בְּגַבְרָא הַהוּא וְאֵשֵׁיצֵי יָתֵיהּ מִגּוֹ עַמֵּיהּ אֲרֵי מִזַּרְעֵיהּ יְהַב לְמֹלֶךְ בְּדִיל לְסָאָבָא יָת מַקְדְּשִׁי וּלְאַחָלָא יָת שְׁמָא דְקוּדְשִׁי׃ וְאִם מִכְבַּשׁ יִכְבְּשׁוּן עַמָּא בֵּית יִשְׂרָאֵל יָת עֵינֵיהוֹן מִן גַּבְרָא הַהוּא בְּדִיְהַב מִזַּרְעֵיהּ לְמֹלֶךְ בְּדִיל דְּלָא לְמִקְטַל יָתֵיהּ׃ וְאֵשַׁוֵּי אֲנָא יָת רוּגְזִי בְּגַבְרָא הַהוּא וּבְסַעֲדוֹהִי וְאֵשֵׁיצֵי יָתֵיהּ

שאת פני רשע לא טוב. טבח בחור בילדותך. וכל איוב דכו' כבא על זה פקחת עיניך: במדה ג' דגשים וסימ' לא תעשו עול במשפט. אך רחוק יהיה. במדה הראשונה אמות עשרים. דדה. אנך. וס' בלשון תרגום תעברון רחיקן אריכין: במשקל ד' דגשים וסימ' לא תעשו עול במשפט. והשיבו לחכם במשקל. לזהב במשקל בזקק. לבזבח הנחשת: ואני אתן ב' וסימ' ואני אתן את שברך. ואני אתן את פני באיש ההוא: באיש ח' קמצין וסימ' ויפצרו באיש בלוט. ויצו אבימלך. ואני אתן את פני. לא יאבה יי' סלח לו. ויחר אף דוד באיש באד. והשמתיהו לאות ולמשלים. ושמתי אני את פני. מה לעשות לאיש: טמא ב' דגשים וס' ב' טמא יטמאנו. לבען טמא את:

בן בנו ובן בתו מנין

5 18 א יח

[margin notes, partly legible:] ו' חס' בליש · ג' פס' · ז' וחס' ל' · ל' · ג' קמצין · ל' דגש' · ל' דגש' · ל' · ל' · מ' ל' בל' · ל' · ל' דגש' · ל' · סיפין ל' · כל כתי' כן · ל' · אל לא תפנו · מדה ג' דגש' · ל'

A Page from the Rabbinical Bible
Leviticus (19.30-20.5)

Bomberg edition, Venice, 1524-1525

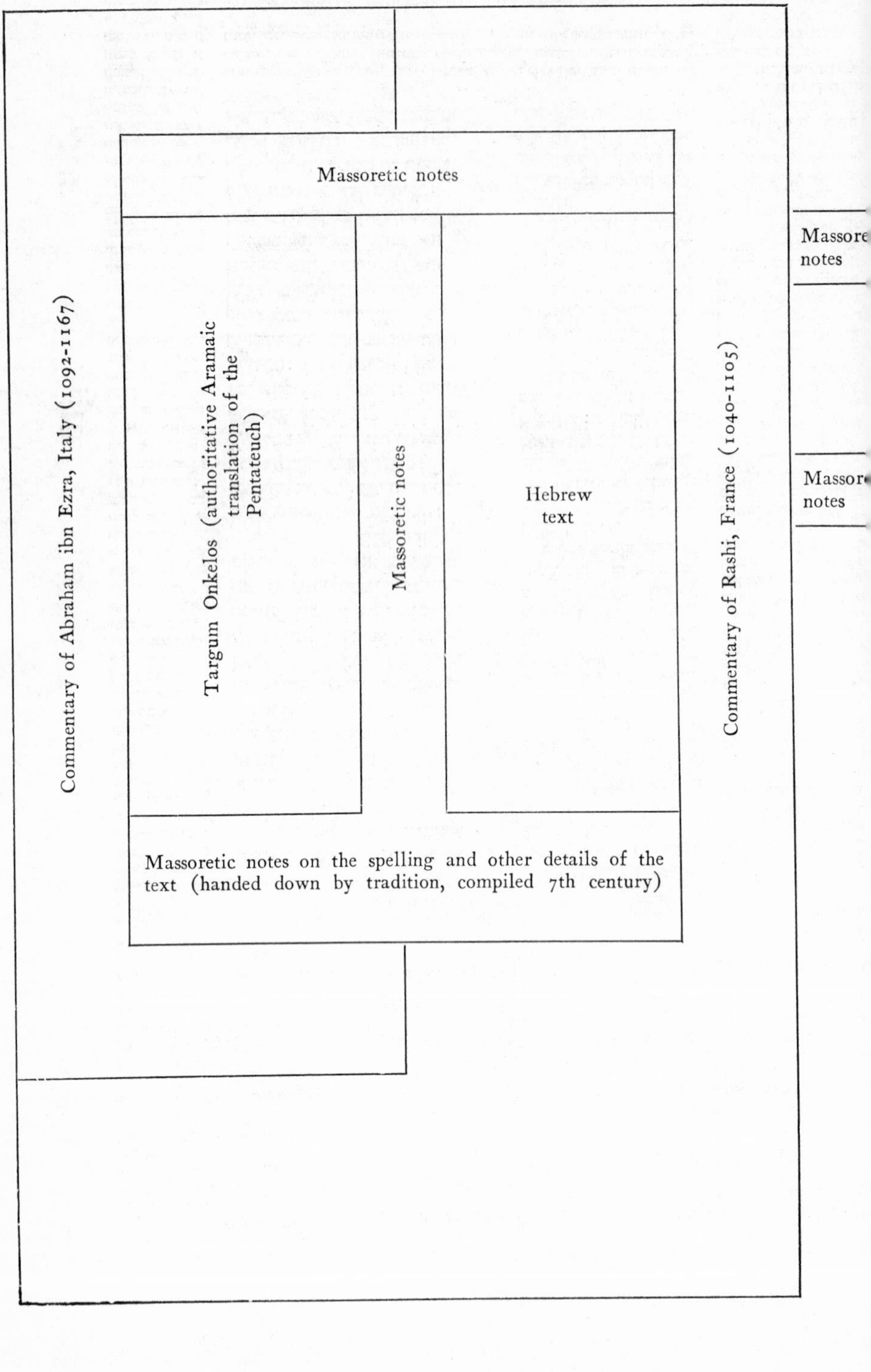

Prophets, as well as in other legal enactments, the Mishna recognized the higher sanctity of the Torah.

Some influential teachers in the mishnaic period opposed the extremely painful forms of biblical interpretations which made elaborate deductions from particles or stylistic repetitions. Thus the school of Rabbi Ishmael laid down the principle that was destined to become very fruitful in later days, that "The Torah speaks in the language of man."[7] For all its fondness for homiletic and allegorical interpretations, the Talmud recognized that the literal meaning of a text must take precedence over its figurative interpretation, declaring, "The literal meaning of a verse may not be disregarded."[8]

Moreover, the masoretes, whose principal activity followed the compilation of the Talmud, amassed a good deal of sound grammatical material during their ceaseless labors to protect the biblical text. In the tenth century the Gaon, Saadia ben Joseph noticed the similarities of biblical and Rabbinic Hebrew. His contemporary, Judah ibn Koreish, recognized the resemblances of Hebrew to its sister tongues Aramaic and Arabic. Between them, these two scholars laid the foundations of comparative Semitic philology.

The scattered and unsystematic linguistic observations of the masoretes were replaced by the scientific grammatical studies of brilliant philologists like Judah Hayyuj and Abulwalid ibn Janah and by the notable commentaries of gifted exegetes like Rashi, the Kimhis, Abraham ibn Ezra, and a host of others. Their scientific works attained a level of achievement that bears favorable comparison with those of our own day.

Thus, imperceptibly, the basis was laid for a human approach to the Bible that would regard it not as the dictation of God to men, but as the record of man's aspiration to God. Religious thinkers might still regard the Bible as the inspired Word of God, but man now became the agent and not merely the recipient of the Divine Revelation.

This revolutionary attitude toward the Bible began to dominate the thinking of most modern men in the eighteenth century. In the past the Bible had been regarded as great because it was holy. It was now regarded as holy because it was great. The lectures of Bishop Robert Lowth of Oxford on *The Sacred Poetry of the Hebrews* and on Isaiah, and the rhapsodic discourses of Johann Gottfried Herder in Germany on *The Oldest Sources of Humanity*, led to a new aesthetic appreciation of the Bible as literature, as the expression of the national spirit of Israel during its most creative period.

Resting upon the foundations of medieval learning, the modern age has built the imposing structure of biblical scholarship, which today includes a score of disciplines. Comparative philology has revealed the relation of Hebrew to other members of the Semitic group, the vocabulary and grammatical structure of which have shed light upon the biblical idiom. The text-critical study of the Bible has often revealed the true meaning of the text and in many instances faulty passages have been corrected. The higher critical study of the Bible has revealed a great deal concerning the sources, composition and mutual relationship of the various books and helped us understand the message of the biblical authors against the background of their times. Ancient civilizations have been brought to light whose literary and material remains have re-created the history of the ancient Orient and illumined almost every page of the Bible. Above all, archaeology and the allied sciences of comparative religion and anthropology have enlarged the frame within which the Bible is to be set.

Our conceptions regarding the development of biblical civilization and its literature are still in flux, to be sure. There are untold variations of attitude among contemporary scholars, varying all the way from the extremes of traditionalism to ultraradical criticism. Yet modern biblical research is beginning to achieve a new synthesis of critical approach and respect for tradition. In large measure this emerging point of view is the result of the extensive and fruitful excavations in the lands of the Fertile Crescent—Egypt, Palestine, Syria, and Iraq. The discoveries made there have offered welcome evidence of the essential credibility of the biblical writers and corrected the vagaries of some critics, who possess more acumen than sympathy and more analytical method than constructive imagination.

Our understanding of biblical tradition, history, law, ethics, poetry, prophecy and wisdom has been completely revolutionized by modern biblical and Semitic scholarship. But our debt to the past remains imponderable. If today a modern reader possesses the means for comprehending the Bible better than the greatest mind in medieval times, it is because we are dwarfs standing on the shoulders of giants.

What is the significance of the Bible for the modern age? On the most obvious level, the Bible is *literature*. Within its covers repose some of the world's greatest masterpieces in poetry and prose. There is scarcely one branch of literary art not represented by a noble example.

But the importance of the Bible goes deeper. It is an indispensable element in the *religious* and *moral* education of the human race. The Bible is the immortal record of God's Revelation through its various stages and forms, as embodied in the life and thought of the chosen spirit of Israel, who sought after God and the good life. Even this is not all. The importance of the Bible is more than historical—it is living religion. It contains the profound and ever-fruitful insights of lawgivers, prophets, poets, and sages who looked deep into the heart of man and the universe and recognized both as the handiwork of God. The modern religious spirit finds God revealed far more impressively in the majestic harmony and order of the universe than in the miracles which earlier generations delighted to chronicle. Similarly, the Bible as the achievement of man bears impressive testimony to the divine inspiration that is its source.

Finally the Bible is *history*, vivid, revealing, unforgettable. It is the thrilling record of the tragic yet glorious experience of the Jewish people during its most vigorous period. Though Israel has always been politically weak and physically negligible, the world has recognized its unique religious genius and moral power. As Santayana has said, "He who does not know the past is doomed to repeat it." A knowledge of this basic aspect of the world's spiritual development is crucial today. One may well doubt whether mankind will have many more chances to repeat the mistakes of yesterday. Hence, understanding the Bible means not merely excavating the past, but laying the foundations of the future.

2. THE BACKGROUND OF THE BIBLE[9a]

A true appreciation of the Bible as literature, religion and history is predicated upon the recognition that it is not an anthology of sacred texts or a collection of edifying tracts written by the like-minded believers of a religious sect. It is, in the words of an acute twentieth-century scholar, "a national literature upon a religious foundation." The Bible reveals all the varied and even contradictory intellectual currents and spiritual tendencies that characterized the life of Israel during the first fifteen hundred years of its collective experience. The biblical period begins with the emergence of the Hebrew tribes upon the stage of history during the middle of the second millennium B.C.E. and continues until the persecutions of Antiochus, which preceded the Maccabean revolt (168 B.C.E.). Radical, conservative and moderate, rationalist and mystic, believer and skeptic, all have found their place within the canon of Scripture. The stimulating variety of attitudes and contents in the Bible is heightened by the colorful influences of the older, neighboring cultures of Egypt, Syria and Mesopotamia. The roots of the Bible are to be sought throughout the Near East as surely as its fruits belong to the world.

A clue to the lively intellectual ferment within Israel that produced the Bible is supplied by the traditional division of the Hebrew Bible into three parts: the Torah, or Law, the Nebiim, or Prophets, and the Ketubim, or Sacred Writings. This tripartite arrangement, which is very ancient, recalls the three principal cultural elements in biblical thought: the priest, or custodian of Torah, the prophet, or speaker of the Word, and the sage, the teacher of Wisdom. These groups are clearly delineated in two biblical passages. Jeremiah declares: "For instruction shall not perish from the priest, nor counsel from the wise, nor the word from the prophet" (18:18). Ezekiel utters his warning: "They shall seek a vision of the prophet, and instruction shall perish from the priest, and counsel from the elders" (7:26).

Each of these three elements must be understood in terms of its individual development, its relationship to the other two strands, and its ultimate incorporation into the common heritage of Israel.

3. TORAH—THE LAW[10a]

The Torah was the particular province of the priest. The Hebrew word *kohen*, "priest," and its Arabic cognate *kahin*, "seer of a spirit, diviner," bear witness to the earliest period of Semitic history. This stage of religion may have preceded the successive eruptions from the Arabian desert into the lands of the Fertile Crescent and Egypt that produced the different Semitic and Hamitic peoples. At all events, in this primitive period, whether before or after the emergence of distinct ethnic groups, there was only one functionary who met all the religious requirements of the clan. He was the diviner, consulted on all individual and group problems, as well as the custodian of the religious cult and the officiant at sacrifices.

With the growth of a more complex social system, and particularly with the transfer from a nomadic or seminomadic life to a settled agricultural economy, the functions of this dignitary were divided. The free spirit of the god, which ancient men believed was most evident and potent in hypnotic trances and similar transports, became the particular province of wandering seers or dervishes, who eked out a precarious existence from the bounty of those who consulted them on the future, particularly with reference to personal problems. On the other hand, more and more elaborate shrines, altars and temples now arose, which were ministered to by priests. The emoluments of the priests were more substantial and their position in society was more respected than that of the wandering seers. As a result, the priesthood early became a hereditary caste, jealously protecting its prerogatives as guardians of the sanctuary. As a matter of fact, the functions of divining the future and revealing the will of the god or gods were never completely surrendered by the priest, yet more and more his activities tended to become formalized through ritual associated with the sacred objects of the shrine.

These priests naturally created and preserved the rituals connected with their sanctuaries. Being the only educated group, they became the custodians of culture. The literature and science of ancient Egypt and Mesopotamia was almost exclusively the work of the priesthood. In Israel during the days of the First Temple, the priests were the medical authorities, the judges in civil and criminal cases, and the arbiters on all religious problems, as well as the custodians of the ancient historical traditions.

The center of all this priestly activity lay in shrines and temples like those at Shiloh, Beth-el, Gilgal, and, pre-eminently, the Temple of Solomon in Jerusalem, which took precedence over these older and lesser sanctuaries, but never succeeded in superseding them completely. In these sanctuaries, ancient historical records and manuals of law were preserved, both for the practical guidance of the priests and for the instruction of their youth.

The Bible contains many of these briefer *torot*, or legal manuals, necessary to the functioning of the priesthood. Such is the torah of the leper, forbidden foods, and the various sacrifices, all in Leviticus. There were also more extensive legal and moral codes of hoary antiquity, often combining ritual enactment, civil and criminal law, moral exhortation and legal procedure. Such is the Book of the Covenant (Ex. 21-23) and the Holiness Code (Lev. 17-26).

In II Kings 24, we read of an even more elaborate code discovered during the reign of King Josiah (621 B.C.E.). Repairs had been undertaken of the Temple buildings and this Torah was found buried in the foundations or hidden in the walls of the sanctuary, as was common in the ancient world. This code is generally identified today, in whole or in part, with Deuteronomy, the fifth book of the Torah. Doubtless, there were many other *torot* of briefer or more extensive compass which have not reached us, especially those of the local sanctuaries. The prophet Hosea seems to refer to such codes when he says, "Though I write him ten thousand *torot*, they are foreign to him" (8:12).[11]

What is the origin of the Five Books, or Pentateuch? To this question tradition gave a very definite answer. It was Moses, the great liberator of Israel, who had bestowed upon his people the Torah he had received from God.

There were, of course, manifest difficulties connected with this view. That Moses could have written the last verses of Deuteronomy, describing his own death, was a problem the Rabbis solved homiletically. Other passages, like Gen. 12:6 and 36:31, for example, which seemed to infer a post-Mosaic date, were noted by medieval Jewish exegetes. Their observations were repeated and reflected by Spinoza in his *Tractatus Theologico-Politicus*, which was the direct stimulus to the modern Higher Criticism of the Pentateuch. Scholars found many repetitions and inconsistencies in the text and were led to the hypothesis of multiple sources embedded in the Torah. Once set in motion, the process of source analysis gained momentum. More and more contradictions in the text were being discovered which could be resolved only by the hypothesis of new sources, subsources, redactors, and redactional schools.

With the assumption that the Pentateuch consisted of multiple documents combined more or less skillfully by redactors, came the tendency to assign increasingly later dates both to the individual sources and to the composite product, many centuries after the Mosaic age. Moses became a legendary, if not mythical, figure and any resemblance between him and the traditional portrait was purely a matter of accident. The Priestly Code, the largest Pentateuchal source, was generally assigned to the days of the Second Temple, and its narratives and legislation were described as an artificial "*Rueckbildung*," or throwback, of Second Temple conditions into earlier ages.

It should be noted that the higher-critical study of the Torah has made important and enduring contributions to our understanding of biblical law and thought. These values need to be salvaged from the exaggerations and errors into which the critics were all too often betrayed. They cannot be dismissed as wholly insignificant, a procedure often advocated today, particularly in nonscientific publications intended for the general reader.

Archaeological discoveries throughout the Near East brought to light law codes of high antiquity. The most important of these, the Babylonian Code of Hammurabi (twentieth century, B.C.E.), and the Assyrian, Hittite and Hurrian codes, possess many elements that shed light upon Pentateuchal law and tradition. Thus, aside from its many points of contact with the Code of Hammurabi, the Book of the Covenant (Ex. 21-23) contains much of the customary law of the Semitic peoples, and is, therefore, in part at least older than the Exodus from Egypt.

A similar situation obtains with regard to the most famous code of all, the Decalogue (Ex. 20; Deut. 5). It is, to be sure, unique in its simplicity and comprehensiveness and bears the unmistakable stamp of Israel's faith in one God, Whose likeness is not to be pictured by man. Nonetheless, the moral standards ordained in the Ten Commandments have their parallels in the Egyptian *Book of the Dead*, which describes the cross-examination that the dead undergo in the nether world.

For reasons of this kind, as well as larger historical considerations, scholars are recognizing increasingly that if there had been no tradition of a legislator like Moses it would have been necessary to invent one. Without such a dominating personality, it remains inconceivable how a band of slaves could have engineered a mass escape from a powerful country like Egypt. What is more, this group of cowed and oppressed helots were transformed into a mighty people, fired with the resolution to brave the hazards of the desert and carry on a long drawn-out struggle for the conquest of the strongly defended Promised Land. Moreover, this aggregation of clans possessed a strong sense of unity, a common historical memory and, underlying both, the worship of the same God. All this presupposed a Liberator who was also a Lawgiver. In order to impress upon the people the way of life they were to follow, what was required was not only the exalted principles of the Decalogue, but the more mundane and tangible details of ritual, civil and criminal law.

The great prophets of later times also bore testimony to the existence of an exalted religious and ethical tradition in Israel. Even Amos, the earliest among them, who spoke in the name of one living and universal God, enforcing His law of righteousness throughout the world, did not speak of himself as an innovator. On the contrary, the prophets called upon the people to "return" to their God and His law. Their denunciations of the people would be as pointless as they would be unfair, if the "Knowledge of the Lord" which they demanded were not already part of the heritage of the people, however misunderstood or violated.

Many other features of the Pentateuch, in both its historical and legal sections, which had previously been dismissed as inventions of Second Temple writers, were seen to have very old parallels. This is true of the Tabernacle and the Ark in the wilderness, which have their analogies in the *mahmal* and the *'otfe*, sacred tentlike structures borne in the religious processions of various Arab tribes. So, too, with regard to the elaborate system of sacrifices described in Leviticus, the technical terms of which are known to us from Syrian and Punic documents. Another example, the *'edah* or *kahal*, inadequately rendered "congregation" in our current Bible translations, is discussed below.

Thus the conviction has been gaining ground among scholars that the tradition of the Mosaic authorship of the Pentateuch is not an invention. It may never be possible to establish the precise extent of legal material emanating from his period, but that the Torah contains the work of Moses appears certain.[11a]

The sanctuaries naturally served as the libraries for the legal codes that were necessary to the priest in carrying on his ritual and judicial duties. They would also be the natural locale for collecting the historical traditions of the people, especially since the lives of Abraham, Isaac, Jacob, Joseph, and Moses were bound up with the sacred sites and thus served to validate their sanctity. In addition to these national traditions there were others of even greater antiquity that Israel shared with its kinsmen, as part of their common Semitic heritage. Such were the narratives of Creation, the first human pair, the rise of sin, and the Flood. These tales, retold in Israel, were imperceptibly transformed by the alchemy of the Hebrew spirit to reflect the higher and profounder insights of Israelite religion.

All these traditions were originally repeated orally and probably were chanted in verse form. As time went on, however, poetry gave way to prose, and oral transmission to written forms. It is by no means easy to recapitulate the literary history of these historical traditions or to trace the origin and order of composition of the law codes now incorporated in our Torah. The process was undoubtedly long and complex. Yet for the reasons indicated, a new respect for the credibility of the biblical narratives and the antiquity of biblical law has developed.

In part, the difficulty that modern scholars have in reconstructing the steps leading to the compilation of the Torah stems from the fact that the composition and redaction of these codes and traditions proceeded slowly and anonymously over a period of centuries. Their final editing and integration into a single continuous work is most plausibly to be attributed to the impact of the destruction of the First Temple by the Babylonians and the exile of the people in 586 B.C.E.[12a] This catastrophe constituted a major threat to Jewish survival. Six centuries later, when the Second Temple was destroyed by the Romans, a similar crisis confronted Jewish leaders. At that time the traditions governing the Temple and its services were carefully collected in the mishnaic treatise *Middot*, lest they be forgotten in time. In very much the same spirit, the traditions and laws preserved by the priests of the First Temple seem now to have been assembled and codified in the Torah par excellence, the Five Books of Moses.

The collapse of the Babylonian Empire and the rise of Persia in its stead gave the Jewish people a new lease on life.[13a] Cyrus was magnanimous and farsighted in his policy toward subject peoples. He permitted those Jews who so desired to reconstitute their community life in Palestine, granting them religious and cultural autonomy. The Torah proved an incomparable instrument for uniting and governing the Jewish community. Three-quarters of a century after the Return, Ezra, who was a priest by birth and a *sofer*, or "scribe," by calling, persuaded the struggling Jewish settlement in Jerusalem to accept the Torah as its constitution for all time. Nor was this all. Though himself a priest, Ezra carried through a unique peaceful revolution, which stripped the priesthood of its position of religious and intellectual leadership, leaving it only the conduct of the Temple ritual as prescribed by law. The spectacle of moral corruption and degeneracy that a hereditary priesthood exhibited led Ezra to transfer the spiritual leadership of the people from the priests to the scholars, who represented a nonhereditary, democratic element recruited from all classes. The ritual ministrations of the priests in the Temple went on unimpaired, but the dynamic creative impulse in Judaism was henceforth centered in a less pretentious institution, the synagogue, at once a house of prayer, study and communal assembly.

The importance of this revolution, unparalleled in ancient religion, can scarcely be exaggerated. The Talmud gives Ezra little more than his due when it declares, "Ezra was worthy of giving the Torah had not Moses preceded him."[14] Ezra and his scholarly successors are to be credited, in large measure, with the progressive, evolving and democratic character of normative, traditional Judaism.[15a]

The *Soferim* and the Rabbis not only preserved the Torah, they gave it new life. Their activity made the Bible relevant to the needs of new generations and thus prepared it to serve as the eternal charter of humanity. They gave the Jewish tradition some of its most noteworthy characteristics, its protean capacity for adjustment, and its fusing of realistic understanding and idealistic aspiration. These nameless scribes thus contributed in no small measure to the survival of the Jewish people. But their significance is not limited to the household of Israel. The Christian world, too, owes them a debt of gratitude. As founders of Rabbinic Judaism they helped create the background from which Christianity arose, formulating many of the basic teachings that both religions share in common.

Henceforth, the written Torah was complete, with nothing to be added or removed. The oral Torah would carry the growth and development of the Jewish religion forward to its new phase.

4. THE PROPHETS OF ISRAEL

The second great division of the Bible is called "the Prophets." Like so many other aspects of Israelite life, the prophets represent a unique Hebrew development of elements common to all the Semitic peoples. Reference has been made above to the single official of the primitive Semites who exercised all religious functions which were later divided between the priest and the prophet. We have briefly traced the role of the priest, the custodian of Torah, who represents one line of development. The other is represented at its highest by the Hebrew prophet, the revealer of the Divine Word. In its origins, the institution was infinitely less exalted.

Side by side with the formalized role of the priesthood, with its emphasis upon ritual, there arose a considerably more informal type of religious leadership, the diviner, soothsayer, or "seer," familiar today in the Arab dervish. Not being attached to a sanctuary, he had no fixed locale. He therefore had to depend upon the resources of his own personality for his maintenance and position. He functioned through trances or ecstatic spells, under the influence of which he would mutter or shout his message derived from his god. Self-hypnosis would be induced through dances, rhythmic swaying, music, ceaseless repetitions of the Divine Name, or self-laceration. The diviner was both feared because of his connection with the Divine and despised as a cross between beggar and lunatic. Throughout history, Semitic soothsayers remained on this low level and unquestionably had their counterparts in ancient Israel.

In the Bible, however, this type of functionary is not to be met, except for a few stray allusions during the earlier period of the Judges and the Monarchy. This is due to two factors. In the first instance, the Bible is written from the incomparably higher vantage point of the great prophets, who despised these lowly practitioners of doubtful arts. In the second instance, in the biblical period this functionary had already evolved into a higher type, the *nabi*, or prophet. Other titles by which the prophet was known were *roeh* or *hozeh*, "seer," and *ish haelōhim*, "man of God." The etymology of the word *nabi* is uncertain, being derived by some authorities from the meaning "mutter" and by others from the meaning "announce, proclaim." Probably both derivations are correct, reflecting different stages in the development of prophecy, which began as hypnotic utterances and became the respected announcement of the will of God.

The prophet was not merely the revealer of God to man; he was also man's intercessor before God. In his role as a prophet, Abraham prays for the recovery of Abimelech, the king of Gerar, exactly as, in later periods Moses pleads for Miriam and Aaron, and Samuel prays for Saul. So, too, the sinful king Jeroboam implores "the man of God" to intercede for him, and Elijah and Elisha pray for humbler folk in distress (Gen. 20:7, 17; Num. 12:13; Deut. 9:20; I Sam. 15:11; I Kings 13:6; 17:21; II Kings 4:33).

When prophecy became national in scope, we find such diverse figures as Moses, Samuel, Amos, Isaiah and Jeremiah interceding for Israel (Ex. 15:25; 32:11; Deut. 9-18, 26 and elsewhere; I Sam. 7:5-9; 12:19; Jer. 42:2, 20; Amos 7:2, 5; Is. 37:4). Time and again, Jeremiah is commanded not to pray for his people (Jer. 7:16, 11:14, 14:11), proof positive that Israel's doom is sealed.

According to the Rabbis of the Talmud, the ritual of prayer was ordained as a substitute for the Temple sacrifices after the destruction of the sanctuary. But before prayer became fixed in form, "the service of the heart" was spontaneous and individual. In this sense, prayer may be traced back to the prophets as well as to the priests.

In general, the differentiation of function between prophet and priest was never absolute, each continuing to influence the other throughout the history of Israel.

Thus the Hebrew priest remained the custodian of the *Urim ve-Tumim* which were used as oracles to foretell the future. On the other hand, prophets like Samuel, especially in the earlier period, officiated at sacrifices. Moreover, several of the prophets were priests by descent and vocation. It should be added that the fixed ritual of the priesthood kept it within narrow limits. On the one hand, it prevented the priesthood's sinking to the level of irrationality and charlatanism that often characterized the soothsayer. On the other hand, it lacked the dynamic, personal character of the "seer," which reached its apogee in the great Hebrew prophets.

These great-souled teachers of humanity rejected with scorn the suggestion that they had anything in common with the soothsayers or their successors. Yet the techniques of the great prophets testify to their link with these lowly types. Many of the devices used to induce religious ecstasy are to be found among the greatest of the prophets. Frequently, the prophet would produce a sign as evidence of the truth of his message, or dramatize his theme by strange behavior. Nonetheless, these methods continued to lose ground among the great prophets. As time went on, the conviction among them grew that the truth of their revelation was evident in its content, and did not require buttressing through ecstatic states or hypnotic seizures.

The successive stages of prophecy among the Hebrews may be reconstructed with tolerable completeness. The most primitive soothsayer or dervish is not described in the Bible, except by indirection. Doubtless, these wonder-working mendicants continued to ply their trade, side by side with the higher types of prophet, exactly as astrologists and fortunetellers are contemporaries of Freud and Einstein. Their activity, however, was limited to personal problems and their influence was almost surely local in extent.

From the ranks of the diviners, some individuals were evolving into leaders of tribal and national importance. These were prophets who spoke in the name of the God of Israel and proclaimed His Will to the people. An example is the prophetess Deborah (twelfth century B.C.E.). It was she who nerved a spineless and disunited aggregate of tribes to unite against their common Canaanite foe in the north, inspiring the Hebrew leader Barak to his great victory at the Kishon River (Judg. 4-5). Another was Samuel (eleventh century) who still carried on the personal activities of a diviner, being consulted on matters as petty as the loss of a farmer's asses (I Sam. 9). But Samuel's functions far transcended this lowly role. Like Deborah, he served to unite the tribes against a dangerous enemy, this time the Philistines in the southwest (I Sam. 4:1). He also functioned as a judge and officiant at the rituals conducted at the principal sacred sites (I Sam. 7:15 ff.; 9). His greatest national role was as kingmaker and kingbreaker, a basic factor in the rise and fall of Saul and the ascendancy of David.[16a] Such dominating personalities tended to attract followers, who formed guilds called *Bnai Nebiim* (Sons of the Prophets). These schools of disciples traveled with their master and sought to learn his ways. The most gifted among them ultimately became leaders in their own right.

As the monarchy became a fixed institution, a king would attach a prophet to his court, so that he could be conveniently consulted on matters of state. In the very nature of things, these prophets would tend to be subservient to their masters, proclaiming the messages their overlords wanted to hear. The biblical historians have not transmitted the names of these typical court prophets for posterity. Only the memory of a heroic exception to the rule, a member of this group who proclaimed the truth to his royal master without fear, has been preserved to us. It is

Nathan, who in his deeply moving parable dared to rebuke King David for his adulterous union with Bath-sheba, which he had sealed with the murder of her husband, Uriah (II Sam. 12:1 ff.).

Playing a role similar to that of the court prophets were others who were not attached to the royal court but remained independent figures. Some of them enjoyed great influence, like Ahiah (I Kings 11:31-9, 14:6-16), who set up Jeroboam's dynasty and later announced its doom. Not being completely dependent on the favor of an individual, these leaders could often be independent in attitude.

Incomparably the greatest of these independent figures was Elijah. Emerging suddenly from the wilderness and disappearing in a heavenly chariot, his meteoric career symbolized the two greatest Jewish contributions to civilization, two that really are one: the faith in the One God and the passion for righteousness. In his contest with the priests of Baal on Mt. Carmel, he battled uncompromisingly against the degradation of the God-idea in Israel. In his encounter with the weak-willed King Ahab, whose greed had led him to murder, Elijah stood forth as the courageous champion of social justice. Elijah left no writings behind him. His dramatic actions were far more effective than words in recalling the erring people to the Living God and His teaching. For twenty-seven centuries the awesome figure of the prophet of Gilead has fired the imagination of men.

Such intrepidity of spirit was naturally rare. By and large, even the unattached prophets were responsive to the royal will or the pressure of mass opinion. They were the purveyors of popular religion, highly esteemed, well remunerated, and doubtless attracting many disciples. The prophet Elisha began his career as a follower of Elijah, and some of the latter's intransigence and truth-speaking clung to him. Before long, however, his path diverged from that of his great master. He was a wonder-worker, enjoying the gifts of the populace and the adulation of his followers. He fulfilled all too literally the curse pronounced by Elijah on Ahab's house, by anointing Jehu as king. It is true that Jehu's cold-blooded massacre of Ahab's family and followers may have been carried out without Elisha's knowledge or approval. Nonetheless, the prophet's career shows how easily even the personally independent seer tended to accommodate himself to the *status quo*.

Lacking any pretension to spiritual independence were men of the stamp of Zedekiah ben Kenaanah (I Kings 22:11), who was consulted by the kings of Israel and Judah as to the outcome of their projected war against Syria. For reply he fashioned two iron horns and unhesitatingly proclaimed, "Thus saith the Lord, with these you will gore the Arameans to destruction." Nearly two centuries later, Hananiah ben Azzur triumphantly proclaimed, "I have broken the yoke of the king of Babylonia" (Jer. 28:1 ff.). When Jeremiah, who saw the imminent ruin of the Judean kingdom, placed a yoke on his neck to underscore the need for political submission to the Babylonian Empire, Hananiah unhesitatingly smashed the symbol, doubtless to the resounding applause of the mob.

These enormously popular and, by their lights, influential prophets, have gone down to infamy because they are described in the Bible as "false prophets," a judgment which not only they but virtually all their contemporaries would indignantly have rejected. This unflattering designation has attached to these well meaning preachers of conventional attitudes only because the Bible is written from the standpoint of a few rebels, who were disliked and despised in their own generation.

Almost from the very beginning of prophecy, there was a tradition of nonconformity in Israel. While the priests traced their functions and prerogatives back to Moses and Aaron, the High Priest, there were some spirits who saw in Moses the great prophet whose life was a flaming protest against slavery, tyranny and immorality. Deborah, Samuel, Nathan and Elijah stood in the same great line of opposition to the supineness, lust and greed of the people and its rulers.

These opponents of the *status quo* became especially articulate in the eighth century, the high-water mark of the kingdoms of Israel and Judah. During almost fifty years, the Northern Kingdom was ruled by perhaps its most capable king, Jeroboam II, while Judah enjoyed the presence of an equally able monarch in Azariah or Uzziah.[17a] Between them these kings restored the boundaries of the Solomonic kingdom by successful campaigns to the east, southeast and southwest. The fortifications of Jerusalem were strengthened and the country grew rich because of the spoils of victory, the tolls levied on the great trade routes linking Egypt and the Mesopotamian Valley, and the growing international trade. Luxury grew apace. Winter palaces, summer homes, elaborate furniture and expensive feminine attire became general. A strong sense of national confidence followed in the wake of prosperity. The present was secure; the future would be even more glorious.

The practical leaders, kings, generals, diplomats and merchants alike, did not recognize that the military victories were due to a brief interlude in the international scene, after the Syrian kingdom had fallen and before the new Assyrian power had risen to world dominion. Nor were these realistic observers interested to note that the prosperity was superficial, limited only to the upper levels of society. For the masses, there was ever growing insecurity and outright want. More and more, the independent farmers were being crowded out, their land foreclosed, their children sold into slavery for debt, and they themselves working as tenants on the fields they once had called their own. Moreover, international trade and diplomacy had introduced fashionable foreign cults. Their licentious rites were sapping the moral stamina of the people as surely as economic exploitation was undermining their stake in the country.

These portents of decline, political, social and religious, were so slight that they were noticed by only a few observers, and these, men of little standing or power in their day. In earlier and simpler days, the influence of the prophets had been widely felt. From Moses, through Deborah and Samuel, to Elijah and Elisha, they had been leaders in action. In later times, however, the prophets were looked upon as traitors and enemies of the people, or, more charitably, were dismissed as insane visionaries. As the national decline gathered momentum, the freedom of action of the prophets was restricted, though their freedom of speech could not be denied. Some were driven out, like Amos, or tried for treason, like Micah, or imprisoned, like Jeremiah. Some were killed through lynch law by hired thugs, as was the fate of Jeremiah's colleague, Urijah (Jer. 26:20-24). In rare instances, a member of this group might still influence the course of events. Such was the case with Isaiah, whose efforts were aided both by his aristocratic birth and connections and by the spiritual sensitivity of King Hezekiah. In general, however, these prophets found the door to effective action closed against them.

The period of literary prophecy now began. Several factors conspired to produce this change. The hostility or indifference of the people could not prevent the prophets from expressing God's truth. In Amos's words: "If a trumpet is blown in the city, will not the people tremble? The Lord has spoken, who can but prophesy?" (Amos 3:8).

Jeremiah has left a poignant description of the spiritual compulsion that drove him and his fellows to court men's hatred and even to face death:

> O Lord, Thou hast enticed me, and I was enticed,
> Thou hast overcome me, and hast prevailed;
> I am become a laughing stock all the day,
> Every one mocketh me.
> For as often as I speak, I must cry out,
> "Violence and spoil" do I shout,
> Because the word of the Lord is made a reproach unto me,
> A derision, all the day.
> If I say: "I will not make mention of Him,
> Nor speak any more in His name,"
> Then there is in my heart a burning fire,
> Shut up in my bones,
> Which I weary myself to hold in, but cannot (Jer. 20:7-9).

There were other motives for literary prophecy. Because the prophets exerted little influence on their contemporaries, they or their disciples began writing down their striking utterances out of the very human desire for vindication in the future (Is. 8:16; *cf.* Job 19:23). Doubtless, too, there was the wish to instruct young disciples to carry on the Lord's work, as well as the fear of reprisals for publicly proclaiming the unpopular truth.

It required extraordinary courage for these men, generally despised or ignored, to stigmatize the popular and influential prophets of their day as "false." That position was not reached overnight. In the earlier period, the rebel prophets did not deny the inspiration of their opponents. In the ninth century, Micaiah ben Imlah bravely contradicts Zedekiah's optimistic prophecy, but he explains that his opponent spoke as he did because God Himself has sent a lying spirit to confuse and mislead the king (I Kings 22:19 ff.). A century later, the Judean prophet Micah had outgrown this concept. For him, the false prophets are hirelings, selling their wares to the highest bidder. "When their maw is fed, they proclaim peace, but against him who does not feed them, they declare war" (3:5). A hundred years later, Jeremiah also denies their claim to divine inspiration and stigmatizes his opponent as a liar (28:15).

The free prophets had no professional stake in their calling; theirs was not the kind of message for which men paid. They therefore resented any identification with the conventional prophets. When Amos was called a *nabi* by the priest at Beth-el, he said: "I am neither a prophet nor a member of the prophetic guild" (7:14). Yet poles apart as the free prophets and their conventional rivals were in the content of their message, their techniques, vocabulary and style were similar. Their greatest divergence lay in their destiny. History, the inexorable judge, consigned the conventional prophets to oblivion, and raised the free prophets to immortality as transcendent spiritual teachers of the human race. As critics of society and as heralds of a nobler day, they remain perennially alive.

5. THE MESSAGE OF THE PROPHETS[18a]

The sources of prophetic thought, in both its negative and positive aspects, are of genuine interest today. In attacking the evils of a complex and decadent civilization, the prophets were convinced that they were not innovators, but rather restorers of the pristine tradition of Israel, which had fallen upon evil days. This conviction was fundamentally correct. Two great experiences had come to the Hebrews at the very inception of their history. As time passed by they would have receded in the national consciousness and ultimately been forgotten. That they have not become vague memories was basically the achievement of the prophets and their disciples.

The first great experience was the bondage in Egypt. The experience of common enslavement and liberation of the Hebrew tribes created a sense of the solidarity of Israel. But that was not all. Ever afterward, Hebrew tradition recalled the period of humiliation and suffering in Egypt, and utilized it to develop in the Hebrews a sense of community with the downtrodden and the oppressed. The prophets could count on this ready sense of identification with the underprivileged and the weak.

The second great factor in molding the life and thought of Israel was the desert period, the age of nomadism. Briefly put, the desert played as significant a role in Hebrew history as did the frontier in American history. Professor Turner has pointed out how the existence of untamed and unclaimed land in the United States throughout the eighteenth century influenced the psychology and institutions of the American people. Equally significant in its effect upon Hebrew ideals was the desert, which lies to the east and south of Palestine.

The influence of the desert, however, was complex, for it bore both a real and an ideal character. First and foremost, there was a period of wandering in the wilderness after the escape from Egypt. The well known biblical tradition places the period of wandering at forty years. Modern scholarship is disposed, however, to assume a much longer period before the settlement in Palestine. Whatever the duration, that period was remembered ever after, and as often happens with memory, was idealized by later generations, under the tutelage of the prophets.

The desert was more than a memory of the past. It was also a present reality to the Hebrews, even after the bulk of the tribes had settled in Palestine and progressed to an agricultural and even an urban economy. In Trans-Jordan and southern Palestine, nomadic conditions prevailed throughout the days of the Hebrew kingdoms and long beyond; in fact, down to the present. In describing the allocation of the territory among the twelve tribes, the Bible states that two or three clans at least remained as shepherds on the eastern banks of the Jordan. Thus the memories of nomadic life in the past were reinforced by the existence of similar conditions in the present. It was in the desert at Sinai that the God of Israel had revealed Himself to His people. His power was limitless, but His favorite abode was still the wilderness, vast and terrifying. Centuries after the Israelites had settled in Palestine, it was to the desert that the prophet Elijah fled, not only to seek escape from persecution but to rekindle his ardor for the God of Israel at His mountain.

The desert life, past and present, in both its real and its ideal aspect, exerted an enduring influence upon Hebraic ideals. The life of the Semitic shepherd, by no means lacking in crudity, possesses some noteworthy traits. Nomadic society is fiercely egalitarian. Within the tribe, complete social equality prevails; there are no kings or nobility, no ranks or classes. When a crisis or war threatens, the individual of superior sagacity or prowess emerges as a leader, but he is emphatically *primus inter pares*. When the emergency is over, he reverts to his normal place. The Book of

Judges in the Bible is largely concerned with this type of leadership. It tells, too, of the attempt of an ambitious leader, Abimelech, to establish a hereditary kingship in its stead, an attempt which ended in ignominious failure.

Recent research has demonstrated that this type of primitive democracy was characteristic of all early Semitic societies, indeed of Indo-European groups as well. Under this system, authority is vested in the entire adult male population, which decides questions of war and peace, chooses its leaders and deposes them, and is the supreme legislative and judicial power. In brief, it exercises all the functions of government. Unmistakable traces of this people's assembly (Akkadian *puhrum*, Syrian *mo'ed*) have been discovered in Babylonian epics and Assyrian legal documents, as well as in the Egyptian narrative of Wen-Amon which describes conditions in Syria in the twelfth century B.C.E.

With the evolution of more complex social and economic patterns, and the establishment of a monarchy, the democratic institution of the assembly disappeared, giving way to absolutism in the Babylonian and Assyrian Empires.

The existence of the people's assembly in Israel was overlooked. The terms by which it is referred to in the Bible, *'edah* and, secondarily, *kahal* were erroneously translated "congregation," and thus suggested ecclesiastical connotations wide of the mark. These terms are better translated as "commonalty" or "people's assembly." When a monarchy was established in Palestine, its power was never absolute. During the days of the kingdom the "people's assembly" fought a slowly losing battle to retain its prerogatives. In many respects, which cannot be detailed here, the powers of the *'edah* remained effective to the end; in others, its role became largely symbolic. But the democratic impulse, which gave it birth and which in turn it nurtured, was never wiped out in Israel.

As significant as this primitive democracy is the fact that in the nomadic stage there is virtually no private ownership of wealth. The flocks are owned in common, and rights to wells and pasture grounds are vested in the tribe as a whole. Even after nomadism had given way to settled agricultural life and private ownership of land had become the norm in ancient Israel, as everywhere else, the recollection of the earlier conditions of social equality and common ownership persisted among the Hebrews.

Finally, nomadic society is marked by a strong sense of mutual responsibility. "All for one and one for all" is the law of the tribe. Avenging a crime against any individual member is the duty of the entire tribe. The long-standing feuds among Arab tribes described in the chronicles represent the negative aspect of this conception of tribal brotherhood. The moral code did not extend beyond the tribe, but within the tribe it was all-powerful. Injustice, deception and dishonesty were hotly resented, and indignation found passionate expression in a society where every man was conscious of being the equal of everyone else.

Of themselves these factors—the period of the Egyptian bondage, the nomadic age and the old Semitic inheritance of a primitive democracy—could not have created the basic characteristics of biblical thought. Many peoples have had lowly origins, but most have preferred to forget their past or, better still, to distort it. As for nomadism, it represents a normal stage in social evolution, preceding an agricultural and commercial economy. Among most groups, the end of nomadism meant the surrender of nomadic ideals, and the democracy of the early period disappeared, leaving scarcely a trace

That the same process did not take place in Israel was due to the activity of the prophets. Their role, as will be noted, is not limited to their own activity and writings. Their influence permeated the biblical historians, who recounted the national past from the prophetic standpoint. It also deeply affected the legal codes by which Israelite society was governed. Through history, law and exhortation the Hebrew prophets made it impossible for their fellow countrymen ever to forget that they had been slaves and shepherds. The prophets utilized the Egyptian bondage to inspire the hearts of the people with humanitarian sympathies. Contemporaries of an advanced and often corrupt culture, they recalled the simple laws of justice, freedom and equality by which their nomadic ancestors had lived, and declared those days to have been the most glorious. "I remember for thee the kindness of thy youth, the love of thy bridal state, when thou didst go after Me in the wilderness, in a land unsown" (Jer. 2:1).

In the face of an effete and morally corrupt civilization, nostalgic advocates of the past were not lacking in ancient Israel. There was a clan or guild called the Rechabites, who sought mechanically to revert to a simpler culture, by living only in tents and abstaining from wine, the building of houses, the sowing of seed and the planting of vineyards. Somewhat similar was the institution of the Nazirites, "consecrated to the Lord," who took a vow not to cut their hair, and to abstain from wine, besides avoiding defilement by contact with the dead.

At one with these groups in regarding the nomadic period as a glorious tradition, the prophets were no such ineffectual romantics. On the contrary, they were creative geniuses of the first order, who knew how to utilize the past for the vital needs of the present. Part of the past was dead beyond recall, some of it could be retained, much of it needed to be extended and deepened, while in other respects it had to be transcended completely. The prophets did not urge a return to nomadic conditions, nor did they forbid wine, the dwelling in houses, or the practice of agriculture. They accepted the inevitable social transformation of a settled life. But they demanded the practice of those ideals of nomadism which are valid in every system of society: its concrete sense of mutual responsibility, its passionate attachment to freedom, its instinct for human equality. As Hosea put it, "Sow to yourselves according to righteousness, reap according to mercy, break up your fallow ground. For it is time to seek the Lord, till He come and cause righteousness to rain upon you" (10:12). How the prophets treated the various elements of the nomadic way of life is of more than historical interest. Their procedure points the way to the creative adjustment of tradition to the contemporary scene.

In a nomadic society the strict moral system rested ultimately on the principle of vengeance. When a murder was committed, the relatives of the dead man were enjoined and empowered to exact retribution from the killer and his kinsmen. The prophets transformed vengeance into justice and then proceeded to deepen its meaning to include mercy and loving-kindness. These, they taught, were the attributes of God and must govern the relations of men. More concretely, the Torah limited clan vengeance to cases of premeditated killing and established "the cities of refuge" for accidental murderers (Num. 33:9-34; Josh. 20:1-9). Thus began the long process, still incomplete today, as the tragic incidence of lynchings in America testifies, of bringing human passions and self-interest under the sway of law.

In another direction, also, the prophets transcended nomadic ideals. In the wilderness the clan or tribe is the largest recognized unit, beyond which morality does not apply. Doubtless, there were objective political and economic factors constantly at work breaking down the tribal distinctions in Israel, which were traced back to the twelve sons of the patriarch Jacob. But the process of creating a sense of national solidarity was not easy. Again and again centrifugal forces were in evidence, the most disastrous of which was the division of the Kingdom after the death of Solomon. So powerful were these divisive factors that some scholars doubt whether there ever was a United Kingdom. They regard the reigns of Saul, David and Solomon as a dual monarchy with a single head.

Whatever the truth of this view, it is undeniable that in stimulating the national spirit that ultimately emerged, the prophets played a significant role. They seldom refer to the individual tribes, and even the prime divisions into north and south they regard as a sin and a catastrophe. Amos was a Judean whose principal activity was in Israel, Hosea an Ephraimite who recalled the Davidic dynasty with affection. Jeremiah, who lived long after the destruction of Samaria, looked forward to the restoration of Ephraim to Divine favor, while Ezekiel foretold of a reunion of Judah with their kinsmen from the house of Joseph. The prophets broke the tribal barriers that hemmed Israel in and were therefore the fathers of Jewish nationalism.

In this process of extending the frontiers of solidarity, the Hebrew prophets went beyond the nation to a vision of a united humanity. Unity did not mean uniformity. For the prophets nations were integral elements of God's plan, but their relationship to each other must be governed by His law—justice and mutual co-operation were binding upon all. To use a terminology they themselves would not have recognized, the prophets were the fathers of ethicocultural nationalism. They pointed a way out for mankind between the Scylla of bloodthirsty chauvinism and the Charybdis of lifeless cosmopolitanism, which is sometimes suggested as its remedy. For they demonstrated in their life and thought that national loyalty, properly conceived, is the gateway, not a barrier, to human brotherhood.

It is impossible within the confines of this paper to discuss adequately the insights of Hebrew prophecy in general and the particular contributions of individual figures to such eternal issues as the relationship of God and man, the meaning of history, Israel's role among the nations, the future of society and the character of faith. On these and other problems the prophets have profound contemporary significance, which is all too often ignored through the combination of adulation and neglect which has overtaken the Bible as a whole.

Of the stirring activity of the great prophets, the Bible has preserved only magnificent fragments. It is certain that the prophets whose words have survived must have produced much more than the few hundred verses that have come down to us. There are, moreover, good grounds for assuming that others, less fortunate but perhaps equally worthy, have been completely forgotten. All that has reached us are four books containing prophetic addresses: Isaiah, Jeremiah, Ezekiel, and the Twelve, or Minor, Prophets.

The first three prophetic books follow a broad chronological order. Isaiah belongs to the late eighth century, Jeremiah to the late seventh and early sixth, while Ezekiel is a somewhat younger contemporary of Jeremiah.

Nonetheless, the internal arrangement of these books is not based on historical grounds. Scholars diverge greatly in their views as to the extent of interpolation undergone by each book, Ezekiel in particular being the subject of acute controversy at present. It is, however, universally recognized that beginning with Chapter 40, the Book of Isaiah contains the work of one (and possibly more than one) unknown prophet, who lived nearly two hundred years later, during the Babylonian Exile. In profundity of thought and grandeur of style, this unknown prophet, often called Deutero-Isaiah, eminently deserves his place by the side of Isaiah ben Amoz, who was probably the mightiest intellect among the prophets of Israel. The closing chapters of the Book of Jeremiah consist of oracles against the neighboring nations, which are probably from another hand. The bulk of the book, however, reveals the soul of Jeremiah with a poignant clarity unmatched by any other biblical author.

That historical considerations were not the guiding principle in the arrangement of the prophetic books becomes especially clear in the fourth book of this group. The Hebrew title, the Twelve, is apter than the common English designation, the Minor Prophets. For several of these are minor only in point of size, not significance. The Talmud correctly indicates the reason for joining the work of these twelve prophets, "because each is small, it might have been lost."[19]

This statement is a clue to a principle which has not been adequately evaluated in the arrangement of biblical writings. Since each document was preserved on a scroll, the scribe's tendency was to write the longer text first and then append, often on the remaining section of the same scroll, shorter material, whether or not related in theme. Thus also in the Koran, the longer suras, recognized as later, come first, and the shorter chapters, indubitably the oldest visions of Mohammed, come last. This principle, which sheds light on the organization of material within each biblical book, may explain the position of the Minor Prophets after Isaiah, Jeremiah, and Ezekiel.

The Twelve Prophets include the two earliest literary prophets, Amos and Hosea (middle of the eighth century), and Micah, a younger contemporary of Isaiah. These prophets are among the greatest of the immortal company. The Book of Jonah is an acute satire on the attitude of the popular chauvinist prophets which takes the historical figure of Jonah ben Amittai as its hero to drive home a profound and lasting truth.[20a] Others, like Joel, Obadiah, Nahum, Habakkuk, and Zephaniah, belong to the middle period, while Haggai, Zechariah, and Malachi are representative of the last stage of prophecy in the Persian period, shortly before its disappearance.

These four books, containing the addresses and writings of the prophets, are preceded in the Hebrew Bible by four historical books, Joshua, Judges, Samuel, and Kings, called the Former Prophets. Together, these eight books constitute the second section of the Bible, *Nebiim*, or Prophets. The four historical books contain the history of the Jewish people from their entrance into Palestine until the Babylonian Exile. Superb examples of historical narrative, these works interpret the past experience of Israel in terms of prophetic ideals. They are far more concerned with the religious conditions and the activity of the prophets than with political and economic factors or military and diplomatic events. Thus, the two greatest kings of Judah and Israel, Uzziah and Jeroboam the Second, are dismissed in fourteen verses (II Kings 14:23-15:7), while the prophet Elijah receives more than five chapters (I Kings 17-21) and Elisha eight (II Kings 2-9).

The anonymous historians who created these works, from still older sources now lost, were, on the one hand, disciples of the prophets. On the other, they were deeply influenced by the Torah and its norms for national life, as will be noted below. Hence the historical books, or Former Prophets, which continue the history of Israel begun in the Torah and supply the background for the activity of the prophets, are an ideal link between these two spiritual tendencies.

Both Torah and prophecy find their foil and their complement in the third strand of Hebrew thought, called *Wisdom.*

6. THE VOICE OF WISDOM

The Hebrew priests and prophets have their analogues among all the Semitic peoples, as we have seen. Fundamentally, however, their work was concerned with the life of Israel and therefore it reflects specific national characteristics. Wisdom, on the other hand, is broadly human, dealing with the individual as such. It is therefore even more closely linked to the culture pattern of the ancient Orient.

The connotations of the Hebrew *Hokmah* are far wider than the English rendering "Wisdom" would imply. *Hokmah* may be defined as a realistic approach to the problems of life, including all the practical skills and the technical arts of civilization. The term *hakam*, "sage, wise man," is accordingly applied to the artist, the musician, the singer. Bezalel, the skilled craftsman who built the Tabernacle and its appointments in the wilderness, as well as all his associates, are called "wise of heart" (Ex. 28:3; 35:31; 36:1). Weavers (Ex. 35:25), goldsmiths (Jer. 10:9), and sailors (Ez. 27:8; Ps. 107:27) are *hakamim.*

Above all, the term is applied to the arts of poetry and song, vocal and instrumental. The song in ancient Israel was coextensive with life itself. Harvest and vintage, the royal coronation and the conqueror's return, courtship and marriage, were all accompanied by song and dance. The earliest traditions dealing with the exploits of tribal and national heroes were embodied in song. Snatches of these poems are preserved in the later prose narratives, some being explicitly quoted from older collections, like *The Book of the Wars of the Lord* (Num. 21:14) and *The Book of the Just* (Josh. 10:13; II Sam. 1:18; I Kings 8:53 in the Greek).

The guilds of singers in the Temple, the women skilled in lamentation (Jer. 9:16), the magicians and soothsayers with all their occult arts, are described by the same epithet, "wise" (Gen. 40:8; I Kings 5:10-12; Is. 44:25; Jer. 9:16). Skill in the conduct of war and in the administration of the state (Is. 10:13; 29:14; Jer. 49:7) is also an integral aspect of Wisdom.

All these phases have disappeared with the destruction of the material substratum of ancient Hebrew life. What has remained of Wisdom is its literary incarnation, concerned not so much with the arts of living as with developing a sane, workable attitude toward life. To convey its truths, Wisdom created an educational method and a literature generally couched in the form of the *mashal*, the parable or proverb, brief, picturesque, unforgettable.

It is now clear that the third section of the Bible, called *Ketubim*, the Sacred Writings or Hagiographa, is not a miscellaneous collection, but, on the contrary, has an underlying unity. Basically, it is the repository of Wisdom. The Book of Psalms is a great collection of religious poetry, most of which was chanted at the Temple service with musical accompaniment. Both the composition and the rendition of the Psalms required a high degree of that technical skill which is *Hokmah*. Moreover, in point of content, many Psalms (like 37, 49, 112, 128) have close affinities with the proverbial lore of the Wisdom teachers.

Three other books, Proverbs, Job and Ecclesiastes obviously belong in a Wisdom collection. So does Ben Sira,[21a] or Ecclesiasticus, which was not included in the canon of Scripture, because it clearly betrayed its late origin. Lamentations is a product of *Hokmah* in its technical sense. The Song of Songs is included, not merely because it is traditionally ascribed to King Solomon, the symbol and traditional source of Hebrew Wisdom, but because these songs, whether sung at weddings or at other celebrations, were also a branch of technical song. It has also been suggested that the Song of Songs entered the Wisdom collection because it was regarded as an allegory of the relationship of love subsisting between God and Israel. From this point of view, it would be a *mashal*, which means "allegory" or "fable" as well as "proverb." The Book of Daniel, the wise interpreter of dreams, obviously is in place among the Wisdom books.

The reason for the inclusion of Ruth and Esther is not quite as evident. Perhaps they were included here because both reveal practical sagacity, Esther in saving her people from destruction and Ruth in securing a desirable husband! The three closing books of the Bible, which survey history from Adam to the Persian period, are really parts of one larger work, Chronicles-Ezra-Nehemiah.[22a] It is possible that they may have been included in the Wisdom section merely because they were placed at the end as an appendix to the Bible as a whole. The place of these last-named books in *Ketubim* has also been explained differently. It has been suggested that Chronicles (with its adjuncts) is really an appendix to Psalms, since one of its principal concerns is to describe in detail the establishment of the Temple ritual. Ruth may then have been a supplement to the Psalms, since it concludes with the genealogy of David, the traditional author of the Psalter. Esther may be an appendix to Chronicles, the style of which it seeks to imitate. These links, however tenuous they may appear to the Western mind, will not seem farfetched to anyone familiar with the Semitic logic of association, evidence for which is plentiful in the redaction of the Bible and in the organization of the Mishna and the Talmud.

Wisdom literature in its narrower sense, as it appears in Proverbs or Ecclesiastes, for example, impresses the modern reader as the most secular element in the Bible, being based on clear, realistic observation and logical inference and deduction, rather than on tradition and revelation. Yet in an age permeated by the religious consciousness, the devotee of Wisdom was both unable and unwilling to surrender his claim to Divine inspiration. Thus the *hakam* took his place by the side of the *kohen*, who derived his authority from the Divine Law revealed by Moses, and the *nabi* who spoke out under the direct impact of the Divine. Hence the "wise man," in all the ramifications of the term, could be described, as was Bezalel the craftsman. as "filled with the spirit of God, with wisdom, understanding, knowledge and all manner of skill" (Ex. 31:3).

This conception was given a metaphysical form as well. Each cultivator of Wisdom is endowed with a portion of the transcendental, Divine Wisdom, dwelling in Heaven. This supernal *Hokmah* is described in various poetic figures. Wisdom is the instrument by which God has created the world, or the pattern He has followed in fashioning the universe. She is the beloved playmate of His leisure hours, or the gracious hostess inviting men on the highway to enter her seven-pillared palace (Pr. 8:1 ff.; 8:22 ff.; 9:1 ff.; Ecclus. 1:8 ff. and *passim*). This Hebrew conception of Wisdom as a semidivine figure doubtless draws upon ancient Oriental ideas. In turn it has had wide influence upon such varied elements of thought as Philonian philosophy, Rabbinic speculation, Christian theology, and Gnosticism.

Biblical Wisdom itself was a true Oriental product that had been cultivated for centuries throughout the lands of the Fertile Crescent, Egypt, Palestine, Syria and Babylonia. Everywhere its purposes were similar: the preparation of youth for success in government, agriculture and commerce. Thus Wisdom was part of the cultural inheritance of the Semitic-Hamitic world, which the Hebrews shared with their neighbors and kinsmen.

The tradition that King Solomon was "the wisest of men" and the author of the Song of Songs, Proverbs and Ecclesiastes is no longer airily dismissed by scholars as a mere figment of the folk imagination.[23a] It is seen to reflect the historical fact that the intensive cultivation of Wisdom goes back to his reign, when wide international contacts and internal prosperity contributed to the flowering of culture. Its origins are even more ancient. Embedded in the historical books are gems of Wisdom literature older than Solomon: Jotham's biting fable of the trees and the thornbush (Judg. 9:7), Nathan's parable of the poor man's lamb (II Sam. 12:1), the melancholy comment on the transitoriness of life by the "wise woman of Tekoa" (II Sam. 14:14), not to speak of the later parable of King Joash (II Kings 14:9). Moreover, it is increasingly recognized that the Books of Psalms, Proverbs, and the Song of Songs are anthologies containing a great deal of pre-exilic material, for which parallels of considerable antiquity have been discovered in Babylonia, Syria and Egypt.

Nonetheless, the Golden Age of Hebrew Wisdom literature is the first half of the Second Temple period, roughly between the fifth and the second century B.C.E. This flowering was fostered by both positive and negative factors. After the Babylonian Exile, a far reaching change had taken place in the spirit of the people. It was a chastened folk that returned to Jerusalem after the Proclamation of Cyrus, to rebuild the shattered foundations of the national life. The tragedy of exile had convinced them of the truth of the prophetic message and had imbued them with the desire to fulfil the will of God as revealed in the Torah. Hence, one of the first concerns of the returning settlers was the rebuilding of the Temple. Here, as has been noted, the priests resumed their function as officiants at the ritual, but the spiritual hegemony passed to the scholars, the expounders of the Law.

Prophecy, like the written Torah, had passed its creative phase. It declined and finally ceased to function in the days of the Second Temple. Ultimately the impulse reasserted itself in a strange, scarcely recognizable form, to produce the apocalyptic writings. Various factors contributed to the disappearance of prophecy. The postexilic period as a whole was well described as "an age of small things," with little to stir men's hearts to ecstasy or to wrath. There was neither stimulus nor need for the grand prophetic vision. The Jews were a struggling community under the domination of successive foreign rulers, Persian, Greek, Egyptian and Syrian. The unyielding insistence of the prophets upon national righteousness as the basic premise of national well-being was now an accepted element of Jewish thought, but it was neither particularly novel nor especially relevant to the problems of the hour. For there was little prospect of national greatness and power for Jewish life either in the present or in the recognizable future.

A fundamental revolution in men's thinking now took place. The ancient Semitic outlook, which was shared by the Hebrews, had placed the well-being or decline of the group, the family, tribe or nation in the center of men's thoughts. This collective viewpoint now gave way to a heightened interest in the individual. Prosperity and freedom for a tiny weak people was not likely to be achieved in a world of mighty empires. All that remained was for each human being to strive to attain his personal happiness. What qualities were needed, what pitfalls had to be avoided by a man seeking to achieve success and a respectable place in society? To these perennially modern and recurrent questions, Wisdom now addressed itself with zeal and skill.

The Wisdom literature of the First Temple was sedulously collected and augmented. All signs point to its cultivation by the conservative, upper classes in society, just as the Oral Law was the particular province of the lower and middle classes. These upper strata of society, even the high priestly families among them, whose position and income derived from their services in the Temple, were concerned less with the Will of God than with the way of the world. Their goal in education was utilitarian, the training of youth for careers as merchant princes, landed gentry or government officials. To satisfy this need, a special type of preceptor arose, principally if not exclusively, in Jerusalem, the capital. Like the Sophists in classical Greek, who performed a similar function for the upper class youth of Greek society, these teachers taught "Wisdom" (Hebrew *Hokmah*, Greek *Sophia*).

The Hebrew Wisdom teachers sought to inculcate the virtues of hard work, zeal, prudence, sexual moderation, sobriety, loyalty to authority, and religious conformity—all the elements of a morality making for worldly success. What is more, they did not hesitate to urge less positive virtues on their youthful charges, such as holding one's tongue, and even bribery, as aids in making one's way:

> Where words abound, sin is not wanting,
> But he that controls his tongue is a wise man. (Prov. 10:19)

> A man's gift makes room for him,
> It brings him before great men. (Prov. 18:16)

In brief, this practical Wisdom represented a hardheaded, matter-of-fact, "safe and sane" approach to the problems of living. Of this practical Wisdom the literary repositories are Proverbs in the Bible and Ben Sira or Ecclesiasticus, in the Apocrypha. Both works contain aphorisms and injunctions and observations on life designed to direct youth. Proverbs is more original in style; Ben Sira more derivative. On the other hand, while the literary unit in Proverbs is generally a single verse, Ben Sira has expanded it to a larger form, bordering on our essay.

Among the many preceptors of Wisdom, however, were some whose restless minds refused to be satisfied with these practical goals of what may be termed the lower Wisdom. They sought to penetrate to the great abiding issues: the meaning of life, the purpose of creation, the nature of death, the mystery of evil. In grappling with these ultimate problems they insisted on using the same instruments of observation and common sense that they applied to daily concerns, rather than religious authority and conventional doctrines. Like so many rationalist minds since their day, however, they found unaided human reason incapable of solving these issues. Some, no doubt, finally made their peace with the traditional religion of their day. But others, more tough minded, refused to take on faith what their reason could not demonstrate. Hence their writings reveal various degrees and types of skepticism and heterodoxy.

Several of these devotees of the higher or speculative Wisdom were highly fortunate, for it was given them to transmute the frustration and pain of their quest into some of the world's greatest masterpieces, notably Job and Kohelet. Job is the immortal protest of man against the mystery of suffering. Kohelet expresses the tragic recognition that the basic truth of the universe is beyond men's ken, so that all that remains in life is the achievement of happiness, itself illusory and fleeting. Thus, Wisdom, which began with practical and down-to-earth matters, ended by grappling with the profoundest and most abiding issues of life.

7. THE HIGHER UNITY OF THE BIBLE

The three principal types of religious and cultural activity in ancient Israel were obviously distinct in purpose, emphasis, and technique. Torah and prophecy were principally concerned with the group; Wisdom almost exclusively with the individual. On the other hand, Torah and Wisdom had their gaze fixed on the present, while the prophets used their vision of the ideal world of the future as a touchstone for evaluating the real world of today.

For the priests, ritual was the central feature of the religious life. The Wisdom teachers regarded the Temple service as part of the accepted order of things, but not as especially significant. The prophets, on the other hand, saw righteousness as the goal of religion, and differed among themselves in their attitudes toward ritual. In the brief Book of Amos no favorable reference to sacrifice is to be found. On the other hand, the prophet Ezekiel, himself a priest, drew up a manual on Temple worship after the destruction of the sanctuary. Midway between them stood Isaiah and probably most of the prophets. Isaiah sharply criticized the unholy alliance of piety and plunder in his day. On the other hand, he recognized the Temple in Jerusalem as the seat of God's glory, where he himself had experienced his inaugural vision (ch. 6). In the critical hour when Sennacherib besieged Jerusalem, Isaiah boldly declared that the city of God was inviolate. For the moderate Prophets, ritual was not an end in itself; if it proved a gateway to righteousness, it was acceptable; otherwise it was a snare and a delusion.

It is clear that the activities of priest, prophet, and sage were not carried on in mutual isolation or antagonism. On the contrary, there was a very lively intellectual interchange among them. As a result, the Bible is pervaded by a higher unity, all the more striking because it rests upon the diversity of its component elements.

Doubtless, there were priests in Israel whose interests were purely professional, and for whom religious duty was exhausted in the punctilious fulfillment of the ritual. But the Torah is not the work of priests of this character. On the contrary, it is deeply impregnated with the prophetic spirit. It is profoundly significant that the Torah bears the name of Moses, who is the first of the prophets, "trusted in God's house" beyond any of his successors (Num. 12:7, 8). The great moment of Moses' life is the Divine Revelation on Sinai. His hope for his people is "would that all the Lord's peoples were prophets" (Num. 11:29)!

Moreover, the Torah goes beyond the abstract ethical and religious demands of the prophets and translates these ideals into concrete institutions. The Sabbath law for the protection of the slaves, the six-year period of bond service, the sabbatical year of release from debt, the Jubilee Year for the restoration of real property, the ordinances regarding poor relief, these and countless other elements of biblical legislation are a signal contribution to righteousness in human affairs. All these are explicitly or implicitly motivated by the memories of Egyptian bondage and by the ideals of equality and justice inherited from the wilderness period, the recollection of which the prophets kept alive in the consciousness of the people.

The Ten Commandments are proclaimed in the name of God, who is described as the Redeemer of Israel from the land of bondage, and not as the Creator of heaven and earth, a fact that the medieval philosopher Judah Ha-Levi noted in another connection. The Sabbath rest was enjoined not only upon the Jew, but also upon the slave, "for thou wast a slave in the land of Egypt." The stranger, who in those days, even more than today, had no rights, was not to be oppressed, nor his life embittered, "for ye know the soul of the stranger, for ye were strangers in the land of Egypt" (Ex. 23:9). On the contrary, as is emphasized no less than thirty-six times in the Torah, one law was to be binding upon the alien and the citizen alike. The Golden Rule, "Thou shalt love thy neighbor as thyself" (Lev. 19:18), has its even nobler counterpart in the same chapter, which commands: "And if a stranger sojourn with thee in your land, ye shall not do him wrong. The stranger that sojourneth with you shall be unto you as the home-born among you, and thou shalt love him as thyself; for ye were strangers in the land of Egypt: I am the Lord your God" (Lev. 19:33 f.). Undoubtedly, the persistent effort to limit slavery and the hostility toward the institution manifested by biblical law are the end products of the Hebrews' experience with Egyptian slavery. With extraordinary courage, one biblical code goes further and demands that the Hebrew should not hate the Egyptian, "for thou wast a stranger in his land" (Deut. 23:8). As the Bible became accepted as sacred, these doctrines exerted a continuous educative influence upon the people, giving them a sympathy for the oppressed and a passionate attachment to liberty which was intensified by their later tribulations.

Obviously, these exalted ideals were never universally realized and were often flouted in life. But their enunciation is itself a great achievement. We have only to contrast the Bible with such exalted writings as Plato's *Republic*, which pictures the ideal state of the future as protected by a standing army perpetually on guard against the non-Greek barbarians, or Aristotle's *Politics*, with its reasoned defense of human slavery.

In sum, the spirit of the Torah is best described as "priestly-prophetic." The world's most categorical ethical ideals are to be found in the Decalogue, side by side with ritual enactments. Within the Book of Leviticus, which contains the priestly regulations, the Holiness Code (chs. 17-26) is embedded. Aside from countless ritual ordinances, this code contains the Golden Rule, the demand for loving the stranger and the Jubilee legislation to prevent monopoly in land.

The interplay of both prophetic and priestly elements is particularly evident in Deuteronomy. The insistence upon a single sanctuary (ch. 12 and *passim*) doubtless harmonized with the interests of the Jerusalemite priesthood, though it had obvious religious and moral advantages. On the other hand, the highly varied legislation throughout the book (as *e.g.*, 15, 20, 21, 27) reflects a sympathy for the poor, a hatred of tyranny, and a compassion for the weak, the underprivileged and the alien that is genuinely prophetic in spirit.

Prophecy likewise reveals an intimate relationship with both Torah and Wisdom. The fundamental emphasis of the biblical historians is on the prophetic doctrine that disaster is the inescapable consequence of sin and that national well-being rests upon national righteousness. Interestingly enough, this doctrine is formulated most clearly in Wisdom literature: "Righteousness exalts a people but sin is the shame of a nation" (Prov. 14:34). In retelling the history of Israel in the spirit of the prophets, the Books of Joshua, Judges, Samuel and Kings continue the historical narratives in the Torah. Hence, many scholars refer to the Pentateuch and Joshua as the Hexateuch, while some go even further and include all the historical books under the name Octateuch.

The predilection of the prophets for the techniques of Wisdom needs no elaborate demonstration. The prophets used parables and apothegms with telling effect. Most of their oracles and other addresses are poetic in structure and much of it must have been chanted to musical accompaniment. Prayers and psalms are by no means uncommon in the prophetic books. Moreover, the searching issues that troubled the unconventional Wisdom teachers could not have been overlooked by the profound spirit of the prophets. Jeremiah, Ezekiel and Deutero-Isaiah, in particular, grappled with the agonizing problem of the undeserved suffering of the righteous, both individually and in the collective experience of Israel.

The attitude of Wisdom to the Torah and prophets has already been indicated. Doubtless the Sages looked askance at the emotional basis of prophetic activity, and were skeptical about the prophets' extravagant hopes for the future. Nevertheless, prophetic attitudes penetrated even into their rationalistic circles. Witness the hatred of injustice in Ecclesiastes and Job, the emphasis upon morality as the heart of religion in Psalms 50 and 81, the triumphant affirmation of the coming Divine Judgment on evil in Psalms 75 and 82, and the passionate yearning for purity and freedom from sin throughout the Book of Psalms.

The Bible possesses a unity fashioned out of every current of Hebrew thought and action. It is inexhaustible in the wealth and variety of its contents. Priest, prophet, historian, poet and sage rub shoulders with one another within its covers, as they actually did in their own lifetimes, differing, arguing and influencing one another and unconsciously collaborating in producing the greatest spiritual force in the history of mankind. The prophets' magnificent faith in God's justice, and Job's equally noble protest against undeserved suffering, the Psalmists' mystical absorption in God, and the practical counsel of the Sages in Proverbs, the love of life and the life of love hymned in the Song of Songs and the melancholy reflections of Ecclesiastes—all were authentic expressions of the genius of Israel.

8. The Bible as Literature

The nobility and eternal relevance of the Bible is heightened by its superb literary form. The Bible is a library of masterpieces written by men who are artists not for art's sake, a conception which they would not have favored had they known it, but for life's sake. They were impelled by a single purpose, to tell their message as directly and effectively as possible. With the sure instinct of genius, they utilized the literary techniques and forms of their day and developed them to perfection. Unbeknown to themselves, they produced a gallery of classics in which deceptive simplicity conceals the highest art.

Tolstoy has called the Joseph saga in Genesis the greatest narrative in the world, unrivaled for dramatic power and psychological finesse. Throughout the four books of the Torah in which Moses is the guiding spirit, no formal description of the great leader is to be met with, except for one brief passage where he is described as the "humblest of men" (Num. 12:3). Nonetheless, the character of Moses is one of the most vivid ever drawn. The trajectory of his career is traced through mounting trials and crises with an art as consummate as it is unconscious, an art that Boswell might well have envied but could not surpass.

Over and beyond the sheer perfection of its elements is the architectural structure of Genesis. The majestic opening verse, "In the beginning, God created the heaven and the earth," takes the cosmos as its background. Immediately thereafter, with characteristic Jewish realism, heaven is let alone and the narrative turns to the earth. Concerning itself with the human race, it traces the origin of mankind, its trials and sins culminating in the Flood, from which only Noah and his family survive (2-9). The offspring of two of his sons, Ham and Japhet, are briefly listed and dismissed (10:1-20), so that the descendants of Shem may be treated at greater length (10:21 ff; 11:10 ff.). This serves as a preface to the career of Abraham, with whom the history of Israel begins (12-24). Of his two sons, Ishmael's descendants are briefly noted (25:12 ff.), and the narrative concentrates on Isaac (25:19-27). He, too, has two sons, Esau whose stock is dismissed in one chapter (36), and Jacob, whose personal fortunes and family misfortunes become the fundamental theme of the rest of the book. The Joseph saga then prepares the way for the bondage in Egypt, the liberation by Moses and the giving of the Law at Sinai. With unsurpassed literary art, the Book of Genesis has thus linked Creation and Revelation.

The historian-author of Samuel has painted an unforgettable portrait in the life story of Saul, with its bright early promise and the cloud of mental instability and ruin later descending upon him. At least equally notable is the vivid narrative of David's life with its bright ascendancy, its glorious noonday and its tragic dusk. Surrounding these two principal figures stands an immortal gallery of human nature, Samuel and Jonathan, Michael and Bath-Sheba, Nathan and Solomon, Absalom and Barzillai. Ruth has been described as the most perfect short story ever written. Jonah has been justly called by C. H. Cornill the "noblest book in the Old Testament." For sheer storytelling art, it belongs with the Elijah cycle and Esther. The memoirs of Nehemiah are a revealing picture of the period of the Restoration, with the problems strikingly similar to our own. Oratory has suffered in esteem in modern times, but the tenderness of Deuteronomy, the majesty of Isaiah, and the heartrending pathos of Jeremiah will never lose their power, because they speak from the heart and deep calls to deep.

The poetry of the Bible is perhaps its crowning glory. The moral fervor of the prophets, the passionate tenderness of the love lyrics in the Song of Songs, the grief of Lamentations, and all the human impulses reflected in the Book of Psalms have never been surpassed and rarely equaled. Faith and doubt, victory and defeat, hatred and doom, rebellion and submission, all find matchless expression in the Psalter, the world's most beloved songster. The nature poetry in Psalms (19 and 104) and the great God-speeches in Job have been acclaimed by figures as various as Herder and von Humboldt. The common sense of Proverbs will never cease to charm as well as to instruct young and old, while mature minds grappling with the mystery of life and the existence of evil will find both comradeship and comfort in Ecclesiastes and Job. The one was called by Renan "the most charming book ever written by a Jew." The other was pronounced by Carlyle "the grandest book ever written with pen."

Earlier generations were admonished with regard to the Bible, "turn it over and over, for everything is in it, and grow old and gray with it, but do not swerve from it."[24] That judgment is vindicated anew, as men penetrate ever more deeply into its spirit. For the Bible's goal is righteousness, its weapon is truth, and its achievement is beauty.

NOTES

[1] Baba Batra 15a.

[[2a] Cf. above Judah Goldin, "The Period of the Talmud (135 B.C.E.-1035 C.E.)," pp. 161-164.]

[[3a] Cf. below Alexander Altmann, "Judaism and World Philosophy," *passim.*]

[4] Hagigah 13b.

[5] Yebamot 49b.

[6] Baba Kamma 2b and parallel passages.

[7] Berakot 31b and parallel passages.

[8] Shabbat 63a and parallel passages.

[[9a] Cf. above the chapter by William Foxwell Albright, "The Biblical Period."]

[[10a] Cf. below Louis Finkelstein, "The Jewish Religion: Its Beliefs and Practices," pp. 1743 ff. See also below, Mordecai M. Kaplan, "A Philosophy of Jewish Ethics," p. 1020.]

[11] Reading with the Kethib *ribbo' torothai.*

[[11a] Cf. Albright, *op. cit.*, pp. 11-12.]

[[12a] Cf. *ibid.*, pp. 45 ff. and Goldin, *op. cit.*, pp. 175-177.]

[[13a] Cf. Albright, *op. cit.*, pp. 48 ff.]

[14] Sanhedrin 21b.

[[15a] Cf. Albright, *op. cit.*, pp. 53 ff.]

[[16a] On Samuel, David and Saul, cf. *ibid.*, pp. 23-29.]

[[17a] Cf. *ibid.*, pp. 37-40.]

[[18a] Cf. Kaplan, *op. cit.*, pp. 1032 ff.]

[19] Baba Batra 15b.

[[20a] Cf. above Elias J. Bickerman, "The Historical Foundations of Post-biblical Judaism," pp. 104-105.]

[[21a] Cf. *ibid.*, pp. 95-96, 98-99.]

[[22a] Cf. *ibid.*, pp. 77 ff., and Albright, *op. cit.*, pp. 50 ff.]

[[23a] Cf. below Ralph Marcus, "Hellenistic Jewish Literature," pp. 1101-1103.]

[24] Cf. Abot 5:22.

BIBLIOGRAPHY

In a field in which the literature is enormous, this bibliography makes no pretense to completeness. It consists largely of works in English and is intended to serve as a guide for further reading. Philological studies, detailed commentaries and other technical works beyond the purview of the general reader are generally not included.

A. *Bible Translations and One-Volume Commentaries*

The Authorized and Revised Versions.

The Holy Scriptures—Jewish Version. Philadelphia, 1917.

EISELEN, F. C., *Abingdon Bible Commentary*. New York, Cincinnati, 1929.

MARGOLIS, MAX L., *The Story of Bible Translations*. Philadelphia, 1917.

MOFFATT, JAMES, *A New Translation of the Bible*. New York and London, 1935.

MOULTON, RICHARD G., *The Modern Reader's Bible*. New York and London, 1926.

PEAKE, ARTHUR S. (ed.), *A Commentary on the Bible*. London and New York, 1936.

SMITH, JOHN M. P. (ed.), *The Complete Bible—An American Translation*. Chicago, 1945.

B. *Biblical Criticism*

DRIVER, S. R., *An Introduction to the Literature of the Old Testament* (12th ed.). New York, 1906.

EISSFELDT, OTTO, *Einleitung in das Alte Testament*. Tuebingen, 1934.

MARGOLIS, MAX L., *The Hebrew Scriptures in the Making*. Philadelphia, 1922.

PFEIFFER, ROBERT H., *Introduction to the Old Testament*. New York, 1941.

Driver's classic work is a balanced presentation of the critical position as maintained a generation ago. Eissfeldt's work incorporates the results of the past four decades of Bible study. Pfeiffer's work, which generally adopts radical critical positions, is invaluable because of its succinct summaries of all important views and its rich bibliographical references, especially to recent literature. Margolis's small work presents in popular form a great conservative scholar's views on the composition and canonization of Scripture.

CHEYNE, T. K., *Founders of Old Testament Criticism*. London, 1893.

RUBASCHEFF, S., and SOLOWEITSCHIK, M., *Toledot Bikoret Hamikra*. Berlin, 1925.

Studies in the history of biblical criticism and the progress of investigation.

HOOKE, S. H. (ed.), *Myth and Ritual*. London, 1933.

PEAKE, ARTHUR S. (ed.), *The People and the Book; Essays on the Old Testament*. Oxford, 1925.

ROBINSON, H. WHEELER (ed.), *Record and Revelation, Essays on the Old Testament*. Oxford, 1938.

Collected papers on various phases of Bible studies from the critical point of view.

CASSUTO, U., *La Questione Della Genesi*. Florence, 1934.

———, *Torat Hateudot Ve'Sidduram Shel Sifrei Hatorah*. Jerusalem, 1941.

———, *Me'adam 'ad Noah*. Jerusalem, 1944.

COPPENS, J., *The Old Testament and the Critics* (trans. from the French by Ryan and Tribbe). Paterson, N. J., 1941.

HOFFMANN, DAVID, *Die Wichtigsten Instanzen gegen die Graf-Wellhausensche Hypothese*. Berlin, 1904-1916.

ORR, JAMES, *The Problem of the Old Testament*. New York. 1906.

Cassuto's works in Italian and Hebrew subject the Documentary Hypothesis to the criticism of a leading scholar of our day. Hoffmann's and Orr's works are thoroughgoing critiques of the higher critical position, as expounded a generation ago by a traditionalist Jewish and Protestant scholar, respectively. Coppens's work, translated from the French, is the fair-minded and valuable survey of the various critical theories by a Belgian Catholic scholar.

C. *History and Archaeology*

BERTHOLET, A., *A History of Hebrew Civilization*. London, 1926.

BEVAN, E. R., and SINGER, C., *The Legacy of Israel*. Oxford, 1927.

CAUSSE, A., *Du Groupe Ethnique à la Communauté Religieuse*, Paris, 1937.

FINEGAN, JACK, *Light from the Ancient Past*. Princeton, 1946.

GORDIS, ROBERT, "The Edah—Primitive Democracy in Ancient Israel," in *Professor Alexander Marx Jubilee Volume* (English section). New York, 1949.

GRAHAM, W. C. and MAY, H. G., *Culture and Conscience*. Chicago, 1936.

KAUFMAN, J., *Toledot Ha'Emunah Ha'Israelit*. 7 vols. Tel-Aviv, 1937-1942.

LODS, ADOLPHE, *Israel, from its beginnings to the middle of the eighth century*. New York, 1932.

MAISLER, B., *Toledot Eretz Israel*, Tel-Aviv, 1938.

OESTERLEY, W. O. E., and ROBINSON, T. H., *Hebrew Religion, its Origin and Development* (2nd ed.). London, 1937.

———, *A History of Israel*. Oxford, 1932.

OLMSTEAD, A. T., *A History of Palestine and Syria to the Macedonian Conquest*. New York and London, 1931.

PEDERSEN, J., *Israel: Its Life and Culture*. London, 1926.

SMITH, G. A., *Historical Geography of the Holy Land* (25th ed.), 1932.

SMITH, W. ROBERTSON, *Lectures on the Religion of the Semites*. London, 1927.

WRIGHT, G. E., and FILSON, F. V., *Westminster Historical Atlas to the Bible*. Philadelphia, 1945.

These works deal with the history of the Hebrew people and its religion and civilization in terms of the background of the ancient Orient and in the light of archaeology.

ALBRIGHT, WILLIAM FOXWELL, *Archaeology and the Religion of Israel*. Baltimore, 1942.
———, *The Archaeology of Palestine and the Bible* (3rd ed.). New York, 1935.
———, *From the Stone Age to Christianity*. Baltimore, 1940.
BAILEY, ALBERT EDWARD, *Daily Life in Bible Times*. New York, 1943.
BARTON, G. A., *Archaeology and the Bible* (7th ed.). Philadelphia, 1937.
BURROWS, MILLAR, *What Mean These Stones?* New Haven, 1941.
FRAZER, J. G., *Folk-Lore in the Old Testament*. London, 1918.
GARSTANG, JOHN, *The Foundations of Bible History: Joshua, Judges*. New York, 1931.
GLUECK, NELSON, *The River Jordan*. Philadelphia, 1946.
GRANT, ELIHU (ed.), *The Haverford Symposium on Archaeology and the Bible*. New Haven, 1938.
The Heritage of Solomon. London, 1934.
JACOBSON, DAVID, *The Social Background of the Old Testament*. Cincinnati, 1942.

These works are concerned largely with the bearing of archaeology on the various phases of biblical life and thought.

SMITH, ROY L., *It All Happened Once Before*. New York and Nashville, 1944.
WALLIS, LOUIS, *The Bible Is Human; a study in secular history*. New York, 1942.
———, *God and the Social Process*. Chicago, 1935.
———, *Sociological Study of the Bible*. Chicago, 1927.
WEBER, MAX, *Das antike Judentum*. Tuebingen, 1921.

Works stressing the social and economic aspects of biblical thought.

D. *Torah*

GREENSTONE, JULIUS H., *Numbers With Commentary*. Philadelphia, 1939.
HERTZ, J. H., *The Pentateuch and Haftorahs*. London, 1938.
REIDER, J., *Deuteronomy With Commentary*. Philadelphia, 1937.

E. *The Prophets*

BUBER, MARTIN, *Torat Ha'Nebiim*. Tel-Aviv, 1942.
BUTTENWIESER, MOSES, *The Prophets of Israel*. New York, 1914.
DRIVER, S. R., *Isaiah: His Life and Times*. New York, 1888.
FINKELSTEIN, LOUIS, *The Pharisees*. Philadelphia, 1938.
HAMILTON, EDITH, *The Prophets of Israel*. London, 1936.
HOSCHANDER, JACOB, *The Priests and Prophets*. New York, 1938.
MARGOLIS, M. L., *The Holy Scriptures with Commentary: Micah*. Philadelphia, 1908.
MORGENSTERN, JULIAN, *Amos Studies*. Cincinnati, 1941.
SMITH, GEORGE A., *The Book of the Twelve Prophets*. Garden City, N. Y., 1929.
SMITH, W. ROBERTSON, *The Prophets of Israel*. London, 1907.

Buber approaches the problems in a characteristically philosophical fashion. Finkelstein's study contains three chapters (15-17) dealing with the religious and ethical teachings of the prophets. Edith Hamilton's work is a well-written, deeply personal approach to the prophets. The third book of Morgenstern's study, which is called *The Antecedents of Amos' Prophecy* traces the background of Hebrew prophecy by a highly original biblical scholar of our day. W. Robertson Smith's and Buttenwieser's works are based on the "classic" form of the higher critical theory.

F. *Wisdom*

BUTTENWIESER, MOSES, *The Psalms*. Chicago, 1938.
CHEYNE, T. K., *Job and Solomon; or, The Wisdom of the Old Testament*. New York, 1887.
FICHTNER, JOHANNES, *Die altorientalische Weisheit in ihrer Israelitisch-juedischen Auspraegung*. Giessen, 1933.
FREEHOF, SOLOMON, *The Book of Psalms*. Cincinnati, 1938.
GORDIS, ROBERT, "Mabo Le'Safrut Ha'Hokmah," in *Sefer Hashanah*. New York, 1942.
———, "The Social Background of Wisdom Literature," in *Hebrew Union College Annual*. Cincinnati, 1944.
———, *The Wisdom of Ecclesiastes*. New York, 1945.
———, "Introduction to the Book of Job," in *Morris Raphael Cohen Memorial Volume*. New York, 1950.
JAMES, FLEMING, *Thirty Psalmists*. New York, 1938.
KIRKPATRICK, A. F., *Cambridge Commentary on Psalms*. Cambridge, 1921.
MACDONALD, DUNCAN BLACK, *The Hebrew Philosophical Genius*. Princeton, 1936.
OESTERLEY, W. O. E., *A Fresh Approach to the Psalms*. New York, 1937.
RANKIN, O. S., *Israel's Wisdom Literature*. Edinburgh, 1936.
RANSTON, H., *The Old Testament Wisdom Books and Their Teaching*. London, 1930.

G. *Literary and Religious Appreciation*

BEWER, JULIUS A., *The Literature of the Old Testament* (2nd ed.). New York, 1933.
CHASE, MARY ELLEN, *The Bible and the Common Reader*. New York, 1944.
FOSDICK, HARRY EMERSON, *A Guide to Understanding the Bible*. New York and London, 1938.
MACDONALD, DUNCAN BLACK, *The Hebrew Literary Genius*. Princeton, 1933.
MOULTON, RICHARD G., *The Literary Study of the Bible*. Boston, 1899.
PEAKE, ARTHUR S., *The Bible, Its Origin, Its Significance, and Its Abiding Worth*. London and New York, 1914.

CHAPTER 16

THE INFLUENCE OF JEWISH LAW ON THE DEVELOPMENT OF THE COMMON LAW

By Jacob J. Rabinowitz

1. Introduction

The Jews came to England in considerable numbers after the Norman conquest.[1] They were able to establish themselves under the protection of the king, who welcomed them as a source of income and ready cash. Their financial transactions were numerous and involved large amounts of money. For some time they had a virtual monopoly of the moneylending business, because the taking of interest was prohibited to Christians by the Church.[2] Many a castle was built with funds advanced by Jews to the nobleman who built it, and even some monasteries were built with money borrowed from the Jews.[3] When Aaron of Lincoln—probably the richest Jew in their midst—died, a special branch of the Exchequer was required to handle his financial affairs, so that the king's share of the estate might be collected.[4]

Justice in civil matters between Jew and Jew was administered by the Chapters of the Jews, that is, by Rabbinical courts, in accordance with Jewish law.[5] A special court, the Exchequer of the Jews, which at one time consisted of Jews and Gentiles, had jurisdiction over disputes arising between Jew and Gentile.[6, 6a]

For many centuries before their settlement in England Jews had cultivated the study of law with great devotion and religious fervor. *Dine mamonot*, *i.e.*, that branch of the law which deals with matters relating to property, contract, and torts, as distinguished from ritual law, was particularly favored by men of acute intellect among them. "He who wishes to acquire wisdom should study *dine mamonot*," reads an early talmudic text.[7] Throughout the lands of their dispersion justice was administered among them by Rabbinical courts in accordance with talmudic law as interpreted by leading Rabbis.[8] As a result of centuries of study and practice there developed among them a body of law, and with it a large number of legal forms and devices, far more mature and complex than anything that was known to English lawyers of the twelfth century. Under these circumstances it would be very strange indeed if the Jews did not use the legal forms with which they were familiar, and which were elaborately discussed in their legal literature.

That so little attention has been given to the possible influence of Jews upon the development of the law of the creditor-debtor relationship, a field where their influence should have made itself felt more effectively than in any other legal field, is probably due to the fact that most sources of Jewish law are not available in English. Even where available, it takes years of study to master their intricacies.

Pollock and Maitland have this to say about the possible influence of Jewish law upon English law:

> Whether the sojourn of the Jews in England left any permanent marks upon the body of our law is a question that we dare not debate, though we may raise it. We can hardly suppose that from *Lex Judaica*, the Hebrew Law which the Jews administered among themselves, anything passed into the code of the contemptuous Christians. But that the International *Lex Judaismi* perished in 1290 without leaving any memorial of itself, is by no means so certain.[9]

While it may be conceded that cases of deliberate and conscious adoption by English lawyers of rules and doctrines from the Hebrew law were rare —although this is by no means certain—the adoption of security devices used by the Jews falls into an entirely different classification. Their origin is extrajudicial, they are born of the exigencies and necessities of trade and commerce, where Jew meets Gentile on more or less equal terms, and where religious prejudices are thrust into the background. The judiciary but passes on their effect and validity and is in a limited sense only a party to their creation.

The researches conducted by the present writer have revealed that the *lex judaismi* did leave some important memorials of itself in English law, but that these had come to be so integrated in the English legal system that their origin was completely forgotten.

In the following pages an attempt will be made to present some of the highlights of Jewish influence upon the development of English law.

2. THE JEWISH GAGE

The form of security most frequently used by the Jews in England was known as the "Jewish gage." The nature of this gage has never been fully understood by historians of English law,[10] for the simple reason that its roots are to be found in Hebrew law, with which these historians were totally unfamiliar. The form of security represented by the "Jewish gage" was, as Pollock and Maitland[11] point out, a completely novel institution in England, in that it gave rights in land to a creditor who was not in possession of the land. It was introduced by the Jews and was patterned by them after devices which they had used for many centuries prior to their settlement in England. Only a reference to Hebrew law can give us a clue to its understanding.

The Hebrew device that gave rise to the Jewish gage is not a mortgage in the sense of a pledge of specific property as security for the payment of a debt. It does not form part of the Hebrew law of mortgages, but is rather an integral part of the Hebrew law of execution.[12] It is a general lien in favor of the creditor upon all the real property owned by the debtor at the time the debt is incurred. By virtue of this lien the creditor may follow the property into the hands of a transferee who acquired the property after the lien had attached to it.[13] The lien is implied in law as an incident of every debt evidenced by a *shtar* bond, signed at the instance of the debtor by two witnesses and accompanied by sufficient publicity,[14] and of every judgment of a court of competent jurisdiction.[15] Although a stipulation to the effect that the debtor binds his property for the payment of the debt is usually incorporated in the bond, its omission has no legal effect. In the language of the Talmud,[16] the omission is presumed to be an error of the scrivener.

There is, however, one important limitation upon the right of the creditor to follow the debtor's property into the hands of a transferee. As long as the debtor has free assets sufficient to satisfy the debt in full, the creditor cannot proceed against the property in the hands of a transferee.[17] This limitation of the creditor's right under the lien of the Hebrew *shtar* is an important characteristic of this lien and distinguishes it from a mortgage. The debtor's land, according to Hebrew law, stands surety for the payment of his debts, and just as the surety's liability, under ordinary circumstances, is secondary—that is, he is liable only in case the principal debtor does not possess sufficient assets to satisfy the debt—so the liability of the debtor's land is only secondary.

Originally, the creditor's lien attached only to the debtor's immovable property.[18] At a later period it was held that by inserting a special provision to that effect in the *shtar*, the lien could be extended to the debtor's movable property.[19] At an earlier period the question was raised by the Babylonian scholar, "Master Samuel," as to whether or not the debtor could subject his future acquisitions to the lien of the creditor.[20] By analogy with conveyance of property, some argued that a lien on property to be acquired in the future by the debtor should be ineffective, just as a sale of such property would be ineffective. The conclusion of the Talmud, however, is that the creation of a lien is not to be likened to a conveyance.

In the posttalmudic period the practice became almost universal to incorporate in every *shtar* a lien on the maker's property *movable and immovable, present and future*.[21] This standardized lien clause was introduced by the Jews of England into the bonds they used when advancing money to Gentiles, and was apparently given full force and effect by the English courts. The Latin formula used was *obligo omnia bona mea, mobilia et immobilia.*[22] The legal effect given to this formula by the Exchequer of the Jews was substantially the same as that given to it by Jewish law. The lien of the creditor upon the debtor's land was enforced by the Exchequer of the Jews not only against the debtor himself, but also against a transferee.[23] Similarly, the rule of Jewish law that the lien is enforceable against the transferee only where the debtor does not possess free assets sufficient to satisfy the debt was followed by the Exchequer.[24]

From the Jewish bonds the lien clause found its way into general use; in the thirteenth and fourteenth centuries we find that almost every bond made in England contains the formula: *Obligo omnia bona mea, mobilia et immobilia.*[25] The provision for the binding of the debtor's future acquisition occurs less frequently, but it, too, is found in several bonds in Madox's *Formulare,*[26] and elsewhere,[27] where the lien clause reads: *Obligo omnia bona mea, mobilia et immobilia, presentia et futura.*

The Jewish gage, which, as we have seen, is part of the Hebrew law of execution, the fundamental idea of which is that the entire property of the debtor, movable and immovable, is bound for the payment of his debts, had a profound influence upon the development of English economic life and English law. It was this idea, which gradually gained a foothold in feudal England with its fixity of ownership of land, that resulted, on the economic side, in broadening the base of credit by making land, the principal source of wealth, readily available as security, and, on the legal side, in making land in possession of the debtor liable for the payment of his debts. As Pollock and Maitland have already noted,[28] the statute creating the *writ of elegit,* enacted in 1285, was patterned after the Jewish gage. This writ gave a judgment creditor, or a creditor upon a recognizance, the right to collect his debt from the debtor's real property, to the extent of one-half thereof, by seizing the property through judicial process and holding it until the debt had been paid by the debtor, or until the creditor had satisfied himself out of the rents and profits. The limitation of the creditor's right to one-half of the debtor's property followed an earlier enactment, during the reign of Edward I, which put a similar limitation upon the Jewish creditor.

The idea of the Jewish gage gradually gained a foothold in England, for, contrary to the view of Pollock and Maitland, the *statute of elegit* was not altogether an innovation. According to Pollock and Maitland, prior to 1285 the only remedies available to a creditor against a defaulting debtor were the writs of *fieri facias* and *fieri levare,* the former directing the sheriff to seize the debtor's chattels and make the debt therefrom, and the latter directing him to make the debt from the fruit of the debtor's land.[29] It was only in 1285, these writers assert, that the creditor was given a right in the debtor's land. However, it appears from certain bonds made some twenty-five years before the enactment of the *statute of elegit* that provision was already made then for seizure of the debtor's land by the creditor upon default. Thus in a bond[30] executed about 1260 we find the formula *obligo omnia bona mea, mobilia et immobilia* followed by the clause giving the obligee the right, upon default by the obligor, to seize the latter's land and receive the profits therefrom until the obligation had been fully satisfied, a procedure which was invariably followed in the case of the Jewish gage in which the formula *obligo omnia bona mea*, etc. originated. A similar provision is found in several other bonds[31] enrolled upon the Close Rolls during the reign of Henry III. In still another bond[32] of about the same time we find a specific provision to the effect that the obligation shall constitute a charge upon the obligor's land even in the hands of a transferee. Obviously, then, the creditor's right in the debtor's land was not unknown in England before 1285. What was new in the *statute of elegit* was the extension of this right to all judgment creditors. It may therefore be said that this statute and the practices preceding it, which are the basis of the modern law of execution in England and the United States, are an outgrowth of the *Jewish gage*.

3. THE HEBREW ODAITA AND THE ENGLISH RECOGNIZANCE

Although under Hebrew law a bond attested by two witnesses gave the creditor a lien on the entire property of the debtor, good against the whole world except prior lienors, creditors very often sought further means to facilitate collection of their debts and to overcome procedural difficulties in their enforcement. One of these was the so-called *Odaita*, literally, confession or recognizance. It consisted of a formal declaration by the debtor, before a court of competent jurisdiction, acknowledging the existence of the debt. The declaration was embodied by the court in a document attested by it, and had the force of a judgment.[33]

According to the Talmud, the principle upon which the validity of this device is based is this: an admission against interest is as good as the testimony of "a hundred witnesses."[34] A rule of evidence was thus converted into a means of effecting and initiating jural relationships between the parties, instead of merely proving the existence of such relationships.

The debtor's declaration was sometimes made before two witnesses, rather than before a court, and in such case it was necessary either for the creditor or the debtor to address the witnesses and ask them to bear witness to the declaration about to be made.[35] This safeguard was intended to remove the possibility of the declaration having been made in a jocular manner.

In the twelfth century Maimonides, the great Hebrew philosopher[35a] and codifier of Hebrew law, introduced an innovation into the Hebrew law of recognizances or, perhaps, codified an innovation introduced earlier. He maintained that the requirement for the debtor to address the witnesses with the words "ye be my witnesses, etc." applies only to cases where the declaration is made in the course of a casual conversation. Where the debtor, on the other hand, makes a true or genuine recognizance—*hodaah gemurah*, in Hebrew—this requirement may be dispensed with.[36] As a result of this innovation the phrase "make a true or genuine recognizance" was incorporated in almost every Hebrew recognizance document.

From a certain passage in the Talmud it appears that *Odaita* was in frequent use among Jews during the talmudic period.[37] In the post-talmudic period this form of security became still more frequent, because, according to some authorities,[38] when the debt was evidenced by an *Odaita* the consideration for it could not be inquired into by the court. A totally gratuitous promise, when made in the form of a declaration of a debt, is valid and enforceable, according to these authorities; by his declaration the debtor has precluded himself from attacking the validity of the debt on any ground. Although the prevailing opinion[39] is that a gratuitous promise is valid when accompanied by sufficient formality and solemnity, whether made in the form of a declaration of debt or in the form of an assumption of an obligation, practical draftsmen sought to remove all doubt by drafting most of their documents in the form of a declaration. Only where the declaration form was not feasible, as in the case of a conditional obligation, or of an obligation which could not be reduced to a sum certain (such as the promise to support a child for five years) was the form of an assumption of an obligation used.[40]

The Jews of medieval England used the *Odaita*—recognizance form—in practically all documents written in Hebrew and evidencing transactions between Jew and Jew or Jew and Christian.[41] The Hebrew starrs of acquittance, which are the most numerous of all available Hebrew documents of medieval England, and which the writer will discuss later in more detail, all take the form of a recognizance. The introductory phrase in these documents usually reads: "X recognizes a true recognizance"—a phrase which, as we have seen, is characteristic of the Hebrew *Odaita* and is directly traceable to the rule about the formal requisites for the validity of a recognizance. In the Calendar of the Plea Rolls of the Exchequer of the Jews there are virtually hundreds of entries of starrs of acquittance, and in all of these the recognizance form is used. One of the earliest extant documents evidencing a debt by a Christian to a Jew takes the form of a recognizance.[42] In the thirteenth century all the documents evidencing debts owed by Christians to Jews, take the form of a recognizance. These are found either in full or in abbreviated form in the published records of the Exchequer of the Jews. In a British Museum collection of Hebrew documents, published by the Jewish Historical Society of England, we find a document containing two parallel texts, one in Hebrew and the other in Latin, where the Hebrew phrase *Mode Hodaah Gemurah* is translated *recognosco veram recognicionem.*[43] The Norman-French equivalent of this phrase *reconnusse verreye reconusaunce* is found in Madox's *Formulare Anglicanum*[44] in a document of recognizance, made by a Jew and dated 1275, and in several documents in the Calendar, etc. In the Madox document the introductory phrase reads: *Jeo ke suy ensele de suz reconnusse verreye reconusaunce et testemoine.* The word *testemoine*—testify—is indicative of the procedural origin of the recognizance. As has already been remarked, the recognizance takes the place of testimony by witnesses, on the principle that an admission against interest is as good as the testimony of a hundred witnesses.

On the origin of the Hebrew recognizance, a document found in the Public Records Office in London and published in Meyer D. Davis's collection of Hebrew documents is particularly illuminating. The document reads: "I, the undersigned, recognize a true recognizance that what is written above in the Latin tongue is true and that I made this starr of acquittance to Prior Alexander so that it may be in his hands and in the hands of his assigns as proof of their rights even as a hundred witnesses. And what I have acknowledged I have signed, Jacob, son of Samuel."[45] The phrase "even as a hundred witnesses" is clearly an allusion to the talmudic dictum that an admission against interest is as good as the testimony of a hundred witnesses. From this the recognizance derives its force and validity.

The close resemblance between the form of the Hebrew *Odaita* and that of the recognizance of English law is quite obvious. But the resemblance is not only one of form; it extends to the most fundamental feature of these devices. In the earliest reported cases of recognizances the debtor not only confesses the debt, but also binds his property as security for its payment, a feature which is characteristic of the Hebrew *Odaita*, as well as of other forms of obligation in Hebrew law. Thus in Select Civil Pleas[46] pl. 25 (Hilary Term, 1201), we find: "Miles de Hastings owes to Brian, son of Ralph twenty marks; to wit, ten marks on the Octave of Easter and ten marks at the Nativity of St. Mary the Virgin; and thereof [Miles] places in pledge to him his land of Hokinton, which he holds of the fee of William de Hastings." And again in pl. 174 (Octave of Michaelmas, 1202), it is recorded: "John the vintner demands against Ralph the priest of Elmham thirty-six shillings and four pence; and they make a concord to the effect that Ralph shall give (John) two marks of silver (now), and shall pay him one mark within the octave of S. Edmond, and another within the Octave of Mid-lent; and in case he shall not have paid (them) he has put in pledge to (John) all the lands which he holds as of lay fee in Suffolk."

Further, more direct evidence of the Jewish origin of the recognizance and of its effect in giving the creditor a right in the debtor's land, is found in an entry in the Close Rolls[47] which contains the full text of the instrument executed by the obligor, not just a notation of its tenor and import. Both, the obligor and obligee, were Christians, yet the instrument is a perfect specimen of a Jewish bond, giving the creditor the fullest protection possible under Hebrew law and practice. In the first place, it contains the clause *obligo omnia bona mea, mobilia et immobilia, presentia et futura* which, as we have seen, is characteristic of every kind of Hebrew obligation. Secondly, it contains a provision that in case of default by the debtor the creditor shall have the right to seize the debtor's land and hold it until he had been fully paid, a right which was in all respects identical with that of the Jewish creditor under the "Jewish gage." Thirdly, the provision contained in the instrument, that the surety who guaranteed performance be bound as a principal debtor, is one which is found in Jewish bonds in England, and which goes back to early talmudic times. In an early talmudic text (*c.* second century) we read: "If a man lent his fellow money on a guarantor's security, he may not exact payment from the guarantor [in the first instance]; but if he said, 'on the condition that I may exact payment from whom I will,' he may exact payment from the guarantor [in the first instance]."[48] Later on the two types of undertaking to answer for another's debt, the one imposing upon the accommodating party a primary liability and the other imposing upon him a secondary liability, became so far standardized that they were referred to by two different names, the former being called *Kabblanut* and the latter *Arabut*, very much as these same types of undertaking later came to be called in English and American law by two different names, *suretyship* and *guarantee*. When the Jews came to England they applied this distinction, which had become elementary in Hebrew law, to their transactions with Christians, and wherever possible they made provision that the accommodating party be primarily liable.[49] This provision, which is very convenient from the creditor's point of view, was adopted by Christian creditors, together with the other features of the Jewish bond, when they entered the business of moneylending.

That Jewish security devices should have been adopted by the English is not at all surprising. It must be borne in mind that when the Jews came to England they did not find fixed and established forms of security which they could use. Moneylending on a large scale was unknown in England before the arrival of the Jews. It was the Jew who developed this business, and with it the instruments through which it was carried on. Under these circumstances it was almost inevitable that he used forms of security with which he was familiar, and that these should later be adopted by money-lenders generally.

In this connection it is interesting to note Pollock and Maitland's observations on the nature and origin of the recognizance: "The parties go into the chancery or the exchequer and procure the making of an entry upon the close roll or some other roll. The borrower confesses that he owes a certain sum which is to be paid upon a certain day, and grants that, if default be made, the money may be levied by the sheriff. This practice, which is of some importance in the history of the chancery may have its origin in the fact (for fact it is) that some of its officers were money-lenders on a great scale."[50] The close connection between the Exchequer and the Jews is well known. It was a special branch of the Exchequer, the Scaccarium Judeorum, that had jurisdiction over the financial affairs of Jews and over disputes arising between Jew and Gentile. The money-lending barons of the Exchequer apparently adopted the convenient device of the recognizance from their Jewish wards whose business affairs they were charged with supervising. For convenient it certainly was, since it afforded the easiest way of proving the debt and at the same time bound the debtor's property for its payment.

4. The General Release and the Hebrew Starr of Acquittance

The General Release is a legal form used by lawyers throughout the United States and England whenever a settlement between the contending parties to a controversy is effected out of court. It is one of the most widely used legal forms.

This form contains some very peculiar language to which hardly anyone pays attention. It states, for instance, that the party giving the release releases and discharges the party to whom the release is given from all claims, demands, etc., "from the beginning of the world" to the day when the release is executed; an obvious exaggeration which calls for explanation. Yet no one, as far as the writer is aware, has ever attempted to trace the origin of this form or to account for its peculiarities. It has become part of the daily routine of office practice, and is taken for granted by those using it without arousing their curiosity.

It can be shown that the General Release is an adaptation of an old Hebrew form, introduced by the Jews of medieval England into their dealings with their Christian neighbors; and this accounts for some of its quaint phraseology.

One of the forms most frequently used by the Jews in England was the so-called Starr of Acquittance, the word "starr" being an Anglicized form of the Hebrew word *shtar*. The starr would be executed by the Jewish creditor and delivered by him to his Christian debtor upon payment of the debt owed by the latter to the former.

A large number of such starrs is found in the collection of Hebrew *Shtarot* published by M. D. Davis. Most of these starrs were written in Hebrew, and even when written in Latin or Norman-French they were endorsed in Hebrew by the Jewish creditor, to prevent forgery by the debtor or a plea of forgery by the creditor. In these starrs the creditor, after specifying the debt or claim to which the starr related, would proceed to release the debtor from all other debts "from the creation of the world" to the date of the execution of the instrument, or, sometimes, "to the end of the world." The following is a translation from the Hebrew original of a typical starr of acquittance: "I, the undersigned, recognize a true recognizance that Roger fil. Godward de Sewenington and his heirs are quit from me and my heirs of ten marks and one measure of wheat and of all debts, pledges and challenges from the creation of the world until Pentecost in the 43rd year of the reign of our Lord the King Henry fil. John, and what I have recognized I have signed."[51] The pattern of this starr is exactly like that of the General Release found in fourteenth century documents written in Latin, and in our own time may be found in every formbook used by lawyers through the length and breadth of the United States and England. Both have this outstanding characteristic in common: in addition to specifying the claim or debt immediately preceding the execution of the instrument they include all debts, claims, etc., from the beginning or the creation of the world.

The question naturally arises, who copied from whom? Did the Jewish creditors follow a pattern set for them by English draftsmen, translating it into Hebrew, or did the latter copy from the Jews?

Were there no other evidence as to the origin of the starr of acquittance, the fact that Jews for a long time occupied the position of principal financiers in England, and that they had a highly developed system of law and legal forms of their own, would make it reasonable to suppose that, at least in documents written in Hebrew, they used their own forms rather than adaptations of English forms. But one need not rely solely on this circumstantial evidence. The internal evidence from documents used in England, and the evidence from Hebrew sources outside England, is so abundant and convincing as to leave no doubt of the Hebrew origin of the Starr of Acquittance and its counterpart, the General Release.

To begin with, the phrase "from the beginning of the world" suggests a Jewish origin. It is well known that the Jews count the years of their calendar from the creation of the world. The present year [1959-1960], for example, is 5720, according to Jewish tradition. When the Jewish draftsman wanted to set down a date as far back as possible, it was natural for him to go back to the beginning of his calendar. The exaggeration implicit in this phrase was apparently overlooked because of the absolute certainty it afforded in removing all possible future controversies as to the debts and claims to which the acquittance related, including possible claims against the releasee's predecessors in interest.

Secondly, the starrs, as has already been remarked, were usually written in Hebrew, and even when written in Latin they were endorsed by the creditor in Hebrew. The Hebrew equivalent of the phrase, "from the beginning of the world," found in the modern General Release, is "*mibriat ha-olam,*" literally, from the creation of the world. This phrase occurs uniformly in all the Hebrew starrs, while in the Latin releases there are variations. Along with *a creatione seculi,*[52] which is the exact equivalent of the above Hebrew phrase, we find *a principio seculi,*[53] *ab initio seculi,*[54] *a principio mundi*[55] and *ab origine mundi.*[56] The uniformity of the Hebrew phrase, on the one hand, and the variations in the Latin versions, on the other, suggest that the former was the model and the latter were the copies.

Finally, the essential characteristics of the General Release are found in a Hebrew form occurring in a whole series of Hebrew formbooks and responsa of leading Rabbis, beginning with the tenth century—that is, long before the Jews came to England—down through the centuries almost to our own day. In the earlier sources this form is called *Shtar Abizarya*—the word *abizarya* meaning acquittance—and a distinction is drawn between it and the *Shtar Mehila,* the latter being a release of a specific claim or debt. In the later sources it is called *Mehila Kolelet,* which is the exact Hebrew equivalent of the English term "General Release." Under its former name it is found in a recently published fragment of the formbook of Rab Saadia Gaon[57, 57a] where the creditor releases the debtor from all claims and demands "*from the days of the world until now.*" Under the same name it appears in the formbook of Rab Hai Gaon,[58, 58a] where it is very elaborate, and very nearly approaches our modern General Release. It also appears, still under the name of *Shtar Abizarya,* in the formbook of Rabbi Judah Barzillai,[59] and in the *Sefer Haittur* of Rabbi Isaac b. Abba Mari of Marseilles.[60]

In a thirteenth-century case in the responsa of Rabbi Solomon b. Adreth a similar form was apparently used, but it is no longer referred to as *Shtar Abizarya.* From this responsum it is evident that the form under discussion was in general use, and that it was very comprehensive in scope. Indeed, in the table of contents it is called *Mehila Kolelet*—general release. The responsum reads, in part, as follows: "Question: R sold a field to S with warranty. Many years thereafter R and S had again dealings between them, and S released R from everything and every obligation, as is customary, and he did not remember the obligation of the warranty at the time when he executed the release. Is the obligation of the warranty included in the release?"[61]

A little later in the thirteenth century, in the responsa of Rabbi Asher b. Yehiel,[62] we find reference to a form, the substance of which is that the creditor releases the debtor "from all demands he had against him to this day," the form itself not being quoted by the Rabbi, but only its import stated. In the fourteenth century, in the responsa of Rabbi Nissim Gerondi[63] and in those of Rabbi Isaac b. Shesheth[64] there is reference in the text itself to a release which is called *Mehila Kolelet.*

Finally, in a sixteenth-century formbook, compiled by Rabbi Solomon Jaffe[65] in accordance with the usages prevailing in the Jewish communities of Constantinople and Salonica, we find a most polished specimen of this form under the name *Shtar Mehila.*

In order to show concretely the close resemblance between the form of the General Release now in use in England and in the United States, and the Hebrew forms that have just been mentioned, the writer will quote the material portions from the former and from some of the latter.

The General Release reads, in part, as follows:

Know all men by these presents, that I . . . have remised, released and forever discharged, and by these presents do for myself and my heirs, distributees, executors and administrators, remise, release and forever discharge the said . . . his heirs, distributees, executors and administrators, of and from all manner of action and actions, cause and causes of action, suits, debts, dues, sums of money, accounts, reckonings, bonds, bills, specialties, covenants, contracts, controversies, agreements, promises, variances, trespasses, damages, judgments, extents, executions, claims and demands whatsoever, in law and in equity, which against the said . . . I ever had, now have, or which I or my heirs . . . hereafter can, shall or may have for, upon or by reason of any matter cause or thing whatsoever *from the beginning of the world* to the date of these presents, and more particularly . . .

The *Shtar Abizarya* in the formbook of Rab Hai Gaon reads, in part, as follows:

X son of Y said to us: Ye be my witnesses and accept "*Kinyan*" [a symbolical delivery of some object, ordinarily a kerchief, which confirms the transaction and imparts to it binding legal force] and hand over [the document attesting the transaction] to A son of B, that of my own free will, without duress, [I have made this declaration] that I have received and accepted and have been fully paid everything he owed me, growing out of all there was between us *from the days of the world* until now. . . . And in accordance with what preceded between them, whether partnership or a loan, business transactions or purchase and sale, inheritance or things other than these, one is to specify accordingly, and then generalize and write of everything that transpires among men: of partnership, of joint venture, of business transactions, of inheritance, of purchase and sale, of deficit and surplus, of profit and loss, of loan and bailment, of pledge and of suretyship, of trespass and of fraud and of all manner and fashion of things in the world. And I cleared and acquitted the above named and his heirs, for myself and my heirs for all generations, of all *claims, challenges and demands* which men may demand of one another.

The introductory paragraph of the *Shtar Mehila* contained in the form-book of Rabbi Samuel Jaffe reads as follows:

> Before us, the undersigned witnesses, X, of his own free will, without duress, but wholeheartedly and willingly, made a true, valid and effective recognizance that he has received total and complete satisfaction of all the demands, rights and complaints that he had, or might have had, against Y and his representatives, *from the day the world was created* to the present day, and particularly of such and such a debt, and such and such a demand.

The similarity between the pattern of the General Release, on the one hand, and that of the two Hebrew forms quoted above, on the other, is obvious and needs no further elaboration. But the similarity is not only one of pattern; it extends to some of the most significant terms and clauses of these forms. In his chapter on Releases, sec. 508, Littleton says: "Also, if a man release to another all manner of demands, this is the best release to him to whom the release is made, that he can have, and shall enure most to his advantage." To this Coke, fol. 291 b, adds: "Demand, *demandum*, is a word of art, and in the understanding of the common law is of so large an extent, as no other one word in the law is, unless it be *clameum*, whereof Littleton maketh mention, sect. 445."

A mere glance at the Calendar of the Plea Rolls of the Exchequer of the Jews will reveal that both of these terms, *claims* and *demands*, occur in starrs found on almost everyone of its pages, while the Hebrew equivalents of these terms may be found in numerous documents in M. D. Davis's collection of Hebrew *Shtarot*. As in the case of the form itself, and perhaps more convincingly, the question as to which was the model and which the copy, the Hebrew terms or their equivalents in Latin and Norman-French, is answered by a reference to the Rab Hai Gaon form quoted above which dates back to the tenth century, and in which the same Hebrew terms signifying claims and demands, as those found in the Hebrew *Shtarot* in England, occur.

5. THE COMMON LAW WARRANTY OF REAL PROPERTY[66]

The warranty clause, commonly used in the United States and England in the conveyance of real property, is also of Jewish origin. The modern warranty clause reads substantially as follows: "The grantor, his heirs and assigns will warrant, defend and acquit the grantee, his heirs and assigns against all men." In English deeds of conveyance of the Middle Ages the last phrase of the above clause often reads, "against all men and women"; sometimes it reads, "against all men and women, Christians and Jews."

A comparison of the medieval warranty clause, of which our modern version is obviously a direct offspring, with the standard Jewish warranty clause used by Jews in the various lands of their dispersion from the Middle Ages down almost to our own day, reveals that the former is an abbreviated adaptation of the latter. The Jewish warranty clause reads substantially as follows:

And whoever shall come from the four winds of the world, man or woman, Jew or Gentile, son or daughter, heir or legatee, near or far, who shall arise and contrive and make any claim or requisition whatsoever on the said William, or his heirs or representatives, regarding the said house with the court and appurtenances, it will be obligatory upon me, my heirs and representatives, to free them and protect them against those claimants, and to maintain their possession of the house, court and appurtenances aforesaid, in peace and comfort (peaceably and quietly), on the surety of all my property, landed or movable, which I now possess or may in future acquire.

It is fairly obvious that the phrase "against all men and women, Christians and Jews" of the medieval English clause was taken almost verbatim from the above Jewish clause. What is more, the terms *defend* and *acquit* also seem to have been taken from the Jewish formula. The Hebrew equivalent of *defend* is found in a number of Hebrew documents from Angevin England and also in the formulary of Rabbi Jehudah Barzillai (eleventh century, Spain). The equivalent of *acquit* is likewise found in many Hebrew documents from Angevin England and in a portion of a warranty clause quoted in the Talmud.

Together with the warranty clause itself, some of the important rules of law connected with warranty were adopted by the English from the Jews. The extension of the benefit of the warranty to the assigns of the grantee is one of these rules. Thus, where A conveys a parcel of real property to B who, in turn, conveys it to C, and X evicts C by virtue of a paramount title, C has an action for breach of warranty not only against B, his immediate grantor, but also against A, his grantor's grantor. The reason for this is that C, who is B's assign, is included within the scope of the warranty given by A to B. The inclusion of assigns within the scope of the warranty was copied by the English from the Jews, together with the other features of the warranty clause.

Another rule in medieval English law of warranty which seems to have been adopted by the English from the Jews was that all real property remaining in the hands of the grantor at the time of the conveyance becomes bound for the warranty, defense and acquittance of the grantee. This rule of law is traceable to the Hebrew legal concept of *ahrayut* which, freely rendered, means that a man's property stands surety for the obligations he assumes in writing, whether the obligation grows out of a loan of money, a warranty incidental to the conveyance of real property, or the endowment of wife by husband. In virtually every Hebrew deed of conveyance in medieval England, as elsewhere, there is a stipulation for a warranty binding the grantor's property, movable and immovable, present and future. The idea of *ahrayut* was apparently taken over by the English together with the Hebrew warranty clause; this resulted in the rule, which prevailed in medieval England, that the obligation of a warranty constitutes a charge upon all the real property remaining in the hands of the grantor at the time he makes the conveyance.

6. THE HEBREW KETUBAH AND ANGLO-AMERICAN DOWER[67]

The origin of the Anglo-American institution of dower, whereby the married woman, upon the death of her husband, is entitled to a life estate in one-third of the real property that the deceased husband owned at any time during the marriage, is shrouded in mystery.

However, certain rules with regard to dower, as well as the formula that was used in medieval England when the husband endowed his wife at the church door, appear to be of Jewish origin.

The outstanding characteristic of dower in Anglo-American law is that it constitutes a charge upon all the real property that the husband owned at any time during the marriage, regardless of who the owner of the property may be at the time of the husband's death. As a result of this rule the practice grew up in England and the United States to have the wife release her dower rights whenever the husband conveys a parcel of real estate. For without such a release the property would be subject to the wife's claim of dower if the husband should predecease her.

The important effect of this rule of law, and of the practice that grew out of it, upon family life and the relations of husband and wife throughout the ages need hardly be emphasized. It served as an effective counterbalance to the rather low position to which the *feme coverte* or married woman was relegated in English law.

The rule that dower constitutes a charge on the husband's property did not become firmly established in English law until about the beginning of the thirteenth century. Glanvil, in his treatise on the laws of England, written about 1187, still hesitates to concede to the widow the right of claiming dower in property transferred by her husband during his lifetime. However, while Glanvil was still hesitating about the rule of law, the common practice, as shown by deeds of conveyance of the time, was to have the wife join in the conveyance, or release her dower rights whenever a conveyance was made by the husband. Legal practice, as is often the case in the early stages of the development of a legal system, preceded legal theory in this respect.

This practice of having the wife join with her husband in the conveyance of real property prevailed among the Jews for at least a thousand years prior to their settlement in England. It grew out of a rule, ascribed by the Talmud to Simeon b. Shatah, which subjected all of the husband's property to a lien in favor of the wife for the payment of her *Ketubah*. A release by the wife of her dower rights is already mentioned in the Mishna. In later times this practice became almost universal among the Jews. In all the available Hebrew documents from Angevin England, evidencing conveyances of real property by Jew to Jew and by Jew to non-Jew, there is not a single instance where there is not a release by the wife of her dower rights.

This practice alone, which the English apparently copied from the Jews, might have been sufficient to give rise to the rule that where the wife fails to release her dower rights the property remains subject to such rights. But there is also evidence that the English endowment formula was copied from the Hebrew *Ketubah* formula. The most definite trace of Hebrew influence upon the development of the English endowment document is found in the medieval English dower *de la plus belle*, which originated in a provision in the Hebrew *Ketubah* giving the wife the right to collect her dower from the best part of her husband's property.

7. THE COMMON LAW MORTGAGE[68]

The form of mortgage used in the United States and England also is of Jewish origin. This form is at variance with both the true economic significance of the transaction and the intention of the parties. Since a mortgage is a pledge of property to secure a debt, one would expect the mortgage instrument to read that if the mortgagor fails to pay the debt on the due date the mortgaged property is to be forfeited to the mortgagee. Instead, the mortgage is, in form, an immediate conveyance of the property by the mortgagor to the mortgagee, with a condition that if the former pays the debt when due the property is to revert back to him.

In the modern form of the mortgage the conveyance and the condition are incorporated in one single instrument. However, in the early stages of the development of the mortgage the conveyance and the condition were incorporated in two separate instruments, and both instruments were delivered to a third, neutral, party to be turned over to the mortgagor should the debt be paid, or to the mortgagee in case it was not paid.

A device identical in all respects with the English mortgage in its earlier stage of development was used by the Jews throughout the Middle Ages.

and was designed to overcome a certain rule of Hebrew law known as *asmakta*.

Briefly stated, in accordance with the doctrine of *asmakta*, where a conveyance is made, or an obligation is assumed, as a penalty for the noncompliance with an undertaking to which it is collateral, the conveyance or the obligation is not valid. There is lacking that finality of determination which is requisite for the validity of an act in law, since the intention of the party purporting to make the conveyance, or to assume the obligation, is to fulfill his main undertaking, and not to effect a transfer of his property, or an assumption of an obligation other than his main obligation. In a mortgage with a forfeiture clause, for example, the intention of the mortgagor is to undertake to pay the mortgage debt, and not to effect a conveyance of his property. The forfeiture clause is intended as a penalty for the nonpayment of a debt, and therefore it is not valid. Only where there is a present conveyance of the property with a condition making the conveyance void in case of repayment of the money by the grantor is the transaction valid.

As a result of this doctrine, the practice grew up among Jews that whenever a transaction in the nature of a mortgage took place, it took the form of an outright conveyance of the property by the mortgagor to the mortgagee and an agreement by the mortgagee that the conveyance shall be void if the borrower returns the money to the lender on the due date. In order to remove all appearance of *asmakta* from the transaction, the conveyance by the mortgagor and the agreement by the mortgagee were delivered to a third party (*shalish*).

The Jews of medieval England used this device in their transactions with non-Jews, and through them it came into general use in England. For a long time the mortgage was used in England in exactly that form in which it had been used by the Jews; that is, two separate instruments were employed and both instruments were delivered to a third party. It was not until the beginning of the fifteenth century that conveyance and condition began to be incorporated in the same instrument and the mortgage assumed the form in which it is still used in the United States and England.

8. THE CONDITIONAL OR PENAL BOND[69]

The conditional or penal bond is a device similar in conception and design to the mortgage in the form of a conveyance with a condition subsequent.

It contains the same logical twist as that involved in the common law mortgage. Instead of the conditional obligation it is intended to be, with the obligation emerging upon the happening of a certain contingency, it takes the form of an absolute obligation which is to become void in case of the nonoccurrence of the contingency upon which the obligation is made to depend.

Thus where a fidelity company undertakes to guarantee the faithful performance of his duties by a person entrusted with the administration of some fund, the company's bond will usually read somewhat like this: "X company is bound to pay $1,000, but the condition of this bond is such that if Y will faithfully perform his duties the obligation of this bond shall be void; otherwise it shall remain in full force and effect."

This device, too, is of Jewish origin and was designed by the Jews to overcome the difficulty of the doctrine of *asmakta* mentioned above.

Maimonides in his Code of Hebrew Law cites the following device which was used by the "sages of Spain" to remove the flaw of *asmakta* from conditional obligations: The obligor would undertake an immediate and absolute obligation, and the obligee, on his part, would undertake to release the obligor upon the nonoccurrence of the contingency upon which the obligation was to depend. The doctrine of *asmakta* not being applicable to releases and defeasances, this device accomplished the purpose of a conditional obligation in a legally valid manner by inverting the condition and attaching it to the release instead of the obligation.

The Maimonides device, in the form of two separate instruments—one an absolute obligation and the other a conditional avoidance of the obligation—is mentioned in the responsa of Rabbi Solomon b. Adreth and is found in a Hebrew document from Angevin England, evidencing a transaction between two Jews and dated 1251. As in the case of the mortgage, both instruments were delivered to a third party. Numerous examples of the use of this device by English Jews in their transactions with non-Jews are found on the rolls of the Exchequer of the Jews.

From the Jews the device passed into general use among Englishmen, who used it for the purpose of overcoming a rule known in English law as the rule against penalties, which is similar to the Hebrew doctrine of *asmakta* and which, there is reason to believe, was developed through the influence of that doctrine.

The English device, in its original form, was in every detail identical with its Hebrew counterpart. Two instruments were used and both instruments were delivered to a third party. The modern form in which both, the obligation and the condition, are incorporated in a single instrument came into use at the beginning of the fifteenth century, about the same time that the mortgage assumed its present form.

9. TRIAL BY JURY

The generally accepted view of the origin of trial by jury is that it developed from the inquest that was used by the Frankish kings on the

Continent for the purpose of determining questions of ownership of land to which the king laid claim and other disputed issues, relating mainly to fiscal matters, between the king and his subjects. It was the royal prerogative to have such questions decided by a verdict of the *best men* of the neighborhood, instead of by the then prevailing modes of trial, such as the ordeal, combat, or the oath with oath helpers.

The first important step in the development of the jury system in England, according to this view, was a series of ordinances, known as assizes, by which Henry II extended to his subjects, in certain specified types of cases dealing with possession of land, the royal prerogative of trial by inquest. Another important step was taken when judges began to allow the parties, in cases not covered by the assizes, to have their case decided by a verdict of their neighbors or, as the phrase went, to *put themselves upon the country*. The final step was to compel the parties to *put themselves upon the country*.[70]

Pollock and Maitland were apparently aware of the break in the continuity of the story, which is presented by the transition from trial by jury in a few selected types of cases, as a result of an ordinance, to trial by jury in nearly all cases, by consent, real or fictitious, of the parties. In their *History of English Law*, they say:

> Trial by jury, in the narrowest sense of that term, trial by jury as distinct from trial by an assize, slowly creeps in by another route. The principle from which it starts is simply this, that if in any action the litigants by their pleadings come to an issue of fact, they may agree to be bound by the verdict of a jury and will be bound accordingly. In course of time the judges will in effect drive litigants into such agreements by saying, "You must accept your opponent's offer of a jury or you will lose your cause"; but in theory the jury only comes in after both parties have consented to accept its verdict. In course of time the jury, which has its roots in the fertile ground of consent, will grow at the expense of the assize, which has sprung from the stony soil of ordinance.[71]

But the question still remains, how did it happen that "the fertile ground of consent" was substituted for "the stony soil of ordinance." Where did the principle of consent, which apparently developed simultaneously with the assizes,[72] or, perhaps, even preceded them, come from?

An indirect answer to this question is contained in the following passage from Pollock and Maitland:

> We have seen . . . that the verdict of jurors becomes a common mode of proof only because litigants "put themselves" upon it, and that the summons of a jury . . . is always in theory the outcome of consent and submission. Both litigants have agreed to be bound by a verdict of the country. They

might perhaps have chosen some other test. We may, for example, see a plaintiff and a defendant putting themselves upon the two witnesses named in a charter, or upon the word of some one man.[73]

The similarity, in principle as well as in idiom, between *putting oneself* upon a jury and *putting oneself* upon some witness or witnesses seems to be significant. This similarity not only points to the broad principle upon which trial by jury was based, namely, that parties may choose the means of deciding the issues between them and that they will be bound by such choice, but it also furnishes a clue to a hitherto unknown influence upon the development of the jury system in England.

An institution which is quite similar to the jury system in medieval England is found among the Jews at a very early time. It is the lay court, usually consisting of three judges, which derives its jurisdiction from the fact that the parties voluntarily submitted their controversy to it. The binding effect of the decision of such a court is based not on its inherent power, but on the agreement of the parties to be bound by its decision. Moreover, according to Jewish law, parties may agree to be bound by the testimony of certain witnesses, and they will be bound by such testimony, even if the witness happens to be one who would ordinarily be considered incompetent. In other words, the principle of consent in Hebrew law, as in medieval English law, applies to judge and witness alike. Indeed, we find the same term used in the Mishna to signify agreement to be bound by the decision of a judge and by the testimony of a witness. In Mishna (Sanhedrin 3, 2), we read:

> If one suitor said to the other, "I accept my father as trustworthy," or "I accept thy father as trustworthy," or "I accept three herdsmen as trustworthy," R. Meir says: He may retract. But the sages say: He cannot retract.

The rule of the Mishna is interpreted by the leading posttalmudic authorities as applying to witnesses and judges alike.[74] The Talmud,[75] commenting on the phrase "I accept three herdsmen as trustworthy," says that although herdsmen are ignorant of the "affairs of the world," their decision is binding, if the parties accepted them as judges.

The similarity between the principle enunciated in the above Mishna and that underlying the binding effect of a jury's verdict in medieval England is obvious. This similarity, coupled with the fact that the same principle was also applied to the testimony of a witness, both by the Jews of early talmudic times and by Englishmen in the Middle Ages, appears to be of great significance.

What is most significant, however, is that the Hebrew equivalent of the phrase *se ponere super* or *put oneself upon* is found in a responsum by a famous thirteenth-century German rabbi in connection with the submission of a controversy to a lay court. In this responsum, after citing Mishna (Sanhedrin 3, 2), quoted above, the learned Rabbi says:

> The same rule applies to two parties who took upon themselves to abide by the decision of the heads of the community. And if the plaintiff says: "We didn't put ourselves upon them," let the defendant affirm his allegation upon oath . . . In such a case where they put themselves upon the "best men of the town" and the heads of the community it is the custom in our entire realm that whatever one takes upon himself before the heads of the community, who were chosen with the consent of the community, he cannot retract therefrom."[76]

The idiom in this quotation, used by the Rabbi to express the idea of submission of a controversy by the parties, is identical with that used in medieval England to express the same idea in connection with a jury. The combination of similarities between the ideas and between the idioms expressing them makes the possibility of a mere coincidence very remote.

Another indication of the relationship between the English jury and the Jewish lay court is found in an entry on the rolls of the Exchequer of the Jews, dated 1244. This entry reads, in part, as follows:

> . . . and that this is true she puts herself upon the township of London. The Jew does likewise; wherefore let inquest be had on the morrow of the Ascension.[77]

The parties *put themselves* upon the township of London, that is, upon representatives of the community, exactly as in the responsum of the thirteenth-century German Rabbi, quoted above.

A further parallel between the English jury and the Jewish court may be seen in the fact that, as in the case of the members of the jury, an oath was administered to the members of the Jewish lay court in England each time they were selected to try a case or to discharge some other judicial function, such as the assignment of dower to a woman. The oath was administered in the form of an adjuration in the presence of ten persons (a *minyan*), a procedure which is mentioned by Rashi,[78] the famous eleventh-century commentator of the Talmud. Reference to such an oath by the members of a lay court is found in three Hebrew documents from medieval England. The opening sentence in these documents reads: "We were selected and adjured in the presence of ten persons to constitute a *bet din* (a court)."[79] There seems to be no authority in Hebrew law, talmudic or posttalmudic, for an oath to be administered to members of a Jewish lay court. Nor is there any evidence of such practice among the Jews outside of England. It seems likely that this is a case of non-Jewish practice having been adopted by the Jews. This further strengthens the assumption of a close relationship between the two institutions, the Jewish lay court and the English jury, for it seems to indicate that in the thirteenth century, when trial by jury had hardly passed beyond its formative stage, the Jews regarded it as being so much akin to their lay court that they copied a procedure from the jury and applied it to the lay court.

The historical connection between the Jewish lay court and the English jury appears in certain aspects of the history of the Jews in medieval Europe.

As soon as the Jews became an important element in medieval Europe new methods of trial had to be developed in order to meet the case of litigation between Jew and non-Jew. The mode of trial that prevailed in Europe at that time, the ordeal by fire or by water, was entirely alien to the Jew, repugnant to his concept of proof, and altogether unsatisfactory to him. He needed some rational legal framework under which his business undertakings might achieve a degree of security and stability. He could not afford to allow his business transactions to be regulated by totally inadequate archaic rules of substantive and procedural law. One is not likely to be willing to risk his money on the outcome of an ordeal by fire or by water.

In one of the earliest extant charters granted to the Jews in Europe, in addition to provisions of a substantive nature, is a provision that the Jew is not to be subjected to the ordeal by fire or hot water.[80] Substitutes for trial by ordeal had to be provided in litigation between Jews and non-Jews. One of these was to submit the controversy to a body of neighbors, similar to the Jewish lay court. In order to secure impartiality, these bodies were made up of Jews and non-Jews.[81]

In England we find throughout the thirteenth century that cases between Jews and non-Jews are tried by mixed juries, usually six Jews and six non-Jews.[82] There is also good reason to believe that the trial of cases between Jews and non-Jews by mixed juries goes well beyond the thirteenth century. In a charter granted by King John to the Jews in 1201 there is the following provision: "And if a Christian shall have cause of action against a Jew, let it be tried by the Jew's peers."[83] A similar provision is found in a charter by King Richard I, dated 1190,[84] and one of like nature was probably also contained in the charter granted to the Jews by Henry I.[85] This provision for trial by the Jew's peers, *per pares judei*, can hardly have reference to anything else but trial by a mixed jury, for, so far as the writer knows, not a single recorded instance has been found of a case between a Jew and a non-Jew having been tried by a court consisting wholly of Jews.[86]

It seems likely that submission of controversies between Jews and non-Jews to mixed juries had its origin in a charter granted to the Jews by Henry I, and that, consequently, it antedated the assizes of Henry II. In addition to the numerous cases, recorded on the rolls of the Exchequer of the Jews, in which the parties *put themselves* upon a mixed jury, one finds on these rolls a large number of cases in which they *put themselves* upon some witness or witnesses, arbitrators, officials, etc. The following are typical examples:

Elias de Abbacia and Vives, son of Isaac of Stanford, *put themselves upon three Christians and three Jews* of Northampton for the determination of a question relating to 40s. of chattels of commendise and 100s. claimed by the one of the other. The arbitrators are to notify their award to the Justices of the quindene of St. Martin.[87]

Manser of Huntingdon, attached to answer Peytevin of Bedford, for that he will not suffer three of his chirographs to be placed in the Chest according to the Assize, comes before the Justices, and says that the said chirographs were made *sub poena*, and that therefore it was that he would not permit them to be placed in the Chest. Peytevin avers that this is false, and that his real reason was that there was a dispute between them as to a certain debt which Manser demands of him; and that this is true, *he puts himself upon the oath of Master Moses*, and gives ½ mark to have his oath; and Manser does likewise. Master Moses, being summoned, comes before the Justices and, being sworn, says, that the said dispute, and nought else, stands in the way of the chirographs being placed in the Chest . . .[88]

The idea of *putting oneself upon, i.e.*, of the parties voluntarily selecting a method of deciding a disputed issue between them, was deeply ingrained in the Jew's mind, as a result of his many centuries of experience with the lay court. The Jew's commercial and financial activities also contributed to the development of this idea, since a simple and expeditious method of resolving disputes is a necessary concomitant of a high degree of business activity. It is therefore not unlikely that the Jews, who frequently had occasion to resort to litigation, had something to do with the shaping of the ideas that led to the establishment of trial by jury.[89]

10. THE THIRTY-NINTH CLAUSE OF MAGNA CARTA

One of the basic principles of the Anglo-American system of law, and an important component of democracy, as it is understood and practiced in the United States and England, is that of the supremacy of the law. The law is supreme; the ruler and those whom he rules are alike subject to it and bound by its dictates. Government by rule of law, rather than by the arbitrary will of any individual or group of individuals, is the corollary of this principle.

In the United States this principle finds expression in the famous *due process of law* clauses of the Fifth and Fourteenth Amendments to the United States Constitution declaring that no person shall be deprived "of life, liberty, or property, without due process of law."

Through various intermediate stages, the due process clause of the

United States Constitution is traceable to the thirty-ninth clause of Magna Carta, which reads:

Nullus liber homo capiatur, vel imprisonetur, aut disseisiatur, aut utlagetur, aut exuletur, aut aliquo modo distruatur, nec super eum ibimus, nec super eum mittemus, nisi per legale judicium parium suorum vel per legem terrae.

No freeman shall be taken or imprisoned, or disseized, or outlawed, or exiled, or in any way destroyed, nor will we go upon him, nor send upon him, except by the lawful judgment of his peers or by the law of the land.

A whole literature has been written on the meaning of the phrase *or by the law of the land*. Some historians of the English Constitution are of the opinion that the phrase is to be interpreted, rather narrowly, as having reference to matters of judicial procedure. The clause is interpreted by these historians as embodying a guarantee that the then prevailing modes of trial will be observed in cases involving the liberty or property of freemen. The more widely accepted view, however, is that the phrase has reference to both substance and procedure, and that the clause was intended as a guarantee against the arbitrary infringement by the king of the personal liberty and property rights of freemen.[90]

The great principle embodied in the thirty-ninth clause of Magna Carta is found in the medieval legal literature of the Jews, which deals quite extensively with the problem of the limitations of royal power. We shall begin with the *Mishna Torah*, the Code of Hebrew Law, written by Maimonides several decades before Magna Carta was signed by King John.[90a] In the 5th chapter of *Gezela Va-abeda*, sections 13 and 14, it is stated:

13. And in like manner where a king was angered against one of his serfs or servants (*abadav ve-shamashav*) among the inhabitants of the realm and took away his field or court, it is not robbery, and its enjoyment is permitted. He who purchases it from the king acquires title to it, and the original owner cannot reclaim it from him. For, such is the rule with regard to all kings that they may take to themselves the property of their servants when angered against them . . . But where a king took away a court or a field from one of the inhabitants of the realm, not in accordance with the laws which he had enacted, he is a robber, and if a purchaser acquires the property from the king, the original owner may reclaim it from such purchaser.

14. The general rule is: Every law which the king enacts for all, and which is not intended for one person alone, is not robbery. But where he takes away from one person alone, not in accordance with the law known to all, committing an act of brigandage against that person, it is robbery.

It would be hard to find a more forthright statement of the limitation of royal power. Simply stated, Maimonides's rule is, that a law, the effect of which is to deprive an individual of his property rights, is not valid, unless it is regularly promulgated, of general application and known at the time it is sought to be applied. The similarity between this rule and the principle of *the law of the land* of Magna Carta, or of *due process of law* of the United States Constitution, is quite obvious and needs no elaboration. What is more, the exception made by Maimonides to his rule limiting the validity of royal acts, namely, that it does not apply where such acts are directed against the king's *serfs or servants,* is also clearly implicit in the words of Magna Carta, which limits the application of the thirty-ninth clause to freemen.

Maimonides's statement with regard to the limitation of royal power is predicated upon a Talmudic maxim, as interpreted by the leading Jewish jurists of the Middle Ages, which reads: "The law of the kingdom is law."[91] Rabbi Joseph ibn Migas, a leading Jewish authority of the early twelfth century in Spain, expounding this maxim, places the emphasis on the word "law" and says: "The law of the kingdom is law, but the robbery of the kingdom is not."[92]

Nahmanides, the famous thirteenth-century Jewish philosopher and jurist, places the emphasis on the word "kingdom," saying that the law of the *kingdom* is law but not the law of the *king*.[93]

Similar views are expressed by Rabbi Judah, or Sir Leon, of Paris who cites Ri (R. Isaac b. Meir) and Rabbenu Tam (R. Jacob b. Meir), the famous French Tosafists of the twelfth century as his authorities.[94]

The doctrine of the limitation of the royal power was common learning among the Jews of the Middle Ages and was certainly well known among the Jews of England. In fact, Mordecai b. Hillel cites a decision by an unnamed London Rabbi in which this doctrine was involved.[95] The case arose between two Jews and the decision turned on the validity in law of a certain levy by the king. The Rabbi decided that the levy in question was not valid, distinguishing between regular taxes, which are valid, and so-called "dona," or forced gifts, which were often exacted from the Jews of England by the king and which, the Rabbi held, were not a valid exercise of the royal power.

In 1215 the Jews had good reason for offering to the barons advice on how the royal power should be limited. They had but recently been subjected to a veritable reign of terror by a rapacious king whose depredations could not bring but home to them with particular vividness the distinction between *the laws of the kingdom* and the *robbery of the king*. It was in 1210 that John threw the whole Jewish community of England into prison and extorted from them, by the most ruthless and cruel means, the then enormous sum of 66,000 marks.[96] It is, therefore, not at all unlikely that the Jews had some part in the formulation of clause thirty-nine of Magna Carta.

NOTES

[1] Pollock & Maitland, *History of English Law,* I, p. 468 (2nd. ed.); J. M. Rigg, *Select Pleas, Starrs & Other Records from the Rolls of the Exchequer of the Jews. A.D. 1220-1284.* Selden Society Publications, XV, p. x.

[2] Pollock & Maitland, *op. cit.*, I, p. 473.

[3] J. Jacobs, *The Jews in Angevin England*, p. xiv.

[4] *Ibid.*, p. xvii.

[5] Rigg, *op. cit.*, p. xiii. n. 1.

[6] *Ibid.*, p. xx.

[[6a] Cf. Cecil Roth, "The European Age in Jewish History (to 1648)," p. 230.]

[7] *Ibid.*, Mishna, Baba Batra, end.

[8] See Finkelstein, *Jewish Self-Government in the Middle Ages*, pp. 6-7.

[9] Pollock & Maitland, *op. cit.*, I, p. 475.

[10] *Ibid.*, p. 473.

[11] *Ibid.*, p. 469.

[12] Shulhan Aruk, Hoshen Mishpat, ch. 111, sec. 1.

[13] Mishna Baba Batra 10.8; Hoshen Mishpat, ch. 39, sec. 1, and ch. 111, sec. 1.

[14] *Ibid.*

[15] *Ibid.*, ch. 372, sec. 8.

[16] Baba Mezia 15b.

[17] Mishna Gittin, 5.2; Hoshen Mishpat, ch. 111, sec. 8.

[18] Baba Batra, 44b; Hoshen Mishpat, ch. 113, sec. 1.

[19] *Ibid.*

[20] Baba Batra, 157 a-b; Hoshen Mishpat, ch. 112, sec. 1.

[21] See *e.g.*, Sefer Hashtarot (Formulary) of Rabbi Judah Barzillai, No. 34.

[22] Rigg, *op. cit.*, pp. 33, 93, 94, n. 1.

[23] *Ibid.*, pp. 18, 53, 63.

[24] *Ibid.*, p. 65; *Calendar of the Plea Rolls of the Exchequer of the Jews,* I, p. 73; *Calendar of the Close Rolls,* Edw. I, I, p. 389.

[25] Pollock & Maitland, *op. cit.*, n. 1, II, p. 2, n. 2, & p. 225, n. 6; *Madox Formulare Angelicanum*, Nos. 159, 640, 644.

[26] *Madox, op. cit.*, Nos. 119, 643, 645.

[27] *Calendar of the Close Rolls,* 1268-1272, pp. 243, 258, 300, 410-411.

[28] Pollock & Maitland, *op. cit.*, I, p. 475, n. 1.

[29] *Ibid.*, II, p. 596.

[30] *Madox, op. cit.*, n. 25, No. 635.

[31] *Calendar of the Close Rolls,* 1259-1261, pp. 463-464; 1264-1268, pp. 395, 504.

[32] *Ibid.*, 1264-1268, p. 521.

[33] Sanhedrin, 29b; Hoshen Mishpat, ch. 39, sec. 7, and ch. 250, sec. 3.

[34] Gittin, 40b.

[35] Hoshen Mishpat, ch. 81, sec. 6.

[[35a] Cf. below Alexander Altmann, "Judaism and World Philosophy," pp. 973 f.]

[36] Hoshen Mishpat, ch. 81, sec. 8; Yad Hahazakah, Toen, ch. 7. The phrase "*Hodaah Gemurah*" does not appear in the printed editions of Maimonides's Code. It appears in Tur's quotation of the passage from Maimonides. A comparison of a large number of quotations from Maimonides's Code, as found in Tur, has convinced the writer that the author of Tur had before him a revised and corrected version of the code. Certain evidence recently found by the writer points to the conclusion that the phrase *Hodaah Gemurah* did not originate with Maimonides and that it is of considerably earlier date than his Code.

[37] Baba Kamma, 84b.

[38] Ketubot, 101b, Rashi's commentary *ad loc.;* see also the commentary of Rabbi Asher b. Yehiel *ad loc.*

[39] Hoshen Mishpat, ch. 40, sec. 1.

[40] See Hoshen Mishpat, ch. 60, sec. 2.

[41] See, *e. g.*, Meyer D. Davis, ed., *Hebrew Deeds of English Jews,* Nos. 1, 7, 8, 9.

[42] John H. Round, ed., *Ancient Charters,* Pipe Roll Society Publ., X, p. 82.

[43] Abrahams, Stokes and Loewe, *Starrs & Jewish Charters in the British Museum,* pp. 4-5 (1234).

[44] No. 689.

[45] Davis, *op. cit.*, n. 41, No. 193.

[46] Selden Society Publications, III.

[47] *Calendar of Close Rolls,* 1256-1259, p. 493.

[48] Mishna Baba Batra, 10.7.

[49] Davis, *op. cit.*, n. 41, No. 54. This is an assignment of a debt in which it is recited that William de Huneworth is the debtor and Roger Michael of Holt Market is the *kabblan, i.e.*, the surety with primary liability.

[50] *Op. cit.*, II, p. 204, n. 1.

[51] Davis, No. 118.

[52] Rigg, *Select Pleas,* p. 42.

[53] *Ibid.*, p. 72.

[54] *Madox, op. cit.,* No. 142.

[55] *Ibid.*, No. 702.

[56] *Ibid.*, No. 703.

[57] Supplement to *Tarbiz,* publication of the Hebrew University of Jerusalem, I, No. 3, p. 70; (Additional note by Professor Saul Lieberman—On the exact meaning of the term see *ibid.*, p. 22, n. 1; Geiger *apud* Kraus, Additamenta ad librum Aruch completum, p. 2).

[[57a] On Saadia Gaon cf. above Judah Goldin, "The Period of the Talmud," pp. 194 ff.]

[58] *Tarbiz, op. cit.*, p. 22.

[[58a] On Hai Gaon see below Abraham S. Halkin, "Judeo-Arabic Literature," pp. 1132 ff.]

[59] No. 4.

[60] S. v. Mehilah. See *Tarbiz, ibid.*

[61] Responsa of R. Solomon b. Adret, *sub nomine* Toledot Adam, No. 217.

[62] Ch. 76, sec. 3 & 4.

[63] No. 22.

[64] No. 404.

[65] Tikkun Soferim, No. 50.

[66] For a full discussion and citation of authorities, see J. Rabinowitz, "The Origin of the Common Law Warranty of Real Property and of the Inchoate Right of Dower," in *Cornell Law Quarterly,* XXX, 1944, pp. 77-94.

[67] *Ibid.*

[68] For a full discussion and citation of authorities see Rabinowitz, "The Common Law Mortgage and the Conditional Bond," in *University of Pennsylvania Law Review,* XCII, 1943, pp. 179-194.

[69] *Ibid.*

[70] Pollock & Maitland, I, p. 140 f. J. B. Thayer, *A Preliminary Treatise on Evidence,* p. 47 f.

[71] I, p. 149.

[72] See Glanvil, 13, 2. See also, n. 19, *infra.*

[73] II, p. 623.

[74] Maimonides's Code, Sanhedrin 7, 2; Hoshen Mishpat 23, 1.

[75] Sanhedrin 25b.

[76] Teshubot Maimonyot, Shoftim No. 10, quoting a responsum of R. Meir b. Baruch of Rothenburg.

[77] *Calendar of the Plea Rolls of the Exchequer of the Jews,* I, p. 156. Cf. Pollock & Maitland, *op. cit.,* II, p. 624, n. 1. "The verdict of the jurors is not just the verdict of twelve men; it is the verdict of a *pays,* a country, a neighborhood, a community."

[78] Rashi, *Commentary to Shebout* 38b, catchword *Be-Sefer Torah.*

[79] Davis, *Hebrew Deeds* (*Shtarot*), Nos. 3, 15, 156.

[80] ". . . . Et nullatenus volumus, ut praedictos Judeos ad nullum judicium examinandum, id est nec ad ignem nec ad aquam calidam seu etiam ad flagellum, nisi liceat eis secundum illorum legem vivere vel ducere." Aronius, *Regesten zur Geschichte der juden im fraenkischen und deutschen Reiche,* No. 81; Rozière, *Recueil Général des Formules,* I, No. 27 (Charter of Louis the Pious, before 825).

[81] See S. W. Baron, *The Jewish Community,* I, pp. 249-250.

[82] See *e. g., Calendar of the Plea Rolls of the Exchequer of the Jews,* I, pp. 127-128, 145, 169. See also Jacobs, *The Jews in Angevin England.* p. 201, quoting an early case of an inquest by twelve Christians and twelve Jews from the rotuli de Ablatis, ed. Roberts, p. 92 (1199-1200).

[83] Rigg, *Select Pleas,* etc., p. 1.

[84] Rymer, *Foedera,* ed. Clarke, I, 51.

[85] In the preamble to John's charter reference is made to a charter granted to the Jews by his father's grandfather, Henry I. John's charter is stated there to be a confirmation of the one granted to the Jews by Henry I.

[86] In his essay entitled "*Pęr Judicium Parium vel. per Legem Terrae,*" *Magna Carta Commemoration Essays* (p. 102), Professor F. M. Powicke, compares the *per judicium parium* of Magna Carta with the *per pares judei* of John's charter to the Jews, and arrives at the conclusion that neither refers to trial by jury. In support of this conclusion he cites Bracton's *Note Book*

(II, p. 706, case 918), in which a Jew objected to the jurisdiction of the court on the basis of King John's charter, although he was offered to have his case decided by a mixed jury. However, the Jew's objections did not rest upon the *per pares judei* clause of the charter, but upon another clause in the same charter which reads: "And as often as cause of action shall have arisen between Christian and Jew, let him who shall have appealed the other for the deraignment of his cause have witnesses, to wit, a lawful Christian and a lawful Jew." See Selden Society Publication, LX, Introduction, p. clxl.

[87] *Calendar . . . of the Exchequer of the Jews,* I, pp. 11-12 (1219).

[88] *Ibid.*, pp. 106-107 (1244-1245).

[89] It is true that the generally accepted view is that trial by jury as a result of ordinance preceded trial by jury as a result of voluntary submission by the parties. However, it is not at all certain that this was so. Professor Haskins (*Norman Institutions,* p. 224, n. 109) quotes a document from Normandy, dated 1182, in which it is stated that a certain controversy was voluntarily submitted by the parties to twelve sworn men. Also, in a document of considerably earlier date (1124-1130), found in the Cartulary of Ramsey (p. 143), there is reference to submission of a controversy to *twelve* sworn men—the usual number of men on a jury. Incidentally, this number may be of some significance. Stobbe (*Die Juden in Deutschland waehrend des Mittelalters,* p. 143) cites a charter granted to the Jews of Worms in 1312, according to which the Jewish Council (*Judenrath*), consisting of *twelve* members, was to administer justice among the Jews in accordance with Jewish law. He also cites evidence to the effect that already at the time of the first Crusade (1096) the Jewish council of Worms consisted of *twelve* members. It is quite likely that the number of members on the council was deliberately made to correspond to the number of princes of Israel of old (No. 1:16). Indeed, in *Masseket Soferim* 19, 10, a seventh century Rabbinic source, there is reference to "twelve good men of the town [town councilors] corresponding to the twelve tribes of Israel." If the Jews had some part in the development of trial by jury, it may well be that the number of men on a jury was adopted from the Jews.

It should be noted that the number—twelve—of the Jewish community councilors may also be of significance as indicative of the influence of Jewish community organization upon the development of town government in the later Middle Ages in Europe. The same number of town councilors is found in Montpelier in the beginning of the thirteenth century. The *Coutume* of Montpelier of the year 1204 refers to "*duodecim probi et legales viri, jam electi ad consulendum communitatem Montispessulani*" (twelve honest and lawful men just elected to counsel the community of Montpelier). *Thalamus Parvus, Le Petit Thalamus de Montpelier* (Montpelier, 1836), p. 52.

In addition to the number of councilors in Montpelier, their description as *probi et legales viri* also points in the direction of Jewish influence. The meaning of the term *homo* or *vir legalis* (lawful man), which also occurs quite frequently in English medieval records after the Norman Conquest (cf. "a lawful Christian and a lawful Jew" in the clause of King John's charter quoted above, n. 86), has given rise to considerable speculation and differences of opinion among the leading authorities on English institutional history. See Ch. E. Odegard, Legalis Homo, *Speculum,* XV, 1940, pp. 186-193. The writer believes that *homo legalis* is a literal translation of the Hebrew *ish kasher—a worthy man.* The Hebrew word *kasher* ordinarily means that which is in accordance with the law—*lawful.* Thus, meat from an animal slaughtered in accordance with Jewish ritual law, and otherwise not unfit for consumption according to the same law, is said to be *kasher;* a *sukkah* built in accordance with the rules of the law is similarly said to be *kasher.* But when the adjective *kasher* qualifies the noun *ish* or *adam* (a man) it means *worthy.* Cf. Mishna, *Berakot* 2, 7; B. *Moed Katan* 25a; Maimonides, Code, Nahalot 4, 6. Cf. also M. Jastrow, *A Dictionary of The Targumim, The Talmud Babli and Yerushalmi, and the Midrashic Literature,* pp. 677b-678a. It seems that *homo legalis* is a Hebraism which, in the form of *homme loyal,* first found its way through the Jews into the French vernacular and thence, in its Latin form, into the language of official documents.

[90] See McIlwain, "Due Process of Law in Magna Carta," *Columbia Law Review,* XIV, pp. 27f.

[[90a] Cf. Halkin, *op. cit.,* pp. 1134 ff.]

[91] Gittin 10b.

[92] See Sefer Haterumot 47, 8.

[93] *Ibid.*

[94] Haggahot Mordecai, Baba Batra ch. 1, No. 659, s.v. Heshiv. There is some evidence that R. Judah of Paris settled in England about the year 1182. Cf. Jacobs, *The Jews in Angevin England,* p. 76.

[95] Mordecai, Baba Kamma, ch. 10, No. 152.

[96] Rigg, *Select Pleas,* etc., p. xxiv.

BIBLIOGRAPHY

ABRAMS, I., STOKES, H. P., and LOEWE, H. (eds.), *Starrs and Jewish Charters in the British Museum.* Cambridge, 1930-1932.

BARON, SALO W., *The Jewish Community.* (2 vols.) Philadelphia, 1942.

BIGELOW, M. M., *History of Procedure in England from the Norman Conquest.* Boston, 1880.

DAVIS, MEYER D. (ed.), *Hebrew Deeds of English Jews before 1290.* London, 1888.

FINKELSTEIN, LOUIS, *Jewish Self-Government in the Middle Ages.* New York, 1924.

JACOBS, JOSEPH, *The Jews in Angevin England.* New York, 1893.

MALDEN, H. F. (ed.), *Magna Carta: Commemoration Essays.* London, 1917.

POLLOCK, FREDERICK, and MAITLAND, FREDERIC W., *History of English Law before the Time of Edward I.* (2 vols.) Cambridge, 1923.

RABINOWITZ, JACOB, "The Origin of the Common Law Warranty of Real Property and of the Inchoate Right of Dower," in *Cornell Law Quarterly.* XXX, 1944.

———, "The Common Law Mortgage and the Conditional Bond," in *University of Pennsylvania Law Review.* XCII, 1943.

RABINOWITZ, JACOB, "The Origin of Representation by Attorney in English Law," *Law Quarterly Review*, LXVIII, 1952.

RIGG, J. M. (ed.), *Select Pleas, Starrs & Other Records from the Rolls of the Exchequer of the Jews, A.D. 1220-1284*. London, 1902.

ROUND, JOHN H. (ed.), *Ancient Charters, Royal and Private prior to A.D. 1200*. London, 1888.

THAYER, JAMES B., *A Preliminary Treatise on Evidence at the Common Law*. Boston, 1898.

CHAPTER 17

ON MEDIEVAL HEBREW POETRY

By Shalom Spiegel

I.

To some the mere notion of postbiblical Hebrew poetry will seem a presumption. As if the Bible could have a sequel, or as if at the end of the Psalter one could promise: To be continued. The objection will sometimes be stated in purely aesthetic categories. After the heights ascended by Second Isaiah, or the depths plumbed by Job, can aught be said or sung in the Hebrew language, and not be a poor or pitiable anticlimax? It is true, all great poetry leaves us with a sense of discouragement or defeat, diffident to exercise again the craft of the poet. Awed by extraordinary accomplishment, men are prone to invoke the miraculous and to speak of inspiration. Still, poets in every age and culture will pray and strive for the miracle to happen again.

Could a Hebrew poet in postbiblical times expect a similar grace of Heaven, or did the canonization of Scripture forbid it?

The conception of a canon attests and implies a feeling and a belief that the age of direct communication with God is past, and that with the death of the latter prophets, the holy spirit departed from Israel. This doctrine of the sealing of prophecy would appear to put a ceiling to the aspiration of even the most gifted poet ever to rise in postbiblical Hebrew. To be sure, though God may hide His face, His hand is stretched lovingly over Israel, and hints of His revelation may still be disclosed in dreams.[1] Moreover, there persists in all the ages the hope of the ultimate renewal of prophecy in the end of days.[2] But in the concrete here and now, after the completion of the canon, all one could hope for, at best was *bat kol*, the "daughter of the voice," an echo of the glories of the past.[3]

With the expiration of prophecy, Israel was to incline its ear to the words of the Sages.[4] In fact, some took it to apply already to the entire period of the Second Temple in which the Divine Presence, the source of all prophecy, no longer resided.[5] The reliance on the Torah and its scholars became more urgent and insistent after the loss of state and sanctuary, when the very future of Judaism seemed imperiled. Jerusalem lay in ashes, her gates sunk to the ground. Was one still to believe that "the Lord loveth the gates of Zion more than all the dwellings of Jacob" (Ps. 87:2)? If the Holy Writ was to retain any meaning, and Jewish life any hope, was one not driven to conclude, in the face of the disasters that had overtaken the nation, that the gates of Zion (*ziyyon*) henceforth must mean gates marked (*ziyyun*) or distinguished in the Law? "Ever since the Temple was destroyed, the Holy One, blessed is He, has nothing else in His world but the four cubits of *halaka*."[6] To these four cubits of the law the people clung desperately as to its only remnant of freedom and insurance of restoration. All that mattered from now on was the preservation of the Torah, little else was permitted to weigh as much in the scales of Israel. "The elders have ceased from the gate, the young men from their music" (Lam. 5:14): when the elders ceased from the Sanhedrin, the highest seat of Jewish learning and the supreme court of Jewish law, how could the young be allowed to make music or to indulge in song?[7] One was in no mood to encourage the arts or "to rejoice in mirth as other peoples."[8] This, too, like the renewal of prophecy, must wait until God's own good time: Then only will our mouth be filled with laughter, and our tongue with singing, when it will be said among the nations: the Lord hath done great things with Israel![9] Embattled by a hostile world, often reduced to mere subsistence, the synagogue had to maintain an austere economy of spiritual resources and to huddle all its strength for its prime task of keeping the light of the Torah aflame.

The Jewish Middle Ages build upon this twofold legacy of the Rabbinic age. Divine inspiration is relegated to the remote past or the distant future, and the word of the Lord is sought in the present from the disciples of the wise, the scholars of *halaka*.[9a] Certain critical remarks of the Rabbis against prophecy are retained and elaborated, no doubt, to strengthen the hold of the Torah upon the people. A poet as devoted to his calling as Moses ibn Ezra (d. after 1135) writes in his *ars poetica*:[10]

When our sins increased, and we were scattered among the nations because of our evil doings, and God (exalted is He) allowed the period of prophecy to come to a standstill, the Almighty was gracious unto us and sustained us with His servants who transmitted to us His Torah and the words of the prophets from generation to generation. It is from them that we have inherited our faith and institutions. The prophet Zechariah (peace be unto him) whose prophecy was late, foresaw this succession of sages (their memory be blessed) when he said (Zech. 9:12): "Return to the stronghold, ye prisoners of hope; even today do I declare that I will render double unto thee." The words allude to the company of illustrious scholars upon whom the holy spirit has rested. They are the luminaries of the Torah who lead us to goodness in this world and to bliss in the world to come. In this verse the prophet announced to the children of Israel that they will return from Babylon to their homeland, and that there will rise among them, in place of the prophets who will have ceased, men whose wisdom will be double that of the prophets, as was said: "A sage is superior to a prophet."[11] For the prophet delivers his message as it was given to him, and the prophecy as made known to him by God, whereas the Sage hands down what he received from the prophets, and draws one thing from another in accordance with the powers granted to him by the Torah, and contributes from his own mind in conformity to the laws of reason. His is therefore the excellence of originality. This is evident and indicated, I believe, in Scripture (Jer. 18:18): "Instruction shall not perish from the priest, nor counsel from the wise, nor the word from the prophet." Thus Scripture, making three distinctions, awards to the prophet merely "the word," *i. e.*, the word which he is to make known in the name of God. The entire matter was summed up in a wonderful adage of the sage (peace be unto him): "Where there is no vision, the people perish." (Pr. 29:18), hence he immediately exhorted the people to hold on to the words of the wise, when prophecy and prophets will have ended, saying: "But he that keepeth the law, happy is he."

A compatriot and contemporary of this Spanish poet, the great talmudic scholar and head of the academy at Lucena, Joseph ibn Migas (d. 1141) words it more tersely:

> A sage is superior to a prophet, because the prophet reports only what he heard and what was put in his mouth to be said, while the sage reports what was said to Moses from Mt. Sinai, although he did not hear it.[12]

The gift of inspiration is disparaged for the greater glory of the wisdom in the holy Law. This doctrine adhered to by artist and rabbi alike in the period of the highest flowering of the poetic genius in Spain, is characteristic of the whole of the Jewish Middle Ages. In agreement with talmudic teaching, the Sage is accorded what is denied to the seer, continued possession of the holy spirit. "From the day the Temple was destroyed, although prophecy was withdrawn from the prophet, it has not been withdrawn from the wise,"[13] the custodians and interpreters of the law in each age.

Modesty naturally forbade the medieval scholar to boast of or lay claim to inspiration, at least, not openly. But there were exceptions to the rule, and men famed for their learning and piety, dropping all restraint, admit receiving missives from heaven. Rabbi Abraham son of David of Posquières (d. 1198), the keen critic of the code of Maimonides, is audacious or outspoken enough to avow that "the holy spirit appeared in our school."[14] There may be sin of pride in such assertions, but not heresy. "Saintliness leads to the holy spirit"[15] and "God's secret is with them that fear Him" (Ps. 25:14).[16] In reply to some knotty question in the law, a medieval Rabbi will write: "This is what I was shown in heaven,"[17] a legal locution not hackneyed, but not improper. A scholar's faith or fidelity is not impugned because of such revelations.

Nothing of the sort is ever permitted to the medieval poet. To be sure, he had often enough to blow his own bugle (in absence of the modern art of the paid advertisement), but however frivolous or extravagant his self-praise, he never dared to include in it the faintest pretension to the holy spirit. It would have had the effect of a bad joke. There are sundry varieties of religious delusion in the Middle Ages, but we never hear of a poet to have come forward unreservedly as a prophet, as did in Arabic letters Mutanabbi, *i.e.*, "the pretender to prophecy" (d. 965), in the estimate of his countrymen the most famous of all the poets born or made in Islam.[18]

Of course, a true poet will always await and witness anew the miracle of inspiration and sing of its ecstasies. Hebrew literature, also, has some magnificent examples of poetry quivering with the excitement of the unaccountable but unmistaken event. Invariably, however, there is a chaste reticence about such visitations of the Divinity. The experience is stated almost impersonally, in the traditional imagery, as if to hide the new rapture of the poet in the ancient and familiar memories of his people. Hence the ease with which the medieval synagogue could turn these intimate revelations of the individual into collective prayers of Israel. Take for example the lovely nocturne of Judah Ha-Levi (d. after 1140):

My thought awaked me with Thy Name,
Upon Thy boundless love to meditate;
Whereby I came
The fullness of the wonder to perceive,
That Thou a soul immortal shouldst create
To be embound in this, my mortal frame.
Then did my mind, elate,
Behold Thee and believe;
As though I stood among
That hushed and awe-swept throng
And heard the Voice and gazed on Sinai's flame!

I seek Thee in my dreams,
And lo, Thy glory seems
To pass before me, as of old, the cloud
Descended in his sight, who heard
The music of Thy spoken word.
Then from my couch I spring, and cry aloud,
"Blest be the glory of Thy Name, O Lord!"[19]

Quite fittingly, the poem is included in the liturgy of Shabuot, the holiday of revelation, commemorating the covenant established at Sinai. Originally, however, it is the record of a very personal encounter. In answer to long probings into the riddle of soul and body, the poet experiences, half awake and half in a dream, how into the clouds of his soul there descends the glory of God as into a tabernacle: "My heart beheld Thee and believed Thee, as though I were standing at Sinai." Purged of vanity by such undeserved favor of heaven, the poet's lips murmur a benediction, not a boast. The individual experience loses itself in the event basic to all Israel, the inspiration of today reaffirms the dawn of the historic faith, and the new seeks humbly to bring home the old revelation.

The same poet, as others before and after him, is also familiar with some of the formal aspects of inspiration: the feeling of being but a passive tool and mouthpiece, of being "carried away and overpowered" (Jer. 20:7), of saying not what one pleases, but what one cannot help saying. He knows also the sense of exhilaration, when the halting tongue is quickened of a sudden by the onrush of words, heaven born, pouring in effortlessly, infallible in their felicity, so convincing and compelling as to leave simply no other choice. "The speech of a prophet at the time when he is enwrapped by the holy spirit is in every part directed by the divine influence, the prophet himself being powerless to alter one word."[20] The description has personal accents, as has in the same book the impassioned and insistent inquiry into the state of the prophet and the secret of prophecy, but there is a self-imposed censorship and discipline of silence about any such adventures or aspirations of the poet. The restraint reflects a climate of opinion reared on a doctrine which stressed the pathos of distance separating the present from the ancient days when holy men still walked and talked with God.

In the medieval world one was ready to exercise patience and forbearance even with inordinate claims when made in the name of religion, not poetry. Saadia Gaon (d. 942), perhaps under the influence of certain Moslem ideas, evolved a remarkable doctrine that God never fails to provide His people with a "scholar" in each age whom He enlightens and inspires to guide his generation and make them prosper through him. Significantly, the Gaon adds that such was his own experience, having witnessed "what God in His grace has done for me and for the people."[21] The word used is *talmid*, or disciple (of the wise) or scholar in the law, and thus the claim is advanced on behalf of the Torah and its foremost exponent in every age. But since Saadia was also a prolific poet, and his contemporaries could not help being apprised of the opinions he entertained about himself, we hear the resentment voiced that his poetic compositions were written in verse units and supplied with accents and vowel points. Such resemblance to the Sacred Writ was seized upon by his opponents, who denounced it as a pretense to prophecy.[22] The last such instance, on the threshold of the modern era, is that of Moses Hayyim Luzzatto (d. 1747). Under the spell of inspiration, he believed himself to be receiving revelations from a mentor-angel and to write a second *Zohar*, a sequel to the classic book of Jewish mysticism.[22a] But since he was also a gifted poet, he had to contend with the rumor that he had written one hundred and fifty poems to supplant the Psalms of David. In vain did the poet disavow any such claim or comparison, his devout teacher aiding him by testifying that the poems were the product of toil and skill, not inspiration, as could clearly be seen from the many corrections and deletions, in the handwriting of the author, "such as occur in the natural process of composition, when one writes and crosses out and writes again."[23] The suspected manuscript had to be surrendered to a Rabbinic court, a portion was burned and the remainder buried in the ground, and so lost to posterity.[24] It is true, those were the days of the Sabbatian heresies when the guardians of the law may have thought it their duty to be especially severe.

Not only in times of crisis or peril to religion, but throughout the Middle Ages one can detect a latent or patent hostility to the craft of the poet. On second and serious thought, it must have appeared to be dangerous folly for a scattered and threatened community to dissipate its meager resources in toying with verse or enjoying poesy. Nor is it strange that the philosophic spirits in medieval Judaism were just as inimical to the poets, and particularly to the religious poets. Unrestrained fancy and loose talk, so the philosophers contended, could not but offend against the true precepts of an enlightened faith and breed crude or corrupt notions about God.[25] Rationalists and traditionalists alike seemed to concur that the cause of religion is best served, and error best eschewed, by banning poetry altogether from the worship of the synagogue. If piety prompts one to add or amplify praises to God, there is always inspired Scripture to draw upon with profit, or one can at all times safely turn to the Psalter.[26]

2

The advice was heeded. The Psalter served throughout the ages as a primer of prayer and praise, and handbook of devotion. It became the hymnal of the synagogue and the common man's household book of poetry. It would be difficult to overrate the effect of this most widely circulated anthology of Hebrew verse on the language of faith and the habits of piety of countless generations. Multitudes of men at every period of history discovered in the Psalms the stirrings and strivings of their hearts, and clothed in the venerable words of the book their own penitence and hope. This power of the Psalter stems from the belief that it is not merely a collection of priceless poetry, or a formulary of edifying prayers, but that it is part and parcel of the Holy Writ.

There is nothing more precious than the Book of the Psalms which contains everything. Therein are many praises to His Name, hallowed is He, and many a summons to repentance as well as many supplications for forgiveness and mercy . . . By reciting the Psalms, we at once offer prayer and study Holy Scripture, for King David, peace be unto him, long ago beseeched heaven that whoever will read the Psalter should receive as much reward as he who delves in the depths of the Torah.[1]

This, then, was the unique distinction of the Psalter, that it combined the two fundamental elements of all Jewish worship: it served as a pattern of *prayer* and as a repository of guidance and *instruction* in holy living. The two functions are inseparable, of course, and yet it is the latter that carried most weight in the eyes of the believer. His standards of value are succinctly stated in a maxim current in the Middle Ages:

He who prays, speaks to God; but he who reads the Writ, God speaks to him, as it is said (Ps. 119:99): "Thy statutes are (Thy) converse with me."[2]

It is in this double capacity of the Psalter to furnish both request and reply, search and solution, the cry of human want and the answer of Divine bounty, that one must seek the secret of the unrivaled influence exercised by the book in all ages.

Being a part of Scripture, the Psalms share the fate of that widely read Book: they are subject to ever-new and ever-changing rereading by new generations of men. Each period pours its own inner life into the patient and pliant texts of old which engagingly oblige new inquirers with new answers. Devout centuries extract or extort from the familiar documents messages undreamt of or unsuspected by the original writers. Such fresh and fanciful embroidering upon the ancient design is properly called legend, as the Latin *legenda* literally means: that *which will be read* by successive ages into the events or records of the past. The more a book is used, the more it will be abused, fiction prevailing over fact, or—to vary Aristotle[3]—poetry outlasting history.

The Bible, too, had such a posthumous adventure in its passage through the centuries, its text becoming disengaged from the original intention and enriched by the faith and fantasy of innumerable readers. We can follow this afterlife of the Bible in scattered comments or orderly commentaries which mirror the temper and the trends of the Jewish Middle Ages. Moreover, the centrality of Scripture in the medieval scene accounts not only for the natural and unconscious metamorphosis of the biblical legacy in the course of time, but also for the frequency with which so much of the original creation of the Middle Ages was sunk into biblical exegesis. To gain foothold in medieval Israel, every spiritual endeavor had to be related to the chief concern of the people, Torah. Hence medieval expression is so often cast in the form of a commentary on Scripture. Even dissent and revolt are clothed in what is in name or shape but a commentary. The form succeeded in disguising and preserving a great deal of the independent achievement of the Middle Ages. Whatever their usefulness for the study of the Bible itself, the medieval Bible commentaries are invaluable and indispensable for the revelation of the internal life of the Jew in the Middle Ages.

An example from the Psalter will illustrate the vigor and variety of this invisible creativeness passing unchallenged as biblical interpretation.

Psalm 29 is probably a very old hymn, voicing the dread and the wonder of ancient man before the fury of the elements. A storm is gathering out at sea, "upon many waters," and breaks upon the land, tossing the cedars of Lebanon and rocking the snow-capped Hermon to its foundations. The massive mountains seem to shake helplessly like frightened animals. The storm and the winds, the peals of thunder and the "flames of fire" or the lightning flash herald the power of "the God of glory" as He sets out to strike at the insurgent foes. When the tempest dies away in the desert, all rebellion is quelled, and the conqueror can return to His celestial palace, built "upon the flood" or the upper waters above the firmament, there to receive the tribute and honor due to a "king for ever." The heavenly ceremony is pictured after the fashion of earthly courts, or rather in images borrowed from prebiblical myths.[4] We see the lesser divinities, the *bene elim*, or "the sons of the gods," assemble to pay homage to the victorious godhead. With such "praise on high" the Psalm opens, and it ends with a prayer for "peace on earth."

Quite appropriately we find the earliest use of the Psalm in the liturgy of the festival of Sukkot, when prayers for rain were offered.

Already in the age of the *Tannaim*,[4a] the meaning of the Psalm was thoroughly overhauled:

> Rabbi Eleazer of Modaim said: When the Holy One, blessed be He, appeared to give the Torah to Israel, the earth shook and the mountains quaked, and all the sons of the mighty (*bene elim*) trembled in their palaces, as it is said: "And in his palace every one says 'Glory' " (Ps. 29:9). Whereupon the kings of the world assembled and came to Balaam, saying: What is the uproar that we heard? Is a flood to come to destroy the earth? Said he to them: "The Lord sitteth upon the flood" (*ibid.*, 10). The Holy One, blessed be He, swore long ago that He would not bring a flood upon the world for ever. They then said to him: He will not bring a flood of water, but He may bring a flood of fire as it is said: "For by fire will the Lord contend" (Is. 66:16). But he said to them: He is going to bring neither a flood of water, nor a flood of fire. However, He possesses in His storehouse a priceless treasure, the Torah which He is to present to His sons, as it is said: "The Lord will give strength unto His people" (Ps. 29:11). As soon as the kings heard that from him, they joined in the benediction: "The Lord will bless His people with peace" (*Ibid.*).[5]

Rabbi Eleazar of Modaim died during the siege of Bethar (*c.* 135 C.E.) and taught in days when it became clear that the natural base of the

Hebrew polity, the state and the sanctuary, were lost. However impoverished, Israel still possessed a priceless treasure from God's storehouse, the Torah. Hence the new stress on the gift of revelation, and on God's power in history rather than nature. Transposed, as it were, into a new key, the Psalm was employed in the liturgy of the Feast of Weeks, which commemorates the covenant at Sinai, when the Torah was given to Israel.[6] In medieval Spain[7] the custom seems to have originated of reciting the Psalm on the Sabbath, the traditional day of Revelation,[8] as the Torah is being returned to the Ark, or the treasure brought back to His storehouse, a practice still observed in our synagogues.

Echoes of darker centuries survive in the *Midrash to the Psalms*, a collection of homilies from various times, some perhaps going back to days of Roman or Byzantine rule and oppression:[9]

> *Bene elim* or "the sons of the gods"—what does that mean? The sons of the dumb (*bene ilmim*) and of the deaf (*i. e.,* the sons of Israel) who could answer back the Holy One, blessed be He, but they refrain from answering back, and suffer the yoke of the nations for the sanctification of His name. This is what Isaiah said (42:19): "Who is blind, but my servant, or deaf, as my messenger that I sent?"
>
> *Bene elim*—what else can that mean? The sons of those who are slain like rams (*elim*). Abraham said: I slay; Isaac said: I am (ready to be) slain.[10]

Pained and puzzled by the triumph of the wicked, the religious conscience sought solace and support in the examples of patriarchal piety or the songs of the suffering servant. The ways of God were inscrutable. Abraham did not comprehend how a father could be commanded to slay his only son, but he did not refuse or reproach God, he obeyed instead, to be rewarded and relieved in the end. Silently also the servant of the Lord must bear his martyrdom, a spoil and sport of all mankind, and yet it is with his stripes that the world will be healed. It was in the light of such memories or monition that Psalm 29 was reread in the early Middle Ages.

When the swift victories of Islam and the vast realm conquered by the new faith seemed to make the hopes of Jewish repatriation impracticable or illusory, the troubled heart turned again to the Psalter for courage and comfort. Psalm 29 was rendered as summoning the children of Israel to be *bene elim*, sons of might or men of valor, and to persevere in the faith as there was hope in their future. Verse 10 was understood to contain the solemn assurance that just as the Lord guards the universe against the flood, so He remains His people's king forever: "For as I have sworn that the waters of Noah should no more go over the earth, so have I sworn that I would not be wroth with thee, nor rebuke thee. For the mountains shall depart, and the hills be removed, but my kindness shall not depart from thee, neither shall the covenant of my peace be removed, saith the

Lord that hath mercy on thee" (Isa. 54:9 f.). The Psalm was so translated by Saadia, and his version is still current among Arabic-speaking Jews.[11]

In the lands of medieval Christendom, the Psalm was construed as a prophecy about the days of Messianic deliverance, when "the cedars of Lebanon," the proud kingdoms of the earth will be humbled. The Lord will thunder "upon many waters"; these are the rich and rapacious that grab the goods of this world as greedily as waters cover the sea. But in the end, justice will be enthroned for ever, and in His temple all will say "Glory," as it is said: "Then will I turn to the peoples a pure language, that they may all call upon the Name of the Lord, to serve Him with one consent" (Zeph. 3:9).[12]

After the banishment from Spain (1492),[12a] which uprooted the most populous and prosperous community of the Middle Ages, mystical tendencies gained the ascendancy. The Psalter was read fervently as an apocalypse in which every word is infused with references to the events of the imminently expected Messianic catastrophe or redemption. In fact, the Psalms themselves were discovered to be a book of war songs, an arsenal of mystic or magic weapons, "a sharp sword in Israel's hand"[13] to strike at the root of evil and thus precipitate the end. When the crack of doom failed to come, and the Messianic fever wore away, there spread from Safed, a town in northern Galilee, audacious new doctrines such as the cabbala of Isaac Luria (d. 1572), which gave a new answer to the basic and baffling facts of the historic experience of the Jew and a new meaning to his acts of worship.[14, 14a]

The homelessness of the Jewish people was conceived to be but a detail in the general dislocation of the whole of existence due to a primordial flaw or fracture of all creation which the new cabbala called "the breaking of the vessels." Because of it, all realms of being were unhinged and deranged, thrown out of their proper and purposed station, everything in the order of creation was displaced, all were in exile, including God. Supernal lights fell in the abyss of darkness, and sparks of holiness became imprisoned in shells of evil. The unity of the Divine Name was shattered (the new cabbala speaks of the letters YH being torn away from WH in the name YHWH). It was the mission of man and the purpose of religion to restore the broken name of God and so heal the original blemish of all the visible and invisible worlds. By observing the commandments of the Torah and the ordained discipline of worship, every Jew could become a partner in the work of redemption: he could help to lift the fallen lights of God and set free the holy sparks from the powers of evil.

With ardent precision every detail in form and language of the Psalms was instilled with mystic meaning and function. Concretely, in Psalm 29, three times it was said "Give unto the Lord," seven times "the voice of the Lord," eighteen times the Divine Name is spelled, making seventy-two letters or the numerical value of *hesed*, or mercy. The eleven verses of the Psalm equal WH in the tetragram, while the ninety-one words in the whole Psalm correspond to the sum total of YHWH and Adonai.[15] By means of each of these mysteries of prayer, the worshiper who knew the secrets of the holy letters and was capable of utter inwardness (*kavvanah*) in his devotions, could work miracles of *tikkun* or restitution by which sparks scattered in the lower depths could be reassembled, and "the Holy One, praised be He, reunited with His exiled *Shekinah*." Acts of religion determine the fate of the world, and it is the essential distinction and dignity of man that without his free choice the breach of creation could not be mended. Feeble as man is, unlike the angels, he alone knows, in every breath of his, about the struggle of good and evil, and can influence it by his freedom of action. Hence only man, and not any of the celestial beings, can lead the banished glory of God back to the Master, and thus literally "give unto the Lord glory and strength," thereby completing His enthronement as "king for ever."

In this new myth, which burst forth in the heart of Judaism at so late a stage of the historic faith, mystic notions verge on magic, or perhaps revert to the origins of all worship in which prayer and spell commingle. As if the wheel had come full circle, and the new cabbala had recovered, on another plane, the prebiblical rudiments of magic, residual in the Psalms and perhaps irreducible from man's vocabulary of prayer.

These few examples of Rabbinic and cabbalistic interpretation of Scripture will suffice to indicate the amazing freedom with which the Middle Ages were able to make the words of an old text yield new meaning. Even though the syllables and sentences of the Bible remained intact, a new sentiment infused them with new significance, and transformed the Psalm, far beyond the purposes of the first author, into an untrammeled expression of a new religious attitude and outlook. Often it is an original conception that asserts itself in, or despite, the ancient and venerable vocables, which suffer no outward change through the centuries. The new creation escapes notice (also by the historians of literature), for it is deposited invisibly in the same old words of the Writ.

Above all, even a hurried glimpse into biblical lore of the Middle Ages will prove how futile was the endeavor to exorcise error and heresy from the synagogue by advising the faithful to turn with a safe conscience only to inspired Scripture, particularly the Psalms. We saw traditionalists and rationalists agreeing that it would be best to praise God with the songs of King David alone.[16] Little did either of them dream what dangerously novel ideas could nest in the innocent and time-honored words. The letter is too feeble to imprison the spirit. It is useless to try to freeze the tides of spiritual life into permanent retrospection. Ancient meanings cannot be perpetuated through the ages. At best, the sounds may be reproduced, or perhaps only the symbols of script, but a new spirit will transfigure them in each age.

Fortunately, the synagogue discovered quite early how hopeless it would be to invite the great poetry of biblical antiquity to keep new expression suppressed in Judaism. It was better insight to make room in the synagogue, along with the classical heritage, also for new creative endeavor, and thus enlist the genius of the poets to lend freshness and vigor to the religious quest of medieval Jewry.

3

The beginnings of poetry in the synagogue may well go back to the dawn of public prayer, or to the very origin of the synagogue. The Jews were the only people of antiquity who succeeded in divorcing prayer from sacrifice, and so were the first to evolve the modes and manners of public worship as the world knows them now. The new institution of the synagogue was to grapple first with the two basal needs of all congregational service: conformity and nonconformity. Untutored or undisciplined prayer may grow haphazard and slipshod, self-seeking or disreputable, anarchical and antisocial. Regulated for public propriety, or legislated for the good of society, it may become a stale and spiritless convention. The synagogue strove to retain and reconcile both the requirement of agreement and informality. The oldest order of services includes, along with instruction in the Writ meant for the whole congregation, private devotions or confessions. These elements of spontaneous or subjective piety (called *debarim*, words, or *tahanunim*, supplications) originally followed the recitation of the *Shema*, or the creed of Judaism, and thus hark back to a time before the eighteen benedictions or the principal prayer became an established order of the synagogue.[1] Moreover, even when the eighteen benedictions were finally agreed upon, toward the close of the first century C.E., only their sequence was settled, the wording remaining in flux for centuries. As a matter of fact, there continues for generations the deliberate tendency to keep the prayer fresh and fluid, modified with something new each day, to quote a Rabbi of the fourth century.[2]

Probably there was here at work a rejection of the heathen notion of piety which rigidly forbade any deviation from the hallowed formulary of ancestral ritual. Even the slightest change would only weaken the potency of the prayers, believed by the ancients to be missives from the gods themselves and hence especially efficacious and inviolable.

To prevent the confusion of religion with magic, the Rabbis emphasize that there are no set or sacred spells certain to force down the blessing from heaven. On the contrary, prayer must not be fixed,[3] but free, welling out of the depths of a contrite heart and reaching out entreatingly for the unpredictable grace and goodness of God.

Whatever the motives of the Rabbis, the religious and aesthetic benefit was indisputable. By asking with variety of circumstance also variety of words, the synagogue admitted or even invited into its midst the craftsmen of words, or the poets. As a result the common prayers of Judaism gained increasingly in richness of inspiration and beauty of expression.

The Middle Ages followed the Rabbinic age in the endeavor to preserve both obedience to tradition and individual assertion. The standard prayers, the oldest nucleus of the liturgy, always and everywhere became the center of Jewish worship, a bond of union despite geographic dispersal, and a bridge across the ages linking the present to the past. At the same time, each period and place was left free, if not encouraged, to speak its own mind in new compositions added to, or inserted within, the ancient prayers. These additions, called *piyyut*, or poetry, constitute—in contrast to the stable and stationary standard prayers—an ever-changing and restless element in the Jewish liturgy. They enliven with personal accent or local color the established and universal order of services, and unlike the latter, frankly bespeak the soil and sun, season or situation, which nurtured or ripened them. In fact, it was the vigorous and abundant growth of the *piyyut* that was responsible for the development within medieval Judaism of about half a hundred different rites.[4] Within the larger brotherhood of Israel, and the stock of prayers common to all generations, the medieval synagogue attempts and attains both a contemporary note and regional differentiation. The religious expression varies in the Byzantine age and in the era of Islam; in the same century, Franco-German Judaism differs from Spanish Judaism, as do the rites of Aleppo and Yemen, Prague and Amsterdam. Yet there underlies them all, despite the dissimilar and distinctive body of their poetry, the core of ecumenic prayer invariable in all Jewries.

In fine, before the invention of printing slackened or congealed its growth, medieval Judaism essayed and effected a conciliation and concordance of two contrary but complementary necessities of all spiritual life, arriving at a remarkable synthesis of liberty and order, unity and diversity, permanence and change. The old and the new, the recent and the remote, the casual and the constant, blend to enrich and to reinforce each other. It is this peculiar and pregnant amalgam of opposites, of pattern and freedom, system and vitality which imparts to medieval utterance both strength and suppleness, the discipline of a consistent doctrine and accord with the tune of the times.

A few examples of religious verse may serve as illustration, and help to point out some of the forms and functions of medieval Hebrew poetry.

The heart of the Jewish service is the *Shema*, the Jew's acceptance of the

Kingship of Heaven. It begins with a summons to the worshipers: "Bless ye (*bareku*) the Lord!" It is here, before the call is sounded, that the medieval poet asks "leave" (*reshut*) to intersperse the hallowed prayers with his own effort. Such introductions usually strike the note of preparation for the actual prayer. For example, the poet meditates upon what is to be affirmed in the *Shema*. The first words, after the avowal of faith, command to love God "with all thy heart and all thy might" (Deut. 6:5), that is to love Him "in truth" (cf. Jer. 32:41). For in the holy tongue, God's name is Truth (Jer. 10:10), and in the view of the Rabbis, His seal is truth.[5] These are, also, the very last words of the *Shema*: "I am the Lord your God—Truth," in prayer the immediately following word being joined to the last of recited Scripture (Num. 15:41). The beginning and the end of the *Shema* set the theme of one of the magnificent preludes by Judah Ha-Levi:

With all my heart, O Truth, with all my might
    I love Thee; in transparency, or night,
Thy Name is with me; how then walk alone?
    He is my Love; how shall I sit alone?
He is my Brightness; what can choke my flame?
    While He holds fast my hand, shall I be lame?
Let folk despise me: they have never known
    My shame for Thy sake is my glorious crown.
O Source of Life, let my life tell thy praise,
    My song to Thee be sung in all my days![6]

When promptly thereafter the congregation is summoned to praise or bless the Lord, the familiar *bareku* of the prayer book seems now immeasurably widened in its meaning, or perhaps restored to its real meaning. For what is required cannot be the mere mouthing of pious words, but the truth of a whole life given in service to the Truth that is God. Given? Gained is the better word, for what speaks here is not renunciation, nor even resentment over the world's scorn and hate, but the glad surrender of the failing self to the "source of life" wherefrom every breath is borrowed and all our strength supplied.

The first of the benedictions preceding the *Shema* voices gratitude for the gift of light. It is probably a very old practice, going back to the ancient mystics of Palestine, the Essenes,[6a] who, as Josephus records, would not speak before daybreak about profane matters, but would first greet the dawn with prayers that had come down to them from their forefathers, "as if praying for the sun to rise."[7] Adopted into the synagogue, the morning prayer grew to include the glorious words of Second Isaiah (45:7) about the One God "Who formeth (*yozer*) light and createth darkness." The *piyyut* which is here inserted is called *yozer* and usually hymns the wonders of creation. But sometimes, as in the following example, the poet ponders over the darker might of God which the medieval community had so often to experience. Bewildered by the ways of God with men and His incomprehensible neutrality or apparent assent to evil, the distressed heart seeks in the Holy Writ a clue to the uncanny power and purpose of darkness. Four Scriptural passages on the theme of darkness voice the complaint and the comfort, and form the final line and rhyme of each stanza:

O silent Dove, pour out thy whispered prayer,
Stricken amid the tents of Meshekh;
And lift thy soul unto God—
Thy banner, thy chariot and thy horseman—
Who kindleth the light of thy sun:
Is. 45:7 *Who formeth light and createth darkness.*

To the whole He called with His word,
And it arose in a moment, at His bidding,
To show unto all the strength of His glory
In the world which unto life, not waste, He had formed,
When from the east, unto His light
Ex. 10:21 *He called and moved the darkness.*

And the host of His heavens heard
The word: "Let there be Light"; and learned to know
That there is a Rock by whom are cleft
The firmaments, and the earth's foundations laid.
And they gave thanks to their Maker, now understanding
Eccl. 2:13 *The excellency of light over darkness.*

So will He yet light up my gloom,
And help to raise my fallen estate,
And shed radiance over mine assembly.
Then His people shall yet rejoice:
"Behold the light of the Rock of my praise
Mic. 7:8 *Is mine, though I sit in darkness.*"[8]

One must read in Hebrew the assurance of the ancient seer broken off suddenly, in the middle, as if to indicate the yet unfinished processes of history, to understand the triumph of trust which amidst all the terrors of medieval darkness never despairs of a new dawn: "As for me, I will look unto the Lord; I will wait for the God of my salvation: my God will hear me. Rejoice not against me, O mine enemy: though I am fallen, I shall arise; *though I sit in darkness*, the Lord is a light unto me" (Mic. 7:7-8). When the worshiper is returned to the prayer book, the innocent blessing at sunrise of the ancient mystics does not seem innocent at all: it is heavy with the sighs and salted with the tears of yesterday and today.

Toward its close, the benediction of light contains a prayer for the renewal of the light of Zion. On logical grounds, some schoolmen (notably

Saadia) objected to having the praise of creation and the prayer for redemption rolled into one.[9] In vain: the homeless people clung in fervent hope precisely to this correlation between the first wonders of light and the last wonders of the new day of the Lord. Here the poets of the synagogue interpose a composition called *meora*, for it precedes the praise of the Creator of the luminaries (*meorot*). Sometimes the grief and faith of the captivity is worded in a poignant dialogue, as in the selection here presented, between the "curtains of Solomon" and a pilgrim. He remembers them in their former glory, the pride of a palace, and barely believes his eyes to find them now, faded and frayed, in a Bedouin tent:

> Ye curtains of Solomon, how, amid the tents of Kedar,
> Are ye changed? Ye have no form, no beauty!
>
> "The multitudes which dwelt aforetime in our midst,
> Have left us a desolation, a broken ruin, unprotected—
> The holy vessels have gone into exile and become profane,
> And how can ye ask for beauty of a lily among thorns?"
>
> Rejected of their neighbors, but sought of their Lord,
> He will call them each by name, not one shall be missing.
> Their beauty, as in the beginning, He shall restore in the end,
> And shall illume as the sevenfold light their lamp which is darkened.[10]

The rebuff of the world is forgotten in knowing oneself befriended by God Who, in the language of the great Unknown of the first captivity, forgets none among His hosts, calling each by his first name, the faithful on earth as His stars in heaven. "Why sayest thou, O Israel: my way is hid from the Lord, my right is passed over from my God?" (Is. 40:26-31). Again, one comes back to the accustomed prayers with a heart revived through proud memories and new hope.

The second benediction before the *Shema* turns from nature to history, or from creation to revelation. It renders thanks for the gift of the Torah, "the statutes of life," which in His everlasting love God chose to communicate to Israel, and it asks for divine aid properly to understand the commandments and to fulfill them in love. The *piyyut* here ingrafted is called *ahaba* (love), and as its name and place implies, has for its theme the love of God for Israel and of Israel for God. Medieval piety spoke its inmost soul in some of these poems:

> Let my sweet song be pleasing unto Thee—
>   The incense of my praise—
> O my Beloved that are flown from me,
>   Far from mine errant ways!
> But I have held the garment of His love,
> Seeing the wonder and the might thereof.

The glory of Thy name is my full store—
My portion for the toil wherein I strove:
Increase the sorrow:—I shall love but more!
Wonderful is Thy love![11]

Amid all degradation, Israel knows herself borne and sustained by God's boundless love: "Enough for me the glory of Thy Name!" Clinging to the fringe of His love gives bliss and strength enough to endure all the taunt and torment of the world. If the price of mere knowledge be sorrow (Eccl. 1:18), what would not one readily brave for the love of God?

In another *ahaba*, such love is driven to an even bolder extreme:

Since Thou hast been the abode of love,
My love hath camped wherever Thou hast camped.
The reproaches of mine enemies have been pleasant to me for Thy sake:
Leave them, let them afflict him whom Thou dost afflict!
My foes learned Thy wrath, and I loved them,
For they pursued the victim whom Thou didst smite.
From the day that Thou didst despise me, I despised myself,
For I shall not honor what Thou hast despised.
Until the indignation be overpast, and Thou send redemption,
To this, Thine inheritance that Thou didst once redeem.[12]

Divorced from power, unable to retaliate, how was one to remain free from the corrosions of hate in a dark and cruel age? The medieval Jew won such internal freedom in external bondage through his unconditional trust in God: it was His inscrutable will that redemption should be preceded by penance in exile. The evil forces of the world do unknowingly the will of God. The Jew's love for God enables him to recognize in the enemy the instrument of Divine Judgment, "the rod of His anger," and compels the incredible or impossible: love for one's enemy.

But though love is the willing obedience of all wills to the Will of God, the poet never confuses the remediable ills of society with Divine Purpose. He will not acquiesce in injustice, nor suffer the unworldliness of the saints to benefit tyranny. He knows that lazy opportunism and religious perfectionism may alike cripple the attempts at self-liberation.

In an *ahaba* which must have offended the leadership of its day, our poet warns sternly against the perils of political expediency. These were the times when the charities and welfare funds of Jewish Spain were engaged in aiding the refugees from the Moslem south to establish themselves in the Christian north. The kings of Christian Spain welcomed the influx of Jewish commerce and capital for reasons of statecraft and strategy: such exodus could not but weaken the Moslem provinces and facilitate their reconquest. Was it safe, the poet seems to ask, to put confidence in transitory interests of the crown, and disregard the growing enmity of the populace, the lawless independence of the nobility, the unrelenting opposition of the Church? Will not the Jewish confidants of the king see that they build the future of their people upon a smoldering volcano? Will not the Jewish philanthropists recognize the futility of the endeavors to solve the Jewish question through a policy of new migrations in the lands of dispersion?

> The hand of my rescuers is short,
> It cannot save.
> O that my ways were straight before God,
> Maybe He would see how powerless
> Are all my would-be-redeemers . . .
>
> Weary am I to tread
> The old itinerary of woe,
> Find anew the foe cast his greedy eye
> Upon the remnant of my survivors . . .[13]

Piety and political realism prompt this disagreement with the notables of Jewish Spain, and will ultimately influence the poet to leave his home and journey to the Holy Land. But what interests us momentarily is the fact that the current issues and controversies of the times often found their way and vehicle in the *piyyut*.

After the *Shema* there follows in our prayer book the assurance by the congregation that the Divine behest is cherished in the present as it was in the past, and that it will forever endure in the hearts of Israel, for "there is no God *beside* (*zulat*) Thee." Here a poem may be installed, called *zulat* because of its location in this passage of the liturgy. Often it echoes the strife of the environment against the Jew, the subtle or coarse coercion to make him renounce his faith:

> They reproach me
>   When I seek to serve Him,
> And revile me
>   When I give glory to His Name.
> They seek to set me far,
>   O God, from Thy service:
> But my suffering and oppression
>   Are better than Thine estrangement;
> My portion and my pleasure,
>   The sweet fruit of Thy law.
>
> Let my right hand forget—
>   If I stand not before Thee;
> Let my tongue cleave—
>   If I desire aught but Thy law.

My heart and mine eyes
Will not suffer my feet to slip,
For He, the Lord, is One,
There is none beside Him.[14]

The concluding benediction of the *Shema* strikes the third chord of the Jewish faith, redemption, the previous blessings being devoted to creation and revelation, respectively. Here a poem may be embedded named *geulla,* or redemption. Its frequent theme is the pain and plight of the present which seeks relief or redress from the Rock of Israel:

Let Thy favor flow over me,
Even as Thy wrath hath overflowed.
Shall mine failings for ever
Stand between me and Thee?
How long shall I search
For Thee beside me, and find Thee not? . . .
My Redeemer! to redeem my multitudes
Rise and look forth from Thine abiding place.[15]

There are yet other poetic additions to the morning prayer, but the above are in the main the typical. Perhaps mention should be made also of the *ofan* (wheel), a poem deriving its name from the passage in the prayer book that describes the heavenly host, winged and wheeled (as in the visions of Isaiah and Ezekiel), chanting the praises of God on high, as Israel does on earth. Here the poet has occasion to delve into the labyrinth of heaven or the music of the spheres, or the mysteries of the Divine Name, or the very secret of prayer. Sometimes stress is laid on the daily experience of God's ubiquity, which is more wondrous than even the celestial chariot:

O Lord, where shall I find Thee?
Hid is Thy lofty place;
And where shall I not find Thee,
Whose glory fills all space?[16]

The paradoxes of God are then itemized: All-hidden, He is revealed everywhere; transcendent, and enclosed in the breast of lowly man; a God afar off, and yet near at hand (Jer. 23:23); exalted above all praise, He inhabits the praises of Israel (Ps. 22:4).

Oh, how shall mortals praise Thee
When angels strive in vain—
Or build for Thee a dwelling,
Whom worlds cannot contain?

Yet when they bow in worship
Before Thy throne, most high,
Closer than flesh or spirit
They feel Thy Presence nigh.[16]

Such is the miracle of prayer that we forget to think of the very presumption of all prayer. For in the inwardness of the act, the offering of man and the gift of God are indistinguishable. With the Psalmist, one experiences "my prayer" to be "His mercy" (Ps. 66:20). He already answered us, when He prompted our heart to pray. Hence the sense of surprise and gratitude voiced by the medieval poet when he finds that God is invariably ahead of His children in the game of hide and seek:

I have sought Thy nearness,
With all my heart have I called Thee,
And going out to meet Thee
I found Thee coming toward me.[17]

It is by such disclosure of fresh exploration and adventuring away from the beaten track that the poets of the Middle Ages kept the windows in the house of prayer open to the breezes of the green outdoors. Spontaneous piety continually interrupts the order of established service and quickens it with a breath of fragrant life. New expression adds relevance to the legacy of ages, and the timeless is enhanced by the timely.

The poetic embellishments of the standard prayers were, of course, not restricted to the morning service, or to the benedictions of the *Shema*. The *Amidah*, or the prayer proper of the synagogue, is copiously adorned by the poets, especially on distinguished Sabbaths and holidays. Every event of the Jewish liturgical calendar is enriched by poetic compositions which vary in form and structure and show steady growth and intricate development through the centuries. In the course of time the *piyyut* penetrated into every part of the religious life and every portion of the service. Nor was it confined to public worship in the synagogue.[18] It entered the Jewish home, cheered the family at meals, welcoming the Sabbath and bidding it farewell, partaking in the jollities as well as in the trials of the house from birth to death.

4

At least 35,000 poems by 2,836 poets are listed by Israel Davidson in his *Thesaurus of Medieval Hebrew Poetry*,[1] an indispensable reference book for all study of the subject. New discoveries have added to our knowledge of medieval letters, however a vast amount of medieval creation still lies buried in unpublished manuscripts.

The discovery of the Genizah in Cairo[2] brought to light the forgotten remains of the ancient *payyetanim*, or poets, of Palestine. Their activity spans the centuries between the compilation of the Palestinian Talmud, toward the end of the fourth century, and the havoc wrought to Jewish Palestine by the Crusades. We have now the evidence of literary endeavor in the Holy Land and its environs that extends for more than twenty generations. Slowly there emerges the outline of recognizable growth from the artless prayers of the earlier talmudic age to the more stately and studied diction of the first poet known to us by name, Yose ben Yose (*c.* 400 C.E.?), down to the more intricate and involved patterns of speech and poetry characteristic of the Palestinian school of *payyetanim* and their imitators in other lands. The most important single find in that period of literature is the recovery of the lost poetic work of Yannai (*c.* 550 C.E.), the first poet consistently to employ rhyme in Hebrew. It is he, also, who loaded his verses with the lore of the Midrash, so that his *Kerobah*, or poetic elaboration of the *Amidah*, is in fact a rhymed homily on the portion of the Writ read that week in the synagogue.[3] His disciple is said to be Eleazar ben Killir, the most fertile and influential among the early *payyetanim*. There is no season of the sacred year which he did not supply with prolific compositions some of which are still recited on the major holidays. For long generations, late into the Middle Ages, he remained the model and legislator of synagogal poetry. He is remembered especially for his bold or bizarre word formations some of which were criticized by medieval or modern biblical purists. However, we know now that his was not wholly a private idiom, and that many of his forms and locutions occur in other, both earlier and later, poets of the Palestinian school, or even in the nonpoetic remains of Palestinian literature. All of this tends to prove that the Palestinian *piyyut* is also valuable as a surviving witness of the postbiblical Hebrew vernacular.[4]

There are extant fragments of literary production by a score of poets living in the Holy Land or its vicinity, all of them new surprises of the Genizah, *e.g.*, Joseph ben Nisan of Shaveh-Kiriathaim or Nawe in Trans-Jordan, or Pinehas ben Jacob of Kefar, a suburb of Tiberias (*c.* 800 C.E.), or Samuel ben Hoshana whom we encounter in Egypt in 1011, or Solomon ben Amr al-Singari, named so probably from his native town in Kurdistan, a fecund versifier who wrote *Yozerot* and *Kerobot* for all the sabbaths and festivals, his compositions mirroring the mind and mood of Near Eastern Jewry on the eve of the Crusades.[5]

Saadia Gaon (882-942), reared in Egypt and head of the academy in Sura, old seat of Babylonian learning,[5a] is a versatile writer who used Hebrew verse for a variety of purposes. We have from his pen polemical[6] and didactic,[7] liturgic[8] or even philosophic[9] compositions, some facile and fluent, others dark and difficult. An adept student of the Palestinian *piyyut*, he outdid all *payyetanim* by his audacious innovations and playful artificialities of language. The poems of his elder contemporary, the blind and saintly Nissi Nahrawani[10] win by their simplicity and sincerity. The poets of the house of al-Baradani for two or three generations serve as chief *hazzanim* in Bagdad and as supervisors of all the *hazzanim* in Iraq: it is through them that the Palestinian *piyyut* as well as their own creations spread in the East, or even to northern Africa. We can trace such channels of transmission thanks to a letter in the Genizah written in 1106 to Kairuan by the Gaon Hai (d. 1038)[10a] who is also a poet of considerable stature. Some of his *selihot* voice stirringly the sense of homelessness, and hence the helplessness of the medieval Jew.[11]

Recent yields of scholarship permit us to trace poetic development in both Egypt and Babylonia down to the thirteenth century. In the first half of that century, Eleazar Hababli,[12] poet of wealthy patrons in Bagdad, records the conditions of the closing period of the Abbassid caliphate, while in the second half of the century, Joseph ben Tanhum Yerushalmi,[13] house poet of the Nagid in Cairo, sheds light on Jewish ways and worthies in Egypt under the Mamelukes.

From Palestine *piyyut* spread not only to the east and south, but also to the west and north, to Byzantium, Italy, and the German lands. Southern Italy is the first center of Hebrew culture in Europe and several of its poets, such as Shefatiah (d. 886) and his son Amittai, contributed fine lyrics to our prayer book, some recited in the most solemn part of the service on the Day of Atonement.[14] The ritual for the same day preserves a *keroba* by the son of Kalonymos of Lucca, Meshullam. He died in Mayence in the beginning of the eleventh century. Both the style and the structure betoken the influence of the Palestinian *piyyut*, like most creations of the *payyetanim* in Frankish and German territories, from Simon bar Isaac bar Abun in Mayence in the tenth century, and his younger contemporary Gershom the Light of the Exile (d. 1028), to Rabbenu Tam of Rameru (d. 1171) and Ephraim of Regensburg (d. 1175) foremost *payyetan* of medieval Germany, the last two showing acquaintance with elements of meter as developed in Spain.[15]

The first to adapt the Arabian quantitive or metrical scansion to Hebrew verse was Dunash ben Labrat,[16] a disciple of Saadia, active in Cordova in the middle of the tenth century. The first great poet of Hebrew Spain is Samuel Ha-Nagid (993-1056),[16a] the vizier of the Berber kings of Granada, equally distinguished as statesman, grammarian, and talmudic scholar. He is the outstanding representative if not the founder of the knightly and courtly taste and tradition in Hebrew secular poesy. For nearly two decades he used to accompany the armies of his state on their yearly campaigns and to write in his bivouac poetic reports to his family, describing in detail his military exploits or political feuds, the intrigues at the court or the designs of the rival city-states of Andalusia, appending prayers before battle or songs of victory which breathe a robust, almost antique faith. In decisive crises on the battlefield, or dire danger to his very life, he never despairs, firmly convinced that even on the brink of disaster a vow or prayer, and the intercession of his ancestors in the cave of Machpelah, will summon help from heaven, and the stars in their courses will fight against the enemy as in the days of Sisera. Intermingled with such martial verse are solicitous inquiries about the health of his sons or the progress of their education, exhortation and counsel how to win favor in heaven and friends on earth, and what or how best to study, and moving lyrical outbursts of love and longing for Zion, where he would rather be a humble Levite in the courts of God than retain rank and rule among the great on earth. In short, his *diwan*, or collected poetry, is a diary in verse of a scholar-father turned warrior-statesman, a rare and revealing human document which bares the private cares and the public career of an altogether remarkable man of affairs and man of letters in eleventh-century Spain.[17]

His younger contemporary is Solomon ibn Gabirol (b. 1021), who died early in his thirties and yet won immortal fame as one of the foremost thinkers and poets of the Middle Ages. Known as Avicebron to the scholastics, his *Fons Vitae* is a landmark in medieval philosophy,[17a] and he is equally distinguished as one of the most gifted poets in the Hebrew language. The conflict of the genius with his environment, his being forever nettled and lacerated by "the thorns and thistles of the earth,"[18] the mass of the uncreative who set themselves up as "the norm" and dismiss as "abnormal" the endeavor or the behavior of the creative individuality, this perpetual martyrdom of the spirit is unforgettably uttered in his sorrowful lyrics, or impassioned invective, or his landscape pictures of night and storm, the comrades and symbols of his somber and restless soul. Conscious of his gifts, proud of his calling, ascetically devoted to the search of truth, he was constitutionally unable to serve men or stoop before the mighty "like the priest of Edom before his icons."[19] Hence the inevitable misunderstandings and untoward setbacks of his life which must have sowed the seeds of his early disease and death. Pure and chaste are his sacred songs, the finest fruit of medieval devotion. Discontent and discord die away, and rid of resentment and resistance, "humble of spirit, lowly of knee and stature,"[20] he bows before the throne of glory, "like the beggar who cries at the door for grace."[21] But when he rises from prayer, the knowledge of being loved by God gives him such peace and power that nothing can bow him down. Restored to His favor, the lowly self knows itself restored to lordliness, capable again to recollect and redeem the innate kingliness of the soul and her kinship with God:

Thy life to God's life is akin,
    Concealed like His beneath a veil,
Since He is free of flaw or sin,
Like purity thou too canst win,
    To reach perfection wherefore fail?[22]

His religious verse, notably *The Royal Crown*, a lofty poem charting the solar system of medieval science, entered the rites of many Jewries, bringing to humble houses of worship in distant lands glimpses of vision and insights of contemplation which immeasurably enhanced the sense of wonder at the mystery and vastness of the universe, and in the same breath increased the spirit of magnanimity for all that share the sight of the stars and the warmth of the sun:

Thou art God, and all creatures are Thy witnesses and Thy worshipers.
Yet is not Thy glory diminished by reason of those that adore aught beside
Thee,
For the intention of them all is to reach Thee . . .[23]

The sun-kissed summit of Hebrew poetry is Judah Ha-Levi (d. after 1140), the heart and harp of medieval Judaism.[23a] His is the most beloved name among his people who feel that he voiced and embodied the best in Israel. Wittily but reverently, they apply to him the Scripture (Deut. 12:19): "Take heed to thyself that thou forsake not Ha-Levi (the Levite)," and heartily endorse the homage of his contemporary,[24] *kol Jaakob mityahadim,* "the entire household of Jacob keeps faith with *Judah.*" Because he is an authentic mouthpiece of his people and representative of the genius of its faith and art, all the selections from medieval verse in the foregoing chapters were drawn from his poetry, and yet they give no adequate notion of his grandeur. Every translator of his advises in the end: "Dear reader, study Hebrew, and throw my version in the fire!"[25] For no rendering can recapture the music and magic of his Hebrew, abounding in perfect miracles of sense and sound.

He started as a prodigy in the literary salons of Andalusia. A lively lad and singer born, he showed uncanny skill in adapting Hebrew words to the strains and stanzas of the Arabian love ballads then in vogue. He could match with amazing ease the lightsome lilt or the licentious lines of any of the song hits of the day, as a comparison with the *muwassah* by the popular poet of Seville, al-Abyad, will show:

barrid ġalīl	rakīk belīl
ṣabb al-ʿalīl	nofeth kelīl
lā yastaḥīl	yōfī we-lyl-
fīhi ʿan ʿahdi	-ʾoth sefath maddi
wa lā yazāl	hatter we-gal
fī kulli ḥāl	shad kam ke-gal
yarǧū ʾl-wiṣāl	ki-shdē shegal
wa-hwa fī ʾṣ-ṣaddi[26]	hēn we- ʿas daddi[27]

Such amatory verses unexpectedly turn panegyrical, including a toast or tribute to the patron or benefactor whose name and fame they spread abroad on the wings of a favorite tune. The praise or dispraise of song writers could thus make or mar the reputation of their friends or clients.

No wonder that our poet soon became the darling of polite society and the despair of his fellow minstrels, as he facilely mingled frolic with flattery to his hosts or backers, and gaily caroled the delights of the body and the merriments of youth with a seductiveness in the holy language which perhaps a few regretted, and all the others relished. "Why not fill my *kad* (the Hebrew for a *jug* of wine), while my years are not full *kad* (*i.e.*, twenty-four)!"[28] With such inborn gift of mirth and wit and pun, one wonders what would have become of him in another environment or tradition. The poet himself later rued his celebrity as the acknowledged master of the exquisite trifle. But that was the mood of the changed and harsh realities of the Spanish scene, when the *reconquista* and the counter-attacks of Islam plunged the Peninsula into turmoil and strife.

They fight in their frays,
And we fall in defeat,
As is the custom in Israel.[29]

The poet found a theme for his tongue, touched with the live coals of the ancient altar. At first, the poems that welled out of his new heart were dark and penitential, unsparing in remorse and reproof, austere and ascetic. His friends shook their heads, or began inquiring about his health. A few scholars nodded assent. The spokesmen for religion were delighted. Only the poet felt more and more ashamed, precisely for being a religious poet. Was not that the burden of his message that since men cannot save, the Will of God must be done? Done, not sung. So he decides to put lived life behind his written lines. He turns his back on the Jewish court society, its Arabian meters and melodies, its culture of the senses and its Grecian wisdom, its trust in princes and its worship of men, and in obedient servantship of his Lord, seeks a threefold return to the holy language, the holy law and—hardest of all—the Holy Land. Such resolve is not easy, and the poet does not conceal his lapses, love of life, irresolution. But when he braved all and risked all in utter surrender to his God, he came to his own at last. The wintry mind of the aging poet experienced a belated Indian summer of poetic exultation. Never before had all the wells of inspiration burst in such jubilant and masterly song as on the eve of his departure from Spain, or his voyage on the sea, or in Egypt where he falters and nerves himself anew to go whence there is no return. In these last years of his life, he left some of the finest bits of poetry written by the hand of men.[30]

The days of Judah Ha-Levi are the golden age of Spanish literature. We know about fifty names of contemporary Hebrew poets in Spain,[31] among them writers of renown such as Moses and Abraham ibn Ezra.[32] No Hebrew poet in subsequent generations was able to recapture the glories of this classical epoch. Some excellent verse is still written, and some new patterns of literature are adopted from the Arabic, *e.g.*, the *maqamah* ("assembly," often rendered as "miscellany"), a picaresque genre in rhymed prose intersected by verse, a rather curious blend of mime and satire, tract and tale, farce and homily. Its best known examples in Spain are *The Book of Delight* by Joseph Zabara (written *c.* 1190) and the *Tahkemoni* by Judah al-Harizi (d. before 1235).[33]

Of the poets of the thirteenth century Meshullam de Piera deserves to be singled out for his originality and integrity. Rooted in the mystic faith of the circle of Gerona, center of Spanish cabbalism, he writes with mordant scorn of the pedantries and platitudes of both grammarians and philosophers to whom Writ and Prophecy were but a playground for linguistic or allegorical exercises. A proud and independent spirit, unbribable alike in his blame and praise, he walked his own ways with men or even with the Hebrew language. He sets it free from the pinfold of the biblical vocabulary, resolutely employing all its resources from Midrash and Talmud or even medieval science.[34] His most admired friend and compatriot was the illustrious Moses ben Nahman (1194-*c.* 1270), one of the master minds of medieval *halaka*. In his poems one finds the first intimations of mystic ideas in Spanish Hebrew sacred poetry, and his hymn on the descent of the soul, its sojourn as a stranger on earth, and its homeward journey to God, entered the liturgy of the New Year.[35] The *diwan* of Todros (son of Jehudah) Abulafia (d. after 1300) is a kind of poetic diary, containing the memoirs and fragments of autobiography in verse by a courtier in thirteenth century Castile. It mirrors the light and gay mores of the upper stratum of Jewish society, and the inroads of Averroistic enlightenment[35a] which the mystic revival and the classic books of the Spanish cabbala sought to counteract.[36] Little is known about the poet Nahum, whose *meorot* and *geullot* have the fragrance and radiance of dew. Ecstatic faith blends with a delicate feeling for nature: a blossoming twig in the garden stirs the hope for the branch out of the stem of Jesse, and the sunrise, or the spring, whisper in the ear prospects of freedom and deliverance.[37]

The political decline and spiritual breakdown of the Jewish society in its last century in Spain, the tragic chapter of Marranism and defection since the pogroms of 1391 and the disputation at Tortosa in 1414, are reflected in the verses of Solomon de Piera (*c.* 1340-1420), mentor and minstrel of the Jewish aristocrats and apostates in Saragossa.[38] Proud of his historic faith, though contemptuous of its plebeian new leaders, is Solomon Bonafed (d. *c.* 1450), humanist, polemist, satirist who pleaded with the renegades, heartened the vacillating, rebutted the assailants, and generally voiced the conviction, the consternation, and the confidence of the faithful remnant resolved to persevere in the path of their ancestors.[39]

Provence, a bridge and intermediary between the Arabic culture in

Spain and the lands of Christian Europe,[40] saw flowering of Hebrew poetry in the thirteenth century. Preciosity and artificial fanciness seems to be characteristic of this school of poets who delight in toying with language, in ingenious grammar games and all manner of whimsicality to parade their prowess in Hebrew. Abraham Bedershi (*i.e.*, of Béziers) wrote a piece for the Day of Atonement in which only the first half of the letters of the Hebrew alphabet is used, while another of his devotional poems consists of a thousand words each beginning with the same letter.[41] Similar feats of virtuosity are exhibited in the poetic efforts of his son Yedaiah Penini (*c.* 1270-1340) who is best known for his *Behinat Olam* (Scrutiny of the World), one of the most popular and frequently reprinted moral tracts of the Middle Ages.[42] A genuine poet who versed, vagabonded and vilified like a true Provençal troubadour is Isaac Gorni (*i.e.*, of Aire): impecunious and impudent, he never came to good, either in his own time or in the memory of posterity.[43]

A kindred spirit is Immanuel of Rome (*c.* 1270-1330), the greatest poet of medieval Italy.[44] A delightful rogue with an uproarious sense of humor and irrepressible relish for mischief, he can make the holy language utter the naughtiest improprieties, for which he was placed on the list of prohibited authors.[45] Of course, he keeps assuring the reader, as have all poets since Ovid (*crede mihi lasciva est nobis pagina, vita proba est*) that lascivious is only his lay, not life, and that far from being dissolute, he is devout. But there is something to his protestations. Flippant and frivolous, he has his graver moods, and there runs through his poetry a serious strain of religion and asceticism, nourished from native founts of Jewish piety and reinforced by kindred currents in contemporary Christendom.[46] Immanuel introduced into Hebrew the form of the *sonnet* which had just been transferred into Italian from Provençal; otherwise his diction discloses the impact of the Hispano-Arabic patterns of song and scansion. His vision of hell and heaven, the last of his *maqamat*, or miscellanies, is the first attempt at an imitation of Dante in Hebrew letters. It was followed, almost a century later, by the more ambitious effort of Moses da Rieti (1388-d. after 1460), rabbi, physician, and philosopher who in his *Little Shrine*[47] achieved hardly more than a versified survey of the Jewish Sages and the principal philosophers of the past. But his use of the *terza rima* was deft and in his decasyllabic lines (with the *shewa mobile* counted as a vowel) he follows the Italian syllabic-tonic (rather than the Arabian quantitive) meter.[48] No wonder that the Italian Jewish communities were so proud of this Hebrew disciple of Dante that they adopted one of his cantos into the ritual, dividing it into seven parts, one for each day of the week.

Exiles from Spain enrich Hebrew writing in Italy. Judah Abrabanel, known also as *Leone Ebreo*, the celebrated author of the *Dialoghi di Amore*,[48a] excelled in Hebrew verse as well. In a moving elegy, written in Naples in 1503, he depicts the vicissitudes of his life and his sorrow of separation from his firstborn son who was snatched away from his parents in Portugal and forcibly baptized: paternal affection and fidelity to his faith are voiced with fiery passion of feeling and almost frosty perfection of form.[49] The most engaging poet of the Italian Renaissance is Joseph Sarphati (d. 1527), known in his professional life as Giuseppe Gallo, a physician and son of an eminent physician to Pope Julius II and the Medici. He wrote satirical, humorous and erotic verse full of salt and sparkle, small pieces as a rule, since he took delight and pride in brevity. He seems to have been the first to introduce into Hebrew poetry the *ottava rima*, as he was the first to translate a play into Hebrew, the famous Spanish tragicomedy *La Celestina*, of which only his own introductory poem survived.[50] The earliest original attempt at Hebrew drama seems to be the comedy by Judah Sommo (1527-1592), playwright and producer at the court of Mantua who wrote in Italian a dozen or so theatrical pieces, and a pioneering treatise on stagecraft. He also engaged in the favorite fashion of the times of interchanging poems in commendation or condemnation of the female sex, of course gallantly chiming a paean of praise to the noble lady of his heart in his *Magen Nashim* (Shield or Defense of Women).[51]

One will look in vain for such uses or examples of Hebrew poetry in the northern lands of Europe. Massacres by the Crusaders,[52] persecutions and expulsions (from England in 1290, from France in 1306, 1322, and 1394, from Austria in 1421, from Bavaria in 1452), successive waves of pogroms in which during the frightful year of the "Black Death" alone, in 1348-1349, some three hundred Jewish communities were drowned in blood and fire, left their traces in the poetry of the synagogue, in *selihot*, or penitential verse, and *kinot*, or dirges. The sacrifice of Isaac, the *akeda*, or the story of the *ten martyrs* of antiquity,[53] a prefiguration of Israel's passion and pilgrimage of pain through the centuries, is the recurrent theme of the poets in these lands who mingle recent with ancient grief, and draw new hope from the timeless tale. Poets they are sometimes not by choice or inclination, but perforce, under the lash of brute facts or fate. Often it is the scholar in Rabbinic law who feels the duty to appeal to heaven and to report to posterity the plight of his people or the cruelties of hatred and superstition in his day. Accusations of ritual murder (such as wiped out the community of Blois in 1171, and found expression by several poets, among them Rabbi Ephraim of Bonn[54] and Rabbi Barukh of Mayence[55]), the burning of the Talmud (*e.g.*, in Paris in 1244, bewailed by Rabbi Meir of Rothenburg[56]), the charges of poisoning the wells or of desecrating the Host by which mobs were incited to slaughter the Jews (*e.g.*, on the Easter Sunday of 1389 in Prague, mourned by Rabbi Abigdor Kara[57]), such are the topics and pursuits of poetry in these dark centuries and countries.

Poland, where the persecuted found shelter, became in the sixteenth century a stronghold of talmudic studies so that its *payyetanim* are as a rule its leading rabbinic authorities as, for instance, Solomon Luria (d. 1573).[58] In the next century, the bloody Cossack revolts in 1648 in which several hundred communities were wiped out, shook East European Jewry to its depth, taking such heavy toll in lives that altogether the Jewish population in the world sank to its smallest number in history.[59] Again it was the foremost talmudists in their time who believed they were called upon to be the tongue and the graving tool which would keep alive in the memory of the after ages the anguished shrieks of the murdered multitudes and the atrocious details of the carnage: hence the lamentations or chronicles by rabbinic scholars such as Rabbi Yomtob Lipman Heller (d. 1654) and Sabbetai Cohen (d. 1663).[60]

The shores of the Mediterranean, in both Africa and the Balkans, as well as in other Jewish centers of the Ottoman Empire, witnessed a revival of Hebrew poetry in the sixteenth century as a result of the influx of Spanish refugees. Much of the classical heritage of the Middle Ages was preserved, and some good new poetry written in the literary circles that sprang up in Constantinople (*e.g.*, the poet Solomon ben Mazaltob), in Salonica (Saadia Longo, and especially the splendid poet David Onkeneyra), on the islands of the Aegean (Judah Zarko at Rhodes), in Oran, Tlemcen, and Algiers (Abraham and Isaac Mandil Abi Zimra and Abraham Gavison).[61] But it was particularly Safed in Galilee, a city of legists and mystics,[62] which decisively determined the spiritual outlook and also the poetic utterance of the closing centuries of the Jewish Middle Ages. The new cabbala which spread from there over all the scattered communities was the last religious movement in Judaism to reach and affect every country of the Diaspora without exception.[63] This mystic revival influenced the rites and usages of the synagogue, pervaded the liturgy and the prayer book,[64] and imbued Hebrew expression with new fervor and urgency. The hymn *Lekha dodi* (Come, my beloved) by Solomon Alkabez, the teacher and brother-in-law of the famous Safed cabbalist Moses Cordovero (d. 1570), entered all rituals and is sung all over the Jewish world, when Queen Sabbath is welcomed to the tents of Jacob.[65] In almost all the prayer books of Eastern Jewry there will be found also the hymns for the Sabbath meals of Isaac Luria (d. 1572), the inspired visionary of the new cabbala.[66] The sweetest of all mystic singers and the most significant poet of his century is Israel Najera (*c.* 1542-1619) who in over a thousand songs gave utterance to the new temper of devotion and to the feverish Messianic urge of his times. Set to various Turkish, Armenian, Spanish, and new Greek airs, which the wandering minstrel picked up in his younger and gayer life of the road, and suffused with erotic-mystic imagery, these hymns and elegies treat—in alternating mood and melody, now tender, now tearful, now triumphant—of the quarrel and conciliation of the lovers, of estrangement, forgiveness, and renewal of the covenant between the heavenly bridegroom and His earthly spouse, the community of Israel. The stark sensuality at places met with censure. To some such love songs to the *Shekinah* seemed to speak "the language of adulterers,"[67] especially when suited to strains or reminiscent of sounds known to be flagrantly culpable in a carnal way. But all such misgivings were silenced, when Isaac Luria himself endorsed the *piyyutim*, saying that they were listened to with delight in heaven.[68] The liturgy of the Oriental Jews abounds with his poetry, which spread far and wide not only in the Near East and the Balkan Peninsula, but even to Aden, Calcutta, and Cochin-China. His literary influence was likewise far reaching and pervasive,[69] as attested, among others, by the poetry of Shalom Shebesi (d. after 1677), foremost poet of the remote and remarkable tribe of the Jews of Yemen.[70]

The Messianic ardor of the Lurianic cabbala was bound to erupt in movements such as were precipitated by the appearance of Sabbatai Zevi[70a] as the Messiah and Nathan of Gaza as his prophet (1665-1666), and the kindred mystical heresies of that century. One can study the literary reflections of that convulsion best in Italy again. There earlier than anywhere else, within two decades after the death of Luria, a self-styled disciple of his carried on lively propaganda on behalf of the new school.[71] The struggle for or against cabbalism and Sabbatianism is mirrored in the literature and poetry of seventeenth-century Italy which produced such colorful and contradictory personalities as Leon Modena (1617-1648) and the gifted pair of poets and brothers, Jacob (1615-1667) and Immanuel (1618-d. after 1703) Frances, intrepid fighters against all mystic or Messianic delusions.[72] An eager votary of the new cabbala was Moses Zacuto (1625-1697), rabbi in Venice and Mantua, whose secular verse and dramatic works prove that he was sensitive also to other winds of doctrine. His first drama betrays the Spanish background in Amsterdam from where he stems, for its theme—Abraham shattering the idols of his father—carries overtones of the contemporary conflict of the Marranos who sought to return to Judaism.[73] His mystery play on life beyond life[74] is a remarkable artistic attainment. Gifted beyond all others, as well as comprehensive, is Moses Hayyim Luzzatto (1707-1747), poet, dramatist, mystic, and moralist, in all alike distinguished, a self-confessed Messiah in the days of Voltaire, and the reputed father or forerunner of modern Hebrew literature.[75] He still belongs to an age that did not know, nor would have approved, our new compartments and labels: secular and religious. He wrote secular dramas to gladden friends at their wedding which he considered a religious commandment. This was as little ruse on his part as the inclusion of erotic verse as nuptial songs in the prayer books especially of Oriental Jewries. Both are rather the outcome of that all-embracing unity of the Middle Ages in which what is termed the religious included all that was to be found in the nonreligious, and much else besides. Anyhow, the new and the old fuse imperceptibly even in nineteenth-century Italy, as can be seen in the devotional verse of Samuel David Luzzatto (1800-1865), the last of the *payyetanim* to write an *Aboda* or a poetic description of the ritual of the Day of Atonement.[76]

It was also S. D. Luzzatto who toiled most to retrieve for the new age the lost classics of the Middle Ages. For when the poets of the *Haskala* or the era of Enlightenment set about reviving Hebrew,[76a] they found for their endeavors, in Berlin or Vienna, in Zolkiew or Vilna, no usable past. The masters of medieval song had long sunk in oblivion, and even their names faded from memory. "Who is Yannai?" asks in 1829 the best informed scholar of the times.[77] The choicest lyrics of Judah Ha-Levi were clean forgotten until his *diwan* was recovered and parts thereof printed in 1840 and 1864 by S. D. Luzzatto.[78] The bulk of the poetry of Samuel Ha-Nagid remained unknown until our day, and was published for the first time in 1934.[79] Other admirable poets of the Middle Ages are still hidden in the dust of libraries.

NOTES

I

[1] Hagigah 5b, citing Deut. 31:17 f. and Is. 51:16.
[2] Tanhuma, Behaalotka 6.
[3] Tosefta Sotah, 13, 2. Cf. Sotah 48b; Yoma 9b; Sanhedrin 11a.
[4] Seder Olam R. c. 6.
[5] Yer. Taanit II, 1 f. 65a; b. Yoma 21b and parallel passages.
[6] Berakot 8a.
[7] Cf. Mishna Sotah 9, 11; Sotah 48a; Yer. *ibid.*, IX, 12 f. 24b.
[8] Hos. 9:1 and Gittin 7a; Yer. Megillah III, 2 f. 74a.
[9] Ps. 126:2 f. and Berakot 31a.
[[9a] Cf. above Judah Goldin, "The Period of the Talmud," pp. 156, 159, 160.]
[10] Transl. by B. Halper, *Shirat Yisrael* (Leipzig, 1924), pp. 51 f.
[11] Baba Batra 12a.
[12] Shita mekubbezet on Baba Batra 12a. See Abraham J. Heschel, in *Alexander Marx Jubilee Volume* (New York, 1949).
[13] Baba Batra, 12a.
[14] Hasagot on Hilkhot Lulab 8, 5.
[15] Mishna Sotah 9, 15 end.
[16] Sotah 4b.
[17] Examples from the age of the Geonim, see Aptowitzer, in *Tarbiz* 1, 4 (1930), pp. 82 f. In Spain, see Louis Ginzberg, *Genizah Studies,* II, 273; R. Gershom "the Light of the Exile," see S. Assaf, in *Ziyyunim* (Berlin, 1929), p. 119.

[18] R. A. Nicholson, *A Literary History of the Arabs* (Cambridge, 1930), pp. 304 ff.

[19] *Diwan of Jehudah Halevi*, ed. H. Brody, III, 65. Transl. by Solomon Solis-Cohen, in *United Synagogue Recorder*, I, 1921, No. 3.

[20] Judah Ha-Levi, *Kitab al Khazari*, transl. by H. Hirschfeld (London, 1931), p. 251 (ch. 5, 20).

[21] A. Harkavy, *Zikron la-Rishonim* (St. Petersburg, 1891), pt. 5, pp. 166 f.

[22] *Ibid.*, pp. 160 f.

[[22a] Cf. below the chapter by Abraham J. Heschel, "The Mystical Element in Judaism."]

[23] *The Letters of M. H. Luzzatto and his Contemporaries,* ed. by S. Ginzburg (Tel-Aviv, 1937), p. 357.

[24] *Ibid.*, pp. 381, 397.

[25] *e.g.*, Maimonides, *Guide for the Perplexed*, I, ch. 59.

[26] Cf. Jonah of Gerona (d. 1263) and Aaron Ha-Levi (*c.* 1300) quoted by Joseph Caro, *Bet Joseph*, Orah Hayyim 113. See also Shem Tob Falaquera, *Sefer ha-Mebhakkesh,* Haag, 1779, f. 27b.

2

[1] Isaiah Horovitz, *Shne Luhot ha-Berit* (Wilhelmsdorf, 1686), f. 185b.

[2] *Yosippon*, ed. D. Guenzburg (Berditchev, 1913), p. 22; *Iggeret Musar* by Kalonymos b. Kalonymos, ed. Isaiah Sonne, in *Kobez al Yad* 1, 1936, p. 103. See A. M. Habermann, in *Tarbiz,* 13, 1941, p. 55.

[3] Poetics, ch. 9 (1451b).

[4] H. L. Ginsberg, *The Ugarit Texts* (Jerusalem, 1936), pp. 129 ff., and Th. H. Gaster, JQR 37, 1946, 55 ff.

[[4a] Cf. Goldin, *op. cit.*, pp. 166-167.]

[5] Mekilta, ed. Lauterbach, II, 162, 198, 233 f. Sifre Deut. 343, ed. Friedmann p. 142b. Zebahim 116a.

[6] Mas. Soferim, ed. Higger, p. 314.

[7] Jacob b. Asher, *Tur Orah Hayyim,* 284 end.

[8] Shabbat 86b.

[9] Cf. Ch. Albeck in the Hebrew edition of Zunz, *Die gottesdienstlichen Vortraege* (Jerusalem, 1947), pp. 132 f.

[10] Midrash Tehillim, ed. Buber, p. 231.

[11] Saadia's Arabic transl. of the Psalms with Commentary, ed. S. Lehmann (Berlin, 1901), pp. 10 and 32 f.

[12] See the commentaries of David Kimhi (d. 1232) and Menahem Meiri (d. *c.* 1315), ed. J. Cohn (Jerusalem, 1936), pp. 63 f.

[[12a] Cf. above Cecil Roth, "The European Age in Jewish History (to 1648)," pp. 237 ff.]

[13] *Kaf ha-Ketoret* on Ps. 29, quoted from Ms. Paris by Gershom G. Scholem, *Major Trends in Jewish Mysticism* (New York, 1946), p. 408, n. 9, and p. 248.

[14] On the Cabbala of Luria and his school see the excellent chapter by Scholem, *loc. cit.*, pp. 253 ff.

[[14a] Cf. also Heschel, *op. cit.*]

[15] *Siddur Ozar ha-Tefillot* (Vilna, 1923), p. 586. Cf. *Siddur ha-ARI* (Zolkiew, 1781), f. 108 b ff. and *Shaar ha-Kavvanot* (Jerusalem, 1873), f. 64c ff.

[16] See above I, n. 26.

3

[1] Tosefta Berakot 3, 6. See Louis Ginzberg, *A Commentary on the Palestinian Talmud* (New York, 1941), I, p. 68-73.

[2] R. Aha (*c.* 325 C.E.): Yer. Berakot IV, 3f. 8a; cf. also Berakot 29b: Rabba (d. 331) and R. Joseph (d. 333).

[3] Berakot 4, 4, and Abot 2, 13. See Louis Ginzberg, *loc. cit.*, III, 333.

[4] See Israel Davidson in *Festskrift* in honor of Dr. Simonsen (Copenhagen, 1923), pp. 89 ff.

[5] Yer. Sanhedrin I, 1 f. 18a.

[6] Ed. Brody, II, p. 221. Transl. by Judah Goldin in *Menorah Journal*, 33, 1945, p. 196.

[[6a]Cf. Goldin, *op. cit.*, p. 116.]

[7] Josephus *Jewish War* II, 8, 5. See S. J. Rapoport. *Toledoth R. Eleazar ha-Killir*, n. 20.

[8] *Selected Poems of Jehudah Halevi*, ed. H. Brody, transl. by Nina Salaman (Philadelphia, 1924), p. 130. Here, as elsewhere, I have occasionally revised the translation, to bring it closer to the Hebrew.

[9] See *Siddur R. Saadia Gaon*, ed. Davidson-Assaf-Joel (Jerusalem, 1941), p. 37, and Ismar Elbogen. *Der juedische Gottesdienst*, 3 ed., (Frankfort, a. M., 1931), p. 19. See also N. Wieder, in *Saadya Studies* (Manchester, 1943), pp. 254 ff.

[10] *Selected Poems of Jeh. Halevi*, p. 116.

[11] *Ibid.*, 117 and 165.

[12] *Diwan*, ed. Brody, IV, 232.

[13] *Ibid.*, III, 18 f., and I. F. Baer, in *Zion* 1, 1935, p. 23.

[14] *Selected Poems*, p. 97 f.

[15] *Ibid.*, p. 109.

[16] *Ibid.*, p. 134, transl. by Solomon Solis-Cohen, *Judaism and Science* (Philadelphia, 1940), pp. 174 ff.

[17] *Selected Poems*, pp. 134 ff.

[18] Zunz, *Die synagogale Poesie des Mittelalters* (Berlin, 1855), p. 70.

4

[1] 4 vols. (New York, 1924-1933). See also the *Supplement* in *Hebrew Union College Annual*, 12-13, 1937-38, pp. 715 ff.

[2] See S. Schechter, "*A Hoard of Hebrew Manuscripts*" (1897), repr. in his *Studies in Judaism* (Philadelphia, 1908), II, 1-30.

[3] Fragments of Yannai were first identified by Israel Davidson and published in his *Mahzor Yannai* (New York, 1919). All extant compositions were edited by Menahem Zulay, *Piyyute Yannai* (Berlin, 1938). Cf. also his valuable monograph in *Studies of the Research Institute for Hebrew Poetry* (*SI*) (Berlin, 1936), II, 213 ff. The Institute, founded by Salmann Schocken, has in Jerusalem an unrivalled collection of photostats of the scattered remains of

poetry in the Genizah, and its publications have greatly advanced the study of medieval poetry. New fragments of Yannai were found by P. Vidor (in *Jubilee Volume in Honor of Bernhard Heller* [Budapest, 1941], pp. 32 ff.), and Isaiah Sonne, in HUCA, 18, 1944, pp. 199 ff. See also Zulay, in *Haaretz* (Tel-Aviv, February 8, 1947), release No. 100 of the Schocken Institute, and in *Semitic Studies in Memory of Immanuel Loew* (Budapest, 1947), pp. 147 f. On historic and halakic aspects in the research of Yannai, cf. Saul Lieberman, in *Sinai* (Jerusalem, 1939), II, 221 ff.

[4] Some historical and critical problems of this *payyetan* are discussed by the writer in SI, 5, 1939, 269 ff., also in *Encyclopaedia Judaica,* vol. 9, col. 816-820.

[5] See Menahem Zulay, in SI, 3, 1936, pp. 164 ff., and 5, 1939, pp. 109 ff., and in *Sinai,* 9, 1945, pp. 296 ff.

[[5a] Cf. Goldin, *op. cit.*, p. 194.]

[6] I. Davidson, *Saadya's Polemic against Hiwi Albalki* (New York, 1915); *Esa meshali,* ed. B. M. Lewin, in J. L. Fishman's collection *Rav Saadia Gaon* (Jerusalem, 1943), pp. 481 ff. Cf. B. Klar, in *Tarbiz,* 14, 1943, pp. 156 ff. and 15, 1944, pp. 36 ff.

[7] *E. g.*, "Saadia's Piyyut on the Alphabet," ed. by S. Stein, in *Saadya Studies,* (Manchester, 1943), pp. 206 ff.; cf. Zulay, in *Melilah* (Manchester, 1946), II, 162 ff.

[8] The sacred poetry is ed. by Israel Davidson, *Siddur R. Saadia Gaon,* (Jerusalem, 1941). See also Zulay, in *Tarbiz,* 16, 1945, pp. 57 ff.

[9] Parts of a philosophical poem were published anonymously by Joseph Marcus, *Ginze Shirah u-piyyut* (New York, 1933), pp. 81 ff., now identified by Zulay, *Haaretz,* March 9, 1945, release No. 78.

[10] See Zulay, *Haaretz,* September 25, 1946, release No. 96.

[[10a] Cf. below Abraham S. Halkin, "Judeo-Arabic Literature," p. 1132.]

[11] On Joseph and Nahum al-Baradani see J. Mann, *Texts and Studies in Jewish History and Literature* (Cincinnati, 1931), I, 122, and Spiegel, in SI, 5, 1939, p. 272. The poems of Hai Gaon were edited by H. Brody, in SI, 3, 1936, pp. 5 ff.

[12] *Diwan,* ed. H. Brody (Jerusalem, 1935). On his sacred poetry cf. S. Bernstein, in *Sinai* 9, 1945, No. 104, pp. 8 ff.

[13] See J. Mann, *Texts and Studies,* I, 435 ff.; J. Schirmann, in *Kobez al Yad,* 3, 1939, pp. 40 ff.; A. M. Habermann, *Inbe-hen* (Tel-Aviv, 1943), pp. 31 ff.

[14] Ed. by Benjamin Klar, in his *Megillat Ahimaaz* (Jerusalem, 1943), pp. 71 ff. Cf. J. Schirmann, in SI, 1, 1933, pp. 96 ff.

[15] A. M. Habermann edited the *Liturgical Poems* of Simon bar Isaac (Berlin, Jerusalem, 1938), of R. Gershom (Jerusalem, 1944), and of Ephraim of Regensburg in SI, 4, 1938, pp. 119 ff.

[16] Ed. Nehemiah Allony (Jerusalem, 1947).

[[16a] Cf. Halkin, *op. cit.*, p. 1133.]

[17] *Diwan,* ed. D. S. Sassoon (Oxford, 1934); a vocalized ed. by A. M. Habermann (Tel-Aviv, 1945-1947). For a full bibliography see J. Schirmann, *Kirjat Sefer,* 13, 1936, pp. 373 ff., and cf. *idem. Ziyyon,* 1, 1936, pp. 261 ff. and 357 ff., and *Keneset,* 2, 1936, pp. 393 ff. See also Joseph Weiss, preliminary announcement of a contemplated study, *Tarbut hasranit veshirah hasranit* (Jerusalem, 1947).

[17a Cf. below Alexander Altmann, "Judaism and World Philosophy," pp. 970 f.; also Halkin, *op. cit.*, pp. 1139-1140.]

18 *Shire Shelomo b. Jehudah Ibn Gabirol,* ed. Bialik-Ravnitzky (Berlin, 1924), I, 29, 1.42.

19 *Ibid.*, I, 9, 1.33, and correction, III, 3, pp. 115 and 31.

20 *Selected Religious Poems of Solomon Ibn Gabirol,* ed. I. Davidson, transl. into English verse by Israel Zangwill (Philadelphia, 1923), p. 17.

21 *Ibid.*, p. 16.

22 *Ibid.*, p. 69.

23 *Ibid.*, p. 86. A selected bibliography is appended to J. Schirmann, *Shlomo Ibn Gabirol Shirim nivharim* (Tel-Aviv, 1944), pp. 161 f., to which his recent study in *Keneset,* 10, 1946, pp. 244 ff., and José M. Millás Vallicrosa, *S. Ibn Gabirol como poeta y filósofo* (Madrid-Barcelona, 1945), may be added.

[23a On Judah Ha-Levi as philosopher, cf. Altmann, *op. cit.* pp. 972-973.]

24 Jehudah ben Abun of Seville, cf. Brody-Albrecht, *Shaar ha-Shir* (Leipzig, 1905), p. 129, No. 115, line 3.

25 Franz Rosenzweig, *Jehuda Halewi, Zweiundneunzig Hymnen und Gedichte,* p. 153. See also S. Solis-Cohen, "Judah Halevi," in his *Judaism and Science* (Philadelphia, 1940), p. 174.

26 A. R. Nykl, *Hispano-Arabic Poetry* (Baltimore, 1946), p. 246: about the sweet lips of the beloved, "may they refresh the thirsty one, the lover in pain," etc.

27 *Diwan of Jehudah Halevi,* ed. Brody, I, 136: the last lines parody Ez. 23:21. Cf. now S. M. Stern, in *Tarbiz,* 18, 1947, pp. 168 ff.

28 *Diwan,* ed. Brody, II, 309.

29 *Ibid.*, IV, 131, lines 9 f.

30 The best study on the life of Judah Ha-Levi is by J. Schirmann, in *Tarbiz,* 9, 1938, pp. 35 ff., 219 ff.; 10, 1939, pp. 237 ff.; on his age by I. F. Baer, in *Zion,* 1, 1935, pp. 6 ff.; cf. also his paper in *Schocken Almanach 5699* (1939), pp. 74 ff., and his Hebrew book on the *History of the Jews in Christian Spain* (Tel-Aviv, 1945), p. 49 ff. See also Salo W. Baron, in *Jewish Social Studies,* 3, 1941, pp. 243 ff.

31 J. Schirmann, in SI, 2, 1936, pp. 119 ff.; 3, 1938, pp. 249 ff., and 6, 1946, pp. 253 ff.

32 *The Diwan of Moses b. Ezra,* ed. H. Brody (Berlin, 1935), and the *Commentary* (Jerusalem, 1941). *Selected Poems,* ed. H. Brody, transl. by S. Solis-Cohen (Philadelphia, 1934). Cf. also Brody, *JQR,* 24, 1934, pp. 309 ff. *The Diwan of Abraham b. Ezra,* ed. Jacob Egers (Berlin, 1886); *Reime und Gedichte,* ed. D. Rosin (Breslau, 1885-1894); *Kobez hokmat RABE,* ed. D. Kahana (Warsaw, 1894). See also Simon Bernstein, in *Tarbiz,* 5, 1934, pp. 61 ff., and 10, 1939, pp. 8 ff., and H. Brody, in SI, 6, 1945, pp. 1 ff. On his life cf. the various papers by J. L. Fleischer and the recent literature surveyed by Alexander Marx, in *Essays and Studies in Memory of Linda R. Miller,* ed. by I. Davidson (New York, 1938), pp. 135 f.

33 Zabara's *Sepher Shaashuim,* ed. Israel Davidson (New York, 1914), rev. Hebrew ed. (Berlin, 1925). An English transl. by Moses Hadas (New York, 1932) (Records of Civilization, v. 16). Cf. Hadas, *JQR,* 27, 1936, pp. 151 ff. Harizi's work, ed. P. de Lagarde (Goettingen, 1883); ed. A. Kaminka (Warsaw,

1899). See J. Schirmann, *Die hebr. Uebersetzung der Maqamen des Hariri* (Frankfort a.M., 1930), pp. 113 ff. (full bibliography) and in *Moznayim,* 11, 1940, pp. 101 ff. Cf. also S. M. Stern, in *Tarbiz,* 17, 1946, pp. 87 ff.

[34] Ed. Brody, in SI, 4, 1938, pp. 12 ff. See Joseph Patai, *Misefune ha-Shirah* (Jerusalem), pp. 44 ff. Cf. Schirmann, in *Haaretz,* Jan. 1, 1940, and J. N. Epstein, in *Tarbiz,* 11, 1940, pp. 218 f.

[35] M. Sachs, *Die religioese Poesie der Juden in Spanien* (Berlin, 1901), Hebrew section p. 50, and the transl. p. 135. See also G. G. Scholem, in *Schocken Almanach 5696* (1935), pp. 86 ff. Another example of his religious verse, A. M. Habermann. *Be-ron yahad* (Jerusalem, 1945), p. 79.

[[35a] Cf. Altmann, *op. cit.*, pp. 974-975.]

[36] *Gan ha-meshalim we-ha-hidot,* ed. David Yellin (Jerusalem, 1932-1936); cf. Brody, SI, 1, 1933, pp. 2 ff. On the poet and his age see I. F. Baer, in *Zion,* 2, 1937, pp. 19 ff.

[37] Brody-Wiener, *Anthologia Hebraica* (Leipzig, 1922), pp. 299 ff., and Habermann, *Be-ron yahad,* p. 83. Cf. D. H. Mueller-Schlosser, *Die Haggadah von Serajevo* (1896), pp. 59 and 64. See J. Schirmann, *Kirjat Sepher,* 22, 1945, p. 128.

[38] *Diwan,* ed. Simon Bernstein (New York, 1942), and sacred verse *HUCA,* 19, 1946, pp. 1-74. Cf. also Brody. *Leket shirim u-piyyutim* (Jerusalem, 1936), pp. 3 ff., whose author is de Piera, and not Bonafed. See next note.

[39] See J. Schirmann, in *Kobez al-yad,* 14, 1946, p. 11, where the literature is summarized. Cf. also *Haaretz,* Aug. 12, 1938, release No. 13, and July 19, 1946, release No. 93.

[40] Zunz, *Zur Geschichte und Literatur,* pp. 439 ff.

[41] *Bakasha beth-El,* cf. Davidson, *Thesaurus,* III, 37, No. 800, and *Eleph alphin* (Dan. 7:11) in *Kerem Hemed,* 4, pp. 59 ff. See I. Davidson, "Eccentric Forms of Hebrew Verse," in *Students Annual,* Jewish Theol. Seminary (New York, 1914), p. 82.

[42] The *mem* prayer, Davidson, *Thesaurus,* III, 178, No. 2353, also the *rehuta, ibid.,* I, 271, No. 5957. See also *Zunz Jubelschrift* (Berlin, 1884), Hebrew section 1-19.

[43] Ed. H. Gross, in *Monat. Ges. Wiss. Judentums* (*MGWJ*) 31, 1882, 510 ff. (cf. *ibid.,* 27, 1878, 476 f.); Steinschneider, in G. J. Polak's edition of Bedershi, *Hotem tokhnit* (Amsterdam, 1865), p. 4; Schirmann, in *Haaretz,* April 4, 1944, release No. 69.

[44] For editions and literature cf. Schirmann, *Die hebr. Uebersetzungen der Maqamen des Hariri,* pp. 121 ff. Cf. also H. S. Lewis, in *Proc. Amer. Academy for Jewish Research,* 6, 1935, pp. 277 ff.

[45] Joseph Caro, *Shulhan Arukh,* Orah Hayyim 307:16.

[46] Cf. Isaiah Sonne, in *Tarbiz,* 5, 1934, pp. 324 ff.

[47] *Mikdash meat,* ed. J. Goldenthal (Vienna, 1851). Selections in J. Schirmann's *Mivhar ha-Shirah ha-Ivrit beitalia* (Berlin, 1934), pp. 195 ff.

[48] Rhine, JQR, n. S. 1, 1911, pp. 349 ff., and especially M. Hack, in *Tarbiz,* 11, 1939, pp. 91 ff.

[[48a] Cf. Altmann, *op. cit.*, pp. 976-977.]

[49] Schirmann, *Mivhar,* pp. 217 ff.

[50] Schirmann, *ibid.*, pp. 223 ff., and in *Haaretz,* Sept. 25, 1942, release No. 57,

and Oct. 8, 1944, release No. 75; Umberto Cassuto, in *Jewish Studies in Memory of G. A. Kohut* (New York, 1935), Hebrew section pp. 121 ff., and in *Gaster Anniversary Volume* (London, 1936), pp. 58 ff. Cf. Cecil Roth, *The History of the Jews in Italy* (Philadelphia, 1946), p. 220.

[51] *Zahot bedihuta de-kiddushin*, ed. Schirmann (Jerusalem, 1946); *Magen Nashim*, *ibid.*, pp. 149 ff.; cf. *idem*, MGWJ, 75, 1931, pp. 97 ff., and *Keneset*, I, 1935, pp. 430 ff.

[52] See A. M. Habermann, *Sefer gezerot Ashkenaz VeZarephat* (Jerusalem, 1946), with an introduction on the age by I. F. Baer.

[53] See Louis Finkelstein, in *Essays and Studies in Memory of Linda R. Miller* (New York, 1938), pp. 29 ff., and Solomon Zeitlin, JQR, 36, 1945, pp. 1 ff. and 209 ff.

[54] S. Bernfeld, *Sefer ha-Demaot* (Berlin, 1924), I, 225 ff., and Habermann, *Sefer gezerot*, pp. 133 ff.

[55] Ed. Habermann, in SI, 6, 1945, pp. 133 ff.

[56] Brody-Wiener, *loc. cit.*, pp. 295 ff.; Habermann, *Be-ron yahad*, p. 169, and *Sefer gezerot*, pp. 183 ff.

[57] S. Bernfeld, *loc. cit.*, II, 159 ff.

[58] Habermann, *Be-ron yahad*, pp. 175 ff. Cf. Davidson, *Thesaurus*, IV, 475.

[59] Salo W. Baron, *A Social and Religious History of the Jews* (New York, 1937), II, 165, and III, 129 f.

[60] Bernfeld, *loc. cit.*, (Berlin, 1926), III, 173 ff. and 169 ff. On the chronicles cf. M. Steinschneider, *Die Geschichtsliteratur der Juden* (Frankfort a.M., 1905), pp. 120 ff. Cf. Simon Bernstein, in *Ha-toren*, 10, 1923, pp. 83 ff.

[61] Sol. b. Mazaltob, in *Shirim u-zemirot* (Constantinople, 1545); cf. I. Zinberg, *Hist. of Jewish Literature* (in Yiddish) (Vilna, 1933), vol. 4, p. 353, n. 7, and p. 492. On the Society of Poets in Salonica cf. J. Patai, pp. 86 ff., who also published the poetry of Onkeneyra, in *Kobez al Yad*, 2, 1937, pp. 77 ff. On Saadia Longo cf. also H. Brody, in *Minha le-David* (Yellin) (Jerusalem, 1935), pp. 205 ff. Jehudah ben Abraham Zarko, *Sefer Lehem Yehudah* (Constantinople, 1560); cf. Schirmann, in *Haaretz*, May 17, 1945, release No. 81. Abraham, and Jacob, and Abraham (Jr.) Gavison, see *Omer ha-Shikhah* (Leghorn, 1748), where also verses by Abraham Abi Zimra (f. 135b, see also 134a, 138a and 106a) and by Mandil (122b, 138b f. and 4b preface) are printed. See also Habermann. *Be-ron yahad*, p. 192. Generally on the state of research in this epoch cf. Schirmann, *Kirjat Sefer*, 12, 1935, pp. 389 ff.

[62] See S. Schechter, *Studies in Judaism* (Philadelphia, 1908), II, 202 ff.

[63] G. G. Scholem, Hebrew lecture on the *Idea of Redemption in the Cabbala* (Jerusalem, 1941), p. 13; and *Major Trends*, pp. 285 f.

[64] Abraham I. Schechter, *Lectures on Jewish Liturgy* (Philadelphia, 1933), pp. 40 ff.

[65] A. Berliner, *Randbemerkungen zum taegl. Gebetbuch* (Berlin, 1909), I, 43 ff. Cf. Simon Bernstein, *Shomere ha-homot* (Tel-Aviv, 1938), pp. 83 ff.

[66] G. G. Scholem, *Major Trends*, pp. 271 f. Cf. Meir Wiener, *Die Lyrik der Kabbalah* (Vienna, 1920), pp. 75 ff. (reviewed by Scholem, in *Der Jude*, 6, 1921, pp. 55 ff.)

[67] See Menahem Lonzano, *Shte Yadot* (Venice, 1618), f. 142ab.

[68] Najera's *Zemirot Yisrael* were recently edited by Judah Fries-Horeb Tel-Aviv, 1946). See also David Yellin in *Jewish Studies in Memory of G. A. Kohut,* (New York, 1935), Hebrew section pp. 59 ff.; I. Davidson in *Jubilee Volume* in honor of *Samuel Krauss* (Jerusalem, 1937), pp. 193 ff. and in *Sefer ha-Shanah liyhude Amerika* (New York, 1939), pp. 282 ff.; Isaac Mendelsohn, in *Horeb,* 9, 1946, pp. 53 ff., and A. Mirsky, in *Sefer Ish ha-Torah Vehamaaseh* in honor of Rabbi M. Ostrowski, (Jerusalem, 1946), pp. 125 ff. On the data of his life cf. S. A. Rosanes (Hebrew), *Hist. of the Jews in Turkey* (Husiatyn, 1914), Pt. III, pp. 173 ff. and 309 ff., and M. D. Gaon, in *Mizrah u-maarab,* 5, 1930, pp. 145 ff.

[69] On the influence of Najera on Joseph Ganso in Brusa, see Simon Bernstein, *Shomere ha-homot,* pp. 114 ff., on Solomon Molkho II, *ibid.,* pp. 163 ff., on the rite of Corfu, see *idem,* in *Horeb,* 5, 1939, pp. 46, 48 ff.

[70] *Kobez shire kodesh* (Jaffa, 1931). See A. Z. Idelsohn and H. Torczyner, *Diwan of Hebrew and Arabic Poetry of the Yemenite Jews* (Cincinnati, 1930), pp. 88 ff. Older literature listed by R. Levy, in *I. Abrahams Mem. Volume* (Vienna, 1927), p. 266, n. 1. See recently on the Yemenite *piyyut* Y. Ratzaby in *Kirjat Sefer,* 19, 1942, pp. 65 ff. and the list *ibid.,* 22, 1946, pp. 247 ff.

[[70a] Cf. above Cecil Roth, "The Jews of Western Europe (from 1648)," p. 260; also, Walter J. Fischel, "Israel in Iran (A Survey of Judeo-Persian Literature)," pp. 1171-1172.]

[71] G. G. Scholem, in *Ziyyon,* 5, 1940, pp. 215 ff., and briefly also in his *Major Trends,* p. 257.

[72] Dr. Simon Bernstein edited *The Diwan of Leo de Modena* (Philadelphia, 1932) and *Immanuel Frances* (Tel-Aviv, 1932) (cf. *M. Wilensky,* HUCA, 18, 1944); also poems by Jacob Frances in his *Mishire Yisrael beitalia* (Jerusalem, 1939), pp. 73 ff.

[73] Cf. A. Berliner, in his ed. of Zacuto's *Yesod Olam* (Berlin, 1874), and J. Schirmann, in *Moznayim,* 4, 1936, pp. 625 ff.

[74] *Tofteh Arukh* (Venice, 1715). See the introduction by D. A. Friedmann to his edition of the play (Berlin, 1922).

[75] Cf. my *Hebrew Reborn* (New York, 1930), pp. 29 ff. and 441 f., where the literature is listed. Add now S. Ginzburg, *The Life and Works of M. H. Luzzatto* (Philadelphia, 1931); Isaiah Sonne, in *Sefer ha-Shanah liyhude Amerika,* 1935, pp. 218 ff., and 1938, pp. 154 ff., and *Horeb,* 6, 1941, pp. 76 ff.; F. Lachower, in *Keneset,* 4, 1939, pp. 365 ff., and Benjamin Klar, in his introd. to Luzzatto's *Sefer ha-Shirim* (Jerusalem, 1945).

[76] Published in *Bikkure halttim,* 1825, pp. 29 ff. See I. Elbogen, *Studien zur Geschichte des jued. Gottesdienstes* (Berlin, 1907), p. 95.

[[76a] Cf. below Hillel Bavli, "The Modern Renaissance of Hebrew Literature," pp. 893-895.]

[77] S. J. Rapoport, in his biography of Killiri, n. 19.

[78] *Betulat Bat Yehudah* (Prague, 1840), and *Diwan R. Yehudah Halevi* (Lyck, 1864).

[79] Ed. D. S. Sassoon (Oxford, 1934).

BIBLIOGRAPHY

DELITZSCH, FRANZ, *Zur Geschichte der juedischen Poesie*. Leipzig, 1836.

DUKES, L., *Zur Kenntnis der neuhebraeischen religioesen Poesie*. Frankfort a.M., 1842.

(Both these works are rather antiquated.)

Still basic and by far the best are the works of

ZUNZ, LEOPOLD, *Die synagogale Poesie des Mittelalters*. Berlin, 1855.

———, *Der Ritus des synagogalen Gottesdienstes*. Berlin, 1859.

———, *Literaturgeschichte der synagogalen Poesie*. Berlin, 1865.

A survey of the major *payyetanim* will be found also in

ELBOGEN, ISMAR, *Der juedische Gottesdienst*, pp. 280-353. Frankfort a.M. 1931.

For an introduction to Spanish poetry, see

YELLIN, DAVID, *Ketabim nibharim* II, pp. 165-352. Jerusalem, 1939.

———, *Torat ha-Shirah ha-Sepharadit*. Jerusalem, 1940.

MILLÁS VALLICROSA, JOSÉ M., *La Poesía sagrada hebraicoespañola*. Madrid, 1940.

See also the relevant chapters in

ZINBERG, ISRAEL, *Die Geschichte fun der Literatur bei Yiden*. Vilna, 1929-1937.

WAXMAN, MEYER, *A History of Jewish Literature*. New York, 1930-1941.